THE NEW CAMBRIDGE HISTORY OF

· JAPAN

*

VOLUME II

Early Modern Japan in Asia and the World, c. 1580–1877

This major new reference work presents an accessible and innovative survey of the latest developments in the study of early modern Japan. The period from about 1580 to 1877 saw the reunification of Japan after a long period of civil war, followed by two and a half centuries of peace and stability under the Tokugawa shogunate, and closing with the Meiji Restoration of 1868, which laid the foundation for a modern nation-state. With essays from leading international scholars, this volume emphasizes Japan's place in global history and pays close attention to gender and environmental history. It introduces readers to recent scholarship in fields including social history, the history of science and technology, intellectual history, and book history. Drawing on original research, each chapter situates its primary source material and novel arguments in the context of close engagement with secondary scholarship in a range of languages. The volume underlines the importance of Japan in the global early modern world.

DAVID L. HOWELL is the Robert K. and Dale J. Weary Professor of Japanese History and Professor of History at Harvard University.

THE NEW CAMBRIDGE HISTORY OF

JAPAN

General Editor
LAURA HEIN, *Northwestern University*

Bringing together leading Anglophone and Japanese scholars in three landmark volumes, *The New Cambridge History of Japan* offers an expansive vision of the archipelago's history from c. 500 to the twenty-first century. With an emphasis on the porousness of Japan's boundaries, it embraces a more global perspective than that of the original *Cambridge History*, published a generation ago. Its analyses of gender, the environment, and urban life enrich our understanding of political, social, and cultural history. Volume I, *Premodern Japan in East Asia*, traces the archipelago's history from c. 500 to the late sixteenth century. Volume II, *Early Modern Japan in Asia and the World*, carries the narrative into the late nineteenth century. The third volume, *The Modern Japanese Nation and Empire*, brings the story into the twenty-first century. The essays throughout are written in accessible, authoritative prose for a diverse global audience ranging from specialists to students and all those interested in Japan's rich history.

Volume I: Premodern Japan in East Asia, c. 500–1600
EDITED BY HITOMI TONOMURA

Volume II: Early Modern Japan in Asia and the World, c. 1580–1877
EDITED BY DAVID L. HOWELL

Volume III: The Modern Japanese Nation and Empire, c. 1868 to the
Twenty-First Century
EDITED BY LAURA HEIN

THE NEW CAMBRIDGE
HISTORY OF
JAPAN

*

VOLUME II
Early Modern Japan in Asia and the World, c. 1580–1877

*

Edited by
DAVID L. HOWELL
Harvard University

General Editor
LAURA HEIN

CAMBRIDGE
UNIVERSITY PRESS

CAMBRIDGE
UNIVERSITY PRESS

Shaftesbury Road, Cambridge CB2 8EA, United Kingdom

One Liberty Plaza, 20th Floor, New York, NY 10006, USA

477 Williamstown Road, Port Melbourne, VIC 3207, Australia

314–321, 3rd Floor, Plot 3, Splendor Forum, Jasola District Centre, New Delhi – 110025, India

103 Penang Road, #05–06/07, Visioncrest Commercial, Singapore 238467

Cambridge University Press is part of Cambridge University Press & Assessment,
a department of the University of Cambridge.

We share the University's mission to contribute to society through the pursuit of
education, learning and research at the highest international levels of excellence.

www.cambridge.org
Information on this title: www.cambridge.org/9781108417938

DOI: 10.1017/9781108283748

First published 2024

Printed in the United Kingdom by TJ Books Limited, Padstow, Cornwall

A catalogue record for this publication is available from the British Library

Library of Congress Cataloging-in-Publication Data
NAMES: Tonomura, Hitomi, editor. | Howell, David L. (David Luke),
1959– editor. | Hein, Laura Elizabeth, editor.
TITLE: The New Cambridge History of Japan.
DESCRIPTION: Cambridge ; New York : Cambridge University Press, [2023–2025] | Includes
bibliographical references and index. | Contents: V. 1. Premodern Japan in East Asia,
c.500–1600 / edited by Hitomi Tonomura – v. 2. Early Modern Japan in Asia and the
World, c. 1580–1877 / edited by David L. Howell – v. 3. The Modern Japanese Nation
and Empire, c.1868 to the Twenty-First Century / edited by Laura Hein.
IDENTIFIERS: LCCN 2023002199 | ISBN 9781316510254 (vol. 1 : hardcover) |
ISBN 9781108417938 (vol. 2 : hardcover) | ISBN 9781108283748 (vol. 2 : ebook) |
ISBN 9781107196131 (vol. 3 : hardcover) | ISBN 9781108164535 (vol. 3 : ebook)
SUBJECTS: LCSH: Japan – History.
CLASSIFICATION: LCC DS835 .N49 2023 | DDC 952–dc23/eng/20230215
LC record available at https://lccn.loc.gov/2023002199

Three Volume Set ISBN 978-1-978-110818246-1 Hardback
Volume I ISBN 978-1-31651025-4 Hardback
Volume II ISBN 978-1-10841793-8 Hardback
Volume III ISBN 978-1-10719613-1 Hardback

Contents

Introduction: Genealogies of Japanese Early Modernity *1*
DAVID L. HOWELL

PART I
THE CHARACTER OF THE EARLY MODERN STATE

1 The End of Civil War and the Formation of the
Early Modern State in Japan *15*
MORGAN PITELKA

2 Politics and Political Thought in the Mature Early Modern
State in Japan, 1650–1830 *58*
KIRI PARAMORE

3 Regional Authority during the Tokugawa Period *97*
DAVID L. HOWELL

4 Tokugawa Philosophy: A Socio-Historical Introduction *128*
FEDERICO MARCON

5 Foreign Relations and Coastal Defense under the
Mature Tokugawa Regime *159*
ROBERT HELLYER

Contents

Contents

Please see List of Contributors to ascertain surnames and personal names.

Figures

Maps

Tables

x

Contributors to Volume II

BURNS, Susan L. (Professor of Japanese History, East Asian Languages and Civilizations, and the College, University of Chicago)

CLULOW, Adam (Professor of History, University of Texas at Austin)

EHLERS, Maren (Associate Professor of History, University of North Carolina at Charlotte)

FRUMER, Yulia (Associate Professor of History of Science and Technology, Johns Hopkins University)

GAUBATZ, Thomas (Assistant Professor of Japanese Literature and Culture, Northwestern University)

GHADIMI, Amin (Associate Professor, Graduate School of Humanities, Osaka University)

GRAMLICH-OKA, Bettina (Professor, Faculty of Liberal Arts, Sophia University)

HELLYER, Robert (Professor of History, Wake Forest University)

HOWELL, David L. (Robert K. and Dale J. Weary Professor of Japanese History and Professor of History, Harvard University)

HSIUNG, Hansun (Assistant Professor, School of Modern Languages, Durham University)

JAUNDRILL, D. Colin (Associate Professor of History, Providence College)

KOMURO, Masamichi (Professor Emeritus, Faculty of Economics, Keio University)

MARCON, Federico (Associate Professor of East Asian Studies and History, Princeton University)

NENZI, Laura (Professor of History, Emory University)

PARAMORE, Kiri (Professor of Asian Studies, University College Cork, National University of Ireland)

PITELKA, Morgan (Bernard L. Herman Distinguished Professor of History and Asian Studies, University of North Carolina at Chapel Hill)

RAVINA, Mark (Mitsubishi Heavy Industries Chair in Japanese Studies and Professor of History, University of Texas at Austin)

STANLEY, Amy (Professor of History, Northwestern University)

TEEUWEN, Mark (Professor of Japan Studies, University of Oslo)

WALKER, Brett L. (Regents Professor, Montana State University)

WALTHALL, Anne (Professor of History Emerita, University of California, Irvine)

Preface

The *Cambridge Histories* series form a distinctive genre, one whose essays differ from the monograph chapter, journal article, or encyclopedia entry. We have endeavored to use that genre to bring 73 essays of contemporary scholarship on premodern, early modern, and modern Japanese history to a new generation. The *Cambridge Histories* are intended to be accessible to diverse but specific audiences – that is, to provide a crash course for colleagues who specialize on other parts of the world, a single location for undergraduate and graduate students who are getting a handle on the diversity of the past, and a topography of Japan studies for the general educated reader with an interest in history. An underlying assumption is that we write for readers across the globe, including in Japan, because Japanese history is and always has been part of global history. The porousness of the boundaries between Japan and its transnational context is one of the overarching themes of the essays in this collection.

Another convention of this genre is to put political history at the center of the narrative, even though "political," narrowly defined, does not usefully capture the contours of public life for many premodern and early modern societies, including in Japan. Nor does it help us see modern people who were poorly represented by their political leaders. We deal with these limitations here by expanding our definition of political history to encompass everything that has to do with public, civic, and state activities. This includes categories such as gender, which we see as profoundly political in this sense. Like all *Cambridge Histories*, however, the selection leans toward political, economic, and social topics, here including considerable environmental and urban history.

Since the *Cambridge Histories'* inception over a century ago, the genre has celebrated narrative over accumulation of facts, encouraged its participants to synthesize with gusto, and urged them to choose a point of view that has obvious relevance in the contemporary world. This three-volume collection represents the efforts of 85 authors and translators to convey why and how their particular topics matter in a variety of comparative, transregional, and cross-disciplinary frameworks. The multiplicity of authors also implies internal diversity: readers can expect that any given volume represents a range of concerns and approaches, for the past holds many different lessons for the present.

When the first edition of the *Cambridge History of Japan* was published from 1988 to 1999, there was a considerable gap between Japanese- and English-language scholarship in terms of questions being asked, modes of argumentation, and intended audiences. This is far less true today, and these volumes owe much to the rich and exciting scholarship appearing in Japanese. Our efforts also rest on the first edition of the *Cambridge History of Japan*. We concur with the general editors (John W. Hall, Marius B. Jansen, Madoka Kanai, and Denis Twitchett) that "Japanese history belongs to the world, not only as a right and necessity but also as a subject of compelling interest."

The Japanese archipelago
Map by Fabian Drixler. The coastlines of Japan derive from Inō Tadataka's survey (1800–1821), in Murayama Yūji, ed., *Dejitaru Inō-zu*, DVD-ROM (Kawade Shobō Shinsha, 2015).

꙳

Introduction

Genealogies of Japanese Early Modernity

DAVID L. HOWELL

I introduce this volume of the *New Cambridge History of Japan* with two questions: How is it that Anglophone scholars have come to refer to the Tokugawa period (1603–1868) and immediately surrounding years as Japan's "early modern" period? And does calling the period early modern suggest something fundamentally different from the term used in Japanese, *kinsei*? When the first *Cambridge History of Japan* was published, in 1991, the answer to the latter question was yes: the *kinsei* of "the Japanese" was "more feudal than modern," whereas the early modernity of "Western historians" was "more modern than feudal."[1] As we shall see, however, the term *kinsei* has nothing to do with feudalism. My interest in these questions is more than philological. The answers tell us something about the global history of conceptualizing historical time, particularly the surprising career of modernity.

Let us trace the genealogy of Japanese early modernity – that is, the history of "early modern Japan" as a historical period and the ironies of its emergence. To put my conclusion boldly, "early modernity" as a concept of periodization is older in East Asian historiography than it is in European historiography. Nuance and qualifiers await us in a few pages, but the use of "early modern" to describe Japan during the three centuries from the late sixteenth to the late nineteenth centuries is more than the imposition of a Eurocentric concept on Japan's historical experience.

To be clear, we employ a conventional periodization scheme for this three-volume iteration of the *New Cambridge History of Japan*: premodern (everything up to about 1580), early modern (about 1580 to about 1880), and modern (everything since about 1880). This division of the volumes reflects the institutional taxonomy of Japanese historical studies in the Anglophone world: we are a community of premodernists, early modernists, and

---

[1] Hall, "Introduction," 8–9, paraphrasing Wakita, "Social and Economic Consequences," 96–98.

modernists. Colleagues in Japan generally divide their country's history into four broad periods: ancient (*kodai*), medieval (*chūsei*), early modern (*kinsei*), and modern (*kindai*), with breaks at around 1185, 1580, and 1870. When they compile monumental multivolume national histories – something they do quite a lot – they generally follow this division, sometimes adding protohistorical and contemporary taxa at either end.[2]

Early Modernity

As a term of periodization, early modernity has a surprisingly short history in studies of Europe and a surprisingly long one in studies of East Asia. As Randolph Starn has pointed out, the use of early modernity to periodize European history is an Anglophone phenomenon; the progression from medieval to early modern to modern, familiar to readers of English, is medieval to modern to contemporary in continental Europe. Starn tells us, moreover, that the first references to "early modern Europe" appeared in print only in the early 1940s and that it took about three decades for the formulation to become a fixture in the historiography of Europe.[3]

Jack Goldstone argues that early modernity was originally the province of social and economic historians who wanted a way to characterize the long transitional period between the unraveling of the medieval world by about the end of the fifteenth century and the emergence of industrial capitalism in the early nineteenth century.[4] They enumerated a checklist of characteristics – such as absolutist governments, the rise of merchant capitalism, and protoindustrialization – that helped to distinguish early modern societies from the feudal ones that preceded them and the fully modern (that is, capitalist) ones that succeeded them. The oldest articulation of this new periodization that I have found is an article by the economic historian Violet Barbour, who in 1940 characterized "this early modern period" of the sixteenth and seventeenth centuries as a time when "living medieval rigidities were breaking down and new ones were forming, but these latter were not to reach full effectiveness until the succeeding period."[5]

Early modernity in its initial iteration was not a Marxist concept per se, but it was particularly suited to a Marxist take on history, which saw the early

---

[2] For example, the authoritative *Iwanami kōza: Nihon rekishi* series, now in its fifth iteration (2013–15), employs this taxonomy in its twenty-two volumes.
[3] Starn, "Early Modern Muddle."
[4] Goldstone, "Problem of the 'Early Modern World.'"
[5] Barbour, "Rigidities Affecting Business," 290.

modern as the time after the feudal mode of production had begun to disinte-grate but before the capitalist mode of production had taken root. In Marxist historiography, early modernity was a precapitalist – hence essentially feu-dal – formation, its forward-looking name notwithstanding. Non-Marxist scholars as well embraced the concept and eventually expanded its bound-aries beyond political economy narrowly defined to include things like the spread of information networks, education, urbanization, secularization, and the emergence of a public sphere. By the time early modernity entered main-stream use among European historians in the 1970s, it was no longer necessar-ily tied to a narrative of transition from feudalism to capitalism. Rather, it had become a term of social and cultural history, employed by scholars whose work was quite distant from that of the Marxists and other functionalists who were its original natural constituency. Nowadays scholars of many persua-sions use the term, and in that sense, it conveys nothing definitive about a user's methods or outlook.

East Asian history early modernized a bit later, but it was not the lag-gard one might expect. In 1953, Lien-Sheng Yang reviewed Naitō Torajirō's *Chūgoku kinseishi*, which he rendered as the *History of [Early] Modern China*.[6] Naitō Torajirō (1866–1934), better known as Naitō Konan, was the most influ-ential Sinologist in early twentieth-century Japan. As Yang's square brackets suggest, Naitō uses "*kinsei*" to mean "modern," but he divides the period into "early" (*zenki*) and "late" (*kōki*) phases, stretching nearly a millennium from the Song to the Qing dynasties. His "early" modern period starts in the tenth century with a checklist of transformations – such as the decline of the aris-tocracy, growth of the commercial economy, and rise of popular culture – that typically feature in taxonomies of global early modernity. So far as I can ascertain, Yang's review was the first appearance of "early modern" as a trans-lation of the Japanese term *kinsei*. The brackets around "early" disappeared, and eventually "early modern" became the standard translation of the term.

I will return to the use of *kinsei* in Japanese-language works shortly, but for now let us note that, as a term of periodization, it first appeared decades before Yang's review and hence decades before the coining of "early modern Europe." The first authors to translate *kinsei* into English as "early modern" surely meant the early part of the modern age rather than a distinct period of history. Nevertheless, their choice of words was significant. They detached

---

[6] Yang, "Review of *Chūgoku kinseishi*." Naitō's son Kenkichi compiled *Chūgoku kinseishi* (1947) from students' notes of lectures his father delivered between 1920 and 1925. Miyakawa, "Outline of the Naitō Hypothesis," 535.

large chunks of East Asian history from the centuries before engagement with the West and posited this pre-Western time as the beginning of modernity. And they did this in China – never a darling of modernization theorists – at least as much as in Japan.

The first English-language book to feature "early modern Japan" in its title appeared in 1968, with the publication of *Studies in the Institutional History of Early Modern Japan*, edited by John W. Hall and Marius B. Jansen; five years more would pass before the appearance of the next example, *Deus Destroyed: The Image of Christianity in Early Modern Japan*, by George Elison (Jurgis Elisonas).[7] For many years, authors of books on Japan in the seventeenth through nineteenth centuries chose "Tokugawa" or "Edo" over "early modern" for their titles. I cannot say precisely when the tide turned – perhaps sometime around the publication in 1991 of volume 4 of the early iteration of the *Cambridge History of Japan*, entitled simply *Early Modern Japan*.[8]

Kinsei and the Language of Modernity

The Japanese term *kinsei* is now conventionally translated into English as "early modern." Sure enough, the *kinsei* of scholars writing in Japanese today corresponds almost exactly to the "early modern" of Anglophone historians: it begins in the late sixteenth century and ends with the Meiji Restoration in 1868, at which point *kindai* or "modern" history begins. In fact, the practice of dividing Japanese history into *kinsei* and *kindai* periods is a relatively recent phenomenon. Historians writing after about the beginning of the twentieth century routinely used *kinsei* to refer to the Tokugawa era, but not until the 1950s did *kindai* become securely established as the term of choice to refer to the years after the Meiji Restoration. Moreover, this terminological division of labor is an arbitrary convention: dictionaries such as the authoritative *Nihon kokugo daijiten* define the terms in nearly identical language as referring to "the age close to the contemporary."

Two reasons explain how the term *kinsei* came to refer to the Tokugawa period. The first is that throughout the Tokugawa era itself, people used *kinsei* to describe the time in which they lived. This sense of "recent times" or "nowadays" carried over into the Meiji period, though now one never hears it in ordinary conversation. The other reason is rooted in the practice of

[7] Hall and Jansen, *Studies in the Institutional History*; Elison, *Deus Destroyed*.
[8] Hall, *Early Modern Japan*. Hall's introduction to this volume was the first direct discussion of the meaning of early modernity for Japanese studies. Wigen, "Mapping Early Modernity."

writing history. Scholars active during the first decades of the twentieth century experimented with new forms of periodization and with new meanings for old terms, including *kinsei*. In the process of their experimentation, *kinsei* became a historical period rather than a generic term for the recent past.

Uchida Ginzō first turned *kinsei* into a historical period. He begins his *Nihon kinseishi*, published in 1903, with a brief discussion of the question of how to date the *kinsei* period.[9] After making the point that one might reasonably start as early as the twelfth century or as late as the Meiji Restoration, he accepts "the general view" (*futsū no kenkai*) and settles on the early Tokugawa period – 1616, to be precise – as the most reasonable starting point. He chooses this date because to him it represents the *end* of a half century of developments of the sort that would make it onto any functionalist's checklist of early modern attributes – the rise of commerce and industry, the spread of a money economy, urbanization, and intellectual vitality, all in the context of political chaos followed by unification. As he puts it, "There is adequate scholarly basis to date the onset of modernity (*kinsei*) from the point at which the changes of the transitional period had run their course." As for the end of *kinsei*, Uchida thinks that 1853 – the year of Matthew Perry's mission to Japan – is a good point; he follows that with a transitional period until the abolition of the Tokugawa domains in 1871, after which he dates the beginning of the contemporary age – *saikinsei* (the "most" *kinsei*). Although he begins by attributing many of Japan's archetypically "early modern" changes to the period immediately preceding the Tokugawa, he planned in his history (he published only the first of a projected eleven volumes) to dwell on many of the same topics, including commerce, urbanization, and intellectual life.[10]

Insofar as he was writing decades before the invention of "early modernity" as a concept, Uchida's *kinsei* necessarily means "modern" history, but not the sort of modernity that continuously updates itself to incorporate the present. In another survey of Tokugawa history, published in 1919, he explains that although it would not be wrong to include within *kinsei* the Meiji (1868–1912) and Taishō (1912–26) eras, it is better to distinguish the time since Perry's arrival as *saikinsei*.[11] In any event, Uchida clearly rejected older styles of periodization once prevalent in Japanese historical writing, in which the distance over time from the present was the sole criterion – as

---

[9] Uchida, *Nihon kinseishi*, 1–2.
[10] See the outline contents of the full series, Uchida, *Nihon kinseishi*, v–vi.
[11] Uchida, *Kinsei no Nihon*, 9.

the previously common practice of dividing history into *jōko* (high antiquity), *chūko* (middle antiquity), and *kinko* (recent antiquity) suggests. Instead, Uchida uses *kinsei* as a label meant to capture the particular historical character of the period.[12]

Japanese historians in the late nineteenth and early twentieth centuries were a cosmopolitan lot. They engaged deeply with European historiography, and their ideas attracted the attention of Western scholars. Many of the leading lights of the field, including Uchida, Hara Katsurō, the legal scholar Nakada Kaoru, and the medievalists Fukuda Tokuzō and Asakawa Kan'ichi, had studied in Europe or the United States; Hara, Fukuda, and particularly Asakawa – who spent most of his career at Yale University – published important works in European languages.[13]

The most important result of this engagement was the discovery of a Japanese Middle Ages (*chūsei*) characterized by European-style feudalism. For domestic Japanese purposes, as Thomas Keirstead shows, endowing Japan with a Western-style medieval age allowed scholars to assert a similar Western-style modernity as Japan's proper historical destiny.[14] A comparable, if more drawn-out process, was at work in Western understandings of Japan. Inspired by Asakawa's work, Edwin O. Reischauer emphasizes Japan's unique non-European feudal experience in his consideration of the roots of Japan's successful modernization.[15] As he puts it, "One cannot but compare Japanese success ... with the slow and painful efforts at westernization on the part of the other Asiatic peoples, who for the most part had had longer and often much closer contacts with Western civilization, but lacked the feudal background."[16]

During the half century between the publication of Uchida's book and the first appearance of "early modern Japan" in English, *kinsei* steadily gained acceptance as the standard term to describe the Tokugawa period.[17] For decades, no consensus prevailed on how the term *kinsei* ought to be expressed in English-language histories of Japan. However, even authors who translated *kinsei* as "modern" in their footnotes refrained from calling the Tokugawa period modern in their texts, suggesting that the Tokugawa era has never been "modern" the way that Japan after the Meiji Restoration was. To take

---

[12] Sakamoto, "Edo jidai o 'kinsei' to iu koto."
[13] Keirstead, "Inventing Medieval Japan."
[14] Keirstead, "Inventing Medieval Japan."
[15] Friday, "Futile Paradigm." Asakawa lays out his argument for Japanese feudalism in "Some Aspects of Japanese Feudal Institutions."
[16] Reischauer, "Japanese Feudalism," 46.
[17] Howell, "Nihon kinseishi."

just one example of many, Hall referred in 1955 to "early modern culture" and "modern castle towns" in his footnotes, even while clearly excluding the Tokugawa era from modernity in the text.[18] Eventually, Anglophone scholars sidestepped the problem of direct translation and rendered *kinsei* as "Tokugawa."[19]

What about *"kindai"*? According to Yanabu Akira, the word began appearing regularly as a translation of "modern" around 1890.[20] Before that, dictionaries commonly but not universally rendered "modern" as *kinsei*.[21] For the next half century, *kindai* appeared occasionally as a term of historical periodization, but writers more commonly used it in an abstract sense, along the lines of the English "modernity." *Kindai* was, like "modernity," difficult to define precisely, yet it was freighted with values, positive and negative, in a way that *kinsei* tended not to be.[22] It figures that when a group of intellectuals gathered in 1910 to consider the character of the "modern man," and another panel convened in 1942 to discuss "overcoming modernity," *kindai* rather than *kinsei* was the object of their inquiries.[23]

For a few years in the early postwar period scholars continued to rely on *kinsei* and *saikinsei* to periodize modern history but used *kindai* in adjectival form. Yanabu gives the example of Ienaga Saburō's *Shin Nihonshi* (1949), which characterizes the period since the Meiji Restoration as *saikinsei* but includes chapters on the birth of "modern Japan" (*kindai Nihon*) and the emergence of "modern industry" (*kindai sangyō*).[24] Before long, however, *kindai* entirely supplanted *saikinsei* to describe Japanese history since the Meiji Restoration. The final example of *saikinsei* that I have found is in a history of Tokyo's Nerima ward, published in 1957.[25]

By the time the first postwar edition of the *Iwanami kōza: Nihon rekishi* series appeared in the early 1960s, it had become hard to imagine calling modern history anything but *kindai*. In an essay on periodization produced for that series, Tōyama Shigeki argues that, thanks to the widespread acceptance

---

[18] Hall, "Castle Town": *kinsei* as "early modern" (46 n30, 54 n53), *kinsei* as "modern" (43 n21).
[19] For example, Smith, "Landlords and Rural Capitalists": *kinsei* as "Tokugawa" (166 n8, 169 n19, 171 n30, 179 n59); *kinsei* as "modern" (169 n25).
[20] Yanabu, *Hon'yakugo*, 43–64.
[21] See Yanabu, *Hon'yakugo*, 56–57, for a list of dictionary entries from 1862 to 1911.
[22] On the evolution of the nuances attached to the word "modern" in European languages, see Seed, "Early Modernity."
[23] Yanabu, *Hon'yakugo*, 43, citing "Kindaijin to wa nanzo ya," *Bunshō sekai*, July 1910, and "Kindai no chōkoku," *Bungakukai*, September and October 1942.
[24] Yanabu, *Hon'yakugo*, 53–54.
[25] Tōkyō-to Nerima-ku, *Nerima-ku shi*. *Saikinsei* in this work refers to the period from 1868 to 1945; the postwar years are described as *gensei*, or "present conditions."

of historical materialism, it had become a matter of "common sense" among historians to collapse the seven centuries of warrior rule into a single medieval/feudal (*chūsei/hōken*) age, followed by the modern (*kindai*) era from the Meiji Restoration to the present.[26] Tōyama's "common sense," which tossed out *kinsei* entirely, was shared neither by the editors of the Iwanami series, who grouped its four Tokugawa volumes as *kinsei*, nor indeed by specialists in Tokugawa history – among whom Marxists dominated – who continued to use *kinsei*. Tōyama's invocation of his idiosyncratic common sense was an attempt to relegate the Tokugawa once and for all to premodernity, and its failure settled the issue of periodization. The next iteration of the Iwanami series, published in the mid-1970s, included an essay on periodization by another committed Marxist historian, Araki Moriaki, but his contribution, which addressed debates of concern only to materialists, did not consider the labeling of broad epochs at all.[27]

Early Modern in Any Language

The Tokugawa period became *kinsei* at the beginning of the twentieth century, and it has remained *kinsei* ever since, through many changes in historians' understandings of the era's character. As a term of periodization, *kinsei* has gone from doing modernity's work to doing early modernity's. The seeds of its transformation were there from the beginning, as we see in the convention of ending *kinsei* at the Meiji Restoration and following it with something else – *saikinsei* or *kindai* – more suited to renewing itself to embrace the present. Perhaps it would be sneaky to argue that *kinsei* was destined to be "early modern" even before the idea of "early modernity" had been invented in European historiography. But we cannot disqualify it from being "early modern" just because it was not so from the outset.

The "early modern" destiny of the Tokugawa period is revealed in the contrast with China. As we have seen, the earliest references in English to "early modern" East Asia come from works on China, which reflects Naitō Torajirō's influence on the field. According to Sakamoto Shōzō, Uchida Ginzō profoundly influenced Naitō.[28] Indeed, his influence is evident as early as 1914, when Naitō argued that *kinsei* began in China in the Song dynasty, for that was when absolutism, the rise of commoners, and the

[26] Tōyama and Nagahara, "Jidai kubun ron," 170. Tōyama is credited as the author of the section under discussion here. See also Yanabu, *Hon'yakugo*, 58.
[27] Araki, "Hōsoku ninshiki."
[28] Sakamoto, "Edo jidai o 'kinsei' to iu koto," 114 n15.

emergence of a new culture changed Chinese society. This transformation predated but corresponded to the *kinsei* of Europe, "when the power of ordinary people increased, the discovery of new lands led to economic changes, and social organization changed as well," and of Japan, where "the root structures of society gradually changed," starting as early perhaps as the Kamakura period but in any case no later than the end of the Ashikaga.[29]

In 1955, Miyakawa Hisayuki published in English a sympathetic introduction to the work of Naitō and his principal successor in the so-called Kyoto school of Sinology, Miyazaki Ichisada. Naitō's view of "Chinese history itself [as] the norm of world history" inspired Miyazaki to write a long article on "The Renaissance in the Orient and in the Occident," in which "he compared the early Sung period, the beginning of modern China, with the Renaissance, the beginning of modern Europe."[30] The "modern" in the following quote and elsewhere is Miyakawa's rendering of *kinsei*, but it actually reads a lot like a functionalist definition of early modernity. To see it, replace "modern" with "early modern" and "post-modern" with "modern," in this summary of Miyazaki's *Tōyōteki kinsei* (1950):

> There are scholars who are willing to accept the fact of the important transition from T'ang to Sung but who reject the idea that the Sung is the beginning of the modern period. They are unaware of the universal criteria of modernity which a study of European history suggests; they focus on a few aspects and assert that the modern period in Europe begins with the industrial revolution and the rise of capitalism and, since China did not see such developments under the Sung, they deny its modernity. But China had both a renaissance and a reformation though it had neither a French revolution nor an industrial revolution. The latter are characteristic of post-modern (*sai-kinsei*) rather than of modern Europe....
>
> Developments in post-modern Europe have left Asia behind, but the modern periods of Europe and China are parallel and comparable.[31]

Nevertheless, in English-language scholarship on Chinese history, this usage of *kinsei* (whether rendered as "modern" or "early modern") did not take hold. This may reflect *kinsei*'s toxicity in some Japanese academic circles, for

---

[29] Naitō, *Shina ron*, 7–9. According to Kishimoto, *Higashi Ajia no "kinsei,"* 1–2, Naitō was the first author to think systematically about the meaning of *kinsei* as a term of periodization in Chinese history.

[30] Miyakawa, "Outline of the Naitō Hypothesis," 542, 545; Miyazaki, "Tōyō no runesansu." The translation of the article's title is Miyakawa's.

[31] Miyakawa, "Outline of the Naitō Hypothesis," 546, summarizing Miyazaki Ichisada, *Tōyōteki kinsei* (Kyōiku Taimususha, 1950).

its use identified one with Naitō's Kyoto school, which opposed the Marxist history of the so-called Tokyo school, whose members saw the Song and succeeding dynasties as a feudal (*hōken*) or medieval (*chūsei*) age.[32] During the last decade or so, scholars of China have increasingly adopted the language of early modernity, but the practice of referring to the Ming and Qing dynasties as "late imperial" remains widespread.

The genealogies of early modernity in Japan are two: the translation of the term *kinsei* into English, and the adoption of the phrase "early modern" from European history. In fact, however, despite their separate origins, the two strands have been intertwined for quite some time; *kinsei* in Japanese evolved from its early twentieth-century roots to denote just the sort of placeholder period between the high Middle Ages and the onset of true (read: capitalist) modernity that the term "early modernity" originally suggested in English. *Kinsei*/early modern China lasted for centuries – from the Song until the Qing – while Korea was (until very recently) never *kinsei*/early modern at all because, thanks to the legacy of colonial-era Japanese scholarship, the country was seen as hopelessly stuck in feudal darkness until Japanese colonialism dragged it into the modern world.[33]

Although *kinsei* and "early modern" evolved as terms of historical periodization independently, they did so in response to the historiographical demands of the same functionalist paradigms. It is just that the Japanese started doing it first. Accordingly, early modernity as a period is older in East Asian historiography (i.e. Japanese scholarship on Japan and China) than it is in European historiography. In that sense, we East Asianists can tell our colleagues in Renaissance-Reformation history to keep their paws off our historical era. Early modernity is ours!

Bibliography

Araki Moriaki. "Hōsoku ninshiki to jidai kubunron." In *Sengo Nihon shigaku no tenkai*, edited by Asao Naohiro, Ishii Susumu, Inoue Mitsusada, Ōishi Kaichirō, Kano Masanao, Kuroda Toshio, Sasaki Junnosuke, et al., 59–94. Vol. 24 of *Iwanami kōza: Nihon rekishi*. Iwanami Shoten, 1975.

Asakawa, Kan'ichi. "Some Aspects of Japanese Feudal Institutions." *Transactions of the Asiatic Society of Japan* 46, no. 1 (1918): 76–102.

Barbour, Violet. "Rigidities Affecting Business in the Sixteenth and Seventeenth Centuries." *American Economic Review* 30, no. 1 (1940): 290–97.

[32] Kishimoto, *Higashi Ajia no "kinsei,"* 2–3.
[33] On the legacy of Japanese colonial scholarship, see Pai, *Constructing "Korean" Origins*, and Palais, "Search for Korean Uniqueness."

Elison, George S. *Deus Destroyed: The Image of Christianity in Early Modern Japan.* Cambridge, MA: Harvard University Press, 1973.

Friday, Karl. "The Futile Paradigm: In Quest of Feudalism in Early Medieval Japan." *History Compass* 8, no. 2 (2010): 179–96.

Goldstone, Jack A. "The Problem of the 'Early Modern World.'" *Journal of the Economic and Social History of the Orient* 41, no. 3 (1998): 249–84.

Hall, John Whitney. "The Castle Town and Japan's Modern Urbanization." *Far Eastern Quarterly* 15, no. 1 (November 1955): 37–56.

—— ed. *Early Modern Japan.* Vol. 4 of *The Cambridge History of Japan.* Cambridge: Cambridge University Press, 1991.

—— "Introduction." In Hall, *Early Modern Japan,* 1–39.

Hall, John Whitney, and Marius B. Jansen, eds. *Studies in the Institutional History of Early Modern Japan.* Princeton, NJ: Princeton University Press, 1968.

Howell, David L. "Nihon kinseishi to ārii modan hisutorii: Jidai kubun to hikakushi no kanōsei." *Kokushigaku* 210 (June 2013): 98–122.

Keirstead, Thomas. "Inventing Medieval Japan: The History and Politics of National Identity." *Medieval History Journal* 1, no. 1 (1998): 45–71.

Kishimoto Mio. *Higashi Ajia no "kinsei."* Yamakawa Shuppansha, 1998.

Miyakawa, Hisayuki. "An Outline of the Naitō Hypothesis and Its Effects on Japanese Studies of China." *Far Eastern Quarterly* 14, no. 4 (August 1955): 533–52.

Miyazaki Ichisada. "Tōyō no runesansu to seiyō no runesansu." *Shirin* 25, no. 4 (1940): 465–80, and 26, no. 1 (1941): 69–102.

Naitō Torajirō. *Shina ron.* Bunkaidō Shoten, 1914.

Ōtsu Tōru, Sakurai Eiji, Fujii Jōji, Yoshida Yutaka, and Ri Sonshi (Lee Sungsi), eds. *Iwanami kōza: Nihon rekishi.* 22 vols. Iwanami Shoten, 2013–16.

Pai, Hyung Il. *Constructing "Korean" Origins: A Critical Review of Archaeology, Historiography, and Racial Myth in Korean State-Formation Theories.* Cambridge, MA: Harvard University Asia Center, 2000.

Palais, James B. "A Search for Korean Uniqueness." *Harvard Journal of Asiatic Studies* 55, no. 2 (1995): 409–25.

Reischauer, Edwin O. "Japanese Feudalism." In *Feudalism in History,* edited by Rushton Coulborn, 26–48. Princeton, NJ: Princeton University Press, 1956.

Sakamoto Shōzō. "Edo jidai o 'kinsei' to iu koto." *Nihon rekishi* 769 (June 2012): 105–14.

Seed, Patricia. "Early Modernity: The History of a Word." *CR: The New Centennial Review* 2, no. 1 (Spring 2002): 1–16.

Smith, Thomas C. "Landlords and Rural Capitalists in the Modernization of Japan." *Journal of Economic History* 16, no. 2 (June 1956): 165–81.

Starn, Randolph. "The Early Modern Muddle." *Journal of Early Modern History* 6, no. 3 (2002): 296–307.

Tōkyō-to Nerima-ku. *Nerima-ku shi.* Nerima-ku, 1957.

Tōyama Shigeki and Nagahara Keiji. "Jidai kubun ron." In *Iwanami kōza: Nihon rekishi,* edited by Ienaga Saburō, Ishimoda Shō, Inoue Kiyoshi, Inoue Mitsusada, Kitajima Masamoto, Kitayama Shigeo, Satō Shin'ichi, et al. Vol. 22, 165–226. Iwanami Shoten, 1963.

Uchida Ginzō. *Kinsei no Nihon.* Fuzanbō, 1919. Reprint, Heibonsha, 1975.

—— *Nihon kinseishi.* Fuzanbō, 1903.

Wakita Osamu. "The Social and Economic Consequences of Unification." Translated by James L. McClain. In Hall, *Early Modern Japan*, 96–127.

Wigen, Kären. "Mapping Early Modernity: Geographical Meditations on a Comparative Concept." *Early Modern Japan* 5, no. 2 (December 1995): 1–13.

Yanabu Akira. *Hon'yakugo seiritsu jijō*. Iwanami Shoten, 1982.

Yang, Lien-Sheng. "Review of *Chūgoku kinseishi* (History of [early] modern China), by Naitō Torajirō, and *Chūgoku shigakushi* (History of Chinese historiography), by Naitō Torajirō." *Far Eastern Quarterly* 12, no. 2 (February 1953): 208–10.

PART I

*

THE CHARACTER OF THE
EARLY MODERN STATE

I

The End of Civil War and the Formation of the Early Modern State in Japan

MORGAN PITELKA

To Pacify the Realm

The year 1573 is a notable turning point in Japanese history.[1] We might see it as the rough midpoint of the adult career of the warlord and first "unifier" of the late sixteenth century, Oda Nobunaga (1534–82). Having made his rather showy entrance in 1560 with the defeat of the army of his neighbor Imagawa Yoshimoto, Nobunaga had systematically elevated his name, position, and influence through aggressive military campaigns, political manipulation, and acts of cultural patronage in the years that followed. In the first month of 1573, however, Nobunaga was not the only brash leader striving for power and influence. He faced the opposition of the shogun, Ashikaga Yoshiaki, whom he had installed in 1568 and who now resisted his attempts at control; a diverse array of rival warlords who deplored his vision of a realm pacified in Nobunaga's name; and an armed and organized religious sect set against any attempt to achieve a unified and secular warrior authority. There was little reason at that moment to imagine that stable governance, let alone peace, was possible, or that Nobunaga would be "the first to begin cutting through the thick forest of wars and discord in Japan."[2]

One of the fiercest challengers to Nobunaga was the warlord Takeda Shingen (1521–73), ruler of Kai and Shinano Provinces and an experienced commander. Shingen's record of battlefield prowess made him appear unstoppable. In 1571, for example, he had easily invaded the territory of Nobunaga's ally Tokugawa Ieyasu (1543–1616) and could have eliminated the young warlord, but chose instead to withdraw.[3] Similarly, in early 1573, Shingen handily

---

[1] In fact, Asao Naohiro called out this year as the final one of the medieval period in his essay in the previous iteration of *The Cambridge History of Japan*. Asao, "Sixteenth-Century Unification," 43.

[2] Cooper, *João Rodrigues's Account*, 132.

[3] Nakamura, *Tokugawa Ieyasu monjo*, 1:165.

defeated Ieyasu's armies on a second occasion, this time spread out over a much larger area and well reinforced by Nobunaga's troops. Yet again Shingen opted to pull out his troops rather than destroy his exposed enemy.[4] This was a fortuitous turn for Nobunaga, as Shingen died several months later, apparently of natural causes, without having the chance to mount a direct assault on the Oda armies.

The largely irrelevant Ashikaga shogunate also came to an end in 1573. Ashikaga Yoshiaki, the young shogun whom Nobunaga had installed as part of his initial bid for power, had recently intensified his attempts to establish his independence from Nobunaga, going so far as to turn openly against the warlord and call on rival military men to support him on the battlefield. Nobunaga responded by sending his generals to attack those who had aided Yoshiaki and by personally leading an invasion of the imperial capital of Kyoto to compel the shogun to submit. The Oda lord was relentless in his demonstration of force, burning huge swaths of the northern district of Kyoto and allowing his soldiers to indiscriminately burn down structures (reportedly as many as 7,000 of them) and to slaughter civilian residents.[5] After briefly yielding, Yoshiaki fled to a nearby castle, prompting Nobunaga to attack the fortress with an enormous army, capture the shogun, and send him into exile. "'Let future generations be my judge,' Nobunaga said."[6]

Next the Oda lord turned to two hostile warlords to the north of the capital region: the Asakura, based in Echizen Province, and the Azai, based in Ōmi Province. Both had encouraged the independence of Shogun Yoshiaki and had collaboratively resisted Nobunaga's previous military advances. He laid siege to the Azai stronghold, Odani Castle, and when the Asakura sent forces to assist their allies, Nobunaga led his armies in an invasion of Echizen, toppling castles and fortifications easily with his vastly superior numbers, and either killing local commanders or bringing them into his own forces. Eventually the leader of the Asakura house was killed, and his head was sent to Kyoto for public display. Moving back into Ōmi Province, Nobunaga directed his forces to assault Odani Castle again; within days, the heads of the Azai leader, Hisamasa, and his father, Nagamasa, were likewise sent to the capital to be displayed.

These are hardly the most famous acts of Nobunaga's career, yet 1573 must be seen as a turning point not only in his attempt to pacify Japan but

[4] Morita Kōji, "Mikatagahara no tatakai."
[5] Lamers, *Japonius Tyrannus*, 95.
[6] See Ōta, *Chronicle of Lord Nobunaga*, for the English translation, and Ōta, *Shinchō kōki*, bk. 6, sec. 8, p. 189 for the original Japanese.

also in the shift from a politics of violence at the regional level to a kind of total embrace of warfare across the archipelago, a zenith of the era known in Japanese as Sengoku and in English as "the age of warring states." Nobunaga's successes continued for a decade after this point, with the defeat of the Nagashima confederation, the elimination of the militant Ikkō sect, and the destruction of the Takeda house. Moreover, he embarked on a range of administrative reforms that would be expanded upon by his successors; in 1580, he restructured his warrior organization, ordered the commencement of castle demolition in Yamato, Settsu, and Kawachi Provinces, and required landowners in Yamato to submit reports on their land taxes, all seen as early iterations of what would become key centralizing policies.

Still, the most obvious legacy of Nobunaga was not his centralizing impulse, but his tyrannical and violent tendencies, and in particular his brutality; power, for Nobunaga, was expressed largely through force. When the monks of Mount Hiei sheltered the forces of the Asakura and the Azai in 1571, Nobunaga responded by ordering his armies to burn to the ground the temples scattered across the mountain. Worse than this desecration was his commitment to kill all noncombatants guilty of aiding his enemies:

> One by one they cut off the heads of priests and laymen, children, wise men, and holy men alike. They presented the heads to Lord Nobunaga, saying: "Here is an exalted prelate, a princely abbot, a learned doctor, all the men of renown at the top of Mount Hiei." Moreover, they captured countless beautiful women and boys, and led them before Nobunaga. "We don't care about the evil monks," they shrieked, "but spare us!" Nobunaga, however, absolutely refused to reprieve them. One by one, they had their heads chopped off, a scene horrible to behold. Thousands of corpses lay scattered about like so many little sticks, a pitiful end.[7]

The next day Nobunaga commanded his gunners, who bore arquebuses, to go into the woods and hunt any surviving stragglers. The goal here was not simply sending a political message, as was commonly seen in the practice of displaying the heads of defeated rivals, but rather the spread of terror.

Perhaps unsurprisingly, force was also Nobunaga's undoing. In 1582, Nobunaga's own general Akechi Mitsuhide betrayed his liege, leading to the suicide of both Nobunaga and his heir Nobutada, and bringing to an end the Oda lord's campaign to pacify the realm. The method of Nobunaga's demise – surrounded by hostile warriors while staying in a temple in Kyoto, preparing for a monumental invasion of western Japan – aptly reflects his own occasionally

---

[7] Ōta, *Chronicle of Lord Nobunaga*, 165–66.

Machiavellian approach to achieving peace and fits his reputation as a brutal warlord who would use any means to reach his goals. Nobunaga's violent and untimely death also serves as a useful reminder that the late sixteenth century was hardly a smooth process of "early modern transformation" or even "unification." Rather, the path from an age in which warlords operated as relatively autonomous agents, habitually engaging in acts of riotous medieval pageantry and fierce regional conquest, to one in which one warrior family bullied the assorted powers of the archipelago into an uneasy federation was volatile and contingent.

United under One Sole Leader

In his magisterial *Historia da Igreja do Japão* (1620–21), the Jesuit missionary João Rodrigues (c. 1562–1633) identifies Toyotomi Hideyoshi as the key individual in the transformation of Japan from rule by "tyrants who had usurped the kingdom by force of arms" to being "united under one sole leader in peace and quiet."[8] Hideyoshi, who rose to prominence as a warlord ruling a fief in northern Ōmi and as a general serving Oda Nobunaga, accomplished this goal through an impressive mix of political skill, military guile, and cultural patronage. Many of his attributes were surely learned from Nobunaga: the willingness to deploy violence quickly or when necessary on an unusually massive scale; the intention to carefully control his own vassals and to meticulously manage his growing portfolio of land and armies; and the deep pleasures as well as the utility of collecting and displaying the treasures of the past and present. In the aftermath of Nobunaga's death in 1582, Hideyoshi also revealed new talents, such as the ability to forge alliances with dangerous rivals and thus forestall both war and the expenditure of valuable resources. His brilliant balancing of the twin tools of "conquest and conciliation" made him one of Japan's most influential and successful individual rulers.[9]

Hideyoshi acted swiftly to avenge Nobunaga's death and propel himself to a position of prominence, gathering his forces alongside those of his allies to destroy the turncoat's army in a rapid display of his ability to lead. He moved quickly to cement his influence over the capital city of Kyoto, but many of Hideyoshi's peers were not immediately convinced of his capacity to provide the stability and direction required to pacify the realm. The warlord Shibata Katsuie, in particular, was hostile toward Hideyoshi and

[8] Cooper, *They Came to Japan*, 132–33.
[9] Berry, *Hideyoshi*, 66–67.

seemed to be building a coalition against him. In early 1583, Katsuie and his allies appeared to have outwitted Hideyoshi, attacking some of his troops while he was engaged in a distant campaign and thus was seemingly unable to respond. Hideyoshi's response – driving his most trusted vassals and their men through a harrowing night march in order to launch a successful surprise counterstrike – demonstrated his complete commitment to achieving his goal of pacifying Japan.

After Hideyoshi's elimination of Katsuie, only a few major warlords in central Japan still resisted his calls for unity. The most notable, perhaps, was Tokugawa Ieyasu, another general who had served alongside Oda Nobunaga and who now ruled a large and expanding domain as he absorbed the land and soldiers of the defeated Takeda house. Despite Hideyoshi's growing list of military victories, his forces were unable to defeat Ieyasu's army in the Battles of Komaki and Nagakute in 1584, and in fact the second of these conflicts resulted in the death of three of Hideyoshi's commanders. Hideyoshi here displayed his flexibility; having failed to comprehensively defeat Ieyasu on the battlefield, he turned instead to a war of diplomacy, flattery, and trickery to woo his cooperation. Over the course of a year, Hideyoshi flooded Ieyasu with letters, courted his vassals (and successfully recruited some of them to switch sides), and in the end offered his own mother as a guarantee to ease Ieyasu's fear of a trap. The Tokugawa lord finally gave in, and in 1586 ritually acknowledged Hideyoshi's lordship, and thereafter loyally supported Hideyoshi's activities near and far, no matter how grandiose or unlikely. Again, Hideyoshi had managed to avoid a protracted conflict and instead added an experienced and powerful ally to his roster of supporters. Similarly, in his conquest of Shikoku and his pacification of the province of Etchū, he acquired powerful generals by demonstrating the generous benevolence of an aspiring ruler rather than the petty ruthlessness of a warlord.

Significant expanses of the Japanese archipelago had not yet accepted Hideyoshi's rule, and he turned next to a massive invasion of Kyushu in 1587. Although the campaign occupied half of the year, the result now seems almost predetermined because of the size of Hideyoshi's army, which may have numbered as high as 250,000 men drawn from the ranks of the many generals who had joined his cause during the five years since Nobunaga's death. In addition to swelling the already significant size of his military forces, conquering Kyushu created the opportunity for Hideyoshi to weigh in on the issue of Jesuit activity in Japan. In two edicts issued that year, he first announced that Jesuits had broken the "Buddhist Law in these Precincts of the Sun" and should leave Japan within twenty days. "Japan is the Land of

the Gods. Diffusion here from the Kirishitan [Christian] Country of a pernicious doctrine is most undesirable," he announced.[10] Trade with the Europeans could continue, as well as other interactions that would not "disturb
Buddhism." Next, he clarified his policy for an internal Japanese audience by
outlawing practices of Japanese warrior elites who associated with the Jesuits:
forced conversion of peasants and retainers; slavery, notably the sale of Japanese prisoners and hostages to European merchants trafficking in humans
throughout East Asia; and slaughter of cows and horses for food. He justified
these restrictions in part with reference to the religious uprisings of the Ikkō
sectarians who had beleaguered Nobunaga and represented an institutional
as well as military threat to unification. Religious orders should serve the
state, Hideyoshi implied, rather than external masters of any kind. The fundamental suspicion of Christianity as a vanguard for military invasion that
would motivate the Tokugawa to create broad policies of exclusion and suppression in the seventeenth century thus originated in the earlier aspirations
of the unifiers to exert total control.[11]

The final military barrier to the pacification of the realm was the Hōjō
family, ensconced in a mighty castle in Odawara, where they ruled over the
distant but expansive eastern provinces. Hideyoshi made multiple unsuccessful peace overtures to the Hōjō before launching his assault in 1590. He sent
Tokugawa Ieyasu, who had long been neighbor to the Hōjō and had enjoyed
largely friendly relations, to prepare a base for the assault that included a
tea pavilion for the entertainment of the Toyotomi generals. Indeed, the
campaign took months, reaching its conclusion with a Hōjō surrender in the
seventh month of the year. The heads of Ujimasa, the family patriarch, and
his brother Ujiteru were displayed for all to see in Kyoto, a clear example of
Hideyoshi's communicating to both his fellow warlords and to the general
public in the imperial capital that his military might was not to be challenged.
The realm had now been pacified under one sole ruler.

Hideyoshi's outsized influence extended beyond the battlefield to reshape
social and political procedures as well as cultural practices. He enacted a
range of policies that aimed to demilitarize the population at large and to
create social stability through relative occupational stasis. In 1587, he forbade

[10] Elison, *Deus Destroyed*, 115–16.
[11] It is well established that the unifiers were suspicious of the true motivations of Iberian
missionaries, in particular. See, for example, Fukansai Habian's *Myōtei mondō* (1605), in
which Myōshū notes that "it is said that spreading Christian teaching throughout Japan
in this fashion is nothing but a deceptive ruse to capture Japan." Baskind and Bowring,
Myōtei Dialogues, 191–92. Thanks to Drisana Misra for bringing this quotation to my
attention.

warlords from waging war upon one another in the name of private redress; only conflict that served the needs of the realm – in other words, Hideyoshi – would be authorized. This policy was extended to commoners in the following year in edicts preventing the resolution of private conflicts through violence. Also, in 1588, Hideyoshi issued orders confiscating weapons from the agriculturalists of the archipelago, ostensibly to maintain peace and more pointedly to allow cultivators to focus on their labor. He likewise aimed to separate the warrior population from the farming communities many still were connected to by separating the work of war from the labor of agriculture, and outlawing, in 1591, movement between the two social groupings. Alongside these policies of social governance and national pacification, Hideyoshi ordered a land survey on a scale previously unknown. This survey served to reinforce the centralization of control over land occupancy and production, and to measure possible taxation, corvée labor imposition, and other forms of extraction by the state. Resistance to these measures was not to be tolerated. Hideyoshi's commanders were instructed to cut down commoners who opposed his policies.

A range of cultural practices were similarly transformed through Hideyoshi's intense interest, patronage, and in some cases, spectacular performances. In the world of tea, for example, he worked to amass the largest and most impressive collection of tea utensils since the decline of the Ashikaga shogunate in the late fifteenth century. He then choreographed elaborate opportunities for the display of this assemblage of imported and antique treasures to key constituencies. In 1583, he hosted a massive tea gathering at Daitokuji, one of the most influential religious and cultural centers in Kyoto, at which hundreds of tea practitioners, elite warlords, and members of his own military retinue exhibited their utensil collections and engaged in tea rituals under the guidance of the two tea masters Sen no Rikyū (1522–91) and Tsuda Sōgyū (d. 1591).[12] He staged a similar performance at the imperial court in 1585 after attaining the rank of imperial chancellor (*kanpaku*), an unprecedented accomplishment for a warrior. In 1587, he arranged the famous Grand Kitano Tea Gathering. The event involved hundreds of participants (many of whom attended because the nationwide invitation explicitly threatened those who passed with banishment from the tea world), and this large and heterogeneous group became the audience for Hideyoshi's performance of tea ritual as well as his exhibition of tea utensils. Similarly, in the fields of falconry, Noh theater, warrior banqueting, and even the ritual exchange of gifts,

---

[12] Nagashima, *Tennōjiya kaiki*, 409–11.

Hideyoshi engaged with a combination of personal passion and ruthlessness tinged by the threat of violence to transform practices that had often been the pursuits of private individuals into spectacular displays of power.

The venues for Hideyoshi's activities proliferated over the course of his career, though few have survived into the present. He began construction of a magisterial castle in Osaka in 1583, influenced by Nobunaga's model at Azuchi, and within a year Hideyoshi was able to use the site for tea activities. Construction continued for many years – at great expense and through the toil of tens of thousands of laborers – until the castle ultimately became the most secure fortified structure in Japan, with a huge stone foundation, an inner donjon with numerous palatial structures, including a massive central keep of eight stories (five above ground and three below), and multiple moats and defensive walls. Hideyoshi deliberately chose for this castle a site at the mouth of the Yodo River, the former location of the headquarters of the Ishiyama Honganji, a militant Buddhist sect that had resisted efforts at pacification. The castle became not only the center of the Toyotomi administrative world but an economic hub as well, and the town that rapidly developed around the fortress grew into one of early modern Japan's great cities. Hideyoshi used the castle regularly, as a residence, military headquarters, and stage for a dizzying range of cultural performances. More bluntly, the castle itself served as a baroque pronouncement of the wealth and power of the Toyotomi, articulated in the sumptuous exterior decorations, which included lacquer and gilding on an unprecedented scale.

Hideyoshi also needed a power base in the imperial capital where much of his activity was centered, and so in early 1586 he commenced the construction of a massive fortified palace named Jurakudai, strategically placed in central Kyoto on the former site of the Heian-era imperial palace, another conspicuous act of geographic politicking. The structure was completed after eighteen months and reportedly had stone walls "like a mountain," a main tower "decorated with stars," and a stage – presumably for the performance of Noh plays – in the garden. "The splendor was exceedingly great."[13] Despite its splendor, Jurakudai lasted less than a decade because of its role in one of Hideyoshi's most infamous dramas. In 1591, Hideyoshi made his nephew Hidetsugu (1568–95) heir after his own first son, Tsurumatsu, had tragically died while still a toddler. Hidetsugu received the court title of chancellor and took up residence in Jurakudai, and from this base he played an active role in the ceremonial life of the court and among the elite

[13] Stavros, *Kyoto*, 159.

merchants and warriors of Kyoto. In late 1593, however, Hideyoshi's main concubine Chacha (Yodo-dono) gave birth to another son, Hideyori, which immediately put Hidetsugu's position in doubt. Hidetsugu reportedly increased the size of his guard and tried to guarantee that certain warlords would remain loyal to him. However, his attempts to protect himself only provided Hideyoshi with the pretext he needed to eliminate his nephew and clear the way for his own son. In the seventh month of 1595, he sent Hidetsugu into exile on Mount Kōya and soon thereafter ordered the young man to take his own life. In addition, he arranged for the dismantling of Jurakudai and the murder of Hidetsugu's entire family in an attempt to completely wipe away Hidetsugu's legacy and prevent any possible future challenge to Hideyori.[14]

In fact, this rather gruesome Hidetsugu affair points to a larger shift in the second half of Hideyoshi's career, after he had seemingly accomplished all that a warlord in sixteenth-century Japan could have hoped for: military and political pacification of the realm, the glorification of himself and his family through court promotions, the attainment of unimaginable wealth, and repeated and celebrated cultural accomplishments. In early 1592, Hideyoshi commanded the warlords of Japan to take part in an unprovoked and unnecessary invasion of the Asian continent, with the ostensible goal of conquering the Ming empire. Troops were mobilized from across the archipelago, a castle that would serve as the base of operations was built along the coast of Kyushu, and attacks were launched on Chosǒn Korea, Japan's longtime peaceful neighbor, for failing to "join Japan" in a unified attack on the Great Ming. In the opening days of the conflict, Japan's vanguard army, led by Sō Yoshitoshi and Konishi Yukinaga, took the port city of Pusan, with Korean casualties reported to be as high as 30,000.[15] Although Japanese troops enjoyed initial success and efficaciously captured both Seoul and P'yŏng-yang, resistance from the Korean armed forces and navy in particular was significant, and from late 1592 to early 1593, Chinese reinforcements from the Ming empire arrived and forced the Japanese to withdraw to the southern tip of the peninsula. Hideyoshi issued a set of demands that he expected to be forwarded to the Chinese court, but his generals and negotiators in Korea forged a conciliatory letter requesting, instead, investiture as "King of Japan."[16]

---

[14] See Berry's description and analysis of these events in *Hideyoshi*, 217–23.
[15] Haboush, *Great East Asian War*, 28–29.
[16] See Elisonas's detailed account, "Inseperable Trinity," 282–84.

Amid this instability, Hideyoshi seems to have felt the need to clarify his control over the realm, particularly after the affair with Hidetsugu. In late 1592, while the severed heads of Hidetsugu and thirty members of his family were still on public display in Kyoto, Hideyoshi commanded his chief generals to put brush to paper and sign regulations that were sent out to all of the major warlords. This document and its supplements, titled simply "The Lord's Laws" (*On'okite*), has been referred to by one historian as "a sort of Toyotomi constitution."[17] The document clearly stipulates the power relations between Hideyoshi and his followers and reveals a growing paranoia. "All warlords should obtain permission from his Lordship for marriages," for example, and "Warlords and minor lords must stop accumulating compacts and written oaths" both speak to Hideyoshi's concern that warrior leaders could conceivably use the tried and true techniques of alliance building to create a coalition against him. Other regulations seem to micromanage the lives of his followers to a surprising degree, considering Hideyoshi's own excesses. "Those of humble station as well as members of the warlord class must not maintain great numbers of wives," for example, is unexpected considering how widespread polygamy was among elite warrior families. Another conservative regulation, "Drinking paraphernalia must be limited, and heavy drinking is proscribed," seems to indicate a slide into a form of Confucian moralism, which is relatively unusual for Hideyoshi, who turned more often to the deities of Buddhism and Shinto for legitimacy.[18] A set of supplementary articles was soon released, in which the basic principle of Toyotomi control is extended to the main late-medieval stakeholders: warriors, nobles, temples and shrines, and peasants. They also begin to clarify the relationship between rank and social deportment by stipulating that warrior behavior and conspicuous consumption should correlate with land ownership. Restrictions on the number of spouses, the use of valuable symbols in clothing, and luxuries such as palanquin use and alcohol consumption prefigure the complicated sumptuary regimes that would be established in the seventeenth century, but here come across as rather uncomplicated manifestations of warrior ideas about how rank should manifest in the public sphere. The position of the warlords who signed these documents (sometimes referred to as the Five

---

[17] Berry, *Hideyoshi*, 144–45. Berry also translates a different version of this "code of articles" under the title "The Wall Writings of Osaka Castle," based on the text provided in the 1914 collection *Hōkō ibun*. I have rendered my own translations based on the Bunroku 4/8/2 version presented in Nakamura, *Tokugawa Ieyasu monjo*, 2:270.

[18] Ooms, *Tokugawa Ideology*, 47–50.

Elders, or *gotairō*)[19] is also significant; they acted as a kind of buffer between the outside world and Hideyoshi, receiving and adjudicating special complaints and, if necessary, bringing them to the Toyotomi lord's attention.

It was unsustainable for Japanese troops to continue to occupy the southern portion of the Korean peninsula, and in fact Ming Chinese leaders seem to have embarked on a plan to both prepare for a renewal in hostilities while simultaneously engaging in diplomacy. In 1596, two Chinese envoys traveled to Japan to negotiate with Hideyoshi in person, which the Toyotomi lord interpreted as a sign that the Chinese empire was willing to meet some of his demands. He aimed to host the diplomats in a newly constructed reception hall in Fushimi Castle, located in the southern district of Kyoto. A major earthquake on the thirteenth day of the seventh month of 1596, however, spoiled his plans and toppled the structure as well as a range of buildings across the capital.[20] As one diarist put it, "As for Fushimi, his lordship's castle and gate were destroyed or at least knocked down, and the central keep is completely leveled. A multitude of men, women, and inner guards are dead, of a number that is not yet known."[21] Hideyoshi remained determined and relocated the negotiations to Osaka Castle, expecting acknowledgement of his peer status with the Ming emperor at the least. Instead, he received material and documentary confirmation of his status as a vassal of the Ming.[22] Perhaps worse was the failure of the Korean court to provide a royal prince as hostage. Fearing that failure in Korea could threaten his own standing as hegemon, Hideyoshi relaunched his aggressive war on the Korean peninsula, still claiming the goal of conquering China as his ultimate aim.[23] More than 70,000 samurai who had stayed in Korea since 1593 were joined by a similarly sized force from Japan, and these troops renewed hostilities in the summer of 1597. The Japanese again enjoyed some success, even on the naval front, at the beginning of this second wave of conflicts, but the large relief force sent by the Ming and the Korean troops, combined with the victories of the Korean navy, soon forced the Japanese armies to retreat to their fortresses.[24] The Japanese still enjoyed some further victories but were primarily on the defensive.

---

[19] See Asao, "Sixteenth-Century Unification," 87–89.

[20] See the geologist Iida Kumeji's exhaustive study of the event. Iida, *Tenshō daijishin shi.*

[21] Kurokawa and Noda, "Fushimi jō to jōkamachi," 334–35.

[22] Zoku Gunsho Ruijū Kanseikai, *Tōdaiki,* 68–69. See also Berry, *Hideyoshi,* 232–33; Elisonas, "Inseparable Trinity," 284–85; and Swope, *Dragon's Head and a Serpent's Tail,* 221–26, for useful summaries in English.

[23] Kitajima, "Imjin Waeran," 82–83; Sajima, "Hideyoshi's View of Chosŏn Korea," 102–5.

[24] See Yi, "Role of the Chosŏn Navy," and Nukii, "Righteous Army Activity," for details on Korean activities during the second invasion.

An Unstable Transition

In 1598, Hideyoshi's health began to deteriorate rapidly, and by the middle of the year he seemed unlikely to make a recovery.[25] In the sixth and seventh months, the imperial court engaged in semipublic performances that were intended to appeal to the gods for his recuperation, but he did not improve. In his final months, Hideyoshi became obsessed with somehow guaranteeing that a smooth process of succession would be inscribed in the order of the world he had created; he repeatedly assembled various lords of the realm to promise loyalty and sign oaths of fealty to his only living heir, Hideyori.[26] On the eighteenth day of the eighth month of 1598, the retired regent (*taikō*) Hideyoshi died at the age of sixty-three, leaving behind a polity transformed by the force of his will and personality, but fragile in its makeup.

The documentary record provides little evidence that Hideyoshi's vassals had any intention other than to honor their vows to the Toyotomi lord. However, tension among the two groups of vassals – the Five Elders and the Five Magistrates (*gobugyō*) – emerged immediately after Hideyoshi's passing, implying that at the very least Toyotomi loyalty did not equate to an ethos of cooperation among rivals. For example, Tokugawa Ieyasu's son Hidetada left for Edo on the nineteenth day of the eighth month, apparently an attempt to keep the two senior Tokugawa lords separate in case of an attack on either, while also guaranteeing the stability of Edo in this time of uncertainty. The move was perhaps a wise one, as several sources report that Ishida Mitsunari, one of the Five Magistrates, made preparations to launch an attack on Ieyasu the same day, but then for unknown reasons opted not to engage.[27]

A more pressing matter was the war in Korea. The Five Elders worked together to smother all news of Hideyoshi's death while also recalling Japanese forces from the continent. They sent two envoys to carry out and oversee the retreat.[28] They also sent a stream of letters to warriors in Korea in an effort to coordinate the massive demobilization as well as perpetuate the fiction that Hideyoshi was recovering from his illness and wanted only amity on the continent. They explained that the general Katō Kiyomasa or an alternate would be responsible for arranging peace negotiations, which should include transfer to Japan as hostage a Korean prince or suitable members of the nobility. Three of the Five Magistrates would travel to Hakata and cross over to

---

[25] Nakamura, *Tokugawa Ieyasu monjo*, 2:290–93.
[26] See Berry's narrative of this, including translations of the relevant documents. Berry, *Hideyoshi*, 234–35.
[27] Nakamura, *Tokugawa Ieyasu monjo*, 2:323.
[28] Nakamura, *Tokugawa Ieyasu monjo*, 2:235–326.

Korea if necessary.[29] The speed of this decision is startling; within a week of
Hideyoshi's passing, his chief lieutenants acted to reverse his most ambitious
and farthest-reaching policy, a clear indication of elite warrior opposition to
the six-year-old occupation and war. Although it would take several months
for the Japanese troops to return, and not without sustaining significant
losses, East Asia's largest international conflict since the Mongol invasion of
the thirteenth century finally ended late in the twelfth month of 1598.[30]

The costs of the war were devastating, particularly for Korea. Japanese
troops in the final year of the conflict ritually massacred not only enemy combatants but large numbers of civilians, on previous orders from Hideyoshi. In
a variation on military decapitation, as was standard practice in late medieval
Japanese warfare, Hideyoshi demanded that his forces in Korea "cut off noses
instead of heads," and the generals in command of enormous armies translated this directive into action by issuing quotas to their soldiers.[31] After desecrating military and civilian victims, soldiers submitted their trophies to their
commanders and received receipts as acknowledgement of their exploits.
One extant example from 1597 records that a samurai received a receipt for
submitting 365 noses; this dry and bureaucratic accounting of the unimaginable death and destruction that Japanese armies inflicted on the residents
of the Korean peninsula is relatively typical of the culture of warfare at this
moment in Japanese history, but the effects are amplified by the context of an
unprompted and unprecedented invasion of a neighbor. The army of samurai
took more than noses, as well, systematically looting the cultural heritage of
Korean families and institutions and kidnapping Korean artisans and civilians.
As with the infamous trophy-taking, this was not random plundering, but a
policy promulgated by Hideyoshi to his generals at the beginning of the war
that only increased in urgency once it became clear that a total withdrawal
from the continent would mean no permanent land acquisitions and no further resource extraction. Confucian texts and Confucian scholars, printed
books and metal-type presses, treasured ceramics as well as the potters who
produced them: the Japanese strategy was to plunder not only the material
treasures of Korea but the means of production themselves. All in all, as many
as 100,000 people may have been trafficked from Korea back to Japan as a

[29] See, for example, the elders' letters to Kuroda Nagamasa (329–30), Shimazu Yoshihiro and
his son Tadatsune (331–32), and Mōri Yoshinari plus five of his peers (332–34). Nakamura,
Tokugawa Ieyasu monjo, vol. 2.
[30] The withdrawal was a brutal process, best described by Elisonas, "Inseperable Trinity,"
288–93.
[31] Kitajima, "Imjin Waeran," 85–86.

result of the Imjin War, and although negotiations did result in some repatriations, scholars believe the total number of Koreans who returned was less than 7,000.[32]

The rapid withdrawal from Korea left Japan's military leadership in some disarray, with many generals dissatisfied with the sudden command to retreat and others relieved to be done with a long and unwanted conflict. Japan was at peace through the momentum of Hideyoshi's determination to create stability, but the condition was ephemeral. Although some historians narrate the rise of Tokugawa Ieyasu following Hideyoshi's death as a foregone conclusion, his activities in early 1599 point to his ongoing resolve to work with the other elders and even the Five Magistrates to ensure the stability of the realm. Ieyasu's position was, after all, already quite secure. He was the most powerful landholder in all of Japan, with territory valued at approximately 2,557,000 koku. Closest to him in wealth was Mōri Terumoto, who possessed land valued at approximately 1,205,000 koku, a huge domain that still was less than half the size of Ieyasu's. The land of another elder, Uesugi Kagekatsu, amounted to approximately the same value as Terumoto's. All of the Five Magistrates, by comparison, governed less than 1,000,000 koku of land combined, making them considerably smaller and weaker in terms of both rank and power. Hideyoshi's son Hideyori commanded significant resources in theory but was only a toddler being warily protected by his mother.

Why, then, did Ieyasu begin consolidating more and more power in his own hands over the course of 1599? One factor was perhaps the tension between the rules and regulations of the Toyotomi bureaucracy and Ieyasu's desire to act independently, particularly after so many decades of subservience to warlords who were only slightly older and more powerful than him. Since his emergence onto the field of warrior politics, Ieyasu had been almost continually pledged first to Nobunaga and then to Hideyoshi, a position in the hierarchical warrior society of sixteenth-century Japan that required that he defer to their judgment. Hideyoshi's death was certainly not celebrated by Ieyasu, who favored political constancy over all else, but it did offer him the opportunity to make decisions that otherwise would have been subject to the approval of his liege. For example, Ieyasu wanted to engage in marriage politics freely, without interference from Toyotomi vassals who were observing the laws set down by Hideyoshi but who were also lower ranking than the Tokugawa lord. He therefore arranged secret marriages between

---

[32] Ha, "War and Cultural Exchange"; Haboush and Robinson, *Korean War Captive in Japan*, ix.

his children and the children of a number of warlord allies.[33] This came to the attention of the other elders and the magistrates gathered in Osaka. They determined that they could not overlook this flagrant infringement, so they sent a representative to Ieyasu's residence in Fushimi to make the accusation directly. Ieyasu, however, responded forcefully, rebutting the suggestion that he was defying Hideyoshi's wishes. He argued that he had been appointed as Hideyori's counselor and would never disobey the orders left behind by the Toyotomi lord. Perhaps, he threatened, he should retire immediately and pass on power to his son Hidetada. The marriages were, he concluded, an entirely forgettable incident. When the emissary left, Ieyasu immediately began assembling loyal warriors at his residence until a large army occupied the entire neighborhood. Ieyasu's accusers, overwhelmed by his skilled display of political rhetoric and his obvious military superiority, quickly backed down and announced that Ieyasu's arrangement of marriages was not a problem. The Five Magistrates even went so far as to shave their heads in an act of humble remorsefulness and issued written oaths to Ieyasu reassuring him of their commitment to observing Hideyoshi's wishes.[34] Ieyasu emerged from this conflict in an even more elevated and superior position than he had previously occupied.

Perhaps the most compelling factor in Ieyasu's increasing occupation of the center of the political stage was the outright aggression of the magistrate Ishida Mitsunari, lord of Sawayama in Ōmi Province and one of Hideyoshi's most trusted vassals. Mitsunari was ambitious and may have seen Ieyasu's experience as a threat to Hideyori's future. Ieyasu cannot have been unaware of Mitsunari's hostility but does not appear to have been perturbed by it in the early months after Hideyoshi's death. However, Mitsunari became increasingly menacing in the new year. In the third month of 1599, when Ieyasu was visiting Maeda Toshiie in Osaka, word spread that Mitsunari was planning to attack the Tokugawa lord while he was exposed traveling through the city. Ieyasu, however, had traveled with a sizeable retinue, and Mitsunari's associates apparently lost confidence in the plan. Mitsunari next developed a plot to attack Ieyasu in his own residence in Fushimi. Because it was located in a relatively low spot near the reconstructed Fushimi Castle, Mitsunari reckoned that he could set fire to the buildings from a strategic location on higher ground. Word spread, and generals loyal to Ieyasu convinced him that this threat was serious enough to merit relocating his headquarters. They

---

[33] Kasaya, *Sekigahara kassen to Ōsaka no jin*, 11.
[34] Kasaya, *Sekigahara kassen.*

recommended a well-protected residence on the other side of the Uji River; Ieyasu agreed and moved to this safer location.[35]

Mitsunari's actions only increased the dissatisfaction of a group of generals, led by Katō Kiyomasa, who had previously objected to the Ishida lord's handling of the retreat from Korea. After Maeda Toshiie's death and Mitsunari's increasingly aggressive actions toward Ieyasu, this group decided to launch an attack against Mitsunari with the goal of eliminating him completely. Mitsunari learned that Kiyomasa and company were gathering forces and decided to leave Osaka Castle and move to his residence inside Fushimi Castle. His would-be attackers pursued him to the gates of the castle, resulting in a tense standoff. Ieyasu, again provoked into autonomous action in order to preserve stability, intervened. He sent Mitsunari into confinement in the Ishida lord's own castle, Sawayama, and convinced the generals to back down. In protecting his enemy, Ieyasu ironically seems to have further increased his own reputation and power, and he officially moved out of his temporary residence and entered the main keep at Fushimi. One diarist, writing about Ieyasu's entry into Fushimi Castle, referred to him as "The Lord of the Realm" (*tenka dono*), a term that had previously been applied to the Ashikaga shoguns and then to Nobunaga and Hideyoshi. Another diarist wrote on this occasion that Ieyasu's move inspired "great joy among all men."[36] Certainly Ieyasu's peers mostly responded to this development in a supportive fashion. Mōri Terumoto, for example, perhaps the most powerful elder after Ieyasu, exchanged written oaths of loyalty with Ieyasu soon after the Tokugawa lord moved into Fushimi Castle.[37]

In a very short period after Hideyoshi's death, Ieyasu emerged as the preeminent warlord of Japan. By the middle of 1599, he stood at the top of the political hierarchy, but gave no indication that he intended to challenge the young Toyotomi Hideyori's claim to succeed his father, or to eliminate Ishida Mitsunari or any other Toyotomi loyalists. As far as can be ascertained from the contemporaneous historical record, Ieyasu still considered himself to be a Toyotomi loyalist, albeit one who felt empowered to arrange

[35] Kasaya, *Sekigahara kassen to Ōsaka no jin*, 13–14. See also multiple references to this event in primary sources collected in Fujii Jizaemon, *Sekigahara kassen shiryōshū*, 105–8.
[36] Many primary sources record different versions of these events. I rely here on Kasaya Kazuhiko, who has made a convincing argument about the actual chronology of Mitsunari's banishment and Ieyasu's actions at Fushimi. See Kasaya, *Sekigahara kassen to Ōsaka no jin*, 15–22. On Ieyasu's entry into Fushimi, see Yamashina, *Tokitsune kyōki*, 11:9:194; and Tsuji, *Tamon'in nikki*, 5:83, entry for Keichō 4/intercalary month 3/14 (recording the events of the previous day).
[37] Nakamura, *Tokugawa Ieyasu monjo*, 2:408–9.

his own alliances through marriage. On the seventh day of the ninth month of 1599, Ieyasu traveled to Osaka Castle and – in what must have been an irksome development for Ishida Mitsunari and his allies – stayed in Ishida's residence.[38] Several days later, perhaps at the urging of court representatives who hoped to calm the increasing tension in Kyoto and Osaka, Ieyasu moved out of Mitsunari's residence and into that of his older brother, Ishida Masazumi.[39] It seemed that Ieyasu intended to govern from Osaka Castle, where he could watch over Hideyori. For those who saw Ieyasu's rise as inevitable, as some must have done, this was a logical next step, but for those who felt the Tokugawa lord was disregarding Hideyoshi's wishes, or who hoped to gain something from such a stance, this move was hard to stomach. Plots against Ieyasu seem to have been abundant, and, in one case, he insisted that two potential rivals – Maeda Toshinaga and Hosokawa Tadaoki – send family members as hostages to Edo to guarantee their loyalty to Ieyasu.

One critical observer of Ieyasu's rise and increasing autonomy was Uesugi Kagekatsu, who had joined the council of elders around the time of Hideyoshi's death. Kagekatsu's recently acquired domain of Aizu (1.2 million *koku*) was located to the north of Ieyasu's Kantō provinces, making, in theory at least, a war against the Tokugawa a major opportunity for Uesugi expansion. Ieyasu was aware that Kagekatsu was busy restoring the defenses of his castles and fortifications in Aizu, which may have been the motivation for his request that Kagekatsu visit him in Osaka in the fourth month.[40] Kagekatsu refused, which put some pressure on Ieyasu as he contemplated the post-Hideyoshi landscape of political power and personal alliances.

Kagekatsu's open defiance proved to be the tipping point that moved Ieyasu away from the position of somewhat grudging occupation of the center of the political stage to open pursuit of military supremacy. In the fifth month, he began to make clear his plan to attack Kagekatsu at Aizu in letters asking vassals to fortify and hold their positions in the northern part of Ieyasu's territory, close to the perimeter with Aizu.[41] Next, in the opening days of the sixth month, Ieyasu wrote to vassals and allies whose domains were located between Kagekatsu's territory and the capital region and informed them of his intent to attack Aizu around the seventh month.[42] He assembled his main commanders and organized the approach and attack plan, for

[38] Tsuji, *Rokuon nichiroku*, Keichō 4/9/7 entry, 3:255–56.
[39] Tsuji, *Rokuon nichiroku*, Keichō 4/9/13 entry (recording the events of the previous day), 3:258.
[40] Kuwata, *Tokugawa Ieyasu*, 179–80.
[41] Nakamura, *Tokugawa Ieyasu monjo*, 2:482.
[42] Nakamura, *Tokugawa Ieyasu monjo*, 2:494, 496.

which he received approval from the court.[43] He also made preparations for his own absence from Osaka, meeting with Toyotomi Hideyori and leaving Sano Tsunamasa in charge of the Nishinomaru residence in his absence from Osaka Castle. On the sixteenth day of the sixth month of 1600 (in what is widely seen as the opening move that would lead to the Battle of Sekigahara), Ieyasu departed Osaka Castle to lead the attack on Aizu. He traveled with his personal force of approximately 3,000 hereditary retainers from his days in Mikawa Province as well as significant numbers of Toyotomi retainers who either felt obligated to Ieyasu or hoped to gain from an invasion of Aizu.[44]

Ishida Mitsunari jumped into action after Ieyasu's departure from Osaka Castle. Within days he had contacted various allies and held a secret meeting to plan anti-Tokugawa activities.[45] He also worked with fellow magistrates and elders to issue a document of impeachment targeting Ieyasu that was sent to warlords across Japan. The list of charges alternates between relatively petty accusations ("He has repeatedly ostracized two of the magistrates [Ishida Mitsunari and Asano Nagamasa], despite signing a pledge of cooperation between the elders and the magistrates") and more serious charges ("He has taken all of the warriors' wives and children as hostages but sent those who are his favorites back to their homes"). The primary complaint is surely the charge regarding marriage alliances: "As for marriage arrangements, he has turned his back on the proscription [left by Hideyoshi] and registered more than anyone knows." In a brief postscript, the magistrates enjoined recipients to come quickly to Hideyori's aid, in light of Ieyasu's intention to attack Uesugi Kagekatsu. Also included was a separate letter from the elders Mōri Terumoto and Ukita Hideie, similarly arguing that Ieyasu had turned his back on Hideyoshi's wishes and that all warlords must stand with Hideyori against Ieyasu.[46]

Ieyasu and his son Hidetada were busy preparing to launch their attack on the Uesugi in Aizu when this document of impeachment was disseminated. Less than a week after departing Edo and heading north, however, Ieyasu learned of the scale of Mitsunari's anti-Tokugawa activities and, after an extended consultation with his generals, decided to cancel the attack on Aizu. Ieyasu returned to Edo Castle, where he would continue for the next month the work of planning for a major conflict and sending out letters to

[43] Nakamura, *Tokugawa Ieyasu monjo*, 2:496.
[44] Kasaya, *Sekigahara kassen: Ieyasu no senryaku*, 58–59.
[45] Fujii Jizaemon, *Sekigahara kassen shiryōshū*, 150.
[46] Fujii Jizaemon, *Sekigahara kassen shiryōshū*, 162–64; see also Nakamura, *Tokugawa Ieyasu monjo*, 2:514–17.

key warlords.[47] Mitsunari, meanwhile, dispatched orders to the growing anti-Tokugawa army, or the Western Army as it was named in the sources, to begin moving toward the east.[48] Ieyasu then began sending advance forces west from the Kantō, and they joined together, forming the Eastern Army, and took various fortresses in and around Gifu. Next, Ieyasu played two very different strategy cards in close succession, revealing the importance of both the reliability of family and the need for politics in his efforts against Mitsunari. On the twenty-fourth he ordered Hidetada, who was awaiting orders in the northern part of the Kantō plain, to begin moving to the west along the Nakasendō, the historic highway that cut through the central, more mountainous regions of Japan. This would lead him and the forces under his command – estimated to have consisted of roughly 39,000 men – to eventually join up with the main Eastern Army now waiting in the Gifu region. Ieyasu also sent a flurry of letters on the following day to the generals who had led the troops of the Eastern Army in the toppling of Gifu Castle, expressing his pleasure at their success and his appreciation for their efforts. The letters are virtually identical in content, sent to the leaders of the campaign as well as lesser-known, mid-level commanders.[49] Ieyasu was always a prodigious letter writer, but his activities in the days leading up to Sekigahara, and particularly this surprisingly generous act of epistolary gratitude in the midst of an ongoing conflict, is striking. Letter writing, it is clear, could powerfully influence the formation of alliances, the preparation for war, and indeed the decisions of individual leaders to take one side or another in a battle.

Having made all of these preparations, Ieyasu finally left Edo in the company of 30,000 men and traveled slowly and quietly to Kiyosu to rejoin the main Eastern Army. Mitsunari had set up his forces around a box-shaped canyon near the post town of Sekigahara, and Ieyasu cautiously moved his forces into the center of this pincer, perhaps anticipating the imminent arrival of his son Hidetada and his additional men. The Battle of Sekigahara, as we now name this conflict, unfolded in the early hours of the fifteenth day of the ninth month in an otherwise unremarkable valley near the town. Ieyasu brought his hereditary Tokugawa vassals, long-time allies, and a wide range of warrior bands that had until recently been in service to the Toyotomi. This was a large and experienced, but hardly united, fighting force. Notably absent was Hidetada and his army of 39,000 troops, who would miss the encounter completely because of his own bad judgments along the way. The fighting

---

[47] Fujii Jizaemon, *Sekigahara kassen shiryōshū*, 195.
[48] Fujii Jizaemon, *Sekigahara kassen shiryōshū*, 207–18.
[49] Nakamura, *Tokugawa Ieyasu monjo*, 2:626–30.

began amid the morning mists and proceeded over several hours, with no clear dominant force. The tide was turned by Ieyasu's letter-writing and networking, as he had successfully influenced two major generals in Mitsunari's army to change sides. As a result, the Western Army was pinned back and eventually scattered, with Mitsunari absconding into the hills.[50]

It is tempting to turn immediately to Ieyasu's appointment to the post of shogun, which of course allowed him to establish a new military government in Edo, an event that is seen by many as the key moment in the shift of Japanese history from a medieval to an early modern phase. Ieyasu's victory at Sekigahara, it is commonly understood, made this appointment possible. It would also be sensible to provide a detailed accounting of the land reassignments that Ieyasu oversaw – the allocation of larger, more prosperous fiefdoms for some warlords and the reduction or confiscation of domains for others – which have come over time to be equated with the establishment of the Tokugawa system, a durable balance between centralized power in the hands of the military government in Edo and regional power in the hands of the warlords. The Tokugawa triumph at Sekigahara, such a juxtaposition implies, led directly and seamlessly to Japan's early modernity and thereby was a key stepping stone on the path to the present.

The view from the sources, however, is quite different. As Ieyasu retired to his bed the night after the battle, it is impossible to imagine that he had the feeling that his work was somehow complete. Rather, he faced the prospects of hunting down the escaped Ishida Mitsunari and attacking the Ishida base at Sawayama; dealing with the Mōri, who might very well have chosen to rally around their kinsman Mōri Terumoto, who was protecting Toyotomi Hideyoshi's heir Hideyori at Osaka Castle; putting down other sources of opposition to Tokugawa rule around the country; and dealing with the contentious and complex politics of the warlords, the court, and other sources of institutional authority in these moments of uncertainty. Having witnessed Nobunaga, at the height of his hegemony and after a long string of numerous victories, betrayed and destroyed in a single evening, Ieyasu must have known better than to assume that his rather fortuitous victory in the valley of Sekigahara necessarily would lead to political triumph. Having seen Hideyoshi, who pacified the country and launched a major war in East Asia only to die of disease long before he had accomplished all that he hoped, Ieyasu knew to plan his steps carefully and proceed with caution. It would thus be profoundly ahistorical to conflate the end of battle in the afternoon of the

[50] Fujii Jizaemon, *Sekigahara kassen shiryōshū*, 501–2.

fifteenth day of the sixth month of 1600 with the reassignment of fiefs, a process that would in fact take years, or the appointment of the shogun and the establishment of the Tokugawa military government, an event that would not occur until 1603.

Instead, we must acknowledge the work expended by Ieyasu and his allies to clean up in the aftermath of Sekigahara, and the extensive campaign of social and cultural engagement with the court that was required to prepare for the creation of a new warrior government. These rituals of sociability demonstrate that the medieval practices of political negotiation and alliance-building, which were so significant during the unification efforts of Nobunaga and Hideyoshi, were similarly formative in the birth of the new early modern regime. The documentary record for the two years after Ieyasu's victory is filled with notations of the Tokugawa lord – first based in Osaka and then in Kyoto – sending gifts to the court, going hawking with his peers, exchanging presents of swords and falcons with allies and potential foes, and hosting theatrical performances for a diverse range of elites that emphasized his magnanimous patronage while also creating pleasurable opportunities for socializing and cultural enrichment. This ostensibly "cultural" labor in fact provided the social scaffolding for the confiscation and reassignment of domains that marked the material transition of the world of Sengoku into the first iteration of an early modern political landscape. His predecessor Hideyoshi had, in the words of Mary Elizabeth Berry, "made domainal rule and power sharing the foundation of his settlement,"[51] and Ieyasu signaled with his patronage of the court that he too would seek not to eliminate traditional structures of authority but rather work through them to attain preeminence for his family and stability for the archipelago.

Tokugawa Governance

In the years after his victory, Ieyasu lived in Kyoto and focused his energy, wealth, and significant political capital on strengthening his relationship with the imperial court and on mollifying the concerns of his rivals. Although Nobunaga and Hideyoshi had both chosen to patronize the court without seeking the traditional role of shogun, Ieyasu seemed committed to the goal of attaining this traditional position with its encompassing authority to establish a new polity. Ieyasu's labor was rewarded in the second month of 1603 with his appointment to the position of Barbarian-quelling Generalissimo

---

[51] Berry, *Hideyoshi*, 165.

(*seii tai shōgun*),[52] empowering him to set up a new military government and become the de facto ruler of all Japan. Rather than traveling straight to Edo, Ieyasu responded by visiting the newly constructed castle at Nijō and first hosting visitations by members of the court, followed by days of Noh performances and banquets at the castle. He ended up staying in the capital region for many months, rotating between residences at Fushimi and Nijō, which allowed him to participate in extensive gift exchanges, the hosting of more performances, patronage of the arts, and other debt-paying and community-building rituals. Finally, toward the end of the tenth month, he set out for Edo. From his new role, he oversaw the implementation of policies – some pioneered by warlords of previous generations, others new innovations of his evolving bureaucracy – that would come to serve as part of the foundation of the Tokugawa order. Planning for land surveys (*kenchi*) to be enacted across the archipelago; the issuance of new codes for temples, shrines, and villages; and the expansion of mining operations all occurred in the subsequent months.

In 1605, the growing administration in Edo Castle was stable enough that Ieyasu felt the time was right to retire from the position of shogun, allowing his son and heir Hidetada to guarantee continuity of Tokugawa rule by receiving the same title from the court. In fact the two had laid the groundwork for this transition going back some time, and they used the late-medieval language of the display of military force to make their intended message clear to all observers: Hidetada traveled to Kyoto to receive his elevated court appointment in the company of approximately 100,000 Tokugawa soldiers.[53] With this ritual succession, buttressed by the overwhelming display of his family's undisputed military might, Ieyasu could perhaps hope that the types of succession crises that had harmed the political ambitions of Nobunaga and Hideyoshi would never occur in his family. Of course, the sound strategical thinking displayed in this decision should not distract us from the reality that Ieyasu was, until his death in 1616, an absolute military dictator who trusted almost no one around him, and his family's monopoly on the position of shogun, which would of course continue until 1868, provided stable governance only under the ceaseless threat of mass violence.

The only remaining serious risk to long-term Tokugawa hegemony, other than the possibility of internal strife, was the ongoing health and activity of

---

[52] Nakamura, *Tokugawa Ieyasu monjo*, 3:305–6.
[53] Tōkyō Daigaku Shiryō Hensanjo, *Dai Nihon shiryō*, series 12, vol. 2, beginning on 974, Keichō 10/2/24 entry.

Toyotomi Hideyori and his politically influential mother Chacha (1567–1615), the main concubine of Hideyoshi. Attention usually focuses on Hideyori as the heir of Hideyoshi, but we must take seriously the threat posed to the Tokugawa by his mother as well, a useful example of the constrained but still influential elite women active in the world of late medieval warrior politics. Part of Chacha's power originated in her pedigree; her father was the warlord Azai Nagamasa, whom Nobunaga had destroyed in 1573 as part of his campaign to unify the realm, and her mother was Nobunaga's younger sister, known as Oichi-no-kata. Chacha and her sisters were remarkable survivors. Their mother managed to escape the destruction of Odani Castle with her daughters, and the women took refuge at Kiyosu Castle under the protection of Oda Nobukane, a younger brother of Nobunaga's. After Nobunaga's death in 1582, Chacha's mother married the warlord Shibata Katsuie and took up residence in Kitanoshō Castle. When Hideyoshi's armies assaulted Katsuie in 1583, her mother opted to stay by her new husband's side rather than flee. She and Katsuie committed ritual suicide together in the castle. Her daughters were sent with a trusted vassal to Hideyoshi's camp, where they entered the "protection" of the Toyotomi, effectively hostages. This was a typical practice in which warrior women's bodies were used as bargaining chips, exchanged along with horses, specie, swords, and ceramics as part of the politics of a society at war. Within one year, Chacha, who some records claim was uncommonly beautiful, had become Hideyoshi's second wife, and her other two sisters had been married off into other families (and we will hear more about one of them later).[54]

Such was the tumultuous world of elite warrior women in the late sixteenth century. Chacha's experience as the second wife of the hegemon was mixed. She was of course behind Hideyoshi's main wife Nene (also Nei, Kōtaiin; d. 1624) in rank. However, Nene did not produce a Toyotomi heir, and this opened up a path for increased status and influence for Chacha. She did indeed give birth to her first child, Tsurumatsu, in 1589, but as mentioned earlier, the boy died just two years later. This incident in some sense came to define Chacha. Hideyoshi had refurbished Yodo Castle, located between Kyoto and Osaka, and installed her there before the birth. After Tsurumatsu's death, the castle was shuttered and then largely destroyed, with materials reused in the construction of Fushimi Castle. Despite the brevity of her residence in the castle, Chacha was often referred to as Lady Yodo (Yodo-dono)

---

[54] See Elizabeth Self's excellent dissertation for details on the Azai sisters. Self, "Art, Architecture, and the Asai Sisters."

after this point; in fact, during the Tokugawa period, when she became a figure of popular ridicule, she was rebranded Mistress Yodo (Yodo-gimi). Chacha's ostensible inability to produce and raise a healthy heir thus became constitutive of the historical memory of her identity by associating her with the site of her "failure." In truth, however, she went on to do what none of the other women in Hideyoshi's coterie had been able to accomplish, giving birth to another Toyotomi son in 1593: Hiroimaru, later known as Hideyori. Chacha raised Hideyori and protected him through the turbulent years marking the end of Hideyoshi's life, the withdrawal from Korea, the Battle of Sekigahara, and the naming of Ieyasu as shogun. She and Hideyori became synonymous with Osaka Castle after 1596, and Chacha appears to have bided her time there, planning for the day when her son could reestablish Toyotomi rule in Japan.[55]

For Tokugawa Ieyasu (now the "retired shogun," or ōgosho, though still an active political force) and his son, the shogun Tokugawa Hidetada, Chacha and Hideyori represented a potent threat. Each year, Hideyori grew into the role of a warrior leader who could serve as a legitimate alternative to Tokugawa rule. Other matters occupied Ieyasu and his son for the next decade, including their active involvement in diplomatic affairs and the licensure of various parties to engage in trade with foreign countries. As Adam Clulow discusses in greater detail in Chapter 7 of this volume, the Tokugawa issued "vermilion-seal" permits to merchants and warlords as well as some foreign traders, with numerous such letters sent in 1604 (thirty), 1605 (twenty-eight), 1606 (nineteen), and 1607 (twenty-three).[56] In these early years of Tokugawa rule, Ieyasu and Hidetada clearly intended Japan to play a central role in the early modern economy of East Asia. Ieyasu also played the role of retired sovereign, meeting, for example, Ryukyu's King Shō Nei (r. 1589–1620), who was a hostage of the Shimazu, lords of Satsuma and historical enemies of the Tokugawa (as discussed by Howell, Chapter 18, this volume). The Shimazu were forced to bring their hostage to pay tribute to Ieyasu,[57] presenting the retired shogun with gifts including a sword, 1,000 silver pieces, 100 rolls of silk damask, woolen cloth (rasha), ramie cloth (taiheifu), and 100 rolls of banana fiber cloth (bashōfu).[58] They next traveled to Edo for an audience with Hidetada as shogun, resulting in a double performance of Tokugawa authority over both domestic political

[55] Fukuda, Yodo-dono.
[56] Nakamura, Tokugawa Ieyasu kō den, particularly the chart of shuinsen, 631.
[57] Zoku Gunsho Ruijū Kanseikai, Tōdaiki, 167.
[58] Uehara, Shimazu shi no Ryūkyū shinryaku, 196.

rivals – in this case the Shimazu – and "foreign" powers – represented by King Shō Nei. The shogunate's evolving relationship with the Dutch and the British in this period under the watchful eyes of Ieyasu and Hidetada is discussed by Clulow in Chapter 7 of this volume.

Despite the complex political and economic circumstances not only in Japan but across the East Asian region in these early decades of Tokugawa rule, the threat of the Toyotomi in their colossal fortress of Osaka Castle was the most pressing matter for Ieyasu and Hidetada. Tensions between the Tokugawa and the Toyotomi were amplified in 1614 over a disagreement regarding Hideyori's intention to dedicate a temple bell to the memory of his father.[59] Whether this struggle over ritual propriety was a legitimate conflict or a pretext, Ieyasu and Hidetada opted to launch a major assault on Hideyori and Chacha, who were joined in and around Osaka Castle by an enormous force of *rōnin* and other disenfranchised men, estimated to total 100,000 soldiers. The Tokugawa, now with near total control over the warlords of the archipelago, marshaled a force twice as large. Despite the size of their army, Tokugawa forces found the defenses of the enormous castle to be largely impregnable, and they settled instead for pelting the castle residents with loud canons and thereby forcing a negotiated truce. This was, however, a ruse. In the aftermath of the settlement, the Tokugawa tore down defensive barriers and filled in moats around the fortress. In 1615, Ieyasu and Hidetada returned to Osaka with another enormous army and toppled the now-vulnerable castle. The inhabitants took their own lives (including Hideyori and Chacha), fled, or were captured, and the problem of the Toyotomi was thus eliminated. Ieyasu had approached the challenge of stabilizing the post-Sekigahara world with caution, judiciously creating networks of reciprocity and employing the manifold rituals of sociability and cultural patronage as well as confiscating and reallotting land to reconstruct warrior society around the idea of mutual benefit. However, the comprehensive destruction of Osaka Castle, the single eruption of large-scale violence after Ieyasu became shogun in 1603, illustrates that the Tokugawa were still willing to deploy the tactics pioneered by Nobunaga and weaponized on a regional scale by Hideyoshi when necessary. Other than this notable exception, the story of early Tokugawa rule is largely one of the threat of violence, the display of force, and the pageantry of power rather than the actual exercise of mass killing as had been common in the sixteenth century.

[59] Ono, *Ieyasu shiryō shū*, 120–21.

The Deification of Ieyasu and
Tokugawa Succession

In the wake of their victory at Osaka Castle, the Tokugawa issued two policies that would shape the power relations of the Tokugawa era in complex ways. *Laws for All Warrior Houses* (*Buke shohatto*), a text that posits precedent and Chinese writings on good government as directives for ideal warrior behavior,[60] and *Regulations for the Palace and Nobility* (*Kinchū narabi ni kuge shohatto*), which clarifies the role of Kyoto's courtiers as masters of certain traditional arts and as performers of symbolically significant ritual practices,[61] both aimed to systematize the responsibilities and privileges of two status groups that had, in the late medieval period, acted as often as destabilizing influences as sources of social and political constancy. More broadly, the issuance of these codes by the military government, with Hidetada in the lead role as shogun, served to de-emphasize the personal authority of Ieyasu as one of the larger-than-life figures who had served alongside Nobunaga and Hideyoshi in an age of civil war, and instead to accentuate the legal authority of the shogunate as an institution to govern and regulate society.

In 1616, Ieyasu died of natural causes at his retirement residence in Sunpu, and his body was interred in a shrine located nine kilometers to the southeast on Mount Kunō, a small mountain overlooking Suruga Bay. Before the end of the year, however, his remains were relocated to the far grander locale of the shrine-temple complex on Mount Nikkō, the tallest volcanic peak in eastern Japan and a noted pilgrimage site. Following the precedent set by Hideyoshi, who had arranged for his own deification as a Shinto deity – Toyokuni Daimyōjin, or "Most Bright God of Our Bountiful Country" – at a shrine in Kyoto, Ieyasu had set in motion before his death a process that was subsequently appropriated by various parties, ranging from the shogun Hidetada to priests and scholars who hoped to benefit from controlling the spiritual legacy of the Tokugawa founder. The worship of Ieyasu as the deity Tōshō Daigongen, or "Great Avatar Who Illuminates the East," thereafter proliferated, spreading from the two initial sites at Mount Kunō and Mount Nikkō to a range of private and public shrines across Japan.[62] The warlord who became shogun had now become an object of widespread cultic veneration.

Hidetada was well positioned to successfully continue Tokugawa rule, but his activities and movements in the years after Ieyasu's death demonstrate

---

[60] Bolitho, "Han," 193.
[61] See the translation in Butler, "Tokugawa Ieyasu's Regulations," 532–36.
[62] Nakano, *Shokoku Tōshōgū*, 9–10.

that he did not take this continuity for granted. Indeed, he expended considerable effort shoring up the position of the Tokugawa and laying the groundwork for a smooth succession, both lessons learned from his father. For example, he continued to regularly travel to Kyoto and to use the city as a key site for Tokugawa policy-making and political pageantry, visiting the imperial capital in 1617, 1619, 1623, and 1626. On the first of these visits, he traveled to Kyoto in the company of a large army made up of outside (*tozama*) lords from eastern Japan. The powerful lords of western Japan who were not included in the procession, such as the Shimazu and Fukushima, quickly followed behind Hidetada's force in a parade of their own. In the end, most of the influential lords of Japan ended up joining the Tokugawa leader in the imperial capital, a palpable demonstration of the shogun's authority as supreme military commander of the archipelago. Once assembled in Kyoto, Hidetada again brandished his power as shogun by engaging in a large-scale forced relocation of numerous lords, beginning with the Ikeda house of Himeji and extending, domino-like, across numerous domains in western Japan.[63] He completed his journey to Kyoto with a comprehensive issuance of official shogunal letters acknowledging land grants to warriors, nobles, and shrines and temples. The majority of these grants had been made by Ieyasu in the years after Sekigahara or during his retirement, but not all had been documented under the emerging shogunal bureaucracy in Edo; Hidetada's issuance of vermilion-seal letters verifying land grants set a precedent, and the practice became part of the regular cycle of shogunal rule.

Hidetada's 1619 visit to Kyoto was similarly productive. Again, he chose to use the imperial capital as the stage for the performance of his military supremacy as shogun, and demoted the lord of the Hiroshima domain, Fukushima Masanori (1561–1624), because he had made unauthorized repairs to Hiroshima Castle, which was a direct violation of the codes issued in 1615. When Masanori had been confronted with this violation of shogunal policy, he had made only token modifications to the structure rather than destroying the keep as the shogunate had commanded. Thus, Hidetada ordered the transfer of Masanori from Hiroshima. To ensure compliance, the shogun also launched a large army led by various lords from Shikoku and the central region of Japan toward Hiroshima, though in the end the Fukushima house voluntarily gave up the castle and bloodshed was avoided.[64] Next, the shogun again launched a series of forced relocations of lords to further tinker with the

---

[63] Fujii Jōji, *Edo kaimaku*, 76.
[64] Kasaya, "Tokugawa bakufu no daimyō kaieki"; Kasaya, "Shōgun to daimyō," 72.

military preparedness of the Tokugawa and guarantee the stability of sho-gunal rule. Perhaps most significant among them was the decision to place Osaka Castle under the direct control of the shogunate and the assignment of a trusted vassal to lead the reconstruction effort. The resulting castle became a symbol of Tokugawa authority over Osaka, the emerging financial hub of early modern Japan, and when completed was reportedly two to three times larger than the Toyotomi's original castle on the same site, a rather brazen attempt to bury the memory of Toyotomi rule under an enormous monu-ment to Tokugawa power.[65]

Hidetada oversaw a range of additional policies in his time as shogun that became core components of the early modern system. The shogunate approved the licensure of the Yoshiwara brothel district in Edo, for exam-ple, in 1617, and in the same year, began licensing Kabuki theaters in Kyoto, demonstrating the gradual attempts of the new Tokugawa government to regulate the emerging popular culture of the archipelago's growing urban centers. Similarly, the shogunate under Hidetada continued escalating its restriction of the activities of foreigners, with a particular emphasis on limit-ing the influence of Christianity. Soon after Ieyasu's death, Hidetada clarified earlier anti-Christian injunctions by specifying that helping Christians to hide was as serious a crime as propagating the faith, and thus was punishable by execution. Then, in 1622, in response to news that Christian priests continued to minister in secret in Kyushu, Hidetada ordered executions of both foreign and Japanese Christians in Nagasaki: twenty-five priests and their helpers were crucified while a large number of followers were decapitated. Addi-tional rounds of executions followed, including death by fire for some, with the final toll topping seventy-five Christians killed by the end of the year.[66] Related efforts focusing on the regulation of trade and the Tokugawa shogu-nate's changing relationship with the Dutch and the British are examined in Clulow's chapter in this volume (Chapter 7).

Much of Hidetada's work as shogun involved extending, refining, and securing the general policies started by Ieyasu, who clearly served as the model for his own governance. In line with this general approach to rule, he made early preparations for the transfer of the position of shogun to his son Iemitsu, whom Ieyasu had recommended to succeed Hidetada. Consid-erable intrigue surrounds this succession, illuminating again the powerful role played by women inside the most elite samurai families in ways often

---

[65] Fujii Jōji, *Edo kaimaku*, 82–83.
[66] Hesselink, *Dream of Christian Nagasaki*.

obscured by the historical record. Although Iemitsu was indeed Hidetada's eldest child, he was sickly and withdrawn. The second son, Tadanaga, was reportedly a strapping and gregarious lad, the favorite of Hidetada as well as the preferred choice of his wife Oeyo (also Sūgen'in, 1573–1626). (Oeyo, it is worth noting, was one of the three sisters who escaped the destruction of the Azai by Nobunaga in 1573, and her older sister was Chacha, discussed earlier in this chapter.) However, Iemitsu's wet nurse, Lady Kasuga (1579–1643), advocated for Iemitsu to be named heir, and her argument apparently convinced Ieyasu before his death.[67] Hidetada acceded, despite manifold signs that Iemitsu was not equipped for the strenuous and difficult role of shogun.

The 1623 ritual of succession illustrates why Hidetada and Oeyo were so worried about designating Iemitsu to be the next shogun. Recall that in 1605 when Hidetada was appointed to the position of shogun, he traveled from Edo with an army of 100,000 men to meet his father in Kyoto, and he and Ieyasu engaged in a variety of social and cultural rituals in the imperial capital before the official court ceremony. In 1623, by contrast, Hidetada first arrived in Kyoto early in the sixth month, and his entrance into the city proper was marked by a grand reception of domanial lords, courtiers, and shrine and temple leaders; Iemitsu, however, did not accompany him, and Hidetada had to wait more than a month for Iemitsu to join him because of one of the latter's regular bouts with illness.[68] Previous planned visits to Kyoto to lay the groundwork for this succession had been canceled for similar reasons. Iemitsu finally made it to the city in the middle of the seventh month, and two weeks later – after considerable recuperation from the long journey, as well as meetings with the assembled lords and aristocrats – he received the court appointment of shogun in an elaborate ceremony held in Fushimi Castle. This in turn was followed by weeks of further social and cultural rituals, including a formal visit to the court and a trip to Osaka to see the ongoing construction of the new castle. Iemitsu also accepted a princely gift during this outing – in what was clearly a staged attempt to situate him in a genealogy of famous warrior leaders including Ashikaga Yoshimasa, Oda Nobunaga, and his grandfather – in the form of pieces of the singular resinous wood known as Ranjatai, used in elite incense ceremonies. This famous object, imported to Japan from Southeast Asia during the Nara period, was held in the imperial collection in the Shōsōin storehouse at the Buddhist temple-complex Tōdaiji in Nara and required court permission to handle. Ashikaga Yoshimasa had

---

[67] On Iemitsu and Tadanaga, see Bodart-Bailey, *Dog Shogun*, 13–14.
[68] Fujii Jōji, *Tokugawa Iemitsu*, 33.

cut off a piece in 1465 in a well-known ritual of political culture,[69] and Nobunaga reproduced the ceremony in 1574.[70] Iemitsu could thus return to Edo bearing the court title of shogun while also counting himself as one of the few warrior leaders in history to own fragments of this historical treasure from the imperial storehouse.[71]

In reality, however, Hidetada continued to rule and Iemitsu only gradually became part of the Tokugawa administration in Edo. Hidetada maintained his residence in the Honmaru Palace of Edo Castle, while Iemitsu still lived in the Nishinomaru Palace for more than a year after the shogunal succession. Likewise, Hidetada corresponded with foreign dignitaries as the sovereign ruler of Japan for some time, and furthermore signed many of the enfeoffment letters sent to hereditary lords (*fudai daimyō*) and bannermen in the years after Iemitsu's appointment.[72] Gradually, however, after Iemitsu was allowed to move into the primary shogunal quarters of the Honmaru Palace and Hidetada established himself as the retired shogun in the Nishinomaru Palace, a balance of power was achieved not unlike the dual rule of Hidetada and Ieyasu in the decade after the latter's retirement.

Hidetada was more brazen as retired shogun than his father had been and regularly interfered directly in the affairs of the court, seen in one of his most successful accomplishments: marrying a member of the Tokugawa family into the imperial lineage. His campaign proceeded through multiple stages, beginning in 1618 with initial inquiries, escalating in 1619 with extreme Tokugawa pressure on Kyoto, and finally resulting in success in 1620 with the entry of his daughter, Tokugawa Masako, into the imperial court as a consort of Emperor Go-Mizunoo. This marriage was without precedent, one of the clearest indications that Tokugawa authority even at this early stage was without rival in the history of warrior rule in Japan.[73] The bridal procession from Edo to Kyoto was by all accounts a spectacular display of wealth and power; Masako arrived in Kyoto with an enormous sum of money that made her by far the richest individual in the court, as well as a massive and diverse trousseau of elite material and visual culture that empowered her to be a social and cultural force in Kyoto and in her new family.[74] Hidetada additionally funded the construction and elaborate

[69] Morita Kyōji, *Ashikaga Yoshimasa*, 208.
[70] Ōta, *Shinchō kōki*, bk. 7, sec. 4, pp. 167–68; see also Ōta, *Chronicle of Lord Nobunaga*, 206–7.
[71] Fujii Jōji, *Tokugawa Iemitsu*, 38.
[72] Fujii Jōji, *Edo kaimaku*, 87–88.
[73] Lillehoj, *Art and Palace Politics*, 126.
[74] Lillehoj, *Art and Palace Politics*, 127–30.

decoration of a sumptuous court palace for his daughter, giving her a kind of home base in the capital.

In addition, after Masako's marriage, Hidetada made several visits to Kyoto, twice in the company of Iemitsu, to offer gifts and funding to the court and to engage in diverse forms of pageantry around the capital city. In 1626, for example, the two Tokugawa leaders hosted the emperor and his wife as well as major members of the court in a showy and formal visitation to their head-quarters in the city, Nijō Castle. A huge palace was constructed as a temporary residence for the imperial couple, while the Ninomaru Palace was extended and refurbished, with new gardens added as well. The procession from the court to Nijō included 5,000 participants and countless observers, and it was followed by five days of social and cultural rituals ranging from banquets, kickball (*kemari*) competitions, gift exchanges, and Noh theater to poetry readings.[75] Relations continued to be complex between the Tokugawa and the imperial court, but Hidetada's efforts to secure the cooperation of Kyoto's elites in the acceptance of Masako as a legitimate empress were efficacious, or at least laid the foundation for her own efforts to achieve success. Tōfu-kumon'in, as Masako came to be known, ended up forming a strong bond with her husband, and the two became influential patrons of Buddhism and the arts who helped to lead Kyoto's cultural revival in the mid-seventeenth century. Even after Go-Mizunoo's hasty and politically motivated abdication in 1629, the couple's daughter (Hidetada's granddaughter) ascended to the throne as empress regnant Meishō and ruled until 1643, making the hold of the Tokugawa on the elite institutions of early modern Japan complete.

Hidetada died early in 1632 at the age of fifty-three after a half-year strug-gle with illness. We might expect Iemitsu, the sickly child who was raised in the splendor of Edo Castle and was largely unfamiliar with both the court politics of Kyoto and the harsh realities of the battlefield that had defined his grandfather and father, to have struggled as a truly independent shogun. Sur-rounded by officials appointed by Hidetada and lacking the military authority that had defined the first two shoguns, Iemitsu's position was precarious. Yet, he emerges from the historical record as a remarkably successful ruler who did as much to create the early modern system of Tokugawa rule as any other individual politician of the period. In part this is due to his length of time in office: he served as an independent shogun, freed from the dual polity struc-ture imposed by his father as retired shogun, for nineteen years. But his activ-ism extends beyond mere longevity of rule, seen in his willingness to move

[75] Butler, *Emperor and Aristocracy*, 229–30; Lillehoj, *Art and Palace Politics*, 155–65.

in new directions, counter to the paths carved by the first two shoguns, and indeed to react to new challenges with innovative and long-lasting policies that did much to preserve Tokugawa authority for many generations.

Iemitsu's interaction with the imperial institution, which as described above was a major concern of every warrior leader interested in unifying the realm and bringing an end to civil war since Nobunaga, became the definitive statement on Tokugawa-court relations. He had already journeyed to Kyoto twice, both times in the company of his father, and in 1634 he took what would be not just his final trip to the imperial capital but the final trip of any shogun to the Kansai region until the nineteenth century. The trip was marked by bold statements. Iemitsu traveled in the company of an enormous army, rumored to number 300,000 men; he stayed in the capital for almost two months; and he focused his attention almost entirely on projecting an aura of kingly munificence toward the empress, the court, prominent temples and shrines, and even the townspeople of Kyoto, when he offered a substantial gift of cash to the city's elders along with orders that it be distributed to all residents of the metropolis. He feted nobles with banquets and provided living stipends to aristocratic families on the verge of poverty. Perhaps most importantly, he overwhelmed the retired emperor Go-Mizunoo with luxurious gifts and increases in stipend, transforming a headstrong foe of Tokugawa hegemony into a willing partner. In short, Iemitsu deployed the enormous wealth of the Tokugawa to buy the loyalty of the residents of the capital, or at the very least their cooperation in the project of peaceful shogunal rule.[76]

Iemitsu also invested heavily, perhaps even recklessly, in the veneration of his father and grandfather through massive architectural, decorative, and ritual projects. He sponsored the expansion of the physical plant of the main shrine to Ieyasu at Nikkō from a modest structure to an unprecedented decorative and architectural program, beginning in 1636. The project would end up consuming 568,000 *ryō* of gold, 100 *kanme* of silver, and 1,000 *koku* of rice from the treasury of the Tokugawa.[77] Iemitsu personally made the pilgrimage to Nikkō on at least six occasions and seems to have conceived of the mountain as the ideal site for a complex that would allow worship of his grandfather on an appropriate scale while also inspiring awe at the ongoing authority of the Tokugawa.[78] The structures and landscape that emerged from this substantial investment included interconnected paths, gates, gardens, and buildings, all

[76] Fujii Jōji, *Tokugawa Iemitsu*, 94–101. In English, see Butler, "Court and Bakufu," 235–39.
[77] Hirono, *Tokugawa Iemitsu kō den*, 213–15.
[78] Sonehara, *Shinkun Ieyasu no tanjō*, 66.

marked by remarkable carved and painted decorations. Visitors could gaze upon elaborate Chinese lions, dragons, phoenixes, falcons, and an enormous assortment of plants, rich in symbolic significance from both Chinese and Japanese cultural history.[79]

While still under construction, Iemitsu and his advisers used the Tōshōgū at Nikkō to host the twenty-first memorial celebration in 1636. Such celebrations were more than ancestor worship; in Ieyasu's case, the apotheosis that had occurred after his death, combined with his position as founder of both the Tokugawa lineage and the shogunate, combined to make the memorial meaningful and powerful on a grand, political scale, part of the pageantry that undergirded the military government's authority. The site became both a pilgrimage destination and a cornerstone in the ideology of the Tokugawa state. This becomes apparent when we examine the visits of foreign embassies to Nikkō Tōshōgū. Iemitsu insisted, for example, that the Korean embassy of 1636 visit the ritual site: "If you Three Ambassadors were to make a sightseeing trip [to Nikkō] We would consider it a glory for the entire nation. We should be unable to restrain our joy."[80] The Record of the Tokugawa further claimed that Im Kwang and his entourage "were permitted to make a pilgrimage to Nikkō, just as they had requested."[81] Ryukyuan embassies and Dutch embassies were similarly required to visit the site. By giving the appearance that it was the spontaneous desire of these envoys from abroad to pay homage to "Gongen-sama" and by obtaining gifts and "articles of tribute," such as the Korean bell sent in 1643 or the Dutch chandelier which faces the bell before the Yōmei Gate, to decorate the shrine and further exalt Ieyasu's sanctity, such foreign pilgrimages could not fail to serve as a mechanism for extending the numinous range of the cult of Ieyasu beyond the immediate geographic boundaries of Japan.[82]

Such forced acts of pageantry were not limited to foreign embassies but extended to members of the Tokugawa house as well as other warrior leaders throughout the Tokugawa period. The shogunate transformed the pilgrimage of the shogun or his representative to Nikkō into one of the largest forms of pageantry to occur on a regular basis in early modern Japan. While the shogun himself only visited Nikkō seventeen times during the entire period, a shogunal representative was sent every year.[83] Likewise, the imperial court was

[79] Takafuji, Ieyasu kō, 114–27.
[80] Quoted in Toby, State and Diplomacy, 203.
[81] Toby, State and Diplomacy, 204.
[82] Toby, State and Diplomacy, 204.
[83] Tokugawa Kinen Zaidan, Nikkō Tōshōgū, 8.

required to annually send a representative to worship Gongen-sama on his death anniversary, reinforcing the power of the Tokugawa over the emperor. It was perhaps at times of political crisis that the Nikkō Tōshōgū proved to be most useful. Tokugawa Yoshimune, the eighth shogun and the first to be adopted from a branch family, organized a monumental pilgrimage in 1728, which included 230,830 people in a procession that took approximately four days in each direction.[84] The procession, the rituals at the shrine, and the side activities that Yoshimune pursued on this trip were all conspicuously lavish, indicating that the shogun viewed the trip as an opportunity to advertise not only the ritual, military, and political strength of the shogunate but its financial potency as well. Iemitsu's reconfiguration of the Nikkō Tōshōgū thus created a vital and long-lasting platform for the Tokugawa shogunate to engage in outward-facing rituals of rule, while also allowing for individual members of the Tokugawa family (and perhaps other warriors who were so inclined) to express their devotion to the worship of Ieyasu's avatar, Gongen-sama. (See Teeuwen, Chapter 13, this volume, for more details on the establishment of the Tōshō Daigongen cult.)

Under Iemitsu, the shogunate also continued to display deep distrust of independent religious institutions and instituted new edicts to cement the general persecution of Christianity in particular as a core policy of Tokugawa rule. Ieyasu had already gestured in the direction of increased control of Christianity on several occasions despite his clear interest in global trade. As early as 1605, Ieyasu began working to "prevent the spread of Christianity in his own retinue," prohibiting Christianity among "any samurai receiving income in his fiefs."[85] More substantively, in 1612, Ieyasu responded to a major scandal in Nagasaki (in which the Christian warlord Arima Harunobu tried to bribe the Christian shogunal aide Okamoto) with executions and a general prohibition of Christianity in Tokugawa lands.[86] Forced apostasies, torture, and other forms of prosecution became the norm in Tokugawa law and practice, sealed in a document that Ieyasu's adviser Konchiin Sūden authored in 1614, "Statement on the Expulsion of the Bateren [priests]."[87]

When Iemitsu became shogun in 1623, he accelerated these policies, which increasingly impinged on Japan's thriving trade with Southeast Asia,

[84] Tokugawa Kinen Zaidan, Nikkō Tōshōgū, 39.
[85] Gonoi Takashi, Tokugawa shoki Kirishitanshi kenkyū, quoted in Paramore, Ideology and Christianity, 53.
[86] Zoku Gunsho Ruijū Kanseikai, Tōdaiki, 179. See also Cooper, Rodrigues the Interpreter, 251; Boxer, Christian Century, 314–15.
[87] See Hesselink, Dream of Christian Nagasaki, 144–45; Elisonas, "Christianity and the Daimyo," 367.

conducted both by European and Japanese merchants. Japanese returning from overseas were not allowed back into the archipelago unless they had apostatized, and luggage and cargo were examined more strictly than ever to prevent Christian icons from entering the country.[88] The shogunate progressively came to identify trade as the vector for the dissemination of Christianity and drastically increased licensure requirements in the early 1630s, followed by a ban on Japanese ships traveling overseas entirely in 1635. This was part of a larger attempt to regulate and standardize the practices of foreign trade, which had previously been locally managed, with much of the profits enriching local lords and port town officials.

Iemitsu's concern with centralizing Tokugawa power was made all the more urgent with the outbreak of the Shimabara Rebellion in 1637, the last major military conflict in Japan until the mid-nineteenth century. What started as an isolated peasant uprising over economic precarity rapidly grew into a large-scale rebellion against Tokugawa rule. The conflict centered on Hara Castle in Hizen Province, perhaps the primary region in which Christian missionaries had been active in the late sixteenth and early seventeenth centuries and, as a result, home to many Japanese Christians even in the 1630s.[89] The revolt thus represented many of the most worrisome forces that the Tokugawa feared in the stable world order they had created: class conflict, the influence of outsiders, and foreign religious ideology. The Tokugawa responded with overwhelming force in an imposing display of political organization and military logistics, sending an army of 150,000 soldiers to lay siege to the rebel-occupied castle. Iemitsu's army waited three months for the dwindling supplies and increasing despair to force the rebels into action. When they attempted to sneak out of the castle and steal food, the central army attacked, breaching the castle walls and entering the central keep where they fought the starving but determined insurgents within. Tokugawa forces suffered surprising losses, reportedly more than 20,000 over the course of the entire campaign, but this was a minor setback.[90] The rebels, including those who were unable to move because of malnourishment as well as the many civilian family members who were present, were eventually slaughtered, killed through decapitation, burning, or drowning. Some surely did escape, but the majority of the 23,000 agitators died in the immediate aftermath of the toppling of the castle. Regulations were soon issued to the residents of

---

[88] Hesselink, *Dream of Christian Nagasaki*, 210.
[89] Elison, *Deus Destroyed*, 218. See also Boxer, *Christian Century*, 375–79.
[90] Keith, "Logistics of Power," 164.

the region to effectively address the socioeconomic problems that were likely the primary cause of the revolt: debts were discharged, deforestation was prohibited, market foreclosures were outlawed, and human trafficking was banned.[91] Christianity, of course, was prohibited as well, including "secret prayer," though this was hardly a new policy. The authority of the Tokugawa as national military rulers was clearly – and brutally – articulated in the defeat of the Shimabara rebels, written in the blood of Japanese residents for all to see, a statement not only about the intolerance of foreign religious ideology but more importantly about the willingness and ability of the shogunate to defend its rule even in the most distant regions of the Japanese archipelago.

In 1639, Iemitsu continued to tighten shogunal controls on foreign influ-ence as well as the general population of Japan. The shogunate banned Por-tuguese ships from Japanese waters this year, but only after verifying that the Dutch East India Company could adequately fill the gap and maintain current trading levels; the shogunate then ordered that the Dutch factory at Hirado be transferred to Nagasaki in 1641, with the intention of continuing the lucra-tive trade that had become so important for the Tokugawa.[92] The goal of these policies was not to stifle international exchange or close off Japan com-pletely, but to tightly control the points of entry while allowing trade to flour-ish in the hands of a limited number of trusted collaborators who would not permit Christianity to seep into the archipelago. At the same time, to prevent the internal circulation of Christianity, the shogunate intensified its policies of surveillance and inspection with the establishment of a new inquisition office (*shūmon aratame no yaku*) in 1640.[93] This assortment of rules provided the foundation for the shogunate's overlapping platforms of external regulation of trade through restriction and internal suppression of Christianity through inspection.

This suppression marks the launch of a set of overlapping Japanese poli-cies to exclude Christianity as well as most significant contact with outsid-ers, which would last until the 1850s. Yet these policies must be highlighted as a kind of aberration both in terms of Japan's previous century of global engagement as well as the broader international trends of the day. It is worth asking why, exactly, Tokugawa leaders saw Christianity as such a profoundly

[91] Keith, "Logistics of Power," 168.
[92] For the original text of the edicts of 1635 and 1639, see Kikuchi, *Tokugawa kinreikō*, 6:565–71. On patterns of trade in the seventeenth century, see Innes, "Door Ajar," 376–473. See also Laver, *Sakoku Edicts*.
[93] See Elison, *Deus Destroyed*, 195, and Laver, *Sakoku Edicts*, 65–66. On the first holder of the office, the apostatized Christian Inoue Masashige, see Screech, "17th-Century Japanese Minister's Acquisition"; Hesselink, *Prisoners from Nambu*.

concerning threat. The answer is simply that the rulers of Japan recognized the intersecting trends of Iberian conversion, conquest, and colonization unfolding concomitantly at numerous sites in Asia and the Americas, regions that Japan had come to recognize as neighboring territories. A shipwrecked Spanish pilot had verified for the Japanese in 1596 that Spain intended to subjugate Japan, and English and Dutch agents had amplified this fear in the intervening years.[94] Japanese leaders also became aware of Spanish and Portuguese interest in mapping East Asia alongside the grandiose claims these rulers made to conquering, Christianizing, and colonizing broader and broader swaths of the globe.[95] The enactment of a variety of Tokugawa policies to systematically exclude Christianity from Japan under Iemitsu was thus based on a wide range of evidence gathered over many decades. Ultimately it was also successful in its goal of preventing Japan from suffering the fate of so many other non-Western cultures throughout the early modern world.

Iemitsu also sought to extend the authority of the Tokugawa shogunate at every level of early modern Japanese society. Late medieval warlords had long exchanged family members as hostages, and this practice continued even after the establishment of the shogunate by Ieyasu in 1603.[96] In the 1635 expansion of and revision to the *Laws for All Warrior Houses*, the general requirement that lords (daimyo) should alternate residence in Edo was institutionalized.[97] In 1636, the shogunate clarified that the outside lords (*tozama daimyō*) in particular were required to maintain residences in Edo and to leave family members there as hostages when they returned to their home domains; in 1642, Iemitsu extended this policy to hereditary lords as well.[98] This demand emerged from the right of the Tokugawa, as holders of the court-appointed post of shogun, to command the military service of the lords of the archipelago, and in practice it created the opportunity for pageantry and rituals of obeisance to be observed in Edo Castle. The rotation

---

[94] Boxer, *Christian Century*, 163–67. This suspicion is voiced openly in Fukansai Habian's *Myōtei mondō* (1605), translated by Baskind and Bowring in *Myōtei Dialogues*, 191–92: "Myōshū: 'It is said that spreading Christian teaching throughout Japan in this fashion is nothing but a deceptive ruse to capture Japan.'" My thanks to Drisana Misra for reminding me of these references. See her innovative work on the "global imaginaries" of this period in Japanese history in Misra, "Japanese New Worlds."

[95] See Paramore, *Ideology and Christianity*, and Leuchtenberger, *Conquering Demons*, on this topic.

[96] See Pitelka, *Spectacular Accumulation*, 32–41, on hostage-taking and the experience of Ieyasu, who grew up a hostage of the Imagawa.

[97] It had been mentioned, vaguely, in the earlier 1615 iteration as well. See Ishii, *Kinsei buke shisō*, 454–62.

[98] Fujii Jōji, *Tokugawa Iemitsu*, 109–11. See also, Vaporis, *Tour of Duty*, 11–20.

of residences and the establishment of huge domanial estates in Edo thus became a core policy of control for the Tokugawa, with massive, unanticipated consequences for the shogun's city as well as the culture of Japan during the early modern period, as explored throughout this volume. Similarly, Iemitsu's administration expanded shogunal controls over commoner populations in the late 1640s, likely motivated in part by the devastating effects of the Kan'ei famine, which began in Kyushu in 1638, spread into central Japan, and lasted until 1643. It was Japan's worst famine of the seventeenth century. In 1648, the shogunate issued regulations for commoners in Edo and Osaka, followed in 1649 by the promulgation of the *Keian Legislation* (*Keian furegaki*), a thirty-two-article code regulating the labor and daily life of rural commoners, with a particularly strong focus on frugality.[99]

Although Iemitsu emerges from the historical record as a strong leader who not only consolidated shogunal power for the Tokugawa family in a period of considerable political precarity but expanded the public authority of the position of the shogun, he was less successful than his beloved grandfather in the realm of the production of heirs. This was central to the authority of patriarchal rulers in premodern Japan, where succession disputes launched many of the civil crises that tore apart otherwise strong and stable polities. Ieyasu had many children and deployed them as assets in his attempt to create good government, monopolize power, and maintain stability. Hidetada, too, was both productive as a father and strategic in his placement of his children in key political roles. Iemitsu, by contrast, showed little interest in marriage early on and was focused instead on male sexual partners. The maintenance of one or more lovers, including young men, was of course not uncommon among warrior leaders, but Iemitsu seemed to exclusively prefer male sexual encounters, including relationships with older men.[100] Eventually Iemitsu did take wives and produce offspring, including two sons who would follow him in the position of shogun: Ietsuna, who occupied the office from 1651 to 1680, and Tsunayoshi, who ruled from 1680 to 1709. When Iemitsu died in 1651 after a struggle with a gastrointestinal illness, his heir Ietsuna had already been signing letters in his stead for some time even though he was still just a boy; Iemitsu's duty to continue the Tokugawa lineage, in that sense, had been amply fulfilled.[101] Likewise his filial piety, seen in the elaborate and abundant

---

[99] On debates about the timing of the issuance of *Keian furegaki*, see Fujii Jōji, *Edo kaimaku*, 300–304.

[100] Screech, "Shogun's Lover's Would-Be Swedish Boyfriend."

[101] Fujii Jōji, *Tokugawa Iemitsu*, 216–21.

architectural and visual programs he developed to honor his grandfather and father, was beyond reproach.[102]

Yet as a shogun, Iemitsu is often contrasted with his two predecessors, who unquestionably modeled a particularly masculinist archetype of warrior ruler as father figure. The position of shogun is fundamentally "designated male," yet the form of masculinity that each of these rulers embodied is worth considering.[103] Ieyasu, though hardly as brutal as Nobunaga or Hideyoshi, successfully navigated the hostage-exchanges, familicide, endemic war, and assassination attempts of the late sixteenth and early seventeenth centuries in part through a cold and calculated approach to rule, prioritizing his own safety and power as well as the perpetuation of his lineage as the keys to success, and undoubtedly achieved his goals as patriarch. Hidetada similarly built on his own experiences on the battlefield to deploy the performance of force as a matter of course, and actual violence when necessary. Though perhaps less ruthless than his father, he embraced a model of leadership in which his warrior identity and his position as patriarch of the Tokugawa were constitutive of his identity and ordering the mass executions of Christians was a trivial matter. Even his most famous dalliance with male-male sexuality ended in a notorious act of violence, when he ordered his page and lover Koyama Nagato to commit suicide after an affair.[104]

Iemitsu would seem on the surface to embody a different form of masculinity as shogun. Sickly as a child, prone to delays because of illness, and haunted by dreams of Ieyasu throughout his life, the third shogun appears to veer far from the established patriarchal model of the Tokugawa. Yet Iemitsu was his own man, and he managed his affairs as shogun, the crises that faced the Tokugawa in his years of rule, and indeed the challenges of fulfilling his family duties with steely determination. He followed his father and grandfather in his love of hunting and similarly studied sword-fighting with the famous teacher Yagyū Muneyori.[105] And Iemitsu certainly replicated his father's and grandfather's demonstrated willingness to resort to killing, both in the personal realm – seen in his murder of one of his lovers after learning that the lover had left him for another man[106] – and in the absolutism of many of his political decisions, such as the complete eradication of the Shimabara rebels. Perhaps in Iemitsu's

---

[102] Gerhart, *Eyes of Power*; Gerhart, "Visions of the Dead."
[103] Frühstück and Walthall, "Interrogating Men and Masculinities," 1.
[104] Nishiyama, "Shūdō fūzoku," 342.
[105] Walthall, "Do Guns Have Gender?" 40.
[106] Screech, "Shogun's Lover's Would-Be Swedish Boyfriend," 112. Another example is Iemitsu's elimination of his brother, Tadanaga. See Bodart-Bailey, *Dog Shogun*, 13–14.

career we can see the delineation of a different archetype for a warrior ruler, one more appropriate to the early modern samurai experience of urban culture and bureaucracy but still bearing the vile inheritance of indiscriminate violence passed down from the fighting men of the late sixteenth century. The threat of that violence hovered over early modern Japan like a cloud.

Transformation

Under the rule of the first three Tokugawa shoguns, enormous transformations wracked Japan. The result – the Pax Tokugawa, the long era of surprisingly peaceful governance, balanced between the local and visceral authority of domanial lords and the broader and more performative authority of the shogunate – is the subject of this volume. But the transformations themselves are understudied and only touched upon in this chapter. Our focus on top-down governance has obscured the lived reality of war for so many communities that were destroyed or displaced in the late medieval period. Hidden as well are the experiences of the warrior families who found their livelihoods removed as a result of the era's battles or the land reassignments that followed them. Similarly, the growth of cities over the course of the seventeenth century (see Gaubatz, Chapter 19, this volume) is partially a result of the policies of the first three Tokugawa shoguns, accelerated by the very menace of violence they institutionalized. Too often we have focused on the outcomes of Tokugawa urbanization but not the process. Lastly, the first three Tokugawa shoguns, building on the entrepreneurship of warlords such as Nobunaga and Hideyoshi, did demonstrate interest in stimulating market growth, regulating global exchange, selectively seeking foreign knowledge, and adopting new technologies in order to apply them to improvements in infrastructure. These tendencies were constitutive of Japan's early modern society, shaping the experiences of diverse populations across the archipelago for centuries through an unprecedented Japanese culture of widespread knowledge production and consumerism.

Bibliography

Asao Naohiro. "The Sixteenth-Century Unification." In Hall, *Early Modern Japan*, 40–95.

Baskind, James, and Richard Bowring, eds. *The Myōtei Dialogues: A Japanese Christian Critique of Native Traditions*. Leiden: Brill, 2016.

Berry, Mary Elizabeth. *Hideyoshi*. Cambridge, MA: Harvard University Council on East Asian Studies, 1982.

Bodart-Bailey, Beatrice M. *The Dog Shogun: The Personality and Policies of Tokugawa Tsunayoshi*. Honolulu: University of Hawai'i Press, 2006.

Bolitho, Harold. "The *Han*." In Hall, *Early Modern Japan*, 183–234.

Boxer, Charles R. *The Christian Century in Japan: 1549–1650*. Berkeley: University of California Press, 1951. Reprint, Manchester, UK: Carcanet, 1993.

Butler, Lee A. "Court and Bakufu in Early 17th Century Japan." PhD diss., Princeton University, 1991.

Emperor and Aristocracy in Japan, 1467–1680. Cambridge, MA: Harvard University Asia Center, 2002.

"Tokugawa Ieyasu's Regulations for the Court: A Reappraisal." *Harvard Journal of Asiatic Studies* 54, no. 2 (December 1994): 509–51.

Cooper, Michael. *João Rodrigues's Account of Sixteenth-Century Japan*. London: Hakluyt Society, 2001.

Rodrigues the Interpreter: An Early Jesuit in Japan and China. New York: Weatherhill, 1974.

ed. *They Came to Japan: An Anthology of European Reports on Japan, 1543–1640*. Ann Arbor: Center for Japanese Studies, University of Michigan, 1995.

Elison, George S. *Deus Destroyed: The Image of Christianity in Early Modern Japan*. Cambridge, MA: Harvard University Press, 1973.

Elisonas, Jurgis. "Christianity and the Daimyo." In Hall, *Early Modern Japan*, 301–72.

"The Inseparable Trinity: Japan's Relations with China and Korea." In Hall, *Early Modern Japan*, 253–300.

Frühstück, Sabine, and Anne Walthall. "Interrogating Men and Masculinities." In Frühstück and Walthall, *Recreating Japanese Men*, 1–21.

eds., *Recreating Japanese Men*. Berkeley: University of California Press, 2011.

Fujii Jizaemon. *Sekigahara kassen shiryōshū*. Shinjinbutsu Ōraisha, 1979.

Fujii Jōji. *Edo kaimaku*. Vol. 12 of *Nihon no rekishi*, edited by Kodama Kōta, Hayashiya Tatsusaburō, and Nagahara Keiji. Shūeisha, 1992.

Tokugawa Iemitsu. Yoshikawa Kōbunkan, 1997.

Fukuda Chizuru. *Yodo-dono: Ware taikō no tsuma to narite*. Kyoto: Mineruva Shobō, 2007.

Gerhart, Karen M. *The Eyes of Power: Art and Early Tokugawa Authority*. Honolulu: University of Hawai'i Press, 1999.

"Visions of the Dead: Kano Tan'yū's Paintings of Tokugawa Iemitsu's Dreams." *Monumenta Nipponica* 59, no. 1 (2004): 1–34.

Ha Woo Bong. "War and Cultural Exchange." In Lewis, *East Asian War*, 323–39.

Haboush, JaHyun Kim. *The Great East Asian War and the Birth of the Korean Nation*. New York: Columbia University Press, 2016.

Haboush, JaHyun Kim, and Kenneth R. Robinson. *A Korean War Captive in Japan, 1597–1600*. New York: Columbia University Press, 2013.

Hall, John Whitney, ed. *Early Modern Japan*. Vol. 4 of *The Cambridge History of Japan*. Cambridge: Cambridge University Press, 1991.

Hesselink, Reinier H. *The Dream of Christian Nagasaki: World Trade and the Clash of Cultures, 1560–1640*. Jefferson, NC: McFarland, 2016.

Prisoners from Nambu: Reality and Make-Believe in 17th-Century Japanese Diplomacy. Honolulu: University of Hawai'i Press, 2002.

Hirono Saburō. *Tokugawa Iemitsu kō den*. Nikkō: Nikkō Tōshōgū Shamusho, 1961.

Iida Kumeji. *Tenshō daijishin shi*. Nagoya: Nagoya Daigaku Shuppankai, 1987.

Innes, Robert LeRoy. "The Door Ajar: Japan's Foreign Trade in the Seventeenth Century." PhD diss., University of Michigan, 1980.

Ishii Shirō, ed. *Kinsei buke shisō*. Vol. 27 of *Nihon shisō taikei*. Iwanami Shoten, 1974.

Kasaya Kazuhiko. *Sekigahara kassen: Ieyasu no senryaku to bakuhan taisei*. Kōdansha, 1994.

Sekigahara kassen to Ōsaka no jin. Yoshikawa Kōbunkan, 2007.

"Shōgun to daimyō." In *Shihai no shikumi*, edited by Fujii Jōji, 45–98. Vol. 3 of *Nihon no kinsei*. Chūō Kōronsha, 1991.

"Tokugawa bakufu no daimyō kaieki seisaku o meguru ichi kōsatsu." *Nihon kenkyū* 3 (September 1990): 35–63.

Keith, Matthew E. "The Logistics of Power: Tokugawa Response to the Shimabara Rebellion and Power Projection in Seventeenth-Century Japan." PhD diss., Ohio State University, 2006.

Kikuchi Shunsuke, ed. *Tokugawa kinreikō*. 6 vols. Yoshikawa Kōbunkan, 1931–32.

Kitajima Manji. "The Imjin Waeran: Contrasting the First and Second Invasions of Korea." In Lewis, *East Asian War*, 73–92.

Kurokawa Naonori and Noda Tadao. "Fushimi jō to jōkamachi." In *Momoyama no kaika*, edited by Hayashiya Tatsusaburō, 321–50. Vol. 4 of *Kyōto no rekishi*. Kyoto: Kyoto-shi, 1971.

Kuwata Tadachika. *Tokugawa Ieyasu: Sono tegami to ningen*. Shinjinbutsu Ōraisha, 1963; Reprint, Ōbunsha, 1987.

Lamers, Jeroen. *Japonius Tyrannus: The Japanese Warlord Oda Nobunaga Reconsidered*. Leiden: Hotei, 2000.

Laver, Michael S. *The Sakoku Edicts and the Politics of Tokugawa Hegemony*. Amherst, NY: Cambria Press, 2011.

Leuchtenberger, Jan C. *Conquering Demons: The "Kirishitan," Japan, and the World in Early Modern Japanese Literature*. Ann Arbor: Center for Japanese Studies, University of Michigan, 2013.

Lewis, James B., ed. *The East Asian War, 1592–1598: International Relations, Violence, and Memory*. Abingdon: Routledge, 2015.

Lillehoj, Elizabeth. *Art and Palace Politics in Early Modern Japan, 1580s–1680s*. Leiden: Brill, 2011.

Misra, Drisana Ruchi. "Japanese New Worlds: Intersecting Imaginaries of the Nanban Period (c. 1543–1641)." PhD diss., Yale University, 2023.

Morita Kōji. "Mikatagahara no tatakai." In *Tokugawa Ieyasu jiten*, edited by Fujino Tamotsu, Murakami Tadashi, Tokoro Rikio, Shingyō Norikazu, and Owada Tetsuo, 200–207. Shinjinbutsu Ōraisha, 1990.

Morita Kyōji. *Ashikaga Yoshimasa no kenkyū*. Osaka: Izumi Shoin, 1993.

Nagashima Fukutaro, ed. *Tennōjiya kaiki*. Vol. 7 of *Chadō koten zenshū*, edited by Sen Sōshitsu. Kyoto: Tankōsha, 1957–62.

Nakamura Kōya. *Tokugawa Ieyasu kō den*. Kōdansha, 1965.

Tokugawa Ieyasu monjo no kenkyū. 5 vols. Nihon Gakujutsu Shinkōkai, 1958–62.

Nakano Mitsuhiro. *Shokoku Tōshōgū no shiteki kenkyū*. Meicho Kankōkai, 2008.

Nishiyama Matsunosuke. "Shūdō fūzoku ni tsuite." In *Sei fūzokushi*, edited by Kōza Nihon Fūzokushi Hensanbu, 318–56. Appendix, Vol. 3 of *Kōza Nihon fūzokushi*. Yūzankaku, 1959.

Nukii Masayuki. "Righteous Army Activity in the Imjin War." In Lewis, *East Asian War*, 141–62.

Ono Shinji, ed. *Ieyasu shiryō shū*. Jinbutsu Ōraisha, 1965.

Ooms, Herman. *Tokugawa Ideology: Early Constructs, 1570–1680*. Princeton, NJ: Princeton University Press, 1985.

Ōta Gyūichi. *The Chronicle of Lord Nobunaga*. Translated by Jurgis Elisonas and Jeroen Lamers. Leiden: Brill, 2011.

Shinchō kōki. Edited by Okuno Takahiro and Iwasawa Yoshihiko. Kadokawa Shoten, 1991.

Paramore, Kiri. *Ideology and Christianity in Japan*. London: Routledge, 2009.

Pitelka, Morgan. *Spectacular Accumulation: Material Culture, Tokugawa Ieyasu, and Samurai Sociability*. Honolulu: University of Hawai'i Press, 2016.

Sajima Akiko. "Hideyoshi's View of Chosŏn Korea and Japan-Ming Relations." In Lewis, *East Asian War*, 93–107.

Screech, Timon. "A 17th-Century Japanese Minister's Acquisition of Western Pictures: Inoue Masashige (1585–1661) and His European Objects." In *Transforming Knowledge Orders: Museums, Collections and Exhibitions*, edited by Larissa Förster, 72–106. Leiden: Brill, 2019.

"The Shogun's Lover's Would-Be Swedish Boyfriend: Inoue Masashige, Tokugawa Iemitsu, and Olof Eriksson Willman." In *Sexual Diversity in Asia, c. 600–1950*, edited by Raquel A. G. Reyes and William G. Clarence-Smith, 105–24. Abingdon: Routledge, 2012.

Self, Elizabeth. "Art, Architecture, and the Asai Sisters." PhD diss., University of Pittsburgh, 2017.

Sonehara Satoshi. *Shinkun Ieyasu no tanjō: Tōshōgū to Gongensama*. Yoshikawa Kōbunkan, 2008.

Stavros, Matthew. *Kyoto: An Urban History of Japan's Premodern Capital*. Honolulu: University of Hawai'i Press, 2014.

Swope, Kenneth. *A Dragon's Head and a Serpent's Tail: Ming China and the First Great East Asian War, 1592–1598*. Norman: University of Oklahoma Press, 2009.

Takafuji Harutoshi. *Ieyasu kō to zenkoku no Tōshōgū*. Tōkyō Bijutsu, 1992.

Toby, Ronald. *State and Diplomacy in Early Modern Japan: Asia in the Development of the Tokugawa Bakufu*. Princeton, NJ: Princeton University Press, 1984. Reprint, Stanford, CA: Stanford University Press, 1991.

Tokugawa Kinen Zaidan. *Nikkō Tōshōgū to shōgun shasan*. Tokugawa Kinen Zaidan, 2011.

Tōkyō Daigaku Shiryō Hensanjo, ed. *Dai Nihon shiryō*. Tōkyō Daigaku Shuppankai, 1901–.

Tsuji Zennosuke, ed. *Rokuon nichiroku*. 6 vols. Taiyōsha, 1934. Reprint, Zoku Gunsho Ruijū Kanseikai, 1991.

Tamon'in nikki. 5 vols. Kadokawa Shoten, 1967.

Uehara Kenzen. *Shimazu shi no Ryūkyū shinryaku: Mō hitotsu no Keichō no eki*. Ginowan, Okinawa: Yōju Shorin, 2009.

Vaporis, Constantine Nomikos. *Tour of Duty: Samurai, Military Service in Edo, and the Culture of Early Modern Japan*. Honolulu: University of Hawai'i Press, 2008.

Walthall, Anne. "Do Guns Have Gender? Technology and Status in Early Modern Japan." In Frühstück and Walthall, *Recreating Japanese Men*, 25–47.

Yamashina Tokitsune. *Tokitsune kyōki*. 14 vols. In *Dai Nihon kokiroku*, edited by Tōkyō Daigaku Shiryō Hensanjo. Iwanami Shoten, 1959–91.

Yi Min'ung. "The Role of the Chosŏn Navy and Major Naval Battles during the Imjin Waeran." In Lewis, *East Asian War*, 120–40.

Zoku Gunsho Ruijū Kanseikai, ed. *Tōdaiki, Sunpuki*. Heibonsha, 1995.

2

Politics and Political Thought in the Mature Early Modern State in Japan, 1650–1830

KIRI PARAMORE

This chapter analyzes the history of Japanese politics and political thought between 1650 and 1830. The politics of this period has traditionally been characterized as staid and static – a conservative influence on a stagnant society. Yet the culture of this same period of Japanese history is usually described in the opposite terms – flourishing and dynamic. The Japan of Matsuo Bashō, Chikamatsu Monzaemon, Katsushika Hokusai, and Itō Jinsai was a place of cultural and intellectual diversity, development, and dynamism. Yet the Japan of the Tokugawa state, at exactly the same time, was a place of restrictive regulation, conservativeness, and stasis – or so the story goes.

By examining its political history through the frame of its broader cultural environment, this chapter looks to reconcile these two opposing visions of early modern Japan. Rather than looking at politics exclusively in structural terms, we will also look at the culture of politics, including the significant social role of political thought. For the purposes of this chapter, I define politics as the processes of negotiation between different stakeholders at all levels in society which constituted governance, and political thought as the deliberate expression of political positions (opinions) in those processes of negotiation. Political thought can be found in state proclamations, memorials, advice documents, and political treatises. But politics in early modern Japan also found expression in lewd street performance, graffiti, and urban rioting, the content and claims of which both influenced, and were influenced by, more established genres of political discussion. Analyzing this diversity of sources in combination reveals shared historical trends observable through the period, for instance, a movement toward expression of political opinion in terms of expectations of the future (instead of through examples from the past). This is a process of historical change which has also been noted in the history of other early modern polities. The historical theorist Reinhart

Koselleck has referred to an expansion of "the horizon of expectation" in some early modern societies, linked to an increase in political agency and an acceleration of economic development.[1]

Probably the most globally influential theory to emanate from the field of Japanese history over the last decades, and one which resonates with these broader theories on early modernity, is Hayami Akira's idea of the "industrious revolution."[2] Hayami described the "industrious revolution" as a wide-ranging change in mentalities, rooted in the peasantry, which underlay early modern economic development in Japan. Originated to explain the development of Japan as a nonindustrialized early modern polity, it has since been used by other scholars to analyze the nature of preindustrial economic development in other parts of the world, notably in Europe.[3] Using economic historical and historical demographic research, Hayami emphasized the significant increases in nutrition, clothing, housing, and literacy which this industrious revolution brought about in Japan. But he also noted ethical and political aspects, describing industriousness as "morally configured" labor, "an ethos everyone was called upon to respect," which in turn "people expected would result in a rise in their material standard of living."[4] Interestingly, for Hayami, "perhaps the most significant reason why this ethos of industriousness became so firmly entrenched in daily life ... was that people's rising expectations – for an improved standard of living – were satisfied to a certain extent."[5] This link between a shared labor ethos and a shared *expectation* of material outcomes is a political facet in Hayami's theory of the industrious revolution which appears to resonate with Koselleck's "horizon of expectation."

The political valency of the ethic of economic productivity in early modern Japan has also been noted in other recent scholarship, notably in David L. Howell's studies on early modern Japanese conceptions of identity and status, for instance in his conception of "the politics of the quotidian."[6] In this chapter we try to develop and link some of these ideas, teasing out the relationships between popular ideas of industriousness, political expectation,

[1] Koselleck, *Futures Past*, 257–69.
[2] Hayami, "Introduction," 25–29.
[3] De Vries, *Industrious Revolution*.
[4] Hayami, "Introduction," 27.
[5] Hayami, "Introduction," 28.
[6] Howell, *Geographies of Identity*, 45–78. See also Ehlers, *Give and Take*. This link between the ethics of governance, labor, and productivity was also picked up in some earlier English-language scholarship on Japanese political thought history, for instance Tetsuo Najita, *Visions of Virtue*.

popular political protest action, and written treatises of political thought and state policy, attempting to present a more comprehensive understanding of the mature political culture of early modern Japan.

This chapter is divided into five sections. The first section, "Civil Rule in a Military State," describes the mature apparatus of the Tokugawa state, analyzes its standardization across the country, touches on some of the key economic problems it faced, and outlines the ostensibly determining roles of class, status, and gender in the apparatus. It also touches upon early challenges to that apparatus, and thereby makes clear that this government system was contested, even in the early stages of its development in the mid-1600s.

The second section, "Confucian Debate and 'Political Economy,'" analyzes the rise to prominence of Confucian discursive forms in political debate and the significance of Confucian political thinking being based *outside* the state. It then analyzes the significant change to the horizon of political expectation brought about by the general acceptance in the late-1600s of the Confucian ideal of "political economy" – an ideal through which the state was held responsible for general social welfare.

Section three, "Debating Reform," examines the overt state-led attempts to "reform" Tokugawa public administration, analyzing the economic factors behind them, their relations to Confucian political economic theorization, and to increasingly public instances of debate and performance which also employed political thought to comment on governance in the early 1700s. It shows the influence of private-sphere Confucian political thinking on the central state's reform policies, but also on the arguments made by those who politically resisted those reforms. These forms of resistance found expression not only in public policy writings but also in lewd populist publications and drunken street festivals.

Section four, "Debating Capital," examines various forms of political response, at both state and street level, to the increasing power of mercantile capital, and the prevalence of state debt, particularly in the late 1700s. It discusses concrete interactions between urban commoner street politics (protests/riots) and state policy. It also analyzes the way the street interacted with other nonstate, yet organized, forms of political expression. It demonstrates that political analyses emanating from private academies and schools in the urban areas outside Edo both influenced, and reacted to, the agenda of the urban graffitists and rioters who affected both policy and regime change in the late 1700s.

Section five, "State Building and the Institutionalization of Debate," analyzes the growing integration of merchant capital, popular sentiment, and private academy intellectual specialists into state institutions as part of the creation of a state-led information order in the late 1700s and early 1800s. It concentrates particularly on the significance of the state's integration and propagation of scholarly communicative methodologies which had earlier been employed by the politically influential private academies. It analyzes the role of these methodologies in facilitating broader public debate on issues of governance, firstly outside the government, and then within it.

Civil Rule in a Military State

Many of the most interesting dichotomies inherent in early modern Japanese society were related to the nature of the Tokugawa state as a military state, titularly led by a hereditary warrior caste. Political society was ostensibly based in hereditary military power, yet in reality the central political issues of the era were nearly all economic, requiring merchant economic know-how. Ostensibly power was supposed to be wielded by charismatic individual military leaders, but the demands of such a complicated commercial society, rather, required complex bureaucracies whose governing efficacy was rooted in close cooperation and shared knowledge. This section will reexamine the financial and personnel issues inherent in this dichotomy, thereby also confirming the structural contours of the Tokugawa state as understood in current scholarship.

One dominant issue in early modern Japanese politics which focuses attention on this dichotomy was the finance of state debt. Many other early modern states, for instance in Europe, also had problems with state debt – often linked to the financing of wars by those states.[7] To understand the manifestation of debt as a chronic state problem in early modern Japan, despite this being a particularly peaceful period of Japanese history, it is necessary to touch upon certain particularities in how early modern Japanese states (both the shogunal and domanial states) managed finance and delineated status. The Tokugawa state managed the composite states of Japan (domains) and governed its own core Tokugawa fiefs and the lords and vassals who ruled them through a system which hierarchicalized status and measured both state revenue and expenditure in terms of rice consumption units (*kokudaka*). The Tokugawa state's use of *kokudaka* linked political power directly to rice revenue – both symbolically, through status, and financially, as it was the base of tax revenue and state salary payments to samurai.

---

[7] He, *Paths toward the Modern Fiscal State*; Knights, *Representation and Misrepresentation*, 13–14.

The Tokugawa period, particularly the seventeenth century, witnessed massive economic growth, leading in turn to the creation of a significant manufacturing and service economy and further monetarization. The more the Tokugawa economy thus "developed," however, the more it diversified, and thus the smaller the rice base of the economy became as a proportion of the total. As a result, from the 1650s, most governments in the mature Tokugawa states came to share the same financial problematic linked to the *kokudaka* system: rice, the tax revenue base of the states, and thus also of the entire samurai population, kept shrinking as a percentage of the economy. Yet simultaneously, the increasingly educated and productive population was coming to expect more and more from the state. This created the situation within which the shogunal and domanial states came to rely upon private credit. But their collateral base against this credit, taxation income measured in rice consumption, was vulnerable.

This was the great contradiction of the Tokugawa state: the economic development which it had facilitated undercut the financial base of its hierarchical organization. Simultaneously, urbanization, higher literacy, and excess labor time led to an unprecedented public interaction with cultural production, much of which, coming from China, assumed a Confucian meritocratic moralism, which in turn undercut the legitimacy of the hereditary warrior state system. This was the dynamic context within which increasingly broad and complex political negotiations developed through the early modern period.[8]

Before embarking upon our examination of those negotiations, let us first confirm the position of current historiography on the structural organization of the early modern state. The earliest Tokugawa state was a conquest regime, primarily funded by booty and resource extraction – notably including the mining and overseas export of precious metals. When Tokugawa Ieyasu established the shogunal state at the beginning of the seventeenth century, Japan provided the silver for up to 30 percent of the circulating stock of global trading currency. The Tokugawa regime monopolized the export trade in precious metals, and bullion export provided an important financial base for the state. The state's relationship with the people, ensuring them relative peace through their military capacity to pacify territory and provide order, was based on the same means which ensured the state's control of mining resources: their capacity to monopolize violence. The apparatus of

---

[8] A similar decline in the comparative value of agricultural taxation and thereby of the state treasury has been observed in other early modern polities. For instance, this is sometimes provided as one of the causes of the English Civil War. See Braddick, *State Formation*.

the early Tokugawa state was accordingly military in structure. Power was exercised by individuals in direct hierarchies based on personal loyalty. Until the end of the 1630s, and particularly under the rule of the first two shoguns, Ieyasu and Hidetada, the legitimacy of power originated primarily in the person wielding it, be they the shogun or a senior lieutenant acting on their behalf. This is what in Japanese historiography, following Weberian models, is often referred to as the "charismatic" nature of rule before the mid-1600s.[9]

By the 1640s, however, a more evolved system was emerging where the authority of lieutenants became tied to particular functional responsibilities. Most of the major responsibilities of the shogunate, for instance the governance of its cities, land reclamation projects, water engineering, military responsibilities, regulation of religious institutions, and supervision of the regional domains, were each managed by an office. The heads of these offices were hereditary appointments, senior retainers of the shogunate, usually with the status of a daimyo with a relatively small fief. Above the various agency heads sat a handful of senior councillors (rōjū) – usually also senior retainers of daimyo status, some of them daimyo of other Tokugawa domains – who functioned together as a kind of cabinet. This created what is usually referred to as the "bureaucratic structure" of the Tokugawa shogunate.[10]

Although thus often referred to as a "bureaucratic" structure marking "civil rule" and contrasted against the "charismatic" power of the early shogunate, this system actually preserved many elements of the medieval warrior band order from which it had evolved. For instance, when officers, at any level, were appointed, they were appointed as vassals of the person they directly served, swearing an oath of loyalty to that individual and their family – not to the state or the shogun directly. This arbitrated feudal basis of power also severely limited the pool of people from which appointments could be made. Nearly all of the senior positions (agency heads) within this system were hereditary appointments, drawn from a relatively small pool of the hierarchically highest houses of Tokugawa vassals (those on 10,000 koku or more). The agencies were then staffed by mid-level Tokugawa vassals who also inherited their initial appointments. The number of mid-level Tokugawa vassal families – bannermen (hatamoto) and housemen (gokenin) – from which these staff could be drawn was much larger than the number of officials required, however, meaning most samurai had no involvement in governance. As recent research has demonstrated, the category of bannerman itself was also

[9] Fujii, Edo jidai no kanryōsei, 195–96.
[10] Fujii, Edo jidai no kanryōsei, 195–96.

formalized during the mid-1600s with the aim of bringing Tokugawa house military units under direct shogunal control. The position of *wakadoshiyori* (often translated as "junior councillor") in turn seems to have been created to manage the bannermen, who in turn led the core administrative and military units in the Tokugawa house. In this way, while the senior councillors managed the public or national affairs of the Tokugawa regime (*kōgi*), the junior councillors managed the administration of the Tokugawa house itself (*kasei*).[11]

Another peculiarity of this so-called bureaucracy was that at almost every level, including at the level of the agency heads themselves, multiple officers were appointed. Thus, many agencies had two, three, or more hierarchically equal directors. On the one hand, this significantly limited anyone's capacity to wield power arbitrarily. The system ensured consultation before action as no leader had monopolistic control. On the other hand, this system also ensured that no sole officer ever had ultimate responsibility.[12] The buck did not stop here, there, or anywhere. It was a relatively loose system of governance. These basic structures were also replicated in the domanial states.[13]

All the positions in these shogunal and domanial bureaucracies were occupied by men. Women were excluded from these offices of the shogunate which handled the day-to-day management of the state. However, at the very top of government, this entirely male executive bureaucratic apparatus of daily administration represented only one of three branches in Edo Castle which advised the shogun. In Edo Castle, this executive bureaucratic system, headed by the senior councillors, and made up of various daimyo-level agency heads, was referred to as the *omote*, or front government. It was paralleled by a less formal group of advisers in the shogun's inner chamber, or inner government, in Japanese the *oku*. The third branch of advice in Edo Castle was the shogunal women's chambers, in Japanese the *ōoku*. The advisers in the inner chamber, including those at the very top, were often directly appointed by the shogun, and at many points during the mature Tokugawa shogunate's history these key positions were held by samurai of relatively low hereditary standing. The inner chamber was thus the place in the shogunate administration most open to meritocratic advancement, where advisers from outside the state structures could be brought in, and where political thinking from outside the state (notably from the private academy networks of the

[11] Koike, *Edo bakufu chokugai gundan*, 189–90, 226.

[12] Fujii, *Edo jidai no kanryōsei*, 197–99.

[13] For instance, if we look at the structure of Tokushima, an outside (*tozama*) domain ruled by the Hachisuka house, we see a similar picture. Kasaya, *Kinsei buke shakai*, 196.

cities) was first able to influence government discussions. The third branch of political influence within Edo Castle, the shogunal women's chambers, was made up entirely of women – matriarchs, consorts, and other female attendants, the majority daughters of lordly samurai houses or the imperial house in Kyoto. The most senior members of the women's chamber were often referred to as *onna rōjū* (lady senior councillors), using a title clearly meant to parallel the male senior councillors who formally ran the executive government (*omote*). Contemporaneous shogunate sources even record instances of *onna rōjū* themselves using this term to argue to the shogun that their status was equal to that of the male *rōjū*.[14] Until recently, both narrative and graphic depictions of the governmental hierarchy of the Tokugawa state have tended to show only the *omote* element.[15] Figure 2.1, reflecting more recent Japanese historiography, adds the *oku* and *ōoku* into the structural schema of the state, showing the three-branch structure of power as outlined above. Many of the most significant and controversial political decisions of the mature Tokugawa state, for instance over succession or shogunal reactions to major breakdowns in order, were taken through a process of negotiation between these different branches in Edo Castle.

One notable example of this process was the succession of the eighth shogun, Yoshimune (1684–1751, r. 1716–45). Regarded as one of the most reformist of Tokugawa leaders, Yoshimune was the first Tokugawa shogun to come to power in a negotiated succession. Yoshimune was not an heir to the shogunate but was rather part of the succession of one of the three collateral Tokugawa houses, the house of Kii. The three collateral houses, each of which held a large Tokugawa fief in Owari, Kii, and Mito, respectively, were established early in the shogunate to ensure options for succession if the central line was extinguished – which occurred in 1716. The process of Yoshimune's succession demonstrates the power of the women's chambers, the way the three branches interacted in a crucial decision-making process, and the extent to which major issues in the shogunal government were, already by the early 1700s, being publicly discussed and debated in the streets.

[14] There is a famous example of an argument over this matter at the beginning of the Kansei reforms, in the last decade of the eighteenth century, between the head of the women's chambers, Ōsaki, and Matsudaira Sadanobu directly after he had taken power, partly with her help. This argument, including reference to the *onna rōjū* title, can be found in a contemporary source, Kaiho, *Keizaiwa*, 399–400. See also Sekiguchi, *Goisshin to jendā*, 102–3; Takeuchi, Fukai, and Matsuo, *Tokugawa ōoku jiten*, 88–89.

[15] Examples in English-language scholarship include a chart, "Main Offices of the Tokugawa Bakufu," in Hall, "*Bakuhan* System," 166–67, and a table, "Tokugawa Military Organization," in Totman, *Politics in the Tokugawa Bakufu*, 44.

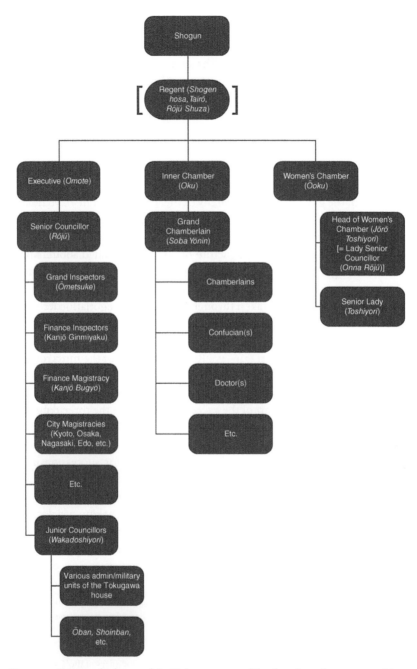

Figure 2.1 Structural schema of the Tokugawa state. The three-branch structure of the chart is inspired by "Tokugawa bakufu shokusei zu," Fukai, *Edojō o yomu*, 12.

As the six-year-old shogun Tokugawa Ietsugu neared death on the night of 18 June 1716, the heads of the three collateral houses, together with other key shogunal figures, assembled at Edo Castle to decide the succession. The official *Records of the Tokugawa House* (*Tokugawa jikki*) narration of the conversation begins with the head of the inner chamber, the grand chamberlain (*soba yōnin*) Manabe Akifusa, opening the meeting by transmitting a decree from the head of the women's chambers, Ten'eiin, that Yoshimune should be appointed shogun. According to the record, Yoshimune himself then humbly declined, giving reasons for the lord of Owari or Mito to be appointed instead. The head of Mito house then said that Yoshimune should accede. When Yoshimune continued to decline, Ten'eiin herself appeared in the meeting, eventually ending the discussion by literally screaming at Tokugawa Yoshimune: "You boy! You cannot decline!"[16] The silence of the ostensible executive of the shogunate, the senior councillors (*rōjū*), who were also present, is as striking as the dominance of Ten'eiin, who appears to have basically decided who would succeed, partly by denying Yoshimune's attempt to have the senior councillors speak.

The succession also seems to have involved mobilization on a wider level than just the castle elite. The diary of Owari retainers who were present in Edo at the time, having accompanied their lord on the road to Edo for the meeting, notes that the Lord of Owari seemed to have been informed of the meeting later than the Lord of Kii. The morning before the meeting, fish and oil merchants in the streets were already loudly proclaiming that the Kii house's Yoshimune would become a fine new shogun and ridiculing the house of Owari. Humorous poems parodying the Owari house and predicting a Kii victory were graffitied on various walls in the city.[17] It appears that the expression of public sentiment was in full swing, and possibly was also being instigated and choreographed.

This gives an impression of a succession question which was most forcefully engaged, and indeed at least according to the official records, seemingly decided predominantly by the women's chamber, with the leading male military leaders of the government in the executive branch rather passive. It also suggests that the succession controversy was at the very least actively followed and commentated upon by the general public, if not the object of a public relations campaign. Graffiti and hearsay among the lower orders were already a part of politics.

Yet although in this example public sentiment appears to have been utilized, and women nobles appear to have played a decisive role, in the first

---

[16] Kuroita, *Tokugawa jikki*, 9:141.
[17] Ōishi, *Kinsei Nihon no shōsha to haisha*, 137–38.

century of Tokugawa rule this potential power of women nobles, and of the broader population, was also clearly contested by many members of the male shogunal elite. For instance, when Ikeda Mitsumasa attempted to construct an alternative bureaucratic system in his Okayama domain in Bizen in the 1650s, one in which ordinary lower-level samurai would play more significant roles, the shogunate cracked down on Ikeda's chief adviser and senior vassal, the Confucian scholar Kumazawa Banzan.[18] The shogunal senior councillor Sakai Tadakatsu instructed the domain lord to stop the reforms and dismiss Banzan, while the shogunate's own Confucian scholar, Hayashi Razan, publicized a number of widely circulated tracts slandering Banzan as a rebel and a Christian, an allegation which these same texts simultaneously leveled against one of the most powerful contemporaneous women members of the Edo Castle women's chambers, Soshin (or as Razan called her, "the witch-nun Soshin").[19] This demonstrates that even the relatively straightforward hierarchies and structures of early Tokugawa rule were the object of political manipulation and contestation, and that the exercise of bureaucratic muscle against opponents was accompanied, even at this early stage, by public propaganda. The structural apparatus, from the beginning, was never taken for granted, neither by its supporters nor by its opponents. Nor was it imagined by either to be isolated from sentiment in broader society.

Confucian Debate and "Political Economy"

The history of these kinds of political controversies of the 1650s and 1660s demonstrates that while the shogunal state itself employed hearsay and propaganda, it had little toleration for the political innovation or debate of others. Political thought, and political thought delivered through Confucian scholarship in particular, was regarded as potentially seditious. As a later top shogunal adviser and Confucian scholar, Arai Hakuseki (1657–1725), pointed out in the early 1700s, in the mid-1600s Confucianism was still regarded by much of the samurai elite as a foreign religious tradition which, like Christianity, more often than not led to seditious words and actions.[20]

Elite attitudes to political thought, however, changed dramatically through the course of the latter seventeenth century. By the reign of Shogun Tokugawa Tsunayoshi (r. 1680–1709), the shogunal state was justifying

---

[18] McMullen, *Idealism, Protest, and the Tale of Genji*, 113–30.
[19] Hayashi Razan, *Sōzoku zengoki*, 3b; Paramore, *Ideology and Christianity*, 90–102.
[20] Arai, *Arai Hakuseki zenshū*, 6:550.

its own reformist policy agenda through the use of Confucian ideology and taking advice from independent Confucian thinkers. This new state approach to Confucianism reflected changes in general society where, particularly in the numerous urban centers of Japan, small Confucian private schools were becoming an increasing part of the recreational, intellectual, and religious landscape – especially in the lives of many low-level samurai. The industrious revolution had created a demand for practical knowledge which was partly met by private academies. Their popularity was also facilitated by the growth in literacy and surplus labor time which accompanied economic growth. By the early 1700s, the literacy rate was around 50 percent for males in many urban areas, and probably higher in the larger scholarly centers of Edo, Kyoto, and Osaka.[21] This created an urban literary landscape of "aesthetic networks" and "libraries of public knowledge" clustered around Confucian learning, thereby incidentally laying the basis for a vibrant political discourse.[22] The growth of Confucianism, not as a state system or ideology, but as a broadly engaged and understood worldview, occurred within this more general cultural blossoming. The central role of Confucian learning in facilitating advanced literacy created a shared vocabulary on issues of ethics and governance which facilitated debate of political issues.

Within that conversation, a shift can be seen through the course of the late seventeenth century from a view which saw the ideal role of government as based on premodern ideas of "supervising agriculture, controlling water" (kannō chisui) to the more expansive Confucian ideal of "ordering the world, succoring the people" (keisei saimin). The term keisei saimin was regularly abbreviated at the time to form the word keizai. Today keizai is the Japanese word for "economy," but at that time it functioned to mean something like "political economy" while also retaining the welfare connotations associated with the full phrase's exaltation to "succor the people" (saimin). The Confucian conception of keizai, "political economy," thus became the new operative term for describing the role of the state and a baseline in discussions of politics.

Dazai Shundai opened his On Political Economy (Keizairoku, 1729), probably the most widely read treatise on contemporary politics in Tokugawa Japan, with the following explanation of the meaning of political economy:

> Governing the state and the realm is called political economy (keizai). It means ordering (kei) the world, and succoring (sai / sukuu) the people. Ordering (kei) stands for ordering governance (keirin). The Book of Changes says,

[21] Rubinger, Popular Literacy.
[22] Berry, Japan in Print; Ikegami, Bonds of Civility; Rubinger, Private Academies.

"the gentleman orders governance"; the *Doctrine of the Mean* says, "order the governance of the realm's Great Way."[23]

This outlook justified a much more comprehensive approach to government responsibility. Military defense and occasional land reclamation projects were no longer enough. Governance was now supposed to deliver general welfare.

Shogun Tokugawa Tsunayoshi as well as later shogunal leaders such as Tokugawa Yoshimune and Matsudaira Sadanobu not only employed this comprehensive political vision to justify their policies but also sometimes used it to form policy and fix problems. Many elements in the reform agendas of both Tsunayoshi and Yoshimune were based on policy advice which originated with independent Confucian thinkers. These Confucian thinkers were usually not directly employed by the shogunal state but rather earned their living primarily in the sphere of private urban education described earlier. From the late 1600s, there began to emerge concrete personal links between the scholars of these schools and the shogunal state leaders. This was partly a result of the leaders themselves, like many other members of the samurai urban population, being drawn into close engagement with Confucian learning practices in private schools. Many senior shogunal officials had themselves attended private Confucian schools and discussion groups and were thus students and sometimes disciples of major private sphere Confucian scholars.

For example, much of the advice of two of the most influential political thinkers of the early 1700s, Ogyū Sorai and Dazai Shundai, made its way into senior government circles through the mediation of former students who now held high state office. Kuroda Naokuni, for instance, a former low official of the inner chamber who enjoyed close relations with both shoguns Tsunayoshi and Yoshimune, had been a student of Sorai's private school in the late 1600s and maintained a close relationship with him and his other students.[24] Kuroda, after a meteoric rise through the ranks, ended his career as senior councillor of the Western Palace and a castle lord on over 30,000 *koku*.[25] Kuroda was one of a number of former Sorai students through which first Sorai and later Shundai passed briefs to senior shogunate members.[26]

---

[23] Dazai, *Keizairoku*, 16.

[24] On the influence and connections of Kuroda Naokuni and his wife, Kuroda Tosako, see Yonemoto, *Problem of Women*, 101–2 (on Naokuni's close relationship with Sorai's patron, Yanagisawa Yoshiyasu [1659–1714]), and 206–7 (on Tosako's influence).

[25] Hayashi Jussai, *Kansei chōshū shokafu*, 11:94–96.

[26] Dazai, *Shundai jōsho nihen*, 703–4. Early in his career Ogyū Sorai had also had multiple interactions with Shogun Tsunayoshi through the mediation of Yanagisawa Yoshiyasu, chamberlain under Tsunayoshi and a notable early patron of Sorai. See Fukai, *Tsunayoshi to Yoshimune*, 27–28.

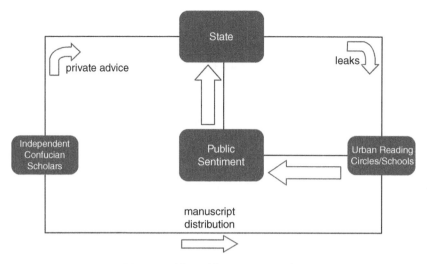

Figure 2.2 The public sentiment cycle.

Other senior shogunate members took advice into the state from other Confucian political scholars, and domain lords took advice from Confucian scholars in their own domains. The advice being received by the state was thus diverse in origin and often contradictory in nature. This multiplicity and diversity of opinion also fed into the public discourse that the open circulation of much of this writing sustained. Crucially, there are many examples of these advice documents later reappearing in the public domain and being widely circulated in manuscript or print form.[27] Thus, there was a circular movement of political opinion between private schools and members of the state apparatus. Confucian political theory and advice, whether articulated in the setting of a school or delivered to a shogun, had thus both a private and public nature (Figure 2.2).

Rulers also had increasing need for political thought from the late 1600s due to the increasing complexity of the financial and administrative challenges faced by the state. This required a much more rigorous approach to financial management. The shogunate's increasing attention to state finances was demonstrated by the increasing breadth and scope of power wielded by a range of new shogunate finance institutions unified under the new finance

---

[27] A classic example is Ogyū Sorai's famous texts *Seidan* (Discourse on politics) and *Taiheisaku* (Policies for a great peace). On the interaction of the policy and public versions of these texts, see Maruyama, "Taiheisaku kō." On the politics of manuscript circulation in early modern Japan, see Kornicki, *Book in Japan*.

office (*kanjōsho*). Ietsuna's and Tsunayoshi's governments in the last decades of the 1600s used this office to devise and administer new policies which began to "extend the hand of shogunate national policy into the territories of all domains."[28] A study commissioned from the shogunal finance office and a new unit Tsunayoshi had appointed within it, the financial inspections unit (*kanjō ginmiyaku*), led to lands enfeoffed to daimyo being targeted for reallocation in what became known as the "Great Genroku Land Reallocation" (*Genroku jikata naoshi*) in the last years of the 1690s. While higher lords were divested, replacements were appointed from the bannerman level of lower retainers. These internal changes were made together with the systematization of village relief, revaluation and reissuance of currency, more central regulation of overseas trade, and other such measures designed to strengthen the shogunate's hand in national policy over the interests of larger landowners and merchant monopolists.[29] Tsunayoshi justified these interventionist, and often reallocative, reforms using the Confucian concept of benevolence, representing himself and the shogunate as carrying out benevolent government, and casting those who he opposed and deposed as driven by profit and lust – negative values from a Confucian perspective.

Debating "Reform"

The engagement of some senior samurai leaders with the private sphere of Confucian scholarly activity, and most importantly with key Confucian frameworks of political thought such as "political economy," significantly affected the way the politics of reform was imagined and articulated. "Reform periods" during the course of the Tokugawa shogunate, notably the three major state-led reforms of the Kyōhō (1716–36), Kansei (1787–93), and Tenpō (1830–44) eras, all attempted centralization, combining increased regulation of domains and general finance to try to counter nonstate monopolistic mercantile activity. These reform periods, and the reform measures emanating from the central state which defined them, were thus often carried out and perceived in relation to attempts to strengthen the shogunate over the increasingly dominant merchant houses. In all three cases of major reform this was to different extents articulated through emphasis on the Confucian ethical virtue of benevolence, expressed primarily through increased state action in social welfare, intervention in the financial system, and a call for a

---

[28] Miyake, "Edo bakufu no seiji kōzō," 26.
[29] Miyake, "Edo bakufu no seiji kōzō," 27–30.

return to a more moral polity which often involved condemnation of luxury and extravagance.[30]

The Confucian packaging of many of the reform measures of the Kyōhō reforms, including these condemnations of decadence, has in some past scholarship fed an at-times Orientalist outlook on the reforms, focusing unduly on their calls for frugality, asceticism, and thrift. The actual role of Confucian ideas in the reforms, however, was much more multifaceted.[31] Although thrift was often advised in public proclamations and lectures aimed at lower samurai, Confucian scholars in the wider private sphere most consistently and vigorously advised the shogunate to improve finances by increasing production. The advice was not to contain the economy but to expand it.[32]

As Ogyū Sorai neatly put it in his famous political advice text *Discourse on Government* (*Seidan*, c. 1725–27), "To govern a state and the realm, first you must create prosperity, that is the basis of governance ... as Confucius said, 'first make the people prosperous, then teach them.'"[33] *Discourse on Government*, which enjoyed wide public circulation, particularly in the second half of the 1700s, was probably based on discussions and advice Sorai gave to Yoshimune in private in the 1720s. Another Sorai text, *Policies for a Great Peace* (*Taiheisaku*), which enjoyed wide circulation somewhat earlier, was likely also based on these discussions with the shogun.[34]

In *Discourse on Government*, Ogyū Sorai repeated Kumazawa Banzan's much earlier Confucian advice that samurai should be returned to the land. But he then went much further, suggesting that once back on the land they should teach the peasants to make consumer goods for the market.[35] A similar employment of the market can be seen in the even more widely read *On Political Economy* by Dazai Shundai. There he recommended "short-term solutions" based on his observation of the handful of domain governments which had relatively good financial situations. These, he noted, had access to some kind of

---

[30] He, *Paths toward the Modern Fiscal State*, 10, describes this kind of "paternalistic justification of state power" as a defining aspect of early modern decentralized fiscal states globally, likening the Japanese case to similar instances in Britain and China.

[31] Notable Kyōhō reforms included using the newly created financial inspection unit to rationalize and centralize control of the intendants (*daikan*) who administered shogunal lands (Ōishi, *Kyōhō kaikaku*, 223; Ōishi, *Kinsei Nihon no tōchi to kaikaku*, 104; Fukai, *Tsunayoshi to Yoshimune*, 141–44) and the successful establishment of new industries to provide import replacement manufacturing (Ōishi, *Kyōhō kaikaku*, 460–500).

[32] Murata, "Yoshimune no seiji," 6–7.

[33] Ogyū, *Seidan*, 303. The paraphrasing of Confucius comes from *Analects*, Book XIII, art. 9; the original and James Legge English translation can be viewed here: https://ctext.org/dictionary.pl?if=en&id=1414

[34] Ogyū, *Taiheisaku*, 447–85.

[35] Ogyū, *Seidan*, 325.

trade advantage, often involving overseas trade. Therefore, Shundai reasoned, the short-term solution for most domanial governments, and by association also the shogunal domains, was to similarly obtain or manufacture tradeable nonagrarian goods for sale, and then to manipulate their release in the market.

> Teach the masses handicraft manufacturing, then when they have time off from agricultural work, have them manufacture things that are useful to people, trade these with other domains, and you should have enough revenue. This is the technique to make a country [domain] richer.[36]

To attain a good price in a timely fashion, Shundai advised, it would be best for the domain government to itself take in hand the selling of these goods in Osaka. The domain could then monopolize the sale of these items, making sure to control the timing of their release to attain the best price.

> The way it is done in the Nagasaki trade, where [the shogunate monopsonistically] buys all the goods from the foreign ships and then sells it domestically, this is the right way to run the market. The various feudal lords should take the products made in their own domains and sell them in other places. What is wrong with this?[37]

This was a plan for the state to extract maximum profit by using the same kind of mercantile monopolies and hoarding techniques (market manipulation) as employed by the contemporaneous merchant houses. Shundai overtly proffered the example of foreign trade at the center of his advice on how to create a more successful "Confucian" government. Yet, while proffering this ultrapragmatic advice for state utilization of the market, in another advice text focused more on individual behavior written about the same time, Shundai railed against "a ruler ... loving profit as much as he loves the people," and complained that "if those above like profit, then vassals beneath them will go for profit and a terrible politics will arise in which profit and the people are set in competition."[38] In other words, the individuals being advised by Shundai, be they domain lords or their samurai retainers, had better not love profit. The state itself, however, should use the market, knowledge, and the industriousness of their population to attain the best margin possible. The approach of the Kyōhō reform government resonated with this kind of advice in looking for the state to engage trade and production issues actively, while at the same time condemning private profit seeking, luxury, and material

---

[36] Dazai, *Keizairoku*, 48.
[37] Dazai, *Keizairoku*, 52.
[38] Dazai, *Shundai jōsho nihen*, 703–4.

decadence as ends in themselves. The overriding aim of reducing state debt makes sense of this seeming contradiction.

Another major, yet often understudied part of the politics of the Kyōhō reforms, however, is the politics of the resistance against those reforms. There was a strong contemporaneous backlash against the reforms and the political and ethical outlook they represented. This was led by dissatisfied hereditary samurai rulers and allied merchant houses but also actively engaged by the masses. Intriguingly, this resistance often utilized Confucian discourse in ways very similar to those used by the reform government's supporters. The nature of resistance to the government reform agenda, just as much as the content of the agenda itself, thereby serves to confirm the connections between hereditary rulers, the wider private works of Confucian academicism, and the common people.

There were plenty of critics of the Kyōhō reforms. The new lord of Owari, Tokugawa Muneharu, the man who would have been shogun in place of Yoshimune if Ten'eiin had not carried the day in 1716, was particularly strident. Soon after coming to power as the new lord of the Tokugawa's largest collateral house in 1730, he authored, self-published, and widely disseminated his own political text, *Onchi seiyō* (1731), in which he attacked all the laws promulgated in the Kyōhō reforms.[39] He even identified laws themselves as a cause of social problems.

> As there are more laws promulgated every year, it is only natural that the number of criminals is also increasing.... If the laws are simplified, it will be easier to abide by them, and there will be fewer criminals.... It is a source of shame if a country has many laws.[40]

This was actually a quintessentially Confucian argument – that the people should be governed through the suasion of culture rather than the coercion of law. But Muneharu's method of demonstrating his displeasure was hardly

---

[39] Shiseki Kenyūkai, *Daimyō chojutsushū*, 5–6. The title *Onchi seiyō* is itself parodic. *Seiyō* means "political program," but *onchi* is an auditory homonym which, depending on the Chinese characters used, would most usually mean "tone deaf" 音痴 (slang for "obstinate," alluding to Muneharu's political stance to the reforms) but could also mean "the lands of a vassal awarded by his lord" 恩地 (alluding to Muneharu's position as a vassal of the Tokugawa shogun). The characters actually used in the title, 温知, form a nonword by combining the character for warm water with the character for knowledge (alluding both to, literally, warm knowledge, but also to the idea of the "popular wisdom" of the bathhouse, one of the main areas of public interaction and gossip in early modern Japan's cities). In this way, the title sets the stage for the work's public reception, both by identifying itself openly as adversarial and by associating itself with an anti-elite populist space (the bathhouse) and a form of "knowledge" based in that space.

[40] Tokugawa, *Onchi seiyō*, cited in Shiseki Kenkyūkai, *Daimyō chojutsushū*, 49.

Confucian. On returning to his home fief in 1731, having failed to convince anyone in Edo to change policy, Muneharu made his position on thrift clear by funding a number of drunken public festivals and opening a new night entertainment area in Nagoya which employed in excess of 1,000 new sex workers. Limiting the number and size of these kinds of areas had been one of the shogunate's most public policies – propagandized by shogunal supporters as a win-win, both reducing needless expenditure and improving morals. Muneharu was sending a clear signal that he rejected both this kind of moralism and the political thought behind it.[41]

Importantly, however, Muneharu himself did not see his critique as a critique of the mainstream Confucian political theory of his day. In fact, it is likely Muneharu had his own inhouse Confucian scholar, the Owari domain Confucian Fukada Shinsai, help him draft the text. *Onchi seiyō* deftly engaged theoretical issues which were being debated at the time in Japanese Confucian circles, discussing the role of the state and the place of morals and emotion in contemporary Confucian terms. One of the main debates in Japanese Confucianism at that time was over the centrality of individual morals. For followers of mainstream Neo-Confucianism, improving the moral state of individuals (self-cultivation) was key to a good society and thus a part of good government. Ogyū Sorai, however, whose works were at peak popularity in the 1730s, had argued that it was not the moral state of rulers but their actions that counted as good government. A good life and a good state for Sorai were realized not by suppressing passions but by harnessing them.[42] Tokugawa Muneharu used some of these concepts in his writing.

Thus, by the 1730s, Confucian political theory was neither a flat morality which people conformed to nor one ideological corner in a political debate between opposing parties. It had rather become the field of political debate. In this example, it was a debate between the Tokugawa shogun and the domanial head of the largest Tokugawa collateral house, the two most powerful men in the country. But it was a debate performed for a larger public. It was a debate not only articulated in widely read texts but performed publicly through Yoshimune's stately demeanor and Muneharu's funding and participation in wild public festivals and parties – including ostentatious appearances in the streets riding on the back of a white ox.[43] In a society of ongoing political tensions, governed through constant negotiation between stakeholders

---

[41] Ōishi, *Kinsei Nihon no shōsha to haisha*, 141.
[42] Ogyū, *Benmei*, 142.
[43] Ōishi, *Kinsei Nihon no shōsha to haisha*, 145–46.

separated into different fiefs, classes, status groups, and genders, Confucian political theory had become a conceptual framework within which those differences could be expressed and performed.

By the end of the Kyōhō period, however, there was also a contradiction emerging in the way certain forms of Confucian thinking worked in real governance. The idea of "benevolent government," in particular, had gained considerable traction under both Tsunayoshi and Yoshimune, but in both cases had also provoked a backlash. In the Confucian ideal, governance was supposed to be delivered naturally and harmoniously through custom and ritual, not imposed by law and force. Yet "benevolent governance" under the mid-Tokugawa state was most often enacted through laws and proclamations. Tokugawa Muneharu was not the only person to see the contradiction in this approach and to use it to attack the reforms. Against the vision of benevolent governance offered up by the likes of Yoshimune was emerging a more laissez-faire approach, which held that the shogunal state could best govern by facilitating rather than disciplining the rising forces of consumerism and mercantile capital.

From the mid-1700s, this more laissez-faire outlook would come to dominate governance. Through most of the second half of the 1700s, the rise of a comparatively openly pro-mercantile shogunal regime under Tanuma Okitsugu provided a different political context of debate and critique from that experienced under Yoshimune. When the Tanuma regime was eventually brought down in the late 1780s, however, it was replaced by a government led by Matsudaira Sadanobu, a grandson of Yoshimune, who then used the benevolence ideology of the Kyōhō reforms to launch his own Kansei reforms. The increasingly public debates of the late 1700s thus often revolved around issues of both social welfare and finance, debating the position of capital within an imagined (and contested) benevolent state.

Debating Capital

The politics of the mid- and late 1700s, and of the early 1800s, was thus characterized both by a more clearly defined relationship to capital and an increasing interaction between elite samurai aristocratic and plebian street politics. The best example of that interaction is the manner in which regime change occurred in the late 1780s, when Tanuma Okitsugu and his followers were removed from power in favor of a new government under Matsudaira Sadanobu, thus leading to the Kansei reforms. The pro-mercantile Tanuma regime was brought down by the political consequences of major instances of organized and directed rioting which occurred in the context of the Tenmei famine (1782–88). These included multiple mass uprisings across Japan, including very serious disturbances in Osaka and Edo.

One of the worst famines in Japanese history, the Tenmei famine resulted in the deaths of up to one million people. Northeast Japan was the worst-hit area. One of the Tanuma regime's financial policies, designed to ensure the value of shogunal ṣalaries on the rice market, had been to keep rice prices artificially high. As part of the same policy of maintaining the monetary value of the state rice system, the regime had also encouraged the cultivation of rice in colder, not necessarily suitable, terrains like the northeast, where rice had thus replaced more robust nonrice food crops like millet. Both these policies exacerbated the famine, particularly in the always-poorer northern areas. As the growing extent of the famine became clear, different domanial governments and merchant houses vied with each other to buy in stockpiles of rice and other grains. This not only caused the grain prices to inflate rapidly but also led to confusion and encouraged hoarding, which inhibited the flow of rice around the country. Northern domains which had ordered relief rice on the Edo markets found the export of their rice out of the city being physically blocked by the troops of city magistrates concerned that their own areas would be left with insufficient supply. Shogunal officials in Osaka trying to ensure that ordered rice was moved to the more severely affected northern and eastern domains were physically attacked. These factors, coupled with a paltry welfare intervention from the shogunate, resulted in the shogunal government, and Tanuma in particular, being blamed for the famine. Frustration against Tanuma's rule and the continuing famine began to manifest, both among large sections of the domain lords and shogunal vassals, but even more dramatically among the general population.

At a popular level, the reactions against Tanuma were represented not only in clandestinely distributed texts but also in an explosion of anti-Tanuma graffiti, and eventually in open rebellion. Graffiti is an inherently transitory medium, but the extent of diary-writing and note-taking among early modern Japanese provides ample record of graffiti from the period. In a modern collection of early modern graffiti compiled from such contemporary sources, one can find nearly a hundred pages of closely copied examples of personalized anti-Tanuma graffiti.[44] In addition, it contains a similar amount of content of graffiti attributing political blame for the Tenmei famine to other lords

---

[44] For example, Yajima, *Edojidai rakusho ruijū*, 10:10–40 and 9:12–42.

or the state in general.[45] This gives some idea of the extent of public reaction and discourse against the government.

Although inherently popular as a medium, and often humorous, it is also interesting to note that much of this political graffiti made its points through relatively high-brow literary allusion and reference to mainstream political thought texts. For example, one of the most widely distributed instances of graffiti, recorded in at least six locations just in this one compilation, was a spoof of the premier text of Neo-Confucianism, *Greater Learning* (J. *Daigaku*, Ch. *Daxue*). In the graffiti version, retitled *Greater Evil* (J. *Daiaku*), the role of the Song dynasty Neo-Confucian commentator Cheng Yi in the original text is replaced by Tanuma, who then, in couplets which rhyme perfectly with the Japanese reading of the original *Greater Learning*, exalts the reader to "throw away virtue," "increase death," and "illuminate the way of greater evil" in a text which thereby reverses the entire content of the original version.[46] The concentration of references to "death" in anti-Tanuma popular writing added a grim flavor to the black comedy of the graffiti, pointing to the seriousness of the underlying issues.

Increasingly, popular reaction turned violent. Local rebellions and riots erupted around the country, both in rural and urban areas. In this context, many of the domanial elite began to fear a complete collapse of the Tokugawa order. In 1784, Tanuma's son Okitomo was stabbed to death by another Tokugawa retainer in Edo Castle. Of even more political significance, however, was Okitomo's funeral procession through the streets of Edo a few days later, which had to be carried out at night due the unpopularity of the regime. Even then it was attacked by crowds of rock-throwing townspeople.[47] Even in Edo, the state could not maintain order. In this context, ranking domain lords, led by the heads of the three collateral Tokugawa houses, pressured Tanuma to go. Late in the summer of 1786, he stood down from the position of senior councillor. But the shogunate bureaucracy remained stacked with his supporters, and they successfully blocked attempts to have Matsudaira Sadanobu take over the government.[48] The hand of change was ultimately forced not by any palace intrigues or hereditary appointments but by a massive commoner uprising in Edo itself.

In the early summer of 1787, severe urban rioting broke out first in Osaka and then in a large number of other cities throughout Japan, most dramatically in Edo. The Edo riot (*uchikowashi*) of 1787 led to the government losing

---

[45] Yajima, *Edojidai rakusho ruijū*, vols. 9–11.
[46] Yajima, *Edojidai rakusho ruijū*, 9:32.
[47] Titsingh and Screech, *Secret Memoirs of the Shoguns*, 149.
[48] Fujita, *Tanuma jidai*, 212–24.

control of the city for three days. In addition to attacking rice merchants and storehouses, rioters particularly targeted the specialist merchants who converted samurai rice salaries into cash (*fudasashi*). The rioters clearly perceived those in control of the financial system as part of the cause of famine and poverty, targeting their businesses and houses for special attention. The violence of the rioters, just like the learned theoretical analysis of Ogyū Sorai, held the link between public debt and the rice taxation and salary system responsible. For those on the street, this link was personified by the particular merchants who transferred samurai rice salary into the currency form used for debt payment. The disciplined symbolism of the performative acts they carried out in the streets, often in front of *fudasashi* houses, made this clear, as Anne Walthall describes in Chapter 20 of this volume. Only in the days after these riots, and through the intercession of shogunal women's chambers figures, notably the *onna rōjū* Ōsaki, was Hitotsubashi Harusada, father of the new, adolescent shogun, Tokugawa Ienari, able to force the resignation of key inner-chamber Tanuma loyalists, notably the chamberlain Yokota Noritoshi, and have Matsudaira Sadanobu appointed as senior councillor and a few months later as shogunal regent.

Matsudaira Sadanobu had been brought to power by a popular urban revolt. His new government recognized that fact by differentiating itself as much as possible from the former regime in order to try to hold public support. The early policies of the Kansei reform government were thus framed as reactions to the famine and public order emergency. They were overtly interventionist measures, such as the establishment of government-supported village grain stores holding 50 percent of local needs – a traditional Chinese institutional response to famine. These were funded by a new tax of 50 *koku* on every 10,000 *koku* of a daimyo's holdings. Despite being introduced as "emergency measures," these basically redistributive 1789 laws on grain provision, together with the village grain store policy, stayed in place until near the end of the Tokugawa period.[49]

Although these interventionist reforms catered to the public sentiment that had blamed the famine on capital, it is important to note that Sadanobu himself did not regard merchants, merchant capital, or the rich as the cause of these problems. Matsudaira Sadanobu, as well as being a senior Tokugawa lord, was an accomplished artist and author who himself wrote treatises on issues of political economy. In discussing the causes of inflation in his "Discourse on Prices," he followed much other Confucian political theory writing

[49] Fukai, "Hōreki, Tenmei kara Kansei," 19–20.

which had pinpointed the disparity between different circulating currencies and the reduction in the population employed in cultivation as the root causes of the economic problems. He also blamed decadence but was adamant that the rich were not to blame for extravagant, decadent living.

> It is simply not true that the decadent all belong to the rich houses. In fact, quite the opposite, none of the rich houses reach these high levels of decadence. Those who do reach this level of extravagance, even when they go into debt, continue to be extravagant. So, to say that those who have money are therefore decadent, and those who do not have money are therefore thrifty: this is just bad logic. Those kinds of arguments make no contribution, and rather make it even more difficult to maintain public order.[50]

In addition to showing Sadanobu's attitude to the rich, the last sentence of this quote also demonstrates the leader's awareness of the power of political argument on the streets and his sensitivity to containing it. In reality, Sadanobu needed both the street and the rich merchants on his side. The shogunate's financial situation inherited from Tanuma was appalling. In 1770, the shogunate had reserves of three million ryō; by 1788, it had only 810,000 ryō. At the same time, in 1788, the shogunate had a deficit for that year of one million ryō.[51]

Sadanobu therefore looked to engage certain chosen merchant leaders both to secure a flow of capital and, perhaps just as importantly, to help facilitate functional price adjustment. The manner of engagement was quite radical. Sadanabu gave the green light to a finance office plan to officially appoint commoner capitalists as associate officers of the shogunal finance office (kanjōsho goyō). The shogunate co-opted the heads of ten merchant houses with considerable financial resources to serve as members of this group. They were expected to use their capital in a fund, also paid into by the shogunate, which would aim to stabilize rice prices but also turn enough humble profit to sustain itself. This fund seemed to work quite well. Ten years after it was set up, the shogunate was no longer paying money in, and the fund was being used to provide low-interest strategic loans. Interestingly, only Edo-based capitalists were co-opted into the finance office in this plan; the merchants of Osaka were excluded. This was part of a broader Sadanobu strategy to rebalance financial activity toward Edo from Osaka. It can thus actually be regarded as a more successful attempt to realize what had also been a Tanuma regime objective: to establish Edo as a national financial center.[52]

---

[50] Matsudaira, "Bukkaron," 10.
[51] Takeuchi, *Kansei kaikaku*, 20.
[52] Takeuchi, *Kansei kaikaku*, 20–22.

The shogunate was also quite careful about the political reception of their selections for co-option. Merchants involved in the salary-rice-to-currency conversion business were blacklisted, as were any other merchant houses which had been specific targets of the Edo rioters.[53] In this way the shogunate showed its deference to the will of the general population as expressed in the riots, on the one hand, while to an extent actually building on some aspects of Tanuma's mercantilist policies, on the other. Sadanobu, like Tanuma, looked not to oppose but to employ the power of merchant houses to achieve state aims.

The history of Japanese governance in the late 1700s has often been portrayed as a contest between the pro-merchant policies of the Tanuma regime (1759–87) against the allegedly anti-mercantile, statist policies of Matsudaira Sadanobu's Kansei reform regime from 1788. These portrayals were heavily wrapped up in the Cold War politicization of Japan's early modern history, when anti-communist sensibilities in US-based Japanese studies championed Tanuma as "a man not afraid to look ahead and make a break with political and economic traditionalism," contrasting his rule against the "triumph of reaction" represented by Matsudaira Sadanobu's Kansei reforms.[54] Japanese historiography has been more balanced and open to the advantages of Sadanobu's regime, but until recently it has similarly emphasized a clash between two opposing visions of government – one laissez-faire and pro-commerce (Tanuma Okitsugu), one statist and anti-mercantile (Matsudaira Sadanobu). The most recent Japanese academic writing looking at their respective periods of influence, however, has questioned seeing them in opposition and rather suggested more attention be given to continuities between the two regimes, particularly in the nature of their relationship with merchant capital.[55] Recent scholarship has demonstrated that the two regimes showed much continuity in fields as diverse as currency provision and adjustment, on the one hand, and colonization and militarization of the far north of Japan, on the other.[56]

The big difference between the Tanuma and Kansei reform regimes' approaches to engaging capital, however, was Matsudaira Sadanobu's tendency to institutionalize the state's relationship with merchants through processes of co-option and state structural expansion. He co-opted merchants

[53] Fukai, "Hōreki, Tenmei kara Kansei," 20–22.
[54] Hall, *Tanuma Okitsugu*, vii, 131.
[55] For this argument and examples of similarities in fields as diverse as colonization of Hokkaido, see Fukai, "Hōreki, Tenmei kara Kansei," 26–27.
[56] Fujita, *Tanuma jidai*, 105–6; Fukai, "Hōreki, Tenmei kara Kansei," 11–13. On Kansei's continuation of northern policy, see Paramore, "Nationalization of Confucianism," 46–50.

by inviting certain merchant house leaders to join the apparatus of the state. Whereas Tanuma's approach was comparatively similar to outsourcing, Sadanobu's practices of co-option were conducted as part of a larger state-building exercise. Although clearly not anti-capital, Sadanobu was also not anti-state. He looked to build state institutions to give direction and advice to government action. The overarching strategy in that state-building exercise was the state's engagement, utilization, and co-option of other social forces and movements. Just as the Kansei reforms' engagement of merchant houses was a way to co-opt that group, so too the exclusion of other merchant houses, and the tenor of policy at the beginning of the reforms, looked to engage the clearly articulated outlooks of the urban rioters who represented the street. Possibly the Kansei reforms' most significant engagement and co-option, however, targeted neither the urban poor nor the rich merchants, but rather the middle layer of educated opinion based in the private school and leisure learning spheres of urban life across Japan.

As we have seen, much of the political discourse at all levels – in popular culture, state institutions, and on the street – was colored by the political writing and analysis of thinkers who earned their living in the private Confucian schools of Japan's urban centers. Possibly one of the Kansei reforms' most significant actions, and certainly their most enduring, was a build-up of educational and knowledge institutions inside the shogunate, which integrated leading figures from this private sphere more closely into state circles, in many cases through direct state appointment and samurai vassalage. This reform and expansion of the state's educational and knowledge institutions also led to new relationships between shogunal and domanial state academies and elites, and crucially to an integration of debate-centered scholarly and political practices from the private sphere into state institutions.

State Building and the Institutionalization of Debate

The Kansei reform government established a wide range of new state knowledge institutions. This led to the creation of a network of shogunal and domanial state schools with a standardized approach to knowledge and a new emphasis on the education and promotion of state officials – a Tokugawa "information order."[57] The Kansei government established national, state-run

---

[57] I use this term following Bayly, *Empire and Information*, and apply it to East Asia in Paramore, "Transnational Archive of the Sinosphere."

shogunal Confucian and medical academies; appointed nonstate Confucian teachers from the west of Japan to take over as professors at these schools, giving them samurai status as relatively senior Tokugawa retainers in the process; integrated the shogunal interpreters from Nagasaki into the activities of the academies to teach Dutch and Chinese; and made attendance at the academies compulsory for all junior officials in the shogunate.

The people and ideas that dominated this new state system were almost exclusively drawn from *outside* the shogunal state system. The scholars whom Matsudaira Sadanobu put in charge of the new institutions of this information order had no standing in the shogunate before his takeover. Sadanobu not only acted upon political advice documents (memorials) written by these figures but appointed them into the shogunate to supervise the knowledge elements in the reforms. In the early 1790s, the shogunal Confucian academy, the Shōheizaka Academy, was repopulated with political thinkers from western Japan, who then oversaw the creation of a new intersection between the state and the sphere of public political debate based in the private academies of the cities. Three of these new appointments, Shibano Ritsuzan, Koga Seiri, and Bitō Jishū, became known as "The Three Kansei Professors." Both Shibano Ritsuzan and Koga Seiri had written biting memorials to previous lords which attacked the very basis of the Tokugawa political system. Seiri, for instance, in a memorial to his previous domain lord written several years before the Tenmei famine and resulting riots, had attacked the entire hereditary basis of state appointment:

> As our country is under a regime of generals, the path of (s)election is closed. Particularly in domains such as ours [Saga], the damage of the hereditary system is not to be avoided. Those with hereditary status are negligent, and those without do not serve. This is why the spirit of the gentleman/samurai cannot be enacted and why custom can so degenerate.[58]

In his widely circulated memorial *Ritsuzan jōsho*, likely written in the 1760s, Shibano Ritsuzan noted ominously,

> "The prince is like a boat, the masses like the water. The water can support a boat well but can also overturn it. The masses can live well under the rule of a prince, or they can destroy him." The winds and waves of the masses rise when the sentiments of the masses are obstructed. For this reason, since antiquity, making sure the sentiments of the masses are communicated has

---

[58] Koga, *Jūjikai*, 160, uses the word *han* to indicate the domain government of Saga; this is an early use of this term, which is now the ordinary way to refer to domains in Japanese.

been the primary business of governance. "Communicating the sentiments of the masses" means ensuring the sovereign is informed about the suffering of the masses.[59]

The invocation of this warning from the classical Confucian text *Xunzi* (an invocation which had also been referred to by Dazai Shundai in his memorials to Kuroda Naokuni) was followed by Ritsuzan's advice on listening to the sentiments of the masses. This linked into Seiri's emphasis on the traditional Confucian idea of remonstrance in another cutting attack on the nature of Japan's governments and ruling class:

> In Japan particularly, the custom of remonstration is not performed. Lines of communication are normally closed, and the sentiments of the masses are not communicated up to those on high. This is because the path of education is not propagated. A sovereign who would leave behind the bad practices of former years and set right the state must first collect the knowledge of many people. To do this, there is nothing more urgent than "opening the channels of communication."[60]

Shibano Ritsuzan's and Koga Seiri's conflation of the traditional Confucian ideas of: (1) remonstrance (the duty of a vassal and/or scholar to speak uncomfortable truth to his lord); (2) communication of the "sentiments of the masses" (which inherently valued commoner opinion); and (3) the Song Neo-Confucian Cheng Yi's idea of "opening channels of communication" (Ch. *kaiyanlu*) communicated a vision of the critical writings and views of the Confucian scholars outside the state as representing the sentiments of the people. This is an interesting conflation of ideas on the role of the (upper-class) gentry and the sentiments of the (lower-class) masses. Ritsuzan, Seiri, and other major political thinkers of this period clearly saw what modern historiography too readily labels "elite" political thought as closely intertwined not only with the welfare of the lower classes but also with their opinions. Of course, as we saw earlier, this view to an extent reflected the reality of the way political opinion circulated in early modern Japan, with street rumor and action interacting with articulated written political opinion.

Although largely ignored in modern political and political thought histories, the contemporaneously most influential figure in the Kansei reforms' expansion of state academicism was Shibano Ritsuzan. In 1790, Matsudaira Sadanobu

---

[59] Shibano, *Ritsuzan jōsho*, 106–7. The quote that opens this section is traditionally attributed to Confucius through *Kongzi jiayu* (House records of Confucius): https://ctext.org/kongzi-jiayu/wu-yi-jie. It is also contained in *Xunzi*.
[60] Koga, *Jūjikai*, 156–57.

elevated Ritsuzan from commoner status into the middle-to-upper ranks of the samurai caste, making him a vassal of the Tokugawa house on a 5,000-*koku* stipend. Sadanobu appointed Ritsuzan as a professor of the state Confucian academy and then issued a nationally distributed decree in which he publicly ordered the official head of that academy to follow Ritsuzan's orders.[61]

Ritsuzan had argued in *Ritsuzan jōsho* that specialist knowledge had to be integrated into the structures of governance.[62] He argued for education and examinations to be institutionalized in the state structures so that the government elite would both share a common ethic and possess a wide range of necessary specialist skills. By 1800, the shogunate had an examination system, people were being appointed on the basis of this system, and a range of state academies across the domains of Japan were beginning to pick up the approach of the Shōheizaka Academy, which Ritsuzan was now basically running.[63]

Once in place, Ritsuzan played a central role advising on further reforms to a range of other state institutions, including a repopulation of the state medical academy. The Kansei reforms established a centralized shogunal medical academy, which worked in parallel with the Shōheizaka Academy.[64] One theme running through the reforms and establishment of all these state knowledge institutions was a new privileging of foreign knowledge, notably including language capacity. The shogunate obliged the hereditary houses of state Chinese and Dutch translators based in Nagasaki to supply language teachers to the academies in Edo. Many of the state's new appointments into the top levels of the academies during the Kansei reforms were scholars who had taken a deep interest in external affairs. In extant copies from the archives of the Shōheizaka Academy, now held in the Imperial Household Library, can be found not only a variety of Qing commentaries on classic works of Confucian political theory but also contemporaneous snippets of field intelligence reports from Qing military commanders on the Chinese frontier with Russia, Dutch medical dictionaries, and Qing Chinese treatises on Europe and the Americas.[65] Koga Seiri's

[61] Backus, "Relationship of Confucianism to the Tokugawa Bakufu," 118.
[62] Shibano, *Ritsuzan jōsho*.
[63] Hashimoto, *Edo bakufu shiken seidoshi*; Paramore, "Nationalization of Confucianism."
[64] Machi, "Development of Scholarship in the Igakkan"; Paramore, "Chinese Medicine, Western Medicine and Confucianism."
[65] Most of the archives of the Shōheizaka Academy were destroyed during the fires which engulfed the University of Tokyo library in the aftermath of the Great Kantō earthquake of 1923. Significant elements of the archives, however, and some contemporaneous copied documents can be found in other collections, notably those of the collateral houses and those now held in the Imperial Household Library. The Qing Heilongjiang border commandery reports were viewed by the author in the Imperial Household Library, Imperial Palace, Tokyo, in 2011.

son, Tōan, a later leader of the academy, wrote major treatises on maritime defense and canon technology. Tōan's son, Koga Kin'ichirō, in turn became learned in Dutch and was appointed the first head of the shogunate's Western learning academy.[66]

Previously, state-affiliated Confucian schools, like that of the Hayashi, had been just one more player in the private education market, attended by whoever could pay. But after the Kansei reforms, the new state Confucian academy, the Shōheizaka Academy, taught only shogunal retainers – actual and potential future state officials. In the same major public proclamation in which he had announced Shibano Ritsuzan's supremacy in the state Confucian academy, Matsudaira Sadanobu had also expressed the hope that the practices and outlooks taught in this academy would be picked up by domain academies. His idea was that this new orthodox state academy system – the shogunal Confucian academy, supported by hundreds of domain state academies – would begin to create a standardization of approach to government and the role of theory and knowledge in government across the regions of Japan.

This was the extension of the intellectual revolution in the private sphere into the structures of the state.[67] As can be seen in Figure 2.3, there was a boom in the establishment of domanial academies during and after the Kansei reforms, and as can be seen in Figure 2.4, the majority of these schools followed the Shōheizaka line.

The new state academicism's emphasis on open communication was supported by the methodology of their scholarly practice. As we will see, from the Kansei reforms period onwards, the practice of so-called social reading (kaidoku) became standardized across the various state academies of Japan. Recent academic literature on both education and political thought in Tokugawa Japan has focused on the significance of this practice for the way both scholarly and political debate developed from the late 1700s through the early to mid-1800s.[68] Social reading was a pedagogical practice based around debate in small groups on the reading of prepared texts. The historian Maeda Tsutomu has described the practice of this debate as following three key principles: being intercommunicative, egalitarian, and associative. Maeda sees the formation of this practice, realized in these three principles, as a direct reaction to the strict vertical hierarchy of the feudal military system.[69]

[66] Makabe, *Tokugawa kōki no gakumon to seiji*.
[67] Matsuda, *Edo no chishiki kara Meiji no seiji e*, 79–80.
[68] Maeda, *Edo kōki no shisō kūkan*; Lan, *Kanbunken ni okeru Ogyū Sorai*.
[69] Maeda, *Edo no dokushokai*, 54.

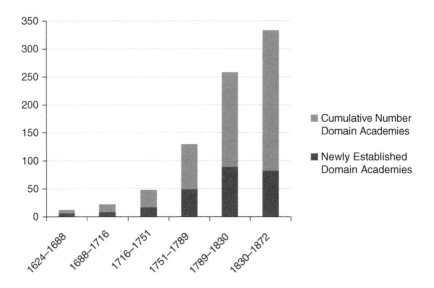

Figure 2.3 Establishment of domain academies during the Tokugawa period. Statistics drawn from Ishikawa, *Nihon gakkōshi*, 281.

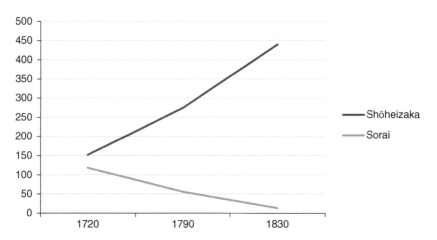

Figure 2.4 Graphic representation of the number of domanial state Confucian teachers associated with Sorai or Shōheizaka (shogunal academy) in the later Tokugawa period. Statistics drawn from Ishikawa, *Nihon gakkōshi*, 259.

Institutionalization of Confucian pedagogy in the state led to standardization of these social reading practices in the shogunal and domanial state knowledge infrastructure. An emphasis on the nature of political communication, and a direct relation of that outlook to the practice of social reading, can be found in many later shogunal and domanial state school regulations.[70] In many of those regulations, there is a particular emphasis on the ethical utility of social reading both as a form of self-cultivation for the individual, and in encouraging a practice of equal, open communication between different ranking members of one domain or bureaucratic unit.[71]

Following the Shōheizaka Academy line has until recently been understood to mean following orthodox Song Neo-Confucian theory. But the latest research has demonstrated that what was most heavily standardized in the shogunal and new domanial academies was not any single political interpretation but rather the debate-centered pedagogical practice of social reading. There was not only a high level of tolerance for other forms of theory but also much encouragement of the use of new ideas. For instance, almost all shogunal academy social readings for which there are records show extensive use of relatively recent scholarly theories from Qing China, most of which were highly critical of Neo-Confucian approaches.[72]

Moreover, in the development of many domanial academies, the social reading practice became directly related to critical discussion of contemporary politics and eventually the direct political debates of the last decades of the Tokugawa period leading into the Meiji Restoration. Maeda Tsutomu has identified such processes, which he calls "the politicization of social reading," in a number of domains and has analyzed the process through contemporaneous samurai diaries and memoirs for Hamamatsu, Kanazawa, Satsuma, and Mito domains.[73] Mito and Satsuma domains would become the platforms for much of the most dynamic political debate leading into the restoration period.

This interrelated state-society discursive space of debate would form the politics of the rest of the nineteenth century. From the very beginnings of the movement to overthrow the shogunate in the late 1830s to the Meiji Restoration and the early decades of politics in Meiji Japan itself, political argument was formed in discussion groups heavily influenced by these methodologies, whose members expressed their political critique through Confucian political theoretical frameworks. Echoing allusions in the work of the former University of Tokyo political-thought historian Watanabe Hiroshi, the historian of

---

[70] For instance, in the rules of the Kanbe domain school Kyōrindō in Monbushō, *Nihon kyōikushi shiryō*, 6:110, and in a range of school rules compiled in Kurokawa, *Gakkō hen*, 21–23. See also Maeda, *Edo no dokushokai*, 238–39.

[71] See, for example, the references to the academy rules of Kaga and Chōshū domains in Maeda, *Edo kyōiku shisōshi*, 465–66, 484, 502.

[72] Maeda, *Edo kyōiku shisōshi*, 292–94.

[73] Maeda, *Edo no dokushokai*, 240–54.

Chinese thought Kojima Tsuyoshi has recently posited Confucianism as "the revolutionary ideology of the Meiji Restoration."[74] Even the political practices of the post-Meiji freedom and people's rights movement of the 1880s, which led to the establishment of constitutional government in Japan, have been linked to the social reading practices of debate.[75]

The general direction of both the knowledge and political economic reforms of Sadanobu's Kansei reign continued on for around twenty years after he stepped down from the shogunal regency in 1793. He had stacked the upper levels of the shogunate bureaucracy with loyalists even more effectively than had Tanuma. From around 1830, shogunal politics would enter a new phase, yet the significance of the Kansei reforms' institutionalization of knowledge would carry on. The specialists who managed the treaty negotiations with the United States in the 1850s, and the interpreters who translated between US Commodore Matthew C. Perry and the shogunate, were all drawn from the Shōheizaka Academy and the shogunal Academy of Western Learning (Bansho Shirabesho), which was set up by Koga Kin'ichirō, Koga Seiri's grandson, and initially staffed entirely with members from the shogunal Confucian academy.[76] The most influential early Meiji political discussion group, and also the forum for the first major liberal political discussions in East Asia, the Meiroku group, was almost all graduates or former teachers of the shogunal academies established in the Kansei reforms or of the Western learning academy which grew from them.

In this sense, the state building of the Kansei reforms left behind a significant legacy in the spheres of knowledge, education, and political debate. The legacy of Kansei's economic reforms is harder to judge. On the one hand, relative stability over the next thirty years was attained. On the other hand, the crisis precipitated by the Tenpō famine of 1833–36 was in many ways a carbon copy of what had happened from 1782 to 1788 in the Tenmei famine, with a similarly horrendous death toll. Interestingly, Ōshio Heihachirō, leader of an armed uprising against the shogunate in Osaka in 1837, which is sometimes alleged as the first spark on the long road toward the overthrow of the Tokugawa state, was a friend and regular correspondent of the leaders of the Shōheizaka Academy in Edo, especially Koga Seiri's son, Tōan.[77]

---

[74] Kojima, *Yasukuni shikan*; Watanabe, *History of Japanese Political Thought*.
[75] Maeda, *Edo no dokushokai*, 359–63, especially direct quotes from movement meeting rules dictating the use of "social reading," 362. Kōno, *Meiroku zasshi no seiji shisō*; Kurozumi, *Kinsei Nihon shakai to jukyō*.
[76] Makabe, *Tokugawa kōki no gakumon to seiji*.
[77] Aiso, *Ōshio Heihachirō shokan*.

Conclusion

How can we characterize the politics and political thought of the mid- and late Tokugawa periods? On the one hand, Japan was governed by regimes where the vast majority of high offices were inherited, presiding over economic inequality so bad that famines leading to the deaths of hundreds of thousands occasionally occurred in a country which was otherwise comparatively wealthy. On the other hand, it was a politics in which "public sentiment" was lauded by theorists and courted by rulers. Public sentiment was not only an important theoretical concept but also clearly part of the political mix in issues of contested succession, reactions to emergencies like famine, and the control of urban disorder. Tokugawa Japan was thereby a polity where, despite the public having no formal role in governance, large sections of the public came together regularly to discuss politics and the theories behind it, and rulers both engaged this discourse and at times submitted to it.

This belied the reality of the larger processes of negotiation lying behind the facade of hereditary samurai rule. These negotiations involved different classes, genders, status groups, and ranks. Confucian political theory provided a shared framework for debates, thereby affecting the form and outcomes of negotiated settlements. Of course, just as in our times, and as it has always been, neither the processes of government nor the debates around them were by any means egalitarian. Gender, status, wealth, rank, chance, and luck all determined unequal access to the process. Although not being egalitarian, neither was the mature early modern Japanese state simply autocratic, despotic, or even feudal.

How then can we characterize the *history* of politics and political thought of early modern Japan? The history of early modern Japan was a history of the expansion of politics. The who, what, why, and how of politics in Japan all broadened between the mid-seventeenth and late nineteenth centuries.

Who? Participation in politics, and expectations of who in society *should* express political opinions, broadened considerably between the mid-seventeenth and late eighteenth centuries. At the beginning of the seventeenth century, any expression of political or even heterodox religious opinion by people not at the top of the military hierarchy was liable to be regarded as seditious. Confucian political thought was frowned upon, and new political structures which looked to engage broader participation, even only among the samurai, were discouraged, as we saw in section one in the example regarding Ikeda Mitsumasa and Kumazawa Banzan. By the early eighteenth century, however, this had changed. Open political debate, including in printed form

and in organized private schools, was widely tolerated. Shogunal and domanial states at times openly engaged advice from this private sphere of debate,
encouraged the use of extra-state political advice and ideas in state reform, and
employed people from the Confucian private educational sphere as advisers.
Often these advisers had themselves been previously responsible for unsolic-
ited opinion pieces which had gained popularity in public political discussion
outside the state. As we saw in the cases of Tokugawa Yoshimune's succession, in the public criticism of the Kyōhō reforms, and particularly toward the
end of the Tanuma regime, debate around state decisions, including critical
debate, was engaged at a broad social level, from domain lords to poor commoners, sometimes in concert. As the eighteenth century progressed, political
participation continued, including through the expression of political ideas in
dynamic forms such as performance and rebellion – as the politics of the Edo
riot and Matsudaira Sadanobu's succession demonstrate.

What? The expectation of what politics and governance should deliver,
and what the responsibilities of the state therefore were, also expanded considerably in this period. In short, expectations of government went from the
very limited view of expecting only security and communal river control (in
the language of the time: "supervising agriculture, controlling water" – *kannō
chisui*), to literally "ordering the world" through the provision of social welfare, notably including protection from the consequences of natural disaster or
economic decline ("ordering the world, succoring the masses" – *keisei saimin*).

Why? In addition to the contract-like expectations of betterment touched
on by Hayami in his theorization of "industriousness," other aspects of Japanese early modernization contributed to this steady expansion of the political.
Excess labor time, especially for the lower samurai, created a kind of otium
allowing more time for both involvement in, and imagination of, the political.
Male literacy, which had expanded toward 50 percent in some areas by the
eighteenth century, was also a major tool of political engagement. Crucially,
the content of written texts was, from the beginning of the literacy boom in
the seventeenth century, inherently transcultural (or what in a modern context would be called transnational). The fact that most texts were Chinese, or
based in a trans-Asian cultural context, meant that political identity was being
imagined not only against domestic but also external others – by global and
thereby inherently pluralist standards. The idea of "political economy," for
instance, is one example of a new standard in Japanese politics which entered
through the transnational literary and cultural world that literate Japanese
were now embedded within. The contemporaneous Chinese imperial state,
the Qing, being Manchu-led, was itself defined in pluralist terms, and from

the late eighteenth century Japanese political thinkers were clearly aware of the pluralist nature of political thought in China. The shared discursive form of political debate in early modern Japan was increasingly integrated into a shared trans-Asian language and literary tradition, which was inherently transnational. Including cultural and ethical norms from other polities which were not of the samurai system, it could not but engender a pluralist political outlook in Japan.

How? The primary justification of political power at the beginning of the seventeenth century, physical force – the capacity to monopolize violence (and thereby ensure security) – in the latter seventeenth century came to be augmented by other justifications of power which gradually began to undermine, or at least relativize, the legitimacy of governance through violence. Hayami's "ethos of industriousness," which all people (including rulers) were "called on to respect," already located moral power and expectation of state action in labor and productivity.[78] The rise of Confucian political thought outlined in this chapter, including its embrace by various shogunal and domanial states, also added in the powerful idea that coercion (law) was an inherently inferior manner of rule, best replaced by suasion (culture). This powerful shared cultural element in political debate thus served to further relativize the base of state power in violence and to suggest an expectation for governance to be anchored in cultural activity and form – which in the Japanese context was based outside the state, in the private Confucian and other urban academies and salons.

The relative stability of macropolitical structures in the mature early modern state belied radical change in the reality of politics between the mid-seventeenth and early nineteenth centuries. By the end of this period, the expansion of political participation, facilitated by surplus labor and encouraged by new transnational (predominantly Chinese) publishing and information networks, had led to an increase in public involvement in the political – perhaps not a Habermasian public sphere, but certainly more publicness than before. The broad acceptance of the Confucian welfare model of "political economy" had also led to an increase in public expectations of what politics could and should deliver. As the connections we discussed between academic political economy analysis, popular protest, riot, graffiti, and state policy demonstrate, a political imagination had emerged couched in a language and philosophy which was new and transnational, and which was shared across large swathes and various strata of Japanese society.

[78] Hayami, "Introduction," 25–29.

Bibliography

Aiso Kazuhiro. *Ōshio Heihachirō shokan no kenkyū*. Osaka: Seibundō, 2003.

Arai Hakuseki. *Arai Hakuseki zenshū*. 6 vols. Kokusho Kankōkai, 1907.

Backus, Robert L. "The Relationship of Confucianism to the Tokugawa Bakufu as Revealed in the Kansei Educational Reform." *Harvard Journal of Asiatic Studies* 34 (1974): 97–162.

Bayly, C. A. *Empire and Information: Intelligence Gathering and Social Communication in India, 1780–1870*. Cambridge: Cambridge University Press, 1996.

Berry, Mary Elizabeth. *Japan in Print: Information and Nation in the Early Modern Period*. Berkeley: University of California Press, 2006.

Braddick, Michael J. *State Formation in Early Modern England, c. 1550–1700*. Cambridge: Cambridge University Press, 2000.

Dazai Shundai. *Keizairoku*. In *Sorai gakuha*, edited by Rai Tsutomu, 7–56. Vol. 37 of *Nihon shisō taikei*. Iwanami Shoten, 1972.

Shundai jōsho nihen. In *Nihon keizai taiten*, Vol. 9, edited by Takimoto Seiichi, 689–708. Shishi Shuppan, 1928.

De Vries, Jan. *The Industrious Revolution: Consumer Behavior and the Household Economy, 1650 to the Present*. Cambridge: Cambridge University Press, 2008.

Ehlers, Maren. *Give and Take: Poverty and the Status Order in Early Modern Japan*. Cambridge, MA: Harvard University Asia Center, 2018.

Fujii Jōji. *Edo jidai no kanryōsei*. Aoki Shoten, 1999.

Fujita Satoru. *Tanuma jidai*. Yoshikawa Kōbunkan, 2012.

Fukai Masaumi. *Edojō o yomu: Ōoku, chūoku, hyōkō*. Genshobō, 1997.

"Hōreki, Tenmei kara Kansei." In *Kinsei 4*, 1–32. Vol. 13 of *Iwanami kōza: Nihon rekishi*.

Tsunayoshi to Yoshimune. Yoshikawa Kōbunkan, 2012.

Hall, John Whitney. "The *Bakuhan* System." In *Early Modern Japan*, edited by John W. Hall, 128–82. Vol. 4 of *The Cambridge History of Japan*. Cambridge: Cambridge University Press, 1991.

Tanuma Okitsugu, 1719–1788, Forerunner of Modern Japan. Cambridge, MA: Harvard University Press, 1955.

Hashimoto Akihiko. *Edo bakufu shiken seidoshi no kenkyū*. Kazama Shobō, 1994.

Hayami, Akira. "Introduction: The Emergence of 'Economic Society.'" In *Emergence of Economic Society in Japan, 1600–1859*, edited by Akira Hayami, Osamu Saito, and Ronald P. Toby, 1–35. Vol. 1 of *The Economic History of Japan, 1600–1900*. Oxford: Oxford University Press, 2004.

Hayashi Jussai, ed. *Kansei chōshū shokafu*. 26 vols. Rev. ed. Zoku Gunsho Ruijū Kanseikai, 1964–67.

Hayashi Razan (as Rō Yōshi). *Sōzoku zengoki* (1651–52). In *Gunsho ikkoku*, Vol. 7, edited by Ōta Nanpo. Naikaku Bunko, National Archives of Japan. https://doi.org/10.20730/100019324

He, Wenkai. *Paths toward the Modern Fiscal State: England, Japan, and China*. Cambridge, MA: Harvard University Press, 2013.

Howell, David L. *Geographies of Identity in Nineteenth-Century Japan*. Berkeley: University of California Press, 2005.

Ikegami, Eiko. *Bonds of Civility: Aesthetic Networks and the Political Origins of Japanese Culture*. Cambridge: Cambridge University Press, 2005.

Ishikawa Ken. *Nihon gakkōshi no kenkyū*. Nihon Tosho Sentā, 1977.

Iwanami kōza: Nihon rekishi, edited by Ōtsu Tōru, Sakurai Eiji, Fujii Jōji, Yoshida Yutaka, and Ri Sonshi (Lee Sungsi). 22 vols. Iwanami Shoten, 2013–16.

Kaiho Seiryō. *Keizaiwa*. In *Honda Toshiaki, Kaiho Seiryō*, annotated by Kuranami Seiji, 373–411. Vol. 44 of *Nihon shisō taikei*, edited by Ienaga Saburō, Ishimoda Shō, Inoue Mitsusada, Sagara Tōru, Nakamura Yukihiko, Bitō Masahide, Maruyama Masao, and Yoshikawa Kōjirō. Iwanami Shoten, 1970.

Kasaya Kazuhiko. *Kinsei buke shakai no seiji kōzō*. Yoshikawa Kōbunkan, 1993.

Knights, Mark. *Representation and Misrepresentation in Later Stuart Britain: Partisanship and Political Culture*. Oxford: Oxford University Press, 2005.

Koga Seiri. *Jūjikai*. In *Nihon Keizai sōsho*, Vol. 17, edited by Takimoto Seiichi, 155–68. Nihon Keizai Sōsho Kankōkai, 1914–17.

Koike Susumu. *Edo bakufu chokugai gundan no keisei*. Yoshikawa Kōbunkan, 2001.

Kojima Tsuyoshi. *Yasukuni shikan: Bakumatsu ishin to iu shin'en*. Chikuma Shobō, 2007.

Kōno Yūri. *Meiroku zasshi no seiji shisō: Sakatani Shiroshi to "dōri" no chōsen*. Tōkyō Daigaku Shuppankai, 2011.

Kornicki, Peter F. *The Book in Japan: A Cultural History from the Beginnings to the Nineteenth Century*. Leiden: Brill, 1998.

Koselleck, Reinhart. *Futures Past: On the Semantics of Historical Time*. New York: Columbia University Press, 2004.

Kuroita Katsumi, ed. *Tokugawa jikki*, Vol. 9. Vol. 46 of *Kokushi taikei*, edited by Kokushi Taikei Henshūkai. Yoshikawa Kōbunkan, 1978.

Kurokawa Mamichi, ed. *Gakkō hen*. Vol. 8 of *Nihon kyōiku bunko*. Dōbunkan, 1910–11. Reprint, Nihon Tosho Sentā, 1977.

Kurozumi Makoto. *Kinsei Nihon shakai to jukyō*. Perikansha, 2003.

Lan Hung-yueh. *Kanbunken ni okeru Ogyū Sorai*. Tōkyō Daigaku Shuppankai, 2018.

Machi, Senjurō. "The Development of Scholarship in the Igakkan (1): The Founding of the Igakkan." *Journal of the Japan Society of Medical History* 45, no. 3 (September 1999): 339–72.

Maeda Tsutomu. *Edo kōki no shisō kūkan*. Perikansha, 2009.

———. *Edo kyōiku shisōshi kenkyū*. Kyoto: Shibunkaku, 2016.

———. *Edo no dokushokai: Kaidoku no shisōshi*. Heibonsha, 2012.

Makabe Jin. *Tokugawa kōki no gakumon to seiji: Shōheizaka Gakumonjo jusha to bakumatsu gaikō hen'yō*. Nagoya: Nagoya Daigaku Shuppankai, 2007.

Maruyama Masao. "Taiheisaku kō." In Rai, *Ogyū Sorai*, 787–829.

Matsuda Kōichirō. *Edo no chishiki kara Meiji no seiji e*. Perikansha, 2008.

Matsudaira Sadanobu. "Bukkaron." In *Rakuokō isho*, Vol. 1, edited by Ema Seihatsu, 56 pp. Yao Shoten, 1893.

McMullen, James. *Idealism, Protest, and the Tale of Genji: The Confucianism of Kumazawa Banzan (1619–91)*. Oxford: Oxford University Press, 1999.

Miyake Masahiro. "Edo bakufu no seiji kōzō." In Kinsei 2, 1–36. Vol. 11 of *Iwanami kōza: Nihon rekishi*.

Monbushō, ed. *Nihon kyōikushi shiryō*. 9 vols. Monbushō Sōmukyoku, 1890–92.

Murata Michihito. "Yoshimune no seiji." In Kinsei 3, 1–34. Vol. 12 of *Iwanami kōza: Nihon rekishi*.

Najita, Tetsuo. *Visions of Virtue in Tokugawa Japan: The Kaitokudō Merchant Academy of Osaka*. Chicago: University of Chicago Press, 1987.

Ogyū Sorai. *Benmei*. In Rai, *Ogyū Sorai*, 37–186.

    Seidan. In Rai, *Ogyū Sorai*, 259–446.

    Taiheisaku. In Rai, *Ogyū Sorai*, 447–85.

Ōishi Manabu. *Kinsei Nihon no shōsha to haisha*. Yoshikawa Kōbunkan, 2015.

    Kinsei Nihon no tōchi to kaikaku. Yoshikawa Kōbunkan, 2013.

    Kyōhō kaikaku no chiiki seisaku. Yoshikawa Kōbunkan, 1995.

Paramore, Kiri. "Chinese Medicine, Western Medicine and Confucianism: Japanese State Medicine and the Knowledge Cosmopolis of Early Modern East Asia." *Journal of Early Modern History* 21, no. 3 (2017): 241–69.

    Ideology and Christianity in Japan. London: Routledge, 2009.

    "The Nationalization of Confucianism: Academism, Examinations, and Bureaucratic Governance in the Late Tokugawa State." *Journal of Japanese Studies* 38, no. 1 (2012): 25–53.

    "The Transnational Archive of the Sinosphere: The Early Modern East Asian Information Order." *Proceedings of the British Academy* 212 (2018): 285–310.

Rai Tsutomu, ed. *Ogyū Sorai*. Vol. 36 of *Nihon shisō taikei*. Iwanami Shoten, 1973.

Rubinger, Richard. *Popular Literacy in Early Modern Japan*. Honolulu: University of Hawai'i Press, 2007.

    Private Academies of the Tokugawa Period. Princeton, NJ: Princeton University Press, 1982.

Sekiguchi Fumiko. *Goisshin to jendā: Ogyū Sorai kara kyōiku chokugo made*. Tōkyō Daigaku Shuppankai, 2006.

Shibano Ritsuzan. *Ritsuzan jōsho*. In *Nihon Keizai sōsho*, Vol. 17, edited by Takimoto Seiichi, 103–54. Nihon Keizai Sōsho Kankōkai, 1914–17.

Shiseki Kenyūkai, ed. *Daimyō chojutsushū*. Vol. 18 of *Naikaku bunko shozō shiseki sōkan*. Kyūko Shoin, 1982.

Takeuchi Makoto. *Kansei kaikaku no kenkyū*. Yoshikawa Kōbunkan, 2009.

Takeuchi Makoto, Fukai Masaumi, and Matsuo Mieko, eds. *Tokugawa ōoku jiten*. Tōkyōdō Shuppan, 2015.

Titsingh, Isaac, and Timon Screech. *Secret Memoirs of the Shoguns: Isaac Titsingh and Japan, 1779–1822*. London: Routledge, 2006.

Totman, Conrad. *Politics in the Tokugawa Bakufu, 1600–1843*. Cambridge, MA: Harvard University Press, 1967.

Watanabe, Hiroshi. *A History of Japanese Political Thought, 1600–1901*. Translated by David Noble. International House of Japan, 2012.

Yajima Shōken, ed. *Edojidai rakusho ruijū*. Vols. 9–11. Yajima Shōken, 1915.

Yonemoto, Marcia. *The Problem of Women in Early Modern Japan*. Oakland: University of California Press, 2016.

3

Regional Authority during the Tokugawa Period

DAVID L. HOWELL

The Tokugawa state is notoriously difficult to characterize. Edwin O. Reischauer popularized the oxymoron "centralized feudalism," which captures the challenge of describing a national government with sweeping authority that nonetheless entrusted rule over the majority of people to autonomous baronies known as domains.[1] One does not see the phrase much nowadays – the regime was neither as centralized nor as feudal as the combination suggests – but the most common alternatives, such as "federalism," "compound state," and "flamboyant state," do not conjure a clear picture of the polity to those who do not already know it well.[2] Better is Takagi Shōsaku's coinage of "garrison state" (*heiei kokka*), which captures the logic of military preparedness that underlay all institutions during the Tokugawa period, but it has yet to catch on with many Anglophone scholars.[3] Specialists, even those writing in English, often resort to the portmanteau *bakuhan*, referring to the *bakufu* (shogunate) and *han* (domains), to describe the state. As a term of convenience, *bakuhan* works as well as anything, but it suffers from the flaw of suggesting that the shogunate and domains together constituted the entirety of the state.

Here I will not introduce my own new term of convenience, oxymoronic or otherwise. On the contrary, I suggest that we embrace the state's complexity, which is suggested graphically in Map 3.1. (For a more straightforwardly schematic overview, Harold Bolitho's chapter on the domains in the earlier iteration of the *Cambridge History of Japan* is an excellent place to look.[4])

---

[1] "Centralized feudalism" is the title of a chapter in Reischauer, *Japanese*, 64–77.
[2] Berry, *Hideyoshi*, for "federal"; Ravina, *Land and Lordship*, following Mizubayashi, *Hōkensei no saihen*, for "compound state"; Brown, *Central Authority and Local Autonomy*, for "flamboyant."
[3] Takagi, *Nihon kinsei kokkashi*, 1, lays out the idea succinctly through a contrast between the late medieval and early modern states. Ehlers, *Give and Take*, 1–2, introduces the term to Anglophone readers.
[4] Bolitho, "*Han*."

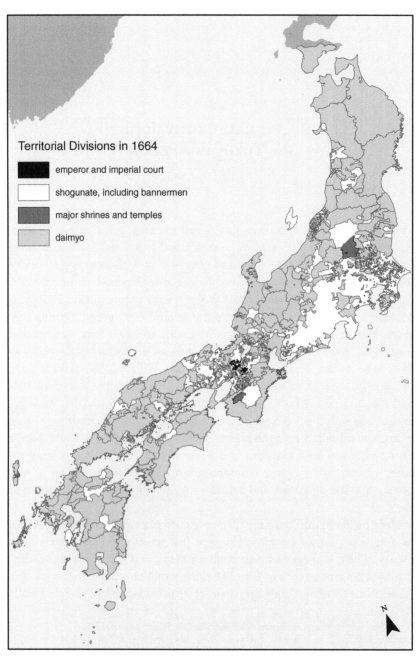

Map 3.1 Territorial divisions in 1664. Map by Fabian Drixler, based on Nishioka and Hattori, *Nihon rekishi chizu*, amended with information from Kokusho Kankōkai, "Kanbun inchi-shū," as well as Kadokawa Nihon Chimei Daijiten, *Shinpan Kadokawa Nihon chimei daijiten*, and Heibonsha Chihō Shiryō Sentā, *Nihon rekishi chimei taikei*. The coastlines derive from Inō Tadataka's survey (1800–1821), in Murayama, *Dejitaru Inō-zu*. For an earlier color version of this map, see Drixler, "Edo and the Architecture of the Great Peace," 22–23.

Scholars have spent plenty of time measuring the relative importance of the shogunate and domains and using their answers to declare that Japan was either *a* state or an assemblage of them; *a* nation or a multitude of not-quite-nations.[5] For our purposes, it is enough to say that Japan was more than the sum of its major institutions, as is clear if we look at the state from the perspective of the people in the countryside, who constituted around 90 percent of the national population.

This chapter focuses on the structures of rule below the national level during the Tokugawa period. Its initial topic is the domains – the *han* of the *baku-han* state – but it will go beyond the domains in their variety and survey as well other subnational jurisdictions, such as the shogun's personal landholdings; fiefs held by shogunal retainers whose holdings were too small to qualify as domains; and lands under the authority of major temples and shrines, members of the imperial aristocracy, and the imperial house itself. Sketching out the institutional structure of the early modern regime is a prerequisite to conveying the nature of the Tokugawa state. It also offers an introduction to a peculiarly early modern form of delegation and control. No political philosopher would ever have conjured the Tokugawa system as a model of governmental organization. Yet it endured for a quarter of a millennium and might have endured longer had it not succumbed to the challenge of Western imperialism. Rather than stick to a top-down view, however, I also look at the state from the vantage point of rural communities and their residents.

A keyword in the latter part of the chapter is governmentality, by which I mean both people's experience of being governed and the ways in which they actively participated in facilitating their own subjecthood to ruling authority. I examine how samurai and commoners collaborated in governing the countryside, using shared-revenue villages (*aikyū mura*) – villages split among multiple overlords – as a site to think about governmentality. Michel Foucault first described governmentality in a discussion of how western European theories of governance evolved from a medieval focus on the control of territory to an early modern emphasis on the control of "things," by which he meant people and institutions.[6] The aim of "government," in Foucault's formulation, lies between the extremes of single-minded expropriation and the altruistic pursuit of the common good. Its "convenient" end is to create a system in which the people subsist on the wealth they produce and the population grows, with benefits accruing to ruler and ruled alike. Rulership entails

---

[5] Toby, "Rescuing the Nation from History."
[6] Foucault, *Essential Foucault*, 229–45.

a mix of law, negotiation, and other tactics to recruit the ruled into participating in their own subjecthood. Because "government" involves much more than the operation of a state on its subjects, governmentality extends beyond the formal institutions of the state. In the context of early modern Japan, the removal of the warrior class from most of the countryside necessarily led to a kind of power-sharing arrangement between the samurai and commoners, in which the use of "laws themselves as tactics" was a common expedient for getting things done.[7]

The Domains and Other Jurisdictions

Let us begin with a clear-cut definition before venturing into the brambles. A domain was an autonomous territory ruled by a lord known as a daimyo, literally a "great name." The shogun enfeoffed daimyo with territories with an assessed yield of at least 10,000 *koku* of rice (or its equivalent); a *koku* was a measurement equal to about 180 liters, or 140 to 150 kilograms, nominally about enough to feed an adult man for a year. The shogun formally invested daimyo with their territories in exchange for their vassalage. During the reigns of the first few shoguns, it was easy to maintain the fiction, or indeed the reality, of some degree of personal connection between shogun and daimyo, but that faded with time. Still, the idea that every daimyo was a vassal of the shogun remained at the core of the institutional order.

At any given time, there were about 260 domains in Tokugawa Japan. *About*. The qualifier hints at the trickiness of the subject. There were *about* 260 domains in part because the number fluctuated over the course of the 268 years from the founding of the shogunate in 1603 to the domains' abolition in 1871, and in part because the definition of a domain, ostensibly so clear-cut, was surprisingly knotty. To be sure, we could come up with a precise list of criteria and pinpoint a precise moment in which to count the domains. Ironically, this would be easiest if we limited our inquiry to the period immediately *after* the Tokugawa shogunate's fall – that is, from 1868 to 1871 – which is the only time the word *han*, now universal in scholarship and everyday discourse, was used to designate the domains in official documents.[8]

---

[7] Foucault, *Essential Foucault*, 237.

[8] *Han* was used in some intellectual discourse before 1868. After Japan annexed the Ryukyu kingdom, it established a Ryukyu han in 1872 after the abolition of the domains elsewhere in Japan. It was abolished in 1879. See Roberts, *Performing the Great Peace*, 10–15, on how many of the terms used today to describe Tokugawa-era institutions – shogun, daimyo, han, tennō (for emperor), and so on – were either not used at all or were not the ordinary terms of reference at the time.

Such an exercise would still beg the question of whether we ought to privilege the domain so exclusively as a unit of subnational political authority.

Daimyo territories varied greatly in size and productivity. A tiny domain with the minimal holding of 10,000 *koku* might barely encompass two dozen villages, while the largest – the Kaga domain, based in Kanazawa and assessed at over a million *koku* – spanned three provinces. The numbers fluctuated over time, but there were usually about fifty domains assessed at 100,000 *koku* or more, another fifty between 50,000 and 100,000 *koku*, and the remaining 160 or so between 10,000 and 50,000 *koku*. Daimyo whose domains had yields of over 20,000 *koku* resided in castles, or at least enjoyed the status of castellans, while their less exalted colleagues had to make do with smaller fortified compounds (*jin'ya*). In general, the territorial extent of a domain meant little since assessed yields lined up only imperfectly with land area; however, daimyo whose domains comprised one or more of Japan's sixty-eight provinces generally received preferential treatment in matters of protocol. Provinces served no administrative function during the Tokugawa period, though people did imagine the national space in terms of them.

A domain's official assessed yield (*omotedaka*) generally reflected the results of land surveys done during the early seventeenth century. Successive decades of population growth, extensive land reclamation, and improved agricultural technology ensured that almost every domain's actual yield (*uchidaka*) was much higher than its official one. For example, at the end of the Tokugawa period, the Sendai domain in northeastern Honshu had an official assessed yield of 620,000 *koku* and an actual yield of about 1.12 million *koku*. This sort of discrepancy had real-world significance, but not for the distinctions of rank and standing that I discuss in this chapter.

Except for close relatives of the ruling Tokugawa house, all daimyo fell into one or the other of two categories: those whose ancestors had allied themselves with the founder of the shogunate, Ieyasu, before the Battle of Sekigahara in 1600 and those who pledged allegiance only after Ieyasu's triumph. The longtime vassals were known as "house," or *fudai*, daimyo – a *fudai* is a hereditary servant – and the relative newcomers "outside" (*tozama*) daimyo. Throughout the Tokugawa period, but particularly during the first century of its rule, the shogunate actively attainted daimyo for infractions real and imagined, moved domains around, increased and decreased domains' official yields, and occasionally elevated lesser men to daimyo rank. These changes affected house and outside daimyo alike, and newly created daimyo were assigned to one category or the other depending on their relationship with the Tokugawa house.

Three domains – Kii, Owari, and Mito – were founded by sons of Ieyasu's and were known as the August Three Houses (*gosanke*). Kii and Owari could provide successors to the shogunal house if the main line died out, while the lord of Mito lived full time in Edo Castle as a shogunal adviser. Yoshimune (r. 1716–51), the eighth shogun, was the first one to come from a collateral house: he was the daimyo of the Kii domain when he succeeded Tokugawa Ietsugu, who had died at the age of six. Yoshimune granted to two of his sons and a grandson three more new domains – Tayasu, Hitotsubashi, and Shimizu – and made them eligible to provide shogunal heirs. These daimyo were known as the August Three Ministers (*gosankyō*), the name a reflection of their identical imperial court ranks, and they ranked just below the lords of the Three Houses. The daimyo of these six houses shared with the shogunal branch the privilege of bearing the Tokugawa surname. There were other domains headed by more distant Tokugawa kin; known as "related houses" (*shinpan*), their lords often bore Ieyasu's original surname, Matsudaira, and served the regime as a subset of the house daimyo.

The distinction between house and outside daimyo was important and enduring. House daimyo, because their forefathers' ascent owed entirely to Ieyasu's patronage, were expected to be unquestioningly loyal to the Tokugawa house. Their domains tended to be smaller on average than the outsiders' ones, but they were concentrated in the most productive and strategically important parts of the archipelago, particularly in the rich hinterlands of Osaka and Kyoto in central Honshu, and Edo in eastern Honshu. They filled the most important positions in the Tokugawa bureaucracy, sitting on the five-man boards of the junior elders (*wakadoshiyori*) and senior councillors (*rōjū*) or as the prime minister (*tairō*).

The outside daimyo, in contrast, tended to have larger domains on the peripheries of the archipelago – in Kyushu, Shikoku, northeastern Honshu, and along the Japan Sea coast. Some of the most prominent among them descended from contenders for hegemony during the civil wars of the sixteenth century. Stereotypically, they offered their fealty to the shogunate grudgingly and received in return a mixture of respect and suspicion. Sure enough, Albert M. Craig writes that, in the Chōshū domain, samurai mothers put their boys to bed with stories of the day they would exact their revenge on the hated Tokugawa.[9] We cannot generalize, however, because even outside daimyo were often closely tied to the Tokugawa house. For example, two prominent outside domains, Kaga and Tosa, were founded by daimyo

---

[9] Craig, *Chōshū in the Meiji Restoration*, 22.

whom Ieyasu had generously rewarded for their support after 1600; outsiders they definitely were, but they owed and paid respect to the shogunate until the eve of the regime's fall.

The higher a domain's assessed yield, the greater its wealth but also the more onerous its obligations to the Tokugawa regime within the structure of the garrison state. The domains did not pay taxes to the shogunate, but every daimyo, as a vassal of the shogun, was expected to provide troops and perform other military services commensurate with his domain's yield. As in the contemporary world, a capacious understanding of national security extended "military" service to include the provision of funds and corvée labor for civil engineering projects ranging from road and bridge repairs to large-scale landfill and riparian projects. During the early Tokugawa period, daimyo eager to win or preserve shogunal favor often went beyond their formal obligations to perform public works,[10] but by the nineteenth century, domains strapped for cash and willing to risk shogunal displeasure often shirked even pressing duties like strengthening coastal defenses; during the last decade of Tokugawa rule, some even declined to provide troops to quell rebellion.[11]

For the purposes of understanding the political economy of early modern Japan, it is probably enough to note the categorical and income distinctions among the daimyo as I have just described them. For people at the time, however, these distinctions were of a set with hierarchies of imperial court rank, lineage, and other markers of prestige.[12] The sum of these hierarchies was revealed most clearly in the seating order at Edo Castle when daimyo assembled for ceremonial audiences with the shogun. Each daimyo waited his turn in one of seven different rooms. In the first sat the lords of the six collateral branches of the Tokugawa house and a few of the most exalted house and outside daimyo. The succeeding rooms accommodated lords of gradually descending status, but for a middling daimyo, placement in one room or another owed as much to his house's relationship to the Tokugawa as to his domain's yield. In the most distant room sat daimyo with domains of 20,000 *koku* or less. Mixed in among the daimyo in the fourth through seventh rooms were select others, including some bannermen (*hatamoto*) and so-called high houses (*kōke*), whose status I discuss later in this section.

As with so many things in early modern Japan, the categories I have sketched out were much more fluid than their apparently strict definitions

---

[10] Roberts, *Mercantilism in a Japanese Domain.*
[11] Kamishiraishi, *Bakumatsu no kaibō senryaku.*
[12] Guidebooks were available: Berry, *Japan in Print.*

suggest. For example, not every daimyo whose domain comprised a province formally held the ceremonial rank of "province holder" (*kunimochi*) and not every official "province holder" governed a whole province. Some provinces were too small to justify the honor; some daimyo were too important not to be granted the status.

This fluidity extended even to domains' assessed yields and indeed the category of daimyo itself. The Tsushima domain had an assessed yield of 100,000 *koku*, but that number reflected its geopolitical importance rather than the actual productivity of its lands. The domain's eponymous home is a mountainous island with little arable land (it also administered some land better suited to agriculture on the mainland), but because Tsushima was critical to the shogunate as an intermediary in diplomacy and trade with Korea, it enjoyed a commensurately high, if fictive, yield. The Three Ministers were likewise granted 100,000 *koku* each, but they did not actually administer fiefs at all. Their income came from widely scattered villages managed as part of the shogun's personal holdings, and their skeletal domanial bureaucracies were staffed by officers seconded from the main Tokugawa house administration.

At the other extreme is Kitsuregawa, an outside domain northeast of Edo. Its lord came from a branch of the once-great Ashikaga house, whose shogunate (1336–1573) had preceded the Tokugawa's. Although assessed at a mere 5,000 *koku*, well below the threshold to be considered a domain, the Tokugawa deferred to its lord's distinguished lineage and accorded it the ritual status of a 100,000-*koku* domain. It received special treatment in other ways, too, most notably in its exemption from the otherwise universal (and often financially ruinous) duty to participate in the alternate-attendance system (*sankin kōtai*), in which daimyo spent about half their time in Edo and half in their domains. Matsumae, situated on the southern tip of Hokkaido and charged with serving as custodian of relations between Japan and the Indigenous Ainu people, began the Tokugawa period with no assessed yield at all. For more than a century, its status remained fuzzy – Matsumae behaved as a domain and its lord as a daimyo, regardless of its actual legal status – but the shogunate did not clearly treat it as having nominally attained the 10,000-*koku* threshold necessary for official domanial status until 1719.

Sometimes existing daimyo spun off cadet lines of their houses as branch domains (*shihan*), much the way the ruling Tokugawa house had created the Three Houses and Three Ministers. Not surprisingly, this practice was most common among the great domains with large holdings, though relatively modest domains occasionally created branches as well. Their motivations varied, but, as in the Tokugawa's own case, a significant advantage to creating branches was to have a ready source of possible heirs should the main branch lack an appropriate successor. Some branch domains were quite substantial. The huge Kaga domain, for example, enfeoffed the lords of the Toyama and Daishōji domains with assessed yields of 100,000 *koku* and 70,000 *koku*, respectively. Others just cleared the 10,000-*koku* minimum for their lords to enjoy daimyo status. A few branch domains even established branches of their own. For example, in 1652, the Chōshū domain's branch, Chōfu, spun off 10,000 *koku* of its 60,000-*koku* assessed yield to create the Suekiyo domain.

Branch domains existed in a variety of relationships with the shogunate and their home domains. Whether, how, and to what degree the parent domains exercised control over their branches varied considerably regardless of the formalities of shogunal recognition. Some branch domains, including Toyama and Daishōji, received formal letters of investiture (*shuinjō*) from the shogunate; the parent domain's yield was reduced commensurately to mark the branch's formal independence. Others were not recognized as free-standing domains but were listed on the parent domain's letter of investiture, thus receiving some measure of legitimation from the shogunate without any adjustment to the parent's assessed income. Still others received no official shogunal recognition at all yet enjoyed a degree of autonomy as fiefs within their parent domains.

Watari, a 24,350-*koku* branch of the Sendai domain ruled by a domain elder (*karō*), is an example of this last type. The head of the Watari fief had his own samurai retainer band, including house elders and other officials. Unlike most samurai, however, the Watari retainers lived in villages on the fief and engaged in agriculture and handicrafts to supplement their miniscule official stipends. Sendai was stripped of much of its territory after its defeat in the military struggle following the Meiji Restoration; the punishment hit the lord of Watari, Date Kunishige, particularly hard: he lost all but about 59 *koku* of his fief, and almost all of his 1,362 retainer households lost their warrior status. They responded to the calamity by emigrating to Hokkaido, where they established a successful agricultural colony. Kunishige was not a daimyo by any ordinary standard other than his large fief, yet his subjects treated him as one;[13] even now, docents at the modest museum in Date City, Hokkaido, refer to the current family head as "his lordship" (*tonosama*).

In addition to the daimyo, there was a host of other fief-holders who controlled land and ruled over commoner villagers. Most of these were bannermen, members of the shogun's personal retainer band below the rank of

[13] Howell, "Early *Shizoku* Colonization of Hokkaidō."

daimyo who, in principle, enjoyed the right to an audience with the shogun.[14] There were 5,200 bannermen at the end of the eighteenth century, of whom nearly half, 2,260, held fiefs while the rest drew stipends from the shogun's granary. Most bannermen's fiefs were small: about 65 percent were below 1,000 *koku* in assessed yield and nearly half of those were valued at under 300 *koku*. Only 11 percent of bannermen held fiefs assessed at 3,000 *koku* or more. Altogether, bannermen held territories assessed at 2.63 million *koku* at the close of the eighteenth century. Incidentally, the great majority of the shogun's retainers (17,240 households in the early eighteenth century) were housemen (*gokenin*), who did not have the right of audience with the shogun. Nearly all of them drew stipends, but 172 were enfeoffed with lands assessed at an average of just under 200 *koku* each.

Bannermen were a diverse lot. Many were descendants of Tokugawa vassals from Ieyasu's earliest days as a minor warlord in Mikawa Province, but there were also some whose ancestors had served other sixteenth-century warlord houses before being absorbed into the Tokugawa forces during Ieyasu's rise to hegemony. After the Tokugawa settlement, the shogunate occasionally took on as direct vassals the younger sons of daimyo and existing bannermen. The regime also incorporated doctors, Confucian scholars, and other particularly talented or useful commoners into its retainer band as bannermen.

Bannermen filled many of the key positions within the shogunal bureaucracy, usually at the rank of magistrate (*bugyō*). They governed major cities, oversaw national finances, supervised mines, regulated religious organizations, and managed diplomacy and coastal defense. As intendants (*daikan*), they administered the shogun's personal landholdings (*tenryō*). Bannermen's fiefs, as we shall see, were often highly fragmented – a village or even just a fraction of a village here and there scattered across a province or two. Unlike daimyo, who generally spent half their time in Edo and half in their domains, most bannermen lived full time in Edo, with the result that, even though they enjoyed the rights of lordship over their fiefs, they often outsourced daily administration to local commoner officials; some never visited their fiefs at all. A few (thirty-three around the end of the Tokugawa period) enjoyed the status of quasi daimyo (*kōtai yoriai*) and lived in fortified compounds in the countryside; they participated in the alternate-attendance system but were generally excluded from holding high offices in the shogunate.

Another group of lords distinct from the daimyo were the high houses, who governed small fiefs of a few hundred to about 4,000 *koku* while serving

---

[14] Fukai, "Hatamoto, gokenin."

the shogunate in important ceremonial roles. They oversaw protocol within Edo Castle, served as masters of ceremony on important ritual occasions, and acted as the shogun's envoys in dealings with the imperial court in Kyoto and with the Ise Shrines and the Tokugawa mausolea at Nikkō. Some high houses descended from branches of the imperial court aristocracy, but most represented the remnants of once-prominent warrior houses that had faced extinction as losers in the civil wars of the sixteenth century. Of these, a number had been closely connected to the Ashikaga shogunate and thus enjoyed great prestige if little military might. Others, such as the Takeda, Imagawa, and Uesugi, traced their roots to major contenders for hegemony, while three high houses descended from sons of the first actual hegemon, Oda Nobunaga (1534–82). Despite their low incomes, high houses enjoyed imperial court ranks comparable to, or even higher than, daimyo.

By far the most famous high-house lord today is Kira Yoshinaka (also read Yoshihisa, 1641–1703), whose quarrel with the daimyo of Akō, Asano Naganori, inspired the *Treasury of Loyal Retainers* (*Chūshingura*), which tells the tale of the vendetta carried out against Yoshinaka by forty-seven of Naganori's retainers. Naganori injured Yoshinaka in Edo Castle and was sentenced the same day to commit *seppuku* – ritual self-disembowelment. Yoshinaka's ancestors had been among the leading retainers of the Ashikaga shogunal house; after Naganori's retainers assassinated him twenty months after the incident at the castle, his grandson and successor was stripped of his high-house status as punishment for Yoshinaka's failure to defend himself properly during the attack on his Edo mansion: even a master of ceremonies was a warrior and expected to behave as one.[15]

Several dozen major Buddhist temples and Shinto shrines around the archipelago held land in fief. For example, around the middle of the seventeenth century, temples and shrines had fiefs in twenty-nine villages in the province of Musashi (where Edo was located), which cumulatively accounted for around 34,000 *koku*, or 3 percent of the province's assessed yield.[16] A handful of religious institutions – Kōfukuji, Kōyasan, Nikkō Tōshōgū, Kan'eiji, and Zōjōji (the last three closely tied to the Tokugawa house) – ruled over territories of 10,000 *koku* or more, and a few dozen more (including the Ise Shrines at about 7,600 *koku*) had smaller fiefs of a few thousand down to a few dozen *koku*. Altogether, religious institutions controlled lands assessed at about 635,000 *koku*. They held administrative rights and obligations very similar to

---

[15] Takeda, Miyoshi, and Namiki, *Chushingura*.
[16] Mori, *Bakuhansei kokka*, 123–25.

those of bannermen – that is, they could levy taxes and punish lawbreakers, but they could not impose the death penalty.

The final category of lord is the imperial house and court aristocracy, which in the mid-Tokugawa period comprised 106 houses. All held some land in fief, though the aristocratic houses (*kuge*) often had minute holdings. Altogether, the aristocracy had holdings of 46,600 *koku*, often distributed across multiple villages in tiny parcels, no doubt to discourage the aristocrats from trying to take advantage of an independent wealth base.

For all their diversity, domains and other jurisdictions functioned like miniature versions of the shogunate, just as the shogunate itself functioned like a massive domain in the administration of its own territories. Each maintained a dual character as a military organization and civil administration, with samurai serving both as warriors and as bureaucrats. Assisting the lord was a small circle of advisers drawn from the ranks of his collateral houses and other leading families; when, as was often the case, the lord was a mediocrity or worse, these advisers governed in his name. Below these men were several tiers of samurai officials who oversaw military affairs (including policing), taxation, rural administration, and other key elements of governance. Just how many tiers and what counted as a key element of governance depended on the size and complexity of the jurisdiction. The large domain of Tosa had 4,101 enfeoffed or stipended retainers around 1780,[17] while a middling bannerman's samurai retinue might number a half dozen or so, only one or two of whom might have regular official duties. The outward-facing side of government belonged entirely to men, but the shogun's and domains' household administrations included their own hierarchies of women from the lord's official consort and recognized concubines down to serving women. They often exercised considerable influence, both official and unofficial, as Kiri Paramore demonstrates in Chapter 2.[18]

Just as scholars have agonized over how best to describe the Tokugawa polity as a whole, they have struggled to characterize the domains. The biggest outside domains could assert their autonomy openly enough for scholars to treat them as quasi-independent regimes. In contrast, house domains habitually deferred to the shogunate in matters big and small, even to the point that the shogunate chastised them for seeking permission to implement routine policies.[19] Bannerman territories and other jurisdictions below the level of domains enjoyed only limited autonomy, which probably suited

[17] Hirao, *Kōchi han zaiseishi*, 78.
[18] Beerens, "Interview with Two Ladies"; Hata, "Servants of the Inner Quarters"; Yonemoto, *Problem of Women*.
[19] Botsman, *Punishment and Power*, 81.

many of the minor lords well enough because they did not have the resources to manage complex administrations.

Even the biggest and most influential domains faced hard limits to their autonomy. Other than the three domains the shogunate deputized as custodians of relations with Korea (Tsushima), Ryukyu (Satsuma), and the Ainu (Matsumae), they could not conduct independent foreign trade or diplomacy. They could not enter into pacts or alliances with one another, which meant that daimyo families' marriages and adoptions required shogunal approval, as did the adoption of heirs. They could not impose tariffs on goods from other domains or impede the movement of people or commodities around the archipelago beyond limits imposed by the shogunate. They enjoyed some control over religious institutions, but they could not contravene core policies related to the proscription of Christianity. Likewise, they enjoyed a measure of agency over the fine points of social-status categories, such as setting the boundaries between samurai and commoners or commoners and outcastes, but social-status institutions applied everywhere, so that a samurai or peasant was recognizable as such throughout the archipelago.

Although they were clearly subordinate to the shogunate, domains privileged their own identities whenever possible, sometimes even when doing so went against the shogunal will. Luke Roberts has demonstrated that the smooth functioning of Tokugawa politics hinged on the maintenance of a gap between surface truths and barely hidden realities, often framed in purely performative acts of submission to the shogunal will. The shogunate often acquiesced to the charade, even as it stood ready to harshly punish open defiance.[20] These open secrets tended to focus on matters important to the domain's ruling house rather than routine matters of political economy.

The tension that characterized every domain's relationship with the shogunate reflected its dual identity as a largely autonomous fief created to support its ruling house's military apparatus and its real-life nature as a subdivision of an increasingly unitary state. The shogunate's agonized response to the Akō vendetta of 1703 reflected its understanding and even encouragement of the domains' distinct identities, while ultimately underscoring the shogunate's primacy.[21] Asano Naganori's retainers, bound to their lord by ties of vassalage but not kinship, had no right in Tokugawa law to kill the man they held responsible for the downfall of the Asano house and with it their own status as Akō samurai. Indeed, launching a blood feud was the last thing the

---

[20] Roberts, *Performing the Great Peace.*
[21] H. D. Smith, "Capacity of Chūshingura"; Bitō, "Akō Incident."

Tokugawa authorities wanted to encourage. At the same time, the public celebrated the loyalty and selflessness of the men who carried out the vendetta, a sentiment that resonated with some in the ruling circle. After nearly a century of peace had transformed the samurai from warriors to government officials, the Akō men seemed to be a throwback to a golden age of the samurai. Accordingly, the men were not executed like common criminals but were instead allowed to die honorably by committing *seppuku*: their loyalty was acknowledged and rewarded, but the Asano's domain was wiped away forever by a shogunate that behaved increasingly as an "absolutist" state as the early modern era progressed.[22]

Local Governance

Tokugawa governments were both understaffed and overstaffed. The number of samurai officials meaningfully employed at any given time was ridiculously small by the standards of our own bureaucratized world, though perhaps not those of the global early modern age. Edo's half million commoners lived under the administration of two Edo town magistrates (*machi-bugyō*), who between them employed about 250 men. A shogunal intendant charged with overseeing a hundred or more villages might have a staff of thirty, including messengers and menials. At the same time, it was not unusual for two or more men to share a title and job responsibilities. Edo's magistrates, for example, maintained two offices and took monthly turns either being open for public business or closed to process accumulated paperwork. Having two men share the magistracy served to check each one's ability to abuse his power. These examples come from the shogunate's bureaucracy, but the basic pattern applied within jurisdictions throughout the archipelago. Even with job sharing there were never enough official positions to go around, with the result that many samurai were underemployed or entirely unemployed, particularly at the lower ranks. Employed or not, the great majority of samurai lived and worked in castle towns or smaller fortified communities. Very few lived in farming or fishing villages, and those who did were of marginal samurai status and did not in any case necessarily participate in village governance.

Commoners mostly looked after themselves. For most Japanese, that meant living in a village community whose leaders took responsibility for allocating and collecting taxes, monitoring the movement of residents in and

[22] White, "State Growth and Popular Protest."

out of the village, tracking births and household size, and coordinating with other village heads as necessary in matters ranging from supplying corvée laborers to negotiating access to irrigation. This arrangement gave villages oversight over basic responsibilities such as paying taxes and maintaining at least superficial social order in exchange for an implicit promise of benevolent rule, meaning that the authorities would not just keep the peace but also show consideration for their subjects' well-being – by lowering taxes when crops failed, for example.

Commoners looking after themselves did not enjoy full autonomy. Rather, they were deputized to participate in their own governance. They carried out their duties under the authorities' supervision, which could be more or less strict depending on the character of the lord. At one extreme was the Satsuma domain in southern Kyushu, where samurai accounted for an unusually high share of the population – about a quarter, in contrast to the national figure of about 6 percent – and were much more common in the countryside than elsewhere. At the other extreme were the territories of bannermen and other minor lords, where jurisdictions were chopped up into tiny parcels that would have been difficult to administer closely even if the lords had the personnel to do so. Between these extremes, the shogunate and large domains posted intendants to oversee rural administration, while smaller domains had a central office in charge of local affairs.

Over time, it became increasingly common for authorities in large jurisdictions to bundle villages into groups of a dozen or more under the authority of a "great village head" (ōjōya or ōnanushi) or village-league representative (sōdai) who oversaw administration of the whole group in addition to serving as the head of his home village. The appointment of such men served as a response to commercialization and the concomitant intertwining of rural economies, which fueled broad regional conflicts over things like the prices of rural cotton and urban night soil that could, in extreme cases, embroil over a thousand villages at a time.[23]

Many village heads enjoyed perquisites, such as the right to use a surname in public and carry two swords while on official business, that blurred the boundary between commoner and samurai. Yet all village heads, even those administering regional village leagues, were commoners. Conversely, all intendants and magistrates were samurai. As with so much else in Tokugawa Japan, however, there were occasional exceptions to these rules. Let us briefly pause to look at the Ōba house, intendants of the Hikone domain's

---

[23] Walthall, "Village Networks."

Setagaya fief. The Ii house of Hikone was one of the Tokugawa's most important vassals. In recognition of their status, the Ii received a supplementary fief of twenty villages in the hinterland of Edo in 1633. Following its usual, albeit idiosyncratic, practice, the Hikone domain employed prominent local families to administer the fief on its behalf. The Ōba, rusticated former samurai whose forebears had once served the Kira house, were one such family. By the latter part of the eighteenth century, they had assumed hereditary control over the Setagaya intendancy, but they remained commoners until the 1830s. Even as samurai, the intendants maintained their long-standing practice of selecting brides from among the daughters of prominent village heads in Edo's western suburbs (beyond the boundaries of the Setagaya fief). Ōba Misa, the daughter of Kaburagi Hidetane, head of Nakanobu village, married her second cousin, the penultimate intendant, Ōba Yoichi, in 1857. When, in 1865, Yoichi died heirless at the age of thirty-nine, the family kept his death secret long enough to adopt Misa's younger brother as heir. As Ōba Hironosuke, he served as the last intendant of Setagaya.[24]

The guiding principle of Tokugawa governance was a place for everyone and everyone in their place. In the countryside, the authorities depended on village officials for its realization. Paperwork fueled the officials' labors. They kept copious records, invariably composed in literary Japanese (*sōrōbun*) and written in a standard cursive style of calligraphy (*o-ieryū*). Other than minor variations in official terminology – a village head might be a *shōya*, *nanushi*, or *kimoiri*, depending on the region – this paperwork, with its standard formats, language, and handwriting, would have been legible throughout the archipelago, even to officials whose spoken dialects of Japanese might have been barely comprehensible to one another. This paperwork served as the regime's principal means of communication with, and knowledge of, its subjects. We know this because millions upon millions of rural documents survive to this day, thanks to both to the sturdiness of *washi* (Japanese paper) and rural elites' practice of constructing fire-resistant storehouses to keep valuables, including family archives.

From the abundance and variety of surviving records, we can conclude that, in principle and nearly in practice, every Japanese person who lived under the mature Tokugawa regime was visible to the state through the medium of documentation. This is not to say that the shogunate or domains maintained searchable, central registries of their subjects or that they even cared to know anything particular about their lives, particularly if those lives

[24] Setagaya-ku, *Ōba Misa no nikki*, 1:285–96.

were law-abiding ones led by women, children, or men other than household heads. But it does mean that, ideally, everyone was knowable and placeable, despite it being an age in which commoners did not ordinarily use surnames in public and no one routinely carried identification.

The principal textual mechanism for keeping track of commoners was the village population register. The register was not a census document per se but rather a statement of the residents' status as parishioners of Buddhist temples (or, in a few domains, Shinto shrines). The shogunate ordered the compilation of these registers as part of its proscription of Christianity in the early seventeenth century.[25] They began with a formulaic affirmation that no one in the village followed a prohibited religion (generally understood to be Christianity, though there were proscribed Buddhist sects as well), and that the enumerated villagers were parishioners of this or that temple. The villagers were then listed by household, with each entry including the name of the household head (ordinarily but not universally a man) and his dependents, such as his wife, children and their spouses, and other cohabiting relatives and servants. One's listing in a register or section of a register marked not only one's legal place of permanent residency but one's social status as well. A commoner was a person listed in a village or urban neighborhood registry; an outcaste was a person listed in an outcaste registry; and so on. (Domains had their own ways of keeping track of samurai and their families.) The entries generally stated the name and age of each resident, along with their relationship to the household head and the name and sect of the temple to which they were affiliated.

People moved around quite a lot during the Tokugawa period. When villagers moved legally to another community (whether within or across domanial boundaries) for reasons of marriage or adoption, the village heads exchanged documents acknowledging the transfer of registry from one household and parish to another. Generally, newborn children were added to the registers in the year following their birth, though sometimes village heads seem to have waited until there was general confidence the infant would survive. The registers did not ordinarily list deaths, but local temples kept mortuary records.

The registers were intended as logs of the parish affiliations of villagers rather than population records per se. Babies who died shortly after birth, whether of natural causes or as victims of infanticide, were generally invisible. The movement of particular individuals into and out of the registers through marriage, adoption, or death cannot always be ascertained without

[25] Hur, *Death and Social Order.*

looking at other documents. And only observers with local knowledge could track individual life courses with confidence because of the dual tendencies of families to reuse names – especially men's names – and for people – especially men – to change their names in tandem with their changing familial roles. Nevertheless, for all practical purposes, they served as annual snapshots of village populations and thus as an important means for the regime to know its subjects.

An unregistered commoner was an unplaced commoner, invisible to the authorities and hence a source of anxiety. Commoners became unplaced when their village heads removed their names from the village registry without arranging for their transfer to another community. This typically occurred when villagers either absconded outright or traveled away from home, nominally temporarily, but never returned. Villages sought to protect themselves from liability for the mishaps and misdeeds of members who were beyond the community's control, even if their whereabouts were in fact known. Liability could mean anything from the hassle and expense of claiming the remains of an absconded villager who had died on the road to legal peril under the principle of communal responsibility for criminal wrongdoing. Removing a villager from the register absolved the community of responsibility. At the same time, the removal took the villager off the tax and corvée rolls – villages paid land taxes and performed labor duties as a communal unit – and went against the regime's desire to keep every possible commoner accounted for. Removal from a village register was thus a drastic action, not undertaken lightly.

Unregistered commoners were called *mushuku*, which literally translates as "undomiciled," but they were not necessarily homeless. With no community or relatives legally bound to take responsibility for them, unregistered commoners represented disorder to the authorities. Although many unregistered commoners were just unlucky people whose circumstances had left them at the margins of society, others were indeed gamblers, gangsters, and criminals. They sought the anonymity of big cities and lightly governed regions like the Kantō plain surrounding Edo, where the landscape of tiny jurisdictions made it hard for the authorities to keep close track of people's movements. As a result, the Kantō had a reputation for being a hotbed of disorder.

In 1805, the shogunate created a special police force, the Kantō Regulatory Patrol, and charged it with controlling crime and disorder in the hinterland of Edo. The agents of this disorder were presumed to be unplaced persons: unregistered commoners and their warrior counterparts, the so-called masterless samurai (*rōnin*) – an ill-defined population of armed men who asserted samurai status for themselves whether they were really from warrior families or not. Members of the patrol enjoyed the extraordinary right to cross domanial and other jurisdictional boundaries in pursuit of their lawless prey. Although there is room to debate how much disorder was really on the rise, there is no doubt that economic change stressed rural communities and that criminal gangs – the forebears of modern-day yakuza – emerged during this time.

Commoners looked after themselves so long as they maintained the facade of social order in their communities. Once the facade was broken, the state readily exercised its power, as Takahashi Satoshi reveals in an example from 1849.[26] A resident of Mishuku, a village in the foothills of Mount Fuji, ran an unlicensed inn, which became the scene of the gangland killing of an unregistered commoner. The village head could have reported the killing, but doing so would have exposed his failure of oversight in letting the villager lodge an unregistered commoner, with repercussions for himself, the innkeeper, and indeed the entire community. The villagers thus decided to bury the dead man at a local cemetery and hope he would not be missed. (Although the victim was unregistered, he was well known to locals.) As an added precaution, they struck the innkeeper from the village registry, declaring that he had absconded; all evidence suggests that he remained in or near the village.

The scheme might have worked if the killing had been the result of a routine quarrel between a couple of unregistered gamblers. In fact, however, it was payback for an earlier gang-related murder, and soon enough investigators from the shogunate were on the scene. The village head endured months of repeated summons to Edo for questioning. He managed to keep up the fiction that the innkeeper had absconded, which helped to protect him and the innkeeper's relatives from criminal liability. Nevertheless, the inquiry was ruinously expensive: on top of hefty expenses for travel and extended stays at a litigants' inn (*kuji yado*) in Edo, he spent a small fortune wining, dining, and bribing officials to get his case moved up the magistrate's docket.

The case reveals some intriguing truths about local governance in early modern Japan. Events that would be front and center of the narrative today – a murder, a hidden body, a fugitive hiding in plain sight – barely figure into the story, at least when narrated from the village head's perspective. The case hinged on his dereliction in allowing lawless sorts like unregistered commoners to frequent his village and his unfortunate but understandable decision to try to cover the mess up.

[26] Takahashi, *Edo no soshō*.

Fractured Sovereignty and Governmentality

Thus far, this chapter has looked high and low at the institutions of regional governance, examining, on the one hand, the domains and similar jurisdictions and, on the other hand, the responsibilities of self-governing village communities. In most places and for most purposes, the connection between these two layers of governance was straightforward: village households interacted with the authorities through their heads, who in turn interacted with their domains through officials tasked with taxation, public works, and other matters of local administration. Sometimes, groups of villages engaged communally with the authorities, but communications and paperwork still flowed up and down in the same manner.

In many places, however, local governance was not at all straightforward. Although bannermen's fiefs and other small jurisdictions worked in principle as domains did – that is, as more or less autonomous polities – in practice, minor lords lacked the resources, personnel, and perhaps even the desire to govern independently. The shogunate often exercised some administrative functions on their behalf, but as lords, the bannermen ultimately held responsibility for their fiefs and their subjects.

One problem for minor lords was that their fiefs were frequently distributed among several dispersed villages. For example, a bannerman named Okano Tōmasa held a fief assessed at 1,671 *koku* spread across five different villages, three of which were located in the hinterland of Edo and two in central Honshu. His holdings in each village ranged from 150 *koku* to 512 *koku*. All were shared-revenue villages, meaning that at least one other lord also drew revenue from, and held some measure of authority over, each of them. Tōmasa and his successors were notorious spendthrifts, but even if they had not been, the pressures of maintaining their families, vassals, and servants left them with little wherewithal to invest in good governance. Indeed, after Tōmasa's death in 1835, perennial money problems forced the family to cede management of its household finances to the heads of its three Edo-area villages, whose residents were the lord's creditors as well as his subjects.[27]

Even more striking is the case of the Tsuda house, a bannerman with a fief assessed at 6,614 *koku* distributed across fourteen villages in the hinterland of Edo. The Tsudas' holdings put them in the top tier of bannermen. They maintained a commensurately large establishment, with two residences in Edo and as many as ninety-six samurai in their retinue. Nevertheless, they

[27] Ōguchi, "Reality behind *Musui Dokugen*."

ruled their holdings without an administrative apparatus and dispatched vassals to the countryside only when necessary; for the most part, "local administration was entrusted to the village headmen of their domain."[28] From 1842 to 1864, the chronically indebted Tsuda lord turned over control of his household finances to a group of commoner officials and merchants from his fief. The managers came from prominent merchant families in Sawara, an important "country place" – administratively a village, but in fact a burgeoning commercial center – in Shimōsa.[29] They imposed austerity measures ranging from reducing the household staff to limiting the lord to fifteen baths per month to save on fuel. They also ensured that loans made to the lord by his own subjects – the managers included – would be repaid before those extended by outsiders. Their most impressive achievement, however, was to create a reserve fund that they used to underwrite public works in and around Sawara even after the village was transferred to the Sakura domain in 1864.[30]

As noted above, bannermen frequently held fiefs spread across multiple communities, many of which were themselves shared-revenue villages, divided between two or more lords. Shared-revenue villages were overwhelmingly concentrated in the economically and strategically important Kantō (near Edo) and Kansai (near Kyoto and Osaka) regions, where they were interspersed among house daimyo domains and territories under direct shogunal control. Villages divided among two to four lords were most common, but there could be more. The record holder seems to be Mibu, now part of the city of Kyoto: around the end of the Tokugawa period, its 1,252 *koku* were shared among seventy-three lords, who claimed stakes ranging from just over 402 *koku* down to a measly 0.038 *koku* (about 5.7 kg of unpolished rice).[31]

Let us now turn to two simple examples of shared-revenue villages in Hitachi, a province northeast of Edo, each of which represents a type in a taxonomy proposed by Shirakawabe Tatsuo.[32] The Mito domain ruled the bulk of the province; nevertheless, 345 other lords also held some claim to territory in Hitachi. Three of them shared dominion over Mimura village. Mimura was huge by early modern standards, with an assessed yield of about 2,422 *koku* at around the beginning of the eighteenth century. The Hitachi Fuchū

---

[28] Sakai, "Outsourcing the Lord's Finance," 59.
[29] T. C. Smith, *Native Sources of Japanese Industrialization*, 22.
[30] Sakai, "Outsourcing the Lord's Finance," 57–72.
[31] *Kyūdaka kyūroku torishirabechō* database.
[32] Shirakawabe, "Hatamoto aikyū chigyō ron." On Mimura and Koido villages, see Onodera, "Sonraku no shakai soshiki."

domain ruled over about 40 percent of it (by assessed yield). The remainder was split between a pair of bannermen, who held about 14 percent and 46 percent each. Each lord's fief comprised specific, mostly contiguous parcels of land, each administered by its own head and other commoner officials. For residents of Mimura, therefore, depending on where in the village they lived, the Hitachi Fuchū daimyo or one or the other of the bannermen would be the lord in whose fief they would be registered. Nevertheless, villagers whose paddies and fields were scattered widely about the village – as was often the case in early modern Japan – might find themselves liable for land taxes and other obligations to two or even all three lords.

Koido, a village about eight kilometers from Mimura, was much smaller than Mimura, just 425 *koku*. At the beginning of the eighteenth century, two bannermen held the village in fief, controlling two-thirds and one-third each. Individual landholders in the village were assigned to one or the other of them. In that respect, it was clear who each individual's overlord was; as in Mimura, separate sets of village officials administered each bannerman's part of the village. However, in contrast to the contiguous parcels administered by each fief holder in Mimura, the bannermen's territories in Koido were distributed like the fat in finely marbled beef – an intricate web of a bit of wet paddy here, a few square meters of dry field there – because that is how their individual subjects' lands were held.

Regardless of how their taxes were distributed or how many sets of village officials they had, shared-revenue villages were still clearly recognizable as communities, their residents tied together not only through agriculture and taxation but also through religious rituals, social ties, and economic interactions. Let us look in some detail at Daikata, a village in Kazusa Province.[33] It was a reasonably prosperous agricultural village in the central part of the Bōsō Peninsula, modern-day Chiba Prefecture. In 1838, its population of 682 was divided among 148 households.[34] Its assessed yield of 1,471 *koku* was divided into four holdings, one of which was controlled directly by the shogunate and the others assigned to bannermen. All three of the bannermen held stakes in other villages as well. Like their counterparts in Koido village, Daikata's commoner households were assigned to one or another of the fief holders, but nearly all of them farmed land and paid taxes to two, three, or all four of the village's lords.

---

[33] Daikata has become something of a model case for studies of shared-revenue villages. See, in particular, Watanabe, *Aikyū sonraku*.

[34] Heibonsha Chihō Shiryō Sentā, *Nihon rekishi chimei taikei*, s.v. "Daikata-mura," https://japanknowledge.com

Daikata, like many other shared-revenue villages in the Kantō region, was first divided among multiple lords during the Genroku era (1688–1704), when the shogunate undertook a major redistribution of fiefs assigned to bannermen and minor house daimyo in the hinterland of Edo. Accordingly, in 1698, the village was split among four bannermen. One, the Ōhashi house, was stripped of its holdings in Daikata in 1758, after which its 141-*koku* stake in the village alternated between the shogunate and the Shimizu domain, one of the Three Ministers established by the shogun Yoshimune; a shogunal intendant oversaw the holding in either case. The remaining three bannerman houses retained their holdings in Daikata until the Meiji Restoration. The bulk of the village's yield – about 65 percent – was assigned to a 2,000-*koku* bannerman who bore Tokugawa Ieyasu's original surname, Matsudaira; at the end of the Tokugawa period, Matsudaira Gonnosuke held 955.056702 *koku* in Daikata. The second-largest stake, about 16 percent, went to the Mita house; its head at the time of the restoration was Un'ichirō, a 580-*koku* bannerman who was assigned 233.258606 *koku*. A stake of approximately 10 percent went to the Kōno house; at the end of the Tokugawa period, Kōno Ryōken was a doctor in the service of the shogun's household (*okuishi*) who drew 140.9935 *koku* of his 600-*koku* income from the village. The shogunate's precise stake was 141.473999 *koku*, likewise just under 10 percent of the village's total yield.

Altogether, Daikata's assessed yield was 1,470.782837 *koku*. That last digit, representing seven-millionths of a *koku* (1.26 ml), amounted to barely an infant's fistful of polished rice, around forty grains.[35] Fractions of a *koku* expressed in ever-smaller units – in an age before decimal points, Daikata's yield would have been read as one thousand, four hundred seventy *koku*, seven *to*, eight *shō*, two *gō*, eight *shaku*, three *sai*, seven *satsu* – abound in the rich documentary records of the time, lending a veneer of precision to the regime's apprehension of its realm.

The *performance* of precision was the key, for the tiny units would have been scarcely credible even if the sum of the individual fiefs in Daikata did not come up three *sai* – around 180 grains of rice! – short of the stated total assessed yield. Here we see Tokugawa institutions working toward the "convenient" ends of governmentality: the state asserted perfect knowledge of its realm's productive capacity, and its subjects took the numbers given to them to find a workable system of assessing and collecting tax levies on themselves without resorting to thimbles to count rice grains down to the last *satsu*.

---

[35] *Kyūdaka kyūroku torishirabechō* database. Rice weight from Webb, "Rice Quality and Grades," 97.

Daikata was not a particularly big place – its area was around 2.3 square kilometers (slightly bigger than Monaco) – but its four fiefs were distributed across six hamlets (*nyūchi*).[36] Dwellings of subjects of the Matsudaira lord could be found in all six hamlets, but the other lords' subjects were concentrated in just one or two hamlets each. The village thus fell between the extremes of the ideal types described earlier in this section: the fiefs were to some extent geographically defined, as in Mimura, but also intertwined, as in Koido. Regardless of the hamlet of their residence or the identity of their lord, villagers held land throughout the community, and officials of the various lords made efforts to coordinate the assessment and collection of tax payments throughout the village. Ultimately, however, each fief's head was responsible for the timely payment of taxes to his lord.

The Maejima house was one of Daikata's wealthiest and most influential. The family built a fortune founded in agriculture, supplemented by the late eighteenth century with substantial income from tenant rents, moneylending, and commercial ventures such as rice dealing.[37] They used some of their wealth to acquire real estate (and possibly a secondary base of operations) in the Asakusa neighborhood of Edo.[38] Perhaps their most noteworthy venture was their business as finance manager (*katte makanai*) for three bannermen, none of whom had any connection to Daikata village. Like the finance managers for the Okano and Tsuda lords, described earlier in this section, the Maejima oversaw the collection and marketing of tax grain on the bannermen's fiefs and looked after the lords' household finances, which often involved negotiating loan terms for their perennially strapped clients.

For generations, the Maejima patriarch served as head (*nanushi*) or associate head (*kumigashira*) of the Kōno fief. The family lived in the hamlet of Miroku, which was home to the great majority of the households assigned to that lord. They helped to oversee a population of about fifty people in the late 1830s, which rose to the high eighties by the 1860s. In 1866, they held about 93 *koku* of land within Daikata as well as additional plots – worth another 20 or 30 *koku* – in several nearby villages. Although they held some land in every Daikata fief, the bulk of their property was divided between the holdings of the Matsudaira lord (about 64 percent) and their own Kōno lord (31 percent).

The Maejima's duties as village officials involved them in the business of three constituencies: the Kōno lord, the residents of Miroku, and Daikata

---

[36] Area calculated on the basis of the current area of Daikata, now a subdivision of Tōgane City, Chiba Prefecture: https://toukei-labo.com/2010/?tdfk=12&city=12213&id=49
[37] For an overview of the Maejima house, see Chiba-ken, "Kaidai."
[38] Watanabe, *Sōbyakushō to kinsei sonraku*, 239–67; Chiba-ken, "Kaidai," 11–17.

village as a whole.[39] Naturally, these often overlapped. When a local shrine was destroyed in a storm, word immediately went around to officials of all four fief holders, but Maejima Jisuke and a colleague from another fief took the lead in overseeing its rebuilding. Presumably Jisuke was involved because the shrine was in his home hamlet of Miroku, but it was an institution important for the whole village, and indeed, the entire community contributed to the cost of reconstruction. In 1809, officials from the three bannerman fiefs drew up a set of laws to govern the community as a whole. Many of the items were boilerplate exhortations – do not gamble, do not fight, do not indulge in luxuries beyond your station – but others addressed problems peculiar to shared-revenue villages, especially those regarding the need to make full and timely payment of taxes on landholdings in fiefs other than one's own lord's.

As in all village communities in early modern Japan, the Maejima and other commoner officials in Daikata sought to resolve problems on their own whenever possible. Bannermen generally had few resources and little incentive to micromanage the affairs of their subjects. Sure enough, the Kōno lord deputized officials in the four villages in which he had a stake to serve as a pair of local intendants (jidaikan), responsible for exercising day-to-day authority in two villages each. When a dispute over irrigation water led to fisticuffs between subjects of different fief holders, the threat of appealing to the bannerman for judgment was enough to get the parties to resolve their differences.[40] This sort of thing no doubt happened all the time.

For all their looking after themselves, however, the residents of Daikata, like other villagers throughout the archipelago, were embedded in webs of authority that revealed the limits of their autonomy. In 1832, the associate head of the Matsudaira fief severely beat a villager (possibly a former head) from the Kōno fief in the house of a villager from the Shimizu fief. The assaulted man's son submitted an appeal for an investigation to the victim's lord, Kōno Ryōi, who duly dispatched two agents (yōnin) to the village. The outcome of the case is not clear. It is possible that, during the two days that elapsed between the assault and the writing of the petition, the villagers tried unsuccessfully to resolve the incident among themselves. But the victim of the assault appeared to be near death, which was reason enough to call in the bannerman's agents. The surviving documents offer no comment on the cause of the assault – merely that it was an "argument" (kōron).[41]

---

[39] In invoking this taxonomy, I follow Nakamura, "Kinsei aikyū mura."
[40] Maejima-ke monjo, sa70 (1848/7).
[41] Maejima-ke monjo, sa86 (1832/3/5) and sa84 (1832/3/7).

Whatever was behind the dispute and however it was ultimately resolved, the lord was in charge at the end.

In taking up shared-revenue villages, I have highlighted the complications of sovereignty in rural spaces in which territoriality and rulership did not necessarily align. Nevertheless, it is important to underscore how Daikata's nature as a singular community often transcended its character as an amalgam of fiefs. Let us close this discussion with a brief survey of Daikata's place among the villages in the district (*gun*) of Yamabe in Kazusa Province. Yamabe was one of nine districts in Kazusa. About two-thirds – 89 of 135 – of its villages were of the shared-revenue type. Fifty-three of the eighty-nine shared-revenue villages were divided between two lords; all of the rest were divided among three to seven lords, except for one, Ōami, which was divided into thirteen fiefs. Altogether, the shared-revenue villages in Yamabe were divided into a total of 274 holdings, or an average of about three each.

Daikata was one of six villages that shared responsibility for staging the annual festival to the communities' tutelary deity at the Hiyoshi Shrine in neighboring Mamezaku village. Daikata participated in two irrigation unions, one in which nine villages drew water from a nearby lake and another in which a subset of that group – Daikata and four other villages – drew water from a local river. From the outset of the Tokugawa period, it was one of five villages organized into a league that may have been tasked originally with maintaining local security but evolved to focus entirely on the rare need to dispose of wayfarers who collapsed and died in the neighborhood. After 1827, Daikata was one of thirty villages in a reform league (*kaikaku kumiai*) based in the neighboring town of Tōgane; reform leagues of two or three dozen villages each were created around the Kantō as part of a shogunal effort to improve public safety in the region. Finally, Daikata was part of a league of thirty-three villages established to support shogunal falcon hunts in the area. Although Ieyasu in particular was an avid falconer, no shogun ever hunted in or around Daikata after the middle of the seventeenth century. Nevertheless, the league remained intact until the end of the Tokugawa period, and Daikata paid dues to support the infrastructure of falcon keepers who waited in vain for a shogunal visit.[42]

Of the eight villages with which Daikata participated in irrigation unions and management of the Hiyoshi Shrine, two were under the same single

---

[42] On shogunal falcon hunting, see Nesaki, *Shōgun no takagari*, and Pitelka, *Spectacular Accumulation*.

lord and the remaining six were shared-revenue villages of two to seven fiefs. Altogether, Daikata and its most important neighbors comprised thirty distinct jurisdictions, most of them subject to the authority of lords too weak and too poor to intervene actively on their behalf. Accordingly, rather than six village officials sorting out the details of the annual shrine festival or nine coordinating access to irrigation, major decisions involved at least two stages of consultation, first within the village and then with neighboring communities. Of course, here I refer only to formal mechanisms of authority; every village had its own webs of social hierarchy, wealth, and lineage – not to mention the gender- and age-inflected dynamics of decision-making within households.

Shared-revenue villages occupied large swaths of literally unmappable territory in some of the most politically and economically important parts of early modern Japan. Their ability to function despite their geographical ambiguity stands in contrast to the Meiji state's eager consolidation of top-down control during the years after its establishment. No doubt the key to shared-revenue villages' apparent stability was that they had an enduring communal identity. Fief holders in shared-revenue villages came and went, but the villages themselves remained. For that matter, domains came and went, but the villages themselves remained. Although the shuffling of daimyo domains, which had been extremely common during the seventeenth century, became less so as the Tokugawa period progressed, the practice never ended (especially among small domains). Bannermen seem to have been reassigned so commonly that it is occasionally difficult for us to know who held a given village at a given time. Yet whatever the disruptions, the village endured. Villagers tilled their fields and pursued their by-employments, and for the most part village heads made sure the taxes were paid and a facade of order maintained.

Secrets

As noted at the start of this chapter, Luke Roberts characterizes the early modern polity in terms of a tension between the convenient falsehoods of the official story – what he calls *omote* (surface) documents – and the messy truths of the (barely) concealed *uchi* (interior). It is a persuasive exposition of the workings of the Tokugawa state, particularly at the level of relations between the shogunate and domains.[43] Although Roberts shies away from generalizing

---

[43] Roberts, *Performing the Great Peace.*

his argument beyond Japan, it is easy enough to find parallel phenomena elsewhere in the early modern world, as any reader of *The Return of Martin Guerre* could tell you.[44] To rephrase Roberts's argument in the language of governmentality, he describes a regime in which the ruling authorities in the shogunate had ceded much everyday control of "things" – people and institutions – to their subjects in the domains: so long as the shogun's authority was not explicitly challenged, there was little incentive to pry off the surface facade. That cession allowed the ambiguities and gaps between jurisdictions to function reasonably smoothly. At the same time, it is easy to see why such an arrangement would be intolerable to the self-consciously modern Meiji state that came to power after 1868.

For all the pervasive high-stakes monkey business at work in Roberts's analysis, fear and violence are not significant themes, except in the case of commoners who exposed open secrets to win official concessions, knowing that doing so would cost a scapegoat or two his life. There were many layers of *omote* and *uchi* – domains were just as happy to trade in convenient falsehoods with their commoners as the shogunate was with the domains – which meant that opacity was a fundamental characteristic of the early modern polity. Not only could the authorities not see what really went on below them, they had strong incentives not to see. When things were stable this was probably fine: so long as villages paid their taxes and maintained the illusion of order, the authorities were not really interested in intervening in their internal disputes, however outrageous the injustices meted out to the weak or discontented.[45] Once the facade of order cracked, however, the authorities had to confront the fact of just how little they really knew about their subjects.

Post-restoration reforms in the countryside sought to resituate agents of central authority in the villages and thereby reassert the sovereign's power. During the years after 1868, a different kind of relationship – a new style of "government" – had to emerge in the countryside, without however having time to evolve organically. From the standpoint of villagers, two key transformations were, first, the state's reassertion of the primacy of sovereignty over territory (knowing and controlling the land) and, second, a deepening of the government of "things" (controlling people and institutions) much more directly than before.

[44] Davis, *Return of Martin Guerre.*
[45] For a chilling example, see Ooms, *Tokugawa Village Practice*, 11–70.

Bibliography

Beerens, Anna. "An Interview with Two Ladies of the Ōoku: A Translation from the *Kyūji shimonroku.*" *Monumenta Nipponica* 63, no. 2 (2008): 265–324.

Berry, Mary Elizabeth. *Hideyoshi.* Cambridge, MA: Harvard University Press, 1982.

Japan in Print: Information and Nation in the Early Modern Period. Berkeley: University of California Press, 2006.

Bitō Masahide. "The Akō Incident, 1701–1703." Translated by Henry D. Smith II. *Monumenta Nipponica* 58, no. 2 (2003): 149–70.

Bolitho, Harold. "The Han." In *Early Modern Japan*, edited by John Whitney Hall, 183–234. Vol. 4 of *The Cambridge History of Japan.* Cambridge: Cambridge University Press, 1988.

Botsman, Daniel V. *Punishment and Power in the Making of Modern Japan.* Princeton, NJ: Princeton University Press, 2005.

Brown, Philip C. *Central Authority and Local Autonomy in Early Modern Japan.* Stanford, CA: Stanford University Press, 1993.

Chiba-ken Sōmubu Monjoka, ed. "Kaidai." In *Tōgane-shi Daikata Maejima-ke monjo mokuroku I*, 1–44. Chiba: Chiba-ken, 1988.

Craig, Albert M. *Chōshū in the Meiji Restoration.* Cambridge, MA: Harvard University Press, 1961.

Davis, Natalie Zemon. *The Return of Martin Guerre.* Cambridge, MA: Harvard University Press, 1983.

Drixler, Fabian. "Edo and the Architecture of the Great Peace." In *Samurai and the Culture of Japan's Great Peace*, edited by Fabian Drixler, William Fleming, and Robert Wheeler, 21–35. New Haven, CT: Yale University Peabody Museum, 2015.

Ehlers, Maren. *Give and Take: Poverty and the Status Order in Early Modern Japan.* Cambridge, MA: Harvard University Asia Center, 2018.

Foucault, Michel. *The Essential Foucault: Selections from the Essential Works of Foucault, 1954–1984.* Edited by Paul Rabinow and Nikolas Rose. New York: New Press, 2003.

Fukai Masaumi. "Hatamoto, gokenin." In *Kokushi daijiten.* Yoshikawa Kōbunkan, 1979–96.

Hata Hisako. "Servants of the Inner Quarters: The Women of the Shogun's Great Interior." Translated by Anne Walthall. In *Servants of the Dynasty: Palace Women in World History*, edited by Anne Walthall, 172–90. Berkeley: University of California Press, 2008.

Heibonsha Chihō Shiryō Sentā. *Nihon rekishi chimei taikei*, 50 vols. Heibonsha, 1979–2005.

Hirao Michio. *Kōchi han zaiseishi.* Kōchi: Kōchi Shiritsu Shimin Toshokan, 1965.

Howell, David L. "Early Shizoku Colonization of Hokkaidō." *Journal of Asian History* 17 (1983): 40–67.

Hur, Nam-lin. *Death and Social Order in Tokugawa Japan: Buddhism, Anti-Christianity, and the Danka System.* Cambridge, MA: Harvard University Asia Center, 2007.

Kadokawa Nihon Chimei Daijiten Hensan Iinkai. *Shinpan Kadokawa Nihon chimei daijiten*, 51 vols. Database format accessed through JapanKnowledge. Net Advance, 2018.

Kamishiraishi Minoru. *Bakumatsu no kaibō senryaku: Ikokusen o kakuri seyo.* Yoshikawa Kōbunkan, 2011.

Kokusho Kankōkai, ed. "Kanbun inchi-shū." In *Chiri-bu*, 1–310. Vol. 9 of *Zokuzoku gunsho ruijū*, Pt. 2. Kokusho Kankōkai, 1906.

Kyūdaka kyūroku torishirabechō. Database, National Museum of Japanese History, Sakura, Chiba, Japan. www.rekihaku.ac.jp/up-cgi/login.pl?p=param/kyud/db_param

Maejima-ke monjo. Chiba Prefectural Archives, Chiba.

Mizubayashi Takeshi. *Hōkensei no saihen to Nihonteki shakai no kakuritsu*. Yamakawa Shuppan, 1987.

Mori Yasuhiko. *Bakuhansei kokka no kiso kōzō: Sonraku kōzō no tenkai to nōmin tōsō*. Yoshikawa Kōbunkan, 1981.

Murayama Yūji, ed. *Dejitaru Inō-zu*, DVD-ROM. Kawade Shobō Shinsha, 2015.

Nakamura Sō. "Kinsei aikyū mura chigyōshu to sonraku kyōdōtai: Kazusa no kuni Yamabe-gun Daikata-mura o jirei to shite." *Aikoku Gakuen Daigaku ningen bunka kenkyū kiyō* 13 (2011): 65–76.

Nesaki Mitsuo. *Shōgun no takagari*. Dōseisha, 1999.

Nishioka Toranosuke and Hattori Shisō, eds. *Nihon rekishi chizu*. Zenkoku Kyōiku Tosho, 1956.

Ōguchi Yūjirō. "The Reality behind *Musui Dokugen*: The World of the *Hatamoto* and *Gokenin*." Translated by Gaynor Sekimori. *Journal of Japanese Studies* 16, no. 2 (1990): 289–308.

Onodera Atsushi. "Sonraku no shakai soshiki ni oyobosu aikyū shihai no eikyō." *Tsukuba Daigaku jinbun chirigaku kenkyū* 15 (1991): 251–67.

Ooms, Herman. *Tokugawa Village Practice: Class, Status, Power, Law*. Berkeley: University of California Press, 1996.

Pitelka, Morgan. *Spectacular Accumulation: Material Culture, Tokugawa Ieyasu, and Samurai Sociability*. Honolulu: University of Hawai'i Press, 2015.

Ravina, Mark. *Land and Lordship in Early Modern Japan*. Stanford, CA: Stanford University Press, 1999.

Reischauer, Edwin O. *The Japanese*. Cambridge, MA: Belknap Press, 1977.

Roberts, Luke S. *Mercantilism in a Japanese Domain: The Merchant Origins of Economic Nationalism in 18th-Century Tosa*. Cambridge: Cambridge University Press, 1998.

   Performing the Great Peace: Political Space and Open Secrets in Tokugawa Japan. Honolulu: University of Hawai'i Press, 2012.

Sakai, Kazuho. "Outsourcing the Lord's Finance: An Origin of Local Public Finance in Early Modern Japan." In *Public Goods Provision in the Early Modern Economy: Comparative Perspectives from Japan, China, and Europe*, edited by Masayuki Tanimoto and R. Bin Wong, 54–72. Oakland: University of California Press, 2019. https://doi.org/10.1525/luminos.63

Setagaya-ku Kyōiku Iinkai, ed. *Ōba Misa no nikki*. 3 vols. Setagaya-ku Kyōiku Iinkai, 1988–91.

Shirakawabe Tatsuo. "Hatamoto aikyū chigyō ron." In *Hatamoto chigyō to sonraku*, edited by Kantō Kinseishi Kenkyūkai, 79–130. Bunken Shuppan, 1986.

Smith, Henry D., II. "The Capacity of Chūshingura." *Monumenta Nipponica* 58, no. 1 (2003): 1–42.

Smith, Thomas C. *Native Sources of Japanese Industrialization, 1750–1920*. Berkeley: University of California Press, 1988.

Takagi Shōsaku. *Nihon kinsei kokkashi no kenkyū*. Iwanami Shoten, 1990.

Takahashi Satoshi. *Edo no sosho: Mishuku mura ikken tenmatsu*. Iwanami Shoten, 1996.

Takeda Izumo, Miyoshi Shōraku, and Namiki Senryū. *Chushingura, the Treasury of Loyal Retainers: A Puppet Play*. Translated by Donald Keene. New York: Columbia University Press, 1971.

Toby, Ronald. "Rescuing the Nation from History: The State of the State in Early Modern Japan." *Monumenta Nipponica* 56, no. 2 (2001): 197–237.

Walthall, Anne. "Village Networks: Sōdai and the Sale of Edo Nightsoil." *Monumenta Nipponica* 43, no. 3 (1988): 279–303.

Watanabe Takashi, ed. *Aikyū sonraku kara mita kinsei shakai: Kazusa no kuni Yamabe-gun Daikata-mura no sōgō kenkyū*. Iwata Shoin, 2016.

Sōbyakushō to kinsei sonraku: Bōsō chiikishi kenkyū. Iwata Shoin, 2007.

Webb, B. D. "Rice Quality and Grades." In *Utilization*, edited by Bor S. Luh, 89–119. Vol. 2 of *Rice*. 2nd ed. New York: Van Nostrand Reinhold, 1991.

White, James W. "State Growth and Popular Protest in Japan." *Journal of Japanese Studies* 14, no. 1 (1988): 1–25.

Yonemoto, Marcia. *The Problem of Women in Early Modern Japan*. Berkeley: University of California Press, 2016.

4

Tokugawa Philosophy
A Socio-Historical Introduction

FEDERICO MARCON

Premise: A Field That Is Not (Yet)

One of the most significant developments in the intellectual life of early modern Japan was the emergence of a class of scholars who, as professionals or amateurs, engaged in the production of a sophisticated, coherent, often original, and well-integrated corpus of texts that deserve the label of "philosophy." This chapter focuses on the historical *event* that was the constitution of a philosophical archive in early modern Japan – a development that should be regarded as qualitatively and quantitatively unprecedented in Japanese history outside Buddhist institutions. From the second half of the sixteenth through the nineteenth century, a growing number of professionals and amateurs engaged in the production of texts and in social practices within different kinds of institutions with the concerted aim of producing authoritative and advanced inquiries on issues and themes that in a European context would be unquestioningly recognized as "philosophical." These included investigations on the nature of reality and the laws that govern it (metaphysics); the motivations, norms, and aims of moral life (ethics); the function and rules of language (philology and linguistics); the principles of good government (politics); the legitimation of cognitive claims (epistemology); and other fields of theoretical inquiry. Scholars' inquiries took the form of commentaries and exegeses of canonical Chinese sources, treatises, essays, collections of lecture notes, encyclopedias, and dictionaries and lexica of philosophical terms. These texts circulated as printed volumes but more often as manuscripts. If many were conceived as texts to be read, others originated from public lectures and lessons offered in educational academies (*shijuku*), as private tutoring, or in cultural circles. Scholars for vocation or advocation embraced research and exegeses, speculation and experimentation, debate and collaboration, and lecturing and publishing as ideal practices of the utmost social value. They cherished accumulation of knowledge and self-reflective inquiries on the validity of one's investigative methodology in the pursuit of an ideal of the "investigation of things and extension of knowledge" (Ch. *gewu zhizhi*, J. *kakubutsu chichi*) that complied quite closely, in methodology and aims, with what in contemporary Europe was commonly known as *philosophia*.

The defense of a philosophical approach to the intellectual archive of Tokugawa Japan is not aimed at forcibly reducing the complexities of those discourses to the categories, scopes, and logic of Western philosophy, as, for instance, was the case of Feng Youlan's pioneering survey on Chinese philosophy.[1] At the same time that it wants to draw scholars' attention to the philosophical archive of Tokugawa thinkers as a historical event in its own right, this chapter also shares with Bryan van Norden the wish that Western departments of philosophy acquire a more pronounced multicultural and less Eurocentric approach.[2] *Philosophia* should be understood as the name of various sorts of cognitive practices that in different historical contexts aimed at developing, via self-reflective analysis, claims that fulfilled a higher standard of epistemological authority. The heuristic advantage of investigating Tokugawa *philosophy (testugaku)* rather than *thought (shisō)* is to draw a renewed historiographical attention to the socio-intellectual formation of that discourse in its own right (with specific logic, styles, terminologies, themes, social organizations, etc.), but also to rediscuss its connotations of nationalistic particularity – which reduced it to ideology or "mentality" and thus excluded it from more comparative and theoretical analyses – with the aim of contributing to a multicultural understanding of the history of various authoritative cognitive practices around the world.[3]

The Social Formation of Tokugawa Philosophy

Inquiring into the formative process of a philosophical archive in the social and intellectual dynamics of sixteenth- and seventeenth-century Japan does not mean that there were no texts or practices of philosophical significance before. Neither does it intend to reduce the subsequent development of Tokugawa philosophy to its own beginnings, in a sort of *reductio ad originem*. It simply aims at tracing the social and intellectual dynamics that led to the establishment, in the course of the seventeenth century, of a socially recognizable figure of "scholar" (*jusha*, lit. "learned person," "Confucianist") whose

---

[1] Feng, *History of Chinese Philosophy*.
[2] Van Norden, *Taking Back Philosophy*.
[3] As, for instance, in Melchiorre, *Filosofie nel mondo*.

intellectual production had the character of what in contemporary Europe would have been granted the name of philosophy. It also gives evidence of why it would be reductive to understand Tokugawa philosophy simply in terms of "Confucianism" (or "Neo-Confucianism") in the same way that it would as well be reductive to study early modern European philosophy in terms of Aristotelianism.

Before the Tokugawa era, the two institutions that housed the authors of philosophical treaties were the Daigakuryō, the formative academy for the court aristocracy in the Nara and Heian periods, and Buddhist temples. The scholars (*hakase*) of the Daigakuryō came from families such as the Sugawara, Ōmi, Kiyohara, and Nakahara, which transmitted within their household lineages the competence over the interpretation of the Five Classics (Ch. *wujing*, J. *gokyō*) and enjoyed teaching monopolies in disciplines associated with that canonical corpus.[4] Buddhist institutions, in the Nara, Heian, and subsequent periods, produced commentaries and abridgments of sutras as well as original treatises on Buddhist philosophy (notable to an Anglophone audience are the works of Kūkai and Dōgen). As the political authority of the imperial court declined in the course of the twelfth century, the Daigakuryō lost much of its institutional function, and as official contacts with the continent (and the flow of texts) diminished, the pedagogical and scholarly activities of the *hakase* sclerotized in the transmission of received exegetical readings of the Five Classics.

The impetus for philosophical investigations inspired by Song philosophy – which would later give terminology, canonical archive, and methodological guidance for inquiries on metaphysics, natural history (in the form of materia medica), medicine, ethics, politics, governance, military strategy, history, mathematics, and so forth – grew within Buddhist institutions in the late Kamakura and Muromachi periods.[5] Thanks to the activities and travels of the Tendai monk Shunjō (1166–1227) and the Rinzai monk Enni (1202–80), among others, large portions of the commentaries and treatises of the Cheng brothers, Zhu Xi, and other Song scholars started to circulate within the temple networks of the Tendai and Rinzai schools of Buddhism. These texts not only offered a new interpretation of Confucianism but also invited a renewed interest in the Four Books (Ch. *sishu*, J. *shisho*), which, with the

---

[4] In the Heian period, the field of studies divided into *kiden* (historiography), *monjō* (lexicography), *myōgyō* (Confucian studies), *myōbō* (jurisprudence), and *sandō* (mathematics, including astronomy and calendrical studies). See Hisaki, *Nihon kodai gakkō*.
[5] Wajima, *Nihon Sōgakushi*; Wajima, *Chūsei no jugaku*; Kawamoto, *Chūsei Zenshū no jugaku gakushū*.

notable exception of the *Analects*, had occupied only a marginal presence in the curriculum of the Daigakuryō. The reading of Zhu Xi's commentaries on the Four Books became part of Tendai training, which expanded its comprehensive approach to doctrine and utilized Song commentaries on the *Analects* and the *Mencius* as instruments for the interpretation of sutras and for meditative purposes. It was however within the Rinzai temple network in Kyoto that Song philosophy acquired a larger following. Chūgan Engetsu (1300–75) contributed to make the Nanzenji monastery one of the centers for the study of Zhu Xi's philosophy. It was from the Gozan monastic network of which Nanzenji was a part, thanks to its ties with the political authority of samurai clans in Kyoto and in other provinces, that Song Confucianism began percolating outside Buddhism.[6] As Hori Isao has put it, "in Rinzai Zen temples, the reading and memorizing of Zhu Xi texts had superseded the recitation of [Buddhist] scripture in the training of the youngsters."[7] Rinzai monks from Nanzenji and from Engakuji in Kamakura also served as lecturers of Chinese classics, medicine, and military science at the Ashikaga Gakkō, located in the Ashikaga district of Shimotsuke (modern-day Tochigi Prefecture), especially after its revitalization by Uesugi Norizane (c. 1410–66).[8]

The lectures of Rinzai monks such as Chūgan Engetsu and Gidō Shūshin (1325–88) on Zhu Xi's commentaries of the Four Books were attended by high-ranking samurai who served under the Ashikaga for the political and ethical guidance they offered. If Gidō's relationship with Shogun Yoshimitsu (1358–1408) represented symbolically the interest of samurai elites for Zhu Xi's philosophy in the Muromachi court, it was the spread of similar forms of lecturing and tutoring by Buddhist monks for the benefit of increasingly autonomous samurai houses (soon to become what historians call *sengoku daimyō*) that paved the way to a structural connection of samurai authority and Song philosophy. Nanzenji, joined later by Tenryūji, Daitokuji, and Engakuji, became a gathering point for monks interested in devoting themselves to the study of Song philosophy as part of their monastic training. From there, Giyō Hōshū (1362–1424) advised the former shogun Ashikaga Yoshimochi and produced the first *kunten* notation of Zhu Xi's *Sishu jizhu*.[9] Keian Genju (1427–1508), a Rinzai monk who trained at Nanzenji and in China, was invited to offer counseling on Confucian classics to the Shimazu family of domanial

---

[6] Collcutt, *Five Mountains*.
[7] Hori, *Hayashi Razan*, 18.
[8] See Maezawa, *Ashikaga gakkō*.
[9] *Kunten* is a system of annotation to render a Chinese text readable as Japanese.

lords in Ōsumi and Satsuma. Thanks to Shimazu's patronage, Genju's teaching of Zhu Xi's philosophy was consolidated in a lineage of scholars in southern Kyushu that continued well into the Edo period with Nanpo Bunshi (1555–1620), the author, alongside exegetical works on Zhu Xi, of the *Teppōki* (1606), a treatise on firearms.

The protracted civil disturbances of the Ōnin era between 1467 and 1477 and the consolidation of the local autonomy of *shugo daimyō* facilitated the spread in different regions of Rinzai monks who responded to the samurai need for tutoring and advising on topics as varied as political administration, military strategy, and ethics grounded on Zhu Xi's reading of the classics. From the Satsuma cluster of Confucian scholars, Minamimura Baiken moved to Tosa and established there a new lineage of philosophical inquiry. Among his disciples, Tani Jichū (1598–1650) abandoned his Buddhist vows and dedicated himself to the teaching of Confucian philosophy to students such as Ogura Sansei (1604–54) and Nonaka Kenzan (1615–64), both of whom served as teachers and advisers for the Okura family of domanial officials in Tosa. Another of Baiken's students, Yamazaki Ansai (1619–82), abandoned his Tendai initiation to devote his life to the study of Zhu Xi's philosophy, which he promoted as lecturer and adviser at the service of the Hoshina domanial lords of Aizu and from his private academy in Kyoto (Ansaijuku). Ansai is today considered one of the most influential of early Tokugawa thinkers.[10]

The widespread interest in Zhu Xi's philosophy in the second half of the fifteenth through the sixteenth centuries affected also the Confucian tradition within the imperial court. The aristocrat Ichijō Kaneyoshi (1408–81) authored treatises grounded in the Song commentaries on the Four Books, while Kiyohara Naritada, *hakase* of the Daigakuryō, abandoned the traditional predilection for the Five Classics and started instead lecturing on the Four Books with explicit reference to Zhu Xi's commentaries. When at the beginning of the seventeenth century Naritada's descendant Hidetaka saw his position of *myōgyō hakase*, or scholar of Confucian classics, threatened by the lecturing

[10] On Ansai, see H. Ooms, *Tokugawa Ideology*; Takashima, *Yamazaki Ansai*; Tajiri, *Yamazaki Ansai no sekai*. Among Ansai's students, we find some of the most influential philosophers of the first half of the Tokugawa period: Satō Naokata (1650–1719), who served as an adviser in various domains; Asami Keisai (1652–1712), who refused multiple invitations of domanial lords because he conceptualized a return of the political authority to the imperial house (*sonnō*); Miyake Shōsai (1662–1741), who served the Oshi domain before becoming an adviser-for-hire for a number of domains; Yusa Bokusai (1659–1734); Tani Jinzai (1663–1718); the aristocrats Ōgimachi Kinmichi (1653–1733) and Tsuchimikado Yasutomi (1655–1717); Shinto priests such as Izumoji Nobunao (1650–1703); astronomers such as Shibukawa Harumi (or Shunka, 1639–1715); and many others.

and tutoring activities of a young former monk named Hayashi Razan, the Kiyohara family's brand of Confucian studies had completely absorbed in their curriculum the approach and ideas of Song philosophy.

Pragmatic reasons were certainly behind the renewed interest in Song philosophy among sixteenth-century Sengoku daimyo. Rinzai monks initiated into Zhu Xi's commentaries advised on military strategies and governmental and administrative techniques in Satsuma, Tosa, and other regions. But they could also provide information on and, possibly, connectivity to Ming China because of the transnational network that Buddhist institutions maintained. Daimyo patronage of scholarship also served the purpose of making symbolic display of the enlightened nature of the new powerhouses. The institution of "house rules" (*kakun*) was an effect of such patronage: they regulated the hierarchical bonds between domanial lords, their retainers, and local strongmen (*kokushi*) with reference to the principles of government contained in the Confucian canon, offering intellectual legitimation to daimyo sovereignty.[11]

The genealogy of Fujiwara Seika and Hayashi Razan, who for decades historians have regarded as the founding fathers of Tokugawa Confucianism, should therefore be understood as only one among many coexisting lineages of philosophical teaching that emerged in the course of the sixteenth century, spreading from the Buddhist network formed around Nanzenji to different provinces. Trained as Rinzai monks in Kyoto (respectively at Shōkokuji and at Kenninji), Seika and Razan left the order to pursue the ideal of the literatus, the scholar-official at the center of the political life in China, which they believed to be a perfect realization of Zhu Xi's philosophy. Fujiwara Seika was initiated to Song philosophy during his novitiate and received further training by Kang Hang (1567–1618), a Chosŏn Confucian official imprisoned during the second of Hideyoshi's campaigns in Korea (1597) whom he met in Fushimi. In Kyoto, Seika strived to earn recognition as a Confucian scholar. He opened a small school where he lectured on Zhu Xi's commentaries wearing a *shin'i*, the formal costume of scholar-officials. Some of the students he trained in turn established scholarly lineages specializing in Song philosophy that prospered throughout the Tokugawa period. Among them, Matsunaga Sekigo (1592–1657) opened a school in Kyoto (the name of which changed from Shunjūkan to Kōshūan and finally Sekigodō) where he trained second-generation scholars of the caliber of Kinoshita Jun'an (1621–99), who would become personal adviser of Shogun Tsunayoshi and teacher of Arai Hakuseki (1657–1725)

---

[11] Spafford, "Language and Contours of Familial Obligation"; Arima and Akiyama, *Bushidō kakunshū*. An English anthology of *kakun* can be found in Wilson, *Ideals of the Samurai*.

and Muro Kyūsō (1658–1734); Andō Seian (1622–1701); Itō Jinsai (1627–1705); and Kaibara Ekiken (1630–1714). Nawa Kassho (1595–1648), born into the family of a wealthy peasant of Himeiji, rose to become scholar-adviser in the service of lord Katō Tadahiro of the Kumamoto domain and, later, of Tokugawa Yorinobu, lord of the Wakayama domain. Hori Kyōan (1585–1643), after studying Song philosophy with Seika and medicine with Manase Shōjun (1559–1605), served as scholar-adviser for the Asano family of the Hiroshima domain and for Tokugawa Yoshinao, lord of the Owari domain, and then opened a school of medicine in Kyoto, which became one of the central training institutions for generations of scholars.[12] Finally, Hayashi Razan (1583–1657), after serving as librarian, secretary, and attendant – a sort of secretarial position formalized under the title of *ohanashishū* – for Tokugawa Ieyasu at Fushimi and tutor for Ieyasu's son Hidetada and grandson Iemitsu, founded in 1632 a private academy in Edo at Shinobugaoka, near Ueno, which he called Senseiden. The school was renamed Shōheikō (or the Shōheizaka Academy) in 1690 and moved to Yushima, where it enjoyed shogunal patronage under Shogun Tsunayoshi. The Senseiden and, later, the Shōheizaka Academy continued to be run by the descendants of Razan and offered training not only to the bureaucratic personnel of the shogunate but also to scholars such as Yamaga Sokō (1622–85) and Ogyū Sorai (1666–1728). Razan continued his collaboration with the first Tokugawa shoguns: he authored the diplomatic correspondence with the Ming and Chosŏn courts; organized an archive of historical documents for the shogunate; collaborated on the edition of a series of shogunal edicts, among which were the *Buke shohatto* (Laws for all warrior houses) and the *Shoshi hatto* (Laws for all *hatamoto* and *gokenin*); and established genealogical affiliations of the Tokugawa family with the Minamoto and certified genealogical lineages for other warrior households. A polymath like many other scholars of the earlier generations, Razan authored commentaries on Zhu Xi's philosophy and treatises on practical learning (military strategy, annals, genealogy), dictionaries propaedeutical to more in-depth exegetical study of the Chinese classics, as well as introductions to the most complex conceptions of Zhu Xi's metaphysics, primers on Shintō mythology and institutions, Chinese history, Buddhist cosmology, and so on.

Razan greatly benefited from the patronage of the Tokugawa, but as the genealogical sketch proposed earlier suggests, he was far from the pioneer of

---

[12] Including Motoori Norinaga, who studied there from 1752 to 1758, specializing in medicine under Hori Gen'atsu and Confucian studies under Hori Keizan, a close friend of Ogyū Sorai. See Jōfuku, *Motoori Norinaga*; Takahashi Masao, *Motoori Norinaga*.

Tokugawa Confucianism that later scholarship portrays him to be. Part of that exaggeration was an effect of the archival invention the Hayashi family itself arranged through the compilation of the *Tokugawa jikki* (True records of the Tokugawa) between 1799 and 1844 under the editorial leadership of Hayashi Jussai (1768–1841) and Narushima Motonao (1778–1862). Part of it was also the official recognition the school received after the 1790 *Kansei igaku no kin* (Prohibition of heterodoxies of the Kansei era), an edict that, in the context of Matsudaira Sadanobu's Kansei reforms, aimed at restricting public lecturing and the publication of philosophical treatises to only the most orthodox interpretation of Zhu Xi's thought. While the implementation of the edict was uneven in the different provinces of the archipelago (it suspended seminars on "heterodox practices" in the Shōheizaka Academy but failed to interrupt the scholarly activity of the many private academies distant from Edo) and hardly of great censorial effect (since it targeted *printed* materials, whereas most philosophical treatises still circulated in manuscript form), it reinforced the institutional image of orthodox Zhu Xi studies.[13] The two combined events of the Kansei edict and the *Tokugawa jikki* reinforced in the early Meiji period the view that Neo-Confucianism constituted the ideological backbone of the Tokugawa shogunate, the replication of which found in Maruyama Masao's work a platform that institutionalized a representation of Razan as the ideological éminence grise behind the Tokugawa regime.[14]

The formalization of Tokugawa authority in a new shogunate in 1603 – a reinvention, rather than a repetition, of the governments of the Minamoto and the Ashikaga – created the social and institutional conditions for the employment of scholars who, as advisers, tutors, physicians, and researchers, became a social reality in early modern Japan. It was in their texts that the event of Tokugawa philosophy unfolded.

The Social Structure of Tokugawa Philosophy

The epistolary exchanges between Fujiwara Seika and Hayashi Razan in the first years of the seventeenth century capture them struggling to self-fashion themselves as literati in the tradition of Chinese scholar-officials (Ch. *shi dafu*) in a social context of great turmoil and creative instability after the Tokugawa's

---

[13] See Backus, "Relationship of Confucianism"; Backus, "Kansei Prohibition of Heterodoxy."
[14] Maruyama, *Nihon seiji shisōshi kenkyū*, translated as *Studies in the Intellectual History of Tokugawa Japan*. H. Ooms, *Tokugawa Ideology*, and Boot, "Adoption and Adaptation of Neo-Confucianism," criticize Maruyama's thesis.

victory at Sekigahara (1600). The obstacles they faced in contriving a professional role for their scholarly expertise was a symptom of a lingering contradiction between the demand for scholarly advice from samurai authorities at the shogunate and domain levels and the lack of institutional legitimation for that role.[15] If some of these advisers never broke ties with the Buddhist institutions that housed them, others were stranded in an indeterminate social limbo, as Seika and Razan were after their voluntary defrocking. Many indeed continued to look like Buddhist monks – for instance, by shaving their heads, like in the case of *machi-isha* (town doctors). This appears to be one of the immediate strategies for many of these new "scholars." In 1605, Ieyasu granted Razan permission to lecture in Kyoto on Zhu Xi's philosophy only if he continued to wear (nondenominational) Buddhist clothes and shaved his head – a habit that continued to be practiced in Razan's academy in Edo until 1696.[16]

A combination of factors contributed to hinder the creation of a social platform for these new scholars to operate with recognized authority. Buddhist institutions had lost, since the Azuchi-Momoyama period, the temporal sway they used to have, and the Tokugawa authorities did not intend to restore it. Furthermore, the consolidation of a close social hierarchy within the warrior class that the Tokugawa developed in the first decades of the shogunate became an impediment to social advancement for all those categories (*rōnin* or various typologies of local strongmen often referred to as *gōshi* or *jizamurai*) that did not fit within the retainer system (*kashin*): there was therefore no space for a "free floating" scholar without apparent ties with an enfeoffed warrior household. Third, there was no institutionalized system of promotion and legitimation of scholarly activities to which the first generation of scholars could model their own professional self-fashioning, because of the absence and impossibility to implement in Japan a selective process similar to the "imperial examinations" (Ch. *keju*) that, in neighboring Ming China and Chosŏn Korea, reproduced at the institutional level an ordering of officials that ostensibly mirrored the ethical and cognitive value system at the heart of Zhu Xi philosophy.[17]

The different strategies that scholars followed to self-fashion themselves professionally in the early seventeenth century were therefore the result of, on the one hand, the absence of a precise institutional role for scholarly labor and, on the other, the active promotion of intellectual cultivations that the Tokugawa themselves advocated in theory, as an ideal upheld in the *Laws for*

---

[15] See Hori, *Hayashi Razan*, 40–48.
[16] Marcon, *Knowledge of Nature*, 58–67.
[17] Elman, *Cultural History of Civil Examinations*.

Warrior Houses, and, in practice, by encouraging the establishment of educational facilities for samurai retainers.[18] The Tokugawa's promotion of scholarship did not simply adhere to an abstract ideal but was also instrumentally linked to the necessity of nurturing a class of trained samurai-functionaries that could reinforce the institutionalization of a legal and administrative system in support of the new political order (*tenka taihei*). The rapid rise of literacy among the samurai and the general population in the second half of the seventeenth century stimulated the demand of teachers for domanial (*hankō*) and commoners' schools (*terakoya*). In turn, the demand for advanced training in specialized knowledge also steadily increased throughout the eighteenth century.[19] As a result, the number of students enrolled in private academies increased, furthering the emergence of new schools first in the major urban centers and castle towns and, by the end of the eighteenth century, in the countryside as well, including, for the first time, women.[20] But cities and towns remained the main centers for the gathering of scholars, students, books, cultural associations, and diatribes, similarly connecting urbanization and the rise of "secular" scholars in early modern Japan and medieval Europe.[21]

The multiplication of schools and academies throughout the seventeenth century accompanied the growth of a second generation of scholars (*jusha*) who were not trained in Buddhist institutions, thus severing the already tenuous link between their philosophical investigations and Buddhist doctrine. Some trained with former monks such as Hayashi Razan and Yamazaki Ansai. Others devoted themselves to scholarly research largely as autodidacts, supported by the increased number of Chinese volumes commercially available via Nagasaki's trade port. This was the case of Nakae Tōju (1608–48), who served as a retainer in the Ōzu domain before opening his own private academy, the Tōju Shoin, where he taught the philosophy of Zhu Xi and Wang Yangming and could count as disciples Kumazawa Banzan (1619–91), Fuchi Kōzan (1617–87), and Nakagawa Kenshuku (1624–58).

For much of the Tokugawa period, the majority of people involved in intellectual labor – as authors of texts, teachers, researchers, or simply as amateur members of one of the many cultural associations (known as *ren* or *kai*) of the period – were of samurai origin.[22] Thinkers of commoner background surely

---

[18] Wajima, *Shōheikō to hankō*.
[19] Rubinger, *Popular Literacy*; Takahashi Satoshi, *Edo no kyōikuyoku*; Umihara, *Kinsei no gakkō to kyōiku*; Tsujimoto, *Kinsei kyōiku shisōshi*.
[20] Rubinger, *Private Academies*; Maeda, *Edo kyōiku shisōshi kenkyū*.
[21] See, for comparison, Le Goff, *Les intellectuels au Moyen Age*.
[22] Maeda, *Edo no dokushokai*; Tanaka, *Edo wa nettowāku*.

participated in the scholarly community early on in the seventeenth century: for instance, Itō Jinsai, the son of a wealthy merchant in Kyoto, received a sufficient endowment from his family to dedicate his life to scholarship (he trained under Matsunaga Sekigo) and counted in his private academy, the Kogidō, established in 1662, a large number of commoners among his students; Nakamura Tekisai (1629–1702) similarly came from a family of cloth-makers and dedicated his scholarly activities to the education of the urban population of artisans, merchants, and shopkeepers. But even when in the eighteenth century intellectual labor found support in the expanding demand for new schools, in a burgeoning publishing industry, and through the support of merchants' patronage – as in the case of merchants' academies such as the Kaitokudō of Miyake Sekian (1665–1730) and Nakai Shūan (1693–1758) – the majority of socially recognized scholars were of samurai origin and devoted their scholarly activities as a form of service to domanial lords, either as a lifelong engagement, as in the case of Kaibara Ekiken for the Kuroda family of domanial lords in Fukuoka, or as "scholars-for-hire" who served domanial lords in forms of temporary or task-oriented employment.

By the turn of the eighteenth century, the steady growth in literacy among commoners transformed them into enthusiastic consumers of cultural products. The result was a diversification of the market for cultural goods as members of different social classes invested their time and resources in cultural activities. By the end of the century, with the emergence of new cultural consumers among the population of large landowning peasants, culture exited the major urban centers of the Kamigata and Kantō areas and spread to the countryside. The value of education, a pillar of the Tokugawa political order, was matched by the social distinction that connoisseurship and erudition acquired as a marker of status. In addition, the increase in the number of volumes reaching Japan from China and from Europe through the Dutch East India Company (VOC) after Tokugawa Yoshimune's relaxation on the censoring activities of the Nagasaki town magistrate (*machi-bugyō*) expanded the themes and topics of inquiry, inviting scholars to investigate Western matters.[23] The participation in cultural activities of members from the various social classes – from samurai to wealthy peasants and merchants – exploded during the second half of the eighteenth century, producing the dynamic popular culture of late Tokugawa Japan.[24] And yet, the number of scholars of common origin remained relatively low, due in part to the lack

---

[23] Iwashita, *Edo no kaigai jōhō nettowāku*; Hsiung (Chapter 11), this volume.
[24] Harootunian, "Late Tokugawa Culture and Thought."

of an institutionalized open system of selection and in part to the financial difficulty of earning a living as a scholar.

Few scholars were able to survive only by teaching and publishing, and those who did had to heavily rely on the patronage of wealthy merchant families, such as the Funabashiya, the Kōnoike, the Tominaga, the Mitsuboshiya (all of which provided the initial capital for the foundation of the Kaitokudō). Kimura Kenkadō, the wealthy son of an Osaka sake brewer and real estate investor, ran a salon that housed and supported the labor and research of artists such as Yanagisawa Kien (1703–58), Maruyama Ōkyo (1733–95), and Ike Taiga (1723–76); scholars such as Katayama Hokkai (1723–90), Kaiho Seiryō (1755–1817), and Ono Ranzan (1729–1810); and literary and artistic figures such as Ueda Akinari (1734–1809), Hiraga Gennai (1728–80), Ōta Nanpo (1749–1823), and Shiba Kōkan (1747–1818).[25] The large majority of Tokugawa scholars relied on employment as scholar-retainers or were practicing physicians who engaged in scholarly pursuits on the side of this profession: such was the case for Hori Keizan (1688–1757), Motoori Norinaga (1730–1801), Sugita Genpaku (1733–1817), and many others. Involvement in cultural circles and private schools provided professional and amateur scholars from the commoner classes indirect and, far more rarely, direct contact with members of the samurai elites. The expanding networks of cultural exchange, even though only occasionally bringing samurai and commoners physically together, created intellectual associations by virtue of shared ideas, interests, practices, and often the same scholar-teachers supervised the activities of different groups.[26]

That said, in terms of audience and themes, the intellectual panorama of Tokugawa Japan maintained, during its first two centuries of development, a marked separation between urban and rural centers and a distinct class orientation. Scholars of commoner origins tended to have an audience and students from the same social class. That was the case of the teachers and students of the Kaitokudō in Osaka, but also of Ishida Baigan's (1685–1744) school of *sekimon shingaku* (lit. "heart-learning") – carried over, after Baigan's death, by his students Tejima Toan (1718–86) and Nakazawa Dōni (1725–1803) – and of the

---

[25] On the Kaitokudō, see Najita, *Visions of Virtue*. On Kimura Kenkadō's patronage, see Nakamura Shin'ichirō, *Kimura Kenkadō no saron*.

[26] The socially mixed composition of *some* cultural associations should not immediately suggest a democratization of learning or the existence in Japan of a horizontal "republic of letters" (an ideal rather than a reality in early modern Europe as well), as Ikegami, *Bonds of Civility*, implies. On the hierarchical structure of the European republic of letters, see Goldgar, *Impolite Learning*.

Kangien of Hirose Tansō (1782–1856).[27] It was nonetheless among urban commoners that women scholars made their debut in an intellectual environment largely dominated by men. The former Buddhist nun Jion-ni Kenka (1716–78), daughter of a wealthy sake brewer from Omi, was among the first disciples of Ishida Baigan and an active promoter of his thought in Edo and then in all the Kantō. As an intellectual, she rejected Baigan's chauvinistic view of a disciplined woman as the moral inhabitant of the household kitchen in her role as "wife" and as a silent and transcendental engine for the development of filial piety in her role as "mother." It was thanks to her activities as an organizer that Nakazawa Dōni established in 1781 a college, the Sanzensha, in the shogunal city, which spread Baigan's ethics of diligence and frugality to commoners and low-ranking samurai of both sexes. Later, women scholars such as Yaguchi Nakako (1790–1846), Bandai Kimiko (1783–1837), and Tagami Tatsuko (1802–67) popularized *shingaku* in the southwestern regions of Honshu and Kyushu via public lectures and certificate-issuing seminars open to students of different classes and sexes.[28]

At the turn of the nineteenth century, these social divisions tended to break asunder, so that, despite the attempt of the shogunate to exercise tighter control on the spread of "heterodox" doctrines (*igaku*) in 1790, it was not uncommon for scholars of non-samurai origin to find employment at the service of a domanial lord, as in the case of Yamagata Bantō (1748–1821), who, born into a family of wealthy peasants of Harima, rose to the position of scholar and adviser for financial matters in the Sendai domain. By the last decades of the period, the institutionalization of Confucian scholarship within the shogunate reinforced its formative role for the state bureaucracy. It also diminished, however, its relevance to the philosophical debate elsewhere.[29]

The absence of a precise institutional frame for scholarly activities in the first two centuries of the Tokugawa period explains also the diverse ways in which transmission and authority operated. It also provides, as the following section will show, the best explanation for the eclectic and diverse character that Tokugawa philosophy had since the beginning. Although it is conventional in many introductory surveys of early modern Japanese thought to divide it into distinct schools, there was no clear separation nor markedly

---

[27] Baigan's school aimed at reframing Zhu Xi's ethical norms to conform to the everyday life experience of commoners, with practices, rituals, and conceptions adopted from Zen Buddhism and Shinto. See Beonio-Brocchieri, *Religiosità e ideologia*; Imai and Yamamoto, *Sekimon shingaku no shisō*.

[28] Robertson, "Shingaku Woman."

[29] Paramore, "Nationalization of Confucianism."

doctrinarian sectarianism among the different thought systems of the period.[30] In Japanese scholarship, the division of Confucianism into discrete and neatly defined schools can hardly be observed in the philosophical archive of the period, but should rather be traced back to the taxonomical divisions operated by Meiji historians, in particular Inoue Tetsujirō (1856–1944), one of the earliest historians of East Asian philosophies, and Tsuda Sōkichi (1873–1961), the scholar who contributed the most to conceive of the study of Japanese intellectual history as "thought" (shisō) rather than "philosophy" (tetsugaku).[31] Inoue distinguished three genealogies of Japanese Confucianism: the first orthodoxly devoted to Zhu Xi Confucianism, the second to Wang Yangming Confucianism, and the third to ancient-learning Confucianism.[32] His neat distinction of schools was only partly consonant with the early Meiji views of Fukuzawa Yukichi (1835–1901) and others who conceived of Tokugawa Confucianism in terms of feudal premodernity or as an alien form of thought. Inoue saw in the political utilitarianism of scholars inspired by Wang Yangming and in the empiricist rationalism of the "ancient learning school" of Jinsai and Sorai forms of indigenous resistance to Zhu Xi's orthodoxy imposed by the Tokugawa authorities.[33] This view not only fueled the scholarly creed on the pragmatic, down-to-earth character of Japanese thought of later literary and intellectual historians such as Katō Shūichi, Minamoto Ryōen, and Bitō Masahide but also found further validation in the interpretive paradigm set up by Maruyama Masao.[34] The best example of retroactive invention of

---

[30] Illustrative examples are Koyasu, Edo shisōshi kōgi; Furuta and Koyasu, Nihon shisōshi dokuhon; Tajiri, Edo no shisōshi; Watanabe, History of Japanese Political Thought; Bowring, In Search of the Way.

[31] Particularly in Tsuda, Bungaku ni arawaretaru waga kokumin shisō.

[32] Inoue dedicated three distinct volumes to the three forms of Confucianism that spread in Tokugawa Japan. In chronological order, they are Nihon yōmeigakuha no tetsugaku (1900), Nihon kogakuha no tetsugaku (1902), and Nihon shushigakuha no tetsugaku (1905).

[33] Inoue's criticism of Ogyū Sorai's Sinophilia appears in Kokumin dōtoku gairon.

[34] On the paradigmatic effect on the field of Tokugawa intellectual history of Inoue and Maruyama scholarship, see Kurozumi, "Tokugawa Confucianism," and Kurozumi, "Nihon shisō to wa nani ka." Katō Shūichi makes the anti-speculative, "down-to-earth" nature of the Japanese mind the heuristic cornerstone of his Nihon bungakushi josetsu. As he puts it in the opening of the introduction, "In every age of their history the Japanese have expressed their thought not so much in abstract philosophical systems as in concrete literary works" (English translation by Chibbett, History of Japanese Literature, 1). The view that jitsugaku was the main thrust of Japanese intellectual investigations originated in the early Meiji period, in the writings of Fukuzawa Yukichi and Nishi Amane. It was influential in Anglophone historiography on Confucianism via the works of intellectual historians Tsuda Sōkichi and Minamoto Ryōen; the latter consolidated his views on the principle of practicality in Jitsugaku shisō no keifu. Bellah, Tokugawa Religion, and de Bary and Bloom, Principle and Practicality, were influential in framing the discussion on the pragmaticism of Tokugawa thought. For a critical assessment of these views on jitsugaku, see Harootunian's review of de Bary and Bloom's Principle and Practicality.

intellectual "schools" is *kokugaku* as the name of either a discrete school of "national learning" or of a scattered movement of "nativist" ideologies.[35] Even though the term can be sporadically found in philosophical texts as early as the seventeenth century, such as the writing of the Shinto priest Yoshimi Yukikazu (1673–1761), it never indicated a school or movement before the last decade of the Tokugawa period. None of the scholars later grouped in this "school" or "movement" used the term *kokugaku* to refer to their scholarship or their relations with other scholars; furthermore, none of the scholars later grouped within this "school" constituted a definite lineage of master-teacher.[36] Despite the nebulous character of the scholarship of those professional and amateur thinkers that would only in the Meiji period be structured into an organic genealogy as *kokugaku*, it was with them that philosophical production moved from the cities to the countryside, where it found among the learned members of the rural elites readers, students, and organizers of cultural associations devoted to Shinto rituals, mythology, and precursors of folklore studies.[37] It was within the intellectual ferment of these new political actors who were to play an important role in the revolutionary decades before and after the Meiji Restoration of 1868 that female thinkers found a new voice and audience, as in the examples of Kurosawa Tokiko (1806–90), Matsuo Taseko (1811–94), and Deguchi Nao (1837–1918).[38]

Given the fact that scholars used to move quite independently from one teacher to another, research topics and texts from different philosophical traditions, and engage in quite harsh diatribes with one another, lines of transmission seemed to be much looser and nonbinding for scholars (*jusha*) than for practitioners of any other cultural form. Very few academies followed the *iemoto* system of vertical transmission more commonly associated with

[35] In the English literature, the notion of a school of "national learning" is defended in Nosco, *Remembering Paradise*, and the idea of a widespread nativist movement in Harootunian, *Things Seen and Unseen*. On the question of "nativism," see Breen, "Nativism Restored." If the idea of a school (or even movement) of "national learning" does not stand the proof of the archives, the question of "nativism" is more complex. Susan Burns, for instance, shows in her *Before the Nation* how not all scholars who would be later framed in a *kokugaku* genealogy can be understood as "nativist." Vice versa, Mark McNally argues in *Pursuing the Way* that nativist themes were supported also by scholars outside *kokugaku*. McNally, *Like No Other*, has more recently contended that "exceptionalism" is a better qualifier than "nativism" for some forms of *kokugaku* thought in late Tokugawa Japan.
[36] Kamo no Mabuchi and Norinaga only met once, and Hirata Atsutane famously met Norinaga only in a dream.
[37] See Harootunian, *Things Seen and Unseen*; Sugi, *Kinsei no chiiki*; *Snow Country Tales*, the English translation of Suzuki Bokushi's *Hokuetsu seppu* (1836–42).
[38] See Nenzi, *Chaos and Cosmos*; Walthall, *Weak Body of a Useless Woman*; E. G. Ooms, *Women and Millenarian Protest*.

artisanal and artistic workshops.[39] Disciples often acquired an autonomous if not openly oppositional stance vis-à-vis their teachers. One famous case was Yamazaki Ansai's Kimon academy, which was characterized by a close reading of the Chen-Zhu commentarial traditions as well as investigations in the rituals and mythology of Shintoism. Not only was the systematicity of Ansai's philosophy not carried over by his main students – Satō Naokata famously rejected Ansai's interest in Shintoism, Miyake Shōsai developed a strange form of metaphysical spiritualism, and Asami Keisai emphasized a strongly normative view of the ethical life in quotidian interactions – but, most importantly, the three "star" students of the Kimon school engaged in incessant quarrels with one another and with their teacher.[40] Scholars, in other words, delinked from institutional normativity, tended to operate in autonomy if not in competition with one another.

The institutionally unregulated and relatively autonomous life of scholars, in turn, affected the processes of legitimation and authorization of scholarly labor. First, the lack of framing institutions – such as the Daigakuryō or Buddhist temple complexes in premodern Japan, the university in Europe, or the examination system in China – determined that the social position of scholars in the larger society affected their status within the smaller scholarly society; this explains why, especially in the first half of the period, scholarly practices tended to have a high degree of class homogeneity in terms of audience and issues. Second, lack of institutional authority transferred the legitimating function to the canonical sources grounding scholars' claims. Profound knowledge of and an ability to quote from the classics was highly valued, to the point that the paratextual organization of scholars' theoretical constructs in the form of commentaries, clarifications, and lexicographical dictionaries tended to be more authoritative than stand-alone treatises.[41] Third, participating in debates or diatribes could also enhance the visibility of individual scholars, whether these were scholar-retainers, physicians, or heads of private academies. And opportunities to engage in public confrontations with other scholars were not rare throughout the period.[42] Famous

---

[39] The term *iemoto* system (*iemoto seido*) refers to an organizational structure of different kinds of cultural and artisanal groups in Tokugawa Japan, and it is usually associated with cultural circles of tea experts (*chadō*). Ikegami, *Bonds of Civility*, 163, explains that "the *iemoto* system ideally aimed at enhancing the authority of the grand master by creating a hierarchical order of professional teachers, semi-professionals, and amateur students."

[40] See H. Ooms, *Tokugawa Ideology*, 194–285; Tajiri, *Yamazaki Ansai no sekai*; Ŏm Sŏk-in, *Higashi Ajia ni okeru Nihon shushigaku*.

[41] On the role of paratextual form in legitimating cognitive claims, see Marcon, "'Book' as Fieldwork."

[42] See Yama, *Edo no shisō tōsō*.

instances are the bitter confrontations on how to judge the vengeful action of the forty-seven *rōnin* of Akō in 1702 among scholars of the most diverse orientations, including Hayashi Hōkō (1644–1732, head of the Shōheizaka Academy), Muro Kyūso, Ogyū Sorai, Satō Naokata, Asami Keisai, and others;[43] and the so-called *kokka hachiron* debate on the political significance of poetry, spurred by the circulation of the "theses" of Kada no Arimaro (1706–51) in 1742.[44] Fourth, proximity to power also played an important role in authorizing the scholarly claims of thinkers, as in the case of Arai Hakuseki, adviser of Manabe Akifusa, domanial lord of Takasaki, who played an important role within the shogunate during the reign of Tokugawa Ienobu, and Ogyū Sorai, adviser of Yanagisawa Yoshiyasu, domanial lord of Kawagoe, and confidante of Shogun Tsunayoshi. Fifth, reputation within cultural associations (some of which centered on temples, such as the network of Sinophiles at Manpukuji of which Sorai was a member) was of great importance in establishing a scholar within the field of cultural production: the acquisition of social capital through these activities contributed to the authority given to a scholar's work. Only later in the period did publications came to play a role in the notoriety and cultural importance of individual scholars, since for a large part of the period the majority of theoretical and philosophical texts circulated in manuscript form, a tendency that continued well into the nineteenth century. Before that, editorial work in prefacing or adding *kundoku* reading to Chinese classics as well as in compiling lexica and encyclopedias tended to be regarded of greater value in establishing the reputation of scholars.

Tokugawa Philosophy: Styles and Themes

The philosophical archive of Tokugawa Japan appears to be as diverse in terms of topics, approaches, and applications as the social organization of its authors and practitioners. Without an overarching institutional frame, scholars pursued research that to a certain extent responded to assigned commissions or to the expectations deriving from the professional role they covered as either samurai retainers, "scholars-for-hire," physicians, or teachers. Kaibara Ekiken, for instance, published works on history (centered around the Kuroda family of domanial lords), education and individual cultivation, public

---

[43] An English anthology of the different positions can be found in de Bary, Gluck, and Tiedemann, *Sources of Japanese Tradition*, 2:438–68; Tucker, "Rethinking the Akō Ronin Debate"; McMullen, "Confucian Perspectives on the Akō Revenge."

[44] See Nosco, "Nature, Invention, and National Learning"; Boot, "Japanese Poetics"; Flueckinger, *Imagining Harmony*, 148–55.

health, communal ethics, agronomy (in collaboration with Miyazaki Yasu-sada, 1623–97), materia medica, and metaphysics that directly responded to domanial commission or that were framed by him as an attempt to improve living conditions, spiritual and material, within the Fukuoka domain. Ishida Baigan, to offer a different example, developed a complex ethical system, both theoretically grounded in a metaphysical order inspired by Zhu Xi's cosmology and pragmatically tailored to the daily challenges of artisans, merchants, shopkeepers, and day laborers, that promised moral respectability to the urban population. At the same time, a high degree of unity and consistency characterized the philosophical landscape of Tokugawa Japan. This derived from the common set of canonical sources – the Four Books and, to a lesser extent, the Five Classics and the large apparatus of commentaries stretching back to Song philosophers – which gave a template to the first generation of thinkers for the development of discrete disciplines and a very coherent terminological dictionary of key heuristic concepts, but which also consti-tuted one of the major sources for the authority and legitimacy of scholarly investigations.

The only apparent contradiction of diversity and uniformity characteris-tic of Tokugawa philosophy – the central tenet of the most recent historio-graphical research, in particular of Kurozumi Makoto – is at odds with the long-held paradigms established by Inoue, Tsuda, and Maruyama, whereby the eclecticism of Tokugawa "Confucianism" resulted from forms of autoch-thonous resistance against the monolith of Zhu Xi's xenogenetic ideology.[45] Often ignored or easily dismissed by historians as unoriginal and superficial, the works of the first generation of scholars such as Fujiwara Seika, Hayashi Razan, and Matsunaga Sekigo were no less sophisticated and engaging than those of the second. Responding to the needs of their patrons, not only was their textual production polymathic, but it established a philosophical termi-nology that would last until the end of the period.

It was not, however, simply a common canon and a common terminology that gave sense and coherency to the philosophical discourse in the first half of the period. Zhu Xi's philosophy offered an organic system of investigation that connected metaphysical concerns with a logically stringent inferential proce-dure that could be applied to the most diverse ambits, from cosmology and natural history to politics and aesthetics. In this regard, the comparison with the Aristotelian organon connecting metaphysics to the different branches

---

[45] See, in particular, Kurozumi, *Kinsei Nihon shakai to jukyō*; Kurozumi, *Fukusūsei no Nihon shisō*; Takeuchi, "Nihon shisō e no shiza"; Koyasu, *Hōhō to shite no Edo*, 7–30. In English, see Kurozumi, "Nature of Early Tokugawa Confucianism."

of the Aristotelian corpus via logic and rhetoric is less interesting if simply aimed at listing convergences and divergences than for the analogously structured form both systems provided to philosophers' speculative labor. In fact, if Song philosophy provided a generative platform, it rarely constricted scholars' investigations to dogmatic orthodoxy, even within the presumed school of Zhu Xi studies of the period, the Shōheizaka Academy, where themes drawn from Buddhist, Shinto, and literary texts were part of its pedagogical curriculum (until the ban on heterodoxy that was part of the 1791 Kansei reforms).[46]

At a metaphysical level, the working premise that Tokugawa philosophers adopted from Song Confucianism was that all phenomena in the universe follow the same rules, as they partake of the same substance, which undergoes a process of diversification into myriads of things (Ch. *wanwu*, J. *banbutsu*), corporeal and incorporeal, by its constant movement, determined by an energetic principle (Ch. *qi*, J. *ki*) forming patterns or structural recurrences (Ch. *li*, J. *ri*). This diversification proceeds in a complex schema of combinatory processes whereby two different tendencies (*yin*, *yang*) exercise a shaping effect on the five elementary constituents of all entities (the five phases, Ch. *wuxing*, J. *gogyo*). Different thinkers developed different understandings of this fundamental metaphysical structure and contrived different applications that provided hypothetical explanations of the causes of phenomena – from the composition of the soil to the medicinal effect of particular herbs, from the dynamics of typhoons to the origins of earthquakes, from the causes of different emotions to the ideal hierarchy of an ordered society. What all scholars shared was the working assumption that if at the basis of all phenomena there were rules that applied to everything (natural phenomena, emotions, communities, deities, etc.), the universe was, at least in principle, knowable. That knowledge was expressible and communicable, and on its basis the individual and communitarian lives of all could be improved. In other words, whether directly engaging metaphysical questions or not at all (as, most distinctly, in the writings of Ogyū Sorai), Tokugawa scholars trusted that investigations of the classics and their triangulation with, or application to, observational practices on social, mental, or natural phenomena could produce authoritative knowledge. This knowledge promised to improve the living conditions of individuals and communities on the basis of an implicit order – usually expressed by formulae such as *"tenchi shizen no ri,"* meaning "patterns/rules (*ri*) that spontaneously or automatically (*shizen*) structured everything in the universe (*tenchi*)" – believed to transcendentally exist behind

---

[46] See Wajima, *Shōheikō to hankō*.

experienceable reality. The pursuit of learning, in whatever form (speculative like that of Satō Naokata and Ishida Baigan, pragmatic like that of Ogyū Sorai and Kumazawa Banzan, or encyclopedic like that of Tominaga Nakamoto and Kaibara Ekiken), always implied the investigation of the reason (kyu ̄ri) behind all phenomena (kakubutsu).

Different thinkers offered different justifications or grounding of their cognitive and ethical claims by appealing to either a universal pattern or schema (the ri plane) or through the specific form this pattern seemed to assume from their observation of the behavior of individual substances (as an effect of ki). The investigation of individual entities – plants, emotions, behaviors, social hierarchies – could be in any case conceptualized as the experienceable effect of an invisible, transcendental logic that could be grasped only inferentially. Similarly, one could appreciate the order of society by meditating on its consonance with a universal pattern (as, for instance, in Satō Naokata) or, vice versa, one could grasp abductively a transcendental pattern behind the investigation of particular instantiations (as in Kaibara Ekiken). Not all thinkers indulged in metaphysical speculations: some surely explored in depth the abstract rules and implications of Zhu Xi's schemata (e.g. Minagawa Kien [1743–1807] and Miura Baien [1723–89]); but others simply assumed them as ultimate reasons beyond observed patterns in natural and social phenomena (e.g. Kaibara Ekiken, Itō Jinsai, or Arai Hakuseki); others tried to either synthesize or compare Song metaphysics with Buddhism (e.g. Ishida Baigan and Tominaga Nakamoto) or with Shinto (e.g. Yamazaki Ansai); and others simply had no interest in discussing metaphysical structures (e.g. Ogyū Sorai). The important point is that metaphysical speculations continued to be practiced: Ishida Baigan's defense of merchants' ethicality was justified by grounding it to ri-ki metaphysics as experienced by individuals' affects and sense of debt toward their parents;[47] Andō Shōeki's (1703–72) ecological thought is exquisitely metaphysical;[48] and so are the assumptions on the fertility of the soil also presented in metaphysical terms by a "pragmatic" thinker such as Satō Nobuhiro (1769–1850).[49] They were not abandoned because of an alleged "down-to-earth" attitude of the "Japanese mind." Ogyū Sorai's justification of a rationalist or instrumentalist approach to politics can similarly be interpreted as a form of metaphysical hypostatization of the "way of the sages" rather than as anti-metaphysical proto-modern empiricism. And metaphysical was the cosmology that Motoori Norinaga inferred from his philological

---

[47] Beonio-Brocchieri, Religiosità e ideologia.
[48] Yasunaga, Andō Shōeki.
[49] Marcon, "Satō Nobuhiro."

analysis of the *Kojiki*: a universe dominated by the movement of impersonal forces (*kami*), the logic of which could not be analytically induced but only emotionally grasped (*mono no aware*).

The interaction of universal and particular – an organizational logic as much as a system of regulative principles behind the heterogeneous appearances of the myriad things – played out differently in the works of different scholars. At the epistemological level, some maintained a strong deductive approach (e.g. Minagawa Kien), others more inductive (e.g. Itō Jinsai). In all cases, however, the assumption that behind visible and invisible phenomena of the universe there were structured tendencies, if not laws, in the modern sense of the terms, rather than chaos did not excuse scholars from giving a sound justification to their claims. Quite the contrary, the investigation of the causes of things involved scholars in repeated attempts of interpretation (*shitchū*), correction (*teisei*), rectification (*kaisei*), and clarification (*keimō*) – terms that often appeared in the titles of scholars' treatises or in methodological prefaces (*hanrei*). Kaibara Ekiken, in his *Taigiroku* (posthumously published in 1714), conceived of doubt (*gi*) as the necessary attitude at the basis of scholars' investigation of things.[50] Itō Jinsai believed that philosophical clarification of the original meaning of the key terms in the Confucian classics was a necessary precondition for their proper understanding.[51] Ogyū Sorai maintained that ethical and political principles had to be justified not simply by the authority of the classics but also by scholars' investigation of the current state of affairs.[52] The correction of mistakes (*go*) and falsehoods (*kyo*) was at the core of most treatises on materia medica, which was sustained by sophisticated empirical and philological evidence triangulating multilingual sources and observational practices.[53] In short, the absence of institutional framing for scholarly activity reinforced scholars' need to justify their claims without clinging to *auctoritates* or certifying schools.

The interaction of universal "rules" or "patterns" and particular "instantiations" not only regulated metaphysical speculations but found generative application also in disciplines as diverse as political philosophy and ethics, medicine, astronomy, and materia medica, as well as literary theory and aesthetics. Kaibara Ekiken, for instance, argued that the variation within the same genus of plants could be determined by the particular composition of the soil in which it grows, so that the "universal" genus of flowering cherry

[50] Kaibara, *Philosophy of Qi*.
[51] Tucker, *Itō Jinsai's Gomō jigi*.
[52] Kojima, "Sorai's Theory of Learning."
[53] Marcon, *Knowledge of Nature*, 239–50.

trees acquired the distinct characteristics of the *yamazakura* variant of cherry tree only when it grew in the peculiar soil of the Yoshino Hills by virtue of the specific composition of elementary substances.[54] Speculations on the logico-metaphysical relations of universal and particular legitimated the application of the ethical assumptions behind the social role of the literatus in China to samurai elites,[55] but also their applicability to artisans, merchants, or peasants, so that the idea of a hierarchy of ethicality in the more orthodox forms of Zhu Xi's philosophy could be transformed into notions of ethical equality that overcame social divisions – as in the ethical systems of Ishida Baigan or Yamagata Bantō – without subverting the legal hierarchy separating samurai and commoners.[56] The preponderance of studies on political philosophy is not just an effect of historiographical discrimination – indeed, the almost exclusive focus on the political writings of Tokugawa scholars in the writings of Maruyama Masao and his student Watanabe Hiroshi at the University of Tokyo exercised an enormous influence not only in Japan but in the Anglophone world as well. It also reflects the large number of thinkers employed as advisers of domanial and shogunal elites in the quality of scholar-retainers or "scholars-for-hire," as mentioned earlier.[57] It reflected, as well, the attempt of the first generations of thinkers to create in Japan the conditions for the emergence of a class of scholars that occupied key governmental positions, analogous to the literati bureaucrats of the Ming and Qing courts. That attempt was destined to fail. Indeed, the scholarly expertise of retainers played an important role in administration, diplomatic exchanges, and education of various domains. But Zhu Xi philosophy hardly qualifies as Tokugawa state ideology, as Maruyama Masao conceived it to be, and politics was performed according to rules that looked at Confucian principles only marginally.[58] The prescriptive division of society in the "four-class system" of samurai, peasants, artisans, and merchants (*shi-nō-kō-shō*) that scholars advocated on the model of Ming China never obtained in Tokugawa Japan, neither de jure (whereby the Tokugawa legislated only the division between samurai and commoners, aristocracy, and religious clergy – as well as groups of outcastes) nor de facto: if it is often difficult to distinguish peasants and artisans from merchants, a certain fuzziness existed at the borders between low-ranking

---

[54] Kaibara, *Yamato honzō*; Marcon, *Knowledge of Nature*, 95–96.
[55] See Nakai, "Naturalization of Confucianism," and Boot, "Adoption and Adaptation of Neo-Confucianism in Japan."
[56] See Sawada, *Confucian Values and Popular Zen*; Beonio-Brocchieri, *Religiosità e ideologia*; Najita, *Visions of Virtue*.
[57] See Paramore (Chapter 2), this volume.
[58] See Roberts's *Performing the Great Peace*.

samurai and commoners.[59] Similarly, if normative views on the dominated position that women were supposed to occupy in society were overarching in scholarly social theories since Kaibara Ekiken's *Onna daigaku*, posthumously printed in 1729 as a single volume from a section of *Wazoku dōjikun* (1710), the gender roles in Tokugawa society were far more complex, as women occupied, within their social classes, roles that gave them importance and a degree of agency at odds with Confucian precepts.[60]

A logic of universal and particular was also at the core of the conceptual and philological work of Itō Jinsai on the Four Books and Kamo no Mabuchi (1697–1769) on Japanese classics, as well as in a new conceptualization of the historical nature not only of languages and societies and their values but also of the ways in which ethical normativity (in terms of virtues and relations regulating society) should be understood (as in the works of Ogyū Sorai and Motoori Norinaga). A consequence of this attention to historicity unfolded in monumental works of historical research, such as the one developed in the Mito domain in the *Dai Nihonshi* (History of Great Japan), the compilation of which began in 1715.[61]

Even though Tokugawa philosophers in the second half of the period tended to specialize in particular fields and disciplines – which included heterogeneous approaches, as in Katayama Kenzan (1730–82) and Minagawa Kien, as well as an expanded corpus of sources, looking at later Ming and Qing thinkers such as Wang Yangming, Song Yingxing, and Fang Yizhi, or Western texts for new heuristic categories, approaches, or technologies – they maintained a marked interdisciplinary approach. Thinkers pursued investigations on what we would call today "scientific" subjects,[62] or on "aesthetics" (e.g. in the theoretical essays of Yosa Buson, 1716–84), "literary theory" (e.g. in Hattori Nankaku, 1683–1759), and linguistics (e.g. in Arai Hakuseki, Ogyū Sorai, Minakawa Kien, and Motoori Norinaga), with a self-conscious attention to the epistemological legitimacy of their research – grounded, as we have seen, in textual rather than institutional authority – but also of their ethico-political or aesthetic consequences. The philosophical production of these thinkers can hardly be reduced to ideology, religion, or as expression of a transcendental "Japanese mind." It is as well reductive to think of it in terms of Confucianism, in the same way in which, for instance, rarely do we read of European philosophy in terms of Aristotelianism or Christian theology. Confucian texts (the Four Books, the Five Classics, and their commentaries) did

---

[59] See Ehlers (Chapter 17), this volume; also, Fukaya, *Edo jidai no mibun ganbō*.
[60] Yabuta and Yanagiya, *Mibun no naka no josei*; Stanley, *Selling Women*.
[61] Kajiyama, *Dai Nihonshi no shigan*. In English, see Koschmann, *Mito Ideology*.
[62] See Frumer (Chapter 10), this volume.

indeed frame and give authority to much of the philosophical explorations of Tokugawa thinkers. That said, we can easily find references to, and syntheses of, concepts and notions taken from Shintoism, Daoism, Buddhism, "Western" philosophy, and even Christianity (e.g. in, indirectly, Hirata Atsutane, 1776–1843). If all scholars were generically known as *jusha*, no matter the object of study or method of analysis or conceptual apparatus they utilized, it would be reductive to automatically translate *ju* 儒 as "Confucian," and we should rather return to its general meaning of "scholarship" or "learning." Tokugawa scholars (as *jusha*, pursuers of learning) carried on investigations that self-consciously justified their own procedures and accounted for the ethico-political consequences of their claims.

Conclusions

It was Nishi Amane (1829–97), a Confucian physician turned philosopher after 1868, who, in an 1862 letter to Matsuoka Rinjirō, invented the term *tetsugaku* to refer to the "study of human nature and the principles of things" (*seiri no gaku* 性理之学). In 1872, he explained that "in the Eastern lands, it is called *ru* [J. *ju*] [儒]; in the Western continents it is called 'philosophy'" [*hirosohi* 斐鹵蘇比]. Both are concerned with clarifying the Way of Heaven and establishing the fundamental norms of human life. In substance they are one. This Way is coeval with the human race, and it can never be destroyed until the end of time."[63] If Amane – as Takano Chōei (1804–50) had done before him[64] – attempted at first to reconcile Asian thought within one historical framework alongside the traditions of European philosophy, he would later reject that view and come to a position closer to those held by Fukuzawa Yukichi, Mori Arinori (1847–89), and Nakamura Masanao (1832–91).[65] In *Hyakugaku renkan* (1874), he affirmed, contrary to the synthetic views he had defended only two years earlier in *Kaidaimon*, that "in our country there is nothing that deserves to be called philosophy; China too does not equal the West in this regard."[66] That judgment, similar to the one Nakae Chōmin (1847–1901) had defended (i.e., that "since olden times to this day there has been no philosophy in Japan"[67]) would become the official view shared by most Meiji intellectuals. The refusal

---

[63] Nishi, *Kaidaimon*, 19. English translation in Steben, "Nishi Amane," 48.
[64] Takano, "*Seiyō gakushi no setsu.*"
[65] On Nishi, see Havens, *Nishi Amane.*
[66] Quoted in Havens, *Nishi Amane*, 108–9.
[67] Quoted in Maraldo, "Contemporary Japanese Philosophy," 738. On the history of "*tetsugaku*," see Godart, "'Philosophy' or 'Religion'?" and Defoot, "Is There Such a Thing as Chinese Philosophy?"

to designate pre-Meiji thought as "philosophy" was indeed common among intellectuals in the late nineteenth century. Not only did Amane's own position become closer to that of Nakae and other Japanese utilitarian positivists such as Miyake Setsurei (1860–1945), Inoue Testujirō and, to a lesser degree, Kiyozawa Manshi (1863–1903), but it would determine a division between Western philosophy and Asian thought that continues to today. "More than anything else," John Maraldo notes, "it was the establishment of philosophy as an academic discipline, taught in the novel institutional setting of a university, that promoted philosophy as a Western discipline."[68] There were exceptions, such as Inoue Enryō's project for a comprehensive "world philosophy," which he struggled to promote through his Tetsugakudō Kōen.[69]

The separation of Western *philosophy* and Asian *thought* has persisted in Japanese academia to this day, with two main consequences. On the one hand, it presented Asian thought in terms of identitarian culturalism, or in terms of specific forms of thinking that are indissolubly connected to Asian cultures. In the case of Japan, it followed a two-step process: first, Inoue Tetsujirō, while assigning to Asian thought the appellation of *tetsugaku* and thus intending to offer it a fundamental regulative role within Asian societies, presented Japanese "philosophy" as eminently particular and exceptional, inherently grounded in Japanese folkish ethos and distinct not only from European but also (and particularly) from Chinese philosophy; second, Tsuda Sōkichi, by normalizing the category of *shisō* in the academic presentation of East Asian thought, established a discipline that was essentially descriptive and philological, aimed at confirming the cultural homogeneity and distinctness of a Japanese way of thinking behind the particularities of individual thinkers.

On the other hand, the separation of *shisō* and *tetsugaku* made philosophy departments in Japan exclusively focused, with some minor exceptions, on Western philosophy, de facto erasing the possibility of generative contacts with other traditions.[70] As Maraldo put it, "departments of 'pure philosophy' in Japanese universities restrict themselves to the study of Western philosophers, while it is uncertain whether professors in departments of 'Chinese philosophy' and 'Indian philosophy' should count as philosophers or as historian-philologists."[71] Consequently, while "philosophy" (*tetsugaku*) maintains institutional legitimacy and authority to produce universal investigations, Asian "thought" (*shisō*) remains particular and culture-specific.

[68] Maraldo, "Contemporary Japanese Philosophy," 738.
[69] Schulzer, *Inoue Enryō*, 77–86.
[70] With the possible exception of the Kyoto school of Nishida Kitarō (1870–1945).
[71] Maraldo, "Contemporary Japanese Philosophy," 755.

Shisō and *tetsugaku* are today in mutual opposition in three respects. First, while *tetsugakushi* (history of philosophy) refers to the historical development of abstract, self-referential, and self-legitimating forms of thought and reasoning, *shisōshi* (history of thought) traces the history of modes of thinking that encompass *Weltanschauungen*, *mentalitées*, folk beliefs, religiosities, and ideologies, all of which are culture-specific, nonuniversal, nonspeculative, nonreflexive, and, therefore, noncritical. Second, while *tetsugakushi* utilizes terminology and an approach that is genealogically conducible back to Western philosophy (as if only Western thought had created the means and the needs for self-reflexivity), *shisōshi* develops from textual analyses that are faithful to the historical terminology of the doctrines it investigates but regimented to historiographical methodologies that depend upon speculative claims deriving from Western philosophy. Third, there is a precise hierarchy of epistemological legitimacy and institutional prestige between the forms of thought that the terms *tetsugaku* and *shisō* refer to, and whether or not the historian adopting one or the other term to refer to early modern speculative traditions is aware of this epistemological hierarchy, this is projected in the way they make sense of these traditions. More precisely, *shisōshi* is a historiography of lesser forms of thought in the sense that it is a historiography of culturally and nationally specific *Weltanschauungen*. On the contrary, *tetsugaku* is the realm of abstraction, of the metalanguage, of critique, of science. In other words, *tetsugaku* deals with the universal, *shisō* with the particular.

If in the Japanese context one can sustain the dubious argument that the terms *tetsugaku* and *shisō* function merely as proper names, the reluctance in Anglophone scholarship to use the term "philosophy" for Tokugawa thought is less justifiable. Philosophy, as meta-discipline, maintains its fundamental function of providing the instruments for the legitimation of transdisciplinary cognitive practices – which also justify historiographical methodologies. Thought, a field for historical research, maintains the role of protecting, with the keen attention of antiquarians, the sanctuary of a distinct national identity.[72]

---

[72] The historiographical problem here is double: the lack of a systematic exegesis of the Tokugawa philosophical archive is accompanied by the reduction of the theoretical investigations of individual thinkers to historically particular expressions of an ahistorical Japanese "way of thinking." See, for instance, H. Nakamura, *Ways of Thinking of Eastern Peoples*. This heuristic process is a sort of orientalizing anthropologization that has as its ultimate aim the description of a dehistoricized *forma mentis* of the Japanese. Apart from the reductive simplifications it produced, this procedure reifies the existence of a homogeneous, collective entity called "Japanese," the variety of which is regimented under a stereotypically distinct style of thought.

Bibliography

Arima Sukemasa and Akiyama Goan, eds. *Bushidō kakunshū*. Hakubunkan Shinsha, 2012.

Backus, Robert L. "The Kansei Prohibition of Heterodoxy and Its Effects on Education." *Harvard Journal of Asiatic Studies* 39, no. 1 (June 1979): 55–106.

——— "The Relationship of Confucianism to the Tokugawa Bakufu as Revealed in the Kansei Educational Reform." *Harvard Journal of Asiatic Studies* 34, no. 34 (1974): 97–162.

Bellah, Robert. *Tokugawa Religion: The Values of Pre-Industrial Japan*. Glencoe, IL: Free Press, 1957.

Beonio-Brocchieri, Paolo. *Religiosità e ideologia alle origini del Giappone moderno*. Milan: Istituto per gli Studi di Politica Internazionale, 1965.

Boot, Willem Jan. "The Adoption and Adaptation of Neo-Confucianism in Japan: The Role of Fujiwara Seika and Hayashi Razan." DLitt diss., University of Leiden, 1983.

——— "Japanese Poetics and the *Kokka hachiron*." *Asiatica Venetiana* 4 (1999): 23–43.

Bowring, Richard. *In Search of the Way: Thought and Religion in Early-Modern Japan, 1582–1860*. Oxford: Oxford University Press, 2017.

Breen, John. "Nativism Restored." *Monumenta Nipponica* 55, no. 3 (Autumn 2000): 429–40.

Burns, Susan. *Before the Nation: Kokugaku and the Imagining of Community in Early Modern Japan*. Durham, NC: Duke University Press, 2003.

Chibbett, David. *A History of Japanese Literature: The First Thousand Years*. London: Macmillan Press, 1979.

Collcutt, Martin. *Five Mountains: The Rinzai Zen Monastic Institution in Medieval Japan*. Cambridge, MA: Council on East Asian Studies, Harvard University, 1981.

de Bary, William Theodore, and Irene Bloom, eds. *Principle and Practicality: Essays in Neo-Confucianism and Practical Learning*. New York: Columbia University Press, 1979.

de Bary, William Theodore, Carol Gluck, and Arthur E. Tiedemann, eds. *1600 to 2000*. Vol. 2 of *Sources of Japanese Tradition*, 2nd ed. New York: Columbia University Press, 2005.

Defoot, Carine. "Is There Such a Thing as Chinese Philosophy? Arguments of an Implicit Debate." *Philosophy East and West* 51 (2001): 393–413.

Elman, Benjamin. *A Cultural History of Civil Examinations in Late Imperial China*. Berkeley: University of California Press, 2002.

Feng Youlan. *A History of Chinese Philosophy*. 2 vols. 2nd ed. Translated by Derek Bodde. Princeton, NJ: Princeton University Press, 1952.

Flueckinger, Peter. *Imagining Harmony: Poetry, Empathy, and Community in Mid-Tokugawa Confucianism and Nativism*. Stanford, CA: Stanford University Press, 2011.

Fukaya Katsumi. *Edo jidai no mibun ganbō*. Yoshikawa Kōbunkan, 2006.

Furuta Hikaru and Koyasu Nobukuni, eds. *Nihon shisōshi tokuhon*. Tōyō Keizai Shinbunsha, 2006.

Godart, Gerard Clinton. "'Philosophy' or 'Religion'? The Confrontation with Foreign Categories in Late Nineteenth Century Japan." *Journal of the History of Ideas* 69, no. 1 (January 2008): 71–91.

Goldgar, Anne. *Impolite Learning: Conduct and Community in the Republic of Letters, 1680–1750*. New Haven, CT: Yale University Press, 1995.

Harootunian, Harry D. "Late Tokugawa Culture and Thought." In *The Nineteenth Century*, edited by Marius B. Jansen, 168–258. Vol. 5 of *The Cambridge History of Japan*. Cambridge: Cambridge University Press, 1989.

"Review of *Principle and Practicality: Essays in Neo-Confucianism and Practical Learning,* by William Theodore de Bary and Irene Bloom." *Journal of Japanese Studies* 7, no. 1 (Winter 1981): 111–31.

Things Seen and Unseen: Discourse and Ideology in Tokugawa Nativism. Chicago: University of Chicago Press, 1988.

Havens, Thomas R. H. *Nishi Amane and Modern Japanese Thought.* Princeton, NJ: Princeton University Press, 1970.

Hisaki Yukio. *Nihon kodai gakkō no kenkyū.* Tamagawa Daigaku Shuppanbu, 1990.

Hori Isao. *Hayashi Razan.* Yoshikawa Kōbunkan, 1964.

Ikegami, Eiko. *Bonds of Civility: Aesthetic Networks and the Political Origins of Japanese Culture.* Cambridge: Cambridge University Press, 2005.

Imai Jun and Yamamoto Shinkō. *Sekimon shingaku no shisō.* Perikansha, 2006.

Inoue Tetsujirō. *Kokumin dōtoku gairon.* Sanshodō, 1930.

Nihon kogakuha no tetsugaku. Fuzanbō, 1902.

Nihon shushigakuha no tetsugaku. Fuzanbō, 1905.

Nihon yōmeigakuha no tetsugaku. Fuzanbō, 1900.

Iwashita Tetsunori. *Edo no kaigai jōhō nettowāku.* Yoshikawa Kōbunkan, 2006.

Jōfuku Isamu. *Motoori Norinaga.* Yoshikawa Kōbunkan, 1990.

Kaibara Ekiken. *The Philosophy of Qi: The Record of Great Doubts.* Translated by Mary Evelyn Tucker. New York: Columbia University Press, 2007.

Yamato honzō (1709). National Diet Library. https://dl.ndl.go.jp/pid/2605899

Kajiyama Takao. *Dai Nihonshi no shigan: Sono kōsei to jujutsu.* Kinseisha, 2013.

Katō Shūichi. *Nihon bungakushi josetsu.* 2 vols. Chukuma Shobō, 1975–80.

Kawamoto Shinji. *Chūsei Zenshū no jugaku gakushū to kagaku chishiki.* Shibunkaku, 2021.

Kojima Yasunori. "Sorai's Theory of Learning." In *Tetsugaku Companion to Ogyū Sorai,* edited by W. J. Boot and Takayama Daiki, 71–84. Cham, Germany: Springer, 2019.

Koschmann, J. Victor. *The Mito Ideology: Discourse, Reform, and Insurrection in Late Tokugawa Japan, 1790–1864.* Berkeley: University of California Press, 1987.

Koyasu Nobukuni. *Edo shisōshi kōgi.* Iwanami Shoten, 1998.

Hōhō to shite no Edo. Perikansha, 1999.

Kurozumi Makoto. *Fukusūsei no Nihon shisō.* Perikansha, 2006.

Kinsei Nihon shakai to jukyō. Perikansha, 2003.

"The Nature of Early Tokugawa Confucianism." Translated by Herman Ooms. *Journal of Japanese Studies* 20, no. 2 (Summer 1994): 337–75.

"Nihon shisō to wa nani ka." In *"Nihon" to Nihon shisō,* edited by Karube Tadashi, Kurozumi Makoto, Satō Hiroo, and Sueki Fumihiko, 3–32. Vol. 1 of *Iwanami kōza Nihon no shisō.* Iwanami Shoten, 2013.

"Tokugawa Confucianism and Its Meiji Japan Reconstruction." In *Rethinking Confucianism: Past and Present in China, Japan, Korea, and Vietnam,* edited by Benjamin A. Elman, John B. Duncan, and Herman Ooms, 370–96. Los Angeles: UCLA Asian Pacific Monograph Series, 2002.

Le Goff, Jacques. *Les intellectuels au Moyen Age.* Paris: Seuil, 1985.

Maeda Tsutomu. *Edo kyōiku shisōshi kenkyū.* Shibunkaku Shuppan, 2016.

Edo no dokushokai. Heibonsha, 2018.

Maezawa Terumasa. *Ashikaga gakkō: Sono kigen to hensen.* Mainichi Shinbunsha, 2003.

Maraldo, John. "Contemporary Japanese Philosophy." In *Companion Encyclopedia of Asian Philosophy*, edited by Brian Carr and Indira Mahalingam, 737–61. London: Routledge, 2000.

Marcon, Federico. "The 'Book' as Fieldwork: 'Textual Institutions' and Nature Knowledge in Early Modern Japan." *British Journal for the History of Science – Themes* 5 (December 2020): 131–48.

The Knowledge of Nature and the Nature of Knowledge in Early Modern Japan. Chicago: University of Chicago Press, 2015.

"Satō Nobuhiro and the Political Economy of Natural History in Nineteenth-Century Japan." *Japanese Studies* 34, no. 3 (December 2014): 265–87.

Maruyama Masao. *Nihon seiji shisōshi kenkyū*. Tōkyō Daigaku Shuppankai, 1952.

Studies in the Intellectual History of Tokugawa Japan. Translated by Mikiso Hane. Princeton, NJ: Princeton University Press, 1974.

McMullen, James. "Confucian Perspectives on the Akō Revenge: Law and Moral Agency." *Monumenta Nipponica* 58, no. 3 (Autumn 2003): 293–315.

McNally, Mark. *Like No Other: Exceptionalism and Nativism in Early Modern Japan*. Honolulu: University of Hawai'i Press, 2015.

Pursuing the Way: Conflict and Practice in the History of Japanese Nativism. Cambridge, MA: Harvard University Asia Center, 2005.

Melchiorre, Virgilio, ed. *Filosofie nel mondo*. Milan: Bompiani, 2014.

Minamoto Ryōen. *Jitsugaku shisō no keifu*. Kōdansha, 1986.

Najita, Tetsuo. *Visions of Virtue in Tokugawa Japan: The Kaitokudō Merchant Academy of Osaka*. Chicago: University of Chicago Press, 1987.

Nakai, Kate Wildman. "The Naturalization of Confucianism in Tokugawa Japan: The Problem of Sinocentrism." *Harvard Journal of Asiatic Studies* 40, no. 1 (June 1980): 157–99.

Nakamura, Hajime. *Ways of Thinking of Eastern Peoples: India, China, Tibet, Japan*. Translated by Philip P. Wiener. Honolulu: East-West Center Press, 1964.

Nakamura Shin'ichirō. *Kimura Kenkadō no saron*. Shinchōsha, 2000.

Nenzi, Laura. *The Chaos and Cosmos of Kurosawa Tokiko: One Woman's Transit from Tokugawa to Meiji Japan*. Honolulu: University of Hawai'i Press, 2015.

Nishi Amane. *Kaidaimon*. In *Nishi Amane zenshū*, Vol. 1, edited by Ōkubo Toshiaki, 19–24. Munetaka Shobō, 1960.

Nosco, Peter. "Nature, Invention, and National Learning: The *Kokka hachiron* Controversy, 1742–46." *Harvard Journal of Asiatic Studies* 41, no. 1 (June 1981): 75–91.

Remembering Paradise: Nativism and Nostalgia in Eighteenth-Century Japan. Cambridge, MA: Council on East Asian Studies, Harvard University, 1990.

Ŏm Sŏk-in. *Higashi Ajia ni okeru Nihon shushigaku no isō: Kimon gakuha no riki shinseiron*. Bunsei Shuppan, 2015.

Ooms, Emily Groszos. *Women and Millenarian Protest in Meiji Japan: Deguchi Nao and Ōmotokyō*. Ithaca, NY: Cornell University Press, 2010.

Ooms, Herman. *Tokugawa Ideology: Early Constructs*. Princeton, NJ: Princeton University Press, 1985.

Paramore, Kiri. "The Nationalization of Confucianism: Academism, Examinations, and Bureaucratic Governance in the Late Tokugawa State." *Journal of Japanese Studies* 38, no. 1 (Winter 2021): 25–53.

Roberts, Luke. *Performing the Great Peace: Political Space and Open Secrets in Tokugawa Japan.* Honolulu: University of Hawai'i Press, 2012.

Robertson, Jennifer. "The Shingaku Woman: Straight from the Heart." In *Recreating Japanese Women, 1600–1945*, edited by Gail Lee Bernstein, 88–107. Berkeley: University of California Press, 1991.

Rubinger, Richard. *Popular Literacy in Early Modern Japan.* Honolulu: University of Hawai'i Press, 2007.

Private Academies of Tokugawa Japan. Princeton, NJ: Princeton University Press, 1982.

Sawada, Janine A. *Confucian Values and Popular Zen: Sekimon Shingaku in Eighteenth-Century Japan.* Honolulu: University of Hawai'i Press, 1993.

Schulzer, Rainer. *Inoue Enryō: A Philosophical Portrait.* Albany: State University of New York Press, 2019.

Spafford, David. "The Language and Contours of Familial Obligation in Fifteenth- and Sixteenth-Century Japan." In *What Is a Family? Answers from Early Modern Japan,* edited by Mary Elizabeth Berry and Marcia Yonemoto, 23–46. Oakland: University of California Press, 2019.

Stanley, Amy. *Selling Women: Prostitution, Markets, and the Household in Early Modern Japan.* Berkeley: University of California Press, 2012.

Steben, Barry D. "Nishi Amane and the Birth of 'Philosophy' and 'Chinese Philosophy' in Early Meiji Japan." In *Learning to Emulate the Wise: The Genesis of Chinese Philosophy as an Academic Discipline in Twentieth-Century China,* edited by John Makeham, 39–72. Hong Kong: Chinese University of Hong Kong Press, 2012.

Sugi Hitoshi. *Kinsei no chiiki to zaison bunka: Gijutsu to shōhin to fūga no kōryū.* Yoshikawa Kōbunkan, 2001.

Suzuki Bokushi. *Snow Country Tales: Life in the Other Japan.* Translated by Jeffrey Hunter with Rose Lesser. New York: Weatherhill, 1986.

Tajiri Yūichirō. *Edo no shisōshi: Jinbutsu, hōhō, renkan.* Chūkō Shinsho, 2011.

Yamazaki Ansai no sekai. Perikansha, 2006.

Takahashi Masao. *Motoori Norinaga: Saisei no igokoro.* Kōdansha, 1986.

Takahashi Satoshi. *Edo no kyōikuyoku.* Chikuma Shinsho, 2007.

Takano Chōei. *"Seiyō gakushi no setsu*: The Theories of Western Philosophers." Translated by Gino K. Piovesana. *Monumenta Nipponica* 27, no. 1 (Spring 1972): 85–92.

Takashima Motohiro. *Yamazaki Ansai: Nihon shushigaku to suika shintō.* Perikansha, 1992.

Takeuchi Seiichi. "Nihon shisō e no shiza." In *"Nihon" to Nihon shisō,* edited by Karube Tadasi, Kurozumi Makoto, Satō Hiroo, and Sueki Fumihiko, 33–58. Vol. 1 of *Iwanami kōza: Nihon no shisō.* Iwanami Shoten, 2013.

Tanaka Yūko. *Edo wa nettowāku.* Heibonsha, 1993.

Tsuda Sōkichi. *Bungaku ni arawaretaru waga kokumin shisō no kenkyū.* 4 vols. Rakuyōdō, 1916–21.

Tsujimoto Masashi. *Kinsei kyōiku shisōshi no kenkyū: Nihon ni okeru "kōkyōiku" shisō no genryū.* Kyoto: Shibunkaku Shuppan, 1990.

Tucker, John Allen. *Itō Jinsai's Gomō jigi and the Philosophical Definition of Early Modern Japan.* Leiden: Brill, 1998.

"Rethinking the Akō Ronin Debate: The Religious Significance of *Chūshin gishi.*" *Japanese Journal of Religious Studies* 26, no. 1–2 (1999): 1–37.

Umihara Tōru. *Kinsei no gakkō to kyōiku.* Shibunkaku Shuppan, 1988.

Van Norden, Bryan W. *Taking Back Philosophy: A Multicultural Manifesto*. New York: Columbia University Press, 2017.

Wajima Yoshio. *Chūsei no jugaku*. Yoshikawa Kōbunkan, 1965.

Nihon Sōgakushi no kenkyū. Yoshikawa Kōbunkan, 1962.

Shōheikō to hankō. Shibunkaku, 1966.

Walthall, Anne. *The Weak Body of a Useless Woman: Matsuo Taseko and the Meiji Restoration*. Chicago: University of Chicago Press, 1998.

Watanabe, Hiroshi. *A History of Japanese Political Thought, 1600–1901*. Translated by David Noble. International House of Japan, 2012.

Wilson, William Scott. *The Ideals of the Samurai: Writings of Japanese Warriors*. Burbank, CA: Ohara Publications, 1982.

Yabuta Yutaka and Yanagiya Keiko, eds. *Mibun no naka no josei*. Yoshikawa Kōbunkan, 2010.

Yama Yoshiyuki. *Edo no shisō tōsō*. Kadokawa Sensho, 2019.

Yasunaga, Toshinobu. *Andō Shōeki: Social and Ecological Philosopher in Eighteenth-Century Japan*. New York: Weatherhill, 1992.

5

Foreign Relations and Coastal Defense under the Mature Tokugawa Regime

ROBERT HELLYER

In 1782, Isaac Titsingh, the chief factor of the Dutch East India Company's (VOC) Nagasaki trading outpost, lamented that his company's trade at the Kyushu port had gradually declined since the VOC had established a compound on the artificial island of Dejima in 1641. The VOC official blamed the shogunate, asserting that the regime's debasement of currency, limits on exports, and manipulation of selling prices for imported goods had combined to make trade far less lucrative.[1] In his assessments, Titsingh illustrated how much diplomacy and trade at Nagasaki, early modern Japan's most important venue for interaction with the outside world, had changed since the early seventeenth century. As Adam Clulow explores in Chapter 7, during the initial decades of the Tokugawa peace, Nagasaki served as the point of entry for embassies from Southeast Asian states as well as a center for the thriving silver-for-silk trade. Chinese, Dutch, and – until the shogunate banned their entry in 1638 – Portuguese ships brought Chinese-produced silk that fed a cottage weaving industry growing especially in the Nishijin district of Kyoto.[2] For their return cargo, the ships carried Japanese silver, in high demand on the China market.[3] As Clulow illustrates, the silver-for-silk trade became a cornerstone of Japan's foreign trade, demonstrating the limits of the "closed country" moniker still often used to describe the Tokugawa-period state's relationship with the outside world.

As this chapter will explore, the shogunate enacted the currency debasement and imposed the trade limits described by Titsingh beginning in the late seventeenth century as its rule over the Japanese realm matured and became more secure. Thereafter, the silver-for-silk trade gradually declined, as did diplomatic and commercial contacts with Southeast Asia. Overall, Japan's

---

[1] Titsingh and Screech, *Secret Memoirs of the Shoguns*, 186.
[2] Innes, "Door Ajar," 491.
[3] A recent study of the Nagasaki silver-for-silk trade within the seventeenth-century global economy is Gunn, *World Trade Systems*.

foreign relations became more contained in four gates or portals. These areas had participated in diplomacy and foreign trade since the early Tokugawa period but, by the mid-eighteenth century, their positions had become codified in the foreign relations structure. At the Nagasaki portal, Chinese and Dutch ships continued to trade but mostly brought medicinal products to exchange for copper and select marine products. At the northern portal, the Matsumae domain dominated relations with the Ainu. In the south, the Satsuma domain maintained indirect control over the Ryukyu kingdom, and to the west, Tsushima, an island situated between the Korean Peninsula and Kyushu, mediated ties with Korea.

The chapter will outline how from the late seventeenth to the early nineteenth century the more mature shogunate supervised and repeatedly recast structures of trade, diplomacy, and maritime defense for the Japanese realm. It will detail the ways in which the Tokugawa regime, despite being Japan's central authority, could not act unilaterally but had to recognize the agency held by Satsuma and Tsushima in their relations with foreign states. In addition, the chapter will explain the monopolistic and market tools employed by the shogunate to control key sectors of Japan's foreign trade, highlighting the similarities to approaches taken by the English East India Company in its commercial activities in East and Southeast Asia. In turn, it will explore the Pacific contexts – notably a common desire among participants to limit the use of silver in trade with China – that shaped the Japanese state's foreign trade, and thus its larger interface with the outside world during much of the Tokugawa period. Finally, it will demonstrate the diversity in imported products that had emerged by the early nineteenth century, reflected in the variety of goods in demand by both male and female Japanese consumers.

The Interdependent Relationships within the Foreign Relations System

In modern international relations, central governments of nation-states exclusively formulate and execute foreign policy, exemplified in the dispatch of ambassadors. Maintaining an embassy in a foreign capital, an ambassador operates as the primary representative of their nation, thereby facilitating veritable national policies. By contrast, in early modern East Asia multiple groups would often conduct a state's foreign relations. Moreover, it was not uncommon for leaders of states to hold multiple loyalties to domestic and foreign sovereigns. In addition, Ming and later Qing hegemony helped to mitigate interstate conflicts and thus the development of a diplomatic order like the Westphalian system that emerged in early modern Europe.[4]

The Sō, the ruling house of Tsushima, offers an example of the "dual loyalties" at the heart of the Japanese foreign relations system. The head of the Sō house was, like all other lords, a Tokugawa vassal. Yet he and his retainers enjoyed a monopoly over Japanese commercial intercourse with Korea and served as the sole diplomatic intermediary between Japan and Korea.

The Sō gained their intermediary position primarily because the Chosŏn court dictated it. Chosŏn leaders renewed diplomatic ties with the Tokugawa regime in 1607, roughly a decade after the Japanese military's withdrawal from Korea at the end of the Imjin War (1592–98). Willing to make peace but still mistrusting Japanese intentions, Chosŏn leaders calculated that the Sō, who had long traded with groups on the Korean Peninsula, would be a more accommodating and pliant partner if granted a monopoly on trade with their kingdom. They therefore made the head of the Sō house a vassal and bestowed commercial and diplomatic privileges, the most prominent being permission for around 500 Tsushima officials and merchants to reside in a walled complex, the Japan House, just outside Pusan.[5]

In his influential monograph, Ronald Toby explains how the Sō served their Tokugawa overlords by assisting in the journey of Korean embassies to and from Edo during the first decades of Tokugawa rule. By directing that the Korean missions travel overland through more populated regions of Japan, shogunal leaders could demonstrate to the elites and commoners who came to view the processions that the recently established Tokugawa regime was legitimate and held the respect of neighboring foreign states.[6]

Tsushima traded with Korea in private and official categories. The private trade, the area of highest volume, involved Tsushima merchants exchanging goods with officially licensed Korean merchants at a market near the Japan House. Chosŏn officials restricted the overall trade volume by limiting the number and size of ships that Tsushima could dispatch and by sanctioning only a handful of trading days per month. Despite these controls, the domain and its merchants profited handsomely as middlemen in the import of Chinese silk as well as Korean ginseng, purchased with Japanese silver. Tsushima officials would use Japanese silver ingots, which circulated as currency

---

[4] Kang, *East Asia before the West*.

[5] For an overview of the Tsushima side of this relationship, see Tashiro, *Kinsei Nitchō tsūkō bōeki shi*. An excellent accounting of the Korean perspective is Lewis, *Frontier Contact*.

[6] Toby, *State and Diplomacy*, 53–76.

throughout much of the realm, to purchase Chinese silk from Korean merchants. (Korean envoys would obtain silk during their annual tribute missions to Beijing.) Primarily through the sale of Chinese silk on the Japanese domestic market, Tsushima enjoyed annual profits averaging between 2,000 to 4,000 *kan* of silver (1 *kan* equals 3.75 kg). Even a 2,000 *kan* profit was substantial, equating to roughly 80,000 *koku* of rice, more than the annual income of most lords.[7]

The Sō undertook the official trade in fulfillment of their status as a vassal of the Chosŏn court. The domain dispatched regular diplomatic missions to the Japan House for meetings with Chosŏn officials and received official seals that legitimized the Sō's trade monopoly. Consistent with established East Asian diplomatic practices, the Sō gave and received specific gifts. The domain proffered tin and copper as well as water buffalo horns (used as military equipment), and in return Chosŏn officials bestowed small amounts of ginseng, and more importantly, a sizeable amount of rice.[8] The domain came to depend upon the Korean rice shipments to supply the Japan House residents, to pay for the cost of envoys on missions traveling between Tsushima and the Japan House, and critically, to feed a significant portion of the domain's population. In 1700, it was estimated that of Tsushima's population of 32,000, 18,000 lived on rice and barley grown on the island and 7,000 from rice grown on Sō lands in Kyushu, with the remaining 7,000 dependent upon Korean rice.[9]

Much like the Sō, the Shimazu, the ruling house of Satsuma, obtained silk by interfacing with the Chinese tribute system. In 1609, the Shimazu had dutifully waited for Tokugawa permission before dispatching a 3,000-man invasion force that quickly subjugated the previously independent Ryukyu kingdom. Thereafter, the Shimazu assumed direct control of Amami Ōshima and two other islands in the northern half of the Ryukyu island chain. On those islands, they deliberately weakened the established political hierarchy and forced islanders to sever political and religious ties with Shuri, Ryukyu's administrative seat, located near the port of Naha on the island of Okinawa.

The Shimazu allowed the Shō, the Ryukyu royal family, to continue to rule over the rest of kingdom. The Shimazu received annual tribute from the

---

[7] Tsuruta Kei estimates that Tsushima garnered between 2,000 and 4,000 *kan* annually during the boom period. Tsuruta, "Establishment and Characteristics of the 'Tsushima Gate,'" 43–44; Tsuruta, *Tsushima kara mita Nitchō kankei*, 83.

[8] Tsuruta, "Establishment and Characteristics of the 'Tsushima Gate,'" 42. For more about the official and private trades, see Tashiro, *Kinsei Nitchō tsūkō bōeki shi*, 58–71.

[9] Tsuruta, *Tsushima kara mita Nitchō kankei*, 56, 65, 79.

Shō and directed them, in the fashion of the system of alternate attendance, to regularly send members of the Ryukyu royal family to the domain's castle town, Kagoshima, and reside in a guarded compound, the Ryukyu House.[10] In so doing, the king codified another "dual loyalty" system that allowed Ryukyu to maintain some autonomous space between Japan and China until the late nineteenth century. The kingdom also dispatched regular tribute missions to the Ming (and later the Qing) court and established a trading outpost in the Chinese port of Fuzhou. These missions provided a vital form of legitimacy as Ryukyuan elites did not view a king as fully ascending to the throne until receiving a mission of investiture from Beijing. As was the case with Korean tribute missions, Ryukyuan officials used their connections to the Chinese tribute network to acquire silk at Fuzhou, paid for with silver, which in turn was delivered to Satsuma.[11] In addition, the Ryukyu court regularly sent missions to Edo to celebrate the ascension of a new shogun. Throughout the journey, Shimazu retainers would escort the Ryukyu contingent, thereby displaying their rule over the kingdom. The envoys dressed in ways to emphasize their "otherness" and thus the perception that the kingdom was, like Korea, a foreign state dispatching envoys to show respect to the Tokugawa shogunate.[12]

At Nagasaki, the silver-for-silk trade continued to thrive. Chinese and Dutch (VOC) ships arrived with silk produced not only in China but also in the northern Vietnamese province of Tonkin.[13] German physician Engelbert Kaempfer described silk as the good in highest demand but noted that "sappanwood [used as a red dye] and hides also guarantee the importer a safe and good reward." He stressed that the Dutch enjoyed their highest profit margins from sugar and a variety of other goods that included "camphor from Borneo."[14] For centuries, peoples throughout West, South, and East Asia had valued Borneo camphor for its aromatic qualities. Many also believed it had medicinal qualities.[15] In the seventeenth century, Dutch and Chinese ships alike also brought large amounts of brown, refined white, and rock sugar.[16]

---

[10] For a short overview of the Ryukyu House's role within the Satsuma-Ryukyu relationship, see Fukase, "Ryūkyū-kan ni miru Satsuryū kankei."

[11] Tomiyama, Ryūkyū ōkoku, 64–71.

[12] For a recent study of the cultural dimensions of Ryukyu's missions to Edo, see Seifman, "Performing 'Lūchū.'"

[13] Iioka, "Rise and Fall of the Tonkin-Nagasaki Silk Trade."

[14] Kaempfer, Kaempfer's Japan, 209–10.

[15] Donkin, Dragon's Brain Perfume, 17–20.

[16] Davidson, Island of Formosa, 445.

The Dutch also dispatched annual missions to Edo modeled on the system of alternate attendance. The VOC's contingent included the chief of the Dutch factory on Dejima, as well as a secretary, the company physician, and a handful of other personnel. Like their Korean counterparts, the Dutch missions traveled primarily overland, notably through the urban centers of Kyoto and Osaka, and then via the Tōkaidō highway to Edo. While at the capital, the group received an audience with the shogun and met with Japanese physicians and astronomers.[17]

Restricting the Silver-for-Silk Trade

By the late 1660s, Tokugawa leaders concluded that, because of prodigious annual outflows of silver, estimated to be four times the amount produced annually by Japanese mines, some restrictions were in order.[18] In 1671, they instructed Nagasaki officials to set prices for imports, thereby advancing previous practices of using market controls to reduce outflows of silver. In 1684, the limitations of that approach were revealed when Qing authorities lifted maritime bans imposed to combat perceived threats to the Chinese coast. Tokugawa leaders realized that the repeal would bring more Chinese junks to Japanese shores seeking to acquire loads of silver. The shogunate therefore set further market-centered restrictions instead of attempting to inspect outgoing vessels to determine the amount of silver in their cargoes. In 1685, the shogunate directed that Nagasaki merchants could purchase up 6,000 *kan* worth of goods from Chinese merchants and 3,000 *kan* from the Dutch. Nonetheless, over the next few years hundreds of Chinese ships, freed from the previous maritime restrictions, arrived at Nagasaki, bringing silk and other products to exchange for Japanese silver.[19] In 1688 alone, 194 junks called, leading Nagasaki officials to refuse 77 of them entry. Instead of returning home, many frustrated Chinese captains clandestinely traded directly with Nagasaki merchants, thereby mitigating the 1685 ceilings and continuing the outflow of silver.[20]

The shogunate made similar moves relating to domain trade, ordering Tsushima to limit its annual sales of imports on the domestic market to 1,080 *kan* and Satsuma to around 1,200 *kan*. Yet Tsushima, far from Nagasaki and other nodes of Tokugawa authority, essentially ignored the directives and continued to export high volumes of silver, with the trade reaching a peak

---

[17] Goodman, *Japan and the Dutch*, 23–29.
[18] Nakai, *Shogunal Politics*, 108.
[19] Zhou, *Qing Opening to the Ocean*, 88.
[20] Yamawaki, *Nagasaki no Tōjin bōeki*, 58, 71–72.

in 1694.[21] The flow of silver through Ryukyu also apparently remained steady, although the shogunate did impose some restrictions, such as allowing Satsuma the privilege of selling Chinese goods imported through Ryukyu via an officially sanctioned wholesaler in Kyoto.[22] Uehara Kenzen notes that Satsuma and Tokugawa leaders saw the arrangement as mutually beneficial: Satsuma could gain a sanctioned presence on the Kyoto market, where silk was in high demand, and the shogunate could count on the domain to help limit the illicit trade through which silver flowed from the realm. Satsuma officials thereafter actively enforced Tokugawa anti-smuggling edicts, particularly by assuring that Chinese goods imported via Ryukyu were sold only through the Kyoto wholesaler. Satsuma officials believed that a show of fealty would protect the domain's trading rights. They also sought to ensure that the silver provided to Ryukyu would translate into more revenue for the domain treasury.[23] As this example shows, decisions about foreign trade often involved mutually beneficial accommodations between Satsuma, Tsushima, and the shogunate.

In the early eighteenth century, Tokugawa leaders began to search for more lasting measures to limit exports of the metal. Arai Hakuseki, an adviser to shoguns Ienobu (r. 1709–12) and Ietsugu (r. 1713–16), became one of the more vocal critics of the silver-for-silk trade. He famously declared that silver and other precious metals were akin to the "bones of the earth" that could not be replenished and thus should be retained for use within the realm instead of being exchanged for "foreign trinkets." Arai played a pivotal role in the promulgation in 1715 of a series of measures that maintained the previous annual ceilings on trade through Nagasaki for Chinese and Dutch ships. Yet the Tokugawa regime went a step further, directing that only thirty Chinese junks and two Dutch merchantmen could call each year. Importantly, the new guidelines, dubbed the Shōtoku edicts by historians for the reign name (1711–16) during which they were issued, also encouraged Chinese and Dutch traders to replace silver with cargoes of copper and marine products, both of which were in demand in China.[24] Moreover, the Tokugawa regime adopted a credential trading system based on Chinese models. Before a Chinese merchant vessel left Nagasaki to return to its home port, shogunal officials issued a document that consisted of half of an official seal. Upon the ship's return the

[21] Tashiro, "Tsushima Han's Korean Trade," 91.
[22] Kagoshima-ken, *Kagoshima kenshi*, 2:726–27.
[23] Uehara, *Sakoku to han bōeki*, 97–102.
[24] Nakai, *Shogunal Politics*, 109–10. For more on the copper export trade, see Shimada, *Intra-Asian Trade in Japanese Copper*.

following year, the captain presented the credential, which Nagasaki officials compared to the other half of the original seal. If both matched, then the whole document served as a ticket to trade. The system allowed the shogunate to close a loophole: the ability of Chinese captains, who arrived after the yearly quota had been filled, to trade by asserting that their vessels had merely "drifted ashore" because of capricious winds or currents. After some initial friction, Qing officials came to accept the credential system and helped to perpetuate its use in Chinese-Japanese trade until the mid-nineteenth century.[25]

The Shōtoku edicts and the credential system also solidified the role of institutions established a few years earlier to help the Tokugawa regime more effectively manage foreign trade through Nagasaki. In 1689, the shogunate had ordered the construction of the Chinese Residence, a compound that would serve as a domicile-cum-trade headquarters for Chinese merchants. Although similar to the existing Dutch compound on Dejima, the Chinese Residence was much larger, consisting of a walled compound of residential barracks, offices, and warehouses surrounded by a palisade and moat. At peak times, it housed close to 5,000 Chinese merchants and sailors, although the average was usually around 2,000 men. As was the case with the Dutch on Dejima, the shogunate prohibited the Chinese from leaving the compound, except to unload goods from their junks or to conduct sanctioned trade with Japanese merchants. Apart from shogunal officials, the only visitors to the all-male residence were courtesans from the nearby Maruyama pleasure quarters.[26]

In 1697, the shogunate took an additional step to regulate more tightly trade at Nagasaki by merging several institutions that oversaw exports and the sale of imports on the Nagasaki market. The following year, the Nagasaki clearinghouse was established. Until its abolition in the mid-1860s, the clearinghouse functioned as the primary regulatory trade organ in Nagasaki. During the decades after its establishment, the office evolved into an institution that supplied export copper and marine products to Chinese and Dutch merchants, and in return received their imports. The clearinghouse then sold the imported goods to Nagasaki merchants through a bidding system or based upon special arrangements. Its officials worked closely with Tokugawa-sanctioned merchants as well as copper and silver mints. Moreover, clearinghouse officials permitted Tsushima representatives to purchase, at a reduced rate, the water buffalo horns (often imported from Southeast Asia) and other goods used in the Sō's official trade with the Chosŏn court.

[25] Peng, *Trade Relations*, 39–67.
[26] Jansen, *China in the Tokugawa World*, 29–30.

Thanks to its comprehensive reach over trade, the clearinghouse allowed shogunal officials to more effectively regulate the outflow of silver and limit smuggling. Shogunal leaders were well aware that, in contradiction of Tokugawa edicts, merchant guilds exploited established contacts with Chinese merchants to continue to use silver to purchase imports (such as had occurred in 1688 when Chinese ships had been refused entry). By placing all shogunal institutions and merchant guilds under the clearinghouse's unified regulatory umbrella, the shogunate established a more viable means to stamp out unsanctioned trade.[27] For good measure, the shogunate also directed several Kyushu domains to use force when necessary to stifle Chinese smuggling that mushroomed on the northern Kyushu coast in the wake of the stricter Tokugawa stance.[28]

As the sole middleman in transactions between Chinese and Dutch merchants and the Nagasaki merchant community, the clearinghouse gained income by adding a 20 percent markup on the Dutch and Chinese imports it sold on the Nagasaki market via royalties from various barter arrangements and through assorted levies. With those profits, the clearinghouse would first pay its expenses, chiefly personnel costs, and earmark some funds for advance payments for future trade. It also allocated large portions of its revenue to the city of Nagasaki. With this measure, the shogunate acted as a "benevolent" feudal overlord in order to assure stable incomes and thus social stability in a city that depended upon foreign trade. In 1714, the clearinghouse garnered roughly 161,000 ryō in profits. It bestowed 70,000 ryō of that amount on the residents of Nagasaki, allocated 15,000 ryō for advance payments of imports, and sent the remaining 76,000 ryō to the Tokugawa treasury.[29] The value of the trade is illustrated by the fact that, in 1747, the lord of the wealthy Kaga domain (present-day Ishikawa and Toyama Prefectures) spent just over 171,000 ryō on expenditures within his domain and to maintain residence in Edo.[30]

Under the guidance of clearinghouse officials, Japan increased its exports of marine products, which Chinese ships had begun carrying as early as 1681.[31] In 1698, Nagasaki officials polled Chinese merchants about their product preferences and found particular interest in dried abalone and sea cucumbers, goods already widely consumed in China. Thereafter marine products, which also included kelp and shark fins, became a mainstay of Nagasaki's export trade.[32]

---

[27] Yamawaki, *Nagasaki no Tōjin bōeki*, 89.

[28] Wilson, *Defensive Positions*.

[29] Arano, *Kinsei Nihon to higashi Ajia*, 99; Innes, "Door Ajar," 343; Yamawaki, *Nagasaki no Tōjin bōeki*, 281.

[30] Tōkyō-to Edo Tōkyō Hakubutsukan, *Sankin kōtai*, 101.

[31] Nagazumi, *Tōsen yushutsunyūhin*, 254.

[32] Wakamatsu, "Nagasaki tawaramono," 140.

Tsushima and Satsuma Define Their Roles in the Realm-Wide Foreign Relations System

During the closing decades of the seventeenth century, Tokugawa leaders began the practice of debasing the silver ingots used as currency throughout the realm – the same ingots exported through Nagasaki, Satsuma, and Tsushima. They implemented these measures as part of a larger push for fiscal renewal, which included attempts to increase mining production. The shogunate soon reaped the fruits of debasement, garnering roughly five million *ryō* in revenue, funds that provided an important boost to the Tokugawa treasury.[33]

Although not expressly intended to limit foreign commerce, the shogunate's debasement measures hindered the trade of Tsushima and Satsuma. Domain officials encountered resistance from their Korean and Ryukyuan trading partners, who knew that Chinese merchants would not welcome the debased silver ingots because of the difficulty of using them on the Chinese market. Of the two domains, Tsushima endured sharper declines in trade profits due to problems associated with debased currencies issued by the shogunate.[34]

In response to the debasement policies and the trade limits instituted during the previous years, the leaders of Satsuma and Tsushima began to appeal for dispensations. They specifically requested that the shogunate allow their domains to export higher quality silver ingots minted before the debasement policies went into effect and for the Tokugawa regime to loosen the limits on domain trade imposed in previous years. Through these appeals and the responses of Tokugawa leaders, we gain insights into not only how the shogunate and the two domains defined the value of foreign trade but also the overall structure of maritime defense.

To promote their domain's case, Tsushima officials first trumpeted the value of ginseng to the realm. Domain officials often played up incidents – such as one samurai's threat to commit ritual suicide if not allowed to purchase the medicinal root – to argue that their import trade was vital to the social wellbeing of the realm.[35] In 1715, Tsushima leaders dispatched Amenomori Hōshū, a Confucian scholar in the domain's employ, to Edo to appeal their case. In a series of memorials, Amenomori stressed that, for the large and economically strong Satsuma, the effects of the restrictions on silver exports would be minimal. Yet Tsushima, charged with the vital task

---

[33] Innes, "Door Ajar," 577–99; Totman, *Early Modern Japan*, 138.
[34] Izuhara Chōshi Henshū Iinkai, *Izuhara chōshi*, 782–85.
[35] Imamura, *Ninjin shi*, 2:470–71.

of maintaining friendly ties with a neighboring independent state, faced a tougher road. He stressed that

> the lord of Tsushima has a limited income and Tsushima is but a small domain. It is therefore difficult for Tsushima to support itself by its own agricultural production. Nonetheless, through its commercial connections, Tsushima defends a border of the realm with a foreign country. This is because the export of silver ingots to Korea and Ryukyu provides a means for collecting information about the outside world.[36]

In a later missive, Amenomori asserted that "Tsushima contributes to the overall defense of the realm by gauging the relative importance of information of foreign countries," thereby defining the island as a "primary strategic bulwark" that helped to protect all of Japan.[37] In effect, Amenomori argued that the domain's diplomatic activities were equivalent to the military levies that the shogunate placed on Kyushu-area lords. While others manned castles or fulfilled specific responsibilities, such as the defense of Nagasaki, the Sō maintained and regulated relations with Korea. Moreover, in stressing the gathering of intelligence via trade, Amenomori no doubt sought to remind Tokugawa leaders of the valuable information about the Ming–Qing transition that Tsushima had provided the shogunate in previous decades.[38] Amid these appeals, shogunal leaders tabled efforts to reduce silver exports through Tsushima and thereafter allowed the domain to continue to use, for several decades, high-quality silver ingots in its trade with Korea.[39]

For their part, Satsuma leaders pushed for special privileges based upon their domain's position as suzerain of Ryukyu. They argued that a steady flow of higher quality currency helped to maintain Ryukyu's tribute trade with the Qing, and thus the economic and political stability of the kingdom. Satsuma leaders also highlighted their domain's role in facilitating the Ryukyuan embassies that periodically traveled from Kagoshima to fete the ascension of a shogun. They suggested that a disruption in those embassies due to problems in the Ryukyu-Qing trade would result in a cascade of issues. The Shimazu's dominance over the kingdom would be weakened, which in turn would tarnish Tokugawa authority by showing that a foreign state no longer displayed the proper fealty and respect to the shogunate. After much back and forth between the domain and Tokugawa officials during the first decade of the eighteenth century, the shogunate permitted the Shimazu to continue

---

[36] Amenomori, quoted in Tashiro, *Kinsei Nitchō tsūkō bōeki shi*, 337 n109.
[37] Amenomori, quoted in Tashiro, *Kinsei Nitchō tsūkō bōeki shi*, 337 n110.
[38] Toby, *State and Diplomacy*, 129–40.
[39] Yamamoto, *Tsushima-han Edo karō*, 232–38.

to export up to 900 *kan* in silver as part of Ryukyu's tribute trade, a ceiling that remained in place until the early nineteenth century. The Tokugawa regime also officially recognized the role of the Shimazu in bringing Ryukyuan missions to Edo by directing that the rank of the Shimazu lord would be raised by one level each time an embassy journeyed to the Tokugawa capital.[40] Moreover, as it did with Tsushima, the shogunate later officially recognized Satsuma as contributing to the overall defense of the realm through its suzerainty over Ryukyu. In 1748, the Nagasaki magistrate characterized Satsuma's defensive role as "containing" Ryukyu, just as it had defined Tsushima as contributing to the overall defense by "containing" Korea. The shogunate thus also exempted the domains from dispatching men for the defense of Nagasaki, a requirement imposed on other Kyushu domains.[41]

As Noell Wilson has shown, the shogunate formulated a realm-wide coastal defense system centered on Nagasaki. The shogunate created an organizational rather than technology-based defense that depended upon coordination with Kyushu domains. Leaders in Edo charged the Saga and Fukuoka domains with protecting against unwanted incursions into Nagasaki from European ships, maintaining surveillance of Dutch activities, and enforcing anti-smuggling measures. When more Chinese ships arrived during the decades after the aforementioned 1688 Qing repeal of maritime prohibitions, Fukuoka spearheaded a multidomain effort that employed lethal force to prevent smuggling in the waters off northern Kyushu.[42]

To buttress these defenses, the shogunate received intelligence about events outside of Japan not only from Satsuma and Tsushima but also from the Dutch factory in Nagasaki. Upon moving to Dejima in 1641, the Dutch accepted, as an obligation to continue to trade, the duty of gathering foreign news and delivering periodic reports, especially about possible Portuguese or Spanish plans for aggression against Japan. Although such concerns faded by the late seventeenth century, the VOC outpost remained an important intelligence source. When a Dutch ship arrived in Nagasaki harbor, interpreters (low-ranking officials trained in the Dutch language) interviewed the chief of the Dutch factory concerning news of the outside world. As Matsukata Fuyuko has shown, the interpreters reported those details to shogunal officials in Nagasaki, but not before sometimes suppressing or adjusting information to make it more palatable for leaders in Edo.[43]

---

[40] Kamiya, *Taikun gaikō*, 137–43.
[41] Arano, *Kinsei Nihon to higashi Ajia*, 217–20.
[42] Wilson, *Defensive Positions*, 1–16.
[43] Matsukata, *Oranda fūsetsugaki*.

The Shogunate's Localization Strategy

As the examples of Satsuma and Tsushima in the previous section illustrate, Tokugawa leaders' ongoing efforts to restrict the outflow of silver by imposing trade quotas had, at best, limited impact. Moreover, the Japanese market continued to demand imported products such as sugar, which Chinese and Dutch ships still brought in significant volumes.[44] In the end, localization, the encouragement of domestic production of imported products, would have a more lasting effect on Japanese foreign trade. Behind much of this effort was the proactive leadership of Shogun Yoshimune (r. 1716–45), who fostered domestic production of Japan's main imports: ginseng, sugar, and silk.

Yoshimune stimulated localization first by initiating surveys of domestic and foreign fauna and flora. In 1718, Tsushima officials used their contacts in Pusan to gather information about Chinese and Korean plants and animals as well as to obtain samples of Korean ginseng. The shogun subsequently ordered Tokugawa officials in Nagasaki to query Chinese and Dutch merchants about their knowledge of ginseng and other medicinal plants.[45] As this knowledge spread throughout the realm, ginseng came to be cultivated in many parts of Japan. Officials around Nikkō, which emerged as a prominent area of ginseng cultivation, later concluded that Tokugawa aid, dating back to Yoshimune's time, had stimulated production and thereby made ginseng more available and affordable throughout the realm.[46]

Yoshimune also played a key role in creating a nascent domestic sugar industry. The shogun tested a sugarcane crop at one of his residences and later acquired sugar-refining know-how from a Chinese ship captain. With his encouragement, Owari and Kii in central Honshu, as well as domains in Shikoku and western Honshu, began to cultivate and refine sugarcane, complementing production in Ryukyu and the Amami Islands. By the 1780s, observers commented that consumption of domestic sugar had surpassed that of imported varieties.[47] Localization of less prominent imports, such as sappanwood, was also achieved.[48]

Most significant of all, production of silk, the highest volume import good of the early Edo period, grew at points throughout the realm. Kären Wigen has traced the development of sericulture and silk reeling in one key area: the southern Shinano region (in present-day Nagano Prefecture). Expanded

[44] Mazumdar, *Sugar and Society*, 99.
[45] Tashiro, *Edo jidai Chōsen yakuzai chōsa*, 65–66, 183–218.
[46] Imamura, *Ninjin shi*, 2:511–12.
[47] Iwao, "Edo jidai no satō bōeki," 16–17; Totman, *Early Modern Japan*, 312–13; Mazumdar, *Sugar and Society*, 175.
[48] Shimada, "Tōsen raikō rūto," 59–71.

production of silk began there in the early eighteenth century and remained a significant industry into the early twentieth century.[49]

The success of localization is reflected in a series of moves made by the Tokugawa regime in 1763. Although issuing no specific order, in that year shogunal officials ended silver exports through Nagasaki.[50] That autumn they also reduced the outflow of copper, another export mainstay since the early seventeenth century. Nagasaki officials informed Chinese and Dutch merchants that because some domestic copper mines were exhausted, their annual export quotas of the metal would be reduced significantly. Moreover, by 1763, Tsushima had, for all intents and purposes, ended its exports of silver, the result of decades of Tokugawa debasement policies and particularly the success of localization of ginseng and silk, two of the domain's key imports for over a century.[51]

The 1764 Watershed

Because of a convergence of trends, 1764 became a watershed in Japan's commercial and diplomatic ties with the outside world. Beginning in that year, the shogunate, definitively mature in its rule, instituted measures that led the Japanese state to interact with the outside world based on judiciously selected and interconnected frameworks of diplomacy, trade, and coastal defense.

The year 1764 proved to be a diplomatic watershed as it was the last time a Korean embassy traveled to Edo. In that year, Shogun Ieharu (r. 1760–86) welcomed a 472-person Korean contingent to celebrate his succession as shogun. Since the first years of the Edo period, embassies from Chosŏn, an independent neighboring kingdom, had formed an essential part of the Tokugawa regime's use of diplomacy to enhance its internal standing and legitimacy. Yet, after 1764, leaders of a more assured shogunate found them less significant. Matsudaira Sadanobu, who emerged as a prominent leader in the shogunate from 1787 to 1793, directed that subsequent missions would not travel to Edo. Seeing an opportunity to economize, he pushed for representatives of the Korean court and the Tokugawa regime to instead exchange official documents at Tsushima. After protracted negotiations, the Korean side eventually agreed to Matsudaira's proposal. In 1811, a Korean embassy traveled to Tsushima, where its chief representative exchanged official letters with an envoy of the

[49] Wigen, *Making of a Japanese Periphery*, 97–98.
[50] Yamawaki, *Nagasaki no Tōjin bōeki*, 319.
[51] Tashiro, *Kinsei Nitchō tsūkō bōeki shi*, 323–29.

shogun as means to congratulate Shogun Ienari (twenty-seven years after his succession). Matsudaira also reduced the scale of diplomatic contacts with the Dutch, directing that their annual missions to Edo should now take place once every five years. Thereafter, each mission consisted of three instead of four men, and the Dutch were instructed to halve the number of gifts presented to the shogun and other officials, thereby reducing the gifts offered in return by the shogunate.[52]

After 1764, shogunal leaders also took a more direct role in foreign trade, assuring the continued inflow of medicinal products and, in a turnabout, overseeing a steady flow of silver and gold (valued at 875 *kan* that year alone) into the realm.[53] To obtain the bullion and medicinal goods, the shogunate continued to export copper through Nagasaki. As economic historian Shimada Ryūto has shown, despite the drop in export volumes, the shogunate pursued a sophisticated policy of manipulating copper prices to assure profits. Tokugawa officials directed that mines sell copper for export at prices substantially lower than what the mines required simply to recoup production costs. Shimada concludes that mines recovered losses accrued in sales to the shogunate by charging higher prices to domestic buyers. In turn, the Nagasaki clearinghouse provided copper to Dutch merchants at rates much lower than the office's acquisition price. He notes that the clearinghouse made up for this shortfall because it acquired imports at prices markedly lower than the value of the goods on the Japanese market. The clearinghouse could therefore gain substantial profits when it sold imported medicinal products and other goods to Nagasaki merchants. Shimada emphasizes that the shogunate implemented this complex price structure to assure a steady level of trade through Nagasaki that would safeguard the livelihoods of Tokugawa officials and the populace of Nagasaki.[54]

In addition, in 1785 the shogunate imposed a monopoly over the export of marine products, especially the valuable trio of sea cucumbers, abalone, and kelp. It created regional clearinghouses – in the western Honshu port of Shimonoseki, as well as in Osaka, Edo, and Hakodate – that facilitated the collection, sale, and transport of all marine products destined for the China market. Asserting feudal prerogative, Tokugawa leaders instructed coastal domains to sell, at established purchase prices, prescribed amounts of marine products each year. Thanks to these new measures, the Nagasaki clearinghouse

---

[52] Kasutani, "Naze Chōsen tsūshinshi wa haishi sareta ka"; Nakamura, *Kinsei Nagasaki bōekishi*, 498.
[53] Nakamura, *Kinsei Nagasaki bōekishi*, 447.
[54] Shimada, *Intra-Asian Trade in Japanese Copper*, 57–59.

enjoyed increased profits: from 795 *kan* in 1784 to 1,432 *kan* annually between 1785 and 1788.[55]

In developing direct controls over the marine products trade, the Tokugawa regime acted much like other states and entities trading in the western Pacific and Southeast Asian waters in the late eighteenth century. For example, in the 1760s, English East India Company (EIC) officials also searched for silver substitutes suitable for trade with the China market. Some dreamed of exchanging British woolens for tea, but found such plans stymied by limited Chinese interest in those wares. Alexander Dalrymple was apparently the first EIC official to conceive of creating an entrepôt, strategically located on maritime trading routes, which would potentially solve the British dilemma of trade with China.[56] Under his initiative and supervision in 1763, the same year that the Tokugawa regime ended silver exports through Nagasaki, the EIC obtained the island of Balambangan just north of Borneo in the Sulu Sea. It thereafter attempted to attract not only EIC vessels and British country traders (merchants engaged in private commerce between India, insular Southeast Asia, and China), but also Chinese and other Asian merchant ships to the island. Dalrymple envisioned that Asian traders would bring a range of other marine products valued in China, such as agar-agar, shark fins, cowries, birds' nests, and pearls. To obtain those goods, Chinese junks would call at Balambangan bearing tea, silks, and porcelains. With such a trade, the EIC could potentially obtain Chinese goods, without using bullion, and ship them for sale on the European market. Dalrymple also hoped that Chinese ships would bring Chinese immigrants, with their knowledge of Asian trading networks and the Chinese market, to populate the island and to supervise much of the trade. After a settlement was established on the island in 1773, the EIC official in charge of it (Dalrymple had been dismissed in a salary dispute) failed to effectively develop the entrepôt model and clumsily tended relations with the Sultan of Sulu, who played a leading role in many of the area's commercial networks. In 1775, a cousin of the sultan eventually led a successful attack on the island, ending the EIC presence there.[57] Nonetheless, the EIC continued attempts to establish other entrepôt for forest and marine products, including on Penang, an island on the western coast of the Malay Peninsula.[58]

---

[55] Hayashi, *Tsūkō ichiran*, 4:130; Nagasaki Kenshi Henshū Iinkai, *Nagasaki kenshi: Taigai kōshō hen*, 577–80; Nakamura, *Kinsei Nagasaki bōekishi*, 447.
[56] Tagliacozzo, "Necklace of Fins," 27.
[57] Fry, *Alexander Dalrymple*, 36–93; Warren, *Sulu Zone*, 17–37.
[58] Among other marine products, Chinese junks transported sea cucumbers, shark fins, and agar-agar from Singapore to Amoy and Canton. Phipps, *Practical Treatise on the China and Eastern Trade*, 281.

As these comparisons illustrate, late eighteenth-century Tokugawa leaders had, in many respects, solved the dilemma of foreign trade that perplexed their forebears since the seventeenth century: how to trade with China without being bled of silver. Under the new frameworks instituted in the second half of the eighteenth century, the shogunate could benefit by exchanging copper and marine products for medicinal goods, as well as some silver and gold. Overall, the Japanese state remained commercially connected with the China market, the dominant economy in East Asia, but in more managed ways.

In fact, the shogunate found itself well positioned to benefit from an expanding and lucrative sector: the import of plant and animal parts, as well as minerals and fossils, used to make medicines. The trade included a vast array of products for women, suggesting that female consumers held an increased level of commercial agency. For example, Chinese ships brought to Nagasaki dinosaur and mammoth fossils, which Japanese physicians prescribed to alleviate uterine bleeding. Dutch vessels also brought Chinese-produced alum, which, after being heated to remove remaining moisture, was used to counteract excessive menstrual bleeding. In addition, imported borax was mixed with other minerals to create a medicine to treat pain and vaginal discharge after childbirth. Chinese ships brought parts of the forsythia plant, used to treat syphilis, and zinc carbonate (an ingredient in modern calamine lotion), which was employed as a cure for conjunctivitis.[59] For their part, the Dutch also delivered narwhal horns cleverly marketed as those of the mythical unicorn. Apothecaries mixed the narwhal horns (or in their place, rhinoceros horns) with ginseng, aloe, musk, bear's gallbladder, and stones from the intestine of cattle to create a medicine for treating childhood diseases. The Dutch imported annually about thirty kilograms of narwhal horns after 1800.[60]

Russian Visitors and Shogunate-Domain Frictions

In the closing decades of the eighteenth century, Russians established colonial, military, and merchant outposts in the North Pacific stretching from Sitka in Alaska to the Sea of Okhotsk north of Ezo (modern-day Hokkaido). The outposts collected furs, especially of the sea otter, to sell in Europe but most profitably to exchange at Canton. Officials in the capital of Saint Petersburg also aimed to expand trade with Japan. Japanese castaways who ended up in Russia described their homeland as rich in gold and silver, while

---

[59] Yamawaki, *Kinsei Nihon no iyaku bunka*, 130–31, 210–11.
[60] Miyashita, *Nagasaki bōeki to Ōsaka*, 5–12.

Russian envoys in Beijing erroneously reported that the Dutch-Japanese trade at Nagasaki consisted of the exchange of skins for Japanese gold, silver, and porcelains. These rumors led many Russians to speculate about selling furs on the Japanese market in exchange for gold and silver.[61]

Such hopes prompted the court at Saint Petersburg to send Adam Laxman as its official envoy to Japan in 1792. Bringing Japanese castaways for repatriation, Laxman called at Nemuro, on the eastern part of Ezo, and requested permission to travel to Edo to appeal his case for an opening of commercial relations. Matsudaira Sadanobu declared that negotiations could only take place at Nagasaki and offered a permit that allowed the bearer to enter the port at a future date. Laxman reluctantly departed, although he remained optimistic that the permit would allow a future Russian mission to establish commercial ties with Japan. In 1804, the Russian government tried again, this time sending Nikolai Rezanov to Nagasaki, bearing the permit that Laxman had received. Officials in Saint Petersburg instructed their envoy to explain to his Japanese counterparts that Russian ships could bring furs, walrus and elephant tusks, fish, leather goods, and woolen cloth to exchange for rice, copper, and silk.[62] Russian officials hoped that trade with Japan could bring profit and simultaneously supply colonies in the Pacific with much needed foodstuffs.[63]

During Rezanov's visit, shogunal officials queried Russians about how many of their vessels might call annually if trade relations were established. They also asked if the Russians would bring sugar, medicines, or other products in demand on the Japanese market. Rezanov answered "only in general terms," revealing the still nascent scope of his plans for bilateral trade.[64] Following a period of internal consultation, the shogunate rejected Rezanov's overtures, proclaiming that "in the instance of commerce, it may appear that adding things which your country has to those which our country lacks would be of mutual benefit. After detailed deliberation, we have concluded that in exchange for foreign items of little value, we would lose useful Japanese goods. All things considered, such trade would not be in the interest of the realm as a whole."[65]

Traditionally historians presented shogunal leaders as formulating this and subsequent responses to Western visitors based on an either/or proposition:

[61] Lensen, *Russian Push toward Japan*, 41.
[62] Rezanov, *Nihon taizai nikki*, 383.
[63] Lensen, *Russian Push toward Japan*, 128.
[64] Langsdorff, *Voyages and Travels*, 1:204.
[65] Lensen, *Russian Push toward Japan*, 155; Hayashi, *Tsūkō ichiran*, 7:193.

retaining a "closed" system created in the early seventeenth century or "opening" to a vibrant, emerging West. In such narratives, the shogunate, Satsuma, and Tsushima are seen as having no existing structures or agendas beyond a shared sense of limiting contacts with the outside world. Moreover, Western nations are assumed to be more economically advanced and thus primed to bring valuable goods from their home markets.[66]

Such interpretations neglect the actual commercial flows connecting the early nineteenth-century western Pacific, many of which involved forest and marine products such as the furs at the heart of the Russian trading enterprises. In 1819, Britain at last developed a successful forest and marine products entrepôt with the founding of Singapore. In the first years of that port, sea cucumbers formed, after pepper, the most important import from surrounding areas of Southeast Asia.[67] In addition, US commercial ships, which emerged as a new force following the birth of the United States with the Treaty of Paris in 1783, did not transport manufactured wares produced in the new nation. Although carrying much Mexican silver, US vessels simultaneously sought marine and forest products throughout the Pacific to exchange for tea, silk, and porcelains at Canton. They therefore acquired North American ginseng, furs in trade with Amerindians, sandalwood from Hawai'i, and sea cucumbers purchased in Fiji, all of which were taken to Canton.[68]

This background helps to explain why shogunal leaders rejected Russian overtures. They saw little benefit in incorporating Russia into a system of foreign trade proactively revised by their predecessors and one that allowed Japan to limit silver exports while acquiring desired goods predominately from China. Tokugawa officials probably calculated that Russia would have disrupted their regime's profitable exports of marine products and imports of medicinal goods.

In fact, during the late eighteenth and early nineteenth centuries, domestic demand for specific medicines expanded. This was the case with Borneo camphor, already mentioned as a significant import for the Dutch. By the nineteenth century, more Japanese sought to obtain it for its presumed medicinal value, both as a means to clear "bad air" and as a medicine for common ailments. Japanese consumers especially prized camphor imported from Borneo, but also readily purchased what were viewed as lower-quality varieties from China. In 1764, Japan imported approximately 140 *kin* annually,

---

[66] For example, Keene, *Japanese Discovery of Europe*.
[67] Phipps, *Practical Treatise on the China and Eastern Trade*, 321.
[68] Hellyer, "West, the East, and the Insular Middle," 401–4.

but consumption grew steadily thereafter. After 1820, Chinese ships brought an annual average of over 1,000 *kin*.[69]

Beginning in the 1820s, Satsuma leaders moved to take greater advantage of such valuable trade flows by making their domain an entrepôt to rival Nagasaki. In this effort, Satsuma officials enlisted the help of large merchant houses involved in coastal smuggling.[70] To extend their domain's commercial reach beyond the Kyushu region, Satsuma leaders granted one house, the Hamazaki, a freer hand in coastal trade in return for a portion of the profits. The Hamazaki assumed responsibility for shipbuilding and transport and stationed their agents throughout the domain and in other key Japanese ports to facilitate the expansion of a trading web that stretched from Ryukyu to Niigata on the Sea of Japan coast and the port of Hakodate in Matsumae. With the domain's blessing, by the 1830s the Hamazaki had built a commercial enterprise that complemented Satsuma's existing commercial network: Satsuma and Hamazaki vessels transported Ryukyuan sugar to Osaka and sugar and sweet potatoes to Niigata. The also called at Matsumae, from which they returned with kelp, sea cucumbers, and abalone.[71]

In addition, Satsuma obtained marine products from other partners, in so doing further circumventing the shogunate's monopoly. Domain agents purchased marine products at peripheral ports around the Tokugawa collection centers of Osaka and Shimonoseki. Satsuma officials also permitted medicine merchants from the Toyama domain on the Sea of Japan coast to sell their goods in Satsuma for a fee paid in marine products.[72]

Satsuma used the marine products to obtain Chinese goods from Chinese junks that illicitly called not at Nagasaki per Tokugawa edicts but at ports along the Satsuma coastline. In addition, the domain shipped kelp, a product of the northern oceans, to Ryukyu, where it had become a part of many islanders' daily fare. The kingdom's tribute missions would also take kelp, along with sea cucumbers, abalone, and shark fins, to China to exchange for medicinal products and other goods.[73]

Satsuma built the final link in its new trading network by securing expanded access to sell imports on the Japanese domestic market. As noted earlier, in the late seventeenth century the shogunate had allowed Satsuma to sell only silk on the domestic market, and then only through a specific

---

[69] Miyashita, *Nagasaki bōeki to Ōsaka*, 17–25.
[70] Miyazato and Sawada, *Kaijō-ō Hamazaki Taiheiji den*, 27.
[71] Miyazato and Sawada, *Kaijō-ō Hamazaki Taiheiji den*, 29–37.
[72] Uehara, *Sakoku to han bōeki*, 273–79.
[73] Ōishi, *Konbu no michi*, 85–89; 91–93.

Kyoto wholesaler. Because of the emergence of domestic silk production in the second half of the eighteenth century, Satsuma enjoyed scant profits from the sale of these goods. In 1801, domain leaders requested permission to sell selected Chinese medicinal products on the domestic market. Shogunal officials, seeking to protect the Tokugawa share of that lucrative import trade, flatly refused.[74] Undeterred, Satsuma officials continued to appeal regularly for concessions, stressing that the measures were necessary to "aid Ryukyu": to stabilize the kingdom's economy and, by implication, maintain the prestige of its tribute relationship with the Qing. During the 1810s and early 1820s, successive typhoons and droughts brought poor harvests and in turn famine to Ryukyu. In light of these events, the domain redoubled its appeals, arguing that these natural calamities required an expansion of sales of imports at Nagasaki to assuage the kingdom's economic woes. In 1825, shogunal officials finally relented, permitting Satsuma to sell sixteen imported goods and medicinal products, including a Chinese variety of medicinal camphor, similar to the more valuable Borneo camphor. In total, the shogunate allowed Satsuma to sell 1,720 *kan* in goods annually, well up from the earlier limit of just over 900 *kan* in effect since 1716. Yet while they granted these concessions, shogunal officials instructed Satsuma not to interfere in the export of marine products and the import of several other valuable medicinal products, which they considered fundamental to the stability of trade through the Nagasaki clearinghouse.[75]

By comparison, Tsushima leaders garnered modest gains from the burgeoning market in imported medicines. Japanese consumers viewed medicinal goods from China as more efficacious, thus reducing profits gained from Tsushima's sales of Korean materia medica. However, the domain found a niche by importing cattle hides, hooves, and horns from Korea. Once again underscoring the gendered divisions of imported products, leather from the tanned hides was often used in armor worn by male samurai. Tashiro Kazui explains that during the first decades of the nineteenth century demand for leather grew as domains sought to strengthen their military readiness as the increasing number of Western vessels visiting Japanese shores made coastal defense a more pressing concern. Osaka craftspeople fashioned the horns and hooves into "flat Korean ivory" and "Korean tortoiseshell," which were used to make combs and hairclips for women that imitated those fabricated from the more expensive tortoiseshell imported by Chinese and Dutch merchants

---

[74] Hayashi, *Tsūkō ichiran*, 8:481.
[75] Nakamura, "Nagasaki kaisho Tenpō kaikakuki," 68–69; Kagoshima-ken, *Kagoshima kenshi*, 2:747–50.

at Nagasaki. These lower-priced hair accessories proved popular in Edo and other urban areas.[76]

Nonetheless, these new commercial initiatives did little to offset the domain's mounting debts to Edo and Osaka merchants. Therefore, Tsushima leaders began to pursue a new path: a sustained campaign to acquire financial aid from Edo. The shogunate often granted the domain's requests, usually after a barrage of petitions that began with laments about Tsushima's woeful economic situation. In the 1810s, Tsushima gained several grants and loans to offset costs related to the reception of the aforementioned Korean embassy in 1811. The shogunate also proffered an annual stipend for twenty years to reduce the economic pain inflicted by the slowdown in trade, an award in addition to one the domain had received annually since 1776. Moreover, shogunal leaders bestowed 10,000 *koku* of rice to offset the reduction in imported rice that resulted from poor harvests in Korea. As an additional reward for the completion of the 1811 embassy, the shogunate awarded lands in Kyushu in 1818 valued at 20,000 *koku*.[77] To cap it off, the shogunate permitted the Sō to be lax in the biennial ritual of alternate residence. Between 1810 and 1842, the lord and his entourage traveled to Edo only five times, a form of fiscal relief to Sō's strained treasury. In the same period, lords from other domains would have made up to fifteen trips, all at significant financial cost.[78] Yet despite the Tokugawa aid and concessions, the domain remained saddled with onerous debts to Osaka and Edo merchants, which in 1835 totaled a whopping 8,530 *kan*.[79]

Foreign Relations Entering the Bakumatsu Period

We can view internal events, such as the aborted uprising of Ōshio Heihachirō in 1837, as well as external shocks, notably in the form of the British victory over the Qing in the Opium War (1839–42), as combining to commence the Bakumatsu period, the closing days of Tokugawa rule that culminated in the Meiji Restoration of 1868. Guided by the commercial, diplomatic, and defensive agendas and frameworks outlined in this chapter, Tokugawa, Satsuma, and Tsushima leaders grappled with one of the more pressing challenges of the Bakumatsu era: the increasing arrival of Western military and merchant ships. In the 1840s, Tsushima officials, faced with a wave of Western ships on their shores, continued to request Tokugawa financial aid. For their part,

[76] Tashiro, "Bakumatsu-ki Nitchō shibōeki," 178–82.
[77] Yamamoto, *Tsushima-han Edo karō*, 156–57; Arano, *Kinsei Nihon to higashi Ajia*, 234–35.
[78] Tsuruta, "Tenpō-ki no Tsushima-han zaisei," 61.
[79] Nagasaki Kenshi Henshū Iinkai, *Nagasaki kenshi: Hansei hen*, 1109.

Satsuma leaders used the visit of French and British ships to Ryukyu to further their domain's trading network at the expense of the Tokugawa-controlled Nagasaki entrepôt. Shogunal leaders struck back, protecting their regime's monopolies on key exports and imports, a stance they maintained as Japan transitioned into the treaty port era in 1859.[80]

Bibliography

Arano Yasunori. *Kinsei Nihon to higashi Ajia*. Tōkyō Daigaku Shuppankai, 1988.

Davidson, James W. *The Island of Formosa: Past and Present*. New York: Macmillan, 1903. Reprint, Taipei: SMC, 1992.

Donkin, R. A. *Dragon's Brain Perfume: A Historical Geography of Camphor*. Leiden: Brill, 1999.

Fry, Howard T. *Alexander Dalrymple (1737–1808) and the Expansion of British Trade*. London: Frank Cass, 1970.

Fukase Kōichirō. "Ryūkyū-kan ni miru Satsuryū kankei." *Kagoshima rekishi kenkyū* 3 (1998): 45–50.

Goodman, Grant K. *Japan and the Dutch, 1600–1853*. Richmond, UK: Curzon Press, 2000.

Gunn, Geoffrey. *World Trade Systems of the East and West: Nagasaki and the Asian Bullion Trade Networks*. Leiden: Brill, 2017.

Hayashi Akira, ed. *Tsūkō ichiran*. 8 vols. Kokusho Kankōkai, 1912–13. Reprint, Osaka: Seibundō Shuppan, 1967.

Hellyer, Robert. *Defining Engagement: Japan and Global Contexts, 1640–1868*. Cambridge, MA: Harvard University Asia Center, 2009.

"The West, the East, and the Insular Middle: Trading Systems, Demand, and Labour in the Integration of the Pacific, 1750–1875." *Journal of Global History* 8, no. 3 (2013): 391–413.

Iioka Naoko. "The Rise and Fall of the Tonkin-Nagasaki Silk Trade during the Seventeenth Century." In *Large and Broad: The Dutch Impact on Early Modern Asia: Essays in Honor of Leonard Blussé*, edited by Nagazumi Yōko, 46–61. Toyo Bunko, 2010.

Imamura Tomo. *Ninjinshi*. 7 vols. Seoul [Keijō]: Chōsen Sōtokufu Senbaikyoku, 1935.

Innes, Robert LeRoy. "The Door Ajar: Japan's Foreign Trade in the Seventeenth Century." PhD diss., University of Michigan, 1980.

Iwao Seiichi. "Edo jidai no satō bōeki ni tsuite." *Nihon gakushiin kiyō* 31, no. 1 (1973): 1–34.

Izuhara Chōshi Henshū Iinkai, ed. *Izuhara chōshi*. Izuhara: Izuhara-chō, 1998.

Jansen, Marius B. *China in the Tokugawa World*. Cambridge, MA: Harvard University Press, 1992.

Kaempfer, Engelbert. *Kaempfer's Japan: Tokugawa Culture Observed*. Edited, translated, and annotated by Beatrice M. Bodart-Bailey. Honolulu: University of Hawai'i Press, 1999.

Kagoshima-ken, ed. *Kagoshima kenshi*. 5 vols. Kagoshima: Kagoshima-ken, 1939–41.

Kamiya Nobuyuki. *Taikun gaikō to higashi Ajia*. Yoshikawa Kōbunkan, 1997.

---

[80] Hellyer, *Defining Engagement*, 150–206.

Kang, David. *East Asia before the West: Five Centuries of Trade and Tribute.* New York: Columbia University Press, 2010.

Kasutani Ken'ichi. "Naze Chōsen tsūshinshi wa haishi sareta ka: Chōsen shiryō o chūshin ni." *Rekishi hyōron* 355 (November 1979): 8–23.

Keene, Donald. *The Japanese Discovery of Europe: Honda Toshiaki and Other Discoverers, 1720–1798.* London: Routledge and K. Paul, 1952.

Langsdorff, Georg Heinrich von. *Voyages and Travels in Various Parts of the World, during the Years 1803, 1804, 1805, 1806, 1807.* 2 vols. London: Henry Colburn, 1813–14.

Lensen, G. A. *The Russian Push toward Japan: Russo-Japanese Relations, 1697–1875.* Princeton, NJ: Princeton University Press, 1959.

Lewis, James B. *Frontier Contact between Chosŏn Korea and Tokugawa Japan.* London: Routledge Curzon, 2003.

Matsukata Fuyuko. *Oranda fūsetsugaki to kinsei Nihon.* Tōkyō Daigaku Shuppankai, 2007.

Mazumdar, Sucheta. *Sugar and Society in China: Peasants, Technology, and the World Market.* Cambridge, MA: Harvard University Asia Center, 1998.

Miyashita Saburō. *Nagasaki bōeki to Ōsaka: Yunyū kara sōyaku e.* Osaka: Seibundō, 1997.

Miyazato Gennojō and Sawada Nobuto, eds. *Kaijō-ō Hamazaki Taiheiji den.* Kagoshima: Hamazaki Taiheiji-ō Kenshōkai, 1934.

Nagasaki Kenshi Henshū Iinkai, ed. *Nagasaki kenshi: Hansei hen.* Yoshikawa Kōbunkan, 1973.

Nagasaki kenshi: Taigai kōshō hen. Yoshikawa Kōbunkan, 1985.

Nagazumi Yōko. *Tōsen yushutsunyūhin sūryō ichiran, 1637–1833.* Sōbunsha, 1987.

Nakai, Kate Wildman. *Shogunal Politics: Arai Hakuseki and the Premises of Tokugawa Rule.* Cambridge, MA: Council on East Asian Studies, Harvard University, 1988.

Nakamura Tadashi. *Kinsei Nagasaki bōekishi no kenkyū.* Yoshikawa Kōbunkan, 1988.

"Nagasaki kaisho Tenpō kaikakuki no shomondai: Sakoku taisei hōkai katei no ichi sokumen." *Shien* 115 (1978): 65–94.

Ōishi Ken'ichi. *Konbu no michi.* Daiichi Shobō, 1987.

Peng, Hao. *Trade Relations between Qing China and Tokugawa Japan, 1685–1859.* Singapore: Springer, 2019.

Phipps, John. *A Practical Treatise on the China and Eastern Trade: Comprising the Commerce of Great Britain and India, Particularly Bengal and Singapore, with China and the Eastern Islands.* London: W. H. Allen, 1836.

Rezanov, Nikolai. *Nihon taizai nikki, 1804–1805.* Translated by Ōshima Mikio. Iwanami Shoten, 2000.

Seifman, Travis. "Performing 'Lūchū': Identity Performance and Foreign Relations in Early Modern Japan." PhD diss., University of California, Santa Barbara, 2019.

Shimada Ryūto. *The Intra-Asian Trade in Japanese Copper by the Dutch East India Company during the Eighteenth Century.* Leiden: Brill, 2006.

"Tōsen raikō rūto no henka to kinsei Nihon no kokusan daitai-ka: Soboku benibana o jirei toshite." *Waseda keizaigaku kenkyū* 49 (September 1999): 59–71.

Tagliacozzo, Eric. "A Necklace of Fins: Marine Goods Trading in Maritime Southeast Asia, 1780–1860." *International Journal of Asian Studies* 1, no. 1 (2004): 23–48.

Tashiro Kazui. "Bakumatsu-ki Nitchō shibōeki to Wakan bōeki shōnin: Yunyū yon hinmoku no torihiki o chūshin ni." In *Kaikoku*, edited by Inoue Katsuo, 171–95. Vol. 2 of *Bakumatsu ishin ronshū*. Yoshikawa Kōbunkan, 2001.

Edo jidai Chōsen yakuzai chōsa no kenkyū. Keiō Gijuku Daigaku Shuppankai, 1999.

Kinsei Nitchō tsūkō bōeki shi no kenkyū. Sōbunsha, 1981.

"'Tsushima Han's Korean Trade, 1684–1710." *Acta Asiatica* 30 (1976): 85–105.

Titsingh, Isaac, and Timon Screech. *Secret Memoirs of the Shoguns: Isaac Titsingh and Japan, 1779–1822.* London: Routledge, 2006.

Toby, Ronald. *State and Diplomacy in Early Modern Japan: Asia in the Development of the Tokugawa Bakufu.* Princeton, NJ: Princeton University Press, 1984. Reprint, Stanford, CA: Stanford University Press, 1991.

Tōkyō-to Edo Tōkyō Hakubutsukan. *Sankin kōtai: Kyodai toshi Edo no naritachi.* Tōkyō-to Edo Tōkyō Hakubutsukan, 1997.

Tomiyama Kazuyuki. *Ryūkyū ōkoku no gaikō to ōken.* Yoshikawa Kōbunkan, 2004.

Totman, Conrad. *Early Modern Japan.* Berkeley: University of California Press, 1993.

Tsuruta Kei. "The Establishment and Characteristics of the 'Tsushima Gate.'" *Acta Asiatica* 67 (1994): 30–48.

"Tenpō-ki no Tsushima-han zaisei to Nitchō bōeki." *Ronshū kinsei* 8 (1983): 60–79.

Tsushima kara mita Nitchō kankei. Yamakawa Shuppansha, 2006.

Uehara Kenzen. *Sakoku to han bōeki: Satsuma-han no Ryūkyū mistu bōeki.* Yaesudake Shobō, 1981.

Wakamatsu Masashi. "Nagasaki tawaramono o meguru shokubunka no rekishiteki tenkai." *Kyōto Sangyō Daigaku Nihon bunka kenkyūjo kiyō* 1 (1996): 128–60.

Warren, James. *The Sulu Zone, 1768–1898: The Dynamics of External Trade, Slavery, and Ethnicity in the Transformation of a Southeast Asian Maritime State.* 2nd ed. Singapore: National University of Singapore Press, 2007.

Wigen, Kären. *The Making of a Japanese Periphery, 1750–1920.* Berkeley: University of California Press, 1995.

Wilson, Noell. *Defensive Positions: The Politics of Maritime Security in Tokugawa Japan.* Cambridge, MA: Harvard University Asia Center, 2015.

Yamamoto Hirofumi. *Tsushima-han Edo karō: Kinsei Nichō gaikō o sasaeta hitobito.* Kōdansha, 1995.

Yamawaki Teijirō. *Kinsei Nihon no iyaku bunka.* Heibonsha, 1995.

Nagasaki no Tōjin bōeki. Yoshikawa Kōbunkan, 1964.

Zhou, Gang. *The Qing Opening to the Ocean: Chinese Maritime Policies, 1684–1757.* Honolulu: University of Hawai'i Press, 2013.

6

The Meiji Restoration

MARK RAVINA

What was the Meiji Restoration? In the narrowest sense, the restoration was a palace coup. In the early hours of the ninth day of the twelfth month of 1867 (3 January 1868), troops from Satsuma domain took control of the Imperial Palace gates, forcing out guards from Aizu and Kuwana. That seizure of power allowed for the return of dissident radical courtiers, who immediately prompted the young emperor Mutsuhito to declare the "revival of ancient kingly rule." Seated behind a bamboo screen on a high platform, the monarch read an edict abolishing the Tokugawa shogunate and establishing a new council of courtiers and daimyo. Tokugawa Yoshinobu, the fifteenth and last Tokugawa shogun, tried to retain power by relying on his imperial titles instead of his shogunal authority. But the new regime was in no mood to compromise, and warfare erupted early the following month. After a few pitched battles, shogunal forces collapsed and Yoshinobu surrendered Edo Castle in the fourth month of 1868. Northeastern daimyo and some shogunal officers fought on, but by the fifth month of 1869 the defeat of the old regime was complete.

Such a narrow focus on the early months of 1868 allows for concision but also leaves much unanswered. Why did a simple coup within the Japanese elite lead to revolutionary change? Initially, the restoration was largely a struggle between southwestern daimyo and northeastern daimyo, and little in those early months foreshadowed years of transformative change. But within a decade, the new Meiji government had reshaped almost every aspect of life in Japan. It dissolved much of the ruling elite, abolishing daimyo domains and forcing the last generation of daimyo into retirement. It eliminated traditional status distinctions, stripping samurai of their hereditary stipends and "emancipating" stigmatized status groups such as *eta* and *hinin*. Samurai lost their hereditary monopolies on military and civil service, and the new government began conscripting commoners into a new national army. The central government took control of taxation as well as civil and criminal law, replacing hundreds of local tax and legal codes with centralized codes, statues, and rulings. The new national tax system redefined property relations along capitalist lines: taxes were paid by the landowner based on the value of the property rather than the harvest yield, and the government lifted restrictions on the sale and alienation of land. The state instituted mandatory primary education and began to standardize textbooks across the country. By 1881, the Meiji state was counting, taxing, drafting, arresting, and educating the Japanese people with unprecedented levels of national consistency and control. In response, the Japanese populace formed a nationwide movement to challenge the government's autocracy. Seizing on the government's vague statements about power sharing and consensus, they demanded an elected assembly and constitutional limits on state power.

In toto, the reforms of the Meiji Restoration comprise an almost canonical nationalist revolution. At the heart of many Meiji reforms was the creation of a new national identity. The scattered, regional institutions of daimyo and lesser lords were replaced by a single national army, navy, and treasury. The Meiji state denounced the hereditary privileges of samurai as a perverse impediment to the inherent unity of the Japanese people. The conscription of commoners was described in terms of the equal freedom and responsibilities of all Japanese men. Education emphasized vernacular Japanese over classical Chinese, traditionally the language of scholarship. The transformation can also be understood as a "bourgeois revolution." The new government's market-oriented reforms and abolition of hereditary privilege catalyzed a shift in power from samurai to landowners and entrepreneurs.

Explaining the restoration as a revolutionary transformation (bourgeois, nationalist, or both) requires an expansive perspective that looks far beyond a coup in Kyoto. In a broad temporal view, the Meiji Restoration can be seen as the result of long-term changes in Japanese social and economic structures. By the eve of the restoration, the core ideological precepts of the Tokugawa system bore little resemblance to lived experience. The samurai, for example, were not rugged self-reliant warriors but urban rentiers enmeshed in a commercial economy. Merchants were not simple transporters of commodities but quasi bankers who provided essential financial services. Indeed, many daimyo domains were deeply in debt to their merchant financiers. As Kiri Paramore observes in this volume (Chapter 2) "this was the great contradiction of the Tokugawa state: the economic development which it had facilitated undercut the financial base of its hierarchical organization." The social order seemed out of order.

Many Tokugawa-era reformers and cultural critics advocated reversing socioeconomic change so that lived experience might conform to expectations and explicit norms. How could samurai learn to resist the temptations of urban life and recover the stoic martial vigor of their forefathers? How might obstreperous commoners somehow relearn the deference of their ancestors? A vocal minority suggested an opposite approach. Perhaps the solution was not to restore status distinctions but to acknowledge that those norms had eroded and to make appropriate changes in laws and regulations? Many of the Meiji state's reforms can be understood as the sudden and complete triumph of this minority view. Better to recognize a commercial economy with new laws than to attempt to restore an imagined "natural" economy. Better to abolish hereditary status distinctions than to defend them. Nationalist discourse, with its emphasis on the centrality of Japanese identity over hereditary rank, catalyzed criticism of the old order: weren't all Japanese equally servants of the emperor?

The Meiji Restoration was also driven by a confrontation with transnational expectations. Changes in the international order, like those in the domestic social order, demanded a radical rethinking of the Japanese state and the Japanese nation. Part of that crisis was imperialist military power, which humiliated the Tokugawa regime. But imperialism was both empowering and debilitating. The new Meiji state quickly mastered the tropes of Western imperialism and deployed them against the Qing, Yi, and Shō dynasties. At heart, Japan's nineteenth-century international crisis was a clash between two international systems. From the perspective of Western diplomats, Tokugawa Japan made no sense. Who was the Japanese sovereign? Who was empowered to sign and enforce treaties? Was it the shogun? The emperor? The king of Ryukyu? Individual daimyo? The Tokugawa state system's web of coincident power and authority maintained domestic peace for over two centuries and was well designed for its international environment: limited but peaceful ties with Korea, China, and Ryukyu. But the privileged actor in nineteenth-century Western international law was the unitary nation-state. From that perspective, the Tokugawa order was not only weak but eccentric and "Oriental," an obscure and illegible network of political powers and obligations. The international order thus necessitated a Japanese nation-state as an alternative to colonial subjugation. By restyling the Japanese emperor as Japan's singular and exclusive sovereign, the Meiji Restoration created a new Japanese state that was legitimate and legible in Western political discourse. By insisting that the Japanese were one people, undivided by caste, estate, or region, the Meiji state created a nation along with the nation-state. Both domestically and internationally, Japan was reconceived as a single sovereign entity, the political expression of a unitary Japanese people.

Connecting these domestic and international faces of the revolution was a reverence for the ancient past. The bold innovations of the restoration were commonly described as a return to or resurrection of ancient ways. In places, this rhetoric had a grain of truth. For example, the ancient Japanese state had conscripted commoners, so the abolition of samurai status could be styled as a return to ancient practice. But the great value of reverence for the ancient past was how it allowed a wide-ranging attack on Tokugawa-era traditions in the name of more ancient traditions. A single reform could be described as new or old, as suited the occasion.

Japan was not unique in linking its modern revolution to ancient precedent. The early American republic and revolutionary France styled themselves as successors to both the Roman empire and Roman democracy. George Washington, for example, contrasted his armies with those of the British monarchy through references to Rome: American and Roman soldiers, unlike their opponents, fought in defense of liberty for their republics.[1] French revolutionary thought and iconography was suffused with references to the classical republican tradition.[2] In nineteenth-century Germany, the transformation of a regional Prussian monarchy into a broader German monarchy was supported symbolically by connecting Kaiser Wilhelm I (1797–1888) with Frederick Barbarossa, the Holy Roman emperor (1122–90).[3] In all these cases, ancient models were yoked to radical change. The Meiji Restoration's veneration of the Japanese past was thus a part of its global present and broader currents of revolutionary nationalism. Indeed, a highly selective reverence for the past is a cornerstone of nationalism.

The Japanese imperial institution was uniquely well suited to this transnational process of reinventing the ancient past. While the Hohenzollern house could be linked metaphorically to ancient Rome, the Japanese imperial house could draw on a canonical genealogy tracing a lineage of 121 sovereigns across twenty-six centuries. The imperial house also benefited, paradoxically, from centuries of remoteness from practical affairs. Since the fourteenth century, when an imperial challenge to warrior rule ended in disaster, emperors were content to reign rather than rule. That left the political face of the imperial institution as something of a blank slate onto which diverse groups could project their aspirations.

[1] Shalev, *Rome Reborn on Western Shores*, 19–22.
[2] Baker, "Transformations of Classical Republicanism."
[3] Kennedy, "Regionalism and Nationalism"; Tebbe, "'Revision' and 'Rebirth.'"

Many late Tokugawa imperial loyalists envisioned a return to a remote past before the appearance of formal state structures. A true restoration of imperial power would make the state unnecessary since people would be connected to the monarch through their local shrines. Accordingly, for many nativists, the most critical office of the ancient Japanese state was the Jingikan (Department of Divinities), the only agency not based on Tang Chinese precedent. The Meiji government revived the Jingikan and dutifully mentioned the "unity of rites and rule" (*saisei itchi*), but the Jingikan remained a minor agency, weakened by internal divisions and overshadowed by powerful organs such as the Army Ministry and Home Ministry.[4] For many nativist activists, the restoration realized their fears rather than their hopes: more Western influence rather than less.

Advocates of a strong state, by contrast, cited precedents from the apex of imperial state power in the seventh through ninth centuries. But that ancient state, known as the *ritsuryō* state for its legal codes, was built on Chinese models, primarily the practices of the Tang dynasty. Rather than restore an unsullied Japanese past, emulation of the ancient *ritsuryō* state legitimized the adoption of foreign models. Much as the ancient throne had reached its pinnacle of power by adapting Chinese models, so too could the modern throne be restored through the adoption of Western models. The question, of course, was what political model? Advocates of powerful democratic institutions could point to Britain, where a beloved monarch presided over a robust parliament with a steadily expanding franchise. Conservatives could point to the successes of the nascent Prussian empire and insist on the primacy of a powerful military and bureaucracy over a weaker elected assembly. The power of imperial loyalism came partly from its ability to contain these diverse visions. With the exception of tiny anarchist and socialist movements, late Tokugawa- and Meiji-era political discourse centered on how, not whether, the emperor should reign over Japan.

Taking account of these forces (domestic instability, a new international order, and a reconceptualization of the imperial house) requires a time frame much longer than the early months of 1868, but how much longer? This chapter begins with the Tenpō crisis of the 1830s, which marks an inflection point on all three issues. In 1838, Tokugawa Nariaki, the daimyo of Mito, evocatively summarized the Tenpō crisis with a four-character phrase: *naiyū gaikan*,

---

[4] Much recent research emphasizes tension within nativism, *kokugaku*, and Mitogaku. See, for example, Teeuwen, "Clashing Models," and Thal, "Redefining the Gods." For an example of a nativist activist and her disillusion with the Meiji state, see Walthall, *Weak Body of a Useless Woman*.

or "domestic troubles and foreign threats."[5] Both contemporary observers and historians have since used the term to refer to the dual crises of the late Tokugawa era. "Domestic troubles" points to a range of long-simmering socioeconomic tensions, which conservatives perceived as a collapse of the moral order. "Foreign threats" refers to looming international crises, both the immediate threat of Western demands on Japan and the broader challenge of a new international order.

Domestically, Japan was wracked by food shortages, sparked by a series of harvest failures. National population registers show a loss of over a million people, more than 4 percent of the population.[6] While the terrible Tenmei famine of the 1780s had been equally severe, the Tenpō famine sparked widespread public outrage at the shogunate and the failure of its relief works. In Osaka, for example, a former police constable, Ōshio Heihachirō, furious that the shogunate was not seizing private storehouses of grain for public relief, called for the destruction of the government he once served. Across Japan, villagers began to treat wealthy local commoners more as targets of protest than as local leaders. That sense of social and political failure foreshadowed the rapid demise of the old order.

Internationally, during the Tenpō era, Japanese observers discovered the full impact of Western imperialism when Britain defeated China in the First Opium War (1839–42). British victory threatened two centuries of frosty but stable peace between the major powers of East Asia. After the consolidation of the Qing dynasty in the mid-1600s, the Tokugawa, the Qing, and the Korean Chosŏn dynasty had managed to avoid war with each other, largely by restricting their trade and diplomatic relations. The Opium War revealed that such conflict avoidance was no longer sustainable. Conventional diplomacy would not stop the imperialist powers from starting wars, and Japan needed a new strategy for this new international environment. Japan would need to talk like a nation-state in negotiations and fight like a nation-state in war. Although the threat of Western imperialism was clear, the shogunate was unable to formulate a sustained response: too many powerful figures were invested in the status quo. That institutional inertia continued even after US naval forces arrived in Edo Bay in 1853 to demand trade and diplomatic relations. Yoshinobu's bold, if frenzied, reform efforts to create a centralized state came too late to save the shogunate, but they anticipated the Meiji government's nation-state building policies.

[5] Ishii, *Tokugawa kinreikō*, 1:204–17.
[6] Jannetta, "Famine Mortality."

Ideologically, the twin crises of the Tenpō era sparked reforms based on new interpretations of imperial sovereignty. In Mito domain, for example, reformers attempted to restore ancient Japanese virtues under the rubric "revere the emperor, expel the barbarian" (sonnō jōi). While the daimyo of Mito, Tokugawa Nariaki, did not involve the imperial house in the management of his domain, he invoked imperial sovereignty to justify a range of new policies: new land surveys, the resettlement of urban samurai in the countryside, and the persecution of Buddhism. The Mito reforms ended in catastrophe: conservatives within the domain became alarmed by Nariaki's radicalism and the shogunate placed him in domiciliary confinement. Nariaki's supporters in Mito were outraged, and the domain lapsed into a protracted struggle that by 1864 had escalated into a localized civil war. Although "Mito thought" wrecked Mito domain, the movement developed some core ideological features of Meiji reforms: most notably, the invocation of the ancient past to justify radical change. Key modern concepts, such as the "imperial body politic" (kokutai), were articulated and refined during the Tenpō era.[7]

When did the Meiji Restoration end? In international affairs, we might mark the end of the Meiji project in 1894, when Japan began successfully renegotiating its unequal treaties, or in 1895, with Japanese victory in the Sino-Japanese War of 1894–95. Those events marked the transformation of the Japanese state from a potential target of Western imperialism to a nascent imperialist power. But we can see the antecedents of that shift as early as 1876, when Japan imposed on Korea an unequal treaty based on Western models. In domestic policy we might break at 1896, with the implementation of a comprehensive civil code. That new legal code formalized the legal equality of all Japanese men, while at the same time establishing gender hierarchies based on samurai-style notions of the family. The code thus both finalized the abolition of the samurai as a distinct estate, while recasting the patriarchal samurai family as a Japanese national tradition. But the overall policy of dissolving the Tokugawa-era status system, while reproducing samurai norms, can be traced to the early years of the restoration. In the famous Charter Oath of 1868, the Meiji emperor declared that "all classes, high and low, shall unite in vigorously carrying out the administration of affairs of state," and that "the common people, no less than the civil and military officials, shall each be allowed to pursue his own calling." By 1876, the Meiji government had effectively dissolved the samurai estate, stripping samurai of their hereditary incomes and their key public emblem of status, the right to wear two

---

[7] Koschmann, Mito Ideology.

swords. Alternately, we might highlight the Meiji Constitution of 1889, which addressed both domestic and international concerns. Domestically, the constitution established an elected assembly, a key demand of the opposition for over a decade. Internationally, the constitution employed Western legal thought to establish the Meiji emperor as the leader of a constitutional monarchy, thereby consolidating the Meiji state's legitimacy.

This chapter ends the Meiji Restoration in September 1877, when the new Meiji government emerged triumphant from an eight-month civil war. That victory ensured that future challenges to the state would be civil rather than military. Key struggles remained, including the drafting of the constitution, the reform of civil law, and treaty revision. But the opposition would contest those issues through rallies, editorials, and elections rather than on the battlefield. After 1877, the Meiji government was no longer a turbulent, revolutionary regime, but a cohesive oligarchy shaping the emergence of a nation-state.

The Domestic Context

The domestic Tenpō crisis was an explosive manifestation of long-standing socioeconomic tensions. A rich and colorful testament to late Tokugawa-era domestic discontent is *An Account of What I Have Seen and Heard*, published in 1816 under the pseudonym Buyō Inshi. The author's true identity remains unknown, but internal evidence suggests that Buyō was an Edo-based samurai of lower or middling rank. Buyō described a decaying social and moral order. He lamented how "the four classes of warriors, farmers, artisans, and merchants, as well as all others, have lost their sense of trust and righteousness, turned toward superficiality, and become obsessed with luxury and greed." The growth of a market economy had eroded warrior virtue, since "those who have the instincts required of a warrior ... detest anything that smacks of greed or profits" and are thus "at a huge disadvantage in the world in which we live." The result was an upside-down world in which "townspeople, idlers and even farmers mock the warriors." Proper relations between men and women had been inverted as well, with wives acting "like masters" and husbands "like servants." Cuckoldry was widespread, but husbands themselves had precipitated this moral collapse by indulging their lusts with concubines and prostitutes. The world, in short, was a cesspool of depravity.[8]

---

[8] Teeuwen and Nakai, *Lust, Commerce, and Corruption*, esp. 42, 61, 73, 365–66.

Buyō was an especially dyspeptic and pessimistic critic, and we can read his condemnation of "luxury and greed" as evidence of a rising and prosperous consumer economy rather than a tragic decline of older ways. But many shared Buyō's concern that lived experience did not correspond to formal expectations, either moral or legal. People were not living in accordance with their hereditary or ascriptive status. The question, for both social critics and policymakers, was whether to restore old norms or to recognize social change and adjust norms accordingly. Much late Tokugawa discourse was nostalgic, looking back toward a pure society, unsullied by avarice and frenzied striving. Of course, as Paramore notes in this volume (Chapter 2), the government could indulge in public moral hectoring while adopting a more pragmatic agenda. Matsudaira Sadanobu's Kansei reforms publicly trumpeted Confucian rectitude but also included sotto voce engagements with new socioeconomic realities. Many domains actively promoted commodity production in order to increase revenue, and several prominent intellectuals, most notably those connected to the Kaitokudō academy, began to conceptualize robust consumer markets as a force to be managed rather than a moral failing to be corrected. Nonetheless, austerity was a recurrent theme in Tokugawa-era policy, and government decrees commonly sought to control consumption through regulation and exhortations to frugality. Whatever their economic impact, those edicts fostered an image of the realm's samurai rulers as arrogant, tiresome meddlers rather than stalwart military leaders. What, for example, was the logic behind Mizuno Tadakuni's edicts regulating the size of children's dolls and banning guides to sumo wrestling?[9]

The reluctance of Tokugawa-era officials to explicitly embrace a market economy is understandable. If the state recognized the centrality of commerce, how could it also justify the hereditary exclusion of commoners from public office? Instead, domains quietly created exemptions to the status system. As Maren Ehlers observes (Chapter 17, this volume), in Hikone domain, commoners with knowledge of rice marketing served as rural intendants (*daikan*), a position nominally reserved for samurai. Rather than openly violate status boundaries, the domain had the commoners dress as samurai while on duty, complete with the distinctive marker of samurai status, two swords. Status distinctions were maintained because those commoners were temporarily transformed into samurai. Domains also struggled to keep lower samurai from falling out of the status system. Many samurai houses fell into

---

[9] For popular perceptions of Mizuno's sumptuary reforms, see Stanley, *Stranger in the Shogun's City.*

genteel poverty due to a steady fall in rice prices over the Tokugawa era, rising living standards, compulsory "loans" to their lords, and poor household management. One of the boldest efforts to address samurai poverty came in Yonezawa domain, where the government promoted weaving by samurai households. That required an artful redefinition of samurai duties. According to domain decree, Yonezawa samurai had once shown their loyalty through courage in combat, but in the 1800s the daimyo of Yonezawa needed revenue more than martial valor. Hence, loyalty meant producing high-quality cloth through a domain-managed putting-out system. Yonezawa samurai were still samurai, but they now served with a loom rather than a sword. Yonezawa's policy was exceptional, the product of both a uniquely long and severe budget crisis and boldly reformist thinking.[10] Most Tokugawa-era reformers were, as in Hikone, content to tinker with the tensions between formal status and lived experience. But reforms such as samurai weaving in Yonezawa foreshadowed the radical changes of the Meiji era.

The Tokugawa shogunate's ambivalence toward commerce was perhaps most evident in commercial law, which was both highly developed and technically secret. In order to consistently adjudicate disputes in Osaka, the shogunate's magistrates compiled an extensive body of case law, effectively comprising a working legal code. Parties to lawsuits commonly retained pettifoggers, who advised them on both the details of litigations and strategies for potential out-of-court settlements. In some cases, these agents had long-standing relations with entire villages; they were the default representatives for residents of those villages who had legal issues in Osaka. But none of these innovations were publicly acknowledged. The Osaka civil and commercial codes were never published but merely circulated as private manuscripts marked "confidential." Criminal law was still more secretive. When a definitive collection of Edo criminal and administrative case law was published, the shogunate seized and destroyed the printing boards and punished the author with internal exile. Because the law was treated as a state secret, the government did not recognize pettifoggers as lawyers, but insisted that Japan's de facto attorneys were only couriers and bail bondsmen. Those agents could convey legal documents and accept responsibility for the appearance of an individual in court, but they were not officially authorized to provide legal advice or representation.[11] One key aspect of Meiji-era legal reform was

[10] Ravina, *Land and Lordship*, 71–114.
[11] Flaherty, *Public Law, Private Practice*; Takikawa, "Kujishi to kujiyado"; Takikawa, *Kujishi kujiyado*, 67–71, 99–175.

simply a new understanding of commercial law as public rather than private knowledge.

The comparative legal scholar James Wigmore highlighted that tension between public and private law in 1897, when discussing Japan's new Civil Code. He noted that the reforms were Japan's first modern comprehensive legal code and, as such, marked Japan's rise as a Western-style "civilized" nation. But looking at commercial activity, rather than commercial law, the code was less remarkable. Wigmore noted, with some hyperbole, that Tokugawa-era economic institutions included "the bank, the exchange, the insurance system, the brokerage contract, and the joint-stock corporation." Accordingly, he declared that "we have no cause to anticipate friction from putting into force a modern commercial Code in a nation which has for two centuries possessed nearly every leading institution and expedient therein regulated." While Wigmore overstated the parallels between Japanese and European economic institutions, he highlighted the critical distinction between the Tokugawa and Meiji polities. Tokugawa-era governments were loath to legitimize commerce through a formal legal code, so the most modern aspects of the economy were managed quietly through unpublished case law verdicts. The Meiji government, by contrast, saw the recognition of commerce as central to its economic power and legitimacy, and boldly declared its codification of new legal norms.[12] As with the abolition of the status system, the Meiji government publicly proclaimed what the Tokugawa system had struggled to conceal.

Economic growth and change also transformed samurai control over rural villages. Tokugawa-era governments treated most villages as largely self-governing, with local commoner elites representing the best interests of their villages to samurai authority. In the early Tokugawa era, those assumptions were idealistic but still plausible, since both wealthy and poor farmers were connected by common interests. Bad harvests tended to hurt all farmers growing similar crops, and with low labor mobility, wealthy local farmers needed poorer villagers as farm labor. But commercialization, and increased labor mobility, eroded those shared interests. Villagers increasingly consumed each other's crops as inputs in commodity production, using mulberry leaves, for example, to feed silkworms. A bumper crop of mulberry might force down prices, delighting those farmers raising silkworms but dismaying mulberry cultivators, especially those who had borrowed to buy fertilizer. Further, when wealthy villagers also served as creditors, bankruptcies represented

[12] Wigmore, "Administration of Justice in Japan."

opportunities rather than collective hardship. Farm labor moved gradually from intergenerational ties between families to short-term labor contracts. Increasingly, economic interests divided villages rather than united them, and commoner elites became the targets rather than the leaders of mass movements.

A similar process occurred in cities. As Ehlers observes (Chapter 17, this volume), the shogunate relied on structures of urban administration that assumed local self-governance: urban neighborhoods (chō) were run by local collectives with their own hierarchies and rules. In the early Tokugawa era, urban districts were often populated by homeowners with plots of similar size. But as early as the 1680s, powerful merchants began accumulating land, not through sale, but through loan defaults in which homes were pledged as collateral. As absentee landlords, those merchants then hired tenement managers, and by the 1850s Edo was run primarily by the agents of landlords rather than communities of homeowners. Thus, in both urban and rural areas, conventional forms of conflict resolution could not contain new social tensions. As a result, conflicts grew increasingly violent as protesters and rioters ransacked the homes and storehouses of the wealthy. Remarkably, even the most explosive Tokugawa-era riots resulted in little loss of life: protesters were more focused on leveling differences by destroying property and loan records than on vengeance through personal violence.

Broad dissatisfaction with the status quo also shaped religious attitudes. Buyō voiced the widely shared notion that Buddhist monks were decadent grifters who used donations to fulfill their own base and worldly desires. "The dharma is as sullied as mud ... it has turned into a Way for stealing from the people and damaging the state. If Śakyamuni were to appear in the world today ... he would punish the monks and put a stop to the whole of Buddhism."[13] It seems doubtful that Tokugawa-era Buddhism was uniquely corrupt, but the trope was pervasive in the 1800s, and many smaller Buddhist temples seemed to have lost congregants and struggled financially. In part, that decline was due to competition from the so-called New Religions of the 1800s, such as Tenrikyō, Kurozumikyō, and Konkōkyō. Those movements drew heavily on existing symbolism and rituals, and some New Religions were similar enough to later be incorporated into state Shinto. But their charismatic leadership offered both relief from social dislocation and a new vision of community. Across Japan they poached congregants from established Buddhist institutions.[14]

---

[13] Teeuwen and Nakai, *Lust, Commerce, and Corruption*, 160–61.
[14] Hardacre, "Conflict between Shugendō and the New Religions"; Hardacre, "Sources for the Study of Religion and Society"; Vesey, "Buddhist Clergy and Village Society."

Buddhism also suffered from the critique that it was a "foreign" religion and threat to local practice. Mito learning, in particular, treated Buddhism as a threat to Japanese society. In his influential treatise *New Theses* (*Shinron*, 1825), for example, the Mito scholar Aizawa Seishisai denounced Buddhism as "barbaric" and seditious. "When transformed by barbarism (*i*) from within," he lamented, "how can the body politic (*kokutai*) survive?" That fierce critique of Buddhism contrasted with Aizawa's embrace of Confucian thought, which he deemed fully consonant with the ways of the ancient Japanese gods. Like other Mito thinkers, Aizawa asserted that Japan had enjoyed virtuous imperial rule in ancient times, before the introduction of Confucian thought. Accordingly, some Mito thinkers criticized Confucianism as prolix and unnecessary, but they saved their fiercest invective for Buddhism.[15]

The most explosive manifestation of these myriad socioeconomic and ideological tensions came in 1837, in a rebellion led by Ōshio Heihachirō (1793–1837), a disillusioned samurai. Ōshio had served with distinction as an Osaka police constable but, despite his successful career, he resigned in 1830 to lead a private academy, where he focused on Ōyōmei (Wang Yangming) learning, a heterodox school of Confucianism. Ōyōmei learning combined a reverence for classical texts with an emphasis on the cultivation of innate virtue. Ōshio was a charismatic teacher, and his academy's students and disciples included both samurai and commoners. In 1836, Ōshio became angered by the government's failure to respond to the Tenpō famine. A harvest failure in northeastern Japan caused a surge in rice prices in Osaka, and the government's relief efforts were not enough to relieve widespread misery. Ōshio was particularly incensed that the government did not seize and distribute private stockpiles of grain. Convinced that he was acting on behalf of "heaven," Ōshio devised a plan to overthrow the shogunate, and on the twenty-ninth day of the second month of 1837 he led a small band to Osaka, where they attacked and looted private storehouses. After a day of sporadic street fighting, the rebels were routed and fled. Ōshio himself committed suicide rather than surrender to police. Ōshio's failed coup was hardly a revolutionary movement, but it shocked and humiliated the shogunate. Mounted officers sent to suppress the rebels were instead thrown to the ground when their horses were startled by gunfire. In the following months, at least two rebellions claimed Ōshio as their inspiration.

Ōshio's grievances against the shogunate resembled Buyō Inshi's lament. Rich merchants dissipated their ill-gotten wealth in brothels and teahouses.

---

[15] Quote adapted from Wakabayashi, *Anti-foreignism and Western Learning*, 166–67. For the original text, see Imai, Seya, and Bitō, *Mitogaku*, 66.

Daimyo abetted this decay by deferring to their merchant creditors as loyal retainers. "Even in the midst of the natural disasters and divine punishments of this age," the warrior elite was failing not only to serve as a moral exemplar but even to feed the poor and succor the needy. But, unlike Buyō, Ōshio felt compelled to take direct action. He planned to seize and distribute rice to the poor as the first step in a radical moral revitalization: "We shall rectify the trends in extravagance and debauchery in a thorough cleansing of the corrupt."[16] He imagined that his rebellion would start a millenarian transformation sanctified by the *kami*, including Amaterasu, and the Buddha. Ōshio's charismatic leadership and concern for the poor echoed the discontents of the New Religions, while his heterodox invocation of an ancient glorious age resembled Mito learning.

Ōshio's rebellion cut across class lines. As a constable, his intellectual circle was almost exclusively samurai, and even in rebellion, his samurai followers fought under a banner with his family crest. But the students at his academy included wealthy commoners, and he aspired to lead a mass uprising. His manifesto explicitly appealed to the poor, and he flew an additional rebel banner reading "save the people" (*kyūmin*) that drew hundreds of ordinary followers. While many of Ōshio's rebels were samurai, their weapons were those of a peasant rebellion: iron tools, guns, and torches rather than swords. Ōshio's rebellion did not efface class distinctions, but his uprising suggests that discontent with the shogunate, and the status quo more broadly, could generate collective action across class and status lines.

The threat of such a general rebellion, linking the top and the bottom of the formal status system, terrified contemporary observers. In any event, while Ōshio's rebellion inspired several smaller uprisings, it did not spark a revolution. On the contrary, the Tokugawa order lasted another two generations. But Ōshio's rebellion helps explain why the Meiji government faced so little resistance when it systematically dismantled the Tokugawa order. The samurai class had lost confidence in its own leadership and institutions. While few samurai shared Ōshio's revolutionary zeal to destroy the status system, they found it difficult to defend the status quo, especially in the face of a foreign crisis.

The International Context

While facing these domestic challenges, the Tokugawa system confronted a collapse of the East Asian international order. In the aftermath of Hideyoshi's disastrous invasion of Korea (1592–98), Japan enjoyed a remarkable period of

[16] Newmark, "Self-Made Outlier."

domestic and international peace from the early 1600s until the foreign crisis of the 1850s. This Pax Tokugawa was supported by diplomatic ingenuity. Diplomats skillfully evaded questions that might prompt a conflict between Edo, Seoul, and Beijing. Was the Japanese shogun the equal, superior, or inferior of the Korean king? What was the rank of the Japanese emperor vis-à-vis the Qing emperor? Early modern diplomatic practice kept the peace by ignoring these questions or by allowing different answers in Edo, Seoul, and Beijing. The most striking example was the Ryukyu entente. Between 1609 and 1872, the Ryukyu archipelago was simultaneously an independent kingdom, a tributary state of the Tokugawa shoguns, a tributary state of the daimyo of Satsuma, and a tributary state of Beijing, first under the Ming dynasty and later under the Qing. As detailed by Robert Hellyer (Chapter 5, this volume), Satsuma, with permission from the Tokugawa, invaded and conquered Ryukyu in 1609. But neither Satsuma nor the shogunate had reason to trumpet that victory in foreign capitals. On the contrary, the primary value of Ryukyu was as an entrepôt with China. As a tributary state, Ryukyu was allowed regular missions to the Chinese capital, and those missions provided Satsuma and the shogunate with indirect access to Chinese luxury goods. Insisting that China recognize Japanese sovereignty over Ryukyu would have had the perverse result of undermining the value of the conquest. Accordingly, Japan sought to conceal its conquest from China, even giving its agents in Ryukyu detailed instructions on how to hide from Chinese emissaries. Since Japan did not openly contest Chinese supremacy, the Qing court chose not to investigate rumors of Japanese control.[17]

Western imperialism shattered such carefully nurtured ententes with seemingly innocuous questions: Who was authorized to conclude treaties on behalf of Ryukyu? Was the Ryukyuan king an independent sovereign? Japan and China had managed stable and peaceful, albeit distant, relations precisely by avoiding those questions. By demanding Western-style treaties, the Western powers forced Japan to recast its claims to Ryukyu. Was Ryukyu culturally Japanese and therefore part of the Japanese nation-state? Or was Ryukyu culturally inferior to Japan and therefore in need of Japanese colonial protection? Or should Japan allow for an autonomous Ryukyuan state? Those varied options gave Japanese statesmen ample agency: they could choose to seize Ryukyu, acknowledge its independence, yield it to the Qing, or negotiate a partition. But they could not choose the status quo, the compromise that allowed Ryukyu to be simultaneously Chinese, Japanese, and independent.

[17] For a detailed and lively discussion of Japan and Ryukyu, see Hellyer, *Defining Engagement*.

Still more pointedly, Western demands for diplomatic relations forced the shogunate to clarify its relationship with the emperor. Was the shogun a unitary sovereign who could conclude treaties on behalf of Japan? Or was he a military vassal of the emperor whose decisions required imperial approval? In its relations with Korea, the shogunate had evaded those questions by referring to the shogun as the *taikun*, or "great lord," of Japan. That term, which entered modern English as "tycoon," dodged the nettlesome question of where the shogun stood in relation to the Korean king, the Qing emperor, and the Japanese emperor. That convention successfully kept the peace between Japan and Korea for over two centuries. But the Western powers saw such conventions as curious evasions of their most pressing question: Who was authorized to conclude treaties on behalf of Japan?

Western treaty demands similarly destabilized the relationship between the shogun and the daimyo. The early Tokugawa shoguns beat the daimyo into submission, extracting oaths of loyalty and degrading their autonomy and military potential. After the mid-1600s, in the absence of interstate conflict, the shogunate was disinclined to continue centralizing power or to maintain its own military. The shogun's power as military hegemon lay in his authority to command daimyo, who would, in turn, command their own forces. Western imperialism thus confronted the shogunate with an unappealing choice. Would it build a national military and challenge long-standing traditions of domain autonomy? Or would it encourage the domains to improve their own militaries, and hope that those forces would remain under indirect shogunal command? The magnitude of that challenge was compounded by shogunal indecision and inconsistency, making the regime appear both belligerent and weak. In its last years, the shogunate moved aggressively to dismantle old hierarchies in favor of a modern national army, but by that time, the southwestern domains of Satsuma and Chōshū were both aggrieved and powerful enough to ignore its commands.[18]

Western imperialism thus destroyed the East Asian international order with both overt aggression and ontological assumptions. The British military shattered the illusion of Qing hegemony when it defeated Chinese forces in the Opium Wars. The US Navy humiliated the shogunate when a heavily armed squadron, led by Commodore Matthew Perry, entered Edo Bay to demand a treaty in 1853. But Western diplomatic norms were toxic even absent military force because they required exclusivity and clarity where Tokugawa order had nurtured plurality and ambiguity. The Western powers had little patience for

---

[18] See Jaundrill's discussion in this volume (Chapter 12).

the interlocking power relations of the shogunate, the daimyo, and the imperial house. Their demand, backed by the specter of violence, for a single Japanese sovereign triggered the collapse of the Pax Tokugawa.

The collapse of the Tokugawa state system and the establishment of the new Meiji state were thus part of sweeping global changes in political norms that characterized the "long nineteenth century." The Meiji Restoration was the product of a world in which the nation-state was increasingly seen as the ideal, if not inevitable, political form: the normative expression of self-determination by "civilized" peoples. Both late-Tokugawa reforms and Meiji reforms aimed at creating a new Japanese polity that would be recognized as sovereign and legitimate in that emerging international order. Indeed, Japanese activists sometimes described their revolution as part of a broader global transformation: old empires (Qing, Ottoman, and Habsburg) were in collapse, while new nation-states (such as the United Kingdom and Germany) were creating new forms of empire. Meiji statesmen were transfixed by these new models of political power. How could the British crown turn ordinary peasants into trustworthy sailors and send them around the world with advanced weapons? How did Otto von Bismarck hammer diverse German lands into a single German state?

Meiji-era nation-building is sometimes described as "Westernization," but Japanese statesmen were highly selective in their emulation of Western models. The language of an East-West binary effaces how often Meiji leaders cited "Western" models as negative examples. They showed no interest in the Habsburg dual-monarchy or the Polish Sejm. They were unimpressed by the Italian Risorgimento, although Japanese populists would later discover Giuseppe Mazzini. Meiji statemen sought to emulate not "the West" but a select set of powerful and ascendant Western political practices. In particular, they were fascinated by the nation-state, a new species of polity, and its new form of empire.

The fading empires of the long nineteenth century were commonly stitched together by dynastic alliances, often the intermarriage of elite households. Those regimes relied on at least a modicum of ethnic pluralism, if only to allow, for example, Habsburg monarchs to rule through Hungarian, Czech, Polish, Slovak, and Italian intermediaries. By contrast, nation-states asserted an essential cultural identity between sovereign and subject, between ruler and ruled. However much, for example, Hungarians might differ from one another, they were, in theory if not in practice, bound together by common ties of culture, language, religion, and tradition. By extension, the Hungarian people could only be ruled by a sovereign (be it a monarch, president, or prime minister) who embraced their common history, language, and heritage. Because nationalist revolutions emphasized this cultural unity, they commonly attacked hereditary status, noble privilege, serfdom, and slavery. While national monarchs might advance the cause of national unity, other hereditary distinctions were understood as impediments.

Nineteenth-century nationalist discourse commonly spoke in two registers. On the one hand, it endorsed a capacious vision of the emancipation of "people" and focused on their "freedom" from conventional status distinctions. But nationalism also endorsed a narrower ethnic sense of "the people." That chauvinist voice meant that nationalism was toxic to multiethnic empires, dissolving them from within. How could a German-speaking Habsburg monarch claim authority over Italy? How could an ethnically Manchu Qing emperor be the sovereign of China? While destabilizing older empires, nationalism simultaneously created a new justification for imperial conquest: since some civilizations were deemed unready for self-determination, colonial conquest could be redefined as enlightened supervision. Described variously as "white man's burden" and "la mission civilisatrice," these new imperial projects established European domination over much of the world's population. Colonialism and national self-determination were thus complementary movements since "advanced" nations were obliged to establish stewardship over less developed parts of the world. In the lofty rhetoric of Western nineteenth- and twentieth-century world politics, all states were equal in their sovereign rights, and the international community comprised a "family of nations." Practically, during the late Tokugawa and Meiji eras, Western international practice reflected a three-part hierarchy. At the top was a small cadre of superpowers, self-appointed custodians of the emerging international order. Second was a group of lesser colonial powers and independent states. Most of the world fell into a third category, colonial and quasi-colonial states deemed unfit for self-rule.

The Meiji Restoration was a Japanese instance of this transnational order, both in its logic of national self-determination and its rhetoric of imperialism and colonialism. Accordingly, the Meiji Restoration generated both a discourse of national liberation and pretexts for Japan to subjugate its neighbors. Like their contemporaries, Japanese nationalist revolutionaries attacked hereditary privilege in the name of freedom and liberation. But national liberation required international belligerence. As an aspiring superpower, Japan needed to "liberate" its neighbors by subjugating them to its enlightened rule. While some interpretations of Meiji imperialism connect it to the invasion of China in the 1930s, it is essential to see Meiji foreign policy in the context of the late-nineteenth-century scramble for colonies. For example, when Japan attacked Taiwan in 1874, it employed Western colonial discourse and Western advisers in justifying the assault. Since Qing China had failed to stop aboriginals from killing shipwreck survivors on Taiwan's Pacific coast, Japan was obliged to bring order and civilization to that lawless frontier. Because Japanese imperialism was mimetic, much Japanese belligerence against China and Korea was lauded in the Western press.[19]

Crisis and Collapse: 1843–1868

In broad outline, the collapse of the shogunate was straightforward. Faced with a foreign policy crisis, the shogunate sought to enhance its own author-ity by invoking its status as an imperial servant. Rather than insist on its own supreme authority in foreign affairs, the shogunate claimed that it was sign-ing unpopular treaties on behalf of the emperor, vastly elevating the polit-ical authority of the imperial institution. Simultaneously, the shogunate encouraged the domains to modernize their armies and rewarded them with a greater voice in national affairs. Those policies backfired, unintentionally creating an anti-Tokugawa coalition. Powerful domains claimed as their own the enhanced imperial mandate and used it to overthrow the shogunate.

The actual political process, however, was vastly more intricate, compli-cated by succession disputes, marriage alliances, assassinations, and battle-field engagements. That turmoil makes institutional actors seem mercurial if not incoherent. We can say, for example, that Chōshū domain and Satsuma domain were sworn enemies as late as 1864, but then suddenly became allies, joining forces to topple the shogunate in 1868. But that alliance was possible only because a civil war had transformed Chōshū itself, crushing an estab-lished elite and bringing to power a faction of radical imperial loyalists. In a similar vein, Satsuma supported Tokugawa Yoshinobu in the 1858 shogu-nal succession dispute, but sought to destroy him when he actually became shogun in 1866. Satsuma policy changed because the daimyo Shimazu Nariakira died in 1859 and was succeeded by Shimazu Hisamitsu, his half-brother and bitter rival. Hisamitsu vacillated between employing his late half-brother's confidants and sending them into internal exile.[20] The impe-rial court itself was the site of coups and countercoups, followed by purges

---

[19] Eskildsen, "Of Civilization and Savages." See also Eskildsen, *Transforming Empire in Japan and East Asia.*

[20] Also, Hisamitsu was effectively the daimyo of Satsuma from 1859 until 1871, when he was technically regent to his half-brother's heir.

of the losing factions. And the throne itself was transformed when Emperor Kōmei died suddenly in early 1867 and was succeeded by his fifteen-year-old son Mutsuhito, the Meiji emperor.

The net effect of that turmoil was a steady weakening of the old guard across political institutions. Within the shogunate, the imperial court, and key domains, lower-ranking, marginalized figures displaced long-established elites. "Low-ranking" and "marginal" are, of course, relative terms. The courtier class itself was a tiny, hereditary, exclusive group, so the term "low-ranking courtier" is almost an oxymoron. But even within those rarified circles, lower-ranking officials eclipsed their higher-born rivals. The court noble Iwakura Tomomi, for example, emerged as the single most powerful courtier in the early Meiji era, eclipsing men from more prestigious houses, such as the Nijō, Sanjō, and Kujō. Among samurai, the Meiji leadership emerged overwhelmingly from men whose low rank would, a generation before, have excluded them from positions of power. That turnover within the old status system produced one of the paradoxes of the Meiji state: hereditary status was dissolved by the elites themselves. Across institutions, Meiji leaders were men who had, years before, chaffed against hereditary hierarchies.

Within that tumultuous environment, the shogunate swung between two conflicting approaches to national unity: autocratic demands for daimyo obedience and conciliatory invitations to daimyo cooperation. In broad outline, the shogunate confronted the daimyo in 1843 under its Tenpō reforms. From 1843 to 1858, it sought consensus. From 1858 to 1860, it again attempted authoritarian control. From 1860 to 1866, it veered again toward consensus. From 1866 to 1868, the last shogun, Tokugawa Yoshinobu, attempted to strengthen and centralize shogunal authority. This pattern of oscillation continued under the new Meiji government. From 1868 to 1871, the new government sought to implement reforms by working through the daimyo. Only in 1871 did the government move decisively to centralize control, dissolving the daimyo and claiming their political authority.

Britain's stunning defeat of the Qing in the First Opium War prompted a bold assertion of shogunal power. In 1843, the shogunal senior councillor Mizuno Tadakuni attempted both military modernization and a substantial expansion of Tokugawa revenue. His reforms addressed a core issue of the Tokugawa state system: How could the shogunate build a modern national military with the income of a regional lord? Mizuno ordered the creation of Japan's first modern artillery division and reorganized coastal defenses. He undertook a massive canal project, from Edo Bay to Inbanuma Lake, designed both to open new farmland and to make Edo less vulnerable to naval blockade.

To pay for these projects, Mizuno asserted direct shogunal control over three regions: the port of Niigata and two broad regions around Edo and Osaka. Displaced vassals would be compensated with cash or other lands, but Mizuno's intent was clear: more revenue for the shogunate. The transfers would also have allowed Mizuno to rationalize the defense of the capital. The areas around Edo and Osaka were controlled by hundreds of Tokugawa vassals who owed traditional military service. But Mizuno wanted modern artillery more than mounted lancers and wanted tax revenue more than ritual obligations of vassalage. His reforms foreshadowed attempts by the last shogun, Yoshinobu, to create a national military supported by a national fisc.

While the logic of Mizuno's reforms was clear, so was the determination of his opposition. Mizuno's fellow daimyo did not share his enthusiasm for reducing daimyo authority in order to strengthen the shogunate, and they lobbied furiously against the plan. Their objections were bolstered by a wave of commoner protests: farmers feared that the land transfer would result in new surveys, uncover unrecorded fields, and increase taxes. In the intercalary ninth month of 1843, less than four months after announcing the land transfer plan, Mizuno was forced out of the shogunal senior council, ending the shogunate's reform effort. Mizuno's fall from power left future shogunal leaders leery of confronting the daimyo. On the contrary, until 1858, shogunal leaders sought to address Japan's foreign crisis through cautious consensus.

That risk averse approach left the shogunate unprepared for its eventual foreign crisis. As early as 1849, the Dutch had warned that the United States planned to demand a trade treaty, and in late 1852, they explicitly described the impending arrival of a heavily armed squadron. The shogunal senior leadership chose to hope that the Dutch were wrong. As a result, when Commodore Perry entered Uraga Bay on 8 July 1853, the government scrambled frantically to respond. A Russian envoy, Admiral Putiatin, arrived in Nagasaki less than three months later and a British delegation the following year. Those challenges in Edo and Nagasaki were compounded by trouble at the periphery. Perry was considering Naha as a possible refueling and resupply station, and Russia was building fortifications on Sakhalin. The Tokugawa strategy of ill-defined borders as buffers, which had kept the peace for centuries, meant nothing to the Western powers or their policy of clearly delineated sovereign territories.

Facing a multilateral crisis, the shogunate redoubled its efforts at consensus. Breaking with the tradition of shogunal primacy in foreign policy, the shogunal leadership sought support from the daimyo and the imperial house. Abe Masahiro, the shogunal senior councillor, requested advice on treaty demands from the daimyo, relying in particular on the daimyo of Satsuma and Mito. The daimyo of Mito argued for war, convinced that samurai spirit could compensate for Japan's inferior technology. Other daimyo, however, were desperate to avoid a conflict. Much daimyo advice failed to recognize the magnitude of the foreign crisis, assuming that foreign demands could be chattered away. Overall, the consensus favored caution over war, so in 1854, Abe concluded a basic treaty with the United States, allowing for the resupply of US ships with "wood, water, provisions and coal, and other articles their necessities may require." But that quest for consensus compounded rather than resolved the crisis. Abe's strategy resolved the immediate challenge but created a new long-term problem: key daimyo now expected regular consultation on national affairs. When the powers promptly demanded more comprehensive trade agreements, Abe resigned, handing the foreign crisis to Hotta Masayoshi.

Hotta intensified Abe's quest for consensus. He sought imperial support for unpopular but seemingly inevitable concessions to the Western powers. The United States, for example, wanted trade and treaty ports, the exchange of diplomatic representatives, and extraterritoriality and freedom of religion for its citizens. But radical imperial loyalists viewed the practice of Christianity and the presence of foreigners as polluting the "land of the gods." In Hotta's mind, imperial sanction would insulate the shogunate from accusations that it was allowing "barbarians" to despoil Japan. Hotta understood his request as pro forma. He was confident that the imperial house would promptly accede since it had never denied a Tokugawa request for approval of a treaty. Of course, the Tokugawa had never before asked.

Hotta's request was a disastrous miscalculation. The imperial house refused to approve the treaty, and while the shogunate eventually compelled a public statement of support, the court leaked that its assent had been coerced. That dissent undermined the shogunate's claim of an imperial mandate and turned loyalist radicals into anti-shogunal activists. Where Abe had established a precedent for consultation with the daimyo on foreign affairs, Hotta added that the shogunate would also engage the imperial court. Those two missteps exacerbated tensions within the early modern order. The shogun was Japan's supreme military commander, responsible for national defense, but he lacked a national army and was now beholden to both the imperial house and the daimyo.

Why did Hotta miscalculate so badly? First, he failed to appreciate the influence of radical imperial loyalists and the xenophobia of the emperor himself. Insulated from practical concerns, the court could not appreciate how rejecting the treaties would lead to war with the imperialist powers. But a confounding factor was a succession dispute within the Tokugawa house itself. The twelfth shogun, Ieyoshi, died less than two weeks after Perry's departure, and his heir, Iesada, was childless and sickly. It was widely (and correctly) assumed that Iesada would not produce a son, so the Tokugawa house needed to arrange the adoption of an heir. One candidate, Tokugawa Yoshitomi, was supported by *fudai* daimyo, lords who traditionally staffed the shogunal administration. Yoshitomi was frail and sickly, but since the *fudai* wanted a pliant shogun, that infirmity was a virtue and, by genealogy, Yoshitomi was the better choice. The rival candidate, Tokugawa Yoshinobu, was understood as a break with convention. Yoshinobu was a more distant Tokugawa relative, but he had a reputation for intelligence and maturity. Most important, his candidacy became an emblem of national unity and out-reach beyond conventional power holders. As the son of the daimyo of Mito, a collateral Tokugawa line, his candidacy represented the shogunate's will-ingness to look beyond the *fudai* lords, and Yoshinobu's vigor and vitality, it was hoped, would represent Japanese determination in treaty negotiations.

Yoshinobu's allies advanced a plan that was both convoluted and ulti-mately counterproductive. They hoped that backing from the imperial house for Yoshinobu might counterbalance Yoshitomi's strong support from within the shogunate. Knowing that Hotta wanted imperial approval for foreign treaties, Yoshinobu's allies wanted imperial approval to be contingent on Yoshinobu's designation as heir. Many of Yoshinobu's supporters actually favored the trade treaties, if only as a stopgap measure while Japan reformed its military. But they argued that imperial approval should be tied to the appointment of a strong shogun. That elaborate plan backfired. The imperial court refused to support the treaties but also failed to support Yoshinobu.

The 1858 treaty-succession dispute was a Pyrrhic victory for anti-foreign imperial loyalists. The imperial court's unprecedented show of independence prompted a furious and punishing reprisal. After Hotta resigned in frustration and humiliation, his successor, Ii Naosuke, reasserted Tokugawa authority through a massive purge of courtiers, daimyo, shogunal officials, and ordinary samurai. Ii was especially incensed that Yoshinobu's supporters had brought the imperial court into a family matter of the Tokugawa house. Ii punished Tokugawa Yoshinobu himself with *kinshin*, restricting the would-be shogun to his residence and banning him from political activity. He levied similar sanctions on several of Yoshinobu's elite supporters, including the lords of Tosa, Uwajima, Fukui, Owari, and Sakura. Yoshinobu's father was punished with lifetime confinement to a single room. Ii also imprisoned, banished, or executed scores of less high-ranking samurai and ordered the imperial court to punish a dozen courtiers. Having silenced the opposition, Ii designated Yoshitomi as shogunal heir, and in late 1858 Yoshitomi became Tokugawa Iemochi, the fourteenth and penultimate Tokugawa shogun. Ii also signed a trade treaty with the United States, known as the Harris Treaty, and authorized similar trade treaties with other Western powers.

But while Ii was determined to reassert conventional shogunal authority, he lacked any broader vision for Japan. His most extensive and thoughtful writings were on the tea ceremony, not foreign or domestic policy. Furthermore, his purges prompted a determined response. On 24 March 1860, Ii was ambushed while riding in his palanquin in Edo. Amidst a swirling snowstorm, his assailants, primarily Mito samurai, killed him with a firearm, but then severed his head with a sword. Ii's assassination stunned the shogunate and inspired a wave of imperial loyalist violence, focused largely on Ii's allies within the imperial court. In addition to a looming foreign crisis, the shogunate also faced what we would now term endemic domestic terrorism.

Ii's death left the shogunate without a clear leader, and the council of elders returned to a policy of consensus, attempting to repair relations with Ii's enemies. Tokugawa Yoshinobu, loser in the 1858 succession dispute, was released from confinement and named guardian (kōken) to the shogun Iemochi, his former rival. The shogunate also employed the time-tested strategy of marriage politics, most notably the marriage of imperial princess Kazunomiya to the shogun Iemochi in 1862. But that strategy had the perverse consequence of infuriating rather than mollifying loyalist radicals.

The shogunate also sought to forge consensus by regularizing consultation with the daimyo through a formal council. Matsudaira Yoshinaga (also known as Shungaku, 1828–90), the lord of Fukui, was given the new title "minister of political affairs" (seiji sōsai), and several other daimyo were designated as "councillors" (san'yo). From 1864 those lords met in Kyoto with select court nobles to form a national council. Daimyo councils met until 1871 and comprised a continuity between late Tokugawa and early Meiji practice.[21] Matsudaira Yoshinaga himself held cabinet-level positions in the early Meiji government, and his writings from the early 1860s foreshadow several Meiji reforms. First, he recommended that the shogunate and the domains all establish bicameral parliaments based on the English and French models. The shogunal parliament would consist of shogunal retainers, daimyo, and high-ranking samurai, while the domanial parliaments would consist

---

[21] Ravina, *To Stand with the Nations of the World*, 104.

of local samurai as well as some farmers and townspeople. He noted that since weighty matters, such as government appointments, were debated in French and English parliaments, public debate would not undermine shogunal authority.

Second, Yoshinaga insisted that the shogunate show greater respect for the imperial court and give it greater financial support. But respect for the court did not preclude demanding reforms. For example, Yoshinaga recommended the forced laicization of imperial family members who had taken Buddhist vows.[22] That reflected not only a hostility toward Buddhism but a paradox within imperial loyalism: it venerated the abstract notion of the court much more than its people or practices. Yoshinaga's critique of the court thus foreshadowed Meiji reforms. While extolling the imperial court's ancient ways, Meiji reformers refashioned the Meiji emperor as a modern monarch who would rank with the monarchs of the Great Powers. That required changes in practices ranging from dress to public ceremonies to funeral rites. The Meiji emperor himself publicly criticized the court as fusty and hidebound. When Yoshinaga suggested that the imperial house abandon its ancient support of Buddhism, he presaged how the Meiji state would retool the emperor system to suit the needs of modern nationalism.

Despite these precursors to Meiji-era policies, the shogunate's attempts to forge consensus were largely a failure. Without clear leadership, the shogunate could not pursue internal reforms, and that undermined its ability to confront both domestic and international crises. The shogunate faced an immediate domestic challenge from imperial loyalists in Chōshū domain. In June and July 1863, Chōshū radicals shelled Western ships in the Straits of Shimonoseki, convinced that they were acting on an imperial command. The Western powers counterattacked, routed Chōshū forces, and destroyed their artillery. The shogunate disavowed Chōshū's actions, but Western notions of sovereignty required a shogunal response: if the shogunate was Japan's national government, it was responsible for the actions of Chōshū. Accordingly, the Western powers demanded that the shogunate pay a massive indemnity or make extensive concessions in trade treaty negotiations. Chōshū radicals intensified their challenge in August, when they staged an abortive coup in Kyoto. The coup failed and the fighting started fires that destroyed over 20,000 homes. That fiasco turned the imperial court against Chōshū.

With the assent of both the imperial court and a daimyo council, the shogunate began a military campaign to punish Chōshū, known as the First

---

[22] Matsudaira Shungaku Zenshū Hensan Iinkai, *Matsudaira Shungaku zenshū*, 2:93–100.

Chōshū Expedition. The army was a coalition force, commanded by the former daimyo of Owari (a Tokugawa collateral house), but with troops from twenty-one southwestern domains, including a large contingent from Satsuma. That combined shogunal army was roughly 150,000 men, and the prospect of a complete military rout changed politics within Chōshū. Conservatives took power from radical imperial loyalists and began a negotiated surrender to the Tokugawa. Chōshū delivered the severed heads of three officials deemed responsible for the failed coup in Kyoto. They expelled to Dazaifu a court official, Sanjō Sanetomi, who had sought refuge in Chōshū. They also agreed to deliver a handwritten apology from their daimyo and to raze the domain's major castle. Hard-liners within the shogunate had expected nothing less than the personal surrender of the daimyo himself in Edo, but commanders on site were convinced that they had fulfilled their mandate. Without military conflict, the expedition decamped late in the twelfth month of 1864.

The First Chōshū Expedition ended in shogunal victory, but the conflict had the perverse long-term consequence of strengthening anti-shogunal forces. The expedition prompted a civil war within Chōshū. Even as shogunal forces were demobilizing, Chōshū radicals insisted that the government had conceded too much, and they organized partisan battalions against their own domain leadership. During that civil war within Chōshū, imperial loyalist rebels took advantage of the anti-hierarchical aspects of imperial loyalism. Since all were equal beneath the emperor, all could fight on the emperor's behalf. In that spirit, the rebels began arming and mobilizing commoners and even *kawata*, an "unclean" status group. Such social leveling anticipated the conscript army of the Meiji era, but with important qualifications: Chōshū rebels wore distinctive uniforms, based on hereditary status distinctions, drilled in segregated military units, and the samurai remained an elite officer class, above the most talented and devoted commoner soldier. Nonetheless, when the rebels took control of their domain in early 1865, they had already abandoned a key aspect of the Tokugawa order: the samurai monopoly on military service. That new Chōshū government was battle-hardened and disinclined to comply with shogunal demands.

The recalcitrance of Chōshū's new government bedeviled the shogunate. How should the shogun deal with a domain that had surrendered, but then changed its mind? A charismatic shogun might have ignored the Chōshū problem as beneath the concern of a sage and merciful lord, whose most pressing concern was national defense. But under a feeble and dying shogun, the regime was acutely sensitive to Chōshū's provocations, and it began moving toward a second military campaign in order to compel Chōshū's overt submission.

That quest to subjugate Chōshū exposed a key vulnerability of Tokugawa rule. The shogunate's military supremacy was dependent on its ability to mobilize the domains against each other. But that ability was disappearing with astonishing rapidity. Particularly striking was the declining animosity between Satsuma and Chōshū. In early 1864, Saigō Takamori, the commander of Satsuma's forces, had envisioned a campaign against Chōshū as a chance to crush a domestic rival. Satsuma and Chōshū had, after all, been openly fighting for control of the Imperial Palace gates. But during the First Chōshū Expedition, Saigō helped negotiate Chōshū's surrender and then vocally opposed further sanctions. By 1866, Satsuma was lobbying the imperial court to forgive Chōshū and secretly helping Chōshū import Western weapons. Saigō's volte-face was triggered by a meeting with Katsu Kaishū, a dissident shogunal officer, who insisted that a punitive campaign against Chōshū was contrary to Japan's national interest. Protracted domestic discord, argued Katsu, could only help foreigners and the most retrograde elements in the shogunate. Won over by Katsu's arguments, Saigō became a vocal advocate for leniency vis-à-vis Chōshū.

The First Chōshū Expedition thus exacerbated rather than resolved the problem of Chōshū's defiance. By the summer of 1866, the shogunate had resolved to launch a second expedition, with the goal of enforcing a punitive surrender and ending Chōshū's insubordination. That Second Chōshū Expedition was a catastrophe. Long-standing shogunal allies such as Aizu domain sent troops, but Satsuma refused, and the expedition force was disorganized, dispirited, and poorly led. The shogunate's planned invasion of Chōshū resulted instead in a rout of expedition forces, with Chōshū invading the neighboring domains of Hiroshima and Kokura. The shogunate declared a cease-fire, using as a pretext the death of Shogun Iemochi on 29 August.

Iemochi's death prompted the ascension of Yoshinobu, loser of the 1858 succession dispute. Yoshinobu's status within the shogunate had been rising since 1860, and in early 1867 he formally became the fifteenth and last shogun. Yoshinobu began dismantling the basic structures of Tokugawa rule, transforming the shogunate into a modern, centralized state. He replaced the Tokugawa council of elders with a Western-style cabinet system. He began replacing hereditary stipends with a modern salary system. Most striking was Tokugawa military reform, where Yoshinobu requested 2,000 French officers to train a new shogunal army. While some of Yoshinobu's reforms resemble the frantic scrambling of a failing regime, they suggest, overall, a coherent plan for a modern state, inspired by Napoleonic France.

French support for the shogunate prompted a British response. Although both countries were technically neutral, Britain sought to counterbalance France by supporting anti-shogunal forces. It allowed a Scottish merchant to sell modern weapons to Satsuma, ignoring a formal arms embargo. The British legation's translator, Ernest Satow, was especially active, using an anonymous newspaper editorial to attack the "worn-out pretense of acknowledging the Tycoon [shogun] to be the sole ruler of Japan." In a meeting with Saigō Takamori, Satow actively encouraged swift action against the shogunate. Saigō thought that time favored an anti-shogunal Satsuma-Chōshū alliance, but Satow insisted that with French support the shogunate was growing stronger and that time favored Yoshinobu.[23]

This combination of official neutrality and effective partisanship continued during the Boshin War (January 1868–June 1869). Yoshinobu himself surrendered in April 1868 after a few pitched battles in the Kansai region. But the last stand of the old regime was a combination of shogunal officers and French advisers. They refused to surrender the shogunal fleet and escaped to Hokkaido, where they resisted until the following summer. Although Whitehall and Quai d'Orsay were formally neutral, there is no mistaking how Japan, like much of the world, was entangled in imperialist power struggles. Remarkably, within less than a decade, the Meiji state would learn the rhetoric of Western imperialism and embark on its own interventions against Korea.

The Creation of the Meiji State: 1868–1877

From 1868 until 1871, the nascent Meiji leadership was tentative and hesitant. Rather than strike decisively at Tokugawa sociopolitical structures, they continued late Tokugawa-style incremental reform. The state continued daimyo councils that resembled, in both spirit and form, late Tokugawa practice: they preserved existing hierarchies and accomplished little. As a group, the daimyo were distinctly unsuited to modern politics. They expected to be advised and flattered, not challenged in negotiations, and they were largely uninterested in practical solutions to daunting political challenges. In the caustic assessment of Ernest Satow, Japan's daimyo were "high-born dummies" whose intellect "was nearly always far below par."[24]

---

[23] Ravina, *To Stand with the Nations of the World*, 109–10.
[24] Satow, *Diplomat in Japan*, 38, 371–72.

The emerging Meiji leadership was well aware of the limitations of daimyo rule. Primarily samurai from the lower and middle ranks of their domains, they had chaffed against the rigid hierarchies of domain rule even as they benefited from their own legal superiority to commoners. But their willingness to challenge ascriptive status was balanced by a fear of seeming disloyal to their lords. Caught between those conflicting motivations, the oligarchy moved cautiously. In the summer of 1869, the government ordered the daimyo to surrender their investitures to the emperor, a symbolic move toward centralization. But the surrender was only symbolic, since the lords were promptly reappointed as domain governors (*chihanji*). Only in August 1871 did the Meiji oligarchy move decisively to dismantle the old regime. It abolished the domains themselves, replacing them with prefectures, and then moved rapidly to consolidate over 300 domains into seventy-six prefectures.[25] The rank of daimyo was dissolved, but the lords were given lofty titles in a new peerage and granted lavish retirement payments in the form of government bonds. A few lords, most notably Shimazu Hisamitsu in Satsuma, grumbled about their loss of privilege, but the vast majority were mollified by the combination of financial and ascriptive compensation. With the daimyo gone, the central government could confront the urgent task of creating powerful national institutions, such as a national tax system, a national military, and nationwide education.

The Meiji leadership embarked on that project of nation-building while effectively split in half. From November 1871 until the autumn of 1873, a "caretaker government" undertook domestic reform, while a massive diplomatic mission visited the United States and European countries with the goals of preparing to renegotiate the unequal treaties and exploring Western institutions and technologies. Having attacked the Tokugawa shogunate for acceding to unequal treaties, Meiji leaders were acutely aware of how the agreements could be used to delegitimize a regime. Rather than entrust the mission to mid-level officials, key members of the Meiji oligarchy left Japan for a tour of major world capitals. The mission is known as the Iwakura Mission for its highest-ranking member, the court noble Iwakura Tomomi, and included Ōkubo Toshimichi from Satsuma and Kido Kōin from Chōshū. The members began to return in the summer of 1873, but Iwakura himself did not arrive in Tokyo until September. The rejoining of the two halves of the government sparked a deep and profound crisis.

---

[25] Technically, seventy-two *ken*, three *fu* (Osaka, Kyoto, and Tokyo), and one *shi* for Hokkaido.

The caretaker government is sometimes described as "traditional," in contrast to the "modern" perspective of the Iwakura Mission. But that distinction is nonsensical. The "caretaker" government laid the foundations for the modern Japanese state. It began national military conscription, insisting that all Japanese men were equal in both their rights and duties. It began compulsory primary education and explicitly denounced gender and class differences in schooling. It began work on legal reform, translating the Napoleonic Code into Japanese. It began the practice of imperial tours, sending the emperor around the country as a symbol of unity and progress. It changed the calendar, abandoning a lunisolar calendar with "leap months" in favor of the Gregorian calendar. When the members of the Iwakura Mission returned, they denounced the caretaker government for its rashness and its radicalism, not its adherence to "tradition."

We can see the radicalism of the caretaker government in its educational reforms. In 1872, it announced universal primary education and declared the equality of men and women as part of a broad assault on conventional hierarchies. "People exert themselves and choose occupations and professions in accordance with their abilities. Since education is the means [*zaihon*, lit. "an asset"] for self-advancement, everyone should study, and should seek to discipline themselves, grow their wealth, and excel in their occupation." Accordingly, education henceforth would be treated as an individual obligation of all people, including "lords, samurai, farmers, artisans, merchants, and women," so that "no village should have an unlettered household, nor any household an unlettered member." The edict directly attacked gender roles as part of its attack on convention: "While higher education will depend on the ability of the student, parents should without fail educate young children without distinction between boys and girls." The caretaker government rejected education as a means of helping the individual to serve the state. That misconception was a "hoary and pernicious" conceit, promoted by samurai in order to justify their lives of "idle speculation and theorizing." The purpose of education, the government declared, was individual self-advancement, not service to the state.[26]

Underlying this boldly individualistic interpretation of education were budgetary concerns. The caretaker government declared its commitment to universal primary education without a plan for financing it, so it hoped to impose the costs on local governments and families. The insistence that "parents should without fail educate young children" was thus both an ideological manifesto and an appeal for funds.

---

[26] The policy was officially Dajōkan edict 214 (Gakusei: Dajōkanfukoku #214).

Despite that cynical motive, the radical egalitarianism of the edict was transformative and catalyzed popular challenges to gender conventions. Young women invoked the government's edict to study foreign languages, mathematics, science, and technology, often despite the opposition of their parents, who feared that an unconventional education would make them arrogant and unfit for marriage. Women also exploited the government's confused and contradictory sumptuary edicts to challenge gender norms on hairstyles and clothing. Wearing men's *hakama*, a blousy trouser, instead of women's kimono, young women could take longer steps, and their bold gait threatened gender conventions and alarmed traditionalists. In a 1907 interview, the Kyoto educator Atomi Kakei recalled how the behavior of Tokyo female students inspired her to found a school dedicated to proper norms and values: "They looked so impudent, walking about with pencils tucked behind their ears, carrying English-language books under their arms, instead of bundled in a wrapping cloth (*furoshiki*)." The tabloid press reported on this behavior with both horror and bemusement. The *Yūbin hōchi shinbun* wondered if women, having donned men's trousers, would soon start to urinate while standing. The *Chōya shinbun* reported that female students were visiting teahouses with their teachers and summoning geisha.[27]

Beneath these lurid tabloid reports was a pervasive concern that challenges to masculine privilege would weaken society. Subsequent educational edicts reversed the caretaker government's assault on gender hierarchies in favor of "traditional" Japanese values. In 1879, for example, the government explicitly repudiated how earlier reforms had emphasized practical skills and Western ways while neglecting the virtues of loyalty and filial piety. Henceforth, Japanese education would focus on the "unique spirit of our nation" and instill in students virtues such as the loyalty of subjects and the chaste obedience of wives. The government thus endorsed as essential Japanese values the Confucian hierarchies rejected seven years earlier by the caretaker government.[28]

The caretaker government was equally radical in other areas of statecraft. It announced conscription with the bold statement that the emergence of a hereditary warrior estate had been a tragic mistake. The Meiji government would address that misfortune by returning to the ancient practice of conscripting commoners while also adopting state-of-the-art weapons and tactics

---

[27] Copeland, "Fashioning the Feminine"; Nakajima, *Meien gakusei no jidai*, 86–87; Patessio, *Women and Public Life*, 33–48.
[28] Ravina, *To Stand with the Nations of the World*, 178; see also Dajōkan, edict 214.

from the West. The edict was explicit that all Japanese men were now equal in both their rights and duties, including the duty of repaying one's debt to the state in blood. In legal affairs, the justice minister, Etō Shinpei, sought the rapid creation of a new court system and a legal code based on the Napoleonic Code. His own assistants advised caution since they had not yet developed suitable translations for key French legal terms. But Etō was convinced that a public legal code, combined with swift and transparent court proceedings, would liberate the commercial energies of the Japanese people. Freed from the constraints of an opaque legal system, the Japanese people would propel Japan to wealth and power through their commercial dynamism.

The caretaker government was thus defined by the urgent and optimistic chaos of a revolutionary regime. Convinced that they were unleashing the boundless energies of the Japanese people, they treated caution as cowardice. They hoped to build a state by liberating a nation. That boldness proved especially dangerous in foreign policy. The caretaker government was determined to establish Japan immediately as a regional power, demanding recognition as an equal from Qing China and Chosŏn Korea. Those demands smashed the perduring peace of the Tokugawa era. In June 1873, for example, the Qing court received foreign minister Soejima Taneomi as part of a delegation of foreign envoys. That ceremony omitted, for the first time, the ritual kowtow, which for centuries had marked foreign nations as tributaries of the "central kingdom." At that event, Soejima strategically placed himself at the head of the Western envoys, aligning Japan with "modern" international law and against traditional East Asian diplomacy.

Emboldened by that success vis-à-vis Qing China, the caretaker government pushed for a confrontation with Korea. Relations between the Tokugawa and Yi dynasties had been limited but peaceful for over two centuries, and the Korean court saw no reason to indulge Japan's sudden adoption of "barbarian" practices. The Yi dynasty had refused to recognize the new Meiji government's representatives and even mocked their new Western-style uniforms. The caretaker government was incensed. Former samurai, eager to show their valor and prove their worth, agitated for war. Foreign ministry officials determined that an attack to avenge an insult to the sovereign was legitimate under Western international law.[29] The caretaker government resolved to send an envoy to Korea, Saigō Takamori, who pledged to win Korean recognition of the Meiji state or die trying.

---

[29] See Moriyama Shigeru's opinion in Dajōkan, "Sada Hokubō hoka futari kichōgo mikomi kenpaku."

The Iwakura Mission members, who began to return in the summer of 1873, were horrified at the caretaker government's rashness. Its domestic policies were a maelstrom of conflicting edicts, and its deficit spending was so large that the finance minister had stopped attending cabinet meetings in protest. But the plan to attack Korea was particularly urgent and alarming. What, the mission members asked, was the endgame? How would an attack on Korea advance Japanese interests? Had the caretaker government budgeted for a war? How would the government respond when Britain or Russia or China joined the conflict? Or had the caretaker government naïvely assumed that a Japan-Korea conflict would remain a tidy bilateral affair? The caretaker government dismissed these concerns, deriding as cowardice the Iwakura Mission's caution.

The Iwakura Mission's restraint was a product of their world tour. At the outset, the mission had been as rash and impatient as the caretaker government. In Washington, they had hoped to make immediate headway on treaty revision, but instead, through naïveté and ambition, managed only to antagonize their US counterparts. Chastised and disheartened, the mission shifted its emphasis from treaty revision to the exploration of Western institutions. In Britain, they were awestruck by the massive scale of modern industry: factories the size of small cities, consuming mountains of coal, supplied by seemingly endless miles of railroad. Britain was an appealing model for Japan: a rich island nation with a global empire. But building the infrastructure behind such an empire would take decades, not months or years. On the continent, they were dazzled by the new German empire. How had Bismarck turned a fractious gaggle of petty nobles into a rising continental empire, powerful enough to humiliate France in the Franco-Prussian War? Perhaps the key was Bismarck's realpolitik: fighting wars only after diplomatically isolating one's enemies. Both the British and the Prussian models suggested the need for a cautious approach to Korea. However grave the Yi dynasty's insult, Japan could not start a war of honor without careful planning and diplomacy.

After weeks of contentious meetings in late 1873, the members of the Iwakura Mission outmaneuvered their rivals and secured an imperial order canceling Saigō's mission to Korea. The caretaker government was incensed, and key members resigned, including Saigō Takamori, Itagaki Taisuke, and Etō Shinpei. In the wake of those resignations, Ōkubo emerged as the most powerful figure in Japanese politics, and he presided over the steady and cautious expansion of state power until his assassination in 1878. In contrast to the caretaker government's enthusiasm for popular energies, the Ōkubo administration assumed that the nascent Japanese nation needed firm guidance from a centralized state. The historian Banno Junji has described the Ōkubo administration as an early form of "developmental despotism," a government focused on the economic well-being of the people but much less mindful of their consent.[30]

One of the greatest accomplishments of the Ōkubo administration was land tax reform, which allowed the Meiji state to tax directly the Japanese people. Unlike Tokugawa-era taxes, which were based on harvest yields, the new land tax was based on the market value of the land and paid in cash, not kind. The government also ended traditional restrictions on the sale of land, thereby formally turning farmland into a capitalist commodity rather than a locus of duties and privileges. Despite fears of widespread resistance, the introduction of the new tax system in 1874 went smoothly, but there were massive protests in 1876 after a drop in rice prices raised the effective tax rate. With characteristic caution, the government suppressed the protests but moderated its policy, reducing the tax rate from 3 percent to 2.5 percent. That mixture of authoritarianism and restraint was a defining feature of the Ōkubo administration. Without acknowledging the legitimacy of popular dissent, it avoided using the full power of the state against rural protests.

The government was equally cautious when it implemented conscription, announced by the caretaker government but effected primarily under the Ōkubo administration. The government began conscription with exemptions that covered over 80 percent of draft-age males, although it still insisted that all men owed military service to the state. Exemptions included household heads, potential household heads, those with a brother in the military, upper-level students, and government officials. The government gradually curtailed those exemptions after the introduction of a national school curriculum helped create a more compliant populace. Only in 1889 did the government finally limit draft exemptions to disability or illness.[31]

The costs of the conscript army mandated the dissolution of Japan's hereditary warrior class. The caretaker government had approved the conversion of samurai stipends into bonds in 1872, but the policy was implemented only in 1876. In March of that year, the government stripped ex-samurai of their most visible hereditary power: the right to wear swords in public. Thereafter, swords were restricted to police and active-duty military officers. In August, the government declared the replacement of hereditary samurai stipends with government bonds. The conversion schedule was sharply progressive,

---

[30] Banno, *Mikan no Meiji ishin*, 166–69, 197–208. See also Banno, *Japan's Modern History*, 75.
[31] Ravina, *To Stand with the Nations of the World*, 180.

inflicting income reductions of over 75 percent on the wealthiest samurai, but only 2 percent cuts on the lowest tier.

As an administrative project, stipend conversion was a remarkable achievement for a new government. The Ōkubo administration floated a massive bond issue, backed by a British loan, without triggering financial turmoil or a spike in commodity prices. As a social project, the impact on individual samurai varied widely. The more samurai held firm to the conceit that commercial affairs were beneath their station, the more they were left adrift in an unfamiliar world. Period tabloids reveled in stories of haughty samurai brought low, forced by poverty into pulling rickshaws or selling their daughters into prostitution. But stipend conversion was an opportunity rather than a disaster for the many ex-samurai who had been quietly supplementing their meager incomes with by-employments such as weaving, lantern-making, and umbrella-making. Relying on their artisanal skills and commercial experience, those former samurai used bonds to turn by-employments into small businesses. The net effect was thus diverse. Former samurai became successful businessmen, violent anti-government activists, and quiet, genteel paupers.

The government contained resistance to its reforms through new censorship laws, with penalties of up to three years for the vague crime of "undermining obedience to national law." Those new laws reversed an earlier Meiji policy of encouraging public debate as part of enlightenment. Ironically, the Iwakura Mission members themselves had criticized the caretaker government in both the Japanese and foreign language presses, thereby stoking interest in the public contest of ideas.[32] But, having legitimized public dissent, the Ōkubo administration struggled to curtail it.

In foreign policy, as in domestic policy, the Ōkubo administration replaced revolutionary frenzy with deliberate statecraft. Eager to dissipate the fury of displaced samurai, in 1874 it staged a punitive raid against Taiwan, nominally in retaliation for the murder of shipwrecked Ryukyuans by Indigenous Taiwanese in 1871. The attack had two goals: gaining international recognition of Ryukyu as Japanese territory and, more ambitiously, staking a colonial claim to Taiwan. The government planned the raid with advice from Charles LeGendre, a former US army officer and diplomat, so it expected international support. When the United States and Britain denounced the raid, the Japanese government shifted rhetoric and insisted that the attack was merely

---

[32] See, for example, Kido's critique of the caretaker government: "Discourse of Kido, Councillor of State, after his Return to Japan," *Japan Weekly Mail*, 8 November 1873, in McLaren, "Japanese Government Documents." See also Ravina, *To Stand with the Nations of the World*, 177.

an investigatory mission. After narrowing its aims, the Ōkubo administration achieved a diplomatic victory. The Qing dynasty agreed to pay a large indemnity to Japan on behalf of the Ryukyuans, establishing the principle that the Ryukyu Islands were Japanese territory.[33]

The raid had the incidental effect of highlighting the virtues of military modernization. Tokugawa-era samurai, having rarely seen combat, focused on individual honor at the expense of good order and discipline. In Taiwan, those attitudes resulted in heavy losses to disease because soldiers considered malaria prophylaxis beneath their dignity. Samurai bravado also amplified the effectiveness of indigenous tactics because samurai who "bravely" broke formation were more easily ambushed.

On Japan's northern frontier with Russia, the Meiji government faced a similar challenge: transforming a buffer zone into a hard and exclusive demarcation. In 1875, Japan and Russia agreed to a clear international border, with Japan ceding Sakhalin in exchange for control of the Kuril Islands up to the Kamchatka Peninsula. That modern sense of borders required the relocation of hundreds of Sakhalin Ainu, since they were now assigned a new binary identity as either Japanese or Russian imperial subjects. In Hokkaido, the government changed the designation of Ainu, abandoning the Tokugawa-era term Ezo, which meant "barbarian," in favor of "former natives" (kyūdo-jin). Inspired by US models, the Ōkubo administration sought to "civilize" the Ainu by discouraging indigenous customs and encouraging sedentary agriculture.

On the continent, the Ōkubo administration continued to press Japanese claims against Korea, but with studied realpolitik rather than revolutionary passion. In September 1875, the government confronted Korea with a provocation carefully modeled on Western gunboat diplomacy. The Japanese navy invaded Korean coastal waters, drew fire from Korean shore batteries, staged a large retaliatory attack, and then claimed status as an aggrieved party. In the ensuing negotiations, Japan extracted major concessions from the Yi dynasty. The Treaty of Kanghwa (1876) declared that Korea "being an independent state enjoys the same sovereign rights as does Japan." That article had the effect of breaking conventional East Asian diplomacy, wherein Yi monarchs were technically vassal kings of the Chinese emperor. The treaty also reproduced a core tension of Western international law: all states were equal, but some more equal than others. Despite the "equality" of Japan and Korea,

---

[33] For a comprehensive survey of the Taiwan expedition, see Eskildsen, *Transforming Empire in Japan and East Asia*.

Japan received extraterritorial privileges in Korean treaty ports: Japanese subjects would be tried only in Japanese courts. The Ōkubo administration thus used Western international practice to begin Japan's encroachment on Korean sovereignty.[34]

Now in the opposition, members of the caretaker government catalyzed the growth of two overlapping movements: violent reaction by former samurai and calls for an elected assembly. Those movements appear, superficially, as polar opposites, united only by a shared antipathy for the Ōkubo administration. Indeed, like all revolutionary movements, the Meiji Restoration inspired unlikely alliances. For example, as justice minister in the caretaker government, Etō Shinpei had insisted on the rapid adoption of the Napoleonic Code, but in the Saga Rebellion of 1874 he joined forces with the xenophobic Patriot's Lament Party (Yūkokutō), who rejected the "foul ways of the barbarians." Like the ephemeral alliance a century later of Iranian communists and Islamic fundamentalists, that coalition was grounded in a common antagonist rather than a common goal. In the case of the Saga Rebellion, the government swiftly and decisively crushed the insurrection, and displayed Etō's severed head on a pike as a warning to other would-be rebels.[35]

At a deeper level, violent samurai reaction and petitions for democratic institutions were different tactics toward a common purpose: giving dissident former samurai a voice in the new Meiji state. Since a franchise limited to tax-paying, literate, adult men would have the effect of empowering most ex-samurai, calls for democratic institutions emerged from ex-samurai dissent. In January 1874, key members of the caretaker government (most notably Itagaki Taisuke, Etō Shinpei, and Soejima Taneomi) issued a public call for an elected national assembly. They attacked the Ōkubo administration for bringing the country to the brink of ruin by undermining the prestige of the throne and ignoring popular grievances. They rejected the idea that the Japanese people were not yet "enlightened" enough to enjoy democratic institutions, insisting that elections were a path to popular enlightenment. The language of the petition fused Western political thought, Confucian discourse, and the rhetoric of samurai honor. Those who have a duty to pay taxes, the petition insisted, also have a right to participate in government affairs, a paraphrase of European thought. But the petition also described the Ōkubo administration's autocracy as "closing paths of speech," a phrase rooted in Song dynasty Chinese discourse.

---

[34] For an overview, see Hamashita, "Tribute and Treaties," 17–50.
[35] Tsutsumi, *Chihō tōchi taisei.*

The petition's vision of suffrage was vague. Who, exactly, were "the people"? In many ways, the petition was similar to Matsudaira Yoshinaga's proposal for a bicameral legislature ten years before. But the 1874 petition was public, and it suggested to Japan's commoners that they could safely voice legitimate, principled dissent. Carefully and gradually, Japanese commoners began to declare publicly their expectations and grievances. By the early 1880s, demands for an elected national assembly became a genuine mass movement, the freedom and people's rights movement (*jiyū minken undō*), cutting across status and regional boundaries.[36]

The nascent democratic movement was also unsure whether "the people" included women. There were limited Tokugawa-era precedents for female suffrage, or more precisely, cases where status was more important than gender. In Tokugawa farm families, women sometimes succeeded as heads of households, especially in the case of widows with young children. In some villages, they could represent their families in village politics, so there are records of farm women voting in village elections.[37] In the 1870s, local political activists debated how to translate that practice into a new political language. Several localities decided that "no taxation without representation" applied to Japanese families, so female heads of household could indeed vote. But the central government's view of political power was more constrained. As the Meiji state expanded the franchise for men, starting with prefectural assemblies in 1879 and then with a national assembly in 1889, it simultaneously restricted localities from extending voting rights to women.[38]

The Meiji state also constrained female political power at the apex of the social order, insisting that only male descendants of the male line could ascend to the throne. That new "tradition" reflected Austro-German influence more than Japanese practice. In the Tokugawa era, for example, Empress Go-Sakuramachi reigned from 1762 to 1771 and later served as guardian for her young heir. Across social strata, the Meiji state fused the more patriarchal aspects of local and European traditions to make modern politics a male sphere.

Calls for a representative assembly and calls for armed rebellion remained entangled until the Satsuma Rebellion of 1877, the last episode of large-scale violent resistance by former samurai. Known in Japanese as the "War of the

---

[36] The petition is reproduced in de Bary, Gluck, and Tiedemann, *1600 to 2000*, 723–24. For an overview of the *jiyū minken undō*, see Kim, *Age of Visions and Arguments*.

[37] Walthall, "Life Cycle of Farm Women," 68–69.

[38] Anderson, *Place in Public*.

Southwest," the Satsuma Rebellion was in scale and scope more a civil war than a "rebellion": the Meiji government mobilized some 60,000 soldiers and sailors and nineteen warships to defeat a force of some 30,000 rebels. The state spent over forty million yen on the war, and covered the expense partly by printing unconvertible currency, which triggered widespread inflation. The fighting began in January, when rebels seized a government armory in the castle town of Kagoshima, and the tide turned decisively against the rebels in April, after the government broke their siege of Kumamoto Castle. But the rebels proved tenacious as a guerrilla force in the Kyushu mountains and were defeated only in late August.

The rebels were motivated by a range of grievances, most notably the compulsory conversion of samurai stipends to bonds and threats to Satsuma's autonomy. Beginning in 1871, the Meiji government steadily expanded national power by appointing non-natives as prefectural governors. But it allowed an exception for Satsuma, and governor Ōyama Tsunayoshi, a Satsuma native, had resisted and blunted central government reforms. The relative autonomy of Kagoshima Prefecture in the early Meiji era was a continuation of the unique status of Satsuma domain within the Tokugawa order. On the question of stipend conversion, however, the Meiji state would not tolerate Satsuma exceptionalism. The Meiji government was willing to placate Satsuma with a special stipend conversion schedule, but it would no longer allow the prefecture a local veto over national policies. The rebels were thus motivated by a defense of regional and hereditary privileges. But the rebellion also drew support from advocates of natural rights, such as a rebel band in Kumamoto who had studied Rousseau's *Social Contract*.

Japanese broadsheets (*nishikie*) captured this duality in their imaginative depictions of Saigō and his rebels. The prints commonly showed Saigō in a Western military uniform, but accompanied by followers in traditional samurai dress, armed with swords and spears. The prints also depicted a rebel banner with the slogan "a new government, rich in virtue." In actuality, such a banner never flew, but the invention reflects how, in the popular imagination, the rebellion contained both a vision of progress and a nostalgia for Confucian values. Editorials in the English-language press also reveal the two faces of the rebellion. The *Tokio Times* celebrated the rebels' defeat as a victory for national unity, comparing the Satsuma rebels to the Confederacy in the US Civil War: "widespread throughout the empire it is accepted and appreciated, as never before, that this is one country;—not a bundle of semi-sovereign and jealous powers, but a nation." But the *Japan Daily Herald* insisted that the scale of the rebellion represented an urgent and unmet demand for political inclusion, "an almost universal feeling throughout the country in favor of popular representation."[39]

The defeat of the Satsuma Rebellion marked a decisive end to military challenges to the Meiji state. The government would still face sporadic outbursts of violence. Indeed, Ōkubo himself died the following year at the hands of assassins who sought, in part, to avenge Saigō's death. That ended the Ōkubo administration per se, but not his vision of Japanese modernization led by the state rather than the nation. In 1881, the Meiji oligarchy forced out Ōkuma Shigenobu, who advocated a British-style constitutional monarchy with a strong parliament. Instead, the oligarchy focused on institutions that would acknowledge but constrain popular political action. The 1889 Japanese constitution came down from the state rather than up from the people and featured an elected assembly (the Diet) with only limited powers. Popular participation was further limited by institutions such as the Privy Council and the *genrō*, an unofficial council of senior political leaders. Those unelected bodies advised the emperor and determined his choice of prime minister. Even during the 1920s, the apex of prewar Japanese democracy, elections influenced but did not determine the formation of the government.

While that vision of a strong state constrained Japanese civil society, it also laid the foundation for Japan as a nascent world power. When observers described Japan as the "Britain of the East" in the early 1900s, they were commending its colonial empire and underlying economic and military prowess, not the nation's robust parliament or vibrant civil society. Japan had subjugated both Taiwan and Korea and won international recognition for those colonial conquests. In world politics, Japan's position in Korea was widely accepted as parallel to France in Vietnam, Britain in India, and the United States in the Philippines. That recognition suggested that Japan had transformed modern imperialism, making it global rather than Western. Perhaps the Great Powers club would admit a non-white, non-Christian member. But others saw Japan's empire as a rebuttal to, rather than an emulation of, Western imperialism. The Japanese philosopher-adventurer Miyazaki Tōten, the African American scholar-activist W. E. B. DuBois, and the Vietnamese nationalist Phan Bội Châu all celebrated Japanese military victories and saw Japan's empire as potentially liberatory. That tension between Japanese emulation and rejection of Western models, including imperialism, emerged from a duality inherent in the Meiji Restoration.

---

[39] Ravina, *To Stand with the Nations of the World*, 196–97.

Bibliography

Anderson, Marnie S. *A Place in Public: Women's Rights in Meiji Japan.* Cambridge, MA: Harvard University Asia Center, 2010.

Baker, Keith Michael. "Transformations of Classical Republicanism in Eighteenth-Century France." *Journal of Modern History* 73, no. 1 (2001): 32–53.

Banno, Junji. *Japan's Modern History, 1857–1937: A New Political Narrative.* Translated by J. A. A. Stockwin. London: Routledge, 2014.

   Mikan no Meiji ishin. Chikuma Shobō, 2007.

Copeland, Rebecca. "Fashioning the Feminine: Images of the Modern Girl Student in Meiji Japan." *US-Japan Women's Journal* 30/31 (2006): 13–35.

Dajōkan. Edict 214. www.mext.go.jp/b_menu/hakusho/html/others/detail/1317943.htm

   "Sada Hokubō hoka futari kichōgo mikomi kenpaku." *Kōbunroku,* honkan-2A-009-00, kō 01697100, kenmei bango 019, National Archives of Japan.

de Bary, William Theodore, Carol Gluck, and Arthur Tiedemann, eds. *1600 to 2000.* Vol. 2 of *Sources of Japanese Tradition,* 2nd ed. New York: Columbia University Press, 2005.

Eskildsen, Robert. "Of Civilization and Savages: The Mimetic Imperialism of Japan's 1874 Expedition to Taiwan." *American Historical Review* 107, no. 2 (2002): 388–418.

   Transforming Empire in Japan and East Asia: The Taiwan Expedition and the Birth of Japanese Imperialism. Singapore: Springer Singapore, 2019.

Flaherty, Darryl E. *Public Law, Private Practice: Politics, Profit, and the Legal Profession in Nineteenth-Century Japan.* Cambridge, MA: Harvard University Asia Center, 2013.

Hamashita, Takeshi. "Tribute and Treaties: Maritime Asia and Treaty Port Networks in the Era of Negotiation, 1800–1900." In *The Resurgence of East Asia: 500, 150 and 50 Year Perspectives,* edited by Giovanni Arrighi, Takeshi Hamashita, and Mark Selden, 17–50. London: Routledge, 2003.

Hardacre, Helen. "Conflict between Shugendō and the New Religions of Bakumatsu Japan." *Japanese Journal of Religious Studies* 21, no. 2/3 (1994): 137–66.

   "Sources for the Study of Religion and Society in the Late Edo Period." *Japanese Journal of Religious Studies* 28, no. 3/4 (2001): 227–60.

Hellyer, Robert. *Defining Engagement: Japan and Global Contexts, 1640–1868.* Cambridge, MA: Harvard University Press, 2009.

Imai Usaburō, Seya Yoshihiko, and Bitō Masahide, eds. *Mitogaku.* Vol. 53 of *Nihon shisō taikei.* Iwanami Shoten, 1973.

Ishii Ryōsuke, ed. *Tokugawa kinreikō.* 11 vols. Sōbunsha, 1959–61.

Jannetta, Ann Bowman. "Famine Mortality in Nineteenth-Century Japan: The Evidence from a Temple Death Register." *Population Studies* 46, no. 3 (1992): 427–43.

Kennedy, Katharine D. "Regionalism and Nationalism in South German History Lessons, 1871–1914." *German Studies Review* 12, no. 1 (1989): 11–33.

Kim, Kyu Hyun. *The Age of Visions and Arguments: Parliamentarianism and the National Public Sphere in Early Meiji Japan.* Cambridge, MA: Harvard University Asia Center, 2007.

Koschmann, J. Victor. *The Mito Ideology: Discourse, Reform, and Insurrection in Late Tokugawa Japan, 1790–1864.* Berkeley: University of California Press, 1987.

Matsudaira Shungaku Zenshū Hensan Iinkai, ed. *Matsudaira Shungaku zenshū.* 4 vols. Hara Shobō, 1973.

McLaren, Walter Wallace. "Japanese Government Documents." *Transactions of the Asiatic Society of Japan* 42, pt. 1 (1914): 567–77.

Nakajima Masukichi. *Meien gakusei no jidai*. Yomiuri Shinbunsha, 1907.

Newmark, Jeffrey. "A Self-Made Outlier in the Tokugawa Public Sphere: Ōshio Heihachirō and His 1837 Osaka Riot." In *Religion, Culture, and the Public Sphere in China and Japan*, edited by Albert Welter and Jeffrey Newmark, 115–43. Singapore: Palgrave Macmillan, 2017.

Patessio, Mara. *Women and Public Life in Early Meiji Japan: The Development of the Feminist Movement*. Ann Arbor: Center for Japanese Studies, University of Michigan, 2011.

Ravina, Mark. *Land and Lordship in Early Modern Japan*. Stanford, CA: Stanford University Press, 1999.

To Stand with the Nations of the World: Japan's Meiji Restoration in World History. New York: Oxford University Press, 2017.

Satow, Ernest Mason. *A Diplomat in Japan*. Philadelphia: Lippincott, 1921.

Shalev, Eran. *Rome Reborn on Western Shores: Historical Imagination and the Creation of the American Republic*. Charlottesville: University of Virginia Press, 2009.

Stanley, Amy. *Stranger in the Shogun's City: A Japanese Woman and Her World*. New York: Scribner, 2020.

Takikawa Masajirō. *Kujishi kujiyado no kenkyū*. Akasaka Shoin, 1984.

"Kujishi to kujiyado." *Jiyū to seigi* 2 (1951): 12–17.

Tebbe, Jason. "'Revision' and 'Rebirth': Commemoration of the Battle of Nations in Leipzig." *German Studies Review* 33, no. 3 (2010): 618–40.

Teeuwen, Mark. "Clashing Models: Ritual Unity vs Religious Diversity." *Japan Review* 30 (2017): 39–62.

Teeuwen, Mark, and Kate Wildman Nakai, eds. *Lust, Commerce, and Corruption: An Account of What I Have Seen and Heard by an Edo Samurai*. Translated by Mark Teeuwen, Kate Wildman Nakai, Miyazaki Fumiko, Anne Walthall, and John Breen. New York: Columbia University Press, 2014.

Thal, Sarah. "Redefining the Gods: Politics and Survival in the Creation of Modern Kami." *Japanese Journal of Religious Studies* 29, no. 3/4 (2002): 379–404.

Tsutsumi Keijirō. *Chihō tōchi taisei no keisei to shizoku hanran*. Fukuoka: Kyūshū Daigaku Shuppankai, 2010.

Vesey, Alexander M. "The Buddhist Clergy and Village Society in Early Modern Japan." PhD diss., Princeton University, 2003.

Wakabayashi, Bob Tadashi. *Anti-foreignism and Western Learning in Early-Modern Japan: The New Theses of 1825*. Cambridge, MA: Council on East Asian Studies, Harvard University, 1986.

Walthall, Anne. "The Life Cycle of Farm Women in Tokugawa Japan." In *Recreating Japanese Women, 1600–1945*, edited by Gail Lee Bernstein, 42–70. Berkeley: University of California Press, 1991.

The Weak Body of a Useless Woman: Matsuo Taseko and the Meiji Restoration. Chicago: University of Chicago Press, 1998.

Wigmore, John H. "The Administration of Justice in Japan." *American Law Register and Review* 45, no. 10 (1897): 628–41.

PART II

*

ECONOMY, ENVIRONMENT, AND TECHNOLOGY

7

International Economy and Japan at the Dawn of the Early Modern Era

ADAM CLULOW

On 25 February 1630, a Dutch East India Company (VOC) official, Willem Janssen, sailed into the port city of Nagasaki.[1] The sprawling harbor was bustling with activity as mariners unloaded goods and small flat-bottomed craft raced between ship and shore. As his vessel slipped into Nagasaki's sheltered waters, Janssen spotted a junk preparing to leave. It carried three ambassadors from Ayutthaya, a powerful polity located in modern-day Thailand. They had recently returned from Edo where they had presented a letter from their royal master assuring the shogun that he would treat Japanese merchants arriving in his territory as his own subjects.[2] Drawing closer to shore, Janssen noted two vermilion-seal trading ships, or *shuinsen*. These were vessels that sailed under the protection of Tokugawa-issued maritime licenses, but which were crewed by a mix of domestic and foreign mariners. The first was owned by a Japanese merchant but had been chartered by a Chinese trader and was heading for Vietnam under the supervision of a Dutch pilot, Vincent Romeijn. The second carried an ambassador from Cochinchina, who had been sent to make contact with the shogun and thereby open up trading links with Japan. This mission had ended in failure, however, and the ambassador was preparing to return home with his gifts undelivered and his letters unread.

As Janssen gazed out across the harbor, his eyes settled on a collection of five Portuguese galliots that were moored in the still waters. Nagasaki was famous as a terminus for Portuguese shipping, which sailed along the rich trading route from Macao to Japan, but rather than taking on goods, these ships were surrounded by guards, their sails lowered and their decks

---

[1] Copie van het journaal van de zending van Willem Jansz. naar Nagasaki, gehouden door Coenraedt Cramer, 1630 februari 23- 1630 maart, Nationaal Archief, Den Haag, Collectie Sweers, nummer toegang 1.10.78, inventarisnummer 5.

[2] Hayashi, *Tsūkō ichiran*, 7:10. For an English translation of this letter, see Satow, "Notes on the Intercourse between Japan and Siam."

conspicuously empty of activity. They had remained in this state since 1628 when an embargo had been placed on Portuguese trade by Tokugawa officials, imprisoning these vessels within the harbor. As Janssen approached the waterfront, he could make out one last vessel. It was a forlorn sight, pulled up to the docks, its masts, sails, and guns stripped out, its hull rotting in the fetid water with no flag or other markings to be seen.[3] This ship, the *Erasmus*, belonged to Janssen's employer, the VOC. It had been seized years earlier as part of a second embargo initiated in response to a violent confrontation between Dutch officials on Taiwan and Japanese *shuinsen* merchants. The *Erasmus* was also the reason for Janssen's visit. He had been dispatched by his superiors in Batavia to secure the release of the vessel and to reopen trading relations with Japan.

Janssen's account of Nagasaki harbor in February 1630 reveals a surprising amount about the nature of Japan's place in wider circuits of trade at the dawn of the early modern era. Most obviously, he described what was clearly a global trading hub. Starting in the sixteenth century, Japan, and especially Kyushu, experienced a surge of maritime exchange that had reshaped ports such as Nagasaki into strikingly cosmopolitan centers.[4] By 1630, when Janssen arrived in Nagasaki, Japan was bound tight to a vast maritime network that for the first time encompassed the entire globe, connecting every inhabited continent. While the open ocean remained a dangerous space filled with hazards, developments in maritime technology had made it possible to dispatch a vessel to trade thousands of miles away and expect that it would return safely.[5] And as the collection of Asian and European vessels assembled in Nagasaki showed, Japan's trade had assumed what can only be described as a "worldwide scale."[6]

Nagasaki was crowded with foreign vessels, ambassadors, and merchants because the archipelago's ports and cities offered a lucrative opportunity for profit. While a vast range of goods were traded, Japan's position in global networks was underpinned by the silver-for-silk exchange – Chinese raw silk and silk goods for Japanese silver – that acted as a powerful magnet drawing in foreign merchants. Rapid developments in mining technology had enabled Japan to emerge alongside Spain's American colonies as one of the two great producers of silver. This increase in silver production was accompanied by an

---

[3] Copie van het journal van de zending van Willem Jansz. naar Nagasaki, 238.
[4] For two excellent overviews of maritime East Asia, see Haneda and Oka, *Maritime History*, and Gunn, *World Trade Systems*.
[5] Reid, *Southeast Asia in the Early Modern Era*, 1.
[6] Iwao, "Japanese Foreign Trade," 1.

insatiable appetite for silk as the Japanese economy expanded after a century of endemic conflict during the Sengoku period.

Janssen's description of the two *shuinsen* preparing for departure highlights the importance of Asian merchants in connecting Japan up to wider circuits of trade. The century from roughly 1540 to 1640 saw the tumultuous opening encounter between Europe and Japan, as first Portuguese, then Spanish, Dutch, and finally English trading vessels arrived in Japanese ports. But while this interaction was both dramatic and copiously documented, Europeans were often less important than they seemed. Although there were periods of intense profitability brought about by favorable political conditions, the story of the European encounter with Japan is filled with false starts, setbacks, and aborted dreams. Arguably the most successful maritime enterprise to arrive in Japanese harbors was not the Portuguese Estado da India, which established the first European empire in early modern Asia, or the VOC, long praised as the world's first multinational corporation, but the Zheng maritime network. At its peak, the Zheng network, which successfully ejected the VOC from its "beautiful colony" on Taiwan, sent dozens of trading vessels to Nagasaki each year.[7]

Finally, Janssen's account of impounded vessels and rotting goods showed just how determined Tokugawa officials in Nagasaki and Edo were to manage international engagement, even if it meant suspending flourishing trade routes. While attention has traditionally focused on the maritime restriction edicts of the 1630s, long mischaracterized as part of a drive toward total isolation, the Tokugawa regime had in fact worked consistently to organize and control foreign trade. The goal was not only to ensure a steady flow of goods into Japanese markets but also to safeguard the elaborate domestic political architecture that had been constructed in the aftermath of the Battle of Sekigahara in 1600. What emerged was a policy of active but channeled engagement that gave rise to the *shuinsen* system itself, the twin embargoes of Portuguese and Dutch shipping that Janssen witnessed, and also the maritime restriction edicts of the 1630s. At the same time, the regime worked to cut ties with any group that it saw as a potential threat or which might inadvertently drag Japan into conflict overseas. The goal was not to close Japan off but rather to construct a framework for "orderly relations" that worked to buttress the Tokugawa system.[8]

---

[7] Blussé, "VOC as Sorcerer's Apprentice," 90.
[8] Cullen, "Nagasaki Trade," 71. In his influential study of Tokugawa foreign relations, Ronald Toby describes a "positive, constructive" policy that "sought actively to reconstitute Japanese relations with the international environment in ways that advanced both international and domestic goals." Toby, *State and Diplomacy*, xvi.

This chapter considers the wave of globalization that broke upon Japanese shores in the sixteenth century and which accounts for the crowded harbor that Janssen described in his diary. It was not the first time the archipelago had experienced a period of heightened interaction, but this phase saw a break from the traditional confines of East Asian diplomacy as Japanese leaders made contact with a range of distant states and colonies.[9] This chapter aims to situate Japan within global networks of trade by exploring the underlying commercial dynamic that drove engagement and the crowded commercial landscape that emerged as a result. The focus is, first, on successive challengers – the Portuguese, *shuinsen* merchants, the Dutch, the English, and the Chinese – all of whom attempted to tap into the lucrative silver-for-silk exchange; and, second, on Tokugawa attempts to channel trade through sanctioned pathways while cutting links with any group that might inject volatility into a precariously balanced system. This attempt to control and regulate overseas interactions led directly to trade embargoes and eventually to the shutting down of the *shuinsen* system. It also underpinned wider Tokugawa attitudes toward its subjects operating overseas. The chapter concludes by examining the Zheng maritime organization, which emerged to challenge the VOC for control over trade routes in East and Southeast Asia.

Silver for Silk

Two basic facts burned themselves on the minds of enterprising merchants approaching the archipelago in the sixteenth century: Japan boasted a prolific supply of cheap silver and a huge appetite for Chinese raw silk. The archipelago was home to rich silver mines, which disgorged significant quantities of precious metals into the region at a time in which demand was artificially inflated. The "land of Japan yields," one observer explained, "every sort of metal … [but the] principal mines are those of silver and may be found throughout the country."[10] Mining booms were nothing new in Japanese history. In the seventh and eighth centuries, there had been an earlier mining boom as the archipelago had entered a new political era characterized by the emergence of strong imperial courts.[11] By contrast, the sixteenth century

---

[9] Mark Ravina identifies three "waves of intense international engagement," including an earlier phase in the seventh and eighth centuries and a later one in the nineteenth century. Ravina, *To Stand with the Nations of the World*, 18–25. See also Batten, *To the Ends of Japan*, 147–52.

[10] Cooper, *João Rodrigues's Account*, 104.

[11] Nagase-Reimer, "Water Drainage," 25.

iteration was defined not by a strengthening but by a collapse of central authority as individual daimyo competed ruthlessly for any advantage in the conflicts that sprawled across the archipelago.[12] Precious metals, especially silver, offered a way to finance protracted conflict, to pay for armies, and to underwrite the construction of massive fortresses capable of resisting assault. The result was to propel a rapid sequence of interlocking innovations that combined to increase production.[13]

Not surprisingly, control of the most prolific mines became an important barometer for daimyo as they vied to expand territory and influence.[14] The Iwami silver mine, which featured prominently on European maps of Japan in this period, propped up the Ōuchi family. They used its riches to build up a gleaming capital in Yamaguchi, which came to rival a crumbling Kyoto.[15] As the Sengoku period ebbed, such mines became a key target for the unification regimes. Hideyoshi's vast military campaigns were paid for in gold and silver, and he worked to gain control of key mines, including the Sado gold and Iwami silver mines.[16] Ieyasu went further, drawing mines scattered across the archipelago under Tokugawa control and issuing detailed regulations governing their operation.[17] The result was a flood of silver pouring out of Japanese mines that effectively financed the process of political consolidation. A significant share of this wealth found its way into the vast treasury amassed by the Tokugawa. In 1609, a visitor to the shogun's court noted in wonder that there were "83 million taels ... of silver alone" in Ieyasu's "hoard."[18] Still more passed through Japanese ports with an estimated 200 tons of silver per year exported in the first decades of the seventeenth century.[19]

Silver was bound to silk, with some estimates suggesting that silk accounted for as much as 70 percent of imports into the archipelago.[20] There was a huge appetite not only for raw silk, which could be processed by weavers inside Japan, but also for silk piece goods.[21] The pace of silk imports jumped dramatically in the early seventeenth century, doubling and then tripling. The

[12] Kobata, "Production and Uses of Gold and Silver," 245. This period also saw the opening of prolific gold mines.
[13] Nagase-Reimer, "Water Drainage," 26. Nagahara and Yamamura, "Shaping the Process of Unification," 80.
[14] Walker, *Toxic Archipelago*, 75.
[15] Conlan, "Failed Attempt."
[16] Kobata, "Production and Uses of Gold and Silver," 257; Asao, "Sixteenth-Century Unification," 61; Iwao, *Sakoku*, 177.
[17] Hellyer, *Defining Engagement*, 34; Laver, *Japan's Economy by Proxy*, 98–99.
[18] Cooper, *João Rodrigues's Account*, 105.
[19] Flynn and Giráldez, "Born with a 'Silver Spoon,'" 201–21.
[20] Cullen, "Nagasaki Trade," 70.
[21] Gunn, *World Trade Systems*, 80.

impact was obvious to foreign visitors who noted that "trade has so increased that the whole nation wears silk robes; even peasants and their wives have silk sashes, and the better-off among them have silken robes."[22]

Japan's silver-for-silk exchange was part of a global silver boom. Dennis Flynn and Arturo Giráldez argue that the "entire world economy was entangled in a global silver web" in this period, creating the first true age of globalization.[23] The engine of this global dynamic was unprecedented Chinese demand for silver. The collapse of the paper currency system and the adoption of the single-whip tax reform in the 1570s sparked a process of "silverization" that pushed up the price of silver in China.[24] Such intense demand coincided with new points of supply originating from two very different parts of the globe. The first was the silver mines of Potosí, located high in the Andes mountains in modern-day Bolivia, in 1545. From there, silver was brought to Acapulco and then transported aboard lumbering galleons to the Spanish colony at Manila. Once in the Philippines, it was injected into the Chinese economy via the dozens of private junks that arrived to trade every year. The second point of supply was Japanese mines, which produced roughly half the volume of the silver flowing out of the Spanish Americas.[25] The fact that Potosí and the silver mines dotted across Japan were part of a wider commodity boom was clear to observers. Tokugawa Ieyasu requested fifty miners from New Spain whose techniques and technologies might, he believed, serve to increase production at key Japanese mines.[26]

In East Asia, the key commercial struggle across this period centered on which group could secure the key role of middleman, that is by becoming the conduit connecting expanding Japanese supplies of silver with unprecedented Chinese demand. The first to do so over an extended period of time were the Portuguese, who took advantage of a political vacuum to claim a significant share of the silver-for-silk exchange.

Macao and Nagasaki

In the sixteenth century, official relations between China and Japan broke down. The *wakō*, the multiethnic pirate-merchants discussed in Peter Shapinsky's chapter in volume 1, were both one cause of this suspension as well as

---

[22] Cooper, *João Rodrigues's Account*, 181.
[23] Flynn and Giráldez, "Cycles of Silver," 405; Flynn and Giráldez, "Path Dependence," 89.
[24] Flynn, "Silver in a Global Context," 226.
[25] Given the incomplete nature of statistics from this period, there are a range of estimates, including some considerably lower. Asao, "Sixteenth-Century Unification," 61.
[26] Innes, "Door Ajar," 90–91.

its beneficiaries, and they profited off a booming illicit trade between China and Japan. The gradual fading of the *wakō* threat was bound up with the emergence of the Portuguese as a maritime presence in East Asia. The result is that it is not possible to draw a clear line between the last phase of a longer piracy cycle and the first decades of Portuguese activity in East Asia. For this reason, Arano Yasunori describes a larger *wakō* phenomenon or environment (*wakōteki jōkyō*) that stretched from the sixteenth into the seventeenth century and encompassed the arrival of the Portuguese.[27]

In their efforts to seize control of the silver-for-silk trade, Portuguese entrepreneurs benefited, first, from a willingness of Chinese officials to look the other way as they established a foothold in Macao and, second, from the embrace of maritime daimyo in Japan eager to draw the profits of long-distance trade to their territories. By the seventeenth century, Portuguese officials could recount a detailed story explaining how sovereignty over Macao had been ceded to them by the Ming government in return for their aid in suppressing dangerous pirates. In fact, the beginnings of the settlement in Macao and its legal status remain murky. What is clear is that, beginning in the 1550s, Chinese officials and Portuguese traders developed what Jack Wills describes as an "astonishingly useful and durable accommodation" that gave the Portuguese some limited territorial rights to Macao in return for opening up a reliable, and readily controllable, conduit for long-distance commerce.[28]

The first Portuguese mariners arrived in Japan in 1543, accompanied by a famous *wakō* captain, Wang Zhi, whose involvement highlights the blurred lines that Arano describes.[29] It quickly became clear that the presence of a Portuguese base in China, combined with the collapse of official trading relations between China and Japan, presented a remarkable opportunity. For Luis Frois, who penned a famous description of Japan in this period, the "discord between China and Japan [was] a great help to the Portuguese who want to go to Japan." Since there were no formal relations, "the Portuguese merchants have a great means of negotiating their worldly business."[30] To make it all work, however, Portuguese mariners required a stable base in Japan capable of anchoring the Macao trading route. Plenty of daimyo were willing to provide one. One observer explained that because "these Japanese lords even though they have much land, are very poor in revenue and ready money,

[27] Arano, *Edo bakufu to higashi Ajia*, 19.
[28] Wills, "Relations with Maritime Europeans," 343.
[29] Murai, "Reconsideration of the Introduction of Firearms," 26. Murai discusses a range of conflicting dates related to the arrival of Wang Zhi.
[30] Quoted in Boxer, *Great Ship from Amacon*, 21.

a man cannot easily describe how pleased they are when a Portuguese ship enters one of their ports, owing to the profits which they derive therefrom."[31] While they sought out new sources of income, individual daimyo always engaged on their own terms. A Portuguese attempt to develop the port of Hirado, which was controlled by the entrepreneurial Matsura family, broke down in the face of a violent dispute that claimed the lives of more than a dozen sailors and merchants. When the Portuguese ship from Macao shifted to another port, the Matsura responded by attacking it.[32]

In the end, the Portuguese settled on Nagasaki as the terminus for their Japan trade. The decision was the product of a symbiotic relationship that developed between a Christian daimyo, Ōmura Sumitada, who wanted trade; Jesuit missionaries who desired a secure base for their activities; and Portuguese merchants looking for a reliable entry point into the Japanese market.[33] In 1580, Sumitada famously ceded the territory to the Jesuits in what became known as the donation of Nagasaki. Despite such language, Nagasaki's exact status was, like Macao, difficult to pin down. In an important study, Reinier Hesselink calls it "a hybrid anomaly" that was "neither a Portuguese colony nor a Japanese domain."[34]

With their twin bases in Macao and Nagasaki, Portuguese trade boomed, reaching a high point in the last decade of the sixteenth century. Jan Huygen van Linschoten, whose account of Iberian trade would go on to spur Dutch dreams of breaking into the Japanese market, explained that a Portuguese ship traveled yearly from Macao to Nagasaki with "silk, and returns only silver, from which they derive great profits."[35] In most years, the vessel departed from Macao for Japan during the summer.[36] On average it reached Nagasaki in two weeks, although the voyage could take up to a month in unfavorable conditions. Once there, it took on a cargo consisting primarily of silver bullion. Robert Fitch, an English traveler who visited Asia at the high point of the exchange, explained that the Portuguese "have a great caracke which goeth thither every yere, and she bringeth from thence every yere above six hundred thousand crusadoes: and all this silver ... they imploy to their great advantage in China."[37] Although it is impossible to obtain precise registries,

---

[31] Quoted in Boxer, *Great Ship from Amacon*, 40.
[32] For a detailed description of Matsura attempts to exploit overseas trade, see Toyama, *Matsura-shi to Hirado bōeki*.
[33] Elisonas, "Christianity and the Daimyo."
[34] Hesselink, *Dream of Christian Nagasaki*, 68.
[35] Van Linschoten, *Itinerario*, 1:110.
[36] Boxer, *Affair of the "Madre De Deus,"* 11.
[37] Quoted in Hakluyt, *Principal Navigations*, 5:498.

the few occasions that one of these vessels was seized suggests a cargo of staggering value.

While the endemic conflicts that rippled across the archipelago did disrupt trade at times, Portuguese merchants prospered in the absence of a single central government. When Tokugawa Ieyasu came to power he brought political stability, but the new regime also enabled a formidable competitor, the *shuinsen* merchants who opened up new trading circuits stretching across East and Southeast Asia.

Japanocentric Diplomacy and the *Shuinsen* System

The creation of the *shuinsen* system formed part of a wider Tokugawa attempt to revive and reconfigure Japan's diplomatic relations. By 1600, Japan was entrenched as a key node on global trading circuits, but it remained a diplomatic pariah in East Asia, where Hideyoshi's disastrous invasion of Korea had violently severed ties with traditional diplomatic partners. The urgent challenge that confronted Tokugawa officials after the Battle of Sekigahara in 1600 was to secure the rapid "normalization of relations with East Asia."[38] Over the next three decades, they would succeed not only in reestablishing relations but in configuring a new order that seemed, at least from certain perspectives, to place Japan at the symbolic center of a wider diplomatic universe.[39]

That the regime was able to do so in such short order was in part because of the active involvement of a handful of key domains.[40] The intersection between overarching Tokugawa control over foreign relations and domanial interests has been the subject of innovative work by Etsuko Hae-Jin Kang, Robert Hellyer, and others, who have highlighted the presence of "multiple voices and agendas" that combined with the center to form a composite Tokugawa diplomatic order.[41] These multiple overlapping agendas are clear in Tokugawa relations with Chosŏn Korea, which were orchestrated by the Sō family that ruled over the small domain of Tsushima.

For the Sō, close links with Korea represented an economic lifeline critical to their survival.[42] By the time Ieyasu came to power, they were determined

[38] Toby, *State and Diplomacy*, 23.
[39] Arano, "Formation of a Japanocentric World Order."
[40] For all its power, the shogunate did not rule over a unified political terrain. See Howell (Chapter 3), this volume. Batten, *To the Ends of Japan*, 43, reminds us that if the regime was not fully centralized, it was also "more centralized than anything seen in Japan since ancient times."
[41] Hellyer, *Defining Engagement*, 12.
[42] Kang, *Diplomacy and Ideology*, 139; Toby, *State and Diplomacy*, 26.

to ensure that the diplomatic chasm between Japan and Korea was rapidly bridged. In service of this goal, officials from Tsushima expertly manipulated both sides, using a combination of negotiation, manufactured compromise, and, when necessary, outright deception. This extended to forging a letter from the "king of Japan" in 1606 while also dispatching two unfortunate convicts, who had supposedly been involved in desecrating royal tombs during Hideyoshi's invasion.[43] Such concessions, even if they had not been authorized by the shogun, served to satisfy Korean preconditions for reengaging and spurred the dispatch of the official embassy that arrived in Japan in 1607. When the diplomatic letter carried by the ambassadors raised new questions, it was hurriedly substituted with a new one. The result was to accelerate the diplomatic timeline, ensuring that relations with Korea were reestablished less than a decade after Hideyoshi's death.

While Tsushima labored to secure Korean cooperation, other diplomatic partners were drawn in by force. In 1609, Satsuma domain received permission from Edo to invade the Ryukyu kingdom, an independent state located in current-day Okinawa.[44] One year later, the captive monarch Shō Nei was dutifully paraded before the shogun, and the kingdom he represented was forced into a new position as vassal state.[45] Without risking its own soldiers, the shogunate gained a powerful symbol in the form of a subordinate ruler arriving in the capital to pay homage directly to the shogun.

These overlapping efforts enabled Edo to move rapidly from a position of isolation to generate a "portfolio of legitimating assets" that served to entrench its authority.[46] The arrival of embassies from Korea and the Ryukyu kingdom, whether voluntary or brought by force, enabled the Tokugawa regime to piece together the building blocks of a new Japonocentric political order. Sometimes called the Japan-centered civilizational order (*Nihon-gata kai chitsujo*), the Tokugawa model was adapted from the Chinese system but reconfigured to place the shogun at the center.[47] The key audience was a domestic one. Ronald Toby, who has produced a pioneering study of this period, argues that the "ability of the early shoguns to produce ostentatious foreign embassies on Japanese soil, thereby demonstrating international legitimacy, was a powerful propaganda tool in the building of domestic legitimacy."[48]

---

[43] Toby, *State and Diplomacy*, 31; Kang, *Diplomacy and Ideology*, 143.
[44] Toby, *State and Diplomacy*, 57.
[45] Even after the conquest, the Shō family retained some measure of independence. See Tomiyama, *Ryūkyū ōkoku*.
[46] Toby, *State and Diplomacy*, 108.
[47] For the clearest description of this process, see Arano, *Kinsei Nihon to higashi Ajia*.
[48] Toby, *State and Diplomacy*, 76.

To be effective, embassies had to be grand productions capable of being displayed at key moments such as the accession of a new shogun. They were often spectacular affairs including large contingents of scholars, musicians, and servants, who were deliberately paraded through the archipelago.[49]

While the Tokugawa regime succeeded, with the help of well-placed domains, in drawing Korea and the Ryukyu kingdom into a new diplomatic order, the possibility of establishing official relations with China shimmered always on the horizon out of reach. The problem was how to do this without undermining carefully constructed notions of Tokugawa centrality. In 1611, a high-ranking shogunal official, Honda Masazumi, dispatched a letter to China. As the first document that touched directly on the possibility of opening ties between China and Japan, the precise meaning of the letter's contents has been the subject of extensive debate. Historians have interpreted the same document very differently: either as showing a willingness to at least pay lip service to a Chinese-dominated hierarchy or an outright refusal to do so.[50] Regardless of how one reads this document, the outcome was the same, and any possibility of formal diplomatic relations was quietly abandoned. Despite this, private Chinese merchants remained a constant presence in ports across Kyushu where they were permitted to trade unhindered.

Alongside normalizing diplomatic relations, the Tokugawa sought to construct a mechanism to manage long-distance commerce. The *shuinsen* system formed part of a new framework designed to channel engagement through clearly defined pathways.[51] The shogunate issued passes (*shuinjō*) authorizing their holders to undertake a single voyage from Japan to a stated destination.[52] Although the bulk went to Japanese merchants, any merchant based in Japan could obtain such a license, and recipients included Ryukyuan, Chinese, and European traders.[53] Between 1604 and 1635, when the system was closed down, the shogunate issued licenses for more than 350 *shuinsen*, permitting these vessels to sail to ports across East and Southeast Asia.

The pass system was created for two primary reasons. The first related to Japan's long history as an international pirate hub, which made it necessary

[49] Toby, *State and Diplomacy*, 203.
[50] Mizuno, "China in Tokugawa Foreign Relations," 110, argues that the Tokugawa never entertained the possibility of taking on a role as an "inferior member of the Sinocentric world order," hence dooming the possibility of formal relations. For an opposing view, see Fujii, "Jūnana seiki no Nihon."
[51] The classic work on the *shuinsen* is Iwao, *Shuinsen bōekishi*. For a more recent work, see Nagazumi, *Shuinsen*.
[52] Innes, "Door Ajar," 112.
[53] Iwao, *Shuinsen bōekishi*, 224.

to provide a mechanism for port authorities to distinguish between Japanese pirates and legitimate merchants. Although they could be counterfeited, the *shuinjō* were a clear marker that could be shown when ships from Japan dropped anchor in a foreign port. Second, requiring Japan-based merchants to obtain a license allowed the Tokugawa to exert control over expanding trade routes. As trade surged, its profits spilled unevenly across the archipelago as individual daimyo, some hostile to the regime, sought out opportunities to send ships, merchants, and even ambassadors to distant harbors. The *shuinsen* system provided a mechanism to ensure that only trusted lords and merchants received passes. As such, it was part of a much wider program designed to secure Tokugawa hegemony over a fractious archipelago by allowing the regime to first strip away the profits from maritime trade and then to suppress this revenue stream altogether.[54] This underlying dynamic has prompted Michael Laver to describe the creation of a licensed system of trade as "the first of several maritime restrictions," suggesting in this way that we can draw a clear line from the *shuinsen* to the edicts of the 1630s.[55]

The immediate impact of the new license system was, however, to trigger a new surge in trade, and *shuinsen* merchants rapidly emerged as a formidable competitor to the Portuguese. On the most basic level, the success of *shuinsen* merchants grew out of the silver-for-silk exchange, which created a profitable underlying dynamic, but other factors worked in their favor. First, they drew on a suite of maritime technologies not available to previous generations of Japanese merchants and mariners. Sixteenth-century descriptions of Japanese vessels were dismissive, returning again and again to the dangers their crews faced when venturing even short distances away from the coast. Although they sailed from Japanese ports, the *shuinsen* looked very different. As Nagazumi Yōko and Peter Shapinsky have argued persuasively, these were hybrid vessels, incorporating Japanese, European, and Chinese maritime technology and frequently carrying foreign pilots and crews.[56]

Second, *shuinsen* merchants could claim a degree of political protection not afforded to their competitors. These vessels were authorized by the shogun, and they functioned as mobile outposts of Tokugawa authority in seas and ports far distant from Japan. Because of this, any attack on a *shuinsen*, regardless of where it occurred, was treated as a challenge to the regime's

---

[54] Innes, "Door Ajar," 117–18, suggests a third reason for the creation of the *shuinjō* system: to divide available trading destinations among Japan-based merchants.

[55] Laver, *Sakoku Edicts*, 32.

[56] Nagazumi, *Shuinsen*, 58–59; Shapinsky, "Polyvocal Portolans," 24, cites a 1622 depiction of a hybrid vessel incorporating a European-style rudder and cabins, a prow seemingly modeled on an *atakebune*, and Chinese sails.

authority.[57] In the few cases when this happened, Edo opted for a dispro-portionate response, including the multiyear embargos described by Janssen in 1630. The result was to inscribe these vessels with an indelible mark of Tokugawa legal authority and to convince all parties that substantial pun-ishment would swiftly follow any violation, even if the actual incident had occurred hundreds of miles away from Japan. If a captain carried a *"chapa, or license"* from Japan, then he could, one European observer noted, pass freely even through blockades because he "feared nothing."[58]

The combination of maritime technology and the protection afforded by Tokugawa licenses allowed *shuinsen* merchants to push aggressively into new markets. The most important of these was in Southeast Asia, where vessels from Japan formed one part of what Anthony Reid famously described as an "age of commerce."[59]

Japanese Merchants and Migrants in Southeast Asia

In the second half of the sixteenth century, Chinese maritime entrepreneurs, including the ubiquitous Wang Zhi, who accompanied the first Portuguese merchants to Japan, started to sail between Southeast Asia and Japan, but the volume of traffic remained relatively limited.[60] This changed decisively with the advent of the *shuinsen* system. The overwhelming majority of these licenses were issued for ships traveling to Southeast Asia, including 85 licenses for Cochinchina, 44 for Cambodia, 52 for the Philippines, and 56 for Siam.[61] The result was that tens of thousands of Japanese merchants and migrants arrived in the region aboard these vessels, opening up new commercial links and establishing enduring communities.[62]

While the existence of Tokugawa records related to the issuance of *shuinjō* makes it possible to construct tables listing the number of vessels that left Japan in this period, we know far less about the nature of the Japanese push into the region. This is in large part because of the absence of contempo-rary travel accounts documenting individual voyages or materials produced on the Southeast Asian side describing what happened when these vessels

---

[57] Arano, "Formation of a Japanocentric World Order," 212.
[58] Blair and Robertson, *Philippine Islands*, 18:229.
[59] Reid, *Expansion and Crisis*.
[60] "Qinhuo Wang Zhi."
[61] For these figures, see Iwao, *Shuinsen bōekishi*. The figure for Cochinchina includes fourteen ships sent to Annan.
[62] Ishizawa, "Les quartiers japonais," suggests that 71,200 men and women left aboard Japanese vessels and roughly another 30,000 on foreign ships in this period.

actually dropped anchor at their intended destinations. One way round this is by considering a different kind of source. The opening up of trading links with Southeast Asia was accompanied by a surge of diplomatic letters dispatched from the shogun to his counterparts across the region. Although attention has traditionally focused on correspondence with East Asian powers such as Korea or China, by far the most letters were sent to Southeast Asia. Between 1601 and 1614, Tokugawa Ieyasu dispatched a total of forty-eight diplomatic missives written in his own name.[63] Of these, forty-one, or more than 85 percent, were directed toward Southeast Asia, and this flow of letters out of Japan was matched by an influx of correspondence coming into the archipelago from the region.

The content of such letters varied considerably. Many were filled with essentially interchangeable diplomatic platitudes, but a surprising number focused on the violent conduct of Japanese merchants in Southeast Asian ports. A typical letter penned in 1606 by the lord of Cochinchina explained that local officials had welcomed the arrival of Japanese merchants and extended them all possible courtesies. Rather than engaging in trade, however, they had run "rampant in my lands stealing goods and money belonging to Fujianese merchants and abusing neighboring residents and women."[64] It was one variation of a much-repeated complaint: that although Japanese merchants arrived seemingly intent on trade, they shifted swiftly and without warning or apparent provocation to violence. Another letter dispatched by the king of Cambodia in 1610 concluded that the "people of your country are cruel and ferocious. They come to engage in commerce but quickly act contrary to this purpose and rampage along the coast."[65]

Such charges are reflected in other sources. Richard Cocks, an English merchant based in Japan, described, for example, the "burning [of] China junckes ... whereof the King of Cochinchina advised the emperour [shogun] of their vnrulynesse."[66] This easy switch between trade and violence was not unique to Japanese merchants and such descriptions closely parallel contemporary accounts of what happened when European vessels arrived in ports across the region.[67] Here Europeans were invariably presented as persistent troublemakers who relied on violence to solve an array of problems. What is different, however, is the way in which the Tokugawa responded to these

---

[63] Fujii, "Jūnana seiki no Nihon."
[64] Kondō, Gaiban tsūsho, 107.
[65] Kondō, Gaiban tsūsho, 184.
[66] Cocks, Diary of Richard Cocks, 2:385.
[67] Clulow, "Like Lambs."

complaints. While vessels carrying Tokugawa trading licenses were assured of protection, the same could not be said of individual merchants from Japan. In a typical letter to Cochinchina, the shogun renounced all legal claims over Japanese merchants while urging his correspondent to prosecute any offenders to the fullest extent of the law. "If there are merchants from my country who visit your country and commit crimes," Ieyasu explained, "then please punish them according to your laws."[68] It was not an isolated instruction. In letter after letter sent to Southeast Asia, the shogun condemned the conduct of Tokugawa subjects, publicly renounced any claim to legal authority over their bodies, and insisted that all offenders should be dealt with according to local law.

Such instructions reveal a very different relationship between the state and its subjects overseas from that which underpinned European expansion. Whereas European rulers generally insisted on their role as "Parent and Protector" even if their subjects were operating in distant lands, the Tokugawa worked to sever any connection with Japanese merchants operating abroad by insisting that all offenders be punished within the framework of the host state's legal system.[69] This was not the result of a latent hostility toward trade, but was in fact entirely consistent with a wider Tokugawa policy designed to limit dangerous overseas interactions that might damage domestic stability by drawing the regime into conflict. The same urge would lead to the end of the *shuinsen* system after a series of episodes made it clear that the Tokugawa might have to go war to defend the integrity of the licenses it had issued. In this way, the "implicit but clear goal of Tokugawa policy was," Mark Ravina argues, "to sever international relations that might undermine Tokugawa hegemony."[70]

The most important legacy of the *shuinsen* system was the opening up of new markets to Japanese penetration. Over time, highly active Japanese communities, or *Nihon machi*, developed in ports scattered across Southeast Asia. These ranged from large communities in the Philippines and Ayutthaya (Siam) that numbered in the thousands to smaller settlements of a few hundred residents in Cochinchina and Cambodia.[71] Although not the largest, one of the most dynamic communities emerged in Ayutthaya, where Japanese

[68] Kondō, *Gaiban tsūsho*, 101.
[69] Clark, *Colonial Conferences*, 47.
[70] Ravina, *To Stand with the Nations of the World*, 28.
[71] We know a great deal about these settlements because of two remarkable books by Iwao, *Nan'yō Nihon machi* and *Zoku nan'yō Nihon machi*. Over a period of almost fifty years, Iwao collected a vast amount of documentation related to the Japanese active in this region.

migrants pioneered an important new trade in deerskins that came to link consumers in Japan's expanding cities with a wider ecological hinterland in Southeast Asia.

Scattered references to a large-scale deerskin trade start to appear in the last decades of the sixteenth century, coming mainly from the Philippines.[72] One observer noted that the Japanese "obtain very large numbers of buckskins, which they call *sichino cava*, and which they prepare in a curious manner."[73] Fueling this trade was a sustained demand for deer leather. In comparison with other kinds of leather, deer leather was both soft and pliable, making it well suited for a range of products. Demand emerged first from the samurai population, which prized deer leather for use in armor. But since Japan was at peace after 1600, this armor was employed primarily for display rather than for use in battle. As Japan's urban population expanded, the locus of demand shifted gradually from the warrior class to a wider swath of the population as the inhabitants of Edo, Osaka, and a host of castle towns rushed to purchase vast numbers of two-toed socks (*tabi*), coin purses (*hayamichi*), and other items made of deerskins.[74]

By the 1610s, Ayutthaya had displaced the Philippines as the key supply point for deerskins. The development of the trade was bound up by Yamada Nagamasa, whose brief but spectacular career saw him rise to high political rank within Ayutthayan politics. Born in Suruga, Yamada left the service of the local daimyo around 1611 to sail to Siam by way of Taiwan.[75] Once there, he found employment in a contingent of several hundred Japanese mercenaries employed by the king. These imported troops, which formed a key prop of royal power, were famous across the region. According to one contemporary observer, the king of Siam's power, "by water and land, consists most of his own Vassals and Natives; he hath indeed some few Strangers, as Moors, Malayers and some five hundred Japanners, the most esteemed for their courage and fidelity."[76]

Although he started his career as a soldier, Yamada juggled multiple identities as a military and political entrepreneur, as leader of the Japanese community, and as a prosperous merchant. His fortunes were closely tied with the steady expansion of the lucrative deerskin trade. By the time he arrived,

---

[72] Iwao, *Early Japanese Settlers*, 6; Borao, "La colonia de japoneses."

[73] Carletti, *My Voyage around the World*, 130.

[74] Laver, "Skins in the Game."

[75] For two revealing studies of Yamada's career, see Owada, *Yamada Nagamasa*, and Polenghi, *Samurai of Ayutthaya*.

[76] Caron and Schouten, *True Description*, 133–34.

Ayutthaya had already emerged as a key node capable of shipping out 150,000 hides in a single year.[77] Once he became head of the Japanese community, Yamada came to assume a large share of this trade with observers noting that "his wealth and power has increased ... so that he can send 3000 piculs of Sappan wood and 50,000 deerskins to Japan this year."[78] Under his leadership, Japanese migrants came to monopolize all phases of the trade. Skins were brought down from the interior to ports where Japanese migrants prepared and processed them into bundles of three sorts – *cabessa*, or top quality, *barriga*, or middle quality, and *pees*, or low quality skins – before they were shipped back to Japan.[79] The extent of the monopoly meant that anyone who wanted to break into the trade was forced to enter into restrictive contracts with Japanese representatives. Even if they did so, rival merchants claimed bitterly that the Japanese reserved top quality goods for themselves, leaving everyone else with the "refuse" of the trade.[80]

Although the deerskin trade did not approximate the scale of the silk-for-silver exchange, it was highly profitable for individual merchants. More importantly, it showed the capacity of *shuinsen* entrepreneurs to rearrange the traditional contours of the commercial landscape by opening up new trading possibilities and regions. The emerging rivalry between the Portuguese and Tokugawa licensed traders was soon joined by two new challengers: the VOC, which arrived in 1609, and the English East India Company (EIC), whose first ship reached Japan in 1613.

The Arrival of the Companies

In 1609, two vessels belonging to the VOC reached Japan. The leaders of the expedition dispatched an envoy to meet with Tokugawa Ieyasu to ask for permission to establish a trading outpost in Japan. This was swiftly granted, and the Dutch factory, as it is usually called, was established in the northwestern corner of Kyushu in the small port city of Hirado. It remained there for just over three decades until Tokugawa officials forcibly relocated it to Nagasaki, where the company's servants were confined to the man-made island of Dejima.

---

[77] Copie missiven door Maerten Houtman uijt Judea in Siam aen den oppercoopman Heijndrick Janssen in Patanij, sedert 18 Maert tot 24 April 1613, VOC 1056: ff. 95–99.
[78] Coolhaas, "Een brief aan Jan Pietersz," 407.
[79] For a superb study of the early deerskin trade, see Cheng, "Emergence of Deerskin Exports."
[80] Coolhaas, "Een brief aan Jan Pietersz."

Although often described as the world's first multinational corporation and the predecessor of modern companies, the VOC wielded a suite of essentially sovereign powers including the rights to conduct diplomacy, to deploy military forces, and to seize control of territory by building fortresses and strongholds. The contradictions between the company's state-like characteristics and its more conventional qualities as a corporation mean that it is often characterized in terms of dualities. Jurrien van Goor, one of the most influential VOC historians, calls it a "hybrid state: run as a business concern but acting like a kingdom."[81] This panoply of powers allowed the VOC to rapidly establish and then entrench itself in Asia. The Dutch acquired their first territorial possession in Southeast Asia in 1605 and quickly came to dominate the trade in precious spices, especially nutmeg and then cloves, which could command huge profit margins.

While the VOC would go on to establish an enduring presence in Japan, its early years were filled with frustration and failure. This stemmed in part from the location of its primary trading point. From the beginning, Ieyasu wanted the Dutch to establish a trading outpost at Uraga near Edo.[82] Despite this invitation, the Dutch elected to establish their factory in Hirado, a minor port on the western edges of Kyushu. This decision, which marooned the company far away from Japan's economic and political centers, provides further evidence of the role of individual daimyo and their capacity to direct Japan's international engagement. Hirado was controlled by the Matsura, a minor daimyo family with a long-standing connection to piracy. Like the Sō in Tsushima, the Matsura saw foreign trade as an economic lifeline to be secured at any cost. As a result, they engaged in an intensive, and ultimately successful, campaign to convince the Dutch that a base in Hirado offered their best chance of breaking into the rich Japanese market. As part of this, the Matsura made grand promises about the domain itself and their family's influence at the shogun's court. These extended to even the most mundane of details, such as the domain's assessed yield (*kokudaka*), which was suddenly magnified in conversation with VOC agents from just over 60,000 to 90,000 *koku*.[83] Over time, the Dutch came to realize that they had been duped, exchanging a position close to Japan's great cities for the unreliable promises of a minor lord eager to extract revenue and gifts.[84]

---

[81] Van Goor, "Hybrid State," 214.
[82] Hendrik Brouwer to Pieter Both, 29 January 1613, VOC 1056.
[83] Stukken van Sweers, van Vliet c.s., 1.10.78, inv. no. 5.
[84] Frustration with the Matsura boiled over in an extensive complaint documenting everything that had gone wrong. Memorie van t' gene tusschen de Heer van Firando met sijne bongoijs ende mij t sedert het jaer 1623 tot het jaer 1626 ghepassert is, VOC 1094.

At the same time, VOC representatives faced a second problem centered on the company's shifting diplomatic identity. When it was created in 1602, the VOC had been authorized to negotiate directly with local rulers across Asia. From the beginning, however, the company struggled to find a stable position within Asian diplomatic orders and to assert its rights to negotiate on the same level as a state. The result was an improvised strategy that hinged on the introduction of a fictive monarch. The first VOC officials to make contact with Japan claimed to represent "our King (*onsen Coninck*) and Princely Excellence, duke maurijtius of Nassau."[85] The king in question was in fact Prince Maurits, the *Stadhouder* of a number of Dutch provinces and the highest-ranking aristocrat in the United Provinces. Although an important actor in Dutch politics, Maurits operated in the shadow of republican institutions and his position in no way approximated a monarch. For VOC agents, however, invoking the "king of Holland" provided a kind of royal disguise that could be draped over the company's activities, thereby obscuring the unfamiliar nature of the organization while also facilitating diplomatic interactions by boosting the status of Dutch envoys and providing them with a ready vehicle for exchange.

Although the "king of Holland" model of diplomatic interaction underpinned the first diplomatic exchanges with Tokugawa Japan, it set in motion a crisis when the company moved to end this framework. By the 1620s, the organization's new headquarters in Batavia had emerged as a diplomatic hub in its own right. The result was a gradual shift away from a reliance on Maurits in favor of a new emphasis on the governor-general as the central figure in VOC diplomacy. By 1627, when the company elected to dispatch a new mission to Japan, its chosen ambassador brought letters and gifts not from The Hague but from Batavia. Arriving at the shogun's court, the ambassador explained that he had come "from the Governor-General in Batavia to thank His Majesty for the friendship we have received and to ask that it continues in the future."[86] When Tokugawa officials discovered, however, that this latest delegation did not originate with the "king of Holland," they were furious. Dismissing the governor-general as nothing more than "a servant or servant of a servant" and hence clearly not qualified to engage in state-to-state diplomacy, they rejected the ambassador and the embassy, which was forced to depart without ever meeting the shogun or

---

[85] Weider, *De Reis van Mahu en De Cordes*, 3:81–84.
[86] 4 October 1627, Daghregister van de reijse gedaen bij Pieter Nuijts ende Pieter Muijser, oppercoopman, als ambassadeurs aen den keijser ende rijcxraden van Japan van 24 Julij 1627 tot 18 Februarij 1628, VOC 1095:456–458v.

presenting its gifts.[87] It triggered a crisis that defied easy resolution. In the end, the Dutch were forced to abandon their use of formal embassies and to carve out a new position within the Tokugawa order by reinventing themselves as loyal vassals whose only ambition was to offer their service to the shogun.[88]

The VOC's ongoing struggles were made worse by its continued inability to break fully into the Japanese market. From the beginning, the VOC was determined to displace the Portuguese as the key middleman between Japanese silver and Chinese silk. Doing so, however, required access to a reliable source of silk. In service of this goal, the company experimented with multiple strategies. At first, VOC officials decided the easiest place to find silk was in the holds of Portuguese vessels traveling between Macao and Nagasaki. Locating a ship on the open ocean before the advent of radar was, however, extraordinarily difficult. It was far simpler to lie in wait off Nagasaki until the carrack, as the Dutch called the Macao-Nagasaki vessel, arrived on its annual voyage. This is what happened in 1617, when a small squadron of VOC ships arrived at Nagasaki determined to wait for their prey. Furious at this development, Hasegawa Gonroku, the Nagasaki governor (bugyō), who like so many of the city's elites had a personal stake in Portuguese trade, ordered the Dutch to retreat. We were "charged," the VOC commander wrote, "expressly by the governor of Nagasaki not to harm [the carrack] in the slightest and to depart immediately ... or we should be prevented by armed force."[89] Dozens of small craft packed with soldiers were assembled to attack the VOC's ships if they moved against the carrack. Although such vessels posed little danger on the open sea, they were a dangerous threat within the close confines of Nagasaki harbor, and the Dutch opted to retreat.

While the attempt to target Nagasaki failed, the VOC proved far more successful in attacking Chinese merchant vessels traveling along the China-Manila trade route. In 1617, for example, VOC ships seized the massive sum of 823,134 guilders' worth of plunder as well as a number of prisoners from at least seven Chinese junks.[90] Amazed by the richness of the loot, one observer wrote enviously of the "great quantities of raw silk, tafities, satins, velvets and Chine wares which they steal from the Chinese, having of late

---

[87] 5 November 1627, Nuijts/Muijser *Dagregister*, 484.

[88] Clulow, *Company and the Shogun*, ch. 3. Nagazumi Yōko was the first to identify the VOC's use of this terminology in her landmark translation of some of the early diaries; Nagazumi, *Hirado Oranda shōkan*, 2:6. See also Katō, *Bakuhansei kokka no seiritsu*.

[89] Jan Dirckz. Lam to the Amsterdam chamber, letter, 11 October 1617, VOC 1066:286v.

[90] Copie van de veroverde goederen in de Manilhas door Jacques Specx in Firando ontfangen, 12 October 1617, VOC 1066:127–31. Katō, *Bakuhansei kokka no keisei*, 72.

robbed many junks, whereby they sell at such rates that none that cometh truly by their goods can make profit here."[91] A year later the VOC captured nine Chinese junks with cargo worth over 600,000 guilders. Such campaigns turned Hirado, Katō Eiichi argues, into a strategic base for VOC privateering rather than a purely commercial outpost.[92] This changed, however, in 1621 when Tokugawa officials moved to restrict such operations by banning what they described as VOC piracy (*bahan*) "on the sea around the land of Japan."[93]

The VOC's great rival, the EIC, which followed the Dutch into Hirado in 1613, struggled as well to gain access to a reliable supply of silk. In his famous diary, Richard Cocks, who had been placed in charge of the company's factory, explained that "it is certain here is silver enough and may be carried out at pleasure; but then we must bring them commodities to their liking, as the Chinas, Portingales and Spainards do, which is raw silk and silk stuffs."[94] But how to gain access to these goods? There seemed only two alternatives: the English "must procure a peaceable trade in China, or else, as the Hollanders do, to trade with them per force."[95] Neither seemed to offer much promise. The Chinese market was locked to newcomers, while the EIC could not muster the powerful fleets assembled by its Dutch counterpart. As a result, Cocks turned to an unlikely savior, Li Dan, the head of the Chinese community in Nagasaki.[96]

In the first decades of the seventeenth century, Li Dan emerged as the "cheefe commander of all the Chinas in Japon, both at Nangasaque, Firando and elsewheare" and a highly successful merchant.[97] Although his background remains murky, Li Dan had, according to one account, fled from his former position as head of the sizable Chinese community in Manila.[98] In Japan, he quickly established himself as an active trader and occasional pirate who was willing to use violence to secure a quick profit.[99] His personal wealth and position as representative of the Chinese community gave him access to powerful Kyushu daimyo and even officials in the upper reaches of the Tokugawa bureaucracy in Edo.[100]

---

[91] Danvers and Foster, *Letters Received*, 3:291.
[92] Katō, "Rengō Oranda Higashi-Indo Kaisha."
[93] Copie remonstrantie van Jacques Specx overgegeven op 't comptoir Firando, 20 September 1621, VOC 1075:89–92, esp. 92v.
[94] Danvers and Foster, *Letters Received*, 5:26.
[95] Danvers and Foster, *Letters Received*, 3:241.
[96] Clulow, "Commemorating Failure."
[97] Thompson, *Diary of Richard Cocks*, 2:309.
[98] Farrington, *English Factory in Japan*, 1:381.
[99] The best study of Li Dan remains Iwao, "Li Tan."
[100] While it was common for individual merchant communities across Asia to have their own self-elected chiefs, the practice was not well established in Japan. Li Dan was Japan's only China captain, and after his death no comparable figure emerged capable of commanding the allegiances of the Chinese community.

While European chartered companies struggled to find their footing, private Chinese merchants proved highly adept at carving out space to operate in Japan's ports. They also consistently outmaneuvered their European counterparts. In his desperation to secure an economic basis for the fledging English factory in Japan, Richard Cocks came to rely on Li Dan's unlikely – and almost certainly entirely fictive – promise that he could secure official permission for English trade from the Ming court. Over a period of around a decade, the China captain managed to convince Cocks that such access lay just over the horizon and could be unlocked if only the chief merchant was willing to commit additional funds. In 1614, for example, Li Dan confided in him that the "Emperour and other greate men in China delight to heare reportes of our nation."[101] While there is no evidence this was in fact true, Cocks was convinced, describing Li Dan in enthusiastic terms as "a very good frend of ours."[102] Soon there was more good news: that certain great men had agreed to receive gifts presented by Li Dan in the name of the English and to work toward opening key ports for trade. But, of course, there was a problem. The current emperor was about to step down, and negotiations would, Li Dan assured Cocks, have to wait until a new ruler had taken the throne.[103] Undeterred, Cocks reported that when it came to "procuring trade into China, I am still of the opinion it will take effect [and look for] good news w'thin few daies."[104]

Not surprisingly, the China captain's negotiations proved extremely expensive. In January 1618, for example, Cocks presented Li Dan's brother with 1,000 taels "tuching our busyness (or entrance) into China."[105] Whenever progress seemed about to be made, new obstacles which could only be overcome via additional investments suddenly appeared. In 1617, for example, Cocks explained to his superiors that "had it not byn for the greate wars betwixt the Tartars and them the last yeare which cauced the Emperour of China to goe into the northermost partes of his kyngdom," permission would already have been procured.[106] But even as he pointed to renewed difficulties, Li Dan was careful to keep encouraging the chief merchant by, in one instance, presenting Cocks with some "small cheanes of gould" that had supposedly been sent by two members of the "Emperor of Chinas Concell."[107]

[101] Farrington, *English Factory in Japan*, 1:263.
[102] Farrington, *English Factory in Japan*, 1:350.
[103] Cocks, *Diary of Richard Cocks*, 1:34.
[104] Farrington, *English Factory in Japan*, 1:381.
[105] Cocks, *Diary of Richard Cocks*, 2:231.
[106] Farrington, *English Factory in Japan*, 1:557; see also 2:890–91.
[107] Cocks, *Diary of Richard Cocks*, 3:27.

The result was to replenish Cocks's optimism and to ensure that he nurtured "as great hope of trad into China as ever I had."[108]

Not everyone was as impressed by Li Dan's grand promises. Another English merchant, George Ball, wrote a highly critical indictment of the chief merchant's behavior. Accurately predicting that Li Dan's promises were "like to prove nothing but the plot of a nimble brayne to serve his own turne," Ball explained that "Mr Cockes, having his imagginations levelled beyond the moone, hath the eyes of his understanding so blynded with the expectation of incredible wonders."[109] It proved an accurate assessment, and in 1622 Cocks was instructed to shut down the EIC factory in Japan. Convinced that Chinese trade could be opened "w'thin a yeare or two to our own content," he wrote unsuccessfully to his superiors pleading for more time.[110]

While the Dutch celebrated the final closure of the English factory in 1623, they were no closer to securing their own reliable source of Chinese silk. After its privateering operations were restricted by Tokugawa edict, the VOC shifted to a new strategy focused on Taiwan, which lay as an unclaimed political space outside the control of neighboring states. Convinced that the island could serve as a viable entrepôt where Japanese silver could be exchanged for Chinese silk, VOC officials set up a base on the bay of Tayouan on the western side of island. This became the site of a ferocious struggle that was waged between Dutch and Japanese merchants for control over trade.

Competition over Taiwan

Described by Ming authorities as lying "beyond the seas" (haiwai) and by Europeans as simply "outside the jurisdiction of China," Taiwan occupied a place on the peripheries of the Chinese political order.[111] The island had featured briefly in Japanese discussions in the late sixteenth century, when Hideyoshi had dispatched an aggressive letter demanding that its nonexistent ruler agree to pay tribute to him. Taiwan reappeared as a potential target in 1609, the same year that Satsuma's forces set sail to the Ryukyu kingdom, when Ieyasu instructed Arima Harunobu, a famous Christian daimyo with a close involvement in maritime trade, to find suitable envoys who could be brought back to the capital.[112] If Arima's men were unable to secure such

[108] Farrington, English Factory in Japan, 1:681.
[109] Farrington, English Factory in Japan, 1:4.
[110] Farrington, English Factory in Japan, 2:891.
[111] Teng, Taiwan's Imagined Geography, 36; Groeneveldt, De Nederlanders in China, 283.
[112] Turnbull, "Onward, Christian Samurai!"

envoys peacefully, they were authorized to seize them with force. The larger goal of the expedition was to secure additional diplomatic satellites for Edo's emerging Japanocentric order, but in fact no amount of violence would have produced the desired outcome. Unlike the Ryukyu kingdom, Taiwan was not unified under one ruler and lacked any overarching domestic political structure. Instead, the local population was divided into hundreds of independent villages organized into loose and shifting alliances with "neither king, governor, nor chief."[113] When Arima's expedition failed to deliver its intended outcome, the shogunate largely abandoned interest in Taiwan.[114]

While such expeditions produced little concrete result, Chinese merchants based in Japan proved far more successful in their attempts to turn Taiwan into a regional trading hub. Even as he made grand promises of opening Chinese trade for the English, Li Dan moved to turn Taiwan into a regional hub under his control. He did so by making use of the framework provided by the *shuinsen* system. In total, Li and his brother received eleven licenses to send ships to the bay of Tayouan. Li Dan's death in 1625 caused the Taiwan trade to pass, however, from the Chinese community to two Japanese merchant-officials, Suetsugu Heizō Masanao and Hirano Tōjirō, who started dispatching ships to the island.[115]

While this was happening, the Dutch made their own attempt to claim part of the island. In 1622, VOC leaders had decided that the best way to access Chinese trade and damage Portuguese interests in the process was simply to attack and seize Macao, the one European settlement located in Chinese territory. The company assembled a formidable fleet including over a thousand sailors and soldiers under the command of Cornelis Reijersen. Despite Macao's weak defenses, the attack faltered, and the fleet was forced to retreat with numerous casualties.[116] Having failed to take the city, Reijersen shifted to his secondary instructions, which required him to establish a fortified base near the coast of China.[117] The choice settled on the Penghu (or Pescadores) Islands that lie in the straits between China and Taiwan. The occupation of these islands met with resistance from Ming officials in Fujian, who viewed them as Chinese territory. By August 1622, the two sides had

[113] Campbell, *Formosa under the Dutch*, 9.
[114] It did sanction one further expedition in 1616 under the control of the Nagasaki magistrate (*daikan*), Murayama Tōan. If anything, Murayama's operation achieved even less than Arima's earlier attempt. After being scattered by a powerful storm, only one vessel belonging to the small fleet successfully reached Taiwan.
[115] Oka, *Namban Trade*, 95.
[116] Blussé, "Dutch Occupation of the Pescadores."
[117] Groeneveldt, *De Nederlanders in China*, 61.

settled on a compromise: if the Dutch destroyed their fort on the Penghu Islands and retreated to Taiwan, trade relations would be opened and a regular supply of goods assured.[118]

For their base, the Dutch chose Tayouan, in part because the bay was already established as a trading node. As VOC officials noted, two or three Japanese junks arrived each year to rendezvous with Chinese junks, which had arrived there laden with silk.[119] Since Japanese merchants and especially Suetsugu Heizō had no intention of relinquishing access to such an important trading hub, the stage was set for an inevitable clash. It came quickly. At first, VOC authorities elected to implement a tax rather than an outright ban and informed Japanese captains that they were now required to pay a levy of 10 percent on all goods taken out of Tayouan.[120] Furious, they responded that they had traded there for a number of years before the Dutch arrived and had transformed the bay, which they saw as a free trading port, into a prosperous hub through their own efforts.

Such clashes reached a climax in 1627 when Hamada Yahyōe, one of Suetsugu Heizō's captains, recruited sixteen Siraya aboriginal men from one of the villages located close to Tayouan. Joined by two Chinese translators, the villagers traveled to Nagasaki, where they were received by Heizō, who set about transforming them into what the Dutch described as "fabricated" ambassadors, who could petition the shogun directly to bring Taiwan into the Tokugawa orbit.[121] When news about the embassy reached the Dutch, it provoked an outraged reaction from VOC agents, who claimed the villagers as their subjects. Although the ambassadors were permitted to travel up to Edo, shogunal officials, who were increasingly looking to limit overseas interaction, made no attempt to use the embassy to draw Taiwan into the Tokugawa order. The situation might have resolved itself without further conflict. Instead, it escalated suddenly as a result of the actions taken by Pieter Nuyts, the VOC governor on Taiwan. In April 1628, Hamada returned to Taiwan carrying the ambassadors. Believing that Hamada's arrival was the beginning of a military campaign to wrest Tayouan from VOC hands, Nuyts ordered his men to search the vessel and confiscate any weapons. Discovering the villagers below deck, the governor threw them into prison and seized the gifts they had received in Edo. When Hamada met with Nuyts to protest

---

[118] Groeneveldt, *De Nederlanders in China*, 287–90.
[119] Nagazumi, "Japanese Go-Shuinjo," 29.
[120] Schouten, "Memorabel verhael," 82–83.
[121] Schouten, "Memorabel verhael," 87. For a detailed analysis, see Clulow, "Fake Embassy."

his actions, things quickly turned violent, and the situation was only resolved with an exchange of hostages.

In Edo, news of what had happened sparked an outraged reaction. Hamada's ships carried a *shuinjō*, one of the regime's prized maritime trading licenses. For Tokugawa officials, the governor's decision to detain Hamada's vessels, strip them of their armament, and arrest their crew was an unacceptable infringement of the shogun's authority. The result was an embargo on Dutch trade that lasted from 1628 to 1632, until VOC authorities, in an unprecedented step, agreed to hand over Nuyts for punishment in Japan. The Taiwan incident, which started out as a dispute over who would control a previously neutral trading hub, sent shock waves running through the Tokugawa system of licensed trading vessels. It was followed almost immediately by a second episode involving a Japanese merchant vessel sailing under the protection of a *shuinjō* in distant waters. The combination was enough to deal a fatal blow to the *shuinsen* system, rearranging the key economic actors and freezing the growth of the Japanese diaspora in Southeast Asia.

The Takagi Incident

In May 1628, while Hamada and his men were under guard on Taiwan, Spanish vessels reached the coast of Ayutthaya. Sailing under the command of Don Juan de Alcaraso, they had been tasked with taking revenge for an attack that had taken place four years earlier, when Ayutthayan forces, including the king's famed Japanese legion, had seized a Spanish vessel.[122] After seizing a number of local trading vessels, Alcaraso's small fleet sighted a Japanese junk owned by Takagi Sakuemon, a member of a prominent Nagasaki merchant family.[123] Although he carried no instructions to expand his campaign to include Japanese shipping, Alcaraso decided to attack. While his actions may have been motivated in part by the involvement of the king's Japanese troops in the original 1624 incident, Alcaraso likely also saw an opportunity to capture a rich prize with minimal danger.[124] The ship was burnt and forty-two prisoners captured. They were later shipped to Manila, where they would become human bargaining chips in negotiations between Spanish and Japanese authorities.[125]

[122] Blair and Robertson, *Philippine Islands*, 22:139.
[123] Hesselink, *Dream of Christian Nagasaki*, 186, 219, suggests that the Takagi family "was the first of Nagasaki's ruling class to apostatize."
[124] Boxer, *Great Ship from Amacon*, 115. Boxer suggests the attack was motivated by a desire for revenge against the Japanese.
[125] Oka, *Namban Trade*, 230.

News of what had happened traveled quickly to Nagasaki and then to Edo, where Tokugawa officials deliberated how to respond to a second attack on a vessel carrying a *shuinjō*. The problem was that since relations with Spain had already been suspended years earlier, there was no one readily at hand to punish. As a result, the decision was made to place an embargo on Portuguese trade with Japan. Although Spanish forces had been responsible for the incident, they insisted that "since the Castilians and Portuguese had the same king, it made no difference which one of them paid."[126] Furious Portuguese protests that they were in no way connected to the assault were ignored, and three galliots from Macao were seized and impounded. They were later joined by two additional Portuguese vessels that were imprisoned when they arrived in Nagasaki in 1629.[127]

In Nagasaki, an ultimatum intended for Portuguese and Spanish authorities was prepared. It declared that, until appropriate reparations had been made, the offenders punished, and the mariners, either living or dead, returned, all "captains, merchants and people with their capital" would be kept under lock and key.[128] Portuguese officials in Macao, which was entirely dependent on the trade route with Nagasaki, pleaded with their counterparts in Manila "to make satisfaction, and send the value of the cargo burned and lost in the said junk, in order to silence the Japanese."[129] At first, it seemed as if Spanish authorities might yield ground. When a group consisting of four theologians and two jurists met to discuss what had happened, they decided that the attack "had been unjust" because its commander lacked any authority to attack Japanese vessels. Because of this, the decision was made to ship the survivors from the Takagi attack back to Nagasaki with a message that "keen regret was felt over the illegal act recently committed by our galleons."[130]

It marked the high point of negotiations. Although they were loaded onto an outgoing vessel, the survivors never reached Nagasaki, and rumors swirled that the ship carrying them had been deliberately attacked and sunk by the Spanish.[131] The next year, Spanish authorities decided to reverse

---

[126] Blair and Robertson, *Philippine Islands,* 24:172. Portugal and Spain had been unified under one crown since 1580, although their operations in Asia remained separated. Dutch agents based in Japan were insistent that the Portuguese and the Spanish shared a king and hence should be treated as one nation. Diary of Pieter Muijser, 11 July 1628–23 September 1629, VOC 1101:176.

[127] Coolhaas, "Een Indisch Verslag uit 1631," 83.

[128] 13 September 1628, diary of Pieter Muijser, VOC 1101.

[129] Blair and Robertson, *Philippine Islands,* 23:55.

[130] Blair and Robertson, *Philippine Islands,* 23:63.

[131] Boxer, *Great Ship from Amacon,* 116; Nagazumi, *Shuinsen,* 83.

their earlier decision, deciding that although the attack on Takagi's vessel could not be fully justified, they had no obligation to do anything as long as Japan remained closed to trade with Manila. Their refusal to compromise forced Portuguese authorities in Macao into action. Desperate to restart trade, they opted to send a grand delegation to Nagasaki in 1630, led by Dom Gonçalo da Silveira.[132] Once in Japan, the ambassador argued that Macao should not be held accountable for Spanish actions. More importantly, he offered to remain in Japan until such time as Tokugawa officials were completely satisfied "even if this should take eight or ten years." It proved a successful strategy, and the seized galliots were released. While trade resumed its flow, there was still the problem of the ambassador who remained under guard in Nagasaki. One way to secure his release was by following the path taken by the VOC by extraditing the original offenders from Alcaraso's expedition to Japan. Spanish authorities, however, proved far less willing to compromise than their Dutch counterparts, and the situation dragged on unresolved for another four years until 1634, when a new shogun finally gave permission for the ambassador from Macao to travel up to Edo and then to leave the archipelago.

Maritime Restrictions and the Rise of the Zheng

These twin assaults struck at the heart of the Tokugawa system of licensed trading vessels. In 1631, shogunal officials made the first significant change to the *shuinsen* framework in decades by introducing *hoshōjō*, licenses issued by Tokugawa authorities rather than by the shogun himself. The change was driven by a determination to secure shogunal prestige and authority in an increasingly turbulent maritime environment.[133] According to Dutch observers, Tokugawa officials "will not allow their passes (as one has been treated badly by the Spaniards of Manila) to be taken on the sea or to strange lands."[134] It proved a temporary fix, and in 1634 the shogunate made another change, deciding that only seven prominent mercantile families would be permitted to receive licenses. A year later, the entire system was shut down.[135] While the decision removed a key domestic competitor to European merchants, it also reduced the regime's exposure to potential conflict, thereby preventing any further assault on shogunal prestige.

[132] Boxer, *Great Ship from Amacon*, 122–23.
[133] Katō, "Bahansen, shuinsen, hōshosen," 50; Laver, *Sakoku Edicts*, 35.
[134] Tōkyō Daigaku Shiryō Hensanjo, *Dagregisters*, 1:108 (hereafter *Dagregisters Japan*).
[135] *Dagregisters Japan*, 1:236.

The Shimabara uprising, which broke out in 1637, triggered more change by prompting the final expulsion of the Portuguese, who had dominated the silver-for-silk exchange for so long. In the final assessment, there is no evidence that the Portuguese had aided the rebels in any way, but they were tied to a broader Christian threat that loomed, Edo believed, menacingly on the horizon. While Tokugawa officials were clear that the Portuguese would not be able to remain in Nagasaki, they were determined to prevent a collapse in long-distance trade. To fill the gap, they turned actively to a combination of European and Asian merchants. In May 1638, Dutch representatives were summoned to a meeting in Edo to confirm whether they could guarantee to make up for any losses in trading volume caused by the closure of the Macao-Nagasaki route.[136] A second, even more expansive discussion took place in July 1639, when a VOC representative, François Caron, was asked to prepare charts showing the sea routes leading to Japan. Once he arrived, these were laid out on the floor and compared with other maps obtained from Portuguese, Japanese, and Chinese sources. Tokugawa officials questioned Caron: Could he guarantee that the company would bring "the silks, silk goods, medicines and dry goods ... in the same way that the Portuguese have done"?[137] While this was happening, they also approached Tsushima and Satsuma, requiring these domains to increase trade in raw silk and silk goods to compensate for any loss caused by the expulsion of the Portuguese.[138]

The shutdown of the *shuinsen* trade and the end of Portuguese trade with Japan seemed to create the opportunity that the VOC had been waiting for. It had seen off three European rivals, first the English, then the Spanish, and now the Portuguese, as well as the *shuinsen* merchants who had once seemed set to dominate trade routes with Japan. At first, VOC trade with Japan did boom, resulting in what Leonard Blussé describes as the "Honeymoon Years," when VOC profits surged.[139] This hinged on a steady increase in VOC silk imports into Japan: from 855,084 guilders in 1635, imports more than doubled to 2,094,375 in 1637, and then increased still further to more than three million guilders in 1638.[140] And as recent figures collected by Suzuki Yasuko show, this was accompanied by a significant surge in silver exports carried by

---

[136] *Dagregisters Japan*, 3:152.
[137] *Dagregisters Japan*, 4:51–59.
[138] Tashiro, "Foreign Relations," 292–93.
[139] Blussé, "No Boats to China," 64.
[140] Blussé, "No Boats to China," 65.

VOC trading vessels, culminating in 1639, when 2.5 million taels of silver were loaded aboard Dutch ships.[141]

The company's trading honeymoon was made possible by a steady flow of silk from China's maritime provinces to Taiwan. This hinged on the cooperation of a remarkable entrepreneur, Zheng Zhilong, and the maritime organization that he had created.[142] Born in Fujian, Zhilong started his career in the Portuguese stronghold of Macao before moving to Hirado, where he rose to prominence through a close connection with Li Dan, the head of the Chinese community discussed earlier.[143] By the 1620s, Zhilong had relocated his operations to the seas around Fujian, where he emerged as one of many pirate captains who prospered in the busy shipping lanes off China's traditional maritime hub. In 1628, the Ming administration, using a well-worn tactic of charging pirates to suppress pirates, co-opted Zhilong by offering him a position as admiral.[144] Armed with this official endorsement, he soon dispensed with his rivals and emerged at the head of a powerful maritime network.

As Zheng Zhilong's influence over the surrounding seas grew, VOC officials became increasingly concerned that he could challenge the company's control over trading routes around Taiwan. Such worries were amplified by the news that Zhilong, who had emerged from the same cosmopolitan maritime world that had given rise to the *shuinsen*, was building a fleet of warships incorporating European and Asian maritime technologies. In 1633, the company launched an attack on Zhilong's base of Xiamen, sinking the bulk of his fleet. It proved a temporary victory. Determined to strike back, Zhilong proceeded to amass a large fleet of 150 vessels that forced the VOC back to the negotiating table.[145]

By the time terms were concluded, Zheng Zhilong had agreed to provide the company with the silk goods it so desperately needed, and it was this guaranteed supply that enabled the VOC trade surge from 1635 onwards. Any expectation of a prolonged golden age for Dutch trade in Japan was shattered, however, in 1641, when Zhilong's own ships started to arrive in Nagasaki harbor, thereby circumventing the Dutch trading hub on Taiwan. In June of that year, VOC agents recorded the arrival in Nagasaki of a richly laden junk

---

[141] Suzuki, *Japan-Netherlands Trade*, 13.
[142] The rise of the Zheng and their role in East Asia has been studied by a number of scholars, including Tonio Andrade (*Lost Colony*; "Beyond Guns, Germs, and Steel"), Cheng Wei-cheng (*War, Trade and Piracy*), Patrizia Carioti ("Zhengs' Maritime Power"), and Xing Hang (*Conflict and Commerce*).
[143] Hang, *Conflict and Commerce*, 43.
[144] Andrade, *How Taiwan Became Chinese*, 46.
[145] Andrade, "Company's Chinese Pirates," 438–39.

belonging to Zhilong.[146] It was followed in subsequent weeks by five more "great junks" carrying significant quantities of silk.[147] The result was a dramatic drop-off in Dutch trade with Japan as imports plunged from six million guilders in 1640 to around half a million in 1643.[148]

While the VOC did succeed over time in securing alternative sources of silk from places such as Tonkin in Southeast Asia, the threat from the Zheng organization did not disappear. Under Zhilong's famous son, Zheng Chenggong, or Koxinga (1624–62), the Zheng organization grew steadily in strength and reach, pushing into Southeast Asia, where Zheng merchants attempted to seize control of the deerskin trade, which had slipped from the hands of Japanese merchants after the closure of the *shuinsen* system.[149] Again and again, Zheng merchants succeeded in encroaching into markets claimed by the VOC. Despite the company's oversized reputation as a business innovator, new research by Tonio Andrade and Xing Hang has shown that the Zheng organization either equaled or exceeded the VOC in terms of revenue and profitability.[150] It was also a formidable military enterprise capable of mustering powerful armies and fleets. This was brought dramatically home to Batavia in 1661, when Koxinga landed his armies on Taiwan, marking the beginning of a campaign that would end nine months later with the surrender of the VOC fort. Although Koxinga died soon after his victory, his son, Zheng Jing, initiated a highly successful state-building program that allowed him to establish a territorial state with a distinct maritime orientation on the west coast of Taiwan and "informal economic hegemony" over large parts of maritime Asia.[151]

Reassessing Japan's International Engagement

This chapter has attempted to provide a broad, if necessarily incomplete, overview of Japan's international economy at the beginning of the early modern period. By way of conclusion, it is worth reflecting on how much new scholarship has overturned past interpretative models that had once seemed so

---

[146] *Dagregisters Japan*, 5:88.

[147] *Dagregisters Japan*, 5:187.

[148] Blussé, "No Boats to China," 67.

[149] In the end, the VOC would outlive the Zheng organization, which embarked on a disastrous military adventure in mainland China in 1674.

[150] Andrade, *Lost Colony*; for a comparative estimate of volumes of trade, see Hang, *Conflict and Commerce*, 293. Hang concludes (244) that "the Zheng consistently matched or outperformed the VOC in revenues and profitability for most of their time in power, and proved more adaptable to changes in the structure of trade."

[151] Hang, *Conflict and Commerce*, 15.

dominant. In 1951, the prolific historian Charles R. Boxer published his most influential work on Japanese history, *The Christian Century in Japan, 1549–1650.*[152] In this much-reprinted volume, Boxer made two central claims that continued to cast a long shadow over the field for decades. First, he argued for the central importance of Europe in Japanese history, creating what he described as a Christian century that seemed set to transform the archipelago. In recent decades, Boxer's vision has receded as work by Arano, Toby, and other scholars has reoriented the focus back toward Japan's Asian partners. European powers such as the Portuguese, the Spanish, the English, and the Dutch were important, but they were never as significant as their abundant archival records seem to suggest. In fact, they consistently struggled to claim a place on the fringes of an Asian maritime order. New research on the Zheng maritime state on Taiwan represents the next stage of this assault on Eurocentric visions, showing an organization that was, in many ways, more successful than any of the European enterprises that Boxer devoted so much attention to.

Second, Boxer argued that the Tokugawa retreat from Christianity pushed it into an absolutist position designed to achieve total isolation. In fact, as this chapter has shown, the Tokugawa never sought to cut Japan off from the outside world. But if Boxer's vision of a sealed society does not hold true, it is also the case that the Tokugawa regime was strikingly consistent in its basic impulse to control, manage, and, where it deemed necessary, limit interactions with the outside world. A string of decisions, including the willingness to hand over Japanese merchants to foreign jurisdictions, the creation and then suspension of the *shuinsen* system, and the expulsion of the Portuguese were all part of a policy that privileged control over all else. Not surprisingly, this did in fact change the nature of Japan's international exchange. The pattern that emerged in the sixteenth century at the beginning of this period of heightened interaction can best be compared to a delta, formed of dozens of individual streams connecting ports throughout Kyushu to wider trade routes. The expansive nature of this delta meant that a broad array of actors including pirates, merchants, mercenaries, Christian refugees, entrepreneurs, and domanial lords were able to access Japan's maritime boom. Across the first decades of the seventeenth century, this delta was channeled into clearly defined courses as the Tokugawa worked to exert control.[153] This process generated winners such as Satsuma and Tsushima, who retained monopoly

[152] Boxer, *Christian Century in Japan.*
[153] Haneda and Oka, *Maritime History*, 221, points to a similar process happening across East Asia as early modern states "increasingly began to place more emphasis on territorial governance than on foreign trade."

rights over trade with the Ryukyu kingdom and Korea respectively, but also losers, including the *shuinsen* merchants and the Japanese diaspora in Southeast Asia, who lost direct access to Japanese ports.[154]

It was this desire to reduce risk that runs like a thread through Tokugawa foreign policy, which was intended above all else to ensure stability and security for the regime. For evidence of this, we can turn from Willem Janssen, whose account of Nagasaki started this chapter, to a second Dutch observer, Leonard Camps, who wrote a penetrating appraisal of Tokugawa policy. For Camps, the most striking feature of Japanese politics was the shogunate's consistent refusal to commit its vast resources to the kind of overseas adventures pursued by European regimes. In his words:

> [The shogun's] ambition doth not extend beyond the bounds of his own Empire, and contenting himself with those confines God and Nature hath prescribed him; he wages no war against his Neighbours, neither suffers his Subjects to molest or disturb any out of his obedience. No foraign Princes fall out by his instigation; neither doth he give or demand help or assistance upon any account. His power and might consists in the vastness of his Kingdom, and multitudes of his Souldiers; he hath arms at will, Castles that seem impregnable, Provisions in abundance, and Treasure without end.[155]

By any measure, the Tokugawa regime's policy of what might be described as cautious engagement was spectacularly successful. Whereas European powers lurched from war to war, the Tokugawa severed contact with any group that might pull it into conflict, thereby creating a stable environment for a regime that endured for over 250 years. It was only in the nineteenth century, when aggressive European powers started to enter Japanese waters, that this security was finally shattered.

Bibliography

Andrade, Tonio. "Beyond Guns, Germs, and Steel: European Expansion and Maritime Asia, 1400–1750." *Journal of Early Modern History* 14, no. 1 (2010): 165–86.

"The Company's Chinese Pirates: How the Dutch East India Company Tried to Lead a Coalition of Pirates to War against China, 1621–1662." *Journal of World History* 15, no. 4 (2004): 415–44.

[154] This led to what is sometimes described as a system of "four gates" (*yottsu no kuchi*), in which foreign relations were mediated through four separate windows: through Satsuma domain to the Ryukyu kingdom, through Tsushima domain to Korea, through Matsumae domain to the Ainu in Ezochi, and through Nagasaki to Chinese and Dutch traders. See Arano, *Kinsei Nihon to higashi Ajia*.

[155] This translation comes from Caron and Schouten, *True Description*, 98–99.

How Taiwan Became Chinese: Dutch, Spanish, and Han Colonization in the Seventeenth
Century. New York: Columbia University Press, 2008.

Lost Colony: The Untold Story of China's First Great Victory over the West. Princeton, NJ:
Princeton University Press, 2011.

Arano Yasunori. Edo bakufu to higashi Ajia. Yoshikawa Kōbunkan, 2003.

"The Formation of a Japanocentric World Order." International Journal of Asian Studies
2, no. 2 (2005): 185–216.

Kinsei Nihon to higashi Ajia. Tōkyō Daigaku Shuppankai, 1988.

Asao Naohiro. "The Sixteenth-Century Unification." In Hall, Early Modern Japan, 40–95.

Batten, Bruce. To the Ends of Japan: Premodern Frontiers, Boundaries, and Interactions.
Honolulu: University of Hawaiʻi Press, 2003.

Blair, Emma H., and James A. Robertson, eds. The Philippine Islands, 1493–1898. 55 vols.
Cleveland: A. H. Clark, 1903–9.

Blussé, Leonard. "The Dutch Occupation of the Pescadores (1622–1624)." Transactions of
the International Conference of Orientalists in Japan 18 (1973): 28–44.

"No Boats to China: The Dutch East India Company and the Changing Pattern of the
China Sea Trade, 1635–1690." Modern Asian Studies 30, no. 1 (1996): 51–76.

"The VOC as Sorcerer's Apprentice: Stereotypes and Social Engineering on the China
Coast." In Leyden Studies in Sinology, edited by W. L. Idema, 87–105. Leiden: Brill, 1981.

Borao, José Eugenio. "La colonia de japoneses en Manila, en el marco de las relaciones de
Filipinas y Japón en los siglos XVI y XVII." Cuadernos CANELA 17 (2005): 25–53.

Boxer, Charles R. The Affair of the 'Madre De Deus': A Chapter in the History of the Portuguese
in Japan. London: Routledge, 1929. In Charles R. Boxer, Portuguese Merchants and
Missionaries in Feudal Japan, 1543–1640. Reprint, London: Variorum Reprints, 1986.

The Christian Century in Japan, 1549–1650. Berkeley: University of California Press, 1951.

The Great Ship from Amacon: Annals of Macao and the Old Japan Trade, 1555–1640. Lisbon:
CEHU, 1959.

Campbell, William. Formosa under the Dutch: Described from Contemporary Records, with
Explanatory Notes and a Bibliography of the Island. London: Kegan Paul, 1903.

Carioti, Patrizia. "The Zhengs' Maritime Power in the International Context of the
Seventeenth Century Far Eastern Seas." Ming-Qing yanjiu 5 (1996): 29–68.

Carletti, Francesco. My Voyage around the World. Translated by Herbert Weinstock. New
York: Pantheon, 1964.

Caron, François, and Joost Schouten. A True Description of the Mighty Kingdoms of Japan and
Siam. Translated by Roger Manley. London: Samuel Broun and John de l'Ecluse, 1663.

Cheng, Wei-chung. "Emergence of Deerskin Exports from Taiwan under VOC (1624–1642)."
Taiwan Historical Research 24, no. 3 (2017): 1–48.

War, Trade and Piracy in the China Seas, 1622–1683. Leiden: Brill, 2013.

Clark, G. N. Colonial Conferences between England and the Netherlands in 1613 and 1615. Leiden:
Brill, 1940.

Clulow, Adam. "Commemorating Failure: The Four Hundredth Anniversary of England's
Trading Outpost in Japan." Monumenta Nipponica 68, no. 2 (2013): 163–87.

The Company and the Shogun: The Dutch Encounter with Tokugawa Japan. New York:
Columbia University Press, 2014.

"A Fake Embassy, the Lord of Taiwan and Tokugawa Japan." Japanese Studies 30, no. 1
(2010): 23–41.

"Like Lambs in Japan and Devils outside Their Land: Diplomacy, Violence, and Japanese Merchants in Southeast Asia." *Journal of World History* 24, no. 2 (2013): 335–58.

Cocks, Richard. *Diary of Richard Cocks, 1615–1622: Diary Kept by the Head of the English Factory in Japan.* 3 vols. University of Tokyo Press, 1978–80.

Conlan, Thomas D. "The Failed Attempt to Move the Emperor to Yamaguchi and the Fall of the Ōuchi." *Japanese Studies* 35, no. 2 (2015): 185–203.

Coolhaas, W. "Een brief aan Jan Pietersz: Coen teruggevonden." *Bijdragen tot de Taal-, Land- en Volkenkunde* 112, no. 4 (1956): 403–15.

—— ed. "Een Indisch Verslag uit 1631, van de Hand van Antonio van Diemen." *Bijdragen en Mededelingen van het Historisch Genootschap* 65 (1947): 2–236.

Cooper, Michael. *João Rodrigues's Account of Sixteenth-Century Japan.* London: Hakluyt Society, 2001.

Cullen, Louis. "The Nagasaki Trade of the Tokugawa Era: Archives, Statistics, and Management." *Japan Review* 31 (2017): 69–104.

Danvers, F. C., and W. Foster. *Letters Received by the East India Company from Its Servants in the East.* 6 vols. London: S. Low, Marston, 1896–1902.

Elisonas, Jurgis. "Christianity and the Daimyo." In Hall, *Early Modern Japan*, 301–72.

Farrington, Anthony. *The English Factory in Japan, 1613–1623.* 2 vols. London: British Library, 1991.

Flynn, Dennis O. "Silver in a Global Context, 1400–1800." In *The Construction of a Global World, 1400–1800 CE*, Pt 2: *Patterns of Change*, edited by Jerry H. Bentley, Sanjay Subrahmanyam, and Merry E. Wiesner-Hanks, 213–39. Vol. 6 of *The Cambridge World History*. Cambridge: Cambridge University Press, 2015.

Flynn, Dennis O., and Arturo Giráldez. "Born with a 'Silver Spoon': The Origin of World Trade in 1571." *Journal of World History* 6, no. 2 (1995): 201–21.

—— "Cycles of Silver: Global Economic Unity through the Mid-Eighteenth Century." *Journal of World History* 13, no. 2 (2002): 391–427.

—— "Path Dependence, Time Lags and the Birth of Globalisation: A Critique of O'Rourke and Williamson." *European Review of Economic History* 8 (2004): 81–108.

Fujii Jōji. "Jūnana seiki no Nihon: Buke no kokka no keisei." In *Kinsei 2*, edited by Asao Naohiro, Amino Yoshihiko, Ishii Susumu, Kano Masanao, Hayakawa Shōhachi, and Yasumaru Yoshio, 1–64. Vol. 12 of *Iwanami kōza: Nihon tsūshi*. Iwanami Shoten, 1994.

Groeneveldt, W. P. *De Nederlanders in China, 1601–1624.* The Hague: Martinus Nijhoff, 1898.

Gunn, Geoffrey C. *World Trade Systems of the East and West: Nagasaki and the Asian Bullion Trade Networks.* Leiden: Brill, 2018.

Hakluyt, Richard, ed. *The Principal Navigations, Voyages, Traffiques and Discoveries of the English Nation.* 12 vols. Glasgow: James MacLehose and Sons, 1903–5.

Hall, John Whitney, ed. *Early Modern Japan.* Vol. 4 of *The Cambridge History of Japan.* Cambridge: Cambridge University Press, 1991.

Haneda, Masashi, and Mihoko Oka, eds. *A Maritime History of East Asia.* Kyoto: Kyoto University Press, 2019.

Hang, Xing. *Conflict and Commerce in Maritime East Asia: The Zheng Family and the Shaping of the Modern World, c. 1620–1720.* Cambridge: Cambridge University Press, 2016.

Hayashi Akira, ed. *Tsūkō ichiran.* 8 vols. Kokusho Kankōkai, 1912–13.

Hellyer, Robert. *Defining Engagement: Japan and Global Contexts, 1640–1868.* Cambridge, MA: Harvard University Asia Center, 2009.

Hesselink, Reinier. *The Dream of Christian Nagasaki: World Trade and the Clash of Cultures, 1560–1640.* Jefferson, NC: McFarland, 2016.

Innes, Robert LeRoy. "The Door Ajar: Japan's Foreign Trade in the Seventeenth Century." PhD diss., University of Michigan, 1980.

Ishizawa, Yoshiaki. "Les quartiers japonais dans l'Asie du Sud-Est au XVIIème siècle." In *Guerre et Paix en Asie du Sud-Est,* edited by Nguyen The Anh and Alain Forest, 85–94. Paris: Harmettan, 1998.

Iwao, Seiichi. *Early Japanese Settlers in the Philippines.* Foreign Affairs Association of Japan, 1943.

———. "Japanese Foreign Trade in the 16th and 17th Centuries." *Acta Asiatica* 30, no. 1 (1976): 1–18.

———. "Li Tan, Chief of the Chinese Residents at Hirado, Japan, in the Last Days of the Ming Dynasty." *Memoirs of the Research Department of the Toyo Bunko* 17 (1958): 27–83.

———. *Nan'yō Nihon machi no kenkyū.* Nan'a Bunka Kenkyūjo, 1941.

———. *Sakoku.* Vol. 14 of *Nihon no rekishi.* Chūō Kōronsha, 1973.

———. *Shuinsen bōekishi no kenkyū.* Yoshikawa Kōbunkan, 1985.

———. *Zoku nan'yō Nihon machi no kenkyū.* Iwanami Shoten, 1987.

Kang, Etsuko Hae-Jin. *Diplomacy and Ideology in Japanese-Korean Relations: From the Fifteenth to the Eighteenth Century.* London: Palgrave Macmillan, 1997.

Katō Eiichi. "Bahansen, shuinsen, hōshosen: Bakuhansei kokka no keisei to taigai kankei." In *Kaikin to sakoku,* edited by Kamiya Nobuyuki and Kimura Naoya, 41–50. Vol. 14 of *Tenbō Nihon rekishi.* Tokyōdō Shuppan, 2002.

———. *Bakuhansei kokka no keisei to gaikoku bōeki.* Azebura Shobō, 1993.

———. *Bakuhansei kokka no seiritsu to taigai kankei.* Kyoto: Shibunkaku Shuppan, 1998.

———. "Rengō Oranda Higashi-Indo Kaisha no senryaku kyoten to shite no Hirado shōkan." In *Nihon zenkindai no kokka to taigai kankei,* edited by Tanaka Takeo, 407–523. Yoshikawa Kōbunkan, 1987.

Kobata, Atsushi. "The Production and Uses of Gold and Silver in Sixteenth- and Seventeenth-Century Japan." *Economic History Review* 18, no. 2 (1965): 245–66.

Kondō Morishige, ed. *Gaiban tsūsho,* edited by Kondō Heijō. Vol. 21 of *Kaitei shiseki shūran.* Kokusho Kankōkai, 1901. Reprint, Kyoto: Rinsen Shoten, 1983.

Laver, Michael S. *Japan's Economy by Proxy.* Amherst, NY: Cambria Press, 2008.

———. *The Sakoku Edicts and the Politics of the Tokugawa Hegemony.* Amherst, NY: Cambria Press, 2011.

———. "Skins in the Game: The Dutch East India Company, Deerskins, and the Japan Trade." *World History Bulletin* 28, no. 2 (2012): 13–16.

Mizuno Norihito. "China in Tokugawa Foreign Relations: The Tokugawa Bakufu's Perception of and Attitudes toward Ming-Qing China." *Sino-Japanese Studies* 15 (April 2003): 108–44.

Murai Shosuke. "A Reconsideration of the Introduction of Firearms to Japan." *Memoirs of the Research Department of the Toyo Bunko* 60 (2002): 19–38.

Nagahara Keiji and Kozo Yamamura. "Shaping the Process of Unification: Technological Progress in Sixteenth- and Seventeenth-Century Japan." *Journal of Japanese Studies* 14, no. 1 (1988): 77–109.

Nagase-Reimer, Keiko. "Water Drainage in the Mines in Tokugawa Japan: Technological Improvements and Economic Limitations." In *Mining, Monies, and Culture in Early Modern Societies: East Asian and Global Perspectives*, edited by Nanny Kim and Keiko Nagase-Reimer, 25–42. Leiden: Brill, 2013.

Nagazumi Yōko. *Hirado Oranda shōkan no nikki*. 4 vols. Iwanami Shoten, 1969.

——— "The Japanese Go-Shuinjo (Vermilion Seal) Maritime Trade in Taiwan." In *Around and About in Formosa: Essays in Honor of Professor Ts'ao Yung-ho*, edited by Leonard Blussé, 27–42. Taipei: Ts'ao Yung-ho Foundation for Culture and Education, 2003.

——— *Shuinsen*. Yoshikawa Kōbunkan, 2001.

Oka, Mihoko. *The Namban Trade: Merchants and Missionaries in 16th and 17th Century Japan*. Leiden: Brill, 2021.

Owada Tetsuo. *Yamada Nagamasa: Shirarezaru jitsuzō*. Kōdansha, 1987.

Polenghi, Cesare. *Samurai of Ayutthaya: Yamada Nagamasa, Japanese Warrior and Merchant in Early Seventeenth-Century Siam*. Bangkok: White Lotus Press, 2009.

"Qinhuo Wang Zhi." In Zheng Ruozeng, *Chouhai tubian*, Vol. 9. N.p., 1563.

Ravina, Mark. *To Stand with the Nations of the World: Japan's Meiji Restoration in World History*. New York: Oxford University Press, 2017.

Reid, Anthony. *Expansion and Crisis*. Vol. 2 of *Southeast Asia in the Age of Commerce, 1450–1680*. New Haven, CT: Yale University Press, 1993.

——— *Southeast Asia in the Early Modern Era: Trade, Power, and Belief*. Ithaca, NY: Cornell University Press, 1993.

Satow, Ernest. "Notes on the Intercourse between Japan and Siam in the Seventeenth Century." *Transactions of the Asiatic Society of Japan* 13 (1884): 168–69.

Schouten, Justus. "Memorabel verhael van den waeren oorspronck, voortganck ende nederganck van de wichtige differenten die tusschen de Nederlanders en de Japansche natie om den Chineeschen handel ontstaen zijn." In *Nederlands Historische Bronnen*, edited by Leonard Blussé, 69–110. The Hague: Martinus Nijhoff, 1985.

Shapinsky, Peter. "Polyvocal Portolans: Nautical Charts and Hybrid Maritime Cultures in Early Modern East Asia." *Early Modern Japan* 14 (2006): 4–26.

Suzuki Yasuko. *Japan-Netherlands Trade, 1600–1800: The Dutch East India Company and Beyond*. Kyoto: Kyoto University Press, 2012.

Tashiro, Kazui. "Foreign Relations during the Edo Period: *Sakoku* Reexamined." *Journal of Japanese Studies* 8, no. 2 (1982): 283–306.

Teng, Emma. *Taiwan's Imagined Geography: Chinese Colonial Travel Writing and Pictures*. Cambridge, MA: Harvard University Press, 2004.

Thompson, Edward, ed. *Diary of Richard Cocks: Cape-Merchant in the English Factory in Japan, 1615–1622, with Correspondence*. 2 vols. London: Hakluyt Society, 1883.

Toby, Ronald. *State and Diplomacy in Early Modern Japan: Asia in the Development of the Tokugawa Bakufu*. Princeton, NJ: Princeton University Press, 1984. Reprint, Stanford, CA: Stanford University Press, 1991.

Tōkyō Daigaku Shiryō Hensanjo, ed. *Dagregisters gehouden door de Opperhoofden van de Nederlandse Faktorij in Japan*. 13 vols. Tōkyō Daigaku Shuppankai, 1974–.

Tomiyama Kazuyuki. *Ryūkyū ōkoku no gaikō to ōken*. Yoshikawa Kōbunkan, 2004.

Toyama Mikio. *Matsura-shi to Hirado bōeki*. Kokusho Kankōkai, 1987.

Turnbull, Stephen. "Onward, Christian Samurai! The Japanese Expeditions to Taiwan in 1609 and 1616." *Japanese Studies* 30, no. 1 (2010): 3–21.

Van Goor, Jurrien. "A Hybrid State: The Dutch Economic and Political Network in Asia." In *From the Mediterranean to the China Sea*, edited by Claude Guillot, Denys Lombard, and Roderich Ptak, 192–214. Wiesbaden: Harrassowitz, 1998.

Van Linschoten, Jan Huygen. *Itinerario: Voyage ofte schipvaert van Jan Huygen van Linschoten naer Oost ofte Portugaels Indien, 1579–1592.* 3 vols. The Hague: Martinus Nijhoff, 1955.

Walker, Brett. *Toxic Archipelago: A History of Industrial Disease in Japan.* Seattle: University of Washington Press, 2010.

Weider, F. C. *De Reis van Mahu en De Cordes door de Straat van Magalhães naar Zuid-America en Japan, 1598–1600.* 3 vols. The Hague: Martinus Nijhoff, 1923.

Wills, John E., Jr. "Relations with Maritime Europeans, 1514–1662." In *The Ming Dynasty, 1368–1644, Part 2,* edited by Denis Twitchett and Frederick W. Mote, 333–75. Vol. 8 of *The Cambridge History of China.* Cambridge: Cambridge University Press, 1998.

8

The Tokugawa Economy
Of Rulers, Producers, and Consumers

KOMURO MASAMICHI AND BETTINA GRAMLICH-OKA

"Economy," it has been said, is an "abstraction: it is temporally and culturally contingent, given form by exchanges that are imbedded in human relations."[1] In line with this premise, this chapter emphasizes the context and interactions that shaped such exchanges. Examining both macroeconomic history and individual economic activities, we describe the development of the Tokugawa economy, illustrating how its patterns and shifts were experienced by producers and consumers in a particular place and time.

Once-popular narratives in economic history that focused on how economic modernization and industrialization were achieved in Japan during the Meiji period and that served to confirm modernization theories are now a thing of the past.[2] Comparative studies in economic history have moved away from approaches that accept underlying teleologies of capitalist modernity. A recent volume edited by Ōtsuka Keijirō and Sugihara Kaoru, for example, engages with the "various paths" of industrialization in emerging economies in Asia and Africa. "The path each country followed," the editors assert, "was diverse, nonlinear, and more locally and regionally rooted than standard economic history and development economics had allowed for."[3] Debates continue, of course, over the extent of the growth in population, production, and hence living standards that characterized Japan's path to industrialization, but they bring new considerations to bear.

The authors wish to thank Michael Burtscher who translated large parts of the chapter, and in particular Kate Wildman Nakai as our critical reader.

[1] Davison, "Early Modern Social Networks," 456.
[2] Revisions of this approach in English scholarship are introduced by Pratt, "Social and Economic Change." The arguments advanced by Hanley and Yamamura in *Economic and Demographic Change* are taken to a more local and complex level in Howell, *Capitalism from Within*; Wigen, *Making of a Japanese Periphery*; Pratt, *Japan's Protoindustrial Elite*. See also Ravina, *Land and Lordship*; Roberts, *Mercantilism in a Japanese Domain*.
[3] Otsuka and Sugihara, *Paths to the Emerging State*, 27. For a recent summary of the literature that promoted views of Japan's experience as an exceptional path within Asia, i.e., a Western path, see Bassino et al., "Japan and the Great Divergence."

The concepts of economic growth and improvement in standards of living have driven much of the research in economic history on Tokugawa Japan. Two publications by Penelope Francks illustrate these trends in English-language scholarship. In *Rural Economic Development in Japan*, Francks describes the push-and-pull "virtuous circle" of the growth of commercial agriculture and rural manufacture that, in combination, generated rising incomes and improved standards of living in the late Tokugawa period.[4] Francks's second study, *The Japanese Consumer*, focuses on an intertwined phenomenon: the increase in the demand for consumer goods in the same rural regions. On the assumption that Tokugawa rulers and the populace alike regarded self-sufficiency as the norm, earlier narratives tended to view this increase from the perspective of how commercialization brought about the breakdown of self-sufficiency. By contrast, scholars such as Francks have begun to consider consumption as something worthy of study on its own terms and to look into how people of the time related to goods as consumers. In *The Japanese Consumer*, Francks suggests that, on the macro level, researchers should investigate the "relationship between growth and change in consumer demand"; on the micro level, she calls for exploring the circumstances under which households came to substitute market-supplied goods for home-produced ones and embrace new products as increasingly ordinary elements in their lifestyles.[5] This approach continues Susan Hanley's earlier emphasis on popular living standards but with the important difference of directing attention to the perception of these products as not "necessities" but "consumer goods."[6] Such approaches have fostered a rather positive picture of Tokugawa Japan's economy as a dynamic entity with many players.

In outlining the framing features of the Tokugawa economic world – including the political setting and macroeconomic indicators – we, too, draw attention to how the proportion occupied by manufacturing industries and distribution mechanisms increased steadily in tandem with expansion of the economy's overall volume. Diverse factors accompanied and further spurred these trends: urbanization (in cities and country towns), greater social mobility,

---

[4] Francks, *Rural Economic Development*. Francks extends Thomas C. Smith's classic "by-employment" model (Smith, "Farm Family By-Employments") with the notion of household "pluriactivity."

[5] Francks, *Japanese Consumer*, 47–73; Francks, "Inconspicuous Consumption," 142. For recent publications on modern Japan and consumption, see the brief overview by Gordon, "Consumption, Consumerism, and Japanese Modernity." For a fuller treatment, see Francks and Hunter, *Historical Consumer*. For a "nascent" consumer society in premodern Japan, see Farris, *Bowl for a Coin*.

[6] Hanley, *Everyday Things in Premodern Japan*.

expanding trade and communication networks, rising incomes, the labor of women as producers for the market, and a popular consciousness increasingly oriented toward ordinary consumption. The expansion of trade, communications, and markets, as well as rising cash incomes, allowed for wide emulation of goods once the preserve of the political elite.

Foundations of the Tokugawa Economy

The foundations of the Tokugawa economy were laid during the Sengoku period, the unification regimes of Oda Nobunaga and Toyotomi Hideyoshi, and the first decades of Tokugawa rule. Five policies that took shape during this span of time from the mid-sixteenth to the mid-seventeenth century were particularly important: consolidation of territorial rule, adoption of the *kokudaka* system, separation of warriors from farmers, establishment of functionally demarcated status hierarchies, and the creation of a unified currency system.

During the Sengoku period regional lords pursued measures aimed at maintaining the military might necessary to survive amid the chaos of unceasing warfare. They sought to secure territories rich in productive resources and reinvested a large part of their revenue from the land in irrigation works, roads, mining, and maintaining public peace. The annual tribute or rent collected from cultivators (on land and in kind) thus gradually shed the character of a private rent channeled into consumption by elite individuals and acquired instead dimensions of a public tax used for broader economic ends.[7] The Tokugawa system of hybrid rule by the shogunal and domanial governments took this development to the next level. Not only the territories under direct shogunal control (about one quarter of the country) but also the domains of many daimyo were of a size that made it possible for them to undertake public works of a significant scale.

The efforts the Sengoku daimyo put into comprehensive river management were of particular importance and served to encourage the development of new rice farming techniques. Paddies originally were limited to places near springs or small streams in basins and valleys or in easily irrigated areas in the foothills. The riparian and engineering projects undertaken by the Sengoku daimyo facilitated the extension of paddy-field cultivation into the alluvial plains along the mid- and lower reaches of big rivers.[8] At the same time, in the temperate regions of western Japan, the introduction of Indica-type "red rice"

---

[7] Hayami, *Nihon ni okeru keizai shakai*, 47, 62.
[8] The riparian works undertaken by Takeda Shingen in the Kōfu basin are especially famous. See Doboku Gakkai, *Meiji izen Nihon dobokushi*.

(*akagome*), which is drought tolerant as well as suited to cultivation in poorly drained fields, made it possible to grow rice in river plains even without large-scale engineering works.[9]

The introduction of the *kokudaka* system took place against the background of progress in rice cultivation techniques. *Kokudaka* was a unified standard based on the putative average yield of individual fields stated in rice equivalents.[10] The *kokudaka* of each field was determined by measuring its size and assessing its productivity per unit area according to a graded scale. To ensure that these measurements and assessments were conducted uniformly, the length of measuring sticks and the size of measuring cups, that is weights and measures, were gradually unified by decree across the country. The first nationwide land surveys conducted in this manner were undertaken at the order of Toyotomi Hideyoshi in the 1590s. A series of similar surveys followed in the early years of the Tokugawa shogunate, and additional surveys and corrections continued throughout the first half of the seventeenth century. The arable lands of individual farmers, as well as the total arable land of each village, constituted by the sum of the individual plots comprised within it, were indexed according to their *kokudaka* yields. Taxes and dues were collected as a set percentage of this assessed total.

The specification of *kokudaka* was not only a means to draw revenue from producers but also a principle of social organization that pervaded the entire Tokugawa society from the individual farmer up to the shogun himself. It is for this reason that historians speak of a "*kokudaka* system." The surveys and *kokudaka* assessment mechanism served to simplify the complicated, multilayered structures of ownership or vested interests in land that had accrued since medieval times. While the surveys in effect recognized the customary rights of farmers to work particular pieces of land, the taxes and dues owed on these lands became fixed as well. At the same time, the values of the holdings of the shogunate, daimyo, lesser warriors, and court nobles, as well as the stipends of non-enfeoffed retainers, were also expressed in terms of *kokudaka*, and military and labor services were determined on that basis. *Kokudaka* assessments were thus not simply the axis of the relationship between proprietary lords and the farmers working their lands; they also served to indicate relations of vassalage and status within warrior houses and the ruling stratum as a whole.

[9] *Seiryōki* (Notes of Seiryō, c. 1628), a chronicle of the life of the Sengoku military leader Doi Kiyoyoshi (or Seiryō, 1546–1629), offers evidence of Sengoku warlords' interest in agricultural implements, fertilizer, and variety selection. See Saitō, "Daikaikon, jinkō, shōnō keizai," 179–87; see also von Verschuer, *Rice, Agriculture, and the Food Supply*, 79–80.
[10] 1 *koku* equaled 5.1 bushels, or 180 liters, said to be the amount needed to sustain one man for a year.

Adoption of *kokudaka* assessments as the foundation of the system of taxation had important long-range economic consequences. The *kokudaka* of rice fields were determined by assessing average yields per unit area. However, fields for produce other than rice, residential lands, forest lands, and fisheries were also assessed in terms of putative rice yields. In other words, *kokudaka* did not express actual yields in rice but fictional ones arrived at through conversion into putative equivalents. In addition, where agricultural productivity increased in the course of the Tokugawa period, actual revenue from the land might come to exceed the official *kokudaka* assessment. These circumstances created a potential for surplus gain accruing to farmers.

The *kokudaka* system also facilitated the separation of warriors, who lived off tax revenue defined in terms of *kokudaka*, from farmers, who generated that revenue. The Sengoku daimyo had sought to extend their control over local warrior powerholders who also engaged in agricultural production – the so-called *jizamurai* (landed samurai) and *kokujin* (men of the province). These local lords posed a challenge to the establishment of integrated territorial rule in two regards. On the one hand, their high degree of autonomy both economically and militarily rendered uncertain their continued submission to the political and military leadership of the Sengoku daimyo. On the other hand, their engagement in farming made it necessary to avoid interrupting agricultural production when mobilizing them for military service. The military undertakings of the Sengoku daimyo were thus subject to severe seasonal constraints. To resolve these issues, the Sengoku daimyo pursued policies of separating small local landholders from farming activities. These efforts proceeded in parallel with the construction of castle towns, where vassals were ordered to live. By the middle of the seventeenth century, the majority of erstwhile landed warriors had been transformed into urban consumers. The Tokugawa shogunate's stipulation that daimyo should maintain permanent establishments in the shogunal capital and reside there at regular intervals spurred rapid growth in the population of Edo and made it a center of consumption.

This far-reaching social reorganization created intertwined sets of norms and expectations. The rights of warriors over land were limited to claims to regulated tax income as an expression of overlordship, and the permanence of the tenure of daimyo and smaller-scale shogunal vassals was constrained by the possibility that the shogunate might confiscate or reduce their holdings or require them to move from one territory to another.[11] The farmers'

---

[11] For the social reorganization, see Bitō, *Edo jidai to wa nani ka*, 73–80; Fujiki, "Tōitsu seiken no seiritsu," 34–39.

rights to use their land, on the other hand, acquired a degree of permanence by the end of the Sengoku period. Farmers were virtually free to sell and buy or mortgage farmland. Once recognized, customary rights of these sorts assumed the aura of "ancestral laws" that even rulers could not easily infringe according to their own whim. The demarcation of status categories likewise served to guarantee individuals in the various sectors of the economy their respective standings and rights in separate status hierarchies. The extremely harsh conditions to which farmers were subject notwithstanding, they as well as the artisans and merchants of the Tokugawa period were thus able to conduct their businesses on the basis of a set of vested rights they could take for granted.

One further important policy pursued by Tokugawa rulers and their immediate predecessors was securing monetary sovereignty. The circulation of goods, creation of infrastructure, and operation of transportation routes all required forms of payment.[12] The Tokugawa government monopolized the issuance of coins valid throughout Japan.[13] Gold and silver coins were issued from 1600 onward, while the Kan'ei tsūhō copper coin was minted from 1636. This was the first Japan-wide monetary issue by a unified government since the minting of the "twelve imperial coins" (kōchō jūnisen) during the Nara period.[14] Gold and copper coins had fixed denominations recognizable by shape. The value of silver coins was initially determined by weight. The shogunate set official exchange rates between gold, silver, and copper currencies but did not interfere with their exchange according to market value. From the end of the eighteenth century onward, the issuance of silver coins exchangeable at fixed rates for gold coins resulted in a stabilization of market exchange rates between gold and silver; eight Nanryō nishugin silver coins, for example, equaled one ryō of gold. (Minted in 1772, these silver coins inaugurated the first gold-standard coinage system in Japan.)

Coins functioned both as metallic and as token money, and their nominal value as specified by the Tokugawa government was an important factor in determining their exchange value. When markets were stable and public trust in money was high, coins were accepted at this nominal value regardless of their metallic content. In times of economic instability, though, the metallic content of coins played a major role in determining the value at which they circulated.

In addition to the gold, silver, and copper coins minted by the Tokugawa government for circulation throughout Japan, from the late seventeenth century onward individual domains began issuing paper bills valid within their

---

[12] For recent concepts and understandings of the functionality of monies in premodern societies, see Kuroda, Global History of Money.

[13] For currency in pre-Tokugawa times, see Sakurai, "Currency and Credit in Medieval Japan."

[14] For Kan'ei tsūhō, see Yasukuni, "Regional versus Standardized Coinage."

own territories alone, referred to as *hansatsu* (domain bills). Many of these notes were convertible into Tokugawa government-issued standard coins at guaranteed rates. Some, however, were based on commodity reserves such as rice. At times the Tokugawa government enacted prohibitions of domain-based paper money or regulations for its issue. Nevertheless, over time more and more domains turned to issuing their own currencies. A survey conducted at the outset of the Meiji period found that about 80 percent of domains followed this practice.[15] There even were domains where domain-issued notes made up a large proportion of the currency in circulation.[16]

Macroeconomic Indicators of the Tokugawa Economy

Given that economic statistical surveys were not yet conducted in the Tokugawa period, it is difficult to assess nationwide macroeconomic trends with any degree of precision, in particular for the seventeenth century. However, fragmentary historical evidence exists on which estimates can be based, and it is possible to extrapolate from regionally and temporally limited materials.[17] Figure 8.1 shows the trends in the relative growth rates of population, arable land, and actual harvests. Current research posits a countrywide population of 12.6 million in 1525 rising to about 17 million around 1600 and over 31 million by 1721. Thereafter the population is held to have fluctuated between 30 to 32 million until around 1850, with one-third of the population living in eastern Japan and two-thirds in the central and western regions. In the last two decades, the population grew to 34 million.[18] Within this general trend, urbanization rates offer a more refined indicator of overall economic development. The urban population is currently estimated to have comprised about 6.1 percent in 1600, increasing to 12.6 by 1721. One century later, the estimates of the numbers living in towns larger than 10,000 inhabitants show a small decline to 12.3 percent of the total population, falling by 1874 to 10.1 percent.[19] Recently,

---

[15] Sakudō, *Nihon kahei kin'yūshi*, 57.

[16] For instance, Fukuzawa Yukichi mentioned that he used only *hansatsu* in his Nakatsu domain (in present-day Ōita Prefecture). Fukuzawa, *Tsūkaron*, 547–48.

[17] For various quantitative data analyses, see Hayami, Saitō, and Toby, *Emergence of Economic Society in Japan*.

[18] Figures are from Saitō, "1600-nen no zenkoku jinkō," 13; Saito and Takashima, "Population, Urbanisation and Farm Output," 2. Their estimates include population data by Hayami and Miyamoto, "Gaisetsu," and Kitō, "Meiji izen Nihon no chiiki jinkō." For pre-Tokugawa estimates, see Farris, *Japan's Medieval Population*.

[19] These numbers are in line with other observations presented by Gaubatz (Chapter 19), this volume.

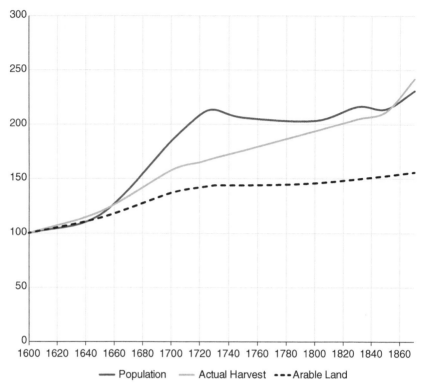

Figure 8.1 Fluctuations in economic variables: population (Saito and Takashima, "Population, Urbanisation and Farm Output," 8; Kitō, *Jinkō de miru Nihonshi*, 78); arable land (Hayami and Miyamoto, "Gaisetsu," 44); actual harvest (Hamano, "Kinsei no seiritsu to zenkoku shijō," 6–9). (The year 1600 is set at 100.)

however, Saitō Osamu and Takashima Masanori have stressed the need to take into account the population patterns in smaller urban centers, such as country towns with less than 10,000 inhabitants. According to their calculations, overall, the size of such centers increased rather than declined.[20] Taken together, these indicators point to a more balanced distribution of production and consumption throughout society in the latter part of the Tokugawa period.

The growth in actual yield (with the productivity of dry fields expressed in rice equivalents) relative to acreage of arable land suggests that expansion in agricultural activity was the result not only of an increase in the area under cultivation but also of more intensive farming techniques made possible by added

---

[20] Saito and Takashima, "Estimating the Shares," 370; Saito and Takashima, "Population, Urbanisation and Farm Output," 7.

labor input, civil engineering projects, and improved fertilization.[21] Although land productivity rose steadily in the seventeenth century, the per capita productivity of agricultural labor decreased as a consequence of rapid population growth. Expansion of the area under cultivation leveled off in the eighteenth century, and the population tended to decrease. The actual yield continued to rise, however. Saitō and Takashima have recently calculated that the actual harvest increased from 30,243,000 *koku* in 1600 to 60,495,000 *koku* by 1804, thus more than doubling both in traditionally more developed western and central Japan and in the eastern provinces.[22] This suggests that both land and labor productivity rose likewise. The increase in actual yield continued unabated in the nineteenth century, and population growth picked up again as well. By comparison to the previous century, there was also an expansion in arable land (even in so-called backward areas such as the eastern regions).

To assess overall economic growth during the Tokugawa period, Saitō and Takashima have also used regional data to bring nonagricultural productivity into their calculations. They estimate that in general the GDP (gross domestic product) level was low in the first 120 years of the Tokugawa period, but that from the 1720s rural-centered development led to sustained growth, signaled by expansion of the nonagricultural sectors. The agricultural sector shrank from 73.7 percent in 1600 to 59.6 percent by 1874, while manufacturing grew steadily from 8.8 percent of the GDP to about 12.3 percent for the same time period. The service sector expanded even more, from 17.5 percent in 1600 to 28.1 percent by 1874.[23] These figures suggest an expansion of nonagricultural productivity in previously less developed regions as well as the traditionally economically advanced centers.[24]

In that prices may be considered "a barometer of economic activity,"[25] price trends also offer evidence of changes in the structure and quantity of production over the course of the Tokugawa period.[26] Both tax levies and warrior income

---

[21] For civil engineering projects that domains, individuals, and communities undertook to raise the agricultural output, see Kanzaka, "Development of Civil Engineering Projects." Fertilizer produced from dried sardines had already been used during the seventeenth century, primarily in the Kyoto-Osaka region. In the eighteenth century, Kujūkurihama on the Bōsō Peninsula east of Edo became the main center of production, and from the latter half of the eighteenth century, the production of herring-based fertilizer began to flourish in Ezo (present-day Hokkaido). See also Howell, *Capitalism from Within*.

[22] Saito and Takashima, "Population, Urbanisation and Farm Output," 9. See also Kanzaka, "Development of Civil Engineering Projects," who argues for a more than 50 percent increase in yield.

[23] Saito and Takashima, "Estimating the Shares," 380–81.

[24] For a similar view, see also Smith, *Native Sources*, 15–49.

[25] Miyamoto, "Prices and Microeconomic Dynamics," 119.

[26] See the studies by Iwahashi, *Kinsei Nihon bukkashi no kenkyū*; Yamazaki, *Kinsei bukkashi*.

were denominated in rice, making it the most important and widely produced commodity in Tokugawa Japan. Approximate real rice prices rose in the first decades of the period until the 1660s, reflecting a shortage in supply and a sharp increase in demand due to continuing population growth and rapid urbanization.[27] From then onward, however, a slight tendency for supply to outweigh demand prevailed until the end of the Tokugawa period, causing rice prices to fall, while those of other commodities climbed, a circumstance described as "low price for rice and high for other commodities" (beika-yasu no shoshiki-daka). This situation exerted pressure on the fiscal policies and household finances of warrior houses, which had to convert income pegged to the rice price into money to cover their expenses. Faced with a decline in revenues, the shogunate undertook various economic reforms beginning in the late seventeenth century, all of which in one way or another attempted to ensure stable rice prices.

The first attempts at market intervention relied heavily on manipulation of the currency – first devaluation and then restoration – and had mixed results. The rapid succession of recoinages caused extreme instability of overall prices for four decades starting around the end of the seventeenth century. The first devaluation, the Genroku debasement of 1695, had as its foremost aim profit from seigniorage (the difference between the nominal value of money and the cost of issuance).[28] The increased amount of coins in circulation also responded to the monetary demands of the growing market and had a moderate inflationary effect. Seeing some success in these measures, in particular the direct profit to be obtained from reminting, the government embarked on further debasements between 1706 and 1711. The price of rice rose by 109 percent. However, the rapid expansion in money supply exceeded the market's capacity, flooding it with 1.3 times as much money as had been in circulation twenty years earlier.[29]

The Shōtoku and Kyōhō monetary reforms between 1714 and 1736, which sought to restore the metallic quality of the currency, had the opposite effect. The currency supply (of higher quality coins) dropped by 33 percent and the price of rice by 65 percent (i.e. the volume of currency was 51 percent larger than prior to the first devaluation in 1695; the price of rice was 26 percent lower). Warrior households, which depended on selling rice to obtain cash, now needed more rice, and domains shipped greater amounts to be marketed in Osaka. The

---

[27] Real rice prices are calculated to reflect supply and demand in ordinary years. As far as possible they thus discount the effects of shortages caused by natural factors such as drought as well as quantitative and qualitative fluctuations of money in circulation.

[28] The technological limitations of mining and the depletion of bullion resulting from the export of large quantities meant that debasement was the only option for bringing more metal currency into circulation.

[29] For the monetary quantity, see Iwahashi, "Tokugawa jidai no kahei sūryō," 258.

deflationary effect was exacerbated by other dimensions of the financial reforms that sought to restrain consumption. At last, with the Genbun recoinage of 1736, the shogunal government reverted to a policy of more moderate currency deval-uation. The total volume of gold and silver coins in circulation increased by 40 percent between 1736 and 1818, and the consequent drop in the value of money spurred a 20 percent increase in the rice price. Researchers have interpreted the success of the shogunate's renewed debasement policy as an indicator that by the mid-Tokugawa period money and the market economy had permeated society.[30]

From the late 1730s until the 1780s, general commodity price levels displayed a downward tendency in comparison to rice. From then on, however, real rice prices declined in comparison to cash crops such as cotton, rapeseed, and raw silk. This indicates an oversupply of rice and heightened the incentive for farm-ers to engage in cultivating cash crops. Until the turn of the nineteenth century, prices for agricultural products tended to be higher than for manufactured goods. Subsequently, however, processed goods began to fetch higher prices, and in the late Tokugawa period (from around 1800 to the opening of the ports in the late 1850s) handicraft manufacture in agricultural villages steadily expanded.[31] By prompting the abandonment of fields subject to relatively heavy taxes (despite the general increase in arable land noted earlier), these develop-ments undermined the foundations of the Tokugawa economic system.[32]

Distribution Systems

Market transactions were integral to the Tokugawa political and economic structure whereby warriors sold tax and stipendary rice to purchase other com-modities.[33] They also were crucial to provisioning the urban centers, where the vast majority of warriors resided. Securing the flow of goods for these trans-actions required connecting five different economic areas: the agricultural villages that produced the staple commodities, domain castle towns, Osaka and Kyoto as the centers of skilled handicraft manufacture and transregional

---

[30] See Iwahashi, *Kinsei Nihon bukkashi no kenkyū*; Shinbo, *Kindai Nihon keizaishi*; Katō, *Kinsei kōki keizai hatten*; Metzler, "Policy Space, Polarities, and Regimes."

[31] The greater volume of historical records available from the eighteenth century on allows for more detailed estimates of general price trends. Miyamoto Matao has compared price trends of agricultural commodities and manufactured goods with the price trends of rice from the 1720s until the end of the Tokugawa period. Miyamoto, "Bukka to makuro keizai no hendō," 94–95; for his data set, see 122–23. Miyamoto, "Prices and Microeconomic Dynamics," 139–41, 157.

[32] Komuro, "Mito-gaku Fujita-ha nōseiron," 225–29.

[33] Miyamoto, "Quantitative Aspects of Tokugawa Economy," 73, 79, includes charts that depict the flow of the economy.

commerce, the new consumer metropolis of Edo, and the remaining gateways for foreign trade.[34]

The majority of goods locally produced in the domains flowed into the castle towns.[35] Tax rice constituted the bulk of these. However, other goods produced by villagers also made their way to the castle towns. These included surplus rice that remained in farmers' hands after the collection of taxes and other grains and goods produced in greater quantity than required for self-consumption or that could not be marketed in the immediate vicinity. The rice collected as land tax was distributed by the territorial lord as stipends to his retainers in the castle town and sold to castle town merchants who marketed it to post station towns, as well as mountain, fishing, and mining villages unable to produce rice themselves. Since the demand for rice within the domains was limited, a large part of tax rice was ultimately shipped to Osaka to be marketed there.

Neither the domains nor the villages were economically self-sufficient. Domain lords and their retainers depended on castle town merchants to obtain goods that could not be secured in their own domains from Osaka and Kyoto in return for the export of tax rice and other local produce. Farmers who marketed their produce in castle towns likewise obtained daily commodities and production materials in exchange. This two-way flow of commodities between Osaka and the castle towns led to the development of methods of payment through bills of exchange (*tegata*) issued between wholesalers in the castle towns and Osaka or Kyoto respectively, allowing accounts to be settled without cash remittances.

As the above description indicates, Osaka and Kyoto were the original hubs of a countrywide economy. This region already had developed a thriving handicraft industry before 1600, and it soon became the main supplier of manufactured goods consumed throughout Japan. Simultaneously, it generated a high demand for surplus agricultural produce from the domains and shogunal territory. The shogunate made sure to put the Osaka-Kyoto region under its direct administration so as to keep the large-scale circulation of goods under its supervision.

Edo, as the political capital, developed quickly as a consumption center in eastern Japan. Originally constructed by Tokugawa Ieyasu at the turn of the seventeenth century, first as his castle town and then as the seat of the new Tokugawa shogunate, it underwent a period of further expansion between the 1630s and 1640s. It was home to a large samurai population, not only the direct

---

[34] For overseas maritime transport and foreign trade, see Hellyer (Chapter 5), this volume.
[35] For a conceptual understanding of the distribution system in the Tokugawa period, see Nakai, *Bakuhan shakai to shōhin ryūtsū*.

vassals of the shogun but also many samurai from the domains. Increasing numbers of daimyo also came to attend on the shogun to display their loyalty to his rule, and by 1642 the shogunate formalized this practice through regulations requiring all daimyo to reside in Edo at regular intervals (typically every other year) and to leave their main wives and heirs there permanently. These lords thus had to maintain extensive residences in Edo staffed by substantial numbers of domain officials, while they themselves periodically led large processions of vassals to the shogunal capital. Edo thereby not only acquired a large samurai population; the number of merchants, artisans, and servants needed to requisition the warrior households expanded vastly as well. Formal population statistics for this period do not exist, but scholars widely agree that Edo had more than one million inhabitants by the early eighteenth century.[36]

In this fashion, Edo grew into a gigantic consumer city in the course of the seventeenth century. Its rice was brought in primarily from northeastern Japan, while the immediate vicinity supplied its vegetables and fresh fish. Many manufactured goods such as vinegar, sake, soy sauce, paper, and textiles, however, had to be obtained from Osaka or Kyoto. To defray outlays for administration and consumption, the shogunal government had to transmit the proceeds from its rice sales in Osaka to Edo. The domain lords likewise had to transfer funds in order to maintain their residences and cover the costs of their sojourns in the shogunal capital. Payments for the vast amount of goods sent to Edo had to be remitted in turn by traders based there to wholesalers in the Osaka-Kyoto region. Money thus had to be transferred between Edo and the Osaka-Kyoto region in both directions, spurring the development of financial tools such as money orders. The shogunate commissioned large trading and moneylending houses in the three cities to transmit its funds from Osaka and Kyoto to Edo.

Next to packhorses over land, the main conduit for interregional trade and the distribution of goods in Tokugawa Japan was coastal shipping from Osaka to Edo. Wholesalers in Osaka began to ship their wares to Edo conjointly on large cargo ships around 1620. In 1694, with the aim of controlling transport fees and spreading out the cost of maritime losses, Edo wholesalers dealing in different kinds of goods brought in from the Kyoto-Osaka region formed shipping syndicates known as the "ten groups of wholesalers" (*tokumi doiya*). In the 1670s, the Edo merchant Kawamura Zuiken investigated and opened sea routes for shipping tax grain from territories under direct shogunal control in northeastern Japan to Edo. These consisted of an eastern route down

---

[36] Kitō, "Edo-Tōkyō no jinkō hatten."

the Pacific coast and one circling the Japanese islands counterclockwise along the Japan Sea coast and passing through Shimonoseki and the Seto Inland Sea before approaching Edo from the south. Commercially organized shipping would make use of these routes, and the entirety of Japan was thus linked by coastal shipping routes.

Trade

The urban Osaka- and Edo-based wholesalers of the first half of the seventeenth century usually operated as receiving wholesalers (*niuke doiya*). They took in large loads of goods, mostly from domain lords, against payment of a storage fee and collected brokerage fees once a transaction was complete. During the second half of the seventeenth century, a new type of wholesale business, the purchasing wholesaler (*shiire doiya*), emerged, and by the end of the seventeenth century it predominated. Purchasing wholesalers would gather information on various goods from production areas and procure items using their own capital and assessments of sales prospects. They would sell these goods after locating the most profitable buyer, a search that expanded steadily from urban centers into local towns and villages. The example of the cotton wholesalers' guild (*toiya nakama*) of Ōdenma-chō in Edo illustrates the shift from the first type of wholesaler to the second, as well as the overall expansion in trade. In the first half of the seventeenth century, it comprised four receiving wholesaler houses. In 1686, by contrast, it registered seventy purchasing wholesaler houses as members.[37]

The growth of the central markets of Osaka, Kyoto, and Edo stimulated production in rural industries. By the mid-Tokugawa period (between 1730 and 1800), small farm households engaged increasingly in commodity production, and local merchants began to assume an active role in purchasing and shipping these commodities to central markets, giving birth to new forms of distribution networks linking urban centers with rural villages.

Expansion in land transport, which had lagged behind to this point, also encouraged involvement in the market. The easing of earlier restrictions on land transport led increasing numbers of farmers to engage in packhorse transport as a side employment, linking rural villages with towns that served as traffic and distribution hubs. Production of cash crops (particularly raw materials for manufactured goods) thereby became an option for more regions than before, leading to a growth in areas producing specialized items such as

---

[37] Matsumoto, *Nihon kinsei toshiron*.

cotton, tobacco, indigo, safflower, rush, wax, rapeseed, paper, and raw silk. During the seventeenth century, cotton production, for example, had been centered in the Kyoto-Osaka region. In the eighteenth century, however, it moved to areas such as the Seto Inland Sea and ultimately spread to the eastern seaboard, Kantō, and even the present-day Nagano region.[38]

The increased quantity of goods flowing into the central markets led to a decline in prices there. Between 1757 and 1771, for example, the average price for raw cotton in Osaka fell by 16 percent from its level in 1727. The decline in the prices of cash crops in the central markets reduced the price gap between central markets and producing areas, which was the urban merchants' source of profit. Wholesalers sought ways to maintain their profit margin by maintaining prices in the central market and lowering the purchase price. Ultimately, the main brunt of market fluctuations was thus felt by the producers.[39]

The main strategy wholesalers in the great urban centers adopted to secure and protect profits was to form chartered trade associations or merchant guilds (kabu nakama) with limited membership. The shogunate tried originally to restrict such arrangements, but in the 1720s it shifted to a policy of granting them recognition.[40] Backed by the authority of the shogunate, the trade associations sought to keep control of the flow of goods from agricultural producers through local acquisition merchants and wholesalers in the castle towns to the wholesalers in the central markets. To this end, the associations frequently sought and obtained edicts prohibiting merchants who were not members to purchase goods directly from producers.[41]

Three factors made this system of control by wholesale merchants possible. For one, the shift of the production of cash crops to more remote regions meant that producers could not easily access markets themselves and had to make use of established transport routes to the urban centers. Second, the cash crops produced by farmers were mostly unprocessed or semi-processed goods that required further refinement by artisans or skilled workers in the urban centers. This was the case, for instance, with the dyeing and weaving of raw and white silk as well as the dyeing of plain cotton. Certainly there were some instances of technology transfer to peripheral areas in the eighteenth century, such as

---

[38] For the changes to trade during the Edo period, see Nakai, "Edo jidai no shijō keitai"; Oka and Yamazaki, *Nihon keizaishi*, 145–46.

[39] See Miyamoto, "Management Systems," 102–3; Wigmore, *Law and Justice*, 1:96–107.

[40] See Wigmore, *Law and Justice*, 1:97.

[41] According to Matsumoto, "Shōnin ryūtsū no hatten," 114–15, the years 1750–80 in particular saw the issuing of many such regulations.

the transmission of silk weaving techniques from Nishijin in Kyoto to Kiryū in the Kantō area, or of cotton weaving techniques from Nishijin to Nōbi in the Nagoya region. By and large, however, such transfers became common only from the 1790s. Until then, rural producers of raw or half-finished goods continued to depend on technologies available only in the metropolitan centers, and the primary market for their goods was thus not the ultimate consumer but intermediate processors. Third, financial constrictions made it difficult for local producers and brokers to skirt existing distribution channels and organize trade between the production areas and the central markets on their own. Collecting payments on the distribution of goods and recovering the costs incurred in long-distance marketing could take considerable time. Local people thus had to rely on a financial backer to advance the necessary funds. The only enterprises capable of procuring such funds were wholesalers benefiting from the trust of metropolitan moneychangers.[42] Reliance on such advance funding, however, also closed the road to free-market participation by the producers. In this manner, control by metropolitan wholesalers over the production and distribution of goods became the norm between the 1750s and 1780s.

From the mid-Tokugawa period, these circumstances gave rise to two competing patterns of long-distance trade. In one, local merchants began to participate in the existing national distribution networks revolving around wholesalers based in the major urban centers. They frequently formed associations or guilds and entered into agreements with metropolitan wholesalers so as to obtain the necessary financing.

A second pattern was for local merchants to operate under a domain monopoly or become part of a *kokueki* (domain benefit) undertaking.[43] The key incentive for domains to become involved in such undertakings was the ever-greater pressure on domain finances caused by the enormous expenditures incurred in Edo. For domain governments, the export of specialized goods and farmers' surplus rice

---

[42] In general, rural industries in peripheral areas did not develop to the point of generating credit systems that could provide financing for distribution expenses. The key source of outside funding for such costs continued to be large merchant houses in Osaka and Kyoto. As is well known, these lent out large sums not only to ailing domains but also to farmers. In the 1860s, the Kōnoike house, for instance, lent 2,500 *kan* of silver to farmers out of a total of 37,000 *kan* in loans (a total sum that exceeded the annual revenue of a major daimyo). Sakudō, *Kinsei hōken shakai no kahei kin'yū kōzō*. Cited by Toby, "Country Bankers," n12.

[43] From the mid-eighteenth century the term *kokueki* came to be used to describe the efforts by domains to secure their prosperity. Economic thought concerned with enriching the domain is thus commonly referred to as *kokueki* thought. For the diverse meanings of *kokueki*, see Gramlich-Oka and Smits, *Economic Thought*; Roberts, *Mercantilism in a Japanese Domain*; Ravina, *Land and Lordship*; Kawaguchi and Ishii, *History of Economic Thought in Japan*.

offered a means of alleviating these pressures by bringing Tokugawa-backed currency into their own territories. Beginning in the 1750s, many domains thus encouraged increased production for central markets, established monopolies, or granted purchase privileges to castle town merchants that left the domain government in control of distribution. They also issued decrees checking the flow of goods into and out of the domain. These *kokueki* policies had the effect of closely tying domain economies to the central markets and stimulating their further commercialization (a development that inadvertently undermined the domanial political structure built upon an agricultural tax base).

For local merchants, domanial pursuit of *kokueki* policies offered an alternative to relying on advance funding from metropolitan wholesalers and a potential foothold for challenging existing distribution networks. Whereas wholesalers in Osaka operated under monopoly rights granted by the Tokugawa government, domains could rely on their own resources to establish wholesale stations in places such as Ōtsu and Fushimi near Kyoto or in Edo, thus avoiding the Osaka region altogether. At the same time, domain authorities' interference in economic distribution impeded producers' free participation in the market and frequently entailed oppression of farmers. This led to an increase in frequency from the late eighteenth century of uprisings opposing monopolies and riots attacking wholesalers.[44]

In the late Tokugawa period, a third option took shape for local merchants seeking to compete with metropolitan wholesalers and domain monopolies: intraregional trade. Together with expansion in the production of specialized goods and handicraft industries, in some regions the division of labor increased (with a significant input of female labor into household by-employment production), and rural markets appeared on a new scale. Commodities like textiles and brewery items were processed and sold locally, and markets for rice grown in the vicinity emerged as well.[45] The agents involved in this kind of production and trade were diverse. In economically relatively advanced regions, they came from the stratum of independent middling farmers and from handicraft manufacturers based in industrially developing small urban areas. In less economically developed regions, wealthy landlords or farmers often doubled as handicraft entrepreneurs. In either case, these were economic actors who engaged in production and trade without receiving advance funds from metropolitan wholesalers or purchasing loans under a domain monopoly. To the extent that they served markets in adjacent regions, they did not need large

---

[44] See Walthall (Chapter 20), this volume.
[45] The Ina valley was a case in point. See Wigen, *Making of a Japanese Periphery*.

funds to finance long-distance distribution. Direct access by producers and local merchants to markets was here comparatively open.[46]

The primary purchasers of the items sold in these rural markets were farmers. In the late Tokugawa period, farm households continued to supply the bulk of their own needs, but the extent to which they purchased additional goods with money gained from commodity production (including handicraft manufacture) and earnings from day labor steadily increased. Farmers who lost their land tended to remain in their villages as petty cultivators paying rent to a landlord for the land they farmed. These petty cultivators could supply themselves with part of their daily needs. The necessities of life that they lacked, on the other hand, had to be purchased with money obtained from household manufacturing as a by-employment or by working as day laborers in nearby towns or post stations. Family members working for a rural handicraft entrepreneur, such as in soy sauce production, might procure earnings as well. In the late Tokugawa period, landless laborers entirely divorced from cultivation also increased in rural areas, although their numbers did not compare to those of active farmers. Those who did not leave for urban centers became wage laborers in rural industries or earned their living in transport. The need of these farmers, petty cultivators, and day laborers for basic provisions that they were unable to produce themselves, such as food grains, sake, soy sauce, cloth, and lamp oil, was one factor spurring the development of markets for these goods in rural areas.[47]

Trends in rice prices furnish collateral evidence for the growth of rural markets. The diversion of farmers' labor into by-employments in rural industries together with the growth of a landless stratum divorced from cultivation resulted in the late Tokugawa period in a decline in the cultivation of wet-field rice and other food grains. Concomitantly, farmers and land tenants engaging in rural production and trade sought to purchase more rice on the market, as did day laborers and the landless. This combination of factors inevitably drove up rice prices in rural markets. It also brought about a change in the sales destinations of the rice collected by territorial lords as taxes. Up to then, surplus tax rice had been sold primarily in central markets such as Osaka. Given the high costs of transportation, however, the rising local demand made it often more profitable

---

[46] For a simplified chart of the late Tokugawa interregional market flow, see Miyamoto, "Quantitative Aspects of Tokugawa Economy," 79.

[47] Many studies exist about the socioeconomic makeup of villages. For instance, Uda Ōtsu village (today part of Osaka) consisted in 1843 of 277 households: 32 percent were nonagricultural, 44 percent combined nonagricultural activities with working small landholdings (23 of the 58 households were nonfarm households headed by a woman or a person unfit for heavy physical labor). Saito, "Rural Economy," 407.

to sell this surplus within the domain. The decline in the quantity of rice supplied to metropolitan markets in turn drove up the rice price there as well.

The third pattern of trade distribution flourished most fully in prosperous regions where there was a substantial stratum of local producers with considerable financial power and wealth. Autonomy over production and distribution in such cases could be strong. And the stronger the autonomy of these economic actors, the greater were their chances of successfully resisting bids for control by metropolitan wholesalers with shogunal backing or domain monopolies.[48]

Such producers were sometimes able to turn to new local sources of funding. Earlier mutual-aid associations (*mujinkō* and *tanomoshikō*) had served as a mechanism for members to pool savings and allocate them in turn, but these could not generate large loans to promote investments on a significant scale.[49] In the late Tokugawa period, however, some small-scale moneylending operations took on more bank-like characteristics. Ronald B. Toby has introduced one such instance, the case of a village head whose family had used its surplus income to build up a moneylending business. During the Tenpō famine of the 1830s, the village head extended this business to generate capital from a network of other "local rural creditors."[50] Up to 60 percent of the loans he made were funded by borrowed capital, enabling him to lend out larger sums than would have otherwise been possible.[51] The banking network was founded on ties of trust and often involved kinship relations. The village head likewise lent most of the funds he gathered not to small farmers but to those with means. He may be considered representative of a village elite that came to engage in banking in the late Bakumatsu and early Meiji periods.

The regional economic communities associated with the third pattern of distribution transcended administrative units and ignored domain boundaries, generating new kinds of regional links.[52] As Tanimoto Masayuki reasons, "Rural-based capital accumulation together with the workings of the regional financial markets contributed to ... region-based industrial development."[53]

---

[48] See the Bunsei tea incident of 1824 and the subsequent thirty-three-year struggle, in which 115 villages of tea producers on shogunal territory filed a suit against wholesalers and merchants for their exploitative business operations. Described in Farris, *Bowl for a Coin*, 114–22.

[49] For treatments, see Kalland, "Credit Institution in Tokugawa Japan"; Crawcour, "Development of a Credit System," 348–49.

[50] Toby, "Country Bankers," 302.

[51] Toby, "Country Bankers," 311.

[52] Kurushima, "Kinsei kōki no 'chiiki shakai'"; Watanabe, *Kinsei sonraku*; Yabuta, *Kokuso to hyakushō ikki*; Wigen, *Making of a Japanese Periphery*. Large temple networks also functioned as a credit institution for rural entrepreneurs to borrow and lend. Yokoyama, "Expanding and Multilayering Networks."

[53] Tanimoto, "Peasant Society in Japan's Economic Development," 244. According to Tanimoto, the tendency for wealthy local farmers to assume responsibility for public works

It should be kept in mind that, viewed on a national scale, the third pattern of distribution did not displace the first and second by any means. Despite new initiatives in financing, lack of funding remained a major obstacle to expanding their operations for most rural producers. The newly developing rural markets nonetheless spurred shifts in the existing hierarchies of the three trade patterns. These were accelerated by a sharp increase in the money supply following the Bunsei and Tenpō recoinages of 1819 and 1837.[54] This contributed to a steady rise in prices (in decline since the 1780s), which, as noted earlier, stimulated increased production, in effect sparking inflation-induced growth.[55] In the first half of the nineteenth century, rulers responded to the rise in prices by initiating various reforms intended to lower them in Edo. Reversing its existing policy of protecting metropolitan wholesalers so as to control distribution and prices, the shogunate ordered the merchant guilds to dissolve as one component of the Tenpō reforms (1841–45). Subsequently domains, too, were ordered to dissolve their associations, although only a few complied. In principle, these measures should have benefited shogunal territories in the Kantō region as they were cheaper suppliers of goods such as soy sauce, oil, and cotton and silk textiles compared to the Osaka-Edo wholesale trade and the domain monopolies.[56] At the same time, however, the shogunate sought to contain the activities of local merchants through absorption into existing distribution networks. This orientation as well as the disruptions caused by the guilds' abrupt dissolution led shogunal leaders to reverse policy once again in 1851 and allow the guilds to revive. By this point in time, however, the shogunate had all but lost its power to control trade.

Consumers

Economic historians list urbanization, expanding trade and communication networks, and rising income as important factors facilitating consumption. By integrating the entire country into wide-ranging networks of supply and commerce, the Tokugawa political structure of shogunal and daimyo territories

projects in place of rulers is further evidence of their growing economic role. Such arrangements, too, were institutionalized under the Meiji government. Tanimoto, "From 'Feudal' Lords to Local Notables," 17.

[54] The quantity of money is estimated to have increased 1.6- to 1.8-fold from 1818 to the opening of the ports in 1854.

[55] For a summary of the debates regarding Shinbo Hiroshi's thesis of "inflationary growth" triggered by the Bunsei recoinage, see Miyamoto, "Prices and Microeconomic Dynamics," 132–35.

[56] The shutting down of the associations briefly helped tea-producing villages in shogunal territory, as described by Farris, *Bowl for a Coin*, 118. For fuller treatments, see Crawcour, "Economic Change in the Nineteenth Century"; Bolitho, "Tempō Crisis."

stimulated and accelerated ordinary consumption. That system's regulations and restrictions likewise gave the Tokugawa economy its frame. This frame, however, was not flexible in accommodating the market forces that gave consumers choices.[57] Consumers also have their own logic.[58]

Although the Tokugawa political structure presumed those of samurai status to be the sole legitimate category of consumer as the recipients of agricultural taxes, the growing commercialization of the economy created a different reality. The higher up in the warrior hierarchy, the higher the privilege (and the duty) to consume and to share (often through gift giving).[59] Status-oriented conspicuous consumption by warriors required lavish outlays in housing, clothing, and food and the display of daimyo processions to Edo, which put an immense burden on domain finances.[60] At a lower level within the warrior class, dependence on stipends of a fixed *kokudaka* geared to the rice price made it difficult for retainers to respond effectively to the changing conditions of an expanding market and money economy. Limited opportunities for seeking financial improvement exacerbated the problem. Contemporaneous scholars, commentators, and diarists relate many cases of low-ranking retainers who had to rely on by-employments to supplement their incomes. Often, just as in tenant-farming households, women undertook a significant part of such by-employments. Inputs of this sort were particularly crucial during crises when lords cut their retainers' stipends or delayed payment.[61] By the nineteenth century, many samurai families were impoverished and could barely keep up the display of a lifestyle in accordance with their status. Those concerned with the collapse of the hierarchical order came up with reform plans to restore samurai solvency. One measure was to elevate material thrift as a virtue and to condemn extravagance and leisure. Lower ranks of samurai were to become "models of personal economy [thrift] to the common people."[62]

---

[57] Howell, "Hard Times in the Kantō," 349, 371.

[58] Thaler, "Behavioral Economics."

[59] Gift economy is left out due to limited space, but see the recent edited volume by Chaiklin, *Mediated by Gifts*.

[60] See, for instance, the discussion by Coaldrake, "Edo Architecture and Tokugawa Law." In 1812, the Tottori domain (320,000 *koku*), for example, spent in twenty-two days about 1,957 *ryō* of gold (c. 2,000 *koku*) on its procession – an amount equivalent to the annual stipend of the highest-ranking retainers of the domain. Travel by the women of daimyo houses could also require substantial expenditures. In 1863, for instance, a daimyo's mother, widow, and two daughters left Edo for Akita, accompanied by fifty-seven female attendants. The trip cost 592 *ryō*. Shiba, "Building Networks on the Fly."

[61] For examples of struggling retainers, see Yamakawa, *Women of the Mito Domain*; Katsu, *Musui's Story*; Vaporis, "Samurai and Merchant."

[62] Garon, *Beyond Our Means*, 124, citing Ooms, *Charismatic Bureaucrat*. Such stratagems in many cases were less than effective. As Fukuzawa Yukichi remarked of the sumptuary

The commercialization of the Tokugawa economy brought new forms of conspicuous and not-so-conspicuous consumption. In the nineteenth century, affluent villagers from Okayama "were not only buying everyday goods but also luxuries such as perfume, cosmetics, and incense; among readily available imported goods were linen from Echigo, medicine from Etchū, expensive furniture from Noto, and sugar."[63] The economic "pluriactivity" of middling farming households, which gave families more cash to spend, created the demand-pull of the "virtuous circle" that Penelope Francks has described.[64] Wealthy farmers and entrepreneurs often engaged as well in forms of consumption that did not directly challenge the privileges of the political elite, such as aesthetic pursuits and erudition. Rural expenditures on learning, connoisseurship, poetry, and leisure trips are well documented.[65]

Urban areas were even more notable centers of consumption. The diaries of city-dwellers describe time and money spent on commodities and on cultural activities such as tea ceremonies, poetry gatherings, and incense parties, as well as on entertaining guests.[66] The many city guides to restaurants, specialized shops, and entertainment districts detail what businesses put up for sale and publishers advertised. In the case of Edo, such guides aimed initially at samurai who had come on their tour of duty but soon began to cater to additional social groups, and to women as well as men.[67] Lawsuits heard by

codes issued in his domain, "Whether these regulations were issued to improve the economic situation or to enforce a system of clothing by rank was not clear, for the two were confused. Since it was just as though [the upper samurai] used the frugality policy as an opportunity to boast of their status, those who were to wear cotton were dissatisfied and did not practice frugality for very long." Shively, "Sumptuary Regulation and Status," 147, citing Fukuzawa, "Kyūhanjō."

[63] Hanley and Yamamura, *Economic and Demographic Change*, 196–97.

[64] Francks, "Rural Industry, Growth Linkages, and Economic Development." See also Kwon, *State Formation*.

[65] Consumption in rural areas has been explored through close readings of the many extant family records, most of which reflect the lives of those who were well off. For details, see Platt, "Elegance, Prosperity, Crisis"; Moriyama, *Crossing Boundaries*; Pratt, *Japan's Protoindustrial Elite*; Wigen, *Making of a Japanese Periphery*.

[66] For records of such activities, see the diaries kept by the merchant wife Kikuchi Tamiko (1795–1864) in Edo; Sugawara, "Kikuchi Tamiko nikki." See also the diaries of Takizawa (Kyokutei) Bakin and his daughter-in-law Michi; Kyokutei, *Kyokutei Bakin nikki*; Takizawa, *Takizawa Michi-jo nikki*. For lives in castle towns, see the records kept by the low-ranking retainer Osaki Sekijō (b. 1841) from Oshi (in present-day Saitama Prefecture), whose picture diary illustrates many gatherings at his home or those of friends; Ōoka, *Bakumatsu-ki kakyū bushi*.

[67] For examples of how the alternate attendance system stimulated consumption, see the diaries by the father and son Toyama Heima and Tamuro, introduced in Vaporis, "Samurai and the World of Goods." The diary by the Kii domain retainer Sakai Hanshirō (b. 1834), who stayed in Edo in 1860–61, describes his many culinary adventures; see Aoki Naomi, *Bakumatsu tanshin funin*. See Nenzi's discussion on guidebooks (Chapter 15), this volume.

the various magistrates offer vivid evidence of fights over commodities and services or rights to provide them.[68] Popular literature and the treatises of commentators and critics contain a wealth of evidence about the up- and downsides of consumer life in Edo in the late Tokugawa period, including its spectacles and theaters and its underbelly of gamblers, brothel owners, and the urban poor.[69]

In that commercial growth undermined the ideal of a stable and static social order, Tokugawa economic development can be described in either positive or negative terms. Economic historians in recent decades have pointed more to the positive aspects that raised the standard of living for many, whereas many social historians note the groups who lost out in the commercialization process, such as low-ranking samurai and landless commoners. Evidence can be given for both perspectives, underlining the complexity of what we call economy.

Adam Smith's famous dictum in *The Wealth of Nations* (1776) that "consumption is the sole end and purpose of all production" alerts us to a further issue that calls for future consideration: seemingly irrational spending.[70] Economic historians have long acknowledged that shogunal and domanial regulations calling for thrift, frugality, saving, self-sufficiency, and the elimination of waste served not only to uphold social hierarchies but also to support a "rational logic" of saving time, investing labor, and adding value. Until recently, however, historians have tended to disregard irrational spending on the consumption of food and drink for pleasure, gifts, leisure, entertainment, status, and comfort.[71] In effect they thereby have echoed the perspective of the Tokugawa regulations, which held that farmers as producers should ipso facto not be irrational consumers and called for restraint in consumption by the lower social ranks, both warrior and otherwise. Yet irrational consumption, if not engaged in out of necessity, was not something random either. Nor were the changes in the consumption patterns of farmers and the lower ranks a simple imitation of their superiors' taste and lifestyle. Rather, such patterns reflected the circumstances and opportunities particular to the consumers' situation. The consumer behavior of the large body of servants

---

[68] For examples of these suits, see Wigmore, *Law and Justice*.

[69] For vivid descriptions of the time, see the volumes by Jones and Kern, *Kamigata Anthology*, and Jones and Watanabe, *Edo Anthology*; Shirane, *Early Modern Japanese Literature*; Teeuwen and Nakai, *Lust, Commerce, and Corruption*; Nishiyama, *Edo Culture*.

[70] For a brief and relevant discussion, see Trentmann, *Empire of Things*, 2.

[71] For a new approach to consider the shogun as consumer, see Oguchi, "Edo Castle as Consumer."

in the Tokugawa period is an example of the sort of issue deserving attention.[72] Servants who flocked to the cities from rural areas sought out their own pastimes there.[73] Servants usually received their wages in advance, but in the nineteenth century some in farming households were given a portion as pocket money for their days off when they could enjoy the theater and fairs at nearby temples and shrines according to their means and tastes.[74]

The task lying ahead is to focus on consumption with the support of large data collections drawn from household account books, diaries, and letters, so as not to rely too heavily on anecdotal evidence alone. Contemporaneous thinkers' writings, too, need to be read more closely with an eye on consumption, since as Frank Trentmann notes, "preferences for [exotic] goods were neither pre-existing nor stable but had to be created."[75] Society changes and so do family patterns, popular culture, and gender roles. Consumer life in Tokugawa Japan was therefore varied and changing as well. With further systematically collected data, we should be able to better evaluate the "diverse, non-linear and more locally and regionally rooted" path taken by Tokugawa Japan.[76]

Bibliography

Aoki Michiko. "Nanushi-ke no nikki ni miru nōson josei no rōdō to kyūjitsu." In *Josei rōdō no Nihonshi*, edited by Sōgō Joseishi Gakkai, 136–49. Bensei Shuppan, 2019.

Aoki Naomi. *Bakumatsu tanshin funin: Kakyū bushi no shoku nikki*. Nihon Hōsō Shuppan Kyōkai, 2005.

Bassino, Jean-Pascal, Stephen Broadberry, Kyoji Fukao, Bishnupriya Gupta, and Masanori Takashima. "Japan and the Great Divergence, 730–1874." *Explorations in Economic History* 72 (2019): 1–22.

Bitō Masahide. *Edo jidai to wa nani ka: Nihon shijō no kinsei to kindai*. Iwanami Shoten, 1992.

Bolitho, Harold. "The Tempō Crisis." In Jansen, *Nineteenth Century*, 116–67.

Chaiklin, Martha, ed. *Mediated by Gifts: Politics and Society in Japan, 1350–1850*. Leiden: Brill, 2016.

Coaldrake, William H. "Edo Architecture and Tokugawa Law." *Monumenta Nipponica* 36, no. 3 (1981): 235–84.

Crawcour, E. S. "The Development of a Credit System in Seventeenth-Century Japan." *Journal of Economic History* 21, no. 3 (1961): 342–60.

"Economic Change in the Nineteenth Century." In Jansen, *Nineteenth Century*, 569–617.

Davison, Kate. "Early Modern Social Networks: Antecedents, Opportunities, and Challenges." *American Historical Review* 124, no. 2 (April 2019): 456–82.

[72] Ōguchi Yūjirō calculates that about 20,000 to 30,000 female servants alone worked for warriors in the city of Edo in 1839. Ōguchi, "Josei no buke hōkō," 182–83.
[73] See Leupp, *Servants, Shophands, and Laborers*, ch. 4.
[74] Aoki Michiko, "Nanushi-ke no nikki ni miru nōson josei no rōdō to kyūjitsu," 146–47.
[75] Trentmann, *Empire of Things*, 4.
[76] Otsuka and Sugihara, *Paths to the Emerging State*, 27.

Doboku Gakkai, ed. *Meiji izen Nihon dobokushi*. Doboku Gakkai, 1936. Reprint, Iwanami Shoten, 1973.

Farris, William Wayne. *A Bowl for a Coin: A Commodity History of Japanese Tea*. Honolulu: University of Hawai'i Press, 2019.

Japan's Medieval Population: Famine, Fertility, and Warfare in a Transformative Age. Honolulu: University of Hawai'i Press, 2006.

Francks, Penelope. "Inconspicuous Consumption: Sake, Beer, and the Birth of the Consumer in Japan." *Journal of Asian Studies* 68, no. 1 (February 2009): 135–64.

The Japanese Consumer: An Alternative Economic History of Modern Japan. Cambridge: Cambridge University Press, 2009.

Rural Economic Development in Japan: From the Nineteenth Century to the Pacific War. London: Routledge, 2006.

"Rural Industry, Growth Linkages, and Economic Development in Nineteenth-Century Japan." *Journal of Asian Studies* 61, no. 1 (2002): 33–55.

Francks, Penelope, and Janet Hunter, eds. *The Historical Consumer: Consumption and Everyday Life in Japan, 1850–2000*. New York: Palgrave Macmillan, 2012.

Fujiki Hisashi. "Tōitsu seiken no seiritsu." In *Kinsei 1*, edited by Asao Naohiro, Ishii Susumu, Inoue Mitsusada, Ōishi Kaichirō, Kano Masanao, Kuroda Toshio, Sasaki Junnosuke, et al., 33–79. Vol. 9 of *Iwanami kōza: Nihon rekishi*. Iwanami Shoten, 1975.

Fukuzawa Yukichi. "Kyūhanjō." Translated by Carmen Blacker. *Monumenta Nipponica* 9, no. 1/2 (1953): 304–29.

Tsūkaron. In *Fukuzawa Yukichi zenshū*, Vol. 4, edited by Keiō Gijuku, 537–66. 2nd ed. Iwanami Shoten, 1959.

Garon, Sheldon. *Beyond Our Means: Why America Spends While the World Saves*. Princeton, NJ: Princeton University Press, 2012.

Gordon, Andrew D. "Consumption, Consumerism, and Japanese Modernity." In *The Oxford Handbook of the History of Consumption*, edited by Frank Trentmann, 485–504. Oxford: Oxford University Press, 2012.

Gramlich-Oka, Bettina, and Gregory Smits, eds. *Economic Thought in Early Modern Japan*. Leiden: Brill, 2010.

Gramlich-Oka, Bettina, Anne Walthall, Miyazaki Fumiko, and Sugano Noriko, eds. *Women and Networks in Nineteenth-Century Japan*. Ann Arbor: University of Michigan Press, 2020.

Hamano Kiyoshi. "Kinsei no seiritsu to zenkoku shijō no tenkai." In *Nihon keizaishi 1600–2015: Rekishi ni yomu gendai*, edited by Hamano Kiyoshi, Ioku Shigehiko, Nakamura Muneyoshi, Kishida Makoto, Nagae Masakazu, and Ushijima Toshiaki, 3–48. Keiō Daigaku Shuppankai, 2017.

Hanley, Susan B. *Everyday Things in Premodern Japan: The Hidden Legacy of Material Culture*. Berkeley: California University Press, 1997.

Hanley, Susan B., and Kozo Yamamura. *Economic and Demographic Change in Preindustrial Japan, 1600–1868*. Princeton, NJ: Princeton University Press, 1977.

Hayami Akira. *Nihon ni okeru keizai shakai no tenkai*. Keiō Tsūshin, 1973.

Hayami Akira and Miyamoto Matao. "Gaisetsu." In *Keizai shakai no seiritsu*, edited by Umemura Mataji, Hayami Akira, and Miyamoto Matao, 1–84. Vol. 1 of *Nihon keizai-shi*. Iwanami Shoten, 1988.

Hayami, Akira, Osamu Saitō, and Ronald P. Toby, eds. *Emergence of Economic Society in Japan, 1600–1859*. Vol. 1 of *The Economic History of Japan, 1600–1900*. Oxford: Oxford University Press, 2004.

Howell, David L. *Capitalism from Within: Economy, Society, and the State in a Japanese Fishery*. Berkeley: University of California Press, 1995.

"Hard Times in the Kantō: Economic Change and Village Life in Late Tokugawa Japan." *Modern Asian Studies* 23, no. 2 (1989): 349–71.

Iwahashi Masaru. *Kinsei Nihon bukkashi no kenkyū: Kinsei beika no kōzō to hendō*. Ōhara Shinseisha, 1981.

"Tokugawa jidai no kahei sūryō." In *Nihon keizai no hatten: Kinsei kara kindai e*, edited by Umemura Mataji, 241–60. Nihon Keizai Shinbunsha, 1976.

Jansen, Marius B., ed. *The Nineteenth Century*. Vol. 5 of *The Cambridge History of Japan*. Cambridge: Cambridge University Press, 1989.

Jones, Sumie, and Adam Kern, with Kenji Watanabe, eds. *A Kamigata Anthology: Literature from Japan's Metropolitan Centers, 1600–1750*. Honolulu: University of Hawai'i Press, 2020.

Jones, Sumie, and Kenji Watanabe, eds. *An Edo Anthology: Literature from Japan's Mega-City, 1750–1850*. Honolulu: University of Hawai'i Press, 2013.

Kalland, Arne. "A Credit Institution in Tokugawa Japan: The *Ura-tamegin* Fund of Chikuzen Province." In *Europe Interprets Japan*, edited by Gordon Daniels, 3–11. Tenterden, UK: P. Norbury, 1984.

Kanzaka Jun'ichi. "The Development of Civil Engineering Projects and Village Communities in Seventeenth- to Nineteenth-Century Japan." In Tanimoto and Wong, *Public Goods Provision*, 150–71.

Katō Keiichirō. *Kinsei kōki keizai hatten no kōzō: Beikoku kin'yū shijō no tenkai*. Osaka: Seibundō, 2001.

Katsu Kokichi. *Musui's Story: The Autobiography of a Tokugawa Samurai*. Translated by Teruko Craig. Tucson: University of Arizona Press, 1988.

Kawaguchi, Hiroshi, and Sumiyo Ishii. *A History of Economic Thought in Japan, 1600–1945*. Translated by Ayuko Tanaka and Tadashi Anno. London: Bloomsbury, 2022.

Kitō Hiroshi. "Edo-Tōkyō no jinkō hatten: Meiji ishin no mae to ato." *Jōchi keizai ronshū* 34, no. 1/2 (1989): 48–69.

Jinkō de miru Nihonshi: Jōmon jidai kara kinmirai shakai made. PHP Kenkyūsho, 2007.

"Meiji izen Nihon no chiiki jinkō." *Jōchi keizai ronshū* 41, no. 1/2 (1996): 65–79.

Komuro Masamichi. "Mito-gaku Fujita-ha nōseiron no ninshiki to shisō." Special issue, *Mita gakkai zasshi* 82, no. 2 (1989): 223–40.

Kuroda, Akinobu. *A Global History of Money*. London: Routledge, 2020.

Kurushima Hiroshi. "Kinsei kōki no 'chiiki shakai' no rekishiteki seikaku ni tsuite." *Rekishi hyōron* 499 (1991): 2–28.

Kwon, Grace. *State Formation, Property Relations, and the Development of the Tokugawa Economy (1600–1868)*. London: Routledge, 2002.

Kyokutei Bakin. *Kyokutei Bakin nikki*. 5 vols. Edited by Shibata Mitsuhiko. Chūōkōron Shinsha, 2010.

Leupp, Gary P. *Servants, Shophands, and Laborers in the Cities of Tokugawa Japan*. Princeton, NJ: Princeton University Press, 1992.

Matsumoto Shirō. *Nihon kinsei toshiron*. Tōkyō Daigaku Shuppankai, 1983.

"Shōnin ryūtsū no hatten to ryūtsū kikō no saihensei." In *Kinsei, ge*, edited by Furushima Toshio, 87–131. Vol. 4 of *Nihon keizaishi taikei*. Tōkyō Daigaku Shuppankai, 1965.

Metzler, Mark. "Policy Space, Polarities, and Regimes." In *Economic Thought in Early Modern Japan*, edited by Bettina Gramlich-Oka and Gregory Smits, 217–50. Leiden: Brill, 2010.

Miyamoto Matao. "Bukka to makuro keizai no hendō." In *Kindai seichō no taidō*, edited by Saitō Osamu and Shinbo Hiroshi, 67–126. Vol. 2 of *Nihon Keizai shi*. Iwanami Shoten, 1989.

"Management Systems of Edo Period Merchant Houses." *Japanese Yearbook on Business History* 13 (1996): 97–142.

"Prices and Microeconomic Dynamics." In Hayami, Saitō, and Toby, *Emergence of Economic Society*, 119–58.

"Quantitative Aspects of Tokugawa Economy." In Hayami, Saitō, and Toby, *Emergence of Economic Society*, 36–84.

Moriyama, Takeshi. *Crossing Boundaries in Tokugawa Society: Suzuki Bokushi, a Rural Elite Commoner*. Leiden: Brill, 2013.

Nakai Nobuhiko. *Bakuhan shakai to shōhin ryūtsū*. Hanawa Shobō, 1961.

"Edo jidai no shijō keitai ni kansuru sobyō." 3 parts in *Nihon rekishi* (1958): 115 (76–83), 116 (30–36), 118 (68–74).

Nishiyama Matsunosuke. *Edo Culture: Daily Life and Diversions in Urban Japan, 1600–1868*. Translated and edited by Gerald Groemer. Honolulu: University of Hawai'i Press, 1997.

Ōguchi Yūjirō. "Edo Castle as Consumer: Procuring Fish for the Shogun's Table." *Monumenta Nipponica* 76, no. 2 (2021), 291–328.

"Josei no buke hōkō." In *Josei rōdō no Nihonshi*, edited by Sōgō Joseishi Gakkai, 181–84. Bensei Shuppan, 2019.

Oka Mitsuo and Yamazaki Ryūzō. *Nihon keizaishi: Bakuhan taisei no keizai kōzō*. Mineruva Shobō, 1983.

Ōoka Toshiaki. *Bakumatsu-ki kakyū bushi no e-nikki*. Suiyōsha, 2019.

Ooms, Herman. *Charismatic Bureaucrat: A Political Biography of Matsudaira Sadanobu, 1758–1829*. Chicago: University of Chicago Press, 1975.

Otsuka, Keijiro, and Kaoru Sugihara, eds. *Paths to the Emerging State in Asia and Africa*. Singapore: Springer, 2019.

Platt, Brian. "Elegance, Prosperity, Crisis: Three Generations of Tokugawa Village Elites." *Monumenta Nipponica* 55, no. 1 (2000): 45–81.

Pratt, Edward E. *Japan's Protoindustrial Elite: The Economic Foundations of the Gōnō*. Cambridge, MA: Harvard University Asia Center, 1999.

"Social and Economic Change in Tokugawa Japan." In *A Companion to Japanese History*, edited by William M. Tsutsui, 86–100. Malden, MA: Blackwell Publishing, 2007.

Ravina, Mark. *Land and Lordship in Early Modern Japan*. Stanford, CA: Stanford University Press, 1999.

Roberts, Luke S. *Mercantilism in a Japanese Domain: The Merchant Origins of Economic Nationalism in 18th-Century Tosa*. Cambridge: Cambridge University Press, 1998.

Saitō Osamu [Saito, Osamu]. "Daikaikon, jinkō, shōnō keizai." In *Keizai shakai no seiritsu*, edited by Umemura Mataji, Hayami Akira, and Miyamoto Matao, 171–215. Vol. 1 of *Nihon keizaishi*. Iwanami Shoten, 1988.

"The Rural Economy: Commercial Agriculture, By-Employment, and Wage Work." In *Japan in Transition: From Tokugawa to Meiji*, edited by Marius B. Jansen and Gilbert Rozman, 400–20. Princeton, NJ: Princeton University Press, 1986.

"1600-nen no zenkoku jinkō: Jūnana seiki jinkō keizaishi saikōchiku no kokoromi." *Shakai keizai shigaku* 84, no. 1 (May 2018): 3–23.

Saito, Osamu, and Masanori Takashima. "Estimating the Shares of Secondary- and Tertiary-Sector Outputs in the Age of Early Modern Growth: The Case of Japan, 1600–1874." *European Review of Economic History* 20 (2016): 368–86.

"Population, Urbanisation and Farm Output in Early Modern Japan, 1600–1874: A Review of Data and Benchmark Estimates." *Hitotsubashi Repository* (2015): 17pp.

Sakudō Yōtarō. *Kinsei hōken shakai no kahei kin'yū kōzō.* Hanawa Shobō, 1971.

Nihon kahei kin'yūshi no kenkyū. Miraisha, 1961.

Sakurai, Eiji. "Currency and Credit in Medieval Japan." *International Journal of Asian Studies* 5, no. 1 (2008): 53–70.

Shiba Keiko. "Building Networks on the Fly: The Travails of Travel for Domain Lords' Women." Translated by Anne Walthall. In Gramlich-Oka et al., *Women and Networks*, 113–42.

Shinbo Hiroshi. *Kindai Nihon keizaishi: Pakkusu Buritanika no naka no Nihon-teki shijō keizai.* Sōbunsha, 1995.

Shirane, Haruo, ed. *Early Modern Japanese Literature: An Anthology, 1600–1900.* New York: Columbia University Press, 2002.

Shively, Donald H. "Sumptuary Regulation and Status in Early Tokugawa Japan." *Harvard Journal of Asiatic Studies* 25 (1964–65): 123–64.

Smith, Thomas C. "Farm Family By-Employments in Preindustrial Japan." *Journal of Economic History* 29, no. 4 (1969): 687–715.

Native Sources of Japanese Industrialization, 1750–1920. Berkeley: University of California Press, 1988.

Sugawara Yukie. "Kikuchi Tamiko nikki." *Edo-ki onna-kō* 6 (1995): 133–51.

Takizawa Michi. *Takizawa Michi-jo nikki.* 2 vols. Edited by Shibata Mitsuhiko and Ōkubo Keiko. Chūōkōron Shinsha, 2012–13.

Tanimoto, Masayuki. "From 'Feudal' Lords to Local Notables: The Role of Regional Society in Public Goods Provision from Early Modern to Modern Japan." In Tanimoto and Wong, *Public Goods Provision*, 17–37.

"Peasant Society in Japan's Economic Development: With Special Focus on Rural Labour and Finance Markets." *International Journal of Asian Studies* 15, no. 2 (2018): 229–53.

Tanimoto, Masayuki, and R. Bin Wong, eds. *Public Goods Provision in the Early Modern Economy: Comparative Perspectives from Japan, China, and Europe.* Oakland: University of California Press, 2019.

Teeuwen, Mark, and Kate Wildman Nakai, eds. *Lust, Commerce, and Corruption: An Account of What I Have Seen and Heard, by an Edo Samurai.* Translated by Mark Teeuwen, Kate Wildman Nakai, Miyazaki Fumiko, Anne Walthall, and John Breen. New York: Columbia University Press, 2014.

Thaler, Richard H. "Behavioral Economics: Past, Present, and Future." *American Economic Review* 106, no. 7 (2016): 1577–1600.

Toby, Ronald P. "Country Bankers." In Hayami, Saitō, and Toby, *Emergence of Economic Society*, 301–34.

Trentmann, Frank. *Empire of Things: How We Became a World of Consumers, from the Fifteenth Century to the Twenty-First.* New York: HarperCollins, 2016.

Vaporis, Constantine N. "Samurai and Merchant in Mid-Tokugawa Japan: Tani Tannai's Record of Daily Necessities (1748–54)." *Harvard Journal of Asiatic Studies* 60, no. 1 (2000): 205–27.

"Samurai and the World of Goods: The Diaries of the Toyama Family of Hachinohe." *Early Modern Japan* 8, no. 1 (2008): 56–67.

von Verschuer, Charlotte. *Rice, Agriculture, and the Food Supply in Premodern Japan.* Translated and edited by Wendy Cobcroft. London: Routledge, 2016.

Watanabe Takashi. *Kinsei sonraku no tokushitsu to tenkai.* Azekura Shobō, 1998.

Wigen, Kären. *The Making of a Japanese Periphery, 1750–1920.* Berkeley: University of California Press, 1995.

Wigmore, John Henry. *Law and Justice in Tokugawa Japan: Materials for the History of Japanese Law and Justice under the Tokugawa Shogunate 1603–1867.* 20 vols. University of Tokyo Press, 1967–86.

Yabuta Yutaka. *Kokuso to hyakushō ikki no kenkyū.* Azekura Shobō, 1992.

Yamakawa Kikue. *Women of the Mito Domain: Recollections of Samurai Family Life.* Translated and with an introduction by Kate Wildman Nakai. University of Tokyo Press, 1992.

Yamazaki Ryūzō. *Kinsei bukkashi kenkyū.* Hanawa Shobō, 1983.

Yasukuni, Ryōichi. "Regional versus Standardized Coinage in Early Modern Japan: The Tokugawa *Kan'ei Tsūhō.*" *International Journal of Asian Studies* 7, no. 2 (2010): 131–57.

Yokoyama Yuriko. "Expanding and Multilayering Networks in Nineteenth-Century Japan: The Case of the Shin-Yoshiwara Red-Light District." Translated by Jeffrey Knot. In Gramlich-Oka et al., *Women and Networks,* 223–45.

9

The Pacific Context of Japan's Environmental History

BRETT L. WALKER

Pacific World

This chapter explores Japan's environmental history within the context of the Pacific world and its natural and human-fashioned features. In the first half of the twentieth century, as the Japanese empire lurched toward a disastrous war with its Pacific rival, the United States, the island country celebrated itself as a maritime empire, initiating, on the eve of the attack on Pearl Harbor, "Marine Memorial Day" in order to "give thanks for the blessings of the sea and pray for the prosperity of maritime Japan." Nationalists viewed Japan as an "ocean empire" (*kaiyō teikoku*) and "maritime nation" (*kaikoku*), one that leveraged its Pacific surroundings to build a national identity.[1] This chapter argues that the nationalists who sold Japan as an "ocean empire" and "maritime nation" were correct in more ways than they ever imagined – Japan's history is intertwined with the rhythms of its Pacific environment in physical and cultural ways. Japan is a Pacific nation, and its history needs to be viewed as part of Pacific world history.

Viewing Japan as a nation shaped by the Pacific is a new concept, but it has analytical benefits. For Japanese, the Pacific has been more than, in the words of US President Theodore Roosevelt, a fluid maritime plane upon which "European peoples," in their desire for empire, "traverse those wastes of water and establish regular communications."[2] As this chapter demonstrates, Roosevelt's "wastes of water" determined the tectonic activity, geographic features, energy supplies, marine creatures, and climate which fueled Japan's early modern and modern history. The Pacific region, characterized by its tectonics and "Ring of Fire" volcanism, shaped Japan in physical ways, defining everything from its topography to the content of its soil and rocks; this, in turn, shaped everything from timber harvests to agriculture and mining. If

[1] Tsutsui, "Pelagic Empire," 29.
[2] Matsuda, "Pacific," 760.

the Atlantic world was a "European invention," one that, according to David Armitage, "Europeans were the first to connect" into a cohesive region of historical analysis, then the connective tissue of the Pacific world is as much natural as human-fashioned.[3] Indeed, Ryan Tucker Jones observes that in the Pacific, the "ecology and lifecycles of ocean creatures also had an impact on human history," one that shapes the story of the Pacific region in important ways. He continues, "In order to understand humans' relations with each other and with the ocean at any place on the North Pacific littoral, then, it is necessary to adopt a circum-Pacific viewpoint attuned to movements above and below the waves."[4] Jones's "above and below the waves" vantage point is precisely what this chapter brings to the study of Japan.

Rather than privilege one natural process over another – say, marine mammal migration over tectonics and volcanism – this chapter paints a comprehensive picture of Japan's early modern and modern history as driven by a spectrum of Pacific forces. The Pacific Ocean itself is a "connective force," with far more tensile strength than the brittle cultural coherency of East Asian or Western civilization. The Pacific world provides coherency to Japanese history in ways that are often neglected but that identify the ingredients of Japan's modern industrial successes and its likely Anthropocene tragedies.[5] By analyzing Pacific tectonics, Pacific highlands and lowlands, Pacific hydrography, Pacific climates, and Pacific politics and culture, this chapter demonstrates that the Pacific Ocean is not only a "connective force" of Japan's history but also the energy source that powers much of it as well.

Pacific Tectonics

The slow grinding of lithospheric plates is an important part of that Pacific engine – the Pacific region is shaped by plate tectonics and its accompanying volcanism. Pacific volcanism is not randomly dispersed, but rather concentrated around the Pacific's Ring of Fire, on which the Japanese islands perch. This is an unchanging and undeniable reality of life on the Japanese islands – earthquakes strike the tectonically dynamic nation 1,500 times per year on average. Specifically, Japan sits on four tectonic plates: the Pacific plate to the north and the Philippine plate to the south, which are constantly being subducted, or drawn under, the Eurasian and North American continental

---

[3] Armitage, "Three Concepts of Atlantic History," 12.
[4] Jones, "Running into Whales," 357, 360.
[5] Jones, "Environment," 121.

plates. Japan teeters on the Eurasian continental plate and remains prone to severe tectonic events, such as volcanoes, earthquakes, and tsunami. These earthquakes are important not only to geologists but to historians, too: often, these tectonic events become the spark that ignites the dry tinder of important historical transformations, ones that redirect Japanese politics and society in important ways.

With plate tectonics, the Earth's crust moves out from vents in the mid-Pacific and travels toward continental plates and subduction zones, where one plate dives beneath another. Such subduction zones prove particularly volatile if rock comprises one plate and basalt the other. The mountainous spine of Japan is a prominent, raised section of the Eurasian continental rim, a cordillera comprised of several prominent volcanoes, including Mount Fuji on Honshu, as well as Mount Aso and Mount Sakurajima on Kyushu. Over geologic and human history such volcanoes have not only become iconographic landmarks of national identity but have created the nutrient-rich soil on which Japanese agrarian communities depend.[6]

Because of its position on the Ring of Fire, most of Japan's volcanoes are subduction volcanoes, which are characterized by explosive pressure in the magma that quickly decompresses on reaching normal atmospheric pressure at the Earth's surface. The result is ash exploding into the atmosphere or moving down the side of the volcano, in a pyroclastic flow, at as much as 200 kilometers per hour. The eruption of Mount Asama in 1783 fits this description, with pyroclastic flows and igneous scoria showers that burned houses ten kilometers away. Japan's earthquakes are also determined by plate tectonics. Normal subduction earthquakes occur constantly as the Pacific plate grinds under the Eurasian continental plate, but sometimes one plate gets stuck and then breaks free, which is the cause of some of the more dramatic earthquakes, such as the Genroku earthquake (1703) and the Ansei earthquake (1855) in the southern Kantō region, and the Great Kantō earthquake (1923).[7]

It is important that historians of Japan pay attention to tectonic geologic calendars as well as historical ones – early modern Japan proved syncretic with its Pacific Ring of Fire geologic context. Such geologic events sometimes precipitated political, social, and economic ones. As Antony R. Berger cautions, scholars should not exclusively focus on anthropogenic environmental change because there are "many examples where environmental change of nonhuman origin (e.g. drought and volcanic eruptions) affected landscapes

---

[6] Freeman, *Pacific*, 16–21.
[7] Barnes, "Vulnerable Japan," 21–27.

in ways that challenged local peoples and led to major societal upheavals."[8] Scholars believe that the eruption of Santorini between 1628 BCE and 1520 BCE, for example, contributed to the collapse of the Minoan society of Crete not long thereafter. Political, social, and economic events in human history often follow, even if imprecisely, major geologic events, and Japan is no exception. Even though tectonic factors remain the product of the "great forces of Nature" and outside anthropogenic forces, they are still intertwined with human history in important ways (see Table 9.1).

Japan's history synchronized to Pacific geologic forces in a number of ways, but earthquakes remain among the most flamboyant. Immediately after the magnitude 7.2 Ansei earthquake of November 1855, for example, the political and cultural aftershocks appeared immediately: anonymous woodblock prints, called *namazue*, depicting a giant catfish swishing away with its tail the fortunes of Edo's elite, proved a harbinger of tough times for the Tokugawa shogunate, which quickly banned the seditious images. The shake struck the capital in the evening, and some 6,500 people died in the city. Observers wrote, the "population was unprepared for a great earthquake. Thinking that Edo was prone only to fires, people built plaster-walled dwellings and erected plaster-walled enclosures with tile roofing. Such construction became the major cause of injuries."[9] The shogunate proved more adept at providing earthquake relief to its military retainers than to the general population, including relaxing required alternate attendance in Edo. Nonetheless, the shogunate still oversaw a massive relief effort for townspeople, which included constructing relief huts, tending to the dead and wounded, controlling prices and wages, and distributing food. As Gregory Smits observes, even though the shogunate brought relief to townspeople relatively expeditiously, the longer-term impact of the Ansei earthquake was more "psychological" and undermined shogunal "power beyond the obvious drain of financial resources."[10]

The Ansei earthquake occurred within the context of the arrival of Commodore Matthew C. Perry (1794–1858), who had arrived on Pacific currents and trade winds only two years earlier, and the subsequent destabilizing debates over the legitimacy of the shogunate and the future of imperial rule. It was followed by a typhoon only ten months later; an influenza outbreak in 1857, which probably killed senior councillor Abe Masahiro (1819–57); and a cholera epidemic the next year, killing 34,000 souls. In 1859, fire burned the

---

[8] Berger, "Abrupt Geological Changes," 3.
[9] Smits, *Seismic Japan*, 103.
[10] Smits, *Seismic Japan*, 137.

Table 9.1 Major seismic events, 1600–1923

Geologic phenomenon	Date	Region	Ferocity
Keichō Nankaidō earthquake and tsunami	1605	Southwestern Japan	M* 7.9
Aizu earthquake	1611	Aizu vicinity	M 6.9
Keichō Sanriku earthquake	1611	Iwate vicinity	M 8.1
Mount Komagatake eruption	1640	Hokkaido	VEI** 5
Kanbun earthquake	1662	Kyoto vicinity	Unknown
Usu eruption	1663	Hokkaido	VEI 5
Mount Tarumae eruption	1667	Hokkaido	VEI 5
Genroku earthquake	1703	Edo vicinity	M 8.2
Mount Fuji Hōei eruption	1707	Central Japan	VEI 5
Hōei earthquake	1707	Southwestern Japan	Unknown
Mount Tarumae eruption	1739	Hokkaido	VEI 5
Great Meiwa earthquake and tsunami	1771	Yaeyama Islands	M 7.4/tsunami: 40m
Mount Asama eruption	1783	Central Japan	Unknown
Mount Unzen eruption	1792	Nagasaki vicinity	Unknown
Mount Unzen earthquake and tsunami	1792	Nagasaki vicinity	M 6.4
Echigo Sanjō earthquake	1828	Niigata vicinity	M 6.9
Zenkōji earthquake	1847	Nagano vicinity	M 7.3
Iga Ueno earthquake	1854	Mie vicinity	M 7.25
Ansei Tōkai earthquake	1854	Suruga Bay	M 8.4
Ansei Nankai earthquake	1854	Southwestern Japan	M 8.4
Ansei earthquake	1855	Edo vicinity	M 7.2
Hietsu earthquake	1858	Atotsugawa fault	M 7.0
Hamada earthquake	1872	Shimane vicinity	M 7.1
Kumamoto earthquake	1889	Kumamoto vicinity	M 6.3
Nōbi earthquake	1891	Central Japan	M 8.0
Meiji Tokyo earthquake	1894	Tokyo	M 6.6
Shōnai earthquake	1894	Yamagata vicinity	M 7.0
Sanriku earthquake	1896	Northeastern Japan	M 8.5
Great Kantō earthquake	1923	Tokyo vicinity	M 8.3

* Magnitude
** Volcano Explosive Index

Edo Castle keep. Then, more political drama rocked the country, including the US-Japan Treaty of Amity and Commerce (1858); the Ansei purge (1858–59); Ii Naosuke's (1815–60) response to *sonnō jōi* (lit. "revere the emperor, expel the barbarians") sympathizers; and the Sakuradamon incident in 1860, when radical samurai killed Ii outside Edo Castle. In 1860, a line from a satirical song poked fun at the Ansei reign name (1854–60), which literally means "safe government." The line chided: "Not calm government, tsunami, earthquake, and great storm, cholera, great fire, and Sakurada trouble." In the popular imagination, the Ansei earthquake epitomized an era of *yonaoshi* (world renewal), when political shifts synchronized with tectonic ones.[11] In the Ansei period, political calamities are impossible to distinguish from the onset of natural ones. In the East Asian conceptualization of dynastic cycles, natural disasters often served as signaling events in regime change, and that is how many Japanese interpreted the seismic events of 1855.

Smits argues that the Ansei earthquake undermined the aura of shogunal strength, or in the words of Edo popular literature, painted them as "cowardly warriors." Indeed, the shogunate failed to subdue the writhing catfish that caused the earthquake, but the myriad deities of the realm did. With popular literature portraying Amaterasu, the Sun Goddess, as bringing order back to Edo, this became a "dress rehearsal among the deities for what actually happened roughly twelve years later when the emperor came to town to stay." Smits summarizes the political ramifications of the Ansei earthquake in this manner: "The stress of earthquakes helped popularize a view that Motoori Norinaga earlier articulated: the imperial line was the pivot of the universe."[12] In other words, this seismic event, the simple shaking caused when one tectonic plate slips under another, resonated politically, socially, and economically throughout nineteenth-century Japan and synchronized with the collapse of the shogunate to usher in the Meiji Restoration of 1868. Earthquakes did not necessarily create political upheaval in Japan, but the Pacific engine certainly powered them.

After the Meiji Restoration, Japanese and foreign architects began building more brick buildings, which, in the case of the Nōbi earthquake of 1891, proved vulnerable to earthquakes. The magnitude 8.0 Nōbi earthquake shook Japan just as the nation was beginning to question the uncritical replication of Western modernity. "Foreigner worship," as nativists cynically labeled it, had gotten out of control; and the more conservative Meiji Constitution (1889) and the Imperial Rescript on Education (1890) evidenced Japan's conservative turn. The shake killed over 7,000 souls, many from falling brick, which nativists associated with Western modernity. In the aftermath of the Nōbi earthquake, observers quickly noticed that most Japanese houses survived the shaking, but foreign buildings, such as the Naniwa cotton textile mill in Osaka, collapsed. After the quake, the "three-story red brick building in the

[11] Smits, *Seismic Japan*, 167–68.
[12] Smits, *Seismic Japan*, 168–69.

usual English factory style" lay in ruins, killing twenty-one people. The Nōbi earthquake quickly synchronized with the mid-Meiji nativist turn. As Gregory Clancey writes, "It was the collapse of the 'foreign' structures that began to bring the 'natural' disaster into technocultural focus."[13]

Clancey continues that, "Red bricks, which for the last twenty years had been among the most visible symbols of progressive Japanese change, were depicted in postdisaster accounts as particularly nefarious, 'flying around' and 'attacking people' in one case and 'raining down like snow and hail' in another."[14] The Nōbi earthquake did not cause Japan's about-face into a more nativist and imperial state in the late Meiji years, but it certainly contributed to a critique of Western culture and technologies that greased the wheels of Japanese ultranationalism. Moreover, the shake nationalized suffering in a manner that solidified the power of the Meiji state and prepared the Japanese for the tough sacrifices ahead – a half century of war. Importantly, once again, the seismic forces of the Pacific synchronized with Japan's conservative reaction to Western modernity and fueled a more reactionary turn in Japanese politics.

If the Ansei earthquake synchronized with Bakumatsu anxieties to usher in the collapse of the shogunate at the hands of "restorationist" forces and the Nōbi earthquake synchronized with a growing sense of Japanese nativism in the mid-Meiji years, the magnitude 8.2 Great Kantō earthquake of September 1923, which killed over 105,000 people, rattled the tensions inherent in Japan's new empire, which included the defeat of China in 1895, the defeat of Russia in 1905, and the annexation of Korea in 1910. The scene in Tokyo was one of unremitting horror. Funaki Yoshie, a patient at a Nihonbashi hospital, was evacuated on a chartered boat on the Sumida River after the massive quake. Many Tokyoites had decided to escape on the Sumida, which was covered with "innumerable boats of all kinds and sizes, all overloaded with people and their personal belongings." Funaki recalled how the terrifying noises continued throughout the night, the awful sounds of the "roaring of the flames and people yelling for water" as they burned to death in the massive conflagration that followed the shake.[15]

Immediately after the quake, Admiral Yamamoto Gonnohyōe (Gonbei, 1852–1933), the prime minister, convened his cabinet, and the Home Ministry declared martial law; some 34,000 troops descended on four prefectures to

---

[13] Clancey, *Earthquake Nation*, 115.
[14] Clancey, *Earthquake Nation*, 115.
[15] Schencking, *Great Kantō Earthquake*, 24–25.

maintain order in the capital area. Gotō Shinpei (1857–1929), former colonial administrator of Taiwan and mayor of Tokyo, became the principal architect of the recovery, but political opposition stymied many of his most grandiose plans. Nonetheless, under the shelter of martial law, officials stood by as rumors of sedition spread in the aftermath of the earthquake. One day after the Great Kantō earthquake, for example, the *Tōkyō nichinichi shinbun* wrote that "Koreans and socialists were planning a rebellious and treacherous plot. We urge the citizens to cooperate with the military and the police to guard against Koreans." One eyewitness remembered that "wild rumors swept through the city and a reign of terror followed that the police, exhausted with their efforts, were powerless to control." Vigilante gangs lumped Korean immigrants together with anarchists and Bolsheviks and accused them of poisoning Tokyo's water. The Imperial Japanese Navy also dispatched fifty naval vessels to the Korea coast, including destroyers and battleships.[16]

The important point is that earthquakes and their accompanying tsunami did not occur in historical vacuums – in this way, geologic and historical calendars had long since synchronized in Japan, well before the Anthropocene. Tectonic events provided the spark that ignited the flames of historical change, whether nativist critiques of shogunal power, nativist critiques of Western modernity, or twentieth-century anxieties regarding ethnicity and imperial subjects. In this manner, Japan proved a Pacific nation, one whose historical events often moved with the same jerking and grinding motion as tectonic plates. As we shall see, Japan's place on the Pacific's Ring of Fire shaped the country in other important ways, including the development of forestry and mining, as well as the nature of its agricultural systems, the evolution of its political economy, and its protocapitalist development in the eighteenth century.

Pacific Highlands and Lowlands

Volcanism and tectonic uplifting that occurred over five million years before present created Japan's mountainous spine, the most prominent ranges being the Hida, Kiso, and Akaishi in central Japan. Tectonic uplifting has determined the human experience in numerous ways as well, including making precious metals and minerals available by thrusting them upward. Coal deposits on Kyushu and Hokkaido, formed 65–25 million years before present, fueled Japan's nineteenth- and twentieth-century industrialization,

[16] Samuels, *3.11*, 53–54.

as did extensive copper deposits in central Japan, such as at the Ashio copper mine. Eventually, because of favorable climatological conditions, a thick blanket of forest covered these mountains in the central and northern reaches of the archipelago, characterized by red pine, red maple, zelkova, chestnut, cedar, and cypress, which the Japanese readily exploited. Such trees played a key role in Japan's early modern history, particularly within the politics of sixteenth-century unification, castle-town construction and urbanization, monument and temple building, and precious-metal refining.

By contrast, in Japan's lowlands – forged more recently by the interplay of plate tectonics, erosion, and alluvial plane formation, as well as global temperature variations and glacial melting – served as the location for the development of Japan's agrarian political economy, which became critical to the entire early modern order.[17] Early modern Japan's political economy revolved around rice, and carpenters built cities and temples with wood. Although Japan's alluvial lowlands constitute only 12 percent of the archipelago, such locations as the Kantō plain, where the Tokugawa family built Edo, became the site of rice-paddy agriculture and, hence, the agrarian landscape of political power.

As Conrad Totman illustrates, political decisions related to Japan's unification under Oda Nobunaga (1534–82), Toyotomi Hideyoshi (1537–98), and Tokugawa Ieyasu (1543–1616) drove Japan's relationship to its forests in the late sixteenth and seventeenth centuries. As castles became more sophisticated in the final years of the medieval period, carpenters required more lumber to build them. In 1576, for example, the seven-story keep in Nobunaga's Azuchi Castle, an architectural space where he enacted his new realm-wide authority, required high-quality lumber, as did the spate of castle construction that began at roughly the same time at Kitanoshō, Kameyama, Himeji, Okayama, and Hiroshima. The castle towns that surrounded the military bastions sprouted up like wild daisies, some ninety of them between 1572 and 1590, and they all required lumber.[18]

In 1590, eight years after the death of Nobunaga and after he had crushed most of his rivals, Hideyoshi began constructing the architectural symbols of his political power, such as Osaka Castle, constructed between 1582 and 1583, and later Jurakudai Palace and Hōkōji in Kyoto. Loggers felled the forests of Yoshino, near Kyoto, and Hideyoshi commandeered lumber from Kumano in Kii, as well as from Hida, Mino, and Suruga in the east, Hyūga in Kyushu,

---

[17] Totman, *Japan*, 10–16.
[18] Totman, *Green Archipelago*, 52–53.

and Akita in the far northeast. Often, Hideyoshi's retainers supplied important pieces of timber to the hegemon as gifts, such as when Ieyasu, master of the Kantō region, supplied the all-important ridgepole for Hōkōji in 1586. Hideyoshi, to satisfy his appetite for castles and palaces, required timber stocks from throughout Japan. If the natural features of the Japanese archipelago, such as the rich mountainous soil and ample precipitation, grew Japan's forests in the first place, it was samurai state-building that exploited them at an alarming pace for monument construction – Japan's Pacific environment was transformed, one tree after another, into the infrastructure of a centralizing state.[19]

With the rise of Ieyasu and the advent of the Edo shogunate in 1603, improved transportation routes, particularly water routes, made accessing remote sources of timber possible. Ieyasu employed official merchants to clear the Ōi River in Suruga as well as the Fuji and Tenryū Rivers in the Tōkai region so that log rafts could navigate them. With large rafts of domain lumber drifting their way through newly improved water routes, Ieyasu built his three main castles at Edo, Sunpu, and Nagoya, as well as other fortifications at Hikone and Zeze in Ōmi, Sasayama and Kameyama in Tanba, and Nijō in Kyoto.

With Ieyasu's death in 1616, Totman submits that the expansion of cities replaced monument building as the main driver in the depletion of timber supplies.[20] Massive urban conflagrations periodically burned large swaths of Edo – the "flowers of Edo," the most famous being the Meireki (1657), Meiwa (1772), and Bunka (1806) fires – and rebuilding required continuous supplies of lumber. The Meireki fire alone burned much of the shogun's Edo Castle, some 500 daimyo mansions, 779 bannermen's residences, 350 temples and shrines, and 400 blocks of the city. It killed around 100,000 people, putting it nearly at a par with the 1923 Great Kantō earthquake. By the end of the seventeenth century, axes and saws had felled much of Japan's most valuable wooded lands in order to build monuments and cities, both of which were closely tied to the political unification and urbanization of Japan under samurai rule.[21]

Because the shogunate oversaw nearly a quarter of all land in Japan, mainly in the central part of the country, the seat of Tokugawa power logically became the most important agent in protecting and replanting forests after the overactive saws and axes of the seventeenth century. But domains also played an important role, often placing forest management within finance ministries, under the jurisdiction of forest magistrates (hayashi bugyō).

[19] Totman, Green Archipelago, 56–58.
[20] Totman, Green Archipelago, 60–63.
[21] Totman, Green Archipelago, 68.

Forests proved financially valuable because they produced lumber, charcoal for cooking and heating homes, wood for smelting, lacquer, and other resources; but domain finance ministries also sought to protect downstream farmland from erosion and flooding. The shogunate and domain lords had a personal interest in managing forests. By 1700, the shogunate and domains had designated *ohayashi* (the lord's forests) as woodlands under the official jurisdiction of the domain family and off limits to commoners. The shogunate and domains even designated certain sizes and types of trees as *tomeki* (reserved trees) and prohibited their felling.[22] Nevertheless, the erosion problem became so severe that the shogunate established an Office of Erosion Control (Doshakata Yakusho) to monitor erosion in the Kinai basin. As Totman argues, early modern Japanese did not have the same notions of land ownership as Europeans, so forest regulation came down to different regimes of land use, but it produced, in the end, a complex system of multiple-use forestry that spared Japan the deforestation that plagued much of Europe.[23]

Simultaneous to forest management, the shogunate and domains drew on lively agronomic traditions and began encouraging planting seedlings to rebuild depleted forests. In 1650, for example, Matsudaira Sadatsuna, the daimyo of Kuwano domain, encouraged loggers to "plant a thousand seedlings for every tree" they harvested.[24] This represented the beginning of early modern Japan's managed forests regime. In 1697, Miyazaki Yasusada (1623–97), in his *Nōgyō zensho* (Agricultural compendium), argued, "Forests are valuable for both farmers and the realm: they should be nurtured in the manner of field crops, with valuable trees being planted and useless ones controlled."[25] As Totman observes, by the second half of the eighteenth century, plantation forestry became common throughout Japan. Throughout the eighteenth and early nineteenth centuries, the shogunate, domains, and villages constantly maneuvered and competed for use of Japan's forests, but the emergent system of plantation forestry ensured that Japan's forests survived the heavy use required by the early modern state and economy – the archipelago, that is, remained green. In the end, however, it was Japan's Pacific topography, flora, and climate that made the entire enterprise possible in the first place.

Jared Diamond, in *Collapse*, has raised Japan's early modern forestry practices as a global "success story," similar to that of sixteenth-century German

---

[22] Totman, *Green Archipelago*, 84–90.
[23] Totman, *Green Archipelago*, 88, 96.
[24] Totman, *Green Archipelago*, 117.
[25] Totman, *Green Archipelago*, 117–18.

principalities.[26] Whereas widespread deforestation had marked the seventeenth century, forest management – overseeing woodlands as agricultural plantations – defined the eighteenth century. "The shift was led from the top by successive shoguns," observes Diamond, "who invoked Confucian principles to promulgate an official ideology that encouraged limiting consumption and accumulating reserve supplies in order to protect the country against disaster."[27] Most likely, the most valuable "Confucian principle" at play in saving Japan's forests was paternalism – passing down ancestral lands to future generations.

The privatized nature of feudal landownership in early modern Japan helped the shogunate avoid a "tragedy of the commons" type scenario: most land in Japan, that is, was linked to warrior family ownership and not commonly held. Warrior families' concern with Confucian paternalism and eagerness to secure the political and financial health of successive generations promoted the long-term foresight required to replant trees on what were often ancestral properties. "Ruin is the destination toward which all men rush, each pursuing his own best interest in a society that believes in the freedom of the commons," wrote ecologist and philosopher Garrett Hardin in his famous article on the tragedy of the commons. "Freedom in a commons brings ruin to all."[28] But early modern Japan had little that qualified as real common land – perhaps periodically redistributed village arable land (*warichi*), if anything; national parks were entirely a post-Meiji phenomenon.[29] Moreover, within this centralized feudalistic order, Japan had no real conception of "freedom in the commons" as a philosophical concept, which likely spared Japan's forests from loggers freely pursuing every last tree in common forests before the next logger felled them.

It was not just Japan's centralized feudalism that allowed it to preserve resources, however. In part, Japan was able to stem overexploitation on the main Japanese islands by exploiting the environments and peoples in the north. As Diamond argues, "part of the Tokugawa solution for the problem of resource depletion in Japan itself was to conserve Japanese resources by causing resource depletion elsewhere, just as part of the solution of Japan and other First World countries to problems of resource depletion today is to cause resource depletion elsewhere."[30] The shogunate and Matsumae

---

[26] Diamond, *Collapse*, 294.
[27] Diamond, *Collapse*, 299.
[28] Hardin, "Tragedy of the Commons."
[29] Brown, *Cultivating Commons*, 101–44.
[30] Diamond, *Collapse*, 300.

domain, on the southern tip of Ezo (Hokkaido), were able to expand trade, fisheries, and mining into the north to supplant what they proved unable to exploit readily on the home islands.

In this regard, assessments that view early modern Japan as an environmental "success story" are complicated by early modern exploitation of Ainu lands. Historians need to give credit where credit is due – early modern Japanese not only did not chop down every last tree to build their monuments to power, as Easter Islanders apparently did, they also replanted them, in a remarkable display of environmental foresight. Nonetheless, it might be more accurate to view early modern Japan as a precursor to the modern world, where conservation at home to promote ecological and economic sustainability often parallels exploitation abroad. While it is true that the shogunate and domains took concrete steps to alleviate deforestation and minimize the overexploitation of domestic resources – as we have seen, less for reasons of Confucian benevolence than Confucian paternalism – they more than compensated by forging an early modern semicolonial order in Ezo, including the exploitation of timber, fisheries (some for export to China), furs, hawks (for falconry), and exotic medicines (for the samurai elite). The creation of massive herring fisheries, where Japanese fishery managers drafted Ainu as laborers, transported massive nitrogen stores from North Pacific coastal waters to Japanese agricultural fields in the Kinai region. There, farmers spread the fish mulch and oil as fertilizer to increase profits in Japan's early modern protocapitalist economy.

As David L. Howell demonstrates in Chapter 18, in the early seventeenth century, Matsumae retainers traded with Ainu chiefdoms, exchanging sake, rice, kettles, and other Japanese goods for dried and salted fish such as salmon, codfish, shark, and abalone; animal pelts such as deer, otter, and bear; pharmaceuticals such as bear gallbladder, fur-seal penis, and medicinal lichens; eagle feathers for arrow fletching; hawks for falconry; and other valuable "hunted commodities." Over the course of the early modern period, Japanese slowly expanded their settlement, known as Wajinchi, and displaced Ainu to live elsewhere. In 1717, 152 Ainu lived in Wajinchi; but that number had decreased to twelve by 1788. Simultaneously, the year-round Japanese population increased from 15,530 in 1716 to 26,564 in 1787.[31] Japanese also expanded their trading activities throughout Ezo, touching some of the most prominent and distant Ainu chiefdoms, such as Menaskur in the east, where Shakushain's War erupted in 1669.[32] Japan's story in Ezo is not necessarily one

---

[31] Howell, *Capitalism from Within*, 31.
[32] Walker, *Conquest of Ainu Lands*, 48–72.

of settler colonialism, unless you view Wajinchi as a process of Japanese settlement and Ainu dislocation (which is certainly how many Ainu viewed it). Certainly, the entirety of Ezo experienced a kind of commercial colonialism, in which Japanese traders, without settling permanently there, penetrated Ainu lands in unprecedented numbers.

Initially, the shogunate and Matsumae domain exhibited considerable interest in gold mining in Ezo. In 1604, shogunal official Honda Masanobu (1538–1616) spoke with Matsumae Yoshihiro (1548–1616), daimyo of Matsumae domain, about opening mines in Ezo, and by 1617, Japanese gold miners had developed placer mines on streams on the Oshima Peninsula. Three years later, Matsumae Kinhiro presented Ezo gold as a gift to Tokugawa Hidetada (1579–1632), the shogun. In 1620, shogunal officials gave Kinhiro permission to expand gold mining operations further into Ezo. In 1628, Japanese miners began extracting large amounts of gold from the Shiriuchi River and, three years later, miners opened placer operations in Shimakomaki, both in western Ezo. In 1633, Japanese miners opened placer mines along the Shibuchari and Kenomai Rivers, both in eastern Ezo and inside Menaskur Ainu territory. Two years later, Japanese miners began extracting gold from streams in Tokachi and Unbetsu, both in the east, as well as Kunnui and the headwaters of the Yūbari River.[33]

Placer mining proved harmful to seasonal Ainu salmon fisheries, and early on caused friction between the Haekur and Menaskur Ainu in the east, as well as with Matsumae domain, key factors in the outbreak of Shakushain's War in 1669. As one Portuguese missionary observed, Japanese placer miners "divert the flow of water along a different course and then dig into the sand which remains, until they reach the living stone and rock beneath the riverbed. And in the sand lodged in the rents and fissures of the rock is found gold as fine as beach gravel."[34] It is not difficult to see how diverting river flows and churning up sediment proved disastrous to salmon runs, contributing to the undermining of independent Ainu life.

Under Matsumae retainers, the trade remained small-scale and was restricted to a variety of prestige items that functioned better in feudal political economies of gift giving than commercial ones. By the eighteenth century, however, Japanese merchant interests had largely taken over the trade, and herring, salmon, kelp, and pelts became more common. These commodities flowed through standard shipping routes along the eastern and western coasts

---

[33] Walker, *Conquest of Ainu Lands*, 82–83.
[34] Walker, *Conquest of Ainu Lands*, 83.

of Japan, where the inhabitants of Osaka, Edo, and other castle towns eventually consumed them. Moreover, the expansion of trade led to the depletion of natural resources, often from overhunting. Echoing the observations of others, Matsumae Norihiro wrote in a memorandum to the shogunate that in the past, Ainu had traded many deer pelts, "but recently it is not like it was before. In all four directions natural resources have become exceedingly scarce," making Ainu subsistence difficult. Clearly, as trade intensified in the eighteenth century, certain "hunted commodities" became scarce.[35]

By the eighteenth century, trade had become so pervasive that it engendered dependency among Ainu chiefdoms as they increasingly incorporated sake and lacquerware into their rituals, integrated rice into their daily diets, covered their bodies in Japanese clothing, and cooked in Japanese iron kettles and pots. For many Ainu, daily life and daily ritual without such Japanese artifacts became incomprehensible. Simultaneously, the environment of Ezo began to reveal signs of stress from the trade, as deer populations fluctuated and many Ainu faced starvation. The important point is this: from the perspective of environmental history, not only was early modern Japan not a "closed country" (sakoku) but neither was it necessarily an insular environmental "success story." Rather, early modern Japan supplemented its own resource deficits with those extracted from semicolonial lands in the north. But Japan also implemented programs that spared valuable resources such as forests from overexploitation.

Matsumae domain had relied on trade in Ezo because it was unable to grow rice, which was the gold standard of the early modern political economy. Most of Japan's agricultural expansion occurred during the late medieval period and the seventeenth century. In the medieval period, the kandaka system, by assessing arable instead of cultivated land for yearly taxes, encouraged farmers to cultivate more land. In the seventeenth century, the shogunate and daimyo began reclaiming lowlands and clearing woodlands for agriculture with corvée labor. Laborers dredged rivers, erected embankments, and dug extensive irrigation canals to bring water to newly created paddies.

As Philip C. Brown observes, paddies and complex irrigation networks were built incrementally over decades and required building and rebuilding in order to function properly and sustain populations. In paddies, pans needed hardening and leveling to function properly, and ridges between paddies needed almost constant maintenance. Hydraulic forces pummeled dikes, and the continual maintenance of such agricultural systems required

---

[35] Walker, *Conquest of Ainu Lands*, 118–19.

the sustained peace that Tokugawa rule afforded. Mostly, Japanese farmers sought to control flooding with new technologies, such as the Shingen dike, which released excess water into catchments at planned intervals. Such irrigation investments meant that farmers could recultivate older, abandoned fields, convert dry fields to paddies, and expand cultivation into new lands, which translated into an overall expansion of land under cultivation. In the end, however, Japan's Pacific environment enabled the entire enterprise – snowpack in the mountains, free-flowing rivers, ample precipitation, and a temperate climate all facilitated the building of Japan's early modern political economy.

The Matsugasaki diversion of 1731 serves as an example of civil engineering that stabilized flooding and increased agricultural production in the Echigo plain on the Sea of Japan coast. The project started in 1727, when an industrious villager submitted a plan to Edo to reclaim parts of Shiunji Lake, north of modern Shibata City, in order to place more land under cultivation. With merchant financing from Edo and Kashiwazaki, laborers engineered a drainage system and diverted the Sakai River. Then, in 1730, a drainage canal diverted flow from the Agano River directly to the Sea of Japan at Matsugasaki. Then nature intervened: in 1731, a flood destroyed the dikes at the head of the diversion canal, expanding it from a pressure-release valve to the mainstream of the Agano River, which is how it stands to this day – now, the Agano no longer flows into the Shinano River, but rather directly into the Sea of Japan. The project alleviated flooding and improved conditions for agriculture, though it rendered the nearby Kaji River unnavigable and useless to commerce.[36] Brown has shown that the effects of such civil engineering projects, when seen collectively, vastly expanded Japan's cultivated land.

In 1600, Japan had approximately 1,621,920 hectares under cultivation. By 1720, that number had increased to about 2,946,240 hectares. Six years after the Meiji Restoration, that number had increased to 3,025,600 hectares. More cultivated land meant more people: early seventeenth-century improvements to agriculture produced enough calories to see Japan's population grow from about 17 million to somewhere around 30 million in the early eighteenth century.[37] Then the population mostly stagnated in the eighteenth and early nineteenth centuries, in what Fabian Drixler identifies as a reversal of the "demographic transition theory," only to begin growing once more in the

[36] Brown, "Floods," 105–6. See also Brown, "Constructing Nature," 100–101.
[37] Brown, "Floods," 99–101; on population, see Saito, "Climate, Famine, and Population," 214 (for the early seventeenth century), and Totman, Early Modern Japan, 250 (for the early eighteenth century).

late nineteenth and early twentieth centuries under the pronatalist policies of the Meiji government.[38]

Not just elaborate civil engineering projects but extensive fertilizer use, double cropping, and crop diversification also characterized early modern agriculture. These developments were, in large part, driven by the potential profits inherent in cash-crop farming. Once more, early modern Japan offers an interesting example of an environmental "success story," in which merchants recycled human waste from cities as agricultural fertilizer. In *Nōgyō zensho*, Miyazaki Yasusada, who we met earlier during the discussion of silviculture, sang the praises of feces, or "night soil," and divided it into two basic categories, with "superior feces" including human biowaste, oil cakes, dried sardines, and pressed whale meat and bones. A good protocapitalist, he cautioned that "superior feces" should only be used on crops that yielded high profits. Hiraga Gennai (1728–80), another agronomist, joked about feces, though "loathsome filth," being turned into fertilizer and hence "nourishing millions."[39]

With limited amounts of arable land and little livestock to produce waste, night soil proved exceedingly valuable. Night soil had become so valuable to Japan's protoindustrial economy that, by the eighteenth century, merchants paid city dwellers to remove their feces and urine. In cities such as Osaka and Edo, night soil was collected, brought to wharves, loaded onto freighters, and brought to surrounding farms. Many merchants complained that wharves reeked of human excrement, but as one Edo official lamented, "it was unavoidable for the manure boats to come into the wharves used by the tea and other ships."[40] Initially, manure boats entered the cities with vegetables to trade for night soil, but by the eighteenth century, vegetables no longer sufficed, and night soil was purchased with silver. Given night soil's high value, it is not surprising that people squabbled over access: often, building owners controlled access to feces, while tenants owned their urine. Fertilizer could cost a farmer 70 percent of the income from a crop, but it still proved a good capital investment. Agricultural output in the seventeenth and eighteenth centuries doubled, while the population proved relatively static at about 31 million.[41] Thus, even as some Japanese farmers transitioned to nonfood crops to profit from consumption in the castle towns – what Thomas C. Smith calls the "agrarian origins of modern Japan" – food output did not necessarily decrease.[42]

[38] See Drixler, *Mabiki*.
[39] Howell, "Fecal Matters," 137–38.
[40] Hanley, "Urban Sanitation," 9.
[41] Totman, *Japan*, 182–86.
[42] Smith, *Agrarian Origins*, ii, writes, "More than any other influence the market lifted economic life in the village out of the context of traditional social groupings.... Economic

Howell demonstrates that the night soil economy functioned like the commercialization of any other valuable resource. Take the village of Hashiramoto, on the western bank of the Yodo River. Wealthy residents contracted with forty-five Osaka landlords to pay twenty-five *momme* in silver annually for access to latrines. Twice each month, Hashiramoto villagers, or more likely hired laborers, traveled to the city to gather the valuable night soil. The work was labor intensive, and they often spent one to three nights making their rounds. Once the night soil arrived in Hashiramoto, the wealthy farmers spread the fertilizer and then sold to neighboring villagers whatever was left over. Sometimes, villagers, such as those from Tokumaru near Edo, exchanged eggplants, fresh and dried daikon radishes, and pickles for the night soil generated by 146 homes in three Edo neighborhoods. Large quantities of night soil also moved on rivers and canals in boats, owned and operated by families who lived aboard them. Apparently, their boats proved so sanitary that they moved excrement out of cities such as Edo and returned with loads of fresh vegetables to sell. These festooned boats made up nearly a quarter of all river traffic in 1872, before the turn to guano and, eventually, nitrogen fixation technologies to manufacture fertilizer.[43]

Modernization focused on the promise of imperialism and chemistry to solve the fertilizer problem, and the Pacific environment, specifically its bird populations, made it possible. As Gregory Cushman has shown, after Alexander von Humboldt (1769–1859) had first speculated about the high phosphorus and nitrogen content of guano, European and US imperialists set their sights on the Pacific to harvest the valuable resource.[44] Between 1840 and 1880, during Peru's "Guano age," the South American country exported thirteen million tons of guano. Eventually, this led to a guano rush throughout the Pacific basin. Whether Chilean conflicts with Bolivia in 1881, the British annexation of Ocean Island, the German annexation of Nauru Island in 1888, or the Japanese exile of the Polynesian Banaban people from Ocean Island to the Caroline Islands during World War II in order to scrape the Pacific island of any bird droppings the British had left behind, guano became one raison d'être of Pacific imperialism. In the early twentieth century, such industrial engineers as Noguchi Jun (1873–1944) emerged when solving the "nitrogen problem" became a national priority of most industrial nations.[45] A graduate

exchange ... became increasingly independent of social organization and created value of its own. Thereafter what goods and services men gave and received, on what occasions and in what amounts, was less a matter of obligation than whether the price was right."
[43] Howell, "Fecal Matters," 143–44.
[44] See Cushman, *Guano*.
[45] On the development of nitrogen fixation processes, see Hager, *Alchemy of Air*.

from Tokyo Imperial University, Noguchi eventually built the Chisso factory in Minamata in 1907 to produce calcium carbide and nitrogenous fertilizers. Starting in the late 1950s, Minamata became the site of Japan's most notorious pollution scandal, when fishers and their offspring developed horrific mercury poisoning, or what became known globally as "Minamata disease."[46] In large part, it was Japan's nineteenth-century quest to replace night soil, fish cake, oil cakes, and guano as fertilizer that led to the contorted bodies of twentieth-century Minamata.[47]

If lumber supplies and rice paddies buttressed Tokugawa power, so too did Japan's gold and silver mines, which financed Japan's sixteenth-century unification and nineteenth-century Western modernization. Like Japan's forests, its rich alluvial lands, and the Pacific's vast guano deposits, the Pacific made mining in Japan possible: hard rock mines prospered from the tectonic uplifting that had brought copper, silver, zinc, and lead closer to the earth's surface, within reach of the enterprising hands, picks, and, eventually, pneumatic shovels of Japanese miners. By the nineteenth century, the Ashio copper mine (in modern-day Tochigi Prefecture) became the most famous of these mines, although the Kamioka mine (in Toyama and Gifu Prefectures) also supplied valuable metals, such as lead and zinc, and later became the site of painful cadmium poisoning in the twentieth century, known as *itai itai byō* (it hurts, it hurts disease). In 1610, farmers discovered surface deposits of copper near Ashio and reported their discovery to a local Buddhist temple. The next year, a shogunal senior councillor presented refined copper to officials in Edo, and they incorporated Ashio into the official holdings of the Tokugawa family. The shogunate placed a magistrate in charge of Ashio, ensuring that the wealth generated from the mine continued to fill Tokugawa coffers. Japan's copper supplies allowed the shogunate to put in place a fairly unified currency system by the end of the seventeenth century, which contributed to Japan's unification under Tokugawa rule. Moreover, the shogunate exported copper cast in the shape of bars to Chinese and Dutch buyers: between 1684 and 1697, it exported 35,931 tons to Chinese buyers and 16,497 tons to Dutch buyers. Eventually, the shogunate placed the Dōza, a Bureau of Copper, first located in Osaka and then in Edo, in charge of copper exports; afterward the Meiji government took over the administrative duties of managing copper.

Timothy J. LeCain argues that the Meiji obsession with Western modernity meant that copper took on a whole new meaning and level of importance

---

[46] George, *Minamata*.
[47] Walker, *Toxic Archipelago*, 152–58.

in the late nineteenth century; but, in a kind of metallurgy-of-desire hypothesis, LeCain suggests that it was copper's molecular structure that made it desirable to modern life. Its availability, malleability, and the fact that it hardens when manipulated and hammered may have served early modern purposes; but its atomic structure – that it has a weakly bonded electron in its outer orbit, which allows it to conduct electricity and heat efficiently – made it attractive to the architects of modern infrastructure. In wires, copper transmitted the energy, heat, and information of industrial civilization and, as a widely available material on the Japanese islands, transmitted Japanese modernity. Not only did engineers make telegraph wires from copper, but naval architects laced together their battlewagons with copper wire: an average pre-dreadnought class battleship, such as Tōgō Heihachirō's flagship *Mikasa* (displacement 15,380 tons), which he used to deliver the bulk of the Russian Baltic fleet to Davy Jones's locker in 1905, contained two million pounds of copper, while the *Musashi* and *Yamato* of World War II fame (displacement 71,659 tons) had somewhere around twice that amount.[48] In short, copper proved a key ingredient for the entire "rich country, strong military" (*fukoku kyōhei*) drive of the Meiji years and beyond, and it occurred naturally in abundance in the Pacific basin. Copper linked Pacific nations such as Chile, Japan, and the United States: copper occurred in abundance in these countries because of the Pacific's tectonics, and the ocean itself provided the transportation for international trade in the desirable element.

In 1870, the Meiji government established the Ministry of Industry (Kōbushō) to drive Japan's rapid industrialization, and copper proved instrumental to their designs. When Itō Hirobumi (1841–1909) articulated the necessity of the ministry shortly after its creation, all of the technological key indicators of modernity – the "mechanical equipment on the western model," as he wrote – required massive amounts of copper. In Itō's words, the industry ministry was to "make good Japan's deficiencies by swiftly seizing upon the strengths of the western industrial arts; to construct within Japan all kinds of mechanical equipment on the western model, including shipbuilding, railways, telegraphy, mines, and buildings; and thus with one great leap to introduce to Japan the concepts of enlightenment."[49] If Tokugawa planners viewed copper through the lens of domestic currency and Chinese and Dutch export markets, Meiji planners sought to bind Japan to its industrial future with endless spools of copper wire. By 1895, under

---

[48] LeCain, *Matter of History*, 244–305.
[49] Walker, *Toxic Archipelago*, 88.

the ministry's auspices, 4,000 miles of copper wire tied Japan inescapably to its modern project.

Extracting this much copper required dramatic changes at the Ashio copper mine; with Meiji technological innovations, the copper itself never changed, but the amount mined certainly did. Miners replaced the shallow surface pits, called *tanuki bori* (raccoon-dog holes), with deeper and more productive shafts, part of a new regime of verticality enabled by a host of new mechanical tools. Eventually, copper extracted from Ashio accounted for nearly half of Japan's domestic copper production. But the Ashio copper mine proved anything but a contained organic machine, as many engineers had portrayed it. Even as early as the 1870s, water in the Watarase River, downstream from the mine, had turned a "bluish white" color. Fish and eels swam dazed in the eerie water, while children who waded in it discovered sores on their legs and feet. The dazed fish portended the collapse of Watarase fisheries in the following years. In 1887, investigators drew connections between the increased production at the mine, polluted water leeching from the mine pit, and the disappearance of fish stocks. If the collapse of local fisheries was not enough, the governor of Tochigi Prefecture, Fujikawa Tamechika (governed 1880–83), learned that silkworms fed mulberry leaves from polluted areas died. The deforestation around the mine also caused uncontrollable flooding, washing toxic mine waste across downstream fields.

The environmental catastrophe at Ashio became, in Fred G. Notehelfer's words, Japan's first pollution incident.[50] In actuality, it was not necessarily qualitatively different from earlier "bad water" episodes around early modern mines. Basically, new technologies allowed miners to tunnel far deeper, and new separation technologies allowed processors to grind ore far finer than ever before – all making toxins brought to the earth's surface with so much labor bioavailable for human and nonhuman bodies. Extracting metals, minerals, and elements from the earth's bowels is dangerous. As the journalist Kōtoku Shūsui (1871–1911) wrote, the Ashio mine "caused poisonous waste to fill the valley and flow in its waters, joining the Watarase River and continuing downstream so that nothing living along the banks escapes its disastrous effects." He continued, "Last year forests at the river's source were recklessly felled by toxic emissions so that now the river runs red with the poisoned earth of the bare mountains." Along with dead fish and sickened bodies, he observed that "as far as the eye can see the once fertile land has been reduced to a wretched sea of withered yellow reeds and white rushes."[51]

[50] Notehelfer, "Japan's First Pollution Incident."
[51] Kōtoku Shūsui cited in Stolz, *Bad Water*, 52.

Farmers sought recourse from the Meiji state, but instead were ignored in favor of Ashio's oligarchical owner. But farmers did find their voice in Japan's first environmental activist, Tanaka Shōzō (1841–1913).

On 18 December 1891, Tanaka gave a thunderous speech in the Diet condemning the mine. He described the dire effects of the "poisonous effluence" on rural communities, and then asked, "Why has the government done nothing for so long?" The answer was because halting the mine meant halting Japan's pursuit of Western progress. Tanaka came to dedicate much of his later life to the Ashio cause. The last stand was at Yanaka village, which engineers had slated for demolition in favor of a catchment basin for heavily polluted water. It proved an apt metaphor for the entire Ashio episode and Meiji priorities more generally. Tanaka failed to save Yanaka: by July 1907, the village was largely dismantled and would soon be submerged in a toxic stew. But the entire episode proved transformative for Tanaka. His new epistemology of *chisan, chisui* (care for mountains, care for water) became one of the first rallying cries for a new environmental philosophy, anticipating the "thinking like a mountain" of Aldo Leopold (1887–1948). In the coming decades, Japan's modern state ignored Tanaka's wisdom in favor of industrialization at any cost, leading to the contorted bodies of Minamata, among other pollution episodes. However, Tanaka still must be seen as among the founding thinkers of modern environmentalism, high on that exalted list with Leopold and Rachel Carson (1907–64).[52]

Pacific Hydrography

Currents shaped the navigation of the Pacific and the distribution of fish and whale populations, both of which figure into Japan's history. Pacific circulations influence atmospheric phenomena, determining the movement and mixture of warm and cold currents. Gyres (circular systems of ocean currents), for example, distribute solar energy from warm waters in the tropics to higher latitudes with colder water. The Kuroshio Current is part of the North Pacific oceanic gyre, and with its clockwise movement serves to distribute warm water northward. In Kuroshio eddies, a lively ecosystem has evolved, serving as havens for plankton and fish larvae. The Pacific serves to redistribute solar energy from warmer climates – both vertically through convective currents and latitudinally through gyres – to areas of the North Pacific, such as the east coast of Japan.

[52] Strong, *Ox against the Storm*.

The Kuroshio is the most prominent of these currents, transporting 50 million tons of seawater past Japan's southeast coast every second – about 6,000 times the amount as the Danube or Volga Rivers. The Kuroshio has wielded great influence on the fisheries, hydrology, and meteorology of Japan. Essentially, the Kuroshio is a thin ribbon of water within the context of the North Pacific – about 100 kilometers wide and with a one-kilometer maximum depth, extending some 3,000 kilometers between the Philippines and the east coast of Japan. The Japanese name Kuroshio, or "black stream," refers to the dark ultramarine color of the relatively warm, high-salinity water within the current.

In terms of its ability to influence the weather and transport energy – both kinetic energy and energy stored in marine life – the Kuroshio has played an important role in everyday life in Japan, for fishers and farmers alike. The Kuroshio evidences the interconnectedness of the entire Pacific Ocean – the current transports forces generated by the earth's rotation, called Coriolis force, as well as kinetic and thermal energy; but it also transports wind-driven force from as far away as Baja California. Near Tokara Strait, the Kuroshio is about 30 sverdrup (or about 30 million cubic meters per second) and peaks in the spring and summer months, not unlike spring runoff in a mountain stream. Then, the Kuroshio increases to about 55 sverdrup near Shikoku. It is no wonder that Japanese fishers and mariners who inadvertently found themselves trapped in the current were quickly whisked out to sea.[53] Such ocean-floor contours as the Izu-Bonin ridge, located due south of Honshu, also influence the Kuroshio and the marine mammals that cruise on this oceanic superhighway.

Near Japan, the Kuroshio merges with the Oyashio Current, or "parent stream," traveling south from the Kamchatka Peninsula with somewhere around 15 to 20 sverdrup of water. Basically, they merge into a biologically rich confluence zone to become what is often called the easterly Kuroshio extension. Within the Kuroshio extension, a distinct and highly volatile line separates two primary water types, warm saline on the right, and colder, but nutrient-rich, Oyashio water on the left. Outstanding pelagic fisheries exist on both sides of this line because fish move between both currents to feed in the Oyashio, and it has long been of interest to Japanese fishers (see Map 9.1).[54]

The mixed water region between the Oyashio and Kuroshio currents is important to understanding the histories of Japan's pelagic and coastal

[53] See Plummer, *Shogun's Reluctant Ambassadors*.
[54] Barkley, "Kuroshio Current," 54, 56, 59; Qiu, "Kuroshio and Oyashio Currents," 1414, 1417, 1422.

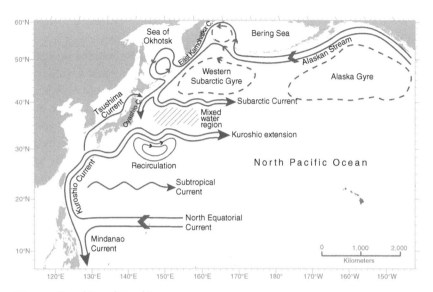

Map 9.1 Kuroshio and Oyashio currents
Map by Center for Geographic Analysis, Harvard University, based on Bo Qiu,
"Kuroshio and Oyashio Currents," in *Encyclopedia of Ocean Sciences* (San Diego: Academic
Press, 2001), 1414. © Elsevier, 2001.

fisheries. The thriving abundance of phytoplankton, diatoms, and zooplankton in the Oyashio and mixed water region support a diverse array of fisheries, including herring, salmon, mackerel, pollock, cod, flounder, rockfish, squid, and shrimp.[55] Early modern Japanese were mainly coastal fishers and whalers, depending on whale migration routes through the narrow Tsushima Strait and along the Pacific coast for opportunities to kill the leviathans. Japan's pelagic fishing and whaling fleets only emerged after the Meiji Restoration of 1868, circling the globe to deliver their catches to the largest fish market in the world, Tokyo's Tsukiji fish market.

In this way, the North Pacific contains major biological hotspots, ones that produce energy in the form of currents and living creatures, and much of this energy is located in higher-level trophic species such as whales. As Jakobina K. Arch observes, early modern Japanese whaling operations, usually with a minimum of 300 laborers but sometimes many more, tended to tap into these important oceanic currents for their quarry. Whales used such currents for navigation to feeding and breeding grounds because they were rich

---

[55] Minoda, "Oceanographic and Biomass Changes," 67–68, 72, 75, 81.

in the zooplankton that baleen whales need to survive. Because early modern Japanese remained principally coastal whalers, their targets were such baleen whales as the North Pacific right whale, the gray whale, and the humpback whale. Other whales, such as faster species from the rorqual family, were pelagic and thus remained out of reach of even the most ambitious Japanese whalers. Whether in the Japan Sea or the Pacific, the contours of the ocean floor and the Oyashio and Kuroshio forced whales into specific geographic areas, where knowledgeable whalers waited for them. Whaling operations in Tosa Bay, the Kumano coast, and Ise and Mikawa Bays drew on the Kuroshio, while the whalers in the Saikai and Chōshū areas drew on the Tsushima Current, a western branch of the Kuroshio, which thrusts from the south into the Japan Sea.[56]

Japan's early modern whaling industry involved killing whales, dragging them to shore, and then processing them within about twenty-four hours, before the cetaceans bloated and spoiled. In such villages as Ogawajima, a small islet off the coast of northern Kyushu, about 800 men crewed the several ten-meter whaleboats that pursued migrating baleen whales. Not only were hundreds of men required to pursue and kill whales on the water, but hundreds more were needed to process them once crews had successfully dragged them ashore. Later, whalers deployed open-water nets to entangle the migrating leviathans before killing them with harpoons. Such harpooning techniques probably originated in the late sixteenth century in the Ise and Mikawa Bay areas. Arch demonstrates that Japan's coastal whaling industry was susceptible to fluctuating whale populations, shifts in migration patterns, and possibly overhunting. In one example, Kii officials appear to have shuttered the Ise whaling operation in 1770 due to a lack of whales. Consequently, the disappearance of migrating whales in one location often caused whaling operations to relocate. In 1606, for example, former whalers from near Ise Bay, led by Wada Yorimoto, established whaling operations in Taiji, the most famous and controversial center of Japanese whaling today. By 1675, whaling near Taiji had become so lucrative that Wada Yoriharu assembled nearby village heads to discuss methods to decrease confrontations over whaling grounds and landing beaches in order to maintain mutual prosperity. But not all regions remained prosperous. In 1641, whaling in Tosa domain ceased because the declining number of whales could not support the 200 laborers involved in the industry. Many of them moved to the northern Kyushu area to exploit the Tsushima Current. Indeed, by 1650, whaling groups operated

[56] Arch, *Bringing Whales Ashore*, xx, 25.

in some seventy-three locations in northern Kyushu, and many of those had connections to Kumano.[57]

Arch argues that the late seventeenth-century transition from harpoon whaling to net whaling, traditionally attributed to Taiji's Wada Yoriharu in 1675, was about expanding the range of target species in the wake of lower whale numbers. Early Japanese whaling operations, similar to their US and European counterparts, focused their killing energy on right whales, a species that now teeters on the brink of extinction. Humpbacks and grey whales swim slightly faster and tend to sink when killed. Nets effectively slowed down these faster whales, ones that could not be easily harpooned, and also kept the giants from sinking once lanced and bleeding to death. The emergence of net whaling corresponded to the slow decline of catches in such locations as Taiji. There, whalers landed ninety-five whales in 1681, but numbers declined thereafter. The net method spread quickly throughout whaling communities in Japan, and Fukazawa Gidayū was using it in northern Kyushu by 1683. Whaling operations around Kyushu managed to kill between twenty and forty whales per year for a thirty-five-year period, even though the region was heavily exploited with the highest concentration of whaling operations in early modern Japan.[58]

Arch observes that within the first three decades of the nineteenth century, coastal whaling operations in Japan began to see fewer whales, largely because of the pelagic fleets of the United States, which had decimated right whales in their summer feeding grounds north of Japan and had started to focus on sperm whales. As whale numbers declined, the US whaling fleet witnessed a 90 percent decrease in harvested whales. Early modern Japan's coastal whaling operations never operated at the scale that the United States' did at this time, but Arch insists that there is still evidence that Japanese whalers felt the squeeze of disappearing whales. For fourteen years between 1823 and 1844, the Koza Whaling Office, in the Kumano area, operated with a financial deficit; the situation became more severe by the 1860s, on the eve of the Meiji Restoration. Eventually, hard times forced the 271 whalers of the Koza Whaling Office to borrow rice to avoid starvation. Similarly, in the northern Kyushu region, the Masutomi whaling group saw its kills decline from 140 to 20 annually between 1805 and 1823.[59] With these unsustainable numbers, many whaling operations went under, much like the lifeless carcasses of their rapidly disappearing prey.

---

[57] Arch, *Bringing Whales Ashore*, 49, 50, 53, 57–60, 62, 63.
[58] Arch, *Bringing Whales Ashore*, 63, 66.
[59] Arch, *Bringing Whales Ashore*, 71–72.

Early modern Japanese integrated many nonhuman animals into Shinto and Buddhist belief systems, and this included whales. Famously, foxes were potent symbols in Inari worship, and Japanese wolves figured prominently in both Shinto and Buddhist iconography.[60] Whales proved no exception. Whalers had integrated killing whales into Buddhist death rituals by the seventeenth century. In some coastal villages, slayed whales were given posthumous Buddhist names, much like people. At Kōganji in Kayoi village, for example, San'yo Shōnin, the head Buddhist priest, created a death registry (*kakochō*) for whales in 1679. The Kayoi whaling group had started net whaling in 1673 in order to increase their harvest, which may have precipitated the Buddhist naming practice. By 1692, Kayoi whalers assisted Buddhist priests in conducting the memorial services. They also established a communal grave for fetal whales, with accompanying Jizō statuary, which honored the unborn, both sapiens and cetaceans. Even after the death of Priest Shōnin, Kōganji continued with the practice of assisting the dead leviathans in their great migration in the afterlife. There are many examples of Buddhist ceremonies commemorating the death of nonhuman animals in early modern Japan – indeed, San'yo Shōnin's activities roughly correspond to Tokugawa Tsunayoshi's (1649–1709) Laws of Compassion for Living Things, with which the shogun principally sought to curtail the abandonment of infants but extended the compassion to dogs throughout the realm – but it is striking that most temples that posthumously named whales intermixed those names with the names of the human dead, blurring the boundary between the human and nonhuman.[61] Along with posthumous names in Buddhist death registries, Japanese also built whale graves and stone memorials along the beaches to pay tribute to dead whales.[62]

Not long after whale numbers plummeted in the 1820s, whaling began to transform from a sustainer of coastal economies to a symbol of national economic strength. This proved particularly true after the Meiji Restoration. In 1875, Nagaoka Moriyoshi (1842–1906), a future House of Peers member and diplomat, trumpeted: "knowledge of the use of whales drives the wealth and power of the nation." Just as pressure on whale populations necessitated the transition from harpoon whaling to net whaling in Japan's seventeenth-century coastal communities, the nineteenth-century crash required a similar technological breakthrough. And just such a breakthrough came with the exploding harpoon, patented by Thomas Welcome Roys (c. 1816–77) of the United States,

---

[60] See Smyers, *Fox and the Jewel*, and Walker, *Lost Wolves of Japan*.
[61] See Bodart-Bailey, *Dog Shogun*.
[62] Arch, *Bringing Whales Ashore*, 153–67.

and the harpoon gun, invented by the Norwegian Svend Foyn (1809–94). In 1899, in the inaugural use of such imported killing technologies, a Japanese steamship bagged three fin whales near Tsushima. From this point forward, successful Japanese whaling operations became those that transitioned from coastal operations to blue water ones.[63] These twentieth-century pelagic whaling fleets are what most people identify with Japan's whaling industry today, not the coastal outfits of the eighteenth century. As Arch has shown, however, it is clear from the historical record that even these smaller operations could have a local effect on whale populations. Early modern extractive economies could deleteriously impact environments just as modern ones do.

Whales were largely consumed in coastal areas because the meat, even if salted, spoiled relatively quickly. But other whale products played an important role in Japan's economic development, given that the emergence of Japan's protocapitalist economy occurred in the arena of cash-crop farming. Much of the energy required for Japan's economic development came from the marine environments of the Pacific Ocean. Agronomist Ōkura Nagatsune (1766–1860), as will be discussed later, experimented with the use of whale oil as an insecticide. Similarly, in 1840, polymath Satō Nobuhiro (1769–1850), in his observations on cultivation, recommended whale oil as a fertilizer. The only better source of fertilizer, he wrote, was herring and fish oil. Satō observed that strengthening Japan in the face of Western imperialism required the "development of natural resources," and exploiting whales on the high seas was an important part of that equation.[64]

In the late nineteenth and early twentieth centuries, Japanese pelagic whaling remained fairly small in scale and was limited to nearby North Pacific waters; but that all changed in 1934, when a Japanese company purchased the Norwegian factory ship *Antarctic* and five catcher boats, older vessels but with updated harpoon guns. The inaugural hunting trip of the *Antarctic Maru* had many experienced Norwegian sailors on board, and the Japanese proved quick studies. Suddenly, as Kurkpatrick Dorsey observes, the Japanese became international players in the pelagic whaling scene, embroiled in the tricky diplomacy of hunting on the high seas.[65] Even though the inaugural sail of Japan's new whaling fleet saw mixed results, by 1938 Japanese whalers operated six floating factories and nearly fifty catcher boats – and, as self-proclaimed upstarts, they refused to sign such international agreements as the 1931 Convention for the Regulation of Whaling. Unlike the situation

[63] Arch, *Bringing Whales Ashore*, 73–75.
[64] Arch, *Bringing Whales Ashore*, 101.
[65] Dorsey, *Whales and Nations*, 57–58.

with Japanese forestry, examined earlier, where private landownership and Confucian paternalism protected forests from overexploitation, or even some of the coastal fisheries examined by Arne Kalland, the high seas proved ripe for a tragedy of the commons type scenario.[66] Diplomats signed a slew of international agreements to implement whale quotas, usually between the Norwegians and British, but few believed that such conventions could protect whales, particularly after Japan entered the bloody fray. British officials tried to get the Japanese to adhere to international conventions, but, drawing on Western bigotry, feared "it is too much to expect the Japs to submit to that." Friction continued between Japanese and European whaling fleets, with Europeans repeatedly accusing the Japanese of wasting whales; the Japanese insisted that their slaughter of whales for meat meant that less oil was extracted per carcass.[67] Japan's pelagic fleet continued to hunt the high seas until the International Whaling Commission's 1982 moratorium on commercial whaling. Today, Japan's "scientific whaling" is done largely in defiance of such international protocols. And given that Japanese whalers, in their 2017 summer hunt in the Southern Ocean, killed 122 pregnant minke whales, the mass fetal graves and Jizō statuary will apparently continue to be necessary.[68]

The Oyashio Current that provided nutrients to the Pacific coast of Japan and nourished migrating whales combined with the Tsushima Current to create excellent fishing grounds near Ezo, today's Hokkaido. Herring fisheries became integral to Japan's protocapitalist development – the nitrogen-, phosphorus-, and potash-rich mulch and oils they provided fertilized the cash crops that birthed Japan's protocapitalist economy. Cash-crop farmers looked to the dried herring and oil to boost their yields in order to profit from selling cotton, tobacco, and soybeans in the cities, which served as hungry consumer centers for enterprising, wealthy farmers called gōnō. The size of early modern Japan's herring fishery is impressive. In 1861, when Thomas Wright Blakiston (1832–91), a British explorer, visited Hakodate, in southern Hokkaido, he was "at once made aware of the principal occupation of the inhabitants, and the consequent trade of the place, by the all-pervading stench of dried fish and seaweed; in the streets, in the houses, on the mountain side, everywhere the same scent haunted me."[69] Dried fish made excellent fertilizer: it was widely available, it rarely burned crops when applied, and it contained excellent levels of nutrients critical to growing plants.

[66] See Kalland, *Fishing Villages*.
[67] Dorsey, *Whales and Nations*, 57–64.
[68] Bando et al., "Results of the Third Biological Field Survey."
[69] Thomas Wright Blakiston cited in Howell, *Capitalism from Within*, 1.

In 1739, Sakakura Genjirō observed that in southern Ezo the "peasants cultivate no fields, but fish herring in place of agriculture.... Matsumae has not seen a poor catch in decades ... and in the span of about twenty days the people earn enough to support themselves for a year."[70] There may not have been poor catches in the first half of the eighteenth century, but, as Howell argues, in the second half of the eighteenth century herring stopped running and fisheries dried up, although without the same disastrous results as the famines devastating northeastern Japan at the same time. Lumbering ships called *kitamaebune*, which held up to 3,000 cubic meters of cargo, made the voyages; in 1857, some 44 percent of these shipments were to the Kinai region, with another 14 percent going to other Japan Sea ports. Dried herring fertilizer only caught on in the Kantō region in the Meiji years, on the eve of the transition to other sources of nitrogen. In 1857, fisheries such as the one at Mashike produced over 11,000 metric tons of herring to be dried, processed, and shipped to Honshu fields. Howell argues that in the nineteenth century, the operators of these coastal fisheries were capitalists, but ones who needed feudalism to survive. By the end of the nineteenth century, he explains, a complete capitalist transformation had largely occurred in the northern herring fisheries.[71] In this manner, the Pacific engine powered Japan's capitalist transition and propelled it into the twentieth century as a leading economic power – capitalistic development that occurred largely independent of Western dispersal.

The trade in *tawaramono*, or "baled goods," also serves as an instructive example of the importance of the Pacific larder. Ainu and Japanese fishers harvested a variety of sea creatures from the Ezo littoral for shipment to Nagasaki, where merchants traded them in China. Hezutsu Tōsaku wrote in 1784 of the thriving trade in *tawaramono* – sea cucumbers, dried abalone, and Shinori kelp comprised most *tawaramono*, but other fish parts were often found in these export bales as well. Under the impetus of Tanuma Okitsugu (1719–88), the lead senior councillor, the shogunate extended licenses to merchants from Edo and Osaka to transport *tawaramono* to Nagasaki, where workers prepared them for export. Even though merchants periodically reported that "these products had become scarce," showing, as with coastal whaling, the possibility of overexploitation, laborers extracted thousands of pounds of dried sea cucumber from the coastal environments of Hokkaido. It was a fertile fishery, one that was made possible by the nutrient-rich currents that swirled around the Japanese islands.

---

[70] Howell, *Capitalism from Within*, 54.
[71] Howell, *Capitalism from Within*, 37, 49.

Like with the herring fisheries, sea cucumber fishery managers had recruited Ainu as laborers. Hezutsu explained that one Ainu fisherman could catch thousands of sea cucumbers in one day, where they were brought to Japanese managers in exchange for rice wine at the local trading post as an incentive. Kushihara Seihō observed that for 500 sea cucumbers, an Ainu fisher received one sixteen-liter bale of rice. Kushihara, a mathematician by training, reckoned that the some 300 Ainu boats working the coastal waters near Sōya hauled approximately 120,000 sea cucumbers to shore each day. With each China-bound *tawaramono* containing about 12,000 dried sea cucumbers, laborers assembled some 300 bales each month for shipment, all overseen by officials from Matsumae domain.[72]

As we have seen, Japanese whalers harpooned baleen whales in coastal waters, dragged their giant carcasses ashore, and processed their massive bodies into food, fertilizer, and insecticides to fuel Japanese bodies and economies in the eighteenth century. Similarly, Japanese fishery managers throughout southern Hokkaido turned the endless shoals of herring there – reportedly so thick that a pole could stand up vertically in the water in their masses of slithering silver bodies – into the dried mulch and pressed oil that provided the nitrogen for Japan's agrarian political and commercial economies. Comprised of a dried menagerie of sea life, *tawaramono*, by contrast, became the material of an international export market that exploited the natural environment of Hokkaido, along with the labor of their Ainu inhabitants, for a trade with China that carried both commercial and diplomatic weight in East Asia. It was the Pacific marine environment more than any other force that drove Japan's political and economic development in the early modern period. In this manner, Japan became a Pacific nation in the eighteenth and nineteenth centuries, entering its modern period increasingly reliant on the great ocean to power its historical emergence as a modern nation.

Pacific Climate

The Pacific determines nearly the entirety of Japan's weather, but global climatological patterns are also important to understanding Japan's seventeenth through nineteenth centuries. When Japan's early modern period began, the Medieval Climate Optimum (950–1250 CE) had since concluded, and climatological volatility became more commonplace in world weather. The origins of the Little Ice Age, as scientists call the global early modern climate, related

---

[72] Walker, *Conquest of Ainu Lands*, 94–97.

to both cosmic and earthly phenomena, but the Pacific context, specifically tectonics in the Ring of Fire, played a critical role in ushering in the Little Ice Age. The Maunder Minimum (1645–1715), or period of sun spot minimum, may have decreased solar radiance and therefore temperatures, but the fact that nearly all of the major volcano eruptions between 1450 and 1902 occurred within the Pacific's Ring of Fire illustrates the importance of Pacific tectonics in understanding Japan's early modern climate and weather.[73] With widespread volcanism remaining the best explanation for the Little Ice Age, the Pacific tectonic context is critical to understanding Japan's early modern environmental history.[74] In this regard, the Pacific could be an engine of widespread human catastrophe as well as political centralization and proto-capitalist development.

Japan's monsoon climate is directly shaped by ocean hydrography. Pacific currents conspire with heating and cooling landmasses in central Asia to create monsoon weather and regular trade winds. Warm temperatures on land continually rise and draw in air and create low-pressure cells. This vertical movement causes monsoonal rains, which have influenced Japanese history in a number of ways, including by providing naturally available irrigation for crops. In Japan, monsoon rains, called *tsuyu*, arrive in the early summer and provide valuable precipitation. On average, Tokyo receives just over 1,500 millimeters of precipitation annually. It is a defining characteristic of Japan's seasonal rhythms, one that influences Japanese economic and cultural life.[75]

In the Pacific atmosphere, convective cells move along the monsoon belt causing air to rise and, by their movement to the poles, contributing to trade winds, rains, and the jet stream. Some 40 percent of global precipitation falls in the areas inhabited by these Hadley cells. In their horizontal circular movement, Hadley cells conspire with the rotation of the globe to create another instance of Coriolis force (as we saw with Pacific currents), which contributes to the creation of cyclone and anticyclone storms. In the South and East China Seas, such cyclones and hurricanes are called typhoons. They often track from the southwest to the northeast across the Japanese archipelago and have contributed to natural disasters throughout Japanese history.[76] Within a typhoon, plunging air pressure sucks up sea levels, creating massive storm surges that have been a defining factor of Japanese life for centuries.[77]

---

[73] Briffa et al., "Influence of Volcanic Eruptions."
[74] Richards, *Unending Frontier*, 58, 67.
[75] Freeman, *Pacific*, 11–14.
[76] Grossman and Zaiki, "Reconstructing Typhoons."
[77] Freeman, *Pacific*, 11–14.

Similarly, the El Niño/Southern Oscillation (ENSO) has influenced Japan's environmental history, possibly contributing to the climatological extremes of the early modern period. ENSO events occur when contrary winds and currents interrupt prevailing easterlies in the North and South Pacific, causing dramatic climatic changes in the Pacific basin and elsewhere in the world. With El Niño, warm surface water prevails in the central and east-central equatorial Pacific, accompanied by high air pressure in the western Pacific and low air pressure in the eastern Pacific. By contrast, La Niña events occur when the high pressure is in the east and the low pressure is in the western Pacific. Such dramatic fluctuations cause changes in rainfall and temperature; but shifting Pacific surface temperatures lead to changes in marine organisms, too. In East Asia, El Niño events often translate into drought because easterly moving warm surface waters bring rainfall away from East Asia, possibly explaining the frequent references to severe drought in early modern weather diaries, ones that intermix with periods of cold, and then blowing winds and torrential rains. Indeed, although *reigai* (cold-weather damage) characterizes nearly all the eighteenth and nineteenth centuries' famine episodes, *kanbatsu* (severe drought) explains the crop failures that occurred between 1626 and 1668. Not all weather damage is the same.

In general, warmer global temperatures characterized the medieval world and cooler temperatures the early modern world, and this fact influenced Japan's history. In Japan, the Maunder Minimum often translated into wetter seasons, ENSO events translated into drier weather, and volcanism translated into colder weather. Importantly, frigid summers correspond with Japan's most horrifying famines, when starving people, in rare instances, reportedly resorted to cannibalism to nourish themselves. Using cherry-blossom viewing dates, Lake Suwa freezing records, and Edo weather diaries, scholars have reconstructed a past climatological picture for Japan's early modern period, which corresponds neatly to the global snapshot of the Little Ice Age. Cherry-blossom viewing records, for example, suggest warmer temperatures between the eleventh and thirteenth centuries and cooler temperatures between the sixteenth and eighteenth centuries, with expected yearly variability. Freezing dates for Lake Suwa place some of the coldest winters on records in the early seventeenth century, roughly corresponding to the eruption of Mount Huaynaputina in Peru in 1600, which altered weather around the globe.[78] Cooler temperatures associated with the Little Ice Age

[78] Mikami, "Climatic Variations," 190–93. Much of this information was later reproduced in Mikami, Zaiki, and Hirano, "History of Climatic Change."

reconfigured Japan's early modern subsistence patterns: cooler temperatures often translated into crop failure and famine. Using archaeobotanical evidence from Lake Karikomi, for example, scholars hypothesize that the practice of *hansaibai* (partial cultivation) of chestnut trees in the Hida and Echizen regions corresponded to the disappearance of other food sources during the Little Ice Age.[79]

Dendroclimatic analysis of hinoki cypress in central Japan presents a more precise chronological picture, one that corresponds to famine patterns in early modern Japan. Hinoki cypress tree rings reveal five extreme cool phases during Japan's early modern period: 1727–49, 1782–1802, 1808–23, 1831–42, and 1852–92.[80] The 1727–49 phase corresponds to the Kyōhō and Kan'en famines. The 1782–1802 phase corresponds to the Tenmei famine (1782–88), which was principally caused by abnormally frigid temperatures in northeastern Japan. Finally, the Tenpō famine (1833–38) corresponds to the 1831–42 phase. In total, ten severe famines ravaged early modern Japan, and volcanism and frigid Little Ice Age temperatures contributed to all of them (see Table 9.2).

Importantly, climatological shifts, specifically the Little Ice Age, shaped the entire early modern world. With decades of upheaval such as the Tenmei famine, there is a concrete relationship between global (the eruption of Mount Laki in Iceland), regional (the Pacific's Ring of Fire), and local (the eruption of Mount Asama) natural phenomena in precipitating severe food shortages, malnutrition, and famine. Not only did famines cause social and economic chaos, but the conservative turn in Edo politics, specifically the rise of Matsudaira Sadanobu (1759–1829) and his Kansei reforms, occurred as a direct result of the horrors of the Tenmei experience – there is a propensity for Japanese politicians, even as recently as the magnitude 9.0 Great East Japan earthquake and tsunami of March 2011, to read morals into these natural disaster stories, often interpreting them as evidence of decaying political and social mores.[81]

In 1615, in an episode known as the Genna famine, cold-weather damage in northeastern Japan led to widespread crop failures, and by the next year Hirosaki domain reported starvation. In 1624, another famine struck the northeast, prompting Aizu domain to prohibit the manufacture of such luxuries as tofu, sake, and rice cakes. In 1626, drought caused famine throughout Japan, and in Kyoto starving people received government handouts. Typically, early

[79] Kitagawa et al., "Human Activity."
[80] Yonenobu and Eckstein, "Reconstruction of Early Spring Temperature."
[81] Walker, *Concise History of Japan*, 298–99.

Table 9.2 Major early modern famines

Era name	Date	Cause	Climatological phase
Genna famine	1615	Cold weather damage in northeastern Japan	Little Ice Age – Phase 1
Kan'ei famine	1641	Drought, flood, and cold weather damage realmwide	Little Ice Age – Phase 1
Enpō famine	1674	Summer/Fall wind and water damage realmwide	Interglacial – Phase 1
Tenna famine	1681	Irregular weather in western Japan	Interglacial – Phase 1
Genroku famine	1695	Cold-weather damage in northeastern Japan	Little Ice Age – Phase 2
Kyōhō famine	1733	Insect damage in south and southwestern Japan	Little Ice Age – Phase 2
Kan'en famine	1749	Cold weather and wild boar damage in northeastern Japan	Interglacial – Phase 2
Hōreki famine	1755	Cold weather damage in northeastern Japan	Interglacial – Phase 2
Tenmei famine	1783–87	Volcanism and cold weather damage in northeastern Japan	Little Ice Age – Phase 3
Tenpō famine	1833–38	Cold weather damage and flood in northeastern Japan	Little Ice Age – Phase 3

Source: Kikuchi, *Kinsei no kikin*, 257–60, and Maejima and Tagami, "Climate of Little Ice Age."

modern Japan's droughts follow what climate scholars call the "hot summer type" of weather phenomenon, in which drought conditions hit the northeast and east in the summer months while sudden periods of dramatic rainfall drench the south. In 1717, for example, drought conditions dried up crops in the northeast and east, with no rain in the Kantō region for a hundred days, while midsummer flooding washed away crops in the south.[82]

In 1641, flooding and cold-weather damage caused crop failures throughout Japan, leading to the Kan'ei famine the next year, which lasted through 1643. The Kan'ei event became so severe that the shogunate was forced to prohibit the selling of human carcasses. The shogunate even permitted daimyo in Edo, who served as part of the alternate attendance system, to return to their home domains. It implemented other tangible famine countermeasures, including prohibitions against rice hording and inflating rice prices. Given the value of rice, the shogunate also implemented the first ever realm-wide

[82] Maejima and Tagami, "Climate Change," 158.

prohibition against sake brewing, ordered daimyo to give detailed reports on crop conditions, and offered exemptions from certain service. It continued to take steps to combat this famine well into 1643.[83]

When it finally came, relief from climatological vagaries proved short lived. By 1666, domains reported wind and water damage to crops, and the shogunate ordered that sake brewing be reduced to half production. Two years later, drought plagued much of the country, and the next year hunger spread among the population. In 1669, while war raged in Ezo between Matsumae domain and the Ainu chief Shakushain, the shogunate provided a 100-day supply of rice gruel in Kyoto and contended with crop failures in domains around Kanazawa. In 1674, during the Enpō famine, late summer and fall weather damage caused crop failures, and by spring the next year, famine victims became so numerous that the shogunate offered relief in badly stricken Yamato, Settsu, and Kawachi Provinces. The situation became so severe that the shogunate constructed a relief operation in the Shin-Yoshiwara pleasure district to administer aid to victims of the famine, and again distributed rice gruel and monetary aid in Kyoto. Agricultural production had barely returned to normal when, in 1680, fall weather damage caused crop failures that led to hunger and death in the western part of the country. The next year, further climatological irregularities and rice shortages from the previous year led to a dramatic spike in hunger, known as the Tenna famine, which was followed by waves of infectious disease in the area around Kyoto. Often, disease accompanied food shortages as malnutrition weakened immune systems.[84]

In 1695, during the Genroku famine, irregularly cold temperatures killed crops in northeastern Japan, causing tens of thousands of deaths in Hirosaki and Morioka domains. The shogunate issued orders against abandoning children and dogs and, under Shogun Tsunayoshi, issued, as we have seen, the Laws of Compassion for Living Things and constructed relief huts for stray people and stray dogs. The shogunate dispatched 30,000 bales of rice to Hirosaki and allowed Morioka domain to forgo its alternate attendance obligation in Edo. Four years later, inclement fall weather still plagued crops in the northeast, and in 1702 Morioka domain reported many famine-related deaths due to cold temperatures and crop failures.[85]

In 1733, during the Kyōhō famine, infestations of plant hoppers devoured crops in central and southwestern Japan, leading to food shortages that killed

---

[83] Kikuchi, *Kinsei no kikin*, 2–46.
[84] See Jannetta, *Epidemics and Mortality*.
[85] Kikuchi, *Kinsei no kikin*, 47–81.

thousands. Agronomist Ōkura Nagatsune, who we met earlier, drew important lessons from the Kyōhō episode decades later, observing that rice crops become vulnerable to insect predation during cooler weather, of which there was much during his lifetime.[86] He experimented with whale and rapeseed oil as insecticides, helping farmers to protect themselves against insect damage. Farmers in western Japan called the ravenous insects Sanemori, a reference to a medieval warrior who had died in the fields of Kaga in the twelfth century. Drawing on Buddhist reincarnation and transmigration of the soul beliefs, western farmers believed that Sanemori had come to seek revenge in the form of plant hoppers. By contrast, farmers in Fukuoka believed it was the spirit of Sugawara no Michizane (845–903), the disgraced Heian statesman who died in exile in Dazaifu. Even the shogunate was unwilling to take chances with these possessed insects and offered prayers at nearby Buddhist temples. Over 10,000 people, oxen, and horses died in the Kyōhō event, and it adversely affected millions of others throughout the country.

In 1749, the Kan'en famine became mainly localized in the northeast and upended such domains as Hachinohe. The Little Ice Age precipitated the Kan'en event, also known as the "wild boar famine," but so did more local climatological phenomena, such as the *yamase* winds. In Hachinohe, the Kan'en episode serves as a classic example of the results of widespread protocapitalization during Japan's early modern period, fueled by the emergence of consumer centers like Edo. As agricultural lands around Edo converted to such cash crops as mulberry and cotton, farmers utilized landscapes further afield to supply foodstuffs such as soybeans to hungry Edo inhabitants. In Hachinohe, farmers slashed and burned upland fields to make room for soybeans. As they did so, they cut down acorn trees and other sources of food for wild boar populations, which turned to human crops in the worsening climatic conditions of the Little Ice Age. In essence, Japan's protocapitalist economy created a landscape that pitted wild boar against humans in a struggle for survival.[87] Only six years after the Kan'en episode, during the Hōreki famine, the northeast again experienced cool temperatures and crop failures, and Morioka domain reported around 50,000 famine deaths.[88]

In 1783, Mount Asama, in central Japan, erupted, as did Mount Laki in Iceland. The massive Icelandic explosion, known as the Skaftá fires, propelled volcanic gases and ash, including sulfur dioxide, some sixteen kilometers into the atmosphere, which then circulated the globe and dramatically influenced

[86] Ōkura, *Jokōroku*; Walker, *Toxic Archipelago*, 46–54.
[87] Walker, "Commercial Growth."
[88] Kikuchi, *Kinsei no kikin*, 29–151.

European and East Asian monsoon climates.[89] Egypt experienced a devastating famine in 1784, for example.[90] In Japan, during the catastrophic Tenmei famine, the ash and gases from these local and global volcanic episodes blocked solar radiance, and temperatures plummeted and crops failed. The Tenmei event fits the "cool summer type" weather phenomenon. Throughout the summer, northerly winds brought cold weather and heavy rains to the far northeast, while heavy rains and flooding inundated the Sea of Japan coast. Cloudy and drizzly weather chilled central Japan and the Kantō region, and persistently cold weather spoiled rice crops before they could ripen. Heavy rains drenched southwestern and western Japan, and cereal crops failed to ripen.[91]

During the Tenmei famine, local opposition to rice transports from the northeast flared into riots and, by the next year, well over 300,000 people had died from famine. As a result of malnutrition, contagious disease also flared throughout the country as the shogunate desperately tried to control rice prices. But the dreadful Little Ice Age weather continued. In the summer of 1786, massive flooding inundated the Kantō region, while in Shikoku violent rainstorms destroyed crops, resulting in high rice prices the next year. In response to the high rice prices, *uchikowashi*, or "smash-and-break," revolts rocked Osaka and Edo and, one month later, Matsudaira Sadanobu became lead senior councillor, initiating a series of conservative initiatives known as the Kansei reforms (1787–93). In many ways, Sadanobu's reforms were responses to the Little Ice Age climatological conditions and the resulting social and economic disorder, as the moral decay he railed against was never disentangled from the environmental chaos of the eighteenth century.[92]

In 1833, again, cold temperatures and floods resulted in crop failures. The next year, during the Tenpō famine, the victims of hunger began piling up in the northeast once more, particularly in Dewa. For the next decade, the Tenpō crisis raged, with rice riots and *ikki* (social insurrections) widespread throughout the country. The Tenpō crisis punished the northeast most severely, with Morioka, Sendai, and other domains reporting heavy casualties and the strongest riots and insurrections, such as the Hie-san-go insurrection (1834) in Hachinohe and the Kitaura insurrection (1834) in Akita. Even during the waning years of the shogunate, the Little Ice Age weather continued to prove relentless, likely influenced by the eruption of Mount Coseguina in

---

[89] Kondo, "Volcanic Eruptions," 776.
[90] Oman et al., "High-Latitude Eruptions."
[91] Maejima and Tagami, "Climate Change," 159.
[92] Kikuchi, *Kinsei no kikin*, 152–92.

Nicaragua in 1835.[93] In 1866, cold temperatures, combined with flooding and wind damage, caused crop damage, and the shogunate imported rice from abroad to feed a hungry population.[94]

As we have seen, it is impossible to disentangle Japan's early modern landscapes of famine from Pacific tectonics and climate. At times, northeastern domains and the shogunate may have fumbled their responses, but their share of the blame is relatively small compared to the natural forces that descended on northeastern Japan predominantly in the eighteenth century. It is also impossible to disentangle Japan's protocapitalist development, its prosperity – albeit unevenly distributed – from these Pacific forces as well. Indeed, urban development in castle towns, the status system, and other historical phenomena facilitated Japan's commercial economy, but it was only possible insofar as the material for such economic growth was naturally occurring. Stories, such as the one an Edo samurai told, of gōnō who "build homes with the most handsome and wonderful gates, porches, beams, alcoves, ornamental shelves, and libraries" existed alongside tales of starvation and cannibalism in the northeast.[95] It is remarkable that the same centuries that witnessed Japan's protocapitalization and political centralization also witnessed such demographic mayhem. But Japan's naturally occurring precipitation – in all its dangerous vagaries – when combined with its rich alluvial lands and abundance of naturally occurring fertilizers, positioned the Pacific nation for capitalistic economic development independent of Western Europe and begs intriguing comparisons.

In 1928, the Marxist Sinologist Karl Wittfogel (1896–1988) wrote of the importance of cultural and natural forces in historical analysis: "Man and his work on one side, nature and its material on the other – this is the fundamental relation, the eternal natural condition of human life upon which every form of this life, and above all its social form, is dependent."[96] Viewing Japan's early modern history through the prism of Pacific forces, as this chapter has done, evokes Wittfogel's integrative approach to understanding political, social, and economic development in conjunction with "nature and its material," in this case, the Pacific environment.

Famously, Wittfogel hypothesized the emergence of "Oriental despotism" in the context of Asian aridity and water scarcity, a mode of production that "first arises when waterworks must be undertaken on a larger scale

[93] Kondo, "Volcanic Eruptions," 776.
[94] Kikuchi, Kinsei no kikin, 193–211.
[95] Smith, Agrarian Origins, 176.
[96] Karl Wittfogel cited in Worster, Rivers of Empire, 27.

(for purposes of protection and irrigation)." He continued that, unlike agriculture in Western Europe, which, with naturally occurring rain, generated progress toward liberal capitalism, "the centralized structure of the highly productive Oriental agrarian order worked in the opposite direction, namely toward the reproduction of the existing order, toward its stagnation." With its Pacific climate, terrain, and currents readily supplying Japan with the material ingredients of protocapitalism, it is not surprising that Japan's *gōnō* became the drivers of Japan's modern economic development, not reliant on the shogunate to provide Oriental despotic large-scale waterworks. As Brown demonstrates, early modern Japan had widespread riparian works, to be sure, but they were largely undertaken at a local level (sometimes with the shogunate's blessing), and often with private capital.[97] Japan's centralizing government, the shogunate, remained preoccupied with other realms of politics and administrative responsibilities. Many consider Wittfogel's Oriental despotism hypothesis to be largely discredited (as communist despots also came from wet areas), but I still find it an instructive lens through which to view the material origins of capitalism. Indeed, Wittfogel's hypothesis may just need more time to mature, as global scarcities of fresh water in the twenty-first century, a resource equally precious as oil, might still create cruel despots of an entirely new order. My point is the Pacific engine made Japan's economic development possible, and it is shortsighted to view Japan's rural experiences – both its landscapes of dislocation, scarcity, and famine, as well as its landscapes of prosperity, abundance, and industriousness – without taking the Pacific context, particularly climate, into consideration.

Conclusion

It has been over twenty-five years since the publication of volumes four and five of the last *Cambridge History of Japan*, which covered "early modern Japan" and the "nineteenth century" respectively. The two volumes explored Japan's political, social, economic, religious, intellectual, and diplomatic history, but were silent on Japan's environmental history, even though Totman had already published his landmark *The Green Archipelago: Forestry in Preindustrial Japan*. The book was a shot across the bow of a field that had largely ignored the physical environment in its historical analysis, even though, as we have seen, there was a rich tradition of Japanese scholars doing so. In fact, perhaps because Japanese scholars drew on Japan's physical environment in

---

[97] Brown, "Floods."

their origins theories, Western scholars have proved reluctant to do so. It was an unfortunate oversight, or maybe just bad timing: with the advent of the Anthropocene Epoch, we now find ourselves on a planet overwhelmingly sculpted by human hands – sometimes advertently and sometimes inadvertently – and that process clearly began in the early modern world, particularly among those countries that today are included among the industrial nations.

Japan's Pacific environment became both an enabler of political, cultural, and economic development and a critical biological indicator of the implications of such historical transformations. As this chapter has illustrated, national unification in the late sixteenth century placed enormous pressure on Japan's forests, as ambitious warlords, in their quest to "take the realm," built wooden monuments to their power, such as Azuchi, Osaka, and Edo Castles. Then, in the eighteenth century, with the Tokugawa grip on power settled, Japan's cities, which started as political constructs but evolved into commercial ones, placed continued pressure on forests, as cities such as Edo, with its million inhabitants, required the housing stock to place roofs over those many heads. As loggers felled more and more trees on shogunal and domanial lands to build those roofs, it became clear that forms of conservation and silviculture were required to ensure the longevity of Japan's valuable, and religiously significant, woodlands. In other words, one measure of the degree to which Japan spawned a "national" government in the seventeenth and eighteenth centuries is the pressure the centralizing process placed on Japan's forests, and the concrete reaction to the deforestation occurring throughout the archipelago. As we have seen, some have hailed Japan's sustainable forestry as one of the precious few environmental "success stories" in human history.

Similarly, ambitious warlords financed the sixteenth-century unification with the riches extracted from gold, silver, and copper mines. Japan's tectonic natural history had made such metals available, and had thrust them close to the surface, where miners extracted, separated, smelted, and then traded them in an international exchange that fed China's insatiable appetite for precious metals. Once the realm was secure in Tokugawa hands, Japan's alluvial plains became the site of the establishment of the political economy, where paddy lands grew the grain on which early modern power fed. To make this system work, national and regional stakeholders undertook massive riparian works that managed water in a manner that allowed farmers to grow their crops. As I have argued, Japan was never an example of Wittfogel's "hydraulic society," where emperors accumulated despotic power through the control of water for irrigation; but farmers nonetheless resculpted their riparian landscape in a manner that brought water to their precious crops – domain wealth and power were measured in grains of rice.

It was in the countryside that Japan's protocapitalist economy began to mature in the eighteenth century. But this was only possible by relocating energy from the Pacific environment to Japan's fields, and this transfer was accomplished through the widespread use of herring mulch, whale oil, and human biowaste on their crops. The swirling Pacific currents that surrounded the archipelago transported important nutrients that migrated up the food chain, all the way up to Japan's urban consumer markets. Japan's weather proved a double-edged sword in this regard – it provided ample natural precipitation, a critical factor in cash-crop farming, but it also came with the eighteenth-century vagaries that often brought malnourished, emaciated, or famished bodies to the land.

In this manner, nature – specifically, the Pacific environment, with its tectonics and seismic activity, its mountainous spine rich with ore and alluvial plains with fertile soil, its thriving coastal waters, and its temperate climate – was ever present in Japan's early modern and nineteenth-century histories. Nature permeated Japanese political life. In Japan, those governments that conformed to the natural rhythms of the Pacific environment, even if by way of analogy, were most legitimate in the eyes of the ruling elite.[98] But as Japan embraced Western modernity in the mid-nineteenth century, Meiji planners replaced that conformity with nature, often expressed through analogy, with control over nature, a trend neatly exemplified by the establishment of the Ueno Zoological Garden. Within the confines of the zoo, nature was controlled more by spectacle than analogy, and Japan's place at the top of the natural heap was made visible through the public enactment of empire.

The Meiji process of asserting control over nature was often cruel. Of course, there is violence inherent in zoos – placing large animals in small cages to be gawked at by wave upon wave of sapiens onlookers, even if for the purpose of promoting the "material sciences" and encouraging the "discovery of advances in agriculture, industry, and commerce," is inherently brutal.[99] But the Japanese and Hokkaido wolves were annihilated within decades of the Meiji Restoration to make way for Western-style livestock ranching and scientific agriculture. In a sense, Meiji planners swept aside centuries of wolf worship, a practice rooted in Buddhist, Confucian, and Shinto beliefs, to make way for Western ways of viewing charismatic carnivores such as

[98] Thomas, *Reconfiguring Modernity*, 43.
[99] Miller, *Nature of the Beasts*, 44.

wolves. East Asian ideas about nature crumbled quickly under the weight of the material requirements of industrialization.

In the final analysis, however, nature may get the last laugh. When Japan took those first steps toward industrialization in the late nineteenth century, the Pacific island nation planted the seeds of the "super storms," extinctions, and sea-level rise that have accompanied the high modernist path. The lesson is that nature is not controllable – remember, at this juncture, the obliterated seawalls of northeastern Japan after the March 2011 earthquake and tsunami. But even to think that it is, and that modern sapiens are somehow separate from it, is dangerous folly. As Japan's early modern and nineteenth-century environmental history demonstrates, the landscape has been shaping people, and people the landscape, for centuries, and no matter how conceited our modern vista may be – we howl in pitiful yearning for our "liberal bodies" to be separated from nature – the reality of our interconnectedness with the natural world will only become more punishing with time.

Bibliography

Arch, Jakobina K. *Bringing Whales Ashore: Oceans and the Environment of Early Modern Japan.* Seattle: University of Washington Press, 2018.

Armitage, David. "Three Concepts of Atlantic History." In *The British Atlantic World, 1500–1800,* edited by David Armitage and Michael J. Braddick, 11–30. Basingstoke: Palgrave Macmillan, 2002.

Bando, Takeharu, Kazuyoshi Nakai, Jun Kanbayashi, Kengo Umeda, Yujin Kin, Futaba Nishimura, Takashi Yoshida et al. "Results of the Third Biological Field Survey of NEWREP-A during the 2017/18 Austral Summer Season." *International Whaling Commission* SC/67B/SCSP/08.

Barkley, R. A. "The Kuroshio Current." *Science Journal* 6 (1970): 54–60.

Barnes, Gina L. "Vulnerable Japan: The Tectonic Setting of Life in the Archipelago." In Batten and Brown, *Environment and Society,* 21–42.

Batten, Bruce L., and Philip C. Brown, eds. *Environment and Society in the Japanese Islands: From Prehistory to the Present.* Corvallis: Oregon State University Press, 2015.

Berger, Antony R. "Abrupt Geological Changes: Causes, Effects, and Public Issues." *Quaternary International* 151 (2006): 3–9.

Bodart-Bailey, Beatrice M. *The Dog Shogun: The Personality and Policies of Tokugawa Tsunayoshi.* Honolulu: University of Hawai'i Press, 2006.

Briffa, K. R., P. D. Jones, F. H. Schweingruber, and T. J. Osborn. "Influence of Volcanic Eruptions on Northern Hemisphere Summer Temperatures over the Past 600 Years." *Nature* 393 (4 June 1998): 450–55.

Brown, Philip C. "Constructing Nature." In Miller, Thomas, and Walker, *Japan at Nature's Edge,* 90–114.

Cultivating Commons: Joint Ownership of Arable Land in Early Modern Japan. Honolulu: University of Hawai'i Press, 2011.

"Floods, Drainage, and River Projects in Early Modern Japan: Civil Engineering and the Foundation of Resilience." In Batten and Brown, *Environment and Society,* 96–113.

Clancey, Gregory. *Earthquake Nation: The Cultural Politics of Japanese Seismicity, 1868–1930.* Berkeley: University of California Press, 2006.

Cushman, Gregory. *Guano and the Opening of the Pacific World: A Global Ecological History.* Cambridge: Cambridge University Press, 2014.

Diamond, Jared. *Collapse: How Societies Choose to Fail or Succeed.* New York: Viking, 2005.

Dorsey, Kurkpatrick. *Whales and Nations: Environmental Diplomacy on the High Seas.* Seattle: University of Washington Press, 2013.

Drixler, Fabian. *Mabiki: Infanticide and Population Growth in Eastern Japan, 1660–1950.* Berkeley: University of California Press, 2013.

Freeman, Donald B. *The Pacific.* London: Routledge, 2010.

George, Timothy S. *Minamata: Pollution and the Struggle for Democracy in Postwar Japan.* Cambridge, MA: Harvard University Asia Center, 2002.

Grossman, Michael, and Masumi Zaiki. "Reconstructing Typhoons in Japan in the 1880s from Documentary Records." *Weather* 64, no. 12 (2009): 315–22.

Hager, Thomas. *The Alchemy of Air: A Jewish Genius, a Doomed Tycoon, and the Scientific Discovery That Fed the World but Fueled the Rise of Hitler.* New York: Three Rivers Press, 2008.

Hanley, Susan B. "Urban Sanitation in Preindustrial Japan." *Journal of Interdisciplinary History* 18, no. 1 (1987): 1–26.

Hardin, Garrett. "Tragedy of the Commons." *Science* 162, no. 3859 (13 December 1968): 1243–48.

Howell, David L. *Capitalism from Within: Economy, Society, and the State in a Japanese Fishery.* Berkeley: University of California Press, 1995.

"Fecal Matters: Prolegomenon to a History of Shit in Japan." In Miller, Thomas, and Walker, *Japan at Nature's Edge,* 137–51.

Jannetta, Ann Bowman. *Epidemics and Mortality in Early Modern Japan.* Princeton, NJ: Princeton University Press, 1987.

Jones, Ryan Tucker. "The Environment." In *Pacific Histories: Ocean, Land, People,* edited by David Armitage and Alison Bashford, 121–42. Basingstoke: Palgrave Macmillan, 2014.

"Running into Whales: The History of the North Pacific from Below the Waves." *American Historical Review* 118, no. 2 (2013): 349–77.

Kalland, Arne. *Fishing Villages in Tokugawa Japan.* Honolulu: University of Hawai'i Press, 1995.

Kikuchi Isao. *Kinsei no kikin.* Yoshikawa Kōbunkan, 1997.

Kitagawa, Junko, Takeshi Nakagawa, Toshiyuki Fujiki, Kentaro Yamaguchi, and Yoshinori Yasuda. "Human Activity and Climate Change during the Historical Period in Central Japan with Reference to Forest Dynamics and the Cultivation of Japanese Horse Chestnut (*Aesculus turbinate*)." *Vegetation History and Archaeobotany* 13 (2004): 105–13.

Kondo, Junsei. "Volcanic Eruptions, Cool Summers, and Famines in the Northeastern Part of Japan." *Journal of Climate* 1, no. 8 (1988): 775–88.

LeCain, Timothy J. *The Matter of History: How Things Create the Past*. Cambridge: Cambridge University Press, 2017.

Maejima, Ikuo, and Yoshio Tagami. "Climate Change during Historical Times in Japan: Reconstruction from Climate Hazard Records." *Geographical Reports of Tokyo Metropolitan University* 21 (1986): 157–71.

"Climate of Little Ice Age in Japan." *Geographical Reports of Tokyo Metropolitan University* 18 (1983): 91–111.

Matsuda, Matt K. "The Pacific." *American Historical Review* 111, no. 3 (2006): 758–80.

Mikami, Takehiko. "Climatic Variations in Japan Reconstructed from Historical Documents." *Weather* 63, no. 7 (2008): 190–93.

Mikami, Takehiko, Masumi Zaiki, and Junpei Hirano. "A History of Climatic Change in Japan: A Reconstruction of Meteorological Trends from Documentary Evidence." In Batten and Brown, *Environment and Society*, 197–212.

Miller, Ian Jared. *The Nature of the Beasts: Empire and Exhibition at the Tokyo Imperial Zoo*. Berkeley: University of California Press, 2013.

Miller, Ian Jared, Julia Adeney Thomas, and Brett L. Walker, eds. *Japan at Nature's Edge: The Environmental Context of a Global Power*. Honolulu: University of Hawai'i Press, 2013.

Minoda, Takashi. "Oceanographic and Biomass Changes in the Oyashio Current Ecosystem." In *Biomass Yields and Geography of Large Marine Ecosystems*, edited by Kenneth Sherman and Lewis M. Alexander, 67–93. Boulder, CO: Westview Press, 1989.

Notehelfer, F. G. "Japan's First Pollution Incident." *Journal of Japanese Studies* 1, no. 2 (1975): 351–83.

Ōkura Nagatsune. *Jokōroku* (1826). In *Nihon nōsho zenshū*, Vol. 15, edited by Nōsangyoson Bunka Kyōkai, 3–56. Nōsangyoson Bunka Kyōkai, 1977.

Oman, Luke, Alan Robock, Georgiy L. Stenchikov, and Thorvaldur Thordarson. "High-Latitude Eruptions Cast Shadow over the African Monsoon and the Flow of the Nile." *Geophysical Research Letters* 33, no. L18711 (30 September 2006).

Plummer, Katherine. *The Shogun's Reluctant Ambassadors: Japanese Sea Drifters in the North Pacific*. Portland: Oregon Historical Society Press, 1991.

Qiu, Bo. "Kuroshio and Oyashio Currents." In *Encyclopedia of Ocean Sciences*, 1413–25. San Diego: Academic Press, 2001.

Richards, John F. *The Unending Frontier: An Environmental History of the Early Modern World*. Berkeley: University of California Press, 2003.

Saito, Osamu. "Climate, Famine, and Population in Japanese History: A Long-Term Perspective." In Batten and Brown, *Environment and Society*, 213–29.

Samuels, Richard J. *3.11: Disaster and Change in Japan*. Ithaca, NY: Cornell University Press, 2013.

Schencking, J. Charles. *The Great Kantō Earthquake and the Chimera of National Reconstruction in Japan*. New York: Columbia University Press, 2013.

Smith, Thomas C. *The Agrarian Origins of Modern Japan*. Stanford, CA: Stanford University Press, 1959. Reprint, New York: Atheneum, 1966.

Smits, Gregory. *Seismic Japan: The Long History and Continuing Legacy of the Ansei Edo Earthquake*. Honolulu: University of Hawai'i Press, 2013.

Smyers, Karen A. *The Fox and the Jewel: Shared and Private Meanings in Contemporary Japanese Inari Worship*. Honolulu: University of Hawai'i Press, 1998.

Stolz, Robert. *Bad Water: Nature, Pollution, and Politics in Japan, 1870–1950*. Durham, NC: Duke University Press, 2014.

Strong, Kenneth. *Ox against the Storm: A Biography of Tanaka Shozo, Japan's Conservationist Pioneer*. New York: Routledge, 2005.

Thomas, Julia Adney. *Reconfiguring Modernity: Concepts of Nature in Japanese Political Ideology*. Berkeley: University of California Press, 2001.

Totman, Conrad. *Early Modern Japan*. Berkeley: University of California Press, 1995.

　The Green Archipelago: Forestry in Pre-Industrial Japan. Berkeley: University of California Press, 1989. Reprint, Athens: Ohio University Press, 1998.

　Japan: An Environmental History. London: I. B. Tauris, 2016.

Tsutsui, William. "The Pelagic Empire: Reconsidering Japan's Expansion." In Miller, Thomas, and Walker, *Japan at Nature's Edge*, 21–38.

Walker, Brett L. "Commercial Growth and Environmental Change in Early Modern Japan: Hachinohe's Wild Boar Famine of 1749." *Journal of Asian Studies* 60, no. 2 (2001): 329–51.

　A Concise History of Japan. Cambridge: Cambridge University Press, 2015.

　The Conquest of Ainu Lands: Ecology and Culture in Japanese Expansion, 1590–1800. Berkeley: University of California Press, 2001.

　The Lost Wolves of Japan. Seattle: University of Washington Press, 2005.

　Toxic Archipelago: A History of Industrial Disease in Japan. Seattle: University of Washington Press, 2011.

Worster, Donald. *Rivers of Empire: Water, Aridity, and the Growth of the American West*. New York: Oxford University Press, 1985.

Yonenobu, Hitoshi, and Dieter Eckstein. "Reconstruction of Early Spring Temperature for Central Japan from the Tree-Ring Widths of Hinoki Cypress and Its Verification by Other Proxy Records." *Geophysical Research Letters* 33, no. L10701 (2006).

10

Scientific Communities and the Emergence of *Science* in Early Modern Japan

YULIA FRUMER

Introduction: sciences and "Science"

Scientific practice is not a modern phenomenon. As long as human society has existed, people have inquired into the nature of the universe, the human body, the flora and fauna, and whatnot. Many were motivated by practical needs, such as calendrical calculations, medicine, or agriculture. They were also curious: What is the nature of rainbows? Why do children resemble their parents? How do plants know to organize their leaves in perfectly symmetrical spirals? As time passed, communities of scholars continued to refine their methods, build instruments, argue about theories, and experiment. And, in the course of this process, they developed agreed-upon standards for investigating nature.

In the nineteenth century, however, things changed in the European scientific landscape. The word "science" came to be used in a different way. It no longer meant just "knowledge," as the original Latin term *sciencia* implied, but something more than that. The new meaning of the word suggested a collective pursuit that crossed disciplinary divides, followed the same philosophical principles, and relied on the same basic experimental methods. There were no longer different sciences, each following its own path. Now, they were all part of "Science," which was larger than the sum of its parts.

A somewhat similar process unfolded in Japan in the Tokugawa period. Japanese scholars were not isolated from European science, as popular myth states, but they did not consider it to be an unquestionable authority, either. The transformation in the understanding of what "science" was came from within, as scholars of different disciplines began reconfiguring their communities. As we shall see in this chapter, they gradually realized that what made them identify one with another was neither social status, nor practical goals, nor even their discipline. Rather, it was the kind of questions they were interested in, the kind of evidence they considered acceptable, the assumptions they shared, and the sources they considered authoritative.

Looking at these factors from the perspective of Tokugawa-period scholars allows us to avoid a teleological narrative of progress and Westernization while not falling into the other extreme of searching for scientific niches that were not "contaminated" by Western science. Instead, we can follow Tokugawa scholars' own rationales and observe the social and intellectual dynamics that brought about the gradual convergence of distant and unrelated fields of study into something that might be called "Science."

Mathematics as a Marker of Professionalism

We can gain a sense of the state of Tokugawa sciences during the seventeenth century by looking at developments surrounding the first calendrical reform of the Tokugawa period. Before the adoption of the modern solar calendar in the Meiji period, calculating a calendar was a complicated business. The Tokugawa calendar was a so-called lunisolar calendar, which combined a solar year of roughly 365 days with twelve whole lunar cycles of waxing and waning. The complicating factor, of course, was that the year is actually 365.25 days long; months, when defined by the appearance of the moon, last 29.53 days, twelve of which do not fit neatly into a solar year. This natural discrepancy already required complex calculations, even without the further hurdles of identifying equinoxes, placing seasonal holidays, and calculating seasonal changes in the amount of light and darkness each day. In this system, it was impossible to create a perfect calendar, and some numbers had to be rounded up. Such tiny deviations would not be perceptible to the human eye, but as time passed, they became larger and larger, and therefore more apparent. Given that Japan's last reform before the Tokugawa period was in the ninth century, by the mid-seventeenth century the calendar was visibly and perceptibly off.[1]

The motivation to reform the calendar was political. Because maintaining the calendar was a government responsibility, an incorrect calendar reflected poorly on the rulers. This concerned Hoshina Masayuki (1611–73), who, at the time, was the most powerful man in Japan, being the uncle and regent of the child shogun Ietsuna (1641–80). Even when Ietsuna became an adult, he still faced an uncertain rule and relied on his uncle for making governing decisions. In order to strengthen Ietsuna's position, Hoshina decided to carry out

---

[1] Frumer, *Making Time*, 59–60.

a calendrical reform. However, instead of appointing professional astronomers to make the calculations, he hired a young, virtually unknown *go* player,
who at the time went by the name Yasui Santetsu II (1639–1715), to lead the
reform efforts. Politically, this decision made perfect sense – as a child, the
go player was raised as a household member of the child-shogun; as an adult
he remained personally loyal to Ietsuna, who still faced a rather precarious
rule. Yet in relation to calendar-making, it was an outrageous move, because
Hoshina passed over what would have been the obvious choice, a member of
the Tsuchimikado family of imperial courtiers.

At the time, the Tsuchimikado family was at the center of the community
of scholars focusing on astronomy and calendar compilation, which were
seen as inherently intertwined and often referred to by a single term, *tenmon-
rekigaku* (lit. "the study of astronomy and the calendar"). The Tsuchimikado
were descendants of Abe no Seimei (921–1005), the famous tenth-century
diviner who learned the esoteric art of *onmyōdō* (the Way of *yin* and *yang*) and
the craft of calendar-making from the Kamo family of courtiers. When Japan
adopted Chinese bureaucratic systems in the seventh century, it established
four related offices: timekeeping, astronomy, calendar compilation, and
onmyōdō divination, the latter entrusted to the Kamo family. After the Seimyō
calendrical reform of 864, however, no algorithmic changes were introduced,
and the work of calendar-makers became rather rote, applying the same algorithm to calculate calendrical templates year after year. Owing to Abe no
Seimei's reputation, however, the Tsuchimikado family thrived as the single
most important locus of calendrical activity, gradually absorbing all duties of
the four offices. By the sixteenth century, the Tsuchimikado were conventionally seen as the calendar-makers, yet their prominence was declining as
their authority was challenged by the emergence of numerous independent
calendar-making centers.

Exposing Tsuchimikado's loss of monopoly on calendar-making, Hoshina's decision to appoint Yasui Santetsu to create a new calendrical algorithm
also reflected recent changes in Japanese scholarly communities. During the
hundred years prior to Hoshina's decision, the Japanese scholarly world had
begun transforming. Following the arrival of the Europeans in the 1540s, the
Japanese occupation of Korea in the 1590s, and later the plight of Ming loyalists fleeing from China in the 1640s, Japanese scholars came into close contact
with scientific communities from abroad. They had more chances to interact
with foreign intellectuals and were exposed to new ideas and new books, and
consequently formulated their own interpretations of (and reactions to) this
new body of knowledge.

The education of young Yasui Santetsu reflected this changing scholarly scene. He studied metaphysics with Hoshina's favorite philosopher, Yamazaki Ansai (1619–82),[2] whose teachings were based on the Neo-Confucian philosophy of Zhu Xi (1130–1200), transmitted through the Korean philosopher Yi T'oegye (also known as Yi Hwang, 1501–70), and interpreted by Japanese scholars. The result was a new metaphysical system, known as Suika Shinto, which stressed the relation between the social moral order and the physical environment of the Japanese archipelago.[3]

Scholars of Yasui Santetsu's generation were unified by questions inspired by Yamazaki Ansai's influential philosophy. Specifically, they were prompted to ponder how they could treat Chinese scholarly treatises as a source of authority when the information contained in these books sometimes contradicted what they had observed in their own studies. Asked equally by members of scholarly communities that otherwise had little in common, this question crossed disciplinary divides to create a common goal. In designing the new calendar, Yasui Santetsu adapted the data and calculations in Chinese calendrical systems to the longitude and latitude of Kyoto. Later in life, when he had become known as Shibukawa Shunkai (or Harumi) – a name bestowed on him for the service of reforming the calendar – he would write books on the Japanese calendar (*Yamato reki*). Despite belonging to a different discipline, his works echoed those of his contemporary, Kaibara Ekiken (1630–1714). Ekiken is known for his magnum opus, *Japanese Pharmacopoeia* (*Yamato honzō*, 1709), in which he adapted the Chinese encyclopedia *Bencao gangmu* (Compendium of materia medica, 1578) to the flora and fauna found in Japan. At this point, the study of plants and the study of the skies were not seen as part of the same scholarly enterprise, yet the common motivation created an initial link between these two communities of scholars.

The teaching of Shunkai's second teacher, Okanoi Gentei, exemplifies the relationship between medicine and astronomy in the mid-seventeenth century.[4] Okanoi was trained as a physician, yet the kind of medicine he engaged with was a metaphysical understanding of the human body as a reflection of the universe. In Neo-Confucian philosophy, man is the nexus of a triad of Heaven-Man-Earth that connects the material and the moral realms. For Okanoi (and many of his contemporaries), the study of the human body was therefore essential to a study of the heavens – a perception that led to his

---

[2] Hayashi, "Igo to tenmon."
[3] Ooms, *Tokugawa Ideology*; Tucker, "Religious Dimensions of Confucianism."
[4] Sugimoto and Swain, *Science and Culture*, 255.

interest in calendrical studies, which he taught to the young Shunkai as part of his medical training.

Shunkai's pivot from such a vision of astronomy – and the subsequent divergence of communities of astronomers and physicians – originated in his study of mathematics. The field of mathematics was thriving at the end of the seventeenth century. The influx of mathematical sources from China, Korea, and Europe introduced Japanese mathematicians to new kinds of mathematical thinking, inspiring them to consider new mathematical theories, such as the calculation of the value of π.[5] At the same time, the booming of commerce and construction in the city of Edo produced a wave of popular mathematics, in which mathematical problems were presented as surveying or taxation problems. Mathematics was considered to be a kind of sophisticated leisure.[6] Having grown up as a *go* player, Shunkai found himself riding the wave of popularity of math, due to his skill in calculating probabilities necessary for the game. Yet popular mathematics and superior *go* abilities were not sufficient for calculating calendrical algorithms, and Shunkai had to develop his mathematical skills by studying under the famous mathematician Seki Takakazu (1642–1708). In so doing, he not only gained mastery of calculation techniques but also entered a community of scholars whose primary concern was not the human arrangement of celestial events into a calendar, but rather sophisticated mathematical calculations.

The affiliation with mathematicians brought Shunkai to an encounter that would transform not only his approach to calendrical science but also the nature of Tokugawa scientific activities in general. During his studies he was introduced to a Korean scholar known in Japanese sources as Yō Razan,[7] who visited Japan on an official mission.[8] Razan brought with him the thirteenth-century Chinese astronomical treatise *Shoushili* (Granting the seasons).[9] Despite being 400 years old at that point, *Shoushili* was a mathematical masterpiece unsurpassed by subsequent calendrical algorithms in China. The treatise offered Shunkai a large set of astronomical data, mathematical methods that were yet unheard of in Japan, and the hint that the geographic

[5] Horiuchi, *Japanese Mathematics.*
[6] Ravina, "*Wasan* and the Physics That Wasn't."
[7] Park An-Ki Nasan (1608–?). The Japanese name is probably derived from a modification of a character 客 (guest) to 容 (used in names to signify dignity and abundance). Thus, the description of Nasan as *Chōsen no kyaku, Razan* (朝鮮の客螺山, Nasan, the guest from Korea) became *Chōsen no Yō Razan* (朝鮮の容螺山, Yong Nasan – Yō Razan, in Japanese pronunciation – from Korea).
[8] Uehara, *Takahashi Kageyasu*, 17; Nakayama, *Nihon no tenmongaku*, 48.
[9] Sivin, *Granting the Seasons.*

location of observers on Earth affects astronomical observations and hence calendrical calculations. The treatise provided Shunkai with the mathematical means to accomplish his goal (inspired by Yamazaki Ansai's philosophy) of creating a calendar specifically suited for the Japanese archipelago. Using the data and the mathematical methods he learned from *Shoushili*, Shunkai came up with an algorithm that served as the foundation of the first calendrical reform of the Tokugawa period. Carried out in the second year of the Jōkyō era (1685), the reform became known as the Jōkyō reform.

Shunkai's focus on mathematics explains his rather complicated relationship with European astronomy. The European astronomy he knew had popular origins. One source of his knowledge was a former Christian convert, Hayashi Kichizaemon, and his student Kobayashi Yoshinobu (1601–84). The former learned Western astronomy from the Jesuits who visited Japan in the sixteenth century, and he continued to engage with astronomy as a devotional practice after the Europeans were banished and Christianity was outlawed in 1639. The two studied a simplified version of Regiomontanus's *De Sphaera* (1472), written by Pedro Gomez, which abbreviated mathematics and mostly focused on cosmology. For Hayashi Kichizaemon and Kobayashi Yoshinobu, cosmology provided legitimization for their Christian worldview, and when the two wrote the book based on their understanding of Gomez, they, too, focused on cosmology. The other source of Shunkai's knowledge of Western astronomy, a popular Chinese book, *Tianjing huowen* (Questions about the heavens, 1675), also focused on cosmology. Written by You Yi, a student of the Jesuit missionary Emanuel Diaz but not a professional astronomer himself, the popular book was smuggled into Japan sometime around the end of the seventeenth century. Despite obviously falling into the category of forbidden books due to its reference to the Jesuits, copies of the book circulated widely in Japan and were openly cited by Japanese scholars, including Shunkai himself.[10] The cosmological discussions and the images in those books made a big impression on Tokugawa readers, and their contents were popularized by the famous writer Nishikawa Joken (1648–1724) in books he published in the early eighteenth century, *Tenmon giron* (1712) and *Ryōgi shūsetsu* (1714). For astronomers and mathematicians, however, these books proved to be frustratingly lacking in mathematical details. "Even though I understand the logic of Westerners," Shunkai wrote, "it is impossible to put it into practice."[11]

---

[10] For example, in Shibukawa Shunkai's 1698 "Tenmon keitō," 118, 125.
[11] This is according to Shunkai's student Tani Shinzan in *Shinzanshū*, cited in Nakayama, *Nihon no tenmongaku*, 75.

In a break from the amateurs fascinated by the European depictions of celestial and terrestrial realms, Japanese mathematicians and astronomers of the early eighteenth century were stirred to action by the possibility of finding previously unknown mathematical methods. In particular, they were inspired by the thirteenth-century *Shoushili* treatise. Among other practices, the treatise introduced methods of calculation that involved sections of an arc – what we might describe as a proto-trigonometry.[12] The description of those methods was enough to excite Japanese mathematicians such as Takebe Katahiro (1664–1739) and Nakane Genkei (1663–1733) but not adequate to answer all the questions such methods provoked, which forced them to attempt to understand the logic that had guided *Shoushili*'s creators.[13]

The close scrutiny of *Shoushili*'s mathematics revealed mistakes in Shunkai's calculations of the calendar – mistakes that could explain the discrepancies between the calendar and observed phenomena, which increased as the years progressed. These mistakes were, in fact, deliberate choices on Shunkai's part: his commitment to Yamazaki Ansai's philosophy dictated his seeking mathematical harmony in nature, and he was averse to what he saw as inharmonious and ugly fractions. For Shunkai, the value of 0.000730485 (of a day) should not have existed in nature and was likely the result of an undetected oversight that concealed the "true" value, 0.00001. Mathematicians such as Takebe Katahiro and Nakane Genkei saw Shunkai's "correction" as a gross error that ought to have been fixed.

Authority of Foreign Scientific Literature

In a curious twist of history, it was Japanese mathematicians' newfound admiration for the thirteenth-century *Shoushili* treatise that stirred their interest in Western astronomy, which they had previously deemed impractical. While searching for new mathematical possibilities suggested by the proto-trigonometry in *Shoushili*, Takebe Katahiro noticed a passage in *Tianjing huowen* that caught his eye. Its author, You Yi, abbreviated all mathematical explanations but mentioned in passing that explanations could be found in another Chinese book, *Xiang xinfa lishu* (Calendrical books expounding new Western methods).[14] The book had yet to find its way to Japan, and even if it had, it would likely have been censored due to its explicit Jesuit content.

---

[12] Sivin, *Granting the Seasons*, 66–67.
[13] See Horiuchi, *Japanese Mathematics*.
[14] Horiuchi, *Japanese Mathematics*, 224.

At the same time, unlike the popular *Tianjing huowen*, *Xiang xinfa lishu* was evidently not deemed profitable enough to smuggle. Nevertheless, Takebe Katahiro had direct access to one person who had authority to ignore the law – the newly appointed eighth Tokugawa shogun, Yoshimune. Takebe Katahiro was Yoshimune's adviser, and the two even conducted astronomical observations together. It did not take much convincing, evidently, to get *Xiang xinfa lishu* imported to Japan. The arrival of the book, and its undeniable mathematical value, provided additional stimulus for Yoshimune's revision in 1720 of the prohibition of Western scientific books. Yoshimune had additional reasons to ease the rules of censorship, which he saw as outdated. Christianity was no longer an urgent threat, while protecting against its influence came at the cost of denying access to much-needed scientific literature – not only from China but also from Holland. Dutch books, such as Dodonaeus's *Herbal* (*Cruydeboeck*, 1554), made a profound impression on Yoshimune with their elaborate illustrations, which suggested to Yoshimune that there was much to learn from the (still incomprehensible) texts as well.

The fact that both Jesuit astronomical treatises written in literary Sinitic (classical Chinese) and works on medicine and flora and fauna written in Dutch were all of foreign origin created a connection between communities that had previously been only tangentially related. Unlike astronomers, scholars of materia medica were motivated not by mathematical pursuits but by classification. Medical doctors who focused on the treatment of wounds were more interested in seeing the human body as flesh and bones, rather than as a mirror of the universe. Yet the common need to gain access to valuable foreign books placed them in the same social network of bureaucrats, booksellers, and printers. Moreover, whether the books arrived from China or from Holland, they mostly came through Nagasaki, which inspired pilgrimages by Edo- and Kyoto-based scholars who hoped to have first access to books and to meet foreigners, who could possibly explain the books' contents. As they traveled to Nagasaki, scholars also met each other, exchanged knowledge of foreign books, and offered new sources of inspiration by revealing yet another set of previously unknown facts and ideas.

And yet astronomers and scholars of medicine and materia medica were still separated by their target languages. The Jesuit astronomical treatises Japanese astronomers read were written in literary Sinitic, the importance of which Hansun Hsiung discusses (Chapter 11, this volume). The mastery of literary Sinitic could not be taken for granted in Japan, yet was not uncommon in scholarly circles. More importantly, the format of Jesuit books, including their mathematical conventions and technical terms, was familiar to Japanese astronomers.

They did not need to waste time on deciphering the basics and could focus on what was new – more sophisticated trigonometry, laws of celestial motion, and observation methods. On the other hand, books relevant to astronomy printed in Dutch translation, such as George Adams's treatise on celestial and terrestrial globes,[15] offered wonderful illustrations, but the explanations that accompanied them were impenetrable to Japanese astronomers. Given the abundance of information on European astronomy in Chinese-language Jesuit treatises, expending energy on studying the difficult Dutch language was lower on astronomers' lists of priorities than it might have been otherwise.

The situation was distinctively different for scholars interested in medicine or in the study of plants and animals. Like astronomers, these scholars too had abundant literature from China, but that literature did not discuss European sciences the way Jesuit astronomical treatises did. If Japanese scholars wanted to read European discussions of taxonomy, distillation methods, or the functions of body parts, they needed to try to understand the Dutch language in which they encountered these discussions. United by the common need to understand the Dutch language, they began forming the movement of Dutch studies (*rangaku*). But, unlike literary Sinitic, Dutch was a language that they had only recently encountered and for which they did not yet have linguistic aids or dictionaries. Even more crucial was the fact that, unlike Chinese, the Dutch language had no shared cultural assumptions with Japanese, so that the world of associations and implications assumed in Dutch words was alien to the Tokugawa Japanese. Professional interpreters in Nagasaki did their best, but they, too, had to work hard to develop an understanding of the words and concepts that went beyond the day-to-day needs of the Dutch trading outpost on Dejima. The first attempt to compile a Dutch–Japanese dictionary ended in 1768, when the author, the chief interpreter Nishi Zenzaburō, died without even finishing the entries for the letter *b*.[16] Interpreters spent years translating just dozens of pages from hefty volumes such as John Jonston's *Natural History of Quadrupeds* (1657), and there, too, they had to rely on previous knowledge, their own interpretation of images, and oral explanations by Dutch merchants, many of whom were of little help with texts that "included so many Latin words."[17] When the famous *Kaitai shinsho* (A new book of

---

[15] Adams, *Treatise.*

[16] Beukers. "Dodonaeus in Japanese," 281–98.

[17] We need to remember that, except for several officers, most of the Dutch residents of Dejima were not educated in the sciences (if educated at all) and hence could hardly be of any help explaining natural history or medical books. Shirahata, "Development of Japanese Botanical Interest," 267–68.

anatomy, based on Adam Kulmus's *Ontleedkundige Tafelen* [Anatomical tables, 1734]), considered the first scientific translation of a Dutch-language book, came out in 1774, the lone person with Dutch language skills among the doctors who worked to produce it refused to attach his name to it. That person, Maeno Ryōtaku, was highly aware of the fact that many passages were left untranslated, and that the Japanese text was more of an extrapolation from doctors' existing knowledge than an actual translation from Dutch.[18] A student of the doctors in the group, Ōtsuki Gentaku, worked on a revised translation between 1790 and 1798, but his version, too, left out passages that were conceptually difficult. During the same period, another Nagasaki interpreter, Shizuki Tadao (1760–1806), began work on a translation of the Dutch version of John Keill's *Introductions to the True Astronomy* (1721), and in 1803 he published the first astronomical text translated from Dutch that Japanese astronomers considered worthy of attention. It was thus not until the early nineteenth century that the linguistic abilities of translators and the understanding of the conceptual bases of European science evolved to a high enough level for translation to become widespread. Only then did astronomers begin sharing physicians' and botanists' interest in Dutch books. They still did not identify themselves as Dutch studies scholars, or *rangakusha*, but received significant assistance from those who did.

Methodology of Observing and Depicting

Even before the end of the eighteenth century, however, various communities of scholars found common interest in their shared focus on observation and depiction as a method of inquiry into the natural world. Scholars of materia medica began focusing more and more on the physical characteristics of plants; doctors influenced by Dutch studies began observing (and later performing) anatomical dissections, and astronomers began measuring the movement of celestial bodies in real-time observations. The latter described their practice as *sokuryō* (測量) – a term that today is used to denote "surveying," but in the Tokugawa period was used in the literal sense of its characters, "measuring by observation," and applied equally to celestial and terrestrial observations.

Scientific literature of European origin undoubtedly played an important role in this development. Western books featured abundant, carefully executed illustrations, which inspired readers' imaginations, encouraged them to inspect images in detail, and prompted them to try to draw what they

---

[18] Sakai, "Translation and the Origins of Western Science."

observed outside the covers of the book. Books describing the Western sciences also came paired with objects and instruments that emphasized seeing and observation, such as looking glasses, specimen jars, microscopes, telescopes, sextants, and theodolites.[19]

Yet Western scientific literature was only one factor that contributed to a new focus on the visual. Already in Ming-period China, images appeared with increasing frequency in books that had been previously primarily textual. The famous encyclopedia of materia medica, *Bencao gangmu*, was only published after the children of its author, Li Shizhen, insisted on the inclusion of images alongside the text. When imported to Japan, such books inspired a whole genre of heavily illustrated encyclopedias, such as the highly popular 1712 *Wakan sansai zue* (Sino-Japanese illustrated encyclopedia), for example. Additional emphasis on lifelike depiction followed a two-year visit to Japan by the Chinese artist Shen Nanpin (1682–1760). Living and teaching in Nagasaki between 1731 and 1733, Shen founded a new school of painting that emphasized three-dimensionality and an attention to minute details. One of Shen's Japanese students was Sō Shiseki (1715–86), famous for his exquisite depictions of marine and mountain fauna. And it was Shiseki's approach to art that prompted his students Odano Naotake (1749–80) and Shiba Kōkan (1747–1818) to begin exploring European modes of painting. Thus, it would be more accurate to say that heavily illustrated Western scientific books were popular in Japan because they answered the already existing preference for detailed depiction.

Nevertheless, the study of European painting further advanced scholars' observation skills. Tokugawa Yoshimune, who was impressed by the Dutch *Herbal*, commissioned local artists to draw images of plants unique to their areas.[20] Odano Naotake was hired by the doctors translating Adam Kulmus's *Ontleedkundige Tafelen* to copy the images in the Dutch book and, in doing so, pointed out to the doctors pictorial details they would have otherwise missed. Satake Shozan (1748–85), daimyo of the Kubota domain, who studied Western painting under Hiraga Gennai (1728–80), went on to write a treatise on the usefulness of Western linear perspective to surveying – a sentiment that was echoed in the mid-nineteenth century by the magistrate of infrastructure for the Kaga domain, Endō Takanori (1784–1864), who wrote a treatise claiming that painting in the Western style was essential to the scientific enterprise.[21]

[19] Screech, *Western Scientific Gaze*.
[20] Marcon, *Knowledge of Nature*.
[21] Onabe, *Zettai tōmei no tankyū*.

We can find a similar focus on observation in the work of the founder of the Asada school of astronomy, Asada Gōryū (1734–99). Gōryū was originally trained as a medical doctor and served as a personal physician of the daimyo of the Kitsuki domain. In the letters he wrote to philosopher Miura Baien (1723–89), whose work was characterized by depictions of cosmological relationships in enigmatic diagrams, Gōryū described his growing interest in European-style anatomy, the observations he made, and the animal dissections he conducted.[22] Once he read the mathematical treatises of Takebe Katahiro and the Jesuit treatises recently imported from China, however, he realized that he was more interested in observing the skies than the insides of bodies. Leaving his post as a domanial physician, Gōryū dove into the study of astronomy, focusing equally on *Shoushili* and the Jesuit astronomical treatises.

Asada Gōryū's astronomical practice *required* drawing as an analytical tool. It emphasized the real-time observation of celestial motion and relied on mathematical calculations using spherical geometry and trigonometry. In order to undertake such calculations, one had to draw a diagram of the earth and indicate on it the path of the observed celestial body. Converting elapsed time into degrees of angles in the diagrams, astronomers of the Asada school made calculations by drawing.

The transformation triggered by the new importance accorded to observation and depiction was apparent in the Kansei calendrical reform of 1798. The reform was carried out by two of Gōryū's students – Takahashi Yoshitoki (1756–1816) and Hazama Shigetomi (1764–1804). The two studied the *Shoushili* system, the Chinese-language Jesuit treatises, and Gōryū's own astronomical theories. Unlike the work of their predecessors, their calculations were no longer purely algebraic, but rather involved spherical geometry and trigonometry that relied on diagrams of the movement of the earth and celestial motion. Their calculations of the beginning and the end of the day were no longer expressed in terms of the time elapsed since local noon, for example, but rather in the position of the sun below the horizon measured in degrees; the seasons, too, were no longer defined by an equal division of the solar year, but rather as degrees of motion in the earth's path around the sun.

Here may be the place to mention the significance of heliocentric theory as a criterion for defining scientific communities. Many readers will be familiar with Thomas Kuhn's famous thesis of paradigm shifts in science. Kuhn based his theory on the example of the scientific revolution in Europe, in which

---

[22] Uehara, Ono, and Hirose, *Tenmon rekigaku shoka shokanshū*, 44–45.

he identifies the sharp conceptual break that had occurred in Europe with the transition from a geocentric to a heliocentric theory.[23] Yet nothing of the sort happened in Japan. The Jesuits who had taught European astronomy in China had been forbidden from mentioning the Copernican theory and instead had taught the hybrid theory of Tycho Brahe, according to which the planets revolved around the sun, but the sun revolved around the earth. Brahe's cosmological model seems "wrong" to our modern sensibilities, but mathematically – for calendrical purposes – it actually worked quite well. Japanese astronomers, who had studied Chinese-language Jesuit treatises, initially based their calculations on the Tychonian model. Yet they were not shocked or surprised when astronomical books and celestial atlases depicting a heliocentric universe began arriving from Holland. They saw the heliocentric model of Copernicus as a natural evolution of the Tychonian one, which required only minor mathematical tweaking. They were much more concerned when they learned of Kepler's first law, which states that orbits are elliptical rather than circular – a distinction that required major changes in their mathematical calculations.[24] But even that concern was not a "paradigm shift" in the Kuhnian sense, only an additional complication to the kinds of calculations to which they had become accustomed. This is because the scientific revolution in Tokugawa Japan was not cosmological but practical. The real paradigm shift for the Japanese occurred when Japanese scholars started perceiving the world in geometrical terms and analyzing it using diagrams. The specific configuration of those diagrams was only secondary.

Breaking the Boundaries of Social Class

Yet it was not only theories and methods that were changing in scientific communities; the social makeup of these communities was changing, too. Like other professionals, scholars belonged to lineages but did not have to be born into a family of scholars to belong to one. Thus, for example, Takahashi Yoshitoki's younger son was adopted into a lineage of astronomers that began with Shibukawa Shunkai and came to be known as Shibukawa Kagesuke. The nonhereditary nature of these lineages allowed the inclusion of people who might previously have been excluded. The famous surveyor Inō Tadataka, for example, was born into the samurai class but was adopted into

---

[23] Kuhn, *Structure of Scientific Revolutions*.
[24] Hazama Shigeyori, "Senkō taigyō sensei jiseki ryakki," in Watanabe, *Tenmon rekigakushijō ni okeru Hazama Shigetomi*, 455.

a merchant family; after amassing a fortune, he was able to leave his business to his son and subsidize his studies under Takahashi Yoshitoki.

Outside of official lineages, too, people born or adopted into the merchant class could engage in scholarly pursuits that had previously been the sole province of the samurai class. Hazama Shigetomi, for example, came from a wealthy family of brewers, and although he was denied an official position at the shogunal astronomical bureau, he was still acknowledged as one of the architects of the Kansei calendrical reform. He was also the designer of several astronomical instruments, most notably the astronomical pendulum clock (*suiyō kyūgi*), which for several decades was considered to be astronomers' most important tool.

Instrument-makers, as a class, were essential to the development of Japanese sciences. Numerous scientific instruments were imported to Japan by the Dutch, but in order to be put to use many needed to be modified. Japanese instrument-makers reverse-engineered armillary spheres, sextants, and theodolites, or, in other cases, studied the depictions and descriptions of such instruments in Chinese-language Jesuit treatises. Replacing Arabic numerals with characters, and correcting for latitude when necessary, they made custom instruments that were easy to use for Japanese astronomers and surveyors.

One of the significant changes instituted by instrument-makers was the standardization of units of measurement. Prior to the early nineteenth century, the value of one *shaku* differed slightly by region and was based on the tools of the main workshop in a given region. When preparing for his first surveying expedition in 1800, Inō Tadataka requested custom-made instruments from Ōno Yasaburō, which effectively forced Inō to adopt Ōno's value for the length of one *shaku*. Once this value was used in the maps produced from Inō's data, it became a standard for the whole of Japan. Today, when we consult historic dictionaries to find that one *shaku* equals 30.34 centimeters, what we are actually seeing is the length of Ōno's particular ruler.[25]

Another contribution of instrument-makers was their subsequent dissemination of scientific information through popular books. One of the instrument-makers who worked on the Kansei calendrical reform, Hosokawa Hanzō, relied on his expertise to write the *Karakuri zue* (Illustrated manual of curious machines). Accompanied by numerous schematics – all drawn based on the rules of linear perspective – the book describes the construction of clocks and automata. The information in *Karakuri zue* was not adequate to allow a

---

[25] Uehara, *Takahashi Kageyasu*, 160–61.

nonprofessional to actually build any of the mechanisms described (and there was not much new in the book for the professional instrument-maker), but it was more than enough to offer readers a taste of the professional knowledge they desired.[26] In another example, clockmakers published books explaining the peculiar ways Europeans measured time. Since clockmakers were the ones who needed to modify European clocks and watches to measure time in local variable hours, they were the best equipped to describe how to translate one system into another, and thus were in the best position to spread knowledge of European-style timekeeping.[27]

In addition to publishing books, instrument-makers inspired others by selling scientific instruments on the general market. After having created custom-made designs for astronomers and surveyors, they found themselves in possession of blueprints and molds, which could be easily reused. They made more of the same instruments and marketed them to a general audience eager to engage in surveying practices similar to those of the professionals or that were described in popular science books.

Instrument-makers and popular science books contributed to the emergence of a wave of scientifically minded amateurs. The ranks of amateurs were quite diverse, including, among others, women. Inō Tadataka, for example, provoked not a small amount of envy when he paired with a scientifically minded partner. The classically educated Ōsaki Ei was already interested in science when she met Inō. Gossiping about her in a letter to Takahashi Yoshitoki, Hazama Shigetomi described how she made observations, took measurements, and served Inō as a right hand. Ei did not accompany Inō on his more arduous surveying expeditions, but nevertheless traveled with him for leisure and used the time for observations and surveying.[28] On the other end of the scientific amateur spectrum were science-crazed daimyo and other high officials. Takahashi Yoshitoki spent not a small amount of time writing back to these high-ranking bureaucrats who had recently bought the newest scientific instruments and were now asking what to do with them.[29]

Such amateurs played a crucial role in the rapid development of scientific fields during the nineteenth century. They further stimulated the market for scientific literature and instrumentation. The rich and powerful among them funded scientific enterprises the central government would not fund.

[26] Yamaguchi, *Nihon no tokei*, 267–68.
[27] Fujimura, *Jimeisho jiban kō.*
[28] Letters compiled in Hazama and Takahashi, "Seigaku shukan shō," 221.
[29] Uehara, Ono, and Hirose, *Tenmon rekigaku shoka shokanshū*, 68.

And, as we will see later in the chapter, the rapidly expanding community of like-minded science enthusiasts provided a fertile background for the formation of schools of science. Unlike the amateurs of the late seventeenth century, they were motivated by similar essential questions and assumptions, falling behind professional astronomy only in the *degree* of their mathematical abilities.

At the same time, there were also groups that were excluded from participation. Most notably, the Tsuchimikado family, who had traditionally been involved in the calendar-making process, was gradually marginalized. In most cases, the Tsuchimikado had not been involved in mathematical computation, but only in mapping annual activities onto the already-devised template. Hazama Shigetomi still maintained a close relationship with the Tsuchimikado, but other astronomers less so. What is more, what was considered to be the Tsuchimikado's skill – prognostication – came under attack. When soliciting expert opinions in preparation for reforming the calendar in 1798, the shogunal regent, Matsudaira Sadanobu, turned to philosopher Nakai Chikuzan (1730–1804), who derided the prognostication section of the calendar as containing "ignorant fables, which greatly damage the public, and easily mislead the ignorant people of this realm, making it hard to enlighten them."[30] From then on, prognostication became a frequent target of criticism by the community of scholars dedicated to improving the calendar. The Tsuchimikado, who had previously been responsible for devising this section, were gradually pushed out.

Institutional Basis for Cross-Disciplinary Learning

The solidification of discrete scientific communities into one unified field of science could not have happened without the emergence of institutions of higher learning. For the first 200 years of the Tokugawa period, the study of a given scientific field was conducted with a teacher, who formed a school characterized by a particular approach or philosophy. Even at the end of the eighteenth century, one had to attach oneself to a teacher in order to master, say, mathematics or surveying, as Inō Tadataka did when he began studying under Takahashi Yoshitoki. Yet with the change of the social composition of scientific communities, accompanied by the emergence of concerns and assumptions shared across the different fields, the organization of learning changed, too.

---

[30] Nakai, *Sōbō kigen*, cited in Okada, *Meiji kaireki*, 37.

In 1726, an academy called the Kaitokudō (Hall of Embracing Virtue) opened in Osaka to serve the population of merchants who yearned for a more thorough education. Originally, the academy had focused on Confucian morals and ethics, but over time the topics of study came to include metaphysics as well as new kinds of knowledge from abroad. In the early nineteenth century, scientific inquiry into the natural world became a fixture in the academy's curriculum and was manifested in publications by its members. For example, in *Yume no shiro* (Instead of dreams), Yamagata Bantō (1748–1821) discusses a variety of natural phenomena and calls for a society guided by astronomy, geography, and mathematics (as opposed to "dreams").[31]

In 1838, a competing Osaka-based academy, Tekijuku, was established by Ogata Kōan (1810–63) to focus exclusively on Dutch sciences. Although the main focus of the academy was medicine, its members studied all topics that could be found in Dutch books, from medicine to astronomy and geography, to the emergent field of botany.[32] One of the new topics found in Dutch books was chemistry. With the first book on chemistry translated by Udagawa Yōan (1798–1846) in 1840, the field of chemistry – which included topics such as electricity – drew the attention of many late Tokugawa scholars who eventually formed the Seimi Kyoku, or Bureau of Chemistry. (*Seimi* 舎密, a transliteration of *chemie*, was the word used for "chemistry" before the invention of the modern term *kagaku* 化学.)

The activities of these schools were enabled by the translation of Dutch scientific literature, which by the 1830s was in full swing and which was rooted in the activities of another institution based in Edo. This institution grew out of the translation needs of the astronomical bureau. Back in 1803, when Takahashi Yoshitoki acquired a Dutch translation of Jérôme Lalande's *Astronomie* (1771), he commented that although he could not understand Dutch, the math in the book suggested it had great potential and therefore should be translated. For the purpose of translation, the bureau hired Baba Sajurō (1787–1822), who was the teenage son of a Nagasaki interpreter. While studying languages, Sajurō was also required to study a given science before attempting to translate a text on that subject. With Sajurō's body of translations ever increasing, more translators were hired by the astronomical bureau, and translation soon occupied the whole department. With a primary objective of translation, the bureau nevertheless served an educational

---

[31] Najita, *Visions of Virtue.*
[32] Marcon, *Knowledge of Nature.*

purpose. Following Sajurō's example, translators were required to study the sciences first. In 1857, extracting the translation department from the astronomical bureau, the government established the translation bureau Hsiung discusses (Chapter 11, this volume). The bureau was first named Bansho Shirabesho (Institute for the Investigation of Barbarian Books) and then renamed Yōsho Shirabesho (Institute for the Investigation of Western Books) in order to avoid the title's derogatory etymology.

All of these institutions would later provide the social, intellectual, and institutional bases for the universities founded during the Meiji period. The Kaitokudō academy and Tekijuku would evolve into Osaka University. The Yōsho Shirabesho would go through several transformations to become Tokyo Imperial University. And the Seimi Kyoku would contribute to the establishment of Kyoto University.

The graduates of these academies would go on to become the intellectual and scientific leaders of the Meiji period. Perhaps the most famous graduate of Tekijuku was Fukuzawa Yukichi (1835–1901), who in the early Meiji period would loudly renounce the Tokugawa past. Itō Keisuke (1803–1901), who led the flora and fauna department at the Bansho Shirabesho, would become the first professor of zoology at Tokyo Imperial University. Others would contribute to the evolution of the Japanese language necessary to engage with modern Western science. Looking for ways to express their new conception of scientific inquiry, late Tokugawa scholars coined terms such as "vacuum" (shinkū), "oxygen" (sanso), "nature" (shizen), and – most importantly – "science" (kagaku).

Conclusion: Toward One *Science*

The story of Tokugawa science is the story of the gradual convergence of diverse scholarly enterprises into one unified field called Science. Early Tokugawa scientific communities benefited enormously from increased interaction with foreign scholars – particularly from China and Korea but also from the lingering influence of the Jesuits who taught Japanese converts before being expelled from the country. Rather than simply adopting foreign-born systems, however, Japanese scholars were encouraged by the interactions with scientific communities abroad to develop their own systems that reflected the physical realities of Japan, a commitment that was shared across disciplines. What separated astronomers from scholars of medicine and materia medica, however, was their methodology. Swept up by the growing popularity of mathematics in the second half of the seventeenth century, astronomers began to see mathematics as a principal skill, as well as a mark of professionalism. For this reason, despite evident curiosity, they initially engaged only glancingly with European astronomy, which they saw as overly focused on cosmology at the expense of the collection of valuable data. Paradoxically, it was engagement with a thirteenth-century Chinese astronomical treatise that paved the way for Japanese mathematicians to take European astronomy seriously. Once Japanese astronomers discovered that Jesuit astronomical treatises published in China contained numerous novel mathematical methods, they increased pressure on Yoshimune to ease censorship laws in 1720 and to allow the importation of scientific literature from China and Holland. The shared quest for foreign books that arrived in Japan through Nagasaki brought astronomers, doctors, and scholars of materia medica into proximity, yet they were still divided by their target languages. Astronomers had the relatively easy task of translating their sources from classical Chinese, while others struggled with the seemingly impenetrable Dutch language.

The Japanese scientific revolution, however, did not take place in the realm of words but in the realm of practice, particularly observation and depiction. Similar to what had happened with astronomy, the initial appreciation of European illustrations came on the heels of artistic trends developed under Chinese influence. Yet serious engagement with European linear perspective and other drawing techniques contributed to the growing emphasis on observation and depiction in scholarly practice across disciplines. Astronomers, scholars of medicine, and those studying flora and fauna all began seeing the world they explored in terms of forms, and they approached observation and the visual representation of those forms as key tools of inquiry.

The conceptual transformations of the late eighteenth century led to social transformations among communities of scholars. Merchant-class origins no longer posed a barrier to scholarship, as money could now pave the way to a life of learning. With the help of instrument-makers and the print industry, which popularized scientific notions, activities, and tools, a wave of amateur scientists invaded previously narrow professional circles. Recognizing that similar questions and assumptions were found across diverse disciplines, late Tokugawa scholars formed academies dedicated to higher learning, creating the conceptual and institutional bases for a new unified field of inquiry into the natural world. No longer disparate communities representing a variety of different sciences, they all now belonged to the community of Science.

Bibliography

Adams, George. *A Treatise Describing the Construction, and Explaining the Use of New Celestial and Terrestrial Globes [...] With a Great Variety of Astronomical and Geographical Problems.* 5th ed. London, 1782.

Beukers, Harmmen. "Dodonaeus in Japanese: Deshima Surgeons as Mediators in the Early Introduction of Western Natural History." In *Dodonaeus in Japan: Translation and the Scientific Mind in Tokugawa Japan,* edited by Willy vande Walle and Kazuhiko Kasaya, 281–98. Leuven: Leuven University Press, 2001.

Frumer, Yulia. *Making Time: Astronomical Time Measurement in Tokugawa Japan.* Chicago: University of Chicago Press, 2018.

Fujimura Heizō. *Jimeisho jiban kō.* Kyoto: Toda Tōzaburō, 1823. National Diet Library.

Hayashi Makoto. "Igo to tenmon." In *Bunkashi no shosō,* edited by Ōsumi Kazuo, 258–87. Yoshikawa Kōbunkan, 2003.

Hazama Shigetomi and Takahashi Yoshitoki. "Seigaku shukan shō." In *Kinsei Kagaku shisō, ge,* 194–222. Vol. 63 of *Nihon shisō taikei.* Iwanami Shoten, 1971.

Horiuchi, Annick. *Japanese Mathematics in the Edo Period (1600–1868): A Study of the Works of Seki Takakazu (?–1708) and Takebe Katahiro (1664–1739).* Basel: Birkhäuser, 2010.

Kuhn, Thomas. *The Structure of Scientific Revolutions.* Chicago: University of Chicago Press, 1962.

Marcon, Federico. *The Knowledge of Nature and the Nature of Knowledge in Early Modern Japan.* Chicago: University of Chicago Press, 2015.

Najita, Tetsuo. *Visions of Virtue in Tokugawa Japan: The Kaitokudō Merchant Academy of Osaka.* Chicago: University of Chicago Press, 1987.

Nakayama Shigeru. *Nihon no tenmongaku: Seiyō ninshiki no senpei.* Iwanami Shoten, 1972.

Okada Yoshirō. *Meiji kaireki: "Toki" no bunmei kaika.* Taishūkan Shoten, 1994.

Onabe Tomoko. *Zettai tōmei no tankyū: Endō Takanori cho "Shahō shinjutsu" no kenkyū.* Kyoto: Shibunkaku, 2006.

Ooms, Herman. *Tokugawa Ideology: Early Constructs.* Princeton, NJ: Princeton University Press, 1985.

Ravina, Mark. "*Wasan* and the Physics That Wasn't: Mathematics in the Tokugawa Period." *Monumenta Nipponica* 48, no. 2 (1993): 205–24.

Sakai, Shizu. "Translation and the Origins of Western Science in Japan." In *The Introduction of Modern Science and Technology to Turkey and Japan,* edited by Feza Gunergun and Kuriyama Shigehisa, 137–57. Kyoto: International Research Center for Japanese Studies, 1996.

Screech, Timon. *The Western Scientific Gaze and Popular Imagery in Later Edo Japan: The Lens Within the Heart.* Cambridge: Cambridge University Press, 1996.

Shibukawa Shunkai. "Tenmon keitō." In *Kinsei Kagaku shisō, ge,* 110–92. Vol. 63 of *Nihon shisō taikei.* Iwanami Shoten, 1971.

Shirahata, Yōzaburō. "The Development of Japanese Botanical Interest and Dodonaeus' Role: From Pharmacopoeia to Botany and Horticulture." In *Dodonaeus in Japan: Translation and the Scientific Mind in Tokugawa Japan,* edited by Willy vande Walle and Kazuhiko Kasaya, 263–79. Leuven: Leuven University Press, 2001.

Sivin, Nathan. *Granting the Seasons: The Chinese Astronomical Reform of 1280, with a Study of Its Many Dimensions and a Translation of Its Records.* New York: Springer, 2009.

Sugimoto, Masayoshi, and David Swain. *Science and Culture in Traditional Japan*. Cambridge, MA: MIT Press, 1978. Reprint, Rutland, VT: Tuttle, 1989.

Tucker, Mary Evelyn. "Religious Dimensions of Confucianism: Cosmology and Cultivation." *Philosophy East and West* 48, no. 1 (January 1998): 5–45.

Uehara Hisashi. *Takahashi Kageyasu no kenkyū*. Kōdansha, 1977.

Uehara Hisashi, Ono Fumio, and Hirose Hideo, eds. *Tenmon rekigaku shoka shokanshū*. Kōdansha, 1981.

Watanabe Toshio. *Tenmon rekigakushijō ni okeru Hazama Shigetomi to sono ikka*. Kyoto: Yamaguchi Shoten, 1943.

Yamaguchi Ryūji. *Nihon no tokei: Tokugawa jidai no wadokei no kenkyū*. Nihon Hyōronsha, 1942.

II

The Problem of Western Knowledge in Late Tokugawa Japan

HANSUN HSIUNG

Glancing at the *Asahi shinbun*'s summer 2000 "Most Outstanding Japanese Scientists of the Last Millennium," two names stand out to the early modernist's eyes: Sugita Genpaku (1733–1817) and Hiraga Gennai (1728–79). Among the twentieth-century Nobel Prize winners and nominees populating the *Asahi*'s list, Sugita and Hiraga were the only two pre-1868 names to crack the top five.[1] That they did so, unlike others of their time, owes itself to a particular understanding of Western knowledge in late Tokugawa Japan. Japanese scientists in the twentieth century may have predicted the existence of mesons and determined the etiology of syphilis, but their successes allegedly rested on an earlier history made possible by figures such as Sugita and Hiraga – a history which has been described as that of the "dawn of Western science in Japan."[2]

Here is that history as Sugita Genpaku himself told it. Following earlier bans on Christianity and the enactment of a series of maritime prohibitions from 1633 through 1641, the Tokugawa shogunate had confined European contact to trade with the Dutch East India Company (VOC), the operational base of which was relocated from the port of Hirado to the salvaged island of Dejima in Nagasaki. Over the next century, Western knowledge, particularly within the field of surgery, began to filter into Japan slowly through this window to a small coterie of the curious, mostly comprising shogunal interpreters (*tsūji*) stationed in Nagasaki. However, their knowledge remained piecemeal and imperfect, premised on an unsteady mastery of the Dutch language and an unsystematic set of live observations and conversations with VOC ship surgeons as they practiced their craft on Dejima. The situation began to change only after the 1740s, when the eighth shogun, Tokugawa Yoshimune (1684–1751), motivated by an interest in natural history, commenced active

---

[1] "Kono 1000-nen 'Nihon no kagakusha.'"
[2] Sugita, *Dawn of Western Science in Japan*.

sponsorship of the study of Dutch. Slowly but surely, a new generation of trailblazers began to carve a path for Western knowledge beyond the Nagasaki community to which its circulation had previously been limited.

Hiraga Gennai was one of these trailblazers. His polymathic studies of Dutch books in the 1760s, covering topics from mining and natural history to perspectival representation, were complemented more famously by his use of Leyden jars to produce static electricity in the 1770s. Then, after the early tremors of Hiraga's discoveries, came an earthquake: the efforts of the physician Sugita Genpaku and his colleagues to translate *Ontleedkundige Tafelen*, the Dutch-language edition of Johann Adam Kulmus's *Anatomische Tabellen* (first ed. 1722). This yielded, in 1774, *A New Book of Anatomy* (*Kaitai shinsho*). In Sugita's own words, *A New Book of Anatomy* awoke Japan to the "transmitted errors" of Chinese knowledge, inciting a movement to "discard Chinese books and take up in particular Dutch books."[3] Gaining momentum, this movement to acquire Western knowledge also gained a name: Dutch learning (*rangaku*).

So, at least, runs the narrative we find in Sugita's manuscript, *An Introduction to Dutch Learning* (*Rangaku kotohajime*). Composed in 1815 on the eve of his death, the manuscript offers a celebratory account of its author's achievements and the intellectual movement his generation inspired, locating in Dutch learning the seeds of a potential displacement of the "Chinese learning" (*kangaku*) which reigned at the time. Perhaps the greatest sign of gradual displacement, for Sugita, was the acceptance of Dutch learning by the shogunate, which in 1811 created a section within its Astronomical Bureau (Tenmongata) dedicated to the translation of Dutch texts, recruiting into service a younger cohort of scholars – among them, Ōtsuki Gentaku (1757–1827) and Udagawa Genshin (1770–1835) – who had been trained by Sugita and his associates.[4]

Little did Sugita know how powerful his prediction of displacement would prove. For in its broad strokes, *An Introduction to Dutch Learning* has functioned as the blueprint for writing anticipatory histories of Japanese modernization. In the half-century that followed, the study of Dutch books became the study of English, French, German, and even Russian books. Dutch learning, by the 1850s, gave way to "Western learning" (*yōgaku*) in general, which thrived not only through private academies across the country but also at the Institute for the Investigation of Barbarian Books (Bansho Shirabesho), created by the

---

[3] Sugita, *Kyōi no gen*, 231.
[4] Sugita, *Dawn of Western Science in Japan*, 66–7.

shogunate in 1856 as a national site for training in European languages.[5] As it grew, Western learning's emphasis on utility (*jitsuyō*) and empiricism (*jitsuri*) is claimed to have provoked Japan's break from a Neo-Confucian metaphysics of nature.[6] By the end of the first decade of the Meiji period, supporters of Western learning obtained a decisive victory over Chinese learning: it was the Institute for the Investigation of Barbarian Books, and not the shogunate's Confucian academy, that became the foundation for Japan's first modern university – Tokyo Imperial University. From that point onward, Japan would follow Western disciplines, methods, and vocabularies; it would create schools, laboratories, and research institutes styled after the West. A Western system of knowledge became synonymous with *modern* knowledge overall.

This interpretation was articulated clearly across the original *Cambridge History of Japan*. Already in 1984, the historian Marius Jansen had declared that "the continuities between the study of the West through Dutch in Tokugawa Japan and the program of modernization in the Meiji period seem self-evident."[7] Self-evidence became more evident in Jansen's editorial decision to include Dutch and Western learning not in the original *Cambridge History*'s fourth volume on early modern Japan, but in its fifth volume on the nineteenth century – referred to in Jansen's own notes as the "modernization" volume.[8] Hirakawa Sukehiro's contribution to the volume, "Japan's Turn to the West," echoed Jansen's thesis: late Tokugawa Dutch and Western learning "anticipate[d] Japan's more ambitious, post-restoration attempts to assimilate modern Western civilization."[9]

Over forty years have passed since Jansen and John Whitney Hall first began their labors on the original *Cambridge History of Japan*; over thirty since the publication of the above-cited fifth volume. Research conducted in the interim has revealed a far more qualified and far less triumphalist portrait of Western knowledge and its impact, attuning us to the complex and fragile negotiations at work in late Tokugawa Japan. Both the study of correspondence networks and rural physicians, for instance, have demonstrated that Dutch learning relied on provisional social and political alliances motivated

---

[5] Although the term "Western learning" only gained currency in the 1850s, the pursuit of other European languages had been already underway since the 1770s. On Dutch versus Western learning, see Satō, *Yōgakushi kenkyū josetsu*, 1–8; Nakayama, *Bakumatsu no yōgaku*, 1–2. On the early study of Latin and French, see Hsiung, "'Use Me as Your Test!'"; Ichikawa, "Du Français au Japonais par le truchement du Hollandais."

[6] Satō, *Yōgakushi no kenkyū*, 3–18.

[7] Jansen, "*Rangaku* and Westernization," 541.

[8] Marius B. Jansen, papers, box 3, folder 3, C0927.

[9] Hirakawa, "Japan's Turn to the West," 436.

more by local imperatives and local moral economies than any grand notions of modern Western science.[10] Meanwhile, a fine-grained focus on the everyday tools and techniques of knowledge-making, especially those of visualization and calculation, has shown Dutch and Western learning's history to be one of protracted and piecemeal integration into a web of existing practices and meanings rather than any epochal paradigm shift.[11] This sense of slow and partial adjustment has been echoed by intellectual histories that stress the common bonds between Western learning and Chinese learning, with the latter equally as dynamic as, and often quite receptive to, the former.[12] Notably, an emphasis on political economy is evident across many of these studies: existing concerns with how to harness natural resources toward productivity preceded later developments typically associated with Western-style "modernization." Utilitarian, empirically oriented research programs in Japan were clearly taking form apart from Western influence, thereby again defusing pretenses of any "revolution" through Western knowledge.[13]

This drive to decenter and deflate claims about Western knowledge has also received impetus from attempts to situate Dutch and Western learning within a broader global modernity – a modernity shaped not by Westernization but by multilateral processes of information exchange across an ever more integrated world.[14] Here, "circulation" has emerged as a keyword for sketching connected histories that undo a binary framework of "Japan" and the "West."[15] Specifically, researchers are now beginning to examine how Western knowledge in the late Tokugawa period was shaped by new patterns of circulation outside of the West itself, looking not only to other parts of East Asia but also to South and Southeast Asia.

This chapter adopts the latter perspective, outlining in particular how the problem of Western knowledge in the late Tokugawa period can be approached as a problem of empire. Empire here appears in two senses. The first section of this chapter recovers the ways in which the historiography of Dutch and Western learning has been animated by modern Japan's imperial project. The second and third sections then analyze Western knowledge

[10] Tazaki, *Zaison no rangaku*; Ogawa, *Bakumatsu-ki Chōshū-han yōgakushi*; Aoki and Iwabuchi, *Chiiki rangaku*; E. G. Nakamura, *Practical Pursuits*; Jannetta, *Vaccinators*; Jackson, *Network of Knowledge*.
[11] Frumer, *Making Time*; Fukuoka, *Premise of Fidelity*; Trambaiolo, "Vaccination and the Politics of Medical Knowledge"; Hsiung, "'Use Me as Your Test!'"
[12] Maeda, *Heigaku to shushigaku, rangaku, kokugaku*; Kishida, *Kangaku to yōgaku*.
[13] Kuriyama, "Between Mind and Eye"; Marcon, *Knowledge of Nature*.
[14] Bayly, *Birth of the Modern World*.
[15] Gänger, "Circulation."

in late Tokugawa Japan through a series of imperial entanglements, raising examples from Dutch-British interactions in Indonesia and the confluence of American and British actors in Qing port towns. Together, these entanglements formed a *transimperial educational commons* – a global infrastructure of knowledge circulation that both configured Japan's access to putatively "Western" texts and also remediated these texts on their journey to Japan. Understanding this transimperial educational commons in turn opens up the problem of Western knowledge in late Tokugawa Japan to new forms of global history, and the final section of this chapter synthesizes future directions for such global historical research.

Dutch Learning's Empire

Let us begin by returning to Sugita Genpaku's canonical work, *An Introduction to Dutch Learning*. Establishing for Dutch learning an orthodox history and historical significance, replete with a pantheon of heroes, their lineages, and the epochal events in which they took part, this text continues to structure standard accounts of late Tokugawa Western knowledge today.[16] As recently as 2018, Japan's public broadcaster, NHK, chose for its New Year's television drama an adaptation of Minamoto Tarō's 1979 manga, *The Heroes* (*Fūunji-tachi*), focused on the lives of Sugita Genpaku and his peers. The drama, tellingly, was subtitled "Dutch learning revolution" (*rangaku kakumei*).[17]

In its own time, however, the role played by *An Introduction to Dutch Learning* appears far more marginal. Neither printed nor widely circulated through scribal publication for much of the late Tokugawa period, manuscript copies of the work had become so rare by the beginning of the Ansei period (1854–60) that many believed the text permanently lost. Chance discovery of a copy held at Yushima Seidō, the site since 1797 of the shogunate's Confucian academy, did result in increased attention on the part of scholars sympathetic to Western learning during the 1860s.[18] Still, it was not until well into the Meiji era that *An Introduction to Dutch Learning* became accessible in print to a wider audience.

Credit for this occurrence is typically attributed to Fukuzawa Yukichi (1834–1901), the most prominent public intellectual of the Meiji period and

[16] Goodman, "Dutch Learning," 361–64, 367–75.
[17] *Fūunji-tachi.*
[18] Fukuzawa, preface to [Sugita,] *Rangaku kotohajime*, 1890 ed., 1–2.

outspoken advocate of Western-style modernization in Japan. And, to an extent, this attribution is not inaccurate. If later testimony is to be trusted, Fukuzawa had already set his sights on having *An Introduction to Dutch Learning* printed since the very start of the Meiji period. Calling on the Sugita household in 1868, he secured permission to carve woodblocks of the manuscript at his own expense.[19] But, in his own words, the time was not yet ripe; the tumult of those early years eclipsed interest in the text. Printing would only occur in 1890, when the newly launched Japanese Society for Medicine (Nihon Igakukai) used Fukuzawa's woodblocks to produce copies as part of a promotional campaign. Fukuzawa's original aims were made apparent in his preface for that edition and in a contemporaneous letter to Nagayo Sensai (1838–1902), architect of modern Japan's public health system and author of the edition's postface. In these documents, Fukuzawa declared his hope that wider circulation would "indicate this fact (*jijitsu*) to the peoples of the world: that [our] current progress is no accident (*gūzen ni arazu*), and that a hundred some years ago, in that one country of the Orient which is Great Japan, Western civilization (*seiyō bunmei*) had already begun to germinate among scholars."[20]

On its surface, Fukuzawa's estimation would seem to correspond to the familiar positioning of *An Introduction to Dutch Learning* as the most "precious and indispensable book for any person who is interested in the modernization of Japan."[21] At the same time, however, Fukuzawa's words tease a dimension obscured by the term "modernization": Meiji Japan's liberal imperialism. It is more than coincidence that the print publication of *An Introduction to Dutch Learning* corresponded with the coming into force of the Meiji Constitution. Six years earlier, Fukuzawa's disciple Fujita Shigekichi (1852–92) had published *The History of the Spread of Civilization into the East* (*Bunmei tōzen shi*, 1884), a narrative centered on the Dutch learning scholars Watanabe Kazan (1793–1841) and Takano Chōei (1804–50). Critical of the shogunate's harsh policies toward Western countries, Watanabe and Takano were arrested, with Watanabe committing suicide and Takano perishing after an attempted prison break. Their tragic heroism, for Fujita, served to crystallize his broader argument that Dutch learning was the source of modern liberalism in Japan.[22]

[19] Fukuzawa, preface to [Sugita,] *Rangaku kotohajime*, 1890 ed., 1–2.
[20] Fukuzawa, preface to [Sugita,] *Rangaku kotohajime*, 1890 ed., 4; Fukuzawa Yukichi to Nagayo Sensai (1 April 1890), in Fukuzawa, *Fukuzawa Yukichi shokan shū*, vol. 6, letter 1466.
[21] Ogata, introduction to Sugita, *Rangaku kotohajime*, 1941 ed., ix–x.
[22] Fujita Shigekichi, *Bunmei tōzen shi*, esp. 119–40. For a discussion of this book's impact, see Satō, "Iwayuru 'yōgaku ronsō,'" 2–3. For a critique of the heroic narrative surrounding Takano et al., see E. G. Nakamura, *Practical Pursuits*, 1–70.

One year after Fujita's book, it was precisely by invoking a world-historical "spread of civilization into the East," against the backdrop of the failed, Japanese-supported Kapsin Coup in Korea, that Fukuzawa would begin his infamous "Datsu-A ron" (Discourse on leaving Asia): only in Japan had liberal reform succeeded, thus necessitating that Japan break with its Asian neighbors and adopt the same imperial stance toward them as Western countries.[23]

In short, at stake in the tale of Dutch learning was less a notion of "Western" modernity in and of itself than the claim that modern world history was experiencing an eastward shift embodied by Japan. Alongside the transmission of knowledge came a transmission of political authority – a *translatio studii et imperii* which, in passing on the mantle of learning, conferred a legitimate right of imperial domination. Fukuzawa had already planted seeds of this reasoning in his *Outline of a Theory of Civilization* (*Bunmeiron no gairyaku*), where he expressed the hope that Japan, and not the West, might one day stand at the apex of the civilized. Dutch learning offered his vision historical credibility. To borrow from Nagayo Sensai's postface to the 1890 edition of *An Introduction to Dutch Learning*, here was a text that should "impress upon the world of nations the glory of our *Eastern* medicine."[24]

To trace the further publication history of *An Introduction to Dutch Learning* is to witness the unfolding of this incipient understanding. The 1890 printing of Fukuzawa's woodblocks was followed two decades later by the anthologization of the text in the 1910s *Library of the Sources of Civilization* (*Bunmei genryū sōsho*). In what had been conceived as a scholarly compilation of historical primary sources, *An Introduction to Dutch Learning* occupied pride of place, standing out of chronological order as the very first entry, only to be followed by a jump back to documents of the Sengoku and early Tokugawa era.[25] Yet both these stirrings were pebbles in the pond. The 1890 edition's more limited print run was intended for the medical community; the later anthology an expensive multivolume set destined for researchers. Sustained interest in *An Introduction to Dutch Learning* among scholars as well as the general public would reach an apex only during a later period. In the end, it was the 1930s and early 1940s that would mark the first heyday of Dutch learning studies.

---

[23] [Fukuzawa,] "Datsu-A ron."

[24] Nagayo, "Kinsei iji enkaku," 16 [86], emphasis added. On Nagayo in the context of imperial biopower, see Rogaski, *Hygienic Modernity*.

[25] Asakura, *Bunmei genryū sōsho*, vol. 1.

The importance of discourses on "science" to Japan's mature imperial project has received significant attention in recent research.[26] Dutch learning was implicated in these discourses, attesting as it seemed to a longer tale of how Japan, since its early modern period, had made modern Western science its own. From scholarly monographs to public radio broadcasts, the period from 1930 to 1945 witnessed the emergence of Dutch learning studies both as a defined academic subfield and as a topic of widespread public fascination. Specialist circles of socioeconomic historians, occupied at the time with debates over how Japan might fit into Marxist theories of stadial development, found in Dutch and Western learning an intellectual index of structural change: To what extent did Western knowledge strengthen Tokugawa "feudalism," and to what extent did it express an emerging bourgeoisie's preference for more pragmatic, empiricist, and outward-looking forms of knowledge? The pattern of argument established by these questions, crystallized polemically first in Takahashi Shin'ichi's 1939 *A Theory of Western Learning (Yōgakuron)*, remained definitive for scholarly battles well into the 1960s, embroiling luminaries of postwar historiography the likes of Hani Gorō, Numata Jirō, and Tōyama Shigeki.[27]

Beyond these specialist circles was a surge of popular interest. Iwanami Shoten's decision in 1930 to republish *An Introduction to Dutch Learning* in its small-format paperback series was perhaps the first sign that the floodgates were opening. Indeed, US occupation authorities later considered the text for censorship. Soon followed the consecration of that work in school textbooks and anthologies of Japanese thought and "spiritual culture."[28] Access was further widened in 1941 by the translation of *An Introduction to Dutch Learning* into contemporary Japanese and German.[29] The former's appearance was accompanied by much public spectacle, including an NHK radio broadcast wherein fifth-generation Kabuki actor Sawamura Tanosuke (1902–68) performed portions of the translation aloud.[30]

---

[26] Mizuno, *Science for the Empire*.

[27] Takahashi, *Yōgakuron*. For an overview of how this "Western learning debate" (*Yōgaku ronsō*) triggered by Takahashi transformed across the post-World War II decades, see Satō, "Iwayuru 'yōgaku ronsō'"; Yamori, "Yōgaku ronsō," 218–19.

[28] See, for example, Tōkyō Tsūshin Daiichi Chūgakkai, *Shinsen kokugo*; Kakiuchi, *Kokubun kagami*; Igarashi, *Shōrōshō: Junsei kokugo tokuhon*; Kakiuchi and Nishio, *Jitsugyō gakkō kokubun*; Dai Nihon Shisō Zenshū Kankōkai, *Dai Nihon shisō zenshū*, vol. 12; Fujita Tokutarō, Fujisawa, and Morimoto, *Nihon seishin bunka taikei*, vol. 10.

[29] Sugita, *Rangaku kotohajime*; Sugita, "Rangaku kotohajime (Die Anfänge der 'Holland-Kunde')."

[30] Takashima, "Rangaku kotohajime."

Against this popular backdrop was concentrated interest in how a proper understanding of Dutch learning might clarify Japan's world-historical position. By the end of the 1930s, researchers were speaking of the need to clarify Dutch learning's "historical mission" (*rekishiteki shimei*) and how the course of its development might serve as grounds on which to construct a "new spirit" (*atarashiki seishin*) of Japan.[31] Their writings burst forth from the pages of history publications into those of popular science periodicals, as well as reviews for international relations.[32] The latter trend grew particularly pronounced once the Japanese empire set its sights on expansion into Southeast Asia. Itazawa Takeo (1895–1962), a founding figure of the study of Dutch-Japanese relations, authored articles on Dutch learning, still widely consulted today, for special issues of foreign policy journals. Next to contributions on finance, demography, and colonial trade, one finds Itazawa's accounts of how the historical relations built by Dutch learning predisposed Japan to become the rightful successor of the Netherlands in Indonesia.[33] Concomitantly, Itazawa began a six-part NHK radio series ostensibly focused on Sugita Genpaku but which served simultaneously as a "history of the overseas development of the Japanese people" (*Nihon minzoku no kaigai hatten shi*). In these broadcasts, Dutch learning became the locus for unpacking deep-seated connections between Japan and the South Pacific.[34] Notably, these activities brought about his eventual purge from the University of Tokyo in 1948.[35]

One might continue to accumulate evidence: as late as 1944, Ministry of Foreign Affairs official Ashino Hiromu (1893–1985) continued to urge readers of the *Diplomatic Review* to take up and study *An Introduction to Dutch Learning*.[36] But this would only belabor a point now apparent: to the extent that Dutch learning has been about a problem of the "modern," that modern has distinctly been a question of Japan's world-historical position as a non-Western empire. For prewar thinkers, this imperial question was one of how Tokugawa contact with Western knowledge in some way authorized, or at least found itself irrevocably figured in, Japan's pursuit of Asian hegemony. Acknowledging this fact thus opens critical potential for us in the present. How can – and why

---

[31] Fujii, "Rangaku no rekishiteki shimei"; Fujiwara, "Atarashiki seishin."
[32] For instance, Nakano Yōzō, "Rangaku kotohajime"; "Nihon bunka to yōgaku no kōshō."
[33] Itazawa, "Rangaku no keitai to yakuwari."
[34] Itazawa, *Sugita Genpaku to Rangaku kotohajime*; Itazawa, *Mukashi no nan'yō to Nihon*.
[35] Maruyama "Itazawa Takeo sensei tsuitō," 229.
[36] Ashino, "*Rangaku kotohajime o yomu*."

might – we rewrite the history of Dutch learning's "modern" as something always already imperial?

The Transimperial Educational Commons

Consider the title page of the *Oranda gogaku genshi – Eerste beginselen der Ned-erduitsche spraakkunst*, or *First Principles of Dutch Grammar* (Figure 11.1). The book was printed in Fukui in the early autumn of 1856 to serve the needs of the Meidōkan domanial academy, established only a year prior by Matsu-daira Shungaku (1828–90). This, in and of itself, attests to the text's signif-icance. Storied in histories of Western learning, it was the Meidōkan that boasted Bakumatsu-period (1853–68) stars Hashimoto Sanai (1834–59) and Yokoi Shōnan (1809–69) as instructors; trained Meiji government elites such as Yuri Kimimasa (1829–1909); and hosted William Elliot Griffis (1843–1928), then a chemistry teacher, who would go on to become one of the leading interpreters of Japan for Western audiences. But a survey of extant copies of the *Eerste beginselen* in Japan also attests to a history beyond Fukui. The book found readers, for instance, in Kaga domain's medical academy, as well as at the shogunate's healthcare facility in what is today the Koishikawa Botanical Gardens. Mito domain's historical bureau, the Shōkōkan, also owned a copy. General interest in the work was sufficient to attract the attention of the Edo commercial publisher Suharaya Ihachi, who reissued it as the *Ranbun kihan Samarangu – Rules of Dutch: Samarang*.[37]

There is at first glance in this history little surprise. By the late 1850s, those in Japan seeking "Western knowledge" had already grown accustomed to the widening availability of Japanese reprints of Dutch books. Domestic reprint-ing was especially important in educational contexts like those of the Meidō-kan. Pedagogy required the provision of multiple copies of assigned texts to students, and the volume of demand foreclosed the use of imported Euro-pean originals, often prohibitively expensive and difficult to obtain in desired quantities. Moreover, transcribing fair copies of Dutch texts for carving onto woodblocks had become a common feature of the political economy of edu-cation. Apprentices at Dutch learning academies frequently performed this labor in exchange for fee waivers; those proficient might even earn surplus pocket change. According to one student at Ogata Kōan's famed Tekijuku

---

[37] Iwasaki Katsumi, *Shōkōkan bunko ransho mokuroku*, no. 186; Miyanaga, "Nihon yōgaku-shi," 43; Itagaki, "Kaga-han no yōgaku ni kōken shita orandago jisho," 29, 42; *Ranbun kihan*.

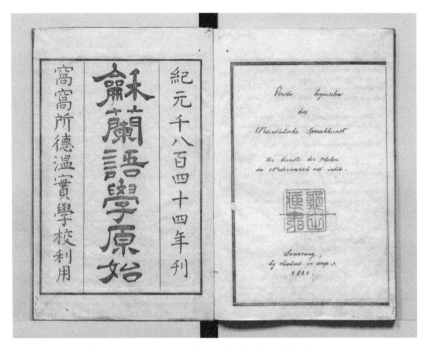

Figure 11.1 *Oranda gogaku genshi*. National Diet Library.

academy, every four pages of Dutch would on average be enough for a haircut, a hot bath, and three servings of soba noodles.[38]

This much has been established in detail by a long tradition of bibliographical studies within Dutch learning research. The minute tracing of collections, native reprints, and patterns for the production and circulation of imported European-language texts comprised a significant enterprise within the activities of the postwar Nichiran Gakkai (Japan-Netherlands Institute) and Rangaku Shiryō Kenkyūkai (Research Group on Dutch Learning Materials). We have, as a consequence, monumental catalogs of the Dutch books known to be owned by the Tokugawa shogunate and similar lists for respective domains.[39] And while on the surface dry, the meticulous study of variant editions enabled by these scholarly aids has resulted in far more nuanced histories

[38] Ishiguro, "Rō-shosei yori," 39; Nakano Misao, "Rangakusha to keizai seikatsu"; Sugi, *Kanzen fukkoku Sugi Kōji jijo den*, 12–16.
[39] Shizuoka Kenritsu Chūō Toshokan Aoi Bunko, *Edo bakufu kyūzō yōsho mokuroku*; Nichiran Gakkai, *Edo bakufu kyūzō ransho sōgō mokuroku*; Mukai, "Bakufu igai no ransho to mokuroku," 41–50.

of reception. Identical titles referenced by Dutch learning practitioners, for example, tended to belie the existence of multiple editions, the differences between which were often responsible for divergent interpretations in Japan. In other cases, especially those of translation, scholars frequently compared editions against one another, juxtaposing their contents. In contrast to those who would hastily search for signs of agentive invention, we now know that patterns of access and circulation, as well as bibliographical practices, were more often than not responsible for differences between Japanese works of Dutch learning and the European-language texts they studied.[40]

Casting the same attentive bibliographical eye onto the *Eerste beginselen* reveals its own surprises. The text in question was made "in service of the schools of the Dutch East Indies" and printed in the port of Semarang in 1844 by Oliphant & Co., Semarang's first printing house and a specialist in "small schoolbooks" (*schoolboekjes*). The printing house enjoyed a close relationship with Dirk Cornelis de Bruin (1814–94), the government official tasked with overseeing colonial education in Semarang. In addition to textbooks on geography and history, it was De Bruin who, though unnamed on the title page, authored the *Eerste beginselen* as part of a four-volume series of graduated language texts for Dutch East Indies schools.[41]

Printing houses like those of Oliphant & Co. were part of broader changes in Dutch colonial policy toward Indonesia during the nineteenth century, forged in interaction with British rule from 1811 to 1815. Arriving in Batavia, Stamford Raffles censured the Dutch for neglecting to elevate colonial society to European standards. His remedy entailed the establishment of a newspaper and a theater, as well as the importation of "school books."[42] Of special concern for Raffles was the perceived lack of education for native females. Given that European males in Indonesia commonly coupled with local females, it was necessary to raise the level of the latter to guarantee standards of childrearing.[43] A significant portion of the schoolbooks imported by the Raffles administration therefore purported to teach proper manners and graces to women.[44]

---

[40] Matsuda, *Yōgaku no shoshiteki kenkyū*; Nomura, "Choyakusha no takken ka"; Hsiung, "Chi no rekishigaku to kindai sekai no tanjō."

[41] Van der Chijs, *Proeve eener Ned. Indische Bibliographie*, 76–123, 246–59; De Bruin, *Fragmentarische herinneringen*.

[42] Taylor, *Social World of Batavia*, 102–10; Tiffin, "Raffles and the Barometer of Civilisation."

[43] Earl, *Eastern Seas*, 18, 26.

[44] *Java Government Gazette*: "New Books for Sale at the Govt. Office" (1:29, 12 September 1812); "New Books for Sale at the Govt. Office" (1:33, 10 October 1812); "School Books," (3:107, 12 March 1814); "School Books," (3:110, 2 April 1814).

A return to Dutch rule by 1816 intensified these projects. Unlike its prior days as a VOC trading station, Indonesia now fell under the direct administrative control of the Netherlands, accelerating the growth of European settler society and tripling the population of Batavia alone by mid-century. The "printing press" (*drukpers*) became a catchword in discussions of "development and civilization." Visiting Oliphant & Co. in 1847, one Dutch observer lamented an earlier "system of government ... wherein the Indians of the archipelago were wronged for centuries"; that "regarded the people not as humans ... but as masses, destined to always remain what they are." It was this administration that had "hate[d] the printing press as the most bitter of enemies."[45] And it was this condition that a new vanguard of schoolbooks, supplied by local publishers such as Oliphant & Co., would now reform.

Dutch actors looked to the overseas colonial market – especially the Batavian secondhand book market – when acquiring items for private trade with Japan. By the first quarter of the nineteenth century, merchants consciously advised one another that higher profits in Japan might be obtained by purchasing books in the East Indies rather than purchasing and moving items from Europe.[46] Through this, the political economy of the colonial print sphere structured Dutch learning scholars' access to texts in Japan.

Japanese actors, too, were aware that the European-language texts made available to them were the product of global changes in a connected educational landscape. Prior research has already remarked on the shared affinity among Dutch learning practitioners for textbooks produced by the Maatschappij tot Nut van't Algemeen (Society for Public Utility), founded in North Holland in 1784 to encourage public elementary education.[47] That Dutch learning scholars regularly studied, recommended, reprinted, and translated the Maatschappij's introductory science texts – for example, the *Volksnatuurkunde*, *Natuurkundig schoolboek*, and *Handleiding tot de kennis der natuur* – has been used in turn to draw parallels between Dutch learning and Enlightenment "popular science" in Europe.[48] To this portrait must be added, however, the Maatschappij's prominence in Dutch colonial print culture. By 1800, branches of the organization had been established in Suriname and the Cape of Good Hope; by mid-century, across different towns and cities in Java.

---

[45] Van Hoëvell, *Reis over Java, Madura en Bali*, 1:104–5.

[46] Nagazumi, *18-seiki no ransho chūmon*, 37.

[47] Ikeda, "Oranda 'Kyōeki kaisha'-hon ni tsuite"; Yoshida, "Jūhasseiki Oranda ni okeru kagaku"; Satō, "Iwayuru 'yōgaku ronsō,'" 12–13.

[48] Yoshida, "Jūhasseiki Oranda ni okeru kagaku," 80–91.

There, the Maatschappij collaborated with local publishers, including Semarang's Oliphant & Co., to reprint and disseminate their works in the field.[49] Dutch learning practitioners such as Koseki San'ei (1787–1839) observed closely the Maatschappij's history, growth, and spread, praising its efforts to spread "affordable and easy-to-understand books on all arts and sciences."[50] Others such as Sakuma Shōzan (1811–64), famed for championing a combination of "Eastern morality" with "Western sciences and techniques" (tōyō no dōtoku, seiyō no gakugei), were equally as observant of these trends, albeit less forthcoming in their admiration. In his search for Dutch works on mathematics, Shōzan complained about the resultant proliferation of elementary-level textbooks, with more advanced works fit for the university level (hogeschool) crowded out of the import market.[51]

Teased already in this brief unraveling of the Eerste beginselen is another history of Dutch learning. The foundations of this other history were already apparent in the work of Nagazumi Yōko, who showed that the decline of the VOC and the escalation of Anglo-Dutch rivalry over Asian maritime trade unmistakably spurred Dutch learning's growth. Dwindling oversight and weak markets for official commodities resulted in increasing VOC tolerance of "private" or kambang trade (wakini bōeki). Listed on the record as "personal belongings," the most lucrative private trade articles were in fact those books, instruments, and artifacts on which Dutch learning subsequently thrived.[52] Anglo-Dutch competition furthermore promoted the activities of local learned societies that would generate the knowledge necessary to exploit natural resources from the region. The Batavian Society of Arts and Sciences (Bataviaasch Genootschap der Konsten en Wetenschappen), for instance, was established in Dutch Indonesia out of a perceived sense of having fallen behind British Bengal's Asiatic Society.[53] These societies propelled the collection and study of botanical specimens, astronomical observations, and climatological data from Japan, creating the grounds for collaboration with Japanese scholars.[54] Tsukahara Tōgo has boldly synthesized these trends

---

[49] See Verslag van den staat der afdeeling Samarang van de Maatschappij.
[50] Koseki, Chūjinsho, 396.
[51] Sakuma Shōzan to Katsu Kaishū (Ansei 3[1856].3.22), in Katsu Kaishū Zenshū Kankōkai, Katsu Kaishū zenshū, Sakuma Shōzan Letter 4.
[52] Nagazumi, "Kaisha no bōeki kara kojin no bōeki"; Nagazumi, "Personal Trade at the Dutch Factory in Japan."
[53] Boxer, Jan Compagnie in War and Peace, 99; Boomgaard, "For the Common Good"; Groot, Van Batavia naar Weltvreden, 45–101.
[54] Tsukahara, "Rangaku, chikyū ondanka"; Tsukahara et al., "Kagakushi no sokumen kara saikentō shita Philipp Franz von Siebold."

by branding Dutch learning a mode of "colonial science."[55] Tokugawa scholars were complicit in a "Batavian paradigm" of knowledge production forged by the Dutch empire.[56]

Such studies from the Japan field offer ripe potential for dialogue with a growing body of scholarship on the circulation of knowledge and information in an "age of global communication."[57] Under the banner of "circulation," these studies have stressed the ways in which knowledge was necessarily mediated and brokered – and thus created anew – in its movement, whether through the transformation of physical artifacts or the performance of multiple translations. Attention to the forgotten middlemen and intermediary artifacts that facilitated circulation in turn highlights the agentive role of a range of non-Western informants, artisans, merchants, scribes, and printers.[58] The outcome, increasingly evident, is a "relocation" of modern knowledge production away from European metropoles and "centers of calculation" into a chain of previously passive "peripheries." In place of an old binary of "West" and "non-West," of "great Western thinkers" against their non-Western *interprètes*, our accounts now seek the multipolar and multisited.[59]

On this basis, the putatively "Western" knowledge studied by late Tokugawa scholars can be seen as a kind of knowledge which took form outside of the "West," shaped by the shifting fate of colonial education between empires. Specifically, putatively "Western" knowledge was forged in the transimperial educational commons.[60] This commons was transimperial because it involved the porting of resources across American, British, Dutch, and Qing networks in the Pacific – by merchants, missionaries and their converts, foreign and native publishers and printers. This commons was educational because the resources circulated and exchanged were above all textbooks – meant for use in schools, for self-study, or, more commonly, for both. Finally, this commons was a commons because well into the 1870s, books circulated outside of any clear intellectual property regimes characteristic of print capitalism. Books in the transimperial educational commons were "textual resources over which one could exercise a common right"

[55] Tsukahara, "'Kagaku to teikokushugi'"; Tsukahara, "Westernization from Different Angles"; Tsukahara, "Tenbō"; Tsukahara, "Unpublished Manuscript."
[56] Legêne, *De bagage van Blomhoff en Van Breugel*; Weber, *Hybrid Ambitions*; Goss, *Floracrats*; van der Velde, *Lifelong Passion*.
[57] Bayly, *Birth of the Modern World*, 19–21; Bayly, *Empire and Information*.
[58] Schaffer et al., *Brokered World*; Fan, *British Naturalists*.
[59] Raj, *Relocating Modern Science*; Raj, "Beyond Postcolonialism"; Subrahmanyam, "Global Intellectual History."
[60] This is a term of my own coinage.

rather than copyright; "they were texts in which everyone could share and have a share."[61]

Adaptation, reprinting, and translation in a transimperial educational commons was an infrastructural condition of possibility for the late Tokugawa study of the West. As a result, we can examine how different forces within the transimperial educational commons shaped the "Western" texts of Dutch and Western learning, and how Japanese readers and translators negotiated with these forces. Among various possibilities, this opens unexplored questions concerning the gendering of Dutch learning texts. Noted already has been the importance to Raffles's initiatives in Batavia of a project that would discipline native female readers according to a regime of genteel motherhood. Compounding this was the centrality of the mother-child relationship as a framework for elementary education: preprimary and primary schooling was a gendered domain. We thus observe two trends. First, among the European-language works studied by Japanese scholars, female authors prevailed. The series of geography textbooks, for example, by Sarah S. Cornell, corresponding member of the American Geographical and Statistical Society, not only was translated, reprinted, and excerpted from the 1860s well into the mid-Meiji period but also served as the principal source for Fukuzawa Yukichi's *All the Countries of the World* (*Sekai kuni zukushi*, 1869) and the frontispiece to his *Conditions of the West* (*Seiyō jijō*, 1866).[62] The *First Lessons in Natural Philosophy* of Mary A. Swift, headmistress of a Connecticut girls' seminary, found widespread popularity after Edo publishers reprinted it in 1867.[63] How was the prevalence of female authorship registered – or, as most cases would suggest, erased – as these texts moved into the male-dominated intellectual world of nineteenth-century Japan? Second, among those texts of "Western knowledge" consumed in Japan, a significant majority had originally been composed and marketed "for women and children." Fukuzawa's popularizing activities again serve as a telling indicator. At the start of his *Illustrated Explanation of the Sciences* (*Kinmō kyūri zukai*, 1868), we find a frontispiece depicting a scene of girls gathered in reading with their teacher (Figure 11.2). This detail is rendered even more curious by the fact that Fukuzawa had envisioned a primarily male readership for his work. What relationship might these male readers have established with the image which greeted them? By understanding how texts of the transimperial

---

[61] Burton and Hofmeyr, "Introduction," 5–6, 19.
[62] Cornell, *Chigaku shoho*; "Cornell's Primary Geography"; Taketani, *US Women Writers*, 41–42.
[63] Swift, *Rigaku shoho*.

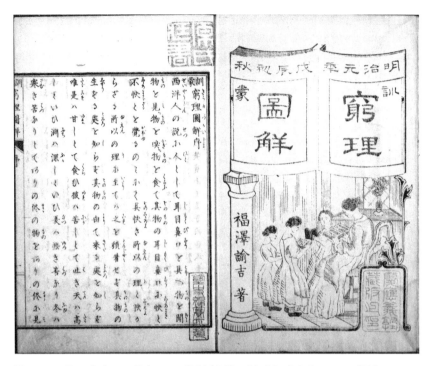

Figure 11.2 Frontispiece to Fukuzawa Yukichi, *Kinmō kyūri zukai*. Courtesy of Fukuzawa Memorial Center for Modern Japanese Studies, Keiō University.

educational commons structured a set of subject positions between women, children, and colonial pupils, we may better understand how Japanese scholars grasped their relationship to other readers situated outside of Western knowledge – readers who were to be disciplined into its regime of knowing.

Analyzing Dutch and Western learning through the transimperial educational commons also allows us to bring late Tokugawa intellectual history into closer conversation with new strands of research on how the circulation of colonial science and medicine constructed modern understandings of race.[64] Slavery remained legal in the Dutch Indies until 1860, forming an integral part of the geographies and travelogues consumed by Japanese scholars, as well as their direct encounters with Dutch trade in Nagasaki.[65] From these emerged a protoanthropology of human difference centered on *kurobō* – "black boys" – a Japanese gloss of the Dutch *zwarte jongen*. Morishima Chūryō (1754–1810), for

[64] Seth, *Difference and Disease*; Poskett, *Materials of the Mind*.
[65] Yamada, "On the Genealogy of *Kokujin*"; Leupp, "Images of Black People," 4–5.

instance, included in the first volume of his *Miscellaneous Stories of the Red-Hairs* (*Kōmō zatsuwa*, 1787) a series of entries concerning the *kurobō* and their customs. From countries of the "South Seas" such as Jakarta, Bengal, Malaya, and Malabar, Morishima tells readers, "young children are abducted and sold to the barbarians," and these children are "by nature quite stupid." Thereafter follow observations on the languages, dress, and hygienic habits of enslaved peoples – including notes on hygiene surrounding defecation.[66] Meanwhile, Ōtsuki Gentaku's *A Clarification of Misunderstandings in Accounts of the Dutch* (*Ransetsu benwaku*, 1787) would seek to explain "black boys" as a product of their "very hot climates." For Ōtsuki, this suggested adaptation: there was no reason to believe that "black boys" should be by necessity "lowly" and "foolish."[67] The concept of "acclimatization" itself was emerging simultaneously in Europe, metamorphosing from an explanation for the survival, death, and change in flora and fauna transplanted to "exotic" environments into a model that might account for human variation.[68] We can therefore see through Dutch and Western learning the ways in which earlier chorographies of civilized and barbarous interacted with contemporaneous shifts in key concepts that would occupy paradigmatic status at the center of colonial science and its explanations of racial difference.

Gender and race are but two examples. Ample room remains to interrogate how European texts consumed in Japan implicated Dutch and Western learning in wider regimes of colonial knowledge production. More locally, within East Asia itself, the transimperial educational commons also challenges established models of Sino-Japanese intellectual relations in the nineteenth century. Indeed, sensitivity to mediation and brokerage in the transimperial educational commons reveals that, more often than not, Japanese scholars consciously favored texts composed in literary Sinitic (*kanbun*) that emerged from the Qing empire's own engagements with Western knowledge, prioritizing these over European-language originals. The next section outlines the dynamics of interaction between late-Tokugawa political needs and the conditions of textual production in China during the mid-nineteenth century.

"Chinese" Textbooks of "Western" Knowledge

Central to the received account of Dutch learning has been a narrative of supersession. Noted already at the start of this chapter was Sugita Genpaku's

---

[66] Morishima, *Kōmō zatsuwa*, 457–58.
[67] Ōtsuki Gentaku, "Misunderstandings about the Dutch," in Goodman, "Dutch Learning," 380–81.
[68] Harrison, "'Tender Frame of Man'"; Osborne, "Acclimatizing the World."

call to "discard Chinese books." Noted frequently, too, in secondary literature is the choice among Dutch learning practitioners to consciously reject the name "Middle Kingdom" (*Chūgoku*) in favor of the Latin-derived "Shina" as a designation for China – this latter term, over the course of Japan's modern history, eventually taking on a pejorative function.[69] Sugita did admittedly entertain, in his late works, the possibility that Chinese knowledge was of benefit to Dutch learning. Nevertheless, supersession persisted in his metaphors. "Chinese [learning] had trained the Japanese mind and had made a foundation whereupon Dutch was able to make a rapid stride," Sugita tells us, and in doing so paints a portrait of edifices past on which a more glorious future is to be erected.[70]

To adopt this trope of Chinese past and European future, however, is to ignore the ways in which regionality continued to shape practices and understandings of circulation integral to intellectual life in Japan. Tokugawa scholars, including those who aggressively pursued Western knowledge, framed their actions in relation to a broader Sinosphere.[71] Indeed, for all his ideological pronouncements, Sugita himself advocated for the use of literary Sinitic when translating Dutch, in the express hope that Dutch learning texts from Japan might find readers on the continent.[72] Western knowledge may have held advantages, but Japan remained resolutely part of a "Chinese" geography of textual exchange.

Thus, even as scholars in Japan voiced increasing interest in Western knowledge in the 1850s, textual circulation through the Sinosphere maintained pivotal importance. Yet the fabric of this Sinosphere, as well as its particular relation to Western knowledge, had also changed radically in the years following the Treaties of Nanjing and Humen (1842–43) in the aftermath of the First Opium War. Ports such as Hong Kong, Ningbo, and Shanghai transformed into major hubs for educational initiatives, spearheaded first by the London Missionary Society and the American Presbyterian Mission. This was followed by Qing attempts in the 1860s to develop institutions that would train experts versed in European languages and sciences, starting with the Beijing Interpreters' College (Jingshi Tongwenguan).[73] The translation,

---

[69] Maeno, *Kanrei higen*, 152; Shimizu, "Ka-i shisō to jūkyū seiki."
[70] Sugita, *Dawn of Western Science in Japan*, 51–52.
[71] For an analysis of Tokugawa intellectual history from the perspective of an "intellectually Confucian-centered, classical Chinese language delivered, trans-Asian Sinosphere," see Paramore, "Transnational Archive of the Sinosphere."
[72] *Yōi shinsho.*
[73] Wright, *Translating Science*; Elman, *On Their Own Terms*, 281–395; Elman, *Cultural History of Modern Science*, 100–131, 158–97.

compilation, and printing of pedagogical texts naturally formed a core part of these efforts. And these texts made their presence ever more felt in Japan after 1858, as new shipping lines and merchant capital bound its treaty ports to those in China. In his 1860 guide to Yokohama, the Western learning scholar Yanagawa Shunsan (1832–70) dedicated a section to the topic of "Imported Books." The imports he described, however, were not European-language texts. "The United States and Britain," he informs readers, "have of late dedicated themselves to the mastery of Chinese learning ... the number of works in Chinese published by them in Shanghai and Hong Kong is overwhelmingly large." Yanagawa then went on to list titles he had encountered, ranging from introductory manuals of natural science, geography, and history to popular miscellanies, magazines, and newspapers. With only one exception, these works were all put out by American Presbyterian Mission and London Missionary Society presses in Hong Kong, Ningbo, and Shanghai, or else produced as textbooks for the Beijing Interpreters' College.[74]

At the very same time as he documented American and British "mastery of Chinese learning," Yanagawa was serving as headmaster (tōdori) of the Institute for the Investigation of Barbarian Books. The institute had opened its doors in 1856, established by the shogunate as its principal Western learning organ. In addition to serving as home to Tsuda Mamichi, Nishi Amane, Katō Hiroyuki, and other key figures who would go on to define the intellectual landscape of the Meiji period, the institute became one of the bases for the foundation of Tokyo Imperial University.[75] We have then a site fraught with symbolism within the genealogy of modern Western knowledge in Japan. That its headmaster, Yanagawa, evinced such interest for new texts coming from China troubles this image. It suggests that in order to truly understand "Japan's turn to the West," we must look to how the Tokugawa shogunate in its closing years, and then a nascent Meiji regime, turned to materials produced in a Sinosphere through which knowledge from American, British, and Qing imperial educational projects circulated.

One might at first attribute this phenomenon to a simple virtue of accessibility. Books on Western knowledge in literary Sinitic, produced in Qing port towns and for new educational institutions, were certainly cheaper than European-language texts. They were also ostensibly easier to master from

[74] Kinkei Rōjin, Yokohama hanjōki, 16a–17a.
[75] Kurasawa, Bakumatsu kyōikushi, 1:77–326; Jansen, "Rangaku and Westernization"; Hsiung, "Daigaku Nankō, Kaisei Gakkō."

a linguistic standpoint.[76] However, this line of reasoning falls apart once we examine a deeper logic behind Yanagawa's interest in these texts – a deeper logic that points to ways in which the dynamics of the transimperial educational commons at times aligned with ideological prerogatives in Japan.

These ideological prerogatives were embedded in the very name of the Institute for the Investigation of Barbarian Books itself. This name was selected only after a series of protracted negotiations that explicitly rejected proposals such as "School (or Institute) of Dutch Learning" (*rangakkō, rangakkan, rangakusho*) and "Institute of Western Learning" (*seiyō gakkō*). In fact, shogunal advisers counseled that references to "Western learning" should be avoided in favor of names signaling that this new institution was to be a site for conducting various forms of research necessary for the Tokugawa state.[77]

Indicative within these debates over naming was an early proposal to call the institute Shokugata-kan.[78] The term was a direct reference to the Zhou dynasty Zhifang Shi, rendered often into English as the "Official of Maps and Tributes" or the "Official in Charge of the Cardinal Directions." As detailed in the *Rites of Zhou*, the Zhifang Shi was a bureaucratic post responsible for producing foreign intelligence and administering tributary relations. Building on this, Japanese shogunal advisers explicitly recommended, in an 1854 policy memo, that "insofar as the function of this institution is primarily to know the condition of the enemy and meet [state] needs, it should follow the Zhifang Shi of the Zhou, and be subordinate to Chinese learning."[79] Put simply, the shogunate viewed the Institute for the Investigation of Barbarian Books not as a site for "Western knowledge" but as an organ of foreign relations – one contained within a paradigm of Chinese learning.

A need to contain the "Western" through the "Chinese" was part of a broadly shared anxiety among Tokugawa officials that any encouragement of Western learning required mechanisms which would guard against scholars "sliding into barbarian [ways]."[80] One of the primary mechanisms agreed upon was to limit admission to the Institute for the Investigation of Barbarian Books to only those applicants who could pass an exam in the Chinese classics.

---

[76] This is the view taken in, for example, Clements, *Cultural History of Translation*, 200–211.

[77] Kurasawa, *Bakumatsu kyōikushi*, 1:80–98; Ōkubo Ichiō to Katsu Kaishū (Ansei 3[1856].4.6), in Katsu Kaishū Zenshū Kankōkai, *Katsu Kaishū zenshū*, Ōkubo Ichiō Letter 3; Tsuboi Shinryō to Sado Miyoshi (Ansei 1[1854].4.11, Ansei 1[1854].10.4, Ansei 2[1855].9.4), in Miyaji, *Bakumatsu ishin fūun tsūshin*.

[78] Kurasawa, *Bakumatsu kyōikushi*, 1:91.

[79] Quoted in Seki, "Hayashi-ke," 26.

[80] Seki, "Hayashi-ke"; Kurasawa, *Bakumatsu kyōikushi*, 1:85–86, 96.

In the words of the scholar Hirose Kyokusō, "Barbarian books may be read only after one has learned to interpret the Four Books and Six Classics."[81] Missionary print in literary Sinitic served as a continuation of this function. According to Ōkubo Ichiō (1817–88), the second headmaster of the Institute for the Investigation of Barbarian Books, these texts were "quite difficult to read unless one was simultaneously versed in both Chinese and Western learning."[82] The crux of the matter was not one of accessibility, whether economic or linguistic. Much to the contrary, missionary print in literary Sinitic was understood as a means to curtail access, limiting readership to those who had proper training in the Chinese classics.

This attitude toward the subordination of Western to Chinese learning paved the way for an unexpected convergence between Tokugawa needs and missionary policies concerning textbook production in China. The case of the American Presbyterian Mission serves as an emblematic example. After it relocated its China mission from Macau to the new treaty port of Ningbo in the summer of 1845 and opened its first school, discussions mounted as to what texts should be used in class. These discussions centered around two questions: whether education should aim to foster English-language literacy, and whether to "expell [sic] altogether from our catalogue of school books, such [books] as all Chinese scholars study" or else "devote a large proportion of time to their study."[83]

The first of these questions was resolved in favor of avoiding English-language education. The argument against English began by highlighting the unique circumstances of the China mission, particularly the prevalence of unscrupulous traders – especially opium traders – in Chinese port towns such as Ningbo. English fluency "would expose the Chinese lad to tempting offers from foreign merchants engaged in the Opium trade, or perhaps from the Chinese themselves engaged in illegal traffic with foreigners."

Missionaries then continued to contrast the China field with that of India. London Missionary Society activities in India had thus far been the most fruitful field for education in English. The Presbyterians, however, and later the London Missionary Society itself, grew skeptical that India policy might apply to China. A legacy of East India Company rule in India had made English a

---

[81] Hirose, *Kyūkei sōdō*, 110.

[82] Ōkubo Ichiō to Katsu Kaishū (Keiō 1[1865].10.19), in Katsu Kaishū Zenshū Kankōkai, *Katsu Kaishū zenshū*, Ōkubo Ichiō Letter 29.

[83] "Committee appointed to consider the propriety of introducing native Chinese works into our schools, and also to recommend such books as may be deemed suitable" (October 1845). Presbyterian Board of Foreign Missions (PCUSA). Board of Foreign Missions Correspondence, vol. 2, no. 125.

"necessary qualification" for natives who hoped to obtain important posts. The growing number of government and native schools catering to this "desire to acquire the language of their rulers" meant that missionaries were "forced to teach English in order to compete."[84] Neither of these conditions obtained for China. Despite increased American and British presence, the Ningbo missionaries deemed it unlikely that English would ever obtain the same prestige as Chinese itself. And this, again, might cause students trained in English, but unable to find a position of social standing, to enter the opium trade as a lucrative substitute. Ultimately, an English education would "enable the opium merchants to carry on their nefarious traffic with the greater advantage" and "thro[w] young men in the way of temptations which must almost certainly result in the shipwreck of their souls." "This consideration," the missionaries admitted, "weighs more heavily upon the mind of your committee than any other which has been presented."[85]

As a result, missionary textbook policy in Chinese port towns and the Tokugawa shogunate's goals fortuitously converged. Written in a manner so as to complement an educational program of cultural-linguistic literacy in literary Sinitic, missionary print promised a means to open access to Western knowledge while confining it to those who already had a firm basis in Chinese learning. Surviving manuscripts confirm that prominent institute scholars often worked through literary Sinitic into European languages rather than directly with European languages themselves. In Mitsukuri Genpo's (1799–1863) journals circa 1859, we discover reading notes from *A Brief Account of the Earth* (*Diqiu shuolüe*, 1856), an introductory geography textbook compiled by the missionary Richard Quaterman Way (1819–95) and printed at the American Presbyterian Mission Press in Ningbo. Next to terms and phrases from the *Brief Account*, Mitsukuri indicated possible Dutch translations. These translations were then compared to terms that appeared in the indices of Dutch publications – in this case, the indices to *The Earth* (*De Aardbol*), a magazine of popular geography and ethnology. Later parts of these reading notes reveal that he compared formulations in the *Brief Account* with passages from the *Chinese-Western Almanac* (*Zhongxi tongshu*), a literary Sinitic text produced by the London Missionary Society in Shanghai. Throughout this, Mitsukuri also worked through Chinese phonology to transcribe approximate English

---

[84] *Report of the Committee in English Instruction* (October 1845), Presbyterian Board of Foreign Missions (PCUSA). Board of Foreign Missions Correspondence, vol. 2, no. 127.
[85] *Report of the Committee in English Instruction* (October 1845), Presbyterian Board of Foreign Missions (PCUSA). Board of Foreign Missions Correspondence, vol. 2, no. 127.

sounds for proper names, especially those of places.[86] Literary Sinitic was a site that mediated the study of Dutch and English.

Moreover, Mitsukuri's work on Way's textbook appears to have been one part of a shogunal project that tasked institute scholars with producing new editions of works on Western knowledge in literary Sinitic for republication in Japan. These new editions bore the imprimatur of shogunal sponsorship, labeled as *kanpan*, or "official prints." The term designated a system whereby the shogunate funded the production of woodblocks, then licensed these out to private printers and publishers. On the one hand, the "official prints" system offered control over textual content; the Tokugawa in the end retained ownership over the physical blocks. On the other hand, the "official prints" system guaranteed that texts which the shogunate deemed important, but which otherwise might not appeal to the immediate commercial interests of publishers, would be regularly printed and disseminated. Over the course of Tokugawa history, the majority of "official prints" comprised approved editions of the Four Books and Six Classics.[87] By the late 1850s, texts of Western knowledge in literary Sinitic had entered this shogunally approved canon.

Missionary works were the first to do so. From this starting point, shogunally approved "official prints" came to include, by the mid-1860s, textbooks produced for use at the Beijing Interpreters' College. Most prominent among these was the *Public Law of the Myriad Countries* (*Wanguo gongfa*, 1864–65), edited by W. A. P. Martin, headmaster and professor at the Interpreters' College. The book notoriously established much of the modern Sino-Japanese legal terminology that persists to this day.[88] Martin's *Introduction to Natural Philosophy* (*Gewu rumen*) was also the object of shogunal attention, appearing as an "official print" through the labor of Yanagawa Shunsan himself.[89] All the while editing and annotating these works for Japanese audiences, scholars at the Institute for the Investigation of Barbarian Books studied reports of ongoing curricular changes at the Beijing Interpreters' College. Whereas the institute lacked any fixed curricular structure, the Beijing Interpreters' College had by 1865 introduced courses of study in disciplinary specializations, namely astronomy, chemistry, mathematics, and political economy. This served as a point of reference when, from 1872 onward, the early Meiji state embarked on reforms to convert the Institute for the Investigation of Barbarian Books

[86] *Chikyū setsuryaku soshō.*
[87] Fukui, *Edo bakufu kankōbutsu*, 3–4.
[88] Liu, *Clash of Empires*, 108–39; Takahara, "Kaiseijo-han 'Bankoku kōhō.'"
[89] Martin, *Kakubutsu nyūmon.*

into a modern university. At this time, we also see several instances of institutional poaching from the Beijing Interpreters' College. Consider, for instance, Émile Lépissier (1826–74). Born in Paris and previously in the employ of the French National Observatory, Lépissier arrived in Beijing in 1867 to take up a professorship in astronomy at the Beijing Interpreters' College.[90] Consider, too, Divie Bethune McCartee (1820–1900), an American Presbyterian missionary who through his friendship with W. A. P. Martin came into the employ of the Beijing Interpreters' College.[91] In 1872, both were hired away to Japan to teach at the Kaisei School (Kaisei Gakkō) – the name given to the new incarnation of the Institute for the Investigation of Barbarian Books. There, Lépissier became Japan's first *professeur de mécanique et d'astronomie*; McCartee became the school's professor of natural history. Notably, within deliberations to hire McCartee, Meiji bureaucrats flagged as an advantage his "skill[s] in Chinese learning."[92] Far from the supersession of China by Japan, Qing institutions served as valuable resources, whether for emulation or poaching. Japanese "Westernization" looked not only to the West itself but to analogous models in the transimperial educational commons.

Western Knowledge and Global Modernity

A similar tale as the above might be told for technologies and expert practices, for here too patterns of circulation within the transimperial educational commons brokered the movement of putatively "Western" knowledge to Japan. Remaining within the world of printing, we note again the confluence of Dutch colonial infrastructures and the missionary field in China. Histories of modern Japan's printing industry point to Motoki Shōzō's (1824–75) activities in Nagasaki in the Bakumatsu period. Motoki's equipment and know-how, however, particularly in the realm of typecasting and electrotyping, came from two exchanges: with George Indermaur (1831–88) of the government printing station in Batavia and with William Gamble (1830–86), head of the Presbyterian Mission Press in Shanghai. Both Indermaur and Gamble made extended visits to Nagasaki in connection with the shogunate's Naval

---

[90] Nakamura and Débarbat, "Tenkyūgi."
[91] Anson Burlingame to US Legation, Peking, 7 March 1865. RG-177-1-2 D.B.M. McCartee Family Papers. On McCartee's career generally, see McCartee, "Western Scholar's Reasons for Coming to China." McCartee also provides a curriculum vitae of his career up to September 1877 in D. B. McCartee to G. Wiley Wells, Esq., 22 September 1877. RG-177-1-2 D.B.M. McCartee Family Papers.
[92] *Gan'yō ruisan.*

Training Institute (Kaigun Denshūjo).[93] A parallel movement of expertise took place in Yokohama through *maibian* – Chinese servants brought over by European settlers. A glance at Yokohama's burgeoning scene of foreign books and newspapers reveals Chinese compositors and press workers, many of whom had earlier cut their teeth in treaty port printing houses on the continent. Longer decades of experience with Western manufacturing processes meant that Yokohama's Chinese servants, often unnamed in the record, were crucial conduits for skills in a range of commercial fields, including Western-style carpentry and furniture-making.[94]

To these examples may be added fresh insights from a new crop of scholars who, furnished with a broader array of languages and a greater desire to speak to historiography outside "East Asian" studies, are extending the geographical scope of the transimperial educational commons.[95] American, British, Dutch, and Qing empires have been the focus of this chapter, but relations between the Tokugawa shogunate and French and Ottoman empires deserve equal attention.[96] Jules Chanoine (1835–1915), arriving in Japan in 1867 at the head of a military mission to train the shogunal army, brought with him years of experience from service in the Taiping Rebellion, as well as a network of colleagues involved in similar programs of military modernization worldwide. Corresponding with military schools in Cairo and Alexandria, Chanoine drew analogies between regions: in his mind, "Yeddo" was "just like Egypt."[97] Missionary education in Beirut also informed the creation of Dōshisha University in Kyoto.[98] An especially fertile direction for future research thus involves linking Japan with semicolonial and "crypto-colonial" spaces. Quasi-autonomous princely states in India, the Egyptian Khedivate, and Ottoman Lebanon, or else countries subject to unequal treaties such as China and Thailand, all embarked on simultaneous projects of "Western knowledge" as part of their defensive foreign policy. A translocal perspective analyzing these sites together as part of a shared moment is necessary.[99]

---

[93] Nakane, *Nihon insatsu gijutsushi*, 201–6; Kawada, "Uiriamu Gamburu"; Kawada, "Oranda denrai no kappan jutsu."
[94] Nishikawa and Itō, *Kaikoku Nihon to Yokohama Chūkagai*, 62–85, 131–50.
[95] The recent translation of Kapil Raj into Japanese has also begun to spur similar discussions among historians of Dutch and Western learning based in Japan. See, for instance, "Rangaku no sotogawa."
[96] Sims, *French Policy Towards the Bakufu and Meiji Japan*.
[97] Colson to Chanoine (4 February 1868), in Chanoine, *Documents*.
[98] Kobiljski, "Le modèle américain ou une modernité partagée?"
[99] Elshakry, "When Science Became Western"; Herzfeld, "Absence Presence."

It is in this sense that the problem of the "modern" resurfaces. For the "early modernity" of the Tokugawa period was, in its latter stages, part and parcel of an emerging condition of global modernity. Sidestepping the teleology of stadial histories, as well as the reification of difference in postmodern and postcolonial histories of "alternate" and "alternative" modernities, the global modern can be understood as a process of coordination and conflict between societies as the speed and density of their interdependencies intensified. In place of normative institutional criteria through which to *compare* societies as "more" or "less" modern, global modernity privileges the complexity and unevenness of their shifting *connections*.[100]

To emphasize these connections is not to discount internal factors. The accepted periodization of Dutch and Western learning, which sees the movement reaching maturity first in the Bunka and Bunsei periods (1804–30), has usefully identified a number of domestic catalysts. Urbanization in particular, accompanied by rural economic crisis and famine, is routinely singled out as the backdrop for a pluralization of the Tokugawa intellectual field, allowing Dutch, Chinese, and national learning (*kokugaku*) to crystallize their identity and mutually position themselves against one another.[101]

Yet precisely this period was also one marked by "world crisis" and an "age of revolutions," the geopolitical rearrangements of which were keenly followed by Dutch learning scholars themselves.[102] Dutch and Western learning were equally a consequence of this conjuncture, arising at a moment when information orders and knowledge networks witnessed rapid global expansion, rendering diverse new texts and resources available to Japan. Moreover, these information orders and knowledge networks were uncontained by any single overarching polarity. The late eighteenth-century world, in C. A. Bayly's words, "was still a multi-centered one," and throughout much of the next century, "European domination was only partial and temporary."[103] Dutch and Western learning grew within this space of indeterminateness – a "caesura" between world systems.[104] Western knowledge in late Tokugawa Japan was thus, ironically, the product of growing entanglements between spaces outside of the "West" itself. New histories of Dutch and Western learning therefore have much to tell us of how Japan attempted to advantageously

[100] Bayly, *Birth of the Modern World*, 1, 11–12.
[101] Najita, "History and Nature"; Iwasaki Chikatsugu, *Nihon kinsei shisōshi*, 2:271–85.
[102] Blussé, *Visible Cities*, 6–8; Armitage and Subrahmanyam, *Age of Revolutions*, esp. xix–xxvi; Bayly, *Birth of the Modern World*, 86–120; Iwashita, *Edo no Naporeon densetsu*.
[103] Bayly, *Birth of the Modern World*, 3.
[104] Yamashita, *Sekai shisutemu ron*, 9; Katsurajima, "'Kinsei teikoku' no kaitai."

negotiate the uncertain shifts and rearrangements of knowledge circulation during the "birth of the modern world." These new histories disturb standard categories of national history (*kokushi*), Oriental history (*tōyōshi*), and Western history (*seiyōshi*) employed in Japan.[105] Instead, they pose a paradox: that the problem of late Tokugawa engagements with Western knowledge can only be solved by examining sites both beyond the West and beyond Japan.

Bibliography

Aoki Toshiyuki and Iwabuchi Reiji, eds. *Chiiki rangaku no sōgōteki kenkyū*. Sakura: Kokuritsu Rekishi Minzoku Hakubutsukan, 2004.

Armitage, David, and Sanjay Subrahmanyam, eds. *The Age of Revolutions in Global Context, c. 1760–1840*. Basingstoke: Palgrave Macmillan, 2010.

Asakura Kamezō, ed. *Bunmei genryū sōsho*. 3 vols. Kokusho Kankōkai, 1913–14.

Ashino Hiromu. "*Rangaku kotohajime o yomu.*" *Gaikō hyōron* 24, no. 3 (1944): 37–40.

Bayly, C. A. *The Birth of the Modern World, 1780–1914*. Malden, MA: Blackwell Publishing, 2004.

   Empire and Information: Intelligence Gathering and Social Communication in India, 1780–1870. Cambridge: Cambridge University Press, 1996.

Blussé, Leonard. *Visible Cities: Canton, Nagasaki, and the Coming of the Americans*. Cambridge, MA: Harvard University Press, 2008.

Boomgaard, Peter. "For the Common Good: Dutch Institutions and Western Scholarship on Indonesia around 1800." In *Empire and Science in the Making: Dutch Colonial Scholarship in Comparative Global Perspective*, edited by Peter Boomgaard, 135–64. Basingstoke: Palgrave Macmillan, 2013.

Boxer, Charles R. *Jan Compagnie in War and Peace, 1602–1799: A Short History of the Dutch East-India Company*. Hong Kong: Heinemann Asia, 1979.

Burton, Antoinette, and Isabel Hofmeyr. "Introduction: The Spine of Empire? Books and the Making of an Imperial Commons." In *Ten Books That Shaped the British Empire*, edited by Antoinette Burton and Isabel Hofmeyr, 1–28. Durham, NC: Duke University Press, 2014.

Chanoine, Jules. *Documents pour servir à l'histoire des relations entre la France et le Japon*. N.p.: n.d.

Chikyū setsuryaku soshō. Manuscript on microfilm. No. 20, Mitsukuri Genpo/Rinshō Kankei Monjo, Kensei Shiryōshitsu, National Diet Library.

Clements, Rebekah. *A Cultural History of Translation in Early Modern Japan*. Cambridge: Cambridge University Press, 2015.

Cornell, Sarah. *Chigaku shoho/Cornell's Primary Geography, for the Use of Schools*. Edo: Watanabe, [n.d.]. Yōgaku Bunko, Waseda University Special Collections, Tokyo.

"Cornell's Primary Geography." 8-E-182. Manuscript. Yōgaku Bunko, Waseda University Special Collections, Tokyo.

---

[105] Haneda, *Atarashii sekaishi e*, 23–30.

Dai Nihon Shisō Zenshū Kankōkai, ed. *Dai Nihon shisō zenshū*. 18 vols. Dai Nihon Shisō Zenshū Kankōkai, 1931–34.

De Bruin, D. C. *Fragmentarische herinneringen uit het level van oud-gouvernements-onderwijzer D. C. de Bruin Sr*. Semarang: Semarang Drukkerij & Boekhandel, 1893.

Earl, George Windsor. *The Eastern Seas, or Voyages and Adventures in the Indian Archipelago in 1832–34*. Singapore: Oxford University Press, [1837].

Elman, Benjamin A. *A Cultural History of Modern Science in China*. Cambridge, MA: Harvard University Press, 2006.

——. *On Their Own Terms: Science in China, 1550–1900*. Cambridge, MA: Harvard University Press, 2005.

Elshakry, Marwa. "When Science Became Western: Historiographical Reflections." *Isis* 101, no. 1 (2010): 98–109.

Fan, Fa-Ti. *British Naturalists in Qing China: Science, Empire, and Cultural Encounter*. Cambridge, MA: Harvard University Press, 2004.

Frumer, Yulia. *Making Time: Astronomical Time Measurement in Tokugawa Japan*. Chicago: University of Chicago Press, 2018.

Fujii Shin. "Rangaku no rekishiteki shimei." *Koten kenkyū* 4, no. 8 (1939): 15–27.

Fujita Shigekichi. *Bunmei tōzen shi*. Self-published, 1884.

Fujita Tokutarō, Fujisawa Chikao, and Morimoto Jikichi, eds. *Nihon seishin bunka taikei*. 10 vols. Kinseidō, 1935–38.

Fujiwara Osamu. "Atarashiki seishin: Rangaku no hattatsu ni tsuite." *Koten kenkyū* 4, no. 8 (1939): 78–97.

Fukui Tamotsu. *Edo bakufu kankōbutsu*. Yūshūdō Shuppan, 1985.

Fukuoka, Maki. *The Premise of Fidelity: Science, Visuality, and the Representation of the Real in Nineteenth-Century Japan*. Stanford, CA: Stanford University Press, 2012.

[Fukuzawa Yukichi]. "Datsu-A ron." *Jiji shinpō* 917, 16 March 1885.

Fukuzawa Yukichi. *Fukuzawa Yukichi shokan shū*. Edited by Keiō Gijuku. 9 vols. Iwanami Shoten, 2001–3.

——. *Kinmō kyūri zukai*. Edo: Keiō Gijuku Dōsha, 1868. Keiō University Library, Tokyo.

Fūunji-tachi: Rangaku kakumei hen. Directed and written by Mitani Kōki. NHK. 1 January 2018.

Gänger, Stefanie. "Circulation: Reflections on Circularity, Entity, and Liquidity in the Language of Global History." *Journal of Global History* 12, no. 3 (2017): 303–18.

Gan'yō ruisan (Meiji 5[1872]/8/15), 88-2. University of Tokyo Semicentennial Collection, University of Tokyo Library, Tokyo.

Goodman, Grant, ed. "Dutch Learning." In *1600 to 2000*, edited by William Theodore de Bary, Carol Gluck, and Arthur Tiedemann, 361–89. Vol. 2 of *Sources of Japanese Tradition*. 2nd ed. New York: Columbia University Press, 2005.

Goss, Andrew. *The Floracrats; State-Sponsored Science and the Failure of the Enlightenment in Indonesia*. Madison: University of Wisconsin Press, 2011.

Groot, Hans. *Van Batavia naar Weltvreden: Het Bataviaasch Genootschap van Kunsten en Wetenschappen, 1778–1867*. Leiden: KITLV, 2009.

Haneda Masashi. *Atarashii sekaishi e: Chikyū shimin no tame no kōsō*. Iwanami Shoten, 2011.

Harrison, Mark. "'The Tender Frame of Man': Disease, Climate, and Racial Difference in India and the West Indies, 1760–1860." *Bulletin of the History of Medicine* 70, no. 1 (1996): 68–93.

Herzfeld, Michael. "The Absence Presence: Discourses of Crypto-Colonialism." *South Atlantic Quarterly* 101, no. 4 (2002): 899–926.

Hirakawa Sukehiro. "Japan's Turn to the West." In *The Nineteenth Century*, edited by Marius B. Jansen, 432–98. Vol. 5 of *The Cambridge History of Japan*. Cambridge: Cambridge University Press, 1989.

Hirose Kyokusō. *Kyūkei sōdō zuihitsu* (1855–57). In *Hyakka zuihitsu*, Vol. 1, edited by Kokusho Kankōkai, 13–184. Kokusho Kankōkai, 1917.

Hsiung, Hansun. "Chi no rekishigaku to kindai sekai no tanjō." *Edo-Meiji renzoku suru rekishi*, edited by Namikawa Kenji and Furuie Shinpei, 52–67. Fujiwara Shoten, 2018.

——— . "Daigaku Nankō, Kaisei Gakkō." In *Yōgakushi kenkyū jiten*, edited by Yōgakushi Gakkai, 180–81. Kyoto: Shibunkaku Shuppan, 2021.

——— . "'Use Me as Your Test!': Patients, Practitioners, and the Commensurability of Virtue." *Osiris* 37 (2022): 273–96.

Ichikawa Shin'ichi. "Du Français au Japonais par le truchement du Hollandais." *Waseda Daigaku daigakuin bungaku kenkyū kiyō* 29 (1993): 15–27.

Igarashi Chikara, ed. *Shōrōshō: Junsei kokugo tokuhon sankōsho*. Vol. 4. Waseda Daigaku Shuppanbu, 1934.

Ikeda Tetsurō. "Oranda 'Kyōeki kaisha'-hon ni tsuite." *Rangaku shiryō kenkyūkai kenkyū hōkoku* 67 (1963): 185–97.

Ishiguro Kyōō [Tadanori]. "Rō-shosei yori (yōsho shahon jidai no kaiko)." *Dokusho sekai* 4, no. 1 (1914): 36–39.

Itagaki Eiji. "Kaga-han no yōgaku ni kōken shita orandago jisho." *Kanazawa Daigaku shiryōkan kiyō* 4 (2006): 27–55.

Itazawa Takeo. *Mukashi no nan'yō to Nihon*. Nippon Hōsō Shuppankai, 1940.

——— . "Rangaku no keitai to yakuwari." In "Ranryō Indo." Special issue, *Taiheiyō* 3, no. 4 (1940): 50–54.

——— . *Sugita Genpaku to Rangaku kotohajime*. Nippon Hōsō Shuppankai, 1940.

Iwasaki Chikatsugu. *Nihon kinsei shisōshi josetsu*. 2 vols. Shin Nihon Shuppansha, 1997.

Iwasaki Katsumi. *Shōkōkan bunko ransho mokuroku*. Self-published, 1939.

Iwashita Testunori. *Edo no Naporeon densetsu*. Chūōkōron Shinsha, 1999.

Jackson, Terence. *Network of Knowledge: Western Science and the Tokugawa Information Revolution*. Honolulu: University of Hawai'i Press, 2015.

Jannetta, Ann. *The Vaccinators: Smallpox, Medical Knowledge, and the "Opening" of Japan*. Stanford, CA: Stanford University Press, 2007.

Jansen, Marius B. Papers. Princeton University Rare Books and Special Collections, Princeton, NJ.

——— . "Rangaku and Westernization." *Modern Asian Studies* 18, no. 4 (1984): 541–53.

Java Government Gazette.

Kakiuchi Shōzō. *Kokubun kagami: Kyōju sankōsho go-gakunen-yō*. Bungakusha, 1933.

Kakiuchi Shōzō and Nishio Minoru. *Jitsugyō gakkō kokubun shinsei kyōju sankōsho*. Vol. 5. Bungakusha, 1935.

Katsu Kaishū Zenshū Kankōkai, ed. *Katsu Kaishū zenshū*. Appendix, *Raikan to shiryō*. Kōdansha, 1994.

Katsurajima Nobuhiro. "'Kinsei teikoku' no kaitai to jūkyū seiki zenhanki no shisō dōkō." In *Kinsei*, edited by Karube Tadashi, Kurozumi Makoto, Satō Hiroo, Sueki Fumihiko, and Tajiri Yūichirō, 367–97. Vol. 3 of *Nihon shisōshi kōza*. Perikansha, 2012.

Kawada Hisanaga. "Oranda denrai no kappan jutsu." *Rangaku shiryō kenkyūkai kenkyū hōkoku* 73 (1960): 293–308.

"Uiriamu Gamburu to Nihon to kappanjutsu." *Gakutō* 48, no. 12 (1951): 3–7.

Kinkei Rōjin [Yanagawa Shunsan]. *Yokohama hanjōki shohen*. [1860?]

Kishida Tomoko. *Kangaku to yōgaku: Dentō to shinchishiki no hazama de*. Osaka: Ōsaka Daigaku Shuppankai, 2010.

Kobiljski, Aleksandra. "Le modèle américain ou une modernité partagée? Les collèges protestants à Beyrouth et Kyoto, 1860–1875." *Monde(s): Histoire, Espaces, Relations* 6 (2015): 1–23.

"Kono 1000-nen 'Nihon no kagakusha' dokusha ninki tōhyō." *Asahi shinbun*, 23 October 2000.

Koseki San'ei. *Chūjinsho* (c. 1839). In *Yōgakusha kōhonshū*, edited by Satō Shōsuke, 382–446. Nara: Tenri Daigaku Shuppanbu, 1986.

Kurasawa Tsuyoshi. *Bakumatsu kyōikushi no kenkyū*. 3 vols. Yoshikawa Kōbunkan, 1983–86.

Kuriyama, Shigehisa. "Between Mind and Eye: Anatomy in Eighteenth-Century Japan." In *Paths to Asian Medical Knowledge*, edited by Charles Leslie and Allan Young, 21–43. Berkeley: University of California Press, 1992.

Legêne, Susan. *De bagage van Blomhoff en Van Breugel. Japan, Java, Tripoli en Suriname in de negetinde-eeuwse Nederlandse cultuur van het imperialism*. Amsterdam: Koninklijk Instituut voor de Tropen, 1998.

Leupp, Gary P. "Images of Black People in Late Mediaeval and Early Modern Japan." *Japan Forum* 7, no. 1 (1995): 1–13.

Liu, Lydia H. *The Clash of Empires: The Invention of China in Modern World Making*. Cambridge, MA: Harvard University Press, 2004.

Maeda Tsutomu. *Heigaku to shushigaku, rangaku, kokugaku: Kinsei Nihon shisōshi no kōzo*. Heibonsha, 2006.

Maeno Ryōtaku. *Kanrei higen* (c. 1777). In *Yōgaku, jō*, 127–80. Vol. 64 of *Nihon shisō taikei*. Iwanami Shoten, 1976.

Marcon, Federico. *The Knowledge of Nature and the Nature of Knowledge in Early Modern Japan*. Chicago: University of Chicago Press, 2015.

Martin, W. A. P. *Kakubutsu nyūmon*. Edited by Yanagawa Shunsan. Hokumonsha, 1870.

Maruyama Tadatsuna. "Itazawa Takeo sensei tsuitō." *Hōsei Daigaku shigakkai* 15 (1962): 222–35.

Matsuda Kiyoshi. *Yōgaku no shoshiteki kenkyū*. Kyoto: Rinsen Shoten, 1998.

McCartee, Divie Bethune. "A Western Scholar's Reasons for Coming to China." *Bibliotheca Sacra* 60 (April 1903): 371–76.

McCartee Family Papers. Presbyterian Historical Society, Philadelphia, PA.

Miyaji Masato, ed. *Bakumatsu ishin fūun tsūshin: Ran'i Tsuboi Shinryō kakei-ate shokan shū*. Tōkyō Daigaku Shuppankai, 1978.

Miyanaga Takashi. "Nihon yōgakushi: Rangaku kotohajime." *Shakai shirin* 49, no. 2 (2002): 1–63.

Mizuno, Hiromi. *Science for the Empire: Scientific Nationalism in Modern Japan*. Stanford, CA: Stanford University Press, 2009.

Morishima Chūryō. *Kōmō zatsuwa* (1787). In Asakura, *Bunmei genryū sōsho*, 1:435–86.

Mukai Akira. "Bakufu igai no ransho to mokuroku." In *Rangaku shiryō kenkyū: Fukan*, edited by Rangaku Shiryō Kenkyūkai, 41–50. Ryūkei Shosha, 1987.

Nagayo Sensai. "Kinsei iji enkaku." Postface to [Sugita,] *Rangaku kotohajime*, 1–16 [71–86].

Nagazumi Yōko. *18-seiki no ransho chūmon to sono rufu*. Monbushō kagaku kenkyūhi hojokin seika hōkokusho, 1995–97.

"Kaisha no bōeki kara kojin no bōeki: 18-seiki Oranda-Nihon bōeki no henbō." *Shakai-keizai shigaku* 60, no. 3 (1994): 321–48.

"Personal Trade at the Dutch Factory in Japan: The Trade Society Organized by Chief Factor Meijlan (1826–1830)." *Memoirs of the Tōyō Bunko* 66 (2008): 1–44.

Najita, Tetsuo. "History and Nature in Eighteenth-Century Tokugawa Thought." In *Early Modern Japan*, edited by John Whitney Hall, 596–659. Vol. 4 of *The Cambridge History of Japan*. Cambridge: Cambridge University Press, 1991.

Nakamura, Ellen Gardner. *Practical Pursuits: Takano Chōei, Takahashi Keisaku, and Western Medicine in Nineteenth-Century Japan*. Cambridge, MA: Harvard University Asia Center, 2006.

Nakamura Tsuko and Suzanne Débarbat. "Tenkyūgi: Hiun no oyatoi gaikokujin tenmon-gakusha Emīru Repishie (1826–1874)." *Tenmon geppō* 109, no. 11 (2016): 799–810.

Nakane Masaru. *Nihon insatsu gijutsushi*. Yagi Shoten, 1999.

Nakano Misao. "Rangakusha to keizai seikatsu." *Rangaku shiryō kenkyūkai kenkyū hōkoku* 182 (1966): 202–5.

Nakano Yōzō. "Rangaku kotohajime." *Kagaku* 21, no. 4 (1934): 234–38.

Nakayama Shigeru, ed. *Bakumatsu no yōgaku*. Kyoto: Mineruva Shobō, 1984.

Nichiran Gakkai, ed. *Edo bakufu kyūzō ransho sōgō mokuroku*. Yoshikawa Kōbunkan, 1980.

"Nihon bunka to yōgaku no kōshō." Special issue, *Kagaku pen* 4, no. 3 (1939).

Nishikawa Takeomi and Itō Izumi. *Kaikoku Nihon to Yokohama Chūkagai*. Taishūkan Shoten, 2002.

Nomura Masao. "Choyakusha no takken ka, genten ransho no chōsa busoku ka: Jirei o chūshin ni." *Itteki* 16 (2008): 1–16.

Ogawa Ayako. *Bakumatsu-ki Chōshū-han yōgakushi no kenkyū*. Kyoto: Shibunkaku, 1998.

Oranda gogaku genshi. Fukui: 1856. National Diet Library.

Osborne, Michael A. "Acclimatizing the World: A History of the Paradigmatic Colonial Science." *Osiris* 15 (2000): 135–51.

Paramore, Kiri. "The Transnational Archive of the Sinosphere: The Early Modern East Asian Information Order." In *Archives and Information in the Early Modern World*, edited by Kate Peters, Alexandra Walshman, and Liesbeth Corens, 285–310. Oxford: Oxford University Press, 2018.

Poskett, James. *Materials of the Mind: Phrenology, Race, and the Global History of Science*. Chicago: University of Chicago Press, 2019.

Presbyterian Board of Foreign Missions (PCUSA). Board of Foreign Missions Correspondence.

Raj, Kapil. "Beyond Postcolonialism ... and Postpositivism: Circulation and the Global History of Science." *Isis* 104, no. 2 (2013): 337–47.

Relocating Modern Science: Circulation and the Construction of Knowledge in South Asia and Europe, 1650–1900. Basingstoke: Palgrave Macmillan, 2007.

Ranbun kihan: Genmei Samarangu. Edo: Suharaya Ihachi, 1856.

"Rangaku no sotogawa: *Kindai kagaku no rirokēshon, Iezusu kaishi to fuhen no teikoku o yomu*." Thematic section, *Yōgaku* 26 (2019): 137–70.

Rogaski, Ruth. *Hygienic Modernity: Meanings of Health and Disease in Treaty-Port China.* Berkeley: University of California Press, 2014.

Satō Shōsuke. "Iwayuru 'yōgaku ronsō' o megutte." *Yōgaku* 1 (1993): 1–14.

Yōgakushi kenkyū josetsu. 2nd ed. Iwanami Shoten, 1976.

Yōgakushi no kenkyū. Chūōkōronsha, 1980.

Schaffer, Simon, Lissa Roberts, Kapil Raj, and James Delbourgo, eds. *The Brokered World: Go-Betweens and Global Intelligence, 1770–1820.* Sagamore Beach, MA: Science History Publications, 2009.

Seki Yoshihisa. "Hayashi-ke ni yoru Kaiseijo shihai ni tsuite no ichi kōsatsu." *Kyūshū kyōiku gakkai kenkyū kiyō* 29 (2001): 21–28.

Seth, Suman. *Difference and Disease: Medicine, Race, and Locality in the Eighteenth-Century British Empire.* Cambridge: Cambridge University Press, 2018.

Shimizu Noriyoshi. "Ka-i shisō to jūkyū seiki: 'Rangakusha' no jugaku shisō to sekai ninshiki no tenkai." *Edo no shisō* 7 (1997): 118–34.

Shizuoka Kenritsu Chūō Toshokan Aoi Bunko, ed. *Edo bakufu kyūzō yōsho mokuroku.* Shizuoka: Shizuoka Kenritsu Chūō Toshokan Aoi Bunko, 1967.

Sims, Richard. *French Policy Towards the Bakufu and Meiji Japan, 1854–95.* Richmond, UK: Japan Library, 1998.

Subrahmanyam, Sanjay. "Global Intellectual History Beyond Hegel and Marx." *History and Theory* 54 (2015): 126–37.

Sugi Kōji. *Kanzen fukkoku Sugi Kōji jijo den.* Nihon Tōkei Kyōkai, 2005.

[Sugita Genpaku]. *Rangaku kotohajime.* With a preface by Fukuzawa Yukichi, 1–4. Hayashi Shigeka, 1890. National Diet Library. https://dl.ndl.go.jp/pid/826051/1/15

Sugita, Genpaku. *Dawn of Western Science in Japan: Rangaku kotohajime.* Translated by Ryōzō Matsumoto. Hokuseido Press, 1969.

Kyōi no gen (1775). In *Yōgaku, jō,* 227–43. Vol. 64 of *Nihon shisō taikei.* Iwanami Shoten, 1976.

Rangaku kotohajime. Translated and with an introduction by Ogata Tomio. Ōzawa Tsukiji Shoten, 1941.

"Rangaku kotohajime (Die Anfänge der 'Holland-Kunde')." Translated by Kōichi Mori. *Monumenta Nipponica* 5, no. 2 (1941): 501–22.

Swift, Mary A. *Rigaku shoho: First Lessons in Natural Philosophy.* Edo: 1867.

Takahara Izumi. "Kaiseijo-han 'Bankoku kōhō' no kankō: Yorozuya Heishirō to Katsu Kaishū o megutte." *Daigakuin kenkyū nenpō* 29 (2002): 299–309.

Takahashi Shin'ichi. *Yōgakuron.* Mikasa Shobō, 1939.

Takashima Haruo. "Rangaku kotohajime." *Dōbutsugaku zasshi* 52, no. 12 (1941): 588.

Taketani, Etsuko. *US Women Writers and the Discourses of Colonialism, 1825–1861.* Knoxville: University of Tennessee Press, 2003.

Taylor, Jean Gelman. *The Social World of Batavia: Europeans and Eurasians in Colonial Indonesia.* 2nd ed. Madison: University of Wisconsin Press, 2009.

Tazaki Tetsurō. *Zaison no rangaku.* Meicho Shuppan, 1985.

Tiffin, Sarah. "Raffles and the Barometer of Civilisation: Images and Descriptions of Ruined Candis in *The History of Java.*" *Journal of the Royal Asiatic Society* 18 (2008): 341–60.

Tōkyō Tsūshin Daiichi Chūgakkai, ed. *Shinsen kokugo.* Tōkyō Tsūshin Daiichi Gakkai, 1930.

Trambaiolo, Daniel. "Vaccination and the Politics of Medical Knowledge in Nineteenth-Century Japan." *Bulletin of the History of Medicine* 88, no. 3 (2014): 431–56.

Tsukahara Tōgo. "'Kagaku to teikokushugi' ga hiraku chihei." *Gendai shisō* 29, no. 10 (2001): 156–75.

———. "Rangaku, chikyū ondanka, kagaku to teikokushugi." *Tōkyō Daigaku Shiryō Hensanjo kenkyū kiyō* 16 (2016): 79–108.

———. "Tenbō: 'Kagaku to teikokushugi' kenkyū no furontia." *Kagakushi kenkyū* 53, no. 271 (2014): 281–92.

———. "An Unpublished Manuscript *Geologica Japonica* by Von Siebold: Geology, Mineralogy, and Copper in the Context of Dutch Colonial Science and the Introduction of Western Geo-sciences to Japan." *East Asian Science, Technology, and Medicine* 40 (2014): 45–80.

———. "Westernization from Different Angles: Review of the Historiography of Science from the Viewpoint of Colonial Science." In *Historical Perspectives on East Asian Science, Technology and Medicine*, edited by Alan K. L. Chan, Gregory K. Clancey, and Hui-Chieh Loy, 279–84. Singapore: Singapore University Press, 2002.

Tsukahara Tōgo, Shinoda Mariko, Itō Kenji, Matsumura Noriaki, Ayabe Hironori, Kakihara Yasushi, Honma Eio, and Sugiyama Shigeo. "Kagakushi no sokumen kara saikentō shita Philipp Franz von Siebold no kagakuteki katsudō." *Narutaki kiyō* 6 (1996): 201–44.

Van der Chijs, J. A. *Proeve eener Ned. Indische Bibliographie (1659–1870). Verhandeling van het Bataviaasch Genootschap van Kunsten en Wetenschappen, Deel XXXVII*. Batavia: Bruining & Wijt, 1875.

Van der Velde, Paul. *A Lifelong Passion: P. J. Veth (1814–1895) and the Dutch East Indies*. Leiden: KITLV, 2006.

Van Hoëvell, W. R. *Reis over Java, Madura en Bali in het midden van 1847*. 2 vols. Amsterdam: P. N. van Kampen, 1849.

Verslag van den staat der afdeeling Samarang van de Maatschappij: tot nut van 't algemeen, sedert hare vestiging op 22 April 1851 tot op heden, den 25 Augustus 1855. Samarang: Oliphant & Co., 1855.

Weber, Andreas. *Hybrid Ambitions: Science, Governance, and Empire in the Career of Caspar G.C. Reinwardt (1773–1854)*. Amsterdam: Leiden University Press, 2012.

Wright, David. *Translating Science: The Transmission of Western Chemistry into Late Imperial China, 1840–1900*. Leiden: Brill, 2000.

Yamada, Keisuke. "On the Genealogy of *Kokujin*: Critical Thinking about the Formation of *Bankoku* and Modern Japanese Perceptions of Blackness." *Japanese Studies* 39, no. 2 (2019): 213–37.

Yamashita Norihisa. *Sekai shisutemu ron de yomu Nihon*. Kōdansha, 2003.

Yamori Saeko. "Yōgaku ronsō." In *Sengo rekishigaku yōgo jiten*, edited by Rekishi Kagaku Kyōgikai, 218–19. Tōkyōdō Shuppan, 2012.

Yōi shinsho. Vol. 1 (1790), 7b–9a. Manuscript. Fujiwara Collection, Kyoto University Library, Kyoto.

Yoshida Tadashi. "Jūhasseiki Oranda ni okeru kagaku no taishūka to rangaku." In *Higashi Ajia no kagaku*, edited by Yoshida Tadashi, 50–108. Keisō Shobō, 1982.

12

Technology, Military Reform, and Warfare in the Tokugawa-Meiji Transition

D. COLIN JAUNDRILL

Warfare punctuated the Tokugawa-Meiji transition at nearly every turn. From the 1830s, when the looming threat of Western imperialism spurred renewed interest in military reform, to the 1877 suppression of the final rebellion against the Meiji government, the specter of armed conflict haunted the tumults and transformations of the mid-nineteenth century, occasionally bursting to life in spectacular and bloody fashion. Yet, though it may have been integral to the story of the restoration, warfare did not play the principal part in deciding its outcome. This is even true of the January 1868 Battle of Toba-Fushimi, where forces loyal to the just-restored Meiji emperor routed a Tokugawa army. Although the defeat hastened the collapse of the old regime, the shogunate had long since lost the political capital it needed to function as a national government. Likewise, the subsequent Boshin War (1868–69) complicated the fledgling Meiji state's consolidation of power, but the fractious Northern Alliance (Ōuetsu reppan dōmei) never stood much chance of victory. And in the 1877 War of the Southwest – by far the greatest challenge to the post-restoration order – Saigō Takamori's forces marched just 180 kilometers before they were contained and destroyed.

While armed conflict may not have been the deciding factor in the outcome of the Meiji Restoration, it was nonetheless a critical piece in the symphony of transformations that played out over Japan's mid-nineteenth century. As long-term shifts in the political, economic, and social structures undergirding the Tokugawa order accelerated, changes to military institutions and practices kept pace and occasionally played a leading role. Moreover, these various realms of activity overlapped and intertwined, with developments in one sending ripples through the others. After all, none of the major changes in pre-Meiji military affairs – the procurement of foreign weapons, the military recruitment of commoners, and civil war itself – were possible without seismic shifts in the shogunate's foreign policy, the status system, and the accelerating unraveling of elite politics.

The outbreak of civil war in the 1860s represented the first significant armed conflict in the archipelago since the seventeenth century. While various forms of violence persisted throughout the two-hundred-odd years of the Tokugawa peace, warfare – understood as organized violence involving one or more polities – largely faded from view. The notion of military preparedness, however, continued to inform the organization of early modern governing institutions and society at large. Over the course of the seventeenth and eighteenth centuries, the archipelago's militaries evolved into constabulary organizations tasked with keeping the peace and protecting the coastline. Although militaries did not quite atrophy during the Tokugawa era, their changed mission left the shogunate and domains ill-prepared to deal with the challenge of nineteenth-century Western imperialism.

As the shape of the imperial threat came into focus – especially after reports of the First Opium War (1839–42) reached Japan – a diverse array of policy-makers, intellectuals, military experts, and opportunistic would-be reformers advanced proposals to help Japan meet the challenges of the moment.[1] The military initiatives of the late Tenpō era (1830–44), undertaken by both shogunal and domanial administrators, sought to adopt contemporary Western military technology to avoid a Japanese reprisal of the Qing dynasty's defeat. While ambitious, this early round of reforms was hindered by fiscal troubles and fractious internecine politics. Military readiness thus became a secondary priority until the mid-1850s, when a collision with US "gunboat diplomacy" pushed defense concerns back to the foreground. From the mid-1850s to the mid-1860s, military reforms evolved from experimentation with flintlock muskets to the thorough remaking of military organizations, a process that accelerated as the domestic political order unraveled. Between 1864 and 1869, a series of rebellions and civil wars rocked the archipelago and pitted these remade militaries against one another. After 1869, the Meiji government emerged victorious from these various conflicts and began the messy work of reconciling a generation's worth of disparate reform efforts – including the former shogunate's – into a cohesive national force. This process took two decades but eventually produced an army and navy capable of achieving the Meiji state's imperial designs. Japan's military continued to evolve, but by the 1890s it was no longer playing catch-up with the so-called Great Powers. Japan had joined the club.

[1] Wakabayashi, "From Peril to Profit," 60–61.

When reformers began remaking Japan's militaries, they approached the challenge of imperialism with the assumption that their principal problem was a hardware gap with the imperial powers of Europe and the United States. If Tokugawa-era warriors could learn to use contemporary firearms and artillery, Japan could defend itself against foreign encroachment. This attitude faced one major obstacle: seventeenth-century tactics and organization were from the seventeenth century, and they were poorly suited to nineteenth-century weapons systems. New hardware required new software.

Several factors complicated technological reforms. For one, hardware was expensive; many domains with reformist intentions found their plans thwarted by fiscal constraints. When hardware did arrive, it was often of varied composition – a particular problem in an era of rapid technological change. Second, the authorities enacting military reforms operated with imperfect information; military manuals were a limited commodity, officers with practical experience were nonexistent, and thorough training was extremely difficult. Third, the structure of Tokugawa-era militaries was integral to the internal organization of the warrior status group. Disbanding or reconstituting military units was tantamount to reforming Tokugawa society itself. Finally, on a personal level, organizational changes challenged warrior notions of masculinity, which had long romanticized autonomy in the exercise of violence.

This chapter will center on warfare and military reform, with a particular focus on the polities and people responsible for organizing violence during the Tokugawa-Meiji transition. Engagements between armies, however, were not the only form of violence during this era, nor were they the only face of warfare. Terrorism, opportunistic brigandage, and irregular warfare played in the background of – and occasionally intersected with – the military campaigns of the era.[2] At the same time, warfare's impact extended beyond the combat zone. Peasants were conscripted as both soldiers and corvée labor. Outcastes used the uncertainty of the moment to push for emancipation, in at least one instance through military service. And some warrior women volunteered to fight, only to be turned away. Conflict had indeed opened numerous potential avenues of change, most of which closed as the disruption of late Tokugawa segued into the national consolidation of early Meiji.

---

[2] Howell, "Social Life of Firearms"; Siniawer, *Ruffians, Yakuza, Nationalists*, 11–41.

Responses to Imperialism (1800s–1840s)

Before Reform

By the time US Commodore Matthew Perry's flotilla sailed for Edo in 1853, Japan had been preparing for a confrontation with the West for several decades, albeit with few tangible results. In any event, early nineteenth-century Tokugawa Japan was ill-prepared to confront foreign encroachment militarily. Over two hundred years of peace saw large-scale demobilization and the reorientation of armies to peacetime duties. Violence persisted, but military campaigning ceased to be an everyday concern for Tokugawa authorities.

Contrary to the popular image of sword-wielding samurai, the armies of the early modern era were combined-arms forces composed largely of spear-armed infantry supported by bowmen and matchlock musketeers, with heavy cavalry reserved for a prestigious and "decisive" role it was not always asked to play.[3] The social composition of these forces varied widely: some warriors were recruited through feudal modes of vassalage and conscription, but many units – especially infantry (ashigaru / dōshin) – fought as paid professionals under the direct command of daimyo.[4] In this respect, the Japanese armies of this era had more in common with their counterparts in "Military Revolution"–era Europe than they did with their early medieval predecessors.[5]

When Tokugawa Ieyasu (1542–1616) and his successors inherited the armies of this era, they took immediate steps to curtail domains' military autonomy by limiting their capacity to construct fortifications and regulating the size and composition of their armies.[6] The number of warriors under arms decreased dramatically. The shogunate, for instance, which had fielded 20,000 warriors for the Shimabara Rebellion in the 1630s, reverted to a peacetime strength of under 6,000 men mostly engaged in constabulary roles.[7] Thousands of warriors and warrior menials (buke hōkōnin) were released by their employers and became rōnin (masterless samurai), leading to social dislocations throughout the mid-seventeenth century. Despite the decline of warfare, military readiness remained central to the Tokugawa conception of good governance. Every domain owed the shogunate military obligations (gun'yaku), which could be discharged in various ways depending on domains' geographic position, wealth, or relationship to the Tokugawa. The most fundamental

---

[3] Stavros, "Military Revolution," 248–52; Swope, Dragon's Head, 76.
[4] Ikegami, Taming of the Samurai, 141.
[5] Stavros, "Military Revolution."
[6] Hall, "Bakuhan System," 159–60.
[7] Hōya, "Kinsei," 206–8; Bolitho, "Han," 205.

demonstrations of domains' readiness to meet their military obligations were their processions to Edo for alternate attendance (*sankin kōtai*), which were executed as rehearsals for military campaigns.[8] On an individual level, warriors were expected to maintain their martial skills, but full units rarely if ever drilled in anticipation of combat.

Historians once interpreted these shifts as an atrophying of the Tokugawa military establishment, but they are better understood as an adaptation to a changing political and social landscape, as the case of musketry and gunnery (*hōjutsu*) illustrates.[9] In the early seventeenth century, when the threat of warfare still loomed, instruction for musketeers stressed basic, practical skills such as loading, firing, and cleaning weapons.[10] By the latter half of the century, instruction moved beyond battlefield proficiency to emphasize mastery of firearms, which often included the production of ammunition and the practice of proprietary techniques. Marksmanship became an opportunity for warriors to demonstrate "masculine military prowess" at a moment when shogunal and domanial authorities had already severely curtailed warriors' ability to exercise violence autonomously.[11] The turn to the martial arts as a showcase for manly violence spurred a proliferation of martial arts styles (*ryūha*). By the early nineteenth century, there were several dozen styles of sword-fighting, musketry, and most other martial disciplines.[12] Until the mid-nineteenth century, calls for military reform and the restoration of Tokugawa-period warriors' prowess – such as the shogun Yoshimune's Kyōhō reforms (c. 1716–45) – took this variegated vision of the martial arts for granted. Thus, while the musketeer of the late eighteenth century may have been a better marksman than his great-grandfather, he was less prepared for the rigors of battle.

Coastal Defense and Dutch Musketry

Despite the increasing rarefication of the martial arts, security concerns – both internal and external – never lost the attention of governing authorities. Tokugawa leaders had responded to the Shimabara Rebellion and the subsequent expulsion of Portuguese traders by charging Kyushu domains with special responsibilities for coastal defense.[13] Fears of foreign invasion

---

[8] Vaporis, *Tour of Duty*, 13, 78–82.
[9] Bolitho, "Tempō Crisis," 126–27.
[10] Udagawa, *Edo no hōjutsu*, 202.
[11] Walthall, "Do Guns Have Gender?," 42–43.
[12] Hurst, *Armed Martial Arts*, 73.
[13] Wilson, *Defensive Positions*, 35–40.

eventually subsided, then resurfaced in response to Russian diplomatic overtures in 1793 and 1805 (the Laxman and Rezanov missions).[14] After the British frigate HMS *Phaeton* raided the Dutch factory at Nagasaki in 1808, the shogunate increased security at Nagasaki and expanded coastal defense arrangements by charging several of its collateral and vassal domains with the protection of Edo Bay.[15] While concerns over coastal defense subsided briefly, the 1824 landing of a British whaler near Edo prompted Tokugawa authorities to issue a "shell and repel" policy (*ikokusen uchiharai rei*) that instructed domains to fire upon foreign ships. Sightings of unfamiliar vessels increased over the following two decades, but only two domains (Matsumae in 1831 and 1834, Satsuma in 1837) complied with the directive.[16]

Reports of Qing China's defeat in the First Opium War drove Tokugawa authorities to devote more sustained attention to military matters. In 1840, a Nagasaki musketry instructor and Tokugawa functionary named Takashima Shūhan used news of the Qing disaster to argue for the widespread adoption of Western musketry techniques. In a memorial to the shogunate's senior councillors (*rōjū*), Shūhan observed that Western countries relied exclusively on gunpowder weapons (*kahō*), which they had improved significantly after decades of near-constant warfare. China's recent defeat, he argued, was a result of its failure to appreciate advances in military technology – unsubtly implying similar negligence on the part of Japanese (*waryū*) musketry instructors, who continued to prize individual skill with a matchlock. Only by embracing Western weaponry and emphasizing "battlefield effectiveness" (*senjō jitsuyō*) could Tokugawa Japan avoid catastrophe. Shūhan was, of course, happy to offer his expertise even if it meant shouldering the burdens of increased notoriety and income.[17] Although Takashima-*ryū* (Takashima style or school) grew out of the broader Japanese (*waryū*) tradition, Shūhan had studied contemporary European techniques with Johan Wilhelm de Sturler, a Dutch veteran of the Napoleonic Wars then directing the Dutch trading post in Nagasaki.[18] Shūhan had also leveraged his official position to purchase European military manuals, fifty flintlock muskets, and a handful of cannons – not an enormous arsenal, but arguably the most advanced in Japan at the time.[19]

[14] Suzuki, "Seeking Accuracy."
[15] Hōya, "Kinsei," 230; Wilson, "Tokugawa Defense Redux."
[16] Wilson, *Defensive Positions*, 119; Hellyer, *Defining Engagement*, 150.
[17] "Yōhō saiyō no kengi," in Katsu, *Rikugun rekishi*, 11:9–12.
[18] Arima, *Takashima Shūhan*, 48.
[19] "Takashima Shirōdayū buki kōnyū no shinmon," in Katsu, *Rikugun rekishi*, 11:22–32.

Takashima-*ryū* benefited from fortuitous timing. Concern over foreign threats and a renewed emphasis on reform (at both the regional and central levels) created a target-rich environment for opportunistic musketry instructors seeking students and patrons. By late 1840, Shūhan's school claimed over 200 students, including warriors from prominent Kyushu domains such as Satsuma, Kumamoto, and Saga. The school's reach expanded in 1841, when the shogunate ordered Shūhan and 100 of his students to demonstrate his techniques outside of Edo. The artillery exercises and infantry drill impressed the senior councillors, who authorized the propagation of Takashima-*ryū* and ordered Shūhan to impart his techniques to two Tokugawa retainers, Egawa Hidetatsu and Shimosone Nobuatsu. This sudden notoriety provoked a backlash from the shogunate's officially sponsored musketry houses (the Inoue and Tatsuke), who worked with their influential allies to discredit Shūhan and sentence him in 1842 to more than a decade of house arrest. These intrigues led to a pause in the shogunate's patronage of Western-style musketry, but certified teachers of Takashima-*ryū* remained free to accept students and propagate the school. Thus, the Takashima-*ryū* network grew even as defense-related concerns slid down policymakers' agendas.

Domestic Remilitarization and Reform (1850s–1860s)

Despite the shogunate's moves against Takashima-*ryū* in the mid- and late 1840s, domains continued to flirt with Western technology. Saga, for instance, devoted significant attention to reproducing modern artillery. When a pair of Dutch warships – the frigate *Palembang* and corvette *Boreas* – visited Nagasaki harbor in 1844, Saga daimyo Nabeshima Naomasa used the occasion to inspect the larger vessel to assess the latest in Dutch weaponry. Soon after, Saga built Japan's first reverberatory furnace for casting high-quality bronze cannons.[20] Similarly, Satsuma continued to patronize Takashima-*ryū* instructors, going so far as to fake the death of its chief instructor to avert Tokugawa scrutiny. In 1847, the domain created the Hōjutsukan, a school for Western-style musketry. Within two years, Satsuma was conducting military maneuvers with hundreds of men. Beyond these two well-known examples, Shimosone Nobuatsu's Edo school hosted students (including some daimyo) from Kaga, Uwajima, and Morioka, while Egawa Hidetatsu's school in Izu drew students from Aizu, Hikone, Matsushiro, and Kawagoe, among others.[21]

---

[20] Wilson, *Defensive Positions*, 129–32.
[21] Sakamoto, "Shimosone Nobuatsu," 60; Ishii, "Nirayama juku," 24.

Nonetheless, widespread interest in Western-style musketry did not translate into institutional change until the 1850s, when the shogunate's signing of limited treaties with the United States, Britain, Russia, and the Netherlands ensured more routine international contacts and destabilized the domestic balance of power.[22] Suddenly, producing a credible military deterrent became a pressing priority for both Tokugawa officials and their counterparts in the domains – especially those domains that believed the shogunate had failed to uphold its duty to defend the realm against outside incursions. Whereas the earlier Tenpō era had seen a flirtation with new weapons and techniques, the Ansei (1854–60) round of military reforms aimed to incorporate new military technologies into existing institutions. Although these efforts achieved some lasting successes, they tended to founder on the shoals of internecine politics, especially when they challenged the structures of existing military organizations.

The Limits of Technological Reform, 1854–1860

In the wake of the Perry expedition, Tokugawa leaders undertook a three-pronged defense program. First, they sought to upgrade coastal defenses around key harbors, particularly Edo. Although shore batteries had straddled the entrance to Edo Bay (the Uraga Channel) for decades, they were manned by domains with diverse musketry traditions and outdated weapons. Egawa Hidetatsu proposed new batteries situated on reclaimed land immediately off the coast of Shinagawa. His original plan envisioned eleven fortifications, although only six were built. But, in a major departure from previous efforts, all of the batteries would be constructed and run according to "Western methods" (seiyōhō).[23]

The shogunate's second, more ambitious program was the creation of a navy, which would (arguably) represent the first standing fleet in Japan's history. Before the nineteenth century, "naval" forces were generally small units constituted on an ad hoc basis. In 1853, Katsu Kaishū – then a low-ranking Tokugawa functionary and Western musketry practitioner of minor renown – recommended a wide range of military reforms, including the creation of a navy capable of securing Japan's coastline and foreign trade.[24] Planning became reality in 1855, when King Willem III of the Netherlands gifted the steamer Kankō-maru (née Soembing) and a small team of naval instructors to the shogunate. Over the next five years, the Dutch cadre at

---

[22] Auslin, Negotiating with Imperialism, 11–33.
[23] Hōya, "Kinsei," 243; "Yōshiki kagi no shōrei," in Katsu, Rikugun rekishi, 12:263.
[24] Kanazawa, Bakufu kaigun no kōbō, 50–54.

the Nagasaki Naval Institute (Nagasaki Kaigun Denshūjo) trained over 200 students, including warriors from prominent domains such as Satsuma and Saga and future shogunal navy leaders such as Kaishū and Enomoto Takeaki. The fleet grew as the shogunate added the small warships *Kanrin-maru* and *Chōyō-maru*.[25] Although the naval institute closed in 1859, its graduates continued to staff the shogunate's naval training facility in Edo. Ultimately, the shogunate's naval reforms were a qualified success, largely because they had the luxury of painting from a blank canvas.

Efforts to reform the shogunate's ground forces proceeded less smoothly, as institutional inertia and outright opposition hampered progress. In 1854, when Abe Masahiro (then the leading figure among the shogunate's senior councillors) called for the creation of a training facility – the Edo Martial Arts School (Kōbusho) – to rekindle the fighting prowess of Tokugawa vassals, his language recalled the largely empty exhortations of earlier eras of reform.[26] But this time would be different. Although the Kōbusho's curriculum included traditional martial disciplines such as sword-fighting (*kenjutsu*) and polearm-fighting (*sōjutsu*), the musketry instructors were all Takashima-*ryū* alumni, including Egawa Hidetoshi (Hidetatsu's son), Shimosone Nobuatsu, and a recently released Takashima Shuhan. Indeed, many of the shogunate's guard units (*bankata*) were required to participate in musketry exercises at the Kōbusho, and marginal members of the warrior status group were encouraged to participate on a volunteer basis.

By the mid-1850s, "Western-style" (*seiyō-ryū*) musketry – as Takashima-*ryū* became known – had changed in terms of both hardware and software. The participants in Shūhan's 1841 demonstration had used smoothbore flintlocks, which were easier to handle than Japan's ubiquitous matchlocks and were standard-issue weapons in contemporary Europe. But, in the late 1840s, flintlocks began to be supplanted by smoothbore percussion muskets, which used fulminate priming caps to ignite the powder in the weapon's firing pan. Compared to flintlocks, percussion muskets were far less prone to misfiring but required a different loading procedure. They would also prove to be a transitional technology, soon supplanted by muzzle-loading percussion rifles and then "repeating" breech-loading rifles. Thus, Japan's nineteenth-century military reforms occurred during a period of rapid transition in military hardware.[27]

---

[25] Kanazawa *Bakufu kaigun no kōbō*, 71–74; Hōya, "Kinsei," 246.
[26] "Kōbujō toritate no shui," in Katsu, *Rikugun rekishi*, 12:175–76.
[27] For a thorough discussion of the contemporary arms trade, see Fuess, "Global Weapons Trade."

Training warriors in units meant abandoning Takashima-*ryū*'s early focus on individual mastery in favor of large-scale lessons in close-order infantry drill. The change of emphasis required the shogunate's musketry instructors and Dutch studies (*rangaku*) scholars to produce accessible translations of contemporary European military manuals. In essence, the Kōbusho became a prototype military academy rather than a traditional martial arts school. These changes did not go unnoticed by students, some of whom referred to the regimented drill exercises as "imitating beasts" (*chikushō no mane*), a practice certainly unbecoming of warriors. Other students would rather watch swordsmen spar than participate in musketry training. In fact, an 1858 report found that, aside from a core of enthusiastic strivers who saw in Western military science an opportunity for advancement, the Kōbusho had failed to achieve the sweeping reform Tokugawa leaders had envisioned. The curriculum deteriorated even further in 1860, when archery (*kyūjutsu*) and *waryū* musketry instructors joined the instructional cadre. While the return of practices such as dog shooting (*inu oumono*) may have soothed the bruised egos of some warriors, they were poor preparation for the nineteenth-century world of rifles and cannons. Nonetheless, the eventual failure of the Kōbusho illustrates how many warriors saw military reforms as threats to not only their livelihoods but also their sense of identity – both in terms of social status and the putative martial independence that was so central to warrior masculinity.

Reforms at the regional level faced obstacles as varied as the domains themselves. Satsuma daimyo Shimazu Nariakira attempted to convert his entire retainer band into a Western-style three-branch military. When Nariakira died in 1858, however, his successors ended the exclusive patronage of Western-style musketry and announced a return to the domain's traditions. Saga continued its pursuit of the latest military technology, sending students to musketry schools in Edo and assembling the largest domain contingent at the Nagasaki Naval Institute.[28] Chōshū, which became a leader in military reform in the mid-1860s, made only temporizing changes until 1859, when new domanial leadership suggested reorganizing foot soldiers (*ashigaru*) and warrior menials into rifle units – a change that would only be fully realized years later. Even aside from these "usual suspects," large domains such as Kaga, Sendai, Tottori, and Okayama (to name a few) ordered their warriors to train in Western-style musketry techniques, as did several small and medium-sized Tokugawa vassal (*fudai*) domains such

---

[28] "Shohan no gakusei," in Katsu, *Kaigun rekishi*, 8:163–67.

as Kawagoe, Sakura, and Sabae.[29] In other words, engagement with new military technologies and techniques was not limited to western Japan's most prominent domains, although most lacked the political and economic wherewithal to implement them.

Toward Organizational Change: The Bunkyū Reforms (1861–1864)

Mounting tensions in the early 1860s added urgency to reform efforts. For the shogunate, the challenge was twofold. First, it had to deter internal challenges from both resurgent domains and the increasingly violent activism of imperial loyalists, who were responsible for attacks on senior Tokugawa leaders in 1860 and 1862. Second, the shogunate had to satisfy the Kyoto court's demand for resistance to foreign encroachment while simultaneously presenting a strong front to Western imperial powers, whom it also had to court for military assistance. Tokugawa leaders responded to these pressures with an ambitious plan to build a new Western-style army and navy to stand alongside – and effectively replace – the traditional core of the Tokugawa military.

In 1861, the shogunate constituted a reform committee to develop detailed plans for constructing each service. The blueprint for the Tokugawa navy was wildly ambitious, calling for the creation of six fleets (sonae) consisting of fifteen squadrons (kumi), each of which would include three frigates and nine corvettes – a total of 180 warships. Crewing the navy would require 48,000 sailors and 7,500 marines.[30] Moreover, this blueprint envisioned a single shogunal navy with no domain-level counterparts, unlike the federal approach of the proposed plan for the army. Ultimately, the naval plan was aspirational; the committee realized that only a generational investment could produce a force of the size it desired.[31] Nonetheless, despite limited time and capital, the shogunate's Bunkyū (1861–64) naval reform made tangible progress in organization, recruitment, and training. For both the new army and navy, the reform commission implemented a standardized rank and pay structure that reconciled a Western-style – Dutch, in this case – chain of command with the shogunate's existing bureaucratic offices (see Table 12.1).[32] At the same time, a new recruitment drive drew upon untapped reservoirs of manpower within

---

[29] Hōya, "Kinsei," 253.
[30] "Enkai kantai no haichi," in Katsu, Kaigun rekishi, 9:201–17.
[31] "Kaigun hensei no kenpaku," in Katsu, Kaigun rekishi, 9:192–95.
[32] "Shokuhō kaikyū no torishirabe," in Katsu, Kaigun rekishi, 9:184–92; "Ansei igo shinchikan," 1605–7.

Table 12.1 Ranks for officers and noncommissioned officers in the Tokugawa army and navy

Navy	Army	Stipend/Notes
kaigun sōsai (admiral)	rikugun sōsai (field marshal)	rōjū-level post
kaigun fuku-sōsai (lieutenant admiral)	rikugun fuku-sōsai (general)	wakadoshiyori-level post
kaigun bugyō (vice admiral) *overall fleet commander	rikugun bugyō (lieutenant general) *overall commander of army	5,000 koku (plus 300 ryō supplement for navy)
gunkan bugyō (rear admiral) *commands naval squadron (buntai)	kihei bugyō (major general of cavalry) *commands brigade of 3–4 regiments; hohei bugyō (major general of infantry) *commands brigade of 3–4 regiments	3,000 koku (plus 250 ryō supplement for navy)
gunkan gashira (captain) *commander of a ship-of-the-line, frigate, or corvette	kihei gashira (colonel) *commands 1 regiment; hohei gashira (colonel) *commands 1 regiment	2,000 koku (plus 200 ryō supplement for navy)
gunkan gashira nami (lieutenant captain) *commands a corvette or brig	kihei gashira nami (lieutenant colonel) *commands half-regiment; hohei gashira nami (lieutenant colonel) *commands half-regiment; ōzutsugumi gashira (lieutenant colonel) *commands 1 battery of 8 guns	1,000 koku (plus 150 ryō supplement for navy)
gunkan yaku (first lieutenant) *commands a small vessel like a schooner, or is first officer on a ship-of-the-line or frigate	kihei metsuke (major); kihei sashizuyaku tōdori (captain of cavalry) *commands 1 squadron; hohei metsuke (major); hohei sashizuyaku tōdori (captain of infantry) *commands 1 company; may also serve as hohei metsuke yaku (inspector of infantry) or hohei metsuke yaku nami (deputy inspector of infantry) (for 150/100 hyō additional stipend); ōzutsu sashizuyaku tōdori (captain of artillery) *commands a half battery	700 koku; 400 hyō (plus 100 ryō supplement for navy, 100 hyō supplement for cavalry)

gunkan yaku nami (second lieutenant)	kihei sashizuyaku (first lieutenant of cavalry)	hohei sashizuyaku (first lieutenant of infantry)	ōzutsu sashizuyaku (section commander)	300 hyō (plus 70 ryō supplement for navy, 100 hyō supplement for cavalry)
gunkan yaku nami minarai (midshipman)	kihei sashizuyaku nami (second lieutenant of cavalry)	hohei sashizuyaku (second lieutenant of infantry)	ōzutsu sashizuyaku nami (second lieutenant of artillery)	
gunkan jōki kata (chief engineer)				
gunkan soiyaku torishimari (petty officer first class)	kihei metsuke shitayaku (noncommissioned officer of cavalry)	hohei metsuke shitayaku (noncommissioned officer of infantry)		
	kihei gumi hata yaku (cavalry flag bearer)	hohei gumi hata yaku (infantry flag bearer)		
gunkan jōki kata nami (machinist second class)				
gunkan soiyaku (petty officer second class)	kihei sashizuyaku shitayaku (sergeant major)	hohei sashizuyaku shitayaku (sergeant major)	ōzutsu sashizuyaku shitayaku (sergeant major)	
gunkan jōki kata nami minarai (machinist third class)				
gunkan soiyaku nami (petty officer third class)	kihei sashizuyaku shitayaku nami (sergeant)	hohei sashizuyaku shitayaku nami (sergeant)	ōzutsu sashizuyaku shitayaku nami (sergeant)	

Adapted from "Ansei ikō shinchikan," 1607.

the Tokugawa retainer band. Four of the five boat-hand divisions (*funate gumi*) that comprised the shogunate's transport fleet were transferred to the new navy, as were 200 men from the ranks of unemployed retainers.[33] The commission planned for these men to become officer candidates and eventually form the nucleus of the naval officer corps.

Tokugawa leaders had more success building the new army, which the reform committee initially envisioned as a shogunal guard (*shin'ei*) rather than a national force (*zenkoku osonae*). Their blueprint called for a 12,000-man army composed of Western-style infantry, cavalry, and artillery units.[34] The technical and elite units – artillery, cavalry, and light infantry – would draw recruits from unemployed warriors and unprestigious guard units, while the bulk of the infantrymen would be recruited via conscription. In 1862, the shogunate announced that it was calling in the manpower obligations of its retainers, requiring land-holding bannermen to furnish one man for every 500 *koku*, three men for every 1,000 *koku*, and ten men for every 3,000 *koku*. These conscripts (*heifu*) were mostly peasants from vassal holdings in the countryside around Edo, but their ranks also included day laborers and warrior menials from the city.[35] Nearly 5,000 men would serve in the new infantry regiments. To rationalize the military employment of commoners, Tokugawa military leaders made "infantry" (*hohei*) a new category of warrior menial ranking below porters (*koagari*). The new infantrymen would comport themselves as warrior menials during their terms of service, with a single short sword to mark their status.[36] In this case, the "short sword" was actually a socket bayonet for the conscripts' rifles. The social marginality of infantrymen enabled the shogunate's military leadership to implement the kind of experimental reforms that might have provoked resistance from warriors with more clout. The conscripts drilled using European (Dutch, then British) military manuals, and they were subjected to an array of new disciplinary regulations – including a day organized according to the Western clock.[37] Within the next year, several hundred of these new conscripts saw combat in the shogunate's suppression of the 1864 Tengu insurrection in Mito domain. Although the new infantrymen performed unevenly in combat, they managed to impress

---

[33] "Funate gumi o haisu," in Katsu, *Kaigun rekishi*, 9:225; Kanazawa, *Bakufu kaigun no kōbō*, 116–17.

[34] "Shin'ei jōbigun sanpei no tōkei," in Katsu, *Rikugun rekishi*, 13:333–37.

[35] Hōya, "Kinsei," 268–69.

[36] "Heifu kaitei no fure," in Katsu, *Rikugun rekishi*, 13:341–42.

[37] "Hohei tonsho kisoku," in Katsu, *Rikugun rekishi*, 14:267–76.

Tokugawa leaders, who moved to expand recruitment and secure training assistance from Europe.

For the domains, the early 1860s represented an extension of Ansei-era reforms. Experiments with Western-style musketry and organizational reforms continued but had yet to produce the kind of thoroughgoing approach undertaken by the shogunate's leadership. That changed in 1863, when a burgeoning diplomatic crisis collided with domestic political tensions. Earlier that year, Tokugawa leaders had acceded to two sets of demands. First, they paid Britain an indemnity of 440,000 silver dollars to atone for the 1861 burning of the British legation and the 1862 killing of British merchants by Satsuma warriors. Placating the imperial powers was seen as a necessary step to avoid war or a British blockade, responses that Whitehall had indeed considered. At the same time, the shogunate faced pressure from the Kyoto court and its loyalist allies, who demanded that the shogun expel all foreigners from the archipelago and close Yokohama, Nagasaki, and Hakodate to foreign trade. Tokugawa leaders attempted to placate both the emperor's coterie and foreign diplomats. Meanwhile, loyalist-leaning domains had received sufficient sanction to take matters into their own hands. In the fifth month of 1863, Chōshū began firing on foreign ships passing through the Shimonoseki Straits. In the sixth month, separate reprisals by US and French ships destroyed all three of the domain's gunboats and wrecked one of its coastal batteries. That same month, a British flotilla sailed to Satsuma to demand a supplementary indemnity and the punishment of the men directly responsible for the Namamugi incident, in which Satsuma samurai had killed a British merchant outside of Yokohama. At the time, Satsuma was poorly prepared for battle. After Shimazu Nariakira's death in 1858, the domain had rolled back its military reforms, a trend that intensified in the run-up to the confrontation with the British. Although British casualties exceeded Satsuma's, the domain lost its three steamships, and the town of Kagoshima suffered severe damage. The disparity in military power was clear; Satsuma's leaders acceded to British demands and began to pursue a more cordial relationship.[38]

In the aftermath of these incidents, both Satsuma and Chōshū took immediate steps to bolster their military readiness. In 1864, Satsuma founded the Kaiseijo, a new military academy that employed Takashima-*ryū* alumnus Akamatsu Kozaburō as an instructor of British drill. The domain also purchased steamships from Britain, dozens of state-of-the-art Armstrong breechloading cannons from a Russian arms dealer, and thousands of muzzle-loading rifles

---

[38] Hōya, *Bakumatsu Nihon to taigai sensō*, 42–53, 65–77.

from Scottish weapons merchant Thomas Blake Glover.[39] In 1866, as civil war loomed, Satsuma's leaders remade the domain military entirely, creating new army (Rikugunshō) and navy (Kaigunshō) departments while simultaneously organizing warriors into rifle companies. By late 1867, Satsuma had created a 3,000-man force of infantry and artillery. Meanwhile, the domain purchased eleven naval vessels (half of which were resold) between 1864 and 1866, including the small warship *Kenkō-maru*.[40]

Chōshū took a more circuitous route to building a new army. In the wake of the 1863 engagements with foreign warships, the domain's leadership placed the Shimonoseki defenses under the command of Takasugi Shinsaku, an ardent imperial loyalist and military reformer. Takasugi proposed creating a force of "Irregulars" (Kiheitai) capable of using tactics that differed from the regular domain army. The Kiheitai – along with the various auxiliary units (*shotai*) that emerged in its wake – recruited volunteers from all levels of the warrior status group and even allowed the enlistment of commoners, especially those wealthy enough to help outfit the new units. Despite high morale, the Kiheitai and its affiliated units had yet to adopt standards for training, organization, and equipment. As a result, they fared poorly against a punitive expedition mounted by the British, French, Dutch, and Americans in the seventh month of 1864. Surprisingly, conflict in the Shimonoseki Straits was not Chōshū's most pressing problem in the summer of 1864. Just two weeks earlier, the domain had attempted the forcible seizure of the imperial palace in Kyoto, leading to a brutal street fight against warriors from Satsuma and Aizu. The failed coup attempt resulted in Chōshū's branding as an enemy of the court. In retaliation, the shogunate organized a massive punitive expedition of 150,000 soldiers to frighten Chōshū into submission. The domain briefly acquiesced to Tokugawa demands, but within three months, loyalist-leaning officers of the domain's auxiliary units seized control of the domain government and began preparing for war. Chōshū purchased thousands of up-to-date rifles, regularized the structure of the *shotai*, and began organizing foot soldiers and warrior menials into rifle battalions (*daitai*). By the middle of 1866, the domain had assembled twenty infantry battalions in addition to the hundreds of men already in the *shotai*. These new units would soon be involved in the opening phase of a three-year civil war.

[39] Kurihara, *Bakumatsu Nihon no gunsei*, 200–201; Kōshaku Shimazu-ke Henshūjo, *Sappan kaigunshi*, 2:797–811.
[40] "Shokō senpu," in Katsu, *Kaigun rekishi*, 10:228–29.

The Restoration Wars, 1866–1869

The year 1866 was a critical inflection point in Japan's nineteenth-century military revolution. To this point, the shogunate and domains had pursued reforms with a similar motivation – the defense of the realm – but with varied approaches and different strategic priorities. The Tokugawa state aspired to the construction of a national military capable of ensuring foreign and domestic security; the domains focused on the defense of their borders, which they viewed as a responsibility to the realm. Although the substance of these priorities remained largely the same, the political context surrounding them shifted rapidly and radically. For the shogunate, domestic security now included the suppression of challenges to Tokugawa authority. For militarily ambitious domains such as Chōshū and Satsuma, an overweening shogunate joined foreign invasion as a threat to the realm.

When the shogunate launched its invasion of Chōshū in the summer of 1866 – its second attempt to threaten the recalcitrant domain into submission – Tokugawa leaders hoped that a decisive show of force would discourage challenges to their authority. Instead, they ignited the archipelago's first civil war in over 200 years. Until the conflict ended in the spring of 1869, the political and military situation remained dynamic, dominated by complex coalition politics that led to spasmodic outbursts of violence. Although often portrayed as two discrete conflicts – the 1866 Chōshū War and the 1868–69 Boshin War – the Restoration Wars are better understood as a single era of civil war that proceeded in three phases. The first, the Chōshū War of 1866, pitted a single rebel domain against a punitive force organized by the shogunate. The resulting Tokugawa defeat encouraged opponents of the regime, who allied with Chōshū to overthrow the shogunate in a second phase that began with the Battle of Toba-Fushimi in the first month of 1868 and culminated in the peaceful surrender of Edo Castle three months later. The final phase, which involved the forcible subjugation of a loose coalition of northern domains and Tokugawa remnants, ended with the surrender of Hokkaido's Goryōkaku fortress in the spring of 1869.

The Restoration Wars ended in victory for a loyalist coalition that saw military reform as critical to national power and sovereignty. As such, the war's outcome had far-reaching consequences for Japan's modern history. That said, it was a small war relative to contemporary conflicts. Most estimates put total deaths near 8,500, the overwhelming majority of which resulted from three battles: Toba-Fushimi, Ueno, and Aizu-Wakamatsu.[41] This total pales in

---

[41] Hōya, *Boshin sensō*, 287–90.

comparison to the deaths caused by contemporary conflicts like the US Civil War (600,000) or China's Taiping Rebellion (millions) – arguably the most destructive war not only of the nineteenth century but of all human history to that point. Two factors contributed to the relatively low death toll. First, the Restoration Wars (as distinct from the broader process of the restoration) were an elite political conflict between two narrow coalitions. Direct involvement in the war was a high-risk, low-reward proposition for most domains and for most of the civilian populace. The conduct of the war also limited the death toll. Both sides fielded small forces of varied composition with little artillery and even less experience. Their commanders were amateurs learning how to operate armies in real time. As recent scholarship on the US Civil War has shown, amateurism was a consequence of the rapid expansion of the wartime officer corps, and one that imposed significant limits on commanders' ability to use technology and tactics to their maximum capabilities.[42] The same was true of the Boshin War, in which units were often led by neophytes and autodidacts of varying ability. When better-trained forces faced each other ten years later during the Satsuma Rebellion, the results were far more destructive.

Phase 1: The Chōshū War, 1866

By the sixth month of 1866, the shogunate had assembled a seemingly overwhelming force of 10,000 soldiers, not including hundreds of men contributed by allied domains. Although more than half of these soldiers carried firearms, the remainder were outfitted with traditional weapons such as spears and bows. The overall strategy was straightforward. Tokugawa forces would advance into Chōshū along four axes: from Kokura in Kyushu; from Suō Ōshima off the rebel domain's southeastern coast; from the northeast coast near Hamada; and from the east along the road to Hiroshima. The shogunate committed the bulk of its forces – including its modern infantry and artillery units – to this last front. Opposing them were Chōshū's *shotai*, backstopped by the domain's reformed rifle battalions. Most of Chōshū's soldiers carried rifles; some of the *shotai* troopers were even armed with late-model breechloaders.

Unlike the muzzle-loaders that made up the bulk of restoration-era small arms, breechloaders could be reloaded from a prone position – and far more quickly than their predecessors. This seemingly incremental technical improvement would lead to revolutionary changes in infantry tactics over

[42] Hess, *Civil War Infantry Tactics*, xv–xx.

the coming decades. But this transformation was in its infancy in the 1860s. Military experts in the United States and Europe continued to favor tight formations, believing that so-called light infantry tactics required specialized training and were suited only to elite units. During the US Civil War, for instance, trainers for both the Union and Confederacy reverted to obsolete tactics because they believed they lacked the time and capacity to train green volunteers properly. Similarly, officers in European armies continued to extol the material and psychological value of "mass" into World War I.

Tactics and technology collided in novel ways during the Chōshū War. The shogunate's new infantry battalions fought in tight formations – reflecting the contemporary military orthodoxy – while their opponents relied on an improvisational approach that used dispersed formations and aggressive maneuvering. When these newfangled forces fought head-to-head, as they did on the Hiroshima front, Tokugawa forces performed well, although their commanders were unable to parlay these modest victories into greater successes. On the other fronts, Chōshū's troopers seized the offensive and easily routed the inexperienced and traditionally outfitted armies of Tokugawa-aligned domains. With its peripheral fronts secured, Chōshū pivoted to attacking the Tokugawa army's supply lines, which were guarded by obsolete allied-domain forces. These counterattacks forced the shogunate to retreat and seek a cease-fire, which allowed both sides to prepare for the next round.

Brief though it was, the Chōshū War presaged a new era of warfare in the archipelago. Politically, the conflict dashed Tokugawa hopes that a swift victory would bolster the crumbling shogunate; it also burnished Chōshū's reputation with other loyalist-leaning domains, enabling the formation of a militarized anti-Tokugawa coalition. These developments all but ensured further hostilities. On a technological level, the age of the rifle had arrived. Chōshū's riflemen had embarrassed their traditionally equipped enemies. Only the shogunate's Western-style rifle battalions had mounted effective resistance. Tokugawa leaders spent the next year in a frantic attempt to expand their army. A French advisory group, recruited the previous year, arrived in Edo and began training a select cadre of soldiers. Domains – both early adopters and latecomers – accelerated reform programs with a view toward preparing for civil war.

Finally, the Chōshū War accelerated the breakdown of the correlation between social status and military service. The shogunate and reform-minded domains turned increasingly to commoners and warrior menials to fill out the ranks of rifle battalions. The most extreme example was the shogunate's Keiō (1865–68) reforms, which expanded conscription, converted high-income

Tokugawa vassals into a taxpaying peerage, and reconstituted lower-income vassals into a professional soldiery.[43] In essence, these reforms abolished the Tokugawa retainer band as it had existed for two centuries. Gender concerns also intertwined with these organizational changes. After all, shogunal and domain leaders authorized the military recruitment of warrior menials, commoners, and outcastes because it allowed them to avoid offending the prickly martial masculinity of higher-ranking warriors. Sex, however, remained a dividing line for authorities. Although warrior women were notionally "warriors" and many had undergone martial arts training, neither side in the Chōshū War seems to have considered their recruitment. That did not mean women were uninterested in military service, as later events would show.

Phase 2: Overthrowing the Shogunate, 1867–1868

The Chōshū War had severely compromised Tokugawa hegemony. The shogunate and domains spent the next year wrangling over the country's political future. The Tokugawa and their allies seemed to have abandoned any hope of preserving the shogunate as a national government, but they were maneuvering to retain significant influence in any reconstituted polity. Chōshū and its partners in the loyalist coalition, on the other hand, sought to replace the shogunate with a state more dedicated to the prerogatives of the Kyoto court. Both sides' machinations came to a head in the autumn of 1867, when the shogunate and a coalition of imperial loyalist domains moved aggressively to break the political deadlock. On the fourteenth day of the tenth month, the shogun, Tokugawa Yoshinobu, symbolically relinquished his authority to the court and called for the creation of a council of daimyo. Meanwhile, Satsuma and Chōshū, who led the loyalist coalition, intensified their attempts to coax the Kyoto court into authorizing a military campaign against the shogunate. Both sides spent the final month of 1867 rushing military units to the capital region. A month later, the Kyoto court ended negotiations and proclaimed the "restoration of imperial rule" (ōsei fukko). As loyalist forces marched into the capital, Yoshinobu withdrew his forces to Osaka, likely fearing that any conflict risked the Tokugawa being branded as enemies of the court. This move also meant abandoning a substantial manpower advantage and several defensible positions around the city.[44] Political wrangling continued for another month, but in the first month of 1868 the Kyoto court ordered Yoshinobu to appear in person, abdicate, and surrender his lands.

---

[43] Totman, *Collapse of the Tokugawa Bakufu*, 349–54.
[44] Hōya, *Boshin sensō*, 16–23.

Events in eastern Japan accelerated the situation's descent into violence. Satsuma had recruited nearly 300 *rōnin* and loyalist activists to sow chaos in Edo and its environs. In the waning days of 1867, the would-be insurgent heroes split into three groups and attacked the shogunate's administrative outposts (*jin'ya*) in the countryside. Within a matter of days, peasant militias had suppressed the *rōnin*, who fled to the main Satsuma estate in Edo. Eager to make an example, Tokugawa leaders ordered the vassal domains of Shōnai and Matsuyama to attack the compound. After a fierce artillery bombardment directed by Jules Brunet, one of the shogunate's French military advisers, the remaining *rōnin* fled to the *Shōō-maru*, a Satsuma steamship. The Tokugawa corvette *Kaiten-maru* pursued and fired on the *Shōō-maru* but backed off after the Satsuma vessel returned fire.[45] These two engagements may have been small affairs, but they escalated tensions to the breaking point.

On the first day of the (lunar) new year, a proclamation issued in Yoshinobu's name called for the rendition of the "dishonest vassals" (*kanshin*) from Satsuma.[46] Tokugawa forces marched on Kyoto the next day. The shogunate's army numbered over 10,000, including thirteen Western-style infantry battalions, twenty-two artillery pieces, and several hundred troops from allied domains such as Aizu. Loyalist forces had fewer resources at their disposal: Satsuma fielded approximately 3,000 men and twenty artillery pieces; Chōshū, around 1,000 soldiers. Several other loyalist-aligned domains such as Hiroshima, Okayama, and Tottori had soldiers in the capital but opted to sit out the fighting to see who triumphed. Like the shogunate's forces, Satsuma and Chōshū's soldiers were organized into Western-style rifle units.

The shogunate's army planned a two-pronged advance into the capital along the Toba road and through the suburb of Fushimi. The local topography, however, made this plan difficult to implement and negated the Tokugawa manpower advantage.[47] Loyalist leaders, on the other hand, had the comparatively simple task of defending the approaches to Kyoto. The battle began on the third day of the first month, when loyalist forces repulsed the initial Tokugawa thrust. The next day, after the Kyoto court publicly endorsed the loyalist cause, Satsuma and Chōshū counterattacked and began driving Tokugawa forces back toward Osaka.[48] Over the following two days, the shogunate's forces retreated toward Osaka Castle, shedding equipment

[45] Hōya, *Boshin sensō*, 48–60.
[46] For a concise description of the court intrigue, see Ravina, *To Stand with the Nations of the World*, 116–20.
[47] Ōyama, *Boshin no eki*, 1:52–61.
[48] Hōya, *Boshin sensō*, 63–66, 78; Drea, *Japan's Imperial Army*, 7–8.

and deserters in their wake.[49] On the night of the sixth, Yoshinobu gave a rousing speech to his remaining soldiers, then promptly fled for Edo aboard the *Kaiyō-maru*. The surviving soldiers had to make their own ways back east. Wakayama, a Tokugawa branch domain that had already submitted to the loyalist coalition, quietly repatriated hundreds of soldiers.[50] Curiously, although both sides had naval vessels in the capital region, the only naval combat was a small and inconclusive engagement between the shogunate's *Kaiyō-maru* and Satsuma's *Kasuga-maru*.[51] Despite possessing a stronger fleet than their adversaries, Tokugawa leaders seemed unwilling to use their ships in a combat role.[52]

Despite the shogunate's defeat, the war's outcome was not yet a foregone conclusion. The leaders of the new loyalist government faced the challenge of coordinating an offensive campaign with a fractious coalition, albeit one that expanded steadily as the direction of the prevailing political winds became clear. Many of the government's new allies had not enacted military reforms. The fledgling state directed allied domains to reorganize their armies along Western lines, but reform would take time; for most of the war, the loyalist coalition was forced to rely upon a handful of domains for serious operations. The shogunate, meanwhile, still had advantages of its own, including favorable geography and a viable reserve of manpower. Several senior Tokugawa officials argued for continued resistance, but the shogun and his closest advisers lacked the political appetite for a protracted civil war. Yoshinobu announced his abdication and dispatched messengers to negotiate surrender terms with the new government. Meanwhile, the shogunate's remaining leaders attempted to respect Yoshinobu's wishes while maintaining a credible deterrent and preventing Edo from descending into chaos. After Yoshinobu's abdication, several hundred infantrymen mutinied and left Edo to seek employment in Aizu.[53]

In this confusing environment, the shogunate's military leadership failed to develop a coherent strategy for defending Edo. The new government's army occupied the critical pass of Hakone without encountering any resistance. On the sixth day of the third month, soldiers from Tosa and Tottori defeated the Shinsengumi – once a *rōnin* gendarmerie, now organized as a

---

[49] Ōyama, *Boshin no eki*, 1:76–95, 103–5.
[50] Ōyama, *Boshin no eki*, 1:127.
[51] Hōya, *Boshin sensō*, 76.
[52] Schencking, *Making Waves*, 11.
[53] Hōya, *Boshin sensō*, 152.

large rifle company – near Katsunuma in the mountains west of Edo. This engagement was an instructive example of the difference between having new hardware and understanding how to use it. Kondō Isami, the Shinsengumi's leader, deployed his unit on a hill facing the advancing enemy but failed to guard his flanks. More critically, his artillery chief – one of the few trained officers on site – was recruiting in a nearby village when the battle began. In his absence, Kondō's anxious troopers fired their two cannons without accurately calculating range or using the correct ammunition. With the Shinsengumi unable to mount effective resistance and apparently oblivious to their dangerously exposed position, Tosa's soldiers maneuvered around both flanks and attacked, driving a stunned Kondō from the field in confusion.[54]

On the thirteenth day of the third month, the new government's forces arrived outside Edo. After a month of talks, the shogunate agreed to surrender Edo Castle and all war materiel – including the Tokugawa navy and infantry units. The Tokugawa would be relocated to a reduced fief, where it would receive an "appropriate" allotment of military resources.[55] Some shogunal officials rejected the settlement. Ōtori Keisuke, the commander of the remaining Tokugawa infantry units, left Edo with several hundred soldiers. After fighting a few small actions against government forces, Ōtori's troops moved north to defend Aizu domain. Enomoto Takeaki, the shogunate's principal naval commander, left Edo with eight ships, although he was soon persuaded to return and surrender half of his fleet to the new government, with the understanding that the remaining ships would follow when the Tokugawa house was safely relocated to new holdings.

The largest cluster of opposition was the Shōgitai, a group of nearly 2,000 former Tokugawa retainers and other hangers-on who had occupied the temple complex at Ueno Kan'eiji. In the spring of 1868, as the new government was preparing to commit more resources to its campaign against the northern domains, its leaders decided to suppress the Shōgitai rather than leave a sizeable pocket of potential enemies in its rear. Sanjō Sanetomi, then the senior court leader in Edo, ordered Ōmura Masujirō of Chōshū to clear out Ueno.[56] Ōmura had garnered a reputation as a clever operator for his performance against the shogunate's forces in the Chōshū War, but in this instance he opted for brute force. Despite lackluster execution and significant losses, Ōmura's forces took Ueno in a single day, killing approximately 250 of the

---

[54] Hōya, *Boshin sensō*, 152–63; Ōyama, *Boshin no eki*, 1:149–152, 161–62.
[55] Hōya, *Boshin sensō*, 161–62.
[56] Hōya, *Boshin sensō*, 167.

Shōgitai warriors and dispersing the rest.[57] Now firmly in control of Edo, the new government was able to turn its attention to the last pockets of resistance in northern Japan.

Phase 3: The War for the Northeast, 1868–1869

The Meiji government's campaign against Aizu and its northern allies was a war of choice, conducted capably by some and ineptly by others, and remarkable for its brutality. After the surrender of Edo Castle, Aizu's daimyo Matsudaira Katamori had returned to his domain hoping to implement the "armed submission" strategy that had worked for the shogunate. Katamori indicated his willingness to surrender as long as Aizu was afforded the same terms as other domains. The new regime, however, intended to make an example of Aizu, both for personal reasons and as a matter of political calculation. Katamori had been one of the shogunate's staunchest defenders. As the protector (*shugoshoku*) of Kyoto during the tumultuous 1860s, he had been an unwavering adversary of loyalist activists. The new government also blamed him for instigating civil war by encouraging Yoshinobu's failed march on Kyoto.[58] On a more practical level, forcing Aizu's submission mere months after overthrowing the shogunate would burnish the new government's veneer of military might. A second domain, Shōnai, was also considered a high-priority target for leading the attack on Satsuma's Edo compound and dithering in its support of the fledgling Meiji state.

To compel Aizu's submission, the new government's leaders sent a small force to the northeast and ordered Aizu's and Shōnai's most powerful neighbors – Sendai, Yonezawa, and Kubota (Akita) – to ready their armies for war. While complying grudgingly with the government's directives, Sendai convened a meeting of northern daimyo in the hopes of brokering a peaceful settlement. Twenty-seven domains petitioned the government to request leniency for Aizu and Shōnai. Their plea was denied. Soon afterward, government representative Sera Shūzō and several of his party were assassinated in a Fukushima brothel by Aizu warriors. With their hand forced, the twenty-seven northern domains sealed a defensive pact; they were soon joined by several domains from the northern coast. Despite its name, the Northern Alliance had no coordinated plan beyond stopping the government's armies at their borders.[59] This was not necessarily an impossible task;

---

[57] Ōyama, *Boshin no eki*, 1:354–72.
[58] Shimoda, *Lost and Found*, 16.
[59] Hōya, *Boshin sensō*, 187–93.

after all, Chōshū had defended itself successfully in 1866, and the outnumbered loyalist army had defeated the shogunate at Toba-Fushimi just a few months prior. Nonetheless, the absence of a coalition strategy was an invitation for miscommunication and infighting.

This phase of the Restoration Wars again showcased the difference between having technological capabilities and understanding how to use them effectively. The new government possessed several critical advantages: more advanced weaponry in greater quantities; more veteran troops and commanders; and (at least until the final phase of the campaign) naval superiority, which enabled it to move troops more rapidly than its northern opponents. This last advantage also meant that government forces held the strategic initiative; in other words, they could determine when and where battles took place. This was one advantage, however, that commanders exploited inconsistently. On the other side, the northern domains did not start the war on a strong footing. Most had put off military reforms until civil war seemed all but certain. Sendai, one of the alliance's most powerful members, had embraced military reforms in the 1850s, only to abandon them under fiscal pressure a few years later. By the time the war began, it had just one rifle company trained in modern tactics. Although the domain encouraged the purchase and use of rifles, the bulk of its army was a hodgepodge of spears and matchlock muskets.[60] Similarly, Aizu and Shōnai only enacted substantive military reforms after Toba-Fushimi. Both domains demonstrated a willingness to recruit commoners for military service, and although Aizu reorganized its retainer band, it did so with a keen sensitivity for the seniority and social status of warriors.[61] The northern domains had some modern artillery and small arms, but not nearly in the quantities their enemies possessed. They did have the support of several hundred of the former shogunate's infantrymen, but not enough to turn the tide of the war. Moreover, the domains' ability to purchase new weapons and supplies was limited to the port of Niigata, where the Dutch Schnell brothers oversaw a profitable gun-running business.[62]

With some notable exceptions, casualty totals for most engagements during this stage of the war were low compared to contemporary conflicts. Part of the reason for the relatively low toll had to do with the composition of the Northern Alliance. The member domains had allied to help defend Aizu and Shōnai against what they viewed as a vindictive cabal. Domains such

---

[60] Ōyama, *Boshin no eki*, 1:385–86; Hōya, *Boshin sensō*, 175–76.
[61] Hōya, *Boshin sensō*, 177–83.
[62] Bolitho, "Echigo War," 266.

as Yonezawa and Sendai had no interest in fighting to the last soldier; they tended to surrender as their war aims slipped below the horizon of possibility. Second, the belligerents on both sides were still learning how to fight a war with modern weaponry. Commanders often dispersed their artillery, reducing its effectiveness. Moreover, as Hōya Tōru has demonstrated, most small-arms firefights seem to have taken place at the very edge of effective rifle range, with the outcome decided when one side ran low on ammunition and withdrew. Thus, while this stage of the conflict featured a few bloody battles, the war was not nearly as destructive as it might have been.

Fighting in the northeast began in earnest in the fifth month of 1868, when a large alliance force attacked the government's forward outpost at the Shirakawa barrier in present-day Fukushima Prefecture. After two and a half months of maneuvering, a government army under the joint command of Satsuma's Ijichi Masaharu and Tosa's Itagaki Taisuke was poised to strike into Aizu and Sendai territory.

Fighting on other fronts went less smoothly. On the Japan Sea coast, Yamagata Aritomo of Chōshū badly bungled an advance on Niigata despite commanding the largest government force. Yamagata was saved by his deputy, Kuroda Kiyotaka of Satsuma. Kuroda launched a daring direct attack on the port of Niigata that, combined with Shibata domain's decision to betray the alliance, secured the area and brought government forces to Aizu's western borders. On the fourth day of the seventh month, Kubota domain abandoned the alliance and attacked Shōnai's northern borders. Shōnai redirected its forces to its northern border and routed Kubota's outmoded army.[63] Only the collapse of the alliance in the ninth month saved Kubota from disaster.

The conquest of Aizu proved to be the decisive moment of the conflict. In three days of fighting, Itagaki and Ijichi's army – operating in defiance of official orders – broke through the Bonari Pass and arrived on the outskirts of Wakamatsu, Aizu's castle town, where they laid siege to the city.[64] With the outcome of the war increasingly certain, alliance domains began to surrender. Yonezawa capitulated on the fourth day of the ninth month, Sendai on the fifteenth. Shōnai decided to surrender on the following day, although it took a week to convey the message to government representatives.

The siege of Aizu continued for three weeks. Itagaki's army, now reinforced by Yamagata, prepared for a general assault. Meanwhile, Aizu-Wakamatsu's

---

[63] Hōya, Boshin sensō, 242–43.
[64] Ōyama, Boshin no eki, 2:21–22.

population, including commoner conscripts and women warriors, rallied to the defense of the town. Dozens of women volunteered to fight as a "women's corps" (*jōshigun*), which they did over the objections of male comrades worried that women's participation might cast doubts upon their martial prowess. Yamamoto Yaeko (known to later generations as Niijima Yae), the daughter of one of Aizu's musketry instructors, donned male clothing and battled government forces with her Spencer repeater. She was commanding an artillery crew on the fourteenth day of the ninth month when government forces began a massive bombardment in preparation for a general assault on Aizu-Wakamatsu.[65] Aizu's leaders finally surrendered on the twenty-second. While the new government treated other alliance domains in relatively conciliatory fashion, its leaders were pitiless in their handling of Aizu. The domain was transferred to the inhospitable northern edge of Honshu; combatants were imprisoned for months; and in a stroke of appalling cruelty, Aizu's dead were left to rot.[66]

Despite the collapse of the alliance, the war continued for another six months as Tokugawa holdouts gave the conflict a quixotic epilogue. Enomoto Takeaki, the former commander of the shogunate's navy, still retained control of four vessels, including the twenty-six-gun frigate *Kaiyō-maru* and the *Kōtetsu* (née CSS *Stonewall*), an ironclad originally built in France for the American Confederacy. Enomoto had waited to join the Northern Alliance after the Tokugawa house had been safely relocated to its new domain in Numazu. He sailed for Sendai with eight ships late in the eighth month of 1868. By the time he arrived, the domain was preparing to capitulate. Enomoto picked up the remnants of Ōtori Keisuke's shogunal infantry, the Shinsen-gumi, and several hundred Aizu and Sendai warriors who wanted to continue the fight. Now in possession of some 2,500 ground troops, Enomoto moved to southern Hokkaido, where, on the twenty-fifth day of the tenth month, he overran the government garrison at Hakodate's Goryōkaku, a Western-style star fort constructed by the shogunate in 1857. His forces secured most of the Japanese lands (Wajinchi) on the southern tip of the island in a matter of weeks. For six months, he held Hokkaido, hoping that his control of the island would give him leverage to negotiate a semi-autonomous domain for former Tokugawa retainers. Government leaders had a different appraisal of the situation, fearing that any diminution of their claims to sovereignty over

---

[65] Wright, "Female Combatants"; "Women of Aizu," in Walthall and Steele, *Politics and Society*.

[66] Craig, "Introduction," 19–21; Shimoda, *Lost and Found*, 40–76.

Hokkaido would invite interference from Russia. As the weather warmed, government forces landed on Hokkaido, which they secured within a month. Goryōkaku surrendered on the eighteenth day of the fifth month of 1869.

The Early Meiji State: Achievements and Challenges (1868–1878)

As the Restoration Wars came to an end, the Meiji government turned its attention to winning the peace, in a process that shaped the future of Japan's military for the next seventy years. During the first decade of the Meiji era (1868–1912), the lingering threat of civil war drove the new state's leaders to focus on domestic security. In the short term, that meant building ground forces under the government's direct command while curtailing the power of potential challengers to its authority. After a failed attempt to create a national army using a federal model, in 1871 the government created an Imperial Guard (*goshinpei*) and abolished the domain armies. Two years later, it implemented a conscription system designed to fill the army's ranks at relatively low cost. The navy, meanwhile, remained a secondary priority. Modern warships were resource- and capital-intensive projects; Japan lacked the ability to build its own vessels until the late 1880s. For several years, the early Meiji navy made do with incremental additions to its existing fleet – a hodgepodge of Tokugawa leftovers and domain vessels – as well as improvements to coastal defense fortifications.

Japan's military began the 1870s in an uncertain state. Only one question had been settled decisively by the Restoration Wars: that of hardware. Meiji military leaders were not beholden to Japan's martial past; they were committed to a future of rifles, cannons, and ironclad warships. Until Japan developed its own military-industrial capacity in the 1880s, the government had to rely upon foreign powers to procure weapons and ships. Meanwhile, several questions regarding the future(s) of the new army and navy remained contested. What were the embryonic state's strategic priorities, especially vis-à-vis the rest of Asia? Was mobilizing an army for domestic security more important than building a navy for maritime defense? How should the new military recruit and train personnel? The new government answered these questions – often multiple times and in conflicting ways – as it responded to the political and social dislocations of the 1870s. There was no unified blueprint for military development; rather, a complex mix of policy initiatives and crisis responses succeeded just enough for the new government to survive its first decade. When Meiji military leaders embarked on a more comprehensive consideration of these questions in the 1880s, the inheritance of the 1870s shaped their situational awareness. As Japan's pursuit of Great Power status accelerated, the core dynamic of Japan's military establishment – constant competition between an oversized, low-tech conscript army and a technologically sophisticated but undersized navy – remained.

Failure of the Federal Approach, 1868–1872

When the Restoration Wars ended, the Meiji government's army comprised an imperial bodyguard (shinpei) of a few hundred volunteers, most of whom were rusticated warriors (gōshi), rōnin, or commoners. Almost all the 110,000 soldiers recruited for the Restoration Wars belonged to the domains. Moreover, Satsuma, Chōshū, and Tosa had done most of the fighting and suffered 40 percent of the coalition's casualties.[67] An 1868 attempt to raise conscripts from allied domains yielded just 1,800 men – less than one-third of the expected total – most of them domain warriors with little allegiance to the central government.[68] In late 1868, Itō Hirobumi, then serving as the governor of Hyōgo, proposed converting the victorious government army into a standing force. His proposal never received serious consideration, as the new state's leadership understood their relative weakness compared with the domains'.[69] The five years between 1868 and 1873 were a period of organizational whiplash, as the Meiji government adopted a trial-and-error approach to building a national military, often responding to the failure of one experiment by pivoting hard in another direction.

The government first experimented with a federal approach, which envisioned a national army supported by closely regulated domain forces. Meiji leaders procured their embryonic army by once again leaning on the governing Satsuma-Chōshū-Tosa alliance for 1,500 conscripts to help secure the new capital at Tokyo.[70] Then, in the second month of 1870, they ordered all domains to reform their armies in accordance with the Regular Army Organization Regulations (Jōbi hentai kisoku), which set organizational standards and recruitment targets based on domains' assessed yields.[71] Compliance varied widely. Although the government's federal approach yielded some fascinating experiments – such as the Tokugawa house's Numazu Military Academy – it was too uneven a foundation for a national army. The War

---

[67] Senda, Ishin seiken, 55.
[68] Katō, Chōheisei.
[69] Itō, "Hokuchi gaisen," 3–5.
[70] Senda, Ishin seiken, 105.
[71] Yamagata, Horiuchi, and Hirayama, "Rikugunshō enkakushi," 121–22.

Ministry (Hyōbushō) tried to mitigate the problem by mandating a British training model for the navy and a French model for the army.[72] Even that proved insufficient. A month later, the government abandoned the federal approach, instead ordering domains to furnish conscripts (chōhei) and officer candidates to the War Ministry based on their aggregate assessed yields. This effort, too, ended in failure, with the army receiving less than a quarter of its anticipated tally.[73] The domains were simply too unreliable to serve as the fulcrum of the government's defense establishment. In the second month of 1871, the War Ministry ordered Satsuma, Chōshū, and Tosa to contribute 6,000 soldiers for an Imperial Guard. This nucleus of veteran soldiers gave the government the deterrent it needed to abolish the domains, a move that Meiji leaders made in the seventh month. The government also disbanded domain armies, although it required each domain to assign one platoon (40–50 men) to one of four garrisons (chindai) located at strategic points throughout the country: in Tokyo, Sendai, Osaka, and Kumamoto. On paper, the Meiji government had consolidated the disparate domain militaries into a national army. The reality was more complex. Most of the garrison soldiers (chindaihei) were former warriors with complicated loyalties and a keen awareness of their socioeconomic precarity. Low morale, disobedience, and outright mutiny plagued the army throughout the 1870s, until the new conscription law and a stricter disciplinary regime brought the rank and file to heel.

Meanwhile, the navy languished as a subsection of the War Ministry until 1872, when successful advocacy by Satsuma's Ōkubo Toshimichi led to the establishment of separate army (Rikugunshō) and navy (Kaigunshō) ministries. Kawamura Sumiyoshi (Satsuma) served as the first navy minister, but the government soon turned to Katsu Kaishū, who had garnered a reputation as the shogunate's leading naval expert. In reality, Katsu was an enthusiast with little real expertise. In 1860, he had "captained" the vessel that carried a Tokugawa delegation to the United States, but he spent most of the journey fighting seasickness belowdecks. He then served as a figurehead admiral and drafted a series of grandiose naval expansion plans. Even after his appointment by the new government, Katsu continued to play the hits, drafting a wildly unrealistic plan that called for the domestic construction of a hundred warships by 1890.[74] Meiji leaders rejected this plan but did authorize (in 1874)

[72] "Kairikugun no hensei hōshin ni tsuki fukoku," in Yui, Fujiwara, and Yoshida, Guntai heishi, 33–35.
[73] Senda, Ishin seiken, 168.
[74] Schencking, Making Waves, 17.

the purchase of six foreign-built warships, only three of which arrived before 1880. Naval appropriations continued to lag behind the army, partly due to political infighting, but principally because of military and fiscal realities. Domestic security, which in the 1870s meant suppressing anti-government revolts, required the new government to assemble significant ground forces. Naval vessels might be useful for transportation, but they were ill-suited to the threats of the moment. Moreover, fleet expansion required capital and infrastructure investment that was beyond the means of a government still struggling to establish a tax base. Consequently, Japan's small navy spent the early Meiji divided between the two newly established naval districts (*chinjufu*) in Nagasaki and Yokohama.

The Conscription System, 1872–1873

The creation of the Imperial Guard and the consolidation of the domain armies bought the new government time to consider a permanent solution to its military dilemma. Government leaders coalesced around two possible options. The first – advocated by Ōkubo Toshimichi and Saigō Takamori, among others – would create a professional volunteer army drawn principally from the ranks of former warriors. This approach could limit social dislocation by providing disaffected warriors with an avenue of employment, but salaries and other expenses would create a significant fiscal burden. The volunteer approach might also have prolonged the survival of the Tokugawa-era status distinctions the new government was attempting to dismantle.

The second approach – championed by Yamagata Aritomo and his allies within the Army Ministry – would rely on a "universal" military service system (*chōheisei*), which offered several advantages to the Meiji government. For one, it could deliver substantial manpower at low cost. Making military service an obligation not only alleviated the government's fiscal burdens; it also meant that conscripts would cycle through the army on a regular basis, facilitating the creation of a sizeable reserve. Moreover, conscripting young men from varied social backgrounds would help the army escape its reliance on volunteers (*sōhei*), who comprised the majority of Imperial Guardsmen and garrison soldiers prior to 1873. Most *sōhei* were former warriors whose rowdiness and resistance to military discipline posed serious difficulties for the army's leadership. Replacing them with more pliable conscripts would remain a priority through the late 1870s. Finally, Yamagata's coterie in the Army Ministry was committed to the idea of an emperor-centered nation-state and viewed military service as a means of inculcating patriotic consciousness in the country's male youth. Although the pro-conscription faction agreed broadly on the merits of mandatory military service, they differed on the details. Some advocated modeling Japan's conscription system on France's, others on Germany's, and some – such as Chōshū's Yamada Akiyoshi – favored the creation of a national militia system rather than a standing army.[75]

Conscription advocates won the argument. On 5 December 1872, the government issued two statements: a conscription edict (chōhei no mikotonori) from the Meiji emperor and a conscription pronouncement (chōhei kokuyu) from the Council of State (Dajōkan). Both documents glossed conscription with the patina of historical precedent. They invoked the thousand-year-old military system of the Nara period (710–84), which also used conscription, as a historical precedent that portrayed the creation of a national conscript army as a restoration of the ideal relationship between the emperor and his subjects. Warriors were the villains in this understanding of Japan's history, since their privileged status usurped imperial prerogatives. The Meiji military establishment's dim view of warriors persisted until the mid-1880s, when warriors' increasing political and social irrelevance rendered warrior values appropriable as guiding principles for a new disciplinary regime.[76]

The government issued the Conscription Ordinance (Chōheirei) on 10 January 1873. The earlier documents articulated the rationale for the conscription policy; the ordinance provided the details. All male subjects were liable for military service, with able-bodied males between the ages of seventeen and forty automatically enrolled in a national guard (kokumingun), a reserve of last resort. At the age of twenty, males would undergo an examination to determine their fitness to serve. Those who passed would be entered into a lottery, with the "winners" selected for active duty (gen'eki) and a smaller cohort chosen for replacement duty (hojū eki). Active-duty soldiers would serve three years in the regular military and a total of four years in the reserves (kōbigun). The law also included a broad range of exemption categories designed to protect skilled laborers and government employees while also minimizing disruption of the rural tax base.

It is tempting to view the 1873 Conscription Ordinance as a foundational moment for Japan's modern military, but its success was far from certain. In the months immediately following its promulgation, hundreds of former warriors mutinied and deserted. In western Japan, resentment against conscription and other new policies led to a rash of violent uprisings. Beyond

---

[75] Yamada, "Heisei ni tsuki kenpakusho"; Westney, "Military," 179.
[76] "Chōhei no mikotonori to kokuyu," in Yui, Fujiwara, and Yoshida, Guntai heishi, 67–69.

outright resistance, the Meiji government also confronted the staggering complexity of implementing conscription on a nationwide basis. It thus decided to proceed in stages, beginning with the Tokyo garrison in early 1873 before expanding to Osaka and the newly established Nagoya garrison later in the year. Sendai, Hiroshima (also newly established), and Kumamoto conducted exams beginning in 1874. As a result, conscripts only fully replaced unruly *sōhei* in the late 1870s. Fiscal challenges remained significant, leading the army to induct only a scant percentage of examinees. Chronic draft evasion severely limited examiners' ability to be selective.

As the army labored to improve its conscript pool, the navy moved in the opposite direction, choosing instead to rely on volunteers. Two factors made the navy's task comparatively easy. First, it was small. In 1872, for instance, the navy had approximately 1,500 enlisted personnel to the army's 17,000.[77] Second, the navy targeted potential recruits who were accustomed to maritime work. This recruiting strategy allowed the navy to screen for technical skills and functional literacy. Although it did accept conscripts, the navy was able to exercise more selectivity than the army.

As conscription – and military service more generally – became an accepted part of civic life in Meiji Japan, the age of the warrior came to an end. From the late Tokugawa era through the conclusion of the Restoration Wars, warriors had attempted to preserve what remained of the autonomy they viewed as their prerogative. The introduction of Western drill, with its emphasis on coordinated and synchronized movement, had limited the possibility for individual action, while the presence of commoners in the ranks exploded old assumptions about the correlation between social status and fighting ability. Warriors themselves did not disappear. Some rebelled against the new order, but most assimilated to the emerging institutions of Meiji society. As warriors ceased to exist as a social category, a particular vision of martial masculinity disappeared with them. It had, however, yet to be replaced. The early Meiji government had built a national military, but critical questions remained unanswered. What were the Meiji state's strategic priorities? What kind of organizations would the army and navy become? And, finally, what kind of soldiers and sailors would those services require?

Challenges to Change, 1873–1877

The conscription policy dealt a crushing blow to former warriors who saw military careers as a potential lifeline during a time of rapid social and economic

---

[77] Schencking, *Making Waves*, 16; Drea, *Japan's Imperial Army*, 29.

change. In late summer 1873, controversy over a proposed invasion of Korea led to the resignation of Saigō Takamori, Itagaki Taisuke, and several other officials seen as advocates for warrior interests. Discontent mounted among volunteers (sōhei) in the ranks; several hundred Imperial Guardsmen deserted in protest.[78] In Kumamoto, the soldiers of the Eleventh Infantry Battalion smashed and burned their barracks. Another infantry battalion in Kagoshima (Satsuma) also mutinied and deserted.[79] In February 1874, former justice minister Etō Shinpei – who had resigned with Saigō and Itagaki – returned to his home province of Saga and led 2,500 former warriors in a rebellion against the new government. Government reinforcements from the Hiroshima and Osaka garrisons managed to suppress the revolt in a matter of weeks. In a cruel bit of irony, government forces had bolstered their numbers by hiring thousands of former warriors as auxiliaries. After Etō was captured and executed, the new government circulated a photograph of his severed head.[80] The message was clear: armed revolt would be met with the full weight of the Meiji military. Nonetheless, challenges against the new government continued.

Common citizens – the very people the army's leaders thought had been edified by their eligibility for military service – also resisted the conscription policy, and not because of their ignorance of military service. Thousands of commoners had participated in the Restoration Wars. Those who saw front-line service could often aspire to compensation for their efforts, whether in the form of status promotion or steady employment. Early Meiji conscripts faced different circumstances. At age twenty, they were obligated to present themselves for inspection, at which point an army medical examiner would determine their future. Conscripts' households had few avenues to protest the three-year loss of their sons' labor. Moreover, the government's frequent policy shifts provoked anxiety that further impositions would follow. Rumors – that the government intended to order additional conscriptions for an invasion of Korea, or that it intended to conscript young women for sex work – flew through the countryside.[81] One rumor, that the conscription pronouncement's metaphorical description of military service as a "blood tax" referred to a literal bloodletting, gave peasants sufficient pretext to act out against the new policy. The blood tax riots (ketsuzei sōdō), as the uprisings

---

[78] Drea, Japan's Imperial Army, 63.

[79] Matsushita, Nihon rikukaigun sōdōshi, 63–67.

[80] Botsman, Punishment and Power, 163–64; Drea, Japan's Imperial Army, 36–38.

[81] Tōkyō nichinichi shinbun (6 March 1873), in Edamatsu, Sugiura, and Yagi, Meiji nyūsu jiten, 1:477.

became known, swept through western Japan in the summer of 1873, leading to widespread destruction of government buildings, attacks on officials, and the brutalization of recently emancipated outcastes (*burakumin*). The rioters' lists of grievances called for the rollback of several new policies, including the land tax, outcaste emancipation, the Western calendar, and conscription.

After the suppression of the riots, potential conscripts continued to oppose the new policy by exploiting legal loopholes and inefficiencies in the law's implementation to evade military service. In its 1873 incarnation, the Conscription Ordinance included a wide range of exemptions, many of which targeted skilled workers such as government officials and technical students. Other provisions, such as those exempting only children, heads of household, and adopted heirs (*yōshi*), were intended to alleviate the burden of conscription on the rural population. Tens of thousands of peasant households evaded service by using the exemption categories, especially the provision for adopted heirs. They were aided by a veritable genre of conscription law guidebooks printed by popular publishers. These books, with titles such as *Don't Worry about Conscription* (*Chōhei shinpai nashi*) "explained" the evolving conscription policy by pointing out its loopholes in copious detail.[82] Attempts to evade the draft often received help from local officials, who had critical administrative roles in the conscription process. In the early Meiji era, the state lacked the administrative infrastructure to implement policy on the local level; it had no choice but to delegate. Village heads (*kochō*) maintained the conscription and exemption rolls. They recorded recruits' ages and judged whether physical disabilities merited exemptions. In other words, they were perfectly positioned to help recruits evade examinations. In fact, evasion became the norm: until the first revisions to the Conscription Ordinance in 1879, the overwhelming majority of eligible youth claimed exemptions to the examination.

As would-be conscripts resisted the draft, many former warriors once again opted for direct action. In March 1876, the Meiji government announced a series of actions designed to eliminate the remaining status privileges of former warriors. The government mandated the replacement of warrior stipends – which it had paid at a reduced rate since the abolition of the domains – with fixed bonds. It also outlawed the public bearing of swords, a decision that drew a clear line between former warriors and state-sanctioned arms-bearers such as soldiers and police. With yet another economic lifeline cut, many déclassé warriors rebelled. That autumn, three insurrections

---

[82] Yoshida, *Gun'eki kokoroe*; Nakano, *Kaisei chōhei shinpai nashi*.

erupted in southwestern Japan, at Hagi (Chōshū), Akizuki, and Kumamoto. The army suppressed these revolts quickly, although the Kumamoto rebels' surprise night attack resulted in over 300 casualties (including sixty dead) for the garrison.

The Meiji government had benefited from good luck in the years following the Restoration Wars. The few challenges to its military hegemony had been small, disorganized affairs that never evolved into existential threats. The War of the Southwest (the Satsuma Rebellion), which began in February 1877, exceeded all the previous rebellions in scale and in casualties. After his resignation from the government in the fall of 1873, Saigō Takamori and his closest lieutenants returned to Kagoshima, where they created a network of private military academies. Meanwhile, Kagoshima's prefectural government ignored policy directives from the central government, refusing to implement the new land tax, the Conscription Ordinance, or the Western calendrical system. In the wake of the 1876 uprisings, a suspicious Meiji government dispatched several Kagoshima-born police officers to investigate potentially rebellious activities. Most of the spies were captured and forced to confess their participation in a conspiracy to assassinate Saigō. This was casus belli enough for Saigō and his men, who organized an army of 13,000 soldiers from the private military academies and Kagoshima's population of disaffected former warriors. Unlike the instigators of earlier rebellions, the Kagoshima rebels were organized and trained. Several hundred were veterans of the Restoration Wars. Almost all of them carried rifles, including some modern breechloaders. In many ways, they were reminiscent of the army Satsuma had fielded during the Restoration Wars. They did, however, have two main shortcomings: insufficient quantities of artillery and a severely limited capacity for resupply. Saigō's rebel army had to strike quickly, as it was poorly suited to fighting a war of attrition.

Unfortunately for the rebels, that is precisely how the campaign unfolded. On 14 February, Saigō's army marched on the Kumamoto garrison, which they found well ensconced behind the castle walls. After a series of unsuccessful attacks, Saigō left 3,000 troops to continue the siege, then took the bulk of his army to the ridgelines around Tabaruzaka, just north of the city, where he hoped to stall government reinforcements. The decision to commit to a positional defense might have seemed unavoidable to Saigō and his lieutenants, but it put their outnumbered and undersupplied force at a severe disadvantage against an enemy that had time and resources on its side. Using these advantages effectively, however, proved challenging for the Meiji military. Dysfunction and poor coordination hampered offensive efforts both at the command level and on the ground. Without a real general staff to coordinate the campaign, the government's civilian leaders allowed senior military commanders – Yamagata Aritomo, Kuroda Kiyotaka, and Kawamura Sumiyoshi (commanding the navy) – to conduct their own operations, which they did with varying degrees of success. Yamagata spent a month battering away at the rebels' Tabaruzaka position, only succeeding after Kuroda drew some of Saigō's troops away with a landing south of Kumamoto on 19 March. Government forces broke the siege of Kumamoto in early April; government forces spent the next five months chasing a diminishing rebel army around Kyushu. The campaign concluded on 24 September, when 20,000 government soldiers encircled and defeated Saigō and his remaining 400 soldiers. The combined casualty totals – 11,000 dead, 26,000 wounded – exceeded the toll of the Restoration Wars.

The War of the Southwest was a qualified victory for the new government's national military. The campaign validated the army's embrace of contemporary military hardware. Government forces had more artillery, more – and newer – small arms, and better access to critical supplies such as ammunition. Moreover, commanders such as Kuroda and Kawamura were able to use the undersized navy to great effect, stretching rebel forces to the breaking point. The new military's software had proved more problematic. Even veteran commanders such as Yamagata and Kuroda were handling much larger bodies of troops than they had during the Restoration Wars, and the army lacked a specialized cadre of staff officers to handle operational planning and coordination between units. Inexperience with the nuts-and-bolts detail work of military campaigning led to debacles such as the stalemate at Tabaruzaka and Saigō's repeated escapes from government forces' attempts at encirclement. Officers improvised solutions for field medicine and logistics, compensating for the army's undermanned supply corps by contracting thousands of teamsters (*ninpu*) to haul ammunition and rations. Conscripts' performance – which was adequate, if not exceptional – was one of the campaign's few bright spots. Although the army did enlist several thousand auxiliaries from the police force and from among former warriors, it did so not because conscripts were poor soldiers, but to avoid compromising its pool of reserves. The War of the Southwest may have bent the new conscription system, but it did not break it.

An Imperial Military?

The army and navy were key players in the Meiji state's first halting steps toward empire. Late Tokugawa military reform advocates had sought to defend Japan's borders against the perceived threat of Western imperialism. Then, in the 1860s and 1870s, political leaders' understanding of territorial sovereignty adapted to the imperial world. The ambiguous status of Okinawa and Hokkaido was a particular source of concern that the Meiji government moved to address almost immediately after it consolidated power. But despite claiming these regions as Japanese territory, for several decades the new government adopted a colonial approach to their security.

Efforts to claim Hokkaido as Japanese territory predated the restoration. For most of the Tokugawa era, only southern Hokkaido had been considered Japanese (Wajinchi), with most of the island designated Ainu territory (Ezochi), although the shogunate moved to take more direct control over Hokkaido in the mid-nineteenth century.[83] Enomoto Takeaki's attempt to establish a semi-autonomous domain in Hokkaido convinced Meiji leaders that the island's ambiguous territorial status represented a potential opening for other imperial powers, especially Russia. To garrison the island, the government adopted a two-pronged approach that relied upon the division between Japanese and Ainu territory at the same time the government's Hokkaido Development Agency (Kaitakushi) was working to eliminate it. Although the 1873 Conscription Ordinance exempted Hokkaido, an 1876 government order allowed the Hokkaido Development Agency to conscript residents of southern Hokkaido for service in the coastal heavy artillery battalion. Until the creation of Hokkaido's Seventh Division in 1896, the former Wajinchi remained the only territory liable to the conscription law. The rest of the island was garrisoned by the Hokkaido militia (tondenhei), a program in which Japanese settlers (including many former warriors from northeastern Japan) were granted land in exchange for occasional military service. Although soldiers from the militia fought in the War of the Southwest and the Sino-Japanese War, it was never a large unit. Fewer than 7,500 soldiers (in total) served in the militia between 1874 and its abolition thirty years later. While insufficient to repel a potential Russian invasion, the militia was a critical pillar of support for the colonization program in Hokkaido.[84]

At the same time, the Meiji government also moved to clarify the territorial ambiguity of the Ryukyu Islands. Though notionally independent, the Ryukyu kingdom had been controlled by Satsuma domain since the early seventeenth century. Like Hokkaido, Ryukyu's ambiguous territorial status made it a potential vulnerability that the Meiji government moved quickly to remedy. In 1872,

[83] Howell, Geographies of Identity, 130.
[84] Mason, Dominant Narratives, 35–37.

the government asserted its control over Ryukyu by declaring the kingdom a "domain" (*han*). Two years later, a quixotic military expedition to Taiwan failed to secure a Japanese foothold on the island but succeeded in gaining Qing recognition of Japanese claims to Ryukyu. In 1879, Japan annexed Ryukyu and dispatched an infantry company to garrison the islands.[85] Such a small unit may have been inadequate as a defense force for the newly created Okinawa Prefecture, but it sufficed to display a Japanese military presence to outside observers. This colonial arrangement persisted until 1898, when the government extended conscription to Okinawa. Even then, Okinawan conscripts faced discrimination for their perceived failure to assimilate to mainland military culture, resulting in tensions that persisted through World War II.[86]

Coda: Building the Imperial Military (After 1878)

The military's experiences in the field during the 1870s had exposed serious obstacles in the Meiji state's path toward parity with the imperial powers of the era. Although the new national military performed its missions adequately, its ad hoc character remained a disadvantage. Having achieved a measure of domestic stability, the government's leaders used the fifteen years between Saigō's rebellion and the onset of the first Sino-Japanese War to build a blue-water navy and mold the army into an effective fighting force. By the early 1890s, the Meiji state finally had the imperial military it sought.

The navy of the 1880s faced intertwined political and material challenges. The fleet remained a hodgepodge of Tokugawa-period leftovers and surplus vessels from overseas. Pressing the government for additional resources required sufficient political clout to challenge the army, which had always enjoyed strategic and budgetary priority. Kawamura Sumiyoshi, the Satsuma-born commander who served as navy minister between 1878 and 1885, solved this problem by persuading Satsuma-born generals such as Kabayama Sukenori and Saigō Tsugumichi to transfer their commissions to the navy. These politically connected landlubbers (neither had ever commanded a ship) helped press the case for naval expansion.[87] In 1883, the Satsuma lobby persuaded the Meiji emperor to support an expansion proposal that called for the navy to add (through foreign purchases and domestic construction) six vessels annually through 1891. But because the cost of

---

[85] Matsumura, *Limits of Okinawa*, 27–38.
[86] Chatani, *Nation-Empire*, 93–103.
[87] Schencking, *Making Waves*, 31–34.

state-of-the-art armored battleships would make it impossible to purchase the navy's desired quantity of vessels, naval leaders chose to employ a doctrine propounded by the French navy's *jeune école*, which advocated the advantages of light, mobile cruisers and torpedo boats vis-à-vis battleships. Since the navy saw the Qing – not the British or Americans – as their most likely adversary, the *jeune école* concept seemed adequate for the moment. By 1893, the navy had amassed twenty-eight warships and twenty-four torpedo boats, a vast improvement over its early Meiji numbers.[88] The navy's geographic footprint also expanded beyond Yokosuka with the construction of new naval stations (*chinjufu*) at Kure and Sasebo in 1887. The political clout that facilitated this growth came at a cost, however: the navy was littered with ineffective officers tied to the Satsuma clique. It took personnel reforms spearheaded by Admiral Yamamoto Gonnohyōe (Gonbei) to enable the emergence of a professional officer corps. By the 1890s, most naval officers were academy graduates rather than Satsuma holdovers.[89]

Meanwhile, the army embarked on a transformative reform program. At the command level, Yamagata and his protégé Katsura Tarō pushed for a reorganization of the army on the German model. This involved the 1878 creation of an independent general staff responsible for military command (*gunrei*). The chief of the general staff reported directly to the emperor, bypassing the civilian chain of command through a legal theory known as the "independence of supreme command" (*tōsuiken no dokuritsu*). In the mid-twentieth century, the military would use this privileged position to supersede the civilian government. But, at the time, this legal theory was intended to isolate the military from the tumultuous political environment that contributed to factional infighting and disciplinary problems. On a more practical level, the various sections of the general staff would be responsible for the kind of detailed planning and coordination the army had failed to practice in the field. The same year, the army established an inspectorate general for education, a post designed to bring order to its haphazard training regimens. In 1885, the government hired a German military mission to professionalize officer education. And, in 1887, the army created divisions (*shidan*) to replace the unwieldy garrison force structure.[90] At the command level, the army looked increasingly like its European counterparts.

---

[88] Ichinose, "Kindai," 322.

[89] Schencking, *Making Waves*, 22–23.

[90] Garrisons were not designed to operate as single units in the field; divisions were organized to do just that.

Reforms to senior administration were accompanied by a makeover of the rank and file, beginning with the conscription system. Reforms enacted between 1879 and 1889 closed draft loopholes. In the late 1870s, more than 80 percent of potential recruits avoided examination annually; that number fell below 30 percent by 1886. The 1889 reform eliminated exemptions and deferments. The expanded recruiting pool enabled conscription examiners to be far more selective even as the size of the army surpassed 50,000 soldiers by 1885.[91] At Yamagata's direction, the army began to devote vastly increased attention to soldiers' ideological education. In part, this was a response to soldiers' performance in the War of the Southwest. Conscripts had fought capably but did not exhibit the élan displayed by many rebels. More troublingly for senior officers, soldiers had shown a willingness to take political action. In 1878, Imperial Guardsmen demanding back pay mutinied within the palace grounds. Conscripts and noncommissioned officers engaged in activism associated with the freedom and people's rights movement.[92] Military leaders responded to these concerns with a new disciplinary regime aimed at crafting a positive identity for "servicemen" (gunjin). In the 1878 Admonition to Servicemen (Gunjin kunkai) and the 1882 Imperial Rescript to Servicemen (Gunjin chokuyu), Yamagata and his coterie – particularly the philosopher Nishi Amane – spliced the language of the pre-Meiji warrior ethos together with the disciplinary norms that the military aspired to demand of its personnel. For a decade, the army and navy had avoided valorizing warriors, but their disappearance into the past made the language of the warrior estate appropriable for use. The admonition and rescript did just that, positing soldiers and sailors as the new standard-bearers for warrior values such as loyalty (chūsetsu) and martial valor (buyū). But whereas early modern articulations of the warrior ethos allowed for idiosyncratic interpretations of principles such as loyalty, the army's new disciplinary regime was uncompromising: the emperor should be the sole object of servicemen's loyalty, and his will was embodied in the military chain of command.[93] Together, the admonition and rescript defined martial masculinity for the new era, but in terms that emphasized obedience over agency. Acts of disobedience did not disappear after the 1880s – far from it – but they were often couched as expressing a higher and purer loyalty to the sovereign.[94]

The army and navy approached the first Sino-Japanese War as products of the path the Meiji government had navigated through a tumultuous era. The

[91] Tobe, *Gyakusetsu no guntai*, 108.
[92] Tobe, *Gyakusetsu no guntai*, 64–65.
[93] Benesch, *Inventing the Way of the Samurai*, 116.
[94] Orbach, *Curse on This Country*.

army was an oversized presence, both in terms of manpower and the way it permeated civic life. Its senior leaders were convinced – like their counterparts in European armies – of the value of élan over materiel. The navy, on the other hand, fashioned a reputation as an elite service, technologically sophisticated and interested in educated volunteers. It was also small, constantly fighting for strategic priority and accounting for a mere fraction of the army's manpower and budget until the 1910s. Rivalry and poor coordination between the services persisted into the mid-twentieth century, with severe consequences for Japan's aggressive pursuit of a continental empire.[95]

Bibliography

"Ansei igo shinchikan." In *Kan'ibu*, Pt. 77, *Tokugawa-shi shokuin*, Pt. 26, 1605–62. Vol. 24 of *Koji ruien, kan'ibu*. Jingū Shichō, 1896–1914. National Diet Library. https://doi .org/10.11501/897661

Arima Seiho. *Takashima Shūhan*. Yoshikawa Kōbunkan, 1958.

Auslin, Michael. *Negotiating with Imperialism: The Unequal Treaties and the Culture of Japanese Diplomacy*. Cambridge, MA: Harvard University Press, 2006.

Benesch, Oleg. *Inventing the Way of the Samurai: Nationalism, Internationalism, and Bushidō in Meiji Japan*. Oxford: Oxford University Press, 2014.

Bolitho, Harold. "The Echigo War, 1868." *Monumenta Nipponica* 34, no. 3 (Autumn 1979): 259–77.

"The Han." In Hall, *Early Modern Japan*, 183–234.

"The Tempō Crisis." In *The Nineteenth Century*, edited by Marius B. Jansen, 116–67. Vol. 5 of *The Cambridge History of Japan*. Cambridge: Cambridge University Press, 1989.

Botsman, Daniel. *Punishment and Power in the Making of Modern Japan*. Princeton, NJ: Princeton University Press, 2005.

Chatani, Sayaka. *Nation-Empire: Ideology and Rural Youth Mobilization in Japan and Its Colonies*. Ithaca, NY: Cornell University Press, 2018.

Craig, Teruko. "Introduction." In *Remembering Aizu: The Testament of Shiba Gorō*, by Shiba Gorō, edited by Ishimitsu Mahito; translated by Teruko Craig, 1–24. Honolulu: University of Hawai'i Press, 1999.

Drea, Edward. *Japan's Imperial Army: Its Rise and Fall, 1853–1935*. Lawrence: University Press of Kansas, 2009.

Edamatsu Shigeyuki, Sugiura Tadashi, and Yagi Kōsuke, eds. *Meiji nyūsu jiten*. 9 vols. Mainichi Komyunikēshonzu, 1983–86.

Fuess, Harald. "The Global Weapons Trade and the Meiji Restoration: Dispersion of Means of Violence in a World of Emerging Nation-States." In *The Meiji Restoration: Japan as a Global Nation*, edited by Robert Hellyer and Harald Fuess, 83–109. Cambridge: Cambridge University Press, 2020.

Hall, John Whitney. "The *Bakuhan* System." In Hall, *Early Modern Japan*, 128–82.

ed. *Early Modern Japan*. Vol. 4 of *The Cambridge History of Japan*. Cambridge: Cambridge University Press, 1991.

---

[95] Paine, *Japanese Empire*, 178–81.

Hellyer, Robert. *Defining Engagement: Japan and Global Contexts, 1640–1868*. Cambridge, MA: Harvard University Asia Center, 2009.

Hess, Earl J. *Civil War Infantry Tactics: Training, Combat, and Small-Unit Effectiveness*. Baton Rouge: Louisiana State University Press, 2015.

Howell, David L. *Geographies of Identity in Nineteenth-Century Japan*. Berkeley: University of California Press, 2005.

"The Social Life of Firearms in Tokugawa Japan." *Japanese Studies* 29, no. 1 (May 2009): 65–80.

Hōya Tōru. *Bakumatsu Nihon to taigai sensō no kiki: Shimonoseki sensō no butaiura*. Yoshikawa Kōbunkan, 2010.

Boshin sensō. Yoshikawa Kōbunkan, 2007.

"Kinsei." In Takahashi et al., *Nihon gunjishi*, 198–308.

Hurst, G. Cameron. *Armed Martial Arts of Japan: Swordsmanship and Archery*. New Haven, CT: Yale University Press, 1998.

Ichinose Toshiya. "Kindai." In Takahashi et al., *Nihon gunjishi*, 310–98.

Ikegami, Eiko. *The Taming of the Samurai: Honorific Individualism and the Making of Modern Japan*. Cambridge, MA: Harvard University Press, 1995.

Ishii Iwao. "Nirayama juku no hakken: Takashima-ryū hōjutsu shūrenjo." *Chihōshi kenkyū* 19, no. 6 (1969): 21–27.

Itō Hirobumi. "Hokuchi gaisen no hei o shosuru no an." In Yui, Fujiwara, and Yoshida, *Guntai heishi*, 3–6.

Kanazawa Hiroyuki. *Bakufu kaigun no kōbō: Bakumatsu-ki ni okeru kaigun kensetsu*. Keiō Gijuku Daigaku Shuppankai, 2017.

Katō Yōko. *Chōheisei to kindai Nihon, 1868–1945*. Yoshikawa Kōbunkan, 1996.

Katsu Kaishū. *Kaigun rekishi*. Vols. 8–10 of *Katsu Kaishū zenshū*. Kōdansha, 1973–74.

Rikugun rekishi. Vols. 11–14 of *Katsu Kaishū zenshū*. Kōdansha, 1974–75.

Kōshaku Shimazu-ke Henshūjo, ed. *Sappan kaigunshi*. 3 vols. Hara Shobō, 1968.

Kurihara Ryūichi. *Bakumatsu Nihon no gunsei*. Shin Jinbutsu Ōraisha, 1972.

Mason, Michele. *Dominant Narratives of Colonial Hokkaido and Imperial Japan: Envisioning the Periphery and the Modern Nation-State*. New York: Palgrave Macmillan, 2012.

Matsumura, Wendy. *The Limits of Okinawa: Japanese Capitalism, Living Labor, and Theorizations of Community*. Durham, NC: Duke University Press, 2015.

Matsushita Yoshio. *Nihon rikukaigun sōdōshi*. Tsuchiya Shoten, 1974.

Nakano Ryōzui. *Kaisei chōhei shinpai nashi*. Kakumeidō, 1884.

Orbach, Danny. *Curse on This Country: The Rebellious Army of Imperial Japan*. Ithaca, NY: Cornell University Press, 2017.

Ōyama Kashiwa. *Boshin no eki senshi*. 2 vols. Jiji Tsūshinsha, 1968.

Paine, S. C. M. *The Japanese Empire: Grand Strategy from the Meiji Restoration to the Pacific War*. Cambridge: Cambridge University Press, 2017.

Ravina, Mark. *To Stand with the Nations of the World: Japan's Meiji Restoration in World History*. Oxford: Oxford University Press, 2017.

Sakamoto Yasutomi. "Shimosone Nobuatsu no seiyō hōjutsu monjin no sekishutsu." *Nihon rekishi* 582 (November 1986): 58–74.

Schencking, J. Charles. *Making Waves: Politics, Propaganda, and the Emergence of the Imperial Japanese Navy, 1868–1922*. Stanford, CA: Stanford University Press, 2005.

Senda Minoru. *Ishin seiken no chokuzoku guntai*. Kaimei Shoin, 1978.

Shimoda, Hiraku. *Lost and Found: Recovering Regional Identity in Imperial Japan*. Cambridge, MA: Harvard University Asia Center, 2014.

Siniawer, Eiko Maruko. *Ruffians, Yakuza, Nationalists: The Violent Politics of Modern Japan, 1860–1960*. Ithaca, NY: Cornell University Press, 2011.

Stavros, Matthew. "Military Revolution in Early Modern Japan." *Japanese Studies* 33, no. 3 (October 2013): 243–61.

Suzuki Junko. "Seeking Accuracy: The First Modern Survey of Japan's Coast." In *Cartographic Japan: A History in Maps*, edited by Kären Wigen, Sugimoto Fumiko, and Cary Karacas, 129–32. Chicago: University of Chicago Press, 2016.

Swope, Kenneth. *A Dragon's Head and a Serpent's Tail: Ming China and the First Great East Asian War, 1592–1598*. Norman: University of Oklahoma Press, 2009.

Takahashi Noriyuki, Yamada Kuniake, Hōya Tōru, and Ichinose Toshiya, eds. *Nihon gunjishi*. Yoshikawa Kōbunkan, 2006.

Tobe Ryōichi. *Gyakusetsu no guntai*. Chūōkōronsha, 1998.

Totman, Conrad. *The Collapse of the Tokugawa Bakufu, 1862–1868*. Honolulu: University of Hawai'i Press, 1980.

Udagawa Takehisa. *Edo no hōjutsu: keishō sareru bugei*. Tōyō Shorin, 2000.

Vaporis, Constantine. *Tour of Duty: Samurai, Military Service in Edo, and the Culture of Early Modern Japan*. Honolulu: University of Hawai'i Press, 2008.

Wakabayashi, Bob Tadashi. "From Peril to Profit: Opium in Late-Edo to Meiji Eyes." In *Opium Regimes: China, Britain, and Japan, 1839–1952*, edited by Timothy Brook and Bob Tadashi Wakabayashi, 55–75. Berkeley: University of California Press, 2000.

Walthall, Anne. "Do Guns Have Gender? Technology and Status in Early Modern Japan." In *Recreating Japanese Men*, edited by Anne Walthall and Sabine Frühstück, 25–47. Berkeley: University of California Press, 2011.

Walthall, Anne, and M. William Steele, eds. *Politics and Society in Japan's Meiji Restoration: A Brief History with Documents*. Boston: Bedford/St. Martin's, 2017.

Westney, D. Eleanor. "The Military." In *Japan in Transition: From Tokugawa to Meiji*, edited by Marius B. Jansen and Gilbert Rozman, 168–94. Princeton, NJ: Princeton University Press, 1986.

Wilson, Noell. *Defensive Positions: The Politics of Maritime Security in Tokugawa Japan*. Cambridge, MA: Harvard University Asia Center, 2015.

———. "Tokugawa Defense Redux: Organizational Failure in the *Phaeton* Incident of 1808." *Journal of Japanese Studies* 36, no. 1 (Winter 2010): 1–32.

Wright, Diana. "Female Combatants and Japan's Meiji Restoration: The Case of Aizu." *War in History* 8, no. 4 (2001): 396–417.

Yamada Akiyoshi. "Heisei ni tsuki kenpakusho." In Yui, Fujiwara, and Yoshida, *Guntai heishi*, 91–109.

Yamagata Aritomo, Horiuchi Bunjirō, and Hirayama Tadashi, eds. "Rikugunshō enkakushi." In *Gunji-hen, kōtsū-hen*, edited by Yoshino Sakuzō, 106–96. Vol. 23 of *Meiji bunka zenshū*. Nihon Hyōronsha, 1927.

Yoshida Tsunenori. *Gun'eki kokoroe: Kaitei chōheirei (kanatsuki)*. Gyokuyōdō, 1876.

Yui Masaomi, Fujiwara Akira, and Yoshida Yutaka, eds. *Guntai heishi*. Vol. 4 of *Nihon kindai shisō taikei*. Iwanami Shoten, 1989.

PART III

*

SOCIAL PRACTICES AND CULTURES OF EARLY MODERN JAPAN

13

Religion in the Tokugawa Period

MARK TEEUWEN

Recent years have seen much soul-searching among historians of religion about the question how, or indeed whether, the term "religion" should be applied to places where that social category did not exist. Tokugawa-period Japan was such a place, and this makes the question of what constituted religion in Tokugawa society a complicated one. It was first in the Meiji period that a calque created to translate "religion" (shūkyō) became part of Japan's social imaginary and also of its system of governance. It was only at the very end of the nineteenth century that a consensus arose as to what "religion" might mean in the Japanese setting, and what place actors and institutions labeled as religious were to occupy within the framework of the modern state. In short, that consensus branded Buddhism, Christianity, and a range of popular sects as religious, while (nonsectarian) Shinto and Confucianism were excluded from the category. This meant that the former enjoyed legal protection as religions, at the price of being confined to the sphere of private faith. State shrines became public stages for imperial and military "nonreligious" ceremonies, while Confucianism would eventually end up on the wrong side of history, spurned as a stifling remnant of feudalism at odds with modernity. Other groups were relegated to the equally novel category of "superstition," exposing them to police harassment for "swindling the credulous."

The period discussed here predated the arrival of modern concepts of the religious versus the secular realm. Shrines and temples were not subjected to the kind of rules that came to apply to the category of "religion" in modernity, simply because there was no concept of a boundary between secular and religious spheres that needed policing. Yet the institutions, people, and practices that were defined as religious in the Meiji period were, by and large, already part of Tokugawa life. There were also terms that covered, if imperfectly, aspects that would later become part of the modern category of religion, "temples and shrines" (jisha), "sect" or "creed" (shūshi, shūmon), and "faith" (shinjin, shinkō, anjin, kie) most prominent among them. This chapter is an attempt to map the field that temples and shrines, sects, and faith occupied in society before that field was reconceptualized as religion in the late nineteenth century.

I will focus on faith-related practices in cities, towns, and villages, and on the ways such practices were administered by the authorities in different phases of the Tokugawa period. New doctrinal developments, and also the impact of commercial publishing and increased literacy, are central to the history of "religion" in the Tokugawa period, but they are beyond the scope of this chapter. I will begin by exploring the legacy of the wars of the sixteenth century and its relation to the emergence of the system of compulsory temple affiliation and certification. I will then sketch the main features of the landscape of faith as it took shape in the middle of the Tokugawa period, with a stunning multiplicity of actors vying for the favors of the same clientele. How did the warrior regime deal with the many conflicts that arose between these actors? How did the regime seek to harmonize the world of faith among commoners with the need to legitimize and sacralize warrior power, and with the ideal of building a society founded on loyalty and filial piety? Finally, I will try to identify the rationale behind the proactive and reactive policies that the Tokugawa regime pursued during different stages of its development and offer some thoughts on the legacy of Tokugawa understandings of faith to the process of defining "religion" in the Meiji period.

Faith, Loyalty, and the Temple Certification System

The beginning of the Tokugawa period marked the end of well over a century of turmoil and political fragmentation. The second half of the sixteenth century, in particular, was full of paradigm-changing events that had a profound impact on temples and shrines. This impact took the form of destruction, co-optation, and regimentation. In the process, the world of temples, shrines, and faith was changed beyond recognition.

To bring out the scale of this change, it will be useful to sketch some characteristics of late medieval society. The wars of the fifteenth and sixteenth centuries caused the great temple-shrine complexes of early medieval Buddhism to decline. These complexes depended on the control of large portfolios of commended estates and income rights from land, as well as monopolies over key court rituals. However, both these sources of income dried up as the country fell apart and central authority evaporated. In the last decades of the sixteenth century, the new hegemons Oda Nobunaga and

Toyotomi Hideyoshi used their military might to subdue some of the largest of these temple complexes in central Japan, burning the Tendai headquarters on Mount Hiei to the ground in 1572 and destroying the two hubs of Shingon in the 1580s. (Mount Kōya was besieged in 1581, and Negoroji burned in 1585.) These events demonstrated the preeminence of warrior muscle over priestly authority.

That authority had been partly economic and military but drew also on the charisma and perceived efficacy of the Buddhist rituals transmitted within priestly lineages. The slaughter of thousands of monastics at the most hallowed centers of Buddhist expertise signaled the collapse of this charisma. Neil McMullin describes the effect of this collapse as a qualitative change in the relation between the large temple-shrine complexes and the state.[1] The fundamental notion that the twin laws of king and Buddha were mutually dependent on each other was undermined, and the stage was set for the emergence of what McMullin calls a "post-Buddhist Japan." In slightly different terms, Hayashi Makoto argues that the unification wars marked the end of what he calls "Aśokan Buddhism" in Japan: a system where the sovereign supports the sangha; where supporting the sangha is understood as a vital technique to protect the realm; and where it is an accepted fact of political life that the sangha has the power to avert threats to the sovereign and the realm by ritual means.[2]

The military campaigns of the late sixteenth century were disastrous, but their success betrayed the fact that these large complexes had already been much weakened. The rise of warrior power had gradually undermined the economic model on which they were founded: control of lands and farmers spread over large areas; control of city guilds, markets, and toll barriers; and monopolies on court rituals. In parallel with the failure of this model, new forms of Buddhism drawing on alternative sources of funding were growing exponentially. These were forms that appealed to the faith of lay believers and actively solicited their patronage. Temples and shrines had begun to engage in fundraising campaigns (*kanjin*), sending traveling mendicants to towns and villages where they solicited donations for devotional projects. These mendicants fostered local communities of dedicated lay patrons. Small halls of worship were erected in preparation for the mendicants' visits, resulting in the creation of extensive networks of faith across regions.[3] Many of these halls would later be upgraded to full-fledged village temples, with priests who

---

[1] McMullin, *Buddhism and the State*.
[2] Hayashi, "Kinsei tenkanki ni okeru shūkyō hendō," 8.
[3] Goodman, *Alms and Vagabonds*.

retained their connections to the larger temple that had stood behind the original *kanjin* activities.

Networks of devotion soon branched out into other services for lay patrons. One was facilitating pilgrimages to the sites to which patrons had already established links of merit; more will be said about this later in this chapter. The innovation that proved a true game changer, however, was the popularization of Buddhist mortuary rites. Pioneered by Sōtō Zen and Pure Land temples, funerals and memorial services for lay patrons became widespread among ever-broadening segments of the population in the course of the sixteenth century. Such services provided these households with the ritual means to construct and maintain a collective identity rooted in the veneration of shared ancestors. The emergence of this new market is usually attributed to an underlying social shift from the extended families of medieval times to smaller stem families: families where the married heir remains while the other siblings move away, either by establishing junior branches of the stem family or by accepting less-promising fates, such as indentured service in other families. Buddhist priests performed offering rites (*kuyō*) to raise and transfer merit to the ancestors of such families or to individual deceased family members, so as to ensure that the dead had safely passed into a better afterlife, that they might look after the household as its protectors or that they would withhold their wrath against their descendants.

As such mortuary rites spread, this created a basis for the upgrading of *kanjin* halls in villages and towns, and many were redeveloped into mortuary temples. Larger temples sought opportunities for new initiatives, supported the pioneers, offered them their protection when needed, and siphoned off some of their profits. Mortuary temples of this kind mushroomed around the country. Takeda Chōshū calculates that 90 percent of Japan's Pure Land temples were founded after 1501, with 60 percent of these originating between 1573 and 1643 as mortuary temples supported by lay patrons.[4] Nam-lin Hur shows that, at least in Edo, the situation was similar for other sects.[5]

It should be noted, however, that these numbers are beset with many uncertainties. The warrior regime regularly placed restrictions on the building of new temples, causing priests to falsify or aggrandize the history of the village halls that they had converted into full-fledged temples. Also, demographers disagree about the timing of the spread of the stem family system. William Wayne Farris argues that at least in "central and western Japan," stem

---

[4] Hōzawa, "Jidan seido to sōsai bukkyō," 28–29.
[5] Hur, *Death and Social Order*, introduction.

families were widespread even among farmers by the "mid-1500s,"[6] while
Fabian Drixler argues that "the period of [the stem family's] fastest diffusion"
arrived only in the second half of the seventeenth century.[7] Either way, there
is no doubt that temple construction boomed in the late sixteenth and early
seventeenth centuries, and that these new temples, in contrast to their medieval forebears, based their economies on the patronage of lay commoners and
their households.

A similar but perhaps more committal kind of network was created by the
Honganji sect, one of a number of so-called Ikkō groups (officially renamed
Jōdo Shinshū in 1872). These groups held that wholehearted faith in and devotion to Amida was the only road to salvation and promoted the practice of
chanting the *nenbutsu* formula *namu Amida-butsu*. Their teaching was easy to
grasp, easy to practice, and offered followers relief from the fearsome power
of large temple complexes and their threats to unleash demonic forces on
their enemies, or even send them to hell. Honganji, the site of the grave of
the sect's founder (Shinran, 1173–1262), stood at the pinnacle of a network
of branch temples and, below those, practice halls (*dōjō*), all supported by
small communities of local laypeople (*monto*). Honganji patriarchs exerted
considerable authority over these communities by defining all other Buddhist
methods as heterodox and threatening members with expulsion if they broke
sect rules. Some of Honganji's branch temples were surrounded by moated
and walled "temple towns" (*jinaichō*) that functioned as centers of production
and trade. Osaka, in fact, was the temple town of Ishiyama Honganji, the
sect's headquarters from 1533 onward. Like the estates and precincts of medieval temple complexes, these temple towns claimed, and often won, the right
to deny access to warrior officials and tax collectors and independent jurisdiction within their own walls. When temples, or their communities, came
into conflict with warlords or rival temple networks, they frequently formed
armed "leagues" (*ikki*) that proved to have considerable military muscle.[8]

The emergence of groups of laypeople defined by faith in a single sect, to
the exclusion of all others, was a new phenomenon in the sixteenth century.
Warfare, in particular, cemented loyalties. In the case of Honganji and similar
networks, the logic of "with us or against us" gave rise to lay sectarian identities in a manner not seen in earlier centuries. Another such faith-based identity, but of a different nature, arrived in the same century: Christianity, spread

---

[6] Farris, *Japan's Medieval Population*, 251–52.
[7] Drixler, "Imagined Communities of the Living and the Dead," 84.
[8] Tsang, *War and Faith*.

by Portuguese Jesuits (and, later, other orders as well) from 1549 onwards. The Jesuit mission to convert lay Japanese and define them as a congregation by means of the sacraments (baptism, confirmation, the Eucharist, and also ordination) created a new community of faith. This community was different from all others because of its ties to a foreign power that was from the start entangled with trade, and soon also with war. In Nagasaki, the Jesuits possessed a "temple town" that, like the *jinaichō* of the Honganji sect and, before that, the temple complexes of the medieval period, claimed rights of noninterference from court and warrior overlords.

Communities of faith proved formidable enemies for the warrior hegemons who sought to reunify Japan in the late sixteenth century. The breaking point for Honganji came in 1580, when Oda Nobunaga forced it into submission after a decade of bloody fighting. Nichiren groups (at the time known as Hokke) had suffered a similar fate earlier on; soon, Christians too would be under attack. The long war against Honganji was to be especially significant. Warrior leaders, including the founding shogun, Tokugawa Ieyasu, found that Honganji believers who had been absorbed into their vassal bands often proved to have split loyalties. Loyalties of faith tended to override loyalties of vassalage, as Ieyasu experienced personally in a conflict with Honganji-connected temples in his own domain in 1563–64 (the so-called Mikawa uprising). Such conflicts brought military governance into direct conflict with faith. The distrust of faith-based groups that these events inspired would stay with the Tokugawa shogunate throughout its lifetime.

The ban on Christianity was the result of many different circumstances, but misgivings about faith communities with suspect loyalties loomed large. Already in 1587, Toyotomi Hideyoshi issued an edict that expelled foreign priests from the country as part of his campaign to bring all of Japan under his unchallenged authority. After Hideyoshi's death, Tokugawa Ieyasu tolerated the Christian church in the greater interest of accessing the global trading network of the Portuguese and the Spanish. In the first decade of the seventeenth century, the total number of Christians in the country may have reached a high of up to 300,000. An incident in 1612, however, sealed the fate of the Japanese church. A Christian daimyo was found to have conspired with a fellow-Christian shogunal retainer in Nagasaki to manipulate Ieyasu's government. Enraged, Ieyasu decided to root out Christianity among his retainers and in the imperial city of Kyoto. In a letter to the Spanish governor of New Spain, Ieyasu argued that in Japan, loyalty between lord and retainer was based on oaths that invoked the Buddhas and gods; therefore, retainers could not be Christians. In 1612 and 1613, Ieyasu (through his son

Hidetada, who held the title of shogun at this time) issued two edicts ordering the destruction of all churches on shogunal lands and the expulsion of all
Christian clergy from the country. The arrival of Dutch and English traders,
who offered an alternative to the Portuguese and the Spanish, facilitated the
execution of this drastic decision. Persecutions and executions began immediately and intensified further in the 1620s.

The final blow came in 1637–38. Two men were arrested in Shimabara (east
of Nagasaki) on suspicion of Christian practices, and this triggered an armed
uprising that involved thousands of villagers. The rebels burned temples and
shrines, killed Buddhist monks, and ensconced themselves under Christian
banners in the abandoned Hara Castle. It took shogunal troops four months
to quell the uprising, killing some 28,000 villagers and suffering great casualties in the process.[9] After this disaster, which was caused by harsh local taxation in the face of bad harvests as much as by anti-Christian pressures, the
shogunate began hunting in earnest for Christians, not only among warrior
retainers but also among the general populace. Christianity now became the
declared enemy of the social order, an infectious creed of disloyalty and rebellion that had to be weeded out at all costs.[10] Mass executions of Christians
continued until the end of the century and ended with the beheading of about
forty villagers in Mino Province in 1698–99.

Establishing Systems of Control

The perceived conflict between faith and loyalty inspired wide-ranging measures to break up communities whose faith was thought to undermine the
social order. At the same time, attempts were made to ascertain that people
followed faiths that were acceptable to the warrior regime. Ironically, this
concern led the regime to impose on all sects a model that closely resembled
that of the Honganji or Ikkō sect: communities of laypeople united by faith
and temple networks with a tightly organized hierarchical structure, from
head temples at the top down to local branch temples and small worship
halls at the bottom. This kind of structure was alien to most temples even
in the early Tokugawa period. The temple complexes of medieval Japan had
taken the form of clusters of semi-independent sub-temples and "cloisters"
(in) that were not necessarily specialized in a single sectarian teaching or practice. Temples and shrines with roots in that older model had clients and serfs,

[9] Hur, Death and Social Order, 64–67.
[10] Elison, Deus Destroyed; Ōhashi, Senpuku kirishitan.

rather than dedicated lay believers, and they had no tradition of leading lay communities defined by a sect-specific faith.

In 1615, the shogunate issued a flurry of temple laws. Many of these were addressed to the old temple complexes that were rebuilding after the onslaughts of the 1570s and 1580s; the shogunate now stripped away many of their old privileges. At the same time, these laws sought to institutionalize the authority of "head temples" (*honzan, honji*) over their "branch temples" (*matsuji*). New temples, for example, could now only attain official status (expressed in the form of an officially awarded temple name) if they were founded with permission of a head temple. In the Kantō area in particular, head temples were defined as the headquarters not just of networks but of sects, marked out by their own teachings and rituals; the new shogunal temple laws stressed that it was the duty of all priests to study and practice the traditions of the sect to which they belonged. In 1632–33, sects were obliged to submit lists of all their branch temples (*honmatsuchō*) to the authorities, and in 1635, the shogunate created a dedicated magistrate's office to oversee temples, shrines, and various kinds of religious professionals: the magistrate of temples and shrines (*jisha bugyō*). The *honmatsuchō* lists of the 1630s were far from complete, and they attest to the patchwork nature of what has been termed the "system of head and branch temples" (*honmatsu seido*) at this early date. Even so, it is clear that the Ikkō model of the hierarchical sect was now being applied to all temples in the realm, at least as an ideal and as a principle of governance. New registers of branch temples were drawn up in 1692 (for the Ikkō and Tendai sects), and existing ones were updated in the years 1786–95. It became standard procedure for shogunal officials to check these registers whenever a temple became involved in any kind of legal trouble, or even when it merely sought permission to rebuild after a fire.

It was also in the 1630s that the shogunate began to use temples as a means to regulate the faith of laypeople. Again, the model of a faith-based community of lay patrons informed the rationale behind the shogunate's policies at this time. The premises on which this system was built were that temples served dedicated lay believers and that laypeople committed themselves to a single sectarian faith under the guidance of their temple of choice. The assumption was that membership of a Buddhist temple would stop laypeople of all classes from slipping into a "pernicious creed" (*jashūmon*) – notably Christianity. In 1635, Sakai Tadakatsu, senior councillor in the shogunate and daimyo of two large domains, expressed the idea behind this new system as follows: "As proof that they do not belong to the Christian sect, all people [within my domains] must register with a temple, and the temple priests must warrant for them."[11] The first "temple certificates" (*terauke shōmon*, *shūshi tegata*) appeared around the same time. Such documents confirmed that the carrier was a registered patron (*danna, danka*) of the temple that issued the certificate and stated that the temple's priest was prepared to guarantee the carrier's legitimate sectarian identity in case they were accused of being a Christian.[12]

The 1660s were a period of administrative consolidation within the shogunate. In this decade, national laws replaced particularized arrangements within the worlds of warriors, courtiers, and temples alike. While earlier temple laws had addressed specific head temples or sects, the shogunate now issued a unified Law for Temples of All Sects (Shoshū jiin hatto, 1665). This law stressed sectarian purity, banning the mixing of doctrines and practices from different sects and prohibiting priests from accommodating women in their temples if this was not established usage in their sect. It denied temples' medieval rights of noninterference and sanctuary, ordering priests to hand over to the warrior authorities any fugitives who might seek asylum in their temple halls. Particularly striking in this law, however, is the attention it gives to the relation between temples and their lay patrons. Its fourth article states that "patrons will select their temple of affiliation according to their own will; temple priests may not contest each other's patrons." This law further rendered it illegal for temple priests to impose extravagant rites on their patrons and stated that priests who wished to found a new temple needed to secure support not only from their head temple but also from their lay patrons.

The issuance of this law in 1665 coincided with efforts to systematize the nationwide implementation of temple certification of people's faith. In 1664, the shogunate ordered all domains to appoint officials charged with annual "sectarian inspections" (*shūmon aratame*). A further order issued in 1671 then made it obligatory for all domains to compile sectarian census registers (*shūmon ninbe-tsuchō*) that listed all inhabitants of villages, city blocks, and rural districts. These registers were to include each person's age, name, and province of birth, as well as the name, sect, and location of their affiliation temple (*dannadera* and other terms). The census registers were normally drawn up by village or block officials; the information contained in them was then confirmed by the priests of the affiliation temples by way of the temple seal. By a variety of routes, depending on local circumstances, the completed registers were submitted to the local authorities and sent on to the office of the magistrate of temples and shrines in

[11] Tamamuro, *Edo bakufu no shūkyō tōsei*, 76–77.
[12] Tamamuro, *Edo bakufu no shūkyō tōsei*, 78–79.

Edo. Those who fell out of such registers could not obtain a temple certificate, which was necessary for all official business, including travel, service in war- rior or courtier households, and much more. "Unregistered persons" (*mushuku*) who lacked such papers were bound to run into trouble sooner or later, and when apprehended, they might well find themselves placed under the control of local bosses of outcaste communities (*hinin*). And even *hinin* were obliged by law to subject themselves to temple certification.

Looking back on these measures, we can discern two main concerns that dominated the religious policies of the shogunate at this stage: establishing warrior sovereignty and centralized control over temples through clear lines of command and preventing "pernicious sects" from disseminating danger- ous forms of faith among the lay population. Both of these concerns had their roots in major challenges that the new hegemons faced in the decades around 1600: the wars with temples and faith-based communities and networks, and the threat of Christian invaders, Christian disloyalty, and Christian rebellions.

The twin goals of controlling temples and regulating people's faith were not always easily combined. In order to prevent disputes between temples or, even worse, sects, it was paramount to ensure that their portfolios of *danna* patrons were stable, because the number of patrons determined the economic worth of a temple, and often also its hierarchical standing within its own sect. On the other hand, the rationale of faith was premised on the idea that lay patrons were free to affiliate themselves with a temple of their choice so that they could receive its guidance as to how to practice their faith correctly. These two concerns (guaranteeing stable patronage for temples and granting patrons the freedom to choose their own affiliation temple) were combined in the fourth article of the 1665 Law for Temples of All Sects, quoted earlier. By confirming patrons' right to "select their temple of affiliation" based on their faith, the shogunate sought to reduce temples' power over their patrons. In practice, however, patrons' freedom of faith was a dead letter. Whenever a patron sought to break with their temple of birth and change affiliation to another, as the first half of this article would appear to allow, the temple that stood to lose from this change might appeal to the second half of the same article and accuse the receiving temple of conspiring with its new-won lay believer so as to "contest" a patron. In weighing the institutional interests of a temple against the private ones of a layperson, warrior officials invariably found the former more pressing.[13]

---

[13] An example of such a case can be found in Tamamuro, "Local Society and the Temple-Parishioner Relationship." In 1737, a high-ranking samurai in Kumamoto tried

One dominant theme of "religious life" (or, in contemporary terms, of faith) in the Tokugawa period, then, was the relation that virtually the entire population maintained with the temples where they were registered. To gain some idea about how these relations worked in real life, and especially of the dynamics that governed the balance of power between temples and their patrons, it will be useful to look at two concrete examples of the ways in which conflicts between priests and patrons were handled. The first example, from the 1820s, occurred between an Osaka physician, his cash-strapped temple, and the lay association of that temple's patrons. The source is *Ukiyo no arisama* (The ways of the floating world), an anonymous work that offers information about assorted incidents in Osaka based on the private investigations of an anonymous author over a period of some three decades.[14] It should be noted that this author displays a strong dislike of priests throughout his writings. He tells the following tale about an incident that happened in his own neighborhood.

When the Osaka physician called Fujita Annan died, his adopted son Kenzō sent a runner to the family's affiliation temple Enshōji, a branch temple of Nishi Honganji. Kenzō requested that the priest should attend to the funeral, which would be performed the following day. Annan had been an extremely stingy man who never worshipped at the temple if he could avoid it. Even when he was reprimanded for this by the priest, Annan had paid no heed whatsoever. With this in mind, the priest replied that he would send an assistant priest (*bansō*) in his stead. When Kenzō heard this, he was livid. He sent another runner with the message that it was unacceptable to leave the funeral of such an important patron to a mere assistant, as though Annan had been some pauper from a back alley. He demanded that the priest should attend in person. The priest replied: "In fact, the implements necessary for such a service have been pawned for 35 *ryō*. You will have to put up this sum so that these implements can be retrieved from pawn. At the moment, the temple has no cash and cannot do this by itself."

The funeral was on the next day, so Kenzō had no other choice but to pay up. Kenzō confronted the priest to retrieve this sum, but the priest proved determined to keep it. Kenzō then discussed the matter with the temple's lay association. In the end, the case was brought before the Osaka authorities

to change his affiliation from a Sōtō to a Nichiren temple after he had been healed by a Nichiren priest. Article 4 of the Law for Temples of All Sects was adduced by both parties. In the end, this samurai not only lost but was stripped of his domain offices and condemned to house arrest.

[14] *Ukiyo no arisama*, 64.

in a lawsuit. It was deemed a serious offence to blackmail parishioners over the body of a dead man, and according to our author, the priest was expelled from the temple. This constituted an offence on the part of the priest, but people in the neighborhood also considered Fujita's conduct "immoderate."

This incident reminds us that the hold that priests had over their patrons was not only based on the temple certification of faith but also on temples' monopoly on household rituals, which impinged on the standing and reputation of their patrons. It also makes clear that aggravated patrons had ways to protest against abuses if they had the support of their lay fellows.

A typical example of a conflict with the opposite outcome occurred between Jōshinji, a Nichiren temple in Shimōsa Province, and its patron Buhei in 1831.[15] The Jōshinji priest complained to his Nichiren head temple that Buhei never worshipped there, failed to perform memorial rites for his ancestors, neglected his house altar, preferred to invite *yamabushi* mountain practitioners to his house for various rituals, and never turned up for temple chores. The priest therefore sought the head temple's support for denying Buhei his affiliation papers and forewarned the villagers of his intention. The village officials then admonished Buhei, who apologized, swore that he was not a follower of "the banned creed [of Christianity]," and promised to improve his behavior.

These two episodes, and many others of similar import, suggest that temple priests had considerable leverage over their patrons but also that they could never ride roughshod over the communities that they served.

The Multilayered World of Faith beyond Temple Certification

Buhei's story also shows that the relation between temple and patron was only one aspect of the multifarious world of faith in the Tokugawa period. Buhei neglected his temple because he preferred the services of *yamabushi*, as practitioners of Shugendō were commonly called. This raises the question of the relationship between temple priests and other actors with whom they competed, quarreled, and cooperated.

Who were Buhei's *yamabushi*, and how did their activities relate to the system of obligatory temple affiliation? *Yamabushi* or *shugenja* were part of nationwide networks that were at least as strictly organized as those of temple priests. In 1613, the shogunate ordered most local *yamabushi* networks to

[15] Arimoto, *Kinsei Nihon no shūkyō shakaishi*, 15.

join one of two main Shugendō branches, known as the Honzan-ha and the Tōzan-ha, both with head temples in the Kyoto region (Shōgoin and Sanbōin, respectively; smaller independent centers were Mount Haguro in Dewa and Mount Hiko in Bungo). *Yamabushi* engaged in stints of ascetic and ritual training both at regional sites – typically on designated mountains with special facilities for such training – and, if they were affiliated with the Honzan-ha or Tōzan-ha, at the main Shugendō center of Mount Ōmine, located between Yoshino and Kumano. A shogunal order issued in 1662 forced *yamabushi* to give up their itinerant lifestyle and settle in towns and villages; many combined their trade with farming. They offered ritual services that were partly specific to Shugendō but also partly overlapped with those of temples, as well as with those of Shinto priests. One such specific role was that of guide (*sendatsu*), leading groups of lay patrons on pilgrimages to Shugendō mountains. There was more overlap in community rituals, such as praying for rain or good harvests, and rituals against pests affecting crops or against the spread of illnesses. Most contested, because it brought in considerable income, was the right to perform rituals of healing, exorcism, and divination, as well as rites for fire prevention and other this-worldly benefits. These kinds of rites were often referred to as *kaji kitō*, two terms that have different technical meanings but were often understood as a compound that may be translated as "prayer rites."

Many temples had fixed patrons not only for mortuary services (*metsuzai danka*) but also for prayer rites (*kitō danka*). Some, in fact, only had patrons of the latter kind, although the more usual pattern was for temples to offer a menu of prayer rites in addition to funerals and memorial services. In contrast to mortuary services, prayer rituals had no relation to the sectarian inspection system, and it was up to individuals whether they wanted to engage in them at all, and if so, where they might choose to take their custom. At times, however, *yamabushi* claimed a monopoly on prayer rites and accused temple or shrine priests of infringing on their turf. How the ritual market was divided between different local actors was partly a matter of legal contract, partly a matter of established usage, and partly an unregulated terrain that bred conflicts whenever an actor decided to claim exclusive rights.

Tsuzukiya village in Shimotsuke Province had a Sōtō Zen temple (Myōkeiji), a Tōzan-ha temple (Henjōji), and a tutelary shrine (Kurama Jinja). In 1799, the documents that determined the functional boundaries between these three institutions were lost, and in order to prevent trouble an attempt was made to define them anew. The village officials confirmed that Myōkeiji's core task was to take care of "all matters related to the next life" – that is, mortuary rites. Henjōji's domain was defined as the performance of rituals for "peace (*anraku*) in this life and the next," specified further as prayer rites of the *kaji kitō* kind for this-worldly benefits, visits to Shugendō mountains to secure peace for the dead, and prayer vigils (*himachi*, lit. "waiting for the sun") in spring and autumn. Finally, the Shinto priest was to preside over the communal festivals of the village shrine. There were, however, also many overlapping functions that were not so easily agreed upon. For healing rites, it was left to villagers' personal "faith" (*kie*) whether they preferred to engage the Shinto priest or a *yamabushi* from Henjōji. The same applied to various other vigils (e.g. at New Year), rites to house gods (*ujigami*) in villagers' households, the distribution of various amulets (e.g. for safe travel), fire prevention rites, building rites, and more. Rituals at small roadside shrines that dotted the village could be performed by either Myōkeiji or Henjōji, depending on patrons' preferences.[16] Overall, this document conveys a situation where religious figures of different descriptions existed side by side, and where conflicts were avoided by enforcing monopolies on some ritual services while leaving others open to competition. Local agreement played as large a role in this regulatory work as vertical links with head temples in Kyoto and Edo.

Shrine priests appear here as a third group of resident providers of rituals. Shrines were diverse, ranging from a small number of large complexes to countless village shrines (*chinju*) and even smaller roadside "chapels," consisting of little more than a container holding a talisman or an image. Late Edo gazetteers, which list and describe temples and shrines, can give us some idea of the situation of shrines. Helen Hardacre has analyzed such gazetteers for the Kōza and Nishi Tama districts in the provinces of Sagami and Musashi.[17] Her findings show that, in the 1830s, Nishi Tama had 390 shrines, spread among 107 villages that contained just under 8,000 households in total. Most were village shrines, run by the villagers themselves. Almost a fifth of shrines (72 in all) were run by Buddhist temple priests or local *yamabushi*. A comparable proportion (75) had a Shinto priest. There were only 43 shrine priests in Nishi Tama, so a good number of them must have managed more than one shrine. A 1665 shogunal law stipulated that Shinto priests without court rank should submit to the supervision of the priestly Yoshida house in Kyoto,[18] but in the 1830s only 7 out of the 43 priests in Nishi Tama held Yoshida licenses. Some had "supervisors" based at a larger shrine in the area, but the majority

---

[16] Arimoto, *Kinsei Nihon no shūkyō shakaishi*, 34–35.
[17] Hardacre, *Religion and Society*, 68–91.
[18] Many priests holding court rank were under the nominal control of the Shirakawa house, who were the transmitters of court rituals related to the *kami*.

acted without any form of official status. They were local farmers who performed shrine rituals according to customary village practice. In Kōza, almost half of all shrines (173 out of 356) were managed by either Buddhist priests or *yamabushi*. Only two shrines in Kōza had Shinto priests; one of them had a Yoshida license and supervised the other. The others were run by the villagers themselves.

In Tokugawa-period Japan, then, shrines did not function as bases for a non-Buddhist Shinto, in spite of the fact that the Yoshida house propounded such a notion. Temple monks and *yamabushi* often played central roles in village shrine rituals, and many shrines were dedicated to Buddhist or Shugendō deities. The most elaborate shrine rituals were seasonal *matsuri*, most commonly held in spring or in autumn. These often revolved around a parade of the *kami* deities through the locality in palanquins (*mikoshi*), although many villages were too small and poor for such extravagance and used simpler formats. The more substantial shrines sought to mimic the largest festivals of the realm, such as the Gion festival in Kyoto, and served as the community hub from which flamboyant multiday festivities were arranged, with streets or neighborhoods competing with each other to put on the best show. Both large and small shrines also offered various forms of prayer rituals against droughts, storms, pests, fires, and illnesses. Such *kaji kitō*-type rituals, however, were at times contested by *yamabushi*, who were liable to turn up in numbers and disrupt the ritual performances of their competitors by force.

Local temple priests, *yamabushi*, and Shinto priests competed not only with each other but also with representatives of religious centers in the wider region, or even in other parts of the country. Agents called "masters" (*oshi*) or "guides" from famous temples, shrines, and mountains maintained relations with local patrons, often formalized by contract. Nishi Tama, for example, was visited regularly by *oshi* from nearby Mount Mitake in Musashi Province. This site had a shrine and a temple as well as a community of *oshi* who organized "pious associations" (*kō*) in the surrounding districts. Members of these associations held prayer vigils (*himachi*) and other communal rites for their ancestors, who were believed to dwell on Mount Mitake, which was deemed a piece of the Pure Land of Miroku (Maitreya), the next Buddha who will appear in our world to save the sentient beings in a distant future. At the foot of Mount Mitake, a Shinto priest managed a shrine dedicated to the mountain deity Zaō Gongen, where *kagura* dances were offered for patrons in exchange for offerings. The priests of the mountain's main temple, Sesonji, performed *goma* fire offerings, and they also recited various sutras at the Zaō Gongen Shrine. In the course of the Tokugawa period, Sesonji was gradually squeezed out by the Zaō Gongen Shrine, while the *oshi* increasingly challenged the Shinto priest's authority and acted as independent priests. These *oshi* had started out as *yamabushi* but evolved into innkeepers who held rituals in their compounds while serving the needs of the associations they organized in villages. They specialized in talismans that secured good harvests and kept silkworms safe from pests and illnesses. By the mid-1800s, Mount Mitake *oshi* had settled on a schedule whereby they visited their villages three times a year to collect donations. These donations were extracted from the village as a single unit rather than from individual households; this ensured that no households escaped their attention.[19]

The Mount Mitake *oshi* had competition from representatives from even larger centers of worship further afield. Pilgrimages to such sites as Mount Kōya and the Ise Shrines were popular in the region. Ise associations, in particular, were ubiquitous throughout Japan; it has been estimated that by the late eighteenth century, as many as 80 to 90 percent of households in the country were served by an Ise *oshi* every year. These *oshi* ran large compounds in Yamada and Uji, the two towns that had grown up in front of the Outer and Inner Shrines of Ise. They had contracts with thousands or even tens of thousands of patrons, often going back to the sixteenth century, which they vigorously guarded against intruders. *Oshi* sent assistants (*tedai*) on regular rounds of the villages and towns where their patrons lived, exchanging sake cups with village heads and distributing amulets, calendars, and other gifts from Ise. Patrons organized themselves in pious associations that raised funds for regular pilgrimage tours to the shrines. In Ise, they attended *kagura* rituals performed in the compound of their *oshi*, visited one or both of the Ise Shrines, and enjoyed the entertainment offered by a multitude of geisha houses and theaters that had sprung up on the hill between the Outer and the Inner Shrine.

There were often multiple Ise associations in the same village. In the village of Higashi Futami in Harima Province, for example, there were ten, with some run by fishers, some by farmers, and some by merchants.[20] Every five years or so, the members of these associations made joint pilgrimages to Ise, which typically took about two weeks. At home, they shared two "Ise houses" (Iseya) where joint meetings were held and the *oshi* assistants would stay. The Ise associations raised funds from their members, who paid regular fees, and also from rent from dedicated fields, some of which were farmed

---

[19] Hardacre, *Religion and Society*, 95–104.
[20] Onodera, "Higashi Harima ni okeru kinsei no Ise sangū"; Teeuwen and Breen, *Social History of the Ise Shrines*, 153.

by a nearby community of outcastes. Ise pilgrimage was not the only activity organized by these associations. They also played a central role in the "hoe ritual" (*mikuwa onrei*), held at the time of rice planting, and included a group of members who went to watch the Gion festival in Kyoto. They had social and economic functions beyond worship, too. Members might obtain loans from their pious associations when in trouble, and the associations were an arena where the village's fishers, farmers, and merchants (though not the outcastes, and only exceptionally the women) mingled, jostled for primacy, and made the informal arrangements that oiled the machinery of community life.

Pious associations that were catered to by agents from distant sites of faith were a common feature of village and city life. In Higashi Futami, there were also associations dedicated to Sumiyoshi and Ebisu, two deities who were popular among fishers. Many temple and shrine towns copied Ise's general model (which, in its turn, had early medieval antecedents from Kumano) in the course of the eighteenth century. *Oshi* from Izumo Shrine developed pious associations along the Japan Sea coast from Ezo (Hokkaido) to Kyushu in the mid-Tokugawa period.[21] In the course of the eighteenth century, Konpira, on Shikoku, developed from a Shugendō site into a predominantly Shinto center of prayer, entertainment, and prostitution patronized by a nationwide network of associations.[22] Ōyama in Sagami Province followed a similar course: serving as a training site for *yamabushi* in the sixteenth century, Ōyama later turned into a pilgrimage destination that catered to lay worshippers from around the Kantō region. Ōyama was run by an uneasy alliance between Shingon temples and *oshi* who visited patrons and accommodated them in the inns they ran on the mountain.[23] By the end of the period, some of these *oshi* sought to break free from the temples by allying themselves with Shinto heads in Kyoto (in this case, the Shirakawa house) and claiming the mountain for Shinto. *Oshi* were active also at mountains such as Mount Fuji, Mount Hakusan (Kaga Province), Mount Tateyama (Etchū), Mount Atago (Yamashiro), and Mount Hiko (Bungo) and shrines such as Kashima (Hitachi), Taga (Ōmi), and Tsushima (Owari). The activities of these agents of pilgrimage turned Japan into a patchwork of intersecting national and regional networks of worship. Barbara Ambros cites an 1809 list of donations paid to such agents by a warrior family in

[21] Zhong, *Origin of Modern Shinto.*
[22] Thal, *Rearranging the Landscape of the Gods.*
[23] Ambros, *Emplacing a Pilgrimage.*

Musashi Province.[24] This family made annual contributions to eight mountains and shrines and biannual contributions to four more, amounting to a considerable sum of money in total. In some form or other, almost every Japanese must have been tied into this national market of mediated prayer rites and pilgrimages to famous centers of worship.

Temples were also part of this national market. We have already seen that many temples provided *kaji kitō* services in addition to providing their patrons with mortuary rites. Some temples took a more radical path and had no *danka* patrons at all. One such temple was Zenkōji in Shinano Province. This temple was home to an Amida triad of exceptional power, which according to temple legend was the very first Buddha image that arrived in Japan in the sixth century. Zenkōji's Amida, which was kept locked out of sight as a "hidden Buddha," saved worshippers from the sufferings of hell and guaranteed them rebirth in the Pure Land. Zenkōji did not belong to one of the sects of Buddhism but formed a network of its own. So-called Zenkōji *hijiri* (holy men) traveled the country advertising the efficacy of its image to lay believers within designated districts. Thirty-nine Zenkōji branch temples, staffed with guides and proselytizers, catered to the same number of districts. Those who worshipped at Zenkōji in the second week of the year received a vermilion seal on their foreheads, which represented their karmic link to the temple's "living Buddha" in material form. Zenkōji was exceptionally welcoming to and popular among women. This stands in stark contrast to such sites as Mounts Hiei, Kōya, Fuji, and many others, which denied access to women in fear of the pollution of childbirth and menstruation believed to adhere to the female sex.

Zenkōji was known in particular for its spectacular *kaichō* or "viewings." The term *kaichō* literally means "opening the curtains." It designates events where images that are normally hidden are exhibited to a fee-paying public. *Kaichō* offered worshippers the opportunity to see and venerate replicas of Zenkōji's triad in exchange for a donation. *Kaichō* could only be held with permission from the shogunate, which began licensing such fundraising initiatives in the late seventeenth century as an alternative to direct funding for necessary repairs to famous temples. *Kaichō* proliferated in the eighteenth century, as the initially restrictive conditions for permitting them were gradually hollowed out. Zenkōji held sixteen *kaichō* at the temple itself; on seven occasions, the replicas set out on lengthy tours, often over multiple years, to Japan's three cities and/or other parts of the country. These *kaichō* not only brought in large sums of money but also occasioned the founding of Zenkōji

[24] Ambros, "Local Religious Specialists," 330.

pious associations and new local sites of Zenkōji-related worship around the country.[25] Zenkōji was not alone in carrying out these kinds of activities; Sensōji in Asakusa, Edo, was another major site for *kaichō*.[26]

Towns and villages were visited not only by agents of large complexes of temples and shrines but also by what one might call religious vagrants who performed various arts on the road and in the streets while distributing talismans and soliciting small donations. Itinerant mendicants raising money for religious projects (*kanjin*) had been a prominent feature of medieval life. In the Tokugawa period, such projects were funded by other means, and the successors of these mendicants evolved into buskers, offering entertainment as much as preaching, reciting mantras, or securing protection against malicious spirits. The so-called Kumano nuns (*Kumano bikuni*) are an example of this category. Seventeenth-century writers agreed that these nuns had, in the past, practiced austerities in Kumano and Ise while traveling the country to raise funds for those sacred sites by singing Buddhist hymns and preaching. In particular, they were known for carrying around paintings showing the realms of transmigration, notably the various hells, and reciting explanations of those images on street corners. But, by the second half of the seventeenth century, the story goes, these nuns had given up the austerities, lost the ability to preach, and were instead gathering alms by singing songs of a more "vulgar" kind, as well as "hanging around with men" – that is, working as prostitutes.[27] Whether this was a fair assessment of the situation or an expression of prejudice is hard to tell; but this common manner of depicting the *bikuni* certainly reflected the view that the shogunal authorities had of these women. In general, the shogunate had a strong dislike of non-sedentary floaters. In the late 1660s, the magistrate of temples and shrines investigated all itinerant religious figures and banned those without a head temple from collecting alms.[28] Kumano nuns who failed to secure affiliation documents from Kumano ended up on the wrong side of the law. This reduced many of them to poverty and likely drove a good number of them into prostitution.

A similar group of roaming ritualists were the so-called *gannin bōzu*, or simply *gannin* (vow priests), described by Gerald Groemer as "religious street

[25] McCallum, *Zenkōji and Its Icon*; Hur, "Invitation to the Secret Buddha of Zenkōji"; Itō, "Kinsei Kawachi-Ōsaka chiiki ni okeru Zenkōji no fukyō katsudō."
[26] Hur, *Prayer and Play*.
[27] Asai Ryōi, *Tōkaidō meishōki* (1661), quoted in Ruch, "Woman to Woman," 547. See also Hur, *Death and Social Order*, 18–19.
[28] Hur, *Death and Social Order*, 93.

performers."²⁹ When this particular term appeared in the seventeenth century, it already had the connotation of "degraded" religious practitioners: *gannin* were once said to have been performers of austerities who collected funds
for temples and shrines, but now they were simply street singers and dancers,
with a repertoire of "satirical ballads" (*chongare, chobokure*) and mock sutras
(*ahodarakyō*). They would parade through town carrying portable shrines,
dancing to raucous music, and singing while collecting alms from onlookers.
The *gannin* avoided the fate of the Kumano nuns by associating themselves
with the Kyoto temple Kuramadera in the late 1660s; this temple had found a
niche for itself by serving as a last resort for various kinds of practitioners who
lacked affiliation credentials. *Gannin* now organized themselves in guilds,
with "group chiefs" (*kumigashira*) and "liaison chiefs" (*furegashira*), the latter
appointed to transmit regulations from the magistrate of shrines and temples
to the *gannin* under their control. Some *gannin* groups traveled around, performing on stages set up at temple fairs and the like; others settled in ghettos
in the cities (notably Edo), performing in groups in the streets and selling
amulets. These ghettos had numerous flophouses, where not only itinerant
gannin but also other floaters could stay for a minimal fee. The authorities at
times ordered *gannin* to track down and arrest criminals, making good use of
their knowledge of street life. Even in the nineteenth century, however, they
continued to define their activities as performers of rituals and facilitators of
worship. A roster from 1813 cites, among other things, distributing talismans,
performing proxy pilgrimages and vigils, dancing for the "enjoyment of the
gods" (*hōraku*), sutra chanting, performing austerities, appeasing roaming
"hungry spirits" (*segaki*), and soliciting contributions for projects of faith.³⁰

Managing Faith: Proactive and Reactive Patterns

Most Japanese were exposed to, and participated in, a large variety of forms of
worship and ritual, facilitated by an equally large variety of agents. The temple certification system, as we saw in the previous section, was based on the
logic that if laypeople were only solidly grounded in one (officially approved)
faith, this would render them secure from falling into another faith – notably
of the "pernicious" category. A closer look at the reality of village and city
life, however, reveals that the lay population did not typically structure their

²⁹ Groemer, "Arts of the *Gannin*"; Groemer, "Short History of the *Gannin*." For more on a
   wide range of similar street performers, see Groemer, *Street Performers and Society in Urban
   Japan*.
³⁰ Groemer, "Arts of the *Gannin*," 278–79.

religious life according to such a notion. The shogunate, too, made no efforts to impose an exclusive faith on laypeople. Rather, its focus was on preventing conflicts between different agents and institutions, who were all competing for custom from a shared clientele.

In fact, it was groups that *did* have some form of exclusive faith, and therefore disparaged outsiders, that attracted negative attention and, at times, repression. Even in such cases, however, the regime was increasingly passive. In the seventeenth century, the shogunate took a proactive attitude against what it saw as faith-based disloyalty, seeking out "heretics" and establishing a system of punishment and control. In the mid-1660s, there were even some attempts at active religious engineering by prominent daimyo with Confucian agendas. In Mito, Aizu, and Okayama, ideological visions inspired attempts to replace temple certification with shrine affiliation, with the aim of inculcating Shinto-Confucian ethics of loyalty in the domain.[31] Such attempts, however, immediately ran into practical problems (including a lack of shrines and Shinto priests) and were soon abandoned. By the early eighteenth century, the regime appeared content to leave the realm of faith alone unless provoked by some incident that necessitated urgent action. The shogunate reacted when head temples involved them in intra-sectarian conflicts or when it felt that the credibility of its laws was at stake. Proactive measures against faith groups, including Christians, became increasingly rare. At the same time, temples and shrines were discouraged from proselytizing, as strongly defined forms of faith were looked upon as threats to the peaceful coexistence of temples and shrines of many hues.

A striking example of an "exclusivist" faith group that triggered reluctant action from the shogunate was a branch of the Nichiren sect that called itself Fujufuse.[32] The name of this branch refers to its principle neither to "receive" (*fuju*) alms from nor "give" (*fuse*) alms to people who "slander the Dharma" – that is, who are not part of the Nichiren faith group. Not worshipping at Shinto shrines was another of this group's rules, which had their roots in the writings of Nichiren (1222–82) himself. The Nichiren sect had split between what Peter Nosco calls accommodationist and fundamentalist factions when the latter refused to participate in services for Toyotomi Hideyoshi's ancestors in 1595. In 1599, Tokugawa Ieyasu gave Nichiō (1565–1630), the leader of the fundamentalist faction, a chance to resolve the matter in a manner that would preserve his honor and yet signal obedience to the new warrior

---

[31] Köck, Pickl-Kolaczia, and Scheid, *Religion, Power, and the Rise of Shinto*.
[32] Tamamuro, *Edo bakufu no shūkyō tōsei*; Nosco, *Individuality in Early Modern Japan*.

regime; but Nichiō persisted in his refusal. He was exiled but pardoned after two years, until renewed conflict with the accommodationists caused him to be exiled again in 1630 (a month after his death). The accommodationist faction continued to draw the shogunate's attention to the "misdeeds" of the Fujufuse fundamentalists, accusing them of disobedience to the laws of the Nichiren sect. Even in the face of these appeals, the shogunate kept a low profile in this schismatic conflict for decades.

The matter came to a head in that decade of hard decisions, the 1660s. All Nichiren associations were banned, and in 1669 Fujufuse temples were excluded from the temple certification system. This opened the way to the prosecution of individual lay followers of the movement, although this remained rare. Perhaps more importantly, it stimulated the development of covert associations that met in secret and were occasionally visited by under-cover priests. Most Fujufuse believers lived double lives, submitting to cer-tification by recognized (non-Fujufuse) temples while practicing their faith in private. A small minority, however, refused temple certification. These hard-core members had the role of mediating between traveling Fujufuse priests and the larger association. When uncovered, Fujufuse members had the choice of apostatizing or being treated as Christians.

The Fujufuse movement was forced underground for various reasons. The fundamentalists' refusal to perform rites of subservience to the warrior regime was one; the insistent attempts by the accommodationists to force the regime to take action against what they saw as a fractious minority within their sect was another. The authorities, local or national, showed little enthusiasm for hunting down Fujufuse groups, and the exclusivist nature of their faith seemed to cause warrior officials little concern unless concrete circumstances forced their hand. Yet this sect demonstrated to the regime that exclusivist faith, even if it was not Christian, tended to inspire stubborn intransigence and disobedience. It was among "fundamentalists" that faith took precedence over loyalty; in that sense, the Fujufuse were similar to Christians.

They were similar, too, to the Ikkō sect in that among both Nichiren and Ikkō followers faith appears to have been a central aspect of personal iden-tity. In contrast to temple priests of most other sects, Ikkō priests refused to serve as caretakers of village shrines, and they seldom participated in the communal rites against insects or droughts. Ikkō communities tended not to participate in the merrier parts of the Bon festival (the summer festivities for the dead), and in regions with a majority of Ikkō adherents, both *yamabushi* temples and Shinto shrines were thin on the ground. Both Ikkō and Nichiren believers preferred to marry within their own faith communities; if they did not, it was not uncommon, at least in the late Tokugawa period, for women of these faiths to remain *danna* of their temples of birth after marriage rather than reaffiliate with the temples of their husbands.[33]

Like the Nichiren sect, Ikkō temples took care to make their commitment to an accommodationist stance explicit not only in the sect's own laws but also in local regulations drawn up by individual temples. Such laws and regulations tended to stress that "faith" (*anjin*) should be exercised within the framework of the "regulations" (*okite*) of the warrior regime. One nineteenth-century set of guidelines for teaching Nishi Honganji lay followers defined *anjin* as "depending on Amida's vow and attaining rebirth in paradise" and *okite* as "respecting national and local laws and behaving in accord with the five constants of human relations."[34] The five constants refer to the ethical norms for behavior between lord and vassal, father and son, husband and wife, elder and younger brother, and two friends; in many contexts, this phrase served as shorthand for loyalty and filial piety. In spite of the stress on *okite*, however, the Ikkō sect was widely regarded as a potential threat to loyalty. In the domains of Hitoyoshi and Satsuma (in southern Kyushu), for example, the sect had been banned completely already in the sixteenth century because of suspected complicity in uprisings, and this ban remained in force throughout the Tokugawa period.

The need to allay such suspicion rendered it all the more important for the Ikkō sect to expose "fundamentalists" within its own ranks. The Ikkō head temples had problems with covert associations in much the same manner as the Nichiren sect. Involvement with such groups could lead to arrest and punishment, though rarely of the severest kind. Clark Chilson describes a number of cases in some detail.[35] In 1767, an Edo temple that was a branch of Nishi Honganji reported a covert group in its part of the city to the magistrate of temples and shrines. A merchant called Kin'emon was arrested and questioned. Hoping to be rewarded with leniency, he revealed all to the investigators. He had been recruited by a neighbor, who had eased him into the group with great circumspection. After much cautious probing, Kin'emon had finally been initiated into the group in a series of secret gatherings that lasted three days. On the first day, Kin'emon had been taken to a secret location where he and about fifteen other prospective initiates had been served tea and snacks by a dozen or so group members. After some waiting, the lay

[33] Arimoto, *Kinsei Nihon no shūkyō shakaishi*, 290–301.
[34] Arimoto, *Kinsei Nihon no shūkyō shakaishi*, 303.
[35] Chilson, *Secrecy's Power*.

leader (*zenchishiki*) of the group made his appearance. In a short sermon this leader argued that the priests of Nishi Honganji lacked the knowledge and the ambition to guide people to salvation; they were merely after people's money. The covert group, on the other hand, followed a secret tradition of practice that went all the way back to Shinran. On the second day, in a different location, the prospective initiates were told to call out *tasuketamae* ("please save me") countless times, until Amida heard them. There were multiple sessions, with short breaks in between to recuperate. When the leader could see that one of the initiates had received Amida's grace, he would shout: "You have been saved!" Kin'emon attained salvation in the third session. On the third day, the initiates performed a symbolic funeral and celebrated their rebirth as fully saved "Buddhas." They were now full-fledged members of the covert Ikkō group.

As a result of this investigation, dozens of people were banished from Edo, while rumors arose that Christianity was now spreading in the city. Branding covert groups as suspected Christians was by no means rare; in fact, it was almost standard for lower officials to fear the presence of Christianity whenever covert communities of faith came to light. A striking example of this is an incident that occurred in Tashiro (Hizen Province), a district that belonged to Tsushima domain, in roughly the same period.[36] Covert faith groups became an acute problem in Tashiro in the years 1758–63, after similar groups had been uncovered in neighboring domains. When rumors of groups engaging in "unorthodox practices" (*ihō*) began to spread, the two Tashiro intendants (*daikan*) started an investigation using two spies. One spy joined a covert group and reported on its activities and practices (which were similar to those of the Edo group described earlier), while the other collected intelligence among local nonmembers. The first spy underwent eight sessions of *tasuketamae* praying, each lasting many hours, before the leader was finally convinced that he had "seen the light" (*kōmyō*). The resulting report led to many arrests, but the spies reported that none of the detained members showed any signs of giving up their unorthodox faith. Quite to the contrary, the arrests and punishments inspired revelations of Amida's "mercy" in those who faced this ordeal, strengthening their faith.

The Tsushima elders made sure that this investigation was conducted in strict secrecy. This was motivated by a fear that the members of this covert group were practicing some form of Christianity. If gossip about Christians in Tsushima domain reached the ears of the shogunal magistrate in Nagasaki,

---

[36] Ōhashi, "Kinsei chitsujo ni okeru 'ja' no yuragi."

this might trigger potentially disastrous measures against the domain. The standard method to uncover Christians was by forcing suspects to step on Christian images (*efumi*); plates for that purpose were kept by the Nagasaki magistrate. The Tsushima officials discussed whether it might be possible to borrow such a plate, but this would require an explanation and thus alert the magistrate to the situation in Tashiro. In the end, they concluded that this would be too risky.

The Nagasaki magistrate's office gave the Tashiro intendants some hints that they knew about the arrests, but otherwise made a point of looking the other way. The reasons for this were pragmatic: tolerating dubious faith among harmless peasants was less damaging than causing a large and alarming scandal, which would force the shogunate to intervene and establish its authority by means of harsh measures. The consequences of identifying Christians were particularly daunting. Not only were severe punishments unavoidable; there were strict regulations for the surveillance of family members and descendants of Christians (*ruizoku*) that were extremely onerous and costly to implement. After the executions in Mino Province in 1698–99, not a single Christian was identified for almost a century. In 1790, a village head (*shōya*) in Urakami near Nagasaki denounced nineteen villagers as Christians, but upon investigation, the magistrate's office found the evidence to be indecisive and the village head corrupt. The accused villagers were ordered to apologize and then released. In 1805, thousands of suspected Christians were discovered in Amakusa, on shogunal lands administered by nearby Shimabara domain. The arrested villagers worshipped deities they called Deus and Mary (Deiusu, Maruya), and they used phrases such as "amen Deus" (*anmen riyusu*) in their prayers. They admitted that these were heterodox practices but denied that they had anything to do with the banned Christian creed; these were merely practices that had been passed down by their ancestors. The domain and the shogunate feared that large-scale arrests would trigger riots, impacting negatively on tax revenues, and they accepted the villagers' explanation. After performing *efumi* and signing an oath to abandon their "heterodox practices" (*ihō*), the villagers were released. The label *ihō* served to avoid a deadly verdict of "pernicious" behavior (*jahō*), which would have unleashed seventeenth-century cruelty on the villagers and unhinged local communities for generations.[37]

The early nineteenth century saw the appearance of new grassroots faith groups. Some of these groups emerged from semilegal popular practices,

---

[37] Ōhashi, *Senpuku kirishitan.*

often involving spirit (or deity) possession, healing rituals, and divination. None of them were embedded in certified institutions, and their leaders were at times targeted by the authorities as practitioners of fraudulent, heterodox, or even pernicious practices. Among those leaders were a surprising number of women – surprising, because women were largely excluded from public roles also in the world of faith. In the Kansai area, numerous female "fox mediums" performed *kaji kitō* rituals for a rapidly growing clientele, in spite of a 1799 ban on fox magic.[38] Nothing was done to enforce this ban until three such mediums, all middle-aged widows, were found guilty of using "Christian magic" in their practice; they were arrested and executed in Osaka in 1829 together with three implicated men.[39] In Nagoya, a widow called Kino was possessed by Konpira in 1802. By preaching and performing rites for the afterlife, she gathered a considerable number of followers not only among commoners but also among warrior retainers of Owari domain. By 1817, there was even a pious association of followers of Kino in Edo. Kino's success triggered a first bout of repression in 1820; more rounds were to follow in subsequent decades. Yet her group survived, acquiring the name of Nyoraikyō in the 1920s.[40] More well known is Nakayama Miki, a farmer's wife from a village in Yamato Province who began to preach and heal as the medium of an almighty deity that possessed her in 1838. Her rapidly expanding group, which later became Tenrikyō, likewise alarmed the authorities and suffered frequent harassment. Like the 1829 fox mediums, Kino and Miki were suspected of Christian heresy, though they were not found guilty of such charges.

The appearance of all these suspicious faith groups motivated warrior officials to restrict proselytization even on the part of "orthodox" temples. Already in the shogunal temple laws of the seventeenth century, teaching patrons about doctrine was strikingly absent from the list of the duties imposed on temples.[41] Sectarian laws, even within the Ikkō sect, gave detailed instructions about funeral rites, mourning taboos, the need to avoid extravagance, and the pursuit of learning by priests, but had nothing to say about preaching to lay believers. There was always a suspicion that preaching, especially to laypeople who were not one's own patrons, might constitute a breach of the legal principle that "temple priests may not contest each other's patrons." Such negative perceptions of preaching to laypeople culminated in an incident that

---

[38] Nakagawa, "Inari Worship in Early Modern Osaka."
[39] Miyazaki, Nakai, and Teeuwen, *Christian Sorcerers on Trial.*
[40] Kanda, *Nyoraikyō no shisō to shinkō.*
[41] Sawa, *Kinsei shūkyō shakairon*, 277–80.

occurred in Edo in the 1840s. In 1842, the so-called Tenpō reforms included a series of new regulations aiming to improve people's "customs" in Edo by banning all kinds of popular entertainments. As the case of the *gannin* illustrates, many entertainers were, at least in name, religious figures. Preaching, too, had become a specialized métier, performed by professional raconteurs and comedians rather than by regular temple priests. Preaching was therefore among the practices that would henceforth be banned within the three cities of the realm; so were gatherings of Ikkō and Nichiren associations, which, in contrast to other pious associations, often featured preaching.

The Ikkō head temples were concerned that the ban against city preaching might weaken their connection with their patrons, and in 1846 they petitioned the Edo magistrate of temples and shrines to grant them special permission on the grounds that preaching to lay believers was a special tradition of this sect. After lengthy negotiations, the magistrate relented, recognizing that the Ikkō sect "differed from all others" in its tradition of visiting the houses of lay patrons to preach and pray; this decision was relayed also to Kyoto and Osaka.[42] This episode shows that warrior officials tended to see preaching to lay associations in the cities as a threat to public order rather than a defense against pernicious beliefs. It also reminds us that the Ikkō and Nichiren sects were regarded as different from all others, and it reveals that other sects did not attach enough importance to preaching to see the need to protest against this blanket ban. From these (and similar) incidents, we can conclude that proselytization and the teaching of doctrines to lay patrons were at best regarded as unimportant, and often frowned upon by the authorities.

The Place of Faith in Tokugawa Ideology

The shogunate was not in the habit of formulating official views on abstractions like "faith." In warrior writings about "the Way of government" (*seidōron*), issues of faith, or even temples and shrines, hardly feature at all.[43] Yet it is perhaps possible to grasp the outlines of the broader discourse on the role of faith in society from the way it was handled in practice. "Faith" was clearly an ambivalent phenomenon. On one hand, faith was a necessary incentive for the "ignorant people" (*gumin*) to lead ethical lives. Fear of hell

---

[42] Sawa, *Kinsei shūkyō shakairon*, 283–84.

[43] In sixteen texts from this genre, collected in Naramoto, *Kinsei seidōron*, the topic of temples and shrines is raised only in a negative sense: negligent priests should be fired, and temples and shrines should be kept simple, without extravagant ornamentation. Christianity or other dangerous forms of faith are not mentioned at all.

and damnation, or of the wrath of neglected ancestor spirits, could be beneficial by preventing people from falling into lives of dissolution. The mortuary
rituals that temple priests performed for their patrons served to inspire filial
piety and loyalty, and they were expected to foster a moral attitude in all
members of the household. Communal shrine rituals were at times viewed
in a similar manner. In Confucian terms, such rituals were categorized as *rei*
(Ch. *li*), rites that order human society, bring the human realm into harmony
with heaven and earth, and thus serve as the "pillar of the state."[44] Prayer
rituals of the *kaji kitō* kind, on the other hand, were regarded with skepticism,
and temples that specialized in them were less likely to be treated favorably
by the authorities. Rather than supporting the social order, such rituals could
well compromise it if they offered people a way to "bribe" themselves out of
justified heavenly retribution.

While this same discourse admitted that people were easily corrupted if
they lacked all faith, immoderate faith was looked upon with suspicion as
a threat to loyalty. People of immoderate faith attached more importance
to their temple than to their warrior lord. They tended to make excessive
donations to temples while appealing to the warrior officials that they could
not afford their taxes. The ignorant were cheated into paying charlatans for
expensive prayer rituals that were mere chicanery. Tight-knit faith groups
formed covert networks that engaged in suspicious activities, threatening law
and order. Misguided faith could push innocent laypeople into the hands of
corrupt priests and mediums, who were driven by greed and inappropriate
worldly ambition.

The authorities were willing to accommodate acts of faith, for example by
recognizing travel permits (*ōrai tegata*) that identified travelers as pilgrims.
In some cases (e.g. on Shikoku), domain officials even organized systems of
assistance for pilgrims who became ill and had to be escorted home. Faith,
however, had to be legitimate. Officials on Shikoku were on the lookout for
impostors who, while pretending to be "practitioners of austerities," were in
fact petty thieves who "check to see whether people are away from home
working in the fields, take whatever they find, and then flee."[45] Having
the proper papers was all the more important for those who sold religious
services: if some trouble brought them to the attention of the authorities,

---

[44] On the central importance of *rei* as argued by such thinkers as Arai Hakuseki (1657–1725),
Ogyū Sorai (1666–1728), and the Mito scholar Aizawa Seishisai (1782–1863), see Nakai,
Shogunal Politics, 186–90; Maruyama, *Studies in the Intellectual History of Tokugawa Japan*,
106; and Wakabayashi, *Anti-Foreignism and Western Learning*, 127.
[45] Kouamé, "Shikoku's Local Authorities and *Henro*," 419.

paperless "impostors" were dealt with harshly. This was especially problematic for the many female healers and soothsayers that eked out a living in the cities. For most, their business could never be quite legal because they were unable to obtain official accreditation.

Protecting and sponsoring national temples and shrines, on the other hand, was regarded as a central task of a legitimate government. Toyotomi Hideyoshi had granted lands to major temples and shrines as part of his national program of cadastral surveys. The Tokugawa shogunate made these grants permanent with, in most cases, only minor adjustments. Hideyoshi had also sponsored rebuilding projects of temples and shrines that had been destroyed in the fighting of the sixteenth century; again, the Tokugawa shogunate continued this policy. The Ise Shrines, for example, were rebuilt and refurnished in their entirety every twenty years, fifteen times between 1609 and 1869, at great cost. Throughout the Tokugawa period, the shogunate underwrote these ritual rebuilding projects and managed them through its magistrate stationed in Ise.

The third shogun, Iemitsu (1604–51), invested heavily in the deification of his grandfather Ieyasu, enshrined in Nikkō as Tōshō Daigongen or the "Great Avatar Who Illuminates the East." In official shrine records (engi), written by a Tendai prelate whose temple was to oversee the shrine, Ieyasu was described as a manifestation of the "Origin and Source of Heaven, Earth, and Man," also known as Sannō Gongen, the protector deity of Tendai's old headquarters on Mount Hiei. Other texts, with a wider dissemination, depicted Ieyasu as the embodiment of mercy and argued that he had received custody of the realm from the Buddha Amida.[46] Tōshōgū shrines in worship of the deified Ieyasu were built at strategic places in towns and cities around the country; by the late Tokugawa period, there were well over 500 of them. The larger ones among them were prominent stages for warrior ritual and also for festivals that engaged entire towns.[47] Together with the mortuary temples of daimyo lords and prominent retainers, Tōshōgū shrines expressed the "sacred" nature of warrior rule in a visual and spatial manner, even without textual exegesis. Ōkuwa Hitoshi points out that in places where the Ikkō sect had a dominant position (in about a third of the country), the local Tōshōgū often faced the regional head temple of that sect. The effect of this placement strategy was that "faith" was firmly contained within the bounds of sacralized warrior rule. Ikkō faith and shogunal sacred power appeared as allies, with

---

[46] Ōkuwa, "Tokugawa shōgun kenryoku to shūkyō."
[47] Nakano, *Shokoku Tōshōgū no shiteki kenkyū.*

one taking care of the otherworldly realm of life after death, and the other of the prosperity of the realm and its people.[48]

From 1646 onwards, the imperial court sent annual envoys to Nikkō and Ise to present offerings to these two national shrines, dedicated to the divine founder of the shogunate and the originator of imperial rule over the realm.[49] This practice followed a historical pattern that went back to the days of the first shogunate in Kamakura: the court performed rituals for the protection of the state, while the shogunate took responsibility for peace and order – and, in the Tokugawa period, funding. Among court rituals for "the safety of the imperial body, the prosperity of the state, abundant harvests, and peace for the myriad people" were Buddhist rituals performed in the palace chapel (Shingon-in) in the second week of the year and rituals for the pacification of the realm delegated by the court to such imperial temples as Tōdaiji, Yaku-shiji, and Hōryūji. Court Shinto ceremonial served much the same purpose. In this category, there was daily morning worship by the emperor of the imperial ancestor deities and the gods of heaven and earth within the palace (*maichō no gohai*), and the *niiname* ritual of first fruits (revived in 1740). Many of these rituals were tremendously expensive; it was the shogunate that picked up the bill.

Did all this add up to an ideology of faith, or even a coherent policy of sacralization on the part of the shogunate? If so, this ideology was very vague, implicit, and open to pluralism. The warrior regime kept the peace, brought the land in line with the "Way of Heaven," caused the military class to stick to the "Way of lord and vassal," instigated a strict but humane system of rewards and punishments, and inspired commoners to put their households in order, to practice filial piety, and to exert themselves in their proper occupations. As a result, the country flourished, and the "Buddhas and gods" (*busshin*) protected and blessed the realm.[50] Christianity was molded to fit the role of the Other, as the epitome of disloyalty, impiety, inhumaneness, greed, corruption, and a morbid yearning for pain and death rather than prosperity in this life. Beyond the demonization of Christianity, the regime took care to stay out of questions of faith, unless law and order appeared to be at stake.

That is not to say that the shogunate did not interfere in faith-related matters. At times, matters of faith were overruled and disrupted by the interests of civil and military governance. Most intrusive were the extensive periods of public mourning for shoguns, emperors, daimyo, and selected members

[48] Ōkuwa, "Kinsei kokka no shūkyōsei," 130–34.
[49] Sonehara, "Ise Jingū to Tōshōgū," 66.
[50] For a typical example of this very standard discourse, see *Seji kenbunroku* (1816), translated in Teeuwen and Nakai, *Lust, Commerce, and Corruption*, 40.

of their families, which routinely put life on hold for days or even weeks at a time. People of all classes were ordered to refrain from "music and construction" while their leaders performed elaborate rites of mourning.[51] Temple and shrine events, including festivals of all sizes, were stopped in their tracks; in many places, even simple purification rites using *suzu* bells were banned, rendering many acts of worship problematic. Mourning was not a private matter but a public demonstration of loyalty and filial piety. While warrior leaders enacted their legitimacy as filial heirs to power, the public was forced to display humble "restraint." Breaches were interpreted as signs of rebellious disrespect for the authorities – or, even worse, as knowing challenges to the sovereignty of the regime, reminiscent of Fujufuse or even Christian deviance.

The Arrival of "Religion" and Its Effects

The last decades of the Tokugawa period saw the reappearance of the Christian threat, in the form of Western encroachment from all sides: the Russians, the British, the Americans, and the French. In some circles, this led to concerns about the spiritual preparedness of the "ignorant people," who would no doubt be targeted by missionaries in an attempt to sever the ties of loyalty and filial piety that held the realm together. In the early nineteenth century, Confucian scholars of the so-called Later Mito school argued that in order to defend against Christian encroachment, it was necessary to "harness the masses" by proactive measures so as to inculcate in them a coherent teaching that focused on loyalty to the emperor and the Japanese gods.[52] These Mito scholars argued that it was necessary to break with the current policy of pluralism and actively convert the populace to a unified Shinto-Confucian teaching. Buddhists approached the need for unity from another angle. Kiyū Dōjin (1814–91), for example, who served as head of the Pure Land seminary at the shogunal Zōjōji in Edo, argued that Buddhism, Confucianism, and Shinto all "originate from one heart," and he believed that each had a crucial role to play in defending the ignorant people from Christian corruption.[53] The Mito model of imposing a unified faith inspired drastic reforms in the early years of Meiji, but had limited impact on shogunal policies before the restoration.

---

[51] Hirai, *Government by Mourning*.
[52] Paramore, *Ideology and Christianity in Japan*, 118.
[53] Paramore, *Ideology and Christianity in Japan*, 126–27. In the early 1860s, Kiyū edited and wrote prefaces to collections of anti-Christian writings, mostly by Buddhist authors from Ming China, and after the Meiji Restoration he argued vehemently for the usefulness of Buddhism in combatting Christianity.

It was in the 1850s that the concept of "religion" arrived in Japan, in the context of negotiations with Western powers for the right of foreign residents to practice their Christian religion in the treaty ports.[54] This was the start of a protracted conceptual battle over the term "religion" and its implications for the world of faith in Japan. The debate passed through many phases, with frequent dramatic reversals of policy and equally dramatic consequences for many institutions, practitioners, and lay followers. Yet, in spite of all this disruptive experimentation and innovation, it is possible to recognize the lingering influence of Tokugawa-period ideas about faith and its place in the realm.[55] In the Tokugawa period, Confucianism was consistently defined as "learning" (gakumon) and never as faith; also, in contrast to priests and practitioners of all kinds, Confucian teachers were never placed under the jurisdiction of the magistrate of temples and shrines. This helps explain why in the Meiji period, Confucianism did not emerge as a candidate for inclusion in the new category of religion. Buddhism was associated with the old regime, disparaged as a threat to loyalty and filial piety, and actively reduced. Buddhists defended themselves as champions of those same values and as allies in the fight against Christianity. Shinshū leaders, especially, adopted the label of "religion" both to differentiate themselves from "nonreligious" Shinto and to profile themselves as the only Japanese counterpart and rival of the Christian mission. The Buddhist "religion" focused on faith in a well-defined doctrine, combined with family and community rituals; kaji kitō prayer rituals were increasingly rejected as "superstition" and as aberrations from true religious practice. Many of the assorted practitioners of the Tokugawa period, from yamabushi to gannin, were now banned. Shinto was strictly separated from Buddhism, institutionally, spatially, and conceptually. In effect, Shinto ritual came to occupy much the same space that Confucian rites (rei) had filled in the Tokugawa period: as a practice that strengthens hierarchical structures by instilling loyalty and filial piety.

The most striking change, perhaps, was the gradual implementation of what Trent Maxey has called the "political grammar of religion."[56] This grammar systematically separates religion from the public realm so as to create an independent sphere of secular authority that was not vulnerable to the competition between "private" religions. In the Tokugawa period, the world of temples and shrines was not administered on the basis of this grammar.

[54] Josephson, Invention of Religion in Japan.
[55] Teeuwen, "Clashing Models."
[56] Maxey, "Greatest Problem."

The shogunate sought to harness the world of faith so as to foster loyalty and filial piety and bolster its authority as guardian of the realm. Without the concept of "religion," there was no notion of a secular realm beyond religion either. This fundamental difference should alert us to the fact that the conceptual landscape of faith in the Tokugawa period cannot be mapped accurately unless we begin by, to borrow a phrase from Jason Ānanda Josephson, "unlearning religion."[57]

Bibliography

Ambros, Barbara. *Emplacing a Pilgrimage: The Ōyama Cult and Regional Religion in Early Modern Japan*. Cambridge, MA: Harvard University Asia Center, 2008.

"Local Religious Specialists in Early Modern Japan: The Development of the Ōyama Oshi System." *Japanese Journal of Religious Studies* 28, no. 3/4 (2001): 329–72.

Arimoto Masao. *Kinsei Nihon no shūkyō shakaishi*. Yoshikawa Kōbunkan, 2002.

Chilson, Clark. *Secrecy's Power: Covert Shin Buddhists in Japan and Contradictions of Concealment*. Honolulu: University of Hawaiʻi Press, 2014.

Drixler, Fabian. "Imagined Communities of the Living and the Dead: The Spread of the Ancestor-Venerating Stem Family in Tokugawa Japan." In *What Is a Family? Answers from Early Modern Japan*, edited by Mary Elizabeth Berry and Marcia Yonemoto, 68–108. Oakland: University of California Press, 2019.

Elison, George. *Deus Destroyed: The Image of Christianity in Early Modern Japan*. Cambridge, MA: Harvard University Press, 1973.

Farris, William Wayne. *Japan's Medieval Population: Famine, Fertility, and Warfare in a Transformative Age*. Honolulu: University of Hawaiʻi Press, 2006.

Goodman, Janet R. *Alms and Vagabonds: Buddhist Temples and Popular Patronage in Medieval Japan*. Honolulu: University of Hawaiʻi Press, 1994.

Groemer, Gerald. "The Arts of the *Gannin*." *Asian Folklore Studies* 58, no. 2 (1999): 275–320.

"A Short History of the *Gannin*: Popular Religious Performers in Tokugawa Japan." *Japanese Journal of Religious Studies* 27, no. 1/2 (2000): 41–72.

Street Performers and Society in Urban Japan, 1600–1900: The Beggar's Gift. London: Routledge, 2016.

Hardacre, Helen. *Religion and Society in Nineteenth-Century Japan*. Ann Arbor: Center for Japanese Studies, University of Michigan, 2002.

Hayashi Makoto. "Kinsei tenkanki ni okeru shūkyō hendō." In *Kinsei, kindai to bukkyō*, edited by Nihon Bukkyō Kenkyūkai, 2–28. Vol. 4 of *Nihon no bukkyō*. Kyoto: Hōzōkan, 1995.

Hirai, Atsuko. *Government by Mourning: Death and Political Integration in Japan, 1603–1912*. Cambridge, MA: Harvard University Asia Center, 2014.

Hōzawa Naohide. "Jidan seido to sōsai bukkyō." In *Sei to shi*, edited by Shimazono Susumu, Takano Toshihiko, Hayashi Makoto, and Wakao Masaki, 25–52. Vol. 3 of *Shiriizu Nihonjin to shūkyō: Kinsei kara kindai e*. Shunjūsha 2015.

---

[57] Josephson, *Invention of Religion in Japan*.

Hur, Nam-lin. *Death and Social Order in Tokugawa Japan: Buddhism, Anti-Christianity, and the Danka System*. Cambridge, MA: Harvard University Asia Center, 2007.

"Invitation to the Secret Buddha of Zenkōji: *Kaichō* and Religious Culture in Early Modern Japan." *Japanese Journal of Religious Studies* 36, no. 1 (2009): 45–63.

Prayer and Play in Late Tokugawa Japan: Asakusa Sensōji and Edo Society. Cambridge, MA: Harvard University Asia Center, 2000.

Itō Jun. "Kinsei Kawachi-Ōsaka chiiki ni okeru Zenkōji no fukyō katsudō." *Ōsaka Rekishi Hakubutsukan kenkyū kiyō* 14 (2016): 43–52.

Josephson, Jason Ānanda. *The Invention of Religion in Japan*. Chicago: University of Chicago Press, 2012.

Kanda Hideo. *Nyoraikyō no shisō to shinkō*. Tenri: Tenri Daigaku Oyasato Kenkyūjo, 1990.

Köck, Stefan, Brigitte Pickl-Kolaczia, and Bernhard Scheid, eds. *Religion, Power, and the Rise of Shinto in Early Modern Japan*. London: Bloomsbury, 2021.

Kouamé, Nathalie. "Shikoku's Local Authorities and *Henro* during the Golden Age of Pilgrimage." *Japanese Journal of Religious Studies* 24, no. 3/4 (1997): 413–25.

Maruyama Masao. *Studies in the Intellectual History of Tokugawa Japan*. Translated by Mikiso Hane. Princeton, NJ: Princeton University Press, 1974.

Maxey, Trent E. *The "Greatest Problem": Religion and State Formation in Meiji Japan*. Cambridge, MA: Harvard University Asia Center, 2014.

McCallum, Donald F. *Zenkōji and Its Icon: A Study in Medieval Japanese Religious Art*. Princeton, NJ: Princeton University Press, 1994.

McMullin, Neil. *Buddhism and the State in Sixteenth-Century Japan*. Princeton, NJ: Princeton University Press, 1984.

Miyazaki, Fumiko, Kate Wildman Nakai, and Mark Teeuwen, eds. *Christian Sorcerers on Trial: Records of the 1827 Osaka Incident*. New York: Columbia University Press, 2020.

Nakagawa Sugane. "Inari Worship in Early Modern Osaka." In *Osaka: The Merchants' Capital of Early Modern Japan*, edited by James L. McClain and Wakita Osamu, 180–212. Ithaca, NY: Cornell University Press, 1999.

Nakai, Kate Wildman. *Shogunal Politics: Arai Hakusei and the Premises of Tokugawa Rule*. Cambridge, MA: Council on East Asian Studies, Harvard University, 1988.

Nakano Mitsuharu. *Shokoku Tōshōgū no shiteki kenkyū*. Meicho Kankōkai, 2008.

Naramoto Tatsuya. *Kinsei seidōron*. Vol. 38 of *Nihon shisō taikei*. Iwanami Shoten, 1976.

Nosco, Peter. *Individuality in Early Modern Japan: Thinking for Oneself*. Abingdon: Routledge, 2017.

Ōhashi Yukihiro. "Kinsei chitsujo ni okeru 'ja' no yuragi: 'Kakushi/kakure nenbutsu' to 'kirishitan.'" In *Tasha to kyōkai*, edited by Shimazono Susumu, Takano Toshihiko, Hayashi Makoto, and Wakao Masaki, 21–50. Vol. 6 of *Shiriizu Nihonjin to shūkyō: Kinsei kara kindai e*. Shunjūsha, 2015.

Senpuku kirishitan: Edo jidai no kinkyō seisaku to minshū. Kōdansha Sensho Mechie, 2014.

Ōkuwa Hitoshi. "Kinsei kokka no shūkyōsei." *Nihonshi kenkyū* 600 (August 2012): 111–37.

"Tokugawa shōgun kenryoku to shūkyō." In *Shūkyō to ken'i*, edited by Amino Yoshihiko, Kabayama Kōichi, Miyata Noboru, Yasumaru Yoshio, and Yamamoto Kōji, 135–60. Vol. 4 of *Iwanami kōza Tennō to ōken o kangaeru*. Iwanami Shoten, 2002.

Onodera Atsushi. "Higashi Harima ni okeru kinsei no Ise sangū: Akashi-shi Higashi Futami o jirei ni." *Kōtsūshi kenkyū* 35 (1995): 85–95.

Paramore, Kiri. *Ideology and Christianity in Japan*. London: Routledge, 2009.

Ruch, Barbara. "Woman to Woman: Kumano Bikuni Proselytizers in Medieval and Early Modern Japan." In *Engendering Faith: Women and Buddhism in Premodern Japan*, edited by Barbara Ruch, 537–80. Ann Arbor: Center for Japanese Studies, University of Michigan, 2002.

Sawa Hirokatsu. *Kinsei shūkyō shakairon*. Yoshikawa Kōbunkan, 2008.

Sonehara Satoshi. "Ise Jingū to Tōshōgū." In *Shōgun to tennō*, edited by Shimazono Susumu, Takano Toshihiko, Hayashi Makoto, and Wakao Masaki, 55–80. Vol. 1 of *Shiriizu Nihonjin to shūkyō: Kinsei kara kindai e*. Shunjūsha, 2014.

Tamamuro Fumio. *Edo bakufu no shūkyō tōsei*. Vol. 16 of *Nihonjin no kōdō to shisō*. Hyōronsha, 1980.

———. "Local Society and the Temple-Parishioner Relationship within the Bakufu's Governance Structure." *Japanese Journal of Religious Studies* 28, no. 3/4 (2001): 261–92.

Teeuwen, Mark. "Clashing Models: Ritual Unity vs Religious Diversity." *Formations of the Secular in Japan*, edited by Aike P. Rots and Mark Teeuwen. Special issue, *Japan Review* 30 (2017): 39–62.

Teeuwen, Mark, and John Breen. *A Social History of the Ise Shrines: Divine Capital*. London: Bloomsbury, 2017.

Teeuwen, Mark, and Kate Wildman Nakai, eds. *Lust, Commerce, and Corruption: An Account of What I Have Seen and Heard by an Edo Samurai*. Translated by Mark Teeuwen, Kate Wildman Nakai, Miyazaki Fumiko, Anne Walthall, and John Breen. New York: Columbia University Press, 2014.

Thal, Sarah. *Rearranging the Landscape of the Gods: The Politics of a Pilgrimage Site in Japan, 1573–1912*. Chicago: University of Chicago Press: 2005.

Tsang, Carol Richmond. *War and Faith: Ikkō Ikki in Late Muromachi Japan*. Cambridge, MA: Harvard University Asia Center, 2007.

Ukiyo no arisama. In *Sesō*, Pt. 1, edited by Harada Tomohiko and Asakura Haruhiko. Vol. 11 of *Nihon shomin seikatsu shiryō shūsei*. San'ichi Shobō, 1970.

Wakabayashi, Bob Tadashi. *Anti-Foreignism and Western Learning in Early-Modern Japan: The New Theses of 1825*. Cambridge, MA: Council on East Asian Studies, Harvard University, 1986.

Zhong, Yijiang. *The Origin of Modern Shinto in Japan: The Vanquished Gods of Izumo*. London: Bloomsbury, 2016.

14

The Medical Revolution in Early
Modern Japan

SUSAN L. BURNS

In Yuzawa, a small town in Akita Prefecture, there is a modest medical practice called Nanayama Clinic in Kawatsura-chō. The physician in charge is a
direct descendent of a doctor called Nanayama Jundō, who practiced in what
was then Kawatsura village in the early nineteenth century. Nanayama Clinic
is by no means unique: in villages, towns, and cities, there are doctors currently in practice who are the living legacy of medical lineages that formed in
early modern Japan. But they are not the only trace of early modern medical
culture in contemporary Japan. Even today, one can purchase prepared medicines such as Jitsubosan and Hongantan that date back to this period. The
"medical revolution" that gave rise to these lineages and products not only
made medical care and medical knowledge widely available for the first time
in Japan's long history, it also had other profound social, cultural, and political implications. As medicine was transformed from a "base practice" into a
lucrative profession to which many aspired, it became an important means of
social mobility that challenged officially authorized ideas of status. The practice of medicine transformed ordinary villagers into local literati and created
new networks through which information, commodities, and ideas flowed.
This chapter explores this set of transformations, focusing specifically on non-
elite doctors and their patients with the aim of understanding the implications of medicine as discourse and practice for life in early modern Japan.

Revolution from Below

The medical revolution took place without the direct involvement of the
Tokugawa shogunate: it was a "revolution from below" in which the shogunate played only an indirect role. The violence of the late sixteenth century that accompanied the founding of the Tokugawa dynasty created a need
for so-called wound doctors who specialized in treating the damage done to
human bodies by swords, spears, and musket balls. After the founding of the

shogunate, some of these doctors would turn to treating more commonplace ailments, becoming part of a patchwork of providers of medical care that included itinerant priests, practitioners of syncretic Shinto (*yamabushi*), and those who had mastered how to lance a boil or set a broken bone.[1] The social dislocations that followed the establishment of Tokugawa rule also had profound consequences for life in Kyoto, the center of medical education in the late sixteenth century and where many doctors educated in Chinese medicine had served the nobility and warrior elite. As the nobles fell into poverty and the locus of power moved beyond Kyoto, some of these doctors relocated to Edo and the castle towns of the daimyo.[2]

But these were unintended consequences, not the result of purposeful action. Over the course of the long Tokugawa period (1603–1868), the shogunate had no defined "medical policy" as such but instead responded in a piecemeal fashion. In times of epidemic disease, it sometimes distributed medicines, much as it provided relief rice in times of famine, a gesture toward the official ideology of "benevolent rule." It was only in 1722 that the shogunate made an attempt to provide medical care to the poor of Edo, when it established the Koishikawa Hospital (Koishikawa Yōjōsho). However, with a capacity initially of only forty inpatients and a staff of seven part-time doctors, it had little impact on the health of the residents of the sprawling city with a population that would soon reach one million. Even in the early nineteenth century, the Koishikawa Hospital could only provide care to several hundred patients a year.[3]

For the rest of the country, the shogunate did far less. In 1729, the eighth shogun, Yoshimune, ordered shogunal medical officials to edit a medical text intended for ordinary people, following an initiative taken in the Sendai domain three decades earlier. Organized around parts of the body (the head, eyes, lower body, etc.), the *Various Formulas for the Assistance of All* (*Fukyū ruihō*) listed simple prescriptions that could be made by easily obtainable botanicals. The shogunate funded its printing and then offered it to the populace at the cost of about ten *monme* – a cheap price, but one that made its widespread use doubtful. Four years later, after the Kyōhō famine had ravaged the country, the shogunate printed another collection of formulas entitled *Miraculous Formulas to Assist the People of the Realm* (*Kyūmin myōyaku*), but this time it ordered the books to be distributed at no cost to stricken villages.[4] These publications

---

[1] Goble, *Confluences of Medicine*, ch. 5.
[2] Ikeda Toyoko, "Kinsei Kanazawa no iryō," 192–93.
[3] Andō, *Edo no yōjōsho*, ch. 3.
[4] Suzuki, "Hozumi Hoan 'Kyūmin myōyaku.'"

were not just an attempt to help the populace help themselves, however. The project had a strong economic motivation: the popularity of expensive raw drugs imported from China was causing a massive drain of hard currency, and the shogunate sought to stem it by encouraging the use of locally available herbs. To the same end, the shogunate had founded a medical garden in central Edo in 1686.[5]

The shogunate's support for medical education was similarly limited. The shogunal medical institute, called the Igakukan, originated as a private academy called the Seijunkan, which was founded in 1765 by Taki Mototaki, a medical official. It was not until 1791 that the shogunate began to fund the school. By this time, private medical academies were already well established in Kyoto and elsewhere, and at least thirteen domains offered medical education in one form or another.[6] In Sendai the domanial academy began to offer instruction on medicine in 1760, initially to the heirs and students of domanial medical officials and eventually to village and town doctors as well.[7] It was not until the mid-nineteenth century, as confrontation with Western powers loomed, that the shogunate took the lead in medical education, creating a school of Western medicine in Nagasaki in 1857 under the direction of Johannes Pompe van Meerdervoort, a Dutch naval surgeon.

Rather than the shogunate, other factors propelled the transformation of medicine into an integral part of everyday life. The rapid expansion of print culture played an important role. Beginning in the seventeenth century, an extraordinary profusion of medical texts began to be published, including medical treatises, commentaries, dictionaries, formularies, collections of case notes, and health manuals, contributing to the diffusion of medical knowledge not only to aspiring doctors but to other readers as well. Significant too was the new enthusiasm for education: as private Confucian academies began to flourish, first in Kyoto and then elsewhere, established doctors also began to take on students, making medical training available as never before. But other less quantifiable factors were also involved: the rising standard of living in this era of peace and prosperity, the new commodity culture, and the tensions of the status system that made the ambitious or disgruntled pursue social roles beyond those authorized by Tokugawa ideology. The medical revolution was the result of multiple and overlapping social and cultural changes "from below."

---

[5] Marcon, *Knowledge of Nature*, ch. 7.
[6] On domanial medical education, see Yamazaki, *Kakuhan igaku kyōiku*. On the Igakukan, see Machi Senjurō, "Igakukan no kiseki."
[7] Chō, "Sendai-han ni okeru sho ishi," 95–96.

Medical Knowledge

Histories of Japanese medicine in Japan have long taken the form of a developmental narrative organized around the idea of competing "schools."[8] According to this narrative, in the early seventeenth century, medical care was shaped by physicians such as Manase Dōsan (1507–94), who were strongly influenced by the scholarly medical tradition of Ming China. Manase had begun his medical training under Tashiro Sanki, who like Manase himself was a Zen monk. Like many others in this era, Tashiro took advantage of the revived China-Japan trade in the sixteenth century to make his way to China. He spent twelve years there studying the predominant form of medical knowledge of the time, which originated in the Jin–Yuan period. Associated with the Chinese physicians Li Dongyuan and Zhu Danxi, so-called Rishu medicine was mediated by Neo-Confucianism, with the result that the body was newly conceived as a microcosm of the cosmos, and human physiology and disease causality were understood in relation to principles such as yin and yang and the five elements. Manase became a prominent figure in late sixteenth-century Kyoto, teaching hundreds of students and treating prominent figures, including the emperor himself.

Then, in the mid-seventeenth century, the dominance of Rishu medicine was challenged by physicians associated with the "ancient formulas school" (*kohōha*). Gotō Konzan (1659–1733), his students Kagawa Shūtoku (1683–1755) and Yamawaki Tōyō (1706–62), and Yamawaki's student Yoshimasu Tōdō, among others, valorized the earliest Chinese medical texts, works such as *Huangdi neijing* (The Yellow Emperor's classic [of medicine]), the *Shanghan lun* (Treatise on cold damage), and collections of canonical medicinal formulas such as *Jingui yaolüe* (Essential prescriptions from the golden cabinet), which dated from the Han period. They derisively labeled Rishu medicine the "latter-day school" (*goseiha*), implying that it was a derivative form of knowledge. In contrast, Gotō and his followers embraced the description of their work as the ancient formulas school. Rejecting what they described as "empty" theorizing, they advocated for a pragmatic approach that privileged the treatment of symptoms over abstract diagnostic principles. Then, in the eighteenth century, the primacy of the ancient formula school was challenged by the rise of "Dutch medicine" (*ranpō*), which gained a growing number of enthusiasts after the shogunate lifted restrictions on the import of Western texts. A new understanding of human anatomy called into question

---

[8] See, for example, Sakai, *Nihon no iryōshi*, sec. 3, and Hattori, *Edo jidai igakushi*.

the Sino-Japanese understanding of human physiology, and new interest in surgical techniques began to challenge the long reliance on pharmacological treatments.

In reality, medicine in practice was more eclectic, more syncretic, and more heterogeneous than the narrative of competing and successive schools suggests. Several of Manase Dōsan's works would be reprinted in the eighteenth and early nineteenth centuries, suggesting they had a readership even in the heyday of ancient formulas medicine, and even devotees of the *Shanghan lun* were interested in European pharmacology and anatomical knowledge.[9] The book collections amassed by ordinary physicians provides further evidence that intellectual cleavages meant little to many ordinary physicians. To cite but one example, Tomizuka Seisai was a doctor who lived in Minami Iizuka village in what is now Chiba Prefecture in the early nineteenth century. Unlike many doctors in this time, he did not come from a family of doctors but was the first in his family to turn to the practice of medicine. Tomizuka was a dedicated bibliophile, and over the course of his life he amassed an impressive library of 177 titles (492 volumes), seventy-six of which were medical texts. The latter included not only canonical works of the ancient formulas canon, such as commentaries on the *Shanghan lun*, but also works on latter-day medicine. However, more than medical theory, Tomizuka's collection was centered on pharmacology and the treatment of commonplace diseases, among them smallpox, syphilis, and febrile diseases.[10]

As Tomizuka's library reveals, print materials were an integral part of the new medical culture. Significantly, many works were written in simple Japanese rather than literary Sinitic (classical Chinese), the language of scholarship in this era, and compiled information from different sources. A case in point is *Explaining the Names of Diseases* (*Byōmei ikai*), a reference book that drew upon a wide range of Chinese medical texts to explain the cause, symptoms, and treatment of almost 2,000 ailments. It was first published in 1668, but Tomizuka acquired a copy more than 150 years later. Its author, Ashikawa Keishū, may have been a student of Manase, given his familiarity with the Rishu medical literature, but his approach was to link the proper Chinese terminology to commonplace names for diseases and their symptoms: the entry for smallpox, or *tōsō*, begins, "this is what is commonly called *kasa*

---

[9] For evidence of the longevity of Manase's influence, see Kosoto, *Nihon kanpō tenseki jiten*, 139, 180, 247, 261, 338. On the influence of Dutch medicine on ancient formulas physicians, see Burns, "Nanayama Jundō at Work."

[10] Tachibanagawa, "Kinsei mura isha no honbako," 81, 82, 86–87.

[a bumpy rash]," while that for leprosy begins, "this is commonly called *sanbyō* [a reference to the notion that leprosy was the result of karmic retribution]."[11]

Books of this type, written in accessible Japanese and offering easy access to medical knowledge, continued to be published over the course of the early modern period. *A Guide to Medical Treatments* (*Iryō tebikigusa*, 1763–76) was organized around specific disorders and provided an overview of contemporary medical theory by citing the work of well-known doctors associated with both latter-day and ancient formulas medicine and recommending specific formulas; *The Simplified Shanghan lun* (*Kan'i Shōkanron*, 1803) provided an introduction to this challenging text in Japanese; and *An Essential Manual for Doctors* (*Ika hikkei*, 1857) made it possible for doctors to match up symptoms with appropriate medicinal formulas. But doctors did not just acquire medical knowledge via print. It also flowed via manuscripts that were copied, edited, and then copied again. Like Tomizuka, the village doctor Nanayama Jundō had an extensive library of medical works, of which sixty-two titles are extant. Only eleven of these were print editions; the others were copies of books or parts of books.

Medical knowledge in this period was not simply derived from Chinese medical texts. Early modern medical doctors were also innovators in their own right, and some of the most prominent of these medical pioneers came from humble backgrounds. A case in point is Hanaoka Seishū (1760–1835). A native of Kii Province (now Wakayama Prefecture), Hanaoka was the son of a villager. As a young man he traveled to Kyoto to study medicine. His teachers included the ancient formulas physician Yoshimasa Nangai, Tōdō's son and successor, and Yamato Gensui, from whom he learned surgery. Yamato was a student of Irako Dōgyū, who instructed him in the so-called Caspar-style surgery that Irako had learned in Nagasaki. Caspar Schamberger, a German physician employed by the Dutch East India trading outpost at Nagasaki from 1649 to 1655, trained a number of Japanese physicians in European surgical techniques in both Nagasaki and Edo, and they in turn instructed their own students. After three years in Kyoto, Hanaoka returned to Wakayama. Recognizing that few patients could tolerate the pain of surgery, he began to experiment with a variety of sedating herbs until he developed a medicinal compound that acted as a general anesthesia. In 1804, he used the compound, dubbed *mafutsusan* (perhaps "datura boiled powder") on a sixty-year-old woman suffering from breast cancer and was able to successfully perform a

[11] Ashikawa, *Byōmei ikai*, 2:46, 4:3.

mastectomy, the first use of general anesthesia during surgery anywhere in the world.[12]

Although the conventional narrative of successive schools reveals little about what was happening on the ground, it is suggestive of the intellectual and social tensions that surrounded the practice of medicine in this era. In the early Tokugawa period, medicine was regarded as less a scholarly endeavor than a matter of skill (*waza*). The Confucian scholar Kaibara Ekiken (1630–1714) reflected this view when he wrote dismissively of "vulgar doctors" who were unable to read Chinese and knew no more than forty or fifty formulas.[13] To counter this view, some ambitious physicians sought to elevate themselves and their profession. Gotō Konzan, for example, studied with Itō Jinsai, whose intellectual practice focused on the recovery of the "ancient meaning" of the Confucian classics. His interest in Han-period medical texts reflected an engagement with a larger intellectual turn in the second half of the seventeenth century. Gotō's aspiration to be recognized as a "Confucian doctor" points to issues that would become more important as the era progressed: the question of where practitioners of medicine fit within the system of status distinctions that shaped social life in this period and growing concerns about the ethics of medical practitioners. Were they merely technicians of the human body or was medicine something more, a profoundly ethical practice that preserved human lives and thus was deserving of respect? Yamawaki Tōyō spoke to the tensions between these two views when he wrote, "Medicine is a base skill and so how can it be a worthy endeavor on the part of a wise scholar? But even if it is beneath them, how can they not do it? How can they avoid doing it?"[14]

In addition to these general concerns about the nature of medicine as a profession, some new forms of medical practice raised specific moral concerns. A case in point is the so-called Kagawa school, founded by Kagawa Gen'etsu (1700–77), who was renowned for his obstetrical skills.[15] Raised as the adopted son of a villager family in the Hikone domain, Kagawa left his village for Kyoto, where he made a living as a masseur and acupuncturist. At some point, he became interested in childbirth, and he eventually developed a number of techniques for managing obstructed childbirth, the most famous of which he called *kaiseijutsu* (life-saving technique). This involved crushing the skull or dismembering the fetus in order to save the life of the pregnant woman. Not all of Kagawa's techniques were so brutal; he also developed

---

[12] Matsuki, "Hanaoka Seishū no 'mafutsusan' kaihatsu."
[13] Kaibara, *Yōjōkun wazoku dōjikun*, 52.
[14] Quoted in Fuse, *Ishi no rekishi*, 36.
[15] The discussion that follows is based on Burns, "Body as Text."

new methods to manipulate the fetus in instances of breach births, making a safe delivery possible. At a time when maternal death was a not uncommon outcome of childbirth, Kagawa's ability to save lives made him famous, and students began to flock to Kyoto to study with him and his successors. By the mid-nineteenth century, the Kagawa obstetrical techniques were being used in villages, towns, and cities around Japan.[16]

The medicalization of childbirth that accompanied the expansion of the Kagawa school gradually began to reshape the experience of childbirth for some women by introducing new gendered relations of authority to the birth site. Some physicians began to attack the practices of midwives (*toriage baba*), who had long played an important role in managing childbirth. Midwives were typically older women within a local community who had acquired their skills by experiencing childbirth themselves and assisting others. In the Kagawa obstetrical texts of this era, midwives were newly disparaged as unlearned and unskilled, and their practices characterized as dangerous to both maternal and fetal well-being. The rise of the Kagawa school also created new tensions within families and with female patients. In an effort to preserve the secrecy of their techniques (both to preserve their monopoly on these skills and to forestall criticism of their techniques), doctors trained in the Kagawa school were instructed to exclude female family members and friends from the birthing room and to position and drape the laboring woman's body so that she, too, was unable to observe their methods. The new intimacy between the male physician and female patient that resulted seems to have made many uneasy, and Kagawa texts responded by offering advice on how to counter the resistance of patients and their families.

In the early nineteenth century, the Kagawa school became implicated in a growing debate about the value of fetal life. The school expanded during a period of growing concern about population stagnation associated with the two great famines of the early modern period, the Tenmei famine of the 1780s and the Tenpō famine of the 1830s. Both famines caused considerable loss of life, and in their aftermath, domanial and shogunal authorities, among others, concluded that abortion and infanticide were suppressing needed population growth – and agricultural productivity. As a result, these then-commonplace practices of reproductive control began to be excoriated as immoral and inhumane, and some domains developed elaborate procedures to police pregnancy with the aim of ensuring live births.[17] The growing value attached

---

[16] Kyōto-fu Ishikai, *Kyōto no igakushi*, 232.
[17] On the anti-infanticide discourse, see Drixler, *Mabiki*. On the policing of pregnancy in the Sendai and Tsuyama domains, see Sawayama, *Shussan to shintai*.

to fetal life notwithstanding, the Kagawa school's secret techniques, specifically the "life-saving technique," aimed to save the life of the mother, even at the expense of the fetus. The school's rapid rise to prominence suggests that many families were similarly inclined, since by the early nineteenth century even ordinary villagers sought out the services of Kagawa practitioners when their wives and daughters-in-law experienced difficult labors. It was in this context that some critics of the school began to attack Kagawa practitioners for what was characterized as "killing the child." In response, the Kagawa school began to modify its approach, instructing students of the need to fully ascertain the death of the fetus before proceeding with its secret techniques.

Becoming a Doctor

As the evolution of the Kagawa school reveals, the claim that the practice of medicine was an ethical profession was subject to a variety of social and political pressures. Crucial to the transformation of medicine from a "base skill" practiced by "vulgar doctors" to a respectable occupation of learned men was the emergence of a de facto system of medical education in the second half of the eighteenth century. The acquisition of a medical education under one or more established physicians was the key to social mobility and propelled the formation of medical lineages in towns and villages around Japan. An illuminative example is the case of Nagamine Gentai (1783–1847) and his son, both of whom lived in Bitchū (now part of Okayama Prefecture). Nagamine was an apparently untrained doctor who moved from village to village over the course of his adult life, never able to gain the trust of villagers or ingratiate himself with village leaders. His son, who later took the name Chibahara Eishun (1803–43), grew up in poverty, but as a young teen he, too, decided to pursue medicine as a career. However, he aspired to the kind of training his father lacked. He first sought employment as a household servant with a series of local doctors, performing menial tasks in exchange for instruction in order to gain a basic education. Eventually, Chibahara was able to enroll as the formal student of one of them, supporting himself by copying texts for others. After marrying into a family as an adopted son-in-law, Chibahara began to practice medicine while teaching basic skills to children. However, within a few years he left his family to pursue further education, this time in Dutch medicine. He spent several months in Osaka at the Tekijuku, the Dutch learning academy founded by Ogata Kōan, but eventually he made his way to Edo, where he was able to study with Satō Taizen, one of the most famous Dutch medicine scholars in the city. With his medical credentials firmly established, Chibahara found employment as a physician in service to a bannerman named Ina who was then the magistrate of the port city of Sakai.[18]

Chibahara's rags to riches story is extraordinary, but the course of his education was one shared by many. Early schooling usually took place at home or in a local private school (*terakoya*), but once a boy (for it was only boys who trained as doctors) was in his teens, he would begin his medical studies. Some would-be doctors did their early training under their own fathers, while others became students of established doctors in neighboring villages or towns for several years. However, for many, medical education did not stop there: it became increasingly common for students to seek out further training in the great urban cultural centers. Initially, Kyoto was the best-known place for medical training, but physicians in Edo, Osaka, and Nagasaki attracted students as well, with the latter particularly attractive to those who wanted to study Dutch medicine. Leaving home for study, of course, required the approval of local officials. In principle, shogunal and domanial authorities held that only villagers who were the heirs of established physicians or those who were unable to perform agricultural labor because of poor health or disability were allowed to become doctors. In reality, as long as the requisite language about poor health was included, petitions to undertake *yūgaku* (study abroad) seem to have been routinely approved.

As would-be doctors flocked to the cities for medical training, well-known physicians began to attract hundreds, even thousands of students. Nakagami Kinkei (1744–1833) is said to have taught an estimated 3,000 students in his academy in Kyoto over the course of his career. His reputation was based on his clinical expertise; his status as a student of Yoshimasa Tōdō, the pioneering figure of ancient formulas; and the efforts of his students, who published his lectures on medical theory, his commentaries, and collections of his case notes.[19] Other academies were established by physicians who developed new, specialized techniques and their descendants. Kagawa Gen'etsu is estimated to have taught his techniques to several hundred students, and his descendants taught the Kagawa methods to thousands more. Hanaoka Seishū is said to have taught almost 2,000 students after his return to Wakayama.[20]

The relationship between a teacher and student was not exclusive: aspiring physicians often studied with different teachers, in succession or at the

[18] Shibata, "Kinsei kōki ni okeru zaison'i."
[19] Kosoto, *Nihon kanpō tenseki jiten*, 252.
[20] On Kagawa's students, see Kyōto-fu Ishikai, *Kyōto no igakushi*, 332–48. On Hanaoka, see Ueno, "Kishū-han no iryō seisaku," 1.

same time, to cultivate specific skills and wide expertise. While prominent physicians have come to be described as practitioners of Chinese medicine or Dutch medicine, by the early nineteenth century it was increasingly common to study both. Generally, initial training would be in Sino-Japanese medicine and Dutch medicine would come later. But, while a student might have multiple teachers, these relationships were formalized as one form of master-disciple relationship, a process that involved the signing of an oath (*kishōmon*) in which the student promised not to reveal the "secret teachings" (*hiden*) of the teacher.[21] In the age of print culture, many famous doctors published medical treatises, but "secret teachings" continued to be reserved for their enrolled students. Thus, when Kagawa Gen'etsu first published his *Treatise on Childbirth (Sanron)* in 1775, he alluded to his "life-saving technique" but provided no description of how to perform it.[22]

Within these general perimeters, however, medical training took many forms. Nakashima Sōsen (b. 1774) was the third generation of his family to practice medicine in a village near the Seto Inland Sea. In 1801, he journeyed to Kyoto where he studied with Yoshimasa Nangai, who counted among his students Hanaoka Seishū. Then, eighteen years later, he journeyed to Nagasaki. Although it is unclear with whom he had studied, he returned home with thirteen notebooks he had compiled on Dutch medicine.[23] Sōsen provided his son Yūgen (1808–78) with a broader education than he himself had received. From 1833 to 1835, Yūgen studied in Kyoto with no less than seven teachers, including Yoshimasa Nangai, but also physicians known for their expertise in obstetrics, Western medicine, and surgery.[24] Not every would-be doctor had the financial resources, however, to pursue such a lengthy education, nor one of such breadth. Honda Kakuan (1814–66), too, was born into a family of doctors. His family had been practicing medicine for two generations in Yaho village in Musashi Province, less than thirty kilometers from Edo. Honda probably did his initial training under his father, but in his early twenties he studied with a doctor named Yasutomi Fumiyuki, a specialist in obstetrics, in Kōjimachi in the central part of Edo for about a year.[25]

Both Honda Kakuan and Nakashima Sōsen kept journals while they were "studying abroad." Nakashima's suggests that his training was more academic than clinical. He typically divided his day between two teachers, and

[21] Umihara, "Edo jidai no ishi shugyō," 88–89.
[22] Kagawa, *Sanron.*
[23] Nakashima Ika Shiryōkan and Nakashima Monjo Kenkyūkai, *Bizen Okayama no zaison'i*, 11, 13–15.
[24] Nakashima Ika Shiryōkan and Nakashima Monjo Kenkyūkai, *Bizen Okayama no zaison'i*, 16.
[25] Osada, "Bakumatsu-ki zaison ni okeru ishi yōsei no jittai."

his training consisted of listening to lectures, copying texts, and what was known as *rindoku* (reading together); that is, the joint recitation of a text followed by a discussion of its content.[26] In contrast, in addition to reading and copying texts, Honda served as an assistant to Yasutomi, who maintained a busy obstetrical practice among the samurai households in Kōjimachi. Honda accompanied him on his visits to patients and aided him in the preparation of medicines. He also occasionally performed treatments such as moxibustion independently.[27] As these two cases suggest, the training provided via "study abroad" varied greatly. In some cases, it may have involved little in the way of serious study. In a letter to Sugita Genpaku written in 1770, the physician Tatebe Seian notes that every doctor who spent some time in Nagasaki declared himself to be a Dutch medicine doctor, even if he had never read a Dutch medical text or formally studied under a teacher.[28]

The practice of "study abroad" did more than simply educate individual doctors. It also created new networks through which information, books, and technology moved around the country. In the 1850s, a network of Western medicine doctors who had trained at Nagasaki under Philipp Franz von Siebold played a leading role in diffusing not only information on the technique of smallpox vaccination but also the precious biological material necessary to perform the procedure.[29] In addition, the cities offered aspiring doctors opportunities to acquire expertise in disciplines other than medicine. It was not uncommon for students to spend time learning to compose *waka*, *haikai*, or Chinese poetry, or studying with a Confucian or nativist scholar. "Study abroad" thus allowed commoners to become proficient in cultural and intellectual practices that functioned as social capital, transforming them into what historian Tsukamoto Manabu has described as "provincial literati" (*chihō bunjin*).[30]

Regulating Medicine

By the early decades of the nineteenth century, the number of doctors had risen dramatically in both the cities and villages, although it is difficult to discern how many were providing medical care to a specific community at any given moment. A hint at the total number of doctors in Japan at the end of the

[26] For a transcription of Nakashima's Kyoto diary, see Nakashima Ika Shiryōkan and Nakashima Monjo Kenkyūkai, *Bizen Okayama no zaison'i*, 219–31.
[27] Sugano, *Edo no mura isha*, 55–59.
[28] Tatebe and Sugita, *Oranda iji mondō*, 382.
[29] Janetta, *Vaccinators*.
[30] Tsukamoto, *Chihō bunjin*.

Tokugawa period comes from a government survey undertaken by the Meiji government in the early 1870s. It gave the total number of doctors as 28,262, or one doctor for every 840 people.[31] This figure, however, tells us little about the actual distribution of doctors. A guide to Edo doctors published in 1819 lists 1,500 doctors, but this number was limited to those in the employ of the daimyo residing in Edo and "town doctors" (machi'i), commoner doctors with townsman status.[32] The real number is certainly far larger: there were at least 110 doctors in service to the shogunate, and the host of practitioners who pulled teeth; removed cataracts; practiced acupuncture, massage, and moxibustion; set bones; and performed abortions went unmentioned. Care by a doctor was readily available in smaller urban areas as well. In 1811, the authorities of the castle town of Kanazawa recognized 195 doctors, in a population of about 56,355 (1:289), while Nagoya had an estimated 300 doctors for a population of about 73,000 (1:243).[33] The number of doctors practicing outside the cities was also significant. According to a study of villages near the post town of Hachiōji on the Kōshū highway in the period between 1830 and 1850, at least sixty individuals who identified as "doctors" practiced for some period in this area. Another similar study of Tsuru district in Kai Province (now Yamanashi Prefecture) reveals that at least fifty-five doctors were working in villages there in the same period.[34]

The proliferating number of doctors and the wealth and extravagant lifestyle of some began to attract attention as early as the mid-eighteenth century. Quacks and avaricious doctors became stock figures in popular literature, where they were mocked for their arrogance and greed. In this period, doctors were paid not for their services but for the medicines they prescribed, and their frequent recourse to expensive medicines was a common object of criticism. In On Doctors (Isha dangi, first published in 1752), the author who wrote under the pseudonym Fun Tokusai (lit. "Shit Profit") described such doctors: they arrived in a palanquin accompanied by runners to the home of an impoverished patient and prescribed expensive medicines that not only did not save the patient but also so depleted the resources of the family that they were unable to provide a proper funeral.[35] In keeping with the dominant ideology of "benevolent rule," officials, too, expressed concern about

---

[31] Fuse, Ishi no rekishi, 26.
[32] Takei and Nanba, Edo kinsei ika jinmeiroku.
[33] Horisaki, "Kinsei Higashi Ano mura," 120; Ikeda Toyoko, "Kinsei Kanazawa no iryō," 199.
[34] Osada, "Edo kinkō nōson in okeru iryō"; Kawanabe, "Edo jidai, Kōshū ni okeru isha," 83–84.
[35] See, for example, Fun, Isha dangi, and Kyannochō, Hyōkin zatsubyō ron.

poorly trained doctors who endangered the health of ordinary people or exploited them by offering expensive but ineffective treatment. In the 1790s, the shogunate issued the first edicts warning its subjects to be wary of poorly trained and unethical doctors.[36] Then, in 1833, the shogunal medical academy published *First Lessons for Doctors* (*Ika shokun*). Authored by Taki Motonori, the director of the academy, this work admonished doctors to remember that medicine was not about profit or prestige but was "a benevolent skill" intended to "preserve life."[37]

But concern about incompetent and greedy doctors overlapped with other anxieties as well. The popularity of "study abroad" meant that there were large numbers of would-be doctors traveling from place to place, and many sought to recoup the costs of their education and travel by offering to treat patients they encountered on the road. Officials in this period were always concerned about the disruptive potential of outsiders in the villages, and doctors were no exception. At the same time, domanial authorities were also troubled by the success of some resident doctors, whose income and lifestyle increasingly challenged the status norms of the period.

The policies of the Sendai domain are revealing of the tensions that emerged in relation to the conventions of status. As masterless samurai (*rōnin*) who became doctors moved into the villages in the mid-eighteenth century, the domain authorized the creation of a separate household registry (*ninbetsuchō*) that removed them from the ordinary village registry that demarcated cultivator status. Around the same time, commoner doctors began to lay claim to the visible signifiers of higher status. In 1747, domanial authorities issued an edict allowing "town doctors" to wear silk garments, although it subsequently denied them the right to ride in a palanquin unless they suffered from a chronic illness that made walking difficult. Village doctors, too, were initially allowed to adopt grander garments than their cultivator neighbors. In 1755, an edict was issued that permitted them to wear cotton or linen *haori*. Within a few decades, however, authorities attempted to crack down on doctors who were not content with these fabric choices. In 1785, an edict was issued that specifically forbade doctors in the villages from wearing silk garments. A few years later, another edict extended that ban to "town doctors" as well.[38]

Tottori was another domain in which doctors and officials struggled over the markers of status. In the late eighteenth century, villagers began to

---

[36] Umihara, "Kinsei kōki hanryō ni okeru 'iryō,'" 1823.
[37] Taki, *Ika shokun.*
[38] Chō, "Sendai-han ni okeru sho ishi," 95–96.

become formal students of domanial doctors, an arrangement that not only offered them access to training but also a degree of social mobility. As students of domanial officials, they were recognized as *rōnin ishi* (masterless-samurai doctors) and allowed to adopt surnames and wear short swords. However, by the 1810s, officials had become concerned about the number of such doctors who had not only left village registries (and therefore responsibility for the rice tax) but who also had taken to wearing a sword within villages, a development described as "not good for village order." In response, the domain issued an edict that not only reiterated the restriction of medical study to those who were disabled or in poor health but also placed new restrictions on doctors of village origin. They were now required to request permission before taking up a practice within a village, including that of their birth, and forbidden from wearing swords.[39]

In response to growing concern about the social mobility of doctors and questions about the efficacy of the treatments some were offering, domains around the country began to develop policies designed both to improve the quality of medical training and to regulate who practiced medicine. In 1815, Sendai expanded its support for medical education by creating a medical school independent from the domanial academy, a free clinic for the poor (where students of the medical school offered treatment), and a medicinal garden.[40] But it was in the early part of the nineteenth century that medical education at the domanial level expanded dramatically. Eventually, 30 percent of the domains supported medical education in some form. This included twenty-three that had established independent medical schools, while many others created medical courses within the domain academies.[41] Aizu's medical school is typical of those in this era. Established adjacent to its domanial academy, it offered instruction on internal medicine, surgery, pediatric medicine, smallpox, and materia medica. Students who excelled were rewarded with a surname and other privileges.[42]

While the expansion of medical education sought to improve the medical profession, the regulation of doctors sought to control and delimit it. In the early nineteenth century, some domains began to forge policies designed to register doctors, while others created ambitious schemes to "credential" them. One such domain was Wakayama, which had become involved in medical education early on, establishing a medical school in 1791. In 1812,

[39] Hirano, "Mura ni okeru ishi," 151–53.
[40] Chō, "Sendai-han ni okeru sho ishi," 80.
[41] Yamazaki, *Kakuhan igaku kyōiku*.
[42] Umihara, *Edo jidai no ishi shugyō*, 27–28.

as a first step toward exercising oversight over doctors, the domain issued an edict stating that those who wanted to study medicine should do so under either a domanial doctor or a private physician who was at least the third-generation successor within a medical lineage. After the completion of their training, would-be doctors were required to sit for an exam at the medical school, and only those who passed were qualified to practice medicine. In the 1830s and 1840s, this procedure was further elaborated: it became the responsibility of teachers to report to the medical school that their students were prepared to undertake the exam, which was to be held twice a year. The exam system addressed new doctors, but the domain also sought to exercise control over those already in practice. In 1823, it issued an edict requiring all doctors in the villages to submit their names, places of residence, and other information to newly created "directors of doctors" (*ishi torishimari yaku*), who were under the authority of the head of the domanial medical school. The directors were tasked with exercising oversight over the doctors practicing within their respective directive's district. Their responsibilities included investigating doctors who had entered the domain from elsewhere and rumors of unethical behavior on the part of physicians, and collecting obligatory donations that were to be used for the support of the medical school.[43]

The medical policy of the Wakayama domain had the intent to weed out problem doctors. Elsewhere the motives of officials were more complicated. Kokura (now part of Fukuoka Prefecture) is one such case. In 1844, the domain issued an edict requiring all doctors practicing within the domain to submit their names, birthplaces, the date they took up residence in Kokura, their current place of residence, and the names of their teachers. This final requirement was seemingly intended to identify those doctors who had no formal training. Based on this data, officials designated doctors as: (1) doctors of commoner origin who had been granted the right to a surname by the domain; (2) *rōnin ishi* (the students of medical officials) who were residing in villages; (3) doctors who originated from outside the domain; and (4) "district doctors" (*gun'i*, doctors of commoner status who did not have a surname). These categories suggest that the intent of this registration system was to investigate not only the number of doctors and their training but also the status privileges to which they were laying claim.[44]

[43] Ueno, "Kishū-han no iryō seisaku," 2–3.
[44] Ōtaguro, "Kinsei kōki ni okeru murakata no ishi tōsei," 85, 87.

The creation of "doctor meetings" (ishi kaigō) at the district level was another policy initiative of the Kokura domain that had multiple motives. These got underway in the early 1840s, and the monthly gatherings apparently included both "district doctors" and village officials. Eventually, a "director of all district doctors" (gun'i sōtorishimari) was designated and granted the right to use a surname and sword-wearing privileges. The main aim of this new organizational structure seems to have been to create a mechanism for doctors to self-police their profession, allowing them to exclude itinerant and poorly trained doctors from the region. Eventually the "doctor meetings" began to take on an educational role. In 1854, when smallpox vaccination was introduced to Kokura, the "doctor meetings" were used to explain the process of vaccination and to designate those who could perform the procedure.[45]

These efforts on the part of the domains in the first half of the nineteenth century reveal that by this time the medical profession was no longer the unregulated free-for-all that it had once been. As medical training became widely available and the number of doctors multiplied, domanial officials responded by attempting to ensure that doctors had a basic level of competency. As we have seen, this not only reflected their "benevolent" concern about the welfare of the populace, officials were also equally concerned about social order, growing economic and other divides within the villages, and the unrestrained movement of those with valued skills. From the position of officialdom, then, the rise of the medical profession was something of a double-edged sword that both shored up their ideological claim to authority and challenged the foundations of the political order. What then of patients? How did the new availability of medical care by doctors shape their lives?

The Patients' Perspective

Writing more than thirty years ago, the medical historian Roy Porter criticized the focus on physicians and medical knowledge and argued that patient experience was a crucial aspect of medical history that has gone unexamined.[46] Unfortunately, the recovery of the experience of patients in early modern Japan has proven to be elusive. This was in spite of the fact that collections of case notes focusing on specific patients were a popular medical genre. Physicians published their case notes to demonstrate their skill, publicize the treatments they developed, and attract students. Reflecting these

[45] Ōtaguro, "Kinsei kōki ni okeru murakata no ishi tōsei," 92–93.
[46] Porter, "Patient's View."

motives, case notes had a fairly standard narrative form: a patient presents with a baffling array of symptoms, but the knowledgeable physician is able to recognize their cause and begins to treat the patient with a series of medicinal compounds, adjusting the prescription and dosages as the illness progresses until the patient recovers. In this literature, however, patients appear as shadowy collections of symptoms rather than distinct personalities, although a not uncommon figure was the recalcitrant patient who was unwilling to await the results of the doctor's therapies and turned to other, less skilled physicians who promised a faster recovery – inevitably with dire results. Thus, these works provide little insight into how patients understood their conditions or made choices about the medical care on offer.

There was a health literature aimed at a general readership, the genre known as "health cultivation books" (yōjōsho), the most famous example of which was Kaibara Ekiken's *Lessons on Health Cultivation* (*Yōjōkun*, 1713). However, as the term "health cultivation" itself implies, the emphasis of these works was not the treatment of disease or illness, but their prevention through a regime that involved the exercise of self-control over diet, physical exertion, sexual practices, and even posture and mastication. In fact, many of the authors of health cultivation manuals regarded sickness as evidence of a failure to correctly manage one's own health. In the words of Kaibara, "the method of health cultivation involves taking precautions during the time when one is not sick. To attack a sickness after it occurs using medicines or the application of needles means that health cultivation has failed."[47] Given this perspective, it is unsurprising that these works contain little information about the experience of sickness and patients' interaction with physicians.

More fruitful for understanding the perspective of patients are the journals kept by elite commoners, which reveal how families dealt with illness and injury. While these typically lack the thick description of symptoms and other clinical information found in physician-authored case notes, they reveal the multiple ways in which ordinary people responded to illness. The diary of Tomizaemon, the headman of a village at the foot of Mount Fuji, was typical of this period. He chronicled almost daily the events that shaped his daily life, touching upon topics such as work, family, friends, social obligations, and of course his health. The diary includes an account of a serious illness that befell Tomizaemon in the early autumn of 1856. The first mention of his poor health was recorded on the twenty-sixth day of the ninth month. At first Tomizaemon merely rested at home, but on the first day of the tenth month, he called in a doctor called

---

[47] Kaibara, *Yōjōkun wazoku dōjikun*, 28.

Kuwahara Genkai, a resident of a village located about fifteen kilometers from his home. Kuwahara examined him and prepared a medicine, but the very next day, Tomizaemon consulted an itinerant doctor staying in a local temple, and this man also provided him with medicine. On the fourth day, he sent a family member to Kuwahara to get more medicine, and on the fifth he visited with an acquaintance who provided him with an amulet, presumably to ward off his illness. Several days passed with no improvement, and so on the eighth day Kuwahara was called in again to examine Tomizaemon. Two days later, an acquaintance arrived with a gift of medicine, and Tomizaemon roused himself to visit a local temple, where a ritual was performed to expel a malevolent spirit. All these efforts notwithstanding, it was not until the fifteenth of the tenth month that Tomizaemon's condition began to improve. On that day, a priest from a local temple paid Tomizaemon a sick call and brought some medicine. Finally a full month after he had first fallen ill, Tomizaemon wrote that he had recovered.[48]

Thus, even as Tomizaemon was treated by Kuwahara throughout his illness, he also tried the medicines provided by visitors and sought out alternatives to medicalized treatments. This kind of medical pluralism, in which patients relied on multiple practitioners, amulets, exorcisms, and prayers, was the norm. The diary of another villager offers further insight into how families in this era navigated the experience of sickness and forms of treatment available. Suzuki Kyūbeirō lived in Shibasaki, a village located about forty kilometers from Edo in what is now Tachikawa City. This was an area in which a large number of doctors practiced, some of whom had studied with prominent physicians in Edo. Suzuki's diary, in which he made entries almost daily for the period between 1837 and 1858, makes mention of twenty-nine physicians. Because Shibasaki had no resident doctor, Suzuki and his family turned often to Shiratori Isai, a physician who lived in Shimofuda, a village located in what is now Chōfu City. Shiratori had once practiced in Ichigaya in Edo, but in 1838 had relocated to Shimofuda and eventually he married Suzuki's sister. In the two decades chronicled in the diary, Suzuki and members of his immediate family consulted with Shiratori at least fifty times for a variety of ailments, including colds, stomach disorders, and postpartum ailments. This long-standing doctor-patient relationship seems to have been based, at least to some degree, on the familial connection. Even so, when itinerant physicians took up temporary residence in Shibasaki, the Suzuki family consulted them for commonplace illnesses.[49]

[48] Kawanabe, "Edo jidai, Kōshū ni okeru isha," 67–69.
[49] Osada, "Kinsei kōki ni okeru kanja no ishi sentaku," 323–25.

For more serious illnesses, Suzuki's family members were willing to venture much farther, even into Edo itself, a good day's journey from Shibasaki. Suzuki's son Yashichi suffered from a serious eye disease, and on several occasions he traveled to Edo to be treated by Itō Genboku, a former medical official of the shogunate and well-known *ranpō* physician who had studied with the German physician Philipp Franz von Seibold in Nagasaki. Similarly, when Nakashima Jirōbei, Suzuki's brother-in-law, developed a lung ailment in 1852, he, too, made several trips to Edo to be treated by Itō and his students, returning home with several weeks' supply of medicines. When Nakashima's condition did not improve, Suzuki and others urged him to consult another doctor. He refused, but as his condition worsened, he and his family increasingly turned to faith-based alternatives to medical care: copying prayers, making pilgrimages to local shrines and temples, and fasting. Such efforts notwithstanding, Nakashima died six months after he had first sought treatment.[50]

This turn toward nonmedical methods of "healing" can also be seen in the diary kept by Takizawa Rō as she nursed her son Takizawa Tarō, the grandson of the popular author Takizawa Bakin. When Tarō fell ill of a mysterious illness, he was cared for by an evolving cast of doctors while friends brought medicines, charms, and made visits to temples and shrines on his behalf. As his condition worsened, his mother became convinced that the family cat, taken in as a kitten about the time Tarō fell ill, harbored a spirit that had attacked her son, and she gave the animal away in a final desperate attempt to save her son.[51]

It is not surprising, perhaps, that the turn to faith-based and ritual practices was particularly pronounced in times of epidemic disease. Both smallpox and measles, two of the most common infectious diseases in this period, were associated with malevolent deities, and efforts to control them took the form of both household-based and community-wide practices. Because the smallpox deity supposedly disliked the color red and dogs, children were sometimes dressed in red clothing and print images of red dogs were posted in entryways of houses in an attempt to ward off the deity and the disease. Other rituals sought to appease the deity in question: some families set up temporary altars with an image of the deity and offered it sake and other delicacies; in some regions, families prepared written apologies (*owabi sho*) to the deity, appealing to it to spare their relatives. Practices at the community level took the form of expulsion rituals (*hōsō yoke, hōsō nagashi*) that sought to drive the deity from the village.[52] These efforts did not mean, however, that

[50] Osada, "Kinsei kōki ni okeru kanja no ishi sentaku," 328–33.
[51] Nakayama, "Bakumatsu Edo no byōka ni okeru iryō sentaku no jittai," 282–84, 300.
[52] Nakamura, "Mura to iryō," 37–38.

smallpox and measles were not the object of medical care as well. Collections of formularies, treatises on therapies, and books offering advice to parents circulated in great number, attesting again to the pluralistic approach embraced by many.

The turn to ritual practices was particularly heightened when cholera, a previously unknown disease, was introduced to Japan, first in 1822 via Nagasaki and then in 1858 from Kanazawa. Cholera was initially referred to by a variety of terms, which reflected the course of the disease, its symptoms, and its high death rate: these included *bōshabyō* (sudden onset diarrhea disease), *niwakayamai* (sudden onset disease), and *korori* (lit. "sudden death," but also a play on the term *korera*, the phonetic rendering of cholera in Japanese). The latter term in particular took hold and came to be written with the characters for fox (*ko*), wolf (*rō*), and badger (*ri*), reflecting rumors that the disease was the result of the workings of malevolent animal spirits. It was widely believed that foxes and badgers, in particular, could take possession of human bodies and cause physical symptoms and mental derangement. During the 1858 epidemic, which followed the recent "opening" of the country by US Commodore Matthew C. Perry, rumors circulated that an "American fox" was responsible for the disease, and images appeared of a supernatural beast that combined aspects of all three animals. Attempts to ward off the disease reflected this understanding. For example, in Ōmiya in Suruga Province (now Fujinomiya City in Shizuoka Prefecture), villagers, who had heard rumors of the tremendous loss of life in Edo and elsewhere, responded first by firing guns twice a day and setting fires around the village. When cases of the disease occurred nonetheless, they developed a more ambitious strategy. Not only did they rebuild the shrine of the local guardian deity (*dōsojin*), they also sent a delegation to Mount Mitsumine in Chichibu, located almost 150 kilometers away. According to local lore, the mountain god of Mitsumine took the form of a dog deity and was able to dispel fox spirits. The aim of the delegation was to borrow (or rather, rent, since they paid a hefty price) the dog deity to frighten away the fox spirit responsible for the disease.[53]

Such efforts, occurring as they did at the very end of the early modern period, reveal that while the new medical culture had a profound impact on early modern society, it did not necessarily replace or even disrupt long-standing beliefs about disease causation in the minds of many. Although elite physicians made no mention of their patients' reliance on

---

[53] Takahashi, "Bakumatsu minshū no kyōfu to mōsō."

amulets, exorcisms, and prayers, and indeed some explicitly attacked the idea that illness resulted from the workings of deities, spirits, or other forces, the diaries and other records compiled by ordinary people, village leaders, and others reveal that medical care and ritual practices existed side by side.

Marketing Medicines and Vernacular Medical Knowledge

The popularity of ritual and faith-based healing does not mean, however, that ordinary people were untouched by the expansion of the medical profession and medical discourse. In fact, by the early nineteenth century, medical knowledge was widely available, and the manufacturers of commercially prepared medicines, known as "prepared medicine" (*awase kusuri*) and "sold medicines" (*baiyaku*), played an important role in diffusing it. As the diaries examined in the previous section reveal, it was commonplace for visitors to bring medicines as a sick-bed gift, even if the patient was under the care of one or more doctors. In contrast to the more costly customized medicines prepared by a doctor for a particular patient, prepared medicines were produced in volume and were sold at pharmacies and sundry shops or by peddlers. The origin of the formulas of "prepared medicines" was varied: some were based upon the Sino-Japanese pharmaceutical canon; others were folk remedies. Many manufacturers described their products as based on a "secret transmission" (*hiden*) and "family transmission" (*kaden*), suggesting (perhaps spuriously) that they were special formulations not available elsewhere. While prepared medicines were often taken in addition to medicines received from a doctor, for many they were the treatment of first resort because of their comparatively low cost and ready availability. While some were marketed as treatments for mild and chronic conditions including menstrual difficulties and pregnancy-related ills, eye ailments, stomachaches, and colds, others claimed universal efficacy.

The large-scale localized production of prepared medicines began in the late seventeenth century. In Toyama, domanial authorities played a leading role in encouraging the manufacture and sale of prepared medicines, while in Ōmi (now Shiga Prefecture), it was local merchants who pioneered this business. Merchants in Yamato, an area long known for the gathering and cultivation of medicinal herbs, also took the lead in producing medicinal products, which found a ready market in the nearby population centers of Kyoto and Osaka. On the island of Kyushu, the area known as Tashiro in what is now

Saga came to dominate the local market for prepared medicines.[54] By the late eighteenth century, individuals and groups in villages and towns all around Japan were involved in the business of medicine production. Many medicinal products were produced by doctors: the renowned nativist scholar and physician Motoori Norinaga sold at least four different prepared medicines, including one called *mushi osae* that promised relief for colicky babies.[55] But others, too, sought to compete in the booming market for prepared medicines. The popular nineteenth-century authors Takizawa Bakin, Santō Kyōden, and Shikitei Sanba all sold prepared medicines and cleverly incorporated advertisements into their published works.

By the early nineteenth century, many products were being sold far beyond their place of manufacture. The cities in particular were filled with pharmacies: according to shopping guidebooks published in the 1820s, Edo had more than 200 medical shops and Osaka almost as many. Urban consumers thus had available to them a vast array of medicinal products produced all around Japan.[56] But prepared medicines were available in villages and towns as well.

The Toyama domain famously employed peddlers, each with a well-defined sales area, to distribute its medicines far afield, and they pioneered a novel sales technique that came to be known as "use first, pay later," according to which a set of medicines used for common ailments was deposited with a customer without any initial charge until the peddler returned the following year to collect payment only for the products used. Other producers adopted a different strategy, establishing branch shops around the country and forging a network of local distributors or agents.[57] One producer who pursued this strategy was Ishida Teikan (1772–1866) of Kameoka in modern Kyoto Prefecture. He developed a medicine he called Hikan Yakuōen (lit. "the king of medicines for the spleen and liver"). Hikan Yakuōen was a remedy for a childhood illness called "spleen sensitivity," symptoms of which included extreme emaciation and a swollen stomach. Ishida began to sell Hikan Yakuōen around 1807. By 1851, it was being sold by distributors in nine cities and towns, including Edo, Tokyo, Osaka, and Ise, and by 1865, its distribution network had expanded to twenty-nine locations and stretched from Kyushu to Tōhoku.[58]

[54] Kōda, "'Nihon yondai baiyaku,'" 6–8.
[55] Yoshida, "Motoori Norinaga," 1106.
[56] Young, "Family Matters."
[57] On the local manufacture of prepared medicines and the creation of distribution networks, see Yagi, "Kinsei Osaka no awasekusuriya"; Matsusako, "Kinsei chūki ni okeru awasekusuri ryūtsū"; Imai, "Kinsei kōki ni okeru zaikata yakushugyō."
[58] Kajitani, "Kindai izen to ikō ni okeru minshū muke ikujisho."

Producers of prepared medicines offered consumers more than access to cheap and accessible remedies for their ailments. Manufacturers and distributors produced an array of broadsheets and pamphlets to promote their products, making medicinal products the most heavily advertised commodity in this time.[59] Many of these print materials did more than simply list the virtues of the product in question; they also referenced contemporary theories about human physiology and disease causality to explain the efficacy of the product, and as a result played a role in the production of what might be termed vernacular medical knowledge: that is, the ideas about the body, disease, and therapeutics that informed the experiences of ordinary people. Unlike terms such as "folk medicine" and "popular medicine," which suggest a body of knowledge that emerged out of quotidian experience, the term "vernacular medicine" draws attention to the processes, practices, and material sites that allow ordinary people access to professional medical knowledge. Thus, it points to the intersection between general and learned forms of knowledge rather than assuming that these are distinctive domains.[60]

A prime example of how marketing materials became involved in the production of vernacular medical knowledge are the many "efficacy books" (kōnōgaki) that were distributed by manufacturers and distributors of prepared medicines. Mimicking the popular genre of household manuals, these were extended advertisements for a prepared medicine that also offered the reading public useful information about particular kinds of sickness and disease. One of the most popular of these, printed at least seven times between 1813 and 1874, was the forty-page illustrated book called *The Golden Foundation of Rearing Children* (*Yōiku shōni kogane no ishizue*), authored by Ishida Teikan, the manufacturer of Hikan Yakuōen. As its title suggests, the book presented as a child-rearing manual, and indeed it did offer advice on childbirth, breastfeeding, and weaning. However, it also devoted considerable space to explaining the etiology of "spleen sensitivity," the childhood illness for which Hikan Yakuōen was a cure. Ishida explains human physiology in terms redolent of Rishu medical theory: "the foundation of the human body are the five viscera and six organs. The most important of the five viscera and six organs is the spleen. The origin of the myriad things of the material world is earth. Earth nurtures all things, and likewise the spleen takes in food and nurtures the five viscera and six organs. Thus, the spleen is the mother of the five organs and

---

[59] Masuda, *Hikifuda ebira fūzoku shi*, 198; Yamaki, *Nihon kōkoku shi*, 43.
[60] I came to this term via my reading of Fissell's discussion of the "vernacular body" in Fissell, *Vernacular Bodies*. Like Fissell, I am using it as a conceptual category that describes how medical discourse shapes ordinary people's understanding of the body.

can also be called earth."[61] According to Ishida, one of the primary functions of the spleen in an infant and young child was to help the body rid itself of "fetal poison," a substance that was produced as a result of the sexual "heat" of gestation, and which was strengthened if the mother did not practice good prepartum hygiene. Hikan Yakuōen, Ishida claimed, improved the workings of the spleen and nurtured the other viscera without the harsh purgative effects of other remedies for "fetal poison."

Ishida's strategy in *The Golden Foundation of Rearing Children* of embedding claims about his product within a medical discourse was widely adopted by other manufacturers, and it did not always take the form of print materials. The Osaka pharmacy that produced a medicinal compound called Uruyusu provided a handbook to its distributors. The *Instructions for Distributors of Uruyusu* (*Uruyusu hiromekata kokoroe*) offered distributors a good deal of practical advice for promoting the product, including a lengthy explanation of how the drug worked on the body, presumably so that they in turn could inform potential customers. The manufacturer of Uruyusu claimed it was based on a Dutch formula, and to support that claim incorporated roman letters into its advertisements. Its explanation of the pharmacological effects of Uruyusu also referenced Dutch medicine. Uruyusu was a treatment for excess phlegm (*tan*), which was described as the cause of symptoms including heartburn, abdominal pain, coughing, and loss of appetite. Reflecting the theory of the four humors that shaped medical practice in Europe in the early modern period, *Instructions* explained that phlegm, one of the humors, was not simply a substance in the throat that one coughed up, it was the symptom of a "poison" that had accumulated within the body causing a variety of debilitating symptoms. Uruyusu, it was said, worked by causing the phlegm in the organs to be expelled via the urine and feces, and thus restored the consumer to good health.[62]

As medical commodities flowed into the homes and bodies of people in this era, they carried with them new kinds of information, often in print, sometimes via oral transmission. It is difficult, perhaps impossible, to know how consumers made sense of the jumble of contesting information they encountered and how it shaped their understanding of their bodies, sickness, and health. But the fact that medicine producers imagined an inquisitive and receptive audience that wanted such knowledge is significant. The broadsheets and booklets they distributed often contained explicit language

---

[61] Ikeda Teikan, *Shōni yōiku kogane no ishizue.*
[62] Kenjudō, *Uruyusu hiromekata kokoroegaki.*

urging readers to retain these materials for future reference – and many did. For example, the Tabei family were village heads (*nanushi*) in Ōhama village in Musashi. Their extant papers from the early nineteenth century contain at least fifteen examples of medical print. The Sakamoto family of Ketsuka village, also in Musashi, were village officials. Their papers include at least twenty-two different broadsheets.[63] The fact that ordinary people held onto these materials, carefully preserving them to reread, consult, and perhaps to share, points to their participation in the medical marketplace of ideas.

Conclusion

In 1874, the new Japanese government issued an ambitious plan for the rapid creation of a modern medical and public health system to the three major population centers of Tokyo, Osaka, and Kyoto. Among its many provisions, the new medical policy (*isei*) called for the creation of a licensing system for medical professionals, including doctors, midwives, and pharmacists, the establishment of modern educational institutions that would teach "Western medicine," and the founding of a system of hospitals that would make care at the hands of licensed physicians widely available.[64] In this same period, the government also attempted to rein in the burgeoning prepared medicine industry, issuing new restrictions on advertisements and imposing stiff new taxes on manufacturers and retailers, and eventually requiring that pharmacies employ a licensed pharmacist.[65] Both the medical policy and the laws that addressed prepared medicines were concerned with promoting medical modernization, but they were simultaneously about the disestablishment of early modern medicine, with its plurality, syncreticism, and emphasis on self-treatment. The endurance of aspects of early modern medicine in the form of commodities, medical lineages, and forms of clinical practice even until the present cannot, of course, be reduced to a single cause, but it undoubtedly attests to the central place these forms of practice and knowledge had in the realm of everyday life. As we have seen, the medical revolution in the Tokugawa period has profound implications for understanding social mobility, the evolution of the status system, education, and evolving notions of governance, and it also profoundly shaped how people in Japan understood the workings of their bodies, health, and disease.

---

[63] The papers for all three families are held by Saitama Prefectural Archive.
[64] Kōseishō Imukyoku, *Isei hyakunenshi*, 7–10.
[65] Burns, "Marketing 'Women's Medicines,'" 153–54.

Bibliography

Andō Yūichirō. *Edo no yōjōsho*. PHP Shinsho, 2005.

Ashikawa Keishū. *Byōmei ikai*. 7 vols. Kyoto: Uemura Tōemon, 1686. Waseda University Library. www.wul.waseda.ac.jp/kotenseki/html/ya09/ya09_00581/index.html

Burns, Susan L. "The Body as Text: Confucianism, Reproduction, and Gender in Early Modern Japan." In *Rethinking Confucianism: Past and Present in China, Japan, Korea, and Vietnam*, edited by Benjamin Elman, Herman Ooms, and John Duncan, 178–219. Los Angeles: UCLA, Asia Pacific Monograph Series, 2002.

——. "Marketing 'Women's Medicines': Gender, OTC Herbal Medicines, and Medical Culture in Modern Japan." *Asian Medicine* 5, no. 1 (2009): 146–72.

——. "Nanayama Jundō at Work: A Village Doctor and Medical Knowledge in Nineteenth Century Japan." *East Asian Science, Medicine, and Technology* 29 (Autumn 2008): 61–82.

Chō Kizen. "Sendai-han ni okeru sho ishi to sono haaku, dōin." *Rekishi* 109 (2007): 79–108.

Drixler, Fabian. *Mabiki: Infanticide and Population Growth in Eastern Japan, 1660–1950*. Berkeley: University of California Press, 2013.

Fissell, Mary Elizabeth. *Vernacular Bodies: The Politics of Reproduction in Early Modern England*. Oxford: Oxford University Press, 2006.

Fun Tokusai. *Isha dangi*. 5 vols. Kanazawa: Notoya Jisuke, 1759. Waseda University Library. www.wul.waseda.ac.jp/kotenseki/html/ya09/ya09_00645/index.html

Fuse Shoichi. *Ishi no rekishi: Sono Nihonteki tokuchō*. Chūōkōronsha, 1979.

Goble, Andrew. *Confluences of Medicine in Medieval Japan: Buddhist Healing, Chinese Knowledge, Islamic Formulas, and Wounds of War*. Honolulu: University of Hawai'i Press, 2011.

Hattori Toshirō. *Edo jidai igakushi no kenkyū*. Yoshikawa Kōbunkan, 1978.

Hirano Mitasu. "Mura ni okeru ishi no sonzai keitai: Kinsei kōki no Tottori hanryō o rei toshite." *Sundai shigaku* 90 (1994): 150–83.

Horisaki Yoshiaki. "Kinsei Higashi Ano mura to ika Mita-shi: Iryō to bunka kōryū no sugata." *Chita hanto no rekishi to genzai* 18 (2014): 117–30.

Ikeda Teikan. *Shōni yōiku kogane no ishizue*. Kyoto: Ikeda Teikan, 1862. Kyoto University Rare Materials Database. https://rmda.kulib.kyoto-u.ac.jp/item/rb00003260

Ikeda Toyoko. "Kinsei Kanazawa no iryō: Dentō no ishizue to shakaishiteki igi o saguru." In *"Dentō" no ishizue: Kaga, Noto, Kanazawa no chiikishi*, edited by Chihōshi Kenkyū Kyōgikai, 192–212. Yūzankaku, 2014.

Imai Shūhei. "Kinsei kōki ni okeru zaikata yakushugyō no tenkai: Hirano-gumi yakushuya, awasekusuriya o chūshin ni." In *Nihon kindai no seiritsu to tenkai: Umetani Noboru kyōju taikan kinen ronbunshū*, edited by Umetani Noboru Kyōju Taikan Kinen Ronbunshū Kankōkai, 275–96. Kyoto: Shibunkaku, 1984.

Janetta, Ann Bowman. *The Vaccinators: Smallpox, Medical Knowledge, and the "Opening" of Japan*. Stanford, CA: Stanford University Press, 2007.

Kagawa Gen'etsu. *Sanron*. Heian [Kyoto]: Saiseikan, 1775. National Institute of Japanese Literature Kotenseki Database. https://kotenseki.nijl.ac.jp/biblio/100273451/viewer/1

Kaibara Ekiken. *Yōjōkun wazoku dōjikun*. Edited by Ishikawa Ken. Iwanami Shoten, 1963.

Kajitani Shinji. "Kindai izen to ikō ni okeru minshū muke ikujisho no henbō: 'Koji yōiku kogane no ishizue' no kaisetsu oyobi honkoku." *Gaikokugo gaikoku bunka* 3 (2010): 55–181.

Kawanabe Sadao. "Edo jidai, Kōshū ni okeru isha to iryō ishiki." *Yamanashi kenshi kenkyū* 7 (1999): 66–106.

Kenjudō. *Uruyusu hiromekata kokoroegaki*. Osaka: Kenjudō, n.d. Waseda University Library. www.wul.waseda.ac.jp/kotenseki/html/ya09/ya09_00542/index.html

Kōda Hirofumi. "'Nihon yondai baiyaku' ni miru gyōshōken no kōchiku, hatten, tenkan katei: Edo chūki kara Meiji-ki made." *Keieiryoku sōsei kenkyū* 15 (2019): 5–19.

Kōseishō Imukyoku, ed. *Isei hyakunenshi: Kijutsu hen*. Gyōsei, 1974.

Kosoto Hiroshi. *Nihon kanpō tenseki jiten*. Taishūkan, 1999.

Kyannochō Chūkai. *Hyōkin zatsubyō ron*. In *Shoki sharebonshū*, edited by Nakamura Yukihiko, 51–76. Koten Bunkō, 1958.

Kyōto-fu Ishikai, ed. *Kyōto no igakushi, Shiryō-hen*. Kyoto: Shibunkaku, 1980.

Machi Senjurō. "Igakukan no kiseki: Kōshō igaku no kyoten keisei o megutte." *Kyōu* 7 (2004): 35–92.

Marcon, Federico. *The Knowledge of Nature and the Nature of Knowledge in Early Modern Japan*. Chicago: University of Chicago Press, 2015.

Masuda Tajirō. *Hikifuda ebira fūzoku shi*. Seiabō, 1981.

Matsuki Akitomo. "Hanaoka Seishū no 'mafutsusan' kaihatsu to Nihon ni okeru 19 seki shotō no zenshin mayaku." *Nihon ishigaku kenkyū* 62, no. 4 (2016): 413–28.

Matsusako Hisayo. "Kinsei chūki ni okeru awasekusuri ryūtsū: Shohin ryūtsū no ichirei toshite." *Machikaneyama ronsō* 29 (1995): 1–25.

Nakamura Aya. "Mura to iryō: Shinano no kuni o jirei toshite." *Rekishigaku kenkyū* 639 (1992): 36–43.

Nakashima Ika Shiryōkan and Nakashima Monjo Kenkyūkai, eds. *Bizen Okayama no zaison'i Nakashima-ke no rekishi*. Kyoto: Shibunkaku, 2015.

Nakayama Manabu. "Bakumatsu Edo no byōka ni okeru iryō sentaku no jittai: Byōnin Takizawa Tarō no kaigo nikki o tegakari to shite." In *Shūkyō, geinō, iryō*, edited by Kantō Kinseishi Kenkyūkai, 279–305. Vol. 2 of *Kantō kinseishi kenkyū ronshū*. Iwata Shoin, 2012.

Osada Naoko. "Bakumatsu-ki zaison ni okeru ishi yōsei no jittai: Honda Kakuan to sannin no deshi o rei to shite." *Ronshū kinsei* 24 (2002): 44–72.

———. "Edo kinkō nōson in okeru iryō: Jūhasseiki Tama chiiki no iryō o chūshin to shite." *Kantō kinseishi kenkyū* 62, no. 7 (2007): 45–77.

———. "Kinsei kōki ni okeru kanja no ishi sentaku: 'Suzuki Kurō kōshi nikki' o chūshin ni." *Kokuritsu Rekishi Minzoku Hakubutsukan kenkyū hōkoku* 116 (2004): 317–42.

Ōtaguro Mami. "Kinsei kōki ni okeru murakata no ishi tōsei: Kokura-han o jirei toshite." *Nanakuma shigaku* 11 (2009): 83–97.

Porter, Roy. "The Patient's View: Doing Medical History from Below." *Theory and Society* 14, no. 2 (1985): 175–98.

Sakai Shizu. *Nihon no iryōshi*. Tōkyō Shoseki, 1982.

Sawayama Mikako. *Shussan to shintai no kinsei*. Keisō Shobō, 1998.

Shibata Hajime. "Kinsei kōki ni okeru zaison'i no shūgaku katei: Bitchū no zaison'i Chihara Eishun no baai." In *Jitsugakushi kenkyū*, Vol. 2, edited by Jitsugaku Shiryōkai, 175–210. Kyoto: Shibunkaku, 1985.

Sugano Noriko. *Edo no mura isha: Honda Kakuan Sadatoshi fushi no nikki ni miru*. Shin Nippon Shuppansha, 2003.

Suzuki Akira. "Hozumi Hoan 'Kyūmin myōyaku' de shomin keimō." *Kanpō ryōhō* 20, no. 8 (2016): 622–26.

Tachibanagawa Toshitada. "Kinsei mura isha no honbako: Ōami Shirasato-chō no Tomizuka-ke no baai." *Rekishi to minzoku* 7 (1991): 79–96.

Takahashi Satoshi. "Bakumatsu minshū no kyōfu to mōsō: Suruga no kuni Ōmiyachō no korera sōdō." *Kokuritsu Rekishi Minzoku Hakubutsukan kenkyū hōkoku* 108 (2003): 149–64.

Takei Yoshikazu and Nanba Katsudō, eds. *Edo kinsei ika jinmeiroku.* N.p.: 1818.

Taki Motonori. *Ika shokun.* Edo: Seijukan, 1833. Reprint, Tokyo: Seiundō, n.d. Waseda University Library. www.wul.waseda.ac.jp/kotenseki/html/ya09/ya09_00051/index .html

Tatebe Seian and Sugita Genpaku. *Oranda iji mondō* (1795). In *Bunmei genryū sōsho*, Vol. 2, edited by Hayakawa Junzaburō, 382–408. Kokusho Kankōkai, 1914.

Tsukamoto Manabu. *Chihō bunjin.* Kyōikusha, 1977.

Ueno Kaneko. "Kishū-han no iryō seisaku to chiiki shakai." *Mie shigaku* 7 (2007): 1–20.

Umihara Ryō. *Edo jidai no ishi shugyō.* Yoshikawa Kōbunkan, 2014.

——— "Kinsei kōki hanryō ni okeru 'iryō' no tenkai: Echizen no kuni Fuchū o rei toshite." *Shigaku zasshi* 112, no. 11 (2003): 1811–37.

Yagi Shigeru. "Kinsei Osaka no awasekusuriya ni kansuru shiryō." *Ōsaka Rekishi Hakubutsukan kiyō* 11 (2013): 89–103.

Yamaki Toshio. *Nihon kōkoku shi: Keizai, hyōgen, sesō de miru kōkoku hensen.* Nihon Keizai Shinbunsha, 1992.

Yamazaki Tasaku. *Kakuhan igaku kyōiku no tenkai.* Kokudosha, 1955.

Yoshida Yoshiyuki. "Motoori Norinaga no igyō to gakumon." *Nihon nōson igakkai zasshi* 65, no. 6 (2017): 1104–6.

Young, William Evan. "Family Matters: Managing Illness in Late Tokugawa Japan." PhD diss., Princeton University, 2005.

15

Flows of People and Things
in Early Modern Japan
Print Culture

LAURA NENZI

Stretching from the southern tip of modern-day Hokkaido to the islands south of modern-day Kagoshima Prefecture in Kyushu, Tokugawa Japan consisted of a constellation of localities with distinct traditions and customs; at the same time, it was also an increasingly interconnected archipelago.[1] While policies and practices enacted in individual cities, domains, and regions retained idiosyncratic characteristics and could differ substantially from one place to the next, individuals operated at the crossroad of local interests and interregional dynamics. People traveled and communicated, merchandise moved, ideas circulated. Ironically, in a country that had, since the early seventeenth century, imposed strict regulations on foreign and domestic travel, movement was everywhere, both as an idea (that is to say, on paper) and as a practice (that is to say, on the road). The print industry played a key role in popularizing the former and inspiring the latter.

This chapter examines the role and the inventive editorial choices of commercial publishers in promoting, extensively and effectively, the movement of people and things in early modern Japan. A for-profit print industry emerged in the seventeenth century and rapidly expanded both horizontally (with more bookstores and printers in more locations, and greater geographical and thematic coverage) and vertically (catering to an increasingly diversified readership, including the minimally literate). Already in late seventeenth-century Kyoto more than 1,000 commercial publishers printed about 3,800 different titles, 800 of which were in the vernacular.[2] Genres

---

[1] For regional diversity, consider the endless disquisitions on the differences between Edo, Kyoto, and Osaka – from roof tiles to toilets, from methods of time measurement to the right way to skewer an eel – included in Kitagawa's *Morisada mankō* (Morisada's miscellany).

[2] Moretti, *Pleasure in Profit*, 3–4.

available in the late Tokugawa period ranged from fiction to how-to manuals on the basics of divination, tactics for bug extermination, and everything in between; educational primers; abridged versions of the classics; single-page ephemera; and more. With the exception of commentaries on contemporary politics and the ruling samurai families, which were forbidden by publication laws, no topic appeared to be off limits.[3]

Variety abounded in the publications pertaining specifically to the flow of people and things. Aside from predictable formats such as guidebooks and travel itineraries, information about travel sites and regional specialty products also appeared in unexpected places, for example, board games and parodies of sumo rankings, testifying to a pervasive interest in tips on places and products. Taken together, these sources unlock stories of movement and knowledge that are both local and global. At the local level, they illuminate the creative editorial and epistemological tactics with which commercial publishers mapped and marketed a land that was united by a shared past and a prosperous present, and readily available for intellectual and material consumption. They narrate, in short, the democratization of knowledge and the creation of an interconnected archipelago in early modern Japan. More broadly, they reflect the global expansion of the information industry and the rise of tourism in the nineteenth century, shedding any perception of Tokugawa Japan as uniquely removed from dynamics at play the world over.

Guidebooks and Itineraries

The practice of collecting and organizing information about the land did not originate with early modern commercial publishers: domain-sponsored surveys (*fudoki*) and cadastral maps preceded them by centuries. Official maps and *fudoki*, however, had limited circulation; it was the commercial print industry that made knowledge of topography, roads, and resources available on a large scale. It did so by way of publications that – in a variety of formats and price ranges – described the lay of the land, cataloged its regional products, outlined the heritage of its sites, and invited one to visit.

One of the keys to the commercial success of these works was the early seventeenth-century return to the woodblock after a fifty-year-long

---

[3] Censorship laws were enforced inconsistently. Punishment for violating them ranged from reprimands and fines to the confiscation of printing materials, shackles, and exile. Only in one case, the offending author, Baba Bunkō (1718–59), was sentenced to death. Jones with Watanabe, *Edo Anthology*, 103–5.

experiment with movable type.[4] Woodblocks allowed publishers to combine text and image onto the same page, providing room for flexibility and creativity. Moreover, they facilitated mass-production: up to 1,500 copies could be printed before a woodblock became unusable.[5] High-volume production in turn resulted in a significant reduction in cost. Inexpensive publications already circulated in the late seventeenth century: in 1681, an unannotated copy of *The Classic of Filial Piety* (Ch. *Xiaojing*, J. *Kōkyō*) cost as much as a bowl of *chazuke*; in the same year, a skilled tradesman could have purchased the seven-volume guidebook *The Kyoto Sparrow (Kyō suzume)* by spending the equivalent of two days' work.[6] By the second half of the Tokugawa period, peddlers sold single-sheet guides to the local pleasure quarters for one quarter to half the price of a bowl of noodles.[7] Other single-page prints were more expensive, depending on size and color.[8] Multivolume series remained relatively affordable: in the nineteenth century, a reprint of Akisato Ritō's 1780 *Illustrated Guidebook to the Capital (Miyako meisho zue*, six volumes) cost two *bu* – the equivalent of about US$60 today.[9]

In the seventeenth century, the print industry established formats and templates that would last for the next 200 years: the first work to list the famous sites of Edo (*Azuma meguri*, 1643); the first guide to the red-light district of the Yoshiwara (*Azuma monogatari*, 1642);[10] the first commercial illustrated guidebook (Nakagawa Kiun's *Young Folks from the Capital* [*Kyō warabe*, 1658]);[11] early versions of city guides (1680s);[12] and the debut of colored commercial maps (1690s).[13] Book trade catalogs from the late seventeenth century already included books on famous places (*meisho zukushi*).[14]

---

[4] Movable type had been adopted in the late sixteenth century as a result of the encounter with Jesuit missionaries and of the exposure to Korean printing techniques during Toyotomi Hideyoshi's campaigns. See Shively, "Popular Culture," 725–33.

[5] Shirahata, "Printing of Illustrated Books," 71.

[6] Moretti, *Pleasure in Profit*, 95. *The Kyoto Sparrow* cost 7 *monme* in 1681, 4 *monme* and 5 *fun* in 1696. A tradesman's daily wage, in mid-seventeenth century Edo, was approximately 3 silver *monme*, decreasing to 2 *monme* 4 *fun* by 1715.

[7] A bowl of soba in the 1830s sold for 16 *mon* (Shirahata, "Printing of Illustrated Books," 72), while guides to Edo's red-light district cost anywhere between 4 and 8 *mon* (Kitagawa, *Kinsei fūzokushi*, 1:283). Maps of Kamakura and its landmarks in 1860 cost 24 *mon* (Hara, *Edo no tabi*, 196 n6).

[8] Marks, *Publishers of Japanese Woodblock Prints*, 24.

[9] Shirahata, "Printing of Illustrated Books," 72.

[10] Saitō, *Bukō nenpyō*, 1:39–40.

[11] Shirahata, "Printing of Illustrated Travelogues," 200; Nakagawa, *Kyō warabe*.

[12] Berry, *Japan in Print*, 143.

[13] Berry, *Japan in Print*, 99.

[14] Moretti, *Pleasure in Profit*, 92.

Bookstores, which also doubled as printing and publishing facilities, were already part of the urban landscape in the seventeenth century: more than a hundred existed around Teramachi street in central Kyoto.[15] In his chronology of the history of Edo (*Bukō nenpyō*), nineteenth-century chronicler Saitō Gesshin dates the appearance of the first bookstore in Edo – one specialized in old books – to the 1640s.[16] Likewise, a 1692 reference guide to the businesses in Kyoto, Edo, and Osaka catalogs numerous bookstores and categorizes them by the types of books they printed and sold (scholarly books, woodblock-printed books, Chinese books, etc.), showing not only their ubiquitous presence but also an early trend toward specialization.[17]

Whether by direct purchase or by loan from a library, prospective travelers in the seventeenth century could thus use overviews of famous places to gather information before a journey. One month before leaving Edo for Kamakura in 1693, for example, Kii domain doctor Ishibashi Shōan borrowed a copy of Kawai Tsunehisa's *A History of Kamakura: New Edition* (*Shinpen Kamakurashi*), a compendium of the prominent sites and of the history of the former samurai capital commissioned by Mito lord Tokugawa Mitsukuni and published by Kyoto bookseller Ogawa Tazaemon in 1685.[18]

Shinpen Kamakurashi catered to the educated who were already familiar with warrior tales and who would have recognized, and enjoyed, its many references to literary classics: as many as 138 to *Azuma kagami* (Mirror of the East, Kamakura period), 28 to *Genkō shakusho* (a fourteenth-century history of Buddhism), and 25 to the *Taiheiki* (Record of the great peace, fourteenth century), to name a few.[19] Indeed, Shōan had first read it in 1685, when it was published, even though he was not planning on visiting Kamakura at the time: he simply wished to learn more about the city's history. Seven years later, with a real trip forthcoming, Shōan turned to *Shinpen Kamakurashi* once again, this time for a practical purpose. His trip lasted six days; shortly after its completion, Shōan returned the copy of the book.[20]

As Shōan's case indicates, early publications on travel sites often validated existing erudition more than informing anew. In part this was a reflection of the fact that early recreational travelers were mostly of the educated

[15] Moretti, *Pleasure in Profit*, 2, 67.
[16] Saitō, *Bukō nenpyō*, 1:48.
[17] *Yorozu kaimono chōhōki*.
[18] Hara, *Edo no tabi*, 48. On Ogawa Tazaemon, see Fujikawa, "Meisho zue o meguru shoshi."
[19] Hara, *Edo no tabi*, 58.
[20] Hara, *Edo no tabi*, 54–56.

kind – they fashioned themselves as antiquarians and poets, not (yet) as gourmands or bargain-hunters. Titles such as *Famous Sites and Poems Pulling You along the Road* (*Meisho waka no michibiki*, 1682), illustrated by Hishikawa Moronobu, a compendium of poetic sites and the illustrious verses that literary giants had composed about them, were conceived with such wayfarers in mind.[21]

As peace, prosperity, and growing literacy rates generated new opportunities for discovery, however, demand for knowledge of the land increased.[22] It was a different kind of knowledge that readers began to seek, one cognizant of past heritage but also of present-day possibilities. Commercial publishers, sensing an opportunity for greater profit, expanded their catalogues accordingly. First, they aimed for broader geographical coverage. In late eighteenth-century Kyoto, Ogawa Tazaemon joined forces with guidebook author Akisato Ritō and went on to produce illustrated guidebooks to an array of provinces (Yamato, Izumi, Settsu, Kawachi) and roads (the Tōkaidō highway, the Kiso road).[23] The first commercially successful illustrated guidebook was, indeed, Ritō's aforementioned *Illustrated Guide to the Capital*. Comprising more than 250 illustrations, the six-volume series was still selling thousands of copies per year well into the early nineteenth century.[24]

With each new guidebook, another area of the archipelago became incorporated into the catalog of collective knowledge and opened up for sightseeing.[25] By the nineteenth century, travel books not only described most regions but could also be found outside the main cities. While some were local reprints of books first produced in the urban areas, others were entirely original. Their authors were regional literati or teachers familiar with the surrounding area and its history.[26] They started by composing textbooks (*ōraimono*) used in local schools to teach the geography of the region, its heritage, and its industries.[27] Over time, however, some of these publications became legitimate reference works. Likewise, the illustrated maps of Kanazawa's eight views,

---

[21] *Meisho waka no michibiki*.

[22] Jansen, "Japan in the Early Nineteenth Century," 64–65.

[23] *An Illustrated Guidebook to Yamato* (*Yamato meisho zue*, 1791); *An Illustrated Guidebook to Izumi* (*Izumi meisho zue*, 1796); *An Illustrated Guidebook to Settsu* (*Settsu meisho zue*, 1796–98); *An Illustrated Guidebook to the Tōkaidō Highway* (*Tōkaidō meisho zue*, 1797); *An Illustrated Guidebook to Kawachi* (*Kawachi meisho zue*, 1801); and *An Illustrated Guidebook to the Kiso Road* (*Kisoji meisho zue*, 1805). Fujikawa, "Meisho zue o meguru shoshi," 39.

[24] This is by Takizawa Bakin's estimate. See Shirahata, "Printing of Illustrated Travelogues," 199–201.

[25] Berry, *Japan in Print*, 15, calls this catalog "the library of public information."

[26] Hara, *Edo no tabi*, 118–23.

[27] Hara, *Edo no tabi*, 90–96.

which had been printed locally since the early eighteenth century, became templates for Edo-based artists and publishers in the nineteenth.[28] The efforts at expansion and inclusion of the early publishers generated the perception that the process would only move in one direction: on to bigger and broader things. Looking back from the vantage point of the nineteenth century, thus, Saitō Gesshin characterized the early maps (*ezu*) of Edo from the 1620s and 1630s as "narrow" (*semashi*), only "becoming broader" (*hiroku nareri*) after the 1660s.[29] (Gesshin later conceded that Edo maps of the mid-1640s were already "much broader" – *mottomo hiroshi* – than their predecessors.)[30]

Aside from aiming for broader geographical scope, publishers also directed their attention to new typologies of readers. Whereas most early guides had been produced with an educated readership in mind (think Shōan), later ones were made to appeal not just to the poets but also to the pragmatists and did not discriminate between erudite citations and matter-of-fact advice. They still included literary references (the Kamakura section in Akisato Ritō's *Illustrated Guide to the Famous Sites of the Tōkaidō Road* contains quotes from the aforementioned *Azuma kagami*, *Taiheiki*, and *Shinpen Kamakurashi*, as well as from the eighth-century poetry collection *Man'yōshū*, the late thirteenth-century diary *Izayoi nikki*, and the early thirteenth-century anthology *Shinkokinshū*) but also directed travelers to teahouses, restaurants, theaters, and souvenir shops. The wayfarer skimming through the pages of Saitō Gesshin's overview of Edo's famous sites (*Edo meisho zue*), for example, would have been directed to street markets and festivals as well as treated to an aside on the life of poet and craftsman Shimizu Josui (1656–1728).[31] In his chronology of the history of Edo, the same Gesshin quoted from another travel book, *Illustrated Guide to the Famous Sites of the Kii Region* (*Kishū meisho zue*), to trace the history of sugar production in Japan.[32] Such guidebooks, in other words, did not treat travel as an extraordinary event, but rather integrated it into conversations and practices that spanned from the erudite to the everyday. By the nineteenth century, the long-standing and somewhat trite association between travel and hardships survived in routine admonishments about forging the character of youngsters ("send a cherished child on a journey") and rhyming adages

[28] Hara, *Edo no tabi*, 123.
[29] Saitō, *Bukō nenpyō*, 1:42. His definition of "narrow" applies to maps that conceive of the borders of Edo as being limited by Shiba Zōjōji to the south; Kōjimachi and Tameike to the west; Asakusabashi to the north; and the Sumida River to the east. By the time he wrote in the nineteenth century, the city limits had expanded well beyond that.
[30] Saitō, *Bukō nenpyō*, 1:49.
[31] Saitō, *Edo meisho zue*, 1:127–33, and Saitō, *Bukō nenpyō*, 1:129.
[32] Saitō, *Bukō nenpyō*, 1:180.

("in travel, a companion; in life, compassion") cited in collections of travel precautions, but commercial publishers had also shown that travel could be a comfortable, even enjoyable, experience for all.

More than that, they had normalized the idea of moving far and wide across a familiar land previewed from every possible angle. The maps included in their publications offered multiple perspectives, from street level to bird's-eye view, from insect's-eye view to night view, from flat to three-dimensional.[33] Their guidebooks did not impose any rigid sequence and could be read in any order, allowing the readers to choose their itinerary on the page as they would have on the road.[34]

Lavishly illustrated and meticulous in their coverage, guidebooks often comprised multiple volumes, making them excellent references to prepare for a journey, or to roam vicariously through a land rich in history and amenities, but impractical to take along on the road. Mindful of the need to access information while on the move, publishers reduced the size of publications to make them transportable: after the 1770s, for instance, illustrated maps of Nara shrank by up to 50 percent to facilitate portability.[35] Publishers also devised lightweight, pocket-size itineraries (dōchūki) for wayfarers to carry. If guidebooks were "things to read," itineraries were "things to use."[36]

In travel itineraries, size and weight mattered. Bound, horizontal-style booklets of about eight or nine centimeters in width and fifteen to twenty in length, they averaged between thirty and fifty grams in weight. The reduction in size did not entail the narrowing of scope or vision. To the contrary, most itineraries feature striking panoramas and encompassing bird's-eye views. In Along the Road from the Eastern Capital to the Western Provinces: A Pocket-Size Treasure (Tōto yori saigoku suji ryochū kaihō, 1852), some maps unfold over several pages (the map of Edo, for example, offers a view that stretches from Senju in the north to Takanawa in the south); elsewhere, fold-out inserts expand the page as needed without compromising the portability of the itinerary.[37]

Despite the emphasis on direction transpiring from most titles ("From A to B: An Itinerary"), itineraries could also be read backward. A wayfarer

---

[33] Shirahata, "Printing of Illustrated Travelogues," 205. An example of a three-dimensional map is Utagawa Sadahide's 1848 Portrayal of Mount Fuji; see Miyazaki, "Artist's Rendering of the Divine Mount Fuji."

[34] Goree, Printing Landmarks, 11–12.

[35] Goree, Printing Landmarks, 104.

[36] Hara, Edo no tabi, 35.

[37] Imai, Dōchūki shūsei, 31:347–48.

traveling along the Nakasendō highway with a copy of *Gokaidōchū saikenki* (A detailed itinerary of the five main highways, 1858) in their pocket, for example, would have been notified about the requirements of the Usuigawa checkpoint, between the post towns of Matsuida and Sakamoto, on two different pages: one for those reading the itinerary as it was printed and paginated (moving away from Edo), and one for those traveling in the opposite direction, toward Edo. Either way, the traveler would have received much-needed advance notice.[38]

The titles of itineraries and guidebooks announced loudly and clearly the publishers' mission to expand and customize. Many lured with the promise of abundant, up-to-date detail, titillating the fastidious wayfarer with clever buzzwords: *shokoku* (in all provinces!), *dai Nihon* (in Great Japan!), *kuniguni* (province by province!), *tsukushi* (complete list!), or *saiken* (a close inspection!).[39] Others defined their intended readership: next to the works meant to be enjoyed "by all" (*banmin*) were the publications "for women" (*joyō*), "for merchants," or "with poems" for the lyrically inclined. Content and approach varied accordingly.

Let us take a closer look at one such customized itinerary. True to its title, *A Mirror of Merchants along the Roads of All Provinces* (*Shokoku dōchū akindo kagami*, 1827) is a work created for the traveling merchant, one pledging to record, "in detail, each and every wholesaler in every province, the craft of each known master, a site's famous products, current prices [of items] when buying in stock, beautiful shops, remedies tested for generations, and miracle drugs for every ailment, all the way to restaurants, teahouses, and renowned inns." Despite the promise to devote attention also to religious and historical landmarks, it does so minimally: the itinerary is all business.[40] Published in Edo by Hanaya Kyūjirō, this single-volume booklet is small (12.6 x 19.3 cm; 133 pages), transportable, and pragmatic. Visually reminiscent of a modern-day navigation system, it provides a bird's-eye view of the road with

---

[38] The itinerary advises that, while the checkpoint inspects women traveling in both directions, it requires transit permits only of men traveling toward Edo, but not in the opposite direction. It also refers to the checkpoint as the "Yokokawa" checkpoint. Ōshiroya, *Gokaidōchū saikenki.*

[39] Yoshiwara *saiken* were a veritable genre of "data collection" on the pleasure quarter of Edo, its teahouses, its prices, etc. They were first published in the seventeenth century – an event nineteenth-century chronicler Saitō Gesshin thought memorable enough to include in his chronology of Edo's history (*Bukō nenpyō*, 1:39). They were reprinted twice a year, in the spring and fall, to update the content for accuracy. Sold at street corners by specialized peddlers known as *saiken uri*, they were purchased not only as actual guides but also as Edo souvenirs; see Rekishi Misuterii Tanbōkai, "*Yoru no Oedo*" *chizu*, 117.

[40] In Imai, *Dōchūki shūsei*, 38:185–452.

lists of distances and relay points ("from A to E via B, C, and D, the distance is X"). Content-wise, one may think of it as a distant relative of the yellow pages: dry yet informative lists of commercial activities (between two and three per page on average), each including name, address, type of business (e.g. *"ochazuke* restaurant," "drinks and snacks," "hot noodles," "draperies"), crest, and any additional information the publisher deemed relevant – from "prepares meals to go" or "superior white-rice sake" to longer endorsements detailing the efficacy of certain medicines.

The entries "pop up" in the itinerary as the traveler moves along the road. As a result, the wayfarer is guided at every point of the journey, both while moving from one location to the next along the road and after arriving in town, where a selection of shops and restaurants awaits. To put it differently, *A Mirror for Merchants* covers both the road and the destination(s). The focus stays on the practical – where to buy socks in bulk, medicines, or noodles – rather than on the lyrical and intangible. We are a long way away from the spirit of *Famous Sites and Poems Pulling You along the Road.*

Whether marketed as works for all or for select types of readers, travel books thus contained copious amounts of information, multiple illustrations, and could be read in any order. To maximize efficiency and expedite the retrieval of information, publishers added charts, tables of contents, "at a glance" summaries, and "best of" lists. The aforementioned *Pocket-Size Treasure* (1852), for example, features lists of the ten best panoramas in the country, the nine fiercest rivers, and the forty most famous mountains.[41] *From Kanazawa to Kyoto: A Roster of Famous Sites along the Road (Kanazawa yori Kyōto made dōchū meishoki*, 1854) includes a table of contents, a list of the eight famous views of Lake Biwa, a calendar of the major festivals and events in Kyoto, and a chart with the distances between various post towns.[42] Yasumi Roan's 1810 manual *A Collection of Travel Precautions (Ryokō yōjinshū)* provides not only an "all at a glance" table of contents but also meticulous indexes of hot springs and checkpoints (organized by province), charts of lunar phases, directories with the times of sunrises and sunsets, tables of transportation fees, panoramic maps with distances between relay stations, and lists of all the stops along the major pilgrimage circuits.[43]

Publishers of travel books mapped and systematized the realm with methodical precision. They made it quantifiable through charts (of fees, of

---

[41] Imai, *Dōchūki shūsei*, 31:90–93.
[42] Imai, *Dōchūki shūsei*, 31:172–74 and 175–86 (the entire guide is 95–188).
[43] Yasumi, *Ryokō yōjinshū.*

distances) and accessible through icons and symbols. Prefatory notes with legends (*hanrei*) placed at the beginning of travel itineraries explained which icons would be used to indicate key landmarks: for example, towers for castles; torii and stylized halls for shrines and temples; circles for famous sites; triangles for sites of historical relevance; or rectangles surmounted by triangles for post towns.[44] There is not always consistency in the choice of icons, but the transformation of the road and its adjacent landscapes into a sequence of easily decipherable symbols opened up the land to a large number of people, including the minimally literate.

The publishers' efforts at visual narration also relied on scale to communicate importance. In the introduction to his *Illustrated Guidebook to the Capital*, Akisato Ritō explains that the human figures included in his illustrations were meant to give the reader not only a sense of scale but also one of priority – the larger the figures, the more worthy of examination the site.[45] Color coding helped organize information about topography and the built environment: oceans and rivers in blue; mountains and trees in green; houses along the road in light brown; and the road in red, for example.[46] Color coding per se was not new. Early Tokugawa survey maps had used the same technique, and colored commercial maps had circulated since the late seventeenth century. What was innovative was the fact that, by the late Tokugawa era, color coding had become part of a rich yet accessible pictorial vocabulary where scale, icons, and tables narrated the realm and its features in immediately accessible terms for the non-elites.

In their efforts to quantify and systematize the land, Tokugawa-era travel books were comparable to their European counterparts. Consider for example the meticulously titled *The Traveller's Pocket-Companion: Or, a Compleat Description of the Roads, in Tables of Their Computed and Measured Distances, by an Actual Survey and Mensuration by the Wheel, from London to All the Considerable Cities and Towns in England and Wales; together with the Mail-Roads, and Their Several Stages, and the Cross-Roads from One City or Eminent Town to Another. With Directions What Turnings Are to Be Avoided in Going or Returning on Journeys, and Instructions for Riding Post. To Which Is Annexed, a New Survey-Map, Which Shows the Market-Days, and Remarkable Things; the Whole Laid Down in a Manner that Strangers May Travel*

---

[44] Examples from *Pocket-Size Treasure*. See Imai, *Dōchūki shūsei*, 31:88.
[45] Shirahata, "Printing of Illustrated Travelogues," 205.
[46] In *Pocket-Size Treasure*. The version in Imai, *Dōchūki shūsei*, vol. 31, is in black and white; the original is at Ibaraki Prefectural Library. A similar palette is used in *Japan at Close Inspection: An Illustrated Map* (*Nihon saiken ezu*, Edo, 1854–59, author unknown, 18 x 12 cm), in Imai, *Dōchūki shūsei*, 31:193–226. Reprinted in black and white.

without Any Other Guide. Also an Account of the Expences of Sending a Letter or Pacquet by Express from the General Post-Office, with Lots of Time, to Any Part of Great Britain (1741). Authored by an anonymous yet authoritative-sounding "Person Who Has Belonged to the Publick Offices Upwards of Twenty Years," it sold at the price of one shilling and six pence; by comparison, mailing an express letter from London to Oxford at the time cost one pound, seven shillings, and nine pence, more than eighteen times as much.[47] This 158-page guidebook makes many of the same promises as its Japanese equivalents. Here, too, the road is broken down into tables, lists, and measurements; here, too, the approach is multidirectional ("going or returning"). The "copious" table of contents, in which "any place or road may be found," consists of a four-column, thirty-one-page spread that cross-lists departures, destinations, roads, and page numbers. The style echoes that of Japanese itineraries – "from A to B, X miles" – and their step-by-step directions: it instructs wayfarers mechanically to walk "two f. beyond Brailes, the right acute; at the entring Oxfordshire, the left to Stratford; 4 f. beyond North Newton, the right to Doddington" and so forth.[48] *The Traveller's Pocket-Companion* is soberly matter-of-fact – no illustrations adorn it, and there is virtually no discussion of landmarks and merchandise except for a caption to the map on the last page. It is for the traveler, perhaps, but certainly not for the tourist.

With the nineteenth century, publishers the world over acknowledged the rise of popular recreational travel and made guidebooks for *tourists*. In antebellum America, where the emergence of an upper middle class, changes in the market, the availability of commodities, and improvements in transportation technology prompted the emergence of domestic tourism after the 1820s, travel was the second most popular topic for books, after religion.[49] *The Fashionable Tour or, A Trip to the Springs, Niagara, Quebeck, and Boston, in the Summer of 1821*, one of the earliest guidebooks printed in the United States, offered useful information on prices, distances, recreation, and commercial facilities for those who decided to explore the affordable North American version of the European Grand Tour in upstate New York.[50]

In Western Europe, the peace that followed the end of the Napoleonic wars and changes in transportation also favored the development of the tourist industry at around the same time: whereas earlier travels through the

---

[47] *Traveller's Pocket-Companion*, xiv.
[48] *Traveller's Pocket-Companion*, 12.
[49] Mackintosh, *Selling the Sights*, 9. There were important regional differences, with the Northeast and the old Northwest ahead of the Deep South and the Southwest.
[50] Gordon, "What to See and How to See It," 84.

continent were largely inspired by the personal amelioration of the few (the Grand Tour above all), now movement could also be motivated by the quest for leisure of the many.[51] Guidebooks such as the Murray in England (1836–) and the Baedeker in Germany (1850s–) provided a combination of practical advice and educated references.[52] In Russia, many of these changes occurred at the end of the nineteenth century, facilitated by changes in transportation technology in the 1830s and 1840s and by the emancipation reform of 1861. Despite the slight delay, they followed a similar trajectory: there, too, publishers who had hitherto produced heavily footnoted and didactic-oriented reference books turned to the publication of practical and inexpensive guidebooks with appealing titles for increasingly diverse consumers.[53] To tell the story of late Tokugawa travel books, in short, is to tell the story of the global expansion of the information industry and of the rise of recreational travel.

Travel Books by Any Other Name? Board Games and Mock Rankings

Guidebooks, maps, street-guides, and woodblock prints have been the focus of attention in most studies of movement and travel culture.[54] They were not, however, the only sources of information on the land and the commodities associated therewith. Printed works in other unexpected formats also bespeak the creative strategies of publishers to address the expanding curiosity for, and popularity of, famous sites, sightseeing tours, and travel mementos. These included board games (*sugoroku*) and mock sumo rankings (*mitate banzuke*).

Board games came in an array of themes and layouts – from pilgrimage to success in this life or rewards in the next – but the basic structure was similar for all: a departure point (*furidashi*); a journey through various stages (*masu*, or "boxes"), which could be actual geographical landmarks or metaphorical life stages; the possibility of facing unforeseen circumstances, from losing a turn to being redirected to a different "box" or being sent back to square one;

---

[51] Palmowski, "Travels with Baedeker," 105, calls this process the "middle-classification of travel."

[52] Murray especially insisted on directing gazes toward a site's historical heritage, "showing more clearly not just what ought to be seen, but how it should be appreciated." Palmowski, "Travels with Baedeker," 108.

[53] Anisimov, Bekasova, and Kalemeneva, "Books That Link Worlds." See also McReynolds, "Prerevolutionary Russian Tourist."

[54] See Shively, "Popular Culture," 735–41; Goree, *Printing Landmarks*; Traganou, *Tōkaidō Road*.

and finally the arrival at one's destination or life goal (*agari*). Travel-themed games in particular contributed to the dissemination of knowledge about roads and landmarks, events and merchandise, concisely and by way of immediately accessible visual representations. For example, in *Sugoroku of the Excursions to the Famous Sites of Edo in the Four Seasons* (*Edo meisho shiki yusan sugoroku*, illustrated by Utagawa Kuniyasu, nineteenth century), the traveler departs from Nihonbashi on New Year's Day, admiring the first view of Mount Fuji, and moves along a series of seasonally significant landmarks: the plum blossoms in Kameido (early spring); the cherry blossoms in Ueno (late spring); the fireworks at Ryōgoku (summer); the rice plants in Ōji, bush clovers in Hagi, and first autumn winds at Eitaibashi (fall). The final stop is Asakusa twelve months later, in the midst of an impossibly crowded year-end market (winter).[55] Not only a guide to the spaces of the city, this is also an excursion through its rhythms and traditions.

While this may not have been the explicit intent of the publishers, travel-themed board games could be seen as distilled guidebooks. Not unlike guidebooks, they were often produced with a target audience in mind: the tourist seeking famous sites; the travel fiction aficionado wishing to recreate the adventures of fictional characters such as Kita and Yaji along the Tōkaidō highway;[56] the pilgrim on their way to a sacred site (or to paradise, even); or the gourmand eating their way to a destination. Not unlike guidebooks, these games represented the land – be it all of Japan, a region, or a city – in a dizzying variety of ways: as a sequence of stages, a wonderland of vistas, a continuum of commodities, and a symphony of seasonal scenes. And, not unlike guidebooks, they recorded distances between stages and alerted prospective travelers about the presence of important landmarks, facilities, and obstacles: teahouses, towering mountains, bridges, checkpoints, or river crossings, for example. They depicted wayfarers on the go and merchandise on the move – the flow of people and things made available at a glance, with little need for elaborate explanations.

Despite their inventiveness, however, board games aimed for the familiar and predictable. Most had similar titles – *Along the Fifty-Three Stations of the Tōkaidō* (*Tōkaidō gojūsantsugi dōchū sugoroku*) is a classic – and perpetuated standard associations. If the departure point is Nihonbashi – as is almost

---

[55] *Edo meisho shiki yusan sugoroku*.

[56] Kita and Yaji are the protagonists of Jippensha Ikku's *Shank's Mare* (*Tōkaidōchū hizakurige*), a story of travel misadventures originally published in installments between 1802 and 1811.

always the case with games unfolding along the Tōkaidō highway – invariably a daimyo parade will be depicted crossing the bridge; in Mishima, a torii will hint at the presence of the famous shrine. Innovation was not the point; the point, rather, was the celebration of a travelscape that was immediately recognizable, open for business, and accessible to all.

Mock rankings spoofed the lists of winners and losers issued in conjunction with sumo tournaments (*sumō banzuke*, also descriptively known as "lists of victories and defeats," *shōbuzuke*). Such lists ranked wrestlers from highest (*ōzeki*, or champion) to lowest (*maegashira*) and divided them into an Eastern and a Western division – purely symbolic and unrelated to geographical provenance. In the vertical Edo-style rankings, still in use today, Eastern and Western divisions were placed to the right and left of a central divide (*hashira*, or pillar) that named referees, organizers, and judges. In the Kansai-style programs, the Eastern and Western divisions were arranged horizontally, one on top of the other. A similar format was used in Kabuki playbills to announce forthcoming plays – titles, plots, the names of the actors, and the location of the theater, as well as illustrations of key scenes – and in prints that commemorated the parades at major religious festivals, describing the participants and the order in which they had marched.[57]

Mock versions of these lists first appeared in the late eighteenth century and reached the height of popularity in the early nineteenth.[58] Formatted as regular rankings, they substituted wrestlers, festivalgoers, and actors with curious objects, must-see locations, or important events. Some were simple and practical (the best teachers in town, the dos and don'ts in case of an earthquake or a disease outbreak), others whimsical and playful (*Things That Appear to Exist, but Don't, and Things That Do Not Appear to Exist, but Do [Aru yō demo nai mono, nai yō demo aru mono]*): the former include heaven and hell, ghosts and spirits, and women of talent; the latter, a female impersonator's penis, a flea's testicles, and people having children past the age of sixty).[59] They all cataloged, assigned value, and helped prioritize.

Some mock rankings also promoted knowledge of the realm and its sites, from the best festivals or hot springs to the most impressive rivers, mountains, or temples. Some ranked the features of one city (see Figure 15.1), others compared multiple locales. For example, *An Even Comparison of What Makes the Three Cities Proud* (*Makezu otorazu sanganotsu jiman kurabe*, 1840) took many of

[57] Aoki, *Ketteiban*, 7.
[58] Aoki, *Ketteiban*, 11.
[59] Kunkunbō, *Azuma miyage*, vol. 5, frame 8.

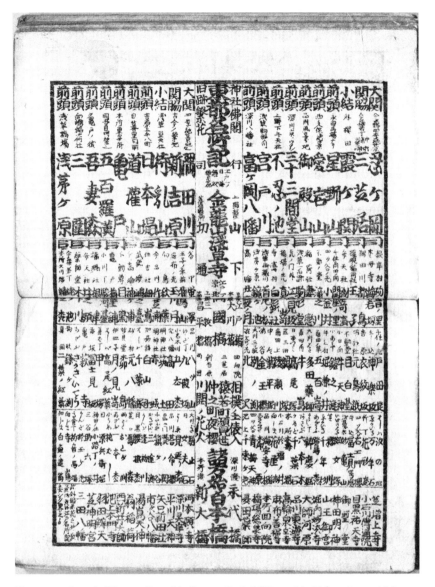

Figure 15.1 *Record of Famous Sites of the Eastern Capital* (*Tōto meishoki*, late 1840s–1860), a mock ranking comparing over 150 famous Edo sites; the champions are the Sumida River and Shinobugaoka (Ueno). In *Edo jiman*, vols. 9–12, frame 46.

Edo's celebrated landmarks (from the Sumida River to the Yoshiwara licensed quarter to Yushima Shrine) and found their correspondents in Osaka and Kyoto (respectively: the Yodo and Kamo Rivers; Shinmachi and Shimabara; Tenman Shrine and Kitano Shrine).[60] Others yet vaunted an all-encompassing coverage of "all provinces" or of "Great Japan." Many openly advertised themselves as virtual travel guides with titles or subtitles such as *Stand-Alone Guide of the Roads from Osaka to All Provinces* (*Ōsaka yori shokoku e dōchū hitori annai*, 1840) or *Compendium of the Famous Sites of All Provinces* (*Kuniguni meisho tsukushi*, Edo, n.d.).[61] Whereas itineraries and board games offered a gradual approach, introducing each landmark as the traveler/reader/player moved along the road, and whereas guidebooks encouraged the reader freely to skip sections and roam, with rankings the emphasis is on established priorities: the best first, the rest to follow. The progressive sense of discovery of itineraries and board games and the serendipitous sightings of guidebooks are replaced here by immediate certainty. The impatient or indecisive traveler, one suspects, would have benefited from these ranked lists in choosing future destinations.

The one-page format and relatively small size of mock rankings (on average, the same as a modern-day newspaper) did not preclude the inclusion of an astonishing amount of information: at over 150 entries, the ranking in Figure 15.1 is impressive but not extraordinary, for other rankings feature over 200 and even as many as 300 entries. Take for example *Mock Sumo [Program] of the Luxuriant Flowers in Each Province of Great Japan* (*Dai Nihon kuniguni hanka mitate sumō*, Osaka, 1840).[62] The "luxuriant flowers" to which the title alludes are splendid locations that the denizens of Osaka ought to visit, as many as 222 (with thirteen more added in the central section). The publisher and the skilled carver of the woodblock even managed to include the distance of each site from Osaka and the name of the province in which each site was located. A typical entry reads: "Second rank [of the Eastern Division], at 75 ri [from Osaka]: Kanazawa in Kaga" or "Third rank [of the Western Division], at 174 ri [from Osaka]: Kumamoto in Higo." (One ri is about 3.9 kilometers.) *Mock Ranking of Famous Places and Historical Sites of Great Japan* (*Dai Nihon meisho kyūseki mitate sumō*) advertised almost 180 spectacular sites throughout the country, from seasonal landscapes to architectural marvels. The champions are Mount Fuji and Lake Biwa; other entries include the cherry blossoms in Yoshino, Suma Beach, Amanohashidate, and the Sumida River.[63]

[60] Reproduced in Aoki, *Ketteiban*, 126.
[61] The former is reproduced in Aoki, *Ketteiban*, 96. The second is mentioned in the same work, 21.
[62] Reproduced in Aoki, *Ketteiban*, 96.
[63] Kunkunbō, *Azuma miyage*, vol. 3, frame 9.

Board games and mock rankings were never meant to replace itineraries and guidebooks but contributed to the collective conversation about the realm, its sites, and its products. With their visual components and simple lists, they simplified the process of gathering information about the movement of people and things.

The Flow of Things

Travel entailed the purchase and consumption of commodities. The print industry thus promoted the notion that the flow of people was to be complemented by the flow of things; that movement had a material aspect to it; and that excursions through sites of past greatness were no different from excursions through centers of present prosperity. The publishers of illustrated guidebooks treated locations associated to the production and sale of goods with the same enthusiasm they reserved for sites made famous by historical events or literary references. Others printed detailed compendia of regional specialty products. Some did both: Osaka bookseller Kawachiya Tasuke, who was behind the publication of illustrated guidebooks to the famous sites of Kii (1811, 1812, 1851) and Shikoku (1814), and of the thirty-three stages of the pilgrimage circuit in the western provinces (1852), also financed the publication of a guide to the agricultural and artisanal products of the Kinai region (*Gokinai sanbutsu zue*, 1813) illustrated by artist Ōhara Tōya (1771–1840).[64]

Directories of regional businesses included in travel itineraries cataloged commercial activities for the benefit of traveling merchants. *A Mirror of Merchants of the Azuma League* (*Azumakō akindo kagami*, 1855) centers on the northern cities of Hirosaki, Morioka, Yamagata, Yonezawa, Tsuruoka, and Sendai.[65] It lists post towns, wholesalers, and retailers, though it occasionally departs from its business focus to direct travelers to hot spring resorts (so they can stay healthy while on the road) and religious landmarks. The introduction celebrates commerce as a veritable vocation (a Way with a capital W, no less) whose benefits are reaped by all:

> The so-called four classes – samurai, farmer, artisan, and merchant – all have their merits. Among them, merchants have, since the age of the gods in the distant past, followed the teachings of Hiruko no Kami [the god of wealth, Ebisu], expanding the Way of Buying and Selling and of the public good around the world.... In these peaceful times, is it not thanks to merchants

---

[64] Fujikawa, "Meisho zue o meguru shoshi," 46–47.
[65] Imai, *Dōchūki shūsei*, 41:235–392.

that grains, clothes, the many utensils and things people use in their daily lives as well as [exotic things like] Chinese and Dutch medicines are delivered to all provinces, even the remote ones?

Having established the universal and quasi-philosophical merits of the marketplace, the focus turns to the actual reader, the merchant planning a business trip, and to what the book can do for them:

> In the castle towns of each province, everywhere in the land, where places prosper, [new] buildings line up one after the other. And yet, many of the merchants who already know what shops [are available], where, and which wholesalers are there, do not ask any further. This [work] organizes [such] information and will be of use as needed. Moreover, acquiring this knowledge will be of great help also to those [who live] along said roads and wish to expand their business. This volume, carved on a woodblock, gives you the opportunity to enjoy your trip, for you will be speaking with those [local] merchants knowing in detail the name of their store and even the emblem on their curtain.[66]

Board games also blended movement with consumerism. Titles such as *Sightseeing the Famous Products of the Eastern Capital* (*Tōto meibutsu yūran sugoroku*, 1861), *Famous Products of Great Edo: A New Edition* (*Shinpan Ōedo meibutsu sugoroku*, 1852), or *A Guide to the Trendy Goods within the City Limits: New Edition* (*Shinpan gofunai ryūkō meibutsu annai sugoroku*, 1847–52) transformed sightseeing into sampling, exploration into shopping. They reimagined the cityscape as a marketplace, the road as a retail paradise. Even when they were not explicitly organized around the topic of regional specialties, some dropped occasional tips on famous merchandise and delicacies.[67]

Meanwhile, mock rankings classified local products just as eagerly as they did famous sites – evaluating the place of the textiles of Kyoto against that of the whale meat from Tosa or the prostitutes of Shinagawa. *Compendium of the Famous Products of All Provinces* (*Kuniguni meibutsu tsukushi*, Osaka, n.d.) lists almost 200 different specialty items from across the country.[68] *Sumo Ranking of the Products of Great Japan* (*Dai Nippon sanbutsu sumō*, Osaka, 1837) ranks the luxury goods and mundane specialties that one could find in Osaka, and in doing so provides a rich gallery of the many commercial items that circulated

---

[66] Imai, *Dōchūki shūsei*, 41:239–40.

[67] See, for example, Odawara and its *uirō* in *Tōkaidō gojūsan eki meishoiri shinpan dōchū sugoroku* (Along the fifty-three stations of the Tōkaidō, landmarks included, new edition, illustrated by Keisai Eisen).

[68] In Aoki, *Ketteiban*, 116.

around the archipelago – silk from Kyoto and Hachijōjima (the two champions), dried bonito from Tosa, kelp from Matsumae, *chirimen* crepe from Tango, sugar from Satsuma, Asakusa seaweed, Suruga bamboo crafts, dried mullet roe (*karasumi*) from Tosa, Seto pottery, Hiroshima oysters, sweetfish from Kyoto, and more.[69]

The extent to which publishers synthesized and simplified information about the land and its products through visual expedients is best exemplified by a map of Japan preserved in a collection of ephemera from around 1840–60. Here, each region or province is transformed into its specialty product: Ise thus becomes a lobster, Owari a giant radish, Shinano a bowl of soba, Tosa a horse, Awa a candle, and so on – the entire archipelago, from the far north (imported Chinese fabrics for Ezo) to the southern islands (potatoes for Ryukyu), is a rich if chaotic assortment of products and commodities.[70]

Because it constantly publicized the importance of sampling regional products and of securing local souvenirs, commercial print culture normalized two ideas. The first was that certain places equaled certain commodities: the two were inseparable. The "famous product" complemented – sometimes even *made* – the "famous site." So extensive was the overlapping of the two that, in writing about a flood that had hit Fukagawa and Susaki in 1791, nineteenth-century chronicler Saitō Gesshin also considered its impact on the local specialty, cold soba noodles (*zaru soba*).[71] The second notion was that local products were meant to circulate: among the joys of travel, a nineteenth-century mock sumo ranking explicitly listed the fact that "people love it when one brings home rare specialty products from each province as souvenirs."[72] It would not have been unthinkable for a nineteenth-century Edoite to dine at a restaurant specializing in food from the fifty-three stages of the Tōkaidō highway,[73] or to find Kyoto's Gion tofu or Osaka's pickled turnips in their neighborhood store; for the fishmongers of Osaka to sell oysters imported from Aki; or for a shop in Osaka Dōtonbori to ship its famed roasted rice cakes (*okoshi*) to all the provinces west of Kyoto.[74] Asakusa seaweed from Shinagawa was shipped throughout the land, while people from all over the country took home the straw knickknacks of Ōmori village as

[69] In Kunkunbō, *Azuma miyage*, vol. 3, frame 12; Aoki, *Ketteiban*, 15 n7.

[70] *Edo jiman*, vols. 9–12, frame 59.

[71] Saitō, *Bukō nenpyō*, 2:8.

[72] *Shibaizuki tabizuki enkutsuron* (1852) in Kunkunbō, *Azuma miyage*, vol. 5, frame 11.

[73] Saitō, *Bukō nenpyō*, 2:133.

[74] Kitagawa, *Kinsei fūzokushi*, 1:199, 249, 263, 288. The author specifically refers to Gion's tofu and to Dōtonbori's rice cakes as "famous specialty products" (*meibutsu*).

souvenirs.[75] Even in the midst of the 1867 social upheaval known as *eejanaika*, during which reports of miracles drove people into the streets to dance in celebration and in defiance of the authorities, someone returned home after an impromptu visit to the Ise Shrines bringing back not only talismans, as expected, but also Ise seaweed "as a souvenir."[76]

Infrastructural innovations facilitated the shipment and transportation of goods. A system of relay couriers (*hikyaku*) had been established in 1663; by the late Tokugawa, couriers were widely used and relatively inexpensive. The cost depended both on distance and on the direction of travel (outbound or returning, uphill or downhill). Transportation fees were a matter of great interest, it appears, for they are discussed not only in travel diaries, itineraries, and guidebooks, but also in ethnographic accounts (such as Tsumura Sōan's *Tankai*, 1795) and collections of curiosities (such as *Morisada's Miscellany*). Sōan informs us that shipping one packhorse load (36 *kanme* equals 135 kg) of luggage from Edo to Kyoto cost about 250 silver *monme* in the late eighteenth century. The other way around, it would cost 13 *monme* per *kanme* of weight – the same packhorse load would thus cost almost twice as much.[77] Morisada reports that, within Edo, "municipal couriers" (*machi hikyaku*) traveling outbound from Nihonbashi to Shiba in the southwest of the city or to Asakusa in the northeast charged 24 *mon*; an inbound or returning trip from Itabashi toward Hongō, however, cost 50 *mon*. Couriers traveling from Edo to other provinces charged by the distance: 100 *mon* per *ri* if going to nearby provinces, 124 per *ri* if going to distant ones.[78]

The detail and extent of the information provided in travel books heightened some travelers' expectations: Osaka merchant Hiranoya Takebei (1801–79), who went to Kyushu on business in 1846, wrote with disappointment about packhorses that failed to show up on time, about locations where he could not hire enough of them to transport his luggage, and about the discrepancy between expectations and reality at a certain landmark ("the shrine looks nothing like the way it is described in the texts"),[79] demonstrating that by the nineteenth century the version of the land as it appeared in printed works – prosperous and perfectly interconnected – was taken to be the standard to which reality had to conform.

---

[75] Saitō, *Shintei Edo meisho zue*, 2:160–63.
[76] Mutō, "Shin hakken no 'eejanaika' shiryō," 25.
[77] Tsumura, "Tankai," 239.
[78] Kitagawa, *Kinsei fūzokushi*, 1:242.
[79] Wakita and Nakagawa, *Bakumatsu ishin Ōsaka chōnin kiroku*, 210, 212, 215.

Movement and Gender

A disjunction between printed works and reality that Hiranoya failed to notice, unsurprisingly, pertained to the experience of female travelers. Women, too, partook in early modern recreational travel: they visited hot spring resorts, temples and shrines, sites of historical and poetic resonance, and busy cities. They read guidebooks (there is evidence that the wives and concubines of the Owari domain lord owned copies of Akisato Ritō's *Illustrated Guide to the Famous Sites of the Tōkaidō Road*),[80] composed poems before famous vistas, and spent money purchasing souvenirs, staying at inns, and hiring porters. They wrote travel diaries and memoirs in which they often reimagined their place in society thanks to the temporary release from the ordinary afforded by movement.[81] In many cases these works were published; at a minimum, they were shared within a circle of friends. Women did not, however, write commercial guidebooks or itineraries. Male authors of guidebooks "for women" decided which sites women should see along the road, and why. Produced under the guise of travel books, some works simply perpetuated gender norms but offered little concrete advice for prospective travelers: their content is more useful to learn about gender expectations than the dynamics of women's journeys.

For example, *Famous Sites of the Capital for Women* (*Onnayō Miyako meisho*), published in Kyoto by Ogawa Genbei in 1815, is a guidebook, textbook, and manual all at once.[82] As a guidebook, it offers a concise history of Kyoto, starting with the capital's transfer from Nagaoka in 794; describes the creation of various landmarks; directs visitors to the capital's iconic sites; and advises on the best places to enjoy the changing of the seasons. Inserts complement the main text with lists of all kinds: the key sites organized by roads that run north-south and roads that run east-west; the provinces of Japan; or twenty-two major shrines, to name a few. Illustrations of famous sceneries (such as the Golden Pavilion or Daimonji-yama) in both color and black and white embellish its pages.

But *Famous Sites of the Capital for Women* is much more than a guide to the city: it is a guide that helps women navigate through life. Flipping through its pages, female readers will improve their writing skills, learning, for example, the most commonly used Chinese characters for textiles, clothing items, fish, birds, insects, trees, and flowers; and the characters most compatible with women's names. They will acquire mathematical skills as well, for the

---

[80] Kornicki, "Women, Education, and Literacy," 30.
[81] Nenzi, *Excursions in Identity.*
[82] *Onnayō Miyako meisho.*

volume features a multiplication table next to a list of the proper poetic names for the months of the year. The schooling in poetry composition extends to include examples of seasonal poems and samples of the verses to pen upon leaving home. Lastly, *Famous Sites of the Capital for Women* is also a how-to manual, with advice on divination and the interpretation of dreams; directories of auspicious days to complete important tasks and of unlucky days when one should abstain from all activities; and instructions on what to do when one has a bad dream, or a good one. With *Famous Sites of the Capital for Women*, a stroll through the famous sites of Kyoto is treated less as an exceptional departure from the quotidian and more as a general education requirement, part and parcel of a woman's upbringing. Like the ability to do math, write, or tell "pine" from "plum," sightseeing was incorporated into the fold of gender education.

At least *Famous Sites of the Capital for Women* contemplated the possibility of sightseeing. Other "guidebooks" for women barely acknowledged their interest in travel and delivered heavy-handed educational lectures instead. Such was the case with a book written by Kyoto author Ikeda Tōri and published in Kyoto and Osaka under the title *Most Valuable for Women: A Comprehensive [List] of the Capital's Landmarks (Joyō shihō: Miyako meisho zukushi, 1824).*[83] Ikeda authored travel guides and educational books; in this particular work, he combines the two genres. Here we find an imbalanced combination of travel advice (minimal), didactics (abundant), and general life coaching. Illustrations throughout the work often depict women outside and on the move – visiting shrines with children, entering huts in seemingly remote locations, enjoying the chirping of insects in the fields, and even traveling to sell firewood. There is a history of the capital (which "originated in the age of emperor Kanmu") and of its landmarks and a gallery of its celebrity denizens. But the reader expecting an actual guidebook will be disappointed: information on distances, specialty products, prices, or directions is missing. There are no maps.

Rather than a tour of Kyoto, this is a tour through the expected life course and educational trajectory of an obedient girl. The volume opens with a disquisition on the ten styles of poetry (*waka jittei*), followed by explanations about the various sizes of paper onto which poems ought to be written; the game of *go* and its origins; the components of various musical instruments (the samisen, the koto); the Tanabata festival; and more. There are sections on "rules for women" (*onna hōshiki*); on Ogasawara-style origami, lest one

---

[83] Ikeda, *Joyō shihō.*

mistakes the male and female styles of folding paper; and on how to tie knots. There is a list of appropriate names for girls based on the five elements and – toward the end of the book, as a telling culmination of sorts – a chart listing compatible and incompatible combinations for prospective couples based on the five elements: an "earth" man, we learn, is suitable for a "fire," "metal," or "wood" woman but never for a "water" or "earth" one. In the end, *Most Valuable for Women* appears to be less about visiting landmarks and more about landing a husband. At a time when women took to the road in significant numbers, some published works suggested that the best course of action for them was actually to stay put.

In Western Europe, the writings produced by women on the move were printed and occasionally *repurposed* as guidebooks (for all, irrespective of gender). In the preface to *The Lady's Travels into Spain* (London, 1774), for example, the editor extols the author, the Countess of Danois, as "perfectly well qualified to describe with accuracy the follies and accomplishments, the vices and virtues of a people amongst whom she resided several years."[84] Her stories, of the "I went, I saw, I sampled, I connected with the past" variety, would have indeed been of great interest for prospective travelers; however, what the countess had originally penned was not a guidebook but a series of detailed letters to her cousin, an enthusiastic armchair traveler.[85]

Published guidebooks in general, it has been argued, empowered European women travelers to escape domesticity and explore, independently, new horizons: as Jan Palmowski points out, the Baedeker and the Murray functioned as "great emancipatory tool[s]" for Victorian women.[86] However, with very few exceptions (Mariana Starke's 1824 *Travels in Europe between the Years 1824 and 1828*, published by Murray, comes to mind), proper guidebooks written by women would not circulate in Europe until the end of the nineteenth century.[87]

The Measure of Success

In the absence of precise statistics and sales records, a good measure of the success of a genre is the existence of parodied versions. While merchants and poets skimmed through the pages of guidebooks to prepare for their journeys,

---

[84] *Lady's Travels into Spain*, vi.
[85] As the countess puts it, addressing her cousin: "you love to travel without going out of your closet." *Lady's Travels into Spain*, 210.
[86] Palmowski, "Travels with Baedeker," 115–16.
[87] Proteau, "'Not Your Ordinary Guidebook.'"

armchair travelers read mock versions of travel guides whose language replicated, tongue-in-cheek, that of legitimate texts, and thus embarked on imaginary adventures along a series of transfigured landscapes, topsy-turvy worlds, and "delusional sites" (*meisho* 迷所, a pun on "famous sites," or *meisho* 名所).[88]

Those with salacious proclivities, for example, figuratively descended upon an eroticized Tōkaidō armed with *A Diary of Rubbing Thighs* (*Hizasuri nikki*, 1855, illustrated by Utagawa Kunimaro). In providing information about roadside amenities, famous sites, and distinct products of each post town, *A Diary of Rubbing Thighs* recasts the road in sexual terms: in Hodogaya, travelers are reminded of the proverb according to which "the women of Sagami go up Shinano hill, but do not go down on the men from Musashi"; at the Hakone hot springs, "the water is so clean one can see all the way to the bottom: the private parts of men and women are visible to the eye"; when the prices of commodities are listed (tea in Kawasaki, for example), they include both the regular cost and the surcharge for "room service." As with any reputable guidebook, *A Diary of Rubbing Thighs* provides anecdotes from the classics and snippets of history but rewrites them to add lascivious (if bogus) detail: the deeds of historical actors and legendary characters such as ninth-century courtier Ariwara no Narihira, twelfth-century warrior Minamoto no Yoshitsune, or even the fictional Oguri Hangan involve exciting encounters with the local girls, bouts with venereal disease, or both. About the Hōjō warrior family of Odawara, travelers should know that the clan founder suffered from erectile dysfunction and "his family jewels and his prick were all shriveled up and useless." The town of Odawara indeed owes its name to his being "inconclusive" (*odawara hyōjō*). Etymological gems of this kind, based on homophones and puns, abound: the site of Senbonmatsu (lit. "1,000 pine trees") near Numazu, for instance, was named after the heroic deed of a local prostitute who "took 1,000 customers in one night, which is to say, she took wood 1,000 times." Even local specialties are revisited in a comical/erotic key: they either provide stamina for all-night lovemaking, like the eel of Hara; can be used as sex toys, like the strings of rice dumplings (*dango*) from Mariko; or – if elongated in shape like the taro stems of Kanbara or "convoluted inside" like the turbo shells of Kurasawa – work as perfectly acceptable surrogates for male and female parts.[89]

One may be tempted to dismiss *A Diary of Rubbing Thighs* and other such guidebook parodies as lowbrow works catering to the unsophisticated. In

---

[88] Goree, "Fun with Moral Mapping."
[89] Higashiōji, *Tōkaidō gojūsantsugi hizasuri nikki*.

fact, they speak volumes about the successful process whereby commercial publishers made knowledge of the realm and its products accessible to all. To enjoy parody, readers would first have had to be familiar with the anecdotes from the historical and literary past that were being spoofed. They would also have had to recognize the guidebook format as an established genre and appreciate the comedic departure from the standard that parodies entail. Lastly, they would have had to be fluent in the idiom of travel – concepts such as "famous place," for instance, or "fifty-three stages," or "local specialty." That by the mid-nineteenth century this was not an unthinkable expectation shows the extent to which the print industry had succeeded in establishing a shared knowledge of an interconnected archipelago.

Conclusion

Educational primers for girls disguised as travel books, mock rankings of specialty items, guides for merchants and poets, board games organized around real-life routes, and excursions in parody all exemplify the extent to which the print industry recognized the pervasiveness of travel as a cultural and social practice. Not just pervasiveness, in fact, but prominence. Consider *Eccentric Debate: Theater Lovers versus Travel Lovers* (*Shibaizuki tabizuki enkutsuron*, 1852), a horizontal mock ranking where "those who like theater" (at the top) argue in favor of their preferred pastime and "those who love travel" respond (at the bottom).[90] Theater fans open up the discussion: "If you watch a play, you will learn and retain wisdom for the rest of your life." To which travel lovers reply: "There is a proverb that says, if you love a child, send them on a journey: travel does you good." Travelers neglect to admire the fall foliage at Yoshino because they are too distracted setting up their gear, quip theater fans; theatergoers are to be pitied, travelers retort, for they are content with a flabby tinfoil prop and never experience the beauty of the real moon shining over the beach in Suma or Akashi. "There is nothing more spring-like than the splendor of the billboard for the *ninokawari* (second month) productions," theater fans rebuke. "When it comes to the pleasures of the springtime, though, nothing beats going on a pilgrimage to Ise under a calm sky," respond travelers. The battle goes on, both sides deploying an arsenal of humor, wit, and lyrical proficiency. When necessary, however, they also bring practical and even scatological concerns into the mix. Who is more pitiful, they argue: a girl traveling by boat who has nowhere to relieve

---

[90] In Kunkunbō, *Azuma miyage*, vol. 5, frame 11.

herself, or a theatergoer who, despite being in the proximity of a toilet, still has to hold it through the end of a long play? The way in which the debate is set up, with the theater side making its point first and the travel side rebutting it afterward, favors the latter: travel enthusiasts always have the last word. Movement, in the end, wins.

Hara Jun'ichirō has identified the Tokugawa-era development of a culture of information (*jōhō bunka*) as one of the leading factors that transformed travel into a bona fide cultural phenomenon, one distinctly different from the wanderings of medieval pilgrims, merchants, and artists.[91] For such a culture of information to develop, the print industry was essential. Thanks to the relentless output of commercial publishers, by the final century of the Tokugawa era knowledge of the land and of its features was extensive and accessible.

It was not just information that was offered widely and cheaply. Publishers produced their own constructions of space, participating in a process whereby borders were redrawn for the travelers' consumption. When publications such as *Edo meisho zue* (1834–36) treated Kanazawa (Musashi Province) as a famous site of Edo and presented it matter-of-factly as part of the larger Edo area,[92] or when Akisato Ritō argued, in *Miyako meisho zue* (1780), that he purposefully incorporated scenic areas of Ōmi Province into the fold of Kyoto in the interest of "draw[ing] sequences that would extend uninterrupted,"[93] they effectively envisioned a land whose contours did not always mirror those from the maps of officialdom. The idea that leisure travelers deserved new conceptions of space was echoed in Europe, where an 1850 testimonial to Thomas Cook acknowledged that "the spirit of pleasurable enterprise is not bounded by landmarks of countries."[94]

Intertwined in a mutually supportive relation, movement and the print industry made each other's success possible. Sometimes the endorsement of an author and a publisher was enough to propel a hitherto unknown site to fame: no one had heard of Koganei village, writes Saitō Gesshin, until geographer Furukawa Koshōken (1726–1807) mentioned its cherry blossoms in his *Shishin chimeiroku* (1794). After that, everyone descended upon Koganei in the spring, brush in hand, and guidebooks (*michishirube*) to the site were published in large amounts.[95] Likewise, late nineteenth-century publishers in

---

[91] Hara, *Edo no tabi*, 34.
[92] Saitō, *Shintei Edo meisho zue*, 2:323–53.
[93] Cited in Shirahata, "Printing of Illustrated Travelogues," 205.
[94] *Testimonial to Mr. T. Cook of Leicester.*
[95] Saitō, *Bukō nenpyō*, 2:25; Furukawa, *Shishin chimeiroku*.

Russia had the power to direct visitors to inhospitable regions by describing them in glowing terms in their guidebooks ("the wholesome but harsh climate of the Arkhangelsk Governorate restores and buoys up the traveller's physical strength").[96] A site ignored by travel guides could languish in a limbo of anonymity and irrelevance. One included, by contrast, was given an identity, associated to a material commodity, linked to a constellation of other sites, represented through images and icons, referenced in charts, and overall elevated to the rank of famous place. Such was the power of the print industry to move people and things, democratize knowledge, and reflect the global expansion of leisure travel and information.

Bibliography

Anisimov, Evgenii V., Alexandra Bekasova, and Ekaterina Kalemeneva. "Books That Link Worlds: Travel Guides, the Development of Transportation Infrastructure, and the Emergence of the Tourism Industry in Imperial Russia, Nineteenth–Early Twentieth Centuries." *Journal of Tourism History* 8, no. 2 (2016): 184–204.

Aoki Michio. *Ketteiban banzuke shūsei*. Kashiwa Shobō, 2009.

Berry, Mary Elizabeth. *Japan in Print: Information and Nation in the Early Modern Period*. Berkeley: University of California Press, 2007.

Edo jiman. 12 vols. 1840–60. National Diet Library. https://dl.ndl.go.jp/info:ndljp/pid/11223544

Edo meisho shiki yusan sugoroku. n.d. National Diet Library. http://dl.ndl.go.jp/info:ndljp/pid/1310735

Fujikawa Reman. "Meisho zue o meguru shoshi no dōkō: Ogawa Tazaemon to Kawachiya Tasuke." *Edo bungaku* 42 (2010): 38–49.

Furukawa Koshōken. *Shishin chimeiroku*. 3 vols. 1794. Waseda University Library. http://archive.wul.waseda.ac.jp/kosho/ru04/ru04_00229/

Gordon, Alan. "What to See and How to See It: Tourists, Residents, and the Beginnings of the Walking Tour in Nineteenth-Century Quebec City." *Journal of Tourism History* 64, no. 1 (2014): 74–90.

Goree, Robert. "Fun with Moral Mapping in the Mid-Nineteenth Century." In *Cartographic Japan: A History in Maps*, edited by Kären Wigen, Sugimoto Fumiko, and Cary Karacas, 108–11. Chicago: University of Chicago Press, 2016.

Printing Landmarks: Popular Geography and Meisho zue in Late Tokugawa Japan. Cambridge, MA: Harvard University Asia Center, 2020.

Hara Jun'ichirō. *Edo no tabi to shuppan bunka: Jisha sankeishi no shinshikaku*. Miyai Shoten, 2013.

Higashiōji Taku, ed. *Tōkaidō gojūsantsugi hizasuri nikki*. Gabundō, 1984.

Ikeda Tōri. *Joyō shihō: Miyako meisho zukushi*. 1824. Tokyo Gakugei University Library. https://d-archive.u-gakugei.ac.jp/libraries/iiif-curation-viewer/index.html?manifest=/iiif/item/10814081/manifest.json&lang=ja

---

[96] Anisimov, Bekasova, and Kalemeneva, "Books That Link Worlds," 194.

Imai Kingo, ed. *Dōchūki shūsei*. 47 vols. Ōzorasha, 1996–98.

Jansen, Marius B. "Japan in the Early Nineteenth Century." In *The Nineteenth Century*, edited by Marius B. Jansen, 50–115. Vol. 5 of *The Cambridge History of Japan*. Cambridge: Cambridge University Press, 1988.

Jippensha Ikku. *Shanks' Mare: Being a Translation of the Tokaido Volumes of Hizakurige, Japan's Great Comic Novel of Travel and Ribaldry*. Translated by Thomas Satchell. Rutland, VT: Tuttle, 1960.

Jones, Sumie, with Kenji Watanabe, eds. *An Edo Anthology: Literature from Japan's Mega-City, 1750–1850*. Honolulu: University of Hawai'i Press, 2013.

Kitagawa Morisada. *Kinsei fūzokushi: Morisada mankō*. 5 vols. Annotated by Usami Hideki. Iwanami Shoten, 1996–2001.

Kornicki, Peter F. "Women, Education, and Literacy." In *The Female as Subject: Reading and Writing in Early Modern Japan*, edited by Peter F. Kornicki, Mara Patessio, and G. G. Rowley, 7–37. Ann Arbor: Center for Japanese Studies, University of Michigan, 2010.

Kunkunbō. *Azuma miyage*. 5 vols. 1852. Waseda University Library. http://archive.wul.waseda.ac.jp/kosho/w006/w006_03156/

The Lady's Travels into Spain; Or, a Genuine Relation of the Religion, Laws, Commerce, Customs, and Manners of That Country. Written by the Countess of Danois, in a Series of Letters to a Friend at Paris. London: Printed for T. Davies, 1774.

Mackintosh, Will B. *Selling the Sights: The Invention of the Tourist in American Culture*. New York: New York University Press, 2019.

Marks, Andreas. *Publishers of Japanese Woodblock Prints: A Compendium*. Leiden: Hotei, 2011.

McReynolds, Louise. "The Prerevolutionary Russian Tourist: Commercialization in the Nineteenth Century." In *Turizm: The Russian and East European Tourist under Capitalism and Socialism*, edited by Anne E. Gorsuch and Diane P. Koenker, 17–42. Ithaca, NY: Cornell University Press, 2006.

Meisho waka no michibiki. 1682. National Diet Library. http://dl.ndl.go.jp/info:ndljp/pid/2534141

Miyazaki Fumiko. "An Artist's Rendering of the Divine Mount Fuji." In *Cartographic Japan: A History in Maps*, edited by Kären Wigen, Sugimoto Fumiko, and Cary Karacas, 98–101. Chicago: University of Chicago Press, 2016.

Moretti, Laura. *Pleasure in Profit: Popular Prose in Seventeenth-Century Japan*. New York: Columbia University Press, 2020.

Mutō Makoto. "Shin hakken no 'eejanaika' shiryō: Amakudariki." *Nagoya-shi Hakubutsukan kenkyū kiyō* 24 (2001): 1–40.

Nakagawa Kiun. *Kyō warabe*. 6 vols. 1658. National Diet Library. http://dl.ndl.go.jp/info:ndljp/pid/2554331

Nenzi, Laura. *Excursions in Identity: Travel and the Intersection of Place, Gender, and Status in Edo Japan*. Honolulu: University of Hawai'i Press, 2008.

Onnayō Miyako meisho. 1815. Waseda University Library. http://archive.wul.waseda.ac.jp/kosho/bunko30/bunko30_g0192/

Ōshiroya Ryōsuke. *Gokaidōchū saikenki*. 2 vols. 1858. Waseda University Library. www.wul.waseda.ac.jp/kotenseki/html/ru03/ru03_03617_0053/index.html

Palmowski, Jan. "Travels with Baedeker: The Guidebook and the Middle Classes in Victorian and Edwardian Britain." In *Histories of Leisure*, edited by Rudy Koshar, 105–30. Oxford: Berg Publishers, 2002.

Proteau, Jasmine. "'Not Your Ordinary Guidebook': Gender and the Redefinition of the Nineteenth-Century Guidebook." *Studies in Travel Writing* 23, no. 2 (2019): 119–38.

Rekishi Misuterii Tanbōkai, ed. *"Yoru no Oedo" chizu.* Kōsaidō Bunko, 2007.

Saitō Gesshin. *Bukō nenpyō.* Edited by Kaneko Mitsuharu. 2 vols. Heibonsha, 1968.

Shintei Edo meisho zue. 6 vols. Edited by Ichiko Natsuo and Suzuki Ken'ichi. Chikuma Shobō, 1996.

Shinpan gofunai ryūkō meibutsu annai sugoroku. 1847–52. National Diet Library. http://dl.ndl.go.jp/info:ndljp/pid/1310567/1

Shinpan Ōedo meibutsu sugoroku. 1852. National Diet Library. http://dl.ndl.go.jp/info:ndljp/pid/1310566

Shirahata Yōzaburō. "The Printing of Illustrated Books in Eighteenth Century Japan." In *Two Faces of the Early Modern World: The Netherlands and Japan in the 17th and 18th Centuries*, edited by Shirahata Yōzaburō and W. J. Boot, 69–83. Kyoto: International Research Center for Japanese Studies, 2001.

——. "The Printing of Illustrated Travelogues in 18th-Century Japan." In *Written Texts –Visual Texts: Woodblock-Printed Media in Early Modern Japan*, edited by Susanne Formaneck and Sepp Linhart, 199–213. Amsterdam: Hotei, 2005.

Shively, Donald H. "Popular Culture." In *Early Modern Japan*, edited by John Whitney Hall, 706–69. Vol. 4 of *The Cambridge History of Japan*. Cambridge: Cambridge University Press, 1988.

Testimonial to Mr. T. Cook of Leicester, Manager of Popular Pleasure Trips. 1850. Leisure, Travel & Mass Culture: The History of Tourism. www.masstourism.amdigital.co.uk

Tōkaidō gojūsan eki meishoiri shinpan dōchū sugoroku. N.d. National Diet Library. http://dl.ndl.go.jp/info:ndljp/pid/1310698

Tōto meibutsu yūran sugoroku. 1861. National Diet Library. http://dl.ndl.go.jp/info:ndljp/pid/1310564

Traganou, Jilly. *The Tōkaidō Road: Traveling and Representation in Edo and Meiji Japan.* New York: Routledge Curzon, 2004.

The Traveller's Pocket-Companion: Or, a Compleat Description of the Roads, in Tables of Their Computed and Measured Distances, by an Actual Survey and Mensuration by the Wheel, from London to All the Considerable Cities and Towns in England and Wales; together with the Mail-Roads, and Their Several Stages, and the Cross-Roads from One City or Eminent Town to Another. With Directions What Turnings Are to Be Avoided in Going or Returning on Journeys, and Instructions for Riding Post. To Which Is Annexed, a New Survey-Map, Which Shows the Market-Days, and Remarkable Things; the Whole Laid Down in a Manner that Strangers May Travel without Any Other Guide. Also an Account of the Expences of Sending a Letter or Pacquet by Express from the General Post-Office, with Lots of Time, to Any Part of Great Britain. By a Person Who Has Belonged to the Publick Offices Upwards of Twenty Years. London: Printed for the Author, and Sold by J. Hodges, 1741. British Library. Microfilm Reel n. 786, ESTC Number T12930. Eighteenth Century Collections Online. www.gale.com/primary-sources/eighteenth-century-collections-online

Tsumura Sōan. "Tankai." In *Nihon shomin seikatsu shiryō shūsei*, Vol. 8, edited by Harada Tomohiko, Takeuchi Toshimi, and Hirayama Toshijirō, 3–278. San'ichi Shobō, 1969.

Wakita Osamu and Nakagawa Sugane, eds. *Bakumatsu ishin Ōsaka chōnin kiroku*. Osaka: Seibundō Shuppan, 1994.

Yasumi Roan. *Ryokō yōjinshū*. 1810. Waseda University Library. http://archive.wul .waseda.ac.jp/kosho/ru03/ru03_02485/ru03_02485.pdf

Yorozu kaimono chōhōki. 1692. National Diet Library. http://dl.ndl.go.jp/info:ndljp/ pid/2532535

16

Labor and Migration in Tokugawa Japan
Moving People

AMY STANLEY

The men and women who built the city of Edo were pulled from the countryside. Their parents and grandparents had been conscripted into armies, and now, in a more peaceful age, tens of thousands of them fought heat and exhaustion on a marshy seaside battlefield. Within decades, they turned a crumbling medieval castle into a magnificent fortress and transformed a cluster of lonely villages into a metropolis of half a million residents, hundreds of city blocks, and an astonishing profusion of stores. Along the way, they learned how to live in a city. According to Miura Jōshin's record of those years, *Things Seen and Heard in the Keichō Era* (*Keichō kenbunroku*), the first migrants to Edo were so unaccustomed to hot water bathing that they were afraid to visit bathhouses. They thought the steam was smoke and that they would be burned alive.[1]

Across the archipelago, their counterparts in other places were building castle towns. In Kanazawa, the daimyo Maeda Toshiie created a fortress out of what had been a Buddhist religious center. As he and his family hunkered down in a hastily erected castle, his conscripted laborers erected walls and dug moats. Powerful merchants, skilled artisans, and purveyors were granted advantageous plots of land, and they hired construction workers to build their homes and stores. Soon, new merchants and laborers flocked to the city and settled, first along main thoroughfares, then along the roads, and finally in immediate outlying areas, until the city took on the shape of a starfish with its arms extended from a compact center. Some of the newcomers sold medicine and rice cakes, jelly candy, and household utensils. Others, poor people with few skills and nothing to sell, worked as day laborers or engaged in unskilled piecework.[2]

---

[1] *Keichō kenbunroku*, quoted in Konno, *Edo no furo*, 15–18.
[2] McClain, *Kanazawa*, 32–45.

Meanwhile, in the mountains, other workers hauled silver out of mines to finance the construction. They, too, were migrants. At Akita domain's Innai silver mine, which first opened in 1606, only the people who did basic manual labor were locals. The rest – prospectors, skilled miners, smelters, refiners, and metalworkers – came from elsewhere. Singing and dancing women came from the city of Kyoto, following the medieval tradition of peripatetic entertainers. Others, who were sent to brothels to work as prostitutes, had been seized by raiding armies in wartime and sold to human traffickers. Together, these men and women – many of them "hicks and bumpkins who only yesterday were covered in mud," according to the mine's chronicle – formed a town of seven or eight thousand people by the 1610s. They, too, had to learn a new way of life, structured by the exigencies of mining.[3]

This pattern was repeated over and over again over the two-and-a-half centuries of the Tokugawa period; people migrated, cities grew, and new patterns of work emerged, and these cycles accumulated until the institutions that structured labor were themselves transformed. By the time of the Ansei earthquake in 1855, Edo encompassed over 1,700 city blocks, nearly five times as many as those early migrants had constructed at the beginning of the seventeenth century.[4] When the city burned, at least 14,000 structures were lost.[5] In the aftermath, men and women gathered to build Edo, just as they had in the beginning. But now, centuries after the original construction, the laborers were no longer rural conscripts under the command of samurai. Instead, they were poor peddlers who temporarily shifted to working construction or manual laborers (ninsoku) under the control of labor bosses (hitoyado).[6]

By this point in the nineteenth century, migrants who came to Edo from the countryside – either to help with the rebuilding or to seek other kinds of work – traveled from places that had changed just as much as the big city. Most peasants still labored in fields or on fishing boats, just as they had in the early Edo period. But others worked in rural towns. They staffed post station inns, wove silk and hemp, brewed sake, processed safflowers, packed cargo onto ships, printed designs onto textiles, dried seaweed, and produced mounds of fluffy cotton batting. There were also those who, like their medieval predecessors, made lives out of wandering. By now, they were greater in number and more diverse. They were itinerant sumo wrestlers, beggars, prostitutes, dancers, acrobats, peddlers, and players.

[3] Stanley, *Selling Women*, 27, 35–36.
[4] "Edo no han'i"; Yoshida Nobuyuki, *Dentō toshi: Edo*, 107.
[5] Smits, "Shaking Up Japan," 1045.
[6] Kitahara, *Jishin no shakaishi*, 222–28.

Over the course of the Tokugawa period, the Japanese landscape had been formed and reformed by the movement of labor as much as by the ravages of floods and fires: first by the demand that drew new people into cities and towns, then by the new physical and social structures that contained them. Meanwhile, the space of the archipelago was traversed in new ways by markets that evaded political boundaries and connected by technologies of communication that linked families and large businesses across wide expanses. The institutions that controlled and mobilized labor were also transformed: while those early deployments of labor in construction and mining had been at least partially controlled by samurai overlords and mediated by status, by the nineteenth century the labor market was more diverse and specialized, involving intermediate layers of bosses and boardinghouses. With the important exceptions of herring fishing in Ezo (Hokkaido), sugarcane farming on the Amami Islands south of Kyushu, and prostitution everywhere, it relied less on forced recruitment, but it was controlled through different kinds of coercion.[7]

Although the mass migrations of the seventeenth century were long past, and the rapid urbanization of the early twentieth century was still far in the future, labor and mobility were tightly linked throughout the Tokugawa period. Merchant houses, samurai households, and small-time labor bosses all moved people from one place to another – from countryside to city, or in circuits through seaports and villages. Work-related mobility became so routine that it inspired new patterns of thinking on the part of ordinary people. Those who watched their neighbors leave, or saw newcomers arrive, could imagine that different types of lifestyles were possible, in new places, and that work would make them attainable.

The World of the "Great Stores" (Ōdana)

Every year, a group of eleven- and twelve-year-old boys traveled from Ōmi Province to the Shirokiya store in the Nihonbashi district of Edo, where they would begin jobs as apprentices. They were all from the area surrounding Nagahama village, which had been the home of the Shirokiya conglomerate's founder, Ōmura Hikotarō (1636–89), who opened the Edo branch of the store in 1662. He had started out dealing in lumber, but then diversified into clothing and dry goods, and his flagship in Nihonbashi was one of the city's representative "great stores" (ōdana), ranking along with the great Mitsui

---

[7] Howell, *Capitalism from Within*; Stanley, *Selling Women*.

Echigoya. Both enterprises counted well over a hundred employees in their Edo branches.[8] As a rule, the store did not recruit management employees from Edo; city natives were restricted to "kitchen" jobs involving manual labor. For important work, the store relied on recruits from elsewhere, particularly Ōmi, so every year two adult men had the unenviable job of escorting an unruly group of future apprentices on a long trip to Edo. According to lore, they carried nearly a hundred pairs of straw sandals so that the boys could change as their shoes wore out.[9] As they traveled from station to station, changing shoes, they were joined by similar groups of village boys heading to city apprenticeships. Other urban firms, including Mitsui Echigoya and the Kyoto-based clothing store Naraya, also recruited new workers from their founders' ancestral villages in the countryside.[10]

This yearly migration of boys was only one of the many ways in which merchant enterprises moved people across space. In one sense, the great stores of Edo and the Kamigata district around Kyoto and Osaka were notable for their staying power. They dominated entire city blocks for hundreds of years. Shirokiya survived as a department store into the twentieth century; Mitsui Echigoya still operates in Nihonbashi under the name Mitsukoshi. But the flagship stores, with their iconic bright banners, relied on the movement of labor to create this impression of permanence. The conglomerates exerted both centripetal and centrifugal forces: they pulled employees into the city and then pushed them out into the provinces.

Once apprentices came to the main stores, they stayed for several years as they learned the trade. At Naraya, they were required to live in the store, unmarried, until they reached their late thirties. While in residence, they were required to dress according to house specifications: usually, the standard was striped cotton livery for younger boys and a steadily increasing range of wardrobe options as they were promoted through the ranks.[11] Typically, these clothing upgrades were associated with carefully organized trips home or to the main store. Shirokiya's Edo apprentices were not permitted to travel until their ninth year in service, when they were finally allowed to join a group trip to Ōmi to see their parents. They always carried the same gifts, prescribed by the store's rules. At the first visit, they could bring handkerchiefs worth three gold *bu* for their parents, and cheaper ones for other friends and relatives. At

---

[8] Nishizaka, *Mitsui Echigoya hōkōnin*, 14; Aburai, *Edo hōkōnin*, 16–19.
[9] Aburai, *Edo hōkōnin*, 16–19.
[10] On Naraya, see Sakurai, "Perpetual Dependency," 118; on Mitsui Echigoya, see Nishizaka, *Mitsui Echigoya hōkōnin*, 101–3.
[11] Aburai, *Edo hōkōnin*, 154–55; Sakurai, "Perpetual Dependency," 120–24, 125, 132.

the sixteen-year visit they could bring striped cloth worth thirty silver *monme*; at retirement they could take home whatever they liked.[12] Although the trips were a kind of vacation, they also allowed the store to advertise its success, and to assure parents of future recruits that their boys would be safe in the company's care.

This style of urban migration and labor organization was quite different from the situation in mining towns, which also tended to draw unmarried male workers from other places. Like the large merchant houses, the prospectors who controlled seams of silver or copper deposits needed to integrate an unsettled population, reconcile them to the rhythms of a new kind of work, and encourage them to cultivate an occupational identity that might keep them in place. Newcomers, who flowed into the mine from the villages or from other mines, often lived communally in barrack-like structures, but they were tied to mine operators, often living in families, who commanded their labor through ties of patronage. The newcomers formed bonds of fictive kinship with other miners who taught them the job, and which obligated them to care for one another when they were ill, elderly, or otherwise unable to work. Eventually, the identity of "miner" became fixed so that recent migrants were of lesser status than those who had come from other places and had already been initiated into the fraternity of miners, which crossed the boundaries of individual towns.[13]

The great merchant households, facing similar problems, approached recruitment and retention differently. They inculcated new recruits in a culture of belonging to the individual firm, using the discipline of literacy, which was largely unavailable to miners. Although most recruits came in knowing how to read and write, they received further instruction during their apprenticeships. At Shirokiya, apprentices were required to spend the evenings studying; they were forbidden to use the time to play board games, which were only allowed on holidays such as the New Year.[14] In addition to learning basic accounting and abacus calculations, apprentices often memorized the precepts of their store's founder, which, ideally, would inculcate loyalty and serve as a guide to conduct, no matter where and in which capacity an employee ended up working. *The Collection of Family Regulations* (*Kanai shikihō-chō*, 1694) compiled by Mitsui Takahira (the son of the Mitsui firm's founder) was supposed to be read aloud to employees twice a month. It contained instructions for everything

---

[12] Aburai, *Edo hōkōnin*, 30–32.
[13] Ogi, *Kinsei kōzan*, 12, 39–41.
[14] Aburai, *Edo hōkōnin*, 192.

from good management and careful inventories to security procedures and the selection of appropriate hair ties.[15] Shirokiya employees were warned not to skip monthly meetings, sleep late, or skulk around in odd corners of the store.[16] At Naraya, the house precepts addressed mundane matters of consumption and hygiene in elevated language. Employees were told that enjoying food was "the worst of disloyalty and unfilial conduct." "You should serve by taking your employment seriously," the rules continued, "without forgetting for a moment the depth of obligation you owe your parents, for it is true that your father and your mother's mercy begins with your birth."[17]

Even when the applications of literacy seemed to be focused narrowly on the business at hand, they also served to build community. New employees at large firms such as Mitsui and Shirokiya memorized their house's proprietary codes: each business had a different set of characters or syllables that it used in place of numbers in its confidential memos. At Shirokiya, apprentices also memorized the secret language that company men used to speak to one another. Sake was *maruya*; cash was *tamahen*.[18] This unorthodox nomenclature was central to their identity as employees of the main firm, and, of course, useless in any other business (unless the clerks went on to share their knowledge as a form of corporate espionage).

Merchant firms, suspicious of their competitors, also tended to be much more careful than mining prospectors about recruitment. Mines were desperate for labor, and they had an open-door policy, taking all comers without asking any questions about their background.[19] It was always far easier to enter a mine than to leave. In contrast, the great stores were picky and more likely to rely on personal ties, as the example of importing boys all the way from a founder's village suggests. But this careful screening applied even when the stores did not engage in long-distance recruitment. Firms that were originally founded in Edo, such as the used clothing dealer and pawnshop operator Minoya, which was based near Nihonbashi in Tōriabura-chō, tended to draw apprentices and clerks from the city and its outskirts. New employees came recommended by business associates or branch households, and their origins tended to overlap with the areas where Minoya bought and sold clothing: the textile weaving town of Kiryū; Tomizawa-chō, the site of

---

[15] Berry, "Family Trouble," 226–27.
[16] Aburai, *Edo hōkōnin*, 140–41.
[17] Sakurai, "Perpetual Dependency," 120.
[18] Aburai, *Edo hōkōnin*, 108–10.
[19] Ogi, *Kinsei kōzan*, 37.

Edo's famous used clothing market; and a cluster of villages in Kazusa Province where the fourth head of the family, who was adopted, had grown up.[20] As the Edo period wore on, even stores that had deep roots in the provinces began to expand their networks. For example, the Kyoto branch of Mitsui Echigoya drew 22 percent of its new employees from its original province of Ise in the first three decades of the eighteenth century. By the 1770s and 1780s, that number had fallen to 4 percent, as more and more hires were made in the city of Kyoto itself.[21] The smaller Kyoto store Naraya, also founded in Ise, followed a similar trajectory.[22]

Whether recruits were fresh from the countryside or sophisticated city natives, the moment of hiring was not an end to mobility. Store employees often found themselves traveling to new places in the course of their work. Newly promoted clerks moved to collect bills from various places in the city, learning the vast metropolis as they passed through unfamiliar neighborhoods. Management employees with more experience went further afield. Shirokiya designated some clerks as "purchasing managers" (kaiyaku) who traveled through the Kantō region visiting markets and buying up silk. They stayed on the road for months at a time, patronizing designated "silk inns" (kinujuku) that stored their inventory and arranged for transportation. The "countryside managers" (inakayaku) went as far as Tōhoku on business trips, and they could be away for the better part of a year.[23]

Employees' pay was variable and usually tied closely to length of service. The Mitsui system is an instructive example. Apprentices were hired on contract, with the promise that they would receive a lump sum at the end of their service, which would climb higher the longer they served. This payment was called "start-up money" (motode), presumably because it allowed retirees to invest in new businesses of their own. But only those who graduated from their apprenticeship would ever see this money, and roughly half did not make it through their term. If they entered the ranks of clerks (tedai), they received "pocket money" (kozukai) at the beginning of every year. This was meant to be spent on necessities: employees were required to spend it all, not save it, and they received more with every year served and every promotion: the amounts ranged from 160 silver monme for first-years to over 2,000 for

---

[20] Iwabuchi, "Ōdana," 147–56. Other stores hired through employee and branch house referrals. Sakurai, "Perpetual Dependency," 118; Nishizaka, Mitsui Echigoya hōkōnin, 53, 58–61, 104–5.

[21] Nishizaka, Mitsui Echigoya hōkōnin, 103–4.

[22] Sakurai, "Perpetual Dependency," 118.

[23] Aburai, Edo hōkōnin, 90–98.

managers. Clerks also received yearly bonuses, and senior employees were granted special allotments (*warigin*) every three years. But the largest payouts were reserved for the end of service, when "retirement money" was added to the originally promised "start-up." Calculated in the abstract, an employee who had completed decades of service could retire with a substantial sum, but most had also accrued debts by overspending their pocket money, so the end-of-term payment was much smaller.[24]

When the clerks finished their terms of service, which could last decades, most of them probably stayed in the cities where the stores were located. Some were fortunate enough to begin branch families, which meant they could marry and establish firms of their own. Unless a clerk was staggeringly lucky and was adopted as heir to the main business, this was probably the best outcome he could imagine. But the vast majority of former clerks were less successful. A surprising number who retired with the backing of their houses ended up failing in business. Others finally returned home to the provinces and lived out the rest of their lives in a place they had not seen for decades. The most common fate was to live somewhere in a city tenement, hopefully finally married, living off the remainder of a meager salary.[25]

This typical life cycle of the large merchant house clerk became a less dominant pattern over the course of the late Edo period, as different kinds of small- and medium-sized businesses started to hire locally and on shorter terms, and even the large heritage firms diversified their employment practices. Saitō Osamu argues that Edo and Osaka diverged on this front: while Osaka enterprises clung to the older model, Edo businesses were more flexible, and that city's population was more dynamic as a result. Edo's workforce, which had been composed of transient armies of apprentices, shifted in the direction of smaller, more stable families. Because families reproduced, Edo's population climbed slightly in the second half of the period, while Kansai cities stayed stable or declined.[26]

But hiring cohorts of young men as store clerks was not the only way in which the large firms mobilized labor. First, and most obvious, many stores were also households, and they required domestic and reproductive work.

---

[24] Nishizaka, *Mitsui Echigoya hōkōnin*, 160–62.

[25] Sakurai, "Perpetual Dependency," 125–32.

[26] Saitō, *Shōka no sekai, uradana no sekai*, 71. Even when the large firms clung to their former practices, they became less influential. For example, as late as 1864, the Kyoto branch of Mitsui Echigoya was still so dependent on male laborers that its presence in Kyoto's Reisen-chō skewed that neighborhood's gender ratio in favor of men, for a total of 206 men and 93 women. Yet the total number of (male) employees had significantly declined over the preceding decades. Nishizaka, *Mitsui Echigoya hōkōnin*, 24, 43.

In general, the "inside" of the household, as opposed to the store, was a more feminine realm, but the gendered division was not absolute. Famously, Mitsui Takatoshi, the founder of the Edo branch of the Mitsui firm, owed his start in life to his mother, Shuhō, a formidable woman who took over the family business in Ise after her husband, whom she had married at the age of thirteen, proved to be more interested in poetry than commerce. A century later, Mine, the mistress of a medium-sized merchant household in Waka-yama, managed properties and collected rent on behalf of her husband, while also raising a son and dealing with cooking, cleaning, and laundry. Her work on the "inside" of the household also benefited the firm: later in life, when she had graduated from mother to mother-in-law, she received an average of sixty-two guests every month. This overwhelming schedule of entertaining was probably crucial to forming the face-to-face relationships that sustained the business.[27]

When it came to servants, however, merchant houses rigorously enforced the distinction between "store" employees and "household" employees. Men worked in both realms, but women only occupied the latter. Like clerks, maidservants tended to be hired through trusted city employment brokers or directly from the individual merchant house's own home territory. Otherwise, if they were migrants, they tended to come from the provinces that surrounded the cities.[28] Unlike the clerks, however, they tended to be hired on very short contracts, for half a year or a year at most, and they moved around fairly often. They were not subject to the same programs of training and acculturation, and they did not need to be literate.

The great merchant households also mobilized labor indirectly. Many operated subsidiary businesses, often run through branch houses, which were loosely connected to the main operation. Mitsui, a famous example, ran money-changing businesses in addition to its original clothing store (see Gaubatz, Chapter 19, this volume). But even smaller outfits diversified their holdings. The used clothing store Minoya also ran a series of pawnshops, which were often established with capital from the main business. Thus, the pawnbrokers' clerks were also employees of Minoya even though they were not affiliated with the primary business.[29]

---

[27] Makita, "Shōka josei no rōdō," 151–53.
[28] Iwabuchi, "Ōdana," 152; Makita, "Shōka josei no rōdō," 157–59; Nagata and Hamano, "Marriage Market in Early Modern Kyoto." Mitsui Echigoya's Kyoto branch manservants tended to come from Nōto and Kaga, even as the store apprentices came from the city itself. Nishizaka, *Mitsui Echigoya hōkōnin*, 62–63.
[29] Iwabuchi, "Ōdana," 143–46.

Beyond their own subsidiary companies, the great merchant houses also held sway over a number of businesses that operated in a penumbra around them. Sometimes this influence was marked on the streetscape. The scroll painting *Kidai shōran*, which portrays the Nihonbashi district around the turn of the nineteenth century, depicts temporary stalls doing business in front of most of the stores facing the main thoroughfare. But Mitsui Echigoya is a notable exception: the street in front of the store's famous blue banners is empty. As Yoshida Nobuyuki suggests, this was a negative manifestation of the firm's power: its deep relationships with the city's peddlers allowed it to prevent small-time operators from blocking its storefront.[30]

Conversely, the great firms stimulated the growth of the smaller businesses that were their suppliers and sometimes their customers. For example, Mitsui Echigoya maintained a complicated relationship with the vendors in Edo's used clothing market, Tomizawa-chō. From its founding in the seventeenth century, Mitsui used the Tomizawa merchants as an outlet for unsold stock – items that had lingered too long on the shop floor or were priced too high to sell. Eventually, Mitsui also started buying items from the Tomizawa brokers so that it could stock its main floor quickly and cheaply. It also started a business selling clothing directly from its stockroom to Tomizawa dealers (and other middlemen who specialized in marketing to specific clienteles). As a result, many of the used clothing dealers, as well as people who depended on them – laundresses and tailors who fixed up old clothes before they were sold, peddlers who bought from the dealers and sold directly to city consumers, middlemen who purchased used clothes and sold them again to vendors outside Edo, and traveling salesmen in the countryside – found themselves indirectly connected to the operation of a great merchant household.[31]

Since most large firms owned land and buildings far beyond their flagship stores and subsidiary businesses, they also employed people in their real estate ventures. Mitsui Echigoya operated between eighty and a hundred Edo city plots during the second half of the Tokugawa period, which it originally accumulated as collateral for its money-lending businesses. These plots typically contained two or three street-facing stores, rows of tenement rooms, and a communal well and outhouse.[32] Beyond Edo, the company also owned several city lots in Osaka.[33] This pattern of diversification through real estate

[30] Yoshida Nobuyuki, *Dentō toshi: Edo*, 252.
[31] Sugimori, "Furugi shōnin."
[32] Yoshida Nobuyuki, *21-seiki no Edo*, 19–21.
[33] Yoshida Nobuyuki, "*Kamiyui Shinza*," 18–19.

holdings was typical even of the smaller "great stores": the used clothing firm Minoya held five Edo lots as well as shares in a hairdressing business.[34] As (typically absentee) landlords, the stores hired building superintendents (*yamori*) who were responsible for collecting rents, dealing with tenants, and handling communication with the city magistrates' offices.[35]

The position of building superintendent is a good example of how the relationship between capital and labor changed over the course of the late Edo period. Originally, the hiring of a superintendent was a straightforward transaction between the landlord (sometimes one of the great merchant firms) and an individual paid to perform the job. But superintendent positions were coveted because they came with both the regular salary from the landlord and the rights to collect various types of fees, including thank-you gifts from tenants and the proceeds from the sale of night soil from tenement latrines. By the nineteenth century, there were about 20,000 superintendent positions in Edo, and investors in the countryside started to buy shares (*kabu*) in them, entitling them to a portion of the associated income. Increasingly, the person who lived in Edo and performed the tasks of the superintendent was separate from the business that held shares in the position.[36]

This movement of provincial capital into the cities was, in some ways, the continuation of the pattern set by firms such as Shirokiya, which originated in Ōmi in the seventeenth century and then set up urban outposts. But by the late Tokugawa period, rather than moving labor from countryside to city in order to operate a business in the capital, rural firms could specialize in investment: they could buy shares in urban businesses or purchase city real estate, keeping most of the personnel and the main base of operation close to home.[37] Yet these rural corporations were still tied into the operations of the older "great stores" that were landlords and the smaller urban firms that were renters.

In that sense, concentrating on employees in flagships of the great stores – the boy apprentices and salesmen writing out receipts on the shop floors – does not account for the complexity of the large merchant households' operations. Nor does it adequately express how many lives and livelihoods they held in their grasp. Building superintendents collected rent for Mitsui, tenement families who made cotton batting worked for Mitsui suppliers, maidservants washed floors in small households affiliated with the main

---

[34] Iwabuchi, "Ōdana," 139.
[35] Yoshida Nobuyuki, "*Kamiyui Shinza*," 18–19.
[36] Yokoyama, *Edo Tōkyō no Meiji ishin*, 76–77.
[37] See the example in Yokoyama, "Expanding and Multi-Layering Networks."

branch of the Mitsui business, used clothing peddlers traveled the countryside selling Mitsui's castoffs, and prosperous rural entrepreneurs bought shares in positions that collected salaries from Mitsui. At first glance, the main enterprise looked like a group of men who started off as apprentices at city stores, learning the house code and wearing cotton uniforms. In reality, it encompassed many more men and women, doing more varied work in far-flung places.

Samurai Households

Like the big mercantile conglomerates, samurai households were institutions that organized labor and moved people across space. The most visible expression of this function was the daimyo retinue: the parade of retainers and laborers, mounted on horses and marching on foot, that accompanied domain lords on their travels. The policy of alternate attendance, which required daimyo to move back and forth between their castle towns and Edo residences, ensured that large groups of warriors traversed the realm on a regular basis. In the most extreme cases, daimyo retinues could contain over 3,000 men.[38] Many of these people did little more than carry spears and boxes, but the ability to recruit, feed, outfit, and transport so many people and animals was a testament to the daimyo's power and an important symbol of his prestige. For the men who traveled on this assignment, bolstering the lord's image in the realm was, in itself, a form of labor.

The kinds of work performed under the status designation and officially recognized occupation of "samurai" could vary widely. In part, this was because the tasks of governance were distributed unevenly. Some men had too much to do, and others were left without any official function and without a sufficient stipend to support them. The occupants of certain positions – the local intendant (*daikan*) or, famously, the Edo city magistrate – were overwhelmed with administrative work. People pointed out that the latter posting was the most onerous in the land, and that those who were appointed to it tended to die of exhaustion while in office. On the other end of the spectrum, a middle-ranking samurai such as Asahi Bunzaemon, who kept a diary of his life in Owari domain at the turn of the eighteenth century, was tragically underemployed. He inspected the tatami mats in the castle and spent a few days a month on guard duty; otherwise, he was free to attend the theater, drink vast quantities of sake during the day, and write all about local gossip.[39]

[38] Vaporis, *Tour of Duty*, 74–77.
[39] Kosaka, *Genroku otatami bugyō*.

Meanwhile, members of the shogunate's reserve force (*kobushingumi*) were even more idle: they actually paid the shogunate a fee for the privilege of being allowed to do nothing.

Other kinds of work also fell under the category of "samurai," because the nominal lord-retainer bond was being used to signal close affiliation, providing social cover for a more straightforward, more temporary economic relationship. This was the case with the employment of sumo wrestlers, who were often brought into daimyo households as low-ranking retainers, probably because the ability to wrestle (unlike, for example, performing Kabuki) seemed to bear some relationship to military skill. At the beginning of the period, sumo wrestlers were either the domain's peasants, who showed unusual ability and were recruited into the retainer band, or existing retainers who also had other functions. By the middle of the era, however, as Edo's sumo scene flourished, daimyo were recruiting directly from the city stables and making temporary retainers out of men who would return to the city after a few years of entertaining the lord and instructing his men in sumo. Unlike other retainers, paid in rice bushels or the rights to fief income, they were paid in cash.[40]

The sumo wrestlers were a highly skilled, outlying example of the more common phenomenon of hiring temporary labor to serve in samurai households. These men were brought in not as stipended retainers but as "servants" (*buke hōkōnin*). Like the designation of "samurai," with which it partially overlapped, this category, too, could contain many different types of work. Some carried palanquins, and the shogunate tended to refer to them as "loincloths" (*rokushaku*) after their manner of dress. Others performed various kinds of menial labor in and around samurai households; they were gardeners, cleaners, cooks, and handymen. A few were better educated and dealt with errands and correspondence; others were hired to work as bodyguards because they were skilled in the martial arts or just generally intimidating. Some men of this nature were hired as "subsidy assistants" and sent to bannermen's fiefs to bully peasants into paying more taxes. Another group – subject to a separate set of rules and often wearing a different type of dress – served as the firefighters attached to daimyo mansions.

Originally, many daimyo brought their servants with them from the provinces when they came to Edo on alternate attendance, and the large, wealthy domain of Kaga followed this practice throughout the period. This

[40] Takano, "Kakae sumō."

was a problem, however, because it was so expensive, and by the nineteenth century, the servants who had been in Edo for a long time made themselves into self-styled labor bosses commanding gangs that were difficult for the domain to control.[41] Other domains entirely abandoned the practice of bringing in local peasants for labor, since those who wanted to abscond to the city soon realized that if they joined the alternate attendance retinue, the domain would subsidize their trip. They often disappeared into Edo and were never heard from again.[42]

To avoid these problems, by the eighteenth century most domains had started hiring servants in Edo and employing them on short-term contracts. These men were dispatched from boardinghouses (*hitoyado*) that gathered rootless, itinerant men, then found them temporary employment and took a cut of their earnings. In the Hongō neighborhood of Edo, where the Nakasendō highway funneled newcomers from the northwest into the heart of the city, boardinghouses dispatched touts to line the streets. They listened for the provincial accents of recent arrivals and led them away, promising work.[43] Although the recruits themselves were usually completely unskilled, the boardinghouses tended to specialize in different markets: some concentrated on daimyo mansions, others supplied only firefighters, and others dispatched day laborers for cart drivers, rice polishers, and construction.

Boardinghouse masters had a rough reputation, which stemmed from the brutal competition to collect fees from a group of highly mobile men with no particular allegiances. Houses were often at odds with one another, as laborers would abscond from one house – still owing money – and flee to a different one. In one notable incident in 1848, two firefighters broke into a boardinghouse, beat up the cook and the master's wife, cut off the master's arm, and poured boiling water on all the household's plants. It turned out that the firefighters were defending the business of a rival boardinghouse, which was run by the heavily tattooed grandson of a famous gambler. Questioned about the incident, he coolly replied, "Taking in bad guys and vagrants is my job."[44]

Samurai households also employed women, but the recruitment mechanisms were different. While Edo did have some boardinghouses for women (*onna yado*), they did not send women to the interior of samurai houses. Instead, women who wished to enter service with Edo bannermen and housemen could find positions via ordinary employment agencies and

---

[41] Morishita, "Kaga-han Edo hantei."
[42] Morishita, "Kaga-han Edo hantei," 194, 196; Miyazaki, *Daimyō yashiki*, 20.
[43] Yoshida Nobuyuki, *Mibunteki shūen to shakai*, 255.
[44] Yoshida Nobuyuki, "Hitoyado," 216–17; Yoshida Nobuyuki, "*Kamiyui Shinza*," 54.

through private recommendations. For example, in 1839, a temple daughter named Tsuneno, who had run away from her village in Echigo, found a job as a maid-of-all-work in a bannerman's household by inquiring at a storefront employment office. She soon discovered that several women had already cycled through the position, probably because of the staggering workload in a household that contained nine women.[45]

The procedure for entering the women's quarters of the shogun or a prominent daimyo was much more complicated. For many women from the countryside, this was a type of finishing school, intended to provide a soon-to-be-married girl with instruction in the manners of her social betters. In fact, families paid dearly for the privilege of placing their daughters, first through providing the kind of education that was likely to yield the girl a good place, then by compensating the go-between who would vouch for her suitability, and finally by paying for all the kimono and accessories that she would need to be presentable in her new post. But this did not mean that the women were idle and decorative. Depending on their status and level of education, they served as messengers, entertainers, chambermaids, fire wardens, and transaction agents.[46]

Most of these posts were "service" in the sense that the women involved performed various tasks and errands on behalf of their employer but some of them also entailed reproductive labor, which was crucial to the perpetuation of the samurai house. If a samurai died without an heir, his household could be dissolved. For high-ranking households with several retainers, or, to an even greater extent, for daimyo, this was a disaster for an entire community that depended on the house for employment. While adoption (even, in some cases, secret post-mortem adoption) was a possible work-around, it was still important for samurai households to produce and sustain children. Even extra sons and daughters could be socially and financially useful if they were placed in advantageous marriages.[47] In order to produce this human capital, both samurai and commoner women – physically located in the "interior" of the house – performed reproductive labor for samurai households. In the best case and cheapest scenario, the household head's wife was able to conceive and bear children, one of whom would go on to inherit his father's family name and stipend. In other cases, samurai households could hire concubines to perform this labor for them.

---

[45] Stanley, *Stranger in the Shogun's City*, 123–31.
[46] Hata, "Servants of the Inner Quarters"; Ōguchi, *Edojō ōoku.*
[47] On adoptions, see Roberts, *Performing the Great Peace*; Yonemoto, "Adoption."

The work of a concubine was straightforward – she would have sex with the head of household and bear his children – but the labor arrangements were not. In the Great Interior of the shogun's castle, women who served the shogun sexually were designated separately from those who performed secretarial or artistic functions, but it was clear that both classes of women were servants. Unless a concubine bore a son who eventually became the shogun, she would never be regarded as a member of the shogun's family or be in the position to command servants herself.[48] In ordinary samurai and commoner households, concubines signed contracts that specified their length of employment and how much they would be paid. Naturally, any children they conceived would belong to their employers' households and would remain there long after their birth mothers had moved on. The concubine contract was such a staple of legal culture that it appeared in the "sample documents" section of children's textbooks and was parodied in books for popular audiences.[49]

Samurai households, like prosperous households in all status groups, also employed wet nurses to perform reproductive labor. Their services sustained babies whose mothers had died or who were otherwise unable or unwilling to nurse. Sometimes this unwillingness was a matter of social status: very elite women were not expected to breastfeed. As a result, shoguns nearly always had wet nurses, and some of them were famous for bestowing favor on these women in recognition of the close attachment they had formed early in life. For example, Tokugawa Iemitsu's wet nurse, Kasuga no Tsubone (1579–1643), used her relationship with the shogun to become a powerful political actor in her own right.[50]

While the shogun's house could choose women based on their high status and social connections, high-ranking samurai families were forced to be more pragmatic. Some turned to their own relations, or to lower-ranking samurai within the same retainer band, while those lucky enough to possess fiefs might try to conscript nursing women from their villages, though this was a significant burden on reluctant peasants. For example, Tōyama Shōemon, a high-ranking samurai in Hachinohe domain, struggled to find adequate milk for his newborn son after his wife died in childbirth. Initially, he tried to conscript lactating peasant women to come to the castle town in a ten-day rotation, but his effort foundered when the village headman responsible for

[48] Hata, "Servants of the Inner Quarters," 175.
[49] Jinbo, "Kinsei hōritsu monjo."
[50] Seigle and Chance, Ōoku, 54–64.

dispatching women faced a shortage and, apparently as a last resort, sent a woman who was not lactating at all. Ultimately, Tōyama had to hire a wet nurse in the castle town.[51]

Tōyama's ultimate solution – a contractual arrangement – was the preferred strategy of most ordinary samurai and commoner families. By the late seventeenth century, labor brokers (*kuchiireya*) in castle towns specialized in recruiting lactating women from the countryside and introducing them to employers, and printed books offered advice on how to choose a wet nurse. These women usually earned more money than other types of servants, because they had to be hired on short notice and their work was desperately needed to sustain the next generation. They also had to be provided with adequate diets to support lactation. As a result, the ability to work as a wet nurse could be a lifeline for young widows and others who found themselves with small children and no means of support. Widows and divorcées fled to the city, babies in tow, to seek positions in this kind of service.[52]

The wives and daughters of samurai engaged in productive as well as reproductive labor alongside their servants. Since many low-ranking warriors were unable to make ends meet on their meager stipends, they supplemented their income with an array of by-employments. Some grew azaleas or raised carp; others made straw sandals or umbrellas. The women of low- and middle-income samurai households often made their own clothes, even spinning their own thread and weaving the cloth themselves. It was this investment in domestic and productive labor that allowed the family to stretch its stipend to pay for food and fuel, to hire maidservants to cook and look after children, and to employ attendants to accompany the head of household when he appeared in public.[53]

Peasant Households

Farm labor of various kinds accounted for the majority of work performed on the archipelago in the Edo period. Planting and harvesting rice necessitated an enormous expenditure of energy on the part of both people and animals (either oxen or horses). Typically, labor began in the early spring, when peasants soaked the rice seeds to prepare them for planting. The soaked

[51] Sawayama, *Edo no chichi to kodomo*, 64–68.
[52] Sawayama, *Edo no chichi to kodomo*, 98–101, 109–11, 114; Katakura, "Bakumatsu ishin-ki no toshi kazoku," 87.
[53] Takiguchi, "Bakushin yashiki to Edo shakai," 80–84; Ujiie, *Hatamoto gokenin*, 96; Yoshida Yuriko, *Kinsei no ie to josei*, 170–73.

seeds were sowed in beds, where they were tended for about thirty days until they grew into seedlings. Then, in late spring, men, women, and children set out to till the rice fields, usually with the assistance of horse- or ox-drawn harrows, and then they opened sluice gates and flooded the paddies. At the beginning of the rainy season, women working in groups transplanted the seedlings to the wet fields. Meanwhile, in dry fields, peasants harvested clover (which was used for fertilizer) and planted vegetables and tobacco, making the fifth month a frenzy of activity. Then came the season for weeding and clearing the undergrowth, and finally the harvest in the fall: cutting the wheat, pulling the rice, picking the vegetables, threshing with Chinese-style flails or "thousand-toothed" threshers, polishing rice grains in stone mortars, and preparing straw-wrapped bundles for tax payment.[54]

At the beginning of the Edo period, large compound households managed this work, and some labor was performed by a class of hereditary servants (*fudai*) that served the same house for generations. By the end of the seventeenth century, the large households had mostly dissolved into smaller independent households. This was possible in part because the increasing popularity of cotton liberated women from the onerous labor required to produce clothing out of hemp and enabled them to contribute directly to agricultural endeavors. Typically, husbands, wives, and even children went out to the fields together. Some children played near the fields or climbed trees; others were engaged in the labor of weeding and sowing seeds. Infants went out to the fields, too, dozing on their mothers' or even their grandfathers' backs. Only toddlers, too unruly to be trusted in the paddies, stayed home with elderly grandparents or, occasionally, all by themselves.[55]

The emergence of smaller family units was not a trend toward small subsistence farming. Instead, over the course of the period, wealthy peasants increasingly managed diversified agricultural and commercial enterprises. For example, in the nineteenth century, the peasant household of the political activist Matsuo Taseko, located in the Ina valley of Shinano Province, derived much of its income from activities other than rice agriculture. In addition to farming, the family brewed sake, raised silkworms, operated a ferry boat service, and lent money to other peasants.[56]

Both these larger enterprises and smaller farming households found themselves in need of labor that the immediate family could not provide. If the

---

[54] Mizumoto, *Mura*, 128–33.
[55] Nagashima, "Kinsei josei rōdō," 33–36; Mizumoto, *Mura*, 127.
[56] Walthall, *Weak Body of a Useless Woman*, 88–96.

head of the household was busy running a brewery, then not only did that business require laborers but someone else needed to be out in the fields all day during the planting and harvesting seasons. If the family raised silkworms, then someone needed to be in the shed day and night during the spring, feeding the voracious insects mulberry leaves, while others were planting seedlings. Even if a family concentrated on rice agriculture, there were times of year when several men and women had to work in tandem, and a family with only a few small children could find itself very short of labor. And, of course, if grandparents were not available, someone needed to feed the babies and watch the toddlers.

This extra labor was supplied by paid servants: farmhands, servants, and nursemaids. Most farmhands were employed through a standard contract system in which the servant signed on for six months to a year of work in return for a designated salary, which was paid up front. Because so many of these contracts are still extant, historians have been able to run studies of how compensation changed over time. Their findings lend credence to the complaints of village headmen, who observed that farm labor had become more and more expensive across the generations. In the Tenpō era (1830–44), one village official in Kōzuke Province complained that in the Genroku era (1688–1704) farmers had been able to hire servants on five-year terms for two gold *bu* or ten-year terms for one or two *ryō*. By his time, in contrast, one year of service cost five to seven *ryō*.[57] Part of the explanation for this phenomenon was that, as the village headmen perceived, agricultural employers were competing with more lucrative job opportunities in the cities, and the population of the countryside, particularly around Edo, was steadily declining. By the eighteenth century, even agricultural laborers could choose to move in order to find the best wages.[58]

Compared to male farmhands, female farmhands tended to travel shorter distances and receive lower wages. Their leisure time was also more constrained (with fewer set vacation days), and they were more likely to be employed in both domestic labor and farm labor simultaneously, with their time divided among tasks as their employers saw fit. This was even true of rural women who had been recruited to work in prostitution at provincial post stations: they divided their time between seeing customers, working in the fields, gathering firewood, and taking care of children, depending on their

---

[57] "Akatsuma-gun ka sesō no hensen kakidome," Tenpō era (1829–43), in Gunma Kenshi Hensan Iinkai, *Gunma kenshi shiryō hen*, 11:929.
[58] Howell, "Hard Times in the Kantō."

health status and the seasonal demands of their employers.[59] Only women with particular skills, or who belonged to specialized occupational groups, received wages that approached those of their male counterparts. For example, groups of women who planted rice seedlings, who circulated among villages, received better wages than women who did general farm labor. Their bargaining power came not only because they formed a collective but because the planting of seedlings was gendered labor, and male planters were considered to be bad luck.[60]

The planting women traveled in narrowly circumscribed areas, but their mobility illustrates an important point: although the typical image of peasant labor involves immobility, being tied to the land, some kinds of agricultural laborers moved as a condition of their employment or simply as part of their lifestyle. In the mountains of Ōno domain, for example, some groups of peasants moved seasonally: in summer, they went up into the mountains to cultivate swidden (*mutsushi*), and in the winter they descended into the valleys.[61] These seasonal patterns of mobility were pronounced elsewhere on the Japan Sea coast, too, because the winters were so harsh. In Nagaoka domain, peasant laborers would come from the countryside into town, where they shoveled rooftops and carved tunnels through the snow.[62]

Other kinds of workers also traveled the countryside, shaping their labor into seasonal patterns. For example, the cattle that peasants used to plow their fields were typically leased from cattlemen who circulated among the villages with their animals. In Echigo Province, some of them moved in a seasonal pattern. During the summer, they would bring their cattle around to villages, and in the process, they would pick up salt from the castle town of Takada (near the coast) and deliver it to Shinano Province, which was inland. In the winter, when the snow made it too difficult to drive cattle, they left the animals in the care of mountain villagers and paid them for the service in salt.[63]

All of this circulating labor supported household-based agricultural production, but much of it was not performed within households. The cattlemen and the laborers who carved tunnels, for example, did not travel with dependents but as single men or groups of men, even if they had wives and children elsewhere. Unlike their counterparts who worked as farmhands, they did not register, even temporarily, in a new household.

[59] Stanley, *Selling Women*, 141–42.
[60] Nagashima, "Kinsei josei rōdō," 38–44.
[61] Ehlers, *Give and Take*, 58.
[62] Sugimoto, *Daughter of the Samurai*, 1–2.
[63] Jōetsu Shishi Hensan Iinkai, *Jōetsu shishi*, 551.

The pattern was different for women. Although they, too, moved across the countryside as single people, they did not tend to circulate, but rather moved from one destination to another. This was an increasingly common phenomenon during the late eighteenth and early nineteenth centuries, when textile production in the countryside provided employment opportunities for single young women. For example, workshops in the silk-weaving town of Kiryū in Kōzuke employed women to spin and weave. Partly as a result of their migration, the population of the town tripled between the mid-eighteenth and the mid-nineteenth centuries.[64] In the cotton-weaving town of Okoshi in Owari Province, weaving households counted ninety-seven female employees in 1852, as opposed to only nine male employees. The numbers in a cotton-weaving town in Settsu Province were less dramatic but similarly skewed: forty-one women and nine men, even as farm labor in the same area continued to be dominated by male servants.[65]

Women also migrated to work as prostitutes in provincial port towns and post stations, where the expansion of travel – both commercial and recreational – created a market for sex. Initially, "pleasure quarters" were an urban phenomenon, catering to the heavily male-dominated populations of the new castle towns in the early seventeenth century. But, in the second half of the period, as more commoners started to traverse the realm, the commercialization of agriculture put cash in the hands of peasants, and the expansion of print culture encouraged rural people to aspire to urban lifestyles, brothel districts sprung up in the small towns of the countryside. Post stations began to rely on the spending of pleasure-seeking travelers (and locals) to supplement their budgets, and ports competed with one another to offer sex and entertainment to passing sailors.[66]

Most of the women who were recruited for this type of work came from peasant families in areas where tax burdens were heavy, harvests were poor, and large families were common. Recruiters would arrive in the villages, typically in early spring, when food stores were running low, or in autumn, just before taxes were due, offering up-front payments for long indenture contracts. The sums were heartbreakingly small by urban standards – often a few *ryō* for many years of service – but they made all the difference to struggling peasants trying to survive another season. The indenture contracts generally followed the same form as those for maidservants, but they had a few

[64] Saitama-ken, *Shinpen Saitama kenshi*, 550; Smith, *Native Sources*, 29.
[65] Yabuta, *Joseishi to shite no kinsei*, 203.
[66] Stanley, *Selling Women*, 103–9.

important differences: special clauses guaranteed that no other parties would come forward to contest the indenture, that the employee could be transferred to another brothel without her consent, and that she could be buried at her employer's discretion if she died during her term. In other words, contracts for indentured service in prostitution were more coercive than those for other kinds of work.[67]

One typical pattern of migration was from Echigo Province, on the Japan Sea coast, to Kantō post stations. A woman named Hatsu, who worked as a "serving girl" at Kizaki station on the Nikkō highway, left a rare written record of her experience. She explained that her parents, peasants from Kanbara district in Echigo, had sold her into service so that they could buy medicine for themselves and her younger sister. After a few months working at a post station brothel, Hatsu herself became ill. She had probably contracted a venereal disease. "At night I was sent out to see customers," she wrote, "and in the afternoon when there were no customers, I was sent to the mountains to gather firewood. Since I had no chance to rest during the day or at night, I could not recover from my illness. I would be viciously beaten if I begged my master to be allowed to rest even a little, so I endured and continued to work."[68]

Hatsu's testimony exposed the brutal exploitation that was typical of the sex industry. Even apologists for the pleasures of the "floating world" usually admitted that it was cruel to women. The pseudonymous social critic Buyō Inshi, who professed to be appalled by the entire business, wrote that working in prostitution was "hell for life." Yet, like most of his contemporaries, he also believed that entering service in a brothel could be a beautiful expression of filial piety. "Indeed she goes bravely off," he mused, "wholeheartedly determined, knowing that she can save her parents from their suffering. These are the true feelings between parents and child. And this is as it should be."[69] It was this conception of work in prostitution as service to a household that allowed samurai and peasant elites to justify a system in which women and girls were bought, sold, and trafficked across the realm. It was only when the illusion of filial devotion faltered – either because the women had lost contact with their families or because they were working as independent streetwalkers rather than in "households" that were actually brothels – that prostitutes themselves became the subject of moral outrage.

[67] Stanley, *Selling Women*, 58–59.
[68] Stanley, *Selling Women*, 142.
[69] Teeuwen and Nakai, *Lust, Commerce, and Corruption*, 321.

Labor Beyond the Household

Throughout the Edo period, even as mobility and migration increased, most labor was organized by households, even if, as in the case of huge merchant firms, those households were atypical in their sheer size and complexity. But there were other, older traditions of itinerant labor that carried over from the medieval period and were institutionalized in a new way in the early modern period, and there were also forms of labor mobilization that relied on bosses who controlled groups of unrelated, often single people. These kinds of labor organizations became typical of the urban underclass, especially in the big cities. By the nineteenth century, groups of migrant laborers were an increasingly conspicuous and troublesome presence, hovering somewhere on the periphery of the status system, often unregistered and undercounted, but a source of keen anxiety for samurai officials.

Some forms of labor had never taken the household as their organizing principle because they had their roots in older itinerant patterns. For example, the bands of actors, sumo wrestlers, and prostitutes who traversed the Inland Sea region followed the precedent of medieval entertainers who had traveled along similar circuits centuries earlier. They visited port cities, castle towns, shrines, and temples, often timing their activities to coincide with religious festivals and temporary markets, and their occupational identities did not encompass the entirety of their work. For example, in 1805, a group of sumo wrestlers found themselves under investigation by the Osaka city magistrate's office after they kidnapped three women from an Osaka teahouse master who was on his way to visit a temporary marketplace at Usa Hachimangū in Kyushu. It turned out that the sumo wrestlers had been called in to settle a debt that the teahouse master owed to a local boss who specialized in supplying women to brothels, and they had taken the women as "collateral." These men did wrestle, but they were also mediators, brokers, human traffickers, and purveyors of information. They used their physical strength, capacity for violence, and connections across the Inland Sea to make themselves useful to local powerbrokers, whose ranks included everyone from underworld figures and village headmen to temple priests and samurai officials. Located outside the formal status system, they structured themselves not as a "household" but as a band of underlings who owed their loyalty to a boss.[70]

A similar evolution – from itinerant occupational group to gang-like organization – took place among the men who served as porters along highways.

---

[70] Kanda, *Kinsei no geinō kōgyō*, 10–12, 229–73.

Lords traveling with their retinues, samurai on official business, and domains sending messages between their own castle towns and Edo all depended on the services of these men, who were dispatched from post towns along the highways and used to carry luggage and palanquins. Many had no fixed address, and they were in some sense public employees: they were paid out of the tax revenue collected by the post stations and lodged in the crowded back-rooms of station warehouses. In the latter half of the Edo period, they faced increasing competition from private express services (*hikyaku*) and developed a sideline occupation: highway robbery. In 1744, one private express association based in Edo complained to the shogunate that these porters would wait in ambush along the roads, and when private express carriers crossed into unpopulated areas, they would rob them of their money and luggage.[71]

Not all groups of male laborers engaged in violence, but they did exist in a liminal space outside the structures of households, villages, and city blocks. Many were subject to three levels of control: they owed their allegiance to the boardinghouse masters who found them their jobs, to the "room bosses" who dominated their workplaces, and finally (and most loosely) to their actual employers. All kinds of migrant laborers, not only the servants of warrior houses, found themselves engaged in these labor organizations. For example, in Edo, udon noodle shops hired their noodle-makers (*udon tōji*) from board-inghouses that specialized in dispatching such men. Because it was relatively difficult to learn how to make udon well, the laborers formed hierarchical rela-tionships in which a noodle boss would teach his underlings the trade, and they would all work in the same kitchen. But these organizations were diffi-cult to control within the framework of households. Established noodle shops tried to keep their workers in place, but workers would often abscond to seek work elsewhere or, eventually, set up their own back-alley establishments.[72]

Rootless groups of male laborers provoked anxiety in samurai authori-ties, who relied on these men to maintain samurai households but loathed their contributions to urban disorder. This concern is reflected in the famous return of people edict (*hitogaeshirei*), issued in 1843 as part of the Tenpō reforms. This edict was intended to stabilize the city of Edo's population and bolster the agricultural workforce by returning recent migrants to the countryside. But a close reading of the text of the edict reveals that it was directed not at migrants in general but at male day laborers without families. "There are those who have started businesses [in Edo] and have wives and

[71] Fukai, "Dōchū no hiyatoi," 215.
[72] "Edo no inshoku sangyō."

children," the edict read. "Subjecting them to a general policy of returning people would cause them hardship. Therefore, as an exceptional display of benevolence, they will be added to the census records in the places where they have been residing for a number of years, and they will not be ordered to return to their villages."[73]

Labor organization outside the framework of the household was also a characteristic of Japan's periphery. Over the course of the eighteenth century, Matsumae domain, which monopolized trade with the Ainu on Hokkaidō, began to operate a series of contract fisheries dedicated to herring, which was increasingly in demand as fertilizer for rice fields. Under the contract fishery system, independent merchants would pay a fee to the domain in exchange for a monopoly on "trade" with local Ainu residents: over time, this trade became, primarily, the operation of fisheries using Ainu as well as migrant Japanese labor. The contract-holding merchants usually did not reside in the territory of the fisheries, and sometimes they were not even individuals but corporations that paid wages to laborers onsite. The Ainu workers in the fisheries typically had few other choices. Their subsistence practices had been undermined by the incursion of Japanese settlers and the policies of Matsumae domain, which prevented them from leaving their territory in Hokkaido. Unable to mount effective resistance to the demands of employers, they were paid very little and subjected to brutal exploitation. The labor practices of contract fisheries anticipated capitalism because they relied on wages rather than kinship or indenture. Nevertheless, Ainu workers' imbrication in the political economy of Matsumae domain, which placed severe limits on their mobility and their ability to make choices, meant that they could not freely sell their labor.[74]

Ainu contract fishers, like urban day laborers, worked for wages outside the conventional structure of the household, but they were held to coercive hierarchical relationships, often cemented by debt and violence, that held them in place. Day laborers, who were not subject to the same type of ethnic discrimination and were not tightly integrated into any domain's political economy, found it much easier to slip these bonds and move on to new opportunities. In that sense, the Ainu fishery workers had much more in common with most women who worked in prostitution, who were held to indenture contracts at brothels and did not receive wages at all. It was their structural and legal disadvantage within the Tokugawa polity – as women or as non-Japanese "others" – that proved as important as the labor relation itself

---

[73] Kinsei Shiryō Kenkyūkai, *Edo machibure shūsei*, 14:321.
[74] Howell, *Capitalism from Within*, 24–48.

in limiting their freedom, even as their labor both fueled and responded to early modern commercialization.

Conclusion

Throughout the early modern period, households were the basic unit of social and legal organization, and most productive and reproductive labor continued to occur within the space of and under the auspices of households. Servants were added to household registers, and even straightforward transactional relationships were mediated by the fiction of kinship. The brothels and workshops that employed dozens of women were registered as "households," their employees regarded as household dependents. The large merchant conglomerates, however anomalous in their structure, were also perceived as houses, and the rules that bound employees were "house codes." At the same time, much of what historians would now perceive as domestic labor was monetized and subject to the pressures of commercialization. Wet nurses and concubines were recruited from faraway villages and paid in cash. The story of the second half of the period is one in which the household structure often remained as a method of organizing labor, but its kinship bonds were displaced by wage relations.

At the same time, while the physical household was rooted in place – situated in a village, a provincial town, or a city neighborhood – the household as a structure for organizing labor did not preclude movement across space, and in many cases actually encouraged migration. Daimyo households could not be maintained without the migration of samurai (and, particularly at the beginning of the period, laborers) to and from Edo. Large merchant households, too, relied on the recruitment of boy apprentices from rural villages. And the continuation of even the smallest peasant household meant that marital partners, usually women, had to be brought in from elsewhere to perform domestic and reproductive labor. Meanwhile, as the commercialization accelerated, knitting together ever-larger economic regions, successful household enterprises also sent people back out across the realm to do business, and failing household enterprises indentured women and children to faraway masters in order to save themselves from ruin. Increasingly, labor entailed travel, and the world of the household – and its various members – expanded out from villages and neighborhoods to encompass larger expanses of space. This became a self-perpetuating phenomenon, as individuals perceived the possibilities of lives and livelihoods far away from home and left for far-flung opportunities in cities and provincial towns.

At the same time, the organization of labor within the structure of the household also caused tension between a legal system based on status – in which each household was registered in a particular place, with a defined occupation and a designation such as "peasant" or "samurai" – and a labor market that was increasingly diversified and integrated across regions. A woman who was registered as a "maidservant" in a provincial town might actually have been a prostitute, a cotton weaver, or a maid-of-all-work; a man who was registered as the head of a peasant household in a village might have been a rice farmer, a sake brewer, a fisher, a pawnshop broker, an innkeeper, or a dealer in silk crepe. An Edo "samurai" might have spent most of his time raising prize azaleas in the courtyard of his residence. At the same time, a son or daughter registered in a particular household may have remained on the rolls long after they had actually left for a job far away, and a city boardinghouse might be full of people who had no urban registration at all. It was not only that a person's actual livelihood and designated occupation did not match; it was also that the "household" container could be a fiction bringing together people in different places who engaged in various kinds of enterprises.

Meanwhile, beginning in the nineteenth century, it was increasingly difficult for samurai authorities to ignore the presence of groups of laborers who were not attached to households at all. Their primary bonds were not those of kinship, even fictive. Instead, their organizations featured coercive and violent relations between bosses and underlings, as well as, occasionally, horizontal bonds of solidarity between workers themselves. To make matters worse, at least from the official perspective, they were literally and figuratively difficult to fix in place, with no registry and often no village or city block to contain them. In some ways, this phenomenon represented a continuity from the medieval past, when, as the historian Amino Yoshihiko points out, samurai authorities could never fully exert control over mobile populations of beggars, fishers, traders, and entertainers.[75] But in the early modern period, these unruly labor organizations were also a portent of a very different, capitalist future. The noodle bosses, sumo wrestling gangsters, and highway robbers that caused the early nineteenth-century version of twentieth-century "social problems" would not survive into the modern era in the same forms. At the same time, like the Ainu laborers in contract fisheries, the women working in brothels, the farmhands paid in cash, and the sumo wrestlers who were samurai retainers in name only, they presaged an era in which a more mobile

---

[75] See Amino, *Rethinking Japanese History*. See also Sakurai and Goodwin in volume 1.

workforce would fully escape the bonds of the status system, and wage labor would come to predominate.

Bibliography

Aburai Hiroko. *Edo hōkōnin no kokoroechō: Gofukushō Shirokiya no nichijō.* Shinchōsha, 2007.

Amino Yoshihiko. *Rethinking Japanese History.* Translated by Alan Christy. Ann Arbor: University of Michigan, Center for Japanese Studies, 2012.

Berry, Mary Elizabeth. "Family Trouble: Views from the Stage and a Merchant Archive." In *What Is a Family? Answers from Early Modern Japan,* edited by Mary Elizabeth Berry and Marcia Yonemoto, 217–38. Oakland: University of California Press, 2019.

"Edo no han'i." Tokyo Metropolitan Archives. www.soumu.metro.tokyo.lg.jp/01soumu/ archives/0712edo_hanni.htm

"Edo no inshoku sangyō." In *Edo: 1838–1841,* edited by Tokyo Metropolitan Archives, 4–5.

Ehlers, Maren. *Give and Take: Poverty and the Status Order in Early Modern Japan.* Cambridge, MA: Harvard University Asia Center, 2018.

Fukai Jinzō. "Dōchū no hiyatoi." In *Hito,* edited by Takahashi Yasuo and Yoshida Nobuyuki, 214–15. Vol. 3 of *Nihon toshishi nyūmon.* Tōkyō Daigaku Shuppankai, 1990.

Gunma Kenshi Hensan Iinkai, ed. *Gunma kenshi shiryō hen.* 27 vols. Maebashi: Gunma-ken, 1977–88.

Hata Hisako. "Servants of the Inner Quarters: The Women of the Shogun's Great Interior." Translated by Anne Walthall. In *Servants of the Dynasty: Palace Women in World History,* edited by Anne Walthall, 172–90. Berkeley: University of California Press, 2008.

Howell, David L. *Capitalism from Within: Economy, Society, and the State in a Japanese Fishery.* Berkeley: University of California Press, 1995.

"Hard Times in the Kantō: Economic Change and Village Life in Late Tokugawa Japan." *Modern Asian Studies* 23, no. 2 (1989): 349–71.

Iwabuchi Reiji. "Ōdana." In *Shiriizu santo: Edo-kan,* edited by Yoshida Nobuyuki, 137–62. Tōkyō Daigaku Shuppankai, 2019.

Jinbo Fumio. "Kinsei hōritsu monjo no gibun." *Hōsei ronshū* 255 (2014): 1–35.

Jōetsu Shishi Hensan Iinkai, ed. *Jōetsu shishi: Tsūshi-hen,* Vol. 4. Jōetsu: Jōetsu-shi, 2004.

Kanda Yutsuki. *Kinsei no geinō kōgyō to chiiki shakai.* Tōkyō Daigaku Shuppankai, 1999.

Katakura Hisako. "Bakumatsu ishin-ki no toshi kazoku to joshi rōdō." In *Josei no kurashi to rōdō,* edited by Sōgō Joseishi Kenkūkai, 85–108. Vol. 6 of *Nihon joseishi ronshū.* Yoshikawa Kōbunkan, 1998.

Kinsei Shiryō Kenkyūkai, ed. *Edo machibure shūsei.* 21 vols. Hanawa Shobō, 2000.

Kitahara Itoko. *Jishin no shakaishi: Ansei daijishin to minshū.* Yoshikawa Kōbunkan, 2013.

Konno Nobuo. *Edo no furo.* Shinchōsha, 1989.

Kosaka Jirō. *Genroku otatami bugyō no nikki: Owari hanshi no mita ukiyo.* Chūōkōronsha, 1984.

Makita Rieko. "Shōka josei no rōdō: Shufu to hōkōnin." In *Josei rōdō no Nihonshi: Kodai kara gendai made,* edited by Sōgō Joseishi Gakkai, 150–62. Bensei Shuppan, 2019.

McClain, James. *Kanazawa: A Seventeenth-Century Japanese Castle Town.* New Haven, CT: Yale University Press, 1982.

Miyazaki Katsumi. *Daimyō yashiki to Edo iseki*. Yamakawa Shuppansha, 2008.

Mizumoto Kunihiko. *Mura: Hyakushōtachi no kinsei*. Iwanami Shoten, 2015.

Morishita Tōru. "Kaga-han Edo hantei ni okeru hōkōnin." In *Buke yashiki: Kūkan to shakai*, edited by Miyazaki Katsumi and Yoshida Nobuyuki, 193–221. Yamakawa Shuppansha, 1994.

Nagashima Atsuko. "Kinsei josei rōdō no tokushitsu to rekishiteki ichi: Nōson, gyoson ("umitsuki mura") o rei ni." In *Josei rōdō no Nihonshi: Kodai kara gendai made*, edited by Sōgō Joseishi Gakkai, 33–47. Bensei Shuppan, 2019.

Nagata, Mary Louise, and Kiyoshi Hamano. "Marriage Market in Early Modern Kyoto, 1843–1868." *History of the Family* 14, no. 1 (2009): 36–51.

Nishizaka Yasushi. *Mitsui Echigoya hōkōnin no kenkyū*. Tōkyō Daigaku Shuppankai, 2006.

Ogi Shin'ichirō. *Kinsei kōzan o sasaeta hitobito*. Yamakawa Shuppansha, 2012.

Ōguchi Yūjirō. *Edojō ōoku o mezasu mura no musume: Namamugi-mura Sekiguchi Chie no shōgai*. Yamakawa Shuppansha, 2016.

Roberts, Luke S. *Performing the Great Peace: Political Space and Open Secrets in Tokugawa Japan*. Honolulu: University of Hawai'i Press, 2012.

Saitama-ken, ed. *Shinpen Saitama kenshi: Tsūshi-hen*, Vol. 4. Urawa: Saitama-ken, 1989.

Saitō Osamu. *Shōka no sekai, uradana no sekai: Edo to Ōsaka no hikaku toshishi*. Riburo Pōto, 1987.

Sakurai Yuki. "Perpetual Dependency: The Life Course of Male Workers in a Merchant House." In *Recreating Japanese Men*, edited by Sabine Frühstück and Anne Walthall, 115–34. Berkeley: University of California Press, 2011.

Sawayama Mikako. *Edo no chichi to kodomo: Inochi o tsunagu*. Yoshikawa Kōbunkan, 2017.

Seigle, Cecilia Segawa, and Linda Chance. *Ōoku: The Secret World of the Shogun's Women*. Amherst, NY: Cambria Press, 2014.

Smith, Thomas C. *Native Sources of Japanese Industrialization, 1750–1920*. Berkeley: University of California Press, 1988.

Smits, Gregory. "Shaking Up Japan: Edo Society and the 1855 Catfish Picture Prints." *Journal of Social History* 39, no. 4 (2006): 1045–78.

Stanley, Amy. *Selling Women: Prostitution, Markets, and the Household in Early Modern Japan*. Berkeley: University of California Press, 2012.

Stranger in the Shogun's City: A Japanese Woman and Her World. New York: Scribner, 2020.

Sugimori Reiko. "Furugi shōnin." In *Akinai no ba to shakai*, edited by Yoshida Nobuyuki, 140–67. Yoshikawa Kōbunkan, 2000.

Sugimoto, Etsu Inagaki. *A Daughter of the Samurai: How a Daughter of Feudal Japan, Living Hundreds of Years in One Generation, Became a Modern American*. New York: Doubleday, 1925.

Takano Toshihiko. "Kakae sumō." In *Bushi no shūen ni ikiru*, edited by Morishita Tōru, 111–38. Yoshikawa Kōbunkan, 2007.

Takiguchi Masato. "Bakushin yashiki to Edo shakai." In *Shiriizu santo: Edo-kan*, edited by Yoshida Nobuyuki, 77–88. Tōkyō Daigaku Shuppankai, 2019.

Teeuwen, Mark, and Kate Wildman Nakai, eds. *Lust, Commerce, and Corruption: An Account of What I Have Seen and Heard by an Edo Samurai*. Translated by Mark Teeuwen, Kate Wildman Nakai, Miyazaki Fumiko, Anne Walthall, and John Breen. New York: Columbia University Press, 2014.

Ujiie Mikito. *Hatamoto gokenin: Odoroki no bakushin shakai no shinjitsu*. Yōsensha, 2011.

Vaporis, Constantine. *Tour of Duty: Samurai, Military Service in Edo, and the Culture of Early Modern Japan.* Honolulu: University of Hawai'i Press, 2003.

Walthall, Anne. *The Weak Body of a Useless Woman: Matsuo Taseko and the Meiji Restoration.* Chicago: University of Chicago Press, 1998.

Yabuta Yutaka. *Joseishi to shite no kinsei.* Azekura Shobō, 1996.

Yokoyama Yuriko. *Edo Tōkyō no Meiji ishin.* Iwanami Shoten, 2018.

"Expanding and Multi-Layering Networks in Nineteenth-Century Japan: The Case of the Shin-Yoshiwara Pleasure Quarters." In *Women and Networks in Nineteenth-Century Japan,* edited by Bettina Gramlich-Oka, Anne Walthall, Miyazaki Fumiko, and Sugano Noriko, 223–45. Ann Arbor: University of Michigan Press, 2020.

Yonemoto, Marcia. "Adoption and the Maintenance of the Early Modern Elite: Japan in the East Asian Context." In *What Is a Family? Answers from Early Modern Japan,* edited by Mary Elizabeth Berry and Marcia Yonemoto, 47–67. Oakland: University of California Press, 2019.

Yoshida Nobuyuki. *Dentō toshi: Edo.* Tōkyō Daigaku Shuppankai, 2012.

"Hitoyado." In *Hito,* edited by Takahashi Yasuo and Yoshida Nobuyuki, 216–17. Vol. 3 of *Nihon toshishi nyūmon.* Tōkyō Daigaku Shuppankai, 1989.

ed. *"Kamiyui Shinza" no rekishi sekai.* Asahi Shinbunsha, 1994.

Mibunteki shūen to shakai=bunka kōzō. Kyoto: Buraku Mondai Kenkyūjo, 2003.

21-seiki no Edo. Yamakawa Shuppansha, 2004.

Yoshida Yuriko. *Kinsei no ie to josei.* Yamakawa Shuppansha, 2016.

17

The Tokugawa Status Order

MAREN EHLERS

In Tokugawa Japan, hierarchy was considered a natural feature of the social order. The samurai commanded fear and deference from subjects while enforcing strict rank distinctions among themselves. Villagers and townspeople too maintained ranks in their communities and displayed them through names, clothes, sandals, houses, and the seats they occupied on ceremonial occasions. Even people on the fringes of society insisted on highly formal shows of deference. The guild of male blind performers (*zatō*), for example, whose members made a living as itinerant musicians, acupuncturists, and masseurs, had constructed a notoriously intricate hierarchy with seventy-three steps and demanded elaborate rituals of submission from members when they encountered a top-ranking leader.[1] The outcaste boss in Edo, a hereditary leader named Danzaemon, wore a *haori* overcoat, *hakama* trousers, and two swords – markers of high status that were normally associated with samurai and not with mostly impoverished people of "polluted" lineage who lived segregated from villagers and townspeople. On occasion, Danzaemon traveled in a palanquin with a substantial retinue, mimicking the style of a small daimyo procession.[2] There were thus hierarchies both within groups and between them, and the authorities reinforced these distinctions by issuing sumptuary decrees, which grew increasingly complicated over time and put the social order on display in everyday life.

This preoccupation with hierarchy seems to confirm what was long considered common knowledge about the Tokugawa status order: at the beginning of the seventeenth century, the shogunate and daimyo stabilized the war-torn country by freezing occupational groups into a hierarchical system and discouraged subjects from challenging their hereditary station. But, since the late 1970s, a more dynamic view has emerged that emphasizes self-governing

[1] Katō, *Nihon mōjin shakaishi*, 196–206.
[2] Amos, *Caste in Early Modern Japan*, 86–90.

occupational groups as the building blocks of the Tokugawa social order and mediators of status. Although these groups performed duties for the authorities and submitted to samurai hegemony, they also used collective action to negotiate their own social standing. This view has translated into new ways to explain social change under the conditions of the status order. Some scholars have highlighted the aspect of gradual erosion of the status order, especially as a result of commercialization.[3] Others emphasize that, signs of erosion notwithstanding, the principles of rule by status remained relevant until the end of the period because they were gradually appropriated by subjects and manipulated by administrators.[4] These two interpretations are compatible in the sense that they both regard the status order as a flexible system subject to competing forces. This chapter draws on both interpretations to introduce the history of the status order in four steps: first, by describing status groups' basic features; second, by tracing the emergence of this order from the sixteenth to the early eighteenth century; third, by characterizing the process of maturation; and fourth, by explaining the reorganization and eventual dismantling of the status order after the Meiji Restoration.

The Status Group and Its Place in Tokugawa Society

Tokugawa subjects were integrated into thousands of corporate groups of locally limited range, organized around an occupation and claiming some sort of collective property. For many of these groups, this property was land. In the countryside, farmers, fishers, and other people who exploited the bounties of nature came together to regulate the use of land and other resources, for example by managing irrigation and access to the commons. In urban areas, townspeople organized into so-called block associations (*chō*; alternatively translated as "neighborhoods"), which typically comprised land on both sides of a block-long street section. These associations were often dominated by people of a particular trade or craft but could comprise a mix of occupations, and they always regulated the sale and use of land. In addition, there were many occupational groups that claimed collective rights on resources other than land. These included guilds (in Japanese often referred to as *nakama*, *za*, or *kumiai*) of merchants, craftspeople, entertainers, and other professionals,

---

[3] Asao, "Jūhasseiki no shakai hendō"; Yoshida Nobuyuki, "Shoyū to mibunteki shūen."
[4] Especially Tsukada Takashi; see his "Mibunteki shūen." For a discussion of Tsukada's and contrasting perspectives, see Ono, "Mibunsei shakairon," 99–100.

and confraternities and other guild-like associations that made a living from begging or the performance of religious rituals. While these latter groups did not regulate landownership, they claimed places or territories (often referred to as *ba*) to monopolize an occupation. Like the land-based status groups, they had a core of stakeholding members who jointly regulated the group's affairs, drew on shared notions of collective property, and shouldered duties vis-à-vis the authorities. Almost every Tokugawa person – with the exception of samurai, imperial courtiers, monks, nuns, and certain types of outcastes – was a member of or affiliated with a village or a block association, but many simultaneously participated in other occupational groups that were not based on the ownership of land.

The structure of these groups was very diverse. Some had one or several hereditary bosses who represented the collective, whereas others let leadership positions rotate among full members or at least among the more senior ones. All occupational groups maintained hierarchies – typically between senior and junior full members, between stakeholders and non-stakeholders, between masters and apprentices, between household heads and dependents, and others. Yet all of them had a body of core members who made collective decisions according to law codes they had worked out within the limitations of domanial and shogunal law and in agreement with other groups. Most of them collected dues from members to fund shared endeavors and defend their interests. Even the social units of the samurai – the retainer bands, which were more hierarchical than the occupational groups among subjects because they were integrated into the lord's extended household (*o-ie*) – had a council of high-ranking vassals at the top and groups (*kumi*) of retainers in the lower ranks.[5]

Seen from a countrywide vantage point, many occupational groups looked like pyramids resting on a foundation of local subunits. But it was in fact the local units that carried the greatest weight within these relatively decentralized structures because they regulated the everyday lives of Tokugawa subjects and served as gatekeepers of status group membership. With between a handful and a few dozen full households each, they were typically small enough for members to supervise and support one another, though some contained even smaller "five-person associations" (*goningumi*) and the like for mutual aid and control. Because of their mutual familiarity, members could serve as guarantors and thus facilitate each other's commercial and social transactions. The land-based groups wielded particular power over members

---

[5] Morishita, *Bushi to iu mibun*, 10–30.

because they were in charge of submitting annual population registers to the government and could turn people into unregistered outlaws by removing them from the register. To be sure, the authorities interfered with registration in various ways, for example by deeming certain categories of people – Christians, for example – unacceptable as residents and creating procedural barriers for register removals, especially of tax-paying households. They also expected villages and *chō* to police themselves and thus made it risky for them to keep deviant people on the register. But governments did not usually challenge the membership structure of existing groups and very rarely forced them to accept newcomers against their will.

These local occupation-based groups were imbedded into the social order through the relationships they maintained with the authorities and other groups.[6] First, many of them formed layered hierarchies with other associations of their own kind. The block associations of a town, for example, clustered in the so-called *machikata* ("town"), whose officials represented all local townspeople vis-à-vis the warrior administration. In larger towns, there was often an additional intermediate layer between the *machikata* and the *chō*. Villages joined overlapping leagues that each regulated a particular facet of social and economic life such as irrigation, transportation, and shrine maintenance. Some of these leagues were imposed by samurai administrators to coordinate the performance of duties, but others were more autonomous, and if the need arose, any of them could serve as a framework for protest movements.[7] Although the leagues and layers of status groups mimicked the spatial structure of feudal rule to a certain extent, their borders did not always coincide with the lines of warrior jurisdictions,[8] and some even produced countrywide hierarchies – a feature that was typical for semi-itinerant craftspeople, entertainers, and clerics.

In addition to these links between peer groups, occupational groups were affiliated with privilege-granting authorities that recognized them as status groups. Because the structure of warrior rule was layered as well, and because old medieval power centers such as monasteries, shrines, and the imperial court retained some authority and continued to confer legitimacy, this resulted in many possible combinations. A group could be recognized by the local daimyo, the shogunate, the imperial court, or a prestigious temple or shrine. Theoretically it could have ties with all of the above, and the

---

[6] Tsukada, *Kinsei Nihon mibunsei*, 353–57.
[7] Walthall, "Village Networks"; Yabuta, *Kokuso to hyakushō ikki*.
[8] Howell, *Geographies of Identity*, 37–38.

guild of male blind performers came close to the maximum of possible connections as it was recognized by both the shogunate and the Koga house of court nobles in Kyoto, and through its local associations also by daimyo and other local authorities. These various relationships reinforced one another and strengthened the guild's position countrywide, yet the local associations only occasionally invoked the authority of their prestigious Kyoto headquarters and created distinct agreements and relationships on the local level. One example of a locally distinct relationship was the control some groups of *zatō* exercised over nearby guilds of female blind performers (*goze*). No such domination existed on the national level because the *goze* did not have a nationwide leadership.[9]

The shogunate and daimyo administrations governed the country by recognizing the occupational groups inside their territories so they could mobilize them in a military emergency. Takagi Shōsaku has used the phrase "garrison state" to characterize the Tokugawa polity because its structure reflected military needs even when the country had been pacified by the early Tokugawa shoguns.[10] Each group had to discharge duties (*goyō*), which could include helping the lord mobilize his military, maintaining his household, administering his territory, or fulfilling his nonmilitary obligations toward the shogunate. It could also include the purveying of commodities; a league of fishing villages on Edo Bay, for example, regularly delivered fresh fish as a duty to the shogun's castle.[11] For members of the land-based communities, the delivery of the land tax also constituted an important obligation, though it was not usually referred to by the term *goyō*. In addition, all status groups were required to maintain order within their ranks and prevent members from disturbing the public peace.

In exchange for these duties, groups received recognition for their occupation. "Occupation" (*shokubun*) in this context referred to the professional activity a group sought to monopolize and which – unlike other livelihoods that might have been present among group members – defined its status (*mibun*), that is, members' public standing in their interactions with the authorities and other groups in society.[12] "Occupation" often had a somewhat fictive quality because not all economic activities that mattered to members were reflected in their status. Recognized groups earned monopolies related to their occupation but also the right to display superficial status markers

[9] Katō, *Nihon mōjin shakaishi*, 160–71, 213–44.
[10] Takagi, *Nihon kinsei kokkashi*, 1.
[11] Yoshida Nobuyuki, *Seijuku suru Edo*, 295–99.
[12] Howell, *Geographies of Identity*, 46–47.

that reflected both their prestige as a self-governing group and individuals' ranks within the group hierarchy. Although it was possible for households to acquire privileges on their own by performing special duties apart from the other group members, these privileges could only be expressed in reference to their occupational community, for example when an "ordinary townsperson" was promoted to the rank of "purveyor merchant" in reward for making donations.

The status order looked quite different from place to place but can be broken down into three broad categories that related to each other in a hierarchical fashion. At the top were the samurai, bound to each other by ties of vassalage that culminated in the shogun. In the middle were the commoners, who comprised a great variety of occupational groups. At the bottom were the "base people" (senmin), in English often rendered as "outcastes," who did not have a countrywide hierarchy and like the commoners were made up of many different occupational groups. Confucian discourse contrasted the base with the "honorable people" (ryōmin) – commoners and samurai – but the stigmatization of base people in Japan was not informed by Confucian ideas, at least not primarily. It resulted from a complex process of marginalization that had begun long before the Tokugawa period and was influenced by Buddhist injunctions against the taking of life as well as Shinto taboos against ritual pollution. Although the barriers between these three categories were not insurmountable (especially not between samurai and commoners), they were relatively high compared to the barriers between the groups within them and gave these categories a caste-like character.

When contemporaries referred to the social order of their time, they often used the term "four estates" (shimin), which was derived from the Chinese Confucian canon. This metaphor described the ideal society as a compound of four types of mutually complementary occupations: warrior officials (shi), farmers (nō), artisans (kō), and merchants (shō). Japanese scholars were familiar with this concept from at least the fourteenth century onward and adapted it to the conditions of their own society, for example by reinterpreting the term shi (the Chinese "gentleman-scholar") as "warrior official" when samurai emerged as Japan's ruling class.[13] Confucian intellectuals often used the "four estates" metaphor to make moral arguments about the state of Tokugawa society. They cited it to insist on the superiority of grain-producing farmers over profit-seeking merchants and to condemn so-called idlers (yūmin) – outcastes, entertainers, prostitutes, and other people of questionable morals who

---

[13] Asao, "Kinsei no mibun," 14–24.

appeared to be excluded from the four estates. But at no point did this metaphor reflect administrative norms and practices. Tokugawa law did not actually rank agriculturists above merchants, and officials distinguished between "townspeople" (*chōnin*) and "villagers" (*hyakushō*, originally "the common people")[14] rather than between farmers, artisans, and merchants. Finally, the status order did not exclude alleged idlers and outcastes but governed them by the same principles as other occupational groups. The only people who were truly without status were vagrants and other people who lacked an affiliation with an occupational group. They were treated as outlaws because they existed outside the structures of mutual surveillance and control.

Both men and women were integrated into the status order through their households. But because popular custom excluded women from the position of household head, women were generally prevented from participating in collective governance. Status groups were constituted of households (*ie*) that shouldered dues and duties, rotated appointments, and shared access to common property. Each stakeholding household functioned as an institution in the context of the status order, but it was often also a self-perpetuating family unit (typically containing a relatively small-sized stem family), and every household, stakeholding or not, was listed in the population register by the name of its head, who was male in most cases and represented other household members including his wife, children, parents, siblings, other live-in relatives, apprentices, and servants. The marginalizing effect this structure had on women can be gauged from the fact that the only occupational groups with female leaders were those that required their members to remain unmarried, namely nunneries and other groups of female clerics as well as guilds of female blind performers (*goze*). The households within these female groups were occupied not by family units but by a master and her apprentices.

Despite their marginal position, women played essential roles in maintaining status groups through the reproductive labor they provided for their households.[15] This could include bearing an heir, but the ability to give birth was not necessarily the most important qualification of a potential wife. An heir could also be acquired through adoption, and many households had much to gain from a wife who contributed to the household economy through her financial knowledge, weaving skills, or farm work. If a household adopted a son-in-law as heir, the wife who remained in her native family was more likely

---

[14] Although *hyakushō* is often translated as "peasant" because of its strong association with farming, the term marked non-farming people as well, for example those living in fishing and mining villages.

[15] Walthall, "Life Cycle of Farm Women," 54–55.

to play a leading role in household affairs and sometimes took on the role of de facto household head. Widows commonly served as temporary household heads under their husband's name until a son reached maturity (sometimes even longer), and they also fulfilled the household's duties as long as this did not require them to perform the labor themselves. For some women, household headship was more than just temporary. In eighteenth- and nineteenth-century Edo, for example, townswomen sometimes appeared as plot owners and household heads on the registers, even in households where a grown man would have been available. Such cases probably reflected the economic circumstances of townspeople, who sometimes preferred adopting a capable son-in-law to succeed them in their trade and who were also more likely to give family women some role to play in business operations. Samurai women, by contrast, do not seem to have been able to own land under their name, perhaps in part because they did not directly participate in their household's official function – performing service for a lord.[16]

Yet even among commoners, female household heads were excluded from the more influential aspects of status group governance such as participation in village assemblies or leadership positions.[17] Single women often faced scrutiny. Governments did not expect women to be living alone and sometimes restricted tenancy by single women. In late eighteenth-century Edo, the city authorities did allow single women to rent apartment space, though they took this for granted only among nuns and *goze*.[18] Their counterparts in Osaka, however, required tenant households to have a male head in the latter half of the Tokugawa period, and some single women in that city adopted a male and declared him household head specifically for the purpose of securing a tenancy.[19]

As this example shows, Tokugawa population registers shaped social customs and allowed authorities to interfere with subjects' households to a certain extent. Toyotomi Hideyoshi laid the groundwork for this system in 1592, when he conducted the first of several surveys of able-bodied men and draft animals to mobilize subjects for military corvée.[20] When the Tokugawa regime embarked on its campaign to eradicate Christianity, it forced the land-based status groups to submit annual registers that listed a Buddhist temple

[16] Yokoyama, *Meiji ishin to kinsei mibunsei*, 283–324.
[17] Nagano, "Nihon kinsei no hyakushō mibun to jendā." Among Osaka's beggar bosses, female household heads were ineligible to perform police duty. Tsukada, *Kinsei Ōsaka no hinin*, 66–74.
[18] Yokoyama, *Meiji ishin to kinsei mibunsei*, 36.
[19] Tsukada, *Ōsaka minshū no kinseishi*, 66–68.
[20] On this and the following, see Yokota, "Kinseiteki mibun seido," 47–67, 71–73.

affiliation for every single subject. Unlike Hideyoshi's earlier registers, the new surveillance rosters, which by 1664 were being enforced countrywide, listed not only able-bodied men but also women, infirm men, minors, tenants, dependents, and beggars by name and often by age, giving administrators an unprecedented tool for monitoring society. The registers allowed them to verify the status of most subjects and track down criminals. They also made status portable. Whenever subjects moved into a new community, they had to transfer their registration by submitting a document of identification issued by their former village head or temple of origin to prove that they were neither Christians nor masterless samurai or unregistered people. The reliance on registers set the Tokugawa status order apart from its Muromachi-era predecessor, which had also ordered subjects by occupation but not involved recording the identity of individual group members or mobilizing all occupational groups for military ends.[21] In 1681, the shogunate charged all daimyo with the annual submission of aggregate population figures from their territories in the categories of vassal, villager, townsperson, *eta*, *hinin*, and so on, indicating the main categories the central authority used to classify the population.[22] Tokugawa officials governed on the assumption that registration corresponded to status. Yet status was never centrally managed or assigned because the land-based status groups were in charge of maintaining the registers and decided whom to include or expel.

The Long Formative Period

The Tokugawa status order was built on, but also disrupted, the legacy of the occupational groups of the late Muromachi period. The sixteenth century was an age of great social upheaval in which samurai, merchants, craftspeople, entertainers, and clerics all strove to expand their autonomy. The greatest innovation was the corporate village (*sōson*), which emerged around the late fifteenth century in the central Kinai region around Kyoto and gradually spread to other parts of the country.[23] *Sō* villages were organized around both land and occupation. Although they existed within the estates (*shōen*) held by tax-collecting proprietors, their formation was not driven by proprietors' interests but by subjects' need to protect themselves and their livelihoods in an age of civil war. Many corporate villages were anchored in a local shrine

---

[21] Yokota, "Kinseiteki mibun seido," 42.
[22] Yokota, "Kinseiteki mibun seido," 71–72.
[23] Tonomura, *Community and Commerce*; Asao, "Sōson kara chō e."

or temple, but their meaning extended far beyond the religious sphere. *Sō* communities dealt with matters of self-defense, agriculture, and commerce and negotiated with overlords and other entities. The language and practices of the *sō*, which circulated widely at the time, were inherited by all Tokugawa status groups to a certain extent, even the samurai: leadership by elders (*toshiyori*); adjudication according to group law; autonomous selection of members; formation of leagues and agreements between groups; shared property; and meetings (*yoriai*) and circulars (*kaibun*) as techniques of collective governance. While a small number of corporate villages were directly recognized as villages by the Tokugawa regime, most Tokugawa-era villages had been no more than hamlets in the sixteenth century and only gradually came into their own as self-governing units. This was because Hideyoshi and his Tokugawa successors did not simply confirm existing structures among subjects but broke up established hierarchies and listed subordinate units as full group members who had to rely on the collective to survive.[24]

The emergence of the Tokugawa status order was a long process that began with Hideyoshi's regime-building intervention and ended only around 1700, when urban growth and land reclamation had slowed down considerably and attainders of daimyo had become rare. There were occasional outbreaks of warfare until the 1630s, and the experience of war thus left a strong imprint on the priorities of the new regime, which sought to mobilize subjects for military campaigns and pacify the country. Hideyoshi took the initiative in the 1580s by drawing a clearer distinction between samurai and villagers. In the sixteenth century, many samurai were living in rural areas, some of them as large landowners, and they often farmed between military campaigns. Hideyoshi ordered all samurai to submit to a master and forced even low-ranking rear vassals to become permanent members of a lord's retainer band. Villagers, on the other hand, were required to disarm and cut their ties of vassalage and were banned from abandoning their land to ensure a stable land tax yield. The separation of samurai and villagers resulted in a redefinition of both categories. Under the new order, samurai were defined as full-time professional warriors who bore arms and answered to a master. Samurai without a master – so-called *rōnin* – had to subject themselves to strict controls while they looked for military employment.[25] Villagers (*hyakushō*), on the other hand, were now understood as farmers without a master who paid land tax and contributed to campaigns through corvée rather than

---

[24] Yamaguchi, *Sakoku to kaikoku*, 65–73.
[25] Yokota, "Kinseiteki mibun seido," 43–46; Asao, "Kinsei Kyōto no rōnin."

armed service. The two categories also began to occupy separate residential spaces. Over the course of the seventeenth century, lords relocated most of their vassals to distinct samurai quarters in the emerging castle towns and made the higher-ranking ones give up control of their fiefs in exchange for stipends. Although many old strongmen remained in the countryside and kept their land, they typically had to abandon their weapons and ties of vassalage.

In the 1580s, Hideyoshi launched a countrywide cadastral survey to dismantle proprietors' tax rights and establish himself as the new fief-granting authority. This survey had a profound effect on the emerging land-based communities among villagers and townspeople, which were now cut into new units and collectively held responsible for tax payments. The survey registered all productive and residential land – both farm and market land – and assigned a productivity value to plots that reflected their tax-paying capacity. The plots were organized into new units called either *mura* (in the countryside) or *chō* (in towns), and the communities that delivered the tax were also called *mura* or *chō* and for the most part coincided with the owners of the land for whose taxes they were responsible. But they had an inner coherence that went beyond the need to pay the land tax. For example, the revenue of one "village" (that is, land unit) could be split up between several tax-collecting overlords, yet the village responsible for delivering these payments remained intact as a self-governing community (see Howell, Chapter 3, this volume). The survey even created "villages" without villagers, that is, units of agricultural land that did not have any settlement on them and whose taxes were forwarded by the heads of nearby villages.[26] Although the latter scenario was exceptional, the fact that it occurred at all highlights the artificiality of the village as a unit of taxation and the need to distinguish it from the village as an economic and social community, whose complexity was not fully visible to the authorities' classification schemes.

The land tax was central to villagers' relationships with fiefholders. It was owed collectively and thus reinforced the village as a status group, pushing villagers to share access to the commons and provide aid to struggling households so the village could meet its assigned burden. But it was ultimately not land tax delivery but duty that defined the status and privileges of villagers as well as members of other occupational communities. The new regime recognized and governed occupational groups on the basis of the duties they performed for their lord and the shogunate. In 1592, Hideyoshi charged the newly recognized villages with providing laborers for corvée (*buyaku*) during

---

[26] Izumi Shishi Hensan Iinkai, *Shinodayama chiiki*, 175–97.

his first invasion of Korea. Although the content of corvée changed over time from battlefield support to construction work and other peacetime jobs, it always remained a duty associated with villagers. The Hideyoshi and Tokugawa regimes assigned corvée obligations to residential plots (within the village) rather than agricultural plots, and until the 1640s, when villagers were allowed to substitute with payments of money and grain, governments treated only households that provided such labor (so-called *yakuya*) as full-fledged villagers (*honbyakushō*).[27]

Townspeople were set apart from villagers by the character of the duties they performed. Because towns were economically more diverse than villages, town residents not only paid land tax on their plots but also performed a range of duties depending on their occupation. Initially, townspeople who performed the same duty often lived together in the same *chō*, especially in newly founded towns, but these homogeneous *chō* quickly disintegrated into more mixed units with residents of different occupations that often had a shared occupational orientation.[28] The block associations were associations of house owners rather than guilds. Their members – the *chōnin* (townspeople) in the narrow sense, excluding tenants – commercially exploited their plots by lending space to merchants and craftspeople, and the *chō* are therefore better described as communities of urban house owners who managed their property with the backing and trust of the *chō* collective. Although they owed land tax on their plots, house owners in the *chō* often received exemptions from the land tax if they shouldered a duty directly for the shogunate (*kuniyaku*), such as post-horse duty or particular types of corvée incumbent on craft guilds, or if they served as purveyors.[29] There were organized craftspeople in the villages as well, and they too were exempted from villagers' corvée if they performed *kuniyaku*. In other words, people of distinct occupations did not always occupy distinct spaces, and not all of their groups were organized around land, but all groups were distinguished from each other by the duties they performed.

The example of Yokoyama valley in Izumi Province illustrates the gradual consolidation of the early modern status order over the seventeenth century in a rural part of the Kinai region. In the late Muromachi period, there was an old monastery called Makiodera in that valley that held the land within it as an estate, backed by powerful temples in the imperial capital. The farmers

[27] Yokota, "Kinseiteki mibun seido," 46–51, 67–68.
[28] Tsukada, "Mibunsei no kōzō"; Yoshida Nobuyuki, "Chōnin to chō"; Berry, *Culture of Civil War*, 210–41.
[29] In many larger towns and cities, *chōnin* were summarily exempted from the land tax.

lived scattered in small hamlets but maintained a confraternity (*miyaza*) around the local Onouto Shrine that facilitated the formation of a corporate village (*sōson*). The most powerful member of this *sōson* was the house of Ikebe, which had once reclaimed most of the land in this area and still represented the farmers vis-à-vis the tax-collecting monastery. Unlike many other landholding strongmen at the time, the Ikebe did not identify as warriors and did not enter any ties of vassalage with more powerful warrior houses.[30] But the situation in the valley changed greatly when Oda Nobunaga destroyed the monastery and Toyotomi Hideyoshi and his successors confiscated and surveyed the land and began to channel tax payments toward themselves and their vassals.

Hideyoshi's first land survey of 1594 still listed the entire valley as a single village. The next one, in 1611, listed fourteen hamlets as "villages," and their number fluctuated until it settled at twelve around the beginning of the eighteenth century. As land reclamation picked up in the 1600s, the new villages began to contest the borders of each other's commons and increasingly turned to their new samurai overlords to mediate their conflicts. They also established village temples that further enhanced their independence from the monastery and provided proof of Buddhist affiliation for the new registers of religious surveillance. Structures of collective decision-making began to appear separately for each village. In the seventeenth century, there had only been two heads for all of the villages in this valley, one from the Ikebe family and one from another prominent household. But by the 1710s, each village had its own procedures for head selection and codified them in village law. In the 1740s, for example, the "villager collective" (*sōbyakushō*) of Butsunami village decided to rotate the headship every three years among its fourteen subgroups (*kumi*) of members. Although villagers continued to be stratified into various ranks and not all residents counted as full members, their communities were now run as self-governing collectives.

The monks of Makiodera, on the other hand, already had a long tradition of self-government and found it curtailed after the confiscation of their estate. The Tokugawa insisted on the integration of all Buddhist temples into sectarian hierarchies, and Makiodera had to accept stronger oversight by the Tendai school, whose Edo headquarters served the Tokugawa as a family temple. This meant that the monks had to tolerate an externally appointed head priest, but they still maintained their own law code under the umbrella of sectarian and shogunal law. During the seventeenth century, the monastic community

---

[30] Izumi Shishi Hensan Iinkai, *Yokoyama to Makiosan*, 110–13, 134–36, 146–49, 234–35.

repeatedly clashed with its new head while also quarreling with the villagers of its former estate over land-related matters, but eventually the monks came to appreciate the head priest's political clout because it strengthened their hand against the villagers. The monks of Makiodera referred to themselves as a *sōchū* or *jichū*, that is, a "general assembly" or "temple assembly" of around seventy subtemples (*shiin*) led by two rotating "elders" (*toshiyori*) – heads of prominent subtemples. These subtemples were the equivalents of hereditary households in other Tokugawa-era status groups. In the case of Makiodera, most novices were recruited from farming families in the Yokoyama valley, some of whom had a long history of supporting a particular subtemple. Every New Year, Makiodera distributed wooden tablets to all villages in the valley as well as talismans to all village households in exchange for their customary support of sutra readings at the temple.[31] Monks and villagers thus reshaped their corporate bodies in opposition to each other but also by rebuilding their reciprocal ties. By the early 1700s, the valley had again settled into a state of relative stability.

If clerics were being integrated into the emerging "garrison state," so too were base people. Since at least the Kamakura period, pariah groups had been a feature of Japanese society, especially in western and central Japan. They suffered discrimination on account of their occupations, which linked them with deviance, poverty, and death-related ritual pollution, but their stigma was reinforced by their duties, which included ritual cleansing and other menial jobs for temples, shrines, the imperial court, and other authorities that acted as their protectors. The warlords of the sixteenth century mobilized base people for war-related duties, particularly leatherworkers (*kawata*, increasingly also known by the derogatory term *eta*, lit. "very polluted"), who supplied raw material for armor, drums, horse gear, and other tools. The second common type of outcaste group in the Tokugawa period was the *hinin* (lit. "nonhuman," a demeaning term for mendicants and often used in the sense of "homeless beggar"), who were typically mobilized as beggar bosses. Leatherworkers and beggar bosses thus shouldered duties that reflected their occupations, but both were also used for additional tasks, especially in punishment, with *hinin* often serving as jail guards and penal assistants and *kawata* as executioners. Besides these two types, there were many other base groups with an artisanal and/or itinerant character such as monkey trainers (*sarukai*), makers of tea brushes (*chasen*), cormorant fishermen (*ugai*), cremators (*onbō*), shamans, and various types of street entertainers.

---

[31] Izumi Shishi Hensan Iinkai, *Yokoyama to Makiosan*, 296.

With the exception of most beggar bosses, who were numerous in towns and cities, many base groups also practiced agriculture. Base people usually lived segregated in their own villages, hamlets, or compounds and thus added another zone to the status-based pattern of residence in Tokugawa Japan.

Whether a particular group was classified as base or not depended on a combination of factors. The most important was customary discrimination on the popular level. This could take many forms, but denial of intermarriage and group membership or co-residence proved the most damaging because outcastes' exclusion from villages and *chō* as well as from respectable occupations turned their stigma into a hereditary condition and perpetuated prejudices about their lifestyle. Another factor was discriminatory legislation by samurai authorities, which distinguished between commoners and base people in many settings, for example by making base people submit separate registers, subjecting them to different punishments and sumptuary and residential regulations, and imposing degrading duties. However, much of this legislation drew upon and reinforced discrimination already present among subjects. A third factor was resistance against discrimination. There were a number of cases at the end of the Tokugawa period of outcastes openly rebelling against discriminatory treatment.[32] But prospects of success were greater if groups pushed back more indirectly and affiliated themselves with a famous monastery, shrine, or courtier family that enhanced their respectability.[33] In combination, these factors produced a wide spectrum of base groups that suffered from varying degrees of exclusion in different aspects of life. There were groups, for example, that were not classified as base by the authorities and whose members intermarried with lower-class commoners yet fell under outcaste rule with regard to their occupation (such as the *gōmune*, street performers living as tenants in Edo's *chō*).[34] Other groups counted as commoners in every possible setting, but because they performed a duty or occupation with base connotations, they were vulnerable to slander and could end up classified as outcastes if they failed to defend their reputation.[35]

In the Tokugawa period, baseness became a hereditary condition. This meant that it could not be erased, no matter whether a base person actually engaged in any stigmatizing activities, and intellectuals began to speculate that outcastes might be of foreign origin.[36] Although governments sometimes

[32] Ooms, *Tokugawa Village Practice*, 264–70.
[33] See, for example, Yoshida Yuriko, "Chiiki shakai"; Yoshida Yuriko, "Manzai to haruta-uchi."
[34] Yoshida Nobuyuki, *Seijuku suru Edo*, 195–211.
[35] Yoshida Yuriko, "Chiiki shakai," 24–25, 27; Yoshida Yuriko, "Manzai to haruta-uchi," 72.
[36] Uesugi, *Meiji ishin to senmin haishirei*, 9–19.

allowed base people to undergo purification rituals to return to commoner status, this opportunity only existed for former commoners who had been forced by poverty to live under beggar boss rule.[37] The registration system made it difficult for outcastes to obfuscate their identity to move into a village or *chō*. Because all changes of residence required a transfer of registration, moving outcastes had to reveal their community of origin, which was known among locals or could be investigated if there was any ground for suspicion. House sales were subject to the approval and review of all titled villagers and *chō* members. Yet the registration system was sufficiently decentralized to allow some base people to "pass" in other places. As we shall see, tenants faced less scrutiny than house buyers and benefited from the anonymity of tenant management, especially in larger cities.

There was no uniform outcaste hierarchy across the entire country. Rather, the shogunate and daimyo facilitated the formation of regional hierarchies around castle towns that reflected local power relationships among base people. The most powerful outcaste boss was Danzaemon, the *kawata* leader of Edo, who enjoyed the shogunate's patronage and had the authority to punish the beggar bosses and monkey trainers under his wing. He was also able to mobilize them for some of his duties for the shogunate.[38] But Danzaemon's influence only extended over the Kantō region around Edo, and the structure of his rule was not representative of the rest of the country. In Osaka and Kyoto, for example, *hinin* and *kawata* existed independently of each other, and there were cities such as Kanazawa where beggar bosses rather than leatherworkers stood at the top of the base people's hierarchy.

Some outcaste groups were constituted as land-based communities. In Izumi Province, the *kawata* village Minami Ōji cultivated over 140 *koku* of taxable land and regulated access to the commons in a similar manner as the commoner villages in the area. Yet Hideyoshi's land survey marginalized rural outcastes because it registered most of their settlements as hamlets, or rather branches (*edamura*), of commoner villages and required them to forward their taxes, registers, and official communications through the "main village." Minami Ōji was a rare case of a *kawata* village paying its land tax directly to the fief holder, but its residents, too, had to defer to their commoner neighbors in certain settings. For example, Minami Ōji belonged to a group of villages clustered around the Shinoda Daimyōjin Shrine that shared irrigation ponds and a commons. But while Minami Ōji had access to the ponds and the commons

[37] Tanaka, "Tottori-han," 21–25.
[38] Tsukada, *Kinsei Nihon mibunsei*, 79–89; Tsukada, *Mibunsei shakai*, 185–207.

and its residents worshipped at the shrine, it did not enjoy the status of a "village of shrine parishioners." Its baseness was on display three times a year during shrine festivals, when the outcastes performed menial tasks instead of celebrating with the other parishioners: providing leather targets for archery, building clay mounds for sumo wrestling, and sweeping the road for the procession of the shrine god.[39]

In this manner, outcastes owned and cultivated land and sometimes organized around the ownership of taxable land. But, primarily, they claimed territories in the manner of trade or craft guilds. *Kawata*, *hinin*, and many other base people delineated turfs, forging relationships with the villages and *chō* within them while distributing access rights among their own households. For the *kawata*, territories primarily served the purpose of carcass collection. In many parts of Tokugawa Japan, farmers abandoned dead livestock at designated dumping sites and made them available to leatherworkers, who relied on this source of raw material because the slaughter of cattle for meat was considered taboo for most of the period. At least during the early history of this system, villagers seem to have regarded the removal of dead animals as an act of cleansing, but as carcasses became increasingly valuable as commodities, the practice developed into a privilege protected by authorities in exchange for leatherworkers' performance of duties. Only *kawata* who held a stake in the turf could pick up carcasses from there for free, and carcass acquisition and leather production often had their own organization separate from each *kawata* village's landholders' collective. Yet even though not all villagers were stakeholders, much of the economy in *kawata* villages, including farm villages such as Minami Ōji, revolved around the manufacturing, sale, and repair of leather, and the monopoly on carcasses thus remained central to *kawata* livelihood until the end of the Tokugawa period.[40]

Beggar bosses claimed territories as well, in their case to maintain access to households of almsgivers. They established permanent, reciprocal relationships with the villages and *chō* inside their turfs, which benefited both sides as commoner and samurai households preferred to bargain with mendicants collectively and strove to establish clear rules regarding acceptable amounts and occasions for begging.[41] The beggar bosses reciprocated by removing polluted items, burying beggar bodies, serving as watchmen, expelling itinerants, and performing other miscellaneous jobs. Warrior authorities recognized the

[39] Izumi Shishi Hensan Iinkai, *Shinodayama chiiki*, 341.
[40] Abele, "Peasants, Skinners, and Dead Cattle"; Mita, *Kinsei mibun shakai*, 305–62.
[41] Ehlers, *Give and Take*, 86–105.

beggar bosses' relationships with villages and *chō* as long as bosses and under-lings refrained from aggressive panhandling and performed duties for their lord in addition to those for villagers and townspeople. Because the beggar bosses were beggars by occupation, rulers put them in charge of supervising homeless migrants in towns and cities. The *hinin* ran town patrols, distributed beggar tags, managed beggar hospices, and expelled suspicious vagrants on behalf of the authorities. In the eighteenth and nineteenth centuries, the beggar bosses' experience in managing beggars and vagrants and their wide-flung social net-works prompted many governments to mobilize them for criminal investiga-tions more generally, and some gradually turned into auxiliary policemen.

The development of *hinin* associations once again highlights the seven-teenth century as a period of consolidation. As daimyo built and expanded their castle towns and were transferred to new fiefs, many of them recog-nized, merged, and granted land to old and new mendicant groups they found on their territories. The leaders of Osaka's four *hinin* associations, which had been given tax-exempt land for dwellings by Hideyoshi and subsequent city authorities, initially included many drifters from other provinces as well as former Christians, perhaps from missionary hospices. But, by the end of the seventeenth century, the four groups had become more closed to outsiders.[42] Although newcomers could still enter the inner circle at that point by marry-ing established guild members, new beggars rounded up from the streets of Osaka no longer joined the guilds proper but were made to live in subordi-nate shelters. By the early eighteenth century, the four *hinin* guilds of Osaka had a clearly defined structure with hereditary duty-performing households. The power of the four guilds also began to radiate outward to the country-side. In the late seventeenth century, villages in the Kinai region began to hire base people as watchmen, and these rural *hinin* gradually came under the influence of the urban beggar boss associations in Kyoto and Osaka and helped them discharge their duties.[43]

The Maturation of the Status Order

The garrison state was intended to stabilize society, and it did keep society stable for over two centuries while the country transitioned from war to peace and navigated major economic changes. One important cause of this

[42] Tsukada, *Ōsaka no hinin*, 23–138. In 1683 and 1691, the group incorporated particularly large numbers of newcomers because the Osaka town magistrate had ordered it to remove all homeless beggars from the streets.
[43] Asao, "Hiden'in to Ōmi no hininban."

stability was the flexibility of the status order. This might sound paradoxical because the status order was very rigid in certain respects, with strict social hierarchies, hereditary privilege, and officials governing on the basis of precedent. But this rigidity was coupled with a high tolerance for superficial compliance. As long as appearances were being upheld and duties performed, officials and status group leaders were willing to accept convenient workarounds and did not mind making exceptions.[44] The second point to consider is that the status order had a built-in flexibility that allowed it to accommodate new divisions of labor. Although individual groups generally became more rigid with time, the principle of government by status – the mobilization of self-governing occupational groups – remained active until the end of the period and led to the recognition of many new associations. The older groups, too, adapted to new circumstances by asserting new privileges and taking on new duties.

For a social order designed for wartime conditions, the end of warfare presented a challenge, and samurai were most directly affected by this change. In the course of the seventeenth century, lords dismissed many lower-ranking retainers and began to hire commoners for special occasions, such as processions or guard duties, which required large numbers of attendants, porters, and guards on a short-term basis. Many young men of town or village background, including non-inheriting younger sons, signed up to serve as low-ranking samurai for a year, a few months, or even a day, and labor agents became a fixture of every castle town (see Stanley, Chapter 16, this volume). These commoners assumed samurai status for the duration of their employment, meaning that they wore two swords, used a surname, and temporarily disappeared from the population register of their *chō* or village, only to return there when their contract expired. The boundary between commoners and low-ranking samurai was thus strictly maintained on the surface but quite porous in practice.[45] Although higher offices were limited to samurai of distinguished lineage and many people of samurai status were underemployed, the idea of samurai status as a role linked to duty performance did not disappear. And for some of these hired hands, the transition became a permanent one as their employers could promote their most talented underlings to higher positions and grant them hereditary samurai status. By the time of the Meiji Restoration, about half of the low-ranking vassal households in Oka domain on Kyushu traced their lineages back to villagers and townspeople,

---

44 Roberts, *Performing the Great Peace.*
45 Asao, "Jūhasseiki no shakai hendō," 60–83.

the majority of whom had been added to the retainer band in the last hundred years of the Tokugawa period.[46]

Most samurai-for-hire performed menial labor. But governments also had a need for educated commoners with special skills and sometimes appointed them to administrative office. Such appointments became especially common in the late Tokugawa period, but as early as 1620, elite townspeople in Hikone domain who had knowledge of rice marketing were serving as rural intendants (*daikan*), a position normally filled by samurai and thus requiring the same status cross-dressing as samurai servants.[47] Although Hikone's intendants remained on the town register, they were allowed to use surnames while on duty and gradually acquired additional status markers, such as the right to carry two swords and wear ceremonial hemp garments on duty-related occasions. When the domain increased the intendants' workload in the 1780s, the men used the occasion to make a failed bid for quasi-samurai status, which would have allowed them to collect their payments in the form of stipends from the domain granary and effectively removed them from the town's population register. More and more commoners were making inroads into samurai status during the latter half of the Tokugawa period because most daimyo houses were deeply in debt and sought to tap commoners' money and commercial and agricultural expertise. But no matter how many status markers these social climbers accumulated, they typically shied away from full transition to samurai status because they could not have held on to their businesses and land as proper vassals. Even Hikone's intendants, who always remained on the town register, had to put their mercantile occupation on hold while serving in the domain administration. The conferral of samurai privileges and offices onto commoners helped perpetuate the status order because it infused administrations with fresh talent, knowledge, and money and satisfied the aspirations of rising mercantile elites. But the privileging of wealthy commoners also bred resentment among low-ranking hereditary samurai, who were excluded from higher office and often suffered from poverty due to sinking stipends. This class produced most of the revolutionaries who launched the Meiji Restoration and dismantled the status order even at the price of abolishing the privileges of the samurai class.

If peace changed the character of samurai duty, it also affected the duties of other status groups. Rulers began to allow groups to deliver payments in lieu of actual duty performance. Early Tokugawa villages, for example, had

[46] Kumagai, "Kinsei daimyō kakyū kashindan," 12–13; Asao, "Jūhasseiki no shakai hendō," 81–83.
[47] Watanabe, "Chōnin daikan."

to perform onerous corvée in fortress and castle town construction, but in the 1640s both villagers and craftspeople were permitted to substitute payments of rice (*bumai*) or money (*bugin*). As castle towns grew and labor markets expanded, it became more convenient for governments to hire experienced workers than to draft labor from towns and villages directly.[48] Yet the duties remained in place, at least on paper, in anticipation of a possible military emergency. There were also cases of status groups acting collectively to hire substitutes. In the late seventeenth century, for example, the block associations of Edo, nudged by the shogunate, began to supply auxiliary firefighters for their own protection. But rather than sending landowners or tenants, the *chō* often employed a certain type of construction worker known as *tobi* for this purpose, who were more skilled than ordinary tenants at performing this dangerous work. In 1720, the shogunate cemented this system by organizing the "town firefighters" into a citywide firefighting organization with multiple companies (see Gaubatz, Chapter 19, this volume).[49] Duty substitutions such as these played a key role in perpetuating the status order because they opened up room for new divisions of labor while upholding the core relationships of the garrison state. But the reliance on hired labor also brought instability. After the 1640s, the status order could no longer function without a large pool of readily available temporary laborers, who were only tenuously integrated into the land-based status groups because many of them lived in tenements or the inns of labor agents. Although the warrior authorities remained ambivalent about labor migration from the countryside to the cities and often took measures to suppress it, they never banned it entirely because they could not afford to jeopardize their labor supply, as officials admitted on occasion.[50]

Status groups thus outsourced the performance of duties. But there was another, more corrosive kind of substitution that gradually spread as a by-product of commercialization: the commodification of stakes. This phenomenon first manifested itself in the *chō*, especially in the larger cities. Contemporaries imagined the *chō* as self-governing, mutually supportive, mutually vigilant groups of house owners, and while this communal ideal always remained somewhat elusive, many *chō* of the early seventeenth century indeed consisted of house owners with plots of similar size.[51] But by

[48] Yokota, "Kinseiteki mibun seido," 67–69.
[49] Wills, "Fires and Fights," 114–22.
[50] Edo's town officials reminded their samurai superiors of this fact, for example, in a consultation about the repatriation of migrants in 1843. See Yokoyama, *Meiji ishin to kinsei mibunsei*, 44.
[51] Yoshida Nobuyuki, "Chōnin to chō," 153–64.

the 1680s and 1690s, powerful merchants in the larger cities had begun to accumulate land in the *chō* to use as collateral in moneylending and operated large tenements to derive income from their plots. To manage these tenements, they often hired caretakers (*yamori*), who performed the role of household head in *chō* self-governance on behalf of absentee landlords. By the mid-eighteenth century, many *chō* in Edo were entirely run by caretakers, and in 1853 only about 3 percent of households in Edo's town quarters were resident landowners.[52]

Caretakers helped maintain the infrastructure of town rule while facilitating the commercial interests of landowners. But they were not as effective as resident landlords in performing the *chō*'s functions of mutual aid and control, transmission of orders and petitions, and registration. Often, the tenements they oversaw were populated by dozens of tenants, and the properties managed by a single caretaker could extend over several *chō*. Control was even weaker if the role of landlord was played by a temple, as was frequently the case in urban areas. By the end of the eighteenth century, over 5,000 townspeople in Edo were living on the grounds of Sensōji, a fief-holding monastery on the outskirts of the city that was organized in a similar way as Makiodera. At the time, Sensōji's thirty-four subtemples derived most of their income from land tenants who operated row houses on their premises. In 1745, the number of townspeople on Sensōji's lands was already so large that the shogunate decided to govern them through Edo's town magistrate rather than the magistrate of temples and shrines. Yet, unlike in the townspeople's quarters proper, there was only a single temple official in charge of communicating with the town magistrate on behalf of thousands of tenants, and shogunal city officials often complained about bad tenant oversight at Sensōji.[53]

Commodification of stakes occurred not just in the *chō* but also within other status groups. By the eighteenth century, status property and membership were often linked by the notion of the share (*kabu*). In the case of trade and craft guilds, a share represented a business right associated (at least ideally) with one member household. Trade and craft guilds were also known as "share associations" (*kabu nakama*) because business rights were the only form of property they claimed, but the term could apply to virtually any status group with hereditary stakeholders. Villagers sometimes spoke of "villager shares" (*hyakushō kabu*) held by members of the village collective. In many places, leatherworkers used the term "share" for their carcass collection rights

---

[52] Iwabuchi, "Kinsei chūkōki Edo"; Yoshida Nobuyuki, "Omotedana to uradana."
[53] Yoshida Nobuyuki, *Kyodai jōkamachi Edo*, 287–314.

(*kusaba kabu*), and guilds of beggar bosses often turned their begging rights into inheritable shares (*bannin kabu*). Even among samurai, some hereditary ranks became informally identified with shares when commoners began to have themselves adopted into samurai households for money, most famously in the case of the shogunate's housemen (*gokenin kabu*).[54]

Shares were not necessarily a symptom of status group decline because they appeared when groups consolidated into stable or hereditary entities. In fact, they often presented an obstacle to commercialization because they allowed members to pass occupational rights onto their descendants. Moreover, groups often regulated the movement of shares by prohibiting pawning, selling, or splitting, and even if they allowed such transactions they could limit them to insiders or supervise them closely by requiring guarantors from within the group.[55] There were groups such as the beggar bosses in Osaka or hairdressers and caretakers in Edo that monopolized certain types of employment – as neighborhood watchmen, communal hairdressers, or caretakers – and appointed underlings or sons as successors without giving the village or *chō* much say in the matter. But, especially in urban areas, shares often did encourage rent-seeking by shareholders. In Edo, for example, guilds of neighborhood hairdressers and neighborhood kiosk owners (*akinai ban'ya*) came to be made up of people who no longer performed the occupation or duties associated with their share and collected rent from the actual operators.[56] Trade in shares also exacerbated wealth gaps within groups. Osaka's guilds of beggar bosses, for example, allowed the trading and pawning of begging rights within the group. These rights were associated with watchman positions in the *chō* and therefore referred to as "watchman shares" (*ban kabu* or *bannin kabu*). In the late eighteenth century, Osaka's beggar boss guilds saw a decline in the number of duty-performing households because some households accumulated shares while others lost theirs and disappeared. Some beggar bosses even moved into townspeople's quarters and stopped performing duty while continuing to collect income from begging shares.[57] The commodification of shares could thus undermine the cohesion and basic functions of self-governing groups.

But commercialization was not just a corrosive force. By creating new divisions of labor, it also stimulated the formation of new occupational associations. Until the end of the Tokugawa period, authorities recognized new

---

[54] Jiang, "Kenkyū nōto."
[55] On guarantors, see Tsukada, "Kasōmin no sekai," 254–55.
[56] Yoshida Nobuyuki, *Seijuku suru Edo*, 289; Tsukada, "Kasōmin no sekai," 254–64; Yoshida Nobuyuki, "Kamiyui."
[57] Tsukada, *Kinsei Ōsaka no hinin*, 66–74; Tsukada, *Ōsaka no hinin*, 147–50.

groups and mobilized them for new duties, and subjects laid claim on new occupations and sought to have them recognized by the government. Most of the new groups took the form of guilds and confraternities because these were not limited by the finite resource of land and could be layered on top of the land-based status groups. Their growth was encouraged by shifts in shogunal policy.[58] Until the late 1600s, the shogunate had insisted on governing townspeople primarily through the *chō* and recognized guilds only in a few occupations that supplied staple commodities, such as lumber, rice, sake, and oil, or performed duties in crime control and other core areas. But by the end of the seventeenth century, many new types of merchants and craftspeople had appeared on the scene, including powerful new moneylenders as well as wholesalers, who formed guilds to insure themselves against the loss of goods in transit. The shogunate co-opted and expanded the wholesalers' self-governing structures and in 1721 pushed ninety-six types of merchants and artisans in Edo to form groups and submit records on group membership. Daimyo pursued similar policies in their territories, and as a result, associations of powerful wholesalers began to dominate the economic and political life of most Japanese town communities. The shogunate repeatedly modified its stance on the recognition of new groups and even issued a ban on all "share associations" between 1841 and 1851 because it suspected them of driving up commodity prices. But even this ban, which was rescinded after ten years because it did not achieve the desired result, could not diminish administrators' reliance on occupational groups.

Subjects eagerly appropriated the logic of the status order for their own ends. Especially for tenants and other people on the fringes of status groups, guilds became a vehicle for making their voices heard because such people had very limited influence within their village or block association and could petition external officials only through their landlords. Once a group had been recognized and was performing duties, it could use its connection to make appeals on completely unrelated matters, for example to request poverty relief or seek official backing in a conflict. But the older groups, too, used the logic of the status order to their advantage. In the eighteenth century, as mentioned, many groups of beggar bosses began to perform new duties as policemen and criminal investigators and demanded to be compensated for their work with new privileges, which could include stipends and additional begging rights, but also new labels and status markers that obscured or at least mitigated their stigma. In many towns, beggar bosses became so important

---

[58] Yoshida Nobuyuki, "Dentō toshi no shūen"; Asao, "Kinsei no mibun," 38–40.

to public safety that the alms they collected assumed the character of a police tax.[59] As late as 1868, the year of the Meiji Restoration, Edo's leatherworker boss Danzaemon and several dozen of his underlings were elevated to "commoner" (*heijin*) status as a reward for mobilizing outcaste troops for the shogunate.[60] These kinds of privileges were coveted by outcastes, but they also caused status anxiety among lower-class commoners, and in that sense created a climate for violent attacks on former base people that occurred after the abolition of outcaste status in 1871. Animus against outcastes was further driven by high population growth in many *kawata* communities, as well as by the economic successes of a small but conspicuous number of leather manufacturers, traders, and beggar bosses.[61]

By the early nineteenth century, many subjects belonged to an occupational group that transcended their village or block association. There were guilds of bathhouse operators, medicine wholesalers, soy sauce brokers, grain dealers, metal casters, lantern makers, toothpick vendors, hairdressers, scrap-metal collectors, fish hawkers, candy peddlers, Shinto clerics, street entertainers, porters, and many more, with structures that reflected the circumstances of their trade and locality. New groups were proliferating in the countryside as well as among base people. In the *kawata* village of Saraike, for example, some residents joined a guild of base cattle traders that specialized in buying old and sick cattle, taking advantage of new cattle-renting services for farmers that had appeared from the middle of the eighteenth century onward.[62] Embedded within the *hinin* village attached to Wakayama town, there was a guild of day laborers during at least the first half of the eighteenth century, whose members unloaded shipments of firewood at the harbor while continuing to derive income from alms.[63] Self-governing associations even emerged among people who performed duties on behalf of others. The *tobi* construction workers mentioned earlier, for example, who served as firefighters on behalf of Edo's townspeople, gradually turned their firefighting brigades into a power base in its own right and attempted to gain recognition from the highest levels by offering to perform duties directly for the shogun.[64] The caretakers of Edo organized through the *chō* to

---

[59] Ehlers, *Give and Take*, 97–102.
[60] Yokoyama, "Meiji ishin to kinsei mibunsei no kaitai," 145–46; Howell, *Geographies of Identity*, 82–83.
[61] Howell, *Geographies of Identity*, 79–109; Mita, "Meiji zenki"; Uesugi, *Meiji ishin to senmin haishirei*, 89–90; Ooms, *Tokugawa Village Practice*, 261–64.
[62] Abele, "Peasants, Skinners, and Dead Cattle," 212–54.
[63] Fujimoto, *Jōkamachi sekai*, 349–54.
[64] Yoshida Nobuyuki, *Kinsei toshi shakai*, 297–301; Wills, "Fires and Fights," 244–62.

regulate access to caretaker positions.[65] By the middle of the eighteenth century, the town elites of Hikone domain who served as rural intendants had established an association (*go-daikan nakama*) that defended their interests as administrators vis-à-vis the domain and collectively vouched for the conduct of appointees.[66] Hikone domain ended its use of townspeople as rural intendants in 1801, but it was not the only example of this kind. In Edo, the *chō* heads (*nanushi*, of whom there were 196 in 1715), commoner officials who represented clusters of *chō*, formed an interest group in the early eighteenth century to discuss administrative matters and protect the dues they collected from the *chō* while promising the shogunate not to extract too much money from the townspeople.[67] Until the Meiji Restoration, the Tokugawa order encouraged subjects to act collectively to assert occupational monopolies, which included claims on administrative positions and could pile up on the backs of existing status groups.

The Dismantling of the Status Order

The Tokugawa status order did not crumble on its own but was actively dismantled by the Meiji government in the years after 1868. The new regime was composed mainly of people of lower samurai background, whose activism against the shogunate was fueled by their frustration with hereditary high-ranking retainers and wealthy commoners and their own inability to attain high office at a time of national crisis. Yet the abolition of the status order was not a foregone conclusion. The Meiji government did not initially plan to end rule by status, and at first merely simplified the status order it had inherited to consolidate its power. But the experiment of a reformed status order foundered after only three years. When the new regime started to remove some of the complexities that had emerged over the years, it actually ended up highlighting the ways in which subjects' aspirations for privileges, overlapping spheres of autonomy, claims on resources, and multiplying channels of control prevented the centralization of power that had become possible after the Restoration Wars. The government thus decided to give up this cumbersome system and encountered relatively little resistance because the framework of the garrison state had already been weakened by various workarounds and substitutions, as well as military reform.

---

[65] Iwabuchi, "Kinsei chūkōki Edo," 224–37.
[66] Watanabe, "Chōnin daikan," 31.
[67] Yoshida Nobuyuki, *Dentō toshi: Edo*, 168–76.

The limitations of rule by status became quickly apparent in the field of urban administration. Immediately after the Meiji Restoration, the administrators of the newly renamed capital of Tokyo were confronted with the challenge of how to control large numbers of unregistered people in the city, including masterless samurai, former shogunal vassals, migrant laborers, and vagrants. For registration, they depended – like their predecessors – on the *chō*, which had in many cases morphed into communities of absentee landowners. Not only were most of Edo's *chō* being managed by caretakers, but caretaker shares had themselves become commodified, creating absentee and deputy caretakers. Moreover, caretakers' fictive "households" had often grown too large and impersonal to exercise any meaningful oversight and register the townspeople through the *chō*. The shogunate had been aware of this problem since at least the 1830s, and the Meiji government finally resolved it with its Household Registration Law (Koseki hō) of 1871, which stipulated that every household, tenant or not, should be registered by its actual location.[68] This law, which came after three years of experimentation, laid the foundation for dismantling the *chō* as self-governing entities. It also denied the category of the unregistered, whose presence had caused popular anxiety and instability in the Bakumatsu years and who had been urged since 1869 to seek registration, with or without the approval of established communities.[69]

The freshly established Meiji regime sought to make the status order more manageable by reducing the growing variety of occupational identities to a handful of general categories.[70] In 1869, following a national order, Tokyo's city government began to assign residents to one of the following status categories: *kazoku* (court nobles), *shizoku* (higher-ranking samurai), *sotsu* (lower-ranking samurai), *shiseki* or *shōseki* (townspeople), "Dan Naoki *shihai-seki*" (people under Dan Naoki's control, that is, the local outcastes), and *shaji-seki* (clerics). The new categories were abstract and no longer assigned through status groups. They made sense to administrators because the privileging of new guilds and the striving for privileges by outcastes and commoners in the course of the Tokugawa period had already reduced the power of villages and *chō* to assign status and had made it extraordinarily difficult for officials to determine the public place of subjects.[71] In urban areas, for example, the proliferation of guilds, confraternities, and privileged

---

[68] Yokoyama, *Meiji ishin to kinsei mibunsei*, 27–61.
[69] Ehlers, *Give and Take*, 156–57.
[70] Yokoyama, "Meiji ishin to kinsei mibunsei no kaitai," 148–53.
[71] On this and the following, see Yokoyama, "Meiji ishin to kinsei mibunsei no kaitai," 135–46.

households had eaten away at the authority of the *chō*. Whereas the *chō* in the first half of the Tokugawa period had played an important role in supervising the trades and crafts of residents – including those organized in guilds – many guilds expanded their autonomy from the *chō* as they began to interact directly with samurai officials. Guild members used their ties with authorities as springboards to attain higher *mibun* (status) – that is, a higher standing in registration, communication with authorities, and appearances in public.

To rein in this complexity and subjects' aspirations, early Meiji officials denied all occupational communities – such as guilds, villages, and *chō* – the power to assign status to subjects.[72] The problem had already been recognized by Tokugawa administrators, who increasingly blocked subjects' demands for more privileges by insisting – contrary to long-standing practice – that there was a difference between status (*mibun*) and occupation (*shokubun*). Officials began to demand that the members of occupational groups that acquired privileges through new duties should limit these to the professional realm and not apply them to their registration or administrative placement. For example, a townsperson with special duties might be called a purveyor or treated as a samurai or accept orders from a courtier family or government office in the context of their occupation, but when it came to status – their registration and procedures of communicating with the authorities – they still counted as a townsperson and had to submit their petitions and other paperwork through the *chō* head. This strategy of separating status and occupation was consciously explored from the late eighteenth century onward, when subjects with special privileges had become too numerous to ignore. By the time of the Meiji Restoration, the habit of regarding status and occupation as two different identities had become so ingrained among administrators that the assignment of general status categories in 1869 no longer seemed a far-fetched idea.

Under the new system of 1869, status was assigned from above rather than through self-governing groups, and for the first time Japan's status order actually had horizontal status categories resembling those of the four estates (*shi-nō-kō-shō*, plus *eta hinin*). Meiji administrators now ordered local officials to remove all ambiguity by forcing people with complicated affiliations – such as commoners under the occupational rule of outcaste bosses, blind professionals, privileged merchants, or temporary samurai – under one of the newly created labels.[73] The most important objective of the new

---

[72] On the following discussion, see Yokoyama, "Meiji ishin to kinsei mibunsei no kaitai," 136–46.

[73] Yokoyama, "Meiji ishin to kinsei mibunsei no kaitai," 150–51; Okumura, "Kindai chihō kenryoku," 95–96.

categories was to facilitate registration, and they continued to be noted on the new household registers (*koseki*) long after rule by status had ended. Meiji officials could now simply draw up new districts for registration without regard for the old status zones such as *chō*, samurai quarters, or temple precincts, into which towns and cities had long been divided. Within each district, all residents could simply be listed by their place of residence and then be marked with one of the new status labels. This was helpful because in Edo, especially, residence had become so mixed that the old administrative structures for townspeople, samurai, and clerics could no longer be easily mapped onto spatial divisions such as *chō* land, samurai land, or temple land. (For example, recall the thousands of townspeople on the grounds of Sensōji's subtemples who fell under the rule of the town magistrate rather than the magistrate of temples and shrines.) By disregarding the status zones, Meiji administrators were able to register all subjects exactly where they resided. But the use of these districts was still limited to the task of registration; it did not imply that the new authorities were ready to give up on rule by status entirely. *Chō*, villages, outcaste groups, guilds, and retainer bands still kept most of their privileges, and the Meiji government continued to rely on these groups to communicate with subjects and governed the members of each category through separate administrative channels. This insistence on keeping the old channels of control intact caused problems when the government began to implement the Household Registration Law of 1871. The first step was to conduct a survey of temporary residents (*kiryū-nin*). For the purpose of that survey, Tokyo's city administrators had to collect residential information from leaders of various status groups such as block associations, retainer bands, and monastic communities, then piece it together and rearrange it by spatial units. They soon complained that it was too complicated to govern people by place of residence if they also had to consider subjects' affiliations with self-governing groups.[74]

In 1871, rule by status finally came to an end. The problems with the Household Registration Law were one major factor behind this decision. But 1871 was also the year in which the new regime made all lords return their lands to the emperor and move to Tokyo, effectively confiscating the daimyo's fiefs. This radical, regime-saving measure called the autonomy of all status groups into question because samurai and people affiliated with court nobles, temples, and other fief-holding entities were released from their ties of vassalage, and many of the authorities that had guaranteed

---

[74] Yokoyama, "Meiji ishin to kinsei mibunsei no kaitai," 157–58.

autonomy and privileges to self-governing groups suddenly disappeared. The new government, meanwhile, had concentrated all fiefs in its hands, and in subsequent weeks quickly appropriated other pockets of autonomy by dismantling the status-based control structures through which it had formerly communicated with subjects. On 3 July (the eighteenth day of the eighth month according to the old lunisolar calendar), it broke down the administrative division between samurai and commoners by stopping to govern the samurai through retainer bands, and ten days later proclaimed the immediate abolition of the status designations of *"eta, hinin,* and other [base people]." This order, which is today known as the outcaste abolition edict (*senmin haishirei*), stated that henceforth, all types of base people should be treated in the same manner as commoners in terms of both status and occupation (see Ian Neary's discussion in volume 3, chapter 18).

The Meiji leadership did not issue the outcaste abolition edict out of a desire to liberate outcastes from their base position. It was primarily interested in eliminating outcastes' structures of self-government and incorporating them into its new, centralized system of government.[75] To be sure, some intellectuals in the Bakumatsu era had advocated outcaste abolition to promote national unity and hoped that moral reform would gradually turn outcastes into useful imperial subjects. Among the early Meiji leaders, there were people who echoed these views, and many leaders leaned toward gradual abolition.[76] The edict of 1871, however, amounted to a sudden leveling of the distinction between commoners and base people and took most subjects by surprise. Many outcastes did perceive the abolition edict as liberating, and some used it in subsequent years to sue their neighbors for discrimination, in some cases successfully.[77] Former commoners, on the other hand, could no longer count on the state to uphold the distinction, and they were forced to make their discriminatory choices more explicit to "protect" their old customs and communities from former outcaste interlopers.[78] Economically, too, the abolition edict had an ambivalent effect on former base people, who did gain freedom of occupation but often saw their livelihoods diminished by the loss of privileges. A few months before the proclamation of the outcaste abolition edict, the government revoked the leatherworkers' carcass collection rights to facilitate modern leather and meat production, and in the early 1870s, local administrators across the country denied former *hinin*'s begging

---

[75] Yokoyama, "Senmin haishirei."
[76] Uesugi, *Meiji ishin to senmin haishirei,* 24–27; Howell, *Geographies of Identity,* 82–84.
[77] Igeta, "Meiji zenki ni okeru buraku."
[78] Howell, *Geographies of Identity,* 88.

rights and issued begging bans, effectively erasing begging as an occupation. The Meiji government also turned against nonbase mendicant groups including the guilds of the blind, not just to revoke their autonomy but also to release subjects from the burden of almsgiving, which many had come to resent during the inflationary years before the Meiji Restoration.[79] The legal abolition of outcastes, mendicants, and many other marginal groups had the added effect of making the Japanese government appear more civilized in Western eyes.

In 1871, the Meiji regime thus gave up on rule by status, in the sense that it stopped relying on self-governing groups for managing, mobilizing, and communicating with subjects. Another big reform begun in 1871 – the issuing of certificates of private landownership – undermined self-governing groups by reshaping subjects' relationship to land.[80] Under the status order, land had been not only the main target of taxation but also an important form of collective property, and the issuing of ownership certificates thus paralleled Hideyoshi's land survey of the late sixteenth century in its significance. It released both residential and agricultural land from the collective grip of the land-based status communities and laid the groundwork for a new tax system that taxed the market value of land and allocated taxes to individual landowners rather than village and *chō* communities. After this reform, land could be traded freely without interference by villages or *chō*, and it could change hands without any regard to government restrictions on the alienation of land from one status zone to another. All subjects could now take up residence wherever they pleased, including former samurai quarters. The start of this reform was soon followed by the revocation of various status-based land tax exemptions that had been enjoyed by groups as well as individual privileged households. After this reform, which took several years to complete, the *chō* and villages ceased to exist as self-governing communities, at least in the eyes of the state.

The privileges of samurai proved the most difficult to deny, but it was here that the need for reorganization was most pressing because the samurai's social units had been heavily impacted by Meiji Restoration warfare. The Boshin War embodied more than just a rift between two opposing camps of samurai over foreign policy and Tokugawa legitimacy. The war also relied on new forms of military mobilization that struck at the heart of the garrison state and rule by status. One factor was the introduction of new styles of

[79] Takano, "Bakuhansei shakai no kaitai," 22–26.
[80] Matsuzawa, *Nihon kindai shakaishi*, 51–69.

Western gunnery and military tactics by the shogunate and many domains in the Bakumatsu era. These new techniques required a reorganization of military units but were obstructed by the old hierarchies of retainer bands, which reflected older forms of warfare.[81] Second, all parties in the struggle mobilized significant numbers of non-samurai for their militaries by raising peasant units as well as units of outcastes, day laborers, even sumo wrestlers and gamblers.[82] Although the Meiji leaders, most of whom were samurai themselves, were hesitant to undermine the privileges of their own class, they had to reorganize the military in ways no longer compatible with the samurai's existing social structures.

The elements of samurai status were dismantled only gradually. In 1871, the government stopped governing the samurai through their status organizations, the vassal bands, and the introduction of universal military conscription in 1872–73 denied the samurai's professional identity as performers of military duty. But the government waited until 1876 to prohibit samurai from wearing swords in public and phase out the payment of stipends to relieve itself of an enormous fiscal burden. This hesitation can be explained with the fear of samurai uprisings, which turned out to be well founded as discontented samurai did rise up against the regime on multiple occasions until 1877. Many of these samurai had fought victoriously in the Restoration Wars and expected to be rewarded rather than demoted by the new regime. That the abolition of samurai privilege succeeded at all seems to have been due to slow and gradual changes in the character of samurai status in the Tokugawa period. Many samurai had already struggled to make ends meet on sinking stipends and appreciated the opportunity to take up new careers. Even high-ranking retainers rarely had any landholdings that would have been worth defending against the centralizing state.[83]

The consequences of withdrawing recognition from thousands of self-governing communities were unpredictable and disruptive, even violent, and it took the Meiji government many years to restructure local government and establish new procedures to mobilize subjects and regulate economic activity. Many of the old villages, chō, and guilds persisted in some form even after losing their public standing and influenced economic and social life in Japan for decades. Yet the fall of the shogunate was a truly revolutionary

[81] Hōya, "Military History of the Boshin War"; Jaundrill, *Samurai to Soldier*, 17–18, 49–54, 60–66, 179–80.
[82] Jaundrill, *Samurai to Soldier*, 49–54, 60–66; Platt, "'Farmer-Soldiers'"; Matsuzawa, *Jiyū minken undō*, 17–23.
[83] Smith, "Japan's Aristocratic Revolution."

moment – not in the sense of one class overthrowing another, but because it paved the way for an entirely new style of governance that radically simplified the relationship between state and subjects, taking into account changes that had been brewing for over two centuries. For the new regime, the fall of the shogunate represented an opportunity to wipe out a convoluted system that gave subjects too much leeway in asserting their interests. For many educated elites, the removal of status distinctions was a liberating experience as they could now take up a career of their choosing and make a mark in the world. But not all samurai fared well after the loss of their privileges, and to samurai and commoners alike, the freedoms granted to lower-ranking groups could feel like social demotion. Millions of humble townspeople, villagers, and mendicants suddenly had to make do without the collective guarantees and privileges of status groups. For outcastes, the fall of the shogunate was a mixed blessing as it brought new freedoms on one hand and a loss of privileges and renewed discrimination on the other. For women, too, the end of the status order had mixed effects. While some women eagerly embraced the new discourse of equality and the new roles they could perform for the nation, the new household registers explicitly subordinated them to men within the structure of the household.[84] For all these discontents, the Meiji Restoration marked the beginning of a long struggle to gain a voice under a new system.

Bibliography

Abele, Michael. "Peasants, Skinners, and Dead Cattle: The Transformation of Rural Society in Western Japan, 1600–1890." PhD diss., University of Illinois at Urbana-Champaign, 2018.

Amos, Timothy D. *Caste in Early Modern Japan: Danzaemon and the Edo Outcaste Order.* London: Routledge, 2020.

Anderson, Marnie. *A Place in Public: Women's Rights in Meiji Japan.* Cambridge, MA: Harvard University Asia Center, 2011.

Asao Naohiro. "Hiden'in to Ōmi no hininban." In *Nihon kokka no shiteki tokushitsu: Kinsei/Kindai,* edited by Asao Naohiro Kyōju Taikan Kinenkai, 3–36. Kyoto: Shibunkaku Shuppan, 1995.

"Jūhasseiki no shakai hendō to mibunteki chūkansō." In *Kindai e no taidō,* edited by Tsuji Tatsuya, 45–94. Vol. 10 of *Nihon no kinsei.* Chūōkōronsha, 1993.

"Kinsei Kyōto no rōnin." In *Asao Naohiro chosakushū,* Vol. 7, 225–50. Iwanami Shoten, 2004.

"Kinsei no mibun to sono hen'yō." In Asao, *Mibun to kakushiki,* 7–40.

[84] Anderson, *Place in Public*; Yokoyama, *Meiji ishin to kinsei mibunsei,* 283–324.

ed. *Mibun to kakushiki*. Vol. 7 of *Nihon no kinsei*. Chūōkōronsha, 1992.

"Sōson kara chō e." In *Shakaiteki shoshūdan*, edited by Asao Naohiro, Amino Yoshihiko, Yamaguchi Keiji, and Yoshida Takashi, 323–62. Vol. 6 of *Nihon no shakaishi*. Iwanami Shoten, 1988.

Berry, Mary Elizabeth. *The Culture of Civil War in Kyoto*. Berkeley: University of California Press, 1994.

Ehlers, Maren. *Give and Take: Poverty and the Status Order in Early Modern Japan*. Cambridge, MA: Harvard University Asia Center, 2018.

Fujimoto Seijirō. *Jōkamachi sekai no seikatsushi*. Osaka: Seibundō, 2014.

Hellyer, Robert, and Harald Fuess, eds. *The Meiji Restoration: Japan as a Global Nation*. Cambridge: Cambridge University Press, 2020.

Howell, David L. *Geographies of Identity in Nineteenth-Century Japan*. Berkeley: University of California Press, 2005.

Hōya Tōru. "A Military History of the Boshin War." In Hellyer and Fuess, *Meiji Restoration*, 153–70.

Igeta Ryōji. "Meiji zenki ni okeru buraku sabetsu to saiban: 'Daishin'in minji hanketsuroku' ni miru." In *Burakushi no kenkyū, Kindai-hen*, edited by Buraku Mondai Kenkyūjo, 323–59. Kyoto: Buraku Mondai Kenkyūjo, 1984.

Iwabuchi Reiji. "Kinsei chūkōki Edo no 'yamori no chōchū' no jitsuzō." In *Toshi to shōnin/ geinōmin: Chūsei kara kinsei e*, edited by Gomi Fumihiko and Yoshida Nobuyuki, 204– 44. Yamakawa Shuppansha, 1993.

Izumi Shishi Hensan Iinkai, ed. *Yokoyama to Makiosan no rekishi*. Vol. 1 of *Izumi-shi no rekishi*. Izumi: Izumi-shi, 2015.

ed. *Shinodayama chiiki no rekishi to seikatsu*. Vol. 4 of *Izumi-shi no rekishi*. Izumi: Izumi-shi, 2015.

Jaundrill, D. Colin. *Samurai to Soldier: Remaking Military Service in Nineteenth-Century Japan*. Ithaca, NY: Cornell University Press, 2016.

Jiang Yingyan. "Kenkyū nōto: Kinsei chūkōki ni okeru bushi mibun no baibai ni tsuite: 'Fujiokaya nikki' o sozai ni." *Nihon kenkyū* 37 (2008): 163–200.

Katō Yasuaki. *Nihon mōjin shakaishi kenkyū*. Miraisha, 1974.

Kumagai Mitsuko. "Kinsei daimyō kakyū kashindan no kōzōteki bunseki: Bungo Oka-han o sozai to shite." *Nihonshi kenkyū* 316 (1988): 1–44.

Matsuzawa Yūsaku. *Jiyū minken undō: "Demokurashī" no yume to zasetsu*. Iwanami Shinsho, 2016.

Nihon kindai shakaishi: Shakai shūdan to shijō kara yomitoku 1868–1914. Yūhikaku, 2022.

Mita Satoko. *Kinsei mibun shakai no sonraku kōzō: Senshū Minami Ōji-mura o chūshin ni*. Kyoto: Buraku Mondai Kenkyūjo, 2018.

"Meiji zenki ni okeru Senshū Izumi-gun Minami Ōji-mura to Shinoda chiiki." In *Mibunteki shūen to chiiki shakai*, edited by Tsukada Takashi and Yoshida Nobuyuki, 83–114. Yamakawa Shuppansha, 2013.

Morishita Tōru. *Bushi to iu mibun: Jōkamachi Hagi no daimyō kashindan*. Yoshikawa Kōbunkan, 2012.

Nagano Hiroko. "Nihon kinsei no hyakushō mibun to jendā." *Keizaigaku ronsan* 40, no. 5–6 (2000): 385–403.

Okumura Hiroshi. "Kindai chihō kenryoku to 'kokumin' no keisei: Meiji shonen no 'kōron' o chūshin ni." *Rekishigaku kenkyū* 638 (1992): 95–106.

Ono Shō. "Mibunsei shakairon to iu shikaku: Kinsei Nihonshi kenkyū kara kangaeru." *Rekishi hyōron* 564 (1997): 89–102.

Ooms, Herman. *Tokugawa Village Practice: Class, Status, Power, Law.* Berkeley: University of California Press, 1996.

Platt, Brian. "'Farmer-Soldiers' and Local Leadership in Late Edo Period Japan." In Hellyer and Fuess, *Meiji Restoration*, 137–52.

Roberts, Luke S. *Performing the Great Peace: Political Space and Open Secrets in Tokugawa Japan.* Honolulu: University of Hawai'i Press, 2012.

Smith, Thomas C. "Japan's Aristocratic Revolution." In *Native Sources of Japanese Industrialization, 1750–1920,* 133–47. Berkeley: University of California Press, 1988.

Takagi Shōsaku. *Nihon kinsei kokkashi no kenkyū.* Iwanami Shoten, 1990.

Takano Toshihiko. "Bakuhansei shakai no kaitai to mibunteki shūen." In *Mibun o toinaosu,* edited by Kurushima Hiroshi, Takano Toshihiko, Tsukada Takashi, Yokota Fuyuhiko, and Yoshida Nobuyuki, 18–28. Yoshikawa Kōbunkan, 2000.

Tanaka Shinji. "Tottori-han ni okeru 'zaichū' hiningashira no seikatsu to 'yaku' (2)." *Kaihō kenkyū Tottori* 3 (February 2001): 11–27.

Tonomura, Hitomi. *Community and Commerce in Late Medieval Japan: The Corporate Villages of Tokuchin-ho.* Stanford, CA: Stanford University Press, 1992.

Tsukada Takashi. "Kasōmin no sekai: 'Mibunteki shūen' no shiten kara." In Asao, *Mibun to kakushiki,* 225–68.

Kinsei Nihon mibunsei no kenkyū. Kobe: Hyōgo Buraku Mondai Kenkyūjo, 1987.

Kinsei Ōsaka no hinin to mibunteki shūen. Kyoto: Buraku Mondai Kenkyūjo, 2007.

"Mibunsei no kōzō." In *Iwanami kōza: Nihon tsūshi,* Vol. 12, edited by Asao Naohiro, Amino Yoshihiko, Ishii Susumu, Kano Masanao, Hayakawa Shōhachi, and Yasumaru Yoshio, 111–35. Iwanami Shoten, 1994.

Mibunsei shakai to shimin shakai: Kinsei Nihon no shakai to hō. Kashiwa Shobō, 1992.

"Mibunteki shūen to rekishi shakai no kōzō." In *Mibun o toinaosu,* edited by Kurushima Hiroshi, Takano Toshihiko, Tsukada Takashi, Yokota Fukuhiko, and Yoshida Nobuyuki, 73–93. Yoshikawa Kōbunkan, 2000.

Ōsaka minshū no kinseishi: Oi to yamai/nariwai/kasō shakai. Chikuma Shobō, 2017.

Ōsaka no hinin: Kotsujiki/Shitennōji/korobi kirishitan. Chikuma Shobō, 2013.

Uesugi Satoshi. *Meiji ishin to senmin haishirei.* Kaihō Shuppansha, 1990.

Walthall, Anne. "The Life Cycle of Farm Women in Tokugawa Japan." In *Recreating Japanese Women, 1600–1945,* edited by Gail Bernstein, 42–70. Berkeley: University of California Press, 1991.

"Village Networks: *Sōdai* and the Sale of Edo Nightsoil." *Monumenta Nipponica* 43, no. 3 (1988): 279–303.

Watanabe Kōichi. "Chōnin daikan: Hikone-han no daikan seido." In *Shihai o sasaeru hito-bito,* edited by Kurushima Hiroshi, 21–61. Vol. 5 of *Shiriizu mibunteki shūen.* Yoshikawa Kōbunkan, 2000.

Wills, Steven. "Fires and Fights: Urban Conflagration, Governance, and Society in Edo-Tokyo, 1657–1890." PhD diss., Columbia University, 2010.

Yabuta Yutaka. *Kokuso to hyakushō ikki no kenkyū.* Azekura Shobō, 1992.

Yamaguchi Keiji. *Sakoku to kaikoku.* Iwanami Shoten, 2006.

Yokota Fuyuhiko. "Kinseiteki mibun seido no seiritsu." In Asao, *Mibun to kakushiki,* 41–78.

Yokoyama Yuriko. "Meiji ishin to kinsei mibunsei no kaitai." In *Kinsei no kaitai*, edited by Rekishigaku Kenkyūkai and Nihonshi Kenkyūkai, 133–62. Vol. 7 of *Nihonshi kōza*. Tōkyō Daigaku Shuppankai, 2005.

Meiji ishin to kinsei mibunsei no kaitai. Yamakawa Shuppansha, 2005.

"Senmin haishirei no seitei riyū to sono rekishiteki ichi." *Fujita sensei taishoku kinen: Tōkyō Daigaku Nihon Shigaku Kenkyūshitsu kiyō bessatsu* (2010): 291–304.

Yoshida Nobuyuki. "Chōnin to chō." In *Kōza Nihon rekishi*, Vol. 5, edited by Rekishigaku Kenkyūkai and Nihonshi Kenkyūkai, 151–64. Tōkyō Daigaku Shuppankai, 1985.

Dentō toshi: Edo. Tōkyō Daigaku Shuppankai, 2012.

"Dentō toshi no shūen." In *Kinsei no kaitai*, edited by Rekishigaku Kenkyūkai and Nihonshi Kenkyūkai, 36–46. Vol. 7 of *Nihonshi kōza*. Tōkyō Daigaku Shuppankai, 2005.

"Kamiyui no shokubun to shoyū." *Shisō* 1084 (2014): 29–45.

Kinsei toshi shakai no mibun kōzō. Tōkyō Daigaku Shuppankai, 1998.

Kyodai jōkamachi Edo no bunsetsu kōzō. Yamakawa Shuppansha, 1999.

"Omotedana to uradana: Shōnin no sekai, minshū no sekai." In *Nihon no kinsei*, Vol. 9, edited by Yoshida Nobuyuki, 305–26. Chūōkōronsha, 1992.

Seijuku suru Edo. Kōdansha, 2002.

"Shoyū to mibunteki shūen." In *Mibun o toinaosu*, edited by Kurushima Hiroshi, Takano Toshihiko, Tsukada Takashi, Yokota Fuyuhiko, and Yoshida Nobuyuki, 94–117. Yoshikawa Kōbunkan, 2000.

Yoshida Yuriko. "Chiiki shakai to mibunteki shūen: Shinano no kuni Shimoina-gun o chūshin to shite." *Buraku mondai kenkyū* 174 (2005): 2–32.

"Manzai to haruta-uchi: Kinsei Shimoina no mibunteki shūen." *Iida-shi rekishi kenkyūjo nenpō* 1 (2003): 50–80.

18

On the Peripheries of the
Japanese Archipelago
Ryukyu and Hokkaido

DAVID L. HOWELL

The Kuroshio flows northward off the Pacific coast of Japan. During the
Tokugawa period, ships disabled in storms rode the current helplessly, often to
their doom. Unlucky crews might have been swept far to the north and east
of the Japanese archipelago, toward the Kuril and Aleutian Islands. Lucky ones
might have made landfall somewhere like the Tosa domain on the southern
coast of Shikoku, which lay closer to the current than other parts of the main
Japanese islands. Luke Roberts relates the story of how, in the summer of 1795,
one such lucky crew found its way to a port at the mouth of the Shimanto River.
The men aboard the small vessel came from the Ryukyu kingdom (modern-day
Okinawa). The shipwrecked men and their hosts had trouble communicating,
but they managed to understand one another well enough to share songs and
stories, paintings and calligraphy, and a wealth of information about the customs
of their homelands. The Ryukyuans even treated their hosts to a dish of "west
ocean rice parched with sugar" – apparently sweetened long-grain rice.[1]

The Tosa officials tasked with taking care of the Ryukyuans surely saw
the men as foreigners. Even aside from all the puzzling over language and
customs, the Ryukyuans' arrival immediately set into motion protocols for
dealing with foreign shipwrecks. Local officials notified their superiors in the
castle town of Kōchi, who sent word to the shogunate's highest appointed
officials, the senior councillors, who in turn oversaw the process of returning
the men home. The shogunate did not repatriate the crew itself, however, but
rather instructed Satsuma, a large and powerful domain in southern Kyushu,
to retrieve the men. Satsuma took responsibility for the castaways because,
since 1609, the kingdom had been the domain's vassal state, kept nominally
independent for reasons that suited both the shogunate and Satsuma.

---

[1] Roberts, "Shipwrecks and Flotsam," 103–10.

Shipwreck stories such as this beg the question of whether Ryukyu belongs in a volume on early modern Japanese history. Should historians emphasize the islands' status as a nominally independent kingdom or focus instead on their subordination to Satsuma and, by association, Japan? The same question applies to Hokkaido, most of which was understood to lie beyond the Tokugawa polity's borders and yet was tied closely both economically and politically to the early modern state.

Any national history project faces the dilemma of what to include when current national boundaries do not coincide with historical ones, but it is particularly vexing in the Japanese case. The identity of the nation with its dominant ethnic group in the modern period has turned every discussion of "Japanese" history into an implicit comment on what and who is meant by "Japanese." The situating of places such as Ryukyu and Hokkaido inside or outside the early modern polity shapes our understanding of their status during the modern era as colonial possessions or integral parts of the Japanese nation. This situating in turn affects the way we understand everything from the indigeneity of the Ainu people of Hokkaido to the status of Okinawan as a full-fledged language or merely a dialect of Japanese.

Most worrisome, however, is the reality that academic choices about history writing inevitably suggest stands on territorial disputes, even when the historian insists that contemporary understandings of sovereignty did not apply in the early modern world. Nowadays, Japan asserts a long history of engagement as the basis of its claim to the so-called Northern Territories – Etorofu, Kunashiri, Shikotan, and the Habomai Islands – which were taken along with the rest of the Kuril Islands by the Soviet Union after World War II.[2] The Ryukyu kingdom's maintenance of tributary relations with the Ming and Qing empires has given rise to outrageous claims that Okinawa properly belongs to China and lamentations of Chiang Kai-shek's failure to "recover" the Ryukyus at the Cairo Conference in 1943.[3]

Ryukyu before the Tokugawa Period

The Ryukyu archipelago is a chain of more than fifty islands that extends for about 1,100 kilometers from the southern tip of Kyushu southwest to Taiwan. The Kuroshio Current isolates most of the archipelago from

[2] See, for example, the Hokkaido prefectural government's presentation of the Northern Territories issue: "What to Know: The Northern Territories."
[3] "Calls Grow in China to Press Claim for Okinawa"; Zhai, "Rewriting the Legacy of Chiang Kai-shek."

Taiwan to the southwest and Japan to the northeast. Geographers divide the Ryukyus into five major groups (the Ōsumi, Tokara, Amami, Okinawa, and Sakishima Islands). Of these, only the Ōsumi Islands, immediately south of Kyushu, have never been subject in any way to the authority of an independent Ryukyuan state. The Tokara and Amami Islands were to varying degrees under Ryukyuan control until the early seventeenth century but were incorporated into the Satsuma domain afterward and are now, along with the Ōsumi Islands, part of Kagoshima Prefecture. The Ryukyu kingdom after 1609 comprised the Okinawa and Sakishima Islands; these island groups, along with the Daitō and disputed Senkaku (Diaoyu) Islands, now make up Okinawa Prefecture. Okinawa is by far the biggest and most important island in the archipelago; other important islands include Amami Ōshima, Miyako, and Ishigaki.

The Amami and Okinawa island groups were populated at least in part by migrants from the Japanese mainland to the north, who brought the Neolithic Jōmon and Yayoi cultures with them between about 3000 BCE and the first centuries of the Common Era. The prehistoric society of the Sakishima Islands reflected no such movement of people or culture, but rather showed cultural affinities with Taiwan and insular Southeast Asia. After a long incubation, during which it was largely isolated from the outside world, Ryukyuan society began to change rapidly around the middle of the eleventh century. The development of trade networks and agriculture supported increasingly complex social and political organization as well as the gradual development of a unitary culture joining Amami and Okinawa in the north with the Sakishima Islands in the south. These changes are reflected in the appearance around the archipelago of stone fortifications that served both military and religious functions. The Gusuku period (c. 1050–1429) is named for these fortifications.[4]

Ryukyuan contacts with Japan and China increased steadily during the Gusuku period. From the twelfth century onward, Ryukyu was a regular destination for traders from both Japan and China, and Ryukyuans themselves began to venture forth in search of commerce. Before then, "the islands had nothing to offer the outside world," as Richard Pearson puts it, but the Chinese invention of gunpowder spurred demand for sulfur, which remained Ryukyu's most important export for centuries.[5] Merchants from the Kyushu port of Hakata brought pottery and other commodities that circulated

---

[4] Akamine, *Ryukyu Kingdom*, 3, 10–19; Pearson, *Archaeology of the Ryukyu Islands*, 134–38.
[5] Pearson, *Archaeology of the Ryukyu Islands*, 138.

throughout the archipelago. Other traders carried ceramics and other goods from China to Kyushu via the Ryukyus.[6]

According to traditional accounts, the protostates of the Gusuku age developed apace until, by the early fourteenth century, three kingdoms had emerged on the island of Okinawa. They struggled among themselves for power and influence, and all responded in 1372 to demands for tribute from the newly established Ming dynasty.[7] Gregory Smits argues that, rather than territorially cohesive regimes, the kingdoms may have been fictive entities that existed mostly to participate in tributary relations.[8] Whatever their precise character, the Chūzan kingdom in central Okinawa was the dominant of the three, and in 1429 it finally eliminated its rivals. Even as it was consolidating its hold over Okinawa, Chūzan extended its reach into the Sakishima Islands, beginning with Miyako around the end of the fourteenth century and expanding into the Yaeyama Islands during the following century. Yaeyama's "independence and prosperity," fueled by a lively trade with Fujian of Chinese ceramics for local shells, marine products, medicinal plants, and woven hemp, came to an end in 1500, when the islands' ruler, Ōyake Akahachi, finally capitulated to Chūzan.[9] By this point, Chūzan – let us now call it the Ryukyu kingdom – had extended its power north to the Amami Islands and influenced if not directly ruled over the Tokara Islands as well. The sixteenth century thus marked the high point of Ryukyuan power.

Smits argues that state-building in Ryukyu owed much to the activities of pirates (wakō) and other adventurers entering the archipelago from the north. Indeed, he concludes that the Shō royal house descended from one Same-kawa, a wakō from Higo Province in western Kyushu.[10] Likewise, Thomas Nelson emphasizes the important influence of medieval Japan on early Ryukyuan religion, economy, and international relations, particularly with Korea.[11] These arguments help to balance the tendency to focus on Ryukyu's far more thoroughly documented Chinese connections.

Akamine Mamoru calls Ryukyu the "cornerstone of East Asia," but a better image may be that of an airline hub through which passengers pass on their way to their final destinations. In Ryukyu's case, some of those passengers had been captured by wakō and put up for sale at Naha's thriving slave

---

[6] Pearson, *Ancient Ryukyu*, 190.
[7] Asato, "Ryūkyū ōkoku no keisei," 128–30.
[8] Smits, *Maritime Ryukyu*.
[9] Pearson, *Ancient Ryukyu*, 265.
[10] Smits, *Maritime Ryukyu*.
[11] Nelson, "Japan in the Life of Early Ryukyu."

market.[12] Their fate is a stark reminder of the human cost of Ryukyu's golden age of independence and prosperity. During the two centuries from the late fourteenth to late sixteenth centuries, maritime traffic in the East China and South China Seas connected Japan, China, Korea, and Southeast Asia via Naha and other Ryukyuan ports.[13] Ryukyu's emergence as a hub owed much to the Ming dynasty's maritime prohibition policies, which limited Chinese travel abroad. The Ming used Ryukyu as its proxy in international trade, as seen in the presence of a community of Fujianese émigrés near Naha who oversaw Ryukyuan trade and diplomacy (except with Japan) and were charged with introducing Chinese culture into Ryukyu.[14] These émigrés and their descendants wielded great influence from their base at Kumemura, a district near both the port at Naha and the royal palace at Shuri, throughout the history of the Ryukyu kingdom and indeed later, but they were not agents of the Ming (or succeeding Qing) state per se. Their presence did, however, help Ryukyu make the most of the Ming tributary system, which represented an opportunity to trade directly with China on advantageous terms. Ryukyu sent far more missions to the Ming than any other tributary – 171 missions in all, nearly twice as many as second-place Annam's eighty-nine.[15]

Ryukyu maintained close ties with Japan during this period as well, though they did not involve nearly as much formal diplomacy as its relations with China did. This difference is not surprising considering that the height of Ryukyuan prosperity coincided with a period of severe disorder in Japan. Yet, whatever the condition of state-to-state relations, merchants, monks, pirates, and other voyagers from the north brought a steady flow of cultural influences, including Buddhism, to the islands. The economic relationship with Japan was important, too. Ryukyuan traders sold spices and other luxury goods from Southeast Asia and China in Japan (and Korea), and in exchange imported copper and ironware.[16]

The integration of the East Asian economy during the sixteenth century undermined Ryukyu's position at the center of it. By the middle of the century, the Portuguese had bases in both China and Japan, and during the decades that followed, Dutch, Spanish, and English commercial interests established themselves in East and Southeast Asia. The Europeans inserted

---

[12] Akamine, *Ryukyu Kingdom*, 30–31. Although he does not discuss Ryukyu, Nelson provides ample evidence of slavery throughout medieval East Asia: Nelson, "Slavery in Medieval Japan."
[13] Kobata and Matsuda, *Ryukyuan Relations*.
[14] Murai, *Ajia no naka no chūsei Nihon*, 129–31.
[15] Murai, "Kenmu, Muromachi seiken," 37.
[16] Nelson, "Japan in the Life of Early Ryukyu."

themselves into the regional carrying trade, using their large ships to transport more cargo and do it more quickly, efficiently, and securely than their Ryukyuan rivals could. The Europeans' arrival alone did not cause Ryukyu's decline, but once they were on the scene it became easy to bypass Ryukyu entirely when transporting goods from Southeast Asia or China to Japan. The kingdom's niche in the regional trading order was further reduced by the Ming dynasty's relaxation of its maritime prohibitions in 1567 and, in the 1580s, the hegemon Toyotomi Hideyoshi's successful assertion of control over shipping to and from Japan.

The Satsuma domain turned its eyes toward Ryukyu as the East Asian world order was changing during the sixteenth century. The few sources that purport to illuminate the prehistory of Satsuma's invasion in 1609 are not reliable; compiled or even composed long after the fact, they attempt to naturalize Satsuma's suzerainty with specious assertions of long-standing claims to the islands.[17] No matter. With the free-for-all world of maritime commerce coming to an end, it made sense for the domain to covet control over all Ryukyuan trade with Japan. Hideyoshi's belief that Ryukyu was his to grant as a fief to whomever he pleased added urgency to Satsuma's desires. The domain managed simultaneously to elbow out rivals for the hegemon's favor and coerce Ryukyu into complying with demands for assistance in Hideyoshi's invasion of Korea, with the result that Hideyoshi acknowledged Satsuma's presumed rights to Ryukyu before he died in 1598.[18]

Satsuma kept up its pressure on Ryukyu after the establishment of the Tokugawa shogunate in 1603. It invaded Ryukyu with the shogunate's permission in the third month of 1609. A small force of Satsuma warriors seized Shuri Castle a few days after landing on Okinawa. Less than two months later the entire archipelago had capitulated, and the king, Shō Nei, and leading members of his court were held captive in Kagoshima. The following year Satsuma took the king to Edo to submit formally to the shogun, Tokugawa Hidetada, who recognized Ryukyu's nominal independence by confirming Shō Nei as king while also granting Satsuma authority to levy taxes on the islands.

Satsuma annexed the islands north of Okinawa but left the Ryukyuan court to administer the rest of the kingdom autonomously. It assigned the kingdom a yield (*kokudaka*) of 89,096 *koku*, which determined the baseline for calculations of annual tribute payments to Satsuma. In 1611, Shō Nei and his council of three top officials (the *sanshikan*) were released from their captivity

[17] Nelson, "Japan in the Life of Early Ryukyu," 369–70.
[18] Kamiya, "Tai-Min seisaku to Ryūkyū shihai," 253–64.

in Kagoshima, but only after they had accepted a fifteen-article proclamation that affirmed Ryukyu's place within the Tokugawa order and unequivocally surrendered the kingdom's control over its trade. Furthermore, the king had to acquiesce to a statement that Ryukyu had always been a tributary of Satsuma's and that it was only through that domain's goodwill that it had been allowed to reestablish itself after its recent chastisement.[19]

Ryukyu during the Tokugawa Period

The Ryukyu kingdom is an example of the complexities of sovereignty in the early modern world. The bottom line is simple: Satsuma controlled Ryukyu, period. China made no territorial claims on the islands, and Japan's hold on them before the 1870s was always exercised through Satsuma. Those of us living in the age of geographically demarcated nation-states may struggle to comprehend how Ryukyu could simultaneously function as an independent kingdom, a colonial appendage of the Satsuma domain, and a tributary of both China and Japan. However, it was hardly the most complexly situated polity in Asia at the time.[20] Indeed, Ryukyu was no odder than vestigial modern examples of ambiguous sovereignty, such as Andorra, a principality without a prince ruled jointly until 1993 by the president of France and the Spanish Bishop of Urgell (who remain the titular heads of state).

After a few decades of uncertainty following the Satsuma invasion, Ryukyu settled into the pattern that would govern it throughout the rest of the Tokugawa period and indeed a few years into the succeeding Meiji era. The kingdom maintained its tributary relationship with China, duly shifting its allegiance to the Qing dynasty after the Ming's collapse in 1644. Officially, it sent tribute missions every other year but in fact contrived to dispatch trade ships to Fuzhou annually.[21] The missions included ambassadors who made the long overland journey from Fuzhou to Beijing as well as traders, students, and interpreters who remained at the Ryukyu House, the kingdom's permanent station in Fuzhou. As in previous centuries, sulfur remained the most important trade item produced in Ryukyu, but now cargoes included Japanese commodities supplied by Satsuma, such as silver, tin, copper, and so-called baled goods (*tawaramono*) – seafood products such as abalone, sea cucumber, and kelp. From China, the Ryukyuans returned with luxury goods

---

[19] Kamiya, "Tai-Min seisaku to Ryūkyū shihai," 266–68. An English translation of the agreements imposed on Shō Nei can be found in Kerr, *Okinawa*, 160–63.

[20] Thongchai, *Siam Mapped*.

[21] Akamine, *Ryukyu Kingdom*, 100–26.

such as silk cloth, tortoiseshells, musk, camphor, spices, medicines, ceramics, and artworks.

Much of the trade was carried out on behalf of the Satsuma domain, but Ryukyuan elites got enough out of the relationship, both economically and geopolitically, to make the hazardous missions worthwhile. Even so, they resisted Satsuma's domination by sabotaging its profits from the trade through such tactics as embezzlement, the deliberate loss of seaborne cargoes, and the importation of shoddy goods.[22] Satsuma was no more virtuous in its evasion of the shogunate's controls on trade. It regularly misdirected trade to Nagasaki and smuggled valuable commodities, such as baled goods from Hokkaido.[23]

Qing representatives traveled to Ryukyu to invest new kings on their succession. During those occasional visits, the Ryukyuan court went to considerable trouble to disguise its subjugation to Satsuma and hence Japan. They took Japanese coins out of circulation, hid Japanese-language documents, and presented any Satsuma men the Chinese might encounter as Ryukyuan subjects from the Tokara Islands.[24] The Qing authorities knew all about Ryukyu's relationship with Satsuma but humored their clients by pretending not to notice the ample evidence that survived these clean-up efforts. The Qing did not care about the Ryukyuans' other entanglements so long as they fulfilled their obligations as a tributary state, and in any event, they were not eager to provoke conflict with Japan by raising uncomfortable questions. The Ryukyuans finally gave up the charade of concealing their ties to Japan only in 1877.

Ryukyu was linguistically, culturally, and physically close to Japan, but during the early modern period its leaders pursued a deliberate policy of Sinicization. It made political sense to play up connections with China to balance the overwhelming power of Satsuma: Chinese suzerainty came with no pretense of actual sovereignty and offered trade access to the richest country in the world. Satsuma encouraged Sinicization so that it too could enjoy the benefits of the tribute trade, which included not only economic gain but ritual privileges in its relations with the Tokugawa shogunate.

Sai On (1682–1761), who effectively ruled Ryukyu from 1728 to 1751, promoted an aggressive policy of Sinicization. Adopted as a young boy into a Kumemura household, he studied in Fuzhou as a youth and later led a tribute mission to Beijing. Sai On, imagining the king as a model Confucian

[22] Taminato and Kaiho, "Bakuhanseika no Ryūkyū to Ezochi," 257.
[23] Hellyer, *Defining Engagement*, 127–31.
[24] Kamiya, "Tai-Min seisaku to Ryūkyū shihai," 279–82.

sage-ruler, asserted Ryukyu's moral parity with its powerful neighbors. Although it is unlikely that external observers shared his vision of Ryukyu, Sai On's construction of a self-consciously Confucian state succeeded domestically, albeit only after a long period of brutal repression. Losers in the struggle over Ryukyu's identity included both Sai On's elite critics, such as the writer Heshikiya Chōbin (1701–34), and others whose association with indigenous practices threatened his rule.[25]

An important but generally unsuccessful element of Sai On's social-engineering project was his attempt to rein in the influence of priestesses and female shamans. Priestesses (*noro*) had been around for centuries – George Kerr once dismissed them as Neolithic "living fossils" – but in 1477, King Shō Shin institutionalized their position within the Ryukyuan state.[26] Under the system devised by the king, a dual hierarchy of priestesses and male officials staffed government offices. The chief priestess (*kikoe-ōgimi*), who was always the king's sister or other close relative, took ritual precedence over the king in some important instances. In the countryside, priestesses served as government officials in addition to overseeing rituals in their jurisdictions of a village or two. Shō Shōken, who served as prime minister from 1666 to 1673, scored some successes in his attempts to weaken the formal power of high-ranking priestesses, but the high priestess remained an official position until the kingdom's demise, and survives unofficially even now. Sai On, for his part, kept up the pressure on the priestesses while attempting to prohibit shamanism. Female shamans (*yuta*) were ubiquitous throughout the archipelago, and households routinely turned to them when faced with illness or other distress. Sai On was disturbed by the shamans' implicit challenge to the state's religious authority, but his prohibition was so manifestly unsuccessful that the court soon gave up any show of enforcing it.[27] Shamanism survived the Japanese government's modernizing projects, the devastation of war, and the US occupation to remain an important part of Okinawan life well into the modern era.[28]

Sai On implemented his vision of a Confucian Ryukyu with little concern for ordinary islanders' welfare. Despite its idyllic facade – all blue ocean and white sand – Ryukyu was a poor place with a weak agrarian base. Satsuma's demands for annual tribute payments equivalent to about 11,000 *koku* of rice, coming on top of the exactions of the Ryukyuan elite, doomed many

[25] Smits, *Visions of Ryukyu*; Steben, "Transmission of Neo-Confucianism."
[26] Kerr, *Okinawa*, 33.
[27] Smits, *Visions of Ryukyu*, 55, 113–16.
[28] Lebra, *Okinawan Religion*, 79–85.

commoners to great hardship. The authorities levied taxes denominated in soybeans and staple grains, but over the course of the early modern era they increasingly exacted payments in raw sugar (*kokutō*) or, where sugarcane cultivation was not feasible, commodities such as banana-fiber cloth (*bashōfu*), linen, and turmeric.[29] On Miyako and other islands in the Sakishima group, the authorities levied a poll tax (*jintōzei*) based on a subject's age, sex, and social status that allowed no room for reduction or even negotiation in hard times. In areas unsuited to sugarcane cultivation, the burden of producing cloth for tax payments fell heavily on women, who engaged in weaving. The poll tax was not finally abolished until 1903.[30]

The tribute trade connected Ryukyu to the broader East Asian regional economy, but it had little impact on ordinary Ryukyuans except for those few who participated in it as sailors and longshoremen. In contrast, the spread of sugarcane cultivation throughout Ryukyu after the middle of the seventeenth century had a transformative impact on commoners' lives. Sugar is a classic tropical commodity, the craving for which, in Sidney W. Mintz's telling, drove the Caribbean slave economy, fueled empire, and transformed British foodways.[31] Although Japanese cuisine has no real equivalent to the sweet tea and even sweeter jam of Mintz's Britain, sugar has been an important ingredient in Japanese cookery since the Tokugawa period.[32] From the latter part of the eighteenth century until the beginning of the twentieth, the Ryukyu Islands supplied the bulk of Japan's sugar. Because Satsuma enjoyed a monopsony over Ryukyuan sugar, it could dictate the price, with the result that it was not unusual for cultivators to lose money on their crops. Ryukyu had no sugar plantations per se, but peasants engaged in communal production under the supervision of local officials, and accordingly had little agency in the process.[33]

As demanding and unpleasant as the work of sugarcane cultivation was for Ryukyuan farmers, conditions were incomparably worse for residents of Amami Ōshima, Tokunoshima, and Kikaijima, three islands in the Amami group that Satsuma turned into monoculture economies. In stages through 1777, Satsuma forced the conversion of virtually all arable land on the three

---

[29] Kurima, "Ryūkyū kinsei no sozei seido." *Kokutō* (lit. "black sugar") is less processed than commercially available brown sugar.
[30] Matsumura, *Limits of Okinawa*, 49–78.
[31] Mintz, *Sweetness and Power*.
[32] Rath, *Food and Fantasy*, 90–96, discusses the early history of sugar in Japanese cuisine, focusing on the late sixteenth and early seventeenth centuries.
[33] Kurima, "Ryūkyū kinsei no sozei seido."

islands to sugarcane production and promised to provide food and other basic necessities to the islanders in exchange. Thereafter, Satsuma supplied the bulk of the domestic sugar to reach the Osaka market; Tokushima and a few other domains produced some sugar as well, and Chinese and Dutch imports, particularly of high-quality white sugar, continued to hold a share.[34] The restoration-era hero Saigō Takamori, who lived in exile on Amami Ōshima from 1859 to 1862, wrote that "the daily life of the islanders seems honestly unendurable." A relatively small class of elites exploited ordinary islanders, about a third of whom were enslaved (*yanchu*), and many of the rest indentured servants. Saigō, no stranger to Satsuma's harsh dominion over its mainland population, lamented that it was "painful to see the extent of tyranny here."[35]

Ryukyu reemerged as a geopolitical hub during the nineteenth century. Beginning with a British sloop, the *Providence*, which was wrecked off Miyako Island in 1797, a steady stream of European vessels made their way to the Ryukyus during the decades leading up to the Meiji Restoration, mostly to take on supplies, which the Ryukyuans readily provided, and often to ask for formal trade, which the Ryukyuans invariably refused. Indeed, the traffic was lively enough that crewmen of the British brig *Brothers* were astonished by the "tolerable English" spoken by some of the Okinawans they encountered at Naha in 1819.[36] By the mid-1840s, the leadership of the Satsuma domain, with the tacit acceptance of the shogunate, was considering ways to open Naha to French trade, but in the end the first formal agreement with a Western power was the "Compact between the United States and Kingdom of Lew Chew," signed on 11 July 1854; the compact did not allow trade per se but did open Naha to all American ships.

Lacking the power to repulse Western vessels, the Ryukyuan authorities had no choice but to tolerate the parade of visitors. Indeed, they earned a reputation for being pleasant and accommodating hosts. They were greatly discomfited, however, when French and British missionaries took up residence. First came the French: in 1846, a priest, Théodore-Augustin Forcade, and his Chinese assistant, Augustin Ko, were left in Naha. Forcade and two successors, who were nominally sent to Okinawa to study Japanese, lived under virtual house arrest, their attempts at language study stymied. Satsuma sent a young man in the guise of a Tokara islander to study French with the

---

[34] Ochiai, "Shift to Domestic Sugar," 96.
[35] Ravina, *Last Samurai*, 82.
[36] Kerr, *Okinawa*, 260–61.

missionaries, but he died within a few months of his arrival, and by the summer of 1848 the French had given up on their mission.[37]

In 1846, a volatile Anglican missionary and doctor, Bernard Jean Bettelheim, landed in Naha with his wife, two small children, and a large quantity of baggage. For the following eight years, they squatted at Gokokuji, a venerable Buddhist temple in Naha, despite the authorities' desperate pleas to every visiting Western ship that they haul the officious man of God away. Officials made it difficult for him to interact with ordinary people, with the result that his proselytizing project ended in utter failure. In the meantime, Bettelheim contrived to insert himself into negotiations with Western visitors, including Matthew Perry, in which he was occasionally useful and always infuriating. He finally left in 1854.[38]

As Jun Uchida and Asano Tomomi show in volume 3, it took eleven years after the Meiji Restoration for the so-called Disposition of Ryukyu (*Ryūkyū shobun*) to play itself out. The Ryukyu kingdom was finally abolished in 1879, but even after that time, the Meiji state left many Ryukyuan institutions in place until as late as 1903, and revanchist officials lobbied the Qing for assistance in resurrecting the kingdom until the Japanese victory in the First Sino-Japanese War of 1894–95 settled the question.

Hokkaido before the Tokugawa Period

Hokkaido is the second largest and least densely populated of Japan's four main islands. Its 83,424 square kilometers and population of 5.2 million (2022) account for about one-fifth of contemporary Japan's land area, but only 4 percent of its population. Today, Hokkaido Prefecture formally comprises Hokkaido and surrounding islands as well as the disputed Northern Territories, which are under Russian control. Until 1869 the island was known in Japanese as Ezogashima (or just Ezo), the "island of the eastern barbarians," a reference to the Indigenous Ainu people. The name Hokkaido, which translates to "northern sea circuit," recalls the "circuits" (*dō*) of seventh – and eighth-century Japan.

Hokkaido is the home of the Ainu people, who, during the Tokugawa period, inhabited Hokkaido, the Kurils, southern Sakhalin, and the northeastern tip of Honshu. Unlike many other Indigenous peoples, the Ainu had no precontact history of isolation from, and ignorance of, their Japanese neighbors to the south. The emergence and development of Ainu culture was inextricably

[37] Kerr, *Okinawa*, 275–79; Lehmann, "French Catholic Missionaries."
[38] Kerr, *Okinawa*, 279–341, describes Bettelheim's antics in detail.

linked to a history of trade conducted over many centuries in an area encompassing the pan–Japan Sea region, south to central Honshu and north to Sakhalin, east to the Kuril Islands and west to continental Northeast Asia.

The archaeologist Utagawa Hiroshi divides the history of Ainu culture before the modern era into two broad periods, the first beginning in the fourteenth century with its emergence out of the preceding Satsumon and Okhotsk cultures, and the second dating from about the end of the eighteenth century, by which time interaction with, and economic dependence on, Japanese society had irrevocably altered the fabric of Ainu life.[39]

The neo-Ainu culture of Utagawa's periodization is the hunting, fishing, and gathering society of the ethnographic literature. According to this literature, the Ainu of recent historical times lived in small, dispersed communities with very little in the way of broad political organization. Although they engaged extensively in trade and other contact among themselves and with outsiders, hunting, fishing, and gathering for immediate subsistence needs was a major focus of their economic lives. Added to the ethnographic literature should be deep involvement in a growing labor economy during the latter part of the Tokugawa period, when commercial fisheries attracted Ainu workers.

Archaeologists mark the birth of Ainu culture in the fourteenth century with the disappearance of pottery manufacture in Hokkaido. The Ainu stopped making pottery once they gained ready access to iron utensils, particularly kettles, from Japan. The volume of iron and ironware imported into Hokkaido rose from about ninety kilograms per year during the Satsumon period to more than a thousand kilograms per year after the transition to Ainu culture. Although the Ainu had some knowledge of metalworking, their dependence on ironware carried with it a concomitant dependence on trade with Japan.[40] The need to procure animal pelts, fish, and kelp to exchange for iron utensils and other Japanese commodities directed productive energy away from the fulfillment of immediate subsistence needs and toward the maintenance of trade networks that extended throughout Hokkaido and beyond, to Sakhalin, the Amur River basin, and the Kuril Islands. Honshu warlords received the pelts of animals available only in the Kurils, such as sea otters and seals, in trade with Ainu in southern Hokkaido and northernmost Honshu. Similarly, Japanese commodities have been unearthed at sites in Sakhalin, the Kurils, and even Kamchatka.[41]

[39] Utagawa, *Ainu bunka seiritsushi*, 320.
[40] Amano, "Satsumon-ki Hokkaidō ni motasareta tetsu"; Fukasawa, *Ainu Archaeology*; Segawa, *Ainu ekoshisutemu no kōkogaku*.
[41] Ōishi, "Chūsei Ōu no reimei," 38–40; Uemura, *Kita no umi*, 3–116.

Behind the increased northward flow of Japanese commodities was the rise of the Andō, a military house based at the northern Honshu port of Tosaminato, who dominated the Tsugaru Strait region during the fourteenth and fifteenth centuries.[42] In their relations with the center, the Andō represented themselves as suzerains of the eastern barbarians, or Ezo. (Whether we can definitively identify these Ezo as Ainu is an open question.) Although this sometimes served to locate them within the medieval institutional order, distinct from the Ezo themselves, in other instances the Andō assumed titles such as "shogun of Hinomoto" that seemed to give them a non-Japanese identity.

Today the Andō's base of Tosaminato is a sleepy fishing village, endowed with a fine natural port but otherwise a most unlikely international commercial crossroads. During the fourteenth and fifteenth centuries, however, the port and subsidiary sites in southern Hokkaido flourished as ships traveled up the Japan Sea coast from central Japan and even Korea to exchange Chinese and Japanese ceramics and Chinese coins for animal pelts and marine products obtained in trade with the Ainu. A striking example of the immense scale of the trade can be seen at the fifteenth-century fortification of Shinoridate in southern Hokkaido, where a cache of 387,514 Chinese coins (by far the largest such cache found in Japan) was unearthed in 1968.[43]

Over time, considerable conflict developed over the terms of exchange, the political organization of trade networks, and, increasingly, the relationship of northernmost Japan with a Japanese state that was itself undergoing a tumultuous transformation. The two centuries from 1457 to 1669 saw southern Hokkaido embroiled in almost continual warfare as these conflicts played themselves out.[44] By the end of the sixteenth century, Japanese authority in southern Hokkaido was unified under the Kakizaki house. In 1593, Kakizaki Yoshihiro submitted to Toyotomi Hideyoshi in exchange for the hegemon's recognition of his monopoly over access to trade with the Ainu. Soon after Hideyoshi's death in 1598, Yoshihiro, now surnamed Matsumae, pledged his fealty to Tokugawa Ieyasu, and in due course the new shogunate recognized the Matsumae as custodians of the relationship between the Ainu and Japan. These acts of feudal submission did not make all of Hokkaido Japanese territory per se, but they did bring the island fully within the purview of the emergent early modern Japanese state and,

[42] Ōishi, "Kita no bushidan."
[43] Kikuchi and Fukuda, Kita no chūsei, 125–31. See also Utagawa, Ainu bunka seiritsushi, 329–31. On coin excavations, see Suzuki, "Shutsudo bichikusen."
[44] Kaiho, Bakuhansei kokka to Hokkaidō, 40, 127–32.

simultaneously, clearly marked the Ainu as living outside of the Tokugawa polity's direct control.

Just as the Tokugawa settlement led to a redrawing of boundaries between Japan and Ryukyu, it dramatically altered the geographies of trade, contact, and even identity in the north. Kakizaki (Matsumae) Yoshihiro's ancestors were Wataritō Ezo, "crossing-party barbarians," described in a fourteenth-century text in ways that modern-day observers might link as they please to a Japanese or Ainu ethnicity: they generally looked and spoke like people of Japan yet were hirsute and used poisoned arrows when hunting.[45] By the end of the sixteenth century, however, the Kakizaki and their retainers claimed an unambiguously Japanese identity. At the same time, the imposition of a new political order fragmented the once-singular world of trade that had encompassed Hokkaido and northernmost Honshu – the world that sustained Tosaminato during the fifteenth century – into three separate units: the Tsugaru and Nanbu domains in Honshu; the Matsumae domain's territory, or Wajinchi, in southernmost Hokkaido; and the Ezochi, which comprised the rest of Hokkaido and an ill-defined expanse extending to the north and east.

The fragmentation of space divided the Ainu population. Hokkaido Ainu traders lost direct access to markets in Honshu and instead found themselves beholden to the Matsumae domain, which established a series of trading posts along the Ezochi coast. Meanwhile, the small communities of Honshu Ainu in the Shimokita and Tsugaru Peninsulas were cut off from their Hokkaido brethren; although they persisted as identifiable communities for some time, they were eventually absorbed into the general populations of the Nanbu and Tsugaru domains.[46] Likewise, the scattered Ainu population of the Wajinchi had well-nigh disappeared by the late eighteenth century.[47]

The Ainu did not submit to this redrawing of economic and political boundaries without a struggle. In 1669, Shakushain, an Ainu chieftain in the Hidaka region of southeastern Hokkaido, led an insurrection against the Matsumae domain with the aim of restoring the Ainu's ability to trade freely, including in Honshu. The shogunate, alarmed by news of the conflict, ordered Tsugaru to mobilize in Matsumae's assistance. Matsumae resorted to low treachery to defeat the Ainu before the Tsugaru forces arrived in Hokkaido: following Ainu conventions of dispute resolution, domain commanders invited Shakushain to a parlay, only to poison him. The leader's death all but ended the war. The Ainu

---

[45] The text, *Suwa daimyōjin ekotoba* (1356), describes the origins of a Shinto shrine in modern-day Nagano Prefecture.

[46] Namikawa, *Kinsei Nihon to hoppō shakai*.

[47] Howell, *Geographies of Identity*, 119.

may have been doomed to failure in any case because Shakushain had never been able to unify all the regional chieftains under him. In any event, Matsumae's triumph in Shakushain's War settled once and for all the Ainu's position as a politically and economically subordinate population to the early modern state.

Hokkaido during the Tokugawa Period

Hokkaido was part of the Tokugawa world from the shogunate's inception, but Shakushain's death marks the real epoch in Ainu history. Not only did the Ainu lose their ability to trade freely in Honshu, but broad, regional chieftainships disappeared, leaving behind only small, kinship-based communities whose territories (*iwor*) were limited to individual river systems. These attenuated communities could not assert autonomy from the systems of trade and interaction established by the Matsumae domain and its agents.

Virtually all Ainu came within the orbit of the Japanese state after Shakushain's War. How any given individual interacted with the state depended greatly on factors such as their region of residence, place in the local community, and gender. During the century or so following the war, Ainu throughout Hokkaido grew increasingly dependent on ties with the Japanese to acquire economically and ritually important commodities such as ironware, lacquerware, sake, rice, tobacco, and cloth. The Matsumae domain directed Ainu to coastal trading posts that the daimyo's leading retainers held in lieu of fiefs. Over time, these trading posts evolved into contract fisheries (*ukeoi basho*) leased to merchants who oversaw the harvesting and processing of maritime products such as herring, kelp, and salmon. During the second half of the eighteenth century, an extensive network of seasonal fisheries developed along the Japan Sea and southeastern Pacific coasts of the Ezochi. They employed Ainu men and women, most of them local, and Japanese men from the Wajinchi and northeastern Honshu. Although commercial fishing was slower to develop on the Pacific and Okhotsk Sea coasts of northeastern Hokkaido, by the end of the century contract fisheries had expanded throughout the island and beyond, into the southern Kurils and Sakhalin.

Historians of Hokkaido during the early modern period tend to divide between those who emphasize the Ainu's character as an autonomous trading people and those who stress their embeddedness within the Tokugawa economy.[48] Each characterization is accurate in its way. Look to the far north

[48] In English, Walker, *Conquest of Ainu Lands*, emphasizes trade, while Howell, *Capitalism from Within*, and Howell, *Geographies of Identity*, stress the Ainu's embeddedness into the Tokugawa economy.

and northeast of Hokkaido and the Ainu's trading activity stands out. Goods like sea otter pelts from the Kurils and Chinese brocades from the Amur River basin passed through Ainu hands on their way to Matsumae and thence to Honshu. Look instead to the south and west and the Ainu's reliance on wage labor is clear. Commercial fisheries on the Japan Sea coast employed Ainu whose labor served as the means to obtain Japanese commodities, some of which – sake and lacquerware, in particular – sustained Ainu ritual and communal life. These regional differences were not absolute, however: Ainu in the northeast worked for wages and those on the Japan Sea coast engaged in trade. And everywhere Ainu devoted considerable time and effort to the hunting, fishing, gathering, and horticulture that lay at the core of Ainu ethnographies, for both trade and wage labor were seasonal employments.

Emphasizing the Ainu's character as a trading people serves as a useful counterpoint to resilient images of them as either a timeless people living in prelapsarian harmony with nature or the abject victims of unspeakable abuse at the hands of Japanese officials and fishery workers. Whatever truth these images have to commend them, they tend to work better as tropes in contemporary political discourse than as the bases for discussions of the complexities of Ainu life in the past. As traders, the Ainu enjoyed considerable agency. Their scope for asserting agency was constrained at the contract fisheries, but even there, evidence of Ainu men serving as supervisors on fishing crews or engaging in nonviolent resistance against poor working conditions undermines the once-prevalent image of them as utterly supine in the face of Japanese cruelty.

It can be difficult to discern Ainu voices in archival sources from the Tokugawa era. The words of Ainu actors, when reported at all, survive only in the formulaic literary language of early modern bureaucracy, their tenor and, surely, much of their meaning lost in the process of translation, first, from Ainu into colloquial Japanese and then into the written idiom. The Ainu are known for their rich bardic tales (*yukar* and *sakorpe*), which offer insights into Ainu understandings of their relationship with the Wajin. They are not historical sources per se – that is, they almost never refer to specific, verifiable historical events – but they do offer rich depictions of trade and other contact between the two peoples. A cherry-picking reader could quickly fill a basket with descriptions of lying and rapacious Wajin trading partners, but in fact the tales feature no shortage of treacherous Ainu and kind-hearted Wajin as well. According to Sakata Minako, however underhandedly some individual Wajin may behave in the tales, as a whole they do not express enmity toward the Wajin: "a common message among them," Sakata argues, is that "a trade partner cannot be an enemy." Moreover, "trade activity indicates friendship in Ainu tradition, and, more remarkably, that ethnic division is no criterion for determining friend or foe in Ainu oral literature."[49]

Ainu participated in ritual relations with representatives of the Matsumae domain and shogunate, deploying constructive mutual misunderstanding to rationalize their role in them.[50] For example, Ainu leaders traveled annually to the Matsumae domain's castle for an *uymam*, or audience, with the daimyo's representatives. The ceremony's origins are not clear, but it may well have taken form only after Shakushain's War.[51] From the Japanese perspective, the ritual was emblematic of a tributary relationship. The Ainu proffered salmon, eagle feathers, bear gall bladders, and other goods as tokens of their submission to the daimyo's suzerainty. In exchange, they received gifts of Japanese commodities such as sake, tobacco, rice, swords, and lacquerware as symbols of the lord's beneficence and compassion. The Ainu, for their part, interpreted the *uymam* as trading expeditions: difficult but lucrative journeys to obtain commodities on favorable terms. Oral tales represent *uymam* as an expression of amity building through reciprocity; thus, from the Ainu's standpoint, "although trade was ceremonially organized, participation in its activities did not mean political defeat or subordination."[52] No doubt each side realized that its partner saw the ritual differently, but they overlooked such discrepancies in the interest of expediency.

The ritual life of Ainu communities adapted to the constraints of the post–Shakushain's War world. The most important ritual of the Ainu is the *iyomante*, or spirit-sending ceremony, in which deities that have taken the form of animals – and thereby brought bounty to the Ainu – are released from their corporeal form and returned to the land of the gods. The *iyomante* has a long history, but its most familiar form, in which Ainu from several neighboring communities came together to send back the spirit of a bear cub, took shape only around the end of the eighteenth century. It served as a vehicle for communal solidarity among multiple *iwor* groups in the absence of overtly political forms of organization. Moreover, by inviting Japanese officials and fishery managers to the *iyomante* as honored guests, the Ainu turned the tables of beneficence on the Japanese.

Finally, there is plenty of evidence that Ainu material culture evolved dynamically within the context of relations with Japan. The abandonment

---

[49] Sakata, "Possibilities of Reality," 182, 183. See also Sakata, *Ainu kōshō bungaku*.
[50] Howell, "Ainu Ethnicity."
[51] Namikawa, *Kinsei Nihon to hoppō shakai*, 53–62.
[52] Sakata, "Possibilities of Reality," 186.

of pottery-making by the first Ainu is the most spectacular example of this evolution, but the integration of Japanese textiles and lacquerware vessels into Ainu daily and ritual life during the Tokugawa period tells a similar story. In short, Ainu culture has a history: however disadvantaged the Ainu may have been in their relations with the Japanese after Shakushain's War, they adapted in ways that preserved Ainu agency.

In its own way, and entirely for its own purposes, the Matsumae domain supported Ainu cultural autonomy. The domain rationalized its monopoly over trade and other contact in the Ezochi by asserting its unique ability to serve as the custodian of relations between the Ainu and the Japanese. To protect its custodianship, the domain structured relations with the Ainu on the principles of separation and dissimilation. Separation meant limiting year-round Japanese residence to the domain's home territory, the Wajinchi, and prohibiting the unauthorized movement of Ainu out of the Ezochi. Dissimilation meant that Ainu living in the Ezochi were not allowed to speak Japanese, take Japanese names, or adopt Japanese customs, particularly the outwardly visible emblems of Japanese identity, such as hairstyles. No doubt many Ainu who worked and lived with Japanese fishers for months every year acquired a good command of Japanese, but that reality was not important so long as the fiction of dissimilation was maintained. Hence, all official interactions between domain officials and Ainu were directed through Japanese interpreters fluent in Ainu.

Matsumae fit awkwardly into the early modern political economy. Unlike nearly every other domain, whose utility to, and standing within, the Tokugawa regime was measured in terms of its agricultural production, Matsumae's raison d'être as a domain was its place as custodian of relations with the Ainu. The Wajinchi's population of around 30,000 people, including a small number of Ainu, supported itself above all through fishing, both in local waters and on seasonal forays along the Hokkaido coast. The domain was home as well to samurai, Buddhist and Shinto clergy, and merchants ranging from small shopkeepers to wealthy operators of contract fisheries and shipping firms. People engaged in agriculture as well, but it was the only domain in which it was too cold to grow rice. The need for that staple made the Japanese inhabitants of Hokkaido just as dependent on long-distance trade as the Ainu.

Lest I paint too rosy a picture of Ainu history during the Tokugawa period, it is important to emphasize that after Shakushain's defeat, the Ainu lived in a constrained environment, cut off from opportunities to trade on their own terms and beholden to contract-fishery operators who controlled both their labor and access to Japanese commodities. The Matsumae domain was generally indifferent to their welfare. It responded to crises such as an uprising in 1789 by mistreated fishery workers with violence and a half-hearted attempt to mitigate the worst abuses. The uprising, at the Kunashiri and Menashi fisheries in the far northeast, was by far the most serious instance of Ainu resistance since Shakushain's War. Violence and cruelty, combined with the fishery operator's ignorance of, or disregard for, Ainu practices of conflict resolution, sparked an attack that cost 130 Japanese fishery workers their lives and led Matsumae to execute thirty-seven Ainu. The domain stripped the fishery operator of his privileges and instituted some modest changes in the contract-fishery system, but the Ainu fishery workers' subordination did not fundamentally change.[53]

The starkest evidence of the imbalance of power between the Japanese and Ainu can be seen in the realm of gender. All evidence suggests that Japanese fishery workers routinely appropriated Ainu women as their "temporary wives" during their sojourns in the Ezochi. We cannot know how many such relationships, if any, were consensual, much less the dynamics between any two given individuals, but ann-elise lewallen argues persuasively that coercion routinely characterized interactions between Japanese men and Ainu women.[54] She notes that Matsuura Takeshirō, an usually sympathetic Japanese observer of Ainu life, corroborated stories of forced "marriages" shared among the Indigenous people; accounts circulated as well of Ainu men – the women's actual husbands – being sent off to work at distant fisheries while their wives' Japanese "husbands" were around. Even if documentary evidence is sparse, the idea that systematic sexual aggression should occur at Hokkaido fisheries is eminently plausible. Large numbers of solitary, mostly young Japanese men lived and worked for weeks or months at a time at the fisheries, far from home and in a position of power over the local Indigenous population. Sexual abuse, violence, and aggression were perhaps inevitable under the circumstances, particularly when the domain authorities evinced so little interest in the everyday lives of their subjects, Ainu or Japanese. In another part of the world, the children born of liaisons between Japanese men and Ainu women might have fed anxieties about miscegenation, but Matsumae's policy of dissimilation – and the structures of identity that underlay it – ensured that nothing like a métis identity ever emerged in Hokkaido. The children born to Ainu women were unequivocally understood to be Ainu by all parties.

[53] Iwasaki, *Nihon kinsei no Ainu shakai*, 169–201.
[54] lewallen, "'Intimate Frontiers.'"

At about the time the contract fishery system became ubiquitous through-out Hokkaido, the shogunate, fearful of Russian aggression, stepped in to take direct control over the island. It did this in two stages, beginning on the Pacific coast in 1799 and expanding to the Japan Sea coast in 1807. The shogu-nate had spurned Russian overtures for trade and suspected the disappointed Russians might try to enlist the Ainu as allies in a plan to conquer Hokkaido. The perceived threat faded in time, and in 1821 Matsumae regained its previ-ous suzerainty over the island. The shogunate stepped in once again in 1855 to assume control over Hokkaido in the wake of Japan's opening to diplomacy and trade with the Western powers, including Russia. Hakodate, in southern Hokkaido, was, along with Shimoda, one of the first two ports to open to Western vessels. During this period, the shogunate exercised exclusive con-trol in Hokkaido and the southern Kurils and shared administration of the southern half of Sakhalin in a Russo-Japanese condominium.

Even as Hokkaido became the site of considerable geopolitical anxiety during the nineteenth century, the basic structure of its political economy changed surprisingly little. The fishing economy grew steadily after the turn of the nineteenth century, particularly after the Tenpō famine of the 1830s drove thousands of impoverished men from northeastern Honshu to seek employment in the herring fishery. The herring-meal fertilizer they produced found a ready market in western Honshu's expanding agricultural economy. In 1855, the shogunate allowed Japanese to settle permanently in the Ezochi, which helped to turn seasonal fishing ports such as Otaru into year-round commercial centers.

In addition to allowing permanent settlement of the Ezochi, the shogunate attempted in a mostly symbolic fashion to incorporate the Ainu into Japan as subjects of the Tokugawa regime. It did this through a combination of shows of benevolence, such as a campaign to inoculate Ainu against small-pox, and efforts to coax them into assimilating into Japanese culture. This reversal of the Matsumae domain's dissimilation policy focused on the same set of mostly visible markers of identity as the domain's policy had: if Ainu – and particularly Ainu men – could be persuaded to adopt Japanese hairstyles, names, and clothing, the shogunate could both assert their Japanese iden-tities to outside observers and find a way to integrate them as commoners into the early modern social status system. Only a relatively limited number of Ainu communities, mostly on the Pacific coast, were the active targets of these assimilation campaigns, and all evidence suggests that many Ainu resisted bitterly even superficial attempts to change the outward markers of their identities.

Hokkaido is often described as modern Japan's first colony.[55] However, when the Meiji state assumed control over the island immediately after the shogunate's fall, it took pains to assert that, far from a colonial acquisition, Hokkaido had always been an integral part of Japan. In 1869, it imposed a political geography dating back to the seventh century by dividing Hokkaido and the Kuril Islands into eleven provinces (*kuni*), further subdivided into eighty-six districts (*gun*). Provinces had not functioned even nominally as administrative units for centuries and would never do so again; districts had a brief comeback later in the Meiji period but were functionally meaningless in 1869. The gesture was purely symbolic, and all the more significant as a result, particularly considering that Ryukyu was never designated a province and the division of Okinawa Prefecture into districts occurred only in 1896.

The state's announcement of the restoration to Ainu communities likewise emphasized the continuity of Japanese control. It included a statement of the emperor's divine ancestry and his superiority over the samurai who had hitherto administered Hokkaido; an expression of regret for the failures of past policies to nurture the Ainu; and a list of modest quantities of rice, tobacco, and sake to be granted to every Ainu woman, man, and child.[56]

The Development Agency (Kaitakushi) administered Hokkaido from 1869 to 1882. It encouraged agricultural settlement and employed foreign experts to facilitate the exploitation of mineral, forest, and animal resources in the island's interior. The state continued after the agency's abolition to promote agricultural immigration, with the result that Hokkaido's population grew from about 58,000 in 1869 to 240,000 in 1882, topped one million in 1901, and stood at about 3.5 million at the end of World War II.

Within this context of rapid growth, the Ainu for a time remained generally invisible to the state, becoming the object of systematic policy-making only during the 1880s. Most Ainu continued their lives as they had before, working as seasonal fishery laborers and engaging in hunting and horticulture until those activities came under pressure from Japanese expansion into the Hokkaido interior. The Development Agency prohibited various iconic Ainu customs, such as the tattooing of women's faces, but never attempted

[55] The classic English-language study of Hokkaido history, Harrison, *Japan's Northern Frontier: A Preliminary Study in Colonization and Expansion*, takes this approach, as its subtitle suggests. For more recent scholarship, see Mason, *Dominant Narratives*, and the essays collected in Mason and Lee, *Reading Colonial Japan*, which treat Hokkaido and Okinawa, along with continental imperial acquisitions, as "colonial Japan."
[56] Several versions of the announcement survive, among them "Ōsei fukko ni yoru tennō shihai tō fukoku no ken."

to enforce the bans. Without discounting the aspirational violence to Ainu culture these gestures represented, we might best see them as a continuation of similarly ineffectual government-sponsored campaigns during the 1870s against "backward" and "barbarous" customs throughout the archipelago, such as dancing during the annual summer *bon* festival to honor the spirits of dead ancestors.[57]

Conclusion

From a geopolitical perspective, Hokkaido's integration into the modern Japanese state was seamless, even if the other parts of the vaguely defined early modern Ezochi – Sakhalin and the Kurils – flipped between Russian and Japanese sovereignty until the end of World War II. Japanese already outnumbered Ainu in Hokkaido by the Meiji Restoration, and by the time the Meiji government enacted the so-called Ainu protection law in 1899, there were thirty or forty Japanese for every Ainu on the island. If Hokkaido was a colony, it was a settler colony whose Indigenous population would, it was believed, inevitably die out sooner or later. Thankfully, it did not.[58]

Okinawa was integrated much more slowly and with far greater difficulty into the modern Japanese nation. The Meiji state tried to placate local elites by keeping key Ryukyuan institutions in place well after the end of Okinawa's twelve-year transition from kingdom to prefecture, even as many of those elites appealed to China for its help in restoring the kingdom. At the same time, officials and intellectuals tried to persuade Okinawans to embrace new identities as Japanese subjects. Many self-consciously progressive islanders took up this call, and poor Okinawan women and men sought better opportunities in the textile mills and factories of western Japan and on the sugarcane plantations of Hawai'i. Ryukyu's ambivalent sovereignty was reconciled through an act of ambivalent integration, Okinawa and its people both fully part of Japan but never fully accepted as such.

Bibliography

Akamine, Mamoru. *The Ryukyu Kingdom: Cornerstone of East Asia*. Translated by Lina Terrell. Edited by Robert Huey. Honolulu: University of Hawai'i Press, 2017.
Amano Tetsuya. "Satsumon-ki Hokkaidō ni motasareta tetsu no ryō to kore ni kansuru shomondai: Ainu-ki to no hikaku ni oite." *Tatara kenkyū* 30 (1989): 1–8.

[57] See Oku, *Bunmei kaika to minshū*, 23–25, for examples.
[58] Howell, "Making 'Useful Citizens' of Ainu Subjects."

Asato Susumu. "Ryūkyū ōkoku no keisei." In *Chiiki to etonosu*, edited by Arano Yasunori, Ishii Masatoshi, and Murai Shōsuke, 111–36. Vol. 4 of *Ajia no naka no Nihonshi*. Tōkyō Daigaku Shuppankai, 1992.

"Calls Grow in China to Press Claim for Okinawa." *New York Times*, 14 June 2013.

Fukasawa, Yuriko. *Ainu Archaeology as Ethnohistory: Iron Technology among the Saru Ainu of Hokkaido, Japan, in the 17th Century*. Oxford: British Archaeological Reports, 1998.

Harrison, John A. *Japan's Northern Frontier: A Preliminary Study in Colonization and Expansion, with Special Reference to the Relations of Japan and Russia*. Gainesville: University of Florida Press, 1953.

Hellyer, Robert. *Defining Engagement: Japan and Global Contexts, 1640–1868*. Cambridge, MA: Harvard University Asia Center, 2010.

Howell, David L. "Ainu Ethnicity and the Boundaries of the Early Modern Japanese State." *Past and Present* 142 (1994): 69–93.

Capitalism from Within: Economy, Society, and the State in a Japanese Fishery. Berkeley: University of California Press, 1995.

Geographies of Identity in Nineteenth-Century Japan. Berkeley: University of California Press, 2005.

"Making 'Useful Citizens' of Ainu Subjects in Early Twentieth-Century Japan." *Journal of Asian Studies* 63, no. 1 (2004): 5–29.

Iwasaki Naoko. *Nihon kinsei no Ainu shakai*. Azekura Shobō, 1998.

Kaiho Mineo. *Bakuhansei kokka to Hokkaidō*. San'ichi Shobō, 1978.

Kamiya Nobuyuki. "'Tai-Min seisaku to Ryūkyū shihai: Ikoku kara 'ikoku' e." In *Bakuhansei kokka to iiki, ikoku*, edited by Katō Eiichi, Kitajima Manji, and Fukaya Katsumi, 247–89. Azekura Shobō, 1989.

Kerr, George H. *Okinawa: The History of an Island People*. Rutland, VT: Tuttle, 1958.

Kikuchi Tetsuo and Fukuda Toyohiko, eds. *Kita no chūsei: Tsugaru, Hokkaidō*. Heibonsha, 1989.

Kobata, Atsushi, and Mitsugu Matsuda. *Ryukyuan Relations with Korea and South Sea Countries: An Annotated Translation of Documents in the Rekidai Hōan*. Kyoto: Atsushi Kobata, 1969.

Kurima Yasuo. "Ryūkyū kinsei no sozei seido." *Nōgyōshi kenkyū* 41 (2007): 51–61.

Lebra, William P. *Okinawan Religion: Belief, Ritual, and Social Structure*. Honolulu: University of Hawai'i Press, 1966.

Lehmann, Jean-Pierre. "French Catholic Missionaries in Japan in the Bakumatsu and Early Meiji Periods." *Modern Asian Studies* 13, no. 3 (1979): 377–400.

lewallen, ann-elise. "'Intimate Frontiers': Disciplining Ethnicity and Ainu Women's Sexual Subjectivity in Early Colonial Hokkaido." In *The Affect of Difference: Representations of Race in East Asian Empire*, edited by Christopher Hanscom and Dennis Washburn, 19–37. Honolulu: University of Hawai'i Press, 2016.

Mason, Michele M. *Dominant Narratives of Colonial Hokkaido and Imperial Japan: Envisioning the Periphery and the Modern Nation-State*. New York: Palgrave Macmillan, 2012.

Mason, Michele M., and Helen J. S. Lee, eds. *Reading Colonial Japan: Text, Context, and Critique*. Stanford, CA: Stanford University Press, 2012.

Matsumura, Wendy. *The Limits of Okinawa: Japanese Capitalism, Living Labor, and Theorizations of Community*. Durham, NC: Duke University Press, 2015.

Mintz, Sidney W. *Sweetness and Power: The Place of Sugar in Modern History*. New York: Viking, 1985.

Murai Shōsuke. *Ajia no naka no chūsei Nihon*. Azekura Shobō, 1988.

"Kenmu, Muromachi seiken to higashi Ajia." In *Chūsei 2*, edited by Rekishigaku Kenkyūkai and Nihonshi Kenkyūkai, 1–42. Vol. 4 of *Kōza Nihon rekishi*. Tōkyō Daigaku Shuppankai, 1985.

Namikawa Kenji. *Kinsei Nihon to hoppō shakai*. Sanseidō, 1992.

Nelson, Thomas. "Japan in the Life of Early Ryukyu." *Journal of Japanese Studies* 32, no. 2 (2006): 367–92.

"Slavery in Medieval Japan," *Monumenta Nipponica* 59, no. 4 (2004): 463–92.

Ochiai Kō. "The Shift to Domestic Sugar and the Ideology of 'The National Interest.'" In *Economic Thought in Early Modern Japan*, edited by Bettina Gramlich-Oka and Gregory Smits, 89–110. Leiden: Brill, 2010.

Ōishi Naomasa. "Chūsei Ōu no reimei." In *Chūsei Ōu no sekai*, edited by Kobayashi Seiji, Ōishi Naomasa, and Irumada Nobuo, 2–40. Tōkyō Daigaku Shuppankai, 1978.

"Kita no bushidan: Andō shi." In *Nihonkai to hokkoku bunka*, edited by Amino Yoshihiko, 318–42. Shōgakkan, 1990.

Oku Takenori. *Bunmei kaika to minshū: Nihon kindai seishinshi danshō*. Shinhyōron, 1993.

"Ōsei fukko ni yoru tennō shihai tō fukoku no ken" (c. 8th month, 1868). Item 1 in "Kisoku kakidome," A4/330. Archives of Hokkaido, Sapporo.

Pearson, Richard. *Ancient Ryukyu: An Archaeological Study of Island Communities*. Honolulu: University of Hawai'i Press, 2013.

Archaeology of the Ryukyu Islands. Honolulu: University of Hawai'i Press, 1969.

Rath, Eric. *Food and Fantasy in Early Modern Japan*. Berkeley: University of California Press, 2010.

Ravina, Mark. *The Last Samurai: The Life and Battles of Saigō Takamori*. Hoboken, NJ: Wiley, 2003.

Roberts, Luke S. "Shipwrecks and Flotsam: The Foreign World in Edo-Period Tosa." *Monumenta Nipponica* 70, no. 1 (2015): 83–122.

Sakata Minako. *Ainu kōshō bungaku no ninshikiron: Rekishi no hōhō to shite no Ainu sanbun setsuwa*. Ochanomizu Shobō, 2011.

"Possibilities of Reality, Variety of Versions: The Historical Consciousness of Ainu Folktales." *Oral Tradition* 26, no. 1 (2011): 175–90.

Segawa Takurō. *Ainu ekoshisutemu no kōkogaku: Ibunka kōryū to shizen riyō kara mita Ainu shakai seiritsushi*. Sapporo: Hokkaidō Shuppan Kikaku Sentā, 2005.

Smits, Gregory. *Maritime Ryukyu, 1050–1650*. Honolulu: University of Hawai'i Press, 2019.

Visions of Ryukyu: Identity and Ideology in Early-Modern Thought and Politics. Honolulu: University of Hawai'i Press, 1999.

Steben, Barry. "The Transmission of Neo-Confucianism to the Ryukyu (Liuqiu) Islands and Its Historical Significance." *Sino-Japanese Studies* 11, no. 1 (1998): 39–60.

Suwa daimyōjin ekotoba (1356). National Institute of Japanese Literature, Tachikawa City, Tokyo. http://kotenseki.nijl.ac.jp/biblio/100128671

Suzuki Kimio. "Shutsudo bichikusen to chūsei kōki no senka ryūtsū." *Shigaku* 61, no. 3/4 (1992): 225–80.

Taminato Tomoaki and Kaiho Mineo. "Bakuhanseika no Ryūkyū to Ezochi." In *Kinsei 2*, edited by Asao Naohiro, Ishii Susumu, Inoue Mitsusada, Ōishi Kaichirō, Kano Masanao, Kuroda Toshio, Sasaki Junnosuke et al., 249–96. Vol. 11 of *Iwanami kōza: Nihon rekishi*. Iwanami Shoten, 1976.

Thongchai Winichakul. *Siam Mapped: The Geo-Body of a Nation*. Honolulu: University of Hawai'i Press, 1994.

Uemura Hideaki. *Kita no umi no kōekishatachi: Ainu minzoku no shakai keizaishi*. Dōbunkan, 1990.

Utagawa Hiroshi. *Ainu bunka seiritsushi*. Sapporo: Hokkaidō Shuppan Kikaku Sentā, 1988.

Walker, Brett L. *The Conquest of Ainu Lands: Ecology and Culture in Japanese Expansion, 1590–1800*. Berkeley: University of California Press, 2001.

"What to Know: The Northern Territories." www.hokkaido-northern-territories.jp/gaiyou/lang_en/

Zhai, Xiang. "Rewriting the Legacy of Chiang Kai-shek on the Diaoyu Islands: Chiang's Ryukyu Policies from the 1930s to the 1970s." *Journal of Contemporary China* 24, no. 96 (2015): 1128–46.

19

The Early Modern City in Japan

THOMAS GAUBATZ

Japan was home to one of the most urbanized societies in the early modern world. By the early eighteenth century, the capital city of Edo (modern Tokyo) had a population of over one million, likely making it the largest settlement on the globe. Osaka, the center of interregional commerce and banking, and Kyoto, the ancient capital and seat of imperial authority, had 300,000–400,000 each. The largest of the provincial castle towns – Nagoya and Kanazawa – had over 100,000 residents, and many more such settlements of varying scales dotted the countryside, serving as centers of administration and trade for their respective domains. In addition, the development of national markets and transportation networks fueled a proliferation of rural market towns, port towns, post towns, mining towns, hot spring towns, and more; it is commonly estimated that, throughout the Tokugawa period, roughly 10 percent of people dwelling in the Japanese archipelago resided in communities that could be described as urban. And with the extension of trade networks and merchant capital into the countryside, rural residents increasingly produced goods for urban markets and consumed commodified forms of culture that were produced in the major cities.

The urbanization of Tokugawa Japan was also remarkable for the pace at which it progressed. Of the major urban centers listed above, few other than the historical capital of Kyoto had predated the founding of the Tokugawa shogunate in 1603; even the shogunal capital of Edo, prior to its selection as the seat of government by Tokugawa Ieyasu, had been little more than a dilapidated castle abutting on fishing villages and unreclaimed marshland. This is not to discount the long and diverse set of urban traditions that had existed in Japan since the emulation of Chinese city planning in the early capitals of Fujiwara, Nara (Heijō), and most permanently at Kyoto (Heian). But the built environment that had once given urban form to the court-centric cosmology of the *ritsuryō* state had been all but annihilated amid the devastation of the late medieval period, and Kyoto's rebirth as a bustling urban center in the decades leading up to the country's unification reflected new social orders and political concerns. The diverse and self-governing towns of late medieval Japan – the merchant town of Sakai and the fortified temple town of Ishiyama Honganji, among others – were likewise forcefully subjugated under the authority of the unifying hegemons of the late sixteenth century; though their sites would form the basis of later urban development, they too would be reorganized according to the social institutions and administrative structures of the Tokugawa polity. The rapid and unprecedented urbanization of the seventeenth century was a uniquely early modern phenomenon, enabled by the vigorous state-building of the shogunate and enduring stability of the Pax Tokugawa, the removal of the warrior class from the land, the development of transportation infrastructure and communication networks on a nationwide scale, and the emergence of a robust domestic market economy.

The overwhelmingly dominant paradigm of spatial and social structure that defined the city in early modern Japan was what modern scholars refer to as the "castle town" (jōkamachi). In its most schematic form, the castle town consisted of a central castle, which acted both as the private residence of the military ruler and as the site of administration and public affairs, abutted most closely by the residences of the lord's direct vassals, followed by neighborhoods of privileged craftsmen and merchants who had been relocated at the lord's mandate to provide skilled labor for construction, military matériel, and luxury goods. These central communities, all of which enjoyed the privilege of patronage by the lord and his direct vassals, were typically protected by a fortified perimeter – wall, earthwork embankment, or moat – with specified gates or bridges as points of entry. Outside of these fortifications were temples and shrines, which enjoyed varying degrees of autonomy and exercised governmental authority over their own local communities, as well as less formal commoner settlements that emerged organically in response to demand for goods and services among the city's non-elite residents; these would gradually be incorporated into the castle town as the processes of urbanization progressed. Finally, situated on the literal and figurative margins of the city, were the so-called outcaste villages of hereditary outcastes and practitioners of those trades stigmatized as unclean, such as the disposal of animal carcasses and treatment of hides. The castle town synthesized a highly rationalized topology of distinct districts – warrior districts (bukechi), commoner districts (chōnin-chi), temple/shrine districts (jisha-chi), and outcaste villages (*eta-mura*) – arranged in a symbolic order and oriented centripetally by the hegemonic authority of the lord's castle.[1]

The paradigm of the castle town originated in the unification period, when it reflected the need for the rapid mobilization of manpower and material force in the event of conflict, but it was gradually adapted to the needs of peacetime governance. The purest expression of this paradigm was in the great provincial castle towns that dotted the landscape.[2] The shogunal seat of Edo had its origins as just such a castle town, though, as we will see in this chapter, its explosive growth over the course of the Tokugawa period strained the limits of that framework and pushed its evolution in new directions. Osaka was a unique case. Toyotomi Hideyoshi's Osaka Castle, built upon the ruins of a subjugated Ishiyama Honganji and modeled on Nobunaga's spectacular but short-lived Azuchi, became the center of the premier castle town of the unification period, only to be devasted once again in Ieyasu's campaigns against Hideyoshi's heir in 1614–15. When the castle was rebuilt under Tokugawa auspices and the city reemerged around it, it retained the schematic spatial orientation of the castle town but with a vastly reduced warrior population. Inhabited almost entirely by commoners, Osaka developed a particularly lively merchant community and culture; due to its role as a central marketplace for provincial rice and other agricultural goods, it earned the title of "the kitchen of the realm" (*tenka no daidokoro*).[3] Kyoto, more than any other early modern city, continued to bear the legacy of a longer urban tradition. This was most conspicuous in the reduced but still culturally active community of the aristocratic court, in the large numbers of religious institutions, in the diversity and cultural vibrancy of its commoner populations, and in the palimpsest-like traces of the distinctive spatialities of the classical and medieval cities. But through the successive efforts of Nobunaga, Hideyoshi, and Ieyasu, Kyoto was reoriented according to the distinctive spatiality of the castle town: one centered symbolically on the hegemon's castle (Hideyoshi's Jurakudai and later Ieyasu's Nijō Castle), incorporating mandatory residences for warrior lords and vassals, and designating districts for religious institutions.[4]

The unique topology of the castle town reflected the division of society into a complex and multivalent hierarchy of status communities, each largely

[1] Yoshida, *Toshi: Edo ni ikiru*.
[2] Matsumoto, *Jōkamachi*. For a detailed study, see McClain, *Kanazawa*.
[3] McClain and Wakita, *Osaka*.
[4] Stavros, *Kyoto*; Sugimori, *Kinsei Kyōto*.

self-governed at the local level and incorporated into the larger political order of the state through overlapping networks of privileges and obligations. The castle town was none other than a spatial projection of the social and institutional logics of status group (*mibun*), with the urban topology of each district reflecting the structure of the local communities that made it up: the warrior districts were structured by the warrior houses (*ie*) within them, the commoner districts by the local communities of the commoner wards (*chō*), and the temple and shrine districts (which themselves often contained and administered their own commoner populations) by their respective religious institutions. This was at least the intent of the shogunal administration, which was motivated initially by an expedient pragmatism – an imperative to arrange resources and personnel rationally for ready mobilization in the event of military action – but came to embrace the status order as an institutional technology of social administration, one which it hoped would lend an objective fixity to the sociopolitical status quo and thus aid the shogunate in sustaining its vision of the realm in perpetuity. The realities of social practice were never entirely apprehended or circumscribed by these systems, but they remained defining structures that individuals and communities were compelled to inhabit and navigate, and that in turn defined the unfolding shapes of early modern urban space and the social processes that such spaces structured and were structured by. Even as social practices pushed against the constraints initially dictated by the status system, transforming communities and ultimately reshaping the urban built environment itself, social structures and processes would continue to be reflected and reinscribed in the organization of urban space. This distinctive and robust homology between urban topology and social organization has been described by Yoshida Nobuyuki with the term "socio-spatial structure" (*shakai-kūkan kōzō*).[5]

The challenge of describing the early modern Japanese city is in making sense of a whole that was simultaneously both more and less than the sum of its parts: a vast social and economic cosmos that contained a diverse and frequently antagonistic mix of local communities and ways of life, setting them into mutual relation but never dissolving the formal distinctions of status that separated them. This challenge is not unique to Japan, but one running throughout urban histories of the non-West since Max Weber's seminal theorization of the urban community as an integrated, legally and administratively autonomous, self-governing community of free and equal citizens – a

---

[5] An excellent introduction to Yoshida's and others' status-based urban histories of early modern Japan is Botsman, "Recovering Japan's Urban Past."

description that was explicitly predicated on the exclusion of the "oriental city" on the grounds that, as Weber remarked regarding Tokugawa Japan, "The city as corporate *per se* was unknown."[6] Japanese urban history of recent decades, driven by revisionist theorizations of the early modern status system, has tended to approach this problem by highlighting the "segmental structure" (*bunsetsu kōzō*) of the city as a heterogeneous composite of status communities of radically different types and structures, and by attending to what Tsukada Takashi describes as the "layered and composite" (*jūsō to fukugō*) nature of the relations between such communities.[7] The early modern castle town is thus best understood not as a unified object defined by a shared urban subjectivity, but rather as a set of spatial frameworks in which the interplay between distinct subjectivities unfolded as a social process, and which was itself reshaped and produced through the unfolding of that process.

In keeping with these premises, this chapter presents a sketch of the shogunal capital of Edo as the site that both exemplified the socio-spatial paradigm of the early modern castle town and threw its tensions, contradictions, and transformations into the clearest relief. By referring to the urban phenomenon as a process, I mean to describe the constant and situational negotiation of social relations between groups with fundamentally distinct values and modes of being; the urban process here is apprehended not according to a linear telos of increasing urban integration or as a symptom or subprocess of modernization, but rather in the dialectical sense of an open-ended unfolding and reshaping through tension and contradiction. Though the communities and subjectivities that comprised Edo's urban cosmos were innumerable, the focus here is on the interplay between three sets of agents: the shogunal administration (the top-down vision of the castle town), the propertied townspeople (*chōnin*), and the diffuse occupational networks that structured life on the urban margins. Prior studies have highlighted the interplay between ruler and ruled – between the "city from above" and the "city from below"[8] – in the shaping of urban space and practice, but have tended to flatten the latter, usually identified with the subjectivity of the townspeople, into a single bloc of resistance (whether implicit or explicit) to the shogunate's feudal authority. But the dominated classes of Tokugawa urban society were themselves diverse, stratified, and as much at odds with one another as with the central authority of the shogunate; their interactions were structured not

[6] Weber, *City*, 82.
[7] Tsukada, *Kinsei Nihon mibunsei*.
[8] McClain, Merriman, and Ugawa, *Edo and Paris*.

by a posited equality as members of a shared urban community but rather by a blunt confrontation between radically divergent communities and lifestyles. The three perspectives sketched here, while hardly sufficient to stand in for the full diversity of the early modern city, reveal the socio-spatial structures of the urban status system not only as a structure of control but equally as a framework for agency, one that agents of differing social positions could navigate and attempt to reshape according to the needs of their communities. The evolution of Edo from an archetypal castle town at the dawn of the Tokugawa period into the diverse and dynamic metropolis of the nineteenth century is likewise neither a narrative of the system's decay and immanent collapse, nor of its stasis and resistance to change, but rather an illustration of its functional logic – and of the human diversity that, despite all of its tensions and contradictions, it was able to sustain and give meaning to.

Castle Town Topography

Early Edo was in many ways simply a magnification of the archetypal castle town. At its geographic and symbolic center was the impressive edifice of Edo Castle, its donjon completed in 1607. Contained within the walls of the castle compound were residences for the collateral houses of Owari, Kii, and Mito, and surrounding the castle were the urban estates of other powerful daimyo lords, interspersed with the more modest residences of shogunal vassals and, farther to the west, neighborhoods of barracks for foot soldiers and other low-ranking warriors. By incorporating daimyo estates into the spatial matrix of the city, the shogunate rendered Edo itself into a microcosm of the Tokugawa polity: like the domains themselves, the estates were nominally sovereign spaces largely exempt from shogunal oversight, though they were (again like the domains) subject to periodic and arbitrary reassignment at the shogun's discretion. To the degree that daimyo estates incorporated the residences of domanial vassals and came also to structure the spatial arrangements and social processes of the commoner populations that were drawn into their orbits, they acted in essence as castle towns in microcosm. Taking such estates together with the residences of shogunal vassals and foot soldiers, by the dawn of the Meiji era, warrior districts collectively came to comprise almost 70 percent of the total surface area of Edo.

The rapid expansion of the city of Edo was in large part a consequence of the shogunate's policy of "alternate attendance" (*sankin kōtai*), wherein each daimyo was required to maintain an Edo estate, of a scale and architectural standard in keeping with his status, where he would live in years of attendance on the shogun and where his wives and heirs would live in perpetuity as virtual hostages. This system of mandatory migration infused the burgeoning capital with an enormous population of largely male residents. While much of this population would only reside in Edo temporarily, the daimyo estates themselves became robust and stable institutions orienting the movement, social relations, and economic activities of thousands of individuals. Equally important to the development of early Edo was the fact that the retainers of daimyo houses were supported by stipends and, as Edo transplants experiencing for the first time the sumptuary demands of social life in the shogun's capital, constituted a perennial market for consumer goods and for the financial services necessary to convert rice-based stipends into cash or lines of credit. Demand was also high for entertainment: in a city where the population was predominantly male, the market for prostitution, both in and outside of the officially licensed brothel districts, expanded rapidly, as did the theater, which also offered its actors as objects of erotic interest (and, through more or less formalized practices of prostitution, sexual release). The newly urbanized samurai class, in its needs for both consumer goods and entertainment, thus fueled the initial explosion of Edo's commoner population, as artisans, merchants, laborers, and entertainers gathered in the city to profit from the economic opportunities of the new warriors' capital and drove the formation of Edo's distinctive urban culture.[9]

To the east of the castle, resting mostly on landfill in what was once the river delta flowing into Edo Bay, was the commoner district of what would eventually be called the "low city" (shitamachi), running from Kanda in the north through Nihonbashi, Nakabashi, Kyōbashi, and Shinbashi, and extending eastward to the Sumida River. These old neighborhoods were the core communities of commoner Edo, many of which enjoyed the privilege of direct patronage by the warrior authorities: in the highly rationalized fashion typical of the castle town, many were originally organized according to trade, having been populated by merchants and artisans summoned directly by Ieyasu for the purpose of providing artisanal expertise, direct access to shipping and trade networks, and financial services. Others had settled spontaneously in response to the growing demands of urban life, including all manner of petty artisans, merchants, street peddlers, and day laborers. Major temples like Sensōji in the northeast at Asakusa and Tōkaiji in the south at Shinagawa initially

---

[9] Vaporis, Tour of Duty.

remained outside the borders of the city proper, while within the city, religious institutions such as the Hie (Sannō) Shrine and the Zōjōji and Kan'eiji temples enjoyed autonomy within their own precincts.

Sites of urban leisure and entertainment had a somewhat more ambivalent place within the castle town paradigm. Since the medieval era, open spaces such as riverbeds, bridges, temple grounds, and marketplaces, due to their place outside of the jurisdiction of any institutional authority, had existed as semisacred sites of free association on the social margins. This was famously the case along the Kamo River in Kyoto, where the performances of troupes of itinerant dancers such as that of Izumo no Okuni pioneered the forms of erotic dance-theater that would later evolve into the Kabuki theater. In Edo, likewise, sites of urban entertainment tended to congeal along the water-ways that marked the city's inner and outer margins – especially along the banks of the Sumida River, whether in the case of the original Yoshiwara pleasure quarters at Nihonbashi Fukiya-chō or the early theater district at Nakabashi. As the case of Izumo no Okuni suggests, women had since the medieval period played a major and visible role in such "unattached" spaces, whether as performers, prostitutes, or consumers; distinctions of gender, like those of status, tended to be more fluid on the social margins. Though some such districts would be relocated during the reconstruction of the city follow-ing the Meireki fire of 1657 (the Yoshiwara district to its permanent location in the northeastern San'ya suburb and the theaters to the licensed districts of Fukiya-chō, Sakai-machi, and Kobiki-chō), entertainment districts would remain closely linked to the landscape and symbolic associations of what Jinnai Hidenobu has called a "city of water."[10]

Liminal, heterotopic spaces such as these thrived in both contrast and com-plementary relation with the highly rationalized and hierarchical socio-spatial order of the castle town. The shogunal authorities, whether out of an ideo-logical anxiety over the morally deleterious effects of leisure and status mix-ing or a practical concern with their potential to house both criminal and politically subversive elements, rapidly took steps to formally incorporate such spaces into their administrative purview as officially recognized enter-tainment districts, subjecting them to stringent systems of licensing and circumscribing them within designated geographical boundaries. In many cases, this incorporation into the socio-spatial order of the castle town also ran parallel with a re-gendering of space and forceful assertion of systems of patriarchal control: in the case of the theater districts, over the course of the

---

[10] Jinnai, *Tokyo*.

seventeenth century, women (and young men) were progressively excised from the stage (though they could continue to move through the theater as an enthusiastic portion of the audience), and in the case of the prostitution districts, working women were forcibly placed under the patriarchal authority of brothel owners. Though the popular culture and urban leisure of the Tokugawa period – the dual "bad places" (akusho) of the licensed prostitution quarters and theater districts – have often been identified with the cultural agency of the townspeople and considered a site of implicit resistance to the status hierarchy, the shogunate for the most part tolerated if not fostered them within their boundaries (with occasional exceptions during conservative reform programs). Commoner sources, in contrast, frequently expressed anxiety toward them, and there on financial rather than moral grounds: many a proper merchant house was ruined at the hands of a household head driven to dissolution by the seductions of urban leisure.[11]

The city would rapidly grow beyond its initial design. One of the historical triggers for the growth of the city was the cataclysmic fire of 1657. More than half of the city was burned, including the great donjon of Edo Castle (never to be rebuilt, though it would continue to loom large in the Edo imagination), and casualties are estimated in the hundreds of thousands. In the face of this tremendous human and material cost, the shogunate proved resilient, using the widespread devastation as an opportunity to reshape the urban framework. In addition to the rezoning and relocation of daimyo estates, the shogunate expanded efforts at land reclamation along the Sumida River and coastal districts. The framework of urban infrastructure was also expanded to the eastern side of the Sumida, where the shogunate would go on to develop new residential space for shogunal vassals as well as new commercial districts for the city's rapidly expanding commoner population. Thus the Sumida, which had originally been conceived as an outer margin and defensive moat for the shogun's city, gradually became one of its symbolic centers, especially in the eyes of the city's commoner populations. The neighborhoods of Honjo and Fukagawa would develop into the city's shipping hub, especially for lumber and construction materials, a function previously held by areas around Nihonbashi and Nakabashi; with this function lost, many of the canals crisscrossing the landfill between the castle and the Sumida River became less critical and were filled in to provide space for appropriation by the commoner populace. Urban development also extended to the outside of the outer moat, which had initially been conceived as the outer fortification

<hr/>

[11] Moriya, Genroku bunka.

of the shogun's castle town; meanwhile, the shogunate took districts that had formerly been administered by rural deputies (Honjo, Fukagawa, Asakusa, Koishikawa, Ushigome, Ichigaya, Yotsuya, Akasaka, Azabu, and so on) and integrated them into the urban administration of the city magistrates, rapidly increasing the number of wards under direct shogunal administration. From an initial count of roughly 300 original wards, the city magistrates would by the early eighteenth century administer 933 wards, a number that would by the mid-nineteenth century nearly double to a maximum of 1,719. Even as early as the turn of the eighteenth century, the fabric of Edo would reach without interruption as far as Sensōji at Asakusa in the north and Tōkaiji at Shinagawa in the south, and would encroach on the surrounding countryside in all directions. Amid this ongoing process of explosive expansion, the very boundaries separating the city proper from its rural hinterland were thrown into question. Even when the senior councillors convened in 1818 to establish conclusively what constituted Edo, in keeping with the logic of "segmental structure," they produced two distinct boundaries: one defining the jurisdiction of the city magistrates over urban commoners and the other defining warrior administration.[12] And just as Edo's outer boundary would become blurred and contested, so would the socio-spatial distinctions separating commoner, warrior, religious, and outcaste communities. This was especially true in the outer and later-developing reaches of the Yamanote area, where commoner communities formed organically around daimyo estates, demonstrating in microcosm the increasing interweaving of status communities and blurring of spatial boundaries.[13]

Perhaps more important than the overall expansion of Edo's surface area and population was the contestation and renegotiation of both social authority and symbolic meaning in many of Edo's diverse spaces. In the aftermath of the Meireki fire, the shogunate established several major firebreaks throughout the city, such as those at Edobashi and Ryōgoku. The firebreak at Edobashi almost immediately became the site of a process of appropriation by diverse commoner populations: ward elders built warehouses as a source of revenue, entrepreneurial merchants set up temporary street stalls, outcastes and itinerant entertainers took advantage of the open space and the crowds it attracted to ply their respective trades and were soon joined by teahouses, archery ranges, vaudeville theaters, and other plebeian entertainments. As James McClain has shown, the firebreak was ultimately reclaimed, through

---

[12] Katō, "Governing Edo."
[13] Iwabuchi, "Kinsei toshi shakai."

complex negotiations of privileges and obligations with the shogunal authorities, as a combination of commoner housing and entertainment district.[14] At
precisely those interstices that had been carved out to serve the interests of
the castle town as a figuration of shogunal authority and administrative totality (preventing the spread of fire across spatial boundaries and allowing space
for the passage of shogunal retinues), there emerged bustling neighborhoods
in which different communities interacted and vied for control over space.
Whereas the shogunate had effectively consolidated other spaces of urban
entertainment such as the prostitution and theater districts into its systems of
spatial administration, pushing them increasingly to the margins of Edo, the
more profoundly heterotopic spaces of Edo's "amusement places" (*sakariba*)
could not be so easily reduced into a rational and hierarchical socio-spatial
structure.[15]

However, this is not to suggest that the evolution of the castle town
beyond its initial design represented the breaking down of the systems of
status or of their reflection in socio-spatial structure, but rather that such systems formed the frameworks through which social relations could be renegotiated. Nor is it to suggest that these negotiations, whether over Edo's
urban space in general or its open spaces in particular, can be reduced to a
narrative of urban commoners laying increasing spatial and symbolic claim
to the warrior's city. Such a narrative is suggested to a degree by cultural representations in the literary or visual arts, which increasingly imagined Edo's
central sites as "famous places," often apprehended from the perspective of
commoners as sites of commerce, leisure, and collective appreciation; but, as
Marcia Yonemoto has observed in a study of the iconography of Nihonbashi,
the relationship between warrior authority and commoner appropriation at
such sites was always an ongoing process of dialectical negotiation.[16] More
importantly, in the background of such harmonious cultural representations,
the city's commoner population itself was increasingly stratified and occupied with its own internal contestations over urban space and status.

Urban Commoner Spaces

The socio-spatial structure of Edo's commoner districts had its most basic
element in the local communities known as *chō* or *machi*, translated here

[14] McClain, "Edobashi."
[15] Regarding *sakariba* as cultural sites, see Takeuchi, *Edo no sakariba*.
[16] Yonemoto, "Nihonbashi."

as "wards." In its most archetypal form, the ward consisted of two rows of storefronts, a few dozen in all, facing one another across a shared avenue of about 100 to 120 meters in length, and set off from neighboring wards by gates at either end; architectural appearances within the ward were in the highly standardized form of the *machiya*, which consisted of a storefront/workspace opening onto the street and a residential space toward the rear of the lot. Though the precise spatial form of both the commoner ward and the commoner house varied regionally and would evolve slightly over the course of the early modern period, together they would constitute a remarkably stable and flexible socio-spatial structure and act as a modular unit of urban development across all of Japan.[17]

If the spatial planning of shogunal administrators was organized around an urban idea that reflected the needs and interests of ruling warlords – one based on a rationalized division of space according to status, on an expedient arrangement of occupationally distinct neighborhoods for distribution of material goods and services, and on the visual symbolism of hierarchical authority – then the ward represented its own urban idea, a bottom-up vision that manifested the social worldview of commoner communities. This urban idea was essentially one of local, collective self-government for the protection of private urban property. The *machiya*, linked to the plot of urban land on which it was built, was the physical projection into urban space of the propertied merchant (or artisanal) household (*ie*), and the ward in its archetypal form consisted of a local community of a few dozen such propertied households. To be an urban commoner (*chōnin*) proper was to be the (typically male) head of such a propertied household and a member of the local self-governing community of a particular ward. Membership in such a community, moreover, demanded adherence to certain social norms. Surviving ward regulations from the seventeenth century suggest a concern for the maintenance of goodwill between members (prohibiting favoritism and cliques, mandating collective decision-making, requiring regular hosting of neighborhood meetings, and dictating collective participation in community rituals such as marriage) and control over community membership (whether by placing conditions of sponsorship or community approval on the sale, purchase, and rental of property, or by explicitly excluding certain trades or social classes). Significantly, such regulations were particularly attentive to socio-spatial structure within the ward, often including conditions stipulating uniformity of architectural appearance – for example, standardizing frontage – as a way

[17] Tamai, *Edo*.

of giving external expression to the idea of the ward as a community whose members share equal public status.[18] The commoner idea of the city was thus a matter of personal membership in a local, self-governing, and nominally egalitarian community. Needless to say, this nominally egalitarian concern only extended as far as male household heads: not to women, children, or renters, who only existed to the ward to the extent that they were attached to a patriarchal household.

Despite possible tensions between this bottom-up vision of local self-government and the top-down vision of a rational, hierarchical city plan projected by warrior authorities, the socio-spatial structure of the ward was rapidly and seamlessly incorporated into the Tokugawa polity. In keeping with the shogunate's treatment of other forms of local community, each ward owed certain duties (*yaku*) to the state, including maintaining basic infrastructure, securing public order by staffing guardhouses and gatehouses, providing miscellaneous forms of corvée labor and regular commitment of manpower to tasks such as firefighting, and paying various taxes, including taxes in kind for those neighborhoods that were originally organized by trade. Assuming that such obligations were met and that there were otherwise no disruptions to the public order, the authorities were not concerned with everyday affairs within any given community. In the case of Edo, the city magistrates (*machi-bugyō*) – the two shogunal representatives responsible for administering Edo's commoner populations – interfaced with the wards through a set of three town elders (*machidoshiyori*), a semi-official position carrying certain perquisites of warrior status that was passed down as a hereditary right among three elite commoner families. These elders would then interface with ward chiefs (*nanushi*), who would pass on shogunal directives to family groups within the wards, and on to each household and its constituent members. In this sense, the shogunate's systems of authority resonated conveniently with the patriarchal structures of the commoner house, as women, children, the elderly, and other non-propertied members of the commoner population need not be administered directly by the state but could be left to the discretion of their respective male household heads. The ward (and ultimately the commoner household itself) thus became one of the terminal units of the shogunate's system of urban status administration.

Despite the egalitarian tendencies occasionally attested in early neighborhood regulations, the commoner ward had always exhibited its own internal

---

[18] Yoshida, *Kinsei toshi shakai*, 45–75.

hierarchies. Foremost among these, though taken for granted at the time, was the gendered hierarchy that (with occasional exceptions) excluded women from householding status, recognizing them only as subordinate members of the patriarchal house. This gendered hierarchy was also articulated in socio-spatial terms, as it suggested that the place of women was within the home, and, especially for more affluent merchant households, in the private residential quarters to the rear of the property rather than the public-facing commercial space of the shop front. However, it should be noted that these distinctions were often quite flexible, especially at the lower end of the socioeconomic spectrum, and, as the period progressed, women were an increasingly public presence in commoner urban space.[19] There were also hierarchies and status differences among the male members of the household: those separating the patriarchal head from his clerks, shop-hands, and servants, only some of whom would ever gain independence as masters of their own households; and those separating eldest sons, who were typically (though by no means exclusively) destined to inherit the position of household head, from younger sons, who would be apprenticed out to other houses, married off as adoptive heirs, or, in the case of large houses, established as the heads of branch houses that were nevertheless still beholden to the main household.

Even among the community of household heads there were inevitably status differentials. This was particularly the case in Edo, where powerful merchants and artisans had been summoned by Ieyasu to provide access to provisions and matériel; these privileged commoner houses naturally came to assume both formal and informal authority among their communities, forming an upper stratum of elite townspeople. And, even from early in the seventeenth century, Edo's commoner districts had a lower stratum of non-propertied residents: renters, who were not considered members of the ward and whose presence was often subject to strict control by ward regulations. Over the course of the seventeenth century, this internal stratification of the ward community was amplified by the broader economic stratification of commoner society and the increasing commodification of urban property, trends that ultimately resulted in the emergence of tremendously wealthy and powerful merchant houses whose influence transcended and in some cases entirely displaced the local authority of the ward community. The most dramatic example of this trend in Edo is no doubt the Mitsui house, whose Echigoya department store would both revolutionize the structure of early

[19] Nakano, "Kinsei shomin no jendā."

modern commerce and radically reshape the socio-spatial structure of Edo's central commoner districts, becoming a national landmark in the process.

The Mitsui house, headed by the energetic patriarch Takatoshi, was originally based in Matsusaka (Ise Province), but by the late seventeenth century had established several branches in Edo – a small dry goods store in Hon-chō 4-chōme that later became a clothier and expanded to two small, rented storefronts in Hon-chō 1-chōme and 2-chōme – as well as locations in Kyoto that served as suppliers for the Edo shops. All were headed by Takatoshi's sons but operated in unison, likely under his careful direction. The Hon-chō 1-chōme and 2-chōme wards consisted mostly of elite clothiers and operated as informal trade guilds, bound together by the collective social and commercial practices of the ward. Most of these clothiers had risen to wealth by doing made-to-order business on exclusive accounts with daimyo and elite commoner houses. In most cases, such sales were accomplished by sending a clerk in person to the client's estate and by taking orders on credit. This practice, based on privileged relationships between elite clothiers and warrior authority, allowed for significant mark-ups, but, as daimyo finances were progressively straitened toward the end of the seventeenth century, such relationships were put under increasing strain, with daimyo occasionally defaulting on payments. Amid this financial climate, the Mitsui Echigoya adopted instead a model of storefront sales with payment in cash, and while this model offered lower profit margins, it also allowed the Echigoya to undercut its competitors (namely, its neighbors, the established businesses of the local Hon-chō community) and furnish more immediate cash flow. These innovations were a smashing success, attracting many daimyo clients who had previously operated on exclusive accounts with Mitsui's neighbors as well as commoner customers from the city at large. Mitsui's epoch-making practice of storefront sales, emblematized by the memorable slogan of "Payment in Cash, No Mark-ups" (*genkin kakene nashi*), effectively established the model of the department store.

Although the historic success of the Mitsui Echigoya is often seen as a story of innovative business practice, it was equally a story of the confrontation between the authority of the ward community and the expanding economic clout of the entrepreneurial merchant house. The Echigoya's Hon-chō neighbors were both envious of its success and wary of the threat that it represented to their traditional business practice, which had allowed them to operate as a cartel and justify mark-ups for elite clients. As such, they quickly conspired to block Mitsui from the Edo market, and even went so far as to request that his landlord install a communal toilet that would drain past the Echigoya's kitchen in an attempt to drive the business from the neighborhood. Likely in response to such harassment, the Echigoya soon purchased property at a new location in the neighboring ward of Suruga-chō, just north of Nihonbashi, and relocated its operations there in 1683. Suruga-chō, however, was a neighborhood of moneylenders, and the ward council, who after all had long been neighbors with the Hon-chō community, shortly declared that a clothier had no place in their community and that the Mitsui house would have to take its business elsewhere. In response, the Mitsui house simply incorporated a moneylending branch into its bustling department store and, relying on the intercession of its own local allies, continued business as usual. The property purchased by Mitsui in and around Suruga-chō was also significant for crossing the boundaries of Suruga-chō proper and the neighboring wards of Muromachi 2-/3-chōme; in its ultimate form it would consist of two enormous storefronts facing one another at the eastern end of Suruga-chō. Within a few decades, the Mitsui house would go on to purchase extensive property in both Suruga-chō and the Hon-chō wards, buying out its competitors and critics and effectively demonstrating the domination of the ward community, and the deformation of its socio-spatial structures, by expanding merchant capital.[20]

By the early eighteenth century, the two Echigoya shops in Edo employed and housed over 500 attendants, including the clerks and shop-hands who worked the floor along with various attendants and servants responsible for maintaining the private operations of such a massive household.[21] The social influence of the Mitsui house extended far beyond the walls of the Echigoya shop and the boundaries of the Suruga-chō ward in other ways too. The shop oriented the labor and movement of a huge range of contractors, whether craftsmen providing service for the shop's operations, merchants supplying groceries and household supplies to support the house's large dependent population, or carpenters and laborers hired for maintenance and reconstruction of the massive Echigoya edifice. In addition, like many other elite merchants, the Mitsui house was able to gather property throughout Edo's commoner districts, which it would then rent out to commoners of lower ranks, whether to middle-class merchants leasing storefront space along a main thoroughfare or to lower-class laborers, craftsmen, and street peddlers who lived in humble tenement housing to the rear of urban lots. Finally, though the nature of the relationship varied locally, Mitsui also provided alms to the local communities around its shops during times of economic hardship or famine, though

[20] Yoshida, *Seijuku suru Edo.*
[21] Nishizaka, "Kinsei toshi to ōdana."

the relationships thus constituted between large merchant houses and the urban poor were always unstable and contested.[22] And this is to say nothing of the multitudes of customers who passed through Echigoya every day. Through such direct and indirect modes of social and economic relation, the Mitsui house thus ultimately shaped the socio-spatial practices of huge portions of the urban population, reorienting the circulation of bodies and labor through its tremendous economic clout. While Mitsui was among the most extreme examples of the expansion of the merchant house, it was not alone in this status: this was the influence of the "great shop" (ōdana) class, which increasingly exerted influence on the socio-spatial structures and practices of Edo's commoner populations as the era progressed. The rising influence of this class through the eighteenth and into the nineteenth century is one reflection of the inherent tension between the community of the ward and its individual households, amplified manifold by the increasing commodification of urban property.

By the end of the Edo period, the class of propertied townspeople made up only a tiny fraction of the commoner population of Edo. While the ward continued to function throughout the Edo period as an administrative apparatus and underlying framework of socio-spatial structure, it was counterbalanced by the steadily increasing stratification of Edo commoner society. At the top sat the ōdana, exemplified by Mitsui as described above. Below them, along with the dwindling minority of small shop owners, was a substratum of merchants who rented modest properties on the main street of a ward, most typically operating a storefront business. Roughly equal in status but assuming a more active role in local administration were the landlords (yanushi), who occasionally owned the property in question but more often were proxy superintendents (yamori) appointed by propertied townspeople who resided elsewhere; in many cases, the landlord also performed duties formerly carried out by property-owning ward members, another reflection of the displacement of the ward community in the course of the commodification of urban property, labor, and administration. And at the bottom of the urban commoner hierarchy was a vast urban working class of laborers, street peddlers, low-ranking craftsmen and performing artists, neighborhood teachers, geisha, and other commoners living at or near a subsistence level. The diverse members of this urban working class resided in what were known as "rear units" (uradana) or "rear tenements" (uranagaya). In its most archetypal form, the tenement consisted of one or more plots of ward property

---

[22] Yoshida, Kinsei kyodai toshi, 181–228.

converted to accommodate various classes of renters: a few units facing the main street of the ward would be converted into modest, rented storefronts of three to six meters, while the majority of the space to the rear of the lot would be converted into a dense matrix of a few dozen humble apartments, the smallest of which were about three by four meters. The shared facilities of the tenement included a well – the site of laundry and thus gossip among the tenement residents – a garbage heap, a communal shrine, and two or three latrines. Most responsibility for daily administration of the affairs of tenement residence fell on the landlord, who in exchange for his troubles enjoyed the income of various gratuities from his residents, as well as incidental income from the sale of night soil to enterprising merchants serving the rural periphery.

In sum, urban commoner society was itself fragmented into a hierarchy of classes and a network of local communities, each of which had its own "segmental structure," and the relationships among which were under a process of constant negotiation. The matrix of socio-spatial structures described above – the ward, the *ōdana*, the tenement – were not the only institutions structuring the urban practices of Edo's commoner populations. In a compelling critique of the tendency in Edo urban studies to overstate the importance of the ward and the influence of the propertied townsperson class, Tsukada Takashi emphasizes the importance of guilds and other professional or status-based organizations, whether formal or informal, as feudalistic collectives organized for shared benefit. He sees them as a form of social organization structuring social and commercial exchange according to their own logics, which interact multifariously with the local hegemonies of the commoner ward or household. Such organizations, and the larger professional networks that were organized around them, were especially important for status communities with less stable forms of urban property: craftsmen, laborers, and especially marginalized groups such as beggars and outcastes. While such communities left less conspicuous traces on the spatial structure of the urban fabric than propertied status communities such as the ward, they still may be taken to represent an alternate form of early modern spatial practice, one that evolved in constant tension with both shogunal and commoner authorities.[23] The remainder of this chapter will use an abbreviated history of the Edo firefighting system to trace the ways in which such occupational networks from the urban margins participated actively in the ongoing socio-spatial processes that constituted the early modern castle town.

---

[23] Tsukada, *Kinsei mibunsei to shūen shakai*, 179–205.

Space and Status in Edo Firefighting

In a city as densely populated as Edo, and constructed almost entirely out of wood, it was perhaps inevitable that fires would be common. There is no need to rehearse here the statistics of how frequently the city burned, to what degree, in what seasons, and in what neighborhoods; it will suffice to observe that, due to the density of the city and thus the rate at which a fire could spread, it was a threat that fundamentally crossed boundaries: a local problem would soon become everyone's problem.[24] Even if fires were more likely to break out in the densely populated commoner districts to the east of the castle, if left unchecked, they could and did rapidly spread to warrior districts, daimyo estates, and even into Edo Castle itself. From the perspective of shogunal administrators, the threat of fire was thus a problem that demanded, if not a unified response in the interest of the castle town as a whole, then at least a comprehensive system that would smoothly integrate the local efforts of Edo's heterogeneous and often conflicting status communities. The process through which something approximating this goal was achieved, however, was long and haphazard, as it required a constant renegotiation of the boundaries of Edo's socio-spatial structures.[25]

The city's initial provisions against fires were a pure expression of the "segmental structure" of the castle town: distinct status communities were responsible for suppressing fires within their spatial boundaries. In the early seventeenth century, the shogunate was primarily concerned with protecting Edo Castle; daimyo estates were left to establish their own private systems of fire prevention, as were the neighborhoods of shogunal vassals and those of the townspeople. After the cataclysmic Meireki fire, the shogunate established a system of regular firefighting units (*jōbikeshi*) staffed by its bannermen and stationed throughout the city, and ordered a selection of daimyo to staff additional brigades to protect other locations of particular shogunal interest: temples, granaries, proprietary temples, major bridges, the shogunal academy, and so on. The daimyo, in turn, expanded the scale of their own firefighting operations into commoner districts surrounding their estates, but, like the shogunate, their concern was ultimately with protecting their own territory, and thus often ineffective when faced with larger blazes.

Firefighting in commoner wards was largely ad hoc throughout the seventeenth century. The first attempt at systematizing it was made by the

---

[24] For a detailed overview, see Nishiyama, "Kasai toshi Edo no jittai."
[25] The following draws from Ikegami, "Edo hikeshi"; Kelly, "Incendiary Actions"; Nakai, *Chōnin*; and Wills, "Fires and Fights."

celebrated city magistrate Ōoka Tadasuke in 1718 amid the wide-ranging social reforms of the Kyōhō era (1716–36). Ōoka required that each ward designate thirty firefighters, and that, in the event of a fire in a given ward, the two wards downwind and two to each side should send their designated teams to fight the blaze. When this system of purely local organization proved ineffective at fighting conflagrations that crossed ward boundaries, Ōoka moved toward coordinating the commoner firefighting system on a larger scale. In 1720, all commoner wards were organized into forty-seven teams, each labeled with a character of the *kana* syllabary: the famous *i-ro-ha* organization. The parameters of the system were amended slightly in 1730, when the existing forty-seven brigades, along with sixteen later additions from the eastern side of the Sumida River, were organized into ten larger divisions to facilitate coordination for larger fires, and the number of firefighters required of each ward was reduced to fifteen. Edo's commoner firefighting system would basically follow these parameters into the modern era, and these teams would end up shouldering the lion's share of all firefighting outside of (and occasionally within) the shogun's castle. But one question remained: given the increasingly stratified and often conflictual internal structure of the wards themselves, who exactly would staff the firefighting teams? This problem would require decades of fitful negotiation between a variety of stakeholders before a stable and more or less functional equilibrium was achieved.

In theory, the new commoner firefighting teams were to be staffed by the ward members themselves, namely the propertied townspeople who shared obligations to one another and to the state. In this regard, the demand to designate a specified number of firefighters to report in the event of any fire was no different from the various other duties (*yaku*) imposed on the various wards and thus passed on to their householding members. However, the ward's propertied upper stratum had little interest in the dangerous business of fighting fires, so they generally passed such responsibilities onto their employees, servants, and tenants. Moreover, it was often observed that, when a fire in fact broke out, the appointed firefighters failed to show up. This was no doubt a result of the self-preservation instincts of a largely untrained, amateur, conscripted firefighting force, but it also turned out that the propertied townspeople who thus conscripted their dependents would generally prefer, in the event of an actual fire, to have all hands protecting their own property: the interests of the individual commoner household only overlapped conditionally with those of the ward community and shogunal administration, and such divergent interests rose quickly to the surface in moments of crisis. Due in part to such desertion, in part to the fact that these were after all amateur squads, and in part to the fact that large blazes required a coordinated response by neighborhoods on a larger scale, the system quickly proved ineffective.

The missing piece to this floundering system came in the hands of an emerging class of day laborers called "hookmen" (tobi). The hookmen, or more literally "kitemen," had earned their name from the curved hook, resembling the beak of a kite, that they wielded masterfully for construction, roofing, or, in the case of firefighting, demolition: since water-pumping systems were too primitive to be effective, firefighting consisted largely of controlled demolition of the burning structures as well as those around them to produce a firebreak. Since the mid-seventeenth century, the hookmen had been grouped with other forms of physical labor under the administration of the Day Laborer's Agency (Hiyōza), but they had gradually emerged as the upper stratum of the class of day laborers, gaining higher wages for their prodigious skill with the eponymous tool, the one piece of property they held to their name. Over time, the hookmen came to be organized under a class of specialized contractors, later called "hookman bosses" (tobigashira), not hookmen themselves but rather townsperson-entrepreneurs; these bosses and their teams developed local neighborhood affiliations, leading to the emergence of a strong sense of territoriality and rivalry with other teams. In other words, the seventeenth and eighteenth centuries saw the gradual formation of the hookmen into a status group in their own right, one defined by social networks and territorial divisions distinct from those of both the castle town and the commoner ward.

While the hookmen were quickly recognized for their bravery in the face of mortal danger and for their technical expertise, they were also seen as problematically inclined toward casual violence. Descriptions of hookman conduct by the city magistrates' office should be read with an eye to the prejudiced view that samurai officials often held toward society's lower ranks, but there is undoubtedly an element of truth to official reports that hookmen were responsible for harassment of commoners, various extortion schemes, catcalling and occasional assault of women in public, and above all fights, both in general and especially at the scenes of fires. Much of this was no doubt a reflection of the aggressive masculine posturing of what were essentially gangs of otherwise unattached young men, but the propensity toward fights was also rooted in the unique territoriality of the hookmen and their bosses, and in the competition over neighborhood contracts. Despite this propensity for unruly behavior, even the warrior authorities themselves had long contracted the hookmen to staff their own firefighting squads, and commoner wards had by the early eighteenth century begun to do the same, hiring hook-men as part of the required numbers designated by the shogunate.

In the decades following Ōoka's efforts to reform the Edo firefighting system, the city magistrates' office received repeated petitions by different groups of entrepreneurial commoners (likely hookman bosses) to contract directly with the shogunate rather than with the individual wards: the goal was to establish a citywide firefighting system staffed by professional hook-men. This was after all the ultimate power play of a marginal status group: to establish institutional privileges through a relationship to authority based on a public occupation (*shokubun*), performing productive labor in service of the Tokugawa state.[26] The various systems proposed were ultimately to be funded by the wards, who predictably responded by rejecting the proposals, largely on the grounds that the planned costs would represent an increase of their own financial obligations. But as the years progressed and fires continued unabated, the city magistrates gradually realized that the hook-men were after all far more adept at fighting fires than amateur commoner squads that often consisted of the young or infirm, and began to petition the wards to employ hired contractors more systematically, albeit still only locally. In fact, by this point most wards were regularly employing hook-men to fight fires as well as for other odd jobs, but they nevertheless fiercely resisted the magistrates' suggestion of systematizing this hiring. The ward heads had no intention of foregoing the services of the hookmen as long as they remained dependent on townspeople's patronage and goodwill. If the hookman bosses sought to achieve privileged status for themselves and their teams by establishing a public "occupation," then the wards sought to deny them the privileges of status, keeping the hookmen in check as a mar-ginal and contingent labor force unprotected by the state. To that end, the propertied townspeople maintained that fire prevention was a duty of the ward, albeit one discharged by hiring hookmen as contractors.[27] Despite this resistance on behalf of the propertied townspeople, in 1787, in response to the ongoing failure of amateur (non-hookman) firefighters to perform competently (or even show up) in the event of a fire, the city magistrates finally dictated that each ward employ a specified number of hookmen as professional firefighters. The precise numbers varied, but the resulting brigades had a composition of about one hookman to every two to three amateur resident firefighters, with the latter only deployed in the event of a

---

[26] Regarding occupation and status, see Howell, *Geographies of Identity*, 45–78.
[27] Yoshida, *Kinsei toshi shakai*, 297–301.

major fire. Though the hookmen had been unable to fully circumvent ward authority, they nevertheless achieved in name the monopoly that they had long been negotiating in practice.

Even in its mature form, the Edo commoner firefighting system always embodied a volatile set of tensions: those between the propertied townspeople and their hookmen contractors, between rival teams of hookmen, and even between individual hookmen, competing to display their skill. These tensions tended to flare up at the scene of a fire. Buyō Inshi, the pessimistic samurai author of *An Account of What I Have Seen and Heard* (*Seji kenbunroku*, 1816), describes the conduct of the hookmen as follows:

> Recently they have begun to engage in a devious practice called "diverting the fire." Pretending as if they are trying to prevent a fire from spreading, they lead the flames to a place where the fire would not likely reach by itself. They do so in hopes that after the fire, they will be employed to rebuild the houses. Quick-witted and rich townspeople manage to save their own houses by secretly bribing the head of the firefighters not to burn them – an unconscionable deed at a time of emergency.[28]

While Buyō's exceedingly caustic appraisal of his contemporary society (both low ranks and high) invites a degree of skepticism, fires were, without a doubt, sites at which the property and privilege of elite commoners were subject to the whims of occupational groups from the urban margins; they were occasions when private grudges and resentments could be given dramatic reprisal, or conversely where superior protection could be secured through bribes. (Then again, the firefighting teams did not always wait for fires to act on their grudges: in a famous incident in 1799, the comic author Shikitei Sanba and his publisher had their houses demolished spontaneously for publishing a satirical account of a firefighter brawl.) Buyō's more significant observation is not of the private grudges and corruption that plagued this convoluted, localized, and segmentally multivalent system but rather of its systemic contradictions. To a certain degree, the hookmen had a vested interest in allowing their territories to burn. In many cases, they were the direct beneficiaries of new construction: in addition to firefighting, they were often contracted by the wards for all manner of odd jobs and construction labor. A fire, if not altogether too destructive, was also a chance to rebuild and thus to profit from the rebuilding.

But the more fundamental contradiction was in the logic of status itself. Contemporary to Buyō Inshi's account, there were rumors that some

---

[28] Teeuwen and Nakai, *Lust, Commerce, and Corruption*, 302.

hookmen, in order to stake a claim of having arrived at the frontline of a fire, even set fires or allowed them to spread. True or not, such rumors were eminently plausible: for the individual hookman, a fire was an opportunity to demonstrate his prowess at his craft, which was not just a matter of earning a monetary reward and prestige among his peers, but could mean advocating for promotion, whether in the form of advancement up the ranks of the firefighting brigades or moving from the reserves hired by a brigade to more stable (and higher paying) employment by a particular ward.[29] For the hookman brigade, a fire was likewise an opportunity to perform the value of its occupation to both community and state, and thus advocate for greater privileges; naturally this led to frequent brawls between competing brigades. In short, the complex spatiality and competing hierarchies of the firefighting system gave rational incentives for various (often violent) actions, both individual and collective, that were at best unrelated to and at worst at odds with the mandate of extinguishing fires.

In light of the frequency of violent conflict between teams of firefighting hookmen, the role of "foremen" (*tōdori*), first established around the turn of the nineteenth century as heads of firefighting brigades, gradually assumed increasing importance as mediators of inter-brigade disputes. Indeed, in the early decades of the nineteenth century, it was as much through conflict mediation as through directing firefighting that the foremen performed the legitimacy of their position, staging lavish reconciliation rituals that made a spectacle both of the potential for firefighter violence and the necessity of strong, well-connected leadership to rein it in. One of the key competencies necessary for such mediation was broad influence in a social network that transcended the spatialities of both ward and brigade territory – that is, facility with the diffuse and informal occupational networks that structured the urban margins. The foremen generally attempted to pass the significant costs of such services on to their ward employers, a practice that often verged into the territory of blunt extortion and protection schemes, leading commoner elites to contend that the foremen, or even the hookmen as a whole, were merely producing the problems that they then claimed to solve. There is an elegant parallel here to the conduct of hookmen surrounding fires, which they might be tempted to allow to spread in order to find a role in putting out. While there are elements here of blunt corruption and mafia-like abuse of local influence, we may also see this as a symptom of the performative logic of occupation intersecting with the complex contradictions of Edo's

---

[29] Minami, *Bakumatsu toshi shakai*, 216–17.

segmental structure: a marginal status group that received privileges based on a mandate to solve shared social problems had every incentive to continue to produce them. And while the commoner elites who were often compelled to pay for such "services" often railed against the hookmen as more problem than solution, the city magistrates, whose concern with the threat of citywide fires far exceeded their solicitude for the private property of wealthy commoners, showed marked leniency in the face of reports of hookmen throwing their weight around.

It is tempting to view Edo's firefighting teams in terms of the centralized public services and municipal employees of the modern era – whether as a progressively developing prototype or as a series of failed attempts. But the foregoing discussion should make clear that firefighting in Edo operated on a different logic, one predicated on the confrontation between distinct categories of social subjectivity. To the degree that the city magistrates who established and administered the firefighting system hoped that it would safeguard the city as a whole (their primary concern always remained protecting Edo Castle and other critical shogunal properties), this concern was only incidentally shared by the local ward governments – who themselves were often divided between a concern for the collective welfare of the ward community (whether or not they imagined that to include the lower, renting classes) and the individual interests of its constituent merchant houses, and who actively worked to undermine any direct relationship between the firefighting teams and the state – and by the firefighting teams themselves, who were perpetually concerned with renegotiating and securing their unstable position in the status hierarchy by defending their territorial monopolies on firefighting, by dramatically performing the utility of their labor, or simply by using their significant expertise at controlled destruction of commoner property to extort favors and settle grudges. The apparent inefficiencies and contradictions of the system – the ways in which the hookmen welcomed fires as a chance to perform their expertise in putting them out and the ways in which the foremen needed the threat of inter-brigade violence in order to perform their expertise in defusing it – were for the most part only problems for the propertied townspeople. From the perspective of the shogunate, the system in its mature form, albeit imperfect and a source of periodic tension, was for the most part effective in avoiding any particularly catastrophic blazes and, like most functions of a society segmented by status, did not require direct oversight. From the perspective of the hookmen, the system afforded a modicum of security along with opportunities for the assertion of agency both at the brigade and individual level, and the benefits of destruction in the wake of a fire – the opportunities for rebuilding – were shared by day laborers and others among society's lower ranks. While a widespread and uncontrolled blaze could threaten the safety of people across the social spectrum, the safely localized fire was feared most of all by those with property to lose; the largely unpropertied underclass residing in Edo's densely packed rear tenements could simply move elsewhere and continue to eke out their livelihoods on the insecure lower fringes of the "floating world." But if the inefficiencies of the firefighting system were felt most of all by the propertied townspeople, then it is also the propertied townspeople who created such inefficiencies by working so strenuously to maintain the hookmen as a contingent labor force, perpetually forced to perform their utility.

On Urban Culture

It is often remarked that "fires and fights" were the "flowers of Edo." While this aphorism tends to be taken as a sardonic comment on the rough-and-tumble quality of life at large in the shogun's city, it would be more precise to take it as one reflection of a plebeian culture in which fires and fights were celebrated as genuine opportunities for the expression of social agency. Similarly, the firefighting hookman became in the nineteenth century one of the archetypes of the "child of Edo" (*Edokko*) – the dyed-in-the-wool Edo local, distinguished by his ready wit, trilled speech, cocksure bravado, short temper, spendthrift habits, gaudy sense of plebeian style, and firm feeling of hometown pride, whether to Edo as such or to the more local communities that made it up.[30] The figure of the "child of Edo" is an object of significant nostalgia, and one often identified with the rising confidence and cultural agency of the townsperson class in the face of warrior hegemony, but while some early articulations of local identity in the eighteenth century were rooted in the culture of the propertied merchant class, the nineteenth-century *Edokko* was a distinctly plebeian figure, one whose wry wit and short fuse were just as likely to be directed at the propertied townsperson elites as they were at warrior authorities. The complex dynamics that shaped the firefighting system, and the competing interests at play, illuminate the social processes of conflict and negotiation upon which the culture and ethos of the *Edokko* were built – in other words, the social processes and stakes concealed within the appearance of a shared urban culture.

Despite the fragmentary and conflictual nature of Edo's segmental social structure, Edo's inhabitants had by at least the mid-eighteenth century come

[30] Smith, "Floating World"; Nishiyama, "Edokko."

to possess, at the level of culture, an emerging collective image of the city, of the shogun's city that was also *their* city: a cultural imaginary of local geography in the form of "famous places" (*meisho*), catalogued in urban guidebooks and immortalized in woodblock prints; a shared history and a set of larger-than-life avatars dramatized on the Kabuki stage, along with a cultish adoration for the local celebrity actors who embodied them; and a body of woodblock-printed literature that circulated across boundaries of status, class, and gender to articulate a shared body of knowledge and a set of aesthetic sensibilities that were understood as defining a uniquely Edo identity. The production of Edo identity was at its peak in the early nineteenth century, when, as a consequence of the expansion of literacy through popular education and the increasing cultural activity of the city's lower classes, the firefighting hookmen became icons of the *Edokko*. This collective vision of a shared urban identity was best expressed in the emergence of the term "Great Edo" (*Ō-Edo*): the name of the city itself became a talismanic icon of the good fortune of all of its people. But my aim in closing with reference to the emergence of such auspicious collective iconography is not to suggest that (the appearance of) a shared culture should stand over and above the fragmented socio-spatial structure and conflictual social processes that gave shape to the early modern city. Rather it is to suggest that such cultural representations, which were rarely as unified or unifying as they seemed or claimed to be, might also be considered as a part of the tense and open-ended negotiation between distinct and often oppositional subjectivities that constituted the urban social process. Rather than resolving the segmental social structure of Edo into a consensus of cultural unity, such representations acted as a symbolic space in which social authority, and indeed the socio-spatial structure that constituted the city itself, could be contested and renegotiated.

For example, some of the richest images of Edo's urban space may be found in the works of Shikitei Sanba (1776–1822). Sanba's *Floating World Bathhouse* (*Ukiyoburo*, 1809–13) and *Floating World Barbershop* (*Ukiyodoko*, 1813–14) depict the premiere publics of early nineteenth-century Edo, emphasizing the roles played by such shared spaces in maintaining norms of community etiquette.[31] Both bathhouse and barbershop were informal institutions of nearly every ward, spaces in which local residents paid a nominal fee to enjoy leisure and community socialization on a daily basis. Using vivid renditions of everyday dialogue and neighborhood chatter to sketch the vibrancy and diversity of

---

[31] For partial translations of these works, see Leutner, *Shikitei Sanba*; Shirane, *Early Modern Japanese Literature*; and Jones with Watanabe, *Edo Anthology*.

urban Edo, Sanba presents a utopian image of community and inclusion in the face of social difference – as he states in his preface to the *Floating World Bathhouse*, "High and low, rich and poor, all go naked into the bath." But contained within this image of the bathhouse as an equalizing space is a nuanced study of the social tensions and power relationships that structured the use of and claims to space, and ultimately of the boundaries of urban community. Sanba gives particular attention to the roles played by tenement-class figures in policing community etiquette and conduct in shared spaces: the exceedingly drunk, violent, or otherwise problematic are ejected by working-class neighborhood toughs (both male and female) – *Edokko* in the fashion of the hookmen – and, especially in the barbershop, members of the propertied classes of the ward (the landlord and wealthy merchants) are incidental figures, passing through or hovering on the fringes of spaces curated by and for the tenement community. Sanba's vision of bath and barber as sites of urban community was rooted in a belief in a shared Edo sensibility, but one that remained predicated upon a recognition of the palpable differences and tensions between social subjectivities, and that above all was structured by the social authority of the tenement class and the social logic of the urban margins.

In this regard, Sanba's work is a fertile symbol of the social logic of the castle town: a model of the city as a space in which distinct status groups negotiated the terms of their interrelational coexistence and established remarkably functional forms of social organization in spite of – that is to say, in recognition of and built upon – differences in public status and private interest. These differences were inherently unequal, built upon hierarchies of both status and class that tended to deepen over time; but, as the example of Edo firefighting shows, the logics of segmental structure still offered robust frameworks for the agency of the socially marginal. If the castle town always remained stratified and fragmented, like all cities, by such hierarchies, then it was equally a place that, to borrow Lewis Mumford's memorable formulation, offered "differentiated opportunities for a common life and a significant collective drama."[32]

Bibliography

Botsman, Daniel. "Recovering Japan's Urban Past: Yoshida Nobuyuki, Tsukada Takashi, and the Cities of the Tokugawa Period." *City, Culture and Society* 3 (2012): 9–14.

Howell, David L. *Geographies of Identity in Nineteenth-Century Japan*. Berkeley: University of California Press, 2005.

---

[32] Mumford, "What Is a City?" 112.

Ikegami Akihiko. "Edo hikeshi seido no seiritsu to tenkai." In *Edo chōnin no kenkyū*, Vol. 5, edited by Nishiyama Matsunosuke, 91–169. Yoshikawa Kōbunkan, 2006.

Iwabuchi Reiji. "Kinsei toshi shakai no tenkai." In *Kinsei 2*, 180–212. Vol. 11 of *Iwanami kōza: Nihon rekishi*.

Iwanami kōza: Nihon rekishi, edited by Ōtsu Tōru, Sakurai Eiji, Fujii Jōji, Yoshida Yutaka, and Ri Sonshi (Lee Sungsi). 22 vols. Iwanami Shoten, 2013–16.

Jinnai Hidenobu. *Tokyo: A Spatial Anthropology*. Translated by Kimiko Nishimura. Berkeley: University of California Press, 1995.

Jones, Sumie, with Kenji Watanabe, eds. *An Edo Anthology: Literature from Japan's Mega-City, 1750–1850*. Honolulu: University of Hawai'i Press, 2013.

Katō Takashi. "Governing Edo." In McClain, Merriman, and Ugawa, *Edo and Paris*, 41–67.

Kelly, William W. "Incendiary Actions: Fires and Firefighting in the Shogun's Capital and the People's City." In McClain, Merriman, and Ugawa, *Edo and Paris*, 310–31.

Leutner, Robert. *Shikitei Sanba and the Comic Tradition in Edo Fiction*. Cambridge, MA: Council on East Asian Studies, Harvard University, 1985.

Matsumoto Shirō. *Jōkamachi*. Yoshikawa Kōbunkan, 2013.

McClain, James L. "Edobashi: Power, Space, and Popular Culture in Edo." In McClain, Merriman, and Ugawa, *Edo and Paris*, 105–31.

Kanazawa: A Seventeenth-Century Japanese Castle Town. New Haven, CT: Yale University Press, 1982.

McClain, James L., John M. Merriman, and Ugawa Kaoru, eds. *Edo and Paris: Urban Life and the State in the Early Modern Era*. Ithaca, NY: Cornell University Press, 1994.

McClain, James L., and Wakita Osamu, eds. *Osaka: The Merchants' Capital of Early Modern Japan*. Ithaca, NY: Cornell University Press, 1999.

Minami Kazuo. *Bakumatsu toshi shakai no kenkyū*. Hanawa Shobō, 1999.

Moriya Takeshi. *Genroku bunka: Yūgei, akusho, shibai*. Kōbundō, 1987.

Mumford, Lewis. "What Is a City?" In *The City Reader*, edited by Richard T. LeGates and Frederic Stout, 110–14. 6th ed. London: Routledge, 2016.

Nakai Nobuhiko. *Chōnin*. Vol. 21 of *Nihon no rekishi*. Shōgakkan, 1975.

Nakano Setsuko. "Kinsei shomin no jendā." In *Jendā-shi*, edited by Ōguchi Yūjirō, Narita Ryūichi, and Fukutō Sanae, 220–66. Vol. 9 of *Shin taikei Nihonshi*. Yamakawa Shuppansha, 2014.

Nishiyama Matsunosuke. "Edokko." In *Edo chōnin no kenkyū*, Vol. 1, edited by Nishiyama Matsunosuke, 1–93. Yoshikawa Kōbunkan, 1973.

"Kasai toshi Edo no jittai." In *Edo chōnin no kenkyū*, Vol. 5, edited by Nishiyama Matsunosuke, 1–90. Yoshikawa Kōbunkan, 1978.

Nishizaka Yasushi. "Kinsei toshi to ōdana." In *Toshi no jidai*, edited by Yoshida Nobuyuki, 173–220. Vol. 9 of *Nihon no kinsei*. Chūōkōronsha, 1992.

Shirane, Haruo, ed. *Early Modern Japanese Literature: An Anthology, 1600–1900*. New York: Columbia University Press, 2002.

Smith, Henry D., II. "The Floating World in Its Edo Locale, 1750–1850." In *The Floating World Revisited*, edited by Donald Jenkins, 5–45. Portland, OR: Portland Art Museum, 1993.

Stavros, Matthew. *Kyoto: An Urban History of Japan's Premodern Capital*. Honolulu: University of Hawai'i Press, 2014.

Sugimori Tetsuya. *Kinsei Kyōto no toshi to shakai*. Tōkyō Daigaku Shuppankai, 2008.

Takeuchi Makoto. *Edo no sakariba: Asakusa, Ryōgoku no sei to zoku.* Kyōiku Shuppan, 2000.

Tamai Tetsuo. *Edo: Ushinawareta toshi kūkan o yomu.* Heibonsha, 1986.

Teeuwen, Mark, and Kate Wildman Nakai, eds. *Lust, Commerce, and Corruption: An Account of What I Have Seen and Heard, by an Edo Samurai.* New York: Columbia University Press, 2014.

Tsukada Takashi. *Kinsei mibunsei to shūen shakai.* Tōkyō Daigaku Shuppankai, 1997.

Kinsei Nihon mibunsei no kenkyū. Kobe: Hyōgo Buraku Mondai Kenkyūjo, 1987.

Vaporis, Constantine Nomikos. *Tour of Duty: Samurai, Military Service in Edo, and the Culture of Early Modern Japan.* Honolulu: University of Hawai'i Press, 2008.

Weber, Max. *The City.* New York: Free Press, 1958.

Wills, Steven. "Fires and Fights: Urban Conflagration, Governance, and Society in Edo-Tokyo, 1657–1890." PhD diss., Columbia University, 2010.

Yonemoto, Marcia. "Nihonbashi: Edo's Contested Center." *East Asian History* 17 / 18 (1999): 49–70.

Yoshida Nobuyuki. *Kinsei kyodai toshi no shakai kōzō.* Tōkyō Daigaku Shuppankai, 1991.

Kinsei toshi shakai no mibun kōzō. Tōkyō Daigaku Shuppankai, 1998.

Seijuku suru Edo. Vol. 17 of *Nihon no rekishi.* Kōdansha, 2002.

Toshi: Edo ni ikiru. Vol. 4 of *Shiriizu Nihon no kinsei.* Iwanami Shoten, 2015.

20

Popular Movements in Early Modern Japan

Petitions, Riots, Martyrs

ANNE WALTHALL

What constituted a popular movement in early modern Japan? In 1600, the Battle of Sekigahara laid the groundwork for a balance of power between the Tokugawa victor, soon to be awarded the title of shogun by the imperial court, and the warlords, called daimyo, who ruled more than 280 domains, but this battle did not end the insurrections by leagues of warriors and farmers that had plagued the country for centuries before.[1] Between 1428 and 1526, for example, local warriors and farmers had launched repeated attacks on Kyoto moneylenders in demanding amnesty from debts.[2] The last insurrection erupted in 1637 in Shimabara in Kyushu between Christians resolved to stick by their beliefs and a military regime determined to eradicate Christianity from Japanese soil. The regime won and celebrated its victory by massacring everyone who had defended the Christian stronghold at Hara Castle. Women and children too were killed, their heads cut off and displayed to all comers.

The vicious suppression of the Christian rebellion proved the futility of armed insurrection and marked the end of joint action by warriors and farmers that had characterized medieval Japan. Starting in the late sixteenth century, the separation between warriors, confined to castle towns, and farmers, officially disarmed, made rebellion impossible, and the later promotion of an ideology of Confucian-inflected benevolent government, however far practice declined from ideal, made it unthinkable. For the next 230 years, until right before the fall of the Tokugawa shogunate in 1867, farmers in mass movements might carry bamboo spears in self-defense, but with rare exceptions, they did not use them against their enemies.[3] They used their guns only as signaling devices. Rulers too refrained from killing protesters during

---

[1] Tsang, *War and Faith*.
[2] Gay, *Moneylenders*, 127–48.
[3] See Uejima and Ueda, *Shibamura sōdō*, 121–23, 140.

an uprising (afterwards was a different matter). This mutual restraint quickly evaporated following the imposition of a new, more highly centralized political order under the titular rule of the Meiji emperor. The first ten years of the Meiji period (1868–1912) saw more uprisings and more violence (murder and arson) than during any single decade since 1637.[4] This chapter focuses on the intermediate period, from 1637 to 1867, when commoners developed a variety of ways to assert their interests and what they perceived to be their rights under a regime that officially paid scant heed to either.

Japanese historians of early modern Japan have paid more attention to social and political movements than have their Western counterparts. Throughout most of the twentieth century, they mined mass movements for traces of rebellion against a despotic feudal regime that might show signs of a semi-proletarian class-consciousness based on class struggle or a revolutionary bourgeois assertion of rights. In recent years, however, they have questioned not how peasants opposed ruling authority but how farmers developed ever more sophisticated techniques to negotiate with their rulers. The vocabulary has shifted to emphasize popular movements (*minshū undō*), whether mass demonstrations plus attacks on the rich or less flamboyant but potentially more consequential deeds based on demands for equality and on a principle of representation that marks a break with medieval forms of direct action.

To the extent that historians in the West have studied early modern agrarian or urban Japan, they have tended to emphasize economic growth and social integration rather than conflict and mass movements. The single exception came in the late 1980s to early 1990s, when six monographs in addition to several essays examined uprisings by farmers and urban riots (see Bibliography). The books differed in scope, those by Vlastos and Kelly dealing with movements in a single domain, those by Bix and White covering the entire country from the 1590s to the 1870s and 1880s, and two by me, one that examined popular movements and the documents they generated in the 1780s and the other that contained translations and analysis of stories about uprisings. After that, the field dried up.

While recognizing the contributions made by my Western colleagues to our understanding of popular movements, I am going to rely on the way Japanese historians have recently interpreted their significance. In particular I draw on the work of Hosaka Satoru, whose forty-year devotion to the collection of records on popular movements has yielded a new interpretation of what constituted protest, how it was organized, and what it meant that is

[4] Esenbel, *Even the Gods Rebel*.

widely recognized in Japan.[5] I start with the petition, since that is the nucleus around which movements coalesced, then highlight the different ways that commoners acted and their principles of organization. This was not risk-free; in addition to executing leaders, the authorities might well imprison or exile others and fine offending villages. Popular movements that skirted the boundary between legal and illegal protest were once deemed less consequential than mass demonstrations or riots, but they have recently been reevaluated for what they reveal about the farmers' political acumen. The analysis of urban riots too has led to new conclusions that speak to rough and ready assertions of social justice and the complexity of urban society. Another place to look for the disjuncture between the official ideology and the status order is in village disputes and uprisings by marginalized groups. In addition, Japan has a rich tradition of commemorating men who sacrificed themselves to save their villages that legitimized action taken on behalf of local interests.

Petitions, Oaths, Contracts, and Circulars

The sheer quantity of documents generated at all levels of society marks one difference between early modern and medieval Japan, a phenomenon that characterizes popular movements as well. It is difficult to enumerate the total number of incidents because they almost always revolved around the presentation of a petition to the ruling authorities that might or might not be deemed illegal. Aoki Kōji counted 3,710 instances of what he termed peasant uprisings (hyakushō ikki) between 1590 and 1877, but because he included legal petitions, this number is probably inflated.[6] Herbert P. Bix counted 3,001 between 1590 and 1871; he too includes legal petitions.[7] On the other hand, he did not include disputes within villages, and these numbered in the thousands. Hosaka puts the number of popular movements that the authorities deemed to be illegal at under 3,000, and even these usually coalesced around a petition. Other documents such as oaths and contracts regulated behavior and expectations within the movement.

Since this was not a regime that permitted popular input in policy, commoners typically relied on the petition to make their voices heard. Ieyasu

---

[5] Hosaka, *Hyakushō ikki to sono sahō*; Hosaka, *Hyakushō ikki to gimin*.
[6] Hosaka, *Hyakushō ikki to sono sahō*, 19. Hosaka took over from Aoki Kōji the compilation and editing of a massive document collection on uprisings covering the period from 1590 to 1860: Aoki and Hosaka, *Hennen hyakushō ikki shiryō shūsei*.
[7] Bix, *Peasant Protest in Japan*, xxi.

and his son Hidetada accepted petitions while out hunting; later shoguns received petitions while on pilgrimage to Ieyasu's shrine at Nikkō, and in the early eighteenth century the shogunate and some domains set up petition boxes to receive complaints.[8] On the other hand, the shogunate issued a decree in 1603, strengthened in 1633, that categorically forbade such direct appeals except under special circumstances. Complaints of malfeasance by lower officials stood a better chance of being accepted than requests to lower taxes.[9] Whether to approve a petition was a decision that the rulers controlled unilaterally. If they deemed a petition to be without merit, the petitioner would be punished.[10] For this reason, when commoners had a grievance, or usually a long list of them, they never knew what their chances of success would be, no matter how standardized the format and language of petitions became.

Petitions in the seventeenth century sometimes revolved around disputes between villages over boundaries or water rights, but the vast majority dealt with taxes. Based on often inaccurate measurements of land and assumptions about how much it could produce, government officials specified the amount that villages were expected to pay in tribute each year along with a variety of ancillary taxes and fees and time spent on the lord's projects as corvée labor. (Taxes were levied village-by-village, not on individuals, a chief factor in making collective action possible and desirable.) Officials understood that the farmers needed to have enough to live on, but any surplus left in the village would corrupt the farmers by giving them a taste for luxury. If the farmers thought their subsistence was threatened, they could petition for redress.

Every petition began with standard phrasing: "In fear and deference we offer up a written petition." It then went on to explain the problem – a lack of rain had stunted the rice crop or, conversely, too much rain and cold weather had prevented it from ripening. The farmers had exhausted themselves in trying to mitigate the damage, but there was no way that the harvest would suffice to pay the yearly tribute, let alone leave enough for their survival. As farmers in a detached portion of the Shirakawa domain explained in 1788: "Although we are afraid to throw off all restraint and forget the great and vast favors you have granted us up to now, it would be more disloyal to become a ghost town, and so humbly we beseech you that through your merciful compassion, the remaining farmers may survive."[11]

[8] Roberts, "Petition Box."
[9] Hosaka, "Hyakushō ikki," 181.
[10] Hosaka, Hyakushō ikki to sono sahō, 73–76.
[11] Walthall, Social Protest, 54.

Farmers often referred to themselves as "honorable farmers" (*ohyakushō*). This term exposed a consciousness of being the people of the realm ruled by the state's public authority, of producing the agricultural products that nurtured rulers and commoners, and of being the hundred names (*hyakushō*, the people).[12] Farmers knew that in the Confucian-inflected ideology of status as defined by their rulers they ranked first among commoners, ahead of artisans, merchants, and marginalized groups such as outcastes, beggars, and entertainers (see Ehlers, Chapter 17, this volume). In return for their hard work, farmers viewed help in maintaining their livelihood as aid originating in their lord's compassion, a humanistic, ethical principle. Rulers too accepted the ideal of benevolent rule (*jinsei*) in dealing with their subjects. As the fifth shogun Tsunayoshi said, "people are the foundation of the state."[13]

These two concepts did not imply reciprocity. Yamasaki Yoshihiro reminds us that the purpose of the early modern state was not to enact benevolent rule but to maintain the system, and for that, it was necessary to keep the farmers alive. As for the farmers, they wanted to improve, not eliminate, domain administration – reform, not revolution.[14] Honorable farmers had an obligation to work hard; the rulers' decision regarding whether or how to bestow compassion was always arbitrary.

In addition to emphasizing how hard they worked and how much they were suffering, the honorable farmers used other rhetorical strategies to make their point. This happened with increasing frequency beginning in the late eighteenth century, when commercial production started playing a larger role in the family farm economy. One of the most potent strategies was to assert that a new government regulation violated past practice. In the farmers' eyes, the past had intrinsic normative value, especially when present practice threatened their livelihood. Farmers always chose a specific past in making this complaint; it was not some mythical golden age. Another strategy was to make invidious comparisons between practices in neighboring domains or the shogun's lands and their own government, especially when it came to tax rates. A third strategy was to use reason backed by experience in making arguments, to develop a rational standard by which to make moral judgments for political purposes. For example, farmers living near Osaka complained that fish fertilizer merchants had raised their prices so high that it cost more to fertilize fields than the harvest was worth. This constituted

[12] Fukaya, Saitō, and Hosaka, *Hyakushō ikki jiten*, 582; Fukaya, *Hyakushō ikki no rekishiteki kōzō*, 64–65.
[13] Yamasaki, *Tokugawa shakai*, 255.
[14] Yamasaki, *Tokugawa shakai*, 85, 86, 205, 255.

wrongdoing on the merchants' part, and because it harmed peasants every-where, "it does not conform to natural principle."[15]

The language of petitions and the development of rhetorical strategies suggest several conclusions: (1) the relationship between farmers and their superiors was based on negotiation and accommodation, not opposition and antagonism; (2) neither side saw anything intrinsically illegal in presenting a petition, even over the heads of lower officials; and (3) even if the ruling authority deemed the contents of a petition or its manner of presentation to be illegal, the logic of the farmers' arguments might force it to accept at least some of the demands. Only rulers could draw the line between legal and ille-gal petitions, and that line could change from one domain to another, from one incident to another, or even during an incident if officials determined as a result of their investigations that the case had no merit. Furthermore, the petition's contents might be deemed legal, and it still might not be accepted. The state used arbitrary decisions to its advantage; petitioners never knew when breaking the rules might get them punished. Confronted with an inher-ently arbitrary system of rule, they created documents for use among them-selves to ensure a united front.

One such document had its origins in the medieval period. This was the written oath to the gods, a covenant that everyone signed together, some-times in blood. They then burned the oath, soaked the ashes in water, and drank it, a way of binding themselves to each other in what they called *ikki* (all for one and one for all).[16] An oath from 1817 states that if anyone betrays the group, he will be punished by the highest gods of heaven, the four heav-enly kings, all of the large and small gods from all the provinces of Japan, and the tutelary deities of the village. In some cases, these oaths were signed in a circle to demonstrate the oath takers' essential equality.[17]

Contracts too provided written evidence of cohesion. Some listed griev-ances and how the farmers planned to resolve them. Uprisings cost money – how would participants raise funds and how would the costs be divided up? Contracts also specified regulations for the participants to follow: no leak-ing the farmers' plans to the authorities, no making a separate agreement with the authorities, no leaving the protest. Those who betrayed the con-tract would suffer not just symbolic punishment by the gods but punishment in the real world. Participants were not to damage crops, they were not to

---

[15] Walthall, *Social Protest*, 87.
[16] Katsumata, *Ikki*, 27–32.
[17] Hosaka, *Hyakushō ikki to sono sahō*, 145–48.

indulge in sake at meetings, they were to be careful of fire and not to steal, they were not to wear inappropriate clothing, and they were not to fake illness and send a substitute.[18]

One type of contract specified the obligations that participants owed their leaders. In 1713 in Shimotsuke, the farmers promised that if the leaders were put in manacles, the farmers would tend their fields; if the leaders were imprisoned, the villagers would support their families; if they were exiled and their possessions sold, the villagers would buy the goods and send the leaders money for their living expenses; if the leaders were executed, the villagers would pay their families 100 *ryō* over two years. A contract from Tajima in 1867 promised that if the leaders were executed, they would be worshipped as gods (*daimyōjin*), and every year two *koku* of rice (10.2 bushels) would be dedicated to paying for memorial services. Like other documents generated during mass movements, these contracts were often signed in a circle.[19]

Farmers used the written word to summon people to act. Just as it was customary for government directives to be passed from one village to another, preparations for mass movements began with circulars going from village to village stating the problem, announcing that meetings held at night would discuss what to do, and warning the village to send men between the ages of fifteen and sixty as participants. This worked so long as village officials were willing to forward the circulars, a premise that became increasingly problematic later in the period. After 1781, posters and flyers took their place. Rather than following a set route from village to village, these were aimed at whoever saw them, and they targeted individuals, rice stores, and rural entrepreneurs deemed threats to the community.[20]

Mass Movements

Mobilizing farmers required preparation, organization, and leadership. There had to be a petition, usually prepared before the uprising, sometimes during its course. Almost all mass movements had a punitive dimension: villages that refused to participate risked retaliation and individuals deemed responsible for the farmers' hardships had their property smashed up in *uchikowashi* (smashing and breaking). Hosaka argues that the relative dearth of reported incidents in the seventeenth century compared to later periods does not

[18] Hosaka, *Hyakushō ikki to sono sahō*, 150–52.
[19] Hosaka, *Hyakushō ikki to sono sahō*, 153–54.
[20] Hosaka, *Hyakushō ikki to sono sahō*, 169–73.

mean the farmers were more submissive. Instead, they were learning new methods of resistance – to present petitions not as individuals but as villages.[21]

A wealth of information from the 1853 mass movement that mobilized around 16,000 farmers in the Sanhei region of the Morioka domain in northeastern Japan documents how the movement was coordinated and sustained from the ground up. It all started in 1847 when the farmers had marched on Tōno, the headquarters for a house elder's fief, with a petition that the domain first accepted and then, after the farmers had returned home, rejected. Having good reason to distrust the authorities, individual organizers, mainly small-scale farmers (*komae byakushō*), decided to induce the farmers to flee to the Sendai domain. After they had done the legwork of getting more farmers committed to resisting the domain and organized planning sessions, men who had broader experience and better contacts took over the leadership. Most of these were village officials, notably Miura Meisuke. He was well educated; well traveled owing to his commercial interests; and, as a member of the village official class, well connected. In addition, he was a big man with a commanding presence and a ready tongue.[22] What sustained him and the other eight leaders was anger at the authorities, pride in coming from a house that had founded the village, and a belief based on knowledge of previous incidents that after death they would be commemorated as righteous men (*gimin*) and worshipped as gods (*daimyōjin*). They thus had a strong sense of mission on behalf of the farmers. One of the leaders told some of the farmers' representatives when they were homesick, "if you had resolved from the beginning to die for the sake of the people, why should you cherish your life now?"[23]

In contrast to individual organizers and leaders, ordinary participants acted collectively as members of their villages. Once local assemblies had agreed to act, the organizers sent circulars to all the villages in the domain urging them to participate and threatening those that did not with arson. Documents from Kanehama village show that each household was supposed to send one man, and twenty-two did so. Nineteen did not. Women headed three of the latter households, and in another eight, women were the de facto heads because the men were working in Hokkaido. Other men were deliberately left behind to handle village administration. No reason was given for why men from the remaining three houses did not join the movement. They later served as messengers, liaison, and observers, suggesting that the village as a unit,

[21] Hosaka, *Hyakushō ikki to sono sahō*, 37.
[22] Bix, "Miura Meisuke."
[23] Hosaka, *Hyakushō ikki to gimin*, 127–28.

not the individual, decided on who should go and who should stay. The village divided the costs of the uprising household by household, with lower assessments on the poorer houses headed by women and a few others. After the Kanehama unit arrived at the border, it decided that eleven men would return to the village; twelve, including the liaison, went on to Sendai. In the case of other villages as well, when men returned home, they did so in groups, not of their individual volition. Hosaka's conclusion is that mass movements were thus not aggregates of individuals in the modern sense, but aggregates of villages.[24] Kurushima Hiroshi points out that the regulations specifying clothing, tools, noisemakers, and flags carried by protesters as well as the requirements for participation resembled those that mobilized farmers for large-scale construction projects. In other words, mass movements reflected the internal dynamics of rural society.[25]

Kanehama village documents attest to the close identification between village and farmer and the structural relations that made it possible for farmers to act collectively. Because the domain's exactions fell on the village, everyone had a responsibility to fulfill them and everyone had an interest in resisting them, even the women, despite economic differences between households. Although some men had temporarily left the village in search of work, their families worked the land alongside other members of the community and occasionally shared communal tasks such as transplanting rice or maintaining irrigation works. Social and quasi-familial ties also contributed to village solidarity. So long as the threat perceived to the farmers' livelihood came from outside, villages constituted the building blocks of mass movements.

These documents also attest to the many months of preparation that went into laying the groundwork for an uprising. Because villages managed their own affairs with samurai administrators sequestered in castle towns, the farmers' activities remained largely invisible. When postwar historians started examining politics and society in early modern Japan, they too had little idea of what the farmers did. This led Albert M. Craig, for example, to claim that the 1831 mass movement in Chōshū was inconsequential because it was "spontaneous and without any element of forethought."[26]

Documents detailing preparations for the 1853 Sanhei uprising reflect patterns of organization underlying all mass movements, whether marches on

---

[24] Hosaka, *Hyakushō ikki to gimin*, 122–25.
[25] Kurushima, "Hyakushō ikki to toshi sōjō," 211, 224.
[26] Craig, *Chōshū*, 56.

castle towns or flights away from it. Especially in the seventeenth century, but even later, villages in mountainous, economically backward areas on the borders between domains might make a collective decision to flee their homes and bring in officials from other domains as mediators, a humiliating experience for their lord. Starting in the 1660s in Kyushu, women joined their men. In the largest such incident, in 1690 in the Nobeoka domain in Hyūga Province, 1,400 men, women, and children took their livestock along as well. In their petition, they demanded administrative reform and that no one be punished for having fled the domain. Domain officials had refused to inspect the harvest for three years, insisting instead that the regular amount of tribute be paid despite wind and flood that had damaged the crops. They had demanded that the tribute be paid in full when the rice was still green, and they had patrolled the villages, giving advice on how to apply fertilizer, for example, that interfered with the farmers' work. If the farmers refused to listen, they were fined. The shogunate intervened and ordered the farmers to go home. It then crucified four leaders, beheaded two, and exiled seven more. On the other hand, it had the domain officials dismissed, reduced the domain lord's rank, and transferred him to Itoigawa on the Japan Sea coast.[27] When Seiriki village and others in the mountains of Awa in Shikoku absconded in 1806, one of the three ringleaders was a woman. She was said to be the person in charge, although she was never punished.[28]

Most mass movements aimed at the domain headquarters, a move toward the local center of authority. In 1686, farmers in the Matsumoto domain in Shinano Province protested when the domain increased the size of the bales for tribute rice and demanded that the rice be hulled. The farmers wanted the size of the bales reduced to the same as in neighboring domains and punishment for tax officials who harassed the farmers. Most of the 224 villages in the domain participated in the march on the castle town, some under threat of arson if they did not, and the protesters smashed up six rice stores that they suspected of being behind the plan to switch from unhulled to brown rice. At first the domain had no choice but to accept the farmers' demands. Two weeks later, officials received orders from the lord in Edo to reject them. They then crucified eight of the uprising's leaders and beheaded another twenty. This was the first of the domain-wide uprisings that erupted at times of trouble over the next 180 years.[29]

[27] Fukaya, Saitō, and Hosaka, *Hyakushō ikki jiten*, 65–67; Hosaka, *Hyakushō ikki to sono sahō*, 62–67.
[28] Kurushima, "Hyakushō ikki to toshi sōjō," 221.
[29] Fukaya, Saitō, and Hosaka, *Hyakushō ikki jiten*, 61–62.

Whereas the overall preparations for mass movements remained the same between the 1696 uprising in Matsumoto and the 1853 flight from Morioka, the farmers' demands changed. As commercial agricultural products such as paper, silk, cotton, and indigo spread, ruling authorities tried to figure out ways to promote and profit from them. In some cases, farmers opposed requirements that they specialize in a single crop, soybeans in Hachinohe in northern Japan, for example, or sugarcane in Amami Ōshima off the coast of Kyushu, that left them with nothing to eat. Because the policies that the farmers attacked were specific to the domain they lived in, mass movements too tended to be confined within domain boundaries or single regions. Even when the shogunate tried to raise taxes during the reign of the eighth sho-gun Yoshimune (1716–45), farmers protested within their local shogunal intendant's jurisdiction, not across the shogun's lands as a whole. As a result, the shogunate collected over 1.8 million *koku* in tribute in 1744, but by the 1770s it collected less than 1.5 million *koku* a year, approximately what it had been collecting in the 1720s. Revenues continued a slow decline thereafter.[30]

Two mass movements in Fukuyama in western Japan highlight how changes in economic conditions shaped farmers' demands. In 1717 the farm-ers marched en masse to the castle town with a petition only once. In 1786, the number of issues had increased dramatically, and the uprising lasted for months with three marches on the castle town. The 1717 petition com-plained about the way a land survey had been done, wanted improvements in the assessment of the yearly tribute and various other fees and burdens, and an investigation into how these taxes and burdens were divided up at the district level. The 1786 petition dealt more with commercial matters, demanding that an office supervising cotton production be abolished and fees for tatami covers be reduced. It itemized demands concerning taxes, in particular their conversion to coin, and it made concrete suggestions regarding village administration and the elimination of waste and fraud at the regional and local levels. News of this movement spread beyond Fuku-yama, sparking uprisings in cotton growing areas in shogunal and banner-man (*hatamoto*) domains nearby.[31]

One of the few mass movements to cross domain boundaries and the larg-est for the entire period was the 1764 protest known as the Tenma uprising, a conflict over post-station duty. It originated in a crisis in the transportation sys-tem felt most severely in the shogun's lands along the Nakasendō, the central

---

[30] Hosaka, *Hyakushō ikki to sono sahō*, 122.
[31] Kurushima, "Hyakushō ikki to toshi sōjō," 227.

highway through the mountains. When the shogunate had set up the system, it had assigned villages near the highway the duty of providing porters and packhorses for official traffic. As traffic increased, it had increased the number of villages responsible for this obligation. By the early 1760s, even this was not enough. A coterie of rural entrepreneurs, wealthy merchants, and moneylenders came up with a plan to have the shogunate assess new levies on villages located too far from the highway to easily send porters and packhorses. With this money, the group would then hire locals and make a profit. In addition, two additional levies came in quick succession, one to pay for the travel and expenses of a Korean delegation come to greet the tenth shogun Ieharu and one to pay for the ceremonies at Nikkō commemorating the sesquicentennial of Ieyasu's death.

The farmers were outraged. At the end of 1764, farmers in Kōzuke started meeting, and rumors spread that they planned to march on Edo with a petition opposing the new levies. Circulars went from village to village, summoning them to assemblies. Then, in Musashi, almost 16,000 men gathered at a riverbed and decided to start their march on Edo on the twenty-second day of the twelfth month. Early that morning they pushed toward Honjō post station. In one village that refused to participate, they smashed up the head's residence and a temple. As the farmers marched toward Edo they gained in numbers. Some reports say 200,000 men participated, but the actual number was probably closer to 70,000–80,000. To pacify the farmers, the shogunate agreed to rescind the new levies on faraway villages. Several officials lost their jobs over this incident that had created an uproar even within the shogun's castle. The protesters then turned their wrath on the men who had come up with the plan in the first place, and other merchants or rural entrepreneurs who they suspected of ill-gotten gains. After the farmers had returned home, the shogunate started searching for ringleaders. One village head accused of writing the circular that summoned farmers to the first meeting was executed. Another 368 men received lighter sentences ranging from exile to fines to manacles.[32]

The Tenma uprising relied on the same principles of organization seen in Morioka in 1853, but it found a greater diversity of targets. Once the shogunate had caved to the farmers' demands, the farmers attacked other commoners. At this point, the village leaders who had first called for resistance to the new levies dropped out, leaving the field to small-scale farmers who attacked

---

[32] Fukaya, Saitō, and Hosaka, *Hyakushō ikki jiten*, 186–88. For a somewhat exaggerated account, see Bix, *Peasant Protest in Japan*, 140–42.

wealthy merchants and rural entrepreneurs based on information regarding their collusion in promoting the new levies or other misdeeds. This pattern was typical of the mass movements that roiled domains, and it has attracted the attention of historians seeking glimmerings of class conflict ever since.

Urban Riots

Participants in both urban riots and farmers' mass movements believed in the legitimacy of their actions, but they differed in who participated and what their goals were. Whereas farmers combined the presentation of a petition with attacks on other commoners for their moral shortcomings, urban people who lived from hand to mouth ignored officials and vented their rage against merchants who hoarded grain and inflated prices.[33] (See Gaubatz, Chapter 19, this volume, for more on the urban poor.) The first peak came in the 1780s when rice riots erupted in over fifty towns and villages, and merchants in the city of Edo suffered attacks for five days. James W. White has argued that this transformation in modes of protest reflects changes in politics and the economy. With the growth of a commercial economy and the erosion of the burden imposed by the yearly tribute, the government lost salience in the lives of farmers and townspeople alike. Instead, the people's oppressors appeared closer at hand in the form of village officials, monopoly wholesale merchants, sake brewers, and rice sellers.[34] Taniyama Masamichi disagrees. According to him, not all people tried to break out of desperate circumstances by relying on violence because they had lost respect for and reliance on government. Some tried to rescue the poor through petitions and other measures to protect residents' livelihoods, and their efforts also deserve recognition. Whether or not mass movements turned violent depended on the situation and the source of injustice perceived as a threat to survival.[35] There existed a clear division between the sexes when it came to interactions with political authorities, but relations within communities were not so differentiated, thus allowing space for women on the margins of protest.

Even though women were more likely to participate in urban riots than in any other form of mass movement, they did not participate in the same way as men. Tsutsumi Yōko has shown that in the castle town of Iida and its environs, women went with children in hand to beg for rice. In the True

[33] This is Kurushima's explanation of Yoshida Nobuyuki's analysis of urban social structure. Kurushima, "Hyakushō ikki to toshi sōjō," 233.
[34] White, *Ikki*, 190.
[35] Taniyama, "Kinsei kōki no minshū undō," 280.

Pure Land (Shinshū) Buddhist communities along the Japan Sea coast, women joined in raising their voices to demand food from merchants and village heads. Sometimes women alone acted collectively to demand food; sometimes men took the lead. Tsutsumi suggests that one precursor for this form of action was the tradition of monthly meetings sponsored by the temples where men and women in sex-segregated groups would read sutras aloud in unison. Sometimes incidents never went beyond group chanting; at other times the chanting preceded smashing up houses.[36] In 1866, just before the opening of hostilities between the shogunate and Chōshū, in the region near Osaka where the shogun's armies had set up camp, women gathered to demand that rice be sold at low prices before men started attacking houses.[37] These cases suggest that some riots were not simply experienced by women but were brought about by them; they prepared the stage for acts of violence.

The most famous example of women shouting in unison is in Kanazawa in 1858.[38] There, despite a poor harvest, the domain had been exporting rice to cover its debts. For days women and children had been coming into the castle town to petition for aid, but none had been forthcoming. Finally, several hundred or perhaps as many as 2,500 women climbed a mountain near the castle and shouted, "We're hungry, we're hungry." After they had done this for two nights running, domain officials opened rice storehouses, and the price of rice dropped. The women had shamed them into action.

Collective begging and shouting in unison constituted a weapon of the weak available to women.[39] For them, the tongue (speech) had a dangerous potency, as it did in late medieval England in a method of communal policing called "the hue and cry." When someone saw an offence being committed, they, no matter their status, were expected to call to those nearby, rousing them to pursue the offender. This practice faded away in the early fifteenth century, in part because judicial courts were increasingly likely to see it as unjustified, especially when used by women, now labeled as scolds.[40] The loss of this avenue of power for English women shows that the right to speak matters. When Japanese women united in speaking up, they deserved the same attention as men who smashed up houses.

---

[36] Tsutsumi, "Ikki, sōjō sekai," 215–17.
[37] Inoue, *Kaikoku to bakumatsu*, 357.
[38] A popular account is in Nagai, *Rekishi o sawagaseta onnatachi*, 40–44.
[39] Tsutsumi, "Ikki, sōjō sekai," 218, notes that in at least one incident in the Kaga domain, men alone participated in shouting together.
[40] Bardsley, *Venomous Tongues*, 38–40, 76–77.

Urban riots did not come out of nowhere. In every case they were preceded by the types of actions taken by women seen earlier: appeals by ward heads and landlords to city magistrates for relief rice to help the destitute; gatherings at night; attempts by groups of buyers to negotiate lower prices with rice stores; and the begging of alms from the wealthy. In Edo in the fifth month of 1787, rioters attacked 80 percent of the stores dealing in foodstuffs, from the shops themselves to residences, storehouses, tools for polishing rice, ledgers, and household belongings. By spreading rice that had been hidden on the street, rioters made a public demonstration of hoarding. They then poured soy sauce and vinegar over it, thus punishing the merchants by making it unfit for sale. Although people who stumbled across a riot might take the rice and goods scattered on the ground, the rioters themselves stole nothing, they were careful not to start fires, and they did not bother the neighbors, showing that as a group they preserved a high level of cohesion based largely on the firefighters' code of conduct. Three days after the riot erupted, people started taking money to rice stores to buy rice at a price they considered fair. They relied on morality prevalent at the time (*tsūzoku dōtoku*) that balanced the legitimacy of commercial enterprises and the ethics of work with notions of responsibility to the community and social justice. The goal was not to wreak havoc but to assert supervision over the food supply.[41]

When commentators reconstructed the 1787 Edo riot, they asserted that it had been led by mythical figures. Diarists reported having seen men of unusual strength, perhaps *tengu*, the half-man, half-bird creatures who could destroy the world of the Buddhist law or embody the mandate of heaven by rewarding good and chastising evil. In the early nineteenth century, writers recalled a beautiful youth and a strong man (Kongōrikishi) who flew about doing extraordinary deeds. These figures provided a way for Edo warriors and commoners to draw on their symbolic world to legitimize violence and to explain the riot in terms that went beyond a simple response to dearth and greed.[42]

The 1866 urban riots erupted in a more complicated political world. Like earlier incidents, they followed a year of disastrous harvests and rising prices, but hardships for the poor had been exacerbated by levies on merchants to pay for the costs associated with the shogun's military campaign against Chōshū that left them less able to help their unfortunate neighbors, by turmoil in domestic markets owing to currency fluctuations caused by foreign purchases of gold, and by disruptions to shipping when Chōshū closed the straits of Shimonoseki

---

[41] Kurushima, "Hyakushō ikki to toshi sōjō," 235–36, 241; Iwata, "Uchikowashi," 152–58.
[42] Walthall, "Edo Riots," 415–16.

to rice transport ships headed for Osaka.[43] At the same time, the printing industry and the spread of literacy brought news to more commoners than ever before. In Edo, satirical verses heaped scorn on the ruling class and, for the first time, posters urged the poor to act. The shogunate did its best to get food to the needy by permitting free trade in rice and other grains, urging the sale of rice at low prices, and distributing relief rice while merchants continued the charity drives that they had started in 1860. Despite these measures, food became scarce, some merchants hoarded rice in the expectation that prices would continue to rise, and flyers called for attacks on privileged merchants, profiteers from foreign trade, and corrupt minor officials.

When the Edo riot broke out in the fifth month of 1866, it did less damage than the one in 1787, but it lasted longer. Merchants who had a reputation for being generous to the poor or who ladled out food to the crowd escaped damage. However, rioters also attacked sake shops, pawnshops, and the offices of merchants who traded with foreigners. Furthermore, the evidence suggests that some warriors as well as children joined the riot for the first time. Although the shogunate dispatched troops to quell it, the chief abbot at the shogun's mortuary temple of Kan'eiji in Ueno took a more effective measure in distributing gold coins to the poor.

Unrest continued even after rioters stopped smashing up houses. Posters satirized the shogunate's attempts to find a viable way to get rice to the destitute. After Shogun Iemochi died in the eighth month, the shogunate directed the townspeople to observe public silence until his funeral rites had been completed. Instead, the poor set up bases at temples whence they launched noisy marches with drums and chants through surrounding neighborhoods to requisition food. When they caught sight of some Americans, they yelled, "We are suffering hardships because trade with barbarians has forced the price of commodities to rise." Women and children threw stones at the foreigners and chased them down the street.[44]

Less than a month after the 1866 riots in Edo, Osaka, and other cities, what is known as the Bushū outburst erupted in the Edo hinterland.[45] The factors behind it were like those for the urban riots, and the goal was the same – to punish the wicked and thereby restore the world (yonaoshi) to harmony and justice. The uprising engulfed the entire province of Musashi; for a week, close to 100,000 farmers divided into multiple units were on the march, wrecking

---

[43] Miyachi, Bakumatsu ishin henkaku shi, 2:28.
[44] Walthall, "Edo Riots," 419–26.
[45] Sippel, "Popular Protest."

the shops, warehouses, residences, and offices belonging to rich merchants and other members of the rural elite. One group even envisioned marching on Yokohama to attack the foreign settlement. The leaders were masterless warriors, farmers, clerks, porters, and two women – O-Washi, "who frightened everyone," and O-Toi, "a truly ugly woman."[46] The uprising ended only when local militia and domain troops from Takasaki confronted the farmers and killed several of them.[47]

Historians once searched mass movements such as that in Musashi or a similar incident in the northeast called the Shindatsu uprising[48] for signs that protesters envisioned a new social order. Calls on the great god of world renewal (*yonaoshi daimyōjin*) were seen as harbingers of a desire for equality and justice. When farmers attacked domain troops with weapons as they did in Kai in 1836 or smashed up 300 enterprises in Mikawa in just a few days, historians discerned the beginnings of class consciousness. But the farmers did not seek a new social order. Their demands for cheaper rice and relief for the poor looked backward to the restitution of an ideal community in which the rich and powerful treated those less fortunate with benevolence. According to Yamasaki, the farmers tried to renew the world specific to the locality in which they lived, not Japan as a whole. Kurushima points out that the typical world renewal movement that paralyzed village administration with attacks on heads and the burning of village records erupted primarily in the silk producing areas of eastern Japan, not the region around Osaka that enjoyed greater prosperity brought by economic development and a greater democratization of village administration.[49]

Principles of Representation

Historians today pay more attention to farmers' initiatives that took advantage of the political order and point to new forms of regional administrative structures. Starting in the late eighteenth century, village leagues in the region centered on Osaka began to oppose commercial policies. In the early nineteenth century, thousands of villages from private domains and shogunal lands repeatedly presented joint petitions through representatives. These province-wide appeals can be seen as akin to class action suits in that they

---

[46] Walthall, "Devoted Wives/Unruly Women," 122.
[47] Miyachi, *Bakumatsu ishin henkaku shi*, 2:30–31.
[48] For a thoughtful analysis of the 1866 Shindatsu uprising, see Vlastos, *Peasant Protests*, 114–41.
[49] Yamasaki, *Tokugawa shakai*, 240; Kurushima, "Hyakushō to mura," 107.

involved the farmers as the plaintiffs versus privileged city brokers as the defendants. In making their appeals, the farmers' representatives relied on litigants' inns in Osaka to mediate for them with the city magistrate's office that had the jurisdiction to try their case. Drawing on their legal expertise developed through generations of experience with higher authority, the inns guided the preparation of documents or sometimes wrote them on the plaintiffs' behalf. Because these lawsuits were nonviolent, stayed within the bounds of legality, and led neither to mass demonstrations nor to the smashing of property, they cannot be seen as an anti-feudal struggle. After a single article by Tsuda Hideo in the 1950s, scholars ignored them until Yabuta Yutaka's work gained influence in the 1990s.[50]

Village leagues appeared in the Kinai region around Osaka because it was highly developed economically and politically fragmented except for the shogunate's regulation of commerce. All the villages that produced cotton or rapeseed were subject to the shogunate's policies that regulated the trade in these items to the advantage of privileged urban merchants and consumers in Edo. Another concern common to villages throughout the region was the cost of the fertilizer produced from herring caught off the coast of Hokkaido. Farmers deplored regulations that depressed the price at which they sold their goods; they liked regulations that lowered the price of fertilizer.

Yabuta analyzes the structural supports that made mass movements over such a wide and administratively diverse region possible as well as the factors that made them successful. Previous scholars had assumed that because peasants are like grains of sand, incapable of building wide-scale organizations, the force behind province-wide appeals must have been cotton merchants living in rural towns. In contrast, Yabuta argues that no, farmers relied on preexisting village networks. Although structured differently depending on the type and size of domain, some being organized on the basic of geographic affinity, others on the basis of domain affiliation, village leagues functioned to maintain law and order, to regulate local issues such as wages for workers and day laborers or the collection of donations by temples, to urge frugality, and to guarantee the necessities of life for the poor.[51] Taniyama and Kurushima argue that the regulations (gijō) established by these leagues constituted a de facto movement toward an autonomous and self-regulating regional administration apart from the political administration by shogun and domains.[52] Moreover,

---

[50] Tsuda, "Hōken shakai"; Yabuta, *Kokuso*.
[51] Yabuta, *Kokuso*, 61, 64, 65.
[52] Taniyama, "Kinsei kōki no minshū undō," 264; Kurushima, "Hyakushō to mura," 72–76.

just as villagers entrusted their village officials with the responsibility of managing tribute payments and village affairs, so too did villages collectively delegate authority to league or district representatives.

Through the village heads, farmers carefully crafted contracts that delegated authority to and requested specific services from their representatives. "Because we want to make a province-wide appeal concerning rapeseed and oil, we are making this request to you as our representative. You are to arrange matters in accordance with the discussions we have already had concerning the petition's intent."[53] The contracts specified the terms of service for the representatives and how the costs associated with the petition would be defrayed, as farmers in Morioka did in 1853. These documents were necessary because it was difficult for farmers to trust people outside their own circle, especially people from other domains, and they feared that outsiders would take financial advantage of them. The contracts also proved that the representatives enjoyed the villagers' support. In return, they had to promise not to betray the cause halfway; that is, they had the collective responsibility to see it through, and they were not to demand reimbursement for expenses aside from those specified in the contracts. Unlike village officials, the representatives were not publicly authorized by the ruling authorities, nor was their position ongoing.

In making their case, the farmers relied on the implicit force of numbers. In the earliest incidents starting in 1773, first neighboring villages united, then they had a district meeting, and then they linked up with neighboring districts. "All of the villages are the same in that they have suffered hindrances" and "we are all farmers exclusively." A circular from 1788 listed which villages and districts were already participating and how the villages addressed in the circular should respond by writing and signing a petition district by district. The villages that received this circular held their own meetings and selected representatives who joined the other representatives in Osaka. In this instance, 200 villages at a time presented petitions, for a total of over 800 villages. In the nineteenth century, the movements became more cohesive, with village leagues taking the lead in organizing the appeals. This made it possible to organize quickly and more broadly. In 1823, 29 representatives for 1,007 villages signed a province-wide appeal focused on cotton. A few months later, the representatives presented another petition concerning rapeseed and rapeseed oil signed by 63 men (including 25 of the original 29) who represented 1,102 villages. In 1864, 54 men represented 1,262 villages in a petition

---

[53] Yabuta, *Kokuso*, 41.

over rapeseed.[54] In negotiations with the city magistrate, the representatives
explained that villages had decided to choose representatives because it would
have been too expensive for everyone to go to Osaka. The threat remained
that if the lawsuit did not go well, then the farmers would take matters into
their own hands.

The province-wide appeals skirted the bounds of illegality in several ways.
First, they targeted not the shogunate directly but the brokers responsible for
implementing its directives, thus pitting the foundation of the realm, the farmers, against mere merchants. Second, the petitions dealt with mutable commercial policy, not the immutable tribute (tax) system. Third, they reflected
a multilayered system of village leagues girded by regulations specifying their
purposes and costs, a new type of regional authority inserted between the
ruling class and villages and necessary to both for the maintenance of law and
order. Not all province-wide appeals were successful; the ones over the sale
of rapeseed were not, but no one was ever punished for them.

Yabuta has pointed out that no other region saw such large-scale, legal
movements based on the grassroots political integration that had accompanied economic development in the Osaka hinterland.[55] In the nineteenth
century, however, relying on representatives became a feature of mass movements in several regions. In the case of the 1853 flight from Morioka, once
it became clear that the negotiations in Sendai would take time, the three
parties to the conflict had to agree on how many farmers would stay and
what their roles would be. The farmers wanted a greater number to remain
behind; the domains wanted a smaller, more easily intimidated group. The
purpose of shrinking the number was to reduce expenses, to allow farmers to
work during the peak growing season, and to lessen the damage to the Morioka domain's reputation. All sides acknowledged that the forty-five men who
stayed behind were general representatives (sōdai), not leaders, so as to avoid
punishment. The villages paid the representatives for the time they spent in
Sendai because they were seen as working on the villages' behalf.[56] The principle of representation functioned effectively in promoting the farmers' interests in two other cases as well, one that dealt with a commercial product, the
other with a political issue.

Like the Kinai region, the Edo hinterland was divided up into a patchwork
of domains. Some villages might have two or even three overlords exacting

[54] Yabuta, *Kokuso*, 69–78.
[55] Yabuta, *Kokuso*, 100.
[56] Hosaka, *Hyakushō ikki to gimin*, 125–26.

tribute but providing minimal security (see Howell, Chapter 3, this volume). In 1827, the shogunate and village officials worked together in designating representatives of village leagues to suppress gamblers, brigands, and other bad apples under the leadership of the Kantō Regulatory Patrol (Torishimari Shutsuyaku). Although not what the shogunate had intended, this system provided the organizational framework for popular movements.

The issue was night soil. Villages in the Edo suburbs found a ready market for vegetables in the city, leading farmers to plant truck gardens rather than cultivate rice paddies. To increase their yields, they needed fertilizer, and the most dependable, high-volume source lay in the city's toilets. By the nineteenth century, urban landlords had discovered that rather than pay farmers to haul their shit away, they could instead sell it to the highest bidder. This was not what the farmers wanted. In the 1790s, over a thousand villages in the Edo hinterland collectively demanded a decrease in the price of night soil.[57] In 1843, the representatives of villages north of Edo took advantage of the shogunate's reforms aimed at reducing prices to appeal to the finance magistrate to lower the cost of night soil. The city magistrate then ordered the heads in charge of commodities to lower the price for cleaning toilets by 10 percent. The fifty-nine villages also set up a district-wide agreement to forbid increases in the price of night soil or usurping anyone's right to clean toilets by offering a higher price. In 1844, two of the heads from this league got representatives from villages in the Tama district to join them in another appeal concerning night soil.[58] Tama lies west of Edo, suggesting that farmers had built networks that crisscrossed the city.

Farmers also relied on representatives to appeal to the authorities concerning political policy, a much more dangerous gamble. In 1840, the shogunate decided on a three-way transfer of daimyo: the lord of Shōnai to be moved to Nagaoka; the Nagaoka lord to move to Kawagoe; and the Kawagoe lord, who had adopted a son of Shogun Ienari (then retired) as his heir, to move to Shōnai, the richest of the three domains. This decree, which came directly from the shogun, threatened everyone in Shōnai, from the lord and his retainers, who faced a 50 percent reduction in income, to merchants, who had loaned them money and would be expected to loan them more to cover the costs of the move, to the farmers who could expect the new lord to order land surveys and increase taxes. In the end, the farmers took the lead in opposing the transfer.

[57] Kurushima, "Hyakushō to mura," 78.
[58] Fukaya, Saitō, and Hosaka, *Hyakushō ikki jiten*, 415; Walthall, "Village Networks."

This movement is famous for a scroll produced afterward that illustrates how the farmers organized their movement. First, they met village by village, sometimes in temples, sometimes in the houses of village officials, to discuss how to oppose the transfer order. They wrote oaths to the gods and Buddhas as farmers had done since the Middle Ages to guarantee good behavior; they also exchanged contracts with each other, promising to support their representatives.[59] At one point, eleven representatives made their way to Edo to petition to the shogun's senior councillors as they left the palace riding in palanquins. Their petition was rejected, and they were turned over to the custody of their domain, not a harsh punishment. Other farmers met in local assemblies that later coalesced into one grand assembly orchestrated to remain orderly with rules for conduct prominently posted on signboards and flags demarcating each village. The center was left open for village representatives. Despite attempts by domain officials to pacify the farmers, they continued to meet while representatives left for Edo and Mito (home of the shogun's senior relative Tokugawa Nariaki) to press their demands.[60]

Like representatives in Morioka, Osaka, and Edo, the Shōnai representatives carried with them contracts specifying their responsibilities and what they could expect in return. Unlike the case in the Osaka region, in addition to specifying the expenses to be covered, these contracts also promised that should the representatives be punished or executed, the villages would take care of their families and provide memorial services for their souls. In other words, the Shōnai farmers knew that their movement could not be considered legal, even if they refrained from violence. They were lucky: once Ienari died in 1841, support for the three-way transfer evaporated.

Historians today value the petitions presented by representatives on behalf of large numbers of villages less for what they achieved politically than for what they imply about the farmers' growing sophistication in circumventing restrictions on voicing grievances and in conceiving of and building a representative form of government. Inoue Katsuo has pointed out that Tokugawa-period farmers were litigious to an extent unimaginable in Japan today, and their willingness to make appeals belies their image as passive and quiescent.[61] As Tanaka Kyūgū commented in 1721, "samurai fight with weapons, farmers with lawsuits."[62] In addition, farmers learned to choose others

---

[59] Inoue, *Kaikoku to bakumatsu*, 94.
[60] See Kelly, *Deference and Defiance*, 76–100.
[61] Inoue, *Kaikoku to bakumatsu*, 71.
[62] Quoted in Ooms, *Tokugawa Village Practice*, 125.

to fight for them – not the village heads lauded in legend as sacrificing themselves for their villagers, but representatives selected and bound by contract for limited periods and specific goals. Another remarkable development that surfaced occasionally in mass movements and disturbances within villages was a notion of equality.

The Nature of Equality

The status system that structured early modern society was predicated on the fundamental inequality of human beings. Members of the hereditary ruling class were superior to farmers. Within villages, heads and other officials whose families had monopolized the positions for generations gave themselves privileges denied ordinary villagers. Yet despite the dominant and pervasive discourse of discrimination expressed in architecture and clothing, behavior and language, protest movements occasionally exposed counter discourses rooted in Buddhism, for example the notion that all are equal in the Pure Land ruled by Amida.

Hosaka has pointed out that concepts of human rights with universal applicability can be seen in Japanese, Korean, and Chinese peasant uprisings. The Taiping Rebellion in China; mass movements that drew their inspiration from Buddhism; and the Donghak movement in Korea, which combined Confucian ethics with Buddhism, Daoism, and geomancy all counted social equality among their principles. A notable expression of this concept comes from Hachiemon from Higashi Zen'yōji village, who was imprisoned for life for leading an 1821 uprising in the Maebashi domain. In prison he wrote a text for his family that stated: "From the single man at the top to all the people below, people are people, and the character for person does not differentiate between them. Even though there is discrimination between noble and base, above and below, this is just a tool of government, and all are equal under heaven."[63]

During village disturbances as well, farmers might envision a different social and political order than the one that constrained their lives. Most disputes attacked village heads' malfeasance, from partiality in dividing up the land tax, to embezzling funds, to misuse of famine relief, to tricking farmers out of their land. In some cases, the farmers wanted to have the position of village head rotate among the landholding villagers, in others they set up a system of electing the head. When women were heads of household, they too

---

[63] Hosaka, *Hyakushō ikki to sono sahō*, 193–94; Inoue, *Kaikoku to bakumatsu*, 112–13.

voted.[64] Since village affairs were too complicated for one man to handle and a council of elders often supported the village head, farmers might demand that one of their own be present at deliberations as their representative.

Farmers also attacked the markers of the status system that set the head and other officials apart from most villagers. In Hozu village, west of Kyoto, the small-scale farmers revolted in 1781 when senior members of the village thrashed one of their number for wearing leather-soled sandals. The farmers broke off relations with those who had done the beating and challenged old village regulations that forbade them such finery, not to mention other locally based sumptuary regulations that marked the gulf between the village elite and those whom they viewed as their inferiors. In the eyes of the small farmers, everyone who lived in the village was a farmer, and status distinctions simply created factions in the community. In similar fashion, farmers in Ikejiri village near Osaka complained that the village's founding families used their prestige to treat the other villagers contemptuously. "Because we are all equally farmers and we are all burdened with the tribute and labor services, we want to be treated as equals."[65]

Farmers who asserted that they were all equally farmers might still discriminate against marginalized people. The district-wide compacts that provided opportunities for farmers in the region around Osaka to institute new forms of representative government also enhanced inequitable treatment of itinerant groups. Some, for example, tried to limit the operations of blind storytellers, alms seekers, and religious practitioners who went from village to village. Beggars too found that villages rejected their traditional responsibilities for them. Twice in mass movements followed by smashing up the houses of local malefactors, the participants attacked outcastes, the first in Kii in 1823, the second in Chōshū in 1831.[66]

On the other hand, the last half of the Edo period found members of the various outcaste groups seeking their own equality with the farmers. Beginning in the late eighteenth century, outcastes began to join farmers' movements, their status uncovered only during the official investigation that followed. The 1782 incident demanding a tax exemption followed by punitive action against cheating moneylenders and the like near Osaka Bay led to Minami Ōji villagers being singled out for unwanted attention (see Ehlers, Chapter 17, this volume). The village leaders protested: "Although we are an *eta* village, we pay tribute and do labor services just like other villages." Their arguments

[64] Aoki, "Kinsei mura shakai."
[65] Walthall, Social Protest, 109–13; Ooms, Tokugawa Village Practice, 203–16.
[66] Inoue, Kaikoku to bakumatsu, 79, 87.

were in vain; the *eta* supervisor from another village placed ninety-three men in manacles for fifteen days. This incident thus forced the villagers to recall the discrimination practiced against them and to admit a consciousness of difference that had disappeared from daily life.[67]

Other outcastes protested discrimination in the marketplace, in cultural practices, and in domain policy. In the region near Edo, a disturbance in 1843 pitted outcastes against a local market that threatened to close its doors to them after one outcaste objected to the money he had been paid for his clog thongs. Over 500 outcastes carrying bamboo spears confronted the Kantō Regulatory Patrol, who mobilized farmers and police armed with muskets to arrest them. For having defied authority, forty-nine outcastes died in prison and an additional fifty-three were also punished. Only five farmers suffered fines and reprimands for their part in provoking the incident. In 1856, the intendant of Nakanojō in Shinano issued new regulations forbidding the outcastes to protect their feet in cold weather, to open umbrellas when it rained, or to loft banners and tall lanterns at festivals. The outcastes responded by claiming that they too were humans who suffered from inclement weather, and they too were Japanese who wanted to express their "gratitude for the benevolence of the great peace and the radiance of the grace bestowed by the country."[68] That same year the Okayama domain tried to reform social practices. In the name of frugality, it ordered outcastes to wear only plain clothing indicative of their status. Well over a thousand people from fifty-three outcaste communities participated in opposition to these new measures in petitions and a march on the castle town.[69]

Not only did outcastes always lose, they also ended up more severely punished than their neighbors. This unequal treatment sometimes led to increased discrimination once other farmers were reminded of the despised people in their midst. Nonetheless, a longer perspective suggests that it is not the outcastes' defeat that matters but that they asserted human rights equal to their fellow farmers.

Commemoration

Localities long retained collective memories of mass movements. Village officials kept records of what had happened, sometimes compiled into chronicles that gave a sober picture of organizers, leaders, and the documents they

[67] Walthall, *Social Protest*, 34–35, 154.
[68] Ooms, *Tokugawa Village Practice*, 265.
[69] Fukaya, Saitō, and Hosaka, *Hyakushō ikki jiten*, 440.

circulated to mobilize villages. In some cases, stories filled with drama drew on the tradition of military tales to paint a picture of insurrection with peasant armies on the march and individuals engaging in armed combat. Wakao Masaki argues that because both chronicles and stories contained elements of the other in a world in which what was considered fact and fiction was not clearly distinguished, defining what constitutes documentary evidence becomes ever more difficult.[70] The most typical form of commemoration was the performance of Buddhist memorial services for executed leaders, beginning in the 1740s, and the erection of monuments to pacify their souls. Over time the leaders might be remembered and the movement itself forgotten, as is the case for the 1696 uprising in Matsumoto. Today people there tell stories about the selfless Kasuke who sacrificed himself for the community as though the mass movement to present a petition and attacks on other commoners had never happened. The same thing happened after the 1764 mass movement opposed to changes in the transportation system. In 1863, at the hundredth anniversary of the leader Heinai's death, he was venerated as an individual who sacrificed himself for the wider community.[71]

The most famous martyr is Sakura Sōgorō. According to legend, Sakura domain officials imposed unbearable taxes in the seventeenth century. Unable to survive, the farmers threatened mass action. Knowing that they would be severely punished, Sōgorō decided to sacrifice himself instead. With a few other village officials, he appealed to district officials. When they refused to accept his petition, he went to Edo to appeal to higher officials and even the lord. When they too rejected his suit, he resolved to petition the shogun, in full awareness that such a deed meant death. His self-sacrifice brought tax relief to the farmers, but the lord was so angry at the humiliation he had suffered at having the faults in his administration exposed that he executed not only Sōgorō but his wife and four sons as well. Sōgorō's angry spirit took revenge by driving the lord mad. In 1752, a later domain lord conferred a posthumous Buddhist name on Sōgorō and erected a shrine to pacify him. It remains a pilgrimage site near Narita Airport to this day. Despite the lack of a factual basis to his story, shrines to his spirit spread across central and eastern Japan. Before the 1859 Minamiyama uprising in the Ina valley north of Nagoya, the leader Ogiso Ihei traveled around the district telling Sōgorō's story to mobilize the farmers.[72] In 2011, I saw a Kabuki play about Sōgorō in Tokyo, and in the lobby was his shrine.

[70] Wakao, *Hyakushō ikki*, 72–73.
[71] Hosaka, "Gimin tanjō," 164–65.
[72] Walthall, "Japanese *Gimin*."

According to Hosaka, legends about the peasant martyrs called *gimin* are largely a product of the Meiji period. Neither the Meiji government nor the popular rights advocates remembered that there had once existed a route for those below to appeal directly to those above. Instead, both sides painted the early modern period in the darkest possible colors to contrast with modern enlightenment. Since many popular rights advocates were local officials, it is not surprising that they came up with the idea of the self-sacrificing village head. Hosaka has uncovered almost 500 instances of monuments or shrines erected to *gimin*, and they are the most common way that early modern mass movements are remembered in Japan today.[73]

Conclusion

The mass movements that erupted during the early modern period speak to farmers' planning skills, to their and the urban poor's sense of justice, and to the continual negotiation of relations between commoners and rulers. It is easy to celebrate their successes: tax exemptions that over time lowered the overall tax rate, the abolition of monopolies that reduced the farmers' profits from commercial agriculture, or the rescission of an unpopular political policy. At the same time, success came at a cost: agricultural work disrupted, villages fined, and men imprisoned, tortured, and executed. And these movements did not always achieve their goals. Sometimes officials refused to accept the farmers' demands, sometimes they accepted them and then reneged on their promises after the farmers had returned home, knowing that the farmers were unlikely to mobilize twice.

The first ten years of the Meiji period saw more mass movements by farmers, more violence, and greater failures than at any time in the early modern period. The farmers' representatives who petitioned for a tax reduction in Shimotsuke in 1869 died in prison without being allowed medicine or visitors. Farmers who delayed paying taxes had their assets seized and property sold. They resented being expected to serve as soldiers as well as to pay taxes, and they loathed arrogant and authoritarian government officials who ordered troops to kill protesters. Confronted with a new and more deadly enemy, farmers armed themselves, killed officials, and burned schools. These movements ended when the government remained intransigent but lowered the new land tax and sent the emperor on progresses around the country.[74]

---

[73] Hosaka, "Gimin tanjō," 160.
[74] Yamasaki, *Tokugawa shakai*, 244–46; Platt, *Burning and Building*, 185–214.

Unlike the system of representation that undergirded mass movements in early modern Japan, when Meiji period citizens were allowed to vote for representatives to prefectural assemblies and later the National Diet, they did so as individuals. The abolition of the status system ostensibly eliminated discrimination based on lineage (with the caveat that former warriors, their lords, and outcastes retained special status) but it did nothing for inequality predicated on wealth. With the advent of modern industry, farmers lost their ideological position as the foundation of the realm, dramatized in the late nineteenth century by the pollution of rivers and prime rice paddies by the Ashio copper mine. The noted activist and village head's son Tanaka Shōzō spent most of his life seeking aid for the victims and environmental remediation. In 1901, he even petitioned the Meiji emperor in the mode of Sakura Sōgorō.[75]

Bibliography

Aoki Kōji and Hosaka Satoru, eds. *Hennen hyakushō ikki shiryō shūsei*. 19 vols. San'ichi Shobō, 1979–97.

Aoki Michiko. "Kinsei mura shakai ni okeru josei no sonsei sanka to 'mura jichi': Mura yakunin sentei no tame no yoriai, irefuda o chūshin ni." *Sōgō joseishi kenkyū* 28 (2011): 57–80.

Bardsley, Sandy. *Venomous Tongues: Speech and Gender in Late Medieval England*. Philadelphia: University of Pennsylvania Press, 2006.

Bix, Herbert P. "Miura Meisuke, or Peasant Rebellion under the Banner of Distress." *Bulletin of Concerned Asian Scholars* 10, no. 2 (April–June 1978): 18–26.

Peasant Protest in Japan, 1590–1884. New Haven, CT: Yale University Press, 1986.

Craig, Albert M. *Chōshū in the Meiji Restoration*. Cambridge, MA: Harvard University Press, 1961.

Esenbel, Selçuk. *Even the Gods Rebel: The Peasants of Takaino and the 1871 Nakano Uprising in Japan*. Ann Arbor, MI: Association for Asian Studies, 1998.

Fukaya Katsumi. *Hyakushō ikki no rekishiteki kōzō*. 2nd ed. Azekura Shobō, 1986.

Fukaya Katsumi, Saitō Jun, and Hosaka Satoru, eds. *Hyakushō ikki jiten*. Minshūsha, 2004.

Gay, Suzanne. *The Moneylenders of Late Medieval Kyoto*. Honolulu: University of Hawai'i Press, 2001.

Hosaka Satoru. "Gimin tanjō no jiki to jōken." In *Kinsei hen*, edited by Aoki Michio and Hosaka Satoru, 160–65. Vol. 5 of *Shinshiten: Nihon no rekishi*. Shinjinbutsu Ōraisha, 1993.

"Hyakushō ikki: Sono kyozō to jitsuzō." In *Kindai e no taidō*, edited by Tsuji Tatsuya, 167–228. Vol. 10 of *Nihon no kinsei*. Chūōkōronsha, 1993.

Hyakushō ikki to gimin no kenkyū. Yoshikawa Kōbunkan, 2006.

Hyakushō ikki to sono sahō. Yoshikawa Kōbunkan, 2002.

Inoue Katsuo. *Kaikoku to bakumatsu henkaku*. Vol. 18 of *Nihon no rekishi*. Kōdansha, 2002.

[75] Strong, *Ox against the Storm*, 132.

Iwanami kōza: Nihon rekishi, edited by Ōtsu Tōru, Sakurai Eiji, Fujii Jōji, Yoshida Yutaka, and Ri Sonshi (Lee Sungsi). 22 vols. Iwanami Shoten, 2013–16.

Iwata Kōtarō. "Uchikowashi no ronri to rinri." In *Kinsei hen*, edited by Aoki Michio and Hosaka Satoru, 152–59. Vol. 5 of *Shinshiten: Nihon no rekishi*. Shinjinbutsu Ōraisha, 1993.

Katsumata Shizuo. *Ikki*. Iwanami Shoten, 1982.

Kelly, William W. *Deference and Defiance in Nineteenth-Century Japan*. Princeton, NJ: Princeton University Press, 1985.

Kurushima Hiroshi. "Hyakushō ikki to toshi sōjō." In *Kinsei 4*, 209–50. Vol. 13 of *Iwanami kōza: Nihon rekishi*.

——— "Hyakushō to mura no henshitsu." In *Kinsei 5*, edited by Asao Naohiro, Amino Yoshihiko, Yamaguchi Keiji, and Yoshida Takashi, 69–110. Vol. 15 of *Iwanami kōza: Nihon tsūshi*. Iwanami Shoten, 1995.

Miyachi Masato. *Bakumatsu ishin henkaku shi*. 2 vols. Iwanami Shoten, 2012.

Nagai Michiko. *Rekishi o sawagaseta onnatachi: Shomin*. Bungei Shunjū, 1976.

Ooms, Herman. *Tokugawa Village Practice: Class, Status, Power, Law*. Berkeley: University of California Press, 1996.

Platt, Brian. *Burning and Building: Schooling and State Formation in Japan, 1750–1890*. Cambridge, MA: Harvard University Asia Center, 2004.

Roberts, Luke S. "The Petition Box in Eighteenth-Century Tosa." *Journal of Japanese Studies* 20, no. 2 (Summer 1994): 423–58.

Sippel, Patricia. "Popular Protest in Early Modern Japan: The Bushū Outburst." *Harvard Journal of Asiatic Studies* 37, no. 2 (December 1977): 273–322.

Strong, Kenneth. *Ox against the Storm: A Biography of Tanaka Shozo, Japan's Conservationist Pioneer*. Victoria: University of British Columbia Press, 1977. Reprint, Folkestone, UK: Japan Library, 1995.

Taniyama Masamichi. "Kinsei kōki no minshū undō." In *Kinsei 5*, 251–86. Vol 14. of *Iwanami kōza: Nihon rekishi*.

Tsang, Carol R. *War and Faith: Ikkō Ikki in Late Muromachi Japan*. Cambridge, MA: Harvard University Asia Center, 2007.

Tsuda Hideo. "Hōken shakai hōkai-ki ni okeru nōmin tōsō no ichi ruikei ni tsuite." *Rekishigaku kenkyū* 168 (February 1954): 1–14.

Tsutsumi Yōko. "Ikki, sōjō sekai no onna to otoko." In *Ikki to shūen*, edited by Hosaka Satoru, 209–28. Aoki Shoten, 2000.

Uejima Hidetomo and Ueda Ryūji. *Shibamura sōdō to Ryūmon sōdō: Yamato no hyakushō ikki*. Nara: Aogaki Shuppan, 2016.

Vlastos, Stephen. *Peasant Protests and Uprisings in Tokugawa Japan*. Berkeley: University of California Press, 1986.

Wakao Masaki. *Hyakushō ikki*. Iwanami Shoten, 2018.

Walthall, Anne. "Devoted Wives/Unruly Women: Invisible Resistance in the History of Japanese Social Protest." *Signs: Journal of Women in Culture and Society* 20, no. 1 (Autumn 1994): 106–36.

——— "Edo Riots." In *Edo and Paris: Urban Life and the State in the Early Modern Era*, edited by James L. McClain, John M. Merriman, and Ugawa Kaoru, 407–28. Ithaca, NY: Cornell University Press, 1994.

——— "Japanese *Gimin*: Peasant Martyrs in Popular Memory." *American Historical Review* 91, no. 5 (December 1986): 1076–1102.

Peasant Uprisings in Japan: A Critical Anthology of Peasant Histories. Chicago: University of Chicago Press, 1991.

Social Protest and Popular Culture in Eighteenth-Century Japan. Tucson: University of Arizona Press, 1986.

"Village Networks: *Sōdai* and the Sale of Edo Nightsoil." *Monumenta Nipponica* 43, no. 3 (Autumn 1988): 293–303.

White, James W. *Ikki: Social Conflict and Political Protest in Early Modern Japan.* Ithaca, NY: Cornell University Press, 1995.

Yabuta Yutaka. *Kokuso to hyakushō ikki no kenkyū.* Azekura Shobō, 1992.

Yamasaki Yoshihiro. *Tokugawa shakai no sokojikara.* Kashiwa Shobō, 2017.

21

Civilization and Enlightenment in Early Meiji Japan

AMIN GHADIMI

The Tokugawa state had once sought to control the mounting forces of early modern globalization by curtailing access to the foreign world. As globalization accelerated at alarming rates during the second half of the nineteenth century, Meiji civilization and enlightenment opened the floodgates before the torrents of European and American power, ideas, things, and people now sweeping the modern world with unprecedented ferocity. Between the Scylla of order and the Charybdis of freedom, of unity and diversity, tradition and science, the state and the people, of autochthony and globality, lurched the *Nippon-maru*, the ship of the Japanese nation, a metaphor that conjures the enlightenment myth of a singular national subject advancing linearly and progressively through time. That ship was powered by a steam engine.

Civilization and enlightenment, *bunmei kaika* in Japanese, encompassed a bewildering range of attempts by state and nonstate actors, over roughly the first decade of the Meiji era (1868–1912), to resolve the epoch-shattering cataclysm of modern globalization by means of deliberate Westernization.[1] At once an era, a mentality, an ideology, a jumble of government policies, an intellectual and popular movement, the material manifestations of these, and the backlash against them, in its totality it revolutionized virtually every dimension of Japanese life. It yielded thunderous progress, dazzling feats of statesmanship and intellect, and unprecedented transformations. It vaulted Japan, in due course, to enviable status as a formidable global power, the very paragon of modernity in the Orient, as the "non-West" was once known. And it unleashed tumult, strife, hate, and bloodshed, a profusion of local, national, and regional problems now infused with global meaning, a perplexity of crises with no indigenous precedent and no known solution.

---

[1] On the historical interchangeability/synonymity of "civilization" and "enlightenment," see Howland, *Translating the West*, 33–40.

Civilization and enlightenment sought to overcome the disruption and derangement wrought by a violently globalizing world by further disrupting and deranging Japanese life. Its successes were sweeping, undeniable. It formed a watershed in global history. And yet it was the inability to stay, the impossibility of quieting, the convulsions of a globalization carried by Western imperialism that constituted its greatest legacy.

Knowing Civilization

That knowledge should be pursued vigorously and liberally across the seas; that that knowledge should be put to use for the profit of the individual and society; that systems of knowing from the past, if they no longer benefited the present, should be dismantled in favor of new knowledge that would civilize and enlighten the people and help them progress – this unrestrained pursuit of knowledge, the education of every Japanese individual and of the unitized national subject, and the release of the generative forces of thought and investigation, was the glittering hallmark of civilization and enlightenment. The Meiji government, then still a volatile fledgling regime with little legitimacy, had made this stentorian promise in 1868: "Knowledge shall be sought throughout the world so as to strengthen the foundations of imperial rule."

The trouble was that seeking knowledge throughout the world destabilized the foundations of imperial rule. To parse new knowledge peacefully, to distinguish between what would enhance or degrade the enlightening polity, required unifying social and epistemological structures, humanistic means of binding freely knowing individuals in a global world into a single community. The past had not endowed the present with those structures. Modern globalization struck the unprepared polity like a historical earthquake, a spiritual earthquake, in the imagery of Carol Gluck. Systems of thought and practice crumbled to the ground, and to decide upon a blueprint for what would rise up instead, to regain an equilibrium that had been lost, as she writes, even as the very foundations of knowing and being kept trembling under every foot, called for an enlightened leadership that could channel the energies of thirty million new national subjects.[2] The capacity of the Meiji leadership to draw up its blueprints from those of the West, to embark on the construction process, and to mobilize the masses to build new foundations – these successes astonish. Yet they did not bring equilibrium. They did not bring peace or stability to Japan or East Asia.

[2] Gluck, "Tanjun na monogatari," 30–31.

To conceive of civilization and enlightenment in this way, as a problem most fundamentally of the globalization of knowledge, indeed of knowing itself and its relationship to order, relies on tacit answers to perennial questions in the study not only of Japan but of history. One question concerns Westernization and globalization. People in the 1870s believed they were Westernizing. To deploy that category here is to recognize its legitimacy: the ideas and practices of civilization and enlightenment were decidedly not indigenous, and their disruptive force came not least from their origins in and association with the rapacious imperialist pursuits of Western Europe and the United States. Westernization thus carried modern globalization, forcing a reckoning with the foundational question of whether people across the world were defined essentially more by sameness or difference. Westernization and globalization were metonymical, perhaps, but more precisely synecdochic.

Globalization implicates modernity. No doubt civilization and enlightenment rested on a bedrock built during the Tokugawa era: literacy, information networks, an emerging civil sphere, intellectual innovation, nationwide travel, protoindustrialization. Even still, it constituted an undeniable break in history, the onset of a new age, an age of modernity that was, in almost every sense, more significant in its departure from the past than in its continuity. The unprecedented force and speed of globalization defined and conditioned this modernity.

Who built modernity? Civilization and enlightenment turned on seeking to constitute the agents of history: to create the modern individual, community, society, nation, and state and to place them in stable relations with one another in a global context. A narrow band of male elites led this all-encompassing endeavor, elites who were visionary and ambitious but also "elitist and tutelary," "proselytizing."[3] Their authority was defined by precarity. Amid turbulent dislocations of agency, determining the protagonists of civilization and enlightenment, and its antagonists, became a destabilizing, strife-ridden process, one that stretched across the globe and extended its reach through politics, thought, society, culture, and more.[4]

Politics and War

On 23 December 1871, not a half-decade after the revolutionary civil war of 1868, not a half-year after the establishment of a centralized national bureaucracy, leading members of the Meiji revolutionary regime departed

---

[3] Hill, *National History*, 53.
[4] "Dislocations" from Gluck, "Tanjun na monogatari," 30.

Yokohama on a whirlwind journey to the West. The embassy included dozens of bureaucrats and experts in virtually every field, whether law, finance, education, military affairs, or the economy, as well as an entourage of students, including five pioneering women, notably Tsuda Ume.[5]

The mission, led by Iwakura Tomomi, had three stated main objectives: to greet Japan's counterparts in the West; to negotiate the revision of the imperialist treaties under which those powers had subjugated Japan; and to learn of the "civilization" of the Occident, of so-called Western civilization. The plan came, to a great extent, from Guido Verbeck, a missionary in Japan originally dispatched from the United States to help revoke the prohibition on Christianity. He wrote a guiding document that he reviewed "clause by clause," in his account, with Iwakura. "It is not necessary to experiment, for there lies the whole of Europe open and ready to be studied and copied by all who like to do so," Verbeck wrote, as if Europe had attained enlightenment. He kindled, too, a quieter "prayer": that the embassy "would bring about, or at least bring nearer, the long longed-for toleration of Christianity."[6]

The Iwakura delegates visited the United States, Britain, France, Belgium, the Netherlands, Germany, Austria, Sweden, Denmark, Italy, Switzerland, and Russia. Visits to Hungary, Spain, and Portugal were canceled. They stopped in Aden, Singapore, Saigon, Hong Kong, and other cities en route home. The United States, where they stayed for 205 days, held an exceptional place in the journey.

Western civilization dazzled them. There were carpets and lace curtains and water closets and elevators at the hotel in San Francisco. The Capitol in Washington was "stunning," "incomparable." London had trains underground. The sewer system in Paris separated clean and dirty water. Everywhere there were post offices, telegraphs, newspapers, and especially schools, at which all children learned "regardless of sex or status." Zoos and museums seemed particularly enlightening. There were gun and shoe factories in the United States, sugar and glass factories in Britain, perfume and chocolate factories in France, an explosives factory in Austria. There were strikes and labor unrest. Kume Kunitake wrote an official chronicle to be published widely for the enlightenment of the masses at home.

The voyagers learned about nationalism, republicanism, democracy, constitutional monarchy, and parliamentarianism, meeting leaders from Ulysses Grant to Queen Victoria to Tsar Alexander II. In Germany, Bismarck

---

[5] Tanaka, *Iwakura shisetsudan*, 25–41.
[6] Griffis, *Verbeck of Japan*, 255–56, 260; Altman, "Guido Verbeck," 59.

personally warned them of the hypocrisy of international law. They wondered about the Bible in the United States. "Balderdash from crazy people," Kume said of the story of a dead man resurrecting. Many were stirred by the Christian ethos of industry, decency, and love.[7]

They bought leather shoes in San Francisco, and their feet hurt. "We laughed and joked with people that civilization and enlightenment actually entails considerable hardship," wrote Sasaki Takayuki, one sojourner. It snowed in Salt Lake City. Kido Kōin (or Takayoshi) bought rubber boots that didn't quite fit him. "Our enlightenment of today is not true enlightenment," he wrote. "In ten years, we will be fighting against its ills." Itō Hirobumi, vice-ambassador, allegedly "set a match to the dress of a nightclub dancer, saying that he wanted to see whether the chiffon she was wearing would burn." Sasaki was aghast at Itō: "This is the way of the world at present, where such manners are practiced, and gaining the upper hand." Kume witnessed a nude woman modeling for artists in Berlin. "Thoroughly detestable," he scoffed.[8] Such was Western civilization.

The sojourners were in Berlin in March 1873, the goal of diplomatic amendments to treaty imperialism by then a pipe dream, when a panicked letter arrived from Sanjō Sanetomi, chairman of the Council of State. He summoned Kido and Ōkubo Toshimichi, two of the foremost statesmen, back home.[9] The caretaker government in Tokyo was spiraling toward disaster.

Political and financial wrangling among government ministries had erupted into an unprecedented public scandal. In 1872, Inoue Kaoru, de facto head of the Ministry of the Treasury, had tried to slash the department budget of Ōki Takatō, the minister of education from Saga. Irate, fellow Saga man and justice minister Etō Shinpei quit the government in January 1873 over his own budgetary disputes. His resignation was denied, and on 2 May, the administrative structure of the government was reshuffled to diminish the power of individual ministries, not least the treasury. Inoue Kaoru and his associate Shibusawa Eiichi counter-resigned. Their resignation manifesto was printed in a foreign-run newspaper in Japan, and internal state budgetary matters spilled into public view. Etō accused Inoue of deliberately leaking information to the press and slapped a fine on him. In the background lurked corruption scandals the justice ministry was gleefully exposing.[10]

[7] Account from Tanaka, *Meiji ishin to seiyō bunmei*; Tanaka, *Iwakura shisetsudan*.
[8] Osakabe, *Yōfuku, sanpatsu, dattō*, 51–55; Takii, *Meiji Constitution*, 17–23.
[9] Account to follow based on Mōri, *Meiji rokunen seihen*.
[10] Kasahara, *Meiji rusu seifu*, 77–109, 134–51; Mōri, *Meiji rokunen seihen*, 96–106; Inada, *Jiyū minken no bunkashi*, 139–41.

Factionalist power struggles were sublimated into a row over the means and meaning of enlightenment. Etō, proclaiming in his resignation manifesto that "the foundation of the wealth and strength of the nation is the peace and security of its citizens," asserted the indispensability of civil law, tacitly his own ministry, in constituting a productive, entrepreneurial populace that would "preserve their rights," engage in industry, and flush the government with cash. Inoue and Shibusawa countered that, even though in but a few years all the "trappings of civilization" had been put into place so that Japan could "rival the nations of Europe and America without a shade of embarrassment," the people remained "unenlightened," "accustomed to the remnants of authoritarianism," with "no knowledge" of "rights and duties." Law, and Etō, only built the "structures" of enlightenment without cultivating its "essence," "an enlightenment based on the power of the people." The two sides seemed to agree more than disagree.

Perhaps the Western enlightenment itself was essentially corrupt and debased, minatory counter-enlightenment movements across the country fulminated. Kagoshima strongman Shimazu Hisamitsu stood at the vanguard of the counter-enlightenment, decrying virtually every dimension of civilization: Christianity, the elimination of status distinctions, the new Western calendar, the idea of formal equality between men and women. Saigō Takamori, leading statesman and revolutionary hero from Kagoshima, had spent almost half a year from late 1872 to April 1873 in Kagoshima, absent from the government, trying to placate Shimazu. Local anti-enlightenment rebellions tore through the archipelago in 1873. Shimazu and his counter-enlightenment band arrived in Tokyo in April in splashily non-Western attire.[11] Was a counterrevolution nigh? The *New York Times* ran a dispatch from a Western observer in Tokyo who noticed that "these chaps were more than ordinarily saucy."[12]

The counter-enlightenment emanated from beyond the sea. The Korean government had, since the Japanese coup d'état of 1868, persisted in rejecting the Meiji emperor as the formal sovereign of Japan, rebuffing Japanese attempts to establish diplomatic relations according to "international law." Long-simmering diplomatic tensions precipitated into an all-out crisis in 1873. During Tokugawa times, the domain of Tsushima, located in the strait separating Kyushu from continental Asia, had enjoyed unique trading privileges with Korea, especially through the Japanese outpost in southern Korea. The

[11] Iechika, *Saigō Takamori*, 393–401.
[12] *New York Times*, 15 June 1873.

dissolution of domains in 1871 eliminated the premise behind this system: all erstwhile domains were now equal, identical. When men from Tokyo landed at the Japanese mission seeking to trade, the Korean regional government accused them of unilaterally violating customs that had stood for centuries. It blockaded and immiserated the Japanese outpost in retaliation. War was imminent. The writing was on the wall, literally. Korean authorities posted a diatribe for their Japanese counterparts to see in May 1873, a manifesto that was relayed back to Tokyo: "They do not feel shameful in adopting institutions from the foreigners and changing their appearance as well as their customs. We should not consider them as 'Japanese' any more nor should we admit them into our territory. ... We may call them a lawless country."[13]

The Tokugawa state had failed in treaty negotiations to secure the status of Karafuto, or Sakhalin, which Japanese settlers coinhabited with Russians and Indigenous Ainu as a result. In 1869, Russian forces, in an apparent attempt to crowd the Japanese out, moved in and built an encampment at Hakkotomari, a hill away from the Japanese settlement at Kushunkotan. Possibly calculated acts of sabotage against Japanese economic and fishing interests persisted. Russian troops, often intoxicated and impoverished, repeatedly inflicted petty theft on Japanese settlers. Rape was undoubtedly endemic; murders were reported. Long mulled, a military dispatch again came to the fore after a particularly damaging arson incident in early 1873 drove Hori Motoi, lead official on Karafuto, to demand intervention. It would almost certainly ignite a war with Russia. Kuroda Kiyotaka, his superior based in Hokkaido who had advocated abandoning Karafuto altogether, told Hori to man up and "endure the unendurable." Then, as the Korea situation ratcheted up, Kuroda changed tune, suspiciously, as if to distract Saigō Takamori. He wrote to Sanjō in September 1873 calling for troops to be sent to Karafuto.[14]

Saigō had written to his colleague Itagaki Taisuke in July 1873 with a befuddling proposition. Professing concern with the deteriorating situation in Karafuto, Saigō deemed an immediate troop dispatch to Korea ill-advised. He proposed instead that he himself go to Korea as an emissary, predicting that he would be assassinated there. A valid pretext would then be established if war with Korea became necessary. His mission was approved.

What was Saigō thinking? Was he trying to instigate or impede war? No one today knows. Even some of his fellow statesmen were flummoxed.[15]

[13] Duus, *Abacus and the Sword*, 37–38.
[14] Akizuki, *Nichi-Ro kankei*, 191–94, 210–14.
[15] Iechika, *Saigō Takamori*, 416.

Whatever his motives, on 15 October, Saigō was reconfirmed as an emissary to Korea. Ōkubo resigned from the government in protest. He and other Iwakura Mission returnees, all home by mid-September, formed a "furtive scheme" to use the emperor to block the Korea dispatch. They invoked, besides urgent domestic concerns, the Russian threat. Thwarted, Saigō, Etō, Itagaki, and hundreds of other statesmen and military officers marched out of the government on 22 October.

The "political upheaval of 1873" sent immediate shockwaves across the archipelago, catalyzing both a cascade of samurai uprisings and the violent, occasionally terroristic, decade-long movement for freedom and people's rights (*jiyū minken undō*). Historians separate the categories conceptually, but they are probably indistinguishable empirically. Irate former samurai, at least one of whom Saigō had earlier sent on a reconnaissance mission to Manchuria, attempted an assassination of Iwakura in January 1874. They failed. That same month, leading defecting oligarchs, minus Saigō, submitted to the state the Proposal for the Establishment of a Popularly Elected Assembly. It was written not by them but by Furusawa Urō, who sometimes used his Christian name, Arthur. Furusawa had studied in Britain, where he learned, in his account, "the liberal doctrines of England" and also "aristocratical haughtiness." Several heavily edited English-language documents in Arthur's own hand strongly suggest that he first wrote the petition in English before it was translated into Japanese. He wrote, separately, a draft letter apparently to a tutor in Britain telling of the prospect of a "constitution of the 19th century copied from yours, putting the first instance in the history of Asia, of ~~getting with of the~~ peoples' ~~getting~~ emancipating themselves from the ~~bondage~~ degrading state of absolute subjection to ... despotism so characteristic from Constantinople eastward to Behring Strait [*sic*]." Liberty, he rhapsodized, arose only from Christianity, and without liberty, life was not worth living.[16]

The parliamentary petition turned on whether the Japanese people were enlightened enough for representative government. Opponents of parliamentarianism protested, Furusawa noted in the proposal, that "to establish a parliament would be no more than to assemble all the ignoramuses of the empire." He insisted that parliamentary government would itself induce civilization, causing men "to advance rapidly into the realm of enlightenment." "Would you have it," his proposal asked, "that we should wait until we ourselves had discovered the principles of steam before we began using steam engines?"[17]

---

[16] Furusawa Urō kankei monjo, no. 36.
[17] McLaren, *Japanese Government Documents*, 427–32.

The response of the Ministry of the Left was anticlimactic: we already had this idea.[18] Debate erupted anyway. Leading intellectual Katō Hiroyuki responded in essence that yes, indeed, to establish a parliament would be to assemble all the ignoramuses of the empire. First, education was necessary to enlighten the people, who remained too "obedient" for representative government. After all, why did Russia not have a parliament yet? Arthur Furusawa accused Katō of "words upside down" and a "mistake in the art of logic" and dumped scrupulously quoted passages from John Stuart Mill's *Considerations on Representative Government* on him to show that a parliament would in fact induce enlightenment. Ōi Kentarō scorned Katō for being "imprisoned by the trajectory of the German past": unlike Germany, Japan had ample precedent in other countries from which to learn; parliamentarianism needed to be accelerated, not delayed.[19] The public sphere became a cacophony of which particular configuration of enlightened European thought which particular intellectual thought best for an incompletely enlightened Japan.

Maybe the ersatz Western intellectuals were themselves the ignoramuses, some suggested. "France is described to us as an enlightened, wealthy, civilized, and warlike country," one petitioner from Kōchi observed. "But is it not enlightenment and civilization … where governors and governed live amicably together, where there are no starving paupers on the street," he asked. "They have tricked us by their international law and deluded us by their false religion."[20] Was France not the uncivilized one?

So began the "public disputes of 1874," propelled by widespread petitioning of the government. From its very first year, the Meiji state had called on "high and low" alike to submit recommendations to the government. Such popular participation constituted a peremptory repudiation of the foundations of status-based Tokugawa governance. People petitioned about everything: tawdry Westernism, civil rights, invading Korea, and colonizing the Caroline Islands, the most peculiar of things.[21]

The most radical Westernizer of the caretaker regime had been, by some accounts, the justice minister Etō, "the father of civil rights" in Japan.[22] In 1871, he wrote a foreign policy manifesto sketching out the future of Japan: It would send Buddhist spies to infiltrate China before invading and seizing that

---

[18] McLaren, *Japanese Government Documents*, 432–33; Matsuzawa, *Jiyū minken undō*, 47–48.
[19] Furusawa Urō kankei monjo, nos. 15-1 to 17; McLaren, *Japanese Government Documents*, 433–39.
[20] McLaren, *Japanese Government Documents*, 449, 454.
[21] Makihara, *Meiji shichinen no dai ronsō*.
[22] Mōri, *Bakumatsu ishin to Saga-han*, loc. 2018–2777, Kindle.

country. Then it would be ready to face Prussia, Russia, and the United States in a four-way struggle for global supremacy. In 1873, Etō reportedly spoke of constructing railroads to subjugate China, capturing Beijing, and seating the Japanese emperor in that city, a new capital of Japan.[23] Etō returned to his native Saga in February 1874 and led an alliance between the Patriot's Lament Party (Yūkokutō), a group of restive samurai resisting enlightenment reforms, and the Attack Korea Party (Seikantō), which inveighed against the use of the Russian excuse to block an invasion of Korea. They rebelled.

A telegram dated 2 February was sent to the Home Ministry in Tokyo on 3 February stating that members of the Attack Korea Party had caused a disturbance at a finance office in Saga. On 6 February, a telegram arrived in Kumamoto, through the telegraph station in Saga, commanding Kumamoto garrison leader Tani Tateki to invade Saga. Tani refused, exhorting the state to desist from demanding military action in hasty telegrams not even written in code.[24] It was of little consequence. In what must be at least a partly apocryphal story, Shima Yoshitake, dispatched by the government in Tokyo to quell forces in Saga, supposedly switched sides aboard the steamship headed south and decided to fight against the state. He joined Etō. The two rose up. The national military departed Kumamoto for Saga on 14 February to smother the rebellion. Etō proclaimed that he was defending the rights of Japan against Korea in order to preserve the civil rights of the Japanese people. Shima declared that once Japan seized Korea, China and Russia were next. Now was the time for a second Meiji Restoration, Etō suggested.[25] They were trounced. Etō fled Saga, sailed around Kyushu, and scurried through Shikoku on a dramatic runaway mission in which he tried to incite a wider civil war. He was caught, tried, and then finally decapitated on 13 April 1874.

Curiosities abound. It is not clear why the initial telegram reporting the disturbance at the finance office was sent from neighboring Fukuoka, not Saga. The state's heavy-handed response seems vastly disproportionate to the communicated problem.[26] The report that it was the Attack Korea Party that had incited the initial conflict appears false: it was seemingly the Patriot's Lament Party, in a dispute over samurai allowances. Telegrams reporting military developments during the war continued to include falsehoods and inaccurate rumors.[27]

---

[23] Matono, *Etō Nanpaku*, 2:288–99.
[24] Ochiai, "Saga no ran to jōhō," 180–84.
[25] Matono, *Etō Nanpaku*, 2:443–45, 464–65.
[26] These concerns are from Mōri, *Bakumatsu ishin to Saga-han*, loc. 2572, Kindle.
[27] Ochiai, "Saga no ran to jōhō," 180–82, 189.

At precisely the moment that the telegraph had made knowledge so easily obtainable, falsehood too spread quickly.

Instant communication technologies had arrived abruptly, disrupting the nature of warfare and of knowledge itself. The first domestic telegraph lines were established between Tokyo and Yokohama in 1869. International links were built between Nagasaki and Shanghai and between Nagasaki and Vladivostok in 1871, connecting Japan through them to Europe. Lines were extended from Tokyo to Nagasaki in February 1873, and telegraph stations were established in Fukuoka and Saga in October 1873 and Kumamoto in March 1875.[28] The way the Saga Rebellion unfolded would have been an impossibility just six months earlier.

Arima Gennai had been on his way from Kumamoto to join the rebel side in Saga when he heard that Etō had been vanquished. His friend Miyazaki Hachirō had petitioned the Meiji state on 9 February 1874: Inasmuch as all nations were supposed to be equal under international law, those that accepted indignities from others were "savage and barbaric." Korea had inflicted indignities on Japan. In a world that "proclaimed civilization and enlightenment" but remained in a state of the strong preying on the weak, Japan needed to "expand its rights over nearby unenlightened countries" so that it could "hold equal rights to powers in Europe and America." Civilized revenge against Korea obstructed, Miyazaki and Arima soon went to the military garrison in Kumamoto to volunteer to fight in Taiwan. By Arima's account, he collected fifty other volunteers.

In late 1871, a group of men sailing from one island in the Ryukyus to another were blown off course and made landfall in southern Taiwan. Fifty-four of them were massacred by Indigenous Taiwanese people. How to respond became a chronic political problem. An initial expedition by Kagoshima was thwarted in 1872. The American Charles Le Gendre, hired into the Japanese foreign ministry that year, offered a characteristic solution: invade and colonize. After all, the Indigenous Taiwanese were but "savages." Foreign minister Soejima Taneomi spent four months in 1873 in the Qing Empire, where he asked about the status of Taiwan. His Qing interlocutors responded that its "barbarian" eastern districts were "beyond the pale of civilization."

In 1874, Saigō Tsugumichi, who unlike his brother Takamori remained in the central state, was placed in charge of the newly formed Bureau of Taiwanese Barbarian Affairs. While his force was waiting in Kyushu in April to set sail on a steamship for Taiwan and retaliate for the massacre, German,

---

[28] Nakamura, *Umi o wataru kikansha*, 3.

British, and now also American officials pressured the state in Tokyo to cease impending hostilities. The mission was called off. Tsugumichi proceeded anyway. Arima, Miyazaki, and their volunteer friends embarked for Taiwan.

The mission was intended as a civilizing colonial settlement. The volunteer and other ad hoc Japanese invaders, named "colonist-soldiers" (shokuminhei), were officially permitted to bring their wives and children. The men could not suffer Taiwan. Arima recalled in his memoirs the hunger, dehydration, and "Taiwan disease" – malaria – he endured as he marauded the villages of the enemy. The settlement failed. The military expedition ended in October 1874 with de facto Chinese recognition of Japanese sovereignty in Ryukyu as well as indemnities paid to Japan. Arima returned home and helped launch the civil rights movement in Kumamoto.[29]

The state was again in turmoil. Kido had resigned in protest of the Taiwan expedition. Shimazu Hisamitsu, who had been recruited into the government in April 1874 to co-opt him, clashed with Ōkubo, who submitted his resignation. Iwakura, fighting with Sanjō, threatened to do the same. As always, corruption scandals lurked just below the surface. Sanjō mediated a solution and retained the statesmen. Outside the regime, Itagaki had joined with other Kōchi civil rights partisans in 1874, notably Kataoka Kenkichi, to found the Risshisha, the Self-Help Society. Other civil rights organizations across Japan, such as that of Kōno Hironaka in today's Fukushima, joined with the Risshisha to form the Aikokusha, the Patriot's Association, in February 1875. Just a month later, in March 1875, Ōkubo and Itō, with the mediation of Arthur Furusawa, brought Kido as well as Itagaki back into the central state. And in April, the regime, under Kido's influence, issued the Rescript for the Gradual Establishment of a Constitutional Polity, undermining the raison d'être of the civil rights movement.

Chaos ensued. Shimazu harped on his counter-enlightenment principles, called for changes in the structure of power in the bureaucracy, and tried to oust Sanjō from power. Itagaki joined Shimazu and fought with Kido, Sanjō, and others on bureaucratic and financial matters. A new crisis in Korea erupted. His designs again obstructed, Itagaki quit the government in October 1875, just months after he rejoined it. Shimazu did the same. The national civil rights organization had already been deflated. The commotion in the government, combined with its flaring foreign tensions, formed what one scholar calls the "political upheaval of 1875," akin to the upheaval just two years earlier.[30]

[29] Orbach, Curse on This Country, 43–52; Suzuki, Ishin no kōsō, 140–41.
[30] Naitō, "Meiji hachinen no seihen," 270–88; Matsuzawa, Jiyū minken undō, 56–66.

Japan relinquished rights to Karafuto in exchange for the Kuril Islands in 1875, bringing tentative peace with Russia and sparking outrage in the Japanese public. War with Korea loomed again. The British-made Japanese steam-powered gunboat the *Un'yō* departed Nagasaki on 14 September on a reconnaissance mission of the seas leading to China. Six days later, as a smaller boat dispatched from the ship went to make landfall near a military encampment on Kanghwa Island, near Seoul, it encountered incoming fire from the Korean side. It returned fire. The next morning, the *Un'yō* unilaterally bombarded the Korean military battery. Japanese troops made landfall and set fire to another battery. Thirty-five Koreans and one Japanese were killed. It was like a rerun of what the civilized British had done in Shimonoseki in 1863: bombard the Japanese port, make landfall, and slaughter fifty-six Japanese men. The Japanese distributed a falsified report among Western diplomats mendaciously claiming that the Korean side had attacked the Japanese ship, with a Japanese flag visibly flying, after it had approached land in pursuit of drinking water. That falsehood became the standard narrative, one outstanding historian has shown.[31]

The extent of premeditation in the incident at Kanghwa Island remains debatable, but it seems probable that it was orchestrated by lower-level Attack-Korea-faction rebels at the helm of the *Un'yō* trying to ignite war.[32] The burgeoning newspaper industry at home battled the incident out. Seki Shingo, an editor at the radical *Hyōron shinbun* who was later imprisoned for sedition, published an editorial setting out the battlelines in what he described as a domestic war over war with Korea. He named newspapers for and against further hostilities. He himself "fired a shot" in favor. "Although those Westerners appear very warm and genuine on the outside," he wrote, "their hearts are more ferocious than those of tigers and wolves." Because "there is no global government," the world was mired in a state of nature. Japan needed to wage war against Korea before Europe and the United States, "whose civilization was still inadequate" and who "disparaged the Japanese," moved to "fly their flags over East Asia" – before, that is, Japan became "the prey of Western beasts."[33] The newspaper *Hyōron*, the word itself a neologism meaning "critique" or "review," pioneered polyphonous opinion journalism in Japan. Foreign wars became a domestic social and cultural issue, waged in public on the home front. The basic infrastructure of total empire and total war had emerged.

[31] Directly from Suzuki, *Ishin no kōsō*, 126–35.
[32] Ochiai, *Chitsuroku shobun*, 186–87.
[33] "Seikanron shasetsu," *Hyōron shinbun* 33 (Oct. 1875): 5–6.

There was no war with Korea, but Japan won. On 10 February 1876, Kuroda Kiyotaka landed on Kanghwa Island, now with a fleet of six warships, two hundred marines, thirty-five artillerymen, and four Gatling guns, as if in an updated recreation of American imperialists arriving in Japan in 1853. "Your country must change and adapt," Kuroda told the Korean side, citing the "enlightenment of the world" visible in the Gatling guns. "We have understood the purport of your military metaphor," the Koreans responded, trying to squirm their way out. They could not. Korea was "opened." Japan and Korea signed a treaty, a civilized medium of "international law," a tool of imperialist subjugation the Japanese learned from the West. They presented a Gatling gun to their Korean interlocutors as a "gift." The Korean officials asked if the gun had been manufactured in Japan or abroad. If the latter, they could not present it to their sovereign.[34]

As in 1873, the counter-enlightenment emerged not only from abroad but from within. Rioting over enlightenment financial policy destabilized localities from 1876 into 1877. Possibly exaggerated stories tell of former Kumamoto samurai among the Shinpūren, the League of the Divine Wind, picking up government-issued allowances with chopsticks, lest physical contact with vile paper currency sully the sanctity of their indigeneity. They purported to surrender all individual autonomy to the divine, construing justice as a heteronomous, autochthonous, and godly concept inaccessible by means of reason and science. To approach the will of the gods required purity, and purity required abnegating all foreign defilement. Having consulted the gods by means of an obscure, superstitious rite they claimed to derive from ancient Japanese texts, they arose in October 1876, destroyed telegraph lines, and assassinated the governor of Kumamoto and the chief of the Kumamoto military garrison. Their pietistic putsch emerged not from benightedness but from their trenchant recognition, and then fanatical repudiation, of the basic rationalist, globalist epistemological conceit of the enlightenment. They well understood that that enlightenment had so insurmountably overcome them, as it had been instantiated in material changes around them, that the feeble intellectual weapons of their past could not rescue them from it. Several of their members called for the cessation of Japanese warmongering in East Asia and for conciliation with their Chinese neighbors. The greater enemy came from elsewhere.

The uprising in Kumamoto ignited a chain of violent rebellions. Agitators from Kumamoto visited Akizuki, in Fukuoka. Former samurai there rose up in solidarity, at least nominally against despotism at home and humiliation

[34] Directly from Suzuki, *Ishin no kōsō*, 123–26, 133.

abroad. The same occurred in Hagi, Yamaguchi, where Maebara Issei, a former bureaucrat in military affairs, cited a litany of grievances to justify sedition, including the dissolution of samurai status, the loss of Karafuto to Russia, the land tax, and meat-eating. He fulminated against Katō Hiroyuki's translation of Johann Kaspar Bluntschli's *Allgemeines Staatsrecht*, which upheld the citizenry as the foundation of the political order: Japan was the kingdom of the emperor. The *Un'yō*, dispatched by the state now to suppress the uprising in Hagi, capsized en route. A rebellion in Chiba and Tokyo was quashed before it could be launched. Saigō Takamori watched with interest.[35]

Belligerents had hoped, as Etō had in 1874, to win the support of Kagoshima rebels and spark a civil war. They did not receive that support. But less than six months later, a Kagoshima faction rose up, led by Saigō. Civil war arrived. It was the second civil war in less than a decade. The first, in 1868, was a political war over who would hold power after the Meiji coup d'état. Now came a war of civilization and enlightenment.

Saigō and his accomplices, notably Kirino Toshiaki, a former top military official in the Kumamoto garrison, and Shinohara Kunimoto, a former army official, had begun establishing a group of private military schools in Kagoshima after the schism of 1873. The ideological manifesto for their academy appeared in the *Hyōron shinbun* in 1875. It decried the indignities that Western states had inflicted on Japan. Upholding the principle of the autonomy and independence of all states, it observed that "international law," with its reciprocal principles of "rights" and "duties," should have obstructed large countries from dominating smaller ones. But Japan failed to resist Western imperialism, and countries that submitted to the "word" of foreigners were "barbaric and savage." Commentary published alongside the manifesto inveighed against those with "western fetishes, who wallow in enlightenment." *Hyōron* was read avidly by would-be rebels at the private academy and provided intelligence to them. It also preached Western revolutionary theory. Saigō himself had once recruited Russian revolutionary Lev Mechnikov to teach in Japan. Foreign instructors were now teaching English and French at the private academy.[36] The Kagoshima rebels opposed Western imperialism but not the West wholesale.

As Kagoshima broke away from the central state, national police chief Kawaji Toshiyoshi dispatched officers to investigate Saigō's private

[35] Ikai, "Shizoku hanran," 290–93; Suzuki, *Ishin no kōsō*, 127; Iechika, *Saigō Takamori*, 488–90.
[36] Ogawara, *Seinan sensō*, 15–24; Mitani, "Kōron kūkan," 76–77; Konishi, *Anarchist Modernity*, 40–43; Ikai, *Saigō Takamori*, 184.

academies at the end of 1876. A member of the reconnaissance mission was captured by the enemy in early 1877. Through torture, the rebels extracted a confession that the state was plotting an assassination of Saigō. It remains unclear whether such a plot actually existed. Perhaps it was a false pretext for war. Concurrently, in early 1877, the state sent a Mitsubishi steamship to Kagoshima to remove to Osaka, in secret, a stockpile of state-managed ammunition and weaponry it saw as a powder keg. Members of the private academy attacked the storage facility and seized munitions on 29 January, raiding several more military stockpiles in early February. The situation spun out of control. A telegram delivered on 18 February from the Kumamoto military garrison reported that Kagoshima forces were invading. On 19 February, a telegram from the central state arrived in Kumamoto declaring war on the Kagoshima army.

Saigō, the nominal leader of the war, failed to offer his own public ideological justification for the rebellion. To this day, historians struggle to account for why war broke out in 1877. "My pen does not move," one biographer of Saigō laments.[37] The turmoil of the times was unfathomable. Like all civil strife, the war turned on petty power struggles but also financial and social upheavals and deep intellectual problems. It involved volatile, complex alliances of convenience, over which journalists at the time themselves puzzled. The civil rights faction in Kumamoto fought for the rebel side, "liberating" territory from the state and holding democratic elections in their newly controlled lands. Hayashi Yūzō, Ōe Taku, and others in the Kōchi civil rights faction, with support from Itagaki, planned and prepared to attack the military garrison in Osaka. The stated aim was to advance civil rights and resist despotism. The state purged the Kōchi faction and imprisoned its leading members.[38] The year before, Ueki Emori, a rising intellectual force in Kōchi, observed that without a bloody revolution, America would have ended up as India. It was a vindictive fight for power, a farrago of ideas, a muddle of factions flummoxed by the incomprehensible changes that had seized people, especially the samurai.

Whatever else it was, the war was gruesome. It became a laboratory for new, civilized technologies of annihilation: landmines, sea mines and torpedoes, rockets, and gas balloons. The imperial armies used rickshaws, an innovation of the times, in their rush from Kokura to the main front at Kumamoto. Steam vessels transferred personnel and matériel. New methods of amphibious warfare helped secure government victory. And long-standing

[37] Banno, *Saigō Takamori to Meiji ishin*, 186.
[38] Ogawara, *Seinan sensō to jiyū minken*, 35–84.

tactics of war persisted: arson, torture, the deployment of child soldiers. Newspapers began frontline wartime journalism, marking a milestone in reportage, engulfing the general populace in the day-to-day affairs of men killing their brothers.[39]

State victory in the civil war stabilized the southwest and buttressed Meiji ascendancy. The nation was welded together. But violence at home and fury over international relations persisted. Ōkubo, leading oligarch of the mid-1870s, was assassinated in 1878. The civil war devastated state finances, influencing the next "political upheaval," that of 1881, which precipitated a switch from a British-style to a Prussian-style model for Japan's constitutional and parliamentary system. Civil rights ideologue Miyazaki Hachirō died for the rebels in the civil war. His brother later described the first day of the civil war as the first day of the revolution.

Thought

"A tenuous balance between conflict and harmony – weighted ever so slightly in favor of harmony – is the usual state of affairs in any community," one eminent historian has written of endemic violence in Japan's 1870s.[40] That balance had been smashed. Despite brutal wars with the Ainu and the subjugation of the Ryukyu kingdom, Tokugawa Japan had remained at peace with its largest neighbors for some 250 years. Now, all of a sudden, Japan was tumbling from cataclysm to cataclysm, mired in relentless wars against its neighbors and its own self. What was this venerable "civilization" that so disrupted the basic equilibrium of national and regional existence?

There was no greater theorist of civilization, or theorist of virtually everything, than Fukuzawa Yukichi. He probably first used the term *bunmei* to describe "civilization" in 1864, in a draft of his text *Conditions of the West*. That text included accounts of the politics and histories of the United States, Britain, and France; a translation of parts of John Hill Burton's *Political and Social Economy*; and a discussion of rights in the tradition of Locke. By 1868, Fukuzawa had derived the term *bunmei kaika* from the American textbook *Mitchell's School Geography* by Samuel Augustus Mitchell and begun using it in his public translations and writings.[41] Textbooks, perhaps even more

[39] Ikai, *Saigō Takamori*, 181–83; Suzuki, *Shin gijutsu*, 10–11, 78; Nagano, *Seinan sensō minshū no ki*, 96–125.
[40] Howell, *Geographies of Identity*, 91.
[41] Craig, *Civilization and Enlightenment*, 45–46.

than highbrow philosophy, formed the intellectual basis of the Japanese enlightenment.[42]

Civilization leapt from space to time across the Meiji divide. In the *ka-i*, or "civilization-barbarism," model of the Tokugawa era, civilization existed in the middle, and barbarism appeared as one moved outward toward the peripheries.[43] The universalist conception of civilization imported from Europe displaced space with time, but then mapped time back onto space: progress over time determined civilization supposedly regardless of location; some nations were more civilized than others because they had progressed further in time. It was, foremost, Fukuzawa who brought this conception to Japan.

In 1869, Fukuzawa translated and published a revised edition of Mitchell's work in his *Handbook of the Myriad Countries (Shōchū bankoku ichiran)*. The book explained: The "best examples of enlightened nations" were the United States, Britain, France, and Germany because they had "made the greatest progress in morals, justice, and refinement" and were "contented and prosperous." The Japanese, half-civilized like the Chinese, Turks, and Persians, stood "a step ahead" of the "barbarous" Arabs. Fukuzawa politely removed Japan from its semi-civilized Chinese and Iranian company in the translation. The "savages" of the world, the "natives of Central Africa, of New Guinea, and Australia," made up the "lowest stage of existence" because they "make war upon each other, and are very cruel and superstitious." France and Germany very cruelly made war upon each other the year after Fukuzawa published the text. Hundreds of thousands of people died. Fukuzawa cited the pluck of French soldiers persisting in the slaughter of Germans as evidence of their "spirit of independence," their civilization.[44]

Fukuzawa modified civilization somewhat in his 1875 magnum opus *An Outline of a Theory of Civilization (Bunmeiron no gairyaku)*, but the basic model of stages remained, as did, this time, the Japanese in semi-civilization, alongside the Chinese, civilized compared to the Ainu. Influenced by and expounding on the theories of Mitchell and Burton as well as Henry Thomas Buckle and François Guizot, Fukuzawa placed "Western civilization as our goal." Japanese inferiority to the West lay in spirit, not just technology, he explained: Japan needed that spirit of civilization, of enterprise and curiosity, that characterized the West. Japan thus wanted education. External civilization – Fukuzawa cited

[42] Hsiung, "Republic of Letters."
[43] Howell, *Geographies of Identity*, 110–12, 150–53.
[44] Craig, *Civilization and Enlightenment*, 46–49, 111.

haircuts and meat-eating – was easy. The essence of civilization, the "reform" of "men's minds," "both the intellectual and moral development of a people" – such was true civilization.[45] It daunted.

The spirit of civilization had to be both national and independent, Fukuzawa continued. "In Japan there is a government but no nation," he lamented, in one of his best-known quips. (See Ravina, Chapter 6, this volume.) Japan needed to construct and defend its national autonomy against the threat of European imperialism: "What has been the outcome in Persia, India, Siam, Luzon, and Java?" he asked. This sense of the autonomous nation was "the first necessary step in the process" toward "the true aim of mankind": that is, the "attainment of the essence of civilization," a spiritual essence.[46]

To build this independent nation demanded radical changes in the intellectual conception of the Japanese polity. It entailed not only a vision of progress toward the future, with Western civilization as its goal, but also a conception of a linear past in which the nation acted as the primary subject of history. Civilization had to constitute, to produce, the Japanese masses as a singular national subject alongside other national subjects in a global system of nation-states. That task required in turn the reconstitution of knowledge itself, the separation of the present from the past, the casting off of the entirety of history as preparation for the enlightened national present, a new stage. It was this enlightenment conception of history, in a world of specious "international law" proclaiming the insidious chimera of equal national sovereignty, that provided the intellectual undergirding for imperialism, the justification for an "enlightened" nation to dominate the less enlightened.

Even with Western civilization as his goal, Fukuzawa acknowledged that Japan could not "be satisfied with the present level of attainment in the West," which continually fought wars, of which there was "no greater calamity."[47] "Is it not wondrous," he wrote privately in 1875 of those "who at present call themselves civilized," "that on Sundays, they shed tears as they listen to the scriptures expounding the love of man, and on Mondays, convert to the creed of self-interest and act like demons?"[48]

Fukuzawa belonged to the Meirokusha, meaning the "Meiji Six Society" or the "Enlightenment Six Society." First conceived in 1873 by Mori Arinori, it published the *Enlightenment Six Journal (Meiroku zasshi)* from February 1874

---

[45] Craig, *Civilization and Enlightenment*, 100–143; Fukuzawa, *Outline of a Theory of Civilization*, loc. 669, 759, 2022, Kindle.
[46] Fukuzawa, *Outline of a Theory of Civilization*, loc. 3530, 4644–4791, Kindle.
[47] Fukuzawa, *Outline of a Theory of Civilization*, loc. 681–87, Kindle.
[48] Craig, *Civilization and Enlightenment*, 136.

to November 1875, featuring the writings of the foremost intellectuals of the day: Fukuzawa and Mori, as well as Nishi Amane, Katō Hiroyuki, Nakamura Masanao, Mitsukuri Rinshō, Tsuda Mamichi, and others.[49] They tended at least to condone Christianity. "There is no religion in the world today that promotes enlightenment as does Christianity," whose "rushing torrent" was something that "cannot be prevented," Tsuda wrote in the *Meiroku*.[50] In his "Fake Petition from a Westerner," Nakamura separately called for the baptism of the emperor as a means of spurring enlightenment. The short essay, printed first in a missionary journal in Shanghai before being republished in Japan, drew the attention and utter alarm of famed intellectual Yoshino Sakuzō decades later.[51] Because of the way the earth rotates, Tsuda explained, enlightenment best moves from east to west, as Christianity once did; it was only "natural" that the United States, though its "culture is rough and shallow," was contributing most to the Japanese enlightenment. For his, or Hegel's, axiom to hold, Tsuda needed to account for why Islam had not displaced Christianity in Europe. "I would respond that the Moslem [*sic*] creed is inferior to the Christian," he offered.[52]

Opposition to Christianity was deep, rife. Kumamoto counter-enlightenment intellectual Sada Kaiseki petitioned the state in 1875. "The nations of Asia and those of Europe differ vastly in their inherent nature," he explained. "Asians do not traverse the myriad nations to obtain colonies." Europeans did, and their first step was to "insert their teachings into a country," just as they were doing in Japan "ever since the revocation of the placard regulating the teachings of the savages."[53]

The reference was to the year 1873, when the Meiji government lifted the ban on Christianity. The state had pursued a flurry of measures and policies until around early 1872 to indoctrinate the masses in a national creed that would obstruct Christian conversions. The 1868 policy of *saisei itchi*, the unity of rites and rule, held the emperor as the head of a combined political and sacerdotal order. *Shinbutsu bunri*, the separation of Buddhism and Shinto, and its subsidiary campaign of *haibutsu kishaku*, the destruction of Buddhism, spurred widespread attacks on and desecration of Buddhist sites and artifacts in support of the national creed. A "Missionary Office" promoted the 1870 Great Promulgation Campaign to "unite the hearts of the masses" in a great state-endorsed doctrine.

---

[49] Braistead, *Meiroku zasshi*, vii–xliv.
[50] Braistead, *Meiroku zasshi*, 39.
[51] Shō, "Kindai Nitchū bunka kōryūshi."
[52] Braistead, *Meiroku zasshi*, 226–27.
[53] Sada, "Yasu kenpaku," 4:437.

The policies did not work. In September 1871, the state's Department of Divinities was downgraded to a ministry; in April 1872, it was again downgraded to a bureau, the Missionary Office was dissolved, and a separate Ministry of Doctrine was formed. The doctrine ministry backed away from totalizing ideological aims and was itself dissolved in 1877. By 1875, the phrase *seikyō bunri*, the separation of doctrine from rule, captured the spirit of governance. The imperial institution would remain sacrosanct, above the multiple competing creeds and doctrines of the world, which would be relegated to the free realm of private conscience, where they could battle for allegiance.[54]

This freedom to know and believe individually unleashed the crushing intellectual suffering of a generation of youth, a "new generation in Meiji Japan," "wandering pilgrims" who, not knowing where to turn to find answers to their questions, flitted from ideology to ideology as the epistemological structures of their parents' world collapsed under the force of globalization. Tokutomi Sohō, "the archetype of the Meiji youth," recalled that the intellectual convulsions of the 1870s had left him with a "mental sickness." He became a Christian, but he "did not feel that intimacy with Christ that is the backbone of Christianity." He left the faith and later became a Japanese nationalist.[55]

A ringing call for religious freedom had come, in English in 1872, from Mori Arinori, dubbed by Itō Hirobumi "the Westerner born of Japan." Mori argued, too, for abandoning the Japanese language. Because the use of Chinese had been "a great drawback to Japanese progress," he called for Japan to adopt English as the national tongue. He proposed a reformed version in which English grammar and spelling actually made sense. Westerners in Japan and professors in Britain and the United States spoke of the "vagaries" of "so unpractical and reckless a visionary" and inveighed against Mori – or *speaked* and *inveyed*, in Mori's English.[56] The problem was not the foolhardy quixotism of Mori. It was that the proprietary rights that heritage Anglophones assumed over an emerging global language, and an emerging global world, were fast slipping away from them.

And it was that Japan's global enlightenment had subverted the most basic structures of Japanese thought. In the first edition of the *Enlightenment Six Journal*, Nishi Amane noted the problem that "it is improper for us to write as we speak as well as improper to speak as we write since the grammars of speech and writing in our language are different." People could not understand their

[54] Maxey, *"Greatest Problem,"* ch. 1.
[55] Pyle, *New Generation*, 119; Irokawa, *Culture of the Meiji Period*; Gluck, "Tanjun na monogatari," 30–31.
[56] Hall, *Mori Arinori*, 195–202.

own language. Some sort of reform was necessary to resolve the linguistic gallimaufry that history had bequeathed to them. Nishi proposed romanizing the Japanese language because "the Western alphabet will greatly assist writers and translators," especially in their adoption of new words; because romanization would enable easier use of the printing press; and because "if we adopt their system, all things of Europe will be entirely ours."[57]

Absorbing knowledge from the West had demanded monumental feats of translation. The sheer deluge of translated works in the 1870s is remarkable: John Stuart Mill's *On Liberty* in 1871, *Considerations on Representative Government* in 1875, and *Utilitarianism* in 1877; an extract of Tocqueville's *Democracy in America* in 1873; Montesquieu's *The Spirit of the Laws* in 1875; Francis Lieber's *On Civil Liberty and Self-Government* in 1876; Rousseau's *The Social Contract* in 1877; and Herbert Spencer's *Social Statics* in 1877.[58]

Translations of Western texts and textbooks, and indeed the invention or redefinition of scores of words including *jiyū* and *minken*, precipitated and spurred the diffuse *jiyū minken undō*, the freedom and people's rights movement. The movement attained its apogee between 1878 and 1881. In 1874, Mitsukuri Rinshō associated the rise of the word *jiyū*, "liberty," with Nakamura's translation of Mill's *On Liberty*; he himself separately took credit for *minken*, his rendering of the French term *droits civils* when he worked on translating the Napoleonic civil code for Etō's justice ministry.[59]

The freedom and people's rights movement did less to spur parliamentarianism and constitutionalism, to which the state was already committed, than to inculcate and normalize what it construed as a salutary culture of confrontation and contestation in the public sphere and on the battlefield: civil society against the state, Japan against its neighbors. The movement marked the origins of, or at least an antecedent to, what in the twentieth century became "imperial democracy." It abetted militancy, terrorism, and imperialism as constituent elements of liberty and resistance to despotism. Nakae Chōmin, dubbed the Rousseau of the Orient, had once plotted a coup attempt to be led by Saigō.[60] The movement contested the protagonists of the enlightenment, even amid shared myths of civilization. Ueki Emori promoted liberalism and individualism and disputed the dominant nationalist conception of civilization advanced by Fukuzawa Yukichi, who himself had endorsed Saigō's supposed anti-despotism. "Civil rights come first; the nation-state comes next,"

---

[57] Braistead, *Meiroku zasshi*, 5, 9.
[58] Anzai, *Jiyū minken undōshi*, 26–27.
[59] Braistead, *Meiroku zasshi*, 117; Mōri, *Etō Shinpei*, 95–101; Anzai, *Jiyū minken undōshi*, 37–54.
[60] Ogawara, *Seinan sensō*, iii.

Ueki wrote. It was a foundational question of civilization: not only who was civilized, but also who civilized.

Intellectual contests arose from the sociological transformations the movement wrought, primarily in the efflorescence of intellectual and civil society organizations. With the "containers" of the Tokugawa status order rent apart, the civil rights movement offered new "containers" – new forms of associational life – to organize an incipient civil society. Activists innovated new political media: speech rallies, lecture circuits, intellectual clubs. People across the country even joined together to write their own proposed draft constitutions.[61]

Newspapers proffered Ueki Emori and his civil rights comrades and nemeses a civilized means to proliferate their ideas and destabilize the national polity. "He who knows not civilization and enlightenment – let me steep him a newspaper and have him drink it": so went a popular refrain of the civilized era. From the early 1870s, fashion dictated that one go to Ginza to eat beef, buy a newspaper at one of the many headquarters newly established there, and take it home to the provinces as a souvenir. Originating in Western colonial settlements, known as "treaty ports," especially at Yokohama, the newspaper industry benefited from the rise of the printing press, especially from 1872; the introduction of electrotyping in 1869 enabled its practical use with the Japanese language. The national postal system, established in 1872 by Maejima Hisoka, spread knowledge. His *Yūbin hōchi shinbun* both collected and disseminated the news through the post.[62]

The Meiji regime enthusiastically promoted newspapers, at first. "Newspapers must take as their purpose the enlightenment of human knowledge," it declared in the seventh month of 1871. "When human knowledge is enlightened," it "guides people to the realm of civilization and enlightenment." Newspapers should be read widely, the state exhorted: their "writing should be extremely easy, and strange characters and odd words must not be used." In distant Kōchi Prefecture, Ueki wrote in his diary in 1874 of frequenting newspaper salons. He was seventeen years old.

The enlightenment darkened. Regulations in April 1873, just prior to the Inoue resignation, tacitly targeted Englishman and newspaper proprietor John Black, who was exploiting extraterritoriality to undermine the government in print. The next month, Black exposed the internal budgetary crisis of the state, throwing it into turmoil. And on 19 October, two days after Ōkubo and his band resigned, the state moved further to curb the newspaper

---

[61] Matsuzawa, *Jiyū minken undō*, 24–27, 98–99; Kim, *Age of Visions and Arguments*.

[62] Suzuki, *Shin gijutsu*, 41–62; Inada, *Jiyū minken no bunkashi*, 15–39, 93, 113–19.

industry. Leaks of confidential information, slander and defamation of the state, the fanning of rumors, the reckless criticism of state ordinances and laws – all were prohibited, seemingly in response to the Etō-Inoue scandal. Newspapers were commanded to issue corrections when they made errors of fact. They were required to submit a copy of each edition to the Ministry of Education. The papers themselves began to radicalize, calling openly for the assassination of government officials and wholesale militant revolution.

In a vicious spiral, the radicalization of the public sphere spurred and then was spurred by the state's restrictions on the press. The intellectual Ono Azusa and his civil society organization, based on the Japanese Students' Society founded in London in late 1873, started its own journal in 1875; besides advocating democracy, they petitioned the Meiji government that year for domestic libel laws. People across Japan "were advancing into the realm of enlightenment," they claimed, but the state failed to protect their honor and dignity in the public sphere, as the British did. Ozaki Saburō, a member of Ono's association, joined Inoue Kaoru in drafting the "two evil laws" of July 1875 curtailing press freedom. The regulations explicitly prohibited encouraging attempts to overthrow the government – because that is exactly what newspapers were doing. The *Hyōron shinbun* reprinted a translation by Mitsukuri Rinshō of an American civics textbook propounding revolutionary theory; anticipating a French revolution in Japan, pundits hailed Mitsukuri in November 1875 as the "Rousseau of the Orient, the Montesquieu of Japan." Dozens of journalists, especially those associated with the *Hyōron*, were tossed in jail, as was Ueki, in 1876, as a teenager, for a submission that editors titled "Monarch Who Makes Monkeys out of Men."[63]

There was terror in the enlightenment: terror in "public opinion" and "public debate," in liberty and rights, which degenerated into slander and sedition without being guided and moderated; terror in a state that meted out cruel violence against its youth to preserve its ascendancy. Knowledge needed enlightened leaders to administer it. For steeping a newspaper and drinking it could prove as toxic as salutary.

Society

It was not for nothing, then, that Fukuzawa construed civilization as a problem of "spirit," a question of the invisible mind more than its visible manifestations, of the journalist more than his journal.[64] Civilization in the

---

[63] Directly from Inada, *Jiyū minken no bunkashi*, 94–95, 134–44, 169–79, 185–204.
[64] Ogawara, *Seinan sensō*, 23.

Tokugawa period had been marked externally, for example by tonsorial and sartorial customs, topknots and swords. These symbols of status demarcated the boundaries of the civilized early modern polity: where the performance of status ended, there too did "Japan" end. To build a homogeneous civil society in the rubble of the status order, Meiji enlighteners called for the internalization and institutionalization of national civilization. Enlightenment would be instilled in the minds and behavior of every man, woman, and child and organized in the bureaucratic apparatus of the state.[65]

Civilization therefore required changes, or professed changes, in the very nature of being, in the relationships among individual, society, and state. Enlighteners sought to construct the autonomous, subjective individual, mediated by the institution of household, in direct relationship with the state. They held him – primarily, but not uniformly, him – as the primary building block of society. The result was the construction of "national society" and the individual self that constituted it.

Households

In the absence of status markers, the bureaucratically recognized household came to determine the boundaries of Japan. The year 1869 saw the implementation of the policy of *hanseki hōkan*, or "the return of domanial registers to the imperial court," which affiliated the population of a domain no longer with the feudal lord but with the central bureaucratic state. Soon after, the newly established Ministry of People's Affairs, supported by Etō Shinpei, began to draft the household registration system, or *koseki*. The system was announced in April 1871 and applied with revisions in early 1872. Only those registered could receive "protection by the government." Those without registration were "nonnationals." The emperor and his family remained above and outside a system designed for his subjects. To this day, the ultimate legal determinant of who is Japanese resides in the household registration system.

The system mandated the adoption and use of family names for all people and collected information about the names, ages, religious affiliations, and relationships of members of a household. Heads of households, the *koshu*, were grouped under broader village or neighborhood leaders, the *kochō*, bureaucratic officials in charge of small, local divisions in the new national "district system" of administration. The *kochō* put the policies of the central state into practice across the country. They did the actual administrative work of enacting enlightenment policies among the 33 million nationals the system

---

[65] Howell, *Geographies of Identity*, 157.

counted in 1872. They spent unfathomable amounts of time copying and distributing state notices by hand until printing presses arrived in the mid-1870s.

Household registration explicitly sought to eliminate hereditary distinctions of occupational status. In mid-1871, the Ministry of the State decreed the abolition of Tokugawa outcaste status, and members of that group were categorized alongside "commoners" in their 1872 registrations. The enactment of special directives to ensure that registration proceeded in Hokkaido and Sakhalin in 1873, and the insistence in 1871 that the Ainu be registered as commoners in the system, indicated the centrality of the *koseki* in constructing the notion of a homogeneous national society.[66] The aggressive settlement and development of Hokkaido, and the atrocious treatment of the Ainu, were themselves a major project of civilization.

Dozens of rebellions protested the bureaucratic elimination of status distinctions and the reconfiguration of society, especially in 1873. Villages in the province of Mimasaka erupted in violence that year. Furious, foremost, with the abolition of outcaste status, incensed that the household registration system would give the state a means to track ordinary people, and convinced of rumors that a "blood tax," the new conscription system, would exploit the new local bureaucracy to draw literal blood from women and give it to foreigners, people torched 263 homes of and murdered eighteen "new commoners."[67] Twenty-seven thousand people were charged with participating in the riot. The same year, when new village administrators in today's Kagawa Prefecture sought to obstruct an incident of vigilante justice, villagers went on an arson rampage, attacking the *kochō* and torching his home. Riots spread, and the homes of 200 other village administrators, four elementary schools, and hundreds of other buildings were burned. The military was dispatched. Seven people were killed. Seventeen thousand were punished for involvement in the rebellion.[68] That was hardly anything compared to the Takeyari Rebellion in Fukuoka, in which almost 64,000 were charged.[69]

Such disturbances reflected outrage and befuddlement over the social bouleversement overtaking everyday people, not least also because of the national land tax, the education system, and the conscript military, known as the "three

---

[66] Account of *koseki* from Endo, *State Construction of "Japaneseness,"* 102–18, 131–36. See also, Matsuzawa, *Chōson gappei*, 52–68; Matsuzawa, *Meiji chihō jichi taisei*, 41–44, 118–19; Okumura, "Shizoku kinōshō"; Suzuki, *Ishin no kōsō*, 88–95.
[67] Howell, *Geographies of Identity*, 79–109.
[68] Fujino, *Minshū bōryoku*, 31–40.
[69] Mogi, "Shinsei hantai ikki."

great reforms" of the early Meiji era. Along with scores of other reforms, many begun in the absence of the Iwakura Mission, they revolutionized social life.

Taxes and Allowances

Under the Tokugawa system, taxes had been levied in kind from villages. The actual value of taxes thus fluctuated with the price of rice. In 1872, with the rise of the household registration system, the Meiji regime lifted the long-standing Tokugawa prohibition on the permanent purchase and sale of land and began to issue "land certificates" to recognize ownership. And in 1873, it instituted a new national land tax, through which taxes were paid from the individual household directly to the central government. This new cash-based legal relationship transformed the nature of the economy. Legal ownership of various kinds, and the investment in and accumulation of capital, were liberalized. Household heads in particular became institutionalized as protagonists of household financial management. The basic structure of society was reorganized around the subjectivity of household heads, not the collective work of villages.[70] A decline in household income could thus increase the real burden of taxes. Tax riots known as the Wappa disturbance seized today's Yamagata Prefecture in 1874, making the area a prototypical "recalcitrant prefecture" and a classic case-study of the convulsions that taxes wrought in local life.

As it collected money, the state had to stop spending money. In the fourth quarter of 1871, for example, state-issued samurai stipends, rewards for military service, and other allowances accounted for 37 percent of state expenditure. It was unsustainable. Government stipends, the hereditary privilege of the samurai, had to be withdrawn. In December 1873, the state instituted a voluntary system in which samurai and nobles could obtain six-year bonds at 8 percent interest as well as cash for trading in their stipends. Mori Arinori had sabotaged an attempt to secure loans in the United States and enforce a mandatory revocation, believing it was inconsistent with civilized Western principles for the state to withdraw rights unilaterally. Kido sneered at Mori's "wallowing in Westernism." In any case, by 1876, it became clear that the state had no choice but to demand compulsory forfeiture of stipends and implement a mandatory bond program. The 1876 scheme was implemented just before the land tax was reduced in 1877 from 3 to 2.5 percent of land value. That change came in response to intense rioting again from late 1876: in Mie Prefecture, 57,000 people were convicted in a rebellion against the tax system. In effect, commoners were profiting at the expense of samurai: commoner taxes were reduced,

[70] Suzuki, *Ishin no kōsō*, 85–88.

and samurai stipends were revoked. Samurai were immiserated. It is not a coincidence that samurai rebellions broke out from 1876. Still, seldom did the rebellions turn on explicit statements against the revocation, which seemed to be a matter of course.

To bring about these fundamental changes in the economy, the state updated ordinances from 1872 innovating the legal and economic status of "limited companies" and called in 1876 for the establishment of banks across the country, which would distribute paper currency and enable a flood of cash to enter the national market. New economic infrastructure spurred industry and facilitated national flows of money, establishing a national financial system.

Ōkuma Shigenobu, the finance minister in 1876 who Shimazu Hisamitsu had tried to oust, construed these transformations as a means of turning idle, unproductive samurai into productive economic actors. He drew on a major trope of civilization: that productivity was its hallmark and that former samurai, with their hereditary guarantees of government salaries, were idle, worthless leeches profiting by doing nothing. Statesman Inoue Kowashi and others tried to defend the samurai as akin to Brahmins in India, people who contributed disproportionately to enlightenment in the absence of a strong middle class comparable to that of the West.[71] But such was civilization: the internalization and institutionalization of profit-seeking, the construction of the entrepreneurial, innovative individual in a capitalist society.

That spirit was promoted by state endorsement of industry and enterprise, exemplified by the 1872 opening of the first state-run factory, the Tomioka silk filature in Gunma. The undertaking was spearheaded by Shibusawa Eiichi, who became the nation's leading pioneering capitalist. Japan's industrial revolution arrived in the late 1880s. Civilization and enlightenment implied, then, two other great watchwords of the era: "the encouragement of productivity and industry" (shokusan kōgyō) and "rich country, strong army" (fukoku kyōhei).

Soldiers

Civilization meant warriors were capitalists and capitalists were warriors. In August 1871, the same Gregorian month as the dissolution of domains, the Meiji regime commanded domains to dissolve their individual standing armies and formed four national military garrisons, or chindai, across Japan, expanded to six in 1873: Tokyo, Nagoya, Sendai, Osaka, Hiroshima, and Kumamoto. Conscription was ordained in January 1873, influenced by

---

[71] Account directly from Ochiai, Chitsuroku shobun, 94–119, 176–99, 208–17; Suzuki, Ishin no kōsō, 170–80, 255–56.

Prussian and French models, and specifically by Albert Charles du Bousquet, a Frenchman in Japanese employ. (See Jaundrill, Chapter 12, this volume.) The system demanded that all men of ability between seventeen and forty be conscripted for seven years, three for active duty. It allowed a long list of exceptions. Only one in thirty men was actually conscripted. Men dodged the draft, for instance, by fraudulently buying other people's family registries. But the government itself wanted a small military: it could not pay for any better.

Conscription made plain the society-building pretenses of the state. Concurrent with conscription, samurai stipends would be slashed, as "warrior" ceased to be an occupation for a hereditary few; the obligation to wear swords would be lifted for all samurai; and "all four estates [would] gradually be enabled to obtain the right to freedom," the state explained. Here appears a great puzzle of civilization and enlightenment: samurai conceived of and carried out reforms from which they themselves appeared to have most to lose. They dissolved their own privileges. Many historians marvel at what they deem to be astoundingly little resistance to such revolutionary reforms, notwithstanding squabbles, debates, and assassinations. Perhaps samurai were truly enlightened. Perhaps they understood that they were merely reconstituting their power, just as they were reconstituting civilization itself, as something less visible and therefore more durable.

Conscription induced a dramatic transformation in both the idea and practice of national life. It offered the reality or the alluring illusion of equality, an escape from social status. It became a universal medical and educational institution, where people took tests and were tested, both mentally and physically. Human life was measured and quantified en masse. The average Japanese male at the start of conscription was 160 centimeters tall.[72]

Education

Civilization meant that everyone studied and was studied, everyone surveilled and was surveilled. Four days after the dissolution of domains in August 1871, the Ministry of Education was established, led by Etō and Ōki Takatō. At the end of that year, Mitsukuri Rinshō and other colleagues began to draft the ordinance that would mandate the education system of September 1872. Calling for the "enlightenment of knowledge" of the individual, the ordinance established a systematic, nationwide system of universal education for both girls and boys. Separate schools for girls were explicitly prescribed.

---

[72] This section is from Katō, *Chōheisei to kindai Nihon*, 45–51; Jaundrill, *Samurai to Soldier*, 95–130.

Schooling was for five hours a day, six days a week. It included three tiers: primary, secondary, and tertiary education. Standard lower primary school, for six- to nine-year-olds, and upper primary school, for ten- to thirteen-year-olds, were mandatory. School was practical, Western.

The education system divided the country into school districts so that, on average, there was one primary school for every 600 children. In 1873, 40 percent of boys attended school; in 1879, almost 60 percent did. The proportion rose from 15 percent to over 22 percent for girls. The gender disparity is acute, but the accomplishment remains signal: in just over a decade from its inauguration, the Meiji government managed to put over one in two boys and almost one in four girls into a national education system. It was, arguably, the single greatest accomplishment of civilization and enlightenment.

The state could not pay for such a vast program. In 1873, state subsidies covered only 12 percent of school costs nationwide. The education ministry demanded that each school district fund the construction and operation of its own schools, a directive that in effect called for taxpayers to pay separately for their own education system. Many parents found the costs crushing. At least 200 elementary schools were torched across Japan between 1872 and 1877.

Rioting and arson often turned on ordinary squabbles: territorialism, jealousy, resentment, and anger at the high salaries of teachers. But intellectual conflagrations engulfed the school system as well. To many, schools embodied all that was wrong in civilization: an overweening state, reckless Westernization, the bureaucratization of life, the flattening of status distinctions.[73] By the end of the 1870s, civil rights activists began to demand "free education" and decried state schools as unjustified "interventionist education" that obstructed individual freedom. Ueki Emori denounced the authoritarianism of Tokugawa education as "slave education" but excoriated too the new state-led "interventionist" system, which was "the greatest hindrance to enlightenment" inasmuch as it "disseminated elements of despotism" across the land.[74] Fights turned, again, on a foundational question: Who civilized?

In 1878, the state ordained the "three new laws," which replaced the now-dysfunctional 1872 district system, reconfigured local geographic organization, established prefectural taxes, and ordained elected representative prefectural senates. The laws marked a dramatic shift toward regional

---

[73] Directly from Yamamoto, *Nihon kyōiku shi*, 72–88; Platt, *Burning and Building*, 7–10, 209–10.
[74] Chiba, "Jiyū minken undō."

self-governance and conceptions of citizenry and away from a bifurcated local system of rulers and the ruled.[75] And in 1879, Tanaka Fujimaro issued the Education Edict of that year, which bore the imprint of the surging civil rights movement and granted greater powers to local governments to determine the content and operation of their schools. Expenditure on and commitment to public education dissipated. The following year, a new education minister proclaimed a new edict rolling back local educational autonomy. State intervention was itself a hallmark of the enlightenment, he said. No civilized country did not have a national state actively "intervening" in educational affairs.[76]

Liberalists lamented its statist character, but the education system and especially the edict of 1872 manifested the individualist spirit of the age. It was a spirit articulated in the 1868 promise that everyone "be allowed to pursue his own calling so that there may be no discontent." And it was embodied in the slogan *risshin shusse*, or rising in the world by autonomous will. That spirit was abetted not least by Nakamura Masanao's early 1870s translation of Samuel Smiles's *Self-Help*.

Education established at least a nominally meritocratic system in which boys could theoretically enter school, then university, and then the national government by dint of their own efforts. The state's 1870 *kōshinsei seido*, or "tributary-student system," based on proposals from Ogura Shohei and Hirata Tōsuke, demanded that each domain send its brightest men to the newly established University–South College, the Daigaku Nankō, a tertiary institution for training in Western learning. Students from across the archipelago arrived in Tokyo to receive systematized university instruction using original-language texts in reading and mathematics as well as law, science, and the humanities. Some people saw disgrace in students devoting their lives to the strange script of savages. A few began stabbing foreign instructors invited to teach in Japan. The system was dissolved in 1871, after the abolition of domains, and under the new Ministry of Education, the renamed South College expanded its educational offerings and continued welcoming foreign instructors. The South College endured, evolved, and merged with other institutions to become the University of Tokyo in 1877, the first holistic university in Japanese history, possibly Asian history, the flagship institution that would train Japan's bureaucrats for decades to come. That year, Ogura Shohei was killed in the civil war fighting for the rebels.[77]

[75] Matsuzawa, *Meiji chihō jichi taisei*, 237–38, 260–63; Matsuzawa, *Chōson gappei*, 112–23.
[76] Yamamoto, *Nihon kyōiku shi*, 89–98.
[77] Shimizu, *Origins of the Modern Japanese Bureaucracy*, 45–61.

Behind virtually every major state-led reform measure, whether at the University–South College or beyond, was an *oyatoi gaikokujin*, a "hired foreigner." Foremost was Guido Verbeck, whose students in Bakumatsu Nagasaki and later at the University–South College included seemingly everyone: Etō, Itō, Ōkuma, Ōkubo, Katō, and more. In 1874, near the peak of hiring foreigners, there were 503 foreign men in the employ of the bureaucracy, 269 from Britain alone.

Foreigners were too expensive. In 1869, Guido Verbeck made 600 yen a month, the same as Iwakura Tomomi's monthly stipend in 1874 and quadruple that of Hoshi Tōru, then an aide in taxation. Of regular expenditures in the Ministry of Public Works, 33.7 percent in 1874 went toward salaries for hired foreigners.[78] Students, meanwhile, were angsty: "To call this a university when its courses hardly surpass those of elementary schools in foreign lands!" one college student cried. "We will be the laughing-stock of generations to come." The state determined to send its own men out instead of bringing foreign men in. After a multitude of decentralized, scattershot study-abroad missions, in 1875, the first eleven students in a merit-based, systematic study-abroad program left Japan, heading to leading American universities such as Columbia and Harvard.[79]

Students brought back cutting-edge knowledge in not only the social but also the natural and mathematical sciences. They took up leading posts at the University of Tokyo and in the bureaucracy. And they transformed Japan. Kaneko Kentarō, who joined Komura Jutarō at Harvard, later became a drafter of the Japanese constitution. Kikuchi Dairoku, who received degrees from the University of London in 1875 and the University of Cambridge in 1877 and eventually became education minister, returned to pioneer Western mathematics as a professor at the University of Tokyo. The education ministry itself had ordained in 1872 that practical, applied "Western math" should displace the more theoretical, impractical "Japanese math" at schools nationwide. And indeed, in 1875, the state issued the Ordinance on Weights and Measures, which standardized Japanese measurements according to those of the West.[80] Japan was to become a global mathematical and scientific juggernaut. Other men who had gone abroad, such as Machida Keijirō of New Haven, Connecticut, or the Risshisha militant Hayashi Yūzō, came home and aligned with the rebels in the 1877 civil war.[81]

---

[78] Umetani, *Oyatoi gaikokujin*, 73–74, 227, 237–39.
[79] Shimizu, *Origins of the Modern Japanese Bureaucracy*, 59–67.
[80] Kanie and Namiki, *Bunmei kaika no sūgaku to butsuri*, 9–33; Ravina, "*Wasan* and the Physics That Wasn't."
[81] Fleming, "Japanese Students Abroad."

Men and Women

Foreign knowledge shattered the hegemony of domestic ideas, not least the very notion of manhood.[82] "There is not a wagon driver, coolie, grocer, or fishmonger these days who, without even knowing its meaning, fails to speak of the equal rights of men and women to any and every one around him," the *Yomiuri shinbun* declared in 1874.[83] In the *Enlightenment Six Journal*, intellectuals raised the call of the equal rights of men and women. Mori Arinori decried the wantonness of men, a characteristic of "barbarians," and expressed sympathy with "a wife's anguish when her husband goes so far as willfully to indulge his carnal desires with wenches and concubines." He called for marriage as a "contractual" legal institution in which men observed exclusive sexual fidelity. "Marriage is only nominal and without reality if the rights and duties of husband and wife are not mutually honored," he wrote. Deploring the practice of "using women as playthings," he reflected, "it is not idle slander that in the eyes of foreigners ours is the most immoral country in the world."[84]

Mori himself became, in 1875, the first Japanese to have a civil, contractual marriage. His wedding became a minor media sensation. The guests stood around in an open parlor and drank whiskey and munched on pastries and cold meat, like civilized people.[85] The marriage did not last.

Men squabbled over the question of women. Katō Hiroyuki sparred with Mori over the "excessive rights" of women, a consequence, Katō claimed, of a "misunderstanding of the principle of equal rights." Katō scorned the Western male custom of obsequiousness toward women, an "uncivil," "evil" set of practices whose "impropriety" Westerners could not understand "since they have been soaked in them for a long time."[86] Why should he follow Westerners in refraining from smoking in front of women? Fukuzawa riposted. He sought to offer a theory that was, in his words, "neither religious nor theoretical but rather a matter deriving from the abacus – the numerical equality of men and women." Drawing from Western bookkeeping, a practice of Western merchants he now sought to deploy as a universal epistemology of balance and morality, Fukuzawa smuggled numbers as a supranational form of universal truth into a discussion of gender equality in the guise of objective, universal positivism.[87]

---

[82] Approach from Sekiguchi, *Goisshin to jendā*, 249–60, 267–70.
[83] Hsiung, "Woman, Man, Abacus," 3.
[84] Braistead, *Meiroku zasshi*, 189, 145, 252–53.
[85] Hall, *Mori Arinori*, 251–53.
[86] Braistead, *Meiroku zasshi*, 376–79.
[87] Hsiung, "Woman, Man, Abacus," 6.

The intellectual question of women's rights, then, assumed a divide between Occident and Orient, even between civilized humanity and barbarous animality, as much as one between men and women. How civilized was Western civilization, really? Were there universal principles transcending the tendentiousness of Western civilization that could govern all human relations? Was everything, even the being of women, culturally contingent? To many women, these were of course urgent epistemological questions but also pressing problems of their very lived existence. When Kusunose Kita, a head of household (*koshu*) from Kōchi, tried to vote in new elections in 1878, she was denied because she was a woman. She withheld tax payments to the government and petitioned for suffrage, her call for rights and her rejection of taxation without representation published in newspapers in 1879. It was perhaps the first "public" document by a woman in the era of civilization. The question of suffrage for female heads of households came up in the Assembly for Prefectural Officials in 1878. The proposition was rejected, but not without historic calls within the state for women's suffrage. Under the intellectual influence of Herbert Spencer and Millicent Garrett Fawcett, male civil rights advocates, most notably Ueki, promoted women's rights and demanded women's suffrage, especially from the 1880s.[88]

By that decade, women themselves, most notably Kishida Toshiko and Fukuda Hideko, née Kageyama, began publicly advocating their rights, leading speaking tours, and writing for newspapers. They found in the freedom and people's rights movement an intellectual framework and social medium for their cause. Kishida promulgated higher education for women, denounced the frivolity of shallow arts that mired women in superficiality and servility, and demanded the edification of women who would be "of benefit to society." She asserted a woman's prerogative to choose her own spouse without the intervention of her parents. And she joined male intellectuals in conjuring women as a yardstick for enlightenment, a testimony to the alleged civilizational superiority of the Occident: the custom of male chauvinism "is an evil practice of the Asian Orient," she said. Her public philippic in 1883 against the "boxing in" of daughters, the failure to expose girls to rigorous education, led to her arrest. Officials interpreted her speech as a political allegory.[89] Fukuda, influenced by Kishida, was in turn arrested in late 1885 just before she could leave for Korea. She had joined a plot to detonate explosives there, overthrow

---

[88] Sekiguchi, *Goisshin to jendā*, 298–304; Anderson, *Place in Public*, 28–42, 80–84, 104–41.
[89] Sekiguchi, *Goisshin to jendā*, 301–2; Anderson, *Place in Public*, 101–2; Yokozawa, *Jiyū minkenka*, 280–81.

the Korean monarchy, and establish a pro-Japanese, enlightenment regime in its stead, all while asserting the rights of women. Partaking in a rising global tide of terrorism, she became Japan's first woman terrorist. She was nineteen years old. The unraveling of an oppressive gendered order, combined with the intellectual grafting of gender differences onto civilizational divides, ignited explosive sociopolitical consequences, almost literally.

Fukuzawa Yukichi might have invoked equal numbers of men and women, but heavily skewed sex ratios in some parts of Japan suggest that parents continued to kill female babies well into the era of civilization. Infanticide, justified centuries earlier in part by the perceived ontological propinquity of infants to animals, had been codified as a form of homicide by 1873 and condemned as a "barbaric" custom in popular discourse.[90] Perhaps that was the civilizing process: the obfuscation, the sweeping under the rug, rather than the real extirpation, of practices loudly denounced as barbaric. Indeed, an initial attempt to codify monogamy in the household registration system had been reversed in 1873 when it could not be sustained; concubinage was explicitly prohibited a decade later, but that practice hardly came to an end.[91]

Neither did the purchase and sale of human beings. The problem of human trafficking came to a head in 1872, when the Maria Luz, a ship carrying indentured laborers from Macau to Peru, docked in Yokohama. The Japanese foreign ministry, urged on by the British consul, ordered Ōe Taku, then the acting governor of Kanagawa, to investigate the matter. The Maria Luz was judged to be in violation of Japanese laws prohibiting human trafficking. Ōe emancipated the Chinese laborers and sent them home. The previous year, he had proposed the emancipation of those of outcaste status in Japan. And indeed, a month after the Maria Luz trials, Inoue Kaoru, drawing from Lincoln's emancipation proclamation, demanded the liberation of prostitutes. Etō's justice ministry decreed the 1872 Emancipation Edict for Female Performers and Prostitutes, which released all prostitutes from contracts.[92] The ministry proclaimed that the purchase and sale of prostitutes degraded them to the level of "cows and horses." It behooved those "moving toward enlightened morals," Tsuda Mamichi said, using the same beastly analogy, to extirpate this practice, now understood as subjugating women.[93] The rhetoric was weighty, revolutionary, as outstanding new research has

---

[90] Drixler, Mabiki, 48, 194–213.
[91] Sekiguchi, Goisshin to jendā, 265, 270.
[92] Botsman, "Freedom without Slavery?"
[93] Sekiguchi, Goisshin to jendā, 271.

revealed. Everywhere, oppressed people were being recognized as such and emancipated.

But were they really? Perhaps that was the enlightenment: it bestowed "freedom" on people, releasing them into a mass society where they would encounter oppression and exploitation less visible and more insidious now that it boasted the shiny veneer of Western civilization.

Enforcement

Civilization did institute means to discipline the population and enforce laws, compelling people to internalize norms and uphold collective standards of social life, not least before a leering, suspicious West. The justice ministry founded a centralized, explicitly Western-style police bureau in 1872 and placed Kawaji Toshiyoshi at the head of Tokyo's force. Kawaji left Japan that year on an investigative tour of Europe. Folded into and reorganized under the Ministry of the Interior in 1874, the national police, now led by Kawaji, became "vanguards of civilization," both inducers and symbols of order.[94] The first modern prison was built in 1872. Harsh corporal punishment, long a symbol in the West of Oriental barbarism, was displaced with punishment intended to reform and discipline individuals – unless you were an "uncivilized" Taiwanese at the turn of the century, in which case you could justifiably be flogged.[95]

Subsumed under the police in 1874 was Tokyo's modern firefighting force, equipped with steam-powered pumps since 1871, which at first were impractical in Tokyo's narrow streets. Kawaji was intent on bringing the nifty hand-pumps he saw in Paris to Japan. Fires had torn through Edo throughout history. The Imperial Palace burned down in 1873. Tsukiji and Ginza went up in flames in 1872, leading to the rise of Japan's first Western-style brick buildings. That year, Tokyo's firefighters collectively got Western haircuts because conventional tied-back hair was "an encumbrance during work."[96]

The enlightenment demanded order. A flurry of decrees, especially under Etō's justice ministry, regulated or prohibited tattooing, public urination, crossdressing, the bathing of men and women together, short hair for women, snake charming, dog fighting, and "wantonly sticking one's head out to peer at or mock passersby from above." Public discipline, a perennial concern in the Tokugawa era, now marked civilization, a move away from

[94] Glasnovich, "Return to the Sword," 87–110; Glasnovich, "Vanguards of Civilization."
[95] Botsman, *Punishment and Power.*
[96] Suzuki, *Machibikeshi tachi no kindai,* 61–66, 79–83.

barbarism. And the bureaucracy quantified barbarism. Almost 4,500 people in Tokyo were arrested in 1876 for peeing in public.[97]

Civilization thus constituted collections of people not only as a subject of history but also as a countable object of knowledge. Drawing from his observations in the United States, Itō Hirobumi led the installation of a statistics division in the treasury ministry in mid-1871. At the end of that year, the regime recruited Sugi Kōji to lead its broader Division of Public Tables. Influenced by Nishi Amane and Tsuda Mamichi, who had both studied in the Netherlands, Sugi was a Dutch-studies scholar with a long-standing interest in statistics.[98] His public tables division published the first-ever official statistical record in 1872. Collective society, which gained greater intellectual coherency with the rise of Spencerian theory around 1880, became luridly visible when cholera swept through the nation in 1877 and again, more severely, in 1879, killing 105,000 people that year.[99] Everything could spread through mass society, whether noxious germs or noisome cultural practices.

Culture

It was an epochal moment in the history of modern Japan. In June 1869, the emperor himself attended the first-ever elections of the Meiji government, in which upper statesmen voted for the head officials of the state. The moment for opening ballots arrived. A scribe of samurai origin attended to his duties. He wore an *eboshi*, a kind of hat. The string affixing it to his head came loose. The hat fell off. He panicked. Sasaki Takayuki diverted eye contact and stifled rising cachinnation. Gotō Shōjirō, about to burst out laughing, excused himself from the room. The emperor withdrew from the scene. Hysterics ricocheted through the hall. Or so recounted Sasaki.[100] Gotō was elected as a junior councillor. He was just over thirty years old.

A hat tumbling during a solemn ceremony might be universally funny. Cultural context made it intolerably hilarious. For one, there was the emperor, before whom one could not giggle. There had been emperors during the Tokugawa era, but people generally did not know or did not care. Civilized revolutionaries relocated the teenaged Meiji emperor from Kyoto to Tokyo and "restored" him to prominence in the name of ancient tradition.

---

[97] Howell, *Geographies of Identity*, 159–63.
[98] Shimamura, *Nihon tōkeishi gunzō*, 11–13, 18.
[99] Johnston, "Shifting Epistemological Foundations," 171–96; Johnston, *Modern Epidemic*, 51–69; Howland, *Translating the West*, ch. 6.
[100] Verbatim from Osakabe, *Yōfuku, sanpatsu, dattō*, 39–40.

The person of the emperor came to embody a "mnemonic site," the symbolic center of the national body that conjured continuity from a fictive ancient past. That fiction was necessary to provide stability amid overwhelming change and to offer legitimacy to a parvenu authority. The emperor thus stood for an "instant of historical rupture," the symbol of a bewilderingly new but purportedly ancient nation around whom the masses could unify and whom they could revere.[101]

The emperor performed the nation in front of hoi polloi to enlighten them, to let them watch the state, and to show them the state was watching. National holidays, starting in 1873, centered around imperial persons, legendary and living. The Meiji emperor himself made processions around the country with the military and bureaucracy in tow, notably in the Six Great Imperial Tours of 1872 to 1885. He was the enlightenment: in 1875, Sanjō called for an imperial visit to Hokkaido to help "the advancement of the narrow and inflexible people into enlightenment." The imperial role revealed the state's conviction that humans could change at the most essential level, that elites could produce a new culture by "reach[ing] into the very souls of the people."[102] That principle was quintessentially modern. But in the strategy lies an anomaly of the Japanese case: as monarchies fell from the Americas and France to Turkey, China, and Russia across the long nineteenth century, Japan "restored" its monarchy.

The tumbling hat of 1869 would still have been funny without the emperor. The *eboshi* was of a style customarily donned by nobility. The scribe was of warrior descent. And he was vanquished by a devious chapeau of another people.[103] The farce lay in civilization itself: warriors suddenly donning the garb of nobility and things going catastrophically, maybe a little predictably, awry.

In the risible mélange of the post-status order, where samurai and nobility, and before long commoners, could all live and serve together in the state and in schools, Western cultural forms fulfilled the imperative, as virtually every other dimension of Westernization did, of overcoming the hodgepodge of a heterogeneous past by transcending and effacing it.[104] Instead of samurai wearing noble *eboshi*, all could wear the clothes of someone entirely else. Civilization and enlightenment did not merge or blend some fanciful preexisting "Japanese culture" with that of the West. It fabricated a national Japanese

[101] Fujitani, *Splendid Monarchy*, 4, 14.
[102] Fujitani, *Splendid Monarchy*, 24–55.
[103] Osakabe, *Yōfuku, sanpatsu, dattō*, 39–40.
[104] Argument from Osakabe, *Yōfuku, sanpatsu, dattō*, 45.

mass culture on a global stage through the homogenizing West, and it used that culture to manage unmanageably diverse people. It did not always work.

On the ninth day of the eighth month of 1871, about a month after the dissolution of the domains, the state issued its edict on hair and clothes, loosening status-based restrictions and ordaining that samurai were free not to wear swords. It further mandated that government officials could wear Western clothes at work, that they would sit on chairs and at tables, and that people could enter government facilities without removing their shoes. Western clothes had already been spreading. The University–South College reasoned in early 1871 that Japanese clothes were impractical when students sat at desks or on chairs and when they conducted chemistry experiments. Companies and institutions, including the post office, the railway, and the customs agency, began mandating Western-style uniforms around 1872. Businesses selling Western clothes began popping up. The fancy Ōkura store, founded in 1872 in Ginza, employed Westerners themselves, such as an Englishman who had tailored for Queen Victoria. Of course, Fukuzawa set up a Western tailoring bureau at his academy, the Keiō Gijuku.[105]

The emperor stood for these changes. He began the Meiji era wearing white make-up on his face and tying his long hair up in customary noble style. He looked, in Western eyes, feminine. In the seventh month of 1871, a senior official in the imperial ministry went to Yokohama and brought back tables, lamps, chairs, and equestrian equipment for him. By the end of the year, he was riding on horseback, listening to Western music, and drinking milk with the empress. And in the fourth month of 1872, having consulted du Bousquet, officials summoned a German tailor in Yokohama to take measurements of a staff officer who had a build similar to that of the emperor. The emperor headed out on his tour of the Japanese west in Western clothes. Ordinary people were unimpressed: it was "as if they have no idea who We are," the emperor marveled in his diary. Regardless, he had transformed from the hereditary head of the nobility into the military head of a nation. Beneath his Western hats, he had kept his hair tied up. The haircut came in March 1873.[106]

Western clothes, like Western civilization, were uncomfortable. A new custom arose of wearing Western clothes at work and sensible clothes at home. Buttons were especially stupid and impractical. Someone forgot to button his pants before appearing in front of the emperor, and we still have a record of this fact. Many men ripped their buttons off in their haste to use the

---

[105] Osakabe, *Yōfuku, sanpatsu, dattō*, 38–43, 68–72.
[106] Directly from Osakabe, *Yōfuku, sanpatsu, dattō*, 62–67. See also Kanbashi, *Shimazu Hisamitsu*, 231.

bathroom. Someone had so much trouble unbuttoning aboard the Iwakura ship to San Francisco that he just did his business outside the urinal. Itō chided the voyagers for "staining the honor" of Japan.[107]

People did not want to change their ways. Officials in Shiga threatened to slap a hair tax on men who refused to chop it off. Police in Aichi were permitted to cut men's hair by force. When Russian emissary Alexei Alexandrovich sailed into Nagasaki harbor in 1872 and again in 1873, the governor of Nagasaki was supposed to greet him in mandated Western clothes. He pointedly did not. And he rebuffed the central state when it reprimanded him. The army implemented a French-style uniform in 1870 and the navy a British-style one. Ninety-seven trainees arriving from Tottori at the Osaka military academy refused to abide by the uniform and remove their swords. They turned around and went home.[108]

The total prohibition of sword-wearing in 1876, the same year samurai stipends were permanently revoked, marked a particularly incisive cut into the samurai past. When Yamagata Aritomo proposed the final edict in 1875, he upbraided "obdurate and benighted" samurai who were "unenlightened to the transformations of the times." "The world changes and times move on," he wrote; prohibiting swords was necessary so that "all the people of the nation gradually progress into the realm of the enlightenment." The Shinpūren erupted in rage over the edict.

And then there were beards. Facial hair was prohibited among Tokugawa samurai. It does not appear that there was an official Meiji ordinance on the matter. Men went ahead. Ōkubo Toshimichi grew out his beard on the Iwakura Mission. Saigō wrote to him, "I saw your picture. You looked utterly hideous. Please stop getting your picture taken."[109]

Civilization and enlightenment changed women's clothes less immediately, though the custom among married women of blackening their teeth faded away over the 1870s. When the empress appeared at a girls' high school in 1875 with high-heeled boots and a pink parasol, she left the students "astounded." Women did cut their hair, much to the ire of men, who insisted that short hair was a guy thing and that women had just not understood true civilization and enlightenment.[110]

The emperor and empress, disrobing themselves of their past, partook of milk and beef in explicit repudiation of long-standing customs not to eat

[107] Takii, *Meiji Constitution*, 11; Osakabe, *Yōfuku, sanpatsu, dattō*, 42, 48–57.
[108] Howell, *Geographies of Identity*, 165; Osakabe, *Yōfuku, sanpatsu, dattō*, 33–34, 84–85.
[109] Osakabe, *Yōfuku, sanpatsu, dattō*, 76.
[110] Howell, "Girl with the Horse-Dung Hairdo," 204–5.

meat. The emperor feted his nineteenth birthday in 1871 with French food. He reflected in his diary that year on his iconoclastic consumption of not only cows and sheep but also rabbits, deer, and other mammals.[111] Rabbits, incidentally, were all the rage in 1870s Japan, not as food but as furry friends. There were rabbit associations, rabbit art, rabbit dealers, and rabbit shows. The *New York Times* described it at the time as "delirium." Ōe Taku, who had taken legal action against the trade of humans, also petitioned against the trade of rabbits. To many, rabbits intimated that humans could not be trusted to make free, rational economic choices. Critiques of pressing social problems became couched in harangues against bunnies, reflecting how any frivolous fad in modern culture operates.[112] In any case, in 1872 the emperor personally visited Dutch doctor Constant van Mansveldt's medical school in Kumamoto during his tour of Kyushu. Mansveldt called on him to spread the custom of meat-eating, which was needed for the Japanese as they "strained their cranial energies" for civilization and enlightenment. Civilization entailed a search for what distinguished man from nature, the construction of humans as distinct from, masters of, nature, not least of trees and forests as well.

Popular writers and of course Fukuzawa Yukichi tried to convince people, both men and women, that eating beef was enlightened. Producers of beef faced intense discrimination. But with cultural taboos on consumption overturned and financial costs slashed, eating beef, especially beef hotpot, became a faddish symbol of civilization. By 1877, there were over 550 beef hotpot restaurants in Tokyo.[113]

"Western food" in general proliferated in restaurants, often attached to hotels, which government officials and intellectuals frequented. The Meiji Six often assembled at the Mikawaya restaurant in Kanda in the early 1870s; a menu in 1877 showed that it served coffee, milk, butter, meat, and curry with rice. Newspapers sent journalists to report on the strange things people were eating. Customers at restaurants trying to use knives and forks sometimes cut their mouths and got blood everywhere.[114]

Civilization accelerated change, life. Rickshaws first carried passengers in Tokyo around 1870. By 1876, there was one rickshaw for every forty people in Tokyo Prefecture and one for every 300 people nationwide. By around 1877, one in every twenty men in Tokyo was a rickshaw driver. Some were

---

[111] Okada, *Meiji yōshoku kotohajime*, 26, 85.
[112] De Ganon, "Down the Rabbit Hole."
[113] Okada, *Meiji yōshoku kotohajime*, 48, 58–63.
[114] Okada, *Meiji yōshoku kotohajime*, 84, 100–104.

former samurai needing money after their stipends were revoked in 1876; others were former outcastes. The Tokugawa order came undone. The use of wheeled vehicles for passengers on city streets marked a repudiation of Tokugawa regulations, under which they could be used only by nobility, even then with extreme restrictions. Neither did the Tokugawa masses generally ride palanquins. They walked. But "the people of the enlightenment" were different, one observer remarked: "A merchant's apprentice unloads his bags at the front [of a rickshaw] and peacefully catches up on sleep aboard the car." Riders of palanquins were "troglodytes, unenlightened." A woman, too, could ride a rickshaw, possibly even with a man in a two-seater, infuriating some. Rickshaws were civilization: fast, new, loud, equalizing, everywhere, loaded with goods, always in a hurry.[115]

And rickshaws were the practical requisite of a bigger, more iconic symbol of civilization: trains. Work on the first train line in Japanese history began in December 1869. The industry arose with British investment under the direction of Edmund Morel, a hired Briton; the British sought to crowd out the Americans and French from an emerging Japanese railway market. The line opened between Yokohama and Shinbashi in October 1872. The journey took just over fifty minutes. Once upon a time, it would have needed a day. Nihonbashi, the center of Tokyo, was almost a forty-minute walk from the train station in Shinbashi. Rickshaws closed the distance.[116]

Trains spurred tourism, leisure, fast business, problems: civilization. Military officials wondered why it was necessary to direct so much scarce money to an expensive enterprise of minor importance. The line went into Yokohama, suggesting to many that it would benefit foreigners more than Japanese. Maybe it was even a means of "giving the land to foreign barbarians." The train itself appeared as "an abominable alien machine," a Christian tool to destroy the Japanese spirit. Some seemed rather confused about what trains actually were: one popular woodblock print pictured a locomotive with square wheels. But the belching train was there to stay, and the industry effloresced in the late 1880s.

Trains contracted time. They demanded punctuality and precision, the measurement of time to the minute. The railway platform would close three minutes before a train departed, the Railway Bureau explained to customers in October 1872.[117] Times needed to change.

---

[115] Suzuki, *Shin gijutsu*, 62–64, 71–88.
[116] Nakamura, *Umi o wataru kikansha*, 56–66; Suzuki, *Shin gijutsu*, 75–79.
[117] Ericson, *Sound of the Whistle*, 8, 11, 58–59, 71.

The system of time in the Tokugawa period separated daytime and night-time each into six parts, meaning each full day had twelve temporal subunits. The measurement of time was thus relative, not absolute. The hour of the rabbit, the division that marked dawn, began in Tokyo at the equivalent of 3:49 am in midsummer and 6:11 am in midwinter; in midsummer, a daytime "hour" lasted two hours and thirty-eight minutes whereas a nighttime "hour" lasted one hour and twenty-two minutes. Imprecision notwithstanding, individual and social life proceeded in relative accord with nature: human activity was organized around daylight.[118]

Gaslights started to enlighten Yokohama's streets in 1872. And on the ninth day of the eleventh month of the fifth year of the Meiji era, the emperor announced that the first day of the sixth year would be 1 January 1873. The Gregorian calendar, and Western timekeeping down to the minute and second, would govern Japanese time. The old calendar included "baseless, unreasonable" elements that had "obstructed the development of human knowledge," the emperor proclaimed. From 1868, working times at the imperial court had already been set from 10 am to 4 pm, and in 1872, the school system's schedules had been premised on Western fixed time. The emperor's edict made such changes official, national.[119] Violent popular rebellions included the new calendar in their litany of grievances with an enlightened government gaslighting them with Western practices utterly at odds with natural agrarian rhythms. In mordant poems, Shimazu Hisamitsu bemoaned the ridiculousness of a calendrical system so divorced from nature that the new year appeared with no sign of renewal: "When the new year arises, the winter deepens – an era that knows not time."[120]

The Modern Prometheus

In May 1880, not a decade after Iwakura Tomomi sailed into the US port of San Francisco, Yoshida Masaharu and a retinue of other low-ranking bureaucrats and commercial leaders arrived at the Iranian port of Bushehr on Japan's first embassy to Iran. The Russo-Turkish War of 1877–78 had heightened alarm, in Japan and in Europe, over rising Russian power. Iran appeared as an emerging flashpoint in Anglo-Russian imperial rivalry – and possibly a good market for Japanese tea, a weak state in which Japan could gain most-favored-nation

[118] Suzuki, *Shin gijutsu*, 92–94.
[119] Steele, "Casting Shadows," 65; Suzuki, *Shin gijutsu*, 100–104.
[120] Takashima, *Shimazu Hisamitsu kō*, 317.

trade status. The Qajar shah Nāṣir al-Dīn greeted the Japanese in Tehran as fellow "Asians" – you are east Asians and we are west Asians, he said – and cross-examined them about their civilization: Were there railroads already in Japan? Did the embassy arrive on a foreign steamship or their own? How was the Japanese army organized? How was the Chinese army organized?[121]

Now Japan was the civilized one. The Yoshida embassy witnessed first-hand the ignominy of an abased Iranian nation. Tehran therefore instilled in Yoshida qualms about Japan's own enlightenment. Persia was an "example": a land that had "cast away its strengths and been left only with its weaknesses" in its "daily-increasing custom of adorning itself with arts and yearning after opulence [or civilization (*ka*)]." He had been invited to a weekly tea party of Western elites in Tehran. "At these gatherings, there isn't a time when their conversations don't revolve around the harms of the Persian government's mimicry of foreign countries or the failure of its political policies or its errors in intercourse," he observed. He thought of home: "Every time I hear these conversations, my mind turns back to the behavior of foreigners in Japan, and I in fact begin to worry about the future of the homeland."[122]

He had every reason to worry. So debilitating had been the wars of the southwest that they at once delayed and made all the more urgent the supreme objective of casting off the imperialist treaties. In the interim, Japanese in the public sphere had repeatedly inveighed – they *inveyed* – against Western colonists who beat up their rickshaw drivers and built buildings on their land without permits and inflicted every manner of indignity on them.[123] But those same Westerners had helped educate their youth and build their railways.

At every step of the way over the decade that separated San Francisco from Bushehr, Japanese people, their Western visitors, and their Asian neighbors fought, in words, with weapons, and by every means between, over every dimension of civilization and enlightenment. At no point was Japan not roiled by strife and disunity. Everywhere was dislocation. Old structures fell and new ones rose and then fell and rose and fell again as the historical earthquake of modern globalization shook with unprecedented, unrelenting force.

And yet the Japanese leadership, its heroes decapitated and assassinated, its composition ever changing, its subjects mutinying and its elites fuming at the buttons on their own pants, gripped the helm of a newly centralized

---

[121] Yamanaka, "Meiji Nihonjin no Perusha taiken," 117–28; Nakaoka, "Yoshida Masaharu Mission," 209, 215–20; Okazaki, "Meiji no Nihon to Iran," 83–85.

[122] Yamanaka, "Meiji Nihonjin no Perusha taiken," 123–25.

[123] Iokibe, *Jōyaku kaisei shi*, 28, 37–39.

nation-state and pulled the *Nippon-maru* together, through, to unquestioned status as the foremost power in the Orient. In short time, the stupendous achievements of civilization and enlightenment shattered the equilibrium not just of the nation but of a global geopolitical, intellectual, social, cultural, and indeed racial and military order that European and American imperialists had constructed for their own benefit. The developments of the enlightenment, each simultaneously a boon and a bane for Japan, inspired other subjugated "colored" peoples across the world to rise up and cast off the yoke of Western civilization, which held them in thralldom, in multiple senses of the word.[124] When Japan crushed Russia in 1905, in what some scholars call World War Zero, W. E. B. Du Bois declared that the global color line had been breached. Japan stole fire from the West. The chimera that resulted turned on the West and also on itself, yielding horrific levels of catastrophe and destruction that the men and women of civilization and enlightenment could scarcely have imagined yet seemed fully to have prognosticated.

One can write a compelling, truthful story not of disorder and strife but of an enlightened leadership winning the consent of its people despite outbursts of violence. The remarkable spirit of initiative and innovation that built Japanese civilization and enlightenment, and the extraordinary brilliance of Japan's enlightened leaders, who peremptorily swept away a past they rightly judged as inadequate for a global present, deserve a distinguished place in the story of the global past. Yet at every point along Japan's tortuous modern route, people looked back at civilization and enlightenment to explain how they had so grievously lost their way: the obscene Western denuding of an essential Japanese aesthetic, perhaps, or maybe the premature truncation of a bourgeois democratic revolution, or the inadequate inculcation of individual subjective autonomy, or the absolutism of the emperor system, or incomplete modernization.

The story of civilization and enlightenment, then, is a story of irresolution. It is the irresolution of the ever-intensifying historical process of modern globalization, in which civilization and enlightenment was but one early, doomed attempt at equilibrium. And it is the irresolution of the historical narrative itself. For if one thing is clear, it is that the enlightenment cannot contain itself. We remain yet too close to the violent, unequal globalization of the West to reckon adequately with the monsters it created. As this volume on the Japanese past now reappears, rewritten, some three decades after its first publication, at a moment when it is no exaggeration to say that Western

---

[124] Mishra, *From the Ruins of Empire*, 2, 7.

civilization and the world it built appear to be collapsing before our eyes; at a moment when globe-encompassing travails have laid bare a "deficit of conceptual resources" in comprehending our shared globality; at a moment when the historians' long-standing taboo of presentism, or specious conceit of extratemporality and extranationality, has been eviscerated; at a moment when mass death has been the consequence of our refusal to adopt equitable, shared frameworks to manage our irrevocable global togetherness – at this moment, one can hardly but marvel at the astonishing, deranging magnitude of the historical earthquake of modern globalization and the deep fractures that civilization and enlightenment entrenched as the ground continued, continues, to tremble.[125] Fukuzawa set Western civilization as Japan's goal, and Japan achieved that goal with stunning success. To many, that itself seemed to be the problem.

When Leroy Lansing Janes, an American hired foreigner in Kumamoto, wrote in 1876 excoriating civilization and enlightenment, he did so to lament that it was civilization, not "Christ, the soul's want," that was filling the hearts of Japan's new generation. Yet his essential critique, which assumed enlightenment notions of linear progress and development to decry that very enlightenment, resembled, reverberated with, the cris de coeur of so many others of radically different stripes, whether in his time or in the decades that followed: the globalization of Western civilization, of which there was no greater example than Japanese civilization and enlightenment, exposed the fatal defects in Western civilization itself. "The sham civilization they would build of a film of Western materialism, dignified by the name of science and civilization, leaving the soul and all its needs unprovided for, is a hollow bubble that would burst one of these days," Janes bewailed, auguring the "violent ruptures and fearful reaction that must occur, till the higher plane of progress is reached."[126]

Bibliography

Akizuki Toshiyuki. *Nichi-Ro kankei to Saharin tō: Bakumatsu Meiji shonen no ryōdo mondai.* Chikuma Shobō, 1994.

Altman, Albert. "Guido Verbeck and the Iwakura Embassy." *Japan Quarterly* 13, no. 1 (1966): 54–62.

Anderson, Marnie S. *A Place in Public: Women's Rights in Meiji Japan.* Cambridge, MA: Harvard University Asia Center, 2010.

Anzai Kunio. *Jiyū minken undōshi e no shōtai.* Yoshida Shoten, 2012.

---

[125] Mishra, "Grand Illusions."
[126] Davis, *Sketch of the Life of Rev. Joseph Hardy Neesima,* 64.

Banno Junji. *Saigō Takamori to Meiji ishin*. Kōdansha, 2013.

Botsman, Daniel V. "Freedom without Slavery?: 'Coolies,' Prostitutes, and Outcastes in Meiji Japan's 'Emancipation Moment.'" *American Historical Review* 116, no. 5 (2011): 1323–47.

Punishment and Power in the Making of Modern Japan. Princeton, NJ: Princeton University Press, 2005.

Braistead, William Reynolds, ed. and trans. *Meiroku zasshi: Journal of the Japanese Enlightenment*. University of Tokyo Press, 1976.

Chiba Masahiro. "Jiyū minken undō ni okeru jiyū kyōiku ron to sono undō: Tosa minken-ha no baai." *Kyōikugaku kenkyū* 50, no. 3 (1983): 52–60.

Craig, Albert M. *Civilization and Enlightenment: The Early Thought of Fukuzawa Yukichi*. Cambridge, MA: Harvard University Press, 2009.

Davis, Jerome Dean. *A Sketch of the Life of Rev. Joseph Hardy Neesima, LL.D., President of Doshisha*. Kyoto: Doshisha University, [1890].

de Ganon, Pieter S. "Down the Rabbit Hole: A Study in the Political Economy of Modern Japan." *Past and Present* 213 (November 2011): 237–66.

Drixler, Fabian. *Mabiki: Infanticide and Population Growth in Eastern Japan, 1660–1950*. Berkeley: University of California Press, 2013.

Duus, Peter. *The Abacus and the Sword: The Japanese Penetration of Korea, 1895–1910*. Berkeley: University of California Press, 1995.

Endo, Masataka. *The State Construction of "Japaneseness": The Koseki Registration System in Japan*. Translated by Barbara Hartley. Melbourne: Trans Pacific Press, 2019.

Ericson, Steven J. *The Sound of the Whistle: Railroads and the State in Meiji Japan*. Cambridge, MA: Council on East Asian Studies, Harvard University, 1996.

Fleming, William D. "Japanese Students Abroad and the Building of America's First Japanese Library Collection, 1869–1878." *Journal of the American Oriental Society* 139, no.1 (2019): 115–42.

Fujino Yūko. *Minshū bōryoku: Ikki, bōdō, gyakusatsu no Nihon kindai*. Chūōkōron Shinsho, 2020.

Fujitani, T. *Splendid Monarchy: Power and Pageantry in Modern Japan*. Berkeley: University of California Press, 1996.

Fukuzawa, Yukichi. *An Outline of a Theory of Civilization*. Translated by David A. Dilworth and G. Cameron Hurst III. New York: Columbia University Press, 2008.

Furusawa Urō kankei monjo. National Diet Library.

Glasnovich, Ryan Sullivan. "Return to the Sword: Martial Identity and the Modern Transformation of the Japanese Police." PhD diss., Harvard University, 2019.

"Vanguards of Civilization: Police Education and Unequal Treaty Revision in Meiji Japan (1868–1912)." *International History Review* 42, no. 6 (2020): 1105–17.

Gluck, Carol. "Tanjun na monogatari no kikensei: Meiji ishin 150-nen ni saishite." Translated by Yamagata Taiju and Matthew Augustine. In *Meiji ishin o toinaosu: Nihon to Ajia no kindaika*, edited by Matthew Augustine, 11–39. Fukuoka: Kyūshū Daigaku Shuppankai, 2020.

Griffis, William Elliot. *Verbeck of Japan: A Citizen of No Country*. Edinburgh: Oliphant, Anderson & Ferrier, 1901.

Hall, Ivan Parker. *Mori Arinori*. Cambridge, MA: Harvard University Press, 1973.

Hill, Christopher L. *National History and the World of Nations: Capital, State, and the Rhetoric of History in Japan, France, and the United States*. Durham, NC: Duke University Press, 2008.

Howell, David L. *Geographies of Identity in Nineteenth-Century Japan*. Berkeley: University of California Press, 2005.

"The Girl with the Horse-Dung Hairdo." In *Looking Modern: East Asian Visual Culture from the Treaty Ports to World War II*, edited by Jennifer Purtle and Hans Bjarne Thomsen, 203–19. Chicago: Center for the Arts of East Asia, University of Chicago and Art Media Resources, 2009.

Howland, Douglas R. *Translating the West: Language and Political Reason in Nineteenth-Century Japan*. Honolulu: University of Hawai'i Press, 2001.

Hsiung, Hansun. "Republic of Letters, Empire of Textbooks: Globalizing Western Knowledge, 1790–1895." PhD diss., Harvard University, 2016.

"Woman, Man, Abacus: A Tale of Enlightenment." *Harvard Journal of Asiatic Studies* 72, no. 1 (June 2012): 1–42.

Iechika Yoshiki. *Saigō Takamori*. Mineruva Shobō, 2017.

Ikai Takaaki. *Saigō Takamori: Seinan sensō e no michi*. Iwanami Shoten, 1992.

Seinan sensō: Sensō no taigi to dōin sareru minshū. Yoshikawa Kōbunkan, 2008.

"Shizoku hanran to Saigō densetsu." In *Meiji ishin to bunmei kaika*, edited by Matsuo Masahito, 275–302. Yoshikawa Kōbunkan, 2003.

Inada Masahiro. *Jiyū minken no bunkashi: Atarashii seiji bunka no tanjō*. Chikuma Shobō, 2000.

Iokibe Kaoru. *Jōyaku kaisei shi: Hōken kaifuku e no tenbō to nashonarizumu*. Yūhikaku, 2010.

Irokawa Daikichi. *The Culture of the Meiji Period*. Translation edited by Marius B. Jansen. Princeton, NJ: Princeton University Press, 1985.

Jaundrill, D. Colin. *Samurai to Soldier: Remaking Military Service in Nineteenth-Century Japan*. Ithaca, NY: Cornell University Press, 2016.

Johnston, William. *The Modern Epidemic: A History of Tuberculosis in Japan*. Cambridge, MA: Council on East Asian Studies, Harvard University, 1995.

"The Shifting Epistemological Foundations of Cholera Control in Japan (1822–1900)." *Extrême-Orient, Extrême-Occident* 37 (2014): 171–96.

Kanbashi Norimasa. *Shimazu Hisamitsu to Meiji ishin: Hisamitsu wa naze tōbaku o ketsui shita ka*. Shinjinbutsu Ōraisha, 2002.

Kanie Yukihiro and Namiki Masatoshi. *Bunmei kaika no sūgaku to butsuri*. Iwanami Shoten, 2008.

Kasahara Hidehiko. *Meiji rusu seifu*. Keiō Gijuku Daigaku Shuppankai, 2010.

Katō Yōko. *Chōheisei to kindai Nihon, 1868–1945*. Yoshikawa Kōbunkan, 1996.

Kim, Kyu Hyun. *The Age of Visions and Arguments: Parliamentarianism and the National Public Sphere in Early Meiji Japan*. Cambridge, MA: Harvard University Asia Center, 2007.

Konishi, Sho. *Anarchist Modernity: Cooperatism and Japanese-Russian Relations in Modern Japan*. Cambridge, MA: Harvard University Asia Center, 2013.

Makihara Norio. *Meiji shichinen no dai ronsō: Kenpakusho kara mita kindai kokka to minshū*. Nihon Keizai Hyōronsha, 1990.

Matono Hansuke. *Etō Nanpaku*. 2 vols. Nanpaku Kenshōkai, 1914.

Matsuzawa Yūsaku. *Chōson gappei kara umareta Nihon kindai: Meiji no keiken*. Kōdansha, 2013.

Jiyū minken undō: "Demokurashii" no yume to zasetsu. Iwanami Shoten, 2016.

Meiji chihō jichi taisei no kigen: Kinsei shakai no kiki to seido hen'yō. Tōkyō Daigaku Shuppankai, 2009.

Maxey, Trent E. *The "Greatest Problem": Religion and State Formation in Meiji Japan.* Cambridge, MA: Harvard University Asia Center, 2014.

McLaren, W. W., ed. *Japanese Government Documents, 1867–1889.* Asiatic Society of Japan, 1914.

Mishra, Pankaj. *From the Ruins of Empire: The Revolt against the West and the Remaking of Asia.* London: Penguin Books, 2013.

"Grand Illusions." *New York Review of Books,* 19 November 2020. www.nybooks.com/ articles/2020/11/19/liberalism-grand-illusions/

Mitani Hiroshi. "Kōron kūkan no sōhatsu: Sōsōki no *Hyōron shinbun.*" In *Nihon rikken seiji no keisei to henshitsu,* edited by Toriumi Yasushi, Mitani Hiroshi, Nishikawa Makoto, and Yano Nobuyuki, 58–85. Yoshikawa Kōbunkan, 2005.

Mogi Yōichi. "Shinsei hantai ikki no kōzō: Fukuoka-ken Takeyari ikki o rei ni." In *Kindai Nihon no shakaishiteki bunseki: Tennōsei-ka no buraku mondai,* edited by Buraku Mondai Kenkyūjo, 132–63. Kyoto: Buraku Mondai Kenkyūjo Shuppanbu, 1989.

Mōri Toshihiko. *Bakumatsu ishin to Saga han: Nihon seiyōka no genten.* Chūōkōron Shinsha, 2008.

——— *Etō Shinpei: Kyūshin kaikakusha no higeki.* Chūōkōronsha, 1987.

——— *Meiji rokunen seihen.* Chūōkōron Shinsho, 1979. Reprint, Chūōkōron Shinsha, 2018.

Nagano Hironori. *Seinan sensō minshū no ki: Taigi to hakai.* Fukuoka: Gen Shobō, 2018.

Naitō Kazunari. "Meiji hachinen no seihen: Umoreta seihen no hakkutsu to kōsatsu." In *"Meiji" to iu isan: Kindai Nihon o meguru hikaku bunmei shi,* edited by Takii Kazuhiro, 269–88. Kyoto: Mineruva Shobō, 2020.

Nakamura Naofumi. *Umi o wataru kikansha: Kindai Nihon no tetsudō hatten to gurōbaru-ka.* Yoshikawa Kōbunkan, 2016.

Nakaoka, San-eki. "The Yoshida Masaharu Mission to Persia and the Ottoman Empire during the Period 1880–1881." *Jōchi Daigaku gaikokugo gakubu kiyō* 24 (1989): 203–35.

Ochiai Hiroki. *Chitsuroku shobun: Meiji ishin to buke no kaitai.* Kōdansha, 2015.

——— "Saga no ran to jōhō." In *Meiji ishin-ki no seiji bunka,* edited by Sasaki Suguru, 175–204. Kyoto: Shibunkaku, 2005.

Ogawara Masamichi. *Seinan sensō: Saigō Takamori to Nihon saigo no naisen.* Chūōkōron Shinsha, 2007.

——— *Seinan sensō to jiyū minken.* Keiō Gijuku Daigaku Shuppankai, 2017.

Okada Tetsu. *Meiji yōshoku kotohajime: Tonkatsu no tanjō.* Kōdansha, 2012.

Okazaki Shōkō. "Meiji no Nihon to Iran: Yoshida Masaharu shisetsudan (1880) ni tsuite." *Ōsaka Gaikokugo Daigaku gakuhō* 70, no. 3 (1985): 71–86.

Okumura Hiroshi. "Shizoku kinōshō, koseki seido, 'kaihōrei': Meiji ishin ki no shakai hensei ni kansuru ichi kōsatsu." In *Kindai Nihon no shakaishiteki bunseki: Tennōsei-ka no buraku mondai,* edited by Buraku Mondai Kenkyūjo, 103–29. Kyoto: Buraku Mondai Kenkyūjo Shuppanbu, 1989.

Orbach, Danny. *Curse on This Country: The Rebellious Army of Imperial Japan.* Ithaca, NY: Cornell University Press, 2017.

Osakabe Yoshinori. *Yōfuku, sanpatsu, dattō: Fukusei no Meiji ishin.* Kōdansha, 2010.

Platt, Brian. *Burning and Building: Schooling and State Formation in Japan, 1750–1890.* Cambridge, MA: Harvard University Asia Center, 2004.

Pyle, Kenneth B. *The New Generation in Meiji Japan: Problems of Cultural Identity, 1885–1895.* Stanford, CA: Stanford University Press, 1969.

Ravina, Mark. "*Wasan* and the Physics That Wasn't: Mathematics in the Tokugawa Period." *Monumenta Nipponica* 48, no. 2 (1993): 205–24.

Sada Kaiseki. "Yasu kenpaku." In *Meiji kenpakusho shūsei*, Vol. 4, edited by Makihara Norio and Mogi Yōichi, 437–47. Chikuma Shobō, 1988.

"Seikanron shasetsu." *Hyōron shinbun* 33 (October 1875): 5–6.

Sekiguchi Sumiko. *Goisshin to jendā: Ogyū Sorai kara kyōiku chokugo made.* Tōkyō Daigaku Shuppankai, 2005.

Shimamura Shirō. *Nihon tōkeishi gunzō.* Nihon Tōkei Kyōkai, 2009.

Shimizu, Yuichiro. *The Origins of the Modern Japanese Bureaucracy.* Translated by Amin Ghadimi. London: Bloomsbury Academic, 2020.

Shō Rō. "Kindai Nitchū bunka kōryūshi no ichi danmen: Nakamura Keiu no 'Gi taiseijin jōsho' o chūshin ni." *Nihon rekishi* 603 (1998): 83–95.

Steele, M. William. "Casting Shadows on Japan's Enlightenment: Sada Kaiseki's Attack on Lamps." *Asian Cultural Studies* 16 (2007): 57–73.

Suzuki Jun. *Ishin no kōsō to tenkai.* Kōdansha, 2010.

——. *Machibikeshi tachi no kindai: Tōkyō no shōbōshi.* Yoshikawa Kōbunkan, 1999.

——. *Shin gijutsu no shakaishi.* Chūōkōron Shinsha, 2013.

Takashima Yanosuke. *Shimazu Hisamitsu kō.* Takashima Yanosuke, 1937.

Takii Kazuhiro. *The Meiji Constitution: The Japanese Experience of the West and the Shaping of the Modern State.* Translated by David Noble. International House of Japan, 2007.

Tanaka Akira. *Iwakura shisetsudan no rekishiteki kenkyū.* Iwanami Shoten, 2002.

——. *Meiji ishin to seiyō bunmei: Iwakura shisetsudan wa nani o mita ka.* Iwanami Shoten, 2003.

Umetani Noboru. *Oyatoi gaikokujin: Meiji Nihon no wakiyaku tachi.* Kōdansha, 2007.

Yamamoto Masami. *Nihon kyōiku shi: Kyōiku no "ima" o rekishi kara kangaeru.* Keiō Daigaku Shuppankai, 2014.

Yamanaka Yuriko. "Meiji Nihonjin no Perusha taiken: Yoshida Masaharu shisetsudan o chūshin ni." *Hikaku bungaku* 35 (1993): 117–28.

Yokozawa Kiyoko. *Jiyū minkenka Nakajima Nobuyuki to Kishida Toshiko.* Akashi Shoten, 2006.

Index

Page numbers in **bold** refer to tables; *italics* refer to figures.

Index